THE
MILITARY
BALANCE
2023

published by

for

The International Institute for Strategic Studies
ARUNDEL HOUSE | 6 TEMPLE PLACE | LONDON | WC2R 2PG | UK

THE **MILITARY BALANCE** 2023

The International Institute for Strategic Studies
ARUNDEL HOUSE | 6 TEMPLE PLACE | LONDON | WC2R 2PG | UK

DIRECTOR-GENERAL AND CHIEF EXECUTIVE **Dr John Chipman**
DIRECTOR FOR DEFENCE AND MILITARY ANALYSIS **Dr Bastian Giegerich**
EDITOR **James Hackett**
ASSOCIATE EDITOR **Alasdair McKay**

MILITARY AEROSPACE **Douglas Barrie** MRAeS
LAND WARFARE **Brigadier (Retd) Benjamin Barry**
MILITARY FORCES AND EQUIPMENT **Henry Boyd**
NAVAL FORCES AND MARITIME SECURITY **Nick Childs**
DEFENCE ECONOMICS **Fenella McGerty**
DEFENCE PROCUREMENT **Haena Jo, Tom Waldwyn**
RESEARCH AND ANALYSIS **Jonathan Bentham, Charlotte Le Breton, Hugo Decis, Joseph Dempsey, Amanda Lapo, Yohann Michel, Robert Mitchell, Meia Nouwens, Ester Sabatino, Dr Simona Soare, Michael Tong, Timothy Wright**

EDITORIAL **Christopher Harder, Jill Lally, Jana Phillips, Nicholas Woodroof, Charlie Zawadzki**
DESIGN, PRODUCTION, INFORMATION GRAPHICS **Alessandra Beluffi, Ravi Gopar, Jade Panganiban, James Parker, Kelly Verity, Jillian Williams, Loraine Winter**
CARTOGRAPHY **Alessandra Beluffi, Kelly Verity**
RESEARCH SUPPORT **Hannah Aries, Anna Blacklaws, Daniel Gearie, Yuka Koshino, Erica Pepe**

This publication has been prepared by the Director-General and Chief Executive of the Institute and his Staff, who accept full responsibility for its contents. The views expressed herein do not, and indeed cannot, represent a consensus of views among the worldwide membership of the Institute as a whole.

FIRST PUBLISHED February 2023

© The International Institute for Strategic Studies 2023
All rights reserved. No part of this publication may be reproduced, stored, transmitted, or disseminated, in any form, or by any means, without prior written permission from Taylor & Francis, to whom all requests to reproduce copyright material should be directed, in writing.

ISBN 978-1-032-50895-5
ISSN 0459-7222

Cover images: The Boeing X-37B Orbital Test Vehicle (DoD/Corbis via Getty Images); Launch of China's third aircraft carrier, the *Fujian* (Li Tang/VCG via Getty Images); The B-21 Raider, the next-generation US bomber, is unveiled at Palmdale, California (Frederic J. Brown/ AFP via Getty Images); Ukrainian soldiers fire a CAESAR self-propelled artillery-piece (Aris Messinis/AFP via Getty Images); K2 main battle tanks and K9 self-propelled artillery pieces delivered to Poland from South Korea (Mateusz Slodkowski/AFP via Getty Images).

The Military Balance (ISSN 0459-7222) is published annually by Routledge Journals, an imprint of Taylor & Francis, 4 Park Square, Milton Park, Abingdon, Oxfordshire OX14 4RN, UK.

A subscription to the institution print edition, ISSN 0459-7222, includes free access for any number of concurrent users across a local area network to the online edition, ISSN 1479-9022.

All subscriptions are payable in advance and all rates include postage. Journals are sent by air to the USA, Canada, Mexico, India, Japan and Australasia. Subscriptions are entered on an annual basis, i.e. January to December. Payment may be made by sterling cheque, dollar cheque, international money order, National Giro, or credit card (Amex, Visa, Mastercard).

Please send subscription orders to: USA/Canada: Taylor & Francis Inc., Journals Department, 530 Walnut Street, Suite 850, Philadelphia, PA 19106, USA. UK/Europe/Rest of World: Routledge Journals, T&F Customer Services, T&F Informa UK Ltd., Sheepen Place, Colchester, Essex, CO3 3LP, UK. Email: subscriptions@tandf.co.uk

Contents

Indexes of Tables, Figures and Maps 4

Editor's Introduction 5

Part One **Capabilities, Trends and Economics**

Chapter 1   **Defence and military analysis** 8
The shadow of war 8

Chapter 2   **Defence and military analysis** 14
Defence budgets and expenditure 14

Chapter 3   **North America** 16
Regional trends in 2022 16;   Arms procurements and deliveries 29;
United States: defence policy and economics 18;   Armed forces data section 32
Canada: defence policy 28;

Chapter 4   **Europe** 50
Regional trends in 2022 50;   Arms procurements and deliveries 69;
Regional defence policy and economics 52;   Armed forces data section 72
Poland: defence policy 66;

Chapter 5   **Russia and Eurasia** 150
Regional trends in 2022 150;   Ukraine: defence policy 165;
Regional defence policy and economics 152;   Arms procurements and deliveries 169;
Russia: defence policy and economics 153;   Armed forces data section 171

Chapter 6   **Asia** 208
Regional trends in 2022 208;   Arms procurements and deliveries 226;
Regional defence policy and economics 210;   Armed forces data section 229
China: defence policy and economics 220;

Chapter 7   **Middle East and North Africa** 302
Regional trends in 2022 302;   Arms procurements and deliveries 312;
Regional defence policy and economics 304;   Armed forces data section 315

Chapter 8   **Latin America and the Caribbean** 364
Regional trends in 2022 364;   Arms procurements and deliveries 373;
Regional defence policy and economics 366;   Armed forces data section 376

Chapter 9   **Sub-Saharan Africa** 420
Regional trends in 2022 420;   Regional defence economics 426;
West Africa: defence policy 422;   Arms procurements and deliveries 431;
East Africa: defence policy 423;   Armed forces data section 433
Central and Southern Africa: defence policy 425;

Part Two **Reference**

Explanatory notes 490
Principal land definitions 494; Principal naval definitions 495; Principal aviation definitions 496

List of abbreviations for data sections 498

International comparisons of defence expenditure and military personnel 500

Index of country/territory abbreviations 506

Index of countries and territories 507

Index of **TABLES**

1 The US DoD budget request by appropriation title, USDm 24
2 US DoD FY2023 budget request vs House and Senate Armed Services and Appropriations Committees' proposed defence budgets, USDbn 25
3 The US DoD total budget request by military service, USDm.........26
4 US National Defense Budget Function and other selected budgets, 2000, 2010–2023 27
5 United States: Next Generation Combat Vehicle (NGCV) 30
6 United States: fixed-wing combat aircraft exports, 2010–22...........31
7 Poland: *Rosomak* wheeled armoured vehicle family 70
8 Spain: selected aerospace procurement since 2010.........................71
9 Russia: defence expenditure, 2015–22 (trillion roubles, current prices) 162
10 Russia: Volume of military-technical cooperation and arms exports (USD billion, current) 164
11 Selected equipment donations to Ukraine, February–September 2022 170
12 Philippines: selected aerospace procurement since 2010.............227
13 Pakistan: selected naval procurement since 2000 228
14 Qatar: selected procurement since 2010....................313
15 Peru: selected procurement since 2010....................374
16 Kenya: defence procurement since 2000 432
17 List of abbreviations for data sections....................498
18 International comparisons of defence expenditure and military personnel....................500
19 Index of country/territory abbreviations....................506
20 Index of countries and territories....................507

Index of **FIGURES**

North America

1 US defence budget as % of GDP....................25

Europe

2 The FREMM frigate: selected national variants 57
3 Europe: selected countries, inflation (%) 2017–27....................60
4 Europe: regional defence spending as % of GDP (average) 62
5 Europe: defence spending by country and sub-region, 2022 63
6 Europe defence budget announcements, 2022 64

Russia and Eurasia

7 Recapitalising Russia's bomber inventory....................158
8 Russia: defence expenditure as % of GDP....................161
9 Ukraine: selected Ukrainian main battle tank (MBT) upgrades.....166

Asia

10 Asia: defence spending by country and sub-region, 2022 216
11 Asia: regional defence spending as % of GDP (average) 217
12 Asia: sub-regional real-terms defence-spending growth, 2021–22 (USDbn, constant 2015)....................219
13 China: defence budget compared with the rest of Asia (total), 2008–22, USDbn, constant 2015 225

Middle East and North Africa

14 Middle East and North Africa: defence spending by country and sub-region, 2022....................310
15 Middle East and North Africa: defence spending as % of GDP (average)....................310

Latin America and the Caribbean

16 Latin America and the Caribbean: defence spending by country and sub-region, 2022....................371
17 Latin America and the Caribbean: regional defence spending as % of GDP (average) 371
18 Latin America: selected countries, inflation (%), 2017–27 372

Sub-Saharan Africa

19 Sub-Saharan Africa: defence spending by country and sub-region, 2022 428
20 Sub-Saharan Africa: regional defence spending as % of GDP (average)....................428
21 Sub-Saharan Africa: total defence spending by sub-region, 2008–22 429

Index of **MAPS**

1 Europe: regional defence spending (USDbn, %ch yoy) 61
2 Russia's full-scale invasion of Ukraine: February–March 2022.......154
3 Russia's full-scale invasion of Ukraine: April–October 2022 155
4 Russia and Eurasia: regional defence spending (USDbn, %ch yoy)..161
5 China and Russia: selected military cooperation activities, 2019–22 211
6 Asia: regional defence spending (USDbn, %ch yoy) 218
7 Middle East and North Africa: regional defence spending (USDbn, %ch yoy)....................309
8 Egypt: defence industry....................314
9 Latin America and the Caribbean: regional defence spending (USDbn, %ch yoy)....................370
10 Sub-Saharan Africa: regional defence spending (USDbn, %ch yoy)....................427

Editor's Introduction

Change in military affairs is often incremental and slow. In many nations there is a formal process in which national-security priorities are assessed, defence policies are produced or updated and restructuring efforts reshape military organisations. Meanwhile, procurement plans lead to the arrival of new or upgraded equipment, changing the size and composition of inventories, which in turn can lead to equipment being retired, stored or destroyed, or sold or transferred to others. War, or other national emergencies, can change the trajectory and pace of change. In 2022, Russia's ill-fated decision to launch a full-scale invasion of Ukraine illustrates how defence transformation can be accelerated or even prompted, especially in Europe.

The Military Balance captures important changes that are under way in military organisations and inventories. Russia's armed forces, of course, have suffered considerable losses in personnel and equipment in the invasion, though Moscow's decision to mobilise means that personnel numbers have increased relative to previous years' figures. The assessment of personnel strength in Ukraine has also changed this year, as that country has looked to boost numbers and improve combat capability after Russia's invasion. Elsewhere, war in East Africa has also led to notable changes in this year's estimate for the personnel numbers of the armed forces of Ethiopia and Eritrea.

Equipment inventories are changing too. Russia failed to gain air superiority over Ukraine and relied mainly on stand-off attacks using its land-attack cruise missiles, depleting its inventory. As a consequence, Moscow has turned to importing Iranian direct-attack munitions. In turn, this is driving closer defence-industrial cooperation between Moscow and Tehran. Russia's tank and artillery fleets have suffered significant attrition. Around 50% of its pre-war fleet of modern T-72B3s and T-72B3Ms is assessed to have been lost. Moreover, the composition of Russia's inventory has changed. As modern vehicles have been destroyed, Russia has looked to maintain its fleet by bringing older vehicles out of store. The war is finally driving out of many East European inventories the Soviet-era equipment that many states have retained since the end of the Cold War. The flow of Western artillery to Ukraine is modernising Kyiv's inventory and delivering improved capability. Meanwhile, Russia's 2022 invasion sharpened Poland's threat perceptions. Warsaw is accelerating its plans to build up its armoured vehicles and artillery, on top of its existing goals of boosting its air and naval power. Indeed, the strategic centre of gravity in Europe has moved further north and east: Germany announced a special EUR100 billion (USD106bn) fund for defence and, like Poland and Finland, joined the group of European nations ordering from the United States the fifth-generation F-35 combat aircraft. Meanwhile, in 2023 Finland will almost certainly formally join NATO, alongside Sweden, a decision that they only took after Russia's 2022 invasion.

Change is under way elsewhere too. In some cases, however, procurement and modernisation plans are being delayed by economic realities. Higher rates of inflation in 2022 eroded the value of many defence investments. Indeed, despite announced increases to defence budgets, in 2022 global defence spending fell for the second year in real terms because of soaring inflation rates. European and Asian defence spending still grew in real terms, and with spending uplifts set to continue into the mid-2020s, these will be more effective as inflation abates. The application of special funds or off-budget expenditure to supplement defence spending has become more prevalent in 2022 as countries seek to rapidly increase investment. Such measures can reduce transparency and accountability while also creating issues for defence economists seeking to accurately track and compare like-for-like international defence budgets.

In China, the 7% nominal increase in the 2022 budget, over 2021 figures, represents a CNY95bn (USD16bn) boost in funding for the People's Liberation Army (PLA), the largest-ever annual increase in absolute terms, even though growth has in recent years stalled in real terms. These funds are enabling the PLA's continued modernisation. The launch of a new aircraft carrier drew headlines, but China also continues to launch more, and more complex, frigates and destroyers. According to the US Department of Defense (DoD), Beijing has also improved its strategic capabilities by introducing new and longer-range submarine-launched ballistic missiles like the JL-3 (CH-SS-N-20). The PLA Navy (PLAN), according to the DoD, likely began 'near-continuous at-sea deterrence patrols', with the JL-3 possibly allowing the PLAN to target the US from longer ranges than before, giving it options to enhance the survivability of its deterrent. And then there is the change to China's land silo-based nuclear deterrent, first publicly observed in the West by open-source analysts. China's air-force inventory is also changing: there are more Y-20 transport aircraft and now YY-20A tankers, and yet more J-20A combat aircraft. Moreover, new J-20As and new Y-20s are now considered to be fitted with locally manufactured engines, respectively the Shenyang WS-10C afterburning turbofan and the Shenyang WS-20, replacing the Russian Saturn AL-31F and Soloviev D-30KP engines. For years, China's inability to domestically manufacture military-specification turbofans had been held as one of the factors limiting the development of its military capability.

This is important as numerical changes to the inventories in *The Military Balance* reflect only one aspect of military capability. The process of generating numerical estimates is made somewhat easier where countries exhibit a degree of transparency in defence affairs, particularly open societies and nations that ascribe to defence-reporting systems – such as to NATO for defence-planning purposes, or to the OSCE and UN for arms-control and confidence-building purposes.

And there is an increasing volume of online reporting and imagery through, for instance, social media, and information from commercial providers of satellite imagery. Data gathered through these sources has to then be assessed alongside other information including from routine open-source monitoring and consultations with other defence specialists. An active conflict sharpens the challenge yet further. And the war in Ukraine illustrates the importance of information warfare, and the risks of this for analysts, as governments actively exploit the information space in order to shape narratives. However, the increasing number of open-source citizen analysts and independent research organisations scrutinising conflict and defence affairs has in recent years provided an increasingly rich source of information, for instance in contributing to assessments of Russian and Ukrainian equipment losses during the current war. The growth in publicly-available courses in analytical techniques, as well as technical tools, has helped this process. The expanding activity of groups like these, and the profusion of open-source data more generally, are leading government agencies to establish units focused on open source. In the case of the war in Ukraine, this volume of information, and the pace at which it has been generated, has meant that analysts have to consider carefully a profusion of often very diverse data, and in many cases reprioritise analytical capacity; this inevitably creates risk for other areas of study. That said, though conflict makes it problematic to judge numbers with precision, assessments can nonetheless be made, including judgements that a particular category of equipment may be in service, but the numerical breakdown between types is unclear. An additional complication is that combat attrition to both formations as well as equipment makes it yet more difficult to generate accurate estimates based on long-established methods, such as on tables of organisation and equipment. However, more information often becomes available over time, enabling more precise judgements.

More broadly, headline numbers remain useful as an indicator, but they have to be scrutinised. For instance, despite significant combat losses, Russia's personnel numbers remained relatively high, but attrition and mobilisation meant that, by the end of the year, the ground forces contained large numbers of relatively inexperienced personnel. And while the numbers of China's fleet of destroyers and frigates, or of heavy transport aircraft, may be relatively uniform, these fleets generally comprise more modern platforms than before.

If anything, these factors highlight the importance of looking beyond numbers to qualitative evaluations of military capability. Equipment holdings may look good on paper, but can they be effectively used? Assessments like these include judgements of industrial sustainability, logistics, maintenance, strategies and plans and training, areas in which Russia's armed forces have in 2022 demonstrated significant deficiencies. Such evaluations may also include difficult-to-gauge factors such as the effect of corruption on industry or the armed forces, military morale or even 'will' among populations. Additionally, they must consider the broader defence-funding burden for states, and where appropriate include assessments of purchasing power parity. Assessments like these require considered methodological approaches. These qualitative factors do not readily lend themselves to comparable assessments between states – a key function of IISS defence data in *The Military Balance*. For this reason, the IISS Defence and Military Analysis Programme has expanded its work in these areas and is looking to devise ways of assessing the broader factors influencing capability, in ways that are comparable between states. We are integrating our judgements into the MilitaryBalance+ database, and this volume illustrates in graphic form one aspect: our approach to identifying important factors that we think influence equipment capability. We are continuing similar work on military-cyber issues and on defence expenditure while exploring other means to deliver in our work further qualitative as well as numerical assessments of global defence data.

MILITARY BALANCE+

THE ONLINE DATABASE

DATA AND ANALYSIS TOOLS

MILITARY BALANCE+, the online database from the IISS Defence and Military Analysis team, provides indispensable information for the private sector, governments, armed forces, academia, the media and more.

- **Perform your analysis on Military Balance+**
  Utilising seven search engines and three data tools you can ask complex questions of the data.

- **Save time and money**
  The Military Balance+ can do in seconds what would otherwise take hours of your researchers' time.

- **Data you can have confidence in**
  All data has gone through a rigorous verification process, meaning you can use it in your work without concern over its validity.

- **Original IISS insight**
  Military Balance+ contains a searchable library of original IISS analysis, charts and graphics.

Deployments
Exercises
Forces
Equipment
Economics
Procurements
Analysis and graphics

173 countries

Data tools

A WORLD OF DEFENCE DATA TO DRIVE YOUR STRATEGY

www.iiss.org/militarybalanceplus

CONTACT

For an online demonstration, trial and subscription information:

Robert Hopgood
Sales Manager for Military Balance+
Direct: +44 (0)20 7395 9911
Mobile: +44 (0)7548 217 063
Email: robert.hopgood@iiss.org

Chapter One: Defence and military analysis

The shadow of war

Russia's full-scale invasion of Ukraine in February 2022 is reshaping the security environment in Europe and has ramifications elsewhere. The scale of Moscow's miscalculation is apparent nearly a year on, but at the outset it was not clear that Russia would face such difficulty. One of the preliminary lessons offered by the war – beyond those for the belligerents – is that defence and intelligence specialists need to sharpen focus on methodologies important to the assessment of military capabilities, and in this case revise how they evaluate Russia's armed forces. Other early take-aways include those related to the importance of aspects of military capability such as intelligence, surveillance and reconnaissance (ISR), longer range artillery and better targeting, and the importance of training and morale. Yet more concern resilience, both civil and military. Meanwhile, although the United States has led international military support for Ukraine, and Washington perceives Russia as the immediate threat, its longer-term focus remains what it views as the challenge from China. Beijing continues to modernise its armed forces at pace. Russia's war also offers lessons for the US armed forces and its defence industry, both for its involvement in Europe, but also in possible contingencies elsewhere, including in Asia.

Military miscalculation

Russia's initial military campaign was launched on a range of assumptions that proved to be ill-judged and over-optimistic: Ukraine's leaders did not flee, and the Ukrainian armed forces did not collapse. Moreover, Russia's strategy was based on a poor understanding of its own armed forces. Russia's recent military operations, and forces with important elements postured for fast and decisive missions, gave its leaders a false sense of confidence. Recent operations took place within relatively permissive operating environments, while training and exercises did not adequately prepare Russian forces for offensive actions against a determined and well-armed opponent. Russian forces displayed lower standards of tactical competence, command, leadership and logistics than their Ukrainian counterparts. The significant investment

in Russia's military power that took place after the latest modernisation phase (the 'New Look') began in 2008 has not brought the desired outcome. While important vulnerabilities in Russian capabilities have been demonstrated, once Russia resorted to artillery-heavy assaults the gap between expectation and performance was – in relation to Russia's weapons – perhaps reduced a little. But in other aspects – such as command and control, maintenance, logistics, planning, reconnaissance and soldier training – significant deficiencies soon became apparent. In the first real test of Russian combat power against a peer adversary for decades, the armed forces have so far come up short.

Military setbacks and the only incrementally-growing resources that Russia is committing to the war have meant that there is a growing gap between military realities and Russia's aims. As of late 2022, though state media control remained tight, and public support ostensibly remained high, some in the Russian security community likely recognised this gap. A crucial issue was whether this was recognised also by President Putin and the military leadership and, if it was, whether they would sustain their intentions or revise goals in line with miltary realities on the ground.

If a key objective of the war was to reassert Russian primacy over its 'near abroad', it has had the opposite effect. The war has reinforced Ukrainian statehood and galvanised its population and armed forces. The effect of the war on Russia's periphery has been varied. Belarus has been drawn closer to Moscow and has been complicit in Russia's actions by offering logistical and material – if not directly physical – support. But in Central Asia, Russia's grip appeared weaker at the end than at the start of 2022, while its ability to be an effective broker elsewhere, such as between Armenia and Azerbaijan, is in doubt. The effect in Europe has been profound. Russia's European strategy, as winter deepened, appeared to focus on weakening Western public resolve by cutting gas supplies. This has caused European states to sharpen their attention on resilience and energy security. It has made more important continued Ukrainian military progress in winter 2022–23 – even if this is at a reduced tempo compared to its mid-September to early November 2022 high point. This is important not only to maintain pressure on a Russian force that is trying to reconstitute, but also to bolster arguments in Western Europe that holding firm during an energy crisis and, indeed, providing continued military support to Ukraine were worthwhile.

Europe refocuses on Russia

The security environment in Europe is shifting sharply against Russia due to further NATO enlargement, decisions by European states to boost their military capability and additional US commitments. In 2019, NATO was described as experiencing 'brain death' by French President Emmanuel Macron, at a time when the then US president, Donald Trump, was at best ambivalent about the value of the Alliance, following decades of various US presidents exhorting Europeans to increase their defence spending.

Russia's 2022 invasion has given NATO a renewed *raison d'être* and impelled Finland and Sweden to formally apply to join the Alliance. It has caused many states to reassess their defence priorities and has in effect shifted further north and east the strategic centre of gravity in Europe. For Germany, Russia's invasion marked a new era in European security, and German Chancellor Olaf Scholz announced a EUR100 billion (USD106bn) fund for defence. And as of the end of 2022, Helsinki and Stockholm were well on the path to NATO membership in 2023. At its Madrid Summit in 2022, NATO agreed a new force model to boost force size and readiness and to replace the NATO Response Force, but as before, a key challenge will be in transforming members' commitments into effective capability. At the same time, European defence expenditure is being increased. This spending trajectory is readily apparent in Russia's immediate European neighbours and at its most obvious in Poland, where the defence minister said the defence budget should increase from 2% to 3% of GDP in 2023. The February 2022 invasion reinforced Warsaw's security concerns and spurred a rapid programme to modernise its land forces with new equipment, including South Korean and US armour.

For at least the next decade, Russia will be central to European security concerns, and will be important in driving defence policy developments and acquisition plans. But these concerns are not universally held. The United States led the Western response to Russia's actions, and while the Biden administration's National Security Strategy did say that Russia was indeed an acute threat, China was still the main challenge for Washington. Moreover, while there is concern across the world about the conflict, many responses were circumspect. China and India remained 'neutral', while several Middle Eastern and African states also hedged. President Xi Jinping of China has claimed that the growth in NATO membership resulted in the Ukrainian crisis – a narrative that was first articulated by Moscow. And in other states there are more hard-headed calculations of how the conflict may directly affect them, for instance in relation to the supply of hydrocarbons or military materiel. Although the leaders of China and Russia in early February 2022 announced a 'no limits' bilateral friendship, the rhetoric may exaggerate the depth and potential of contemporary Sino-Russian relations, and a formal Sino-Russian military alliance or direct Chinese military support for Russia's war in Ukraine both seem unlikely prospects. Nevertheless, the bilateral partnership is now closer and includes an increasingly strong military dimension that goes beyond defence-industrial cooperation.

East Asia

In Asia, the war in Ukraine added complications to an already-deteriorating security environment. Concerns were expressed in some states about the potential problems arising from a dependence on Russia for defence sales and support; Soviet- and Russian-origin equipment comprises a significant portion of the inventories of nations such as India and Vietnam. Meanwhile, China has grown more assertive regarding reunification with Taiwan, while relations between China and the US have become more abrasive. Beijing was harsh in its criticism of the visit to Taipei, in August 2022 by Nancy Pelosi, then-speaker of the US House of Representatives; the visit was accompanied by large-scale Chinese military exercises near Taiwan. Meanwhile, China's military modernisation continued to prompt concern in Washington, which views it as the Department of Defense's 'pacing challenge'. China appears to have expanded its nuclear capabilities, and at the end of the year the Pentagon's annual report on China's military capability noted other important developments including in submarine capability and the integration onto modern Chinese combat aircraft and transport aircraft of domestically produced military-grade jet engines.

Tensions also rose on the Korean Peninsula. By late October 2022, North Korea had launched more ballistic missiles than in any previous year. These activities included, for the first time since 2017, intercontinental ballistic missile-related launches and the launch, in October, of a claimed new intermediate-range ballistic missile; this reportedly overflew Japan. Speculation continued that North Korea was preparing for its seventh nuclear test. Meanwhile, the new South Korean administration has stressed the development of independent national military capabilities and strengthened military cooperation with the US. Large-scale bilateral exercises have resumed, after some years in which these were scaled back to support diplomatic discussions with North Korea. And in July, the government emphasised the importance of South Korea's 'Kill Chain' system and the other two associated systems (Korea Massive Punishment and Retaliation and Korean Air and Missile Defense) which had been renamed amid the short-lived thaw in inter-Korean relations after 2018. Meanwhile, the lifting of US-imposed 'missile guidelines' in 2021 has allowed Seoul to accelerate its development of ballistic missiles with two-ton warheads which could help to provide a powerful precision-strike capability.

In Japan, the war in Ukraine and Taiwan-related developments influenced the defence policy considerations of the Kishida administration. As anticipated, the government released revised versions of the National Security Strategy, National Defense Program Guidelines and Medium-Term Defense Program at the end of 2022 , recasting the latter two as the National Defense Strategy and Defense Buildup Program. The annual defence White Paper noted an 'increasingly severe' security environment and that Japan needed to strengthen its defence capabilities 'dramatically'. Alongside a raft of important defence procurements, including the plan to modify the two *Izumo*-class helicopter carriers to allow shipborne F-35B operations, in December it was announced that Japan would join Italy and the United Kingdom in a programme to develop a new sixth-generation combat aircraft. Governments in Asia and elsewhere are continuing to monitor the war in Ukraine for early lessons relating to military capability and also broader national-security issues.

The Ukraine war: some early lessons

In late 2021 and early 2022, US national-security officials engaged in a series of briefings to Ukrainian and European leaders, relating intelligence assessments about Russia's intent to mount a full-scale invasion. Intelligence assessments were declassified with the judgement that Russia was planning an attack and that Moscow was plotting to stage a 'false flag' attack as a pretext for this. Although for many governments these did not appear to dramatically 'move the needle' in the weeks leading up to 24 February, there is a case to be made that such 'intelligence diplomacy' strategies may in future gain more traction, not least because of what Russia's invasion implied about US intelligence penetration of Russian decision-making circles and the accuracy of its assessment in this case. That said, gaining such information may be more difficult elsewhere.

It is unclear whether governments have integrated this rapid declassification process such that it will automatically be employed in the next crisis, or even that they see a requirement for this. Processes have been established that would make it easier to share intelligence assessments and it is becoming easier to share information with trusted partners. Nonetheless, briefings like these, including the declassification of intelligence information and making this available to the public, have value in keeping populations informed and helping to shape narratives. They are particularly valuable when civilians are being asked to endure degrees of hardship because of wars elsewhere, as in the energy crisis in Europe in the winter of 2022. And they are important when civilians receive information from so many sources, some of varied analytical provenance, that can often provide information faster than governments have traditionally been able to, often because they are restricted by classification constraints. Moreover, there has been a wealth of open-source information on the war in Ukraine produced by citizen analysts and private firms, making use of commercially available satellite systems to deliver imagery-based assessments that were until recently the preserve of governments.

Questions of analysis

The war raises other questions relating to military capability assessments, in that Russia's military power was in many quarters misjudged. A caveat is needed: some elements of the armed forces have been used only sparingly, such as the submarine service, while the strategic-bomber force has for the most part been able to launch its stand-off munitions – even if some of these have appeared to be sub-optimal. However, Russia's military exercises, for instance, were more scripted than they appeared. This was widely understood to be the case for large-scale strategic exercises like *Zapad*, but not so much for Russia's snap exercises – designed to test combat readiness – that had become a feature since Sergei Shoigu became defence minister in 2012. The same goes for Ukraine, where there was generally an underestimation of the capability of its still-nascent non-commissioned officer (NCO) corps and, more broadly, of the fighting potential and 'will' of its armed forces and society. This calls for stricter application of structured analytical techniques to avoid cognitive biases like mirror-imaging. But this is challenging when it is difficult to gain access to armed forces and harder still when these forces are themselves deceived by their own reporting. It calls for techniques, possibly including environmental scanning, that could lead to thorough study of societies as well as their armed forces, and for more regular and more qualitative assessments of military capability.

For instance, while Russia has sunk considerable sums into its post-2008 military-modernisation process, it may be that the effectiveness of these investments has been reduced by the impact of Russia's political culture and of corruption. Alongside poor military and political leadership, further revelations of entrenched corruption in Russia's armed forces will not help to improve mutual trust. In advanced Western armed forces this is seen as an important factor in helping to enable effective military leadership at all levels. Indeed, the war has highlighted the importance of the human factor in war and reinforced the value of investing in personnel, including the competence of commanders at all levels and adequate individual and collective training, without which investments in equipment can be wasted.

After 2014, Ukraine's armed forces embarked on a programme to train and professionalise its troops, including the development of a professional NCO cadre. With the support of NATO and individual member states, through vehicles such as NATO's Ukraine Defence Education Enhancement Programme (DEEP), four areas were addressed for bilateral support from allies: basic training; train-the-trainer courses; the development of a professional NCO career system; and the creation of professional military education systems for NCOs. Reports on the progress of Ukraine's military reform were in many cases mixed, though the demonstration under fire of Ukraine's military adaptability and resilience indicates not only that more structured analysis would have been helpful here, but also that such reforms can bring results in traditionally hierarchical post-Soviet armed forces. However, it is important to also consider that the impressive performance of Ukraine's forces has been against a Russian adversary that has proven surprisingly poor, so caution should be taken in judging whether all of Ukraine's forces have improved to the same degree, or that they have overcome all of the challenges associated with their post-Soviet heritage.

However, in Russia, achieving effective change in this regard will require political will, as well as improvements in education and training. But devolving and encouraging independent decision-making seems to conflict with the type of control and governance that has characterised President Putin's rule. This may be a risk in other authoritarian states too, perhaps including China, though circumstances are different there (for instance, China has had prominent anti-corruption initiatives), and again, much depends on the quality of the enemy these forces would face. Nonetheless, this is a problem for the Russian armed forces moving forward. The ground forces now need to rebuild while engaged in a high-intensity fight. Many of its most experienced troops were lost in the early months of the war, and it is unclear not only how Russia will address the issue of adequately training and then integrating new troops into existing units, but also whether its military culture can change enough in future so that its troops can become militarily effective against a peer adversary.

Military matters

The war in Ukraine has shown how important it is for armed forces to be able to adapt. Both Russian and Ukrainian forces adapted during combat, though with varying degrees of success. After failing in its initial attempt to seize the country with a dispersed set of multiple axes of advance and an optimistic 'thunder run' approach, Russia reshaped its offensives towards the east. Russia's failure to gain control of the air meant it had to resort to greater use of stand-off weaponry and, towards the end of 2022, to augment these with uninhabited aerial vehicles (UAVs) and direct-attack munitions sourced from Iran. Ukraine, for its part, has also rapidly sourced and used direct-attack munitions and has developed a capacity to fuse information from small UAVs to improve the capability of its artillery forces. It also dispersed its air force and maintained combat effectiveness and has also developed a capability to attack Russian targets at-reach using UAVs and missiles. These include the attacks on the Russian Black Sea

Fleet flagship *Moskva* and some of Russia's strategic-bomber bases, and at closer ranges using direct-attack munitions. Attacks like these have highlighted risks to static locations including supply bases and headquarters and also troop concentrations; it appears to be increasingly difficult to hide on the battlefield.

The war has also been a stark reminder of the importance of magazine depth, evidenced by high usage rates for guided weapons and artillery ammunition and the severe attrition of armour. It indicates that any future military capability that relies exclusively on precision weapons will not only likely be costly, but will also need careful replenishment planning. This may require some production lines to remain open that would otherwise close, and government and industry to work together on suitable procurement mechanisms. It may also require striking a balance between mass and capability. There is greater concern over supply-chain issues because of the war – concerns which had already been expressed during the coronavirus pandemic. There are now additional concerns relating to sourcing and traceability in the lower levels of the supply chain. Along with interest in supply chain assurance, this is also leading to a reconsideration in some countries over what supply chains and components may need to be onshored. At the same time, industrial capacity issues highlight potential near-term difficulties in increasing production to replace Western materiel supplied to Ukraine.

Moreover, concerns over supply-chain vulnerabilities form only one aspect of resilience. There is also now greater focus than for decades on the resilience of critical national infrastructure and of societies to state-based threats, including from physical attack as well as from cyber and broader disinformation threats. However, effectively tackling these challenges requires long-term government attention, including in the education sphere, and a joined-up approach within government and between government, the private-sector business community and broader society.

The war has illustrated the continuing importance of the combined-arms approach to warfare – including the integration of UAV and counter-UAV capabilities into land units, and also how increasingly pervasive surveillance can pose risk for manoeuvre forces. Furthermore, it has highlighted the importance of long-range precision artillery and also the armour versus anti-armour fight. Fitting active-protection systems to armoured vehicles can reduce the threat

from anti-armour systems, but not eliminate it. Urban operations have highlighted the continued importance of capabilities, and training, suitable for this terrain. Meanwhile, the war suggests that both unguided and smart ammunition have complementary roles. Large amounts of both conventional unguided ammunition and precision weapons have been expended. Anti-armour weapons illustrate the benefits but also the costs of precision, with concerns expressed not only over whether Ukraine may run out of stocks of Western supplied anti-armour systems, but also about national stocks and defence-industrial capacity in countries that have supplied such systems to Ukraine.

Neither combatant in Ukraine has secured overall air superiority. Ground-based air defence has proved effective in limiting freedom of action and losses have been inflicted, while Russia's comparative lack of modern short- and medium-range air-launched precision-guided munitions has been exposed. The importance of ISR has also been highlighted, alongside the ability to rapidly distribute information from the sensor to the shooter. And the vulnerability of helicopters to air defences has been apparent on both sides. But while air forces have looked to the war for lessons in 2022, some key developments in aerospace technology have more direct relevance elsewhere. The unveiling in December of the new US strategic bomber, the B-21, was clearly focused on Asia-Pacific contingencies; it was anticipated that China's next-generation bomber would also be shown. In areas such as combat-aircraft design and manufacture, a problem for Washington's allies and partners is that its requirements mean its designs will be at a price point that few of them will be willing or able to accept. In turn, this may lead groups of nations to team up in order to deliver advanced capabilities. However, the more diverse their requirements, the harder it will be to produce systems on time that are affordable and able to meet all their needs.

In the maritime domain, Russia's navy has been embarrassed by Ukrainian tactics, but it was not really configured to face an opponent with very limited naval capability but adept at using naval guerrilla tactics. Rather, it was designed to hold at bay an opponent with significant naval dependence. For all the setbacks, Russia was at the end of 2022 still essentially enforcing a distant blockade of Ukraine's trade. This underscores global energy and resource interdependence, and the importance of maritime trade flows and sea lanes of communication, as well as the potential of blockades. More broadly, for navies as for land and air forces, Ukraine has brought home the need to consider attrition, magazine depth and sustainment ability. It has also brought home the threat of unconventional tactics and emerging technologies, and critical undersea infrastructure vulnerabilities.

Money counts

In the wake of the disruption caused by the coronavirus pandemic, the global economic climate is again fraught. Surging inflation, commodity-price spikes, supply-chain crises and heightened economic uncertainty resulting from Russia's invasion of Ukraine have derailed an economic recovery that, in some countries, was far from complete. Inflation rates increased globally in 2021 as a result of higher energy costs, a recovery in demand and ongoing pandemic-related supply-chain disruptions.

The war had led some countries in Europe to increase their defence spending, and others elsewhere to take the opportunity to revise defence strategies. In 2022, around 20 countries in Europe pledged to increase defence spending, with varying degrees of size and immediacy. Nonetheless, the difficult global economic environment that will persist in the short term will impose constraints on public expenditure, not least the higher cost of debt financing in light of increased interest rates designed to curb inflation.

Global defence expenditure grew in nominal terms in 2021 and 2022 but higher rates of inflation meant expenditure fell in real terms in both years. In recent years, high inflation eroded defence spending in real terms in countries in Sub-Saharan Africa, Latin America and the Caribbean, the Middle East and North Africa and Russia and Eurasia, but this trend is now more widespread. Europe and Asia were the only regions globally to continue to exhibit defence-spending growth in real terms in 2021 with Russia and Eurasia joining them in 2022 as war fuelled above-inflation increases in the region.

For some governments, such as those in Europe and Asia, security challenges continue to sharpen even as the value of their defence investments is being undercut. This makes it more important not only to spend wisely and ensure that procurements deliver on time and on budget, but also to see that full use is made of the possibilities deriving from collaborative equipment development and from defence and military partnerships.

Chapter Two: Defence budgets and expenditure

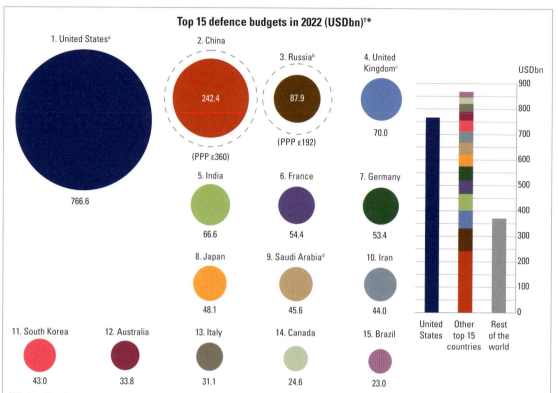

Top 15 defence budgets in 2022 (USDbn)†*

1. United States[a] — 766.6
2. China — 242.4 (PPP ε360)
3. Russia[b] — 87.9 (PPP ε192)
4. United Kingdom[c] — 70.0
5. India — 66.6
6. France — 54.4
7. Germany — 53.4
8. Japan — 48.1
9. Saudi Arabia[d] — 45.6
10. Iran — 44.0
11. South Korea — 43.0
12. Australia — 33.8
13. Italy — 31.1
14. Canada — 24.6
15. Brazil — 23.0

[a] OMB adjusted figure. [b] Total defence expenditure including military R&D funding, military pensions, paramilitary forces' budgets, and other MoD-related expenses such as housing. [c] Includes Armed Forces Pension Scheme and military aid to Ukraine. [d] Excludes security expenditure. Note: Unless otherwise indicated, US dollar totals are calculated using average market exchange rates for 2022, derived using IMF data. The relative position of countries will vary not only as a result of actual adjustments in defence spending levels, but also due to exchange-rate fluctuations between domestic currencies and the US dollar. The use of average exchange rates reduces these fluctuations, but the effects of such movements can be significant in a number of cases. Dashed line reflects an estimate for the value of the Chinese and Russian defence budget in PPP (purchasing power parity) terms to take into account the lower input costs in these countries. These PPP figures are not used in any regional or global totals in this publication and should not be used in comparison with other international data.

©IISS

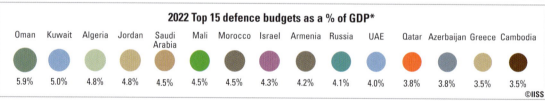

2022 Top 15 defence budgets as a % of GDP*

Oman	Kuwait	Algeria	Jordan	Saudi Arabia	Mali	Morocco	Israel	Armenia	Russia	UAE	Qatar	Azerbaijan	Greece	Cambodia
5.9%	5.0%	4.8%	4.8%	4.5%	4.5%	4.5%	4.3%	4.2%	4.1%	4.0%	3.8%	3.8%	3.5%	3.5%

©IISS

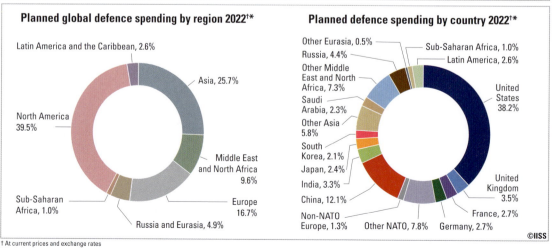

Planned global defence spending by region 2022†*

- Latin America and the Caribbean, 2.6%
- Asia, 25.7%
- North America, 39.5%
- Middle East and North Africa, 9.6%
- Sub-Saharan Africa, 1.0%
- Russia and Eurasia, 4.9%
- Europe, 16.7%

Planned defence spending by country 2022†*

- Other Eurasia, 0.5%
- Russia, 4.4%
- Other Middle East and North Africa, 7.3%
- Saudi Arabia, 2.3%
- Other Asia, 5.8%
- South Korea, 2.1%
- Japan, 2.4%
- India, 3.3%
- China, 12.1%
- Non-NATO Europe, 1.3%
- Other NATO, 7.8%
- Germany, 2.7%
- France, 2.7%
- United Kingdom, 3.5%
- United States, 38.2%
- Latin America, 2.6%
- Sub-Saharan Africa, 1.0%

©IISS

† At current prices and exchange rates
* Analysis only includes countries for which sufficient comparable data is available. Notable exceptions include Cuba, Eritrea, Libya, North Korea and Syria.

Defence and military analysis: Defence budgets and expenditure

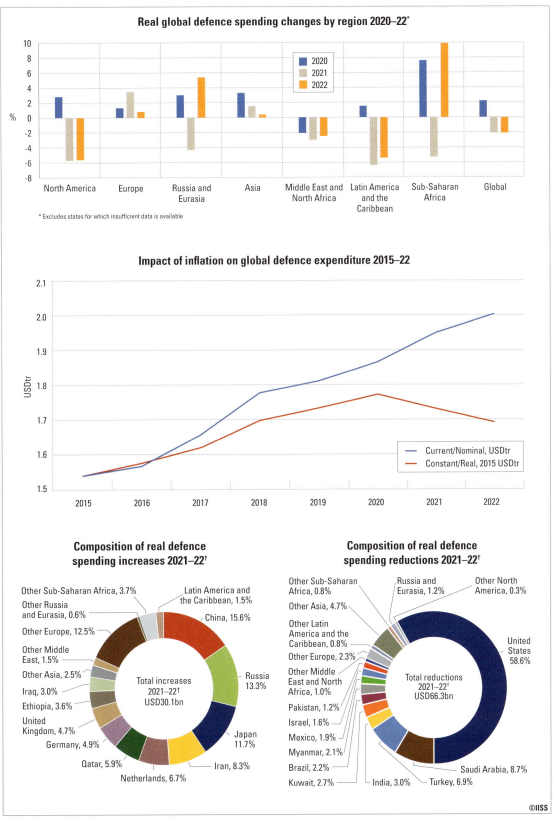

Chapter Three
North America

- According to the 2022 National Defense Strategy (NDS), released in unclassified form in October, Russia is an 'acute' threat but China is the pacing challenge for the Department of Defense. The modernisation of China's armed forces remains the principal driver of US policy attention and capability development.

- The US has led the international response to Russia's 2022 invasion of Ukraine. US officials have played key roles in coordinating defence assistance to Ukraine, and the US has delivered significant stocks, including anti-armour weapons, various air and missile defence systems, and HARM anti-radiation missiles and artillery (particularly HIMARS rocket artillery).

- The US Army is focused on regenerating its capability for large-scale combat operations under its Multi-Domain Operations (MDO) concept. Integrating lessons drawn from Ukraine delayed the official publication of MDO as army doctrine, though the updated document – FM 3-0, Operations – was eventually published in October.

- The US Navy 'Navigation Plan' outlined goals, including 12 nuclear-powered aircraft carriers, 66 tactical submarines, 96 large and 56 small surface combatants, as part of a force design for 373 crewed vessels, plus approximately 150 uninhabited surface and subsurface platforms, to be achieved by 2045.

- The US Air Force unveiled the Northrop Grumman B-21 *Raider* bomber in December 2022, but a timeline for the public display of a prototype crewed element of the Next-Generation Air Dominance project remains unclear.

- The FY2023 DoD budget request prioritises the Pentagon's plan to build advantage by investing in innovation and modernisation as well as industrial capability. The Pentagon is also looking to improve recruitment and retention, and the FY2023 budget includes a 4.6% pay raise for both military and civilian personnel.

- Canada and the US agreed to upgrade infrastructure and systems associated with the North American Aerospace Defense Command.

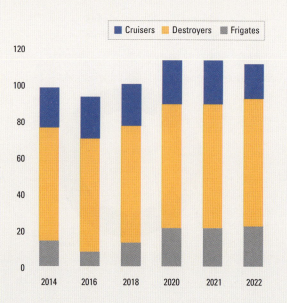

US cruisers, destroyers and frigates, 2014–22

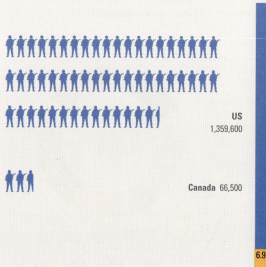

Active military personnel
(25,000 per unit)

US 1,359,600
Canada 66,500
Global total 20,773,950
Regional total 1,426,100
6.9%

Regional defence policy and economics   18 ▶
Arms procurements and deliveries   29 ▶
Armed forces data section   32 ▶

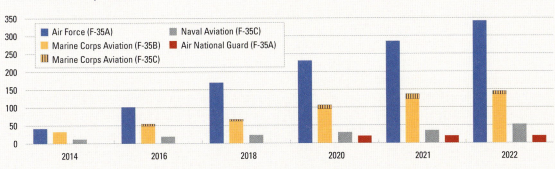

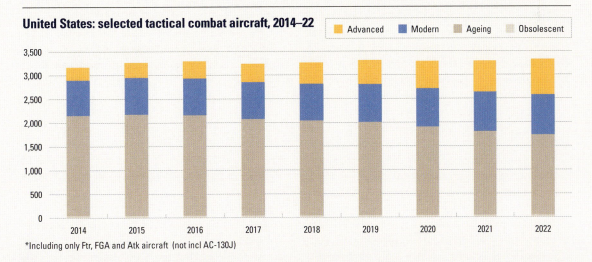

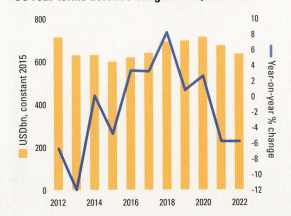

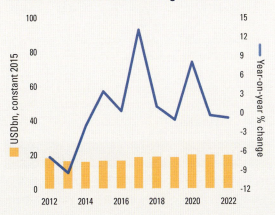

North America

Canada and the United States took strides to deepen cooperation over continental defence in 2022. It is increasingly acknowledged that both have important defence and security interests in the Arctic, the Atlantic and the Pacific. The year also saw the release of major strategic documents by the US. The unclassified versions released in the public domain are shorter than the classified versions for government but still contain important insights into US priorities. Washington also released an Arctic strategy. For its part, Canada stepped up its maritime deployments to the Indo-Pacific and Europe and made progress on some key defence acquisitions, such as the future fighter programme. Both nations delivered defence assistance to Ukraine in the wake of Russia's full-scale invasion, with the US leading contributions from NATO Allies and partner states in terms of both political coordination and material assistance. Washington also increased its deployments to Europe, with forces increasing by over 20,000 in 2022. At the same time debates in the US over prioritisation continue, notwithstanding Russia's actions in Ukraine, because of China's military modernisation and deepening concern over its activities in the Indo-Pacific more generally, but particularly in relation to Taiwan. China is Washington's 'pacing challenge' and its principal security concern.

Shared continental security concerns led both states to re-establish in 2022 the Cross Border Crime Forum, which includes counter-terrorist and cyber-security collaboration as well as law enforcement cooperation over borders, travel and transportation. Both states, but especially the US, also remain concerned by security challenges from transnational organised criminal groups, including drug cartels active in Latin America. Importantly, Ottawa and Washington in 2022 took steps to upgrade the capabilities of the North American Aerospace Defense Command (NORAD) following a Joint Statement on NORAD Modernisation in 2021.

THE UNITED STATES

The Biden administration has led the international response to Russia's 2022 invasion of Ukraine, both politically and materially. Well before Moscow's troops crossed their start line, administration officials were briefing Ukraine's leaders with Washington's assessment of President Vladimir Putin's intent, with similar disclosures to other European leaders. And a public campaign saw the rapid declassification of intelligence pointing to indicators of Russian activity, alongside the significant amount of information derived from commercially available sources that was made available by civilian analysts. US officials have played key roles in coordinating defence assistance to Ukraine, and the US has delivered significant stocks including anti-armour weapons, various air- and missile-defence systems, and HARM anti-radiation missiles and artillery – particularly HIMARS rocket artillery. Nonetheless, the president has maintained a solid 'red line' against the commitment of any US forces. Military trainers were withdrawn from Ukraine in advance of 24 February. Meanwhile, the administration has been firm about the US commitment to NATO, deploying additional troops to Romania, Poland and the Baltic states, as well as bolstering the air and naval presence in Europe and being central to the movement to bring Finland and Sweden into the Alliance, following their application to join.

According to the 2022 National Defense Strategy (NDS), released in unclassified form in October, Russia is an 'acute' threat, but China is the pacing challenge for the Department of Defense (DoD). Indeed, the report continued, the 'most comprehensive and serious challenge to U.S. national security is the PRC's coercive and increasingly aggressive endeavor to refashion the Indo-Pacific region and the international system to suit its interests and authoritarian preferences'. The US is concerned by China's policy and military posture in relation to Taiwan, which it sees as part of this broader pattern of destabilising and coercive behaviour. In late October, Secretary of State Antony Blinken said Beijing had decided that the status quo over Taiwan was 'no longer acceptable, that they wanted to speed up the process by which they would pursue reunification', with the possibility that if pressure on Taiwan did not speed reunification Beijing could use force to meet its goals. Yet this view is not uniformly espoused in the administration, and there remains considerable debate internally over the likelihood of Chinese aggression against Taiwan, the most plausible time period and the form that any such attack might take. While the administration has sent select equipment to Ukraine, but not personnel, the president has leaned in a more assertive direction in East Asia. Without formally abandoning US 'strategic ambiguity' over Taiwan, President Joe Biden had, by October, stated on more than one occasion that he would likely send US combat forces to help Taiwan defend itself in the event of a Chinese attack.

The modernisation of China's armed forces remains the principal driver of US policy attention and capability development. Washington believes Beijing 'has modernized and expanded nearly every aspect' of the People's Liberation Army (PLA) and that China is focused on offsetting US military advantage. The NDS says that the PLA is 'rapidly advancing and integrating its space, counterspace, cyber, electronic, and informational warfare capabilities to support its holistic approach to joint warfare', and that it is also speeding and expanding nuclear modernisation.

To deliver a force able to 'strengthen and sustain deterrence, and to prevail in conflict if necessary', the DoD says in the NDS that it will prioritise a force that possesses capabilities that can 'penetrate adversary defenses at range', that 'securely and effectively provides logistics and sustainment to continue operations in a contested and degraded environment', that maintains information and decision advantage and is able to rapidly mobilise force and generate combat power. Integrated with the NDS were unclassified versions of the Nuclear Posture Review (NPR) and Missile Defense Review. DoD did not release an unclassified space strategy. The NPR reflects international tensions in its language and also seems to balance the revived move to retire older systems such as the B83 gravity bomb, as well as the cancellation of the development agreed by the Trump administration of the nuclear-armed sea-launched cruise missile, with maintenance of other developments agreed during the Trump-era. These include the low-yield warhead for *Trident* II (the W76-2), the life extension to the B61 gravity bomb (the B61-12) and the developmental Long-Range Standoff weapon. Also prominent were commitments to upgrade all legs of the nuclear triad, make nuclear command and control more resilient, and expand the capability of the National Nuclear Safety Agency to produce 'plutonium pits' for nuclear weapons. For its part, the Missile Defense Review reflected a growing diversity and sophistication of threats, indicating the need for sensors and command-and-control systems to be able to operate more seamlessly and rapidly across the threat landscape, though with minimal detail overall in the unclassified version on plans for meeting these challenges.

Meeting ambition

A key challenge for the DoD will lie in delivering on the ambitions contained in its strategy documents, not simply in terms of military capability development and maintaining the funding needed to support these but also in relation to the broader capabilities required to support its ambitions – for instance in national defence industry, the supply chain and innovation. Moreover, the DoD and the national security establishment and industry need to meet these requirements at the right timescale – not only during what the Biden administration's 2022 National Security Strategy called the 'decisive decade' of the next ten years, but beyond that. At the same time, it must cope with the prioritisation problem highlighted by actual and potential threats to security in Europe as well as in the Indo-Pacific. But these are not new problems. And much of the rhetoric in the Biden administration's strategic documents will be familiar to readers of recent versions, even if there was more on the importance of allies and partners than before. Indeed, in early November 2022, Under Secretary of Defense Colin Kahl described the 2022 NDS as in some ways just the next iteration of the 2018 version, issued under the leadership of president Donald Trump and secretary of defense Jim Mattis. But after nearly two years in office, perhaps the most striking aspect of the Biden administration's defence and military policy, under Secretary of Defense Lloyd Austin, is its broad continuity – from the Trump administration as well as the last major military initiatives of the Obama years and the bipartisan agreement on how to size, structure, modernise and fund the US defence establishment.

In practical terms, these conceptual and rhetorical initiatives help justify the significant emphasis on research, development, test and evaluation (RDT&E). The RDT&E budget is now greater than USD130 billion annually, an historic high that considerably exceeds the full investment budget of the rest of NATO combined. These investments have reached such a scale largely because systems that have been at the conceptual or laboratory level for years are now reaching advanced prototyping and field-testing phases, with low-level production to follow.

Investments have also led to the creation of a Pacific Deterrence Initiative to complement the European Deterrence Initiative developed after Russia's aggressions against Ukraine from 2014. The Pacific Deterrence Initiative's funding stands at about USD6bn compared with USD4bn for Europe in the president's 2023 budget request. The plan helps with infrastructure modernisation, enhanced training initiatives – including in the Indo-Pacific with the other 'Quadrilateral Security Dialogue' nations of India, Japan and Australia – and greater targeted experimentation and research (including with Australia and the United Kingdom under the AUKUS arrangement of 2021). To date, however, it has not led to significant changes to US posture, at least in the broader Indo-Pacific. Modest alterations continue, such as deployment changes of a few thousand troops at most in Guam and in Australia. Moreover, according to analysts, it remains unclear if the Pentagon is moving quickly enough to address acute gaps and vulnerabilities, such as shortages of sensors and munitions that would be useful in helping Taiwan fend off possible Chinese attack and vulnerabilities in military and national infrastructural command and control, or alternatives to forward-located airfields and aircraft carriers that could survive possible Chinese pre-emption in any war.

Meanwhile, the documents also note the challenge from what the NDS termed 'persistent threats' from North Korea, Iran and violent extremist organisations. Their persistence perhaps helps explain why the shift towards great-power competition has been constrained in scope, pace, and overall strategic effect within the DoD. Under the updated force-planning construct, the joint force is intended to 'simultaneously defend the homeland, maintain strategic deterrence and deter and, if necessary, prevail in conflict'. However, the precise force-sizing construct remains unclear from the public document. Risk-mitigation efforts 'rooted in integrated deterrence' are seen as key to deterring 'opportunistic aggression' if the US is involved in an 'all domain conflict'. Cooperation with allies is seen as key, as is the US nuclear deterrent and other capabilities such as space and cyber. But the force is also meant to have the ability to 'respond to small-scale, short-duration crises without substantially impairing high-end warfighting readiness'. Washington is looking to build strength in key areas, including surveillance and decision systems, 'particularly in the space domain', hardening its command-and-control networks and developing systems that can 'mitigate adversary anti-access/area-denial capability'. It was noteworthy that the NDS also highlighted the need to improve logistics and sustainment, reinforcing the US ability to 'quickly mobilise and deploy' forces in the face of denial operations.

But the sustainment reference points to other concerns, including not only those highlighted by growing strategic competition with China but also those deriving from the war in Ukraine, and related to security of supply and weapons stocks. It is significant that in 2022 defence officials have paid numerous visits to US defence plants at varying positions in the supply chain. Measures being considered include mitigating vulnerabilities in the current supply chain and improving innovation and planning for procurement mechanisms that can help industry develop or maintain the capability to boost production. But although investments may be growing, and US strategic logic increasingly shifts to a paramount focus on China, there remains much continuity in force structure and in strategy. While the defence debate suggests a desire for greater change, actual adjustments have so far occurred more slowly.

This may change with the influx of greater resources into the Pentagon. Since the mid-2010s, there has been a notable defence-budget build-up in the US. The process began under former secretary of defense Mattis, whose 2018 NDS called for 'additional resources in a sustained effort to solidify our competitive advantage'. That objective has been largely attained over the ensuing half decade even if, during the Biden years, it has been sustained more by Congress than by the administration. Vast spending on COVID-19 relief made it hard even for fiscal hawks and defence doves to turn off the tap, while inflation pressures have further strengthened the argument in the course of 2022 for large defence outlays. And Congress has added tens of billions of dollars to the requested defence budget in each of the first two years of the Biden presidency. Nonetheless, these sums need to be focused correctly, provide quality and quantity, and deliver on the range of technologies and systems for this and the next generation of US armed forces.

US Army

The US Army is focused on regenerating its capability for large-scale combat operations under its Multi-Domain Operations (MDO) concept. These plans pre-date Russia's full-scale invasion of Ukraine in February 2022, but that conflict has influenced thinking in key areas. These include the importance of being able to conduct effective combined-arms warfare at scale, precision long-range firepower and mobile air- and missile-defence capabilities. Integrating lessons drawn from Ukraine delayed the official publication of MDO as army doctrine, though the updated document – FM 3-0, Operations – was eventually published in October.

Moving into 2022, the army had already identified a number of 'critical gaps' in the design of its current divisional structures, and new divisional structures proposed under its Waypoint 2028–2029 initiative are intended to help overcome these shortcomings. Under these proposals, the 1st Cavalry Division (and likely the 1st Armored Division) will restructure as 'Penetration Divisions', each retaining three Armored Brigade Combat Teams (ABCTs), but with the addition of an organic engineering brigade, a dedicated division-level armoured cavalry squadron and an extra artillery battalion to be equipped with the forthcoming 155mm M1299 Extended Range Cannon Artillery system. These changes are intended to make the revised formations better able to conduct breakthrough operations against peer opponents in defensive positions. The Army National Guard is also expected to form its own Penetration Division, with the realignment of existing brigades under the 34th Infantry Division's headquarters.

The remaining nine active force ABCTs and medium-weight Stryker Brigade Combat Teams (SBCTs) based in the continental US (CONUS) seem set to be redistributed into three 'heavy divisions' comprising two ABCTs and one SBCT each. These divisions will lack the dedicated division-level assets available to the two Penetration Divisions and serve instead as general-purpose heavy armoured and mechanised formations.

With the Optionally Manned Fighting Vehicle programme still in the prototyping stage, and not expected to begin being issued to units until 2029, the army is now taking delivery of upgraded M2A4 *Bradley* variants, and the first unit set was issued in early 2022. Development efforts in the Robotic Combat Vehicle uninhabited ground vehicle programme have been refocused, with work on medium-weight fire-support platforms deferred in favour of lighter, reconnaissance-oriented systems.

Under Waypoint 2028–2029, the 10th Mountain and 25th Infantry Divisions will likely become 'Light Divisions' and the 82nd Airborne and 101st Air Assault Divisions 'Joint Forcible Entry Divisions'. All of these divisions will receive a new light tank battalion operating the General Dynamics *Griffin* II design selected to fulfil the Mobile Protected Firepower (MPF) programme requirement in June 2022. Original plans to assign an MPF company to each Brigade Combat Team have been dropped following concerns about overloading brigade headquarters staff. The 82nd and 101st will also receive a dedicated cavalry squadron for divisional reconnaissance, but the Light Divisions will not. The newly formed 11th Airborne Division, created from US Army Alaska in mid-2022, may retain a tailored structure due to its role as the army's dedicated Arctic and extreme cold-weather operations formation.

All of the new divisional designs will also receive a new combat support brigade with engineer, chemical, biological, radiological and nuclear, military police battalions and a short-range air-defence battalion operating the new M-SHORAD system to counter helicopters and UAVs. M-SHORAD was first fielded in Germany in 2021, and the first CONUS-based M-SHORAD battalions began activating in 2022. The army plans to take delivery of its first platoon of M-SHORAD Increment 2 (Directed Energy) systems by the end of 2022 to go alongside the already-issued production models of the M-SHORAD Increment 1 (Kinetic Effect) system.

There has been a significant short-term expansion of the army's presence in Europe following Russia's invasion of Ukraine. By May 2022, this had grown to 45,000 personnel, with a full corps headquarters, two division headquarters, two further ABCTs and one airborne brigade combat team deployed in addition to regular forward-based and rotational forces. Balancing these deployments, the army has also continued to adjust its long-term posture elsewhere. Having previously ended its ABCT rotations to the Middle East, the transfer of the Korea Rotational Force deployment from an ABCT to an SBCT in late 2022 means that the vast majority of the army's heavy armour is now concentrated in Europe and CONUS. In the Pacific, the army has instead focused on lighter forces, and longer-range missile capabilities, with the establishment of an additional brigade-level Multi-Domain Task Force (MDTF) included in the president's FY2023 budget. This third MDTF was officially established in Hawaii at the end of September 2022.

The army's new theatre-missile capabilities, including the short-range Precision Strike Missile (PrSM), will not start to be fielded until 2023, although deliveries of the first modernised M270A2 multiple-launch rocket system, one of the intended launch platforms for PrSM, began in mid-2022. The Future Attack Reconnaissance Aircraft programme, intended to replace the retired OH-58D *Kiowa* helicopter, appears to be behind schedule, with the competitive demonstration phase now delayed until at least late 2023. On 5 December 2022, the army announced it had selected the Bell-Textron V-280 *Valor* as their chosen option to replace the ubiquitous UH-60 *Black Hawk* under the Future Long-Range Assault Aircraft programme.

US Navy

The US Navy is still struggling to deal with the growing challenge from China and multiple other demands. Several proposals to address the navy's future fleet size and structure have been forthcoming. These involve varying combinations of large and small surface combatants and uninhabited vehicles of various descriptions.

Perhaps the most notable is the new Navigation Plan from the Chief of Naval Operations, Admiral Michael Gilday. Released in July 2022, the goals outlined included 12 nuclear-powered aircraft carriers, 66 tactical submarines, 96 large and 56 small surface combatants (as part of a force design for 373 crewed vessels, to be achieved by 2045), and approximately 150 uninhabited surface and subsurface platforms.

Gilday also argued that industrial capacity needs to increase, as it is the greatest obstacle to growing the fleet. However, the US Navy is also facing friction with Congress over its shipbuilding plans and its efforts to decommission older vessels in order to focus on newer capabilities and future programmes.

Five of the US Navy's *Ticonderoga*-class cruisers were among the ships decommissioned in FY2022, and nearly 40 more vessels are slated by the navy for decommissioning in FY2023, although Congress was seeking to prevent a significant number of these planned retirements. All the *Ticonderoga*s are scheduled to leave the fleet by 2027, a significant loss of vertical launch system firepower that will not be replaced straight away by the arrival of new Flight III *Arleigh Burke*-class destroyers, despite various proposals to try to accelerate destroyer construction.

In 2022, one new destroyer commissioned up to November, while two Flight IV *Virginia*-class nuclear-powered guided-missile submarines joined the fleet, plus the 12th *San Antonio*-class landing platform dock, to a slightly improved design. A keel-laying ceremony took place in June 2022 for the first of the new *Columbia*-class nuclear-powered ballistic-missile submarines, although concerns are mounting as to whether these vessels – the navy's top procurement priority – will remain on schedule. The ceremonial keel laying for the third *Gerald R. Ford*-class carrier, the new USS *Enterprise*, took place in August. The same month, construction began on the first of the *Constellation*-class frigates.

Efforts to maintain and refurbish the existing fleet continue to be challenged by high operational demands as well as maintenance backlogs. The Ukraine war saw the extended deployment to the Mediterranean of an aircraft carrier (initially the USS *Harry S. Truman*, replaced by the USS *George H. W. Bush*), while in early 2022 the navy surged four additional destroyers into the European theatre. Separately, in June, the Biden administration announced that two additional destroyers would be forward deployed to Europe, bringing the total forward-deployed presence to six.

In the Indo-Pacific, deployments remained at a high tempo, including a number of freedom-of-navigation transits of the Taiwan Strait during 2022. The latest *Rim of the Pacific* exercise included significantly greater integration of uninhabited platforms. The LHA USS *Tripoli* also carried out a further test of the 'Lightning carrier' with a record 20 Lockheed Martin F-35B *Lightning* II aircraft aboard, potentially adding options to US Navy aviation operations at sea.

The latest update to the US Marine Corps' Force Design 2030 plan to make the force more agile included an increased emphasis on reconnaissance and counter-reconnaissance to both strike and hide. The first Marine Littoral Regiment was formed in March with the re-designation of the 3rd Marine Regiment. The plan intends to make the marines more expeditionary, more focused on long-range missile strikes, less dependent on centralised command, control, communications and intelligence support, and generally more focused on China. The USMC is looking to diversify its footprint in the Asia-Pacific region in particular, and the goals of USMC Commandant General David Berger include helping joint-force commanders better monitor China and deter it from committing various 'gray zone' micro-aggressions as well as possible larger attacks in places such as Taiwan. The plan received considerable criticism from a number of senior retired USMC officers. Differences between the navy and the marines also appeared to be holding up plans for a new light amphibious ship for dispersed operations, particularly in the Pacific.

For the US Coast Guard, top procurement priorities are a new class of medium-sized Offshore Patrol Cutters (OPCs) and new icebreakers. After delays, the first of up to 25 OPCs was due for completion in late 2022. A detailed design and construction contract for a second new heavy icebreaker, or Polar Security Cutter, was awarded at the end of 2021, with the first ship scheduled for delivery in the spring of 2025.

US Air Force

The US Air Force turned 75 in 2022, while the average age of a key fleet component – the Boeing KC-135 tanker – is 59. Although the KC-135 is a comparative outlier, the air force continues to grapple with the challenges of recapitalising a swathe of ageing types in its combat and support fleets at the same time as attempting to build combat capacity. There remains also a 1,650 shortfall in pilots and the wider demands of recruitment and retention.

The USAF continues to view China as the pacing challenge, but it is also confronted by the 'acute threat' of Russia. While the latter is more immediate, the former is more sustained and technologically demanding. Russia's war on Ukraine has reinforced concerns over Moscow's willingness to use military force, but the performance of its Aerospace Forces (VKS) in the conflict has so far been lacklustre at best.

The USAF is trying to employ a strategy centred on combat aircraft fleets to address the immediate challenge of Russia and the longer-term and more demanding issue of the build-up of Chinese airpower. It is far from a simple task, with the confluence of several long-term issues compounding the difficulty.

The combat aircraft fleet continues to decline in number and, along with the overall cut, the service will also see the number of types fielded reduced to four, the latter by design. Combat aircraft types will be reduced to the Boeing F-15EX *Eagle* II, Lockheed Martin F-16 *Fighting Falcon*, Lockheed Martin F-35A *Lightning* II, and Next Generation Air Dominance (NGAD) aircraft. The F-15C/D *Eagle*, F-15E *Strike Eagle* and Lockheed Martin F-22A *Raptor* will be retired over

the course of the next decade or so. The air force's plan to cut the size of the F-22A fleet, removing 33 Block 20 aircraft during FY2023 to free up additional funding for NGAD, met with political opposition.

The fall in total fleet numbers is due to ongoing and historical issues with the Lockheed Martin F-35 *Lightning* II. The aircraft's entry into service was delayed by years and it is now being bought at lower production rates than first envisaged. The F-35A, however, will provide a central element of the mass of the air force's future combat capability. Before then, however, several technical and financial concerns will need to be addressed. The air force is looking to the Block 4 development of the aircraft, combined with Technical Refresh 3 to allow the F-35 to operate against the advanced threats now envisaged. The air force has cautioned that these aircraft need to be affordable and delivered in time.

While there has been no indication yet of when a prototype, or prototypes, of the crewed element of NGAD will be made public, roll-out of the Northrop Grumman B-21 *Raider* bomber took place in December 2022. As of September 2022, six test aircraft were on the production line. The B-21 will operate alongside the KC-135 which, irrespective of its age, will remain in the inventory beyond 2040. The McDonnell Douglas KC-10 *Extender*, operated in far smaller numbers, will be retired during FY2024.

The KC-46A has now been cleared to refuel both the F-22A and F-35 (currently up to 97% of US aircraft) and was deployed on operations to Europe and the Middle East in 2022. However, the revised refuelling vision system required for initial operating capability (IOC) has been delayed again, this time to October 2025. Despite this, the USAF is reportedly considering dropping the KC-Y tanker programme contest altogether and bringing forward the planned KC-Z programme instead.

The first of 351 T-7A *Red Hawk* training aircraft, intended to replace the T-38C *Talon*, was delivered in April 2022. Boeing also delivered the first test MH-139A helicopters in August 2022 following a lengthy Federal Aviation Administration certification process. The MH-139 will replace the USAF ICBM force's venerable UH-1N models.

The HH-60W Combat Search and Rescue (CSAR) programme of record was cut by one-third in the president's FY2023 budget (from 113 to 75 helicopters) as the USAF reportedly re-examines its future CSAR requirements. This, in turn, has significantly increased the HH-60W's unit cost.

The USAF expects to divest an initial batch of A-10 attack aircraft in 2023, although retiring the whole fleet remains politically contentious. Nearly the entire C-130H fleet remained grounded well into October due to engine issues. The AIM-260 Joint Advanced Tactical Missile has not yet officially achieved its projected 2022 IOC, although it is reportedly in live-fire testing. The hypersonic AGM-183A Air-launched Rapid Response Weapon (ARRW) achieved its first successful live firings from a B-52 bomber in summer 2022, but the USAF has delayed any production decision on the system to 2023. In late 2022 the USAF selected a Raytheon and Northrop Grumman team to develop prototypes of its planned scramjet Hypersonic Attack Cruise Missile design.

Supply-chain issues delayed the planned launch of 28 Tranche 0 small satellites as part of the USSF proliferated low Earth orbit constellation test and demonstration phase from September 2022 to perhaps March 2023. Earlier in 2022, the USSF awarded contracts for the follow-on Tranche 1 satellites for the communications Transport Layer and missile-warning Tracking Layer constellations.

DEFENCE ECONOMICS

On 28 March 2022, the DoD submitted its Fiscal Year (FY) 2023 budget request to Congress with a top line DoD budget of USD773bn. Biden called the request 'one of the largest investments in our national security in history'.

The proposed discretionary budget request included USD29.8bn for Department of Energy atomic-energy defence activities and USD10.6bn for 'defense-related activities' carried out by the FBI and other government agencies. Defence-related discretionary spending amounts to USD813bn, with total DoD funding reaching USD827bn when mandatory spending is included.

Inflation, growth and purchasing power

According to the DoD announcement, the USD773bn top line request constitutes a 4.1% increase over the enacted 2022 defence budget of USD742bn, which itself included USD25.6bn in additional funding over President Biden's FY2022 request. However, some have questioned the accuracy of the announced 4.1% increase due to two developments that complicate year-on-year comparisons.

Firstly, Washington authorised USD14.3bn in supplemental defence spending during FY2022, which was tied to the US armed forces' withdrawal from Afghanistan (USD6.5bn), support for Ukraine (USD6.5bn) and other priorities. This additional spending increased the FY2022 DoD budget from USD742bn to USD757bn. Against this number, the Biden administration's FY2023 DoD budget only constitutes a 2.2% increase over FY2022. However, it is possible that additional DoD funds will be used to support Ukraine in FY2023, as the war has become a strategic priority for the Biden administration. In May, Congress passed a USD40bn Ukraine aid package that provided a framework for continuing military, economic and humanitarian support. In September, the administration requested an additional USD11.7bn for Ukraine as part of an emergency funding package to hedge against the likelihood of a 'continuing resolution', or temporary funding measure, starting in FY2023.

Even more important to the discussion of year-on-year growth is the impact of inflation on budget growth and purchasing power. Inflation estimates for the FY2023 budget request are tied to the GDP Price Index and an assumed average inflation rate of 2.2% during 2023. The defence budget's buying power will be eroded if inflation exceeds 2.2% on average over the course of 2023, as other indices and forecasts suggest.

Table 1 The US DoD budget request by appropriation title, USDm

Requests/ Enacted budget by Appropriation Title (USDm)	2022 DoD Requested	2022 Base Enacted	2023 DoD Base Requested	Change between FY2022 Enacted and FY23 Requested
Military Personnel	163,699	166,714	173,883	+7,169
Operations and Maintenance	292,299	294,550	309,343	+14,793
Procurement	143,256	145,212	145,939	+727
Research, Development, Testing, and Evaluation	107,456	118,787	130,097	+11,310
Military Construction	7,143	13,375	10,198	-3,177
Family Housing	1,401	1,525	1,956	+431
Revolving Management and Trust Funds	1,394	2,112	1,583	-529
Totals	**716,648**	**742,275**	**773,000**	**+30,725**

Source: Defense Comptroller, FY23 Defense Budget Overview Book, Appendix A, April 2022

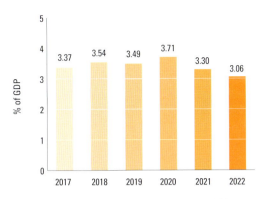

[1] Figures refer to the National Defense (050) Budget Function (Budget Authority) as a % of GDP

▲ Figure 1 **US defence budget** as % of GDP[1]

As the FY2023 budget passed through Congress, various uplifts were proposed for the defence budget amid concerns over the effects of inflation on the DoD's purchasing power and on its ability to meet the challenges of an increasingly tense security environment. During summer 2022, three of the four congressional committees charged with marking up the administration's FY2023 budget recommended funding increases ranging from USD37bn to USD44bn. The House and Senate armed services committees agreed on the FY2023 National Defense Authorization Act (NDAA) on 6 December with a final figure of USD878bn for defence, USD45bn above the presidential request. However, Congress failed to pass the FY2023 spending bill by 30 September 2022, the end of the US fiscal year. Instead, it enacted a continuing resolution that would maintain funding levels for all government departments until 16 December 2022. The resolution also prevents the DoD from using the level funding for new or accelerated production or certain multi-year procurements.

Pacing, acute and persistent challenges
The FY2023 budget is linked to the threat perceptions and objectives articulated in the 2021 Interim National Security Strategic Guidance and the NDS. A classified version of the NDS was sent to Congress on the same day as the FY2023 budget was released in March 2022, with the unclassified version released in October.

According to the budget-release document and March 2022 NDS fact sheet, the USD773bn proposed budget is principally designed to provide the capabilities to deter and compete with China – identified as the United States' 'most consequential strategic competitor' and pacing challenge. The budget must also balance the Pentagon's focus on China with the need to meet other kinetic and non-kinetic threats to the US homeland as well as US allies, interests and personnel.

For its part, Russia constitutes an immediate and acute threat, while the NDS summary and budget document commit the US to working with NATO allies and Kyiv to repel Russia's invasion of Ukraine. 'Persistent threats' from Iran, North Korea and violent extremist groups are also of concern as are pandemics and other 'transboundary challenges'. The budget '[devotes] more than USD3bn to address the effects of climate change' by improving installation resilience and adaptation to climate challenges.

Integrated deterrence, campaigning and building advantage
The FY2023 budget request stresses three activities and investment areas central to realising the NDS. Integrated deterrence – a point of emphasis for the DoD throughout the Biden administration – revolves around integrating and coordinating activities across all domains and all instruments of national power.

In the FY2023 defence budget, integrated deterrence is supported through emphasis on the modernisation, development and procurement of capabilities in several areas. Most notably, the FY2023 budget allocates USD34.4bn to modernise all three legs of the US nuclear triad – up from USD27.7bn in the FY2022 request. It also includes USD24.7bn in funding for capabilities to defend against and defeat missile threats, up from USD20.4bn in the FY2022 DoD request.

Meanwhile, key FY2023 investments in campaigning (which the NDS describes as 'the conduct and sequencing of logically linked military activities to achieve strategy-aligned objectives over time') include the USD6.1bn Pacific Deterrence

Table 2 **US DoD FY2023 budget request vs House and Senate Armed Services and Appropriations Committees' proposed defence budgets, USDbn**

Committee / Organisation	Recommended DoD Budget
House Appropriations Committee	762 billion
Department of Defense Request	773 billion
House Armed Services Committee	839 billion
Senate Armed Services Committee	847 billion
Senate Appropriations Committee	850 billion

Source: "Senate appropriators seek $850 billion for defense, largest total of 4 key committees", Breaking Defense, 28 July 2022

Initiative and the USD4.2bn European Deterrence Initiative, both of which intersect with the broader integrated deterrence approach.

The FY2023 DoD budget request also prioritises DoD's plan to build advantage by investing in innovation and modernisation as well as industrial capability. The DoD's RDT&E requests have been important in funding modernisation projects in recent years. The FY2023 RDT&E request, at USD130bn, was USD11bn higher than the USD119bn enacted in FY22, itself a record amount. Priorities within this broad category of spending include investment in science and technology, artificial intelligence, microelectronics, 5G, and an Industrial Base Analysis and Sustainment (IBAS) programme to strengthen the US defence-related supply chain. The FY2023 budget's IBAS programme will focus on building capacity in chemical production, bio-manufacturing and rare-earth element supply chains.

A people-friendly budget

The Pentagon is also looking to improve recruitment and retention, and the FY2023 budget includes a 4.6% pay rise for military and civilian personnel – the largest in 20 years for military personnel – among several other programmes to 'cultivate [the US] military and civilian workforce, grow [DoD] talent, build resilience and force readiness'.

The pay rise and funding of a USD15/hour minimum wage for the federal workforce also serves as a measure to offset the effects of what could be a prolonged period of inflation volatility. Personnel investments also include several measures to 'ensure accountable leadership' and build a more diverse and equitable workforce. These include USD479 million to implement the recommendations of the Independent Review Commission on Sexual Assault in the Military; USD34m to help the DoD deter, detect and address 'extremism in the ranks'; and development and implementation of talent-management initiatives that improve racial and gender diversity at key points in the military-career lifecycle.

Military departments and armed services

The FY2023 request reveals uplifts to the budgets of the DoD's military departments, though the Department of the Air Force (including the US Space Force (USSF)) and the Department of the Navy (including the US Marine Corps (USMC)) receive significantly larger increases than the Department of the Army.

The Department of the Air Force technically has the highest budget and received the biggest increase in funding, at USD11.8bn. Modernisation efforts across both the US Air Force (USAF) and the USSF are crucial to supporting the air force's seven 'operational imperatives': 1) establishing space resiliency; 2) achieving an operationally optimised Advanced Battle Management System (ABMS), the air force's contribution to the DoD's Joint All-Domain Command and Control (JADC2); 3) advancing development of the sixth-generation Next Generation Air Dominance family of systems; 4) achieving more target engagements at scale; 5) defining optimised, resilient basing, sustainment and communications; 6) defining the family of systems supporting the B-21 long-range strike capability; and 7) transitioning to a wartime posture against a peer competitor.

Nonetheless, funding issues threaten to slow air force and space force modernisation precisely as there is increasing demand for USAF capabilities to help maintain deterrence in the Indo-Pacific. It should also be noted that the overall Department of the Air Force FY2023 budget is distorted by USD40.2bn in pass-through funding (USD41.4bn in FY22), which is allocated to, but not controlled by, the USAF and which usually funds classified or non-disclosed programmes. Moreover, of the remaining USD194bn, USD170bn goes to the air force (22% of the total FY2023 budget request) while USD24.5bn (3% of the total budget request) goes to the space force. This means the overall USAF budget is less than that of the US Army.

As a result, the USAF is increasingly looking to divest legacy systems to free up funds to reinvest in more modern capabilities. The FY2023 budget calls for the retirement of 150 aircraft, the transfer of 100 MQ-9 *Reaper* uninhabited aerial vehicles (UAVs) to another government agency, as well as the divestment of 1,463 aircraft during the Future Years

---

Table 3 **The US DoD total budget request by military service, USDm**

Requested/ Enacted budget by service (USDm)	FY22 Enacted	FY2023 Requested Budget (USDm)	Difference between FY2022 and FY2023	% of Total Base Topline Request for FY2023
Army	174,854	177,315	+2,461	22.9
Navy	221,302	230,848	+9,546	28.9
Air Force	222,279	234,116	+11,837	30.3
Defense Wide	138,125	130,721	-7,404	16.9
Total	**756,560**	**773,000**	**+16,640**	**100**

Source: Defense Comptroller, FY23 Defense Budget Overview Book, Appendix A, April 2022

Defense Program (FYDP). The same FYDP calls for the procurement of just 467 aircraft, just under 90 of which are to be procured in FY2023, including 15 F-35A and F-15EX combat aircraft.

The FY2023 budget increases the Department of the Navy's budget by USD9.5bn over the enacted FY2022 budget with more funding across military personnel, maintenance and operations, procurement, and RDT&E. Procurement funding is set at USD27.9bn for nine battle-force ships, including two Block V *Virginia*-class attack submarines, two *Arleigh Burke*-class destroyers, one *Constellation*-class frigate, incremental funding for the *Columbia*-class ballistic-missile submarine, and four support and logistics ships. Another USD16.8bn is dedicated to the procurement of 96 fixed-wing, rotary-wing, and uncrewed aircraft with plans to buy 15 F-35Bs and 13 F-35Cs. The budget also includes USD4.7bn for weapons procurement.

As with the USAF, the US Navy (USN) and the USMC budgets include platform retirements to free up funds for modernisation. For the USN, the budget envisions the retirement of 12 ships in FY2023 and 24 over the course of the FYDP, including 16 before the end of their service life. The USMC budget stresses the need to continue the retirement of 'legacy capabilities and excess capacity' while the force 'reallocates savings for initiatives that support readiness' and the USMC's Force Design 2030.

The Department of the Army budget has the least overall growth, at USD2.5bn. This reflects the continuing transition from 20 years of counter-terrorism and counter-insurgency operations to preparing for high-intensity large-scale operations.

Interestingly, even though the RDT&E budget is the highest it has ever been, both army RDT&E and procurement funding have decreased in the FY2023 budget request. Funding for military personnel sees the biggest increase, at USD2.9bn, reflecting the strong emphasis placed in the budget request on 'the army's most enduring advantage': its 'highly qualified and capable people'. The army budget request also

Table 4 US National Defense Budget Function and other selected budgets, 2000, 2010–23

USD in billions, current-year dollars	National Defense Budget Function		Atomic Energy Defense Activities	Other Defense Activities	Total National Defense			Department of Homeland Security	Department of Veterans' Affairs	Total Federal Government Outlays	Total Federal Budget Surplus/Deficit
					Discretionary						
FY	BA	Outlay	BA	BA	BA	BA	Outlay	BA	BA		
2000	290.3	281.0	12.4	1.3	304.0	300.8	294.4	13.8	45.5	1,789.0	236.2
2010	695.6	666.7	18.2	7.3	721.2	714.1	693.5	45.4	124.3	3,457.1	-1,294.4
2011	691.5	678.1	18.5	7.0	717.0	710.1	705.6	41.6	122.8	3,603.1	-1,299.6
2012	655.4	650.9	18.3	7.7	681.4	669.6	677.9	45.9	124.0	3,526.6	-1,076.6
2013	585.2	607.8	17.5	7.4	610.2	600.4	633.4	61.9	136.0	3,454.9	-679.8
2014	595.7	577.9	18.4	8.2	622.3	606.2	603.5	44.1	165.7	3,506.3	-484.8
2015	570.8	562.5	19.0	8.5	598.4	585.9	589.7	45.3	160.5	3,691.9	-442.0
2016	595.7	565.4	20.1	8.3	624.1	606.8	593.4	46.0	163.3	3,852.6	-584.7
2017	626.2	568.9	21.4	8.7	656.3	634.1	598.7	62.3	178.8	3,981.6	-665.4
2018	694.5	600.7	23.3	9.0	726.8	700.9	631.2	103.0	191.8	4,109.0	-779.1
2019	712.6	654.0	24.0	9.1	745.7	718.8	686.0	61.4	194.2	4,447.0	-983.6
2020	738.8	690.4	26.0	9.7	774.5	756.6	724.6	114.2	233.3	6,553.6	-3,132.4
2021	719.5	717.6	29.4	10.8	759.6	741.7	753.9	123.2	255.4	6,822.4	-2,775.3
2022*	727.0	741.0	29.5	10.1	766.6	753.7	779.7	71.4	257.9	5,851.6	-1,415.0
2023*	784.0	767.6	31.8	11.1	827.0	813.4	808.6	76.5	296.7	5,792.0	-1,153.9

Notes

FY = Fiscal Year (1 October–30 September)

* (request)

[1] The National Defense Budget Function subsumes funding for the DoD, the Department of Energy Atomic Energy Defense Activities and some smaller support agencies (including Federal Emergency Management and Selective Service System). It does not include funding for International Security Assistance (under International Affairs), the Veterans Administration, the US Coast Guard (Department of Homeland Security), nor for the National Aeronautics and Space Administration (NASA). Funding for civil projects administered by the DoD is excluded from the figures cited here.

[2] Early in each calendar year, the US government presents its defence budget to Congress for the next fiscal year, which begins on 1 October. The government also presents its Future Years Defense Program (FYDP), which covers the next fiscal year plus the following five. Until approved by Congress, the budget is called the Budget Request; after approval, it becomes the Budget Authority (BA).

CANADA

Canada's defence minister, Anita Anand, said at the June 2022 IISS Shangri-La Dialogue that Canada is 'an Atlantic, Arctic and Pacific nation'. The challenges that this presents for the country were underscored during the year, with perceived security concerns emerging on all three fronts.

Following the invasion of Ukraine, the government unveiled in April an uplift of CAD8bn (USD6.3bn) in defence spending over five years. Accompanying the budget move was the announcement of a new defence policy review – billed as an update of the 2017 review proposition entitled 'Strong, Secure, Engaged' – because of the requirement 'to reassess Canada's role, priorities and needs in the face of a changing world'.

In Europe, Canada sought to adjust and bolster, to a degree, its contributions. Its training mission in Ukraine, *Operation Unifier*, was paused weeks before the start of hostilities with the intention to relocate it outside Ukraine. It was announced in August that up to 225 personnel would resume the training effort based in the United Kingdom, initially for four months. Canadian military aid to Ukraine has included M777 howitzers, replacement barrels and funding for 20,000 rounds of 155mm ammunition. It also redeployed its military air transport detachment in the Middle East of two C-130J *Hercules* transport aircraft to the UK to help with the Ukraine military aid effort.

Under its *Operation Reassurance* mission to support NATO, Canadian personnel deployed to Poland for several months to support the reception of Ukrainian refugees there. Other modest enhancements included the addition of a battery of four M777 howitzers and personnel to join the 540 Canadian personnel leading the NATO Enhanced Presence Battlegroup in Latvia. Canada also deployed two *Halifax*-class frigates on NATO operations during 2022 as well as two *Kingston*-class mine-countermeasures vessels. Ottawa also assigned a CP-140M *Aurora* (P-3 *Orion*) Maritime Patrol aircraft to NATO from February to July and deployed from August to December 2022 a new rotation of six CF-18 (F/A-18) *Hornet* combat aircraft to the enhanced NATO Air Policing Mission in Romania.

More broadly for Canada, Russia's 2022 invasion increased security concerns over the Arctic and may have helped to stimulate a renewed focus in Ottawa on the defence and security aspects of Canada's interests there.

The significant modernisation and upgrading that Canada announced in June to its NORAD capabilities was partly a reflection of this. The government said it would invest in an Arctic over-the-horizon radar system, a polar over-the-horizon radar system, and a new network of sensors called *Crossbow* distributed across northern Canada. These plans also reignited debates in Canada over missile defence more broadly. Prime Minister Justin Trudeau attended Canada's signature Arctic exercise *Operation Nanook* in August. NATO Secretary-General Jens Stoltenberg undertook his first official visit to Canada's Arctic at the same time. Meanwhile, Canada hosted the first meeting since 2014 of chiefs of defence of Arctic nations (without Russia). The Canadian Navy has enhanced its presence in the region, including extended deployments by the first two of its new *Harry DeWolf*-class Arctic Offshore Patrol Ships; the third of the class was delivered to the navy in September.

Meanwhile, Canada sought to enhance its presence in the Indo-Pacific, including a two-frigate deployment during 2022. One of the ships, HMCS *Vancouver*, joined a US Navy destroyer on a transit of the Taiwan Strait in September. The same vessel undertook operations to support implementation of UN sanctions against North Korea, maintaining a task also performed by Canadian vessels in previous years.

At the end of March, Ottawa finally chose the Lockheed Martin F-35A *Lightning* II as its preferred bidder for its future combat aircraft programme. But the delivery targets are challenging, with a requirement for the first nine aircraft to be in service by December 2027 and all 88 of the planned aircraft to be in service by 2031.

Concerns remain over costs and the timetable for the navy's new Canadian Surface Combatant, for which Lockheed Martin is the prime contractor with a heavily modified version of the UK Type-26 Global Combat Ship design. Likewise, the new *Protecteur*-class Joint Support Ships appeared to be further delayed, with deliveries of the two vessels now expected in 2025 and 2027 respectively. As a result, Canada has extended the lease on its interim converted auxiliary *Asterix*.

Arms procurements and deliveries – North America
Significant events in 2022

FEBRUARY — LOCKHEED'S AEROJET ACQUISITION FALLS THROUGH

Objections by the US Federal Trade Commission (FTC) halted Lockheed Martin's (LM) planned USD4.4bn acquisition, through its wholly-owned subsidiary Mizar Sub, of Aerojet Rocketdyne Holdings (Aerojet). A month before, the FTC had expressed concern that the buyout might harm competition, saying that Aerojet was the 'last independent supplier of key missile propulsion inputs' including solid propellant rocket motors (SRM). Northrop Grumman is the only other company competing against LM and Raytheon Technologies for missile programme contracts. Industrial consolidation means that Aerojet and Northrop Grumman currently hold over 90% of the SRM market in the US; two decades ago there were six SRM manufacturers. A February 2022 Pentagon report expressed concern regarding a lack of competition in several sectors, including SRM.

MARCH — CANADA FUTURE FIGHTER DECISION

Canada selected the Lockheed Martin F-35A *Lightning* II as the preferred bid to replace its ageing fleet of CF-18 *Hornets*. A contract for 88 aircraft is due to be awarded by the end of 2022. A shortlisting process in December 2021 eliminated Boeing's F/A-18E/F *Super Hornet*, with the final competitors being the F-35 and Saab's *Gripen* E. The project is valued at CAD15–19bn (USD11.74–14.87bn) and first deliveries are expected as early as 2025. However, this is not the first time Canada has selected the F-35. It joined the concept phase of the US Joint Strike Fighter programme in 1998 and, while in 2006 it postponed an acquisition decision, Ottawa agreed in July 2010 to buy the aircraft, with deliveries planned from 2016. The deal was cancelled in 2012, reportedly on cost grounds, and since then Canada has acquired 18 F/A-18A/B *Hornets* from Australia.

MAY — *JAVELIN* PRODUCTION RAMPS UP

In an interview, the CEO of Lockheed Martin discussed a plan to increase *Javelin* missile production from 2,100 to nearly 4,000 systems annually. The same month, it was announced that the Javelin Joint Venture (JJV), a partnership between Lockheed Martin and Raytheon Technologies, had been awarded two production contracts, worth USD309m, for *Javelin* missiles and support functions. After Russia's full-scale invasion of Ukraine, the US – along with other states – increased the number of *Javelin* systems that it shipped to Ukraine. In September, another contract, worth USD311m, was awarded for 1,800 *Javelins* to replenish US Army stocks. Meanwhile, there is focus also on the supplier base, so that firms can not only expand production but also mitigate dependencies on components from overseas. In November 2022, the US government announced that it had so far sent more than 8,500 *Javelins* to Ukraine. Production increases are also planned elsewhere: for example, the Pentagon is seeking to increase HIMARS production from 60 to 96 units a year.

AUGUST — F-35 ENGINE DECISION HEATS UP

GE Aviation announced that its prototype engine for the Adaptive Engine Transition Program (AETP), the XA100, passed the final tests as part of a USD1.01bn R&D contract awarded in 2016. The AETP seeks to improve the F-35's power generation, fuel efficiency and operational capability. The XA100 is designed to fit in the F-35A and F-35C without any structural modification, but it is not compatible with the F-35B. GE's competitor Pratt & Whitney supplies the F-135, the current F-35 engine, and is developing a modernisation package for it and a new engine prototype, dubbed XA101. Both prototypes are intended to provide 25% more fuel efficiency and 10% more thrust as well as greater power for future software blocks, which will be needed in future F-35 developments. An appraisal of whether the new engine or the upgrade should be pursued is due to be completed by February 2023.

Table 5 🇺🇸 United States: Next Generation Combat Vehicle (NGCV)

In 2014, the US cancelled the Ground Combat Vehicle programme, which had been designed to produce a series of replacement armoured vehicles for its Armored and Stryker Brigade Combat Teams, including for the 1980s-era M2 *Bradley* infantry fighting vehicle. Two years later, the army proposed the NGCV as the replacement programme. Indeed, the NGCV is now envisaged as one of the army's 'big six' modernisation priorities, but it encompasses five programmes at different stages of development.

The *Bradley* replacement effort is now called the Optionally Manned Fighting Vehicle (OMFV). This is in the concept-design phase and contracts were awarded to five industry teams in 2021. The army intends to give the next-stage contracts to three teams in 2023 with the aim to award a low-rate initial production (LRIP) contract in 2027.

The Armored Multi-Purpose Vehicle (AMPV) and the Mobile Protected Firepower (MPF) programmes are both now in low-rate production. The former will replace support versions of the M113 family of tracked vehicles with five variants and is potentially worth over USD15 billion. The AMPV has an improved version of the *Bradley* hull and, with approximately 5,000 M113s in US service, the programme has potential for expansion.

OMFV and AMPV are direct replacements for systems already in service, but the MPF project is intended to give Infantry Brigade Combat Teams (IBCTs) a direct precision-fire capability that they have not had before. Following a four-and-a-half-year 'middle-tier acquisition-rapid prototyping phase', the army selected General Dynamics' *Griffin*, which is based on the Austrian–Spanish ASCOD chassis. Vehicles will undergo further tests before unit deliveries begin in 2025.

The army has been experimenting with uninhabited ground systems for many years and in 2018 announced that it would pursue a Robotic Combat Vehicle (RCV) programme in three weight categories. In 2020, contracts were awarded to two industry teams for experimental prototype trials vehicles in the Light and Medium categories. These trials also featured modified M113 and *Stryker* vehicles acting as surrogates for Heavy RCVs. In mid-2022, the army announced that it would prioritise the Light variant and use it to inform development of the other two.

The least developed, yet potentially most expensive, of these programmes is the Decisive Lethality Platform (DLP), which is intended to replace the M1 *Abrams* main battle tank. The *Abrams* is currently undergoing SEPv3 upgrades; a further SEPv4 variant is planned later in the decade, and the army is exploring either a further iteration of *Abrams* or a brand-new design.

Programme		Classification	Replacing	Status	Quantity to be acquired	DoD-estimated total acquisition cost (USD billions)	Potential contractors	First unit equipped	Notes
Decisive Lethality Platform (DLP)		Main battle tank	M1 *Abrams*	Technical-analysis phase			tbd	tbd	Extent of programme likely dependent on RCV-H success
Optionally Manned Fighting Vehicle (OMFV)		Infantry fighting vehicle	M2 *Bradley*	Concept-design phase			tbd	2029	LRIP decision expected 2027
Armored Multi-Purpose Vehicle (AMPV)		Armoured personnel carrier (tracked)	M113	LRIP	2,897	15.33	BAE Systems Land & Armaments	2023	First LRIP contract awarded February 2019
Mobile Protected Firepower (MPF)		Light tank	New capability	LRIP	504	6.65	General Dynamics Land Systems	2025	First LRIP contract awarded June 2022
Robotic Combat Vehicle (RCV)	Heavy (RCV-H)	Heavy uninhabited ground vehicle	New capability	Tests conducted with surrogate systems			tbd	tbd	To weigh 18.1–27.2 tonnes
	Medium (RCV-M)	Medium uninhabited ground vehicle	New capability	Experimental prototype testing			tbd	tbd	To weigh 9.1–18.1 tonnes; EMD decision in FY2024
	Light (RCV-L)	Light uninhabited ground vehicle	New capability	Experimental prototype testing			tbd	2028	To weigh no more than 9.1 tonnes; EMD decision in FY2023

DoD = Department of Defense (US); EMD = engineering, manufacturing and development; tbd = to be decided

Table 6 🇺🇸 United States: fixed-wing combat aircraft exports, 2010–22

Country	Equipment	2010	2011	2012	2013	2014	2015	2016	2017	2018	2019	2020	2021	2022†
Australia	F-35A					2				8	8	14	12	12
Denmark	F-35A												4	2
Egypt	F-16C/D			7	20									
Iraq	F-16C/D					4	10	7	6	11				
Israel	F-35I							2	7	5	6	4	6	3
Italy	F-35A							6*	2*	2*	1*	2*	1*	3*
	F-35B									1*	1*	1*	1*	1*
Japan	F-35A							2	3 & 1*	4*	6*	6*	6*	4*
Korea, Republic of	F-15K	2	2	3										
	F-35A									6	7	11	12	4
Kuwait	F/A-18E/F												12	16
Morocco	F-16C/D	3	13	6										
Netherlands	F-35A			1	1						6 & 2*	5*	7*	8*
Norway	F-35A						2	2	6	6	6	6	6	3
Pakistan	F-16C/D	14	14	1										
Qatar	F-15QA												4	4	14
Saudi Arabia	F-15SA							4	29	19	21	11		
Singapore	F-15SG	4		2				8						
Turkey	F-16C/D		3	11										
	F-35A										2	2		
United Arab Emirates	F-16E/F	3	3	1										
United Kingdom	F-35B			2	1			5	6	3	1	3	3	3
Total = 579		**26**	**35**	**34**	**22**	**2**	**6**	**39**	**61**	**62**	**78**	**79**	**78**	**57**

*Final assembly outside the US †January–October

Canada CAN

Canadian Dollar CAD		2021	2022	2023
GDP	CAD	2.49tr	2.81tr	
	USD	1.99tr	2.20tr	
per capita	USD	52,015	56,794	
Growth	%	4.5	3.3	
Inflation	%	3.4	6.9	
Def exp [a]	CAD	32.8bn	35.5bn	
	USD	26.2bn	27.7bn	
Def bdgt [b]	CAD	29.1bn	31.5bn	
	USD	23.2bn	24.6bn	
USD1= CAD		1.25	1.28	

[a] NATO figure
[b] Department of National Defence and Veterans Affairs

Real-terms defence budget trend (USDbn, constant 2015)

Population 38,232,593

Age	0–14	15–19	20–24	25–29	30–64	65 plus
Male	8.1%	2.7%	2.8%	3.4%	23.4%	9.2%
Female	7.7%	2.6%	2.7%	3.1%	23.6%	10.8%

Capabilities

Canada's armed forces are focused principally on territorial defence, as well as contributing important capabilities to international missions, chiefly through NATO. The 2017 defence review reaffirmed commitments not only to NATO, but also to modernising capabilities, including cyber power. The review promised to increase regular and reserve forces, with particular enhancements in the areas of cyber and intelligence. In April 2022 the government announced a boost in defence spending over five years as a result of Russia's invasion of Ukraine and a new policy review to update thinking in light of the changed global environment. Canada's deployments, although relatively small in scale, underscore a determination to maintain both international engagement and power-projection capability. Canada's leadership of a NATO battlegroup in Latvia highlights a continuing capability to deploy medium-sized land formations. It has also contributed to NATO's air-policing mission and enhanced its European deployment in April 2022. Meanwhile, the deployments of frigates to the NATO theatre and the Pacific demonstrate continuing blue-water naval capabilities. In March 2022 it extended for a further year its coalition contribution to military capacity-building in Iraq, Jordan and Lebanon, with most personnel based in Kuwait. In June additional funding was announced including for NORAD modernisation. The 2017 review pledged to finally deliver on a range of delayed procurements. It raised the target for a future fighter capability to 88 aircraft and in March 2022 it was announced that the F-35A *Lightning* II had been selected. In the interim, Canada has been supplementing its existing fighter force with second-hand Australian F/A-18 *Hornets*. Despite continuing cost concerns, design work has progressed on the future Canadian Surface Combatant programme, based on the UK Type-26 frigate design, while the navy has received three of its six new Arctic Offshore Patrol Ships intended to enhance its Arctic operating capability. There is renewed focus on recruitment and retention, amid reports of personnel shortages and readiness problems; the Chief of Defence said in October that the force was reconstituting. Canada maintains a well-developed range of mainly small and medium-sized defence firms. The strongest sector is in combat vehicles and components, though the government is using its latest naval procurements to establish a long-term national shipbuilding strategy.

ACTIVE 66,500 (Army 22,500 Navy 12,600 Air Force 12,100 Other 19,300) **Gendarmerie & Paramilitary 4,500**

RESERVE 34,400 (Army 26,800 Navy 4,100 Air 2,000 Other 1,500)

ORGANISATIONS BY SERVICE

Space
EQUIPMENT BY TYPE
SATELLITES • SPACE SURVEILLANCE 1 *Sapphire*

Army 22,500
FORCES BY ROLE
MANOEUVRE
  Mechanised
  1 (1st) mech bde gp (1 armd regt, 2 mech inf bn, 1 lt inf bn, 1 arty regt, 1 cbt engr regt, 1 log bn)
  2 (2nd & 5th) mech bde gp (1 armd recce regt, 2 mech inf bn, 1 lt inf bn, 1 arty regt, 1 cbt engr regt, 1 log bn)
COMBAT SUPPORT
  1 engr regt
  3 MP pl
AIR DEFENCE
  1 AD regt
EQUIPMENT BY TYPE
ARMOURED FIGHTING VEHICLES
  MBT 82: 42 *Leopard* 2A4 (trg role); 20 *Leopard* 2A4M (upgraded); 20 *Leopard* 2A6M (52 *Leopard* 1C2 in store)
  RECCE ε120 LAV-25 *Coyote*
  IFV 550 LAV 6.0
  APC 443
    APC (T) 268: 235 M113; 33 M577 (CP)
    APC (W) 175 LAV *Bison* (incl 10 EW, 32 amb, 32 repair, 64 recovery)
  AUV 507: 7 *Cougar*; 500 TAPV
ENGINEERING & MAINTENANCE VEHICLES
  AEV 23: 5 *Buffalo*; 18 *Wisent* 2
  ARV 12 BPz-3 *Büffel*
ANTI-TANK/ANTI-INFRASTRUCTURE
  MSL • MANPATS TOW-2
  RCL 84mm *Carl Gustaf*
ARTILLERY 287
  TOWED 163 **105mm** 126: 98 C3 (M101); 28 LG1 MkII; **155mm** 37 M777
  MOR 124: **81mm** 100; **SP 81mm** 24 LAV *Bison*
UNINHABITED AERIAL VEHICLES • ISR • Light 5 RQ-21A *Blackjack*

Reserve Organisations 26,800

Canadian Rangers 5,300 Reservists

Provide a limited military presence in Canada's northern, coastal and isolated areas. Sovereignty, public-safety and surveillance roles

FORCES BY ROLE

MANOEUVRE
  Other
  5 (patrol) ranger gp (209 patrols)

Army Reserves 21,500 Reservists

Most units have only coy-sized establishments

FORCES BY ROLE

COMMAND
  10 bde gp HQ
MANOEUVRE
  Reconnaissance
  18 recce regt (sqn)
  Light
  51 inf regt (coy)
COMBAT SUPPORT
  16 fd arty regt (bty)
  3 indep fd arty bty
  10 cbt engr regt (coy)
  1 EW regt (sqn)
  4 int coy
  10 sigs regt (coy)
COMBAT SERVICE SUPPORT
  10 log bn (coy)
  3 MP coy

Royal Canadian Navy 12,600

EQUIPMENT BY TYPE

SUBMARINES 4
  SSK 4 *Victoria* (ex-UK *Upholder*) (of which 1 in long-term refit) with 6 single 533mm TT with Mk 48 HWT
PRINCIPAL SURFACE COMBATANTS • FRIGATES 12
  FFGHM 12 *Halifax* with 2 quad lnchr with RGM-84L *Harpoon* Block II AShM, 2 8-cell Mk 48 mod 0 VLS with RIM-162C ESSM SAM, 2 twin 324mm SVTT Mk 32 mod 9 ASTT with Mk 46 LWT, 1 Mk 15 *Phalanx* Block 1B CIWS, 1 57mm gun (capacity 1 CH-148 *Cyclone* ASW hel)
PATROL AND COASTAL COMBATANTS 2
  PSOH 2 *Harry DeWolf* (capacity 1 CH-148 *Cyclone* ASW hel)
MINE WARFARE • MINE COUNTERMEASURES 12
  MCO 12 *Kingston* (also used in patrol role)
LOGISTICS AND SUPPORT 10
  AORH 1 *Asterix* (*Resolve*) (capacity 2 CH-148 *Cyclone* ASW hel)
  AX 9: **AXL** 8 *Orca*; **AXS** 1 *Oriole*

Reserves 4,100 reservists

24 units tasked with crewing 10 of the 12 MCOs, harbour defence & naval control of shipping

Royal Canadian Air Force (RCAF) 12,100

FORCES BY ROLE

FIGHTER/GROUND ATTACK
  4 sqn with F/A-18A/B *Hornet* (CF-18AM/BM)
ANTI-SUBMARINE WARFARE
  2 sqn with CH-148 *Cyclone*
MARITIME PATROL
  2 sqn with P-3 *Orion* (CP-140M *Aurora*)
SEARCH & RESCUE/TRANSPORT
  3 sqn with AW101 *Merlin* (CH-149 *Cormorant*);
    C-130H/H-30 (CC-130) *Hercules*
  1 sqn with C295W (CC-295)
TANKER/TRANSPORT
  1 sqn with A310/A310 MRTT (CC-150/CC-150T)
  1 sqn with KC-130H
TRANSPORT
  1 sqn with C-17A (CC-177) *Globemaster*
  1 sqn with CL-600 (CC-144B)
  1 sqn with C-130J-30 (CC-130) *Hercules*
  1 (utl) sqn with DHC-6 (CC-138) *Twin Otter*
TRAINING
  1 OCU sqn with F/A-18A/B *Hornet* (CF-18AM/BM)
  1 OCU sqn with C-130H/H-30/J (CC-130) *Hercules*
  1 OCU sqn with CH-148 *Cyclone*
  1 OCU sqn with Bell 412 (CH-146 *Griffon*)
  1 sqn with P-3 *Orion* (CP-140M *Aurora*)
TRANSPORT HELICOPTER
  5 sqn with Bell 412 (CH-146 *Griffon*)
  3 (cbt spt) sqn with Bell 412 (CH-146 *Griffon*)
  1 (Spec Ops) sqn with Bell 412 (CH-146 *Griffon* – OPCON Canadian Special Operations Command)
  1 sqn with CH-47F (CH-147F) *Chinook*

EQUIPMENT BY TYPE

AIRCRAFT 110 combat capable
  FGA 96: 71 F/A-18A (CF-18AM) *Hornet*; 25 F/A-18B (CF-18BM) *Hornet*
  ASW 14 P-3 *Orion* (CP-140M *Aurora*)
  SAR 7 C295W (CC-295)
  TKR/TPT 5: 2 A310 MRTT (CC-150T); 3 KC-130H
  TPT 42: **Heavy** 5 C-17A (CC-177) *Globemaster* III; **Medium** 26: 7 C-130H (CC-130) *Hercules*; 2 C-130H-30 (CC-130) *Hercules*; 17 C-130J-30 (CC-130) *Hercules*; **Light** 4 DHC-6 (CC-138) *Twin Otter*; **PAX** 7: 3 A310 (CC-150 *Polaris*); 4 CL-600 (CC-144B/C)
  TRG 4 DHC-8 (CT-142)
HELICOPTERS
  ASW 22 CH-148 *Cyclone*
  MRH 68 Bell 412 (CH-146 *Griffon*)
  SAR 14 AW101 *Merlin* (CH-149 *Cormorant*)
  TPT • Heavy 15 CH-47F (CH-147F) *Chinook*

34   THE MILITARY BALANCE 2023

RADAR 53
  AD RADAR • NORTH WARNING SYSTEM 47: 11 AN/FPS-117 (range 200nm); 36 AN/FPS-124 (range 80nm)
  STRATEGIC 6: 4 Coastal; 2 Transportable
AIR-LAUNCHED MISSILES
  AAM • IR AIM-9L *Sidewinder*
  ARH AIM-120C AMRAAM
BOMBS
  Laser-guided: GBU-10/-12/-16 *Paveway* II; GBU-24 *Paveway* III
  Laser & INS/GPS-guided GBU-49 *Enhanced Paveway* II
  INS/GPS-guided: GBU-31 JDAM; GBU-38 JDAM

NATO Flight Training Canada
EQUIPMENT BY TYPE
AIRCRAFT
  TRG 45: 26 T-6A *Texan* II (CT-156 *Harvard* II); 19 *Hawk* 115 (CT-155) (advanced wpns/tactics trg)

Contracted Flying Services – Southport
EQUIPMENT BY TYPE
AIRCRAFT
  TPT • Light 7 Beech C90B *King Air*
  TRG 11 G-120A
HELICOPTERS
  MRH 9 Bell 412 (CH-146)
  TPT • Light 7 Bell 206 *Jet Ranger* (CH-139)

Canadian Special Operations Forces Command 1,500
FORCES BY ROLE
SPECIAL FORCES
  1 SF regt (Canadian Special Operations Regiment)
  1 SF unit (JTF 2)
COMBAT SERVICE SUPPORT
  1 CBRN unit (Canadian Joint Incident Response Unit – CJIRU)
TRANSPORT HELICOPTER
  1 (spec ops) sqn, with Bell 412 (CH-146 *Griffon* – from the RCAF)
EQUIPMENT BY TYPE
NBC VEHICLES 4 LAV *Bison* NBC
HELICOPTERS • MRH 10 Bell 412 (CH-146 *Griffon*)

Canadian Forces Joint Operational Support Group
FORCES BY ROLE
COMBAT SUPPORT
  1 engr spt coy
  1 (close protection) MP coy
  1 (joint) sigs regt
COMBAT SERVICE SUPPORT
  1 (spt) log unit
  1 (movement) log unit

Gendarmerie & Paramilitary 4,500

Canadian Coast Guard 4,500
Incl Department of Fisheries and Oceans; all platforms are designated as non-combatant
EQUIPMENT BY TYPE
PATROL AND COASTAL COMBATANTS 72
  PSOH 1 *Leonard J Cowley*
  PSO 1 *Sir Wilfred Grenfell* (with hel landing platform)
  PCO 13: 2 *Cape Roger*; 1 *Gordon Reid*; 9 *Hero*; 1 *Tanu*
  PBF 1 Response Boat-Medium (RB-M)
  PB 56: 9 *Baie de Plaisance*; 9 Type-300A; 36 Type-300B; 1 *S. Dudka*; 1 *Vakta*
AMPHIBIOUS • LANDING CRAFT 4
  UCAC 4 Type-400
LOGISTICS AND SUPPORT 32
  ABU 6
  AG 4
  AGB 18
  AGOS 4
HELICOPTERS • MRH 7 Bell 412EP **• TPT** 19:
  Medium 1 S-61; **Light** 18: 3 Bell 206L *Long Ranger*; 15 Bell 429

DEPLOYMENT

CYPRUS: UN • UNFICYP (*Operation Snowgoose*) 1

DEMOCRATIC REPUBLIC OF THE CONGO: UN • MONUSCO (*Operation Crocodile*) 7

EGYPT: MFO (*Operation Calumet*) 55; 1 MP team

IRAQ: NATO • NATO Mission Iraq 16

KUWAIT: *Operation Inherent Resolve* (Impact) 200

LATVIA: NATO • Enhanced Forward Presence (*Operation Reassurance*) 540; 1 mech inf bn HQ; 1 mech inf coy(+); 1 cbt spt coy; LAV 6.0; M777

MALI: UN • MINUSMA (*Operation Presence*) 5

MIDDLE EAST: UN • UNTSO (*Operation Jade*) 4

POLAND: *Operation Unifier* 40 (UKR trg)

ROMANIA: NATO • Enhanced Air Policing 170; 6 F/A-18A Hornet (CF-18AM)

SERBIA: NATO • KFOR • *Joint Enterprise* (*Operation Kobold*) 5

SOUTH SUDAN: UN • UNMISS (*Operation Soprano*) 8

UNITED KINGDOM: Air Task Force Prestwick (ATF-P) 55; 3 C-130J-30 *Hercules* (CC-130J); *Operation Unifier* 170 (UKR trg)

FOREIGN FORCES

United Kingdom BATUS 400; 1 trg unit; 1 hel flt with SA341 *Gazelle* AH1
United States 150

United States US

United States Dollar USD		2021	2022	2023
GDP	USD	23.0tr	25.0tr	
per capita	USD	69,227	75,180	
Growth	%	5.7	1.6	
Inflation	%	4.7	8.1	
Def exp [a]	USD	794bn	822bn	
Def bdgt [b]	USD	760bn	767bn	827bn

[a] NATO figure

[b] National Defense Budget Function (50) Budget Authority. Includes DoD funding, as well as funds for nuclear weapons-related activities undertaken by the Department of Energy. Excludes some military retirement and healthcare costs

Real-terms defence budget trend (USDbn, constant 2015)

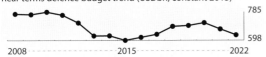

Population	337,341,954				
Age	0–14	15–19	20–24	25–29	30–64	65 plus
Male	9.3%	3.2%	3.3%	3.5%	22.0%	7.9%
Female	8.9%	3.1%	3.2%	3.3%	22.4%	9.8%

Capabilities

The United States remains the world's most capable military power, with a unique ability to project power on a global basis. In October 2022, the Biden administration issued a new National Security Strategy clearly prioritising China as the 'most consequential geopolitical challenge' facing the US, with Russia an immediate but mainly regional threat. These priorities were echoed in a new National Defense Strategy (NDS) that was accompanied by a new Nuclear Posture Review (NPR) and a new Missile Defense Review (MDR). The NDS emphasised homeland defence, integrated deterrence and 'campaigning' to tackle sub-conflict competition that is already under way. It reflected the fact that the force structure is under strain, requires recapitalising with an emphasis on new technology, and needs improved resilience, including of the industrial base. Russia's further invasion of Ukraine in February 2022 led the US to bolster its presence in Europe and also supply large amounts of military and other aid to Ukraine. The NPR reaffirmed broad nuclear modernisation plans but cancelled the proposed nuclear-capable sea-launched cruise missile capability. It also stated that the US would consider using nuclear weapons only 'in extreme circumstances' but did not institute a 'no first use' policy. The MDR reinforced increasing US concern about growing air and missile threats. The US maintains an all-volunteer force, including significant reserves, with high levels of training throughout all commands and services. The Pentagon is trying to improve readiness. Modernisation priorities include a renewal of strategic nuclear capabilities, including a new class of ballistic-missile submarine and a new long-range bomber, as well as improved naval capabilities likely to include both crewed and uninhabited platforms. The US Army is focused on regenerating its capability for large-scale combat operations under its Multi-Domain Operations concept, and the updated doctrine document 'FM 3-0, Operations' was published in October. The US continues to actively develop its defensive and offensive cyber capabilities. The country has the world's most capable defence industry, active in all sectors and with a dominant position in the international defence market, and in the wake of Russia's 2022 invasion of Ukraine there has been focus on issues relating to defence-industrial capacity and security of supply.

ACTIVE 1,359,600 (Army 464,900 Navy 346,300 Air Force 325,100 Space Force 8,400 US Marine Corps 174,550 US Coast Guard 40,350)

RESERVE 817,450 (Army 506,600 Navy 98,250 Air Force 173,400 Marine Corps Reserve 33,050 US Coast Guard 6,150)

ORGANISATIONS BY SERVICE

US Strategic Command
HQ at Offutt AFB (NE)

US Navy
EQUIPMENT BY TYPE
SUBMARINES • STRATEGIC • SSBN 14 *Ohio* with up to 20 UGM-133A *Trident* D-5/D-5LE nuclear SLBM, 4 single 533mm TT with Mk 48 ADCAP mod 6/7 HWT

US Air Force • Global Strike Command
FORCES BY ROLE
MISSILE
  9 sqn with LGM-30G *Minuteman* III
BOMBER
  5 sqn with B-52H *Stratofortress*
  2 sqn with B-2A *Spirit* (+1 ANG sqn personnel only)
EQUIPMENT BY TYPE
SURFACE-TO-SURFACE MISSILE LAUNCHERS
  ICBM • Nuclear 400 LGM-30G *Minuteman* III (1 Mk12A or Mk21 re-entry veh per missile)
AIRCRAFT
  BBR 66: 20 B-2A *Spirit*; 46 B-52H *Stratofortress*
AIR-LAUNCHED MISSILES
  ALCM • Nuclear AGM-86B

Strategic Defenses – Early Warning
EQUIPMENT BY TYPE
RADAR
  NORTH WARNING SYSTEM 50: 14 AN/FPS-117; 36 AN/FPS-124
  SOLID STATE PHASED ARRAY RADAR SYSTEM (SSPARS) 5 AN/FPS-132 Upgraded Early Warning Radar located at Beale AFB (CA), Cape Cod SFS (MA), Clear SFS (AK), Thule AB (GL) and RAF Fylingdales (UK)
  SPACETRACK SYSTEM 7: 1 AN/FPS-85 Spacetrack Radar at Eglin AFB (FL); 6 contributing radars at Cavalier SFS (ND), Clear SFS (AK), Thule AB (GL), RAF Fylingdales (UK), Beale AFB (CA) and Cape Cod SFS (MA); 3 Spacetrack Optical Trackers located at Socorro (NM), Maui (HI), Diego Garcia (BIOT)
  PERIMETER ACQUISITION RADAR ATTACK CHARACTERISATION SYSTEM (PARCS) 1 AN/FPQ-16 at Cavalier SFS (ND)
  DETECTION AND TRACKING RADARS 5 located at Kwajalein Atoll, Ascension Island, Australia, Kaena

36 THE MILITARY BALANCE 2023

Point (HI), MIT Lincoln Laboratory (MA)
GROUND BASED ELECTRO OPTICAL DEEP SPACE SURVEILLANCE SYSTEM (GEODSS) Socorro (NM), Maui (HI), Diego Garcia (BIOT)
STRATEGIC DEFENCES – MISSILE DEFENCES
SEA-BASED: *Aegis* engagement cruisers and destroyers
LAND-BASED: 40 ground-based interceptors at Fort Greely (AK); 4 ground-based interceptors at Vandenburg SFB (CA)

Space

EQUIPMENT BY TYPE
SATELLITES 144
COMMUNICATIONS 47: 6 AEHF; 6 DSCS-III; 2 *Milstar*-I; 3 *Milstar*-II; 5 MUOS; 5 SDS-III; 2 SDS-IV; 1 *TacSat*-4; 1 *TacSat*-6; 6 UFO; 10 WGS SV2
POSITIONING, NAVIGATION & TIMING 30: 12 NAVSTAR Block IIF; 7 NAVSTAR Block IIR; 7 NAVSTAR Block IIRM; 4 NAVSTAR Block III
METEOROLOGY/OCEANOGRAPHY 4 DMSP-5
ISR 14: 5 FIA *Radar*; 5 *Evolved Enhanced/Improved Crystal* (visible and infrared imagery); 2 NRO L-71; 2 NRO L-76
ELINT/SIGINT 31: 6 *Mentor* (advanced *Orion*); 2 *Mercury*; 2 *Nemesis*; 1 *Sharp* (NRO L-67); 3 *Trumpet*; 4 Improved *Trumpet*; 12 Naval Ocean Surveillance System (NOSS); 1 NRO L-85
SPACE SURVEILLANCE 8: 6 GSSAP; 1 SBSS (Space Based Surveillance System); 1 ORS-5
EARLY WARNING 10: 4 DSP; 6 SBIRS *Geo*
REUSABLE SPACECRAFT 1 X-37B OTV
COUNTERSPACE • EW Counter Communications System (CCS)

US Army 464,900

FORCES BY ROLE
Sqn are generally bn sized and tp are generally coy sized
COMMAND
4 (I, III, V & XVIII AB) corps HQ
1 (2nd) inf div HQ
1 (56th) arty comd
SPECIAL FORCES
(see USSOCOM)
MANOEUVRE
Armoured
2 (1st Armd & 1st Cav) armd div (3 (1st–3rd ABCT) armd bde (1 armd recce sqn, 2 armd bn, 1 armd inf bn, 1 SP arty bn, 1 cbt engr bn, 1 CSS bn); 1 SP arty bde HQ; 1 log bde; 1 (hy cbt avn) hel bde)
1 (1st) inf div (2 (1st & 2nd ABCT) armd bde (1 armd recce sqn, 2 armd bn, 1 armd inf bn, 1 SP arty bn, 1 cbt engr bn, 1 CSS bn); 1 SP arty bde HQ; 1 log bde; 1 (cbt avn) hel bde)
1 (3rd) inf div (2 (1st & 2nd ABCT) armd bde (1 armd recce sqn, 2 armd bn, 1 armd inf bn, 1 SP arty bn, 1 cbt engr bn, 1 CSS bn); 1 lt inf bn; 1 SP arty bde HQ; 1 log bde; 1 (cbt avn) hel bde)
Mechanised
1 (4th) inf div (1 (3rd ABCT) armd bde (1 armd recce sqn, 2 armd bn, 1 armd inf bn, 1 SP arty bn, 1 cbt engr bn, 1 CSS bn); 2 (1st & 2nd SBCT) mech bde (1 armd recce

sqn, 3 mech inf bn, 1 arty bn, 1 cbt engr bn, 1 CSS bn); 1 SP arty bde HQ; 1 log bde; 1 (hy cbt avn) hel bde)
1 (7th) inf div (2 (1st & 2nd SBCT, 2nd ID) mech bde (1 armd recce sqn, 3 mech inf bn, 1 arty bn, 1 cbt engr bn, 1 CSS bn))
2 (2nd & 3rd CR) mech bde (1 armd recce sqn, 3 mech sqn, 1 arty sqn, 1 cbt engr sqn, 1 CSS sqn)
Light
1 (10th Mtn) inf div (3 (1st–3rd IBCT) lt inf bde (1 recce sqn, 3 inf bn, 1 arty bn, 1 cbt engr bn, 1 CSS bn); 1 log bde; 1 (cbt avn) hel bde)
1 (25th) inf div (2 (2 & 3rd IBCT) inf bde (1 recce sqn, 2 inf bn, 1 arty bn, 1 cbt engr bn, 1 CSS bn); 1 log bde; 1 (cbt avn) hel bde)
5 (Sy Force Assist) inf bde(-)
Air Manoeuvre
1 (11th) AB div (1 (1st IBCT) inf bde (1 recce sqn, 3 inf bn, 1 arty bn, 1 cbt engr bn, 1 CSS bn); 1 (2nd AB BCT) AB bde (1 recce bn, 2 para bn, 1 arty bn, 1 cbt engr bn, 1 CSS bn))
1 (82nd) AB div (1 (1st AB BCT) AB bde (1 recce bn, 1 mech coy; 3 para bn, 1 arty bn, 1 cbt engr bn, 1 CSS bn); 2 (2nd & 3rd AB BCT) AB bde (1 recce bn, 3 para bn, 1 arty bn, 1 cbt engr bn, 1 CSS bn); 1 (cbt avn) hel bde; 1 log bde)
1 (101st) air aslt div (3 (1st–3rd AB BCT) AB bde (1 recce bn, 3 para bn, 1 arty bn, 1 cbt engr bn, 1 CSS bn); 1 (cbt avn) hel bde; 1 log bde)
1 (173rd AB BCT) AB bde (1 recce bn, 2 para bn, 1 arty bn, 1 cbt engr bn, 1 CSS bn)
Other
1 (11th ACR) trg armd cav regt (OPFOR) (2 armd cav sqn, 1 CSS bn)
COMBAT SUPPORT
3 MRL bde (2 MRL bn)
1 MRL bde (1 MRL bn; 1 SSM bn (forming))
1 MRL bde (5 MRL bn)
4 engr bde
2 EOD gp (2 EOD bn)
10 int bde
2 int gp
4 MP bde
1 NBC bde
3 (strat) sigs bde
4 (tac) sigs bde
1 (1st MDTF) cbt spt bde (1 (I2CEWS) cbt spt bn)
2 (2nd & 3rd MDTF) cbt spt bde(-)
COMBAT SERVICE SUPPORT
2 log bde
3 med bde
1 tpt bde
ISR
1 ISR avn bde
HELICOPTER
2 (cbt avn) hel bde
1 (cbt avn) hel bde HQ
AIR DEFENCE
6 SAM bde

Reserve Organisations

Army National Guard 329,750 reservists

Normally dual-funded by DoD and states. Civil-emergency responses can be mobilised by state governors. Federal government can mobilise ARNG for major domestic emergencies and for overseas operations

FORCES BY ROLE

COMMAND

8 div HQ

SPECIAL FORCES

(see USSOCOM)

MANOEUVRE

Reconnaissance

1 armd recce sqn

Armoured

5 (ABCT) armd bde (1 armd recce sqn, 2 armd bn, 1 armd inf bn, 1 SP arty bn, 1 cbt engr bn, 1 CSS bn)

Mechanised

2 (SBCT) mech bde (1 armd recce sqn, 3 mech inf bn, 1 arty bn, 1 cbt engr bn, 1 CSS bn)

Light

14 (IBCT) inf bde (1 recce sqn, 3 inf bn, 1 arty bn, 1 cbt engr bn, 1 CSS bn)

6 (IBCT) inf bde (1 recce sqn, 2 inf bn, 1 arty bn, 1 cbt engr bn, 1 CSS bn)

1 (Sy Force Assist) inf bde(-)

4 inf bn

Air Manoeuvre

1 AB bn

COMBAT SUPPORT

8 arty bde

1 SP arty bn

8 engr bde

1 EOD regt

3 int bde

3 MP bde

1 NBC bde

2 (tac) sigs bde

17 (Mnv Enh) cbt spt bde

COMBAT SERVICE SUPPORT

10 log bde

17 (regional) log spt gp

HELICOPTER

8 (cbt avn) hel bde

5 (theatre avn) hel bde

AIR DEFENCE

3 SAM bde

Army Reserve 176,850 reservists

Reserve under full command of US Army. Does not have state-emergency liability of Army National Guard

FORCES BY ROLE

SPECIAL FORCES

(see USSOCOM)

COMBAT SUPPORT

4 engr bde

4 MP bde

2 NBC bde

2 sigs bde

3 (Mnv Enh) cbt spt bde

COMBAT SERVICE SUPPORT

9 log bde

11 med bde

HELICOPTER

2 (exp cbt avn) hel bde

Army Stand-by Reserve 700 reservists

Trained individuals for mobilisation

EQUIPMENT BY TYPE

ARMOURED FIGHTING VEHICLES

MBT 2,645: ε540 M1A1 SA *Abrams*; 1,605 M1A2 SEPv2 *Abrams*; ε500 M1A2 SEPv3 *Abrams*; (ε2,000 more M1A1/A2 *Abrams* in store)

ASLT ε100 M1128 *Stryker* MGS (being divested 2022)

RECCE 1,745: ε1,200 M3A2/A3 *Bradley*; 545 M1127 *Stryker* RV (ε800 more M3 *Bradley* in store)

IFV 2,959: ε14 LAV-25; ε2,500 M2A2/A3 *Bradley*; 21 M2A4 *Bradley*; 334 M7A3/SA BFIST (OP); 83 M1296 *Stryker Dragoon* (ε2,000 more M2 *Bradley* in store); 7 *Stryker* MCWS (in test)

APC 10,477

  APC (T) 4,930: 130 AMPV (in test); ε4,800 M113A2/A3 (ε8,000 more in store)

  APC (W) 2,613: 1,348 M1126 *Stryker* ICV; 280 M1130 *Stryker* CV (CP); 167 M1131 *Stryker* FSV (OP); 258 M1133 *Stryker* MEV (Amb); 21 M1251A1 *Stryker* FSV (OP); 46 M1254A1 *Stryker* MEV (Amb); 68 M1255A1 *Stryker* CV (CP); 425 M1256A1 *Stryker* ICV

  PPV 2,934: 2,633 *MaxxPro Dash*; 301 *MaxxPro* LWB (Amb)

AUV 21,516: ε12,500 JLTV; 2,900 M1117 ASV; 465 M1200 *Armored Knight* (OP); 5,651 M-ATV

ENGINEERING & MAINTENANCE VEHICLES

AEV 567: 149 M1150 ABV; 250 M9 ACE; 152 M1132 *Stryker* ESV; 16 M1257A1 *Stryker* ESV

ARV 1,274+: 360 M88A1; ε914 M88A2 (ε1,000 more M88A1 in store); some M578

VLB 383: ε230 M60 AVLB; 93 M1074 Joint Assault Bridge; 20 REBS; 40 *Wolverine* HAB

MW 3+: *Aardvark* JSFU Mk4; some *Husky* 2G; 3+ *Hydrema* 910 MCV-2; M58/M59 MICLIC; M139; *Rhino*

NBC VEHICLES 234 M1135 *Stryker* NBCRV

ANTI-TANK/ANTI-INFRASTRUCTURE

MSL

  SP 1,133: 120 M1134 *Stryker* ATGM; 13 M1253A1 *Stryker* ATGM; ε1,000 M1167 HMMWV TOW

  MANPATS FGM-148 *Javelin*

RCL 84mm *Carl Gustaf*

ARTILLERY 5,096

SP 155mm 689: 486 M109A6; 203 M109A7 (ε850 more M109A6 in store)

TOWED 1,267: **105mm** 821 M119A2/3; **155mm** 446 M777A2

MRL 227mm 594: 368 M142 HIMARS; 226+ M270A1/A2 MLRS

MOR 2,507: **81mm** 990 M252; **120mm** 1,076 M120/M1064A3; **SP 120mm** 441; 363 M1129 *Stryker* MC; 78 M1252A1 *Stryker* MC

SURFACE-TO-SURFACE MISSILE LAUNCHERS

SRBM • Conventional MGM-140A/B ATACMS; MGM-168 ATACMS (All launched from M270A1 MLRS or M142 HIMARS MRLs)

38 THE MILITARY BALANCE 2023

AMPHIBIOUS

PRINCIPAL AMPHIBIOUS SHIPS 7

LSL 7 *Frank Besson* (capacity 24 *Abrams* MBT)

LANDING CRAFT 70

LCT 34 LCU 2000 (capacity 5 M1 *Abrams* MBT)

LCM 36 LCM 8 (capacity either 1 M1 *Abrams* MBT or 200 troops)

AIRCRAFT

ISR 46: 8 EMARSS-G; 4 EMARSS-V; 7 EMARSS-M; 19 RC-12X *Guardrail* (5 trg); 8 RO-6A ARL-E

SIGINT 2 CL-600 *Artemis*

ELINT 9: 4 EMARSS-S; 4 EO-5C ARL-M (COMINT/ELINT); 1 TO-5C (trg)

TPT 156: **Light** 152: 113 Beech A200 *King Air* (C-12 *Huron*); 28 Cessna 560 *Citation* (UC-35A/B); 11 SA-227 *Metro* (C-26E); **PAX** 4: 1 Gulfstream IV (C-20F); 2 Gulfstream V (C-37A); 1 Gulfstream G550 (C-37B)

TRG 4 T-6D *Texan* II

HELICOPTERS

ATK 740: ε250 AH-64D *Apache*; ε490 AH-64E *Apache*

SAR 356: 19 HH-60L *Black Hawk*; 337 HH-60M *Black Hawk* (medevac)

TPT 2,768: **Heavy** 450 CH-47F *Chinook*; **Medium** 1,857: ε20 UH-60A *Black Hawk*; ε900 UH-60L *Black Hawk*; 931 UH-60M *Black Hawk*; 6 UH-60V *Black Hawk*; **Light** 524: 457 UH-72A *Lakota*; 2 UH-72B *Lakota*; 65 UH-1H/V *Iroquois*

UNINHABITED AERIAL VEHICLES 416

CISR • **Heavy** ε180 MQ-1C *Gray Eagle*

ISR • **Medium** 236 RQ-7B *Shadow*

AIR DEFENCE

SAM 1,187+

Long-range 480 M902/M903 *Patriot* PAC-3/PAC-3 MSE

Short-range *Iron Dome*; NASAMS

Point-defence 471+: FIM-92 *Stinger*; 18 M-SHORAD; 453 M1097 *Avenger*

GUNS • **Towed** • **20mm** *Phalanx* (LPWS)

MISSILE DEFENCE • **Long-range** 42 THAAD

AIR-LAUNCHED MISSILES

ASM AGM-114K/L/M/N/R *Hellfire* II; AGM-179A JAGM; AGR-20A APKWS

US Navy 346,300

Comprises 2 Fleet Areas, Atlantic and Pacific. 6 Fleets: 2nd – Atlantic; 3rd – Pacific; 4th – Caribbean, Central and South America; 5th – Arabian Sea, Persian Gulf, Red Sea; 6th – Mediterranean; 7th – Indian Ocean, East Asia, W. Pacific; plus Military Sealift Command (MSC); Naval Reserve Force (NRF). For Naval Special Warfare Command, see US Special Operations Command

EQUIPMENT BY TYPE

SUBMARINES 67

STRATEGIC • **SSBN** 14 *Ohio* (opcon US STRATCOM) with up to 20 UGM-133A *Trident* D-5/D-5LE nuclear SLBM, 4 single 533mm TT with Mk 48 ADCAP mod 6/7 HWT

TACTICAL 53

SSGN 51:

4 *Ohio* (mod) with 22 7-cell MAC VLS with UGM-109E *Tomahawk* Block IV LACM, 4 single 533mm TT with Mk 48 ADCAP mod 6/7 HWT

4 *Los Angeles* Flight II with 1 12-cell VLS with UGM-109E *Tomahawk* Block IV LACM, 4 single 533mm TT with Mk 48 ADCAP mod 6/7 HWT

22 *Los Angeles* Flight III with 1 12-cell VLS with UGM-109E *Tomahawk* Block IV LACM, 4 single 533mm TT with Mk 48 ADCAP mod 6/7 HWT

10 *Virginia* Flight I/II with 1 12-cell VLS with UGM-109E *Tomahawk* Block IV LACM, 4 single 533mm TT with Mk 48 ADCAP mod 6/7 HWT

8 *Virginia* Flight III with 2 6-cell VPT VLS with UGM-109E *Tomahawk* Block IV LACM, 4 single 533mm TT with Mk 48 ADCAP mod 6/7 HWT

3 *Virginia* Flight IV with 2 6-cell VPT VLS with UGM-109E *Tomahawk* Block IV LACM, 4 single 533mm TT with Mk 48 ADCAP mod 6/7 HWT

SSN 2 *Seawolf* (one other damaged in collision in 2021, repair to begin in 2023) with 8 single 660mm TT with UGM-109E *Tomahawk* Block IV LACM/Mk 48 ADCAP mod 6/7 HWT

PRINCIPAL SURFACE COMBATANTS 122

AIRCRAFT CARRIERS • **CVN** 11:

1 *Gerald R. Ford* with 2 octuple Mk 29 mod 5 GMLS with RIM-162D ESSM SAM, 2 Mk 49 mod 3 GMLS with RIM-116C RAM Block 2 SAM, 3 Mk 15 *Phalanx* Block 1B CIWS (typical capacity 75+ F/A-18E/F *Super Hornet* FGA ac; F-35C *Lightning* II FGA ac; E-2D *Hawkeye* AEW&C ac; EA-18G *Growler* EW ac; MH-60R *Seahawk* ASW hel; MH-60S *Knight Hawk* MRH hel)

10 *Nimitz* with 2 8-cell Mk29 GMLS with RIM-162 ESSM SAM, 2 21-cell Mk 49 GMLS with RIM-116 RAM Block 2 SAM, 3 Mk 15 *Phalanx* Block 1B CIWS (typical capacity 55 F/A-18E/F *Super Hornet* FGA ac; F-35C *Lightning* II FGA ac; 4 EA-18G *Growler* EW ac; 4 E-2C/D *Hawkeye* AEW ac; 6 MH-60R/S *Seahawk*/ *Knight Hawk* hel)

CRUISERS • **CGHM** 19:

17 *Ticonderoga* with *Aegis* Baseline 5/6/8/9 C2, 2 quad lnchr with RGM-84D *Harpoon* Block 1C AShM, 16 8-cell Mk 41 VLS (of which 2 only 5-cell and fitted with reload crane) with RGM-109E *Tomahawk* Block IV LACM/SM-2 Block III/IIIA/IIIB/IV SAM/SM-3 Block IA/B SAM/SM-6 Block I SAM, 2 triple 324mm SVTT Mk 32 ASTT with Mk 54 LWT, 2 Mk 15 *Phalanx* Block 1B CIWS, 2 127mm guns (capacity 2 MH-60R *Seahawk*/MH-60S *Knight Hawk* hels)

2 *Zumwalt* with 20 4-cell Mk 57 VLS with RGM-109E *Tomahawk* Block IV LACM/RIM-162 ESSM SAM/SM-2 Block IIIA SAM/ASROC A/S msl, 2 155mm guns (capacity 2 MH-60R *Seahawk* ASW hel or 1 MH-60R *Seahawk* ASW hel and 3 *Fire Scout* UAV)

DESTROYERS 70:

DDGHM 42:

5 *Arleigh Burke* Flight IIA with *Aegis* Baseline 5/9 C2, 12 8-cell Mk 41 VLS with RGM-109E *Tomahawk* Block IV LACM/SM-2 Block III/IIIA/IIIB/IV SAM/SM-3 Block IA/B SAM/SM-6 Block I SAM/ASROC A/S msl, 2 triple 324mm SVTT Mk 32 ASTT with Mk 54 LWT, 2 Mk 15 *Phalanx* Block 1B CIWS, 1 127mm gun (capacity 2 MH-60R *Seahawk*/MH-60S *Knight Hawk* hels)

37 *Arleigh Burke* Flight IIA with *Aegis* Baseline 6/7/9 C2, 12 8-cell Mk 41 VLS with RGM-109E *Tomahawk* Block IV LACM/SM-2 Block III/IIIA/IIIB/IV SAM/SM-3 Block IA/B SAM/SM-6 Block I SAM/ASROC A/S msl, 2 triple 324mm SVTT Mk 32 ASTT with Mk 54 LWT, 1 Mk 15 *Phalanx* Block 1B CIWS, 1 127mm gun (capacity 2 MH-60R *Seahawk*/MH-60S *Knight Hawk* hels) (of which 1 vessel also with 1 Mk 15 SeaRAM with RIM-116C RAM Block 2 and 3 vessels also with 1 Optical Dazzling Interdictor, Navy (ODIN) LWS)

DDGM 28 *Arleigh Burke* Flight I/II with *Aegis* Baseline 5/9 C2, 2 quad lnchr with RGM-84D *Harpoon* Block 1C AShM, 12 8-cell Mk 41 VLS (of which 2 only 5-cell and fitted with reload crane) with RGM-109E *Tomahawk* Block IV LACM/SM-2 Block III/IIIA/IIIB/IV SAM/SM-3 Block IA/B SAM/SM-6 Block I SAM/ASROC A/S msl, 2 triple 324mm SVTT Mk 32 ASTT with Mk 54 LWT, 2 Mk 15 *Phalanx* Block 1B CIWS (of which 5 vessels with 1 Mk 15 SeaRAM with RIM-116C RAM Block 2, 1 Mk 15 *Phalanx* Block 1B instead of 2 *Phalanx*), 1 127mm gun, 1 hel landing platform

FRIGATES 22:

FFGHM 6 *Independence* with 2 quad lnchr with NSM (RGM-184A) AShM, 1 11-cell SeaRAM lnchr with RIM-116C Block 2 SAM, 1 57mm gun (capacity 2 MH-60R/S *Seahawk*/*Knight Hawk* hel and 3 MQ-8 *Fire Scout* UAV)

FFHM 16:

10 *Freedom* with 1 21-cell Mk 49 lnchr with RIM-116C RAM Block 2 SAM, 1 57mm gun (capacity 2 MH-60R/S *Seahawk*/*Knight Hawk* hel or 1 MH-60 with 3 MQ-8 *Fire Scout* UAV)

6 *Independence* with 1 11-cell SeaRAM lnchr with RIM-116C Block 2 SAM, 1 57mm gun (capacity 2 MH-60R/S *Seahawk*/*Knight Hawk* hel and 3 MQ-8 *Fire Scout* UAV)

PATROL AND COASTAL COMBATANTS 89

PCFG 5 *Cyclone* with 1 quad Mk 208 lnchr with BGM-176B *Griffin B* SSM

PBF 84: 32 Combatant Craft Assault; 2 Combatant Craft Heavy; 30 Combatant Craft Medium Mk 1; 20 Defiant 40 (40PB)

MINE WARFARE • MINE COUNTERMEASURES 8

MCO 8 *Avenger*

COMMAND SHIPS

LCC 2 *Blue Ridge* with 2 Mk 15 *Phalanx* Block 1B CIWS (capacity 3 LCPL; 2 LCVP; 700 troops; 1 med hel) (of which 1 vessel partially crewed by Military Sealift Command personnel)

AMPHIBIOUS

PRINCIPAL AMPHIBIOUS SHIPS 31:

LHA 2 *America* with 2 8-cell Mk 29 GMLS with RIM-162D ESSM SAM, 2 Mk 49 GMLS with RIM-116C RAM Block 2 SAM, 2 Mk 15 *Phalanx* Block 1B CIWS (capacity up to 29 ac/hel incl: 6-13 F-35B *Lightning* II FGA ac (possible 20 as full '*Lightning* carrier'); 4 AH-1Z *Viper* atk hel; up to 12 MV-22B *Osprey* tpt ac; 2 MH-60S *Knight Hawk* MRH; 4 CH-53E *Sea Stallion* tpt hel; 2 UH-1Y *Iroquois* tpt hel; up to 1,800 troops)

LHD 7 *Wasp* with 2 8-cell Mk 29 GMLS with RIM-7M/P *Sea Sparrow* SAM, 2 Mk 49 GMLS with RIM-116C RAM Block 2 SAM, 2 Mk 15 *Phalanx* Block 1B CIWS (capacity up to 23 ac/hel incl: 6 AV-8B *Harrier* II FGA or F-35B *Lightning* II FGA ac (possible 20 F-35B as full '*Lightning* carrier'); 4 AH-1Z *Viper* atk hel; 4 CH-53E *Sea Stallion* hel; up to 6 MV-22B *Osprey* tpt ac; 3 UH-1Y *Iroquois* tpt hel; 3 LCAC(L); 60 tanks; 1,687 troops)

LPD 12 *San Antonio* with 2 21-cell Mk 49 GMLS with RIM-116C RAM Block 2 SAM (1 vessel also fitted with 1 Solid-State Laser Technology Maturation (SSL-TM) LWS) (capacity 2 CH-53E *Sea Stallion* hel or 2 MV-22 *Osprey*; 2 LCAC(L); 14 AAV; 720 troops)

LSD 10:

4 *Harpers Ferry* with 2 Mk 49 GMLS with RIM-116C RAM Block 2 SAM, 2 Mk 15 *Phalanx* Block 1B CIWS (capacity 2 CH-53E *Sea Stallion* hel; 2 LCAC(L); 40 tanks; 500 troops)

6 *Whidbey Island* with 2 Mk 49 GMLS with RIM-116C RAM Block 2 SAM, 2 Mk 15 *Phalanx* Block 1B CIWS (capacity 2 CH-53E *Sea Stallion* hel; 4 LCAC(L); 40 tanks; 500 troops)

LANDING CRAFT 145:

LCU 32 LCU 1610 (capacity either 1 M1 *Abrams* MBT or 350 troops)

LCM 8 LCM 8

LCP 33 Maritime Positioning Force Utility Boat (MPF-UB)

LCAC 72: 68 LCAC(L) (MLU ongoing) (capacity either 1 MBT or 60 troops); 4 *Ship to Shore Connector* (SSC) (capacity 1 MBT or 145 troops)

LOGISTICS AND SUPPORT 13

AFDL 1 *Dynamic*

AGOR 6 (all leased out): 2 *Ocean*; 3 *Thomas G. Thompson*; 1 *Kilo Moana*

ARD 2

AX 1 *Prevail*

ESB 3 *Lewis B. Puller* (capacity 4 MH-53/MH-60 hel)

UUV (1 *Cutthroat* for testing)

MISSILE DEFENCE • Long-range 3 8-cell Mk 41 VLS with SM-3

Naval Reserve Forces 98,250

Selected Reserve 55,500

Individual Ready Reserve 42,750

Naval Inactive Fleet

Notice for reactivation:

60–90 days minimum (still on naval-vessel register)

EQUIPMENT BY TYPE

PRINCIPAL SURFACE COMBATANTS

FRIGATES • FFH 1 *Freedom* with 1 57mm gun

AMPHIBIOUS 4

LHA 2 *Tarawa*

LSD 2 *Whidbey Island*

LOGISTICS AND SUPPORT 4

AOE 2 *Supply*

ARS 2 *Safeguard*

Military Sealift Command (MSC)

Fleet Oiler (PM1)
EQUIPMENT BY TYPE
LOGISTICS AND SUPPORT 16
AOR 16: 1 *John Lewis* with 1 hel landing platform; 15 *Henry J. Kaiser* with 1 hel landing platform

Special Mission (PM2)
EQUIPMENT BY TYPE
LOGISTICS AND SUPPORT 21
AGM 2: 1 *Howard O. Lorenzen*; 1 Sea-based X-band radar
AGOR 6 *Pathfinder*
AGOS 5: 1 *Impeccable* (commercial operator); 4 *Victorious*
AGS 1 *Waters*
ARC 1 *Zeus*
AS 4 *Arrowhead* (long-term chartered)
ATF 2: 1 HOS *Red Rock* (leased); 1 MV *Hercules*

Prepositioning (PM3)
EQUIPMENT BY TYPE
LOGISTICS AND SUPPORT 14
AG 2: 1 *V Adm K.R. Wheeler*; 1 *Fast Tempo*
AKR 5: 2 *Bob Hope*; 1 *Stockham*; 2 *Watson*
AKRH 5 *2nd Lt John P. Bobo*
ESD 2 *Montford Point*

Service Support (PM4)
EQUIPMENT BY TYPE
LOGISTICS AND SUPPORT 12
AH 2 *Mercy* with 1 hel landing platform
ARS 2 *Safeguard*
AS 4: 1 *Dominator*; 2 *Emory S. Land*; 1 *Malama* (long-term chartered)
ATF 4: 1 *Gary Chouest*; 1 MV *Ocean Valour*; 2 *Powhatan*

Sealift (PM5)
(At a minimum of 4 days' readiness)
EQUIPMENT BY TYPE
LOGISTICS AND SUPPORT 18
AOT 1 *Maersk Peary* (long-term chartered)
AK 4: 2 *LTC John U.D. Page*; 1 *Maj. Bernard F. Fisher*; 1 *CPT David I. Lyon*
AKR 13: 5 *Bob Hope*; 2 *Gordon*; 6 *Watson*

Fleet Ordnance and Dry Cargo (PM6)
EQUIPMENT BY TYPE
LOGISTICS AND SUPPORT 16
AOE 2 *Supply*
AKEH 14 *Lewis and Clark*

Expeditionary Fast Transport (PM8)
EQUIPMENT BY TYPE
LOGISTICS AND SUPPORT 14
AP 2 *Guam*
EPF 12 *Spearhead*

Dry Cargo and Tankers
EQUIPMENT BY TYPE
LOGISTICS AND SUPPORT 6

AK 2: 1 *Sea Eagle*; 1 SLNC *Corsica* (long-term chartered)
AOT 4: 2 *Empire State*; 1 SLNC *Pax*; 1 SLNC *Goodwill* (long-term chartered)

US Maritime Administration (MARAD)

National Defense Reserve Fleet
EQUIPMENT BY TYPE
LOGISTICS AND SUPPORT 20
ACS 2: 1 *Flickertail State*; 1 *Keystone State*
AGOS 2 *General Rudder*
AGM 2: 1 *Pacific Collector*; 1 *Pacific Tracker*
AK 8: 2 *Cape Ann* (breakbulk); 1 *Cape Chalmers* (breakbulk); 1 *Cape Jacob*; 2 *Cape May*; 1 *Del Monte* (breakbulk); 1 *Savannah*
AP 4: 1 *Empire State* VI; 1 *Golden Bear*; 1 *Kennedy*; 1 *State of Maine*
AX 2: 1 *Freedom Star*; 1 *Kings Pointer*

Ready Reserve Force
Ships at readiness up to a maximum of 30 days
EQUIPMENT BY TYPE
LOGISTICS AND SUPPORT 40
ACS 4: 1 *Flickertail State*; 1 *Gopher State*; 2 *Keystone State*
AK 2 *Wright* (breakbulk)
AKR 34: 1 *Adm W.M. Callaghan*; 4 *Algol*; 1 *Cape Arundel*; 4 *Cape Capella*; 1 *Cape Decision*; 4 *Cape Ducato*; 1 *Cape Edmont*; 1 *Cape Henry*; 2 *Cape Hudson*; 2 *Cape Knox*; 4 *Cape Island*; 1 *Cape Orlando*; 1 *Cape Race*; 1 *Cape Trinity*; 2 *Cape Trinity*; 2 *Cape Victory*; 2 *Cape Washington*

Naval Aviation 98,600
10 air wg. Average air wing comprises 8 sqns: 4 with F/A-18; 1 with MH-60R; 1 with EA-18G; 1 with E-2C/D; 1 with MH-60S
FORCES BY ROLE
FIGHTER/GROUND ATTACK
22 sqn with F/A-18E *Super Hornet*
10 sqn with F/A-18F *Super Hornet*
1 sqn with F-35C *Lightning* II
1 sqn (forming) with F-35C *Lightning* II
ANTI-SUBMARINE WARFARE
12 sqn with P-8A *Poseidon*
1 (special projects) sqn with P-8A *Poseidon*
12 sqn with MH-60R *Seahawk*
3 ASW/ISR sqn with MH-60R *Seahawk*; MQ-8B *Fire Scout*
ELINT
1 sqn with EP-3E *Aries* II
ELINT/ELECTRONIC WARFARE
13 sqn with EA-18G *Growler*
AIRBORNE EARLY WARNING & CONTROL
3 sqn with E-2C *Hawkeye*
6 sqn with E-2D *Hawkeye*
COMMAND & CONTROL
2 sqn with E-6B *Mercury*
MINE COUNTERMEASURES
2 sqn with MH-53E *Sea Dragon*
TRANSPORT
2 sqn with CMV-22B *Osprey* (forming)
2 sqn with C-2A *Greyhound*

North America **41**

TRAINING

1 (FRS) sqn with EA-18G *Growler*

1 (FRS) sqn with C-2A *Greyhound*; E-2C/D *Hawkeye*; TE-2C *Hawkeye*

1 sqn with E-6B *Mercury*

2 (FRS) sqn with F/A-18E/F *Super Hornet*

1 (FRS) sqn with F-35C *Lightning* II

1 (FRS) sqn with MH-53 *Sea Dragon*

2 (FRS) sqn with MH-60S *Knight Hawk*; HH-60H *Seahawk*

2 (FRS) sqn with MH-60R *Seahawk*

1 (FRS) sqn with P-3C *Orion*; P-8A *Poseidon*

6 sqn with T-6A/B *Texan* II

2 sqn with T-44C *Pegasus*

5 sqn with T-45C *Goshawk*

2 hel sqn with TH-57B/C *Sea Ranger*

1 hel sqn with TH-73A

1 (FRS) UAV sqn with MQ-8B *Fire Scout*; MQ-8C *Fire Scout*

TRANSPORT HELICOPTER

13 sqn with MH-60S *Knight Hawk*

2 tpt hel/ISR sqn with MH-60S *Knight Hawk*; MQ-8B *Fire Scout*; MQ-8C *Fire Scout*

ISR UAV

1 sqn with MQ-4C *Triton*

EQUIPMENT BY TYPE

AIRCRAFT 988 combat capable

FGA 704: 10 F-16A *Fighting Falcon*; 4 F-16B *Fighting Falcon*; 52 F-35C *Lightning* II; 5 F/A-18B *Hornet*; 16 F/A-18C *Hornet*; 4 F/A-18D *Hornet*; 327 F/A-18E *Super Hornet*; 286 F/A-18F *Super Hornet*

ASW 126: 14 P-3C *Orion*; 112 P-8A *Poseidon*

EW 158 EA-18G *Growler**

ELINT 9 EP-3E *Aries* II

AEW&C 74: 20 E-2C *Hawkeye*; 54 E-2D *Hawkeye*

C2 16 E-6B *Mercury*

TKR/TPT 3: 1 KC-130R *Hercules*; 1 KC-130T *Hercules*; 1 KC-130J *Hercules*

TPT • Light 54: 4 Beech A200 *King Air* (C-12C *Huron*); 6 Beech A200 *King Air* (UC-12F *Huron*); 8 Beech A200 *King Air* (UC-12M *Huron*); 27 C-2A *Greyhound*; 2 DHC-2 *Beaver* (U-6A); 7 SA-227-BC *Metro* III (C-26D)

TRG 576: 44 T-6A *Texan* II; 231 T-6B *Texan* II; 7 T-38C *Talon*; 55 T-44C *Pegasus*; 237 T-45C *Goshawk*; 2 TE-2C *Hawkeye*

TILTROTOR • TPT 27 CMV-22B *Osprey*

HELICOPTERS

ASW 271 MH-60R *Seahawk*

MRH 258 MH-60S *Knight Hawk* (Multi Mission Support)

MCM 28 MH-53E *Sea Dragon*

ISR 3 OH-58C *Kiowa*

TPT 13: **Heavy** 2 CH-53E *Sea Stallion*; **Medium** 3 UH-60L *Black Hawk*; **Light** 8: 5 UH-72A *Lakota*; 2 UH-1N *Iroquois*; 1 UH-1Y *Venom*

TRG 116: ε10 TH-57B *Sea Ranger*; 76 TH-57C *Sea Ranger*; 30 TH-73A

UNINHABITED AERIAL VEHICLES • ISR 114

Heavy 64: 5 MQ-4C *Triton*; 19 MQ-8B *Fire Scout*; 36 MQ-8C *Fire Scout*; 4 RQ-4A *Global Hawk* (evaluation and trials); **Medium** 35 RQ-2B *Pioneer*; **Light** 15 RQ-21A *Blackjack*

AIR-LAUNCHED MISSILES

AAM • IR AIM-9M *Sidewinder*; **IIR** AIM-9X *Sidewinder* II; **SARH** AIM-7 *Sparrow* (being withdrawn); **ARH** AIM-120C-5/C-7/D AMRAAM

ASM AGM-65F *Maverick*; AGM-114B/K/M *Hellfire*; APKWS

AShM AGM-84D *Harpoon*; AGM-119A *Penguin* 3; AGM-158C LRASM

ARM AGM-88B/C/E HARM/AARGM

ALCM • Conventional AGM-84E/H/K SLAM/SLAM-ER

BOMBS

Laser-guided: GBU-10/-12/-16 *Paveway* II; GBU-24 *Paveway* III; GBU-51 LCDB

Laser & INS/GPS-guided: EGBU-12 *Paveway* II; EGBU-24 *Paveway* III; GBU-52 LCDB; GBU-54 Laser JDAM

INS/GPS-guided: GBU-31/-32/-38 JDAM; AGM-154A/C/C-1 JSOW

Naval Aviation Reserve

FORCES BY ROLE

FIGHTER/GROUND ATTACK

1 sqn with F/A-18E/F *Super Hornet*

ANTI-SUBMARINE WARFARE

1 sqn with P-3C *Orion*

1 sqn with P-8A *Poseidon* (forming)

1 sqn with MH-60R *Seahawk*

ELECTRONIC WARFARE

1 sqn with EA-18G *Growler*

TRANSPORT

6 log spt sqn with B-737-700 (C-40A *Clipper*)

1 log spt sqn with Gulfstream V/G550 (C-37A/B)

5 sqn with C-130T/KC-130T *Hercules*

TRAINING

2 (aggressor) sqn with F-5F/N *Tiger* II

1 (aggressor) sqn with F-16C *Fighting Falcon*

TRANSPORT HELICOPTER

1 sqn with MH-60S *Knight Hawk*

EQUIPMENT BY TYPE

AIRCRAFT 64 combat capable

FTR 31: 2 F-5F *Tiger* II; 29 F-5N *Tiger* II

FGA 24: 12 F-16C *Fighting Falcon*; 10 F/A-18E *Super Hornet*; 2 F/A-18F *Super Hornet*

ASW 4: 2 P-3C *Orion*; 2 P-8A *Poseidon*

EW 5 EA-18G *Growler**

TKR/TPT 11 KC-130T *Hercules*

TPT 40: **Medium** 19 C-130T *Hercules*; **PAX** 21: 17 B-737-700 (C-40A *Clipper*); 1 Gulfstream V (C-37A); 3 Gulfstream G550 (C-37B)

HELICOPTERS

ASW 5 MH-60R *Seahawk*

MRH 12 MH-60S *Knight Hawk*

MCM 6 MH-53E *Sea Dragon*

US Marine Corps 174,550

3 Marine Expeditionary Forces (MEF), 3 Marine Expeditionary Brigades (MEB), 7 Marine Expeditionary Units (MEU) drawn from 3 div. An MEU usually consists of a battalion landing team (1 SF coy, 1 lt armd recce coy,

42 THE MILITARY BALANCE 2023

1 recce pl, 1 armd pl, 1 amph aslt pl, 1 inf bn, 1 arty bty, 1 cbt engr pl), an aviation combat element (1 medium-lift sqn with attached atk hel, FGA ac and AD assets) and a composite log bn, with a combined total of about 2,200 personnel. Composition varies with mission requirements

FORCES BY ROLE
SPECIAL FORCES
(see USSOCOM)
MANOEUVRE
Reconnaissance
3 (MEF) recce coy
Amphibious
1 (1st) mne div (2 armd recce bn, 1 recce bn, 3 mne regt (4 mne bn), 1 amph aslt bn, 1 arty regt (3 arty bn, 1 MRL bn), 1 cbt engr bn, 1 EW bn, 1 int bn, 1 sigs bn)
1 (2nd) mne div (1 armd recce bn, 1 recce bn, 3 mne regt (3 mne bn), 1 amph aslt bn, 1 arty regt (2 arty bn), 1 cbt engr bn, 1 EW bn, 1 int bn, 1 sigs bn)
1 (3rd) mne div (1 recce bn, 1 mne regt (2 mne bn, 1 AD bn, 1 log bn), 1 arty regt (2 arty bn), 1 cbt spt bn (1 armd recce coy, 1 amph aslt coy, 1 cbt engr coy), 1 EW bn, 1 int bn, 1 sigs bn)
COMBAT SERVICE SUPPORT
3 log gp

EQUIPMENT BY TYPE
ARMOURED FIGHTING VEHICLES
IFV 488 LAV-25
APC • APC (W) 207 LAV variants (66 CP; 127 log; 14 EW)
AAV 1,360: 1,200 AAV-7A1 (all roles); ε160 ACV (in test)
AUV 6,929: 1,725 *Cougar*; ε4,500 JLTV; 704 M-ATV
ENGINEERING & MAINTENANCE VEHICLES
AEV 42 M1 ABV
ARV 105: 60 AAVRA1; 45 LAV-R
MW 38 *Buffalo*; some *Husky* 2G
VLB ε30 M60 AVLB
ANTI-TANK/ANTI-INFRASTRUCTURE
MSL
SP 106 LAV-AT
MANPATS FGM-148 *Javelin*; FGM-172B SRAW-MPV; TOW
ARTILLERY 1,459
TOWED 812: **105mm**: 331 M101A1; **155mm** 481 M777A2
MRL 227mm 47 M142 HIMARS
MOR 600: **81mm** 535 M252; **SP 81mm** 65 LAV-M; **120mm** (49 EFSS in store for trg)
UNINHABITED AERIAL VEHICLES
ISR • Light 100 BQM-147 *Exdrone*
AIR DEFENCE • SAM • Point-defence FIM-92 *Stinger*

Marine Corps Aviation 34,700
3 active Marine Aircraft Wings (MAW) and 1 MCR MAW
FORCES BY ROLE
FIGHTER/GROUND ATTACK
4 sqn with AV-8B *Harrier* II
1 sqn with F/A-18C *Hornet*
5 sqn with F/A-18C/D *Hornet*
5 sqn with F-35B *Lightning* II
1 sqn with F-35C *Lightning* II

COMBAT SEARCH & RESCUE/TRANSPORT
1 sqn with Beech A200/B200 *King Air* (UC-12F/M *Huron*); Beech 350 *King Air* (UC-12W *Huron*); Cessna 560 *Citation Ultra/Encore* (UC-35C/D); Gulfstream IV (C-20G)
TANKER
3 sqn with KC-130J *Hercules*
TRANSPORT
16 sqn with MV-22B *Osprey*
TRAINING
1 sqn with F/A-18C/D *Hornet*
2 sqn with F-35B *Lightning* II
1 sqn with MV-22B *Osprey*
1 hel sqn with AH-1Z *Viper*; UH-1Y *Venom*
1 hel sqn with CH-53E *Sea Stallion*
ATTACK HELICOPTER
6 sqn with AH-1Z *Viper*; UH-1Y *Venom*
TRANSPORT HELICOPTER
6 sqn with CH-53E *Sea Stallion*
1 sqn with CH-53K *King Stallion* (forming)
1 (VIP) sqn with MV-22B *Osprey*; VH-3D *Sea King*; VH-60N *White Hawk*
CISR UAV
1 sqn with MQ-9A *Reaper*
ISR UAV
2 sqn with RQ-21A *Blackjack*
AIR DEFENCE
2 bn with M1097 *Avenger*; FIM-92 *Stinger*

EQUIPMENT BY TYPE
AIRCRAFT 417 combat capable
FGA 417: 135 F-35B *Lightning* II; 10 F-35C *Lightning* II; 134 F/A-18C *Hornet*; 79 F/A-18D *Hornet*; 53 AV-8B *Harrier* II; 6 TAV-8B *Harrier*
TKR/TPT 46 KC-130J *Hercules*
TPT 20: **Light** 18: 2 Beech B200 *King Air* (UC-12F *Huron*); 2 Beech B200 *King Air* (UC-12M *Huron*); 7 Beech 350 *King Air* (C-12W *Huron*); 7 Cessna 560 *Citation Encore* (UC-35D); **PAX** 2 Gulfstream IV (C-20G)
TRG 3 T-34C *Turbo Mentor*
TILTROTOR • TPT 273 MV-22B *Osprey*
HELICOPTERS
ATK 134 AH-1Z *Viper*
TPT 288: **Heavy** 135: 129 CH-53E *Sea Stallion*; 6 CH-53K *King Stallion* (in test); **Medium** 25: 11 VH-3D *Sea King* (VIP tpt); 8 VH-60N *White Hawk* (VIP tpt); 6 VH-92A (in test); **Light** 128 UH-1Y *Venom*
UNINHABITED AERIAL VEHICLES
CISR • Heavy 2 MQ-9A *Reaper*
ISR • Light 40 RQ-21A *Blackjack*
AIR DEFENCE
SAM • Point-defence FIM-92 *Stinger*; M1097 *Avenger*
AIR-LAUNCHED MISSILES
AAM • IR AIM-9M *Sidewinder*; **IIR** AIM-9X *Sidewinder* II; **SARH** AIM-7P *Sparrow*; **ARH** AIM-120C AMRAAM
ASM AGM-65E/F IR *Maverick*; AGM-114 *Hellfire*; AGM-176 *Griffin*; AGM-179A JAGM; AGR-20A APKWS
AShM AGM-84D *Harpoon*
ARM AGM-88 HARM
LACM AGM-84E/H/K SLAM/SLAM-ER

BOMBS
Laser-guided GBU-10/-12/-16 *Paveway* II
Laser & INS/GPS-guided: EGBU-12 *Paveway* II; GBU-49 Enhanced *Paveway* II; GBU-54 Laser JDAM
INS/GPS guided GBU-31/-32/-38 JDAM; AGM-154A/C/C-1 JSOW

Reserve Organisations

Marine Corps Reserve 33,050
FORCES BY ROLE
MANOEUVRE
Reconnaissance
2 MEF recce coy
Amphibious
1 (4th) mne div (1 armd recce bn, 1 recce bn, 2 mne regt (3 mne bn), 1 amph aslt bn, 1 arty regt (2 arty bn, 1 MRL bn), 1 cbt engr bn, 1 int bn, 1 sigs bn)
COMBAT SERVICE SUPPORT
1 log gp

Marine Corps Aviation Reserve 12,000 reservists
FORCES BY ROLE
FIGHTER/GROUND ATTACK
1 sqn with F/A-18C/C+ *Hornet*
TANKER
2 sqn with KC-130J *Hercules*
TRANSPORT
2 sqn with MV-22B *Osprey*
TRAINING
1 sqn with F-5F/N *Tiger* II
ATTACK HELICOPTER
2 sqn with AH-1Z *Viper*; UH-1Y *Venom*
TRANSPORT HELICOPTER
1 sqn with CH-53E *Sea Stallion*
EQUIPMENT BY TYPE
AIRCRAFT 24 combat capable
FTR 12: 1 F-5F *Tiger* II; 11 F-5N *Tiger* II
FGA 12: 5 F/A-18C *Hornet*; 7 F/A-18C+ *Hornet*
TKR/TPT 17 KC-130J *Hercules*
TPT • Light 7: 2 Beech A200 *King Air* (UC-12F); 2 Beech 350 *King Air* (UC-12W *Huron*); 3 Cessna 560 *Citation Encore* (UC-35D)
TILTROTOR • TPT 24 MV-22B *Osprey*
HELICOPTERS
ATK 26 AH-1Z *Viper*
TPT 30: **Heavy** 8 CH-53E *Sea Stallion*; **Light** 22 UH-1Y *Venom*

Marine Stand-by Reserve 700 reservists
Trained individuals available for mobilisation

US Coast Guard 40,350
9 districts (4 Pacific, 5 Atlantic)
EQUIPMENT BY TYPE
PATROL AND COASTAL COMBATANTS 334
PSOH 23: 1 *Alex Haley*; 13 *Famous*; 9 *Legend* with 1 Mk 15 *Phalanx* Block 1B CIWS, 1 57mm gun (capacity 2 MH-65 hel)
PCO 62: 14 *Reliance* (with 1 hel landing platform); 48 *Sentinel* (Damen 4708)

PCC 12 *Island*
PBF 174 *Response Boat-Medium* (RB-M)
PBI 63 *Marine Protector*
LOGISTICS AND SUPPORT 65
ABU 52: 16 *Juniper*; 4 WLI; 14 *Keeper*; 18 WLR
AGB 12: 9 *Bay*; 1 *Mackinaw*; 1 *Healy*; 1 *Polar* (1 *Polar* in reserve)
AXS 1 *Eagle*

US Coast Guard Aviation
EQUIPMENT BY TYPE
AIRCRAFT
SAR 44: 11 HC-130H *Hercules*; 15 HC-130J *Hercules*; 5 HC-144A; 13 HC-144B
TPT 16: **Medium** 14 C-27J *Spartan*; **PAX** 2 Gulfstream V (C-37A)
HELICOPTERS
SAR 142: 44 MH-60T *Jayhawk*; 49 AS366G1 (MH-65D) *Dauphin* II; 49 AS366G1 (MH-65E) *Dauphin* II;

US Air Force (USAF) 325,100
Almost the entire USAF (plus active-force ANG and AFR) is divided into 10 Aerospace Expeditionary Forces (AEF), each on call for 120 days every 20 months. At least 2 of the 10 AEFs are on call at any one time, each with 10,000–15,000 personnel, 90 multi-role ftr and bbr ac, 31 intra-theatre refuelling aircraft and 13 aircraft for ISR and EW missions

Global Strike Command (GSC)
2 active air forces (8th & 20th); 8 wg
FORCES BY ROLE
SURFACE-TO-SURFACE MISSILE
9 ICBM sqn with LGM-30G *Minuteman* III
BOMBER
4 sqn with B-1B *Lancer*
2 sqn with B-2A *Spirit*
5 sqn (incl 1 trg) with B-52H *Stratofortress*
COMMAND & CONTROL
1 sqn with E-4B
TRANSPORT HELICOPTER
3 sqn with UH-1N *Iroquois*

Air Combat Command (ACC)
2 active air forces (9th & 12th); 12 wg. ACC numbered air forces provide the air component to CENTCOM, SOUTHCOM and NORTHCOM
FORCES BY ROLE
FIGHTER
3 sqn with F-22A *Raptor*
FIGHTER/GROUND ATTACK
4 sqn with F-15E *Strike Eagle*
3 sqn with F-16C/D *Fighting Falcon* (+6 sqn personnel only)
3 sqn with F-35A *Lightning* II
GROUND ATTACK
3 sqn with A-10C *Thunderbolt* II (+1 sqn personnel only)
ELECTRONIC WARFARE
1 sqn with EA-18G *Growler* (personnel only – USN aircraft)
2 sqn with EC-130H *Compass Call*

ISR
2 sqn with E-8C J-STARS (personnel only)
5 sqn with OC-135/RC-135/WC-135
2 sqn with U-2S
AIRBORNE EARLY WARNING & CONTROL
5 sqn with E-3 *Sentry*
COMBAT SEARCH & RESCUE
2 sqn with HC-130J *Combat King* II
1 sqn with HH-60G *Pave Hawk*
2 sqn with HH-60W *Jolly Green* II (forming)
TRAINING
1 (aggressor) sqn with F-16C *Fighting Falcon*
1 (aggressor) sqn with F-35A *Lightning* II
1 sqn with A-10C *Thunderbolt* II
1 sqn with E-3 *Sentry*
2 sqn with F-15E *Strike Eagle*
1 sqn with F-22A *Raptor*
1 sqn with RQ-4A *Global Hawk*; TU-2S
1 UAV sqn with MQ-9A *Reaper*
COMBAT/ISR UAV
9 sqn with MQ-9A *Reaper*
ISR UAV
2 sqn with RQ-4B *Global Hawk*
2 sqn with RQ-170 *Sentinel*
1 sqn with RQ-180

Pacific Air Forces (PACAF)

Provides the air component of PACOM, and commands air units based in Alaska, Hawaii, Japan and South Korea. 3 active air forces (5th, 7th, & 11th); 8 wg

FORCES BY ROLE
FIGHTER
2 sqn with F-15C/D *Eagle*
2 sqn with F-22A *Raptor* (+1 sqn personnel only)
FIGHTER/GROUND ATTACK
5 sqn with F-16C/D *Fighting Falcon*
2 sqn with F-35A *Lightning* II
GROUND ATTACK
1 sqn with A-10C *Thunderbolt* II
AIRBORNE EARLY WARNING & CONTROL
2 sqn with E-3 *Sentry*
COMBAT SEARCH & RESCUE
1 sqn with HH-60G *Pave Hawk*
TANKER
1 sqn with KC-135R (+1 sqn personnel only)
TRANSPORT
1 sqn with B-737-200 (C-40B); Gulfstream V (C-37A)
1 sqn with C-17A *Globemaster* (+1 sqn personnel only)
1 sqn with C-130J-30 *Hercules*
1 sqn with Beech 1900C (C-12J); UH-1N *Huey*
TRAINING
1 (aggressor) sqn with F-16C/D *Fighting Falcon*

United States Air Forces in Europe - Air Forces Africa (USAFE-AFAFRICA)

Provides the air component to both EUCOM and AFRICOM. 1 active air force (3rd); 5 wg

FORCES BY ROLE
FIGHTER/GROUND ATTACK
2 sqn with F-15E *Strike Eagle*
3 sqn with F-16C/D *Fighting Falcon*
2 sqn with F-35A *Lightning* II (forming)
COMBAT SEARCH & RESCUE
1 sqn with HH-60G *Pave Hawk*
TANKER
1 sqn with KC-135R *Stratotanker*
TRANSPORT
1 sqn with C-130J-30 *Hercules*
2 sqn with Gulfstream V (C-37A); Learjet 35A (C-21A); B-737-700 (C-40B)

Air Mobility Command (AMC)

Provides strategic and tactical airlift, air-to-air refuelling and aeromedical evacuation. 1 active air force (18th); 12 wg and 1 gp

FORCES BY ROLE
TANKER
3 sqn with KC-10A *Extender*
1 sqn with KC-46A *Pegasus*
1 sqn with KC-46A *Pegasus* (forming)
8 sqn with KC-135R/T *Stratotanker* (+2 sqn with personnel only)
TRANSPORT
1 VIP sqn with B-737-200 (C-40B); B-757-200 (C-32A)
1 VIP sqn with Gulfstream V (C-37A); Gulfstream 550 (C-37B)
1 VIP sqn with VC-25 *Air Force One*
2 sqn with C-5M *Super Galaxy*
8 sqn with C-17A *Globemaster* III (+1 sqn personnel only)
5 sqn with C-130J-30 *Hercules* (+1 sqn personnel only)
1 sqn with Learjet 35A (C-21A)

Air Education and Training Command

1 active air force (2nd), 10 active air wg and 1 gp

FORCES BY ROLE
TRAINING
1 sqn with C-17A *Globemaster* III
1 sqn with C-130J-30 *Hercules*
4 sqn with F-16C/D *Fighting Falcon*
5 sqn with F-35A *Lightning* II
1 sqn with KC-46A *Pegasus*
1 sqn with KC-135R *Stratotanker*
5 (flying trg) sqn with T-1A *Jayhawk*
10 (flying trg) sqn with T-6A *Texan* II
10 (flying trg) sqn with T-38C *Talon*
5 UAV sqn with MQ-9A *Reaper*

EQUIPMENT BY TYPE
SURFACE-TO-SURFACE MISSILE LAUNCHERS
ICBM • **Nuclear** 400 LGM-30G *Minuteman* III (1 Mk12A or Mk21 re-entry veh per missile)
AIRCRAFT 1,574 combat capable
BBR 123: 45 B-1B *Lancer*; 20 B-2A *Spirit*; 58 B-52H *Stratofortress* (46 nuclear capable)
FTR 214: 45 F-15C *Eagle*; 4 F-15D *Eagle*; 165 F-22A *Raptor*
FGA 1,063: 218 F-15E *Strike Eagle*; 2 F-15EX *Eagle* II; 410 F-16C *Fighting Falcon*; 91 F-16D *Fighting Falcon*; 342 F-35A *Lightning* II

ATK 135 A-10C *Thunderbolt* II
CSAR 16 HC-130J *Combat King* II
EW 7 EC-130H *Compass Call*
ISR 38: 2 E-9A; 4 E-11A; 26 U-2S; 4 TU-2S; 1 WC-135R *Constant Phoenix*
ELINT 22: 8 RC-135V *Rivet Joint*; 9 RC-135W *Rivet Joint*; 3 RC-135S *Cobra Ball*; 2 RC-135U *Combat Sent*
AEW&C 31: 7 E-3B *Sentry*; 1 E-3C *Sentry*; 23 E-3G *Sentry*
C2 4 E-4B **TKR** 156: 126 KC-135R *Stratotanker*; 30 KC-135T *Stratotanker*
TKR/TPT 70: 36 KC-10A *Extender*; 34 KC-46A *Pegasus*
TPT 336: **Heavy** 182: 36 C-5M *Super Galaxy*; 146 C-17A *Globemaster* III; **Medium** 105: 10 C-130J *Hercules*; 95 C-130J-30 *Hercules*; **Light** 23: 4 Beech 1900C (C-12J); 19 Learjet 35A (C-21A); **PAX** 26: 4 B-737-700 (C-40B); 4 B-757-200 (C-32A); 9 Gulfstream V (C-37A); 7 Gulfstream 550 (C-37B); 2 VC-25A *Air Force One*
TRG 1,126: 178 T-1A *Jayhawk*; 443 T-6A *Texan* II; 505 T-38A/C *Talon*
HELICOPTERS
MRH 4 MH-139A *Grey Wolf* (in test)
CSAR 62: 52 HH-60G *Pave Hawk*; 10 HH-60W *Jolly Green* II
TPT • **Light** 62 UH-1N *Huey*
UNINHABITED AERIAL VEHICLES 261
CISR • **Heavy** 210 MQ-9A *Reaper*
ISR • **Heavy** 27: 10 RQ-4B *Global Hawk*; ε10 RQ-170 *Sentinel*; ε7 RQ-180
AIR DEFENCE
SAM • **Point-defence** FIM-92 *Stinger*
AIR-LAUNCHED MISSILES
AAM • **IR** AIM-9M *Sidewinder*; **IIR** AIM-9X *Sidewinder* II; **SARH** AIM-7M *Sparrow*; **ARH** AIM-120C/D AMRAAM
ASM AGM-65D/G *Maverick*; AGM-114K/M/N/R *Hellfire* II; AGM-130A; AGM-176 *Griffin*; AGR-20A APKWS
AShM AGM-158C LRASM
ALCM
Nuclear AGM-86B (ALCM)
Conventional AGM-158A JASSM; AGM-158B JASSM-ER
ARM AGM-88B/C HARM
EW MALD/MALD-J
BOMBS
Laser-guided GBU-10/-12/-16 *Paveway* II, GBU-24 *Paveway* III; GBU-28
Laser & INS/GPS-guided EGBU-24 *Paveway* III; EGBU-28; GBU-49 Enhanced *Paveway* II; GBU-54 Laser JDAM
INS/GPS-guided GBU-15 (with BLU-109 penetrating warhead or Mk84); GBU-31/-32/-38 JDAM; GBU-39B Small Diameter Bomb (250lb); GBU-43B MOAB; GBU-57A/B MOP
Multi-mode guided GBU-53/B *Stormbreaker*

Reserve Organisations

Air National Guard 105,100 reservists
FORCES BY ROLE
BOMBER
1 sqn with B-2A *Spirit* (personnel only)

FIGHTER
5 sqn with F-15C/D *Eagle*
1 sqn with F-22A *Raptor* (+1 sqn personnel only)
FIGHTER/GROUND ATTACK
10 sqn with F-16C/D *Fighting Falcon*
1 sqn with F-35A *Lightning* II
GROUND ATTACK
4 sqn with A-10C *Thunderbolt* II
ISR
1 sqn with E-8C J-STARS
COMBAT SEARCH & RESCUE
3 sqn with HC-130J *Combat King* II
3 sqn with HH-60G *Pave Hawk*
TANKER
1 sqn with KC-46A *Pegasus*
16 sqn with KC-135R *Stratotanker* (+1 sqn personnel only)
3 sqn with KC-135T *Stratotanker*
TRANSPORT
1 sqn with B-737-700 (C-40C)
6 sqn with C-17A *Globemaster* (+2 sqn personnel only)
10 sqn with C-130H *Hercules*
1 sqn with C-130H/LC-130H *Hercules*
4 sqn with C-130J-30 *Hercules*
TRAINING
1 sqn with C-130H *Hercules*
1 sqn with F-15C/D *Eagle*
4 sqn with F-16C/D *Fighting Falcon*
1 sqn with MQ-9A *Reaper*
COMBAT/ISR UAV
10 sqn with MQ-9A *Reaper*

EQUIPMENT BY TYPE
AIRCRAFT 596 combat capable
FTR 157: 123 F-15C *Eagle*; 14 F-15D *Eagle*; 20 F-22A *Raptor*
FGA 354: 288 F-16C *Fighting Falcon*; 46 F-16D *Fighting Falcon*; 20 F-35A *Lightning* II
ATK 85 A-10C *Thunderbolt* II
CSAR 12 HC-130J *Combat King* II
ISR 13 E-8C J-STARS
ELINT 11 RC-26B *Metroliner*
TKR 162: 138 KC-135R *Stratotanker*; 24 KC-135T *Stratotanker*
TKR/TPT 12 KC-46A *Pegasus*
TPT 197: **Heavy** 50 C-17A *Globemaster* III; **Medium** 144: 99 C-130H *Hercules*; 35 C-130J-30 *Hercules*; 10 LC-130H *Hercules*; **PAX** 3 B-737-700 (C-40C)
HELICOPTERS • **CSAR** 18 HH-60G *Pave Hawk*
UNINHABITED AERIAL VEHICLES • **CISR** • **Heavy** 24 MQ-9A *Reaper*

Air Force Reserve Command 68,300 reservists
FORCES BY ROLE
BOMBER
1 sqn with B-52H *Stratofortress* (personnel only)
FIGHTER
2 sqn with F-22A *Raptor* (personnel only)
FIGHTER/GROUND ATTACK
2 sqn with F-16C/D *Fighting Falcon* (+1 sqn personnel only)
1 sqn with F-35A *Lightning* II (personnel only)
GROUND ATTACK
1 sqn with A-10C *Thunderbolt* II (+2 sqn personnel only)

46   THE MILITARY BALANCE 2023

ISR
1 (Weather Recce) sqn with WC-130J *Hercules*
AIRBORNE EARLY WARNING & CONTROL
1 sqn with E-3 *Sentry* (personnel only)
COMBAT SEARCH & RESCUE
1 sqn with HC-130J *Combat King* II
2 sqn with HH-60G *Pave Hawk*
TANKER
4 sqn with KC-10A *Extender* (personnel only)
1 sqn with KC-46A *Pegasus*
1 sqn with KC-46A *Pegasus* (personnel only)
6 sqn with KC-135R *Stratotanker* (+2 sqn personnel only)
TRANSPORT
1 (VIP) sqn with B-737-700 (C-40C)
2 sqn with C-5M *Super Galaxy* (+2 sqn personnel only)
3 sqn with C-17A *Globemaster* (+9 sqn personnel only)
6 sqn with C-130H *Hercules*
1 sqn with C-130J-30 *Hercules*
1 (Aerial Spray) sqn with C-130H *Hercules*
TRAINING
1 (aggressor) sqn with A-10C *Thunderbolt* II;
    F-15C/E *Eagle*; F-16 *Fighting Falcon*; F-22A *Raptor*
    (personnel only)
1 sqn with A-10C *Thunderbolt* II
1 sqn with B-52H *Stratofortress*
1 sqn with C-5M *Super Galaxy*
1 sqn with F-16C/D *Fighting Falcon*
5 (flying training) sqn with T-1A *Jayhawk*; T-6A *Texan*
    II; T-38C *Talon* (personnel only)
COMBAT/ISR UAV
2 sqn with MQ-9A *Reaper* (personnel only)
ISR UAV
1 sqn with RQ-4B *Global Hawk* (personnel only)
EQUIPMENT BY TYPE
AIRCRAFT 133 combat capable
BBR 18 B-52H *Stratofortress*
FGA 54: 52 F-16C *Fighting Falcon*; 2 F-16D *Fighting Falcon*
ATK 61 A-10C *Thunderbolt* II
CSAR 4 HC-130J *Combat King* II
ISR 10 WC-130J *Hercules* (Weather Recce)
TKR 62 KC-135R *Stratotanker*
TKR/TPT 9 KC-46A *Pegasus*
TPT 98: **Heavy** 42: 16 C-5M *Super Galaxy*; 26 C-17A
Globemaster III; **Medium** 52: 42 C-130H *Hercules*; 10
C-130J-30 *Hercules*; **PAX** 4 B-737-700 (C-40C)
HELICOPTERS • CSAR 16 HH-60G *Pave Hawk*

Civil Reserve Air Fleet
Commercial ac numbers fluctuate
AIRCRAFT • TPT 517 international (391 long-range
and 126 short-range); 36 national

Air Force Stand-by Reserve 16,850 reservists
Trained individuals for mobilisation

US Space Force 6,400
New service established December 2019, currently in
the process of being stood up. Tasked with organising,
training and equipping forces to protect US and allied
space interests and to provide space capabilities to the joint
Combatant Commands

EQUIPMENT BY TYPE
SATELLITES see Space
COUNTERSPACE see Space
RADAR see Strategic Defenses – Early Warning

US Special Operations Command (USSOCOM) 65,800
Commands all active, reserve and National Guard Special
Operations Forces (SOF) of all services based in CONUS

Joint Special Operations Command
Reported to comprise elite US SOF, including Special
Forces Operations Detachment Delta ('Delta Force'),
SEAL Team 6 and integral USAF support

US Army Special Operations Command 35,000
FORCES BY ROLE
SPECIAL FORCES
5 SF gp (4 SF bn, 1 spt bn)
1 ranger regt (3 ranger bn; 1 cbt spt bn)
COMBAT SUPPORT
1 civil affairs bde (5 civil affairs bn)
1 psyops gp (3 psyops bn)
1 psyops gp (4 psyops bn)
COMBAT SERVICE SUPPORT
1 (sustainment) log bde (1 sigs bn)
HELICOPTER
1 (160th SOAR) hel regt (4 hel bn)
EQUIPMENT BY TYPE
ARMOURED FIGHTING VEHICLES
APC • APC (W) 28: 16 M1126 *Stryker* ICV; 12 *Pandur*
AUV 640 M-ATV
ARTILLERY 20
MOR • 120mm 20 XM905 EMTAS
AIRCRAFT
TPT 12: **Medium** 7 C-27J *Spartan* (parachute training);
Light 5 C-212 (parachute training)
HELICOPTERS
MRH 51 AH-6M/MH-6M *Little Bird*
TPT 139: **Heavy** 67 MH-47G *Chinook*; **Medium** 72 MH-
60M *Black Hawk*
UNINHABITED AERIAL VEHICLES
CISR • Heavy 24 MQ-1C *Gray Eagle*
ISR • Light 29: 15 XPV-1 *Tern*; 14 XPV-2 *Mako*
TPT • Heavy 28 CQ-10 *Snowgoose*

Reserve Organisations

Army National Guard
FORCES BY ROLE
SPECIAL FORCES
2 SF gp (3 SF bn)

Army Reserve
FORCES BY ROLE
COMBAT SUPPORT
2 psyops gp
4 civil affairs comd HQ
8 civil affairs bde HQ
32 civil affairs bn (coy)

US Navy Special Warfare Command 10,500

FORCES BY ROLE
SPECIAL FORCES
  8 SEAL team (total: 48 SF pl)
  2 SEAL Delivery Vehicle team

Reserve Organisations

Naval Reserve Force

FORCES BY ROLE
SPECIAL FORCES
  8 SEAL det
  10 Naval Special Warfare det
  2 Special Boat sqn
  2 Special Boat unit
  1 SEAL Delivery Vehicle det

US Marine Special Operations Command (MARSOC) 3,500

FORCES BY ROLE
SPECIAL FORCES
  1 SF regt (3 SF bn)
COMBAT SUPPORT
  1 int bn
COMBAT SERVICE SUPPORT
  1 spt gp

Air Force Special Operations Command (AFSOC) 16,800

FORCES BY ROLE
GROUND ATTACK
  3 sqn with AC-130J *Ghostrider*
TRANSPORT
  4 sqn with CV-22B *Osprey*
  1 sqn with Do-328 (C-146A)
  1 sqn with MC-130H *Combat Talon*
  3 sqn with MC-130J *Commando* II
  3 sqn with PC-12 (U-28A)
TRAINING
  1 sqn with M-28 *Skytruck* (C-145A)
  1 sqn with CV-22A/B *Osprey*
  1 sqn with HC-130J *Combat King* II; MC-130J
    Commando II
  1 sqn with Bell 205 (TH-1H *Iroquois*)
  1 sqn with HH-60W *Jolly Green* II; UH-1N *Huey*
COMBAT/ISR UAV
  3 sqn with MQ-9 *Reaper*

EQUIPMENT BY TYPE
AIRCRAFT 31 combat capable
  ATK 31 AC-130J *Ghostrider*
  ISR 22 MC-12 *Javaman*
  CSAR 3 HC-130J *Combat King* II
  TPT 109: **Medium** 49: 8 MC-130H *Combat Talon* II; 41
  MC-130J *Commando* II; **Light** 60: 20 Do-328 (C-146A); 5
  M-28 *Skytruck* (C-145A); 35 PC-12 (U-28A)
TILT-ROTOR 51 CV-22A/B *Osprey*
HELICOPTERS
  CSAR 7 HH-60W *Jolly Green* II
  TPT • **Light** 34: 28 Bell 205 (TH-1H *Iroquois*); 6 UH-1N *Huey*

UNINHABITED AERIAL VEHICLES • CISR • Heavy
50 MQ-9 *Reaper*

Reserve Organisations

Air National Guard

FORCES BY ROLE
ELECTRONIC WARFARE
  1 sqn with C-130J *Hercules*/EC-130J *Commando Solo*
ISR
  1 sqn with MC-12W *Liberty*
TRANSPORT
  1 flt with B-737-200 (C-32B)

EQUIPMENT BY TYPE
AIRCRAFT
  EW 7 EC-130J *Commando Solo*
  ISR 13 MC-12W *Liberty*
  TPT 5: **Medium** 3 C-130J *Hercules*; **PAX** 2 B-757-200
  (C-32B)

Air Force Reserve

FORCES BY ROLE
TRAINING
  1 sqn with AC-130J *Ghostrider* (personnel only)
  1 sqn with M-28 *Skytruck* (C-145A) (personnel only)
COMBAT/ISR UAV
  1 sqn with MQ-9 *Reaper* (personnel only)

DEPLOYMENT

ARABIAN SEA: US Central Command • US Navy • 5th Fleet 1,000: 2 SSGN; 2 DDGHM; **Combined Maritime Forces** • TF 53: 3 AKEH; 1 AOR

ARUBA: US Southern Command • 1 Forward Operating Location

ASCENSION ISLAND: US Strategic Command • 1 detection and tracking radar at Ascension Auxiliary Air Field

AUSTRALIA: US Pacific Command • 1,700; 1 SEWS at Pine Gap; 1 comms facility at Pine Gap; 1 SIGINT stn at Pine Gap; **US Strategic Command** • 1 detection and tracking radar at Naval Communication Station Harold E. Holt

BAHRAIN: US Central Command • 4,700; 1 HQ (5th Fleet); 10 PCFG; 4 MCO; 1 ESB; 1 ASW flt with 2 P-8A *Poseidon*; 1 EP-3E *Aries* II; 2 SAM bty with M902/M903 *Patriot* PAC-3/PAC-3 MSE

BELGIUM: US European Command • 1,150

BRITISH INDIAN OCEAN TERRITORY: US Strategic Command • 300; 1 Spacetrack Optical Tracker at Diego Garcia; 1 ground-based electro-optical deep space surveillance system (GEODSS) at Diego Garcia **US Pacific Command** • 1 MPS sqn (MPS-2 with equipment for one MEB) at Diego Garcia with 2 AKRH; 3 AKR; 1 AKEH; 1 ESD; 1 naval air base at Diego Garcia, 1 support facility at Diego Garcia

BULGARIA: NATO • Enhanced Vigilance Activities 150; 1 armd inf coy with M2A3 Bradley

CANADA: US Northern Command • 150

CENTRAL AFRICAN REPUBLIC: UN • MINUSCA 10

COLOMBIA: US Southern Command • 70

CUBA: US Southern Command • 650 (JTF-GTMO) at Guantanamo Bay

CURACAO: US Southern Command • 1 Forward Operating Location

DEMOCRATIC REPUBLIC OF THE CONGO: UN • MONUSCO 3

DJIBOUTI: US Africa Command • 4,000; 1 tpt sqn with C-130H/J-30 *Hercules*; 1 tpt sqn with 12 MV-22B *Osprey*; 2 KC-130J *Hercules*; 1 spec ops sqn with MC-130H/J; PC-12 (U-28A); 1 CSAR sqn with HH-60G *Pave Hawk*; 1 CISR UAV sqn with MQ-9A *Reaper*; 1 naval air base

EGYPT: MFO 426; elm 1 ARNG inf bn; 1 ARNG spt bn

EL SALVADOR: US Southern Command • 100; 1 ASW flt with 2 P-8A *Poseidon*; 1 Forward Operating Location (Military, DEA, USCG and Customs personnel)

GERMANY: US Africa Command • 1 HQ at Stuttgart **US European Command** • 39,050; 1 Combined Service HQ (EUCOM) at Stuttgart–Vaihingen

US Army 24,700

FORCES BY ROLE
1 HQ (US Army Europe & Africa (USAREUR-AF)) at Wiesbaden; 1 arty comd; 1 spec ops gp; 1 recce bn; 1 mech bde(-); 1 MRL bde (3 MRL bn); 1 fd arty bn; 1 (cbt avn) hel bde; 1 (cbt avn) hel bde HQ; 1 int bde; 1 MP bde; 1 sigs bde; 1 (MDTF) cbt spt bde(-); 1 spt bde; 1 SAM bde; 1 (APS) armd bde eqpt set

EQUIPMENT BY TYPE
M1A2 SEPv2/v3 *Abrams*; M2A3/M3A3 *Bradley*; M1296 *Stryker Dragoon*, M109A6; M119A3; M777A2; M270A1; M142 HIMARS; AH-64D *Apache*; CH-47F *Chinook*; UH-60M *Black Hawk*; HH-60M *Black Hawk*; M902 *Patriot* PAC-3; M1097 *Avenger*; M-SHORAD

US Navy 400

USAF 13,400

FORCES BY ROLE
1 HQ (US Air Forces in Europe and Africa) at Ramstein AB; 1 HQ (3rd Air Force) at Ramstein AB; 1 FGA wg at Spangdahlem AB with (1 FGA sqn with 24 F-16C/D *Fighting Falcon*); 1 tpt wg at Ramstein AB with 14 C-130J-30 *Hercules*; 2 Gulfstream V (C-37A); 5 Learjet 35A (C-21A); 1 B-737-700 (C-40B)

USMC 550

GREECE: US European Command • 400; 1 ELINT flt with 1 EP-3E *Aries* II; 1 naval base at Makri; 1 naval base at Souda Bay; 1 air base at Iraklion

GREENLAND (DNK): US Strategic Command • 100; 1 AN/FPS-132 Upgraded Early Warning Radar and 1 Spacetrack Radar at Thule

GUAM: US Pacific Command • 9,000; 4 SSGN; 1 MPS sqn (MPS-3 with equipment for one MEB) with 2 AKRH; 4 AKR; 1 ESD; 1 AKEH; 1 tkr sqn with 12 KC-135R *Stratotanker*; 1 tpt hel sqn with MH-60S; 1 ISR UAV unit with 2 MQ-4C *Triton*; 1 SAM bty with THAAD; 1 air base; 1 naval base

HONDURAS: US Southern Command • 400; 1 avn bn with 4 CH-47F *Chinook*; 12 UH-60 *Black Hawk*

HUNGARY: NATO • Enhanced Vigilance Activities 150; 1 armd inf coy with M2A3 Bradley

ICELAND: US European Command • 100; 1 ASW flt with 2 P-8A *Poseidon*

IRAQ: US Central Command • *Operation Inherent Resolve* 2,000; 1 mech inf bde(-); 1 atk hel bn with AH-64E *Apache*; MQ-1C *Gray Eagle*; 1 spec ops hel bn with MH-47G *Chinook*; MH-60M *Black Hawk*; 1 CISR UAV sqn with MQ-9A *Reaper*; **NATO** • NATO Mission Iraq 12

ISRAEL: US Strategic Command • 100; 1 AN/TPY-2 X-band radar at Mount Keren

ITALY: US European Command • 13,050

US Army 4,250; 1 AB bde(-)

US Navy 3,600; 1 HQ (US Naval Forces Europe-Africa (NAVEUR-NAVAF/6th Fleet) at Naples; 1 LCC; 1 ASW sqn with 5 P-8A *Poseidon* at Sigonella

USAF 4,800; 1 FGA wg with (2 FGA sqn with 21 F-16C/D *Fighting Falcon* at Aviano; 1 CSAR sqn with 8 HH-60G *Pave Hawk* at Aviano); 1 CISR UAV sqn with MQ-9A *Reaper* at Sigonella; 1 ISR UAV flt with RQ-4B *Global Hawk* at Sigonella

USMC 400; 1 tpt sqn with 6 MV-22B *Osprey*; 2 KC-130J *Hercules*

JAPAN: US Pacific Command • 55,600

US Army 2,600; 1 corps HQ (fwd); 1 SF gp; 1 avn bn; 1 SAM bn with M903 *Patriot* PAC-3 MSE

US Navy 20,000; 1 HQ (7th Fleet) at Yokosuka; 1 base at Sasebo; 1 base at Yokosuka

FORCES BY ROLE
3 FGA sqn at Iwakuni with 10 F/A-18E *Super Hornet*; 1 FGA sqn at Iwakuni with 10 F/A-18F *Super Hornet*; 2 ASW sqn at Misawa/Kadena with 5 P-8A *Poseidon*; 2 EW sqn at Iwakuni/Misawa with 5 EA-18G *Growler*; 1 ELINT flt at Okinawa – Kadena AB with 2 EP-3E *Aries* II; 1 AEW&C sqn at Iwakuni with 5 E-2D *Hawkeye*; 2 ASW hel sqn at Atsugi with 12 MH-60R;1 tpt hel sqn at Atsugi with 12 MH-60S

EQUIPMENT BY TYPE
1 CVN; 3 CGHM; 4 DDGHM; 4 DDGM; 1 LCC; 4 MCO; 1 LHA; 2 LPD; 2 LSD

USAF 13,000

FORCES BY ROLE
1 HQ (5th Air Force) at Okinawa – Kadena AB; 1 ftr wg at Misawa AB with (2 FGA sqn with 22 F-16C/D *Fighting Falcon*); 1 wg at Okinawa – Kadena AB with (2 ftr sqn with 27 F-15C/D *Eagle*; 1 tkr sqn with 15 KC-135R *Stratotanker*; 1 AEW&C sqn with 2 E-3B *Sentry*; 1 CSAR sqn with 10 HH-60G *Pave Hawk*); 1 tpt wg at Yokota AB with 10 C-130J-30 *Hercules*; 3 Beech 1900C (C-12J); 1 Spec Ops gp at Okinawa – Kadena AB with (1 sqn with 5 MC-130J *Commando* II; 1 sqn with 5 CV-22B *Osprey*); 1 ISR sqn with RC-135 *Rivet Joint*; 1 ISR UAV flt with 5 RQ-4A *Global Hawk*

USMC 20,000

FORCES BY ROLE
1 mne div; 1 mne regt HQ; 1 arty regt HQ; 1 recce bn; 1 mne bn; 1 amph aslt bn; 1 arty bn; 1 FGA sqn with 12 F/A-18D *Hornet*; 2 FGA sqn with 10 F-35B *Lightning* II;

1 tkr sqn with 12 KC-130J *Hercules*; 2 tpt sqn with 12 MV-22B *Osprey*

US Strategic Command • 1 AN/TPY-2 X-band radar at Shariki; 1 AN/TPY-2 X-band radar at Kyogamisaki

JORDAN: US Central Command • *Operation Inherent Resolve* 3,000: 1 FGA sqn with 18 F-15E *Strike Eagle*; 1 CISR UAV sqn with 12 MQ-9A *Reaper*

KOREA, REPUBLIC OF: US Pacific Command • 30,400

US Army 21,500

FORCES BY ROLE

1 HQ (8th Army) at Pyeongtaek; 1 div HQ (2nd Inf) located at Pyeongtaek; 1 mech bde; 1 (cbt avn) hel bde; 1 MRL bde; 1 AD bde; 1 SAM bty with THAAD

EQUIPMENT BY TYPE

M1A2 SEPv2 *Abrams*; M2A3/M3A3 *Bradley*; M109A6; M270A1 MLRS; AH-64D/E *Apache*; CH-47F *Chinook*; UH-60L/M *Black Hawk*; M902 *Patriot* PAC-3; THAAD; FIM-92A *Avenger*; 1 (APS) armd bde eqpt set

US Navy 350

USAF 8,350

FORCES BY ROLE

1 (AF) HQ (7th Air Force) at Osan AB; 1 ftr wg at Osan AB with (1 ftr sqn with 20 F-16C/D *Fighting Falcon*; 1 atk sqn with 24 A-10C *Thunderbolt* II); 1 ftr wg at Kunsan AB with (2 ftr sqn with 20 F-16C/D *Fighting Falcon*); 1 ISR sqn at Osan AB with U-2S

USMC 200

KUWAIT: US Central Command • 10,000; 1 ARNG armd bn; 1 ARNG (cbt avn) hel bde; 1 spt bde; 1 CISR UAV sqn with MQ-9A *Reaper*; 1 (APS) armd bde set; 1 (APS) inf bde set

LIBYA: UN • UNSMIL 1

LITHUANIA: US European Command • 250; 1 radar unit

MALI: UN • MINUSMA 10

MARSHALL ISLANDS: US Strategic Command • 20; 1 detection and tracking radar at Kwajalein Atoll

MEDITERRANEAN SEA: US European Command • 6th Fleet 6,000; 1 CVN; 1 CGHM; 2 DDGHM; **NATO** • SNMG 2; 300; 1 DDGHM

MIDDLE EAST: UN • UNTSO 2

NETHERLANDS: US European Command • 450

NIGER: US Africa Command • 800; 1 CISR sqn with MQ-9A *Reaper*

NORWAY: US European Command • 1,100; 1 (USMC) MEU eqpt set; 1 (APS) SP 155mm arty bn set

PERSIAN GULF: US Central Command • US Navy • 5th Fleet 500: 1 DDGHM; 6 (Coast Guard) PCC

PHILIPPINES: US Pacific Command • *Operation Pacific Eagle – Philippines* 200

POLAND: NATO • Enhanced Forward Presence 700; 1 armd bn with M1A2 SEPv2 *Abrams*; M2A3 *Bradley* **US European Command** • 15,000; 1 corps HQ; 2 div HQ; 2 armd bde with M1A2 SEPv2 *Abrams*; M3A3 *Bradley*; M2A3 *Bradley*; M109A6/7; 1 AB bde with M119A3; M777A2; 2 SAM bty with M902 *Patriot* PAC-3; 1 FGA sqn with 12 F-22A *Raptor*; 1 CISR UAV sqn with MQ-9A *Reaper*

PORTUGAL: US European Command • 250; 1 spt facility at Lajes

QATAR: US Central Command • 10,000: 1 ISR sqn with 4 RC-135 *Rivet Joint*; 1 ISR sqn with 4 E-8C JSTARS; 2 tkr sqn with 12 KC-135R/T *Stratotanker*; 1 tpt sqn with 4 C-17A *Globemaster*; 4 C-130H/J-30 *Hercules*; 2 SAM bty with M902/M903 *Patriot* PAC-3/PAC-3 MSE **US Strategic Command** • 1 AN/TPY-2 X-band radar

ROMANIA: US European Command • 4,000; 1 air aslt bde with M119A3; M777A3; 1 *Aegis Ashore* BMD unit with three 8-cell Mk 41 VLS launchers with SM-3

SAUDI ARABIA: US Central Command • 2,000; 1 FGA sqn with 12 F-16C *Fighting Falcon*

SERBIA: NATO • KFOR • *Joint Enterprise* 660; elm 1 ARNG inf bde HQ; 1 ARNG recce bn; 1 hel flt with UH-60

SINGAPORE: US Pacific Command • 200; 1 log spt sqn; 1 spt facility

SLOVAKIA: NATO • Enhanced Vigilance Activities 400; 1 SAM bty with M902 *Patriot* PAC-3

SOMALIA: US Africa Command • 100

SOUTH SUDAN: UN • UNMISS 8

SPAIN: US European Command • 3,250; 4 DDGM; 1 air base at Morón; 1 naval base at Rota

SYRIA: US Central Command • *Operation Inherent Resolve* 900; 1 armd inf coy; 1 mne bn(-)

THAILAND: US Pacific Command • 100

TURKEY: US European Command • 1,700; 1 tkr sqn with 14 KC-135; 1 air base at Incirlik; 1 support facility at Ankara; 1 support facility at Izmir **US Strategic Command** • 1 AN/TPY-2 X-band radar at Kürecik

UNITED ARAB EMIRATES: US Central Command • 5,000: 1 ISR sqn with 4 U-2; 1 AEW&C sqn with 4 E-3B/G *Sentry*; 1 tkr sqn with 12 KC-10A; 1 ISR UAV sqn with RQ-4 *Global Hawk*; 2 SAM bty with M902/M903 *Patriot* PAC-3/PAC-3 MSE

UNITED KINGDOM: US European Command • 10,000

FORCES BY ROLE

1 ftr wg at RAF Lakenheath with (2 FGA sqn with 23 F-15E *Strike Eagle,* 1 FGA sqn with 21 F-35A *Lightning* II; 1 FGA sqn with F-35A *Lightning* II (forming)); 1 ISR sqn at RAF Mildenhall with OC-135/RC-135; 1 tkr wg at RAF Mildenhall with 15 KC-135R/T *Stratotanker*; 1 spec ops gp at RAF Mildenhall with (1 sqn with 8 CV-22B *Osprey*; 1 sqn with 8 MC-130J *Commando* II)

US Strategic Command • 1 AN/FPS-132 Upgraded Early Warning Radar and 1 Spacetrack Radar at Fylingdales Moor

FOREIGN FORCES

Germany Air Force: trg units with 40 T-38 *Talon*; 69 T-6A *Texan* II; • Missile trg at Fort Bliss (TX)

Netherlands 1 hel trg sqn with AH-64D *Apache*; CH-47D *Chinook*

Singapore Air Force: trg units with F-16C/D; 12 F-15SG; AH-64D *Apache*; 6+ CH-47D *Chinook* hel

Chapter Four
Europe

- The war in Ukraine has caused many states to reassess their defence priorities, and it has effectively shifted the strategic centre of gravity in Europe further to the north and east. Poland has accelerated its project to recapitalise and expand its ground forces' armour and artillery capabilities. This change has been accompanied by a rapid increase in defence expenditure: a new spending level was set at 3% of GDP from 2023.
- As part of efforts to close Germany's long-standing defence-capabilities gap, Germany's Chancellor Olaf Scholz announced in February the creation of a EUR100bn (USD106bn) special fund to finance Bundeswehr investment and equipment projects.
- Russia's February 2022 invasion of Ukraine has reinvigorated NATO. At its Madrid summit in June 2022, NATO agreed a new force model to boost force size and readiness and to replace the NATO Response Force. The assumption under the new three-tier model is that the new force would be able to deploy at least 300,000 troops no later than 30 days. But as before, a key challenge will be in transforming members' commitments into a capability.
- Finland and Sweden were on the path to NATO membership in 2023. For NATO, their accession implies an expanded collective defence obligation. Nevertheless, NATO will benefit from Northern Europe becoming a more integrated space in terms of deterrence and defence. It means that, bar Russian coastlines in the Gulf of Finland and in Kaliningrad, the shores of the Baltic Sea will be controlled by NATO members.
- One outcome of the drive to deliver security assistance to Ukraine is that legacy equipment and ageing ammunition stocks are being flushed out of European inventories. This will be more pronounced in Central and Eastern European countries, where many states had retained Soviet-era legacy equipment in their inventories. It creates an opportunity to accelerate military modernisation and consider expanding equipment commonality.

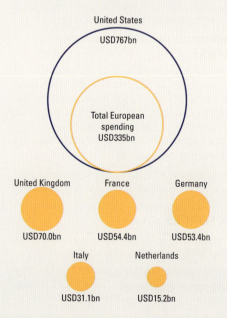

Europe defence spending, 2022 – top 5

United States USD767bn
Total European spending USD335bn
United Kingdom USD70.0bn
France USD54.4bn
Germany USD53.4bn
Italy USD31.1bn
Netherlands USD15.2bn

Active military personnel – top 10
(15,000 per unit)

Country	Personnel
Turkey	355,200
France	203,250
Germany	183,150
Italy	161,050
United Kingdom	150,350
Greece	132,200
Spain	124,150
Poland	114,050
Romania	71,500
Bulgaria	36,950

Global total 20,773,950
Regional total 1,948,260 (9.4%)

Regional defence policy and economics　52 ▶

Arms procurements and deliveries　69 ▶

Armed forces data section　72 ▶

Europe: selected tactical combat aircraft, 2022*

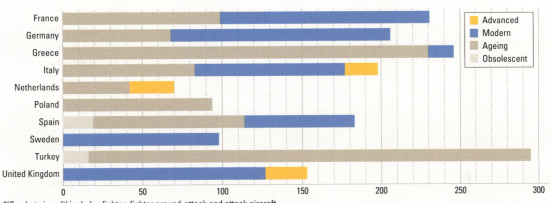

*'Combat aircraft' includes fighter, fighter ground-attack and attack aircraft

Europe: selected main battle tank fleets, 2022

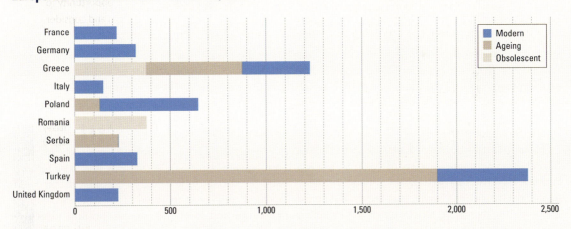

Europe: medium transport aircraft, 2022

Operator	Equipment	Total	Operator	Equipment	Total
Austria	C-130K *Hercules*	3	**Norway**	C-130J-30 *Hercules*	4
Bulgaria	C-27J *Spartan*	3	**Poland**	C-130H/C-130E *Hercules*	7
Denmark	C-130J-30 *Hercules*	4	**Portugal**	C-130H/C-130H-30 *Hercules*	5
France	C-130H/C-130H-30/C-130J-30 *Hercules*	16	**Romania**	C-130B/C-130H *Hercules*/C-27J *Spartan*	12
Germany	C-130J-30 *Hercules*	3	**Slovakia**	C-27J *Spartan*	2
Greece	C-130B/C-130H *Hercules*/C-27J *Spartan*	23	**Sweden**	C-130H *Hercules*	5
Italy	C-130J/C-130J-30 *Hercules*/C-27J *Spartan*	33	**Turkey**	C-130B/C-130E *Hercules*/C-160D *Transall*	24
Lithuania	C-27J *Spartan*	3	**United Kingdom**	C-130J/C-130J-30 *Hercules*	14
Netherlands	C-130H/C-130H-30 *Hercules*	4			

Europe

Russia's full-scale invasion of Ukraine, which began on 24 February 2022, has profoundly affected defence-policy debates in Europe, both at the national and at the multilateral level. It is leading some nations to reconsider the likely character of a potential war in Europe and resulting capability requirements, including doctrine, equipment and personnel, and also dispositions. Between January and the end of July, 20 European states announced defence spending increases. Estonia, Latvia, Lithuania and the United Kingdom declared ambitions to raise their defence spending to 2.5% of GDP. The UK ambition was briefly raised to 3% by 2030 (the figure for which Poland is aiming) but by late year, and amid a changed economic outlook, the new administration of Rishi Sunak reduced the target back to 2% of GDP. Germany announced a special EUR100 billion (USD106bn) fund to pay for defence-modernisation needs. NATO and European Union members also agreed to several packages of sanctions against Russia and began to deliver substantial military assistance to Ukraine. Russia's invasion caused other notable shifts in government policy and public opinion. Finland and Sweden applied for NATO membership, and Denmark held a referendum on 1 June which effectively ended Copenhagen's opt-out from the military aspects of the EU's Common Security and Defence Policy (CSDP).

Finland and Sweden are likely to formally join NATO at some point in 2023. At NATO's Madrid Summit, held from 28–30 June, the Alliance formally invited the two nations to join, after they both applied the preceding month. By October, 28 NATO member states had ratified the required accession documents, with only Hungary and Turkey remaining. Finland and Sweden had previously collaborated closely with NATO, including on operations and through frameworks such as the UK-led Joint Expeditionary Force (JEF). In capability terms, both countries bring valuable assets into the Alliance, albeit in limited numbers. Taken together, their defence spending amounts to less than 5% of the combined spending of European NATO nations. For NATO, the accession of Finland and Sweden implies an expanded collective-defence obligation. This would include protecting Finland's 1,340-kilometre land border with Russia. Nevertheless, NATO will benefit from Northern Europe becoming a more integrated space in terms of deterrence and defence. It means that, bar Russian coastlines in the Gulf of Finland and in Kaliningrad, the shores of the Baltic Sea will be controlled by NATO members. However, both Finland and Sweden will likely need to make additional defence investments due to demand signals from the NATO Defence Planning Process (NDPP), notwithstanding their history of partnering with NATO members. Filling billets in NATO's multinational command structure will increase the burden on the cohort of staff officers. At the same time, both states will need to consider how they would enable the inflow of a large number of NATO forces in the event of a collective defence contingency on NATO's eastern flank. No decisions have yet been made on permanent NATO structures in Finland and Sweden. But, at the very least, NATO states will likely want to discuss the prepositioning of equipment and command and control (C2) arrangements that, while primarily staffed by Finland and Sweden, include a multinational layer that could expand quickly if required. This will also require Finland's and Sweden's exercise posture to evolve further. Currently both states conduct some exercises with NATO members, but closer ties with Alliance members will mean closer integration with NATO exercise cycles.

NATO: new posture, new strategy

Russia's full-scale invasion of Ukraine reinvigorated the NATO Alliance. Furthermore, Russia's actions strengthened unity among Alliance members over threat perceptions, sharpened focus on deterrence and defence (underpinned by a new force model), and triggered applications to join NATO by Finland and Sweden. This followed a year in which the Alliance had to weather two crises. In August 2021, the fall of Kabul to the Taliban, after the collapse of the Afghan government and security forces, damaged NATO's standing and also suggested a degree of strategic failure. (Alliance members had withdrawn their troops earlier, in April 2021.) Then, in September 2021, France was caught off guard by the Australia–UK–US defence trilateral known as AUKUS, which caused significant upset in Paris.

A new Strategic Concept, agreed at NATO's 28–30 June summit in Madrid, elaborated on some of these changes, stating that 'the Euro-Atlantic area is not at peace' and that Russia is 'the most significant and direct threat to Allies' security and to peace and stability in the Euro-Atlantic area'. The document also said that terrorism is 'the most direct asymmetric threat to the security of our citizens and to international peace and prosperity', reflecting NATO's 360-degree approach and the need to demonstrate concern for the security priorities of NATO's southern member states. China was, for the first time, explicitly assessed in a NATO Strategic Concept, and Beijing's ambitions and policies were considered to 'challenge [NATO] interests, security and values'. The Strategic Concept did not create any new core tasks for NATO – some had mooted resilience as a potential addition – but the task list has been reordered with deterrence and defence, crisis prevention and management, and cooperative security all folded under the overarching theme of collective defence. The summit declaration stated that NATO had 'set a new baseline for our deterrence and defence posture. NATO will continue to protect our populations and defend every inch of Allied territory at all times.' However, realising this ambition will require significant and coordinated efforts by member states.

NATO members began to increase defence spending in the years after Russia first invaded Ukraine in 2014, and additional uplifts were announced by some after February 2022. Madrid saw additional commitments to 'build on' the 2014 defence investment pledge, agreed at that year's Wales Summit, and to 'decide next year on subsequent commitments beyond 2024'. As well as this, important outcomes evident after Madrid relate to additional forward-deployed personnel, more prepositioned equipment and a much-increased ambition for high-readiness forces. These efforts are intended to increase the defence and deterrence posture on the eastern flank. That said, certain media reports at the time of the Madrid Summit suggested that some of NATO's eastern members had hoped for an even greater effort to underpin a strategy of forward defence, making permanent some of the rotational deployments by NATO allies to their countries. However, despite NATO's new-found unity, member states disagree on the extent to which Russia threatens the Alliance and the desirability of accepting the costs – and loss of flexibility – that a larger and more permanent presence would demand.

NATO's enhanced forward presence has expanded from four battlegroups – in Estonia, Latvia, Lithuania and Poland – to eight with new multinational deployments in Bulgaria, Hungary, Romania and Slovakia. At the time of the Madrid Summit, these comprised some 9,600 personnel from 24 NATO nations. Furthermore, Canada, France, Germany and the UK have indicated that they will pre-assign forces to reinforce the countries where they already lead NATO's forward-presence battlegroups. These pre-assigned forces are up to brigade-level strength, but it is unclear whether dedicated assets exist to enable their rapid deployment, when needed, from their respective home bases.

NATO also agreed a new force model to increase the scale and readiness of its forces and to replace the NATO Response Force (NRF). Founded in 2002 and expanded in 2015 to include up to 40,000 personnel, the NRF concept includes the ambition to be able to deploy initial elements within five days and the whole force no later than 30 days. In contrast, the new force model is based on a three-tier structure. The first tier, intended to be deployable in less than ten days, encompasses at least 100,000 troops. The second tier, ready at 10–30 days' notice, comprises 200,000 troops, and the third tier, ready at 30–180 days' notice, comprises an additional 500,000. As such, the assumption is that the new force model would generate at least 300,000 troops at a readiness level comparable to the NRF of old (i.e., deployed no later than 30 days).

These forces are intended to be drawn together across multiple domains, including cyber elements, and will be pre-assigned to specific defence plans. NATO plans to transition to this new force model in 2023, even though the details of the composition and exact scale are still being discussed. Germany was the first country to publicly outline its intended offer to this new force model, suggesting that by 2025, Berlin would provide approximately 30,000 troops, 65 aircraft and 20 naval vessels for the high-readiness component (within the first 30 days). However, unless the US force posture in Europe changes significantly, it is likely that most of the high-readiness forces will need to be European. In the past, similar initiatives, including both the NRF and the NATO Readiness Initiative (agreed in 2020), suffered from the tendency of allies to make offers to contribute, while finding it time-consuming and challenging to actually meet the required standards. These issues are unlikely to disappear now that the ambition has increased significantly.

Defence-policy decisions by Germany and Poland also attracted headlines. In July, Warsaw signed agreements to purchase up to 1,000 Hyundai Rotem K2 *Black Panther* main battle tanks, 672 Hanwha Defense K9 *Thunder* 155mm self-propelled artillery pieces and 48 Korea Aerospace Industries (KAI) FA-50 *Fighting Eagle* light fighter ground-attack aircraft from South Korea. They will be acquired in stages that include technology transfer and local production, and initial deliveries began in 2022. Polish licensed production of the K2 and K9, in their Poland-specific variants, is set to start in 2026, and there are plans for follow-on joint development work by the two nations. If it is fully implemented, the scale of the deal will challenge South Korea's defence-industrial base, but it will also test Poland. With these orders coming alongside significant procurements from United States and European manufacturers, Warsaw will need to not only generate the required funding but also fulfil its plans to grow its armed forces, and at the same time maintain, sustain and enable the capability these purchases are intended to generate. While it is apparent that Russia's conventional military capability has been diminished as a result of its war on Ukraine, Warsaw clearly continues to see Moscow as a direct threat. This is evidenced by the speed with which Poland entered into initial negotiations with South Korea and Warsaw's interest in early delivery.

In Europe, arguably the most significant gap between the potential and actual delivery of defence capability is in Germany. In a speech on 27 February, German Chancellor Olaf Scholz argued that Russia's invasion of Ukraine amounted to a new era (in German, *Zeitenwende*) for European security, which will mean radical shifts in policy. As part of efforts to close Germany's long-standing defence-capabilities gap, Scholz announced the creation of a EUR100bn

(USD106bn) special fund to finance Bundeswehr investment and equipment projects. Germany's defence budget stood at 1.3% of GDP in 2021. Initially, there were expectations among some allies – and some observers in Germany – that the special fund would come on top of moves to raise the regular defence budget to 2% of GDP, in line with NATO recommendations. However, deliberations in Berlin since Scholz's announcement suggest that over the coming years it is instead likely to be used to reach 2% through successive drawdowns from the fund. In 2022, the German government announced its intention to purchase up to 70 additional *Eurofighter* aircraft, some 35 F-35A *Lightning* IIs and about 60 CH-47F *Chinook* heavy transport helicopters. According to government plans, close to 41% of the special fund will be invested in air capabilities, followed by around 25% in the Bundeswehr's digitisation needs (primarily around C2), 20% in land systems and just under 11% in the maritime domain. It seems that the requirement for a wide-ranging replenishment of munitions stocks will have to be funded by the regular budget. It is likely that much of the special fund will be invested in programmes that were already planned before 24 February and had been indicated in both Bundeswehr and NATO planning documents, but which had not received adequate funding due to the limitations placed by Germany's core defence budget. Furthermore, it is not clear that Scholz's *Zeitenwende* speech has yet translated into a true shift in mindset. Berlin's Central and Eastern European partners have been disappointed by Germany's hesitance over supplying heavy weapons to Ukraine and extending into the energy and financial sectors meaningful sanctions against Russia. Nevertheless, Germany's defence-policy debate has evolved rapidly in 2022, and the country will adopt its first-ever national-security strategy in early 2023.

Supporting Ukraine

Ukraine's efforts to defend itself have been actively supported by NATO and EU members, though the level and speed of support has varied. Assistance has included ammunition, intelligence, some maintenance and repair support, as well as funding. Equipment donations have ranged from Soviet-era legacy equipment to more sophisticated systems in active service with NATO armed forces. They have also included refurbished equipment that was either in deep storage or has been purchased from

industry stocks. The EU used its European Peace Facility (EPF) to commit EUR3.1 billion (USD2.6bn) by October 2022 – half of the EPF budget for 2021–27 – and approve, for the first time ever, the supply of lethal weapons to a third country. (The EPF is an off-budget instrument, established in March 2021, to fund partner nations' equipment and infrastructure needs.) To help with the coordination and logistics of the national contributions to Ukraine, a US European Command (EUCOM) Control

Centre Ukraine/International Donor Coordination Centre (ECCU/IDCC) was established in March 2022 under US and UK leadership, with a Ukrainian liaison element. This helps match Ukrainian requests with donor offers and assists with the delivery of equipment to Ukraine and training requirements for Ukrainian personnel. The EU agreed on 17 October to launch the EU Military Assistance Mission (EUMAM Ukraine), which initially aims to train 15,000 Ukrainian soldiers on the territory of EU member states and is, at first, mandated for two years. Meanwhile, one notable effort has been the training programme set up in July by the UK, with the aim of training in the UK up to 10,000 Ukrainian recruits and existing personnel every 120 days. The programme, run by the UK's 11th Security Force Assistance Brigade, involves some 1,000 UK personnel. Since it started, Canada, Denmark, Finland, the Netherlands, Norway and Sweden have indicated they would participate in the effort.

One side effect of the drive to deliver security assistance to Ukraine is that legacy equipment and ageing ammunition stocks are being flushed out of European inventories. While these effects will be more pronounced in Central and Eastern European countries, where many states had retained Soviet-era legacy equipment in their inventories, this creates an opportunity to accelerate the pace of military modernisation and to consider expanding equipment commonality within the broader context of rising budgets. However, it is questionable whether (particularly) Europe's defence industries will be able to deliver at the timescales needed by customers. Another potential problem is that additional funding might tempt governments to either invest in their national defence-industrial base, where it exists, or pursue industrial-policy goals rather than focus on immediate capability needs. Careful calibration will be needed to balance national programmes and industrial capacity, given the desire by some to strengthen Europe's defence-industrial and technology base and the instinct of others to cement existing international partnerships through arms orders.

The war in Ukraine has caused many states to reassess their defence priorities, and it has effectively shifted further north and east the strategic centre of gravity in Europe. For NATO, this will likely make it harder to maintain its 360-degree approach. The clear positioning of Russia as the key threat in the new Strategic Concept, when viewed alongside the mixed legacy of crisis-management operations – including arguable failure in Afghanistan and a sense in some capitals that the EU might be a more appropriate vehicle for dealing with instability and state fragility on NATO's southern periphery – is making it harder to ensure that the southern flank receives appropriate attention. Nevertheless, finding credible ways to do so will be needed for unanimity over NATO's engagement on the eastern flank. The Strategic Concept characterises China's attempts to undermine and reshape the international order as a systemic challenge to Euro-Atlantic security. But China has not been placed directly into a deterrence and defence framework because a number of NATO allies do not believe that Beijing poses a military threat to their security. That said, the return of war to Europe has not displaced the ambitions of several European governments to play a growing security and defence role in the Indo-Pacific, though resources to achieve this will be limited. The UK has demonstrated intent, with the deployment of two *River*-class offshore-patrol vessels (OPVs) to the region, as well as the planned deployment of a new amphibious Littoral Response Group in 2023 and a frigate later in the decade. But while the Indo-Pacific tilt, announced in March 2021 by the UK government, is likely to remain only a modest driver of British military planning, the UK deployed forces in 2022 – including four *Typhoon* combat aircraft and an A330 Multi-Role Tanker Transport (MRTT) – to take part in Australia's *Pitch Black* air exercise. Germany also sent aircraft to *Pitch Black*. Following on from the Indo-Pacific deployment of the frigate *Bayern* in 2021 and early 2022, Berlin sent six Eurofighter *Typhoon*s, four A400M transport aircraft and three A330 MRTTs to *Pitch Black* and to Australia's navy-led *Kakadu* drill. Additional engagements with Japan, Singapore and South Korea were planned in the framework of this deployment. For its part, France maintains warships and troops in the region and routinely deploys additional vessels and aircraft. In 2022, it deployed to the region several *Rafale* combat aircraft and tanker and transport aircraft as part of a force-projection exercise, including some to take part in *Pitch Black*.

EU defence initiatives

In March 2022, the EU published its 'Strategic Compass for Security and Defence'. The process was initiated in June 2020, with a threat analysis presented in November 2020 and most of the writing completed in 2021. The document was intended to provide strategic guidance for EU activity in relation to crisis management, resilience, military capability development and multinational partnerships. However, despite last-minute edits and additions, the profound change to Europe's security landscape resulting from Russia's war in Ukraine means that the Strategic Compass cannot but look like it has been overtaken by events. Josep Borrell, EU High Representative of the Union for Foreign Affairs and Security Policy and Vice-President of the European Commission, wrote in its Foreword that the Compass should help to 'turn the EU's geopolitical awakening into a more permanent strategic posture'. Initiatives outlined in the strategy include the establishment of an EU Rapid Deployment Capacity (RDC) to deliver a 5,000-strong crisis-management capability for operations in non-permissive environments and to be fully operational by 2025. It also called for the development of an EU Space Strategy for Security and Defence, as well as for investment in common solutions for strategic enablers and in technology to drive defence innovation and next-generation capabilities, using the European Defence Fund (EDF) and Permanent Structured Cooperation (PESCO). The RDC is meant to be built on modified EU Battlegroups and forces and capabilities earmarked by member states. However, this approach has so far only generated limited success in an EU context. For instance, EU Battlegroups have been fully operational on paper since 2007 but have not been used once despite there, arguably, being no shortage of crises. Nonetheless, a military rapid-response concept document was in the drafting stages in mid-2022 to further inform RDC architecture and planning. As of summer 2022, the EU was also working on its first military strategy to assist the planning of EU operations and deliver military-specific guidance.

The return of war to Europe has triggered a raft of other initiatives that may generate some effect in the future, particularly in relation to the defence-industrial sector. In March 2022, the European Commission was tasked with assessing, in coordination with the European Defence Agency, European defence-investment gaps and outlining measures to strengthen Europe's defence-industrial base. The findings were presented on 18 May and indicated that EU members should increase stocks of weapons and munitions, replace remaining Soviet-era equipment in their inventories and invest in air and missile defence. As a result, in July the Commission proposed a regulation to establish the European Defence Industry Reinforcement through Common Procurement Act (EDIRPA). EDIRPA is meant to have a EUR500 million (USD528m) budget between 2022 and 2024, and the plan is that it would effectively subsidise EU member states' procurement from the EU budget. In the longer run, steps like these towards directly incentivising joint procurement will inform and reinforce the European Defence Investment Programme (EDIP), another proposal the Commission planned to launch before the end of 2022. Overall, these initiatives are likely to encourage more intra-EU collaborative defence development and procurement, objectives that are already features of the EDF and PESCO.

Sub-regional defence: the V4 and the JEF

As well as national efforts and cooperation at the NATO and EU level, European states also use mini-lateral and other sub-regional defence formats to advance their defence-policy aims, although they have variable focus on the war in Ukraine. While the Visegrad Four (V4) seems largely to be continuing to implement existing work programmes with limited adjustments, others, like the UK-led JEF, have a greater operational focus. For instance, the work programmes for the V4 presidencies by Hungary (2021–22) and Slovakia (2022–23) reflected a focus on preparing the V4 Battlegroup that is due to go on standby for EU operations in the first half of 2023. The Battlegroup will be working on military-mobility projects within the context of the Strategic Compass, while also scaling up joint training and exercise activity to improve readiness and interoperability. In contrast, the JEF nations (Denmark, Estonia, Finland, Iceland, Latvia, Lithuania, the Netherlands, Norway, Sweden and the UK) announced in March a set of enhanced exercises focused on the High North, the North Atlantic and the Baltic Sea, reflecting key areas of concern for their governments. In May, the Standing Joint Force Headquarters (SJFHQ) based in Northwood, UK, began deploying forces to Lithuania and Latvia to help coordinate the military activities of JEF nations in the Baltic Sea (the decision to do so was made in February, just before Russia's invasion of Ukraine). Then, in July, JEF governments announced additional exercises while Finland and Sweden awaited ratification of their NATO membership.

Figure 2 The FREMM frigate: selected national variants

In 2002, France and Italy agreed to jointly develop and acquire a new generation of multi-mission frigates (European multi-mission frigates, FREMM). Twenty-seven vessels were originally planned (17 French and ten Italian). While the different national versions share a common basic hull form and major common components, they differ significantly in detail design, and each navy operates different FREMM variants. The first vessel (for the French Navy) was launched in April 2010 and commissioned in November 2012. France has successfully exported one FREMM to Morocco and another to Egypt, while Italy has delivered two to Egypt and, in 2021, won an order for six from Indonesia. A much-modified version of the Italian FREMM was chosen by the US Navy (USN) as the basis for its FFG(X) (subsequently reclassified FFG-62) new-generation small surface combatant (or frigate). The USN plans to procure 20 of the vessels. The export successes of the FREMM family have been due largely to the fact that it represents a modern, capable and proven design that also remains relatively cost-effective.

FREMM family basic dimensions/characteristics:
- France: 142m x 19.8m, 6,200 tonnes full-load displacement; crew complement: 108–118
- Italy: 144m x 19.7m, 6,700 tonnes; crew complement: 145–167
- US: 151m x 19.7m, (est.). 7,200 tonnes, crew complement: 200 (est)

FREMM customers:
- France: 8
- Italy: 8 (two general purpose (GP) variants under construction)
- Morocco: 1
- Egypt: 3
- US: three on order (with 20 planned)
- Indonesia: six on order

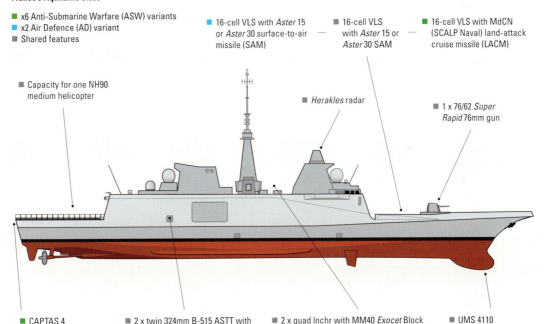

French and Italian versions
Differences between the Italian and French vessels reflect divergent national requirements as well as ambitions to maximise domestic defence industrial workshare. France's *Aquitaine* class was originally to have comprised eight anti-submarine warfare (ASW) variants and nine land-attack variants. However, ASW numbers were reduced to six, the land-attack variant was cancelled and two air defence vessels were added. France's ASW FREMMs have 16 vertical launch system (VLS) tubes for air defence missiles (either A43 or A50 launchers) and 16 A70 VLSs for land-attack missiles. France's air defence FREMMs are equipped with 32 A50 tubes, while Italy's two FREMM variants, comprising four ASW and six general-purpose (GP) ships, have 16 A50 tubes for air defence. For anti-surface warfare, the French FREMMs all carry up to eight MM40 *Exocet* anti-ship missiles (AShMs) on slanted deck launchers, while the Italian GP frigates carry eight *Teseo* AShMs and the ASW versions four *Teseo* missiles and four MILAS anti-submarine missiles.

THE MILITARY BALANCE 2023

Italy's *Bergamini* class

- ■ x4 Anti-Submarine Warfare variants
- ■ x4 General Purpose variants (two under construction)
- ■ Shared features

- ■ *Kronos* radar
- ■ 16-cell VLS with *Aster* 15 and *Aster* 30 SAM
- ■ 1 x 76/62 STRALES (*Davide*) 76mm gun
- ■ 1 x 127/54 LW – *Vulcano* 127mm gun
- ■ Capacity for two NH90 medium helicopters
- ■ 1 x 76/62 STRALES (*Davide*) 76mm gun
- ■ CAPTAS 4 variable-depth sonar
- ■ 2 x triple 324mm B-515 ASTT with MU90 lightweight torpedo
- ■ 1 x quad lnchr with *Otomat* (*Teseo*) Mk2a long-range AShM
  1 x quad lnchr with MILAS anti-submarine missile
- ■ UMS 4110 hull-mounted sonar
- ■ 2 x quad lnchr with *Otomat* (*Teseo*) Mk2a long-range AShM

The US Navy's *Constellation* class

- ■ AN/SPY-6(V)3 *Enterprise* Air Surveillance Radar (EASR)
- ■ 32-cell Mk 41 VLS likely with RIM-162 ESSM and SM-2
- ■ 1 x 57/70 Mk3 (Mk 110) 57mm gun
- ■ Capacity for one MH-60R *Seahawk* medium helicopter and one UAV
- ■ CAPTAS 4 variable-depth sonar
- ■ 1 x 21-cell Mk 49 GMLS with RIM-116C RAM Block II
- ■ 4 x quad lnchr with *Naval Strike Missile* (RGM-184A) long-range AShM

The US Navy's FFG-62

In 2020, the US Navy chose Italy's ASW FREMM design as the basis for its future *Constellation*-class (FFG-62) small surface combatant or frigate programme. The basic FREMM design has been heavily modified to meet the USN's requirements for larger and better armed and protected platforms, with an emphasis on survivability and surface warfare capability; the programme is also intended to secure workshare for US defence industry. The *Constellation*-class will have a larger crew, 32 Mk 41 VLS tubes for *Evolved SeaSparrow* and SM-2 missiles (with some critics pressing to raise this to 48), 16 AShMs and a version of the *Aegis* combat system. The *Constellation*-class will carry the same towed-array sonar as the French and Italian vessels, the CAPTAS 4 variable-depth sonar, but no bow-mounted sonar.

Sources: IISS; Fincantieri, Naval Group, seaforces.org; navalanalyses.com; Congressional Research Service

©IISS

Studies in capability generation: the regeneration of UK maritime-patrol aircraft capability

In February 2020, the arrival at Royal Air Force (RAF) Lossiemouth of a Boeing P-8A *Poseidon* heralded the regeneration of the UK's fixed-wing maritime-patrol aircraft (MPA) capability after a decade's gap. The UK Ministry of Defence (MOD) declared initial operating capability (IOC) in April 2020 with two aircraft. The UK's MPA capability had been shelved following the retirement in March 2010 of the RAF's existing *Nimrod* MR2 MPA fleet and the subsequent cancellation in the Strategic Defence Review of October that year of the replacement *Nimrod* MRA4 programme.

The gap in capability that resulted from the *Nimrod's* demise was widely criticised. The UK had been one of the leading MPA operators globally. Critically, as far as the government was concerned, the MRA4 programme had overrun and was over budget. Furthermore, there were doubts over whether the airframe would even be certified airworthy. However, concerns quickly emerged about the UK's ability to sustain a comprehensive maritime-surveillance picture amid reports of increased Russian naval (and especially submarine) activity in and around UK and NATO waters, particularly the challenge of supporting and protecting UK ballistic-missile submarines when transiting to and from their home base in Scotland. Although the House of Commons Defence Committee was critical, then-minister of state for the armed forces Nick Harvey told the committee in 2012 that the MOD believed it was carrying an 'acceptable level' of risk. Moreover, he added that the capability could one day be regenerated, stating, 'we have not, as yet, taken a view that we would not want to come back into this in the slightly longer term'.

That time came in 2015, when the National Security Strategy and Strategic Defence and Security Review announced that the UK would 'buy nine new Maritime Patrol Aircraft, based in Scotland, to protect our nuclear deterrent, hunt down hostile submarines and enhance our maritime search and rescue'. There seems little doubt that the start of Russia's invasion of Ukraine the year before, and the fact that European states subsequently began reassessing the risk of a major conflict in Europe, hastened this apparent U-turn. At the time, the UK government did not confirm the preferred aircraft. Speculation ranged from the Boeing P-8 *Poseidon* to the Airbus C295, to the Kawasaki P-1 and to uninhabited platforms, with these all offering differing levels of capability. The government finally committed publicly to the P-8 *Poseidon* in July 2016 when then-prime minister David Cameron made the announcement at the Farnborough international air show.

Project *Seedcorn*

The *Nimrod* MRA4 airframes were quickly broken up in the first months of 2011, and over the next few years the UK relied on other technical capabilities, such as signals intelligence, while allies also provided information as well as, on occasion, deploying MPAs to the UK to support maritime-surveillance operations. However, while Harvey's remarks in 2012 indicated that officials had not ruled out reinstating a dedicated maritime-patrol and anti-submarine warfare capability, the UK MOD was taking steps to sustain the required skills under Project *Seedcorn*.

Seedcorn began in 2012 and was renewed for a further three years in 2015. It saw UK personnel – many of whom had worked on *Nimrod* – posted to Australia, Canada, New Zealand and, most significantly, the US to maintain and develop skills in maritime patrol, anti-submarine warfare, anti-surface warfare and intelligence, surveillance and reconnaissance. These countries all operated the P-3 *Orion*, but importantly the US Navy (USN) was, by the early 2010s, in the initial stages of transitioning its capability to the new Boeing P-8 *Poseidon*, based on the 737 airliner. In retrospect, the UK's posting of personnel to the US provided an indication of the UK's likely direction of travel towards regaining its MPA capability, in the form of the P-8A.

In 2012, RAF personnel were sent to Naval Air Station Jacksonville, in Florida, to work with USN aircrew and mission specialists on the P-8 *Poseidon*, operating with the USN's Patrol Squadron 30 (VP-30) training establishment. This was one year before the USN itself declared that the *Poseidon* had reached IOC. RAF personnel comprised pilots, tactical coordinators and weapons-system operators. The year 2012 also saw UK personnel fly the P-8A during Exercise *Joint Warrior* off Scotland. The programme even resulted in an all-UK crew flying a US *Poseidon*.

Over the years, more personnel trained with US forces, with some rising to become instructors in VP-30. UK personnel were also posted to the USN's VX-1 test and evaluation squadron at Naval Air Station Patuxent River. The effect of *Seedcorn* was broader, as the RAF reported in 2022 that UK personnel had also been involved in training Australian, Canadian, New Zealand and US personnel. Bar Canada, all these nations are, or will shortly be, *Poseidon* operators; Boeing is, meanwhile, offering the aircraft for Canada's project to replace its CP-140 *Aurora* aircraft.

From the mid-2010s, USN P-8s occasionally flew from RAF Lossiemouth. This airbase, in northern Scotland, had been earmarked by the UK MOD for investment to accommodate the new aircraft and related facilities. The first aircraft to arrive in the UK were based at RAF Kinloss (formerly the main *Nimrod* base) while works at Lossiemouth continued; *Poseidon* was moved to Lossiemouth in October 2020. The UK's P-8s arrived in rapid succession. The ninth, and final, aircraft was flown in to Lossiemouth in January 2022. According to analysts, this pace means that the RAF still lacks enough crew for the fleet. Nonetheless, the RAF still plans to declare full operational capability in October 2024. The P-8-related facilities at Lossiemouth will also be of broader use. In 2018, Norway and the UK announced a cooperation agreement relating to maritime-patrol aircraft, with Norway receiving its fifth and final P-8 in 2022. Germany has also ordered the type and may well seek a similar arrangement. Both of these nations, plus the US, are likely to make use of Lossiemouth. In addition, Germany, Norway and the UK will all be looking to benefit in terms of support functions as well as the operational advantages of using the same aircraft as the USN. Project *Seedcorn* is now being used to grow the UK's capability on the Boeing E-7A *Wedgetail* airborne early warning and control aircraft. As of late 2022, personnel were embedded with the Royal Australian Air Force.

DEFENCE ECONOMICS

Macroeconomics

European economies were buffeted by strong economic headwinds in 2022, and these are set to continue into 2023. Russia's invasion of Ukraine in early 2022 caused widespread damage and disruption to European economies. Europe's short-term economic outlook is constrained by soaring energy prices, security-of-supply issues, high inflation and rising – and increasingly expensive – government debt levels. According to the International Monetary Fund (IMF), real GDP growth in the Eurozone will slow to 3.1% in 2022 and drop even lower to 0.5% in 2023, compared to the pandemic-related 6.3% contraction in 2020 and 5.2% growth in the recovery year of 2021. The UK saw real GDP contract by 9.3% in 2020, recover strongly by 7.4% in 2021 and, while it is projected to grow by 3.6% in 2022, the projection of 0.3% growth in 2023 points to a more challenging short-term outlook for both the UK and the Eurozone. In 2022, the Eurozone performed stronger than expected, partly because tourism picked up in Italy and Spain. But significant downside risks are weighing on growth, not least the disruption to gas supplies from Russia and the impact this will have on industrial production.

Europe's economic foundations are weaker now than they were coming into 2020, when the continent was hit by the first wave of COVID-19 infections. Fiscal deficits extended from an average of 0.3% of GDP in 2019 to 6.5% in 2020 and have remained elevated ever since at 3.6% in 2021 and 2.7% of GDP in 2022. These figures indicate that Europe had not fully recovered from the economic fallout of the pandemic when Russia invaded Ukraine. Private consumption and investment were still below pre-pandemic levels.

As a proportion of GDP, European debt levels extended from an average of 59.8% in 2019 to 71.5% in 2020; they remained high at 68.7% in 2021 and 64.8% in 2022. This level of debt was sustainable while

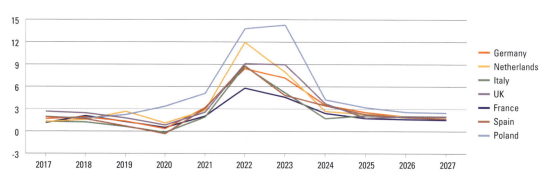

Source: IMF World Economic Outlook, October 2022   ©IISS

▲ Figure 3 **Europe: selected countries, inflation (%) 2017–27**

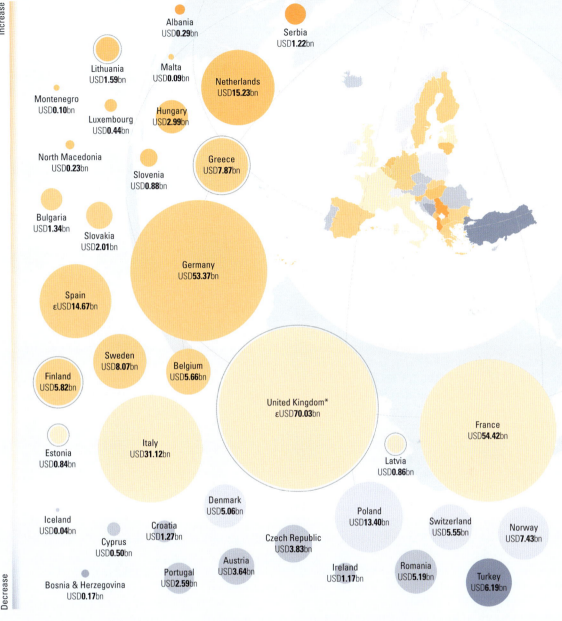

▲ Map 1 **Europe: regional defence spending** (USDbn, %ch yoy)[1]

Sub-regional groupings referred to in defence economics text: Central Europe (Austria, Czech Republic, Germany, Hungary, Poland, Slovakia and Switzerland), Northern Europe (Denmark, Estonia, Finland, Latvia, Lithuania, Norway and Sweden), Southern Europe (Cyprus, Greece, Italy, Malta, Portugal and Spain), Southeastern Europe (Bulgaria, Romania and Turkey), the Balkans (Albania, Bosnia-Herzegovina, Croatia, Montenegro, North Macedonia, Serbia and Slovenia) and Western Europe (Belgium, France, Iceland, Ireland, Luxembourg, the Netherlands and the United Kingdom).

interest rates were low and borrowing was cheap. The IMF has characterised the war as a supply shock in economic terms, arguing its effects have aggravated the policy challenges created by the pandemic. As such, the IMF says that these new shocks are better addressed by fiscal policy than monetary policy, as the latter needs to be employed to stem inflation. Countries in the region are using monetary policy to stem rising inflation, with the effect that interest rate increases will make borrowing less manageable.

Inflation across the region was a concern even before the February invasion. Rates increased globally in 2021 due to higher energy costs, a recovery in demand and ongoing pandemic-related supply-chain disruptions. Despite countries continuing to commit increasing amounts of funding to defence in 2021, surging rates of inflation in all regions resulted in a negative global trend in real terms. The impact was more acute in 2022 as inflation soared, driven by the commodity crisis, supply disruptions and heightened economic uncertainty resulting from the war in Ukraine. The disruption to energy supply caused the oil price to spike, after February, to levels in excess of USD100 per barrel. The US Energy Information Administration (EIA) expects the price of Brent crude oil to average USD105 per barrel throughout 2022 and remain high at USD95 per barrel in 2023.

In its October 2022 World Economic Outlook Update, the IMF revised upward its projection for global inflation in light of rising food and energy prices and lingering supply–demand imbalances. The year saw several countries, particularly in Eastern Europe, face double-digit inflation rates. In September 2022, rates reached 9.9% in the Eurozone and 10.1% in the UK. Policymakers in Europe now face the challenge of easing the impact of higher inflation by managing effectively fiscal and monetary instruments, but without allowing wage–price spirals (where the demand for higher wages drives up costs for suppliers with these costs then passed on to the consumer). Should wage–price spirals occur, inflation will increase further.

Defence spending

European defence spending grew significantly in 2021, with regional spending increasing by 3.5% in real terms, a rate higher than in any other region. Indeed, 2021 was the seventh consecutive year of real growth. It had been projected that, in the short term, European defence spending growth would be subdued in light

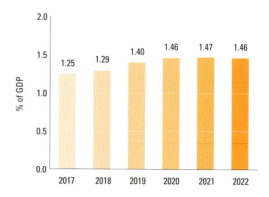

▲ Figure 4 **Europe: regional defence spending** as % of GDP (average)

of fiscal pressure following the pandemic. However, Russia's decision to invade Ukraine on 24 February caused a marked change of course. In the weeks and months that followed, around 20 countries pledged to increase defence spending, though the relative scale – and timelines – differed. Announcements spanned the region – from the UK, France, Germany and Italy to Poland and Romania as well as most Nordic and all Baltic states.

The most notable uplift was the announcement on 27 February by Chancellor Olaf Scholz that Germany would establish a special fund for defence in 2022, amounting to EUR100 billion (USD106bn), and the defence budget would reach 2% of GDP 'from now on'. The announcement came at the end of a period in which Germany's defence spending had seen increases averaging 4.4% in real terms since 2016. Germany's defence budget for 2022 was a 7.3% increase over the 2021 figure, rising to EUR50.4bn (USD53.4bn). However, the financial plan to 2026, approved on 1 July 2022, shows spending remaining flat at this level. As such, in order to reach 2% of GDP 'from now on', the defence budget will need to be supplemented by the special fund if the core budget is not increased to meet the target.

This presents a significant divergence from trend in Germany. Therefore, the uplift will have to be managed effectively to ensure that funds are allocated according to strategic imperatives and managed well thereafter. Moreover, increased investment without a capability development plan raises questions over the ability of the armed forces and defence-industrial base to absorb new resources.

Details of the special fund (*Sondervermögen Bundeswehr*) were announced in June 2022. The EUR100bn (USD106bn) falls to EUR82bn (USD87bn)

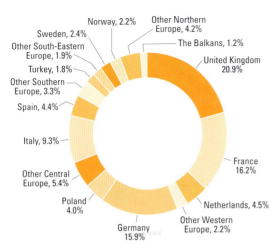

Other Western Europe – Belgium, Iceland, Ireland, Luxembourg
Other Central Europe – Austria, Czech Republic, Hungary, Slovakia, Switzerland
Other Northern Europe – Denmark, Estonia, Finland, Latvia, Lithuania
Other Southern Europe – Cyprus, Greece, Malta, Portugal
The Balkans – Albania, Bosnia-Herzegovina, Croatia, Montenegro, North Macedonia, Serbia, Slovenia
Other South-Eastern Europe – Bulgaria, Romania

©IISS

▲ Figure 5 **Europe: defence spending by country and sub-region, 2022**

after VAT and the costs of interest on borrowing are taken into account. Air procurement takes up 40.8% of the fund with major programmes being the *Eurofighter* and F-35 combat aircraft, the Future Combat Air System (FCAS), heavy transport helicopters, uninhabited systems, space surveillance and ground-based air defence. A significant 25.3% of the funding is to be used for 'management ability/digitisation' procurement with programmes including the digitisation of land-based operations, battle management systems, tactical wide area networks, data centre networks and satellite communications. Land procurement accounts for 20.3%, with this covering the retrofitting of all remaining *Puma* infantry fighting vehicles (IFVs) in the first phase as well as a successor IFV. Naval procurement comprises only 10.8% with major programmes including K130 corvettes, F126 frigates, the Type-212CD diesel-electric submarine being jointly developed with Norway, the Future Naval Strike Missile and the submarine-launched Interactive Defence and Attack System for Submarines, which is being developed by Diehl and ThyssenKrupp Marine Systems and is designed to defeat airborne anti-submarine warfare threats.

The UK also pledged to increase funding for defence, with then-prime minister Boris Johnson announcing at the Madrid NATO Summit that the country's defence budget would reach 2.5% of GDP by 2030. As part of her leadership campaign, the target was increased further to 3% of GDP in the same time frame by the next leader in London, prime minister Liz Truss, in July 2022. The viability of this commitment was questionable given other draws on public spending and caution was expressed at the time about the need for increases to be accompanied by greater oversight and targeted industrial development to help ensure higher funding translated into improved capability.

Truss resigned in October 2022 and the 3% commitment was not repeated by her successor, Rishi Sunak, and his Chancellor Jeremy Hunt in the Autumn Statement, released on 17 November 2022. Pursuing a more fiscally conservative path, the target was reduced back to the NATO minimum of 2% of GDP. The statement did concede that defence spending needed to increase, but said that this would be considered as part of an update to the Integrated Review. The outlook for defence spending in the UK is therefore more subdued and likely to see cuts in real terms as inflation rates remain high.

Other notable announcements in the region include the EUR700 million (USD740m) increase in Finland's 2022 defence budget, with EUR2.2bn (USD2.3bn) also added for defence over the 2023–26 fiscal plan first published in April 2022, the USD340m uplift to the Norwegian budget for border defence, and sizeable uplifts in Estonia and Lithuania as both move towards their goal of spending 2.5% of GDP. Latvia's budget will rise from 2.2% of GDP to 2.5% in 2025. Authorities in Italy have considered increasing military spending by EUR1.5bn (USD1.6bn), with the longer-term goal to raise spending to 2% of GDP from 1.4%. The right-wing coalition government, elected in September 2022, stated in their election manifesto that the country would respect NATO commitments, including the pledge to increase defence spending to 2% of GDP, but progress is likely to be slow in light of economic realities.

In March 2022, the Polish government announced its intention to increase the defence budget from 2.1% to 3% of GDP in 2023. The official budget for 2023 was approved in August and enacted this uplift with an increase in defence funding from PLN58bn (USD13.4bn) to PLN97bn (USD20.8bn); this will bring the budget to 2.8% of GDP. In addition, in March the president signed into law homeland-defence legislation (the Law on the Defence of the Fatherland).

64 THE MILITARY BALANCE 2023

▼ Figure 6 Europe defence budget announcements, 2022

Denmark

2022 defence budget:
USD5.1bn / 1.3% GDP
6 March 2022 – Prime Minister Mette Frederiksen: defence budget will reach 2% of GDP by 2033.

Latvia

2022 defence budget:
USD0.9bn / 2.1% GDP
1 March 2022 – Cabinet approves increase in defence from 2.2% to 2.5% of GDP by 2025.

Norway

2022 defence budget: USD7.4bn / 1.5% GDP
18 March 2022 – NOK3bn (USD313m) added to 2022 defence budget for border defence. Long-Term Defense Plan (April 2020) to reach 2% of GDP by 2028.

Lithuania

2022 defence budget: USD1.6bn / 2.3% GDP
14 March 2022 – State-budget amendment to add EUR298m to 2022 defence budget; aim to increase defence budget to 2.5% of GDP by end of 2022.

Germany

2022 defence budget:
USD53.4bn / 1.3% GDP
27 February 2022 – Chancellor Olaf Scholz: EUR100bn special fund for defence, with budget increasing to 2% of GDP.

Finland

2022 defence budget:
USD5.8bn / 2.1% GDP
5 April 2022 – EUR2.2bn additional funding for defence in the 2023–26 fiscal plan. EUR700m more for 2022.

Estonia

2022 defence budget: USD0.8bn / 2.1% GDP
25 March 22 – Government approved EUR476m uplift to defence between 2022–26 to boost air-defence capabilities. This is intended to increase the budget to over 2.5% of GDP. EUR15.7m added to 2022 budget.

2022 defence budget as % of GDP*

| <2.0 | >2.0 |

*Only countries with announcements shaded

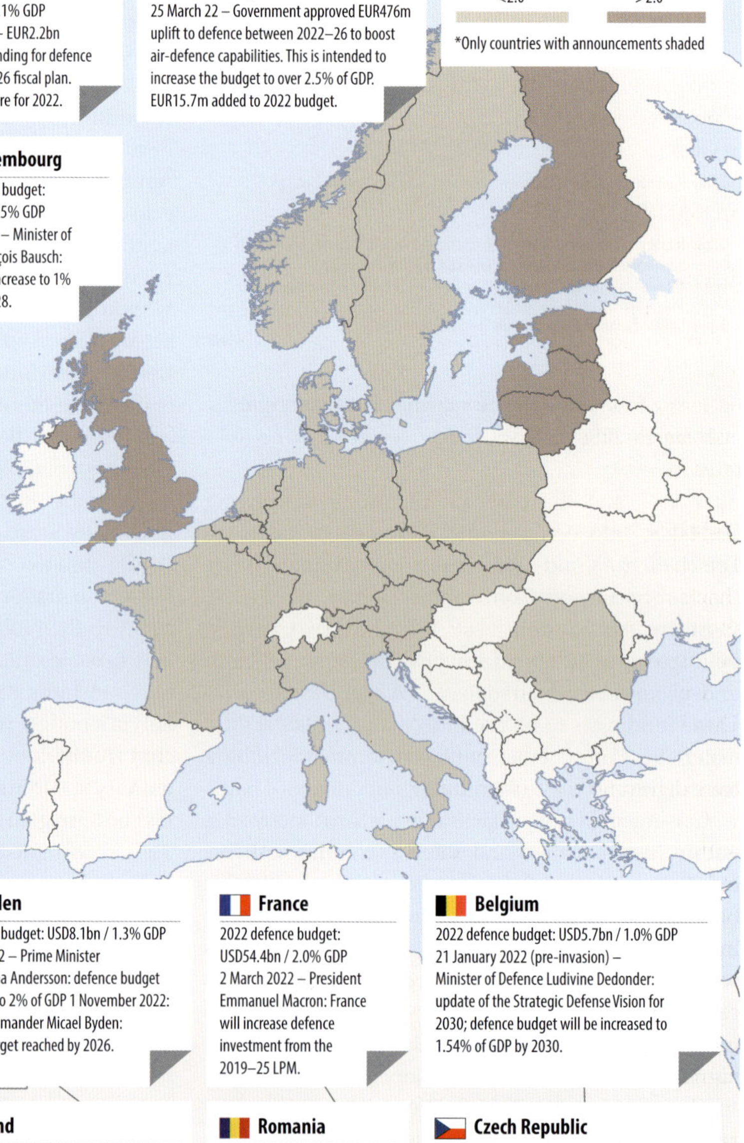

Slovenia

2022 defence budget:
USD0.9bn / 1.4% GDP
16 March 2022 – Minister of Defence Matej Tonin: defence budget will reach 2% of GDP by 2030.

Luxembourg

2022 defence budget:
USD0.4bn / 0.5% GDP
24 June 2022 – Minister of Defence François Bausch: budget will increase to 1% of GDP by 2028.

United Kingdom

2022 defence budget: USD70bn / 2.2% GDP
30 June 2022 – Then-prime minister Boris Johnson: defence budget will increase to 2.5% of GDP by 2030. Liz Truss pledge to reach 3% of GDP while briefly Prime Minister not reiterated by her replacement, Rishi Sunak.

Netherlands

2022 defence budget: USD15.2bn / 1.5% GDP
7 March 2022 – Prime Minister Mark Rutte: the Netherlands is already working towards a 2% of GDP goal and will now look at implementing further increases to defence.

Slovakia

2022 defence budget: USD2.0bn / 1.8% GDP
12 July 2022 – Minister of Defence Jaroslav Nad: first draft of 2023 budget increases defence budget to 2% of GDP.

Italy

2022 defence budget:
USD31.1bn / 1.6% GDP
31 March 2022 – Government considering increasing 2022 defence budget by EUR1.5bn. Long-term goal to reach 2% of GDP by 2028.

Sweden

2022 defence budget: USD8.1bn / 1.3% GDP
10 March 2022 – Prime Minister Eva Magdalena Andersson: defence budget will increase to 2% of GDP 1 November 2022: Supreme Commander Micael Byden: 2% of GDP target reached by 2026.

France

2022 defence budget:
USD54.4bn / 2.0% GDP
2 March 2022 – President Emmanuel Macron: France will increase defence investment from the 2019–25 LPM.

Belgium

2022 defence budget: USD5.7bn / 1.0% GDP
21 January 2022 (pre-invasion) – Minister of Defence Ludivine Dedonder: update of the Strategic Defense Vision for 2030; defence budget will be increased to 1.54% of GDP by 2030.

Austria

2022 defence budget:
USD3.6bn / 0.8% GDP
7 March 2022 – Chancellor Karl Nehammer: need to increase defence budget from 0.7% to 1% of GDP.

Poland

2022 defence budget: USD13.4bn / 1.9% GDP
3 March 2022 – Minister of National Defence Mariusz Błaszczak: defence budget should increase from 2% to 3% of GDP in 2023. Uplift then enacted in the 2023 budget.

Romania

2022 defence budget:
USD5.2bn / 1.7% GDP
1 March 2022 – President Klaus Iohannis: Romania should raise budget from 2% to 2.5% of GDP.

Czech Republic

2022 defence budget: USD3.8bn / 1.3% GDP
6 April 2022 – Government approves plans to accelerate procurement over 2022–24. Minister of Defence Jana Černochová seeks to bring the 2% of GDP target forward by one year from 2025 to 2024.

©IISS

This established an Armed Forces Support Fund. It will be funded through the National Economy Bank (BGK), a state development bank designed to support national economic and industrial growth, with up to PLN40bn (USD8.5bn) made available to fund foreign acquisitions for defence. In July, Poland signed a major procurement deal with South Korea for up to 1,000 Hyundai Rotem K2 *Black Panther* main battle tanks, 672 Hanwha Defense K9 *Thunder* 155 mm self-propelled artillery systems and 48 KAI FA-50 *Fighting Eagle* light fighter ground-attack aircraft.

Defence investments across Europe will increase significantly over the next decade if all of the announced increases occur. The average allocation of GDP to defence among European NATO members would reach an estimated 1.8–1.9% of GDP by 2032, up from 1.6% in 2022 and 1.3% back in 2014.

Despite these announcements, in 2022 European defence spending was still effectively flat in real terms, due to soaring inflation rates. Spending uplifts are set to continue into the 2020s and will be more effective as inflation abates. However, they will be tempered by other public-spending constraints, not least the higher costs of debt servicing as interest rates increase.

Defence industry

The challenges facing aerospace and defence supply chains sharpened from 2021–22 due to labour shortages and disruptions to global shipping caused by ongoing COVID-19-related lockdowns in China, as well as Russia's full-scale invasion of Ukraine. They have been exacerbated by the higher cost of raw materials, components, energy and labour, which have driven up costs of production.

Countries like the UK have made adjustments within their defence budgets to accommodate for inflation, setting aside funding to cover cost uplifts. But any further disruption to supply chains or increased costs for raw materials and components will create further inflationary pressure. Higher costs for skilled personnel will also push up industry expenses, which will feed through to higher contract values.

The primary focus for defence establishments, amid the wave of defence spending increases, is on equipment modernisation and enhancing overall capability. As such, the proportion of European defence budgets devoted to investments is set to increase. A key example is Poland, where the amount allocated to capital spending will jump to 40% in 2023,

having remained steady at 30% for the previous five years. This is notwithstanding the extra-budgetary Armed Forces Support Fund that will be used for the acquisition of foreign equipment.

With defence spending increasing swiftly and significantly, there is a sharpening focus on the absorptive capacity of domestic defence industries. Related to this, there are now questions over the amount that countries will invest in developing their domestic defence sector or whether the immediacy of the security threat posed by Russia will lead some to simply buy off-the-shelf to speed up capability acquisition. That said, a balanced combination of both is perhaps necessitated by the fragmented nature of the European defence-industrial base. As one example, Poland's deal with South Korea includes technology transfer and local production.

Looking beyond the immediate efforts to raise defence spending, Russia's actions have refocused attention on how best to achieve scalable agile production and establish increased stockpiles with more strategic positioning across NATO: both require more weapons systems, such as missiles and other munitions. It is likely, therefore, that higher sales in the short term will focus on upgrades and modifications to existing equipment in order to ensure readiness and sustainment.

The replacement of equipment donated to Ukraine is both a driver and a concern for defence industry. For some states, particularly those in the east, donating equipment designed in the Soviet-era – even if this was later upgraded – creates an opportunity to modernise their inventory, and an opportunity for defence industry. For others, such as the UK, it raises questions over the cost of resupply and the industrial capacity to do so. In 2022, the UK donated lethal equipment, including NLAW and *Javelin* anti-armour systems, multiple-launch rocket systems and *Starstreak* air-defence systems, and non-lethal equipment, including helmets, body armour and night vision goggles. Replacing equipment creates extra demand for defence firms in Europe. In June, the UK defence secretary held talks with defence suppliers over how to increase production. However, rising inflation and the higher factor input costs of raw materials will make it difficult to rapidly increase capacity, adding to the challenges for scalable and agile production. As a result, it may become more expensive to replace equipment, creating further upward pressure on defence spending.

POLAND

A transformative moment

Russia's 2022 invasion of Ukraine has prompted important changes to Poland's defence posture. It has vindicated the long-standing Polish concern about Russia's willingness to use its military power to subjugate a neighbouring nation. In the days immediately after 24 February, Poland was preoccupied with a potential Russian escalation against NATO and an increased risk of attacks on Polish territory. These anxieties grew when Poland became the hub for deliveries of weapons for Ukraine, via Rzeszów–Jasionka Airport, close to the Ukrainian border. For Poland, the material and human cost of Russia's war on Ukraine, and the nature of Moscow's military operations there, has changed Poland's perceptions of Russia.

Indeed, towards the end of 2022, a broad consensus emerged among Poland's political class that Russia had evolved into a serious long-term threat, despite being temporarily weakened militarily by the war. It is assumed by Poland's leaders that Moscow's desire to erase Ukraine's sovereignty will persist as a policy regardless of the outcome of the war. Warsaw also fears that Russia may be able to rebuild the core of its ground forces' capacity relatively quickly and thereby continue to pose an existential threat to its neighbours, with Poland, as a flank nation, first in line.

A change to budgeting

This change in Poland's threat perception has been accompanied by a rapid increase in defence expenditure. Before 24 February, Warsaw planned to incrementally increase the defence budget from 2.2% of GDP in 2022 to 2.6% of GDP in 2026. This was amended in March, and a new spending level was set at 3% of GDP from 2023. In May, an extra-budgetary fund (Funduszu Wsparcia Sił Zbrojnych, FWSZ) was also established, having been announced in 2021, and is intended to finance investments by issuing sovereign bonds. The plan is that in 2023 the fund will bring an additional USD6.3–8.4 billion to the baseline USD20.8bn defence budget, potentially increasing Poland's total defence expenditure to over USD29bn. The latter figure would come close to 4% of GDP which would, according to this measure, make Poland the highest defence spender in NATO.

Early lessons from the war in Ukraine

The course of military operations in Ukraine has led Poland to double down on its technical modernisation and force transformation priorities. From the Polish perspective, while anti-armour weapons, man-portable air-defence systems and armed uninhabited aerial vehicles (UAVs) enabled effective Ukrainian defences in the immediate aftermath of 24 February, Russia's attack was ultimately blunted by armour, firepower, air-defence and personnel strength.

Meanwhile, Poland donated a significant amount of its own weapons to Ukraine. Transfers involved around 230 T-72 main battle tanks (MBTs), constituting the bulk of Poland's inventory; an unspecified number of other systems, such as PT-91 MBTs (a Polish derivative of the T-72), post-Soviet BMPs and various artillery systems, including 54 new Polish-designed *Krab* self-propelled howitzers. However, these donations led to gaps in the inventories of Poland's armoured and mechanised brigades and affected Polish stocks.

New acquisitions

The scale of Poland's weapons transfers to Ukraine, early operational lessons learned from the war and the change in Poland's threat perceptions have all informed Warsaw's decision to dramatically accelerate defence investments.

In the months following 24 February, Poland launched several ambitious armaments programmes. Although the total cost of these projects is unclear at the time of writing, because some terms of the contracts and technical features of the equipment have yet to be finalised, they could be worth between USD30–40bn. Moreover, this figure comes on top of existing flagship programmes that are already under way, and it also does not include planned investments like the long-delayed programme for new submarines. The total value of Polish investments in 2022–35 may reach USD135bn.

Land systems comprise most of the new investments. In July, in an historic turn to an Asian prime contractor, Poland signed a framework agreement with South Korea regarding the delivery and licensed production of up to 1,000 K2 MBTs and 672 K9 *Thunder* self-propelled howitzers. The first contracts were signed in August for 180 K2s and 212 K9s to be delivered in the 2022–26 timeframe. They are designed to fill the most pressing gaps in Polish armoured capabilities. In December, the first vehicles arrived by sea at Gdinya, in Poland. The total value of both contracts is USD6.06bn. Contracts are also expected for the licensed production of further vehicles after 2026. These will be more advanced versions, tailored to Polish needs and dubbed K2PL and K9PL. It is noteworthy that the government highlighted security of supply issues in justifying the choice of South Korea as a strategic partner. This suggests that the bilateral defence relationship may be driven, at least in part, by a view that South Korean munitions and spares could be useful should the war in Europe escalate.

In May, Poland sent a letter of request to the US regarding the potential acquisition of up to 500 M142 HIMARS launchers. This would equal 80 standard US Army batteries and, if the contract were to proceed at this scale, could be worth well over USD10bn. However, in October, Poland signed a framework contract for the delivery of 288 K239 *Chunmoo* launchers from South Korea in 2023–28, stating that the US would be unable to deliver the desired number of HIMARS systems in this timeframe. In July, Poland secured an agreement for the delivery in 2023–24 of 116 M1A1 SA *Abrams* MBTs from US Army stocks. The main motivation behind the *Abrams* decision was to quickly fill the gap in Poland's armoured brigades; it will be partly financed by the US through the Foreign Military Financing system. Meanwhile, Poland's 2021 request for 250 M1A2 SEPv3 *Abrams* remains on track. General Dynamics Land Systems said in August that it had received the order. The same month saw an Abrams Tank Training Academy open in Poland.

In a move to strengthen close-air-support capability, hitherto reliant on some Soviet-era Mil Mi-24 helicopters, Poland announced in September its interest in purchasing 96 AH-64E *Apache* attack helicopters. A letter of request was sent to the US and included a proposal to lease US Army-owned helicopters until the new helicopters could be delivered. It is difficult to estimate the total value of the programme, but it could be in the region of USD12–15bn. A smaller contract, worth USD1.7bn, was signed in July with Italian firm Leonardo for the acquisition of 32 AW149 multi-role helicopters (with some close-air-support capability). Intelligence, surveillance and reconnaissance capability will be augmented with MQ-9A *Reaper* systems, which were leased in October from the US as a 'bridging' option, enabling both the rapid provision of a new capability and the establishment of a training package, in advance of the acquisition process.

Against this backdrop, new investments in the air force seem less ambitious. Seeking a replacement for its ageing fleet of Soviet-era MiG-29 *Fulcrum* and Su-22 *Fitter* combat aircraft, in September Poland signed a contract worth approximately USD3.02bn for 48 FA-50 *Fighting Eagle* multi-role aircraft as part of its broader partnership with South Korea. The first batch of 12 FA-50s will be delivered in 2022–23 in a baseline lead-in jet-trainer configuration. This will be followed by 32 upgraded FA-50PL aircraft from 2025–28, including features such as an active electronically scanned array radar and designed to serve in both air-to-air and ground-attack roles.

Force transformation

The scale of the investment in new capabilities is accompanied by an ambitious plan to increase the armed forces to 300,000 personnel by 2035. This total is intended to comprise around 187,000 professionals (as of 2022, this number stood at approximately 114,000), augmented by 50,000 voluntary Territorial Defence Force personnel (32,000 as of the end of 2021) and a further 50,000 personnel recruited under a new type of one-year service. While this plan may resemble conscription, with troops undergoing one month of basic training and up to 11 months of specialist training, the roles are salaried (troops will be paid more than conscripts of previous years) and are designed for volunteers only.

The new personnel plan stems from the decision to establish two more divisions (making six divisions in total) and to strengthen existing mechanised divisions with an additional armoured brigade each. These are understood to be key assumptions of Poland's 'Model 2035' concept, which is informing modernisation and transformation plans. The process of establishing the fifth division began in September. It will be deployed in eastern Poland, between the 16th Mechanised Division, which is generally focused towards the north and northeast (including the Suwalki Gap and the border with Russia's Kaliningrad exclave), and the 18th Mechanised Division, which is responsible for defending eastern and southeastern Poland. The latter unit is still being developed and will be equipped with the M1A1 SA and M1A2 SEPv3 *Abrams* MBTs and, in the future, the AH-64 *Apache* – in effect resembling US Army structures. The intent is for the unit to provide defence and deterrence against potential Russian–Belarussian operations from the direction of Brest, in Belarus.

Sustainability

Poland's technical-modernisation and force-transformation plans can be seen as an attempt to develop a posture capable of at least blunting, and possibly also stopping, potential Russian aggression against NATO's eastern flank below the nuclear level. The security guarantees under Article 5 of the Washington Treaty are undisputed by Poland's political class. So too is the broader strategic relationship with the US, which involves US deployments to Poland. And Poland welcomed, as a step in the right direction, the overhaul to NATO's defence and deterrence posture vis-à-vis Russia at the 2022 summit in Madrid. Nonetheless, Warsaw seems to be considering a scenario in which the military response to a potential Russian escalation by the US and NATO may be slower than required – perhaps because of a military contingency in the Indo-Pacific. This is also important in the context of the longstanding US calls for its European allies to take on a greater share of the burden of defence and deterrence in Europe. The 2022 Madrid Summit was followed by a process of updating not only NATO's capability plans but also the requirements that will be expected of allies.

However, questions have been raised over the sustainability of Poland's plans. Concerns include personnel shortages and inadequate infrastructure, as well as doubts about the capacity of Poland's economy to continue funding defence at such a historically high level. The high level of inflation (17.2% year-on-year as of September 2022) and a possible recession are important factors that may limit Polish investment ambitions. In October, the issue of bonds worth USD3.2bn, intended to provide money for the extra-budgetary modernisation fund, was suddenly halted. According to analysts, this may suggest only limited interest by financial markets. These investments will also be required in areas other than equipment purchases. Poland's new systems will need a separate modernisation effort for military infrastructure, such as training and maintenance facilities. Moreover, there are doubts over whether the armed forces can attract enough young people to reach the 300,000 target, even with the flexibility offered by new types of service.

Arms procurements and deliveries – Europe

Significant events in 2022

JANUARY — POLAND: PROCUREMENT REORGANISATION

Poland transformed its Armaments Inspectorate (IU), the organisation responsible for procurement and offsets, into the Armaments Agency (AU). The reform is intended to simplify procedures and responsibilities. The government originally wanted the organisation to control the state-owned defence conglomerate Polska Grupa Zbrojeniowa (PGZ), though this idea was shelved. Since its inception in January, the AU has already overseen the signing of significant import contracts such as the USD13.35bn package of equipment with South Korea and the USD1.15bn deal for M1A2 SEPv3 *Abrams* main battle tanks (MBT) with General Dynamics. These deals all include significant work for local industry.

MAY — OTO MELARA FOR SALE

Rheinmetall offered EUR190–210m (USD200.82–221.96m) for a 49% stake in the Oto Melara division of Italian firm Leonardo, with an option to acquire an additional 2% of shares. Oto Melara has a dominant position within the naval gun sector and a smaller share of the armoured-vehicle gun market. Leonardo announced its intention to sell in 2021, saying it would also sell torpedo producer Whitehead Alenia Sistemi Subacquei, in order to focus on aircraft, electronics and helicopters. Initially, Leonardo offered all of Oto Melara for sale. KNDS and Fincantieri each expressed interest in Oto Melara in late 2021, and while the firms are reportedly willing to spend around EUR650m (USD687.03m) or EUR450–550m (USD475.64–581.33m) respectively for a 100% stake, neither has yet made an offer. However, reports indicated that any sale may be held up until Rome receives assurances regarding Italy's role in the Franco-German Main Ground Combat System MBT programme.

JUNE — NORWAY NH90 CANCELLATION

Norway announced that it was cancelling its 2001 contract for 14 NH90 NATO Frigate Helicopters (NFH) for the Norwegian Armed Forces and the Coast Guard. Although deliveries were originally expected to begin in 2005 and be completed in 2008, the first NH90 only arrived in November 2011. In cancelling the contract, Oslo cited delivery delays and an inability by NHIndustries to meet Norwegian requirements. NHIndustries said it considered the termination to be 'legally groundless'. 13 out of 14 helicopters have been delivered, but only eight are in fully operational configurations. Norway is looking to return to NHIndustries the helicopters that have been delivered and is seeking a refund of NOK5bn (USD521.01m).

JULY — *TEMPEST* COLLABORATION

The United Kingdom said that, by 2027, it aims to fly the test demonstrator of its Future Combat Air System (FCAS) programme, also known as *Tempest*. It also outlined a roadmap for a strategic partnership with Japan's F-X programme, with the nature of the bilateral collaboration between the *Tempest*/F-X projects to be decided before the end of 2022. Both countries already cooperate on multiple aerospace research projects including a new air-to-air missile (JNAAM), sensors (JAGUAR) and propulsion systems. Italy and Sweden also participate in the *Tempest* programme, which is led by BAE Systems and involves Rolls-Royce and the UK divisions of Leonardo and MBDA. Tempest and F-X are intended to start replacing the *Typhoon* and the F-2 from the late 2030s.

NOVEMBER — FCAS/SCAF TENTATIVE AGREEMENT

France and Germany announced that discussions on the next phase of the French–German–Spanish FCAS/SCAF programme, planned to replace the *Rafale* and the Eurofighter, had been concluded. A research and technology study (Phase 1A) was completed in 2020–21, but the companies subsequently struggled to establish clear leadership, division of labour and intellectual property rules. The next stage, Phase 1B, is intended to define the architecture of the aircraft demonstrator and was originally planned for 2021–24, while Phase 2, covering the construction and testing of the demonstrator, was due to take place in 2024–27. The first flight of a demonstrator is not now expected until 2028, with the aircraft entering service in the 2050s. Despite the three governments hailing the announcement, Dassault head Eric Trappier described it as a "pseudo-political announcement" suggesting there was much yet to be done before Phase 1B could start. The trilateral relationship is already strained in part because Germany announced it would buy the F-35A in March; there is speculation that Spain may follow suit and buy the F-35 to replace its F/A-18A *Hornet*s.

Table 7 Poland: *Rosomak* wheeled armoured vehicle family

Selected *Rosomak* vehicle contracts*

Date	Variant	Type	Quantity	Value	Delivery dates	Contract type	Notes
Apr 2003	WB; base vehicle	Infantry fighting vehicle (IFV); armoured personnel carrier (APC)	570	PLN4.63bn (USD1.46bn)	2004–13	Production	Originally 690 vehicles for PLN4.93bn (USD1.27bn)
Dec 2010	WSRiD	Reconnaissance	2	PLN49.85m (USD16.53m)	2012–13	Conversion	Conducted by Elbit Systems
Oct 2013	Base vehicle	APC	307	PLN1.65bn (USD522.05m)	2014–20	Production	
Jun 2014	WRT	Armoured engineering vehicle	33	PLN233.56m (USD74.06m)	2016–17	Conversion	
Dec 2014	WPT	Armoured recovery vehicle	18	PLN230m (USD72.93m)	By end of 2025	Conversion	Development extended Dec 2018
Apr 2016	*Rak*	120mm mortar	96	PLN968.32m (USD245.4m)	2017–19	Conversion	To equip eight companies (coy)
Mar 2018	WD	Command post (CP)	7	PLN80m (USD22.15m)	2018	Conversion	
Sep 2019	WD	CP	2	PLN24.7m (USD6.43m)	2020	Conversion	
Nov 2019	*Rak*	120mm mortar	24	PLN275.5m (USD71.75m)	2021	Conversion	To equip two coy
May 2020	*Rak*	120mm mortar	60	PLN703.1m (USD180.3m)	2022–24	Conversion	To equip five coy
Sep 2020	RSK	Nuclear, biological and chemical defence	11	PLN524.4m (USD134.47m)	2028–29	Production	
Sep 2020	*Rosomak-S*	APC	60	PLN105.5m (USD27.05m)	2021–ongoing	Conversion	
Dec 2020	WD	CP	8	PLN73.7m (USD18.9m)	2021–22	Conversion	
Jul 2022	ZSSW-30	IFV turret	70	PLN1.7bn (USD409.87m)	2023–27	Turret production	
Sep 2022	AWR	Reconnaissance	30	PLN1.59bn (USD383.35m)	2024–26	Production	

*As of end of September 2022

AWR = artyleryjskie wozy rozpoznawcze [artillery reconnaissance vehicles]; RSK = rozpoznania skażeń kołowy transporter opancerzony [contamination recognition wheeled armoured vehicle]; WB = wozów bojowych [combat vehicles]; WD = wozach dowodzenia [command vehicles]; WPT = wozu pomocy technicznej [technical assistance vehicle]; WR = wozy rozpoznawcze [reconnaissance vehicles]; WRT = wóz rozpoznania technicznego [technical reconnaissance vehicle]; WSRiD = wielosensorowy system rozpoznania i dozorowania [multisensor surveillance and recognition system]; ZSSW = zdalnie sterowany system wieżowy [remote-controlled turret system]

Over 870 *Rosomak* armoured vehicles have been produced since Poland selected the vehicle in 2002. They are manufactured, by a firm now also called Rosomak, at a factory in Siemianowice Śląskie. Based on Finnish company Patria's Armoured Modular Vehicle (AMV), the family of variants in Polish service has over time had an increased level of local content. A 2003 contract for 690 vehicles was reduced to 570, increasing the number of infantry fighting vehicles (IFVs) but delaying others, such as reconnaissance (recce) and command-post variants. Deliveries began in 2004 and up-armoured *Rosomaks* were deployed to Afghanistan in 2007. Licensed production was extended for another ten years in 2013 and was followed the same year by a contract for 307 additional base vehicles for conversion to variants under separate contracts. Today, as well as IFVs, the army also operates variants in the armoured engineering (WRT), mortar, command post, armoured ambulance and armoured personnel carrier (APC) roles. Some APCs can transport infantry squads equipped with *Spike*-LR. Development of recce and recovery vehicles has taken longer (bar two recce versions delivered for use in Afghanistan), with deliveries now likely to be complete by the mid-2020s if the projects continue. A contract to deliver 70 Polish-designed ZSSW-30 turrets will be completed within the same time frame. These will be installed on base vehicles rather than replacing the IFVs already in service. The turret will be equipped with *Spike* beyond-line-of-sight missiles, unlike the Oto Melara *Hitfist*-30P turret that was licence-produced in Poland. (An earlier initiative to install *Spike* onto those turrets had been halted.) In September 2022, Rosomak announced that its production licence had been extended by five years, to the end of 2028. This will allow production of the delayed recce variants and possibly additional vehicles fitted with ZSSW-30 turrets.

Europe 71

Table 8 Spain: selected aerospace procurement since 2010

Spain maintains a sophisticated defence-industrial base, largely centred on aerospace systems through part-ownership of European defence giant Airbus. Spain's state-owned industrial holding company, the Sociedad Estatal de Participaciones Industriales (SEPI), holds 4.1% of Airbus shares, though the governments of France and Germany hold more, at 10.9% each. In the 2010s, Spain's aerospace procurement was generally limited to small-scale contracts, mostly due to budgetary constraints caused by delays to long-running international projects. However, once the economic impact of the coronavirus pandemic became clear, the government signed several large deals that are partly intended to support the aerospace sector. After Airbus announced redundancies in Spain, in 2020, the government agreed to buy a number of aircraft in order to reinforce the industrial base. Madrid agreed to acquire three A330 transport aircraft

(to be converted into the MRTT configuration in 2023–25), 36 H135 light transport helicopters (with an additional 59 in future), 20 *Eurofighter* combat aircraft and four C295 light transport aircraft. Contracts have been signed for all, apart from the C295s. Also, Spain is participating with other European Union members in Phase II of the Future Combat Air System (FCAS) programme, the *Tiger* MkIII attack helicopter project and the Medium-Altitude Long-Endurance Remotely Piloted Aircraft System (MALE RPAS) uninhabited aerial vehicle (UAV) venture. These will secure substantial local workshare into the 2020s and beyond. Although Spain has denied claims that it is interested in the F-35, speculation persists that the air force would like to acquire these to replace its F/A-18 *Hornet*s. Following Germany's decision to acquire the F-35, any Spanish purchase would likely add to French unease over its partners' commitment to the FCAS programme.

Contract Date	Equipment	Type	Quantity	Value		Contractor	Deliveries
Feb 2010	H135	Light transport helicopter	12	n.k.	M	Airbus	2010–12
Nov 2012	SH-60F *Seahawk***	Anti-submarine warfare (ASW) helicopter	2	EUR24.51m (USD31.51m)		US government surplus	2015
Dec 2013	H135 (EC135T2)	Light transport helicopter	8	EUR45m (USD59.77m)	M	Airbus	Mar 2014–Feb 2015
Feb 2016	MQ-9A *Reaper*	Heavy combat, intelligence, surveillance and reconnaissance (CISR) uninhabited aerial vehicle (UAV)	4	EUR161m (USD178.16m)		General Atomics Aeronautical Systems (GA-ASI)	Dec 2019–Nov 2020
Jul 2016	H215 (AS332 C1e) *Super Puma*	Search and rescue (SAR) helicopter	1	EUR15m (USD16.60m)	M	Airbus	Oct 2016
Dec 2016	SH-60F *Seahawk***	ASW helicopter	2	EUR40m (USD44.26m)		US government surplus	Aug 2017–Apr 2018
c.2017	H215 (AS332 C1e) *Super Puma*	SAR helicopter	2	EUR30m (USD338.78m)	M	Airbus	Nov 2017
Dec 2017	SH-60F *Seahawk***	ASW helicopter	2	EUR28m (USD31.62m)		US government surplus	n.k.
Q2 2019	NH90 TTH	Medium transport helicopter	16	EUR1.38bn (USD1.55bn)	M	NHIndustries	2023–28*
	NH90 NFH	ASW helicopter	7				
May 2019	*Spainsat* NG	Communications satellite	2	EUR850m (USD1bn)	M	Airbus	2023–24*
Nov 2019	SH-60F *Seahawk***	ASW helicopter	2	EUR35.97m (USD40.27m)		US government surplus	n.k.
Jan 2020	PC-21	Training aircraft	24	EUR225m (USD256.79m)		Pilatus Aircraft	Sep 2021–Jun 2022
Nov 2021	A330 MRTT	Tanker/transport aircraft	3	EUR810m (USD958.66m)	M	Airbus	Nov 2021–2025*
Dec 2021	H135	Light transport helicopter	36	EUR310m (USD366.89m)	M	Airbus	2022–26*
Feb 2022	MALE RPAS	Heavy CISR UAV	12	EUR1.43bn (USD1.51bn)	M	Airbus	2029*
Jun 2022	*Eurofighter*	Fighter ground-attack aircraft	20	EUR2.04bn (USD2.16bn)	M	Eurofighter	2026–30*

*planned

**second-hand

M = multinational

Albania ALB

Albanian Lek ALL		2021	2022	2023
GDP	ALL	1.89tr	2.06tr	
	USD	18.3bn	18.3bn	
per capita	USD	6,373	6,369	
Growth	%	8.5	4.0	
Inflation	%	2.0	6.2	
Def exp [a]	ALL	23.1bn	32.6bn	
	USD	224m	289m	
Def bdgt [b]	ALL	25.2bn	32.2bn	40.3bn
	USD	245m	286m	
USD1=ALL		103.21	112.79	

[a] NATO figure
[b] Excludes military pensions

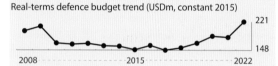

Real-terms defence budget trend (USDm, constant 2015)

Population 3,095,344

Age	0–14	15–19	20–24	25–29	30–64	65 plus
Male	9.3%	3.1%	4.0%	4.6%	21.7%	6.5%
Female	8.4%	2.8%	3.7%	4.4%	23.8%	7.6%

Capabilities

The MOD's Defence Directive for 2022, published in February, listed priorities including improved conditions for personnel, equipment modernisation, institutional reform, strengthening civil defence capabilities, better cyber security and greater contributions to regional operations and engagements. An Integrity Plan 2022–2025 indicated broader efforts to bring Albania's armed forces closer to NATO standards. Tirana is looking to improve the readiness and capability of its infantry battalion, including with new equipment, and is trying to improve recruitment and retention with enhanced benefits and educational and training opportunities. Salary increases were announced in 2022. The Development Plan 2022–2031 will determine future military structures, capacities, capabilities and obligations. Limited modernisation is underway, including the acquisition of helicopters and the installation of an airspace-surveillance system. Additional helicopter aircrew graduated in 2022. A ground-based air defence capability may also be developed. Other priorities include increasing communications and cyber defence capabilities. Albania contributes to NATO, UN and EU missions but does not possess an independent expeditionary capability. In March 2022, a forward-deployed headquarters for US Special Operations Command Europe was established in Albania. NATO allies Greece and Italy police Albania's airspace, and Tirana is upgrading Kuçova Air Base into a NATO tactical air base. A cyber-attack in mid-year, attributed to Iran by Albania and NATO Allies, affected government infrastructure and NATO and individual allies subsequently offered additional security assistance. Albania has little in the way of a domestic defence industry, with no ability to design and manufacture modern military platforms. Nevertheless, the country has some publicly owned defence companies that are capable of producing small arms, explosives and ammunition.

ACTIVE 7,500 (Land Force 2,350 Naval Force 700 Air Force 650 Support Command 1,650 Other 2,150)

ORGANISATIONS BY SERVICE

Land Force 2,350
FORCES BY ROLE
SPECIAL FORCES
 1 spec ops regt (1 SF bn, 1 cdo bn)
MANOEUVRE
 Light
 3 lt inf bn
COMBAT SUPPORT
 1 mor bty
 1 NBC coy
EQUIPMENT BY TYPE
ARMOURED FIGHTING VEHICLES
 APC • PPV 40 *MaxxPro Plus*
ARTILLERY • MOR 32: **82mm** 20; **120mm** 12

Naval Force 700
EQUIPMENT BY TYPE
All operational patrol vessels under 10t FLD

Coast Guard
EQUIPMENT BY TYPE
PATROL AND COASTAL COMBATANTS 14
 PB 9: 4 *Iliria* (Damen Stan Patrol 4207); 3 Mk3 *Sea Spectre*; 2 *Shqypnia*
 PBR 5: 2 Type-227; 1 Type-246; 2 Type-2010

Air Force 650
EQUIPMENT BY TYPE
HELICOPTERS
 TPT 16: **Medium** 4 AS532AL *Cougar†*; **Light** 12: 1 AW109; 3 Bell 205 (AB-205); 2 Bell 206C (AB-206C); 4 Bo-105; 2 H145

Military Police
FORCES BY ROLE
COMBAT SUPPORT
 1 MP bn
EQUIPMENT BY TYPE
ARMOURED FIGHTING VEHICLES
 AUV 8 IVECO LMV

Support Command 1,650
FORCES BY ROLE
COMBAT SUPPORT
 1 engr bn
 1 cbt spt bn
COMBAT SERVICE SUPPORT
 1 log bde (1 tpt bn, 1 log bn)
 1 maint unit

DEPLOYMENT

BOSNIA-HERZEGOVINA: EU • EUFOR (*Operation Althea*) 1
BULGARIA: NATO • Enhanced Vigilance Activites 30; 1 inf pl
LATVIA: NATO • Enhanced Forward Presence 21; 1 EOD pl
SERBIA: NATO • KFOR 61
SOUTH SUDAN: UN • UNMISS 2

Austria AUT

Euro EUR		2021	2022	2023
GDP	EUR	403bn	443bn	
	USD	477bn	468bn	
per capita	USD	53,332	52,062	
Growth	%	4.6	4.7	
Inflation	%	2.8	7.7	
Def bdgt [a]	EUR	3.55bn	3.45bn	3.39bn
	USD	4.20bn	3.64bn	
USD1=EUR		0.84	0.95	

[a] Includes military pensions

Real-terms defence budget trend (USDbn, constant 2015)

Population 8,913,088

Age	0–14	15–19	20–24	25–29	30–64	65 plus
Male	7.2%	2.4%	2.6%	3.2%	24.5%	9.0%
Female	6.8%	2.3%	2.6%	3.1%	24.6%	11.5%

Capabilities

Austria remains constitutionally non-aligned, but is an EU member and actively engaged in the EU's CSDP. Defence-policy objectives are based on the 2013 National Security Strategy, the 2014 Defence Strategy and the 2017 Military Strategy, including providing military capabilities to maintain sovereignty and territorial integrity, to enable military assistance to the civil authorities and to participate in crisis-management missions. Authorities are now shifting emphasis from international operations to homeland defence, and capabilities needed to counter hybrid threats at home. Assets for international deployments may eventually be embedded in the EUFOR Crisis Response Operation Core. In June 2021, plans to streamline Ministry of Defence structures were announced. Implementation began in May 2022. There is a plan to group Cyber, CIS and EW capabilities together in one directorate. While not a NATO member, Austria joined NATO's Partnership for Peace framework in 1995. A September 2019 defence ministry report defined recapitalisation requirements until 2030. It warned that the gap between requirements and available resources was growing and would ultimately undermine the ability of the armed forces to implement its missions. The level of ambition for crisis response is to be able to deploy and sustain a minimum (on average) of 1,100 troops. The September 2019 report also called for the Eurofighter fleet to be upgraded rather than replaced. In October 2022, plans were mooted to procure a small number of additional Eurofighters, two-seaters from the German inventory, and upgrade the existing fleet. There is cooperation with Italy over helicopter procurement. Austria's defence-industrial base is comprised of some 100 companies with significant niche capabilities and international ties in the areas of weapons and ammunitions, communications equipment and vehicles.

ACTIVE 23,300 (Land Forces 13,000 Air 2,800 Support 7,500)

Conscript liability 6 months recruit trg, 30 days reservist refresher trg for volunteers; 120–150 days additional for officers, NCOs and specialists. Authorised maximum wartime strength of 55,000

RESERVE 112,250 (Joint structured 36,050; Joint unstructured 76,200)
Some 12,000 reservists a year undergo refresher trg in tranches

ORGANISATIONS BY SERVICE

Land Forces 13,000

FORCES BY ROLE
MANOEUVRE
  Armoured
    1 (4th) armd inf bde (1 recce/SP arty bn, 1 tk bn, 2 armd inf bn, 1 spt bn)
  Mechanised
    1 (3rd) mech inf bde (1 recce/SP arty bn, 3 mech inf bn, 1 cbt engr bn, 1 spt bn)
  Light
    1 (7th) lt inf bde (1 recce bn, 3 inf bn, 1 cbt engr bn, 1 spt bn)
    1 (6th) mtn inf bde (3 mtn inf bn, 1 cbt engr bn, 1 spt bn)

EQUIPMENT BY TYPE
ARMOURED FIGHTING VEHICLES
  MBT 56 *Leopard* 2A4
  IFV 112 *Ulan*
  APC 153
    APC (T) 32 BvS-10
    APC (W) 121: 71 *Pandur*; 50 *Pandur* EVO
  AUV 216: 66 *Dingo* 2; 150 IVECO LMV
ENGINEERING & MAINTENANCE VEHICLES
  ARV 65: 27 4KH7FA-SB *Greif* (11 more in store); 28 *Dingo* 2 ARV; 10 M88A1
NBC VEHICLES 12 *Dingo* 2 AC NBC
ANTI-TANK/ANTI-INFRASTRUCTURE
  MSL • **MANPATS** *Bill* 2 (PAL 2000)
ARTILLERY 105
  SP 155mm 48 M109A5ÖE
  MOR 120mm 57 sGrW 86 (40 more in store)

Air Force 2,800

The Air Force is part of Joint Forces Comd and consists of 2 bde; Air Support Comd and Airspace Surveillance Comd

FORCES BY ROLE
FIGHTER
  2 sqn with Eurofighter *Typhoon*
ISR
  1 sqn with PC-6B *Turbo Porter*
TRANSPORT
  1 sqn with C-130K *Hercules*
TRAINING
  1 trg sqn with PC-7 *Turbo Trainer*
TRANSPORT HELICOPTER
  2 sqn with Bell 212 (AB-212)
  1 sqn with OH-58B *Kiowa*
  1 sqn with S-70A *Black Hawk*
  2 sqn with SA316/SA319 *Alouette* III
AIR DEFENCE
  2 bn
  1 radar bn

EQUIPMENT BY TYPE
AIRCRAFT 13 combat capable
  FTR 13 Eurofighter *Typhoon* (Tranche 1)

TPT 11: **Medium** 3 C-130K *Hercules*; **Light** 8 PC-6B *Turbo Porter*
TRG 16: 12 PC-7 *Turbo Trainer*; 4 DA40NG
HELICOPTERS
  MRH 18 SA316/SA319 *Alouette* III
  ISR 10 OH-58B *Kiowa*
  TPT 32: **Medium** 9 S-70A-42 *Black Hawk*; **Light** 23 Bell 212 (AB-212)
AIR DEFENCE
  SAM • **Point-defence** *Mistral*
  GUNS 35mm 24 GDF-005 (6 more in store)
AIR-LAUNCHED MISSILES • **AAM** • **IIR** IRIS-T

Special Operations Forces
FORCES BY ROLE
SPECIAL FORCES
  2 SF gp
  1 SF gp (reserve)

Support 7,500
Support forces comprise Joint Services Support Command and several agencies, academies and schools

DEPLOYMENT
BOSNIA-HERZEGOVINA: EU • EUFOR (*Operation Althea*) 167; 1 inf bn HQ; 1 inf coy; 1 hel unit
CYPRUS: UN • UNFICYP 3
LEBANON: UN • UNIFIL 171; 1 log coy
MALI: EU • EUTM Mali 5; **UN** • MINUSMA 2
MIDDLE EAST: UN • UNTSO 4
SERBIA: NATO • KFOR 244; 1 recce coy; 1 mech inf coy; 1 log coy; **UN** • UNMIK 1
WESTERN SAHARA: UN • MINURSO 4

Belgium BEL

Euro EUR		2021	2022	2023
GDP	EUR	506bn	558bn	
	USD	599bn	590bn	
per capita	USD	51,849	50,598	
Growth	%	6.2	2.4	
Inflation	%	3.2	9.5	
Def exp [a]	EUR	5.28bn	6.53bn	
	USD	6.24bn	6.90bn	
Def bdgt [b]	EUR	4.66bn	5.36bn	5.99bn
	USD	5.52bn	5.66bn	
USD1=EUR		0.84	0.95	

[a] NATO figure
[b] Includes military pensions

Real-terms defence budget trend (USDbn, constant 2015)

Population	11,847,338					
Age	0–14	15–19	20–24	25–29	30–64	65 plus
Male	8.8%	2.9%	2.9%	3.1%	23.0%	8.7%
Female	8.4%	2.7%	2.8%	3.0%	22.8%	11.0%

Capabilities
In July 2016, the government published its Strategic Vision for Defence for 2030. This was updated in June 2022, when the Security/Service, Technology, Ambition, Resilience (STAR) Plan was approved by parliament. A month later, in July, a new military programming law was approved which heralded increased defence budgets out to 2030. These are intended to address three key areas: to increase personnel numbers, strengthen the defence technological and industrial base, and deliver major equipment investments. Recruitment and retention criteria are under scrutiny, after retirements and establishment reductions in recent decades. Investments are planned for the motorised brigade, medical support and mobility, with over half of the STAR Plan's investments slated for the land domain. There is focus on 'dual capability' investments that can used in contingencies at home as well as for miliary operations. A Cyber Command was inaugurated in October, falling under the authority of the military intelligence service. NATO, EU and UN membership are central to defence policy. Belgium often cooperates with neighbours and has committed with Denmark and the Netherlands to form a composite combined special-operations command. The air force is forming a joint A400M unit with Luxembourg. Investment projects include fighter aircraft, frigates, mine-countermeasures vessels (being procured jointly with the Netherlands), UAVs and land-combat vehicles. The army has ordered French *Griffon* and *Jaguar* wheeled armoured vehicles as well as the US JLTV. CAESAR NG self-propelled artillery pieces are being procured and will likely arrive from 2027. The air force has selected the F-35 to replace its F-16s and deliveries are planned from 2023, with IOC expected in 2025. It is also procuring UAVs and is looking to buy light utility, heavy transport and search-and-rescue helicopters. Belgium has an advanced, export-focused defense industry, focusing on components and subcontracting, though in FN Herstal it has one of the world's largest manufacturers of small arms.

ACTIVE 23,200 (Army 8,500 Navy 1,400 Air 4,900 Medical Service 1,450 Joint Service 6,950)

RESERVE 5,900

ORGANISATIONS BY SERVICE

Land Component 8,500

FORCES BY ROLE
SPECIAL FORCES
1 spec ops regt (1 SF gp, 1 cdo bn, 1 para bn, 1 sigs gp)
MANOEUVRE
Mechanised
1 mech bde (1 ISR bn; 3 mech bn; 2 lt inf bn; 1 arty bn; 2 engr bn; 2 sigs gp; 2 log bn)
COMBAT SUPPORT
1 CIMIC gp
1 EOD unit
1 MP coy
COMBAT SERVICE SUPPORT
1 log bn
EQUIPMENT BY TYPE
ARMOURED FIGHTING VEHICLES
ASLT 18 *Piranha* III-C DF90
RECCE 30 *Pandur Recce*
IFV 19 *Piranha* III-C DF30
APC • APC (W) 78: 64 *Piranha* III-C; 14 *Piranha* III-PC (CP)
AUV 655: 219 *Dingo* 2 (inc 52 CP); 436 IVECO LMV
ENGINEERING & MAINTENANCE VEHICLES
AEV 14: 6 Pionierpanzer 2 *Dachs*; 8 *Piranha* III-C
ARV 13: 4 *Pandur;* 9 *Piranha* III-C
VLB 4 *Leguan*
ANTI-TANK/ANTI-INFRASTRUCTURE
MSL • MANPATS *Spike*-MR
ARTILLERY 60
TOWED 105mm 14 LG1 MkII
MOR 46: **81mm** 14 Expal; **120mm** 32 RT-61

Naval Component 1,400

EQUIPMENT BY TYPE
PRINCIPAL SURFACE COMBATANTS • FRIGATES 2
FFGHM 2 *Leopold* I (ex-NLD *Karel Doorman*) with 2 quad lnchr with RGM-84 *Harpoon* AShM, 1 16-cell Mk 48 mod 1 VLS with RIM-7P *Sea Sparrow* SAM, 2 twin 324mm SVTT Mk 32 ASTT with Mk 46 LWT, 1 *Goalkeeper* CIWS, 1 76mm gun (capacity 1 med hel)
PATROL AND COASTAL COMBATANTS
PCC 2 *Castor* (FRA *Kermorvan* mod)
MINE WARFARE • MINE COUNTERMEASURES
MHC 5 *Flower* (*Tripartite*)
LOGISTICS AND SUPPORT 2
AGOR 1 *Belgica*
AXS 1 *Zenobe Gramme*

Air Component 4,900

FORCES BY ROLE
FIGHTER/GROUND ATTACK/ISR
4 sqn with F-16AM/BM *Fighting Falcon*
SEARCH & RESCUE
1 sqn with NH90 NFH

TRANSPORT
1 sqn with *Falcon* 7X (VIP)
1 sqn (BEL/LUX) with A400M
TRAINING
1 OCU sqn with F-16AM/BM *Fighting Falcon*
1 sqn with SF-260D/M
1 OCU unit with AW109
TRANSPORT HELICOPTER
2 sqn with AW109 (ISR)

EQUIPMENT BY TYPE
AIRCRAFT 53 combat capable
FTR 53: 44 F-16AM *Fighting Falcon*; 9 F-16BM *Fighting Falcon*
TPT 8: **Heavy** 6 A400M; **PAX** 2 *Falcon* 7X (VIP, leased)
TRG 32: 9 SF-260D; 23 SF-260M
HELICOPTERS
ASW 4 NH90 NFH (opcon Navy)
TPT 11: **Medium** 4 NH90 TTH; **Light** 7 AW109 (ISR) (7 more in store)
AIR-LAUNCHED MISSILES
AAM • IR AIM-9M *Sidewinder*; **IIR** AIM-9X *Sidewinder* II; **ARH** AIM-120B AMRAAM
BOMBS
Laser-guided: GBU-10/-12 *Paveway* II; GBU-24 *Paveway* III
Laser & INS/GPS-guided: GBU-54 Laser JDAM (dual-mode)
INS/GPS guided: GBU-31 JDAM; GBU-38 JDAM; GBU-39 Small Diameter Bomb

Medical Service 1,450

FORCES BY ROLE
COMBAT SERVICE SUPPORT
4 med unit
1 fd hospital
EQUIPMENT BY TYPE
ARMOURED FIGHTING VEHICLES
APC • APC (W) 10: 4 *Pandur* (amb); 6 *Piranha* III-C (amb)
AUV 10 *Dingo* 2 (amb)

DEPLOYMENT

DEMOCRATIC REPUBLIC OF THE CONGO: UN • MONUSCO 1

IRAQ: *Operation Inherent Resolve* 6; **NATO** • NATO Mission Iraq 7

LITHUANIA: NATO • Enhanced Forward Presence 150; 1 mech inf coy with *Piranha* DF30/DF90

MALI: EU • EUTM Mali 15; **UN** • MINUSMA 53

MEDITERRANEAN SEA: NATO • SNMCMG 2: 50; 1 MHC

MIDDLE EAST: UN • UNTSO 1

MOZAMBIQUE: EU • EUTM Mozambique 3

ROMANIA: NATO • Enhanced Vigilance Activities 250; 1 mech inf coy with *Piranha* IIIC

FOREIGN FORCES

United States US European Command: 1,150

Bosnia-Herzegovina BIH

Convertible Mark BAM		2021	2022	2023
GDP	BAM	38.6bn	43.8bn	
	USD	23.4bn	23.7bn	
per capita	USD	6,712	6,818	
Growth	%	7.5	2.5	
Inflation	%	2.0	10.5	
Def bdgt	BAM	318m	313m	324m
	USD	192m	169m	
USD1=BAM		1.65	1.85	

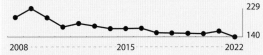
Real-terms defence budget trend (USDm, constant 2015)

Population	3,816,459					
Age	0–14	15–19	20–24	25–29	30–64	65 plus
Male	6.8%	2.3%	2.9%	3.2%	26.6%	7.0%
Female	6.4%	2.2%	2.7%	2.9%	26.8%	10.2%

Capabilities

The armed forces' primary goals are to defend territorial integrity and contribute to peacekeeping missions and potential tasks relating to aid to the civil authorities. Bosnia-Herzegovina joined NATO's Partnership for Peace in 2006 and a Membership Action Plan was presented in 2010. Its aspiration to join NATO has been delayed due to unresolved defence-property issues, and continuing ethnic tensions have seen the ethnic Serb community threaten to withdraw from national structures including the armed forces. The country is reforming its armed forces and modernising its equipment in accordance with its Defence Review, Development and Modernisation Plan for 2017–27 and its NATO aspirations. The armed forces are professional and represent all three ethnic groups. However, low salaries may negatively affect recruitment and retention. Bosnia-Herzegovina contributes to EU, NATO and UN missions, but the armed forces have no capacity to deploy independently and self-sustain beyond national borders. The inventory comprises mainly ageing Soviet-era equipment, though some new helicopters have been procured from the US. Bosnia-Herzegovina has little in the way of a domestic defence industry, with only the capability to produce small arms, ammunition and explosives.

ACTIVE 10,500 (Armed Forces 10,500)

RESERVE 6,000 (Armed Forces 6,000)

ORGANISATIONS BY SERVICE

Armed Forces 10,500
1 ops comd; 1 spt comd
FORCES BY ROLE
MANOEUVRE
　Light
　　3 inf bde (1 recce coy, 3 inf bn, 1 arty bn)
COMBAT SUPPORT
　1 cbt spt bde (1 tk bn, 1 engr bn, 1 EOD bn, 1 int bn, 1 MP bn, 1 CBRN coy, 1 sigs bn)
COMBAT SERVICE SUPPORT
　1 log comd (5 log bn)
EQUIPMENT BY TYPE
ARMOURED FIGHTING VEHICLES
　MBT 45 M60A3
　APC • APC (T) 20 M113A2
ENGINEERING & MAINTENANCE VEHICLES
　VLB MTU
　MW *Bozena*
ANTI-TANK/ANTI-INFRASTRUCTURE • MSL
　SP 60: 8 9P122 *Malyutka*; 9 9P133 *Malyutka*; 32 BOV-1; 11 M-92
　MANPATS 9K11 *Malyutka* (RS-AT-3 *Sagger*); 9K111 *Fagot* (RS-AT-4 *Spigot*); 9K115 *Metis* (RS-AT-7 *Saxhorn*); HJ-8; *Milan*
ARTILLERY 224
　TOWED 122mm 100 D-30
　MRL 122mm 24 APRA-40
　MOR 120mm 100 M-75

Air Force and Air Defence Brigade 800
FORCES BY ROLE
HELICOPTER
　1 sqn with Bell 205 (UH-1H *Iroquois*); Mi-8MTV *Hip*; Mi-17 *Hip* H
　1 sqn with Bell 205 (UH-1H *Huey* II); Mi-8 *Hip*; SA-341H/SA-342L *Gazelle* (HN-42/45M)
AIR DEFENCE
　1 AD bn
EQUIPMENT BY TYPE
AIRCRAFT
　FGA (7 J-22 *Orao* in store)
　ATK (6 J-1 (J-21) *Jastreb*; 3 TJ-1(NJ-21) *Jastreb* all in store)
　ISR (2 RJ-1 (IJ-21) *Jastreb*‡ in store)
　TRG (1 G-4 *Super Galeb* (N-62)‡ in store)
HELICOPTERS
　MRH 9: 4 Mi-8MTV *Hip*; 1 Mi-17 *Hip* H; 1 SA-341H *Gazelle* (HN-42); up to 3 SA-342L *Gazelle* (HN-45M)
　TPT 17: **Medium** 8 Mi-8 *Hip* **Light** 9: 6 Bell 205 (UH-1H *Iroquois*) (of which 2 MEDEVAC); 3 Bell 205 (UH-1H *Huey* II) (1 UH-1H *Huey* II in store)
AIR DEFENCE
　SAM
　　Short-range 20 2K12 *Kub* (RS-SA-6 *Gainful*)
　　Point-defence 9K34 *Strela-3* (RS-SA-14 *Gremlin*); 9K310 *Igla-1* (RS-SA-16 *Gimlet*)
　GUNS • TOWED 40mm 47: 31 L/60, 16 L/70

FOREIGN FORCES
Part of EUFOR – *Operation Althea* unless otherwise stated
Albania 1
Austria 167; 1 inf bn HQ; 1 inf coy; 1 hel unit
Bulgaria 110; 1 inf coy
Chile 7
Czech Republic 2
France 5
Germany 25
Greece 7

Hungary 192; 1 inf coy
Ireland 5
Italy 346; 1 inf bn HQ; 1 inf coy; 1 ISR coy
Macedonia, North 1
Poland 38
Portugal 1
Romania 203; 1 inf coy
Slovakia 53
Slovenia 16
Spain 3
Switzerland 20
Turkey 242; 1 inf coy

Bulgaria BLG

Bulgarian Lev BGN		2021	2022	2023
GDP	BGN	133bn	157bn	
	USD	80.3bn	85.0bn	
per capita	USD	11,746	12,505	
Growth	%	4.2	3.9	
Inflation	%	2.8	12.4	
Def exp [a]	BGN	2.11bn	2.48bn	
	USD	1.28bn	1.34bn	
Def bdgt [b]	BGN	2.10bn	2.48bn	2.97bn
	USD	1.27bn	1.34bn	
USD1=BGN		1.65	1.85	

[a] NATO figure
[b] Excludes military pensions

Real-terms defence budget trend (USDm, constant 2015)

Population	6,873,253				
Age	0–14	15–19	20–24	25–29	30–64	65 plus
Male	7.3%	2.6%	2.5%	2.7%	25.4%	8.3%
Female	6.9%	2.4%	2.3%	2.4%	24.9%	12.3%

Capabilities

The armed forces' main priority is defending state sovereignty and territorial integrity. The Programme 2032 long-term development plan was adopted in 2021, involving significant re-equipment and modernisation and a focus on artificial intelligence and cyber capability. Bulgaria signed a ten-year Defence Cooperation Roadmap with the US in 2020 to assist force development. There are several bilateral defence cooperation agreements with regional states. Bulgaria's airspace is protected by joint activities with NATO's Air Policing Mission, due to the country's limited numbers of combat aircraft. In September, the defence ministry announced it had allocated funds to purchase a further eight F-16C/Ds, on top of the eight agreed earlier. These aircraft are not expected to arrive until 2025. Bulgaria's MiG-29s are due for retirement in 2023, and the government in October said it was looking at options to improve their availability, including by securing additional engines from Poland. The government also received offers for interim combat aircraft from Sweden and France, with offers requested also from Israel and the US. In 2022, Bulgaria established and led a NATO multinational battle group. In an attempt to cope with personnel shortfalls, the military retirement age and salaries have been increased, yet several roles needed to strengthen the armed forces remain understrength. Training is understood to be prioritised for units intended for international operations and those with certain readiness levels declared to NATO and the EU. Bulgaria regularly trains and exercises with NATO partners and regional allies. There are also plans for acquisitions to enable the formation of battalion battlegroups within its mechanised brigades. The navy is looking to procure a multi-purpose patrol vessel and modernise its frigates to boost its presence in the Black Sea. T-72 modernisation is underway, and the local upgrade of 40 T-72s for the ground forces is expected to be complete in 2023, with this including upgraded battle management systems. Bulgaria's defence industry exports small arms but has limited capacity to design and manufacture platforms.

ACTIVE 36,950 (Army 17,000 Navy 4,450 Air 8,500 Central Staff 7,000)

RESERVE 3,000 (Joint 3,000)

ORGANISATIONS BY SERVICE

Army 17,000
FORCES BY ROLE
MANOEUVRE
　Reconnaissance
　1 recce bn
　Mechanised
　2 mech bde (4 mech inf bn, 1 SP arty bn, 1 cbt engr bn, 1 log bn, 1 SAM bn)
　Light
　1 mtn inf regt
COMBAT SUPPORT
　1 arty regt (1 fd arty bn, 1 MRL bn)
　1 engr regt (1 cbt engr bn, 1 ptn br bn, 1 engr spt bn)
　1 NBC bn
COMBAT SERVICE SUPPORT
　1 log regt
EQUIPMENT BY TYPE
ARMOURED FIGHTING VEHICLES
　MBT 90 T-72M1/M2†
　IFV 160: 90 BMP-1; 70 BMP-23
　APC 120
　　APC (T) 100 MT-LB
　　APC (W) 20 BTR-60
　AUV 44: 17 M1117 ASV; 27 Plasan *SandCat*
ENGINEERING & MAINTENANCE VEHICLES
　AEV MT-LB
　ARV T-54/T-55; MTP-1; MT-LB
　VLB BLG67; TMM
ANTI-TANK/ANTI-INFRASTRUCTURE
　MSL
　　SP 24 9P148 *Konkurs* (RS-AT-5 *Spandrel*)
　　MANPATS 9K111 *Fagot* (RS-AT-4 *Spigot*); 9K111-1 *Konkurs* (RS-AT-5 *Spandrel*); (9K11 *Malyutka* (RS-AT-3 *Sagger*) in store)
　GUNS 126: **85mm** (150 D-44 in store); **100mm** 126 MT-12

78 THE MILITARY BALANCE 2023

ARTILLERY 176
SP 122mm 48 2S1
TOWED 152mm 24 D-20
MRL 122mm 24 BM-21
MOR 120mm ε80 *Tundza/Tundza Sani*
SURFACE-TO-SURFACE MISSILE LAUNCHERS
SRBM • Conventional 9K79 *Tochka* (RS-SS-21 *Scarab*)
AIR DEFENCE
SAM • Point-defence 9K32 *Strela* (RS-SA-7 *Grail*)‡;
24 9K33 *Osa* (RS-SA-8 *Gecko*)
GUNS 400
SP 23mm ZSU-23-4
TOWED 23mm ZU-23-2; **57mm** S-60

Navy 4,450

EQUIPMENT BY TYPE
PRINCIPAL SURFACE COMBATANTS • FRIGATES 3
FFM 3 *Drazki* (ex-BEL *Wielingen*) (of which 2†) with 1
octuple Mk 29 GMLS with RIM-7P *Sea Sparrow* SAM,
2 single 533mm ASTT with L5 mod 4 HWT, 1 sextuple
Bofors ASW Rocket Launcher System 375mm A/S mor,
1 100mm gun (Fitted for but not with 2 twin lnchr with
MM38 *Exocet* AShM)
PATROL AND COASTAL COMBATANTS 4
CORVETTES • FS 1 *Smeli* (ex-FSU *Koni*) with 2 RBU
6000 *Smerch* 2 A/S mor, 2 twin 76mm guns
PCF 1 *Molnya*† (ex-FSU *Tarantul* II) with 2 AK630M
CIWS, 1 76mm gun
PCT 2 *Reshitelni* (ex-FSU *Pauk* I) with 4 single 406mm TT,
2 RBU 1200 *Uragan* A/S mor, 1 76mm gun
MINE COUNTERMEASURES 9
MHC 3: 2 *Mesta* (ex-NLD *Alkmaar*); 1 *Tsibar* (Tripartite –
ex-BEL *Flower*)
MSC 3 *Briz* (ex-FSU *Sonya*) (of which 1†)
MSI 3 *Olya* (ex-FSU)† (3 more non-operational)
AMPHIBIOUS • LANDING CRAFT
LCM 2 *Vydra*† (capacity either 3 MBT or 200 troops)
LOGISTICS AND SUPPORT 9: 3 **AGS**; 2 **AOL**; 1 **ARS**;
2 **ATF**; 1 **AX**

Naval Aviation

EQUIPMENT BY TYPE
HELICOPTERS
ASW 2 AS565MB *Panther*
MRH 1 AS365N3+ *Dauphin 2*

Air Force 8,500

FORCES BY ROLE
FIGHTER/ISR
1 sqn with MiG-29/MiG-29UB *Fulcrum*
TRANSPORT
1 sqn with An-30 *Clank*; C-27J *Spartan*; L-410UVP-E;
PC-12M
TRAINING
1 sqn with L-39ZA *Albatros**
1 sqn with PC-9M
ATTACK HELICOPTER
1 sqn with Mi-24D/V *Hind* D/E

TRANSPORT HELICOPTER
1 sqn with AS532AL *Cougar*; Bell 206 *Jet Ranger*; Mi-17
Hip H
EQUIPMENT BY TYPE
AIRCRAFT 26 combat capable
FTR 14: 11 MiG-29 *Fulcrum*; 3 MiG-29UB *Fulcrum*†
FGA (Some MiG-21bis *Fishbed*/MiG-21UM *Mongol* B
in store)
ATK 6: 5 Su-25K *Frogfoot* K; 1 Su-25UBK *Frogfoot* B
ISR 1 An-30 *Clank*
TPT 7: **Medium** 3 C-27J *Spartan*; **Light** 4: 1 An-2T *Colt*;
2 L-410UVP-E; 1 PC-12M
TRG 12: 6 L-39ZA *Albatros**; 6 PC-9M (basic)
HELICOPTERS
ATK 6 Mi-24V *Hind* E (6 Mi-24D *Hind* D in store)
MRH 5 Mi-17 *Hip* H
TPT 18: **Medium** 12 AS532AL *Cougar*; **Light** 6 Bell 206
Jet Ranger
UNINHABITED AERIAL VEHICLES • EW *Yastreb*-2S
AIR DEFENCE
SAM 20
Long-range 20: 12 S-200 (RS-SA-5 *Gammon*);
8 S-300PMU (RS-SA-10 *Grumble*)
Short-range S-125M *Neva*-M (RS-SA-3 *Goa*); 2K12 *Kub*
(RS-SA-6 *Gainful*)
AIR-LAUNCHED MISSILES
AAM • IR R-3 (RS-AA-2 *Atoll*)‡; R-73 (RS-AA-11A
Archer); **SARH** R-27R (RS-AA-10 *Alamo* A)
ASM Kh-29 (RS-AS-14 *Kedge*); Kh-25 (RS-AS-10 *Karen*)

Special Forces

FORCES BY ROLE
SPECIAL FORCES
1 spec ops bde (1 SF bn, 1 para bn)

DEPLOYMENT

BOSNIA-HERZEGOVINA: EU • EUFOR (*Operation Althea*)
110; 1 inf coy

IRAQ: NATO • NATO Mission Iraq 2

MALI: EU • EUTM Mali 4

SERBIA: NATO • KFOR 30

FOREIGN FORCES

Albania NATO Enhanced Vigilance Activities: 30; 1 inf pl
Greece Enhanced Vigilance Activities: 30; 1 AT pl
Italy NATO Enhanced Vigilance Activities: 750; 1 mech
inf BG
Spain NATO Enhanced Air Policing: 130; 6 Eurofighter
Typhoon
United Kingdom NATO Enhanced Vigilance Activities:
120; 1 lt mech inf coy
United States NATO Enhanced Vigilance Activities: 150;
1 armd inf coy

Croatia CRO

Croatian Kuna HRK		2021	2022	2023
GDP	HRK	431bn	494bn	
	USD	67.7bn	69.4bn	
per capita	USD	16,785	17,318	
Growth	%	10.2	5.9	
Inflation	%	2.6	9.8	
Def exp [a]	HRK	8.67bn	9.37bn	
	USD	1.36bn	1.32bn	
Def bdgt [b]	HRK	8.99bn	9.07bn	8.43bn
	USD	1.41bn	1.27bn	
USD1=HRK		6.36	7.13	

[a] NATO figure
[b] Includes military pensions

Real-terms defence budget trend (USDm, constant 2015)

Population 4,188,853

Age	0–14	15–19	20–24	25–29	30–64	65 plus
Male	7.3%	2.5%	2.8%	3.1%	23.5%	9.2%
Female	6.8%	2.3%	2.6%	2.9%	24.0%	13.0%

Capabilities

Principal tasks for the armed forces include defending national sovereignty and territorial integrity as well as tackling terrorism and contributing to international peacekeeping missions. The defence ministry is working on a new long-term development plan and a new defence strategy. Croatia reformed its armed forces, to create a small professional force, prior to joining NATO in 2009. There have been recent moves to improve conditions of service and to increase the proportion of the budget focused on equipment investment. Zagreb has defence cooperation agreements with Bosnia-Herzegovina, Hungary and Romania, and personnel frequently train with regional and international allies. Croatia hosts the NATO Multinational Special Aviation Programme and training centre and participates in EU and NATO missions, including NATO's Enhanced Forward Presence in Poland. The inventory is mainly composed of ageing Soviet-era equipment. In May 2021, Croatia announced the purchase of second-hand *Rafale* F3-R fighters from France. Maintenance personnel were training in France as of November 2022, with pilot training expected to start in 2023. The army will re-equip with *Bradley* IFVs, acquired from the US, and the year saw a modest boost to rotary-wing capability with the US donation of two UH-60M helicopters. The authorities are also looking to acquire short- and medium-range air-defence systems. Croatia has a small defence industry, focused on small arms, ammunition, explosives and naval systems.

ACTIVE 16,700 (Army 11,100 Navy 1,650 Air 1,600 Joint 2,350)

Conscript liability Voluntary conscription, 8 weeks

RESERVE 21,000 (Army 21,000)

ORGANISATIONS BY SERVICE

Joint 2,350 (General Staff)
FORCES BY ROLE
SPECIAL FORCES
  5 SF gp

Army 11,100
FORCES BY ROLE
MANOEUVRE
  Armoured
    1 armd bde (1 tk bn, 2 armd inf bn, 1 SP arty bn, 1 ADA bn, 1 cbt engr bn)
  Mechanised
    1 mech bde (3 mech inf bn, 1 lt mech inf bn, 1 fd arty bn, 1 ADA bn, 1 cbt engr bn)
  Other
    1 inf trg regt
COMBAT SUPPORT
  1 arty/MRL regt
  1 engr regt
  1 NBC bn
  1 sigs bn
COMBAT SERVICE SUPPORT
  1 log regt
AIR DEFENCE
  1 ADA regt
EQUIPMENT BY TYPE
ARMOURED FIGHTING VEHICLES
  MBT 74 M-84
  IFV 102 M-80
  APC 184
    APC (T) 11: 7 BTR-50; 4 OT M-60
    APC (W) 132: 6 BOV-VP; 126 Patria AMV (incl variants)
    PPV 41: 21 Maxxpro Plus; 20 RG-33 HAGA (amb)
  AUV 133: 10 IVECO LMV; 123 M-ATV
ENGINEERING & MAINTENANCE VEHICLES
  ARV 22: 12 JVBT-55A; 1 M-84AI; 1 WZT-2; 2 WZT-3; 5 *Maxxpro Recovery*
  VLB 5 MT-55A
  MW 4 MV-4
ANTI-TANK/ANTI-INFRASTRUCTURE • MSL
  SP 20 BOV-1
  MANPATS 9K11 *Malyutka* (RS-AT-3 *Sagger*); 9K111 *Fagot* (RS-AT-4 *Spigot*); 9K111-1 *Konkurs* (RS-AT-5 *Spandrel*); 9K115 *Metis* (RS-AT-7 *Saxhorn*)
ARTILLERY 157
  SP 21: **122mm** 8 2S1 *Gvozdika*; **155mm** 13 PzH 2000
  TOWED **122mm** 24 D-30
  MRL **122mm** 18: 6 M91 *Vulkan*; 12 BM-21 *Grad*
  MOR 94: **82mm** 54 LMB M96; **120mm** 40 M-75/UBM 52
AIR DEFENCE
  SAM • Point-defence 9+: 3 9K35 *Strela*-10M3 (RS-SA-13 *Gopher*); 6 9K35 Strela-10CRO; 9K310 *Igla*-1 (RS-SA-16 *Gimlet*)
  GUNS SP **20mm** 6 BOV-3 SP

Navy 1,650
Navy HQ at Split

EQUIPMENT BY TYPE
PATROL AND COASTAL COMBATANTS 5
  PCFG 1 *Končar* with 2 twin lnchr with RBS15B Mk I AShM, 1 AK630 CIWS, 1 57mm gun
  PCG 4:
    2 *Kralj* with 4 single lnchr with RBS15B Mk I AShM, 1 AK630 CIWS, 1 57mm gun (with minelaying capability)
    2 *Vukovar* (ex-FIN *Helsinki*) with 4 single lnchr with RBS15B Mk I AShM, 1 57mm gun
MINE WARFARE • MINE COUNTERMEASURES 1
  MHI 1 *Korcula*
AMPHIBIOUS • LANDING CRAFT 5:
  LCT 2 *Cetina* (with minelaying capability)
  LCVP 3: 2 Type-21; 1 Type-22
LOGISTICS AND SUPPORT • AKL 1 PDS 713
COASTAL DEFENCE • AShM 3 RBS15K

Marines
FORCES BY ROLE
MANOEUVRE
  Amphibious
    1 indep mne coy

Coast Guard
FORCES BY ROLE
Two divisions, headquartered in Split (1st div) and Pula (2nd div)
EQUIPMENT BY TYPE
PATROL AND COASTAL COMBATANTS • PB 5: 4 *Mirna*; 1 *Omiš*
LOGISTICS AND SUPPORT 3:
  AAR 1 *Faust Vrancic* (YUG *Spasilac*)
  AKL 1 PT-71†
  AX 1 *Andrija Mohorovicic* (POL Project 861)

Air Force and Air Defence 1,600
FORCES BY ROLE
FIGHTER/GROUND ATTACK
  1 (mixed) sqn with MiG-21bis/UMD *Fishbed*
TRAINING
  1 sqn with PC-9M; Z-242L
ISR HELICOPTER
  1 hel sqn with Bell 206B *Jet Ranger* II; OH-58D *Kiowa Warrior*
TRANSPORT HELICOPTER
  2 sqn with Mi-8MTV *Hip* H; Mi-8T *Hip* C; Mi-171Sh
EQUIPMENT BY TYPE
AIRCRAFT 8 combat capable
  FGA 8: 4 MiG-21bis *Fishbed*; 4 MiG-21UMD *Fishbed*
  TPT • Light (2 An-32 *Cline* in store)
  TRG 21: 17 PC-9M; 4 Z-242L
HELICOPTERS
  MRH 25: 10 Mi-8MTV *Hip* H; 15 OH-58D *Kiowa Warrior*
  TPT 23: **Medium** 15: 3 Mi-8T *Hip* C; 10 Mi-171Sh; 2 UH-60M *Black Hawk*; **Light** 8 Bell 206B *Jet Ranger* II
AIR DEFENCE • SAM
  Point-defence 9K31 *Strela*-1 (RS-SA-9 *Gaskin*); 9K34 *Strela*-3 (RS-SA-14 *Gremlin*); 9K310 *Igla*-1 (RS-SA-16 *Gimlet*)
AIR-LAUNCHED MISSILES
  AAM • IR R-60; R-60MK (RS-AA-8 *Aphid*)
  ASM AGM-114R *Hellfire*

Special Forces Command
FORCES BY ROLE
SPECIAL FORCES
  2 SF gp

DEPLOYMENT
HUNGARY: NATO • Enhanced Vigilance Activities 60
INDIA/PAKISTAN: UN • UNMOGIP 8
IRAQ: NATO • NATO Mission Iraq 10
LEBANON: UN • UNIFIL 1
POLAND: NATO • Enhanced Forward Presence 4
SERBIA: NATO • KFOR 147; 1 inf coy; 1 hel unit with Mi-8 *Hip*
WESTERN SAHARA: UN • MINURSO 8

Cyprus CYP

Euro EUR		2021	2022	2023
GDP	EUR	23.4bn	25.3bn	
	USD	27.7bn	26.7bn	
per capita	USD	30,957	29,535	
Growth	%	5.6	3.5	
Inflation	%	2.2	8.0	
Def bdgt	EUR	482m	470m	465m
	USD	571m	497m	
USD1=EUR		0.84	0.95	

Real-terms defence budget trend (USDm, constant 2015)

Population	1,295,102					
Age	0–14	15–19	20–24	25–29	30–64	65 plus
Male	8.0%	2.8%	3.5%	4.4%	26.4%	5.9%
Female	7.6%	2.4%	2.9%	3.7%	24.6%	7.7%

Capabilities

The National Guard is focused on protecting the island's territorial integrity and sovereignty, and safeguarding Cyprus's EEZ. Its main objective is to deter any Turkish incursion, and to provide enough opposition until military support can be provided by Greece, its primary ally. Cyprus has been enhancing its defence cooperation with Greece, including on cyber defence. Nicosia has also pledged deeper military ties with Israel, while France has renewed and enhanced its defence-cooperation agreement with Cyprus. In 2018 Cyprus also signed a memorandum of understanding on enhancing defence and security cooperation with the UK. Having reduced conscript liability in 2016, Nicosia began recruiting additional contract-service personnel, as part of the effort to modernise and professionalise its forces. Cyprus exercises with several international partners, most notably France, Greece and Israel. External deployments have been limited to some officers joining EU and UN missions. Cyprus has little logistics capability to support operations abroad. Equipment comprises a mix of Soviet-era and modern European systems and in 2022 an announcement was made relating to the procurement of H145M helicopters from France. Cyprus has little in the way of a domestic defence industry, with no ability to design and manufacture modern equipment. However, the government is looking for opportunities to cooperate with defence firms in Greece.

ACTIVE 12,000 (National Guard 12,000)
Gendarmerie & Paramilitary 250
Conscript liability 15 months

RESERVE 50,000 (National Guard 50,000)
Reserve service to age 50 (officers dependent on rank; military doctors to age 60)

ORGANISATIONS BY SERVICE

National Guard 12,000 (incl conscripts)
FORCES BY ROLE
SPECIAL FORCES
1 comd (regt) (1 SF bn)
MANOEUVRE
Armoured
1 armd bde (2 armd bn, 1 armd inf bn)
Mechanised
4 (1st, 2nd, 6th & 7th) mech bde
Light
1 (4th) lt inf bde
2 (2nd & 8th) lt inf regt
COMBAT SUPPORT
1 arty comd (8 arty bn)
COMBAT SERVICE SUPPORT
1 (3rd) spt bde
EQUIPMENT BY TYPE
ARMOURED FIGHTING VEHICLES
MBT 134: 82 T-80U; 52 AMX-30B2
RECCE 79 EE-9 *Cascavel*
IFV 43 BMP-3
APC 294
APC (T) 168 *Leonidas*
APC (W) 126 VAB (incl variants)
AUV 8 BOV M16 *Milos*
ENGINEERING & MAINTENANCE VEHICLES
ARV 2+: 2 AMX-30D; BREM-80U
ANTI-TANK/ANTI-INFRASTRUCTURE
MSL
SP 33: 15 EE-3 *Jararaca* with *Milan*; 18 VAB with HOT
RCL 106mm 144 M40A1
GUNS • TOWED 100mm 6 M-1944
ARTILLERY 412
SP 155mm 48: 24 NORA B-52; 12 Mk F3; 12 *Zuzana*
TOWED 60: **105mm** 48 M-56; **155mm** 12 TR-F-1
MRL 22: **122mm** 4 BM-21; **128mm** 18 M-63 *Plamen*
MOR 282: **81mm** 170 E-44 (70+ M1/M9 in store); **120mm** 112 RT61
AIR DEFENCE
SAM 22+
Medium-range 4 9K37M1 *Buk* M1-2 (RS-SA-11 *Gadfly*)
Short-range 18: 12 *Aspide*; 6 9K331 *Tor*-M1 (RS-SA-15 *Gauntlet*)
Point-defence *Mistral*
GUNS • TOWED 60: **20mm** 36 M-55; **35mm** 24 GDF-003 (with *Skyguard*)

Maritime Wing
FORCES BY ROLE
COMBAT SUPPORT
1 (coastal defence) AShM bty with MM40 *Exocet* AShM
EQUIPMENT BY TYPE
PATROL AND COASTAL COMBATANTS 6
PCC 2: 1 *Alasia* (ex-OMN *Al Mabrukha*) with 1 hel landing platform; 1 OPV 62 (ISR *Sa'ar* 4.5 derivative)
PBF 4: 2 Rodman 55; 2 *Vittoria*
COASTAL DEFENCE • AShM 3 MM40 *Exocet*

Air Wing
EQUIPMENT BY TYPE
HELICOPTERS
ATK 11 Mi-35P *Hind* E (offered for sale)
MRH 7: 3 AW139 (SAR); 4 SA342L1 *Gazelle* (with HOT for anti-armour role)

Paramilitary 250

Maritime Police 250
EQUIPMENT BY TYPE
PATROL AND COASTAL COMBATANTS 10
PBF 5: 2 *Poseidon*; 1 *Shaldag*; 2 *Vittoria*
PB 5 SAB-12

DEPLOYMENT

LEBANON: UN • UNIFIL 2

FOREIGN FORCES

Argentina UNFICYP 251; 2 inf coy; 1 hel flt
Austria UNFICYP 3
Brazil UNFICYP 2
Canada UNFICYP 1
Chile UNFICYP 6
Ghana UNFICYP 1
Greece Army: 950
Hungary UNFICYP 13
India UNFICYP 1
Norway UNFICYP 2
Pakistan UNFICYP 3
Paraguay UNFICYP 12
Russia UNFICYP 6
Serbia UNFICYP 8
Slovakia UNFICYP 300; 2 inf coy; 1 engr pl
United Kingdom 2,260; 2 inf bn; 1 hel sqn with 4 Bell 412 *Twin Huey* • *Operation Inherent Resolve* (*Shader*) 500: 1 FGA sqn with 10 *Typhoon* FGR4; 1 A330 MRTT *Voyager* KC3; 2 C-130J-30 *Hercules* • UNFICYP (*Operation Tosca*) 253: 2 inf coy

TERRITORY WHERE THE GOVERNMENT DOES NOT EXERCISE EFFECTIVE CONTROL

Data here represents the de facto situation on the northern section of the island. This does not imply international recognition as a sovereign state.

Capabilities

ACTIVE 3,000 (Army 3,000) Gendarmerie & Paramilitary 150
Conscript liability 15 months

RESERVE 15,000
Reserve liability to age 50

ORGANISATIONS BY SERVICE

Army ε3,000
FORCES BY ROLE
MANOEUVRE
Light
 5 inf bn
 7 inf bn (reserve)
EQUIPMENT BY TYPE
ANTI-TANK/ANTI-INFRASTRUCTURE
 MSL • MANPATS *Milan*
 RCL • 106mm 36
ARTILLERY • MOR • 120mm 73

Gendarmerie & Paramilitary

Armed Police ε150
FORCES BY ROLE
SPECIAL FORCES
 1 (police) SF unit

Coast Guard
EQUIPMENT BY TYPE
PATROL AND COASTAL COMBATANTS 6
 PCC 5: 2 SG45/SG46; 1 *Rauf Denktash*; 2 US Mk 5
 PB 1

FOREIGN FORCES
TURKEY
Army ε33,800
 FORCES BY ROLE
 1 corps HQ; 1 SF regt; 1 armd bde; 2 mech inf div; 1 mech inf regt; 1 arty regt; 1 avn comd
 EQUIPMENT BY TYPE
 ARMOURED FIGHTING VEHICLES
  MBT 287 M48A5T1
  IFV 145 ACV AIFV
  APC • APC (T) 488: 70 ACV AAPC (incl variants); 418 M113 (incl variants)
 ANTI-TANK/ANTI-INFRASTRUCTURE
  MSL
   SP 66 ACV TOW
   MANPATS *Milan*
  RCL 106mm 219 M40A1
 ARTILLERY 656
  SP 155mm 178: 30 M44T; 144 M52T1; 4 T-155 *Firtina*
  TOWED 84: 105mm 36 M101A1; 155mm 36 M114A2; 203mm 12 M115
  MRL 122mm 18 T-122
  MOR 376: 81mm 171; 107mm 70 M30; 120mm 135 HY-12

PATROL AND COASTAL COMBATANTS • PB 1
AIRCRAFT • TPT • Light 3 Cessna 185 (U-17)
HELICOPTERS • TPT 3: Medium 2 AS532UL *Cougar*
 Light 1 Bell 205 (UH-1H *Iroquois*)
AIR DEFENCE
 SAM Point-defence FIM-92 *Stinger*
 GUNS • TOWED 150: **20mm** 122: 44 Rh 202; 78 GAI-D01; **35mm** 28 GDF-003

Czech Republic CZE

Czech Koruna CZK		2021	2022	2023
GDP	CZK	6.11tr	6.89tr	
	USD	282bn	296bn	
per capita	USD	26,849	28,095	
Growth	%	3.5	1.9	
Inflation	%	3.8	16.3	
Def exp [a]	CZK	84.9bn	89.2bn	
	USD	3.91bn	3.83bn	
Def bdgt [b]	CZK	85.4bn	89.1bn	112bn
	USD	3.94bn	3.83bn	
USD1=CZK		21.68	23.30	

[a] NATO figure
[b] Includes military pensions

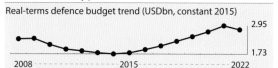
Real-terms defence budget trend (USDbn, constant 2015)

Population 10,705,384

Age	0–14	15–19	20–24	25–29	30–64	65 plus
Male	7.7%	2.5%	2.4%	2.8%	25.1%	8.8%
Female	7.3%	2.4%	2.2%	2.6%	24.2%	12.1%

Capabilities

The 'Long Term Outlook for Defence 2035' and the 'Czech Armed Forces Development Concept 2030', both published in 2019, discussed the evolving security environment, among other issues. In January 2022, the defence ministry released a priorities list that included recruiting more personnel, a commitment to spend 2% of GDP on defence by 2025, to streamline the acquisition process and to establish an investment fund for strategic modernisation projects by 2024. After Russia's February 2022 invasion of Ukraine, Prague announced a boost to defence spending and has donated a significant amount of materiel to Kyiv. In response, allies have donated equipment to the Czech armed forces including, from Germany, 14 *Leopard* 2A4 MBTs. A Defence Cooperation Agreement was agreed with the US in April 2022. The US has granted funds under the Foreign Military Financing programme in part to help replace equipment donated to Ukraine. Modernisation priorities include infantry fighting vehicles (IFV) for a heavy brigade, self-propelled howitzers, multi-role helicopters, transport aircraft, short-range air-defence systems and UAVs. In July, the government cancelled a tender for new IFVs, and opened negotiations with Sweden for the CV90. Prague has entered into negotiations with the US to acquire 24 F-35s as a long-term replacement for its leased *Gripen* combat aircraft, and it is reported that the ministry is looking to acquire *Heron* 1 UAVs from Israel. The armed forces deploy on a variety of international crisis-management operations, including NATO's Enhanced Forward Presence, Air Policing and contributing to NATO's Very High Readiness Joint Task Force. There are plans to upgrade military training and simulation facilities by 2025. The defence-industrial base includes development and manufacturing capability, in particular small arms, vehicles, and training and light attack aircraft. The holding company Czechoslovak Group brings together several companies across the munitions, vehicles and aerospace sectors.

ACTIVE 26,600 (Army 14,700 Air 5,850 Other 6,050)

ORGANISATIONS BY SERVICE

Army 14,700
FORCES BY ROLE
MANOEUVRE
  Reconnaissance
  1 ISR/EW regt (1 recce bn, 1 EW bn, 1 ISR UAV bn)
  Armoured
  1 (7th) mech bde (1 tk bn, 2 armd inf bn, 1 mot inf bn)
  Mechanised
  1 (4th) rapid reaction bde (2 mech inf bn, 1 mot inf bn)
  Airborne
  1 AB regt
COMBAT SUPPORT
  1 (13th) arty regt (2 arty bn)
  1 engr regt (2 engr bn, 1 EOD bn)
  1 CBRN regt (2 CBRN bn)
COMBAT SERVICE SUPPORT
  1 log regt (2 log bn, 1 maint bn)

Active Reserve
FORCES BY ROLE
COMMAND
  14 (territorial defence) comd
MANOEUVRE
  Armoured
  1 armd coy
  Light
  14 inf coy (1 per territorial comd) (3 inf pl, 1 cbt spt pl, 1 log pl)
EQUIPMENT BY TYPE
ARMOURED FIGHTING VEHICLES
  MBT 30 T-72M4CZ (up to 89 T-72M1 in store)
  RECCE 50: 34 BPzV *Svatava*; 8 *Pandur* II (KBV-PZ); 8 *Pandur* II (KBV-PZLOK)
  IFV 227: 120 BMP-2; 107 *Pandur* II (incl 17 CP, 14 comms, 4 amb); (up to 98 BMP-1; 65 BMP-2 all in store)
  APC • PPV 1 *Titus*
  AUV 141: 21 *Dingo* 2; 120 IVECO LMV
ENGINEERING & MAINTENANCE VEHICLES
  AEV 4 *Pandur* II (KOT-Z)
  ARV 13+: 10 VPV-ARV (12 more in store); VT-55A; 3 VT-72M4
  VLB 6 MT-55A (3 more in store)
  MW *Bozena* 5; UOS-155 *Belarty*
NBC VEHICLES BRDM-2RCH
ANTI-TANK/ANTI-INFRASTRUCTURE
  MSL • MANPATS 9K111-1 *Konkurs* (RS-AT-5 *Spandrel*); FGM-148 *Javelin*; *Spike*-LR

RCL 84mm *Carl Gustaf*
ARTILLERY 96
  SP 152mm 48 M-77 *Dana* (up to 38 more in store)
  MOR 48: **81mm** *Expal*; **120mm** 40 M-1982; (45 more in store); **SP 120mm** 8 SPM-85

Air Force 5,850
Principal task is to secure Czech airspace. This mission is fulfilled within NATO Integrated Extended Air Defence System (NATINADS) and, if necessary, by means of the Czech national reinforced air-defence system. The air force also provides CAS for army SAR, and performs a tpt role

FORCES BY ROLE
FIGHTER/GROUND ATTACK
  1 sqn with *Gripen* C/D
  1 sqn with L-159 ALCA; L-159T1*
TRANSPORT
  2 sqn with A319CJ; C295M/MW; CL-601 *Challenger*; L-410FG/UVP-E *Turbolet*
TRAINING
  1 sqn with L-159 ALCA; L-159T1*; L-159T2*
ATTACK HELICOPTER
  1 sqn with Mi-24/Mi-35 *Hind* D/E
TRANSPORT HELICOPTER
  1 sqn with Mi-17 *Hip* H; Mi-171Sh
  1 sqn with Mi-8 *Hip*; Mi-17 *Hip* H; PZL W-3A *Sokol*
AIR DEFENCE
  1 (25th) SAM regt (2 AD gp)
EQUIPMENT BY TYPE
AIRCRAFT 38 combat capable
  FGA 14: 12 *Gripen* C; 2 *Gripen* D
  ATK 16 L-159 ALCA
  TPT 15: **Light** 12: 4 C295M; 2 C295MW; 2 L-410FG *Turbolet*; 4 L-410UVP-E *Turbolet*; **PAX** 3: 2 A319CJ; 1 CL-601 *Challenger*
  TRG 8: 5 L-159T1*; 3 L-159T2*
HELICOPTERS
  ATK 17: 7 Mi-24 *Hind* D; 10 Mi-35 *Hind* E
  MRH 5 Mi-17 *Hip* H
  TPT • Medium 30: 4 Mi-8 *Hip*; 16 Mi-171Sh; 10 PZL W3A *Sokol*
AIR DEFENCE • SAM
  Point-defence 9K35 *Strela*-10 (RS-SA-13 *Gopher*); 9K32 *Strela*-2‡ (RS-SA-7 *Grail*) (available for trg RBS-70 gunners); RBS-70
AIR-LAUNCHED MISSILES
  AAM • IR AIM-9M *Sidewinder*; **ARH** AIM-120C-5 AMRAAM
BOMBS
  Laser-guided: GBU-12/-16 *Paveway* II

Other Forces 6,050
FORCES BY ROLE
SPECIAL FORCES
  1 SF gp
MANOEUVRE
  Other
  1 (presidential) gd bde (2 bn)
  1 (honour guard) gd bn (2 coy)

COMBAT SUPPORT
1 int gp
1 (central) MP comd
3 (regional) MP comd
1 (protection service) MP comd

DEPLOYMENT

BOSNIA-HERZEGOVINA: EU • EUFOR (*Operation Althea*) 2

CENTRAL AFRICAN REPUBLIC: UN • MINUSCA 3

DEMOCRATIC REPUBLIC OF THE CONGO: UN • MONUSCO 2

EGYPT: MFO 18; 1 C295M

IRAQ: *Operation Inherent Resolve* 60; **NATO** • NATO Mission Iraq 3

LATVIA: NATO • Enhanced Forward Presence 81; 1 mor pl

LITHUANIA: NATO • Enhanced Forward Presence 135; 1 AD unit

MALI: EU • EUTM Mali 90; **UN** • MINUSMA 5

SERBIA: NATO • KFOR 8; **UN** • UNMIK 2

SLOVAKIA: NATO • Enhanced Vigilance Activities 400; 1 mech inf bn HQ; 1 mech inf coy

SYRIA/ISRAEL: UN • UNDOF 4

Denmark DNK

Danish Krone DKK		2021	2022	2023
GDP	DKK	2.50tr	2.73tr	
	USD	398bn	387bn	
per capita	USD	68,202	65,713	
Growth	%	4.9	2.6	
Inflation	%	1.9	7.2	
Def exp [a]	DKK	33.2bn	37.8bn	
	USD	5.27bn	5.36bn	
Def bdgt [b]	DKK	33.8bn	35.7bn	40.2bn
	USD	5.37bn	5.06bn	
USD1=DKK		6.29	7.05	

[a] NATO figure
[b] Includes military pensions

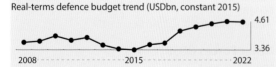
Real-terms defence budget trend (USDbn, constant 2015)

Population 5,920,767

Age	0–14	15–19	20–24	25–29	30–64	65 plus
Male	8.4%	3.0%	3.2%	3.5%	22.4%	9.4%
Female	7.9%	2.8%	3.0%	3.3%	22.0%	11.0%

Capabilities

Denmark maintains a compact but effective force, with a focus on contributing to larger NATO operations. Ties to NATO, NORDEFCO and other regional neighbours have increased. In late 2019 the government agreed an action plan to ensure the promotion of Danish interests in the EU's European Defence Fund. Russia's February 2022 invasion of Ukraine was the driving factor behind the June 2022 vote in which Denmark ended its 'opt out' of EU military cooperation under CSDP. It has also spurred Denmark to increase defence spending, and further increase defence cooperation with Norway and Sweden. The January 2022 Foreign and Security Policy Strategy expressed concerns about cyber and hybrid attacks, as well as pandemic preparedness. Current defence-modernisation priorities include the acquisition of the F-35A, and the upgrade of armoured vehicles within the mechanised brigades. Other acquisition priorities include EW equipment, MALE UAVs and ASW capabilities, while authorities are also considering requirements for GBAD and longer-range artillery systems. The defence agreement for 2018–23 envisages increased defence spending to deal with a deteriorating security environment. The Danish armed forces consist primarily of professional personnel, supplemented by a substantial number of conscripts. The new defence agreement foresees retaining national service and that the annual conscript intake should rise modestly. The authorities are examining measures to improve recruitment and retention. The Danish armed forces have little ability to deploy independently but have contributed to a number of larger multinational deployments. Denmark is largely reliant on imported defence equipment but maintains a small defence industry focused on exports to Europe and North America. The Danish defence industry is mainly active in defence electronics and the design and manufacture of components and subsystems, including subcomponents for the F-35.

ACTIVE 15,400 (Army 8,000 Navy 2,250 Air 3,000 Joint 2,150)
Conscript liability 4–12 months, most voluntary

RESERVES 44,200 (Army 34,400 Navy 5,300 Air Force 4,500)

ORGANISATIONS BY SERVICE

Army 8,000

Div and a bde HQ transforming into operational formations

FORCES BY ROLE
COMMAND
1 (MND-N) div HQ
MANOEUVRE
Mechanised
1 (1st) mech bde (1 ISR bn, 3 mech inf bn, 1 SP arty bn, 1 cbt engr bn, 1 sigs bn, 1 log bn)
1 (2nd) mech bde (1 recce bn, 1 tk bn, 1 lt inf bn)
COMBAT SUPPORT
1 CBRN/construction bn
1 EOD bn
1 int bn
1 MP bn
2 sigs bn
COMBAT SERVICE SUPPORT
1 log bn
1 maint bn
1 spt bn

AIR DEFENCE
1 AD bn

EQUIPMENT BY TYPE
ARMOURED FIGHTING VEHICLES
MBT 44: 15 *Leopard* 2A5 (to be upgraded to 2A7V);
29 *Leopard* 2A7V
IFV 44 CV9035 MkIII
APC 286
APC (W) 286: 81 *Piranha* III (incl variants); 205 *Piranha* V
AUV 158: 84 *Eagle* IV; 59 *Eagle* V; 15 HMT-400
ENGINEERING & MAINTENANCE VEHICLES
AEV 3 *Wisent*
ARV 8 *Wisent*
VLB 6 BRP-1 *Biber*
ANTI-TANK/ANTI-INFRASTRUCTURE
MSL • MANPATS *Spike*-LR2
RCL 84mm *Carl Gustaf*
ARTILLERY 50
SP 155mm 15 CAESAR 8×8
MOR 35: **TOWED 120mm** 20 Soltam K6B1; **SP 120mm**
15 *Piranha* V with *Cardom*-10
AIR DEFENCE • SAM • Point-defence FIM-92 *Stinger*

Navy 2,250

Three naval squadrons, headquartered at naval bases in Frederikshavn and Korsør

EQUIPMENT BY TYPE
PRINCIPAL SURFACE COMBATANTS 5
DESTROYERS • DDGHM 3 *Iver Huitfeldt* with 4 quad lnchr with RGM-84L *Harpoon* Block II AShM, 4 8-cell Mk 41 VLS (to be fitted with SM-2 SAM), 2 12-cell Mk 56 VLS with RIM-162B ESSM SAM, 2 twin 324mm TT with MU90 LWT, 1 *Millennium* CIWS, 2 76mm guns (capacity 1 AW101 *Merlin*/MH-60R *Seahawk* hel)
FRIGATES • FFGHM 2 *Absalon* (flexible support ships) with 4 quad lnchr with RGM-84L *Harpoon* Block II AShM, 3 12-cell Mk 56 VLS with RIM-162B ESSM SAM, 2 twin 324mm TT with MU90 LWT, 2 *Millennium* CIWS, 1 127mm gun (capacity 2 AW101 *Merlin*/MH-60R *Seahawk* hel; 2 LCP, 7 MBT or 40 vehicles; 130 troops)
PATROL AND COASTAL COMBATANTS 12
PSOH 4 *Thetis* 1 76mm gun (capacity 1 MH-60R *Seahawk*)
PSO 3 *Knud Rasmussen* with 1 76mm gun, 1 hel landing platform (ice-strengthened hull)
PCC 5 *Diana* (1 other non-operational)
MINE WARFARE • MINE COUNTERMEASURES 6
MCI 4 MSF Mk I
MSD 2 *Holm*
LOGISTICS AND SUPPORT 12
ABU 2 *Gunnar Thorson* (primarily used for MARPOL duties)
AE 1 *Sleipner*
AGS 2 *Holm*
AKL 2 *Seatruck*
AX 1 *Søløven* (DNK *Flyvefisken*)
AXL 2 *Holm*
AXS 2 *Svanen*

Air Force 3,000

Tactical Air Command

FORCES BY ROLE
FIGHTER/GROUND ATTACK
2 sqn with F-16AM/BM *Fighting Falcon*
ANTI-SUBMARINE WARFARE
1 sqn with MH-60R *Seahawk*
SEARCH & RESCUE/TRANSPORT HELICOPTER
1 sqn with AW101 *Merlin*
1 sqn with AS550 *Fennec* (ISR)
TRANSPORT
1 sqn with C-130J-30 *Hercules*; CL-604 *Challenger* (MP/VIP)
TRAINING
1 unit with MFI-17 *Supporter* (T-17)

EQUIPMENT BY TYPE
AIRCRAFT 50 combat capable
FTR 44: 34 F-16AM *Fighting Falcon*; 10 F-16BM *Fighting Falcon* (30 operational)
FGA 6 F-35A *Lightning* II
TPT 8: **Medium** 4 C-130J-30 *Hercules*; **PAX** 4 CL-604 *Challenger* (MP/VIP)
TRG 27 MFI-17 *Supporter* (T-17)
HELICOPTERS
ASW 9 MH-60R *Seahawk*
SAR 8 AW101 *Merlin*
MRH 8 AS550 *Fennec* (ISR) (4 more non-operational)
TPT • Medium 6 AW101 *Merlin*
AIR-LAUNCHED MISSILES
AAM • IR AIM-9L *Sidewinder*; **IIR** AIM-9X *Sidewinder* II; **ARH** AIM-120B AMRAAM
BOMBS
Laser-guided GBU-24 *Paveway* III
Laser & INS/GPS-guided EGBU-12 *Paveway* II
INS/GPS guided GBU-31 JDAM

Control and Air Defence Group

1 Control and Reporting Centre, 1 Mobile Control and Reporting Centre. 4 Radar sites

Special Operations Command

FORCES BY ROLE
SPECIAL FORCES
1 SF unit
1 diving unit

Reserves

Home Guard (Army) 34,400 reservists (to age 50)
2 (local) def region

Home Guard (Navy) 5,300 reservists (to age 50)
EQUIPMENT BY TYPE
PATROL AND COASTAL COMBATANTS 30
PB 30: 18 MHV800; 12 MHV900

Home Guard (Air Force) 4,500 reservists (to age 50)
EQUIPMENT BY TYPE
AIRCRAFT • TPT • Light 2 BN-2A *Islander*

DEPLOYMENT

ESTONIA: NATO • Enhanced Forward Presence 155; 1 tk sqn with *Leopard* 2A7

IRAQ: *Operation Inherent Resolve* 39; **NATO** • NATO Mission Iraq 125; 1 SF gp; 1 trg team

LATVIA: NATO • Enhanced Vigilance Activities 803; 1 mech inf bn with CV9035 MkIII; *Piranha* V

MALI: UN • MINUSMA 2

MIDDLE EAST: UN • UNTSO 10

NORTH SEA: NATO • SNMG 1; 170; 1 FFGHM

SERBIA: NATO • KFOR 35

UNITED KINGDOM: *Operation Interflex* 130 (UKR trg)

Estonia EST

Euro EUR		2021	2022	2023
GDP	EUR	31.4bn	36.9bn	
	USD	37.2bn	39.1bn	
per capita	USD	27,962	29,344	
Growth	%	8.0	1.0	
Inflation	%	4.5	21.0	
Def Exp [a]	EUR	633m	771m	
	USD	749m	815m	
Def bdgt [b]	EUR	658m	786m	1.14bn
	USD	779m	830m	
FMA (US)	USD	10.0m	8.8m	9.8m
USD1=EUR		0.84	0.95	

[a] NATO figure
[b] Includes military pensions

Real-terms defence budget trend (USDm, constant 2015)

Population	1,211,524					
Age	0–14	15–19	20–24	25–29	30–64	65 plus
Male	8.1%	2.6%	2.2%	2.4%	24.1%	7.6%
Female	7.7%	2.4%	2.0%	2.2%	24.4%	14.1%

Capabilities

Estonia has small active armed forces and is reliant on NATO membership as a security guarantor. Security policy is predicated on the goals of ensuring sovereignty and territorial integrity, and Tallinn remains concerned by Russian security policy and military activity. In the wake of Russia's February 2022 full-scale invasion of Ukraine, Estonia boosted defence spending and transferred military equipment to Ukraine, including ammunition, anti-armour systems and artillery. The MoD publishes medium-term development plans annually. Covering a four-year period, these are intended to ensure that the goals of long-term National Defense Development Plan (NDPP) will be achieved within the planned timeframe. The NDPP for 2031, adopted in December 2021, focuses on improving territorial defence and indirect fire and anti-tank capabilities, as well as boosting maritime and surveillance systems. Rocket artillery systems are being procured from the United States, medium-range air defence systems will be jointly procured with Latvia and short-range air-defence systems with Poland. Estonia signalled its intention in 2022 to join the European *Sky Shield* initiative, to boost air defence capacity. As well as capability development, modernisation spending is directed toward improving infrastructure and readiness. The active armed forces are supplemented by a reserve component and modernisation plans include the creation of a supplementary reserve and additional active and conscript personnel. The NATO battlegroup based in Estonia, present since mid-2017 as part of the Alliance's Enhanced Forward Presence, was bolstered in 2022. Amari air base hosts a NATO Air Policing detachment. Estonia is a member of the UK-led Joint Expeditionary Force. Tallinn also hosts NATO's Cybersecurity Centre of Excellence. There is limited organic capability to deploy abroad, though Estonian forces take part in EU, NATO and UN missions on a small scale. The country has a niche defence-industrial capability, including robotics, ship repair and digital systems.

ACTIVE 7,200 (Army 4,100 Navy 400 Air 400 Other 2,300)
Conscript liability 8 or 11 months (depending on specialisation; conscripts cannot be deployed)

RESERVE 17,500 (Joint 12,000; Territorial Defence 5,500)

ORGANISATIONS BY SERVICE

Army 1,500; 2,600 conscript (total 4,100)

4 def region. All units except one inf bn are reserve based

FORCES BY ROLE
MANOEUVRE
  Mechanised
  1 (1st) bde (1 recce coy, 1 armd inf bn; 2 mech inf bn, 1 arty bn, 1 AT coy, 1 cbt engr bn, 1 spt bn, 1 AD bn)
  Light
  1 (2nd) inf bde (1 inf bn, 1 spt bn)

EQUIPMENT BY TYPE
ARMOURED FIGHTING VEHICLES
  IFV 44 CV9035EE (incl 2 CP)
  APC • **APC (W)** 136: 56 XA-180 *Sisu*; 80 XA-188 *Sisu*
ENGINEERING & MAINTENANCE VEHICLES
  AEV 2 Pionierpanzer 2 *Dachs*
  ARV 2 BPz-2
  VLB 2 *Biber*
ANTI-TANK/ANTI-INFRASTRUCTURE
  MSL • **MANPATS** FGM-148 *Javelin*; *Spike*-SR/-LR
  RCL 84mm *Carl Gustaf*; **90mm** PV-1110
ARTILLERY 168
  SP 155mm 6 K9 *Thunder*
  TOWED 122mm 36 D-30 (H 63)
  MOR 126: **81mm** 60 B455/NM 95/M252; **120mm** 66 2B11/M/41D
AIR DEFENCE
  SAM • **Point-defence** *Mistral*
  GUNS • **TOWED 23mm** ZU-23-2

Reserve

Reserve units subordinate to 2nd inf bde and territorial defence

FORCES BY ROLE
MANOEUVRE
  Reconnaissance
    1 recce coy
  Light
    3 inf bn
    4 (territorial) inf bn
  COMBAT SUPPORT
    1 arty bn
    1 AT coy
    1 cbt engr bn
  AIR DEFENCE
    1 AD bn

Navy 300; 100 conscript (total 400)
EQUIPMENT BY TYPE
PATROL AND COASTAL COMBATANTS • PB 2 *Roland*
MINE WARFARE • MINE COUNTERMEASURES 4:
  MCCS 1 *Tasuja* (ex-DNK *Lindormen*)
  MHC 3 *Admiral Cowan* (ex-UK *Sandown*)

Air Force 400
FORCES BY ROLE
TRANSPORT
  1 sqn with M-28 *Skytruck*
TRANSPORT HELICOPTER
  1 sqn with R-44 *Raven* II
EQUIPMENT BY TYPE
AIRCRAFT
  TPT • Light 2 M-28 *Skytruck*
  TRG 1+ L-39C *Albatros* (leased)
HELICOPTERS • TPT • Light 2 R-44 *Raven* II

Other 1,300; 800 conscript (total 2,100)
Includes Cyber Command, Support Command and Special Operations Forces
FORCES BY ROLE
SPECIAL FORCES
  1 spec ops bn
COMBAT SUPPORT
  2 MP coy
  1 sigs bn
COMBAT SERVICE SUPPORT
  1 log bn

Gendarmerie & Paramilitary

Border Guard
Subordinate to the Ministry of the Interior
EQUIPMENT BY TYPE
PATROL AND COASTAL COMBATANTS 4 (all to be transferred to Navy in Jan 2023)
  PCO 1 *Kindral Kurvits* (FIN *Tursas* derivative)
  PB 3: 1 *Pikker*; 1 *Raju* (Baltic 4500WP); 1 *Valve*
AMPHIBIOUS • LANDING CRAFT • LCU 3
AIRCRAFT • TPT • Light 1 Beech 305ER *King Air*
HELICOPTERS • MRH 3 AW139
UNINHABITED AERIAL VEHICLES • ISR • Light
  some S-100 *Camcopter*

DEPLOYMENT
IRAQ: *Operation Inherent Resolve* 10 • NATO Mission Iraq 40
LEBANON: UN • UNIFIL 1
MALI: EU • EUTM Mali 10; **UN** • MINUSMA 2
MIDDLE EAST: UN • UNTSO 3
MOZAMBIQUE: EU • EUTM Mozambique 1

FOREIGN FORCES
All NATO Enhanced Forward Presence unless stated
Denmark 155; 1 tk sqn
France 219; 1 inf coy
Germany NATO Baltic Air Policing: 150; 4 Eurofighter *Typhoon*
United Kingdom 1,750; 1 armd BG; 1 lt inf BG; 1 SP arty bty; 1 MRL bty; 1 cbt engr coy

Finland FIN

Euro EUR		2021	2022	2023
GDP	EUR	251bn	266bn	
	USD	298bn	281bn	
per capita	USD	53,774	50,818	
Growth	%	3.0	2.1	
Inflation	%	2.1	6.5	
Def bdgt [a]	EUR	5.00bn	5.51bn	6.62bn
	USD	5.91bn	5.82bn	
USD1=EUR		0.84	0.95	

[a] Includes military pensions

Real-terms defence budget trend (USDbn, constant 2015)

Population	5,601,547					
Age	0–14	15–19	20–24	25–29	30–64	65 plus
Male	8.3%	2.8%	2.8%	3.1%	22.2%	10.1%
Female	8.0%	2.7%	2.6%	3.0%	21.6%	12.9%

Capabilities
Finland's armed forces are primarily focused on territorial defence. The country's long border with Russia has focused attention on Russia's military capabilities and plans. In October 2020, the government's report on foreign and security policy assessed a security environment that is rapidly changing and deteriorating. In May 2022, following Russia's invasion of Ukraine, Finland applied for NATO membership. An EU member state, key multilateral defence relationships have hitherto included NORDEFCO and the Northern Group, while there is also strong bilateral cooperation with Sweden and the US. In 2022 Finland signed a mutual security agreement with the UK and is looking to deepen defence ties with the US by negotiating a Defence Cooperation Agreement. The country participates in UN peacekeeping missions and contributes to NATO operations. Legislation limits the number of personnel deployed on international crisis-management operations to an upper ceiling of 2,000 troops. Finland maintains a largely conscript-based force and

88 THE MILITARY BALANCE 2023

intends to increase the number of personnel in the defence forces. There are plans to boost readiness by increasing the number of reservists participating in refresher training. In December 2021 the F-35 was selected for the air force's HX Fighter Program to replace its F/A-18s. Under the Squadron 2020 project, the navy will replace patrol boats and minelayers with corvette-sized vessels. Finland's defence industry consists largely of privately owned SMEs, concentrating on niche products for international markets, but it also features some internationally competitive larger companies producing wheeled armoured vehicles and turreted mortar systems.

ACTIVE 19,250 (Army 13,400 Navy 3,150 Air 2,700)
Gendarmerie & Paramilitary 2,700
Conscript liability 165, 255 or 347 days (latter for NCOs, officers or those on 'especially demanding' duties)

RESERVE 238,000 (Army 185,000 Navy 24,000 Air 29,000) Gendarmerie & Paramilitary 12,000
18,000 reservists a year conduct refresher training: total obligation 80 days (150 for NCOs, 200 for officers) between conscript service and age 50 (NCOs and officers to age 60)

ORGANISATIONS BY SERVICE

Army 4,400; 9,000 conscript (total 13,400)
FORCES BY ROLE
Finland's army maintains a mobilisation strength of about 285,000. In support of this requirement, two conscription cycles, each for about 9,000 conscripts, take place each year. After conscript training, reservist commitment is to the age of 60. Reservists are usually assigned to units within their local geographical area. All service appointments or deployments outside Finnish borders are voluntary for all members of the armed services. All brigades are reserve based

Reserve Organisations 185,000
FORCES BY ROLE
SPECIAL FORCES
1 SF bn
MANOEUVRE
Armoured
2 armd BG (regt)
Mechanised
2 (Karelia & Pori Jaeger) mech bde
Light
3 (Jaeger) bde
6 lt inf bde
COMBAT SUPPORT
1 arty bde
1 AD regt
7 engr regt
3 sigs bn
COMBAT SERVICE SUPPORT
3 log regt
HELICOPTER
1 hel bn
EQUIPMENT BY TYPE
ARMOURED FIGHTING VEHICLES
MBT 100 *Leopard* 2A6; (100 *Leopard* 2A4 in store)
IFV 212: 110 BMP-2MD; 102 CV9030FIN
APC 613
 APC (T) 142: 40 MT-LBu; 102 MT-LBV
 APC (W) 471: 260 XA-180/185 *Sisu*; 101 XA-202 *Sisu*

(CP); 48 XA-203 *Sisu*; 62 AMV (XA-360)
AUV 6 SISU GTP (in test)
ENGINEERING & MAINTENANCE VEHICLES
AEV 5 *Dachs*
ARV 36: 9 BPz-2; 15 MTP-LB; 12 VT-55A
VLB 31: 12 BLG-60M2; 10 *Leopard* 2L AVLB; 9 SISU *Leguan*
MW 6+: *Aardvark* Mk 2; KMT T-55; 6 *Leopard* 2R CEV; RA-140 DS
ANTI-TANK/ANTI-INFRASTRUCTURE
MSL • MANPATS NLAW; *Spike*-MR; *Spike*-LR
ARTILLERY 682
SP 122mm 59: 23 K9 *Thunder*; 36 2S1 *Gvozdika* (PsH 74)
TOWED 288: **122mm** 234 D-30 (H 63); **155mm** 54 K 83/ GH-52 (K 98)
MRL 56: **122mm** 34 RM-70; **227mm** 22 M270 MLRS
MOR 279+: **81mm** Krh/71; **120mm** 261 Krh/92; **SP 120mm** 18 XA-361 AMOS
HELICOPTERS
MRH 7: 5 Hughes 500D; 2 Hughes 500E
TPT • Medium 20 NH90 TTH
UNINHABITED AERIAL VEHICLES
 ISR
  Medium 11 ADS-95 *Ranger*
AIR DEFENCE
 SAM 60+
  Short-range 44: 20 *Crotale* NG (ITO 90); 24 NASAMS II FIN (ITO 12)
  Point-defence 16+: 16 ASRAD (ITO 05); FIM-92 *Stinger* (ITO 15); RBS 70 (ITO 05/05M)
 GUNS 407+: **23mm** ItK 95/ZU-23-2 (ItK 61); **35mm** GDF-005 (ItK 88); **SP 35mm** 7 *Leopard* 2 ITK *Marksman*

Navy 1,400; 1,750 conscript (total 3,150)
FORCES BY ROLE
Naval Command HQ located at Turku; with two subordinate Naval Commands (Gulf of Finland and Archipelago Sea); 1 Naval bde; 3 spt elm (Naval Materiel Cmd, Naval Academy, Naval Research Institute)
EQUIPMENT BY TYPE
PATROL AND COASTAL COMBATANTS 20
PCGM 4 *Hamina* with 4 RBS15 Mk3 (MTO-85M) AShM, 1 8-cell VLS with *Umkhonto*-IR (ITO2004) SAM, 1 57mm gun
PBG 4 *Rauma* with 6 RBS15 Mk3 (MTO-85M) AShM
PBF 12 *Jehu* (U-700) (capacity 24 troops)
MINE WARFARE 8
 MINE COUNTERMEASURES 3
  MCC 3 *Katanpää* (ITA *Gaeta* mod)
 MINELAYERS • ML 5:
  2 *Hameenmaa* with 1 8-cell VLS with *Umkhonto*-IR (ITO2004) SAM, 2 RBU 1200 *Uragan* A/S mor, 1 57mm gun (can carry up to 120 mines)
  3 *Pansio* with 50 mines
AMPHIBIOUS • LANDING CRAFT 52
LCM 1 *Kampela*
LCVP 1 *Utö*
LCP ε50
LOGISTICS AND SUPPORT 7
AG 3: 1 *Louhi*; 2 *Hylje*
AX 4: 3 *Fabian Wrede*; 1 *Lokki*

Coastal Defence

FORCES BY ROLE
MANOEUVRE
Amphibious
1 mne bde
COMBAT SUPPORT
1 cbt spt bde (1 AShM bty)
EQUIPMENT BY TYPE
COASTAL DEFENCE
AShM 4 RBS15K
ARTY • **130mm** 30 K-53tk (static)
ANTI-TANK/ANTI-INFRASTRUCTURE
MSL • **MANPATS** Spike (used in AShM role)

Air Force 2,050; 1,000 conscript (total 3,050)

3 Air Comds: Satakunta (West), Karelia (East), Lapland (North)
FORCES BY ROLE
FIGHTER/GROUND ATTACK
2 sqn with F/A-18C/D *Hornet*
ISR
1 (survey) sqn with Learjet 35A
TRANSPORT
1 flt with C295M
4 (liaison) flt with PC-12NG
TRAINING
1 sqn with *Hawk* Mk50/51A/66* (air-defence and ground-attack trg)
1 unit with G-115EA
EQUIPMENT BY TYPE
AIRCRAFT 107 combat capable
FGA 62: 55 F/A-18C *Hornet*; 7 F/A-18D *Hornet*
ELINT 1 C295M
TPT • **Light** 11: 2 C295M; 3 Learjet 35A (survey; ECM trg; tgt-tow); 6 PC-12NG
TRG 73: 28 G-115EA; 29 *Hawk* Mk50/51A*; 16 *Hawk* Mk66*
AIR-LAUNCHED MISSILES
AAM • **IR** AIM-9 *Sidewinder*; **IIR** AIM-9X *Sidewinder*
ARH AIM-120C AMRAAM
ALCM • **Conventional** AGM-158 JASSM
BOMBS
INS/GPS-guided GBU-31 JDAM; AGM-154C JSOW

Gendarmerie & Paramilitary

Border Guard 2,700

Ministry of Interior. 4 Border Guard Districts and 2 Coast Guard Districts
FORCES BY ROLE
MARITIME PATROL
1 sqn with Do-228 (maritime surv); AS332 *Super Puma*; Bell 412 (AB-412) *Twin Huey*; Bell 412EP (AB-412EP) *Twin Huey*;AW119KE *Koala*
EQUIPMENT BY TYPE
PATROL AND COASTAL COMBATANTS 43
PSO 1 *Turva* with 1 hel landing platform
PCC 2 *Tursas*
PB 40

AMPHIBIOUS • **LANDING CRAFT** 6
UCAC 6
AIRCRAFT • **TPT** • **Light** 2 Do-228
HELICOPTERS
MRH 3: 1 Bell 412 (AB-412) *Twin Huey*; 2 Bell 412EP (AB-412EP) *Twin Huey*
TPT 9: **Medium** 5 AS332 *Super Puma*; **Light** 4 AW119KE *Koala*

Reserve 12,000 reservists on mobilisation

DEPLOYMENT

IRAQ: *Operation Inherent Resolve* 75; 1 trg team; **NATO** • NATO Mission Iraq 5
LEBANON: UN • UNIFIL 161; 1 inf coy
MALI: EU • EUTM Mali 12; **UN** • MINUSMA 4
MIDDLE EAST: UN • UNTSO 14
MOZAMBIQUE: EU • EUTM Mozambique 4
SERBIA: NATO • KFOR 20
SOMALIA: EU • EUTM Somalia 12
UNITED KINGDOM: *Operation Interflex* 20 (UKR trg)

France FRA

Euro EUR		2021	2022	2023
GDP	EUR	2.50tr	2.63tr	
	USD	2.96tr	2.78tr	
per capita	USD	45,188	42,330	
Growth	%	6.8	2.5	
Inflation	%	2.1	5.8	
Def exp [a]	EUR	47.8bn	49.6bn	
	USD	56.6bn	52.4bn	
Def bdgt [b]	EUR	49.7bn	51.5bn	55.1bn
	USD	58.8bn	54.4bn	
USD1=EUR		0.84	0.95	

[a] NATO figure
[b] Includes pensions

Real-terms defence budget trend (USDbn, constant 2015)

Population	68,305,148					
Age	0–14	15–19	20–24	25–29	30–64	65 plus
Male	9.3%	3.1%	3.0%	2.9%	21.5%	9.2%
Female	8.9%	3.0%	2.9%	2.8%	21.6%	11.9%

Capabilities

In November 2022, France published a new National Strategic Review (RNS), which highlighted the deteriorating security environment, the need to strengthen resilience in France and the importance of the NATO Alliance and European strategic autonomy. An updated Military Planning Law was under discussion at

THE MILITARY BALANCE 2023

the end of 2022. France plays a leading military role in the EU, NATO and the UN, and maintains globally deployed forces. In 2018, Paris launched the European Intervention Initiative, in order to foster a common strategic culture and develop the ability to jointly deploy quickly in case of crises. France is also expanding its capabilities in non-traditional domains, having set up a space command, developed a space strategy, formalised an offensive cyber doctrine and in February 2022 adopted a seabed warfare strategy. Deployments abroad have demonstrated the ability to support expeditionary forces independently, although some strategic and intra-theatre military air-transport requirements have been dependent on allies and external contractors. In October 2021, the French armed forces issued a new 'Strategic Outlook' document, illustrating a sharpened focus on improved readiness for high-intensity warfare. The 2019-25 Military Planning Law sought to increase the maintenance budget and accelerate modernisation to, among other concerns, mitigate the effect of operations on equipment availability in light of lessons from overseas deployments. The 2022 RNS discussed issues relating to weapons stocks, security of supply and industrial capacity, in light of the war in Ukraine. In 2022, France reorganised its presence in the Sahel, effectively leaving Mali, and transferred some forces to Niger. France has a sophisticated defence industry, exemplified by companies such as Dassault, MBDA and Nexter, with most procurements undertaken domestically. France has called for greater European defence-industrial cooperation and aims to increase its exports to Europe. It is also seeking to invest in future technologies and supports start-ups and innovation in the defence realm.

ACTIVE 203,250 (Army 114,800 Navy 34,850 Air 40,200, Other Staffs 13,400) Gendarmerie & Paramilitary 100,500

RESERVE 41,150 (Army 25,750 Navy 5,400 Air 5,300 Other Staffs 4,700) Gendarmerie & Paramilitary 30,300

ORGANISATIONS BY SERVICE

Strategic Nuclear Forces

Navy 2,200

EQUIPMENT BY TYPE
SUBMARINES • STRATEGIC 4
SSBN 4 *Le Triomphant* with 16 M51 SLBM with 6 TN-75 nuclear warheads, 4 single 533mm TT with SM39 *Exocet* AShM/F17 mod 2 HWT
AIRCRAFT • FGA 20 *Rafale* M F3 with ASMPA msl

Air Force 1,800

Air Strategic Forces Command

FORCES BY ROLE
STRIKE
1 sqn with *Rafale* B with ASMPA msl
1 sqn with *Rafale* B with ASMPA msl (forming)
TANKER
2 sqn with A330 MRTT; C-135FR; KC-135 *Stratotanker*
EQUIPMENT BY TYPE
AIRCRAFT 20 combat capable
FGA 20 *Rafale* B
TKR/TPT 15: 5 A330 MRTT; 10 C-135FR
TKR 3 KC-135 *Stratotanker*

Paramilitary

Gendarmerie 40

Space

EQUIPMENT BY TYPE
SATELLITES 13
COMMUNICATIONS 4: 2 *Syracuse*-3 (designed to integrate with UK *Skynet* & ITA *Sicral*); 1 *Syracuse*-4; 1 *Athena-Fidus* (also used by ITA)
ISR 6: 1 CSO-1; 1 CSO-2; 1 *Helios* 2A; 1 *Helios* 2B; 2 *Pleiades*
ELINT/SIGINT 3 CERES

Army 114,800

Regt and BG normally bn size

FORCES BY ROLE
COMMAND
1 corps HQ (CRR-FR)
2 div HQ
MANOEUVRE
Reconnaissance
1 recce regt
Armoured
1 (2nd) armd bde (2 tk regt, 3 armd inf regt, 1 SP arty regt, 1 engr regt)
1 (7th) armd bde (1 tk regt, 1 armd BG, 3 armd inf regt, 1 SP arty regt, 1 engr regt)
1 armd BG HQ (UAE)
Mechanised
1 (6th) lt armd bde (2 armd cav regt, 1 armd inf regt, 1 mech inf regt, 1 mech inf regt, 1 SP arty regt, 1 engr regt)
1 (FRA/GER) mech bde (1 armd cav regt, 1 mech inf regt)
1 mech regt HQ (Djibouti)
Light
1 (27th) mtn bde (1 armd cav regt, 3 mtn inf regt, 1 arty regt, 1 engr regt)
3 inf regt (French Guiana & French West Indies)
1 inf regt HQ (New Caledonia)
2 inf bn HQ (Côte d'Ivoire & Gabon)
Air Manoeuvre
1 (11th) AB bde (1 armd cav regt, 4 para regt, 1 arty regt, 1 engr regt, 1 spt regt)
1 AB regt (La Réunion)
Amphibious
1 (9th) amph bde (2 armd cav regt, 1 armd inf regt, 2 mech inf regt, 1 SP arty regt, 1 engr regt)
Other
4 SMA regt (French Guiana, French West Indies & Indian Ocean)
3 SMA coy (French Polynesia, Indian Ocean & New Caledonia)
COMBAT SUPPORT
1 MRL regt
2 engr regt
2 EW regt
1 int bn
1 CBRN regt
5 sigs regt

Europe 91

COMBAT SERVICE SUPPORT
5 tpt regt
1 log regt
1 med regt
3 trg regt
HELICOPTER
1 (4th) hel bde (3 hel regt)
ISR UAV
1 UAV regt
AIR DEFENCE
1 SAM regt

Special Operation Forces 2,200

FORCES BY ROLE
SPECIAL FORCES
2 SF regt
HELICOPTER
1 hel regt

Reserves 25,750 reservists

Reservists form 79 UIR (Reserve Intervention Units) of about 75 to 152 troops, for 'Proterre' – combined land projection forces bn, and 23 USR (Reserve Specialised Units) of about 160 troops, in specialised regt

EQUIPMENT BY TYPE
ARMOURED FIGHTING VEHICLES
MBT 215 *Leclerc*
ASLT 245 AMX-10RC
RECCE 64: 24 EBRC *Jaguar*; 40 ERC-90D *Sagaie*
IFV 706: 599 VBCI VCI; 107 VBCI VPC (CP)
APC 2,499
  APC (T) 49 BvS-10
  APC (W) 2,430: 373 VBMR *Griffon*; ε2,000 VAB;
  57 VAB VOA (OP)
  PPV 20 *Aravis*
AUV 1,503: 1,416 VBL/VB2L; 72 VBL Ultima; 15
VBMR-L *Serval*
ENGINEERING & MAINTENANCE VEHICLES
AEV 110: 38 AMX-30EBG; 72 VAB GE
ARV 44: 27 AMX-30D; 17 *Leclerc* DNG; VAB-EHC
VLB 48: 20 EFA; 18 PTA; 10 SPRAT
MW 16+: AMX-30B/B2; 4 *Buffalo*; 12 *Minotaur*
NBC VEHICLES 26 VAB NRBC
ANTI-TANK/ANTI-INFRASTRUCTURE • MSL
SP 177: 64 VAB *Milan*; 113 VAB with MMP
MANPATS *Eryx*; FGM-148 *Javelin*; *Milan*; MMP
ARTILLERY 245+
SP 155mm 90: 32 AU-F-1; 58 CAESAR
TOWED 155mm 12 TR-F-1
MRL 227mm 11 M270 MLRS
MOR 132+: **81mm** LLR 81mm; **120mm** 132 RT-F-1
AIRCRAFT • TPT • Light 13: 5 PC-6B *Turbo Porter*;
5 TBM-700; 3 TBM-700B
HELICOPTERS
ATK 67: 20 *Tiger* HAP (to be upgraded to HAD);
47 *Tiger* HAD
MRH 104: 18 AS555UN *Fennec*; 86 SA341F/342M *Gazelle*
(all variants)
TPT 167: **Heavy** 8 H225M *Caracal* (CSAR); **Medium** 124:
24 AS532UL *Cougar*; 2 EC225LP *Super Puma*; 52 NH90
TTH; 46 SA330 *Puma*; **Light** 35 H120 *Colibri* (leased)

AIR DEFENCE • SAM • Point-defence 12+: *Mistral*;
12 VAB ARLAD
AIR-LAUNCHED MISSILES
ASM AGM-114 *Hellfire* II; HOT

Navy 34,850

EQUIPMENT BY TYPE
SUBMARINES 9
STRATEGIC • SSBN 4 *Le Triomphant* opcon Strategic
Nuclear Forces with 16 M51 SLBM with 6 TN-75 nuclear
warheads, 4 single 533mm TT with SM39 *Exocet* AShM/
F17 mod 2 HWT
TACTICAL • SSN 5
  4 *Rubis* (1 more severely damaged by fire) with 4 single
  533mm TT with SM39 *Exocet* AShM/F17 mod 2 HWT
  1 *Suffren* with 4 single 533mm TT with MdCN (SCALP
  Naval) LACM/SM39 *Exocet* AShM/*Artémis* (F-21) HWT
PRINCIPAL SURFACE COMBATANTS 22
AIRCRAFT CARRIERS • CVN 1 *Charles de Gaulle* with
4 8-cell *Sylver* A43 VLS with *Aster* 15 SAM, 2 sextuple
Sadral lnchr with *Mistral* SAM (capacity 30 *Rafale* M
FGA ac, 2 E-2C *Hawkeye* AEW&C ac, 8 AS365 *Dauphin*/
NH90 NFH hel)
DESTROYERS • DDGHM 4
  2 *Aquitaine* (FREMM FREDA) with 2 quad lnchr with
  MM40 *Exocet* Block 3 AShM, 4 8-cell *Sylver* A50 VLS
  with *Aster* 15 SAM/*Aster* 30 SAM, 2 twin 324mm
  B-515 ASTT with MU90 LWT, 1 76mm gun (capacity
  1 NH90 NFH hel)
  2 *Forbin* with 2 quad lnchr with MM40 *Exocet* Block
  3 AShM, 4 8-cell *Sylver* A50 VLS with *Aster* 30
  SAM, 2 8-cell *Sylver* A50 VLS with *Aster* 15 SAM, 2
  twin 324mm ASTT with MU90 LWT, 2 76mm gun
  (capacity 1 NH90 NFH hel)
FRIGATES 17
FFGHM 11:
  4 *Aquitaine* (FREMM ASM) with 2 8-cell *Sylver*
  A70 VLS with MdCN (SCALP Naval) LACM, 2
  quad lnchr with MM40 *Exocet* Block 3 AShM, 2
  8-cell *Sylver* A43 VLS with *Aster* 15 SAM, 2 twin
  324mm B-515 ASTT with MU90 LWT, 1 76mm gun
  (capacity 1 NH90 NFH hel)
  2 *Aquitaine* (FREMM ASM) with 2 8-cell *Sylver* A70
  VLS with MdCN (SCALP Naval) LACM, 2 quad
  lnchr with MM40 *Exocet* Block 3 AShM, 2 8-cell
  Sylver A50 VLS with *Aster* 15 SAM/*Aster* 30 SAM,
  2 twin 324mm B-515 ASTT with MU90 LWT, 1
  76mm gun (capacity 1 NH90 NFH hel)
  3 *La Fayette* with 2 quad lnchr with MM40 *Exocet*
  Block 3 AShM, 1 octuple lnchr with *Crotale* SAM, 1
  100mm gun (capacity 1 AS565SA *Panther* hel)
  2 *La Fayette* with 2 quad lnchr with MM40 *Exocet*
  Block 3 AShM, 2 sextuple *Sadral* lnchr with
  Mistral 3 SAM, 1 100mm gun (capacity 1 AS565SA
  Panther hel)
FFH 6 *Floreal* with 1 100mm gun (fitted for but not
with 1 twin *Simbad* lnchr with *Mistral* SAM) (capacity 1
AS565SA *Panther* hel)

PATROL AND COASTAL COMBATANTS 20
FSM 6 *D'Estienne d'Orves* with 1 twin *Simbad* lnchr with *Mistral* SAM, 2 twin 533mm ASTT, 1 100mm gun
PSO 4 *d'Entrecasteaux* (BSAOM) with 1 hel landing platform
PCO 6: 3 *La Confiance*, 1 *Lapérouse*; 1 *Le Malin*; 1 *Fulmar*
PCC 4: 1 *L'Audacieuse*; 3 *Flamant*
MINE WARFARE • MINE COUNTERMEASURES 16
MCD 4 *Vulcain*
MHC 3 *Antarès*
MHO 9 *Éridan*
AMPHIBIOUS
PRINCIPAL AMPHIBIOUS SHIPS 3
LHD 3 *Mistral* with 2 twin *Simbad* lnchr with *Mistral* SAM (capacity up to 16 NH90/SA330 *Puma*/AS532 *Cougar*/*Tiger* hel; 2 LCT or 4 LCM/LCU; 13 MBTs; 50 AFVs; 450 troops)
LANDING CRAFT 40
LCU 2 *Arbalète* (EDA-S) (capacity 1 *Leclerc* MBT or 2 *Griffon*/*Jaguar*)
LCT 4 EDA-R (capacity 1 *Leclerc* MBT or 6 VAB)
LCM 11 CTM
LCVP 25
LOGISTICS AND SUPPORT 33
ABU 1 *Telenn Mor*
AG 2 *Chamois*
AGB 1 *Astrolabe* with 1 hel landing platform
AGE 2: 1 *Corraline*; 1 *Thetis* (*Lapérouse* mod) (used as trials ships for mines and divers)
AGI 1 *Dupuy de Lome*
AGM 1 *Monge*
AGOR 2: 1 *Pourquoi pas?* (used 150 days per year by Ministry of Defence; operated by Ministry of Research and Education otherwise); 1 *Beautemps-beaupré*
AGS 3 *Lapérouse*
AORH 2 *Durance* with 3 twin *Simbad* lnchr with *Mistral* SAM (capacity 1 SA319 *Alouette* III/AS365 *Dauphin*/*Lynx*)
ATS 4 *Loire* (BSAM)
AXL 10: 8 *Léopard*; 2 *Glycine*
AXS 4: 2 *La Belle Poule*; 1 *La Grand Hermine*; 1 *Mutin*

Naval Aviation 6,500

FORCES BY ROLE
STRIKE/FIGHTER/GROUND ATTACK
2 sqn with *Rafale* M F3
1 sqn with *Rafale* M F3/F3-R
ANTI-SURFACE WARFARE
1 sqn with AS565SA *Panther*
ANTI-SUBMARINE WARFARE
2 sqn with NH90 NFH
MARITIME PATROL
2 sqn with *Atlantique* 2
1 sqn with *Falcon* 20H *Gardian*
1 sqn with *Falcon* 50MI
AIRBORNE EARLY WARNING & CONTROL
1 sqn with E-2C *Hawkeye*
SEARCH & RESCUE
1 sqn with AS365N/F *Dauphin* 2
TRAINING
1 sqn with EMB 121 *Xingu*
1 unit with SA319B *Alouette* III (to be WFU end of 2022)
1 unit with *Falcon* 10MER
1 unit with CAP 10M

EQUIPMENT BY TYPE
AIRCRAFT 60 combat capable
FGA 42 *Rafale* M F3-R
ASW 18: 9 *Atlantique*-2 (standard 6); 9 *Atlantique*-2 (being upgraded to standard 6)
AEW&C 3 E-2C *Hawkeye*
SAR 4 *Falcon* 50MS
TPT 25: **Light** 10 EMB-121 *Xingu*; **PAX** 15: 6 *Falcon* 10MER; 5 *Falcon* 20H *Gardian*; 4 *Falcon* 50MI
TRG 6 CAP 10M
HELICOPTERS
ASW 27 NH90 NFH
MRH 40: 3 AS365F *Dauphin* 2; 6 AS365N *Dauphin* 2; 2 AS365N3; 16 AS565SA *Panther*; 1 H160B; 12 SA319B *Alouette* III (to be WFU end of 2022)
UNINHABITED AERIAL VEHICLES
ISR • Light 4 S-100 *Camcopter*
AIR-LAUNCHED MISSILES
AAM • IIR *Mica* IR; **ARH** *Mica* RF
ASM AASM
AShM AM39 *Exocet*
LACM Nuclear ASMPA
BOMBS
Laser-guided: GBU-12/16 *Paveway* II

Marines 2,200

Commando Units 750

FORCES BY ROLE
MANOEUVRE
Reconnaissance
1 recce gp
Amphibious
2 aslt gp
1 atk swimmer gp
1 raiding gp
COMBAT SUPPORT
1 cbt spt gp
COMBAT SERVICE SUPPORT
1 spt gp

Fusiliers-Marin 1,450

FORCES BY ROLE
MANOEUVRE
Other
2 sy gp
7 sy coy

Reserves 6,000 reservists

Air and Space Force 40,200
FORCES BY ROLE
STRIKE
1 sqn with *Rafale* B with ASMPA msl
1 sqn with *Rafale* B with ASMPA msl (forming)
SPACE
1 (satellite obs) sqn
FIGHTER
1 sqn with *Mirage* 2000-5
1 sqn with *Mirage* 2000B

Europe   93

FIGHTER/GROUND ATTACK
3 sqn with *Mirage* 2000D
1 (composite) sqn with *Mirage* 2000-5/D (Djibouti)
2 sqn with *Rafale* B/C
1 sqn with *Rafale* B/C (UAE)
ELECTRONIC WARFARE
1 flt with C-160G *Gabriel* (ESM); Beech 350ER *King Air*
AIRBORNE EARLY WARNING & CONTROL
1 (Surveillance & Control) sqn with E-3F *Sentry*
SEARCH & RESCUE/TRANSPORT
5 sqn with CN235M; SA330 *Puma*; AS555 *Fennec* (Djibouti, French Guiana, French Polynesia, Indian Ocean & New Caledonia)
TANKER
1 sqn with A330 MRTT
TANKER/TRANSPORT
1 sqn with C-135FR; KC-135 *Stratotanker*
TRANSPORT
1 VIP sqn with A310-300; A330
2 sqn with A400M
1 sqn with C-130H/H-30 *Hercules*
1 sqn with C-130H/H-30/J-30 *Hercules*; KC-130J *Hercules*
1 sqn (joint FRA-GER) with C-130J-30 *Hercules*; KC-130J *Hercules*
2 sqn with CN235M
1 sqn with *Falcon* 7X (VIP); *Falcon* 900 (VIP); *Falcon* 2000
3 flt with TBM-700A
1 gp with DHC-6-300 *Twin Otter*
TRAINING
1 OCU sqn with *Mirage* 2000D
1 OCU sqn with *Rafale* B/C
1 OCU sqn with SA330 *Puma*; AS555 *Fennec*
1 (aggressor) sqn with *Alpha Jet**
4 sqn with *Alpha Jet**
1 sqn with Grob G120A-F
2 sqn with Grob G120A-F; PC-21
1 sqn with EMB-121
TRANSPORT HELICOPTER
2 sqn with AS555 *Fennec*
2 sqn with AS332C/L *Super Puma*; SA330 *Puma*; H225M
ISR UAV
1 sqn with MQ-9A *Reaper*
AIR DEFENCE
3 sqn with *Crotale* NG; SAMP/T
1 sqn with SAMP/T

EQUIPMENT BY TYPE
SATELLITES *see* Space
AIRCRAFT 261 combat capable
FTR 34: 27 *Mirage* 2000-5; 7 *Mirage* 2000B
FGA 155: 65 *Mirage* 2000D; 51 *Rafale* B; 39 *Rafale* C (*Rafale* being upgraded to F3-R standard)
ISR 2 Beech 350ER *King Air*
ELINT 2 C-160G *Gabriel* (ESM)
AEW&C 4 E-3F *Sentry*
TKR 3 KC-135 *Stratotanker*
TKR/TPT 17: 5 A330 MRTT; 10 C-135FR; 2 KC-130J *Hercules*
TPT 114: **Heavy** 19 A400M; **Medium** 16: 5 C-130H *Hercules*; 9 C-130H-30 *Hercules*; 2 C-130J-30 *Hercules*; **Light** 70: 1 Beech 350i *King Air*; 19 CN235M-100; 8 CN235M-300; 5 DHC-6-300 *Twin Otter*; 22 EMB-121

Xingu; 15 TBM-700; **PAX** 9: 2 A310-300; 1 A330; 2 *Falcon* 7X; 2 *Falcon* 900 (VIP); 2 *Falcon* 2000 (2 A340-200 in store)
TRG 127: 72 *Alpha Jet**; 18 Grob G120A-F (leased); 17 PC-21; 13 SR20 (leased); 7 SR22 (leased)
HELICOPTERS
MRH 37 AS555 *Fennec*
TPT 35: **Heavy** 10 H225M *Caracal*; **Medium** 25: 1 AS332C *Super Puma*; 4 AS332L *Super Puma*; 20 SA330B *Puma*
UNINHABITED AERIAL VEHICLES
CISR • **Heavy** 8 MQ-9A *Reaper*
AIR DEFENCE • **SAM** 60: **Long-range** 40 SAMP/T; **Short-range** 20 *Crotale* NG
AIR-LAUNCHED MISSILES
AAM • **IR** R-550 *Magic* 2; **IIR** Mica IR; **ARH** *Meteor*; Mica RF
ASM AASM; *Apache*
LACM
Nuclear ASMPA
Conventional SCALP EG
BOMBS
Laser-guided: GBU-12/-16 *Paveway* II
Laser & INS/GPS-guided GBU-49 Enhanced *Paveway* II

Security and Intervention Brigade

FORCES BY ROLE
SPECIAL FORCES
3 SF gp
MANOEUVRE
Other
24 protection units
30 (fire fighting and rescue) unit

Reserves 5,300 reservists

Gendarmerie & Paramilitary 100,500

Gendarmerie 100,500; 30,300 reservists

EQUIPMENT BY TYPE
ARMOURED FIGHTING VEHICLES
APC • **APC (W)** 80: 60 VXB-170 (VBRG-170); 20 VAB
ARTILLERY • **MOR 81mm** some
PATROL AND COASTAL COMBATANTS 43
PB 42: 1 *Armoise*; 2 *Athos*; 4 *Géranium*; 3 *Maroni*; 24 VCSM; 9 VSMP
HELICOPTERS • **TPT** • **Light** 60: 25 AS350BA *Ecureuil*; 20 H135; 15 H145

DEPLOYMENT

BOSNIA-HERZEGOVINA: EU • EUFOR (*Operation Althea*) 5

BURKINA FASO: 300; 1 SF gp; 1 C-130H; 1 DHC-6-300; 2 *Tiger*; 3 AS532UL *Cougar*; 2 H225M; 2 SA342 *Gazelle*

CENTRAL AFRICAN REPUBLIC: 160; **EU** • EUTM RCA 13; **UN** • MINUSCA 5

CHAD: 1,500; 1 mech inf BG; 1 FGA det with 3 *Mirage* 2000D; 1 tkr/tpt det with 1 A330 MRTT; 1 C-130H; 2 CN235M

CÔTE D'IVOIRE: 900; 1 inf bn; 1 (army) hel unit with 2 SA330 *Puma*; 2 SA342 *Gazelle*; 1 (air force) hel unit with 1 AS555 *Fennec*

CYPRUS: *Operation Inherent Resolve* 30: 1 *Atlantique*-2

DEMOCRATIC REPUBLIC OF THE CONGO: UN • MONUSCO 4

DJIBOUTI: 1,500; 1 combined arms regt with (2 recce sqn, 2 inf coy, 1 arty bty, 1 engr coy); 1 hel det with 4 SA330 *Puma*; 3 SA342 *Gazelle*; 1 LCM; 1 FGA sqn with 4 *Mirage* 2000-5; 1 SAR/tpt sqn with 1 CN235M; 3 SA330 *Puma*

EGYPT: MFO 1

ESTONIA: NATO • Enhanced Forward Presence (*Operation Lynx*) 219; 1 lt inf coy

FRENCH GUIANA: 2,100: 2 inf regt; 1 SMA regt; 2 PCO; 1 tpt sqn with 3 CN235M; 5 SA330 *Puma*; 4 AS555 *Fennec*; 3 gendarmerie coy; 1 AS350BA *Ecureuil*; 1 H145

FRENCH POLYNESIA: 950: 1 inf bn; 1 SMA coy; 1 naval HQ at Papeete; 1 FFH; 1 PSO; 1 PCO; 1 AFS; 3 *Falcon* 200 *Gardian*; 1 SAR/tpt sqn with 2 CN235M; 3 SA330 *Puma*

FRENCH WEST INDIES: 1,000; 1 inf regt; 2 SMA regt; 2 FFH; 1 AS565SA *Panther*; 1 SA319 *Alouette* III; 1 naval base at Fort de France (Martinique); 4 gendarmerie coy; 1 PCO; 1 PB; 2 AS350BA *Ecureuil*

GABON: 350; 1 inf bn

GERMANY: 2,000 (incl elm Eurocorps and FRA/GER bde); 1 (FRA/GER) mech bde (1 armd cav regt, 1 mech inf regt)

GULF OF GUINEA: *Operation Corymbe* 1 LHD

IRAQ: *Operation Inherent Resolve* 6; **NATO •** NATO Mission Iraq 3

JORDAN: *Operation Inherent Resolve* (*Chammal*) 300: 4 *Rafale* F3

LA REUNION/MAYOTTE: 1,750; 1 para regt; 1 inf coy; 1 SMA regt; 1 SMA coy; 2 FFH; 1 PCO; 1 LCM; 1 naval HQ at Port-des-Galets (La Réunion); 1 naval base at Dzaoudzi (Mayotte); 1 Falcon 50M; 1 SAR/tpt sqn with 2 CN235M; 5 gendarmerie coy; 1 SA319 *Alouette* III

LEBANON: UN • UNIFIL 571; 1 mech inf bn(-); VBL; VBCI; VAB; *Mistral*

MALI: EU • EUTM Mali 13; **UN •** MINUSMA 26

MEDITERRANEAN SEA: *Operation Inherent Resolve* 100: 1 DDGHM

MOZAMBIQUE: EU • EUTM Mozambique 6

NEW CALEDONIA: 1,450; 1 mech inf regt; 1 SMA coy; 6 ERC-90F1 *Lynx*; 1 FFHM; 1 PSO; 1 PCO; 1 base with 2 *Falcon* 200 *Gardian* at Nouméa; 1 tpt unit with 2 CN235 MPA; 3 SA330 *Puma*; 4 gendarmerie coy; 2 AS350BA *Ecureuil*

NIGER: 1,200; 1 mech inf coy; 1 hel flt with 3 NH90 TTH; 1 FGA det with 3 *Mirage* 2000D; 1 tkr/tpt det with 1 C-135FR; 1 C-130J-30 *Hercules*; 1 UAV det with 6 MQ-9A *Reaper*; 1 ISR det with 1 *Atlantique*-2

QATAR: *Operation Inherent Resolve* (*Chammal*) 70; 1 E-3F *Sentry*

ROMANIA: NATO • Enhanced Vigilance Activities 750; 1 armd BG with *Leclerc*; VBCI; 1 SAM bty with SAMP/T

SAUDI ARABIA: 50 (radar det)

SENEGAL: 400; 1 *Falcon* 50MI

UNITED ARAB EMIRATES: 700: 1 armd BG (1 tk coy, 1 arty bty); *Leclerc*; CAESAR; • *Operation Inherent Resolve* (*Chammal*); 1 FGA sqn with 7 *Rafale* F3

WESTERN SAHARA: UN • MINURSO 3

FOREIGN FORCES

Germany 400 (GER elm Eurocorps)
Singapore 200; 1 trg sqn with 12 M-346 *Master*

Germany GER

Euro EUR		2021	2022	2023
GDP	EUR	3.60tr	3.81tr	
	USD	4.26tr	4.03tr	
per capita	USD	51,238	48,398	
Growth	%	2.6	1.5	
Inflation	%	3.2	8.5	
Def exp [a]	EUR	53.0bn	55.6bn	
	USD	62.8bn	58.8bn	
Def bdgt [b]	EUR	46.9bn	50.5bn	58.6bn
	USD	55.5bn	53.4bn	
USD1=EUR		0.84	0.95	

[a] NATO figure
[b] Includes military pensions

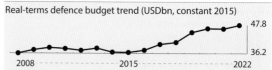
Real-terms defence budget trend (USDbn, constant 2015)

Population	84,316,622					
Age	0–14	15–19	20–24	25–29	30–64	65 plus
Male	7.0%	2.3%	2.6%	2.9%	24.4%	10.3%
Female	6.7%	2.3%	2.5%	2.7%	23.6%	12.7%

Capabilities

The 2016 defence White Paper committed Germany to a leadership role in European defence. It also emphasised the importance of NATO and the need for the armed forces to contribute to collective-defence tasks. Work on a national security strategy began in March 2022 under the leadership of the foreign ministry and this is scheduled to be released in early 2023. Following Russia's full-scale invasion of Ukraine in February 2022, the government-initiated preparations for a EUR100 billion special purpose vehicle to invest in modernisation of the Bundeswehr over the next five years; the funding was approved in early June. The 2018 Konzeption der Bundeswehr underlines that collective- and territorial-defence tasks will drive military-modernisation efforts and are of equal standing with international crisis-management operations. The key implication for defence modernisation is that Germany will need to invest in readiness and return to fully equipping operational units. Germany is aligning its defence-planning process with capability goals derived from multinational guidance. Close military cooperation has been established with the Czech Republic, France, the Netherlands and Romania, including the affiliation of units. The defence ministry has announced its objective to increase authorised active personnel numbers.

Europe 95

In July 2020, the government launched a new voluntary conscript initiative, with 1,000 posts, focused on homeland-security tasks. Volunteers serve for seven months plus five months as reservists over the course of six years. This is in addition to the existing voluntary conscript model that requires between seven and 23 months of military service. In September 2022, Germany set up a Territorial Operations Command to strengthen the armed forces' homeland security functions and take on command-and-control functions for forces deployed in Germany. The armed forces are struggling to improve readiness levels in light of increasing demands on NATO's eastern flank. Germany is scheduled to again become the lead nation for NATO's Very High Readiness Joint Task Force land component in 2023, with the earmarked units prioritised for modernisation and upgrades. Germany has indicated that it intends to provide, from 2025, some 30,000 personnel and some 85 vessels and aircraft at 30 days' notice for NATO's New Force Model, agreed at the Alliance's 2022 Madrid summit. Shortages of spare parts and maintenance problems are reported in all three services. Germany's defence-industrial base is able to design and manufacture equipment to meet requirements across all military domains, with strengths in land and naval systems. The government is pursuing a policy of closer defence-industrial cooperation in Europe.

ACTIVE 183,150 (Army 62,950 Navy 15,900 Air 27,200 Joint Support Service 27,900 Joint Medical Service 19,850 Cyber 14,250 Other 15,100)
Conscript liability Voluntary conscription only. Voluntary conscripts can serve up to 23 months

RESERVE 32,650 (Army 7,600 Navy 1,450 Air 3,750 Joint Support Service 12,500 Joint Medical Service 4,000 Cyber 1,350 Other 2,000)

ORGANISATIONS BY SERVICE

Space
EQUIPMENT BY TYPE
SATELLITES 8
COMMUNICATIONS 2 COMSATBw (1 & 2)
ISR 6: 1 SARah; 5 SAR-*Lupe*

Army 62,950
FORCES BY ROLE
COMMAND
elm 2 (1 GNC & MNC NE) corps HQ
MANOEUVRE
Armoured
1 (1st) armd div (1 (9th) armd bde (1 armd recce bn, 1 tk bn, 2 armd inf bn, 1 mech inf bn, 1 cbt engr bn, 1 spt bn); 1 (21st) armd bde (1 armd recce bn, 1 tk bn, 1 armd inf bn, 1 mech inf bn, 1 cbt engr bn, 1 spt bn); 1 (41st) mech inf bde (1 armd recce bn, 2 armd inf bn, 1 mech inf bn, 1 cbt engr bn, 1 sigs coy, 1 spt bn); 1 tk bn (for NLD 43rd Bde); 1 SP arty bn; 1 sigs coy)
1 (10th) armd div (1 (12th) armd bde (1 armd recce bn, 1 tk bn, 2 armd inf bn, 1 cbt engr bn, 1 sigs coy, 1 spt bn); 1 (37th) mech inf bde (1 armd recce bn, 2 tk bn, 2 armd inf bn, 1 engr bn, 1 sigs coy, 1 spt bn); 1 (23rd) mtn inf bde (1 recce bn, 3 mtn inf bn, 1 cbt engr bn, 1 spt bn); 1 SP arty bn; 1 SP arty trg bn; 2 mech inf bn (GER/FRA bde); 1 arty bn (GER/FRA bde); 1 cbt engr coy (GER/FRA bde); 1 spt bn (GER/FRA bde))

Air Manoeuvre
1 (rapid reaction) AB div (1 SOF bde (3 SOF bn); 1 AB bde (2 recce coy, 2 para regt, 2 cbt engr coy); 1 atk hel regt; 2 tpt hel regt; 1 sigs coy)
COMBAT SUPPORT
1 engr bn(-) (Joint GER-UK unit)
EQUIPMENT BY TYPE
ARMOURED FIGHTING VEHICLES
MBT 321: 223 *Leopard* 2A5/A6; 98 *Leopard* 2A7/2A7V (55 *Leopard* 2A4 in store)
RECCE 220 *Fennek* (incl 24 engr recce, 50 fires spt)
IFV 680: 258 *Marder* 1A3/A4; 72 *Marder* 1A5; 350 *Puma*
APC 812
APC (T) 112: 75 Bv-206S; 37 M113 (inc variants)
APC (W) 700: 341 *Boxer* (inc variants); 359 TPz-1 *Fuchs* (inc variants)
AUV 683: 247 *Dingo* 2; 363 *Eagle* IV/V; 73 *Wiesel* 1 Mk20 (with 20mm gun)
ENGINEERING & MAINTENANCE VEHICLES
AEV 51 *Dachs*
ARV 170: 95 BPz-2 1; 75 BPz-3 *Büffel*
VLB 59: 22 *Biber*; 7 *Leopard* 2 with *Leguan*; 30 M3
MW 30: 6 *Fuchs* KAI; 24 *Keiler*
NBC VEHICLES 44 TPz-1 *Fuchs* NBC
ANTI-TANK/ANTI-INFRASTRUCTURE • MSL
SP 102 *Wiesel* ATGM with TOW or MELLS
MANPATS *Milan*; *Spike*-LR (MELLS)
ARTILLERY 245
SP 155mm 109 PzH 2000
MRL 227mm 38 M270 MLRS
MOR 98: **120mm** 58 Tampella; **SP 120mm** 40 M113 with Tampella
HELICOPTERS
ATK 51 *Tiger*
TPT 102: **Medium** 82 NH90; **Light** 20: 13 H135; 7 H145 (SAR)
UNINHABITED AERIAL VEHICLES
ISR 123: **Medium** 35 KZO; **Light** 87 LUNA
AIR-LAUNCHED MISSILES • ASM HOT; PARS 3 LR

Navy 16,250
EQUIPMENT BY TYPE
SUBMARINES 6
SSK 6 Type-212A (fitted with AIP) with 6 single 533mm TT with DM2A4 HWT
PRINCIPAL SURFACE COMBATANTS 11
DESTROYERS • DDGHM 3 *Sachsen* (F124) with 2 quad lnchr with RGM-84C *Harpoon* Block 1B AShM, 4 8-cell Mk 41 VLS with SM-2 Block IIIA SAM/RIM-162B ESSM SAM, 2 21-cell Mk 49 GMLS with RIM-116 RAM SAM, 2 triple 324mm SVTT Mk 32 ASTT with MU90 LWT, 1 76mm gun (capacity 2 *Sea Lynx* Mk88A hel)
FRIGATES • FFGHM 8:
4 *Baden-Württemberg* (F125) with 2 quad lnchr with RGM-84C *Harpoon* Block 1B AShM, 2 21-cell Mk 49 GMLS with RIM-116C RAM Block 2 SAM, 1 127mm gun (capacity 2 NH90 hel)
4 *Brandenburg* (F123) with 2 twin lnchr with MM38 *Exocet* AShM, 2 8-cell Mk 41 VLS with RIM-7P *Sea Sparrow* SAM, 2 Mk 49 GMLS with RIM-116 RAM SAM, 2 twin 324mm SVTT Mk 32 ASTT with Mk 46 LWT, 1 76mm gun (capacity 2 *Sea Lynx* Mk88A hel)

THE MILITARY BALANCE 2023

PATROL AND COASTAL COMBATANTS 5
CORVETTES • FSGM 5 *Braunschweig* (K130) with 2 twin lnchr with RBS15 Mk3 AShM, 2 21-cell Mk 49 GMLS with RIM-116 RAM SAM, 1 76mm gun, 1 hel landing platform
MINE WARFARE • MINE COUNTERMEASURES 23
MHO 10: 7 *Frankenthal* (2 used as diving support); 3 *Frankenthal* (mod. MJ332CL)
MSO 1 *Ensdorf*
MSD 12 *Seehund*
AMPHIBIOUS • LANDING CRAFT 1
LCU 1 Type-520
LOGISTICS AND SUPPORT 23
AG 4: 2 *Schwedeneck* (Type-748); 2 *Stollergrund* (Type-745)
AGI 3 *Oste* (Type-423)
AGOR 1 *Planet* (Type-751)
AOR 2 *Rhön* (Type-704)
AORH 3 *Berlin* (Type-702) (fitted for but not with RIM-116 RAM SAM) (capacity 2 *Sea King* Mk41 hel)
AORL 6 *Elbe* (Type-404) with 1 hel landing platform (2 specified for PFM support; 1 specified for SSK support; 3 specified for MHO/MSO support);
ATF 3: 1 *Helgoland*; 2 *Wangerooge*
AXS 1 *Gorch Fock*

Naval Aviation 1,850

EQUIPMENT BY TYPE
AIRCRAFT 6 combat capable
ASW 6 AP-3C *Orion*
TPT • Light 2 Do-228 (pollution control)
HELICOPTERS
ASW 22 *Lynx* Mk88A
SAR 24: 11 *Sea King* Mk41; 13 NH90 NFH (*Sea Lion*)
UNINHABITED AERIAL VEHICLES • ISR • Light 2 *Skeldar* V-200 (*Sea Falcon*)

Naval Special Forces Command

FORCES BY ROLE
SPECIAL FORCES
1 SF coy

Sea Battalion

FORCES BY ROLE
MANOEUVRE
Amphibious
1 mne bn

Air Force 27,200

FORCES BY ROLE
FIGHTER
3 wg (2 sqn with Eurofighter *Typhoon*)
FIGHTER/GROUND ATTACK
1 wg (2 sqn with *Tornado* IDS)
1 wg (2 sqn with Eurofighter *Typhoon* (multi-role))
ISR
1 wg (1 ISR sqn with *Tornado* ECR/IDS; 2 UAV sqn with *Heron*)
TANKER/TRANSPORT
1 (special air mission) wg (3 sqn with A319; A321; A321LR; A340; A350; AS532U2 *Cougar* II; *Global* 5000; *Global* 6000)

TRANSPORT
1 wg (3 sqn (forming) with A400M *Atlas*)
1 sqn (joint FRA-GER) with C-130J-30 *Hercules*; KC-130J *Hercules*
TRAINING
1 sqn located at Holloman AFB (US) with *Tornado* IDS
1 unit (ENJJPT) located at Sheppard AFB (US) with T-6A *Texan* II; T-38C *Talon*
1 hel unit located at Fassberg
TRANSPORT HELICOPTER
1 tpt hel wg (3 sqn with CH-53G/GA/GE/GS *Stallion*; 1 sqn with H145M)
AIR DEFENCE
1 wg (3 SAM gp) with M902 *Patriot* PAC-3
1 AD gp with ASRAD *Ozelot*; C-RAM Mantis and trg unit
1 AD trg unit located at Fort Bliss (US) with MIM-104C/F *Patriot* PAC-2/3
3 (tac air ctrl) radar gp

Air Force Regiment

FORCES BY ROLE
MANOEUVRE
Other
1 sy regt
EQUIPMENT BY TYPE
AIRCRAFT 226 combat capable
FTR 138 Eurofighter *Typhoon*
ATK 68 *Tornado* IDS
ATK/EW 20 *Tornado* ECR*
ISR 1 A319CJ (Open Skies)
TPT 58: **Heavy** 38 A400M; **Medium** 3 C-130J-30 *Hercules*
PAX 16: 1 A321; 2 A321LR; 2 A340 (VIP); 2 A350 (VIP); 2 A319; 4 *Global* 5000; 3 *Global* 6000
TRG 109: 69 T-6A *Texan* II, 40 T-38C *Talon*
HELICOPTERS
MRH 16 H145M
TPT 73: **Heavy** 70 CH-53G/GA/GS/GE *Stallion*; **Medium** 3 AS532U2 *Cougar* II (VIP)
UNINHABITED AERIAL VEHICLES • ISR • Heavy 6 *Heron* 1
AIR DEFENCE
SAM 50
Long-range 30 M902 *Patriot* PAC-3
Point-defence 20 ASRAD *Ozelot* (with FIM-92 *Stinger*)
GUNS 35mm 12 C-RAM *Mantis*
AIR-LAUNCHED MISSILES
AAM • IR AIM-9L/Li *Sidewinder*; **IIR** IRIS-T; **ARH** AIM-120B AMRAAM
LACM Taurus KEPD 350
ARM AGM-88B HARM
BOMBS
Laser-guided GBU-24 *Paveway* III; GBU-48 Enhanced *Paveway* II
Laser & INS/GPS-guided GBU-54 Laser JDAM

Joint Support Service 27,900

FORCES BY ROLE
COMBAT SUPPORT
3 MP regt
2 NBC bn

COMBAT SERVICE SUPPORT
6 log bn
1 spt regt

EQUIPMENT BY TYPE
ARMOURED FIGHTING VEHICLES
AUV 451: 206 *Dingo* 2; 245 *Eagle* IV/V
ENGINEERING & MAINTENANCE VEHICLES
ARV 35: 23 BPz-2; 12 BPz-3 *Büffel*
NBC VEHICLES 35 TPz-1 *Fuchs* A6/A7/A8 NBC

Joint Medical Services 19,850
FORCES BY ROLE
COMBAT SERVICE SUPPORT
4 med regt

EQUIPMENT BY TYPE
ARMOURED FIGHTING VEHICLES
APC • APC (W) 109: 72 *Boxer* (amb); 37 TPz-1 *Fuchs* (amb)
AUV 42 *Eagle* IV/V (amb)

Cyber & Information Command 14,250
FORCES BY ROLE
COMBAT SUPPORT
4 EW bn
6 sigs bn

DEPLOYMENT

BALTIC SEA: NATO • SNMCMG 1: 100; 1 MHO; 1 AORL
BOSNIA-HERZEGOVINA: EU • EUFOR • *Operation Althea* 55
ESTONIA: NATO • Baltic Air Policing 150; 4 Eurofighter *Typhoon*
FRANCE: 400 (incl GER elm Eurocorps)
IRAQ: *Operation Inherent Resolve* 80; **NATO** • NATO Mission Iraq 15
JORDAN: *Operation Inherent Resolve* 150; 1 A400M
LEBANON: UN • UNIFIL 82; 1 FSGM
LITHUANIA: NATO • Enhanced Forward Presence 1,000; 1 mech inf bde HQ; 1 armd inf BG with *Leopard* 2A6; *Fennek*; *Marder* 1A3; *Boxer*
MALI: EU • EUTM Mali 55; **UN** • MINUSMA 490; 1 sy coy; 1 hel sqn with 5 CH-53G; 1 UAV sqn
MEDITERRANEAN SEA: NATO • SNMG 2: 40; 1 AOR
NIGER: *Operation Gazelle* 200 (trg)
POLAND: 95 (GER elm MNC-NE)
SERBIA: NATO • KFOR 68
SLOVAKIA: NATO • Enhanced Vigilance Activities 480; 1 inf coy; 1 SAM bty with M902 *Patriot* PAC-3
SOUTH SUDAN: UN • UNMISS 14
UNITED STATES: Trg units with 40 T-38 *Talon*; 69 T-6A *Texan* II at Goodyear AFB (AZ)/Sheppard AFB (TX); NAS Pensacola (FL); Fort Rucker (AL); Missile trg at Fort Bliss (TX)
WESTERN SAHARA: UN • MINURSO 4

FOREIGN FORCES

France 2,000; 1 (FRA/GER) mech bde (1 armd cav regt, 1 mech inf regt)
United Kingdom 185
United States
US Africa Command: Army; 1 HQ at Stuttgart
US European Command: 39,050; 1 combined service HQ (EUCOM) at Stuttgart-Vaihingen
Army 24,700; 1 HQ (US Army Europe & Africa (USAREUR-AF) at Wiesbaden; 1 arty comd; 1 SF gp; 1 recce bn; 1 mech bde(-); 1 fd arty bn; 1 MRL bde (3 MRL bn); 1 (cbt avn) hel bde; 1 (cbt avn) hel bde HQ; 1 int bde; 1 MP bde; 1 sigs bde; 1 spt bde; 1 (MDTF) cbt spt bde(-); 1 SAM bde; 2 (APS) armd bde eqpt set; M1A2 SEPv2/v3 *Abrams*; M3A3 *Bradley*; M2A3 *Bradley*; M1296 *Stryker Dragoon*; M109A6; M119A3; M777A2; M270A1; M142 HIMARS; AH-64D *Apache*; CH-47F *Chinook*; UH-60L/M *Black Hawk*; HH-60M *Black Hawk*; M902 *Patriot* PAC-3; M1097 *Avenger*; M-SHORAD
Navy 400
USAF 13,400; 1 HQ (US Air Forces Europe & Africa) at Ramstein AB; 1 HQ (3rd Air Force) at Ramstein AB; 1 FGA wg at Spangdahlem AB with (1 FGA sqn with 24 F-16C *Fighting Falcon*); 1 tpt wg at Ramstein AB with 14 C-130J-30 *Hercules*; 2 Gulfstream V (C-37A); 5 Learjet 35A (C-21A); 1 B-737-700 (C-40B)
USMC 550

Greece GRC

Euro EUR		2021	2022	2023
GDP	EUR	183bn	210bn	
	USD	216bn	222bn	
per capita	USD	20,263	20,876	
Growth	%	8.3	5.2	
Inflation	%	0.6	9.2	
Def exp [a]	EUR	6.76bn	7.45bn	
	USD	8.01bn	7.87bn	
Def bdgt [b]	EUR	6.50bn	7.44bn	5.25bn
	USD	7.69bn	7.87bn	
USD1=EUR		0.84	0.95	

[a] NATO figure
[b] Includes military pensions

Real-terms defence budget trend (USDbn, constant 2015)

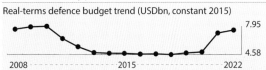

Population 10,533,871

Age	0–14	15–19	20–24	25–29	30–64	65 plus
Male	7.3%	2.8%	2.9%	2.8%	22.8%	10.2%
Female	6.9%	2.5%	2.5%	2.5%	24.1%	12.8%

Capabilities

Greece's 2014 National Military Strategy identifies safeguarding sovereignty and territorial integrity as principal defence objectives; in recent years there has been renewed focus on Eastern Mediterranean security. The armed forces would also be expected to support Cyprus in the event of a conflict. The Force Structure 2020-2034 document set out plans to increase military responsiveness and sustainability, which included the establishment of a special warfare command. Greece is a NATO member and has led the EU's Balkan Battlegroup. The port at Alexandroupoli has become a key hub for NATO members' moving military equipment for military exercises in southern Europe. There is close cooperation with the US. The Mutual Defense Cooperation Agreement, amended in 2022, is the cornerstone of US–Greece defence cooperation and provides for a naval-support facility and an airfield at Souda Bay in Crete. A strategic partnership was agreed with France in 2021 that includes a mutual-assistance clause. There are also defence-cooperation agreements with Cyprus, Egypt and Israel while ties are developing with the UAE and Saudi Arabia. The armed forces still contain conscripts but most personnel are regulars and Athens is looking to move to a fully professional force. Greece's deployments involve limited numbers of personnel and focus on the near abroad, although the country contributes to EU, NATO and UN missions. Athens is in the process of acquiring *Rafale* combat aircraft and frigates from France as part of a its defence partnership. F-16s are being upgraded. There has been significant investment in the new international flight training centre in Kalamata, reportedly run by Israel's Elbit systems. Greece hosts, and takes part in, a wide range of international exercises. There is an extensive defence industry focused on the domestic market, capable of manufacturing and developing naval vessels, subsystems, ammunition and small arms.

ACTIVE 132,200 (Army 93,500 Navy 16,700 Air 22,000) Gendarmerie & Paramilitary 4,000
Conscript liability 9 to 12 months

RESERVE 289,000 (Army 248,900 Navy 6,100 Air 34,000)

ORGANISATIONS BY SERVICE

Army 48,500; 45,000 conscripts (total 93,500)

FORCES BY ROLE
COMMAND
2 corps HQ (incl NRDC-GR)
1 armd div HQ
3 mech inf div HQ
1 inf div HQ
SPECIAL FORCES
1 SF comd
1 cdo/para bde
MANOEUVRE
Reconnaissance
4 recce bn
Armoured
4 armd bde (2 armd bn, 1 mech inf bn, 1 SP arty bn)
Mechanised
10 mech inf bde (1 armd bn, 2 mech bn, 1 SP arty bn)
Light
2 inf regt
Air Manoeuvre
1 air mob bde
1 air aslt bde
Amphibious
1 mne bde

COMBAT SUPPORT
2 MRL bn
3 AD bn (2 with I-*Hawk,* 1 with *Tor* M1)
3 engr regt
2 engr bn
1 EW regt
10 sigs bn
COMBAT SERVICE SUPPORT
1 log corps HQ
1 log div (3 log bde)
HELICOPTER
1 hel bde (1 hel regt with (2 atk hel bn), 2 tpt hel bn, 4 hel bn)

EQUIPMENT BY TYPE
ARMOURED FIGHTING VEHICLES
MBT 1,228: 170 *Leopard* 2A6HEL; 183 *Leopard* 2A4; 500 *Leopard* 1A4/5; 375 M48A5
IFV 175: up to 169 BMP-1; 6 *Marder* 1A3
APC • APC (T) 2,107: 74 *Leonidas* Mk1/2; 1,846 M113A1/A2; 187 M577 (CP)
AUV 596 M1117 *Guardian*; 242 VBL
ENGINEERING & MAINTENANCE VEHICLES
ARV 262: 12 *Büffel*; 43 BPz-2; 94 M88A1; 113 M578
VLB 52: 34 M48/M60 AVLB; 10 *Biber*; 8 *Leopard* 1 with *Leguan*
MW *Giant Viper*
ANTI-TANK/ANTI-INFRASTRUCTURE
MSL
SP 556: 195 HMMWV with 9K135 *Kornet*-E (RS-AT-14 *Spriggan*); 361 M901
MANPATS 9K111 *Fagot* (RS-AT-4 *Spigot*); *Milan*; TOW
RCL 687+: **84mm** *Carl Gustaf*; **90mm** EM-67; **SP 106mm** 687 M40A1
ARTILLERY 3,526
SP 599: **155mm** 442: 418 M109A1B/A2/A3GEA1/A5; 24 PzH 2000; **175mm** 12 M107; **203mm** 145 M110A2
TOWED 463: **105mm** 233: 214 M101; 19 M-56; **155mm** 230 M114
MRL 144: **122mm** 108 RM-70; **227mm** 36 M270 MLRS
MOR 2,320: **81mm** 1,700; **107mm** 620 M30 (incl 231 SP)
SURFACE-TO-SURFACE MISSILE LAUNCHERS
SRBM • Conventional MGM-140A ATACMS (launched from M270 MLRS)
AIRCRAFT • TPT • Light 12: 1 Beech 200 *King Air* (C-12C) 2 Beech 200 *King Air* (C-12R/AP *Huron*); 9 Cessna 185 (U-17A/B)
HELICOPTERS
ATK 28: 19 AH-64A *Apache*; 9 AH-64D *Apache*
MRH 60 OH-58D *Kiowa Warrior*
TPT 127: **Heavy** 25: 19 CH-47D *Chinook*; 6 CH-47SD *Chinook*; **Medium** 14 NH90 TTH; **Light** 88: 74 Bell 205 (UH-1H *Iroquois*); 14 Bell 206 (AB-206) *Jet Ranger*
UNINHABITED AERIAL VEHICLES
ISR • Medium 4 *Sperwer*
AIR DEFENCE
SAM 155+
Medium-range 42 MIM-23B I-*Hawk*
Short-range 21 9K331 *Tor*-M1 (RS-SA-15 *Gauntlet*)
Point-range 92+: 38 9K33 *Osa*-M (RS-SA-8B *Gecko*); 54 ASRAD HMMWV; FIM-92 *Stinger*
GUNS • TOWED 727: **20mm** 204 Rh 202; **23mm** 523 ZU-23-2

National Guard 38,000 reservists

Internal security role

FORCES BY ROLE
MANOEUVRE
Light
1 inf div
Air Manoeuvre
1 para regt
COMBAT SUPPORT
8 arty bn
4 AD bn
HELICOPTER
1 hel bn

Navy 14,300; 2,400 conscript (total 16,700)

EQUIPMENT BY TYPE
SUBMARINES • SSK 10:
3 *Poseidon* (GER Type-209/1200) with 8 single 533mm TT with SUT HWT
1 *Poseidon* (GER Type-209/1200) (fitted with AIP technology) with 8 single 533mm TT with UGM-84C *Harpoon* Block 1B AShM/SUT HWT
2 *Glavkos* (GER Type-209/1100) with 8 single 533mm TT with UGM-84C *Harpoon* Block 1B AShM/SUT HWT
4 *Papanikolis* (GER Type-214) (fitted with AIP) with 8 single 533mm TT with UGM-84C *Harpoon* Block 1B AShM/SUT HWT
PRINCIPAL SURFACE COMBATANTS 13
FRIGATES • FFGHM 13:
4 *Elli* Batch I (ex-NLD *Kortenaer* Batch 2) with 2 quad lnchr with RGM-84C/G *Harpoon* Block 1B/G AShM, 1 octuple Mk 29 GMLS with RIM-7M/P *Sea Sparrow* SAM, 2 twin 324mm SVTT Mk 32 mod 9 ASTT with Mk 46 mod 5 LWT, 1 Mk 15 *Phalanx* CIWS, 1 76mm gun (capacity 2 Bell 212 (AB-212) hel or 1 S-70B *Seahawk* hel)
2 *Elli* Batch II (ex-NLD *Kortenaer* Batch 2) with 2 quad lnchr with RGM-84C/G *Harpoon* Block 1B/G AShM, 1 octuple Mk 29 GMLS with RIM-7M/P *Sea Sparrow* SAM, 2 twin 324mm SVTT Mk 32 mod 9 ASTT with Mk 46 mod 5 LWT, 1 Mk 15 *Phalanx* CIWS, 2 76mm gun (capacity 2 Bell 212 (AB-212) hel or 1 S-70B *Seahawk* hel)
3 *Elli* Batch III (ex-NLD *Kortenaer* Batch 2) with 2 quad lnchr with RGM-84C/G *Harpoon* Block 1B/G AShM, 1 octuple Mk 29 lnchr with RIM-7P *Sea Sparrow* SAM, 2 twin 324mm SVTT Mk 32 mod 9 ASTT with Mk 46 LWT, 1 Mk 15 *Phalanx* CIWS, 1 76mm gun (capacity 2 Bell 212 (AB-212) hel)
4 *Hydra* (GER MEKO 200) with 2 quad lnchr with RGM-84G *Harpoon* Block 1G AShM, 1 16-cell Mk 48 mod 2 VLS with RIM-162C ESSM SAM, 2 triple 324mm SVTT Mk 32 mod 5 ASTT with Mk 46 LWT, 2 Mk 15 *Phalanx* CIWS, 1 127mm gun (capacity 1 S-70B *Seahawk* ASW hel)
PATROL AND COASTAL COMBATANTS 36
PCGM 7 *Roussen* (*Super Vita*) with 2 quad lnchr with MM40 *Exocet* Block 3 AShM (of which 2 still fitted with Block 2), 1 21-cell Mk 49 GMLS with RIM-116 RAM SAM, 1 76mm gun

PCFG 10:
5 *Kavaloudis* (FRA *La Combattante* IIIB) with 2 twin lnchr with RGM-84C *Harpoon* Block 1B AShM, 2 single 533mm TT with SST-4 HWT, 2 76mm gun
4 *Laskos* (FRA *La Combattante* III) with 2 twin lnchr with RGM-84C *Harpoon* Block 1B AShM, 2 single 533mm TT with SST-4 HWT, 2 76mm gun
1 *Votsis* (ex-GER *Tiger*) with 2 twin lnchr with RGM-84C *Harpoon* AShM, 1 76mm gun
PCF 1 *Votsis* (ex-GER *Tiger*) with 1 76mm gun
PCO 8:
2 *Armatolos* (DNK *Osprey*) with 1 76mm gun
2 *Kasos* (DNK *Osprey* derivative) with 1 76mm gun
4 *Machitis* with 1 76mm gun
PBF 4 *Aeolos* (ex-US Mk V FPB)
PB 6: 3 *Andromeda* (NOR *Nasty*); 2 *Stamou*; 1 *Tolmi*
MINE WARFARE • MINE COUNTERMEASURES 3
MHO 3: 1 *Evropi* (ex-UK *Hunt*); 2 *Evniki* (ex-US *Osprey*)
AMPHIBIOUS
LANDING SHIPS • LST 5 *Chios* (capacity 4 LCVP; 300 troops) with 1 76mm gun, 1 hel landing platform
LANDING CRAFT 15
LCU 5
LCA 7
LCAC 3 *Kefallinia* (*Zubr*) with 2 AK630 CIWS (capacity either 3 MBT or 10 APC (T); 230 troops)
LOGISTICS AND SUPPORT 27
ABU 2
AG 5: 3 *Atlas* I; 2 *Pandora*
AGOR 1 *Naftilos*
AGS 2: 1 *Stravon*; 1 *Pytheas*
AORH 1 *Prometheus* (ITA *Etna*) with 1 Mk 15 *Phalanx* CIWS
AORL 1 *Axios* (ex-GER *Luneburg*)
AOT 4 *Ouranos*
AWT 6 *Kerkini*
AXS 5

Coastal Defence

EQUIPMENT BY TYPE
COASTAL DEFENCE • AShM 2 MM40 *Exocet*

Naval Aviation

FORCES BY ROLE
ANTI-SUBMARINE WARFARE
1 div with S-70B *Seahawk*; Bell 212 (AB-212) ASW

EQUIPMENT BY TYPE
AIRCRAFT 1 combat capable
ASW 1 P-3B *Orion* (4 P-3B *Orion* in store undergoing modernisation)
HELICOPTERS
ASW 14: 3 Bell 212 (AB-212) ASW; 11 S-70B *Seahawk*
AIR-LAUNCHED MISSILES
ASM AGM-114 *Hellfire*
AShM AGM-119 *Penguin*

Air Force 18,800; 3,000 conscripts (total 21,800)

Tactical Air Force

FORCES BY ROLE
FIGHTER/GROUND ATTACK
1 sqn with F-4E *Phantom* II

3 sqn with F-16CG/DG Block 30/50 *Fighting Falcon*
2 sqn with F-16CG/DG Block 52+ *Fighting Falcon*
1 sqn with F-16CG/DG Block 52+ *Fighting Falcon*;
F-16V(C/D) *Viper*
2 sqn with F-16C/D Block 52+ ADV *Fighting Falcon*
1 sqn with *Mirage* 2000-5EG/BG Mk2
1 sqn with *Mirage* 2000EG/BG; *Rafale* B/C F-3R

AIRBORNE EARLY WARNING
1 sqn with EMB-145H *Erieye*

EQUIPMENT BY TYPE
AIRCRAFT 240 combat capable
FGA 240: 34 F-4E *Phantom* II; 69 F-16CG/DG Block 30/50 *Fighting Falcon*; 55 F-16CG/DG Block 52+; 28 F-16C/D Block 52+ ADV *Fighting Falcon*; 2 F-16V(C/D) *Viper*; 19 *Mirage* 2000-5EG Mk2; 5 *Mirage* 2000-5BG Mk2; 16 *Mirage* 2000EG; 2 *Mirage* 2000BG; 2 *Rafale* B F3-R; 8 *Rafale* C F3-R
AEW 4 EMB-145AEW (EMB-145H) *Erieye*
AIR-LAUNCHED MISSILES
AAM • IR AIM-9L/P *Sidewinder*; R-550 *Magic* 2;
IIR IRIS-T; *Mica* IR; **ARH** AIM-120B/C AMRAAM; *Mica* RF
ASM AGM-65A/B/G *Maverick*
LACM SCALP EG
AShM AM39 *Exocet*
ARM AGM-88 HARM
BOMBS
Electro-optical guided: GBU-8B HOBOS
Laser-guided: GBU-10/12/16 *Paveway* II; GBU-24 *Paveway* III; GBU-50 Enhanced *Paveway* II
INS/GPS-guided GBU-31 JDAM; AGM-154C JSOW

Air Defence
FORCES BY ROLE
AIR DEFENCE
6 sqn/bty with M901 *Patriot* PAC-2
2 sqn/bty with S-300PMU1 (RS-SA-20 *Gargoyle*)
12 bty with *Skyguard*/RIM-7 *Sparrow*/guns; *Crotale* NG/GR; *Tor*-M1 (RS-SA-15 *Gauntlet*)

EQUIPMENT BY TYPE
AIR DEFENCE
SAM 81
Long-range 48: 36 M901 *Patriot* PAC-2; 12 S-300PMU1 (RS-SA-20 *Gargoyle*)
Short-range 33: 9 *Crotale* NG/GR; 4 9K331 *Tor*-M1 (RS-SA-15 *Gauntlet*); 20 RIM-7M *Sparrow* with *Skygaurd*
GUNS 59: **20mm** some Rh-202; **30mm** 35+ *Artemis*-30; **35mm** 24 GDF-005 with *Skyguard*

Air Support Command
FORCES BY ROLE
SEARCH & RESCUE/TRANSPORT HELICOPTER
1 sqn with AS332C *Super Puma* (SAR/CSAR)
1 sqn with AW109; Bell 205A (AB-205A) (SAR); Bell 212 (AB-212 - VIP, tpt)
TRANSPORT
1 sqn with C-27J *Spartan*
1 sqn with C-130B/H *Hercules*
1 sqn with EMB-135BJ *Legacy*; ERJ-135LR; *Falcon* 7X; Gulfstream V

EQUIPMENT BY TYPE
AIRCRAFT
TPT 27: **Medium** 23: 8 C-27J *Spartan*; 5 C-130B *Hercules*; 10 C-130H *Hercules*; **Light** 2: 1 EMB-135BJ *Legacy*; 1 ERJ-135LR; **PAX** 2: 1 *Falcon* 7X (VIP); 1 Gulfstream V
HELICOPTERS
TPT 31: **Medium** 12 AS332C *Super Puma*; **Light** 19: 12 Bell 205A (AB-205A) (SAR); 4 Bell 212 (AB-212) (VIP, Tpt); 3 AW109

Air Training Command
FORCES BY ROLE
TRAINING
2 sqn with T-2C/E *Buckeye*
2 sqn with T-6A/B *Texan* II
1 sqn with P2002JF; T-41D

EQUIPMENT BY TYPE
AIRCRAFT • TRG 103: 12 P2002JF; 28 T-2C/E *Buckeye*; 20 T-6A *Texan* II; 25 T-6B *Texan* II; 18 T-41D

Gendarmerie & Paramilitary

Coast Guard and Customs 4,000
EQUIPMENT BY TYPE
PATROL AND COASTAL COMBATANTS 124
PCO 1 *Gavdos* (Damen 5009)
PCC 3
PBF 54
PB 66
AIRCRAFT • TPT • Light 4: 2 Cessna 172RG *Cutlass*; 2 TB-20 *Trinidad*
HELICOPTERS • SAR 3 AS365N3

DEPLOYMENT

BOSNIA-HERZEGOVINA: EU • EUFOR (*Operation Althea*) 7
BULGARIA: NATO • Enhanced Vigilance Activities 30; 1 AT pl with M901
CYPRUS: Army 950; 1 mech bde (1 armd bn, 2 mech inf bn, 1 arty bn); 61 M48A5 MOLF MBT; 80 *Leonidas* APC; 12 M114 arty; 6 M110A2 arty
IRAQ: NATO • NATO Mission Iraq 2
LEBANON: UN • UNIFIL 109; 1 FFGHM
MALI: EU • EUTM Mali 2
MEDITERRANEAN SEA: EU • EUNAVFOR MED • *Operation Irini*; 190; 1 FFGHM
MOZAMBIQUE: EU • EUTM Mozambique 8
SAUDI ARABIA: Air Force 100; 1 SAM bty with M901 *Patriot* PAC-2
SERBIA: NATO • KFOR 113; 1 inf coy

FOREIGN FORCES

United States US European Command: 400; 1 ELINT flt with 1 EP-3E *Aries* II; 1 naval base at Makri; 1 naval base at Souda Bay; 1 air base at Iraklion

Hungary HUN

Hungarian Forint HUF		2021	2022	2023
GDP	HUF	55.3tr	62.9tr	
	USD	182bn	185bn	
per capita	USD	18,732	18,983	
Growth	%	7.1	5.7	
Inflation	%	5.1	13.9	
Def exp [a]	HUF	928bn	958bn	
	USD	3.06bn	2.81bn	
Def bdgt [b]	HUF	794bn	1.02tr	1.58tr
	USD	2.62bn	2.99bn	
USD1=HUF		303.14	340.84	

[a] NATO figure
[b] Includes military pensions

Real-terms defence budget trend (USDbn, constant 2015)

Population 9,699,577

Age	0–14	15–19	20–24	25–29	30–64	65 plus
Male	7.4%	2.7%	2.7%	3.0%	23.6%	8.3%
Female	7.0%	2.5%	2.5%	2.9%	24.2%	13.2%

Capabilities

Hungary published a new National Security Strategy in April 2020 and a new National Military Strategy in June 2021. The strategy documents speak of a deteriorating security environment, marked by great-power competition and an increasing military component. The security strategy also characterises mass migration as a key concern for Hungary. Hungary is implementing the Zrinyi 2026 national-defence and armed-forces modernisation plan. Second editions of the doctrines on SOF, CBRN and CIMIC were published in 2021. A new Cyber- and Information Operations Centre was established in January 2022, and a Military Cyberspace Operations Doctrine was published in 2022. A doctrine for NEO operations is expected in 2023. Hungary coordinates policy with other member states of the Visegrád Group, including on defence, and hosts the NATO Centre of Excellence for Military Medicine. The armed forces participate in international crisis-management missions, notably in the Balkans and Iraq, but have very limited organic capacity to deploy forces beyond national borders. Announced equipment-modernisation priorities focus on individual-soldier equipment and fixed- and rotary-wing aircraft. While the air-force-related elements of Zrinyi 2026 had been a focus of attention, and current air procurements include transport and trainer aircraft, at the end of 2018 the ministry also initiated land procurements, including for main battle tanks (Leopard 2A7), Lynx IFVs and PzH2000 self-propelled artillery. PzH 2000 deliveries began in mid-2022. Hungary's defence-industrial base is limited, though the defence ministry has set up an inter-ministerial working group to boost domestic capacity in the small-arms sector. In 2020, a new defence procurement agency, reporting to the national armaments director, began its work and is intended to coordinate defence and security acquisitions.

ACTIVE 32,150 (Army 10,450 Air 5,750 Joint 15,950)
RESERVE 20,000

ORGANISATIONS BY SERVICE

Hungary's armed forces have reorganised into a joint force

Land Component 10,450 (incl riverine element)

FORCES BY ROLE
SPECIAL FORCES
  1 SF bde (4 spec ops bn)
MANOEUVRE
  Reconnaissance
  1 ISR regt
  Mechanised
  1 (5th) mech inf bde (3 mech inf bn, 1 cbt engr coy,
    1 sigs coy, 1 log bn)
  1 (25th) mech inf bde (1 tk bn; 2 mech inf bn, 1 arty bn,
    1 AT bn, 1 log bn)
COMBAT SUPPORT
  1 engr regt
  1 EOD/rvn regt
  1 CBRN bn
  1 sigs regt
COMBAT SERVICE SUPPORT
  1 log regt

EQUIPMENT BY TYPE
ARMOURED FIGHTING VEHICLES
  MBT 56: 12 Leopard 2A4HU; 44 T-72M1
  IFV 121: 120 BTR-80A/AM; 1 KF41 Lynx (in test)
  APC 322
    APC (W) 260 BTR-80
    PPV 62: 50 Ejder Yalcin 4×4 (Gidran); 12 MaxxPro Plus
ENGINEERING & MAINTENANCE VEHICLES
  AEV 5 BAT-2
  ARV 9: 1 BPz-3 Buffel; 8 VT-55A
  VLB 8 BLG-60; MTU; TMM
NBC VEHICLES 14 BTR-80M-NBC
ANTI-TANK/ANTI-INFRASTRUCTURE
  MSL • MANPATS 9K111 Fagot (RS-AT-4 Spigot); 9K111-1 Konkurs (RS-AT-5 Spandrel)
ARTILLERY 33
  SP 155mm 2 PzH 2000
  TOWED 152mm 31 D-20
  MOR 82mm
PATROL AND COASTAL COMBATANTS • PBR 4
MINE COUNTERMEASURES • MSR 3 Nestin

Air Component 5,750

FORCES BY ROLE

FIGHTER/GROUND ATTACK
  1 sqn with *Gripen* C/D

TRANSPORT
  1 sqn with A319; *Falcon* 7X

TRAINING
  1 sqn with Z-143LSi; Z-242L; AS350 *Ecureuil*

ATTACK HELICOPTER
  1 sqn with Mi-24V/P *Hind* E/F

TRANSPORT HELICOPTER
  1 sqn with H145M

AIR DEFENCE
  1 SAM regt (9 bty with *Mistral*; 3 bty with 2K12 *Kub* (RS-SA-6 *Gainful*))
  1 radar regt

EQUIPMENT BY TYPE

AIRCRAFT 14 combat capable
  FGA 14: 12 *Gripen* C; 2 *Gripen* D
  TPT • **PAX** 4: 2 A319; 2 *Falcon* 7X
  TRG 8: 2 Z-143LSi; 6 Z-242L

HELICOPTERS
  ATK 8: 6 Mi-24V *Hind* E; 2 Mi-24P *Hind* F
  MRH 20 H145M (incl 2 SAR)
  TPT • **Light** 2 AS350 *Ecureuil*

AIR DEFENCE
  SAM • **Point-defence** 16 2K12 *Kub* (RS-SA-6 *Gainful*); *Mistral*

AIR-LAUNCHED MISSILES
  AAM • **IR** AIM-9 *Sidewinder*; **ARH** AIM-120C AMRAAM
  ASM AGM-65 *Maverick*; 3M11 *Falanga* (RS-AT-2 *Swatter*); 9K114 *Shturm*-V (RS-AT-6 *Spiral*)
  BOMBS • **Laser-guided** *Paveway* II

DEPLOYMENT

BOSNIA-HERZEGOVINA: EU • *Operation Althea* 192; 1 inf coy

CYPRUS: UN • UNFICYP 13

IRAQ: *Operation Inherent Resolve* 133; **NATO** • NATO Mission Iraq 3

LEBANON: UN • UNIFIL 16

LITHUANA: **NATO** • Baltic Air Policing; 80; 4 *Gripen* C

MALI: EU • EUTM Mali 20

SERBIA: **NATO** • KFOR 469; 1 inf coy (KTM)

WESTERN SAHARA: UN • MINURSO 6

FOREIGN FORCES

Croatia NATO Enhanced Vigilance Activities: 60
United States NATO Enhanced Vigilance Activities: 150; 1 armd inf coy

Iceland ISL

Icelandic Krona ISK		2021	2022	2023
GDP	ISK	3.25tr	3.68tr	
	USD	25.6bn	27.7bn	
per capita	USD	69,422	73,981	
Growth	%	4.4	5.1	
Inflation	%	4.5	8.4	
Sy Bdgt [a]	ISK	5.53bn	5.56bn	5.58bn
	USD	43.5m	41.8m	
USD1=ISK		126.99	133.02	

[a] Coast Guard budget

Real-terms defence budget trend (USDm, constant 2015)

Population 357,603

Age	0–14	15–19	20–24	25–29	30–64	65 plus
Male	10.3%	3.2%	3.2%	3.5%	22.3%	7.7%
Female	9.9%	3.1%	3.2%	3.4%	21.9%	8.5%

Capabilities

Iceland is a NATO member but maintains only a coastguard service. In 2016, the country established a National Security Council to implement and monitor security policy. The Coast Guard controls the NATO Iceland Air Defence System, as well as a NATO Control and Reporting Centre that feeds into NATO air- and missile defence and air-operations centres. Increased Russian air and naval activities in the Atlantic and close to NATO airspace have led to complaints from Iceland. Iceland considers its bilateral defence agreement with the US as an important pillar of its security policy and also participates in the security-policy dialogue of NORDEFCO. Iceland joined the UK-led Joint Expeditionary Force in 2021. Iceland hosts NATO and regional partners for exercises, transits and naval task groups, as well as a NATO Icelandic Air Policing mission. Despite there being no standing armed forces, Iceland makes financial contributions and on occasion deploys civilian personnel to NATO missions. Iceland hosts US Navy P-8A *Poseidon* maritime patrol aircraft, in a rotational deployment based at Keflavik air base.

ACTIVE NIL Gendarmerie & Paramilitary 250

ORGANISATIONS BY SERVICE

Gendarmerie & Paramilitary

Iceland Coast Guard 250

EQUIPMENT BY TYPE
PATROL AND COASTAL COMBATANTS 2
  PSO 2: 1 *Freyja*; 1 *Thor*
LOGISTICS AND SUPPORT • **AGS** 1 *Baldur*
AIRCRAFT • **TPT** • **Light** 1 DHC-8-300 (MP)
HELICOPTERS • **TPT** • **Medium** 3 H225 (leased)

FOREIGN FORCES

Icelandic Air Policing: Aircraft and personnel from various NATO members on a rotating basis
United States 100; 2 P-8A *Poseidon*

Ireland IRL

Euro EUR		2021	2022	2023
GDP	EUR	426bn	492bn	
	USD	505bn	520bn	
per capita	USD	100,129	102,217	
Growth	%	13.6	9.0	
Inflation	%	2.4	8.4	
Def bdgt [a]	EUR	1.07bn	1.11bn	1.17bn
	USD	1.27bn	1.17bn	
USD1=EUR		0.84	0.95	

[a] Includes military pensions and capital expenditure

Real-terms defence budget trend (USDbn, constant 2015)

Population	5,275,004				
Age	0–14	15–19	20–24	25–29	30–64	65 plus
Male	10.6%	3.2%	3.0%	2.9%	23.5%	6.6%
Female	10.1%	3.1%	3.0%	2.9%	23.3%	7.7%

Capabilities

The armed forces' core mission is defending the state against armed aggression. A 2015 White Paper broadened the scope of the national-security risk assessment beyond military and paramilitary threats, noting inter- and intra-state conflict, cyber-attacks, terrorism, emergencies and natural disasters, among others. A White Paper update was issued in 2019 and Ireland's next strategy document is intended be a Strategic Defence Review. Ireland is active in EU defence cooperation and continues to contribute to multinational operations. A Commission on the Defence Forces report, published in February 2022, looked to address immediate requirements and set a longer-term vision beyond 2030. In July, the government decided to move to 'Level of Ambition 2', as set out in the Commission's capability framework. This will build on 'current capability to address specific priority gaps in [Ireland's] ability to deal with an assault on Irish sovereignty and to serve in higher intensity Peace Support Operations.' Spending will rise and personnel numbers are to increase by 2,000 above the current establishment. A High Level Action Plan detailed government responses to recommendations in the Commission report and an implementation report was expected by end-2022. The Commission recommended the creation of a Chief of Defence post and that the air corps and naval service become services on a level with the army. Early actions for late 2022 include planning for military radar capabilities, including primary radar and the establishment of an Office of Reserve Affairs intended to develop a regeneration plan for the Reserve Defence Force. A 2020–24 Equipment Development Plan indicated priorities including a mid-life upgrade for *Piranha* armoured personnel carriers and the two *Roisin*-class offshore patrol ships. Other stated priorities include the procurement of two C295 maritime patrol aircraft and upgrades to the 84mm anti-tank system. In 2023, the country will receive two ex-New Zealand coastal patrol craft to replace decommissioned vessels. Ireland has a small, specialist defence industry focused on areas including drivetrain technologies for land systems.

ACTIVE 8,200 (Army 6,750 Navy 750 Air 700)

RESERVE 1,600 (Army 1,450 Navy 150)

ORGANISATIONS BY SERVICE

Army 6,750

FORCES BY ROLE
SPECIAL FORCES
1 ranger coy
MANOEUVRE
Reconnaissance
1 armd recce sqn
Mechanised
1 mech inf coy
Light
1 inf bde (1 cav recce sqn, 4 inf bn, 1 arty regt (3 fd arty bty, 1 AD bty), 1 fd engr coy, 1 sigs coy, 1 MP coy, 1 tpt coy)
1 inf bde (1 cav recce sqn, 3 inf bn, 1 arty regt (3 fd arty bty, 1 AD bty), 1 fd engr coy, 1 sigs coy, 1 MP coy, 1 tpt coy)
EQUIPMENT BY TYPE
ARMOURED FIGHTING VEHICLES
RECCE 6 *Piranha* IIIH 30mm
APC 101
APC (W) 74: 56 *Piranha* III; 18 *Piranha* IIIH
PPV 27 RG-32M
ANTI-TANK/ANTI-INFRASTURCTURE
MSL • MANPATS FGM-148 *Javelin*
RCL 84mm *Carl Gustaf*
ARTILLERY 131
TOWED • 105mm 23: 17 L118 Light Gun; 6 L119 Light Gun
MOR 108: 81mm 84 Brandt; 120mm 24 Ruag M87
AIR DEFENCE
SAM • Point-defence RBS-70

Reserves 1,400 reservists

FORCES BY ROLE
MANOEUVRE
Reconnaissance
1 (integrated) armd recce sqn
2 (integrated) cav sqn
Mechanised
1 (integrated) mech inf coy
Light
14 (integrated) inf coy
COMBAT SUPPORT
4 (integrated) arty bty
2 engr gp
2 MP coy
3 sigs coy
COMBAT SERVICE SUPPORT
2 med det
2 tpt coy

Naval Service 750

EQUIPMENT BY TYPE
PATROL AND COASTAL COMBATANTS 6
PSO 6: 2 *Roisin* (of which 1 in refit) with 1 76mm gun; 4 *Samuel Beckett* with 1 76mm gun
LOGISTICS AND SUPPORT • AXS 2

Air Corps 700

2 ops wg; 2 spt wg; 1 trg wg; 1 comms and info sqn

EQUIPMENT BY TYPE
AIRCRAFT
  MP 2 CN235 MPA
  TPT • Light 5: 1 Learjet 45 (VIP); 4 PC-12NG
  TRG 8 PC-9M
HELICOPTERS:
  MRH 6 AW139
  TPT • Light 2 H135 (incl trg/medevac)

DEPLOYMENT

BOSNIA-HERZEGOVINA: EU • EUFOR (*Operation Althea*) 5

LEBANON: UN • UNIFIL 338; 1 mech inf bn(-)

MALI: EU • EUTM Mali 20; UN • MINUMSA 12

MIDDLE EAST: UN • UNTSO 12

SERBIA: NATO • KFOR 13

SYRIA/ISRAEL: UN • UNDOF 130; 1 inf coy

Italy ITA

Euro EUR		2021	2022	2023
GDP	EUR	1.78tr	1.89tr	
	USD	2.10tr	2.00tr	
per capita	USD	35,473	33,740	
Growth	%	6.6	3.2	
Inflation	%	1.9	8.7	
Def exp [a]	EUR	28.0bn	28.8bn	
	USD	33.2bn	30.4bn	
Def bdgt [b]	EUR	28.3bn	29.4bn	27.9bn
	USD	33.5bn	31.1bn	
USD1=EUR		0.84	0.95	

[a] NATO figure
[b] Includes military pensions

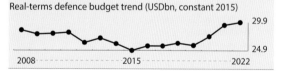
Real-terms defence budget trend (USDbn, constant 2015)

Population	61,095,551					
Age	0–14	15–19	20–24	25–29	30–64	65 plus
Male	6.3%	2.4%	2.4%	2.6%	24.4%	10.1%
Female	6.0%	2.4%	2.4%	2.6%	25.4%	12.9%

Capabilities

Italy is concerned by security challenges in the Euro-Atlantic environment, as well as from Europe's southern flank. A defence White Paper was issued in 2015. The latest three-year defence plan for 2022–24 outlined modernisation goals. Command structure reforms are intended to improve cross-domain command and control. In July 2021, Italy issued its first directive for defence industrial policy. Italy has taken part in NATO's air-policing missions in the Baltic states, Iceland and Romania and since early 2017 has deployed to Latvia as part of the Enhanced Forward Presence. The EUNAVFOR-MED force is headquartered in Rome, while the US Navy 6th Fleet is based in Naples. The country takes part in and hosts NATO and other multinational exercises, continues to support NATO, EU and UN operations abroad and is planning to increasingly focus on Europe's southern flank. Force mobility is enabled by a fleet of medium transport aircraft and tankers, and there are plans to procure fixed-wing aircraft to support special forces. The White Paper and the latest multi-year planning document detailed upgrades to main battle tanks and infantry fighting vehicles as well as the procurement of armoured fighting vehicles to replace the *Dardo* and the M113s. The expected retirement of much of the naval fleet has triggered a long-term replacement plan which includes the acquisition of two attack submarines and two next-generation destroyers to replace the ageing *Luigi Durand de la Penne*-class vessels as well as eight new offshore patrol vessels. F-35As have been ordered for the air force and F-35Bs for both the air force and naval aviation, some of which have been already delivered. Italy signed a MoU with UK and Sweden relating to the development of the UK-led *Tempest* programme and in 2022 increased the funds allocated for the project. Italy takes part in European defence-industrial cooperation activities, including PESCO projects, and has an advanced defence industry capable of producing equipment across all domains. There are particular strengths in shipbuilding and in aircraft and helicopter manufacturing. The country hosts Europe's F-35 final assembly and check-out facility at Cameri.

ACTIVE 161,050 (Army 93,100 Navy 28,700 Air 39,250) **Gendarmerie & Paramilitary 176,100**

RESERVES 17,900 (Army 13,400 Navy 4,500)

ORGANISATIONS BY SERVICE

Space
EQUIPMENT BY TYPE
SATELLITES 8
  COMMUNICATIONS 3: 1 *Athena-Fidus* (also used by FRA); 2 *Sicral*
  ISR 7: 4 *Cosmo* (*Skymed*); 2 *Cosmo* SG; 1 OPTSAT-3000

Army 93,100
Regt are bn sized
FORCES BY ROLE
COMMAND
  1 (NRDC-ITA) corps HQ (1 spt bde, 1 sigs regt, 1 spt regt)
MANOEUVRE
  Mechanised
  1 (*Vittorio Veneto*) div (1 (*Ariete*) armd bde (1 cav regt, 2 tk regt, 1 armd inf regt, 1 SP arty regt, 1 cbt engr regt, 1 log regt); 1 (*Pozzuolo del Friuli*) amph bde (1 cav regt, 1 amph regt, 1 arty regt, 1 cbt engr regt, 1 log regt); 1 (*Folgore*) AB bde (1 cav regt, 3 para regt, 1 arty regt, 1 cbt engr regt, 1 log regt); 1 (*Friuli*) air mob bde (1 air mob regt, 2 atk hel regt))
  1 (*Acqui*) div (1 (*Pinerolo*) mech bde (1 cav regt, 3 armd inf regt, 1 fd arty regt, 1 cbt engr regt, 1 log regt); 1 (*Granatieri*) mech bde (1 cav regt, 2 mech inf regt); 1 (*Garibaldi Bersaglieri*) mech bde (1 cav regt, 1 tk regt, 2 armd inf regt, 1 SP arty regt, 1 cbt engr regt, 1 log regt); 1 (*Aosta*) mech bde (1 cav regt, 1 armd inf regt, 2 mech inf regt, 1 fd arty regt, 1 cbt engr regt, 1 log regt); 1 (*Sassari*) lt

mech bde (1 armd inf regt, 2 mech inf regt, 1 cbt engr regt, 1 log regt))

Mountain

1 (*Tridentina*) mtn div (2 mtn bde (1 cav regt, 3 mtn inf regt, 1 arty regt, 1 mtn cbt engr regt, 1 spt bn, 1 log regt))

COMBAT SUPPORT

1 arty comd (1 arty regt, 1 MRL regt, 1 NBC regt)

1 AD comd (3 SAM regt)

1 engr comd (2 engr regt, 1 ptn br regt)

1 EW/sigs comd (1 EW/ISR bde (1 CIMIC regt, 1 EW regt, 1 int regt, 1 STA regt); 1 sigs bde with (7 sigs regt))

COMBAT SERVICE SUPPORT

1 log comd (3 log regt, 4 med unit)

HELICOPTER

1 hel bde (3 hel regt)

EQUIPMENT BY TYPE

ARMOURED FIGHTING VEHICLES

MBT 150: 149 C1 *Ariete*; 1 C1 *Ariete* AMV (in test)

ASLT 262: 255 B1 *Centauro*; 7 *Centauro* II

IFV 434: 165 VCC-80 *Dardo*; 269 VBM 8×8 *Freccia* (incl 20 CP and 44 with *Spike*-LR)

APC 380

APC (T) 148 Bv-206S

APC (W) 199 *Puma* 6×6

PPV 33 VTMM *Orso* (incl 16 amb)

AUV 1,842: 10 *Cougar*; 1,798 IVECO LMV (incl 82 amb); 34 IVECO LMV 2

AAV 15: 14 AAVP-7; 1 AAVC-7

ENGINEERING & MAINTENANCE VEHICLES

AEV 25 *Dachs*; M113

ARV 70: 69 BPz-2; 1 AAVR-7

VLB 30 *Biber*

MW 34: 6 *Buffalo*; 3 *Miniflail*; 25 VTMM *Orso*

NBC VEHICLES 14: 5 VBR NBC; 9 VBR NBC Plus

ANTI-TANK/ANTI-INFRASTRUCTURE

MSL • MANPATS *Spike*

ARTILLERY 769

SP 155mm 67 PzH 2000

TOWED 173: **105mm** 25 Oto Melara Mod 56; **155mm** 148 FH-70

MRL 227mm 21 M270 MLRS

MOR 508: **81mm** 283 Expal; **120mm** 204: 62 Brandt; 142 RT-61 (RT-F1) **SP 120mm** 21 VBM 8×8 *Freccia*

AIRCRAFT • TPT • Light 6: 3 Do-228 (ACTL-1); 3 P.180 *Avanti*

HELICOPTERS

ATK 35 AW129CBT *Mangusta*

MRH 14 Bell 412 (AB-412) *Twin Huey*

TPT 144: **Heavy** 16 CH-47F *Chinook*; **Medium** 56 NH90 TTH (UH-90A); **Light** 72: 2 AW169LUH (UH-169B); 29 Bell 205 (AB-205); 28 Bell 206 *Jet Ranger* (AB-206); 13 Bell 212 (AB-212)

AIR DEFENCE

SAM 20+

Long-range 20 SAMP/T

Point-defence FIM-92 *Stinger*

AIR-LAUNCHED MISSILES

ASM *Spike*-ER

Navy 28,700

EQUIPMENT BY TYPE

SUBMARINES • SSK 8:

4 *Pelosi* (imp *Sauro*, 3rd and 4th series) with 6 single 533mm TT with A184 mod 3 HWT

4 *Salvatore Todaro* (Type-212A) (fitted with AIP) with 6 single 533mm TT with *Black Shark* HWT

PRINCIPAL SURFACE COMBATANTS 18

AIRCRAFT CARRIERS • CVS 2:

1 *Cavour* with 4 8-cell *Sylver* A43 VLS with *Aster* 15 SAM, 2 76mm guns (capacity mixed air group of 20 AV-8B *Harrier* II; F-35B *Lightning* II; AW101 *Merlin*; NH90; Bell 212)

1 *G. Garibaldi* with 2 octuple *Albatros* lnchr with *Aspide* SAM, 2 triple 324mm ASTT with Mk 46 LWT (capacity mixed air group of 18 AV-8B *Harrier* II; AW101 *Merlin*; NH90; Bell 212)

DESTROYERS • DDGHM 4:

2 *Andrea Doria* with 2 quad lnchr with *Otomat* (*Teseo*) Mk2A AShM, 6 8-cell *Sylver* A50 VLS with *Aster* 15/*Aster* 30 SAM, 2 single 324mm B-515 ASTT with MU90 LWT, 3 76mm guns (capacity 1 AW101 *Merlin*/ NH90 hel)

2 *Luigi Durand de la Penne* (ex-*Animoso*) with 2 quad lnchr with *Otomat* (*Teseo*) Mk2A AShM/*Milas* A/S msl, 1 Mk 13 mod 4 GMLS with SM-1MR Block VI SAM, 1 octuple *Albatros* lnchr with *Aspide* SAM, 2 triple 324mm B-515 ASTT with Mk 46 LWT, 1 127mm gun, 3 76mm guns (capacity 1 NH90 or 2 Bell 212 (AB-212) hel)

FRIGATES 12

FFGHM 10:

4 *Bergamini* (GP) with 2 quad lnchr with *Otomat* (*Teseo*) Mk2A AShM, 2 8-cell *Sylver* A50 VLS with *Aster* 15/*Aster* 30 SAM, 2 triple 324mm B-515 ASTT with MU90 LWT, 1 127mm gun, 1 76mm gun (capacity 2 AW101/NH90 hel)

4 *Bergamini* (ASW) with 2 twin lnchr with *Otomat* (*Teseo*) Mk2A AShM, 2 twin lnchr with MILAS A/S msl, 2 8-cell *Sylver* A50 VLS with *Aster* 15/*Aster* 30 SAM, 2 triple 324mm B-515 ASTT with MU90 LWT, 2 76mm gun (capacity 2 AW101/NH90 hel)

2 *Maestrale* with 4 single lnchr with *Otomat* (*Teseo*) Mk2 AShM, 1 octuple *Albatros* lnchr with *Aspide* SAM, 2 triple 324mm SVTT Mk 32 ASTT with Mk 46 LWT, 1 127mm gun (capacity 1 NH90 or 2 Bell 212 (AB-212) hel)

FFH 2 *Paolo Thaon di Revel* (*Pattugliatori Polivalenti d'Altura* (PPA)) with 1 127mm gun, 1 76mm gun (capacity 2 NH90 or 1 AW101)

PATROL AND COASTAL COMBATANTS 16

PSOH 10:

4 *Cassiopea* with 1 76mm gun (capacity 1 Bell 212 (AB-212) hel

4 *Comandante Cigala Fuligosi* with 1 76mm gun (capacity 1 Bell 212 (AB-212)/NH90 hel)

2 *Sirio* (capacity 1 Bell 212 (AB-212) or NH90 hel)

PB 6: 2 *Angelo Cabrini*; 4 *Esploratore*

MINE WARFARE • MINE COUNTERMEASURES 10

MHO 10: 8 *Gaeta*; 2 *Lerici*

AMPHIBIOUS

PRINCIPAL AMPHIBIOUS SHIPS • LHD 3:

- 2 *San Giorgio* (capacity 3-4 AW101/NH90/Bell 212; 3 LCM; 2 LCVP; 30 trucks; 36 APC (T); 350 troops)
- 1 *San Giusto* with 1 76mm gun (capacity 2 AW101 *Merlin*/NH90/Bell 212; 3 LCM; 2 LCVP; 30 trucks; 36 APC (T); 350 troops)

LANDING CRAFT 24: 15 **LCVP**; 9 **LCM**

LOGISTICS AND SUPPORT 53

ABU 5 *Ponza*

AFD 9

AGE 3: 1 *Leonardo* (coastal); 1 *Raffaele Rosseti*; 1 *Vincenzo Martellota*

AGI 1 *Elettra*

AGOR 1 *Alliance*

AGS 3: 1 *Ammiraglio Magnaghi* with 1 hel landing platform; 2 *Aretusa* (coastal)

AKSL 6 *Gorgona*

AORH 2: 1 *Etna* with 1 76mm gun (capacity 1 AW101/ NH90/Bell 212 hel); 1 *Vulcano* (capacity 2 AW101/NH90/ Bell 212)

AORL 1 *Stromboli* with 1 76mm gun (capacity 1 AW101/ NH90 hel)

AOT 4 *Panarea*

ARSH 1 *Anteo* (capacity 1 Bell 212 (AB-212) hel)

ATS 6 *Ciclope*

AWT 3: 1 *Bormida*; 2 *Simeto*

AXS 8: 1 *Amerigo Vespucci*; 5 *Caroly*; 1 *Italia*; 1 *Palinuro*

Naval Aviation 2,000

FORCES BY ROLE

FIGHTER/GROUND ATTACK

1 sqn with AV-8B *Harrier* II; TAV-8B *Harrier* II

ANTI-SUBMARINE WARFARE/TRANSPORT

5 sqn with AW101 ASW *Merlin*; Bell 212 ASW (AB-212AS); Bell 212 (AB-212); NH90 NFH

MARITIME PATROL

1 flt with P-180

AIRBORNE EARLY WANRING & CONTROL

1 flt with AW101 AEW *Merlin*

EQUIPMENT BY TYPE

AIRCRAFT 13 combat capable

FGA 13: 9 AV-8B *Harrier* II; 1 TAV-8B *Harrier* II; 3 F-35B *Lightning* II

MP 3 P.180 *Avanti*

HELICOPTERS

ASW 56: 8 AW101 ASW *Merlin*; 7 Bell 212 ASW; 41 NH90 NFH (SH-90)

AEW 4 AW101 AEW *Merlin*

TPT 22: **Medium** 20: 10 AW101 *Merlin*; 10 NH90 MITT (MH-90); **Light** 2 Bell 212 (AB-212)

AIR-LAUNCHED MISSILES

AAM • IR AIM-9L *Sidewinder*; **ARH** AIM-120 AMRAAM

ASM AGM-65 *Maverick*

AShM *Marte* Mk 2/S

Marines 3,000

FORCES BY ROLE

MANOEUVRE

Amphibious

1 mne regt (1 recce coy, 2 mne bn, 1 log bn)

1 (boarding) mne regt (2 mne bn)

1 landing craft gp

Other

1 sy regt (3 sy bn)

EQUIPMENT BY TYPE

ARMOURED FIGHTING VEHICLES

AAV 17: 15 AAVP-7; 2 AAVC-7

AUV 70 IVECO LMV

ENGINEERING & MAINTENANCE VEHICLES

ARV 1 AAVR-7

ANTI-TANK/ANTI-INFRASTRUCTURE

MSL• MANPATS *Spike*

ARTILLERY

MOR 22: **81mm** 16 Expal; **120mm** 6 RT-61 (RT-F1)

AIR DEFENCE • SAM • Point-defence FIM-92 *Stinger*

Air Force 39,250

FORCES BY ROLE

FIGHTER

4 sqn with Eurofighter *Typhoon*

FIGHTER/GROUND ATTACK

1 (SEAD/EW) sqn with *Tornado* ECR

1 sqn with F-35A *Lightning* II; *Tornado* IDS

1 sqn with F-35A/B *Lightning* II

FIGHTER/GROUND ATTACK/ISR

1 sqn with AMX *Ghibli*

MARITIME PATROL

1 sqn (opcon Navy) with ATR-72MP (P-72A)

TANKER/TRANSPORT

1 sqn with KC-767A

COMBAT SEARCH & RESCUE

1 sqn with AB-212 ICO; AW101 SAR (HH-101A)

SEARCH & RESCUE

1 wg with AW139 (HH-139A); Bell 212 (HH-212)

TRANSPORT

2 (VIP) sqn with A319CJ; AW139 (VH-139A); *Falcon* 50; *Falcon* 900 *Easy*; *Falcon* 900EX

2 sqn with C-130J/C-130J-30/KC-130J *Hercules*

1 sqn with C-27J *Spartan*

1 (calibration) sqn with P-180 *Avanti*/Gulfstream G550 CAEW

TRAINING

1 OCU sqn with Eurofighter *Typhoon*

1 sqn with MB-339PAN (aerobatic team)

1 sqn with MD-500D/E (NH-500D/E)

1 OCU sqn with *Tornado*

1 OCU sqn with AMX-T *Ghibli*

1 sqn with MB-339A

1 sqn with M-346

1 sqn with SF-260EA; 3 P2006T (T-2006A)

1 sqn with AW101 SAR (HH-101A); Bell 212 (HH-212)

ISR UAV

1 sqn with MQ-9A *Reaper*; RQ-1B *Predator*

AIR DEFENCE

2 bty with *Spada*

Europe **107**

EQUIPMENT BY TYPE
AIRCRAFT 231 combat capable
FTR 94 Eurofighter *Typhoon*
FGA 60: 31 AMX *Ghibli*; 8 AMX-T *Ghibli*; 17 F-35A *Lightning* II; 4 F-35B *Lightning* II
ATK 34 *Tornado* IDS
ATK/EW 15 *Tornado* ECR*
MP 4 ATR-72MP (P-72A)
SIGINT 1 Beech 350 *King Air*
AEW&C 3 Gulfstream G550 CAEW
TKR/TPT 4 KC-767A
TPT 78: **Medium** 33: 11 C-130J *Hercules* (5+ KC-130J tanker pods); 10 C-130J-30 *Hercules*; 12 C-27J *Spartan*; **Light** 37: 17 P-180 *Avanti*; 20 S-208 (liaison); **PAX** 8: 3 A319CJ; 2 *Falcon* 50 (VIP); 2 *Falcon* 900 *Easy*; 1 *Falcon* 900EX (VIP)
TRG 115: 21 MB-339A; 28 MB-339CD*; 16 MB-339PAN (aerobatics); 2+ M-345; 22 M-346; 26 SF-260EA
HELICOPTERS
MRH 54: 13 AW139 (HH-139A/VH-139A); 2 MD-500D (NH-500D); 39 MD-500E (NH-500E)
CSAR 12 AW101 (HH-101A)
SAR 17 AW139 (HH-139B)
TPT • Light 14 Bell 212 (HH-212)/AB-212 ICO
UNINHABITED AERIAL VEHICLES 12
CISR • Heavy 6 MQ-9A *Reaper* (unarmed)
ISR • Heavy 6 RQ-1B *Predator*
AIR DEFENCE • SAM • Short-range SPADA
AIR-LAUNCHED MISSILES
AAM • IR AIM-9L *Sidewinder*; **IIR** IRIS-T; **ARH** AIM-120C AMRAAM; *Meteor*
ARM AGM-88 HARM
LACM SCALP EG/*Storm Shadow*
BOMBS
Laser-guided *Lizard* 2
Laser & INS/GPS-guided GBU-49 Enhanced *Paveway* II; GBU-54 Laser JDAM
INS/GPS-guided GBU-31/-32/-38 JDAM; GBU-39 Small Diameter Bomb

Joint Special Forces Command (COFS)

Army
FORCES BY ROLE
SPECIAL FORCES
1 SF regt (9th *Assalto paracadutisti*)
1 STA regt
1 ranger regt (4th *Alpini paracadutisti*)
COMBAT SUPPORT
1 psyops regt
TRANSPORT HELICOPTER
1 spec ops hel regt

Navy (COMSUBIN)
FORCES BY ROLE
SPECIAL FORCES
1 SF gp (GOI)
1 diving gp (GOS)

Air Force
FORCES BY ROLE
SPECIAL FORCES
1 wg (sqn) (17th *Stormo Incursori*)

Paramilitary

Carabinieri
FORCES BY ROLE
SPECIAL FORCES
1 spec ops gp (GIS)

Gendarmerie & Paramilitary 176,100

Carabinieri 108,000
The Carabinieri are organisationally under the MoD. They are a separate service in the Italian Armed Forces as well as a police force with judicial competence

Mobile and Specialised Branch
FORCES BY ROLE
MANOEUVRE
Other
1 (mobile) paramilitary div (1 bde (1st) with (1 horsed cav regt, 11 mobile bn); 1 bde (2nd) with (1 (1st) AB regt, 2 (7th & 13th) mobile regt))
HELICOPTER
1 hel gp
EQUIPMENT BY TYPE
ARMOURED FIGHTING VEHICLES
APC • APC (T) 3 VCC-2
AUV 30 IVECO LMV
PATROL AND COASTAL COMBATANTS • PB 66
AIRCRAFT • TPT • Light: 2 P.180 *Avanti*
HELICOPTERS
MRH 15 Bell 412 (AB-412)
TPT • Light 31: 19 AW109; 2 AW109E; 2 AW139; 8 MD-500D (NH-500D)

Customs 68,100
(Servizio Navale Guardia Di Finanza)
EQUIPMENT BY TYPE
PATROL AND COASTAL COMBATANTS 166
PCO 2 *Monti* (Damen Stan Patrol 5509)
PCF 1 *Antonio Zara*
PBF 140: 19 *Bigliani*; 5 *Corrubia*; 9 *Mazzei*; 79 V-2000; 12 V-5000; 6 V-6000; 10 V-7000
PB 23 *Buratti*
LOGISTICS AND SUPPORT • AX 1 *Giorgio Cini*
AIRCRAFT
MP 8: 4 ATR-42-500MP; 4 ATR-72-600 (P-72B)
TPT • Light 2 P.180 *Avanti*
HELICOPTERS
TPT • Light 53: 10 AW109N; 17 AW139; 6 AW169M; 8 Bell 412HP *Twin Huey*; 4 MD-500MC (NH-500MC); 8 MD-500MD (NH-500MD)

DEPLOYMENT

BOSNIA-HERZEGOVINA: EU • EUFOR (*Operation Althea*) 346; 1 inf bn HQ; 1 inf coy; 1 ISR coy

BULGARIA: NATO • Enhanced Vigilance Activities 750; 1 mech inf BG with *Centauro* B1; VBM *Freccia* 8×8; PzH 2000

DJIBOUTI: 92

EGYPT: MFO 75; 3 PB

GULF OF ADEN & INDIAN OCEAN: EU • *Operation Atalanta* 150; 1 FFGHM

GULF OF GUINEA: Navy 190; 1 FFGHM

INDIA/PAKISTAN: UN • UNMOGIP 2

IRAQ: *Operation Inherent Resolve* (*Prima Parthica*) 712; 1 inf regt; 1 trg unit; 1 hel sqn with 3 NH90; **NATO** • NATO Mission Iraq 610

KUWAIT: *Operation Inherent Resolve* (*Prima Parthica*) 417; 4 Eurofighter *Typhoon*; 2 MQ-9A *Reaper*; 1 C-27J *Spartan*; 1 KC-767A; 1 SAM bty with SAMP/T

LATVIA: NATO • Enhanced Forward Presence (*Baltic Guardian*) 250; 1 armd inf coy with C1 *Ariete*; *Centauro* B1; VCC-80 *Dardo*

LEBANON: MIBIL 22; **UN** • UNIFIL 868; 1 mech bde HQ; 1 mech inf bn; 1 MP coy; 1 sigs coy; 1 hel sqn

LIBYA: MIASIT 160; 1 inf coy; 1 CRBN unit; 1 trg unit

MALI: EU • EUTM Mali 9; **UN** • MINUSMA 2

MEDITERRANEAN SEA: EU • EUNAVFOR MED: 70; 1 PSOH; **NATO** • SNMG 2: 170; 1 FFGHM; **NATO** • SNMCMG 2: 50; 1 MHO

MOZAMBIQUE: EU • EUTM Mozambique 15

NIGER: MISIN 220; 1 inf coy; 1 engr unit; 1 CRBN unit; 1 med coy; 1 trg unit; 1 ISR unit

PERSIAN GULF: EMASOH 150; 1 FFGHM

POLAND: NATO • Baltic Air Policing: 135; 4 Eurofighter *Typhoon*

SERBIA: NATO • KFOR 715; 1 arty regt BG HQ; 1 Carabinieri unit

SOMALIA: EU • EUTM Somalia 150

WESTERN SAHARA: UN • MINURSO 2

FOREIGN FORCES

United States US European Command: 13,050

Army 4,250; 1 AB bde(-)

Navy 3,600; 1 HQ (US Naval Forces Europe-Africa (NAVEUR-NAVAF)/6th Fleet) at Naples; 1 ASW Sqn with 5 P-8A *Poseidon* at Sigonella

USAF 4,800; 1 FGA wg with (2 FGA sqn with 21 F-16C/D *Fighting Falcon* at Aviano; 1 CSAR sqn with 8 HH-60G *Pave Hawk*); 1 CISR UAV sqn with MQ-9A *Reaper* at Sigonella; 1 ISR UAV flt with RQ-4B *Global Hawk* at Sigonella

USMC 400; 1 tpt sqn with 6 MV-22B *Osprey*; 2 KC-130J *Hercules*

Latvia LVA

Euro EUR		2021	2022	2023
GDP	EUR	32.9bn	38.4bn	
	USD	38.9bn	40.6bn	
per capita	USD	20,546	21,482	
Growth	%	4.5	2.5	
Inflation	%	3.2	16.5	
Def exp [a]	EUR	696m	806m	
	USD	824m	852m	
Def bdgt [b]	EUR	696m	806m	878m
	USD	824m	852m	
FMA (US)	USD	10.0m	8.8m	9.8m
USD1=EUR		0.84	0.95	

[a] NATO figure

[b] Includes military pensions

Real-terms defence budget trend (USDm, constant 2015)

674

231

2008 — 2015 — 2022

Population	1,842,226

Age	0–14	15–19	20–24	25–29	30–64	65 plus
Male	7.8%	2.6%	2.3%	2.6%	24.0%	7.2%
Female	7.3%	2.4%	2.1%	2.4%	25.3%	14.1%

Capabilities

Latvia has small armed forces focused on maintaining national sovereignty and territorial integrity and the country depends on NATO membership as a security guarantor. Russia is Latvia's overriding security concern. In the wake of the February 2022 invasion of Ukraine, Latvia boosted defence spending and transferred military equipment to Ukraine. A national service law was approved in September 2022 and will take effect in January 2023. Two intakes are planned annually. Males between 18-27 will be obliged to serve, with females serving voluntarily. Posts will be filled by volunteers but from late 2023 any unfilled quota will be filled compulsorily. Service will last for 11 months. The September 2020 State Defence Concept highlighted challenges including from new technologies and low military spending in Europe, and the resulting effect on capabilities and crisis response. It emphasised societal resilience and comprehensive defence as well as the significance of a NATO presence in the region. The NATO battlegroup based in Latvia, present since 2017 as part of the Alliance's Enhanced Forward Presence, was bolstered in 2022. Latvia is also a member of the UK-led Joint Expeditionary Force. There is no capacity to independently deploy and sustain forces beyond national boundaries, although the armed forces have taken part in NATO and EU missions. Improvements are being made to logistics and procurement systems. A National Cyber Security Center is planned to be established in January 2023 under the auspices of the Ministry of Defence. Capability-development plans include medium-range air defence (jointly with Estonia), rocket artillery and coastal defence. Acquisition requirements include air, land and naval systems, transport assets and ammunition. Latvia has only a niche defence-industrial capability, with cyber security a focus.

ACTIVE 6,600 (Army 1,800 Navy 500 Air 500 Joint Staff 2,300 National Guard 1,200 Other 300)

RESERVE 15,500 (National Guard 10,000 Other 5,500)

ORGANISATIONS BY SERVICE

Joint 2,300
FORCES BY ROLE
SPECIAL FORCES
 1 SF unit
COMBAT SUPPORT
 1 MP bn

Army 1,800
FORCES BY ROLE
MANOEUVRE
 Mechanised
 1 mech inf bde (2 mech inf bn, 1 SP arty bn, 1 cbt spt bn (1 recce coy, 1 engr coy, 1 AD coy), 1 CSS bn HQ)

National Guard 1,200; 10,000 part-time (11,200 total)
FORCES BY ROLE
SPECIAL FORCES
 1 SF unit
MANOEUVRE
 Light
 1 (2nd) inf bde (4 inf bn; 1 engr bn)
 3 (1st, 3rd & 4th) inf bde (3 inf bn; 1 sy bn; 1 spt bn)
COMBAT SUPPORT
 1 cyber unit
 1 NBC coy
 1 psyops pl
EQUIPMENT BY TYPE
ARMOURED FIGHTING VEHICLES
 MBT 3 T-55 (trg)
 RECCE 170 FV107 *Scimitar* (incl variants)
 APC • APC(W) 8 Patria 6×6
ANTI-TANK/ANTI-INFRASTRUCTURE
 MANPATS *Spike*-LR
 RCL 84mm *Carl Gustaf*; **90mm** Pvpj 1110
ARTILLERY 112
 SP 155mm 59 M109A5ÖE
 TOWED 100mm (23 K-53 in store)
 MOR 53: **81mm** 28 L16; **120mm** 25 M120

Navy 500 (incl Coast Guard)
Naval Forces Flotilla separated into an MCM squadron and a patrol-boat squadron. LVA, EST and LTU have set up a joint naval unit, BALTRON, with bases at Liepaja, Riga, Ventspils (LVA), Tallinn (EST), Klaipeda (LTU). Each nation contributes 1–2 MCMVs
EQUIPMENT BY TYPE
PATROL AND COASTAL COMBATANTS 5
 PB 5 *Skrunda* (GER *Swath*)
MINE WARFARE • MINE COUNTERMEASURES 4
 MCCS 1 *Vidar* (ex-NOR)
 MHO 3 *Imanta* (ex-NLD *Alkmaar/Tripartite*)

LOGISTICS AND SUPPORT 1
 AXL 1 *Varonis* (comd and spt ship, ex-NLD)

Coast Guard
Under command of the Latvian Naval Forces
EQUIPMENT BY TYPE
PATROL AND COASTAL COMBATANTS 6
 PB 6: 1 *Astra*; 5 KBV 236 (ex-SWE)

Air Force 500
Main tasks are airspace control and defence, maritime and land SAR and air transportation
FORCES BY ROLE
TRANSPORT
 1 (mixed) tpt sqn with An-2 *Colt*; Mi-17 *Hip* H
AIR DEFENCE
 1 AD bn
 1 radar sqn (radar/air ctrl)
AIRCRAFT • TPT • Light 4 An-2 *Colt*
HELICOPTERS • MRH 2 Mi-17 *Hip* H
AIR DEFENCE
 SAM • Point-defence FIM-92 *Stinger*; RBS-70
 GUNS • TOWED 40mm 24 L/70

Gendarmerie & Paramilitary

State Border Guard
EQUIPMENT BY TYPE
PATROL AND COASTAL COMBATANTS 3
 PB 3: 1 *Valpas* (ex-FIN); 1 *Lokki* (ex-FIN); 1 *Randa*
HELICOPTERS
 TPT • Light 6: 2 AW109E *Power*; 2 AW119Kx; 2 Bell 206B (AB-206B) *Jet Ranger* II

DEPLOYMENT

IRAQ: *Operation Inherent Resolve* 1; **NATO** • NATO Mission Iraq 1

MALI: EU • EUTM Mali 5; **UN** • MINUSMA 1

MIDDLE EAST: UN • UNTSO 1

SERBIA: NATO • KFOR 136; 1 inf coy

FOREIGN FORCES
All NATO Enhanced Forward Presence/Enhanced Vigilance Activities unless stated
Albania 21; 1 EOD pl
Canada 639; 1 mech inf bn HQ; 1 mech inf coy(+); 1 cbt spt coy; 1 spt coy;
Czech Republic 81; 1 mor pl
Denmark 803; 1 mech inf bn
Italy 250; 1 armd inf coy
Macedonia, North 9
Montenegro 11
Poland 177; 1 tk coy
Slovakia 152; 1 arty bty
Slovenia 42
Spain 504; 1 armd inf coy(+); 1 arty bty; 1 cbt engr coy; 1 SAM bty
United States US European Command: 800; 1 AB bn

Lithuania LTU

Euro EUR		2021	2022	2023
GDP	EUR	55.4bn	64.4bn	
	USD	65.5bn	68.0bn	
per capita	USD	23,386	24,032	
Growth	%	5.0	1.8	
Inflation	%	4.6	17.6	
Def exp [a]	EUR	1.11bn	1.50bn	
	USD	1.31bn	1.58bn	
Def bdgt [b]	EUR	1.10bn	1.50bn	1.91bn
	USD	1.31bn	1.58bn	
FMA (US)	USD	10.0m	8.8m	9.8m
USD1=EUR		0.84	0.95	

[a] NATO figure

[b] Includes military pensions

Real-terms defence budget trend (USDm, constant 2015)

1206

288

2008 ---- 2015 ---- 2022

Population	2,683,546					
Age	0–14	15–19	20–24	25–29	30–64	65 plus
Male	7.9%	2.5%	2.7%	3.0%	23.0%	7.2%
Female	7.5%	2.3%	2.5%	2.7%	24.9%	13.9%

Capabilities

Lithuania's armed forces are focused on maintaining sovereignty and territorial integrity but the country relies on NATO membership for its security. Like the other Baltic states, it is reliant on NATO's air-policing deployment for a combat-aircraft capacity. A new National Security Strategy was adopted in December 2021, which reflected the worsening regional security environment. Russia is the country's predominant security concern, with this focus sharpened by Russia's 2022 invasion of Ukraine. The authorities signalled an increase in defence spending. Lithuania has transferred to Ukraine some military equipment and has also repaired combat-damaged equipment. The authorities are looking to improve readiness and the mobilisation system is being reformed. In mid-2022 the government raised the upper limit for conscript numbers. The numbers of reservists called to annual exercises is also to increase. Lithuania has a limited medium-airlift capability for use in supporting its forces on multinational deployed operations. It takes an active part in NATO and EU operations. Improvements to defence infrastructure are planned, alongside plans to bolster air surveillance and anti-tank capabilities. Lithuania signalled its intention in 2022 to join the European Sky Shield initiative, to boost air defence capacity. Vilnius is also looking to acquire new rocket artillery capabilities, in common with other Baltic states, and acquire additional self-propelled artillery as well as loitering munitions. The NATO battlegroup based in Lithuania, present since 2017 as part of the Alliance's Enhanced Forward Presence, was bolstered in 2022. Šiauliai air base hosts a NATO Air Policing detachment. Lithuania is a member of the UK-led Joint Expeditionary Force. A Regional Cyber Defence Centre was set up in 2021 and a cyber range was opened in 2022, both coming under the National Cyber Security Centre, itself under the defence ministry. Lithuania has a small defence-industrial base, with niche capabilities, for instance in helicopter support and maintenance and repair.

ACTIVE 23,000 (Army 14,500 Navy 700 Air 1,500 Other 6,300) **Gendarmerie & Paramilitary 14,150**

Conscript liability 9 months, 18–23 years

RESERVE 7,100 (Army 7,100)

ORGANISATIONS BY SERVICE

Army 8,850; 5,650 active reserves (total 14,500)

FORCES BY ROLE

MANOEUVRE

Mechanised

1 (1st) mech bde (4 mech inf bn, 1 arty bn, 1 log bn)

Light

1 (2nd) mot inf bde (3 mot inf bn, 1 arty bn)

COMBAT SUPPORT

1 engr bn

COMBAT SERVICE SUPPORT

1 trg regt

EQUIPMENT BY TYPE

ARMOURED FIGHTING VEHICLES

IFV 30 Boxer (Vilkas) (incl 2 trg)

APC • APC (T) 236: 214 M113A1; 22 M577 (CP)

AUV ε100 JLTV

ENGINEERING & MAINTENANCE VEHICLES

AEV 8 MT-LB AEV

ARV 6: 2 BPz-2; 4 M113

ANTI-TANK/ANTI-INFRASTRUCTURE

MSL

SP 10 M1025A2 HMMWV with FGM-148 Javelin

MANPATS FGM-148 Javelin

RCL 84mm Carl Gustaf

ARTILLERY 118

SP 16 PzH 2000

TOWED 105mm 18 M101

MOR 84: **120mm** 42: 20 2B11; 22 M/41D; **SP 120mm** 42 M113 with Tampella

AIR DEFENCE • SAM • Point-defence GROM

Reserves

National Defence Voluntary Forces 5,650 active reservists

FORCES BY ROLE

MANOEUVRE

Other

6 (territorial) def unit

Navy 700

LVA, EST and LTU established a joint naval unit, BALTRON, with bases at Liepaja, Riga, Ventpils (LVA), Tallinn (EST), Klaipeda (LTU)

EQUIPMENT BY TYPE

PATROL AND COASTAL COMBATANTS 4

PCC 4 Zemaitis (ex-DNK Flyvefisken) with 1 76mm gun

MINE WARFARE • MINE COUNTERMEASURES 4

MHC 2 Skalvis (ex-UK Hunt)

MCCS 1 Jotvingis (ex-NOR Vidar)

LOGISTICS AND SUPPORT • AAR 1 Šakiai

Air Force 1,500

FORCES BY ROLE
AIR DEFENCE
 1 AD bn
EQUIPMENT BY TYPE
AIRCRAFT
 TPT 6: **Medium** 3 C-27J *Spartan;* **Light** 3: 1 Cessna 172RG; 2 L-410 *Turbolet*
HELICOPTERS
 MRH 3 AS365M3 *Dauphin* (SAR)
 TPT • **Medium** 3 Mi-8 *Hip* (tpt/SAR)
AIR DEFENCE • SAM 4+
 Short-range 4 NASAMS III
 Point-defence FIM-92 *Stinger;* RBS-70

Special Operation Force

FORCES BY ROLE
SPECIAL FORCES
 1 SF gp (1 CT unit; 1 Jaeger bn, 1 cbt diver unit)

Logistics Support Command 1,400

FORCES BY ROLE
COMBAT SERVICE SUPPORT
 1 log bn

Training and Doctrine Command 1,500

FORCES BY ROLE
COMBAT SERVICE SUPPORT
 1 trg regt

Other Units 2,600

FORCES BY ROLE
COMBAT SUPPORT
 1 MP bn

Gendarmerie & Paramilitary 14,150

Riflemen Union 10,600

State Border Guard Service 3,550
 Ministry of Interior
 EQUIPMENT BY TYPE
 PATROL AND COASTAL COMBATANTS • PB 3: 1 *Lokki* (ex-FIN); 1 KBV 041 (ex-SWE); 1 *Bakauskas* (Baltic Patrol 2700)
 AMPHIBIOUS • LANDING CRAFT • UCAC 2 *Christina* (*Griffon* 2000)
 HELICOPTERS • TPT • Light 5: 1 BK-117 (SAR); 2 H120 *Colibri;* 2 H135

DEPLOYMENT

CENTRAL AFRICAN REPUBLIC: EU • EUTM RCA 1
IRAQ: NATO • NATO Mission Iraq 34
MALI: EU • EUTM Mali 2; **UN** • MINUSMA 45
MOZAMBIQUE: EU • EUTM Mozambique 2
SERBIA: NATO • KFOR 1
UNITED KINGDOM: *Operation Interflex* 15 (UKR trg)

FOREIGN FORCES

All NATO Enhanced Forward Presence unless stated
Belgium 150; 1 mech inf coy
Czech Republic 135; 1 AD unit
Germany 1,000; 1 mech inf bde HQ; 1 armd inf bn(+)
Hungary NATO Baltic Air Policing: 80; 4 *Gripen* C
Luxembourg 6
Netherlands 270; 1 armd inf coy
Norway 270; 1 armd inf coy(+)

Luxembourg LUX

Euro EUR		2021	2022	2023
GDP	EUR	73.3bn	77.7bn	
	USD	86.8bn	82.2bn	
per capita	USD	136,701	127,673	
Growth	%	6.9	1.6	
Inflation	%	3.5	8.4	
Def exp [a]	EUR	341m	464m	
	USD	404m	490m	
Def bdgt	EUR	348m	420m	543m
	USD	412m	444m	
USD1=EUR		0.84	0.95	

[a] NATO figure

Real-terms defence budget trend (USDm, constant 2015)

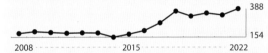

Population	650,364					
Age	0–14	15–19	20–24	25–29	30–64	65 plus
Male	8.6%	2.8%	3.1%	3.6%	25.2%	7.1%
Female	8.1%	2.6%	3.0%	3.5%	23.9%	8.6%

Capabilities

Luxembourg maintains a limited military capability to participate in European collective security and crisis management. 'Defence Guidelines for 2025 and Beyond,' published in late 2017, express support for NATO and EU security policy and contributions to international missions. Defence spending is to rise to 1% of GDP by 2028, and acquisition priorities in this timeframe include ISR, air transport and surveillance, cyber defence and uninhabited capabilities. There are plans to improve space situational awareness, SATCOM and Earth observation capabilites. In 2022, Luxembourg joined the NATO Cooperative Cyber Defence Centre of Excellence. Luxembourg has contributed troops to NATO's Enhanced Forward Presence. It is part of the European Multi-Role Tanker Transport Fleet programme, in which it partially funds one A330 MRTT. It has contributed its A400M to an airlift squadron formed jointly with Belgium. The Belgian and Dutch air forces are responsible for policing Luxembourg's airspace. Sustaining the army's personnel strength depends on better recruiting and retention. A review is considering a specialist reserve of civilian experts. Industrial cooperation inside the EU framework and in NATO is a priority. There is a small but advanced space industry and some foreign defence firms have a presence, but the country is otherwise reliant on imports. A strategy for defence industry, innovation and research is to be developed as part of the new defence guidelines.

ACTIVE 410 (Army 410) Gendarmerie & Paramilitary 600

ORGANISATIONS BY SERVICE

Army 410
FORCES BY ROLE
MANOEUVRE
  Reconnaissance
  2 recce coy (1 to Eurocorps/BEL div, 1 to NATO pool of deployable forces)
EQUIPMENT BY TYPE
ARMOURED FIGHTING VEHICLES
  AUV 48 *Dingo 2*
ANTI-TANK/ANTI-INFRASTRUCTURE
  MSL • MANPATS NLAW; TOW
ARTILLERY • MOR 81mm 6+
AIRCRAFT • TPT • Heavy 1 A400M
HELICOPTERS • MRH 2 H145M (jointly operated with Police)

Gendarmerie & Paramilitary 600
  Gendarmerie 600

DEPLOYMENT

IRAQ: NATO • NATO Mission Iraq 1
LITHUANIA: NATO • *Enhanced Forward Presence* 6
MALI: EU • EUTM Mali 21; **UN** • MINUSMA 2
MEDITERRANEAN SEA: EU • EUNAVFOR MED 2 *Merlin* IIIC (leased)

Macedonia, North MKD

Macedonian Denar MKD		2021	2022	2023
GDP	MKD	723bn	821bn	
	USD	13.9bn	14.1bn	
per capita	USD	6,714	6,816	
Growth	%	4.0	2.7	
Inflation	%	3.2	10.6	
Def exp [a]	MKD	10.6bn	13.7bn	
	USD	204m	235m	
Def bdgt	MKD	10.8bn	13.3bn	
	USD	207m	229m	
USD1=MKD		52.07	58.21	

[a] NATO figure

Real-terms defence budget trend (USDm, constant 2015)

Population 2,130,936

Age	0–14	15–19	20–24	25–29	30–64	65 plus
Male	8.3%	2.8%	3.4%	3.7%	25.2%	6.5%
Female	7.8%	2.6%	3.1%	3.5%	24.8%	8.3%

Capabilities

The armed forces' primary goals are safeguarding the state's territorial integrity and sovereignty, as well as contributing to operations under the EU, NATO and UN umbrellas. North Macedonia formally became NATO's 30th member on 27 March 2020. In the same month, it enacted a new Defence Strategy with a focus on capability development, and improved planning based on NATO and EU standards, among other areas. A 2019–2028 Defence Capability Development Plan (DCDP) consolidated long-term development goals aimed at developing collective defence, cooperative security and crisis-management capabilities. A Mid-Term Defence Capabilities Development Plan, adopted in January 2020, is intended to help implement the DCDP. The 2022 annual procurement plan, adopted in April, noted government-to-government contracts relating to JLTV vehicles, 105mm artillery systems, VSHORAD systems, and the overhaul of utility helicopters, among other matters. Work on MoD restructuring is under way. The armed forces are fully professional and the country aims to train all units, particularly those with deployable capability, to NATO standards. A number of units are earmarked for participation in NATO-led operations, The armed forces have increased their participation in NATO joint exercises since joining the Alliance. Participation in international peacekeeping missions has increased logistics capability. The country has modest maritime and air wings, and relies on Soviet-era equipment. There is little in the way of a domestic defence industry, with no ability to design and manufacture modern equipment.

ACTIVE 8,000 (Army 8,000) Gendarmerie & Paramilitary 7,600

RESERVE 4,850

ORGANISATIONS BY SERVICE

Army 8,000
FORCES BY ROLE
SPECIAL FORCES
1 SF regt (1 SF bn, 1 ranger bn)
MANOEUVRE
Mechanised
1 mech inf bde (4 mech inf bn, 1 arty bn, 1 NBC coy, 1 sigs coy)
COMBAT SUPPORT
1 engr bn
1 MP bn
1 sigs bn
COMBAT SERVICE SUPPORT
1 log bde (3 log bn)

Reserves
FORCES BY ROLE
MANOEUVRE *Light*
1 inf bde
EQUIPMENT BY TYPE
ARMOURED FIGHTING VEHICLES
IFV 11: 10 BMP-2; 1 BMP-2K (CP)
APC 198
APC (T) 46: 9 *Leonidas*; 27 M113; 10 MT-LB
APC (W) 152: 56 BTR-70; 12 BTR-80; 84 TM-170 *Hermelin*
AUV 2 *Cobra*
ANTI-TANK/ANTI-INFRASTRUCTURE
MSL • **MANPATS** *Milan*
RCL 82mm M60A
ARTILLERY 131
TOWED 70: **105mm** 14 M-56; **122mm** 56 M-30 M-1938
MRL 17: **122mm** 6 BM-21; **128mm** 11
MOR • **120mm** 44

Marine Wing
EQUIPMENT BY TYPE
PATROL AND COASTAL COMBATANTS 2
PB 2 *Botica*†

Aviation Brigade
FORCES BY ROLE
TRAINING
1 flt with Z-242; Bell 205 (UH-1H *Iroquois*); Bell 206B
ATTACK HELICOPTER
1 sqn with Mi-24V *Hind* E
TRANSPORT HELICOPTER
1 sqn with Mi-8MTV *Hip*; Mi-17 *Hip* H
AIR DEFENCE
1 AD bn
EQUIPMENT BY TYPE
AIRCRAFT
TPT • **Light** 1 An-2 *Colt*
TRG 5 Z-242
HELICOPTERS
ATK 2 Mi-24V *Hind* E (8: 2 Mi-24K *Hind* G2; 6 Mi-24V *Hind* E in store)

MRH 6: 4 Mi-8MTV *Hip*; 2 Mi-17 *Hip* H
TPT • **Light** 6: 2 Bell 205 (UH-1H *Iroquois*); 4 Bell 206B *Jet Ranger*
AIR DEFENCE
SAM • **Point-defence** 8+: 8 9K35 *Strela*-10 (RS-SA-13 *Gopher*); 9K310 *Igla*-1 (RS-SA-16 *Gimlet*)
GUNS 40mm 36 L/60

Gendarmerie & Paramilitary 7,600

Police 7,600 (some 5,000 armed)
incl 2 SF units
EQUIPMENT BY TYPE
ARMOURED FIGHTING VEHICLES
APC • **APC (T)** M113; **APC (W)** BTR-80; TM-170 *Heimlin*
AUV *Ze'ev*
HELICOPTERS
MRH 1 Bell 412EP *Twin Huey*
TPT 3: **Medium** 1 Mi-171; **Light** 2: 1 Bell 206B (AB-206B) *Jet Ranger* II; 1 Bell 212 (AB-212)

DEPLOYMENT

BOSNIA-HERZEGOVINA: EU • EUFOR (*Operation Althea*) 1
CENTRAL AFRICAN REPUBLIC: EU • EUTM RCA 1
IRAQ: NATO • NATO Mission Iraq 4
LATVIA: NATO • Enhanced Forward Presence 9
LEBANON: UN • UNIFIL 3
SERBIA: NATO • KFOR 65

Malta MLT

Euro EUR		2021	2022	2023
GDP	EUR	14.7bn	16.2bn	
	USD	17.4bn	17.2bn	
per capita	USD	33,667	32,912	
Growth	%	10.3	6.2	
Inflation	%	0.7	5.9	
Def bdgt [a]	EUR	71.8m	82.7m	73.9m
	USD	85.0m	87.4m	
USD1=EUR		0.84	0.95	

[a] Excludes military pensions

Real-terms defence budget trend (USDm, constant 2015)

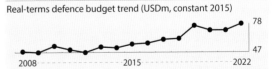

Population 464,186

Age	0–14	15–19	20–24	25–29	30–64	65 plus
Male	7.5%	2.3%	2.7%	3.5%	24.2%	10.2%
Female	7.0%	2.2%	2.5%	3.1%	22.8%	12.0%

Capabilities

The principal roles for the armed forces are maintaining external security and support for civil emergencies and the police. There is also focus on maritime security in the Mediterranean. The Armed Forces of Malta Strategy Paper 2016–2026 laid out defence-policy objectives, including operational and organisational reforms. Malta is neutral but is a member of NATO's Partnership for Peace programme. The country also participates in bilateral and multilateral exercises. Although deployment capacity is limited, Malta has contributed to European missions. Italy has assisted Malta in meeting some security requirements, including air surveillance, while the European Internal Security Fund is funding some modernisation. Although there is some shipbuilding and ship-repair activity and a small aviation-maintenance industry, these are not defence-specific and Malta relies on imports to equip its armed forces.

ACTIVE 1,700 (Armed Forces 1,700)

RESERVE 260 (Volunteer Reserve Force 110 Individual Reserve 150)

ORGANISATIONS BY SERVICE

Armed Forces of Malta 1,700
FORCES BY ROLE
SPECIAL FORCES
 1 SF unit
MANOEUVRE
 Light
 1 (1st) inf regt (3 inf coy, 1 cbt spt coy)
COMBAT SUPPORT
 1 (3rd) cbt spt regt (1 cbt engr sqn, 1 EOD sqn, 1 maint sqn)
COMBAT SERVICE SUPPORT
 1 (4th) CSS regt (1 CIS coy, 1 sy coy)
EQUIPMENT BY TYPE
ARTILLERY • MOR 81mm L16
AIR DEFENCE • GUNS 14.5mm 1 ZPU-4

Maritime Squadron 500
Organised into 5 divisions: offshore patrol; inshore patrol; rapid deployment and training; marine engineering; and logistics

EQUIPMENT BY TYPE
PATROL AND COASTAL COMBATANTS 8
 PCO 1 *Emer*
 PCC 1 *Diciotti* (ITA *Saettia* mod) with 1 hel landing platform
 PB 6: 4 Austal 21m; 2 *Marine Protector*
LOGISTICS AND SUPPORT • AAR 2 *Cantiere Vittoria*

Air Wing
1 base party. 1 flt ops div; 1 maint div; 1 integrated log div; 1 rescue section

EQUIPMENT BY TYPE
AIRCRAFT
 TPT • Light 5: 3 Beech 200 *King Air* (maritime patrol); 2 BN-2B *Islander*
 TRG 3 *Bulldog* T MK1
 HELICOPTERS MRH 6: 3 AW139 (SAR); 3 SA316B *Alouette* III

DEPLOYMENT

LEBANON: UN • UNIFIL 9

Montenegro MNE

Euro EUR		2021	2022	2023
GDP	EUR	4.96bn	5.80bn	
	USD	5.87bn	6.13bn	
per capita	USD	9,433	9,850	
Growth	%	13.0	7.2	
Inflation	%	2.4	12.8	
Def exp [a]	EUR	77.0m	94.7m	
	USD	91.2m	100m	
Def bdgt [b]	EUR	77.0m	94.7m	113m
	USD	91.2m	100m	
USD1=EUR		0.84	0.95	

[a] NATO figure
[b] Includes military pensions

Real-terms defence budget trend (USDm, constant 2015)

Population 604,966

Age	0–14	15–19	20–24	25–29	30–64	65 plus
Male	9.3%	3.1%	3.3%	3.1%	22.9%	7.4%
Female	8.7%	2.9%	3.1%	2.9%	23.6%	9.5%

Capabilities

According to its defence strategy, Montenegro intends to develop an integrated defence system, capable of defending and preserving independence, sovereignty and national territory. A key concern of the authorities is integrating Montenegro into relevant NATO and EU structures. A NATO member since 2017, Montenegro has accepted NATO's capability targets and has been aligning its defence-planning process with NATO standards. Reform and professionalisation of the armed forces have been slow, and developments have been focused on structural issues around improving recruitment, outflow and professional development. The armed forces are not designed to have an expeditionary capability, and as such have little logistics capability to support deployments beyond national borders. Personnel have deployed to EU, UN- and NATO-led operations, although a planned increased in Montenegro's small contribution to KFOR stalled due to internal opposition; similar debates are reportedly taking place as authorities look to discuss what role Montenegro should play in NATO crisis response activities. Podgorica intends to replace ageing Soviet-era equipment. Procurement priorities include light and medium helicopters and light armoured vehicles, as well as improved communications capacities in accordance with NATO standards. A contract for 67 Oshkosh 4x4 JLTVs is expected to be fulfilled by 2023; the first vehicles arrived in October 2020. Future plans include the formation of a special-forces unit and an intelligence unit in the land forces. The country's defence industry is capable of producing small arms and ammunition.

ACTIVE 2,350 (Army 1,275 Navy 350 Air Force 225 Other 500) **Gendarmerie & Paramilitary 4,100**

RESERVE 2,800

ORGANISATIONS BY SERVICE

Army 1,275

FORCES BY ROLE
MANOEUVRE
  Reconnaissance
  1 recce coy
  Light
  1 mot inf bn
COMBAT SUPPORT
  1 cbt spt bn
  1 sigs coy
COMBAT SERVICE SUPPORT
  1 med bn
  1 spt bn
EQUIPMENT BY TYPE
ARMOURED FIGHTING VEHICLES
  APC • APC (W) 8 BOV-VP M-86
  AUV 20 JLTV
ANTI-TANK/ANTI-INFRASTRUCTURE
  SP 9 BOV-1
  MSL • MANPATS 9K111 *Fagot* (RS-AT-4 *Spigot*); 9K111-1 *Konkurs* (RS-AT-5 *Spandrel*)
ARTILLERY 135
  TOWED 122mm 12 D-30
  MRL 128mm 18 M-63/M-94 *Plamen*
  MOR 105: **82mm** 73; **120mm** 32

Reserve
FORCES BY ROLE
MANOEUVRE
  Light
  2 inf bn
COMBAT SUPPORT
  1 arty bn

Navy 350
1 Naval Cmd HQ with 4 operational naval units (patrol boat; coastal surveillance; maritime detachment; and SAR) with additional sigs, log and trg units with a separate coastguard element. Some listed units are in the process of decommissioning
EQUIPMENT BY TYPE
PATROL AND COASTAL COMBATANTS • PCF 2 *Rade Končar*†
LOGISTICS AND SUPPORT • AXS 1 *Jadran*†

Air Force 225
Golubovci (Podgorica) air base under army command
FORCES BY ROLE
TRAINING
  1 (mixed) sqn with G-4 *Super Galeb*; Utva-75 (none operational)
TRANSPORT HELICOPTER
  1 sqn with SA341/SA342L *Gazelle*

EQUIPMENT BY TYPE
AIRCRAFT • TRG (4 G-4 *Super Galeb* non-operational; 4 Utva-75 non-operational)
HELICOPTERS
  MRH 16: 1 Bell 412EP *Twin Huey*; 2 Bell 412EPI *Twin Huey*; 13 SA341/SA342L (HN-45M) *Gazelle*
  TPT • Light 2 Bell 505 *Jet Ranger* X

Gendarmerie & Paramilitary ε4,100

Special Police Units ε4,100

DEPLOYMENT

LATVIA: NATO • Enhanced Forward Presence 11
MALI: EU • EUTM Mali 2
SERBIA: NATO • KFOR 1

Multinational Organisations

Capabilities

The following represent shared capabilities held by contributors collectively rather than as part of national inventories

ORGANISATIONS BY SERVICE

NATO AEW&C Force
Based at Geilenkirchen (GER). Original participating countries (BEL, CAN, DNK, GER, GRC, ITA, NLD, NOR, PRT, TUR, US) have been subsequently joined by five more (CZE, ESP, HUN, POL, ROM)
FORCES BY ROLE
AIRBORNE EARLY WARNING & CONTROL
  1 sqn with B-757 (trg); E-3A *Sentry* (NATO standard)
EQUIPMENT BY TYPE
AIRCRAFT
  AEW&C 16 E-3A *Sentry* (NATO standard)
  TPT • PAX 1 B-757 (trg)

NATO Alliance Ground Surveillance
Based at Sigonella (ITA)
EQUIPMENT BY TYPE
UNINHABITED AERIAL VEHICLES
  ISR • Heavy 5 RQ-4D *Phoenix*

NATO Multinational Multi-Role Tanker Transport Fleet (MMF)
Based at Eindhoven (NLD). Six participating countries (BEL, CZE, GER, NLD, NOR & LUX)
EQUIPMENT BY TYPE
AIRCRAFT • TKR/TPT 7 A330 MRTT

Strategic Airlift Capability
Heavy Airlift Wing based at Papa air base (HUN). 12 participating countries (BLG, EST, FIN, HUN, LTU, NLD, NOR, POL, ROM, SVN, SWE, US)

EQUIPMENT BY TYPE
AIRCRAFT • TPT • **Heavy** 3 C-17A *Globemaster* III

Strategic Airlift International Solution
Intended to provide strategic-airlift capacity pending the delivery of A400M aircraft by leasing An-124s. 11 participating countries (BEL, CZE, FIN, FRA, GER, HUN, NOR, POL, SVK, SVN, SWE)

EQUIPMENT BY TYPE
AIRCRAFT • TPT • **Heavy** 2 An-124-100 (3 more available on 6–9 days' notice)

Netherlands NLD

Euro EUR		2021	2022	2023
GDP	EUR	856bn	937bn	
	USD	1.01tr	991bn	
per capita	USD	57,997	56,298	
Growth	%	4.9	4.5	
Inflation	%	2.8	12.0	
Def exp [a]	EUR	11.8bn	14.8bn	
	USD	14.0bn	15.7bn	
Def bdgt [b]	EUR	11.7bn	14.4bn	15.4bn
	USD	13.9bn	15.2bn	
USD1=EUR		0.84	0.95	

[a] NATO figure
[b] Includes military pensions

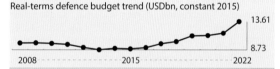
Real-terms defence budget trend (USDbn, constant 2015)
2008 — 2015 — 2022
13.61
8.73

Population	17,400,824					
Age	0–14	15–19	20–24	25–29	30–64	65 plus
Male	8.2%	2.9%	3.1%	3.2%	22.7%	9.3%
Female	7.8%	2.7%	3.0%	3.1%	22.7%	11.2%

Capabilities

The 2018 defence review tasked the armed forces with territorial defence, supporting national civil authorities, improving air transport and ISR capabilities, and boosting integrated air and missile defence. A new White Paper was issued in June 2022. Authorities are looking to improve readiness and deployability, combat power and institutional agility and adaptability. Training is slated to improve and efforts will be made to meet the establishment strength set for units. Defence spending is set to rise. A National Cyber Security Strategy 2022-2028 was published in September 2022. Dutch forces have increasingly integrated with NATO allies, particularly Germany. The army contributes to a Dutch–German tank battalion and there is also cooperation in the air and naval domains. The Dutch armed forces have air-policing agreements with France, Belgium and Luxembourg and the country is a member of the Joint Expeditionary Force and the European Intervention Initiative. The Netherlands, Belgium and Denmark have committed to forming a composite special-operations command. Dutch forces are fully professional and well trained and the Netherlands can deploy and sustain a medium-scale force for a single operation, or a small-scale joint force for an extended period. The Netherlands makes significant contributions to NATO and EU military operations. An agreement is in place with Belgium on the joint acquisition of new frigates and minehunters. Spending plans outlined in June indicated plans to increase the number of F-35A combat aircraft, set up a third airbase to operate the type, and double the number of MQ-9 *Reaper* UAVs. There are plans to replace C-130s with KC-390s, remanufacture AH-64D to AH-64E, and modernise the CH-47 fleet. A MLU is planned for CV90, *Fennek*, and the PzH2000. Replacement of the *Walrus* class submarines is likely delayed. There are plans to boost defence innovation and research and to expand the Defence Space Security Centre. The country has an advanced domestic defence industry focusing on armoured vehicles, naval ships and air-defence systems, and also hosts a range of international aerospace-company subsidiaries. Damen Schelde Naval Shipbuilding exports frigates, corvettes and fast-attack craft, while DutchAero manufactures engine components for the F-35.

ACTIVE 33,600 (Army 15,350 Navy 7,350 Air 6,400 Other 4,500) Military Constabulary 6,500

RESERVE 6,000 (Army 3,900 Navy 1,100 Air 800 Other 200) Military Constabulary 300

Reserve liability to age 35 for soldiers/sailors, 40 for NCOs, 45 for officers

ORGANISATIONS BY SERVICE

Army 15,350
FORCES BY ROLE
COMMAND
  elm 1 (1 GNC) corps HQ
SPECIAL FORCES
  4 SF coy
MANOEUVRE
  Reconnaissance
  1 ISR bn (2 armd recce sqn, 1 EW coy, 2 int sqn, 1 UAV bty)
  Mechanised
  1 (43rd) mech bde (1 armd recce sqn, 2 armd inf bn, 1 engr bn, 1 maint coy, 1 med coy)
  1 (13th) mech bde (1 recce sqn, 2 mech inf bn, 1 engr bn, 1 maint coy, 1 med coy)
  Air Manoeuvre
  1 (11th) air mob bde (3 air mob inf bn, 1 engr coy, 1 med coy, 1 supply coy, 1 maint coy)
COMBAT SUPPORT
  1 SP arty bn (3 SP arty bty)
  1 AD comd (1 AD sqn; 1 AD bty)
  1 CIMIC bn
  1 engr bn
  2 EOD coy 1 (CIS) sigs bn 1 CBRN coy
COMBAT SERVICE SUPPORT
  1 med bn
  5 fd hospital
  3 maint coy
  2 tpt bn

Europe 117

Reserves 3,900 reservists

National Command

Cadre bde and corps tps completed by call-up of reservists (incl Territorial Comd)

FORCES BY ROLE
MANOEUVRE Light
3 inf bn (could be mobilised for territorial def)

EQUIPMENT BY TYPE
ARMOURED FIGHTING VEHICLES
RECCE 197 *Fennek*
IFV 117 CV9035NL (32 more in store)
APC • APC (W) 200 *Boxer* (8 driver trg; 52 amb; 36 CP; 92 engr; 12 log)
AUV 248: 98 *Bushmaster* IMV; 150 *Fennek*
ENGINEERING & MAINTENANCE VEHICLES
AEV 10+: *Dachs*; 10 *Kodiak*
ARV 25+: BPz-2; 25 BPz-3 *Büffel*
VLB 22: 16 *Leopard* 1 with *Legaun*; 2 *Leopard* 2 with *Leguan*; 4 MLC70 with *Leguan*
MW *Bozena*
NBC VEHICLES 6 TPz-1 *Fuchs* NBC
ANTI-TANK/ANTI-INFRASTRUCTURE
MSL • MANPATS *Spike*-MR
ARTILLERY 122
SP 155mm 21 PzH 2000 (27 more in store)
MOR 101: **81mm** 83 L16/M1; **120mm** 18 Brandt
AIR DEFENCE • SAM 42+
Long-range 18 M902 *Patriot* PAC-3
Short-range 6 NASAMS II
Point-defence 18+: FIM-92 *Stinger*; 18 *Fennek* with FIM-92 *Stinger*

Navy 7,350 (incl Marines)

EQUIPMENT BY TYPE
SUBMARINES 4
SSK 4 *Walrus* with 4 single 533mm TT with Mk 48 ADCAP mod 7 HWT
PRINCIPAL SURFACE COMBATANTS 6
DESTROYERS • DDGHM 4:
3 *De Zeven Provinciën* with 2 quad lnchr with RGM-84C *Harpoon* Block 1B AShM, 5 8-cell Mk 41 VLS with SM-2 Block IIIA/RIM-162B ESSM SAM, 2 twin 324mm SVTT Mk 32 ASTT with Mk 46 LWT, 1 *Goalkeeper* CIWS, 1 127mm gun (capacity 1 NH90 hel)
1 *De Zeven Provinciën* with 2 quad lnchr with RGM-84C *Harpoon* Block 1B AShM, 5 8-cell Mk 41 VLS with SM-2 Block IIIA/RIM-162B ESSM SAM, 2 twin 324mm SVTT Mk 32 ASTT with Mk 46 LWT, 2 *Goalkeeper* CIWS, 1 127mm gun (capacity 1 NH90 hel)
FRIGATES • FFGHM 2 *Karel Doorman* with 2 quad lnchr with RGM-84C *Harpoon* Block 1B AShM, 1 16-cell Mk 48 mod 1 VLS with RIM-7P *Sea Sparrow* SAM, 2 twin 324mm SVTT Mk 32 ASTT with Mk 46 LWT, 1 *Goalkeeper* CIWS, 1 76mm gun (capacity 1 NH90 hel)
PATROL AND COASTAL COMBATANTS
PSOH 4 *Holland* with 1 76mm gun (capacity 1 NH90 hel)
MINE WARFARE • MINE COUNTERMEASURES 6
MHO 6 *Alkmaar* (*Tripartite*)

AMPHIBIOUS
PRINCIPAL AMPHIBIOUS SHIPS • LPD 2:
1 *Rotterdam* with 2 *Goalkeeper* CIWS (capacity 6 NH90/AS532 *Cougar* hel; either 6 LCVP or 2 LCM and 3 LCVP; either 170 APC or 33 MBT; 538 troops)
1 *Johan de Witt* with 2 *Goalkeeper* CIWS (capacity 6 NH90 hel or 4 AS532 *Cougar* hel; either 6 LCVP or 2 LCM and 3 LCVP; either 170 APC or 33 MBT; 700 troops)
LANDING CRAFT 17
LCU 5 LCU Mk II
LCVP 12 Mk5
LOGISTICS AND SUPPORT 9
AGS 3: 1 *Hydrograaf*; 2 *Snellius*
AK 1 *Pelikaan*
AKR 1 *New Amsterdam* (capacity 200 containers and 300 vehs) (leased)
AORH 1 *Karel Doorman* with 2 *Goalkeeper* CIWS (capacity 6 NH90/AS532 *Cougar* or 2 CH-47F *Chinook* hel; 2 LCVP)
AS 1 *Mercuur*
AXL 1 *Van Kingsbergen*
AXS 1 *Urania*

Marines 2,650

FORCES BY ROLE
SPECIAL FORCES
1 SF gp (1 SF sqn, 1 CT sqn)
MANOEUVRE
Amphibious
2 mne bn
1 amph aslt gp
COMBAT SERVICE SUPPORT
1 spt gp (coy)

EQUIPMENT BY TYPE
ARMOURED FIGHTING VEHICLES
APC • APC (T) 65 BvS-10 *Viking* (incl 20 CP)
ENGINEERING & MAINTENANCE VEHICLES
ARV 8: 4 BvS-10; 4 BPz-2
MED 4 BvS-10
ANTI-TANK/ANTI-INFRASTRUCTURE
MSL • MANPATS *Spike*-MR
ARTILLERY • MOR 81mm 12 L16/M1
AIR DEFENCE • SAM • Point-defence FIM-92 *Stinger*

Air Force 6,400

FORCES BY ROLE
FIGHTER/GROUND ATTACK
1 sqn with F-16AM/BM *Fighting Falcon*
1 sqn with F-35A *Lightning* II
1 sqn (converting) with F-35A *Lightning* II
ANTI-SUBMARINE WARFARE/SEARCH & RESCUE
1 sqn with NH90 NFH
TANKER/TRANSPORT
1 sqn with C-130H/H-30 *Hercules*
1 sqn with Gulfstream IV
TRAINING
1 OEU sqn with F-35A *Lightning* II
1 sqn with PC-7 *Turbo Trainer*
1 hel sqn with AH-64D *Apache*; CH-47D *Chinook* (based at Fort Hood, TX)

ATTACK HELICOPTER
1 sqn with AH-64D *Apache*
TRANSPORT HELICOPTER
1 sqn with AS532U2 *Cougar* II; NH90 NFH
1 sqn with CH-47D/F *Chinook*
EQUIPMENT BY TYPE
AIRCRAFT 70 combat capable
FTR 42 F-16AM/BM *Fighting Falcon*
FGA 28 F-35A *Lightning* II
TPT 5: **Medium** 4: 2 C-130H *Hercules*; 2 C-130H-30 *Hercules*; **PAX** 1 Gulfstream IV
TRG 13 PC-7 *Turbo Trainer*
HELICOPTERS
ATK 28: up to 27 AH-64D *Apache* (being remanufactured to E standard); 1+ AH-64E *Apache*
ASW 19 NH90 NFH (of which 8 not fitted with sonar)
TPT 32: **Heavy** 20 CH-47F *Chinook*; **Medium** 12 AS532U2 *Cougar* II
UNINHABITED AERIAL VEHICLES • CISR • Heavy 3
MQ-9 *Reaper* (unarmed)
AIR-LAUNCHED MISSILES
AAM • IR AIM-9L/M *Sidewinder*; IIR AIM-9X *Sidewinder* II; ARH AIM-120B AMRAAM
ASM AGM-114K *Hellfire*
BOMBS
Laser-guided GBU-10/GBU-12 *Paveway* II; GBU-24 *Paveway* III (all supported by LANTIRN)
INS/GPS guided GBU-39 Small Diameter Bomb

Gendarmerie & Paramilitary 6,500

Royal Military Constabulary 6,500

Subordinate to the Ministry of Defence, but performs most of its work under the authority of other ministries
FORCES BY ROLE
MANOEUVRE
  Other
  1 paramilitary comd (total: 28 paramilitary unit)
EQUIPMENT BY TYPE
ARMOURED FIGHTING VEHICLES
  APC • APC (W) 24 YPR-KMar

DEPLOYMENT

IRAQ: *Operation Inherent Resolve* 183; 2 trg unit; **NATO** • NATO Mission Iraq 2
LEBANON: UN • UNIFIL 1
LITHUANIA: NATO • Enhanced Forward Presence 270; 1 mech inf coy
MALI: EU • EUTM Mali 6; **UN** • MINUSMA 10
MEDITERRANEAN SEA: NATO • SNMCMG 2: 50; 1 MHO
MIDDLE EAST: UN • UNTSO 12
NORTH SEA: NATO • SNMG 1: 230; 1 DDGHM
ROMANIA: NATO • Enhanced Vigilance Activities 200; 1 air mob inf coy
SLOVAKIA: NATO • Enhanced Vigilance Activities 125; 1 SAM bty with M902 *Patriot* PAC-3
SYRIA/ISRAEL: UN • UNDOF 1

UNITED KINGDOM: *Operation Interflex* 90 (UKR trg)
UNITED STATES: 1 hel trg sqn with AH-64D *Apache*; CH-47D *Chinook* based at Fort Hood (TX)

FOREIGN FORCES

United States US European Command: 450

Norway NOR

Norwegian Kroner NOK		2021	2022	2023
GDP	NOK	4.14tr	4.84tr	
	USD	482bn	505bn	
per capita	USD	89,042	92,646	
Growth	%	3.9	3.6	
Inflation	%	3.5	4.7	
Def exp [a]	NOK	72.5bn	80.6bn	
	USD	8.44bn	8.40bn	
Def bdgt [b]	NOK	64.5bn	71.3bn	75.8bn
	USD	7.50bn	7.43bn	
USD1=NOK		8.59	9.60	

[a] NATO figure

[b] Includes military pensions

Real-terms defence budget trend (USDbn, constant 2015)

Population 5,553,840

Age	0–14	15–19	20–24	25–29	30–64	65 plus
Male	9.2%	2.9%	3.1%	3.4%	23.6%	8.3%
Female	8.7%	2.8%	2.9%	3.3%	22.2%	9.6%

Capabilities

Norway sustains small but well-equipped and highly trained armed forces. Territorial defence is at the heart of security policy. A new Long Term Defence Plan was published in October 2020, arguing that the security environment had deteriorated faster than expected. It envisages a gradual increase in personnel numbers and further measures to strengthen readiness and capability in the High North. Following Russia's further invasion of Ukraine, in February 2022, Norway announced that it will allocate further funds to strengthening its defence in the North. A US Marine Corps contingent has deployed to Vaernes, on a rotational basis, since January 2017 and a second location was in 2018 added at Setermoen. In April 2021 Norway and the US signed a Supplementary Defense Cooperation Agreement which, among other things, provides authorities for US forces to access specific Norwegian facilities and conduct mutual defence activities. Four locations were mentioned as 'focal points' for increased cooperation: Evenes, Rygge and Sola air stations and Ramsund naval station. Norway signed a cooperation agreement with the European Defence Agency in 2006. At any one time, around one-third of troops are conscripts. Senior officers reportedly expressed concerns in 2019 that Norway's force structure was too small for defence requirements. Norway maintains a small presence in a range of international crisis-management missions. Equipment recapitalisation is ongoing, but large procurements will stretch budgets. Norway retired its fleet of F-16s in

Europe 119

early 2022, with the F-35 taking over responsibility for air defence. New submarines are being procured as part of a strategic partnership with Germany. There are plans to strengthen Brigade North with new equipment and manoeuvre and support units. In June 2018, it was announced that a planned upgrade to Norway's main-battle-tank fleet would be pushed to the mid-2020s. Norway has an advanced and diverse defence-industrial base with a high percentage of SMEs and a mix of private and state-owned companies.

ACTIVE 25,400 (Army 8,300 Navy 4,600 Air 4,300 Central Support 7,400 Home Guard 800)

Conscript liability 19 months maximum. Conscripts first serve 12 months from 19–28, and then up to 4–5 refresher training periods until age 35, 44, 55 or 60 depending on rank and function. Conscription was extended to women in 2015

RESERVE 40,000 (Home Guard 40,000)

Readiness varies from a few hours to several days

ORGANISATIONS BY SERVICE

Army 3,900; 4,400 conscript (total 8,300)

The armoured infantry brigade – Brigade North – trains new personnel of all categories and provides units for international operations. At any time around one-third of the brigade will be trained and ready to conduct operations. The brigade includes one high-readiness armoured battalion (Telemark Battalion) with combat-support and combat-service-support units on high readiness

FORCES BY ROLE
MANOEUVRE
Reconnaissance
1 armd recce bn (forming)
1 ISR bn
1 (GSV) bn (1 (border) recce coy, 1 ranger coy, 1 spt coy, 1 trg coy)
Armoured
1 armd inf bde (2 armd bn, 1 lt inf bn, 1 arty bn, 1 engr bn, 1 MP coy, 1 CIS bn, 1 spt bn, 1 med bn)
Light
1 lt inf bn (His Majesty The King's Guards)
EQUIPMENT BY TYPE
ARMOURED FIGHTING VEHICLES
MBT 36 *Leopard* 2A4 (16 more in store)
RECCE 21 CV9030
IFV 91: 76 CV9030N; 15 CV9030N (CP)
APC 390
   APC (T) 315 M113 (incl variants)
   APC (W) 75 XA-186 *Sisu*/XA-200 *Sisu*/XA-203 (amb)
AUV 165: 20 *Dingo* 2; 25 HMT *Extenda*; 120 IVECO LMV (36 more in store)
ENGINEERING & MAINTENANCE VEHICLES
AEV 34+: 20 CV90 STING; 8 M113 AEV; NM109; 6 *Wisent*-2
ARV 12: 6 BPz-2; 6 *Wisent*-2
VLB 36: 26 *Leguan*; 1+ *Leopard* 2 with *Leguan*; 9 *Leopard* 1
MW 9 910 MCV-2
NBC VEHICLES 6 TPz-1 *Fuchs* NBC
ANTI-TANK/ANTI-INFRASTRUCTURE
MANPATS FGM-148 *Javelin*
RCL 84mm *Carl Gustaf*

ARTILLERY 167
SP 155mm 24 K9 *Thunder*
MOR 143: **81mm** 115 L16; **SP 81mm** 28: 16 CV9030; 12 M125A2
AIR DEFENCE
SAM • Medium-range NASAMS III

Navy 2,350; 2,250 conscripts (total 4,600)

Joint Command – Norwegian National Joint Headquarters. The Royal Norwegian Navy is organised into five elements under the command of the Chief of the Navy: the fleet (*Marinen*), the Coast Guard (*Kystvakten*), the recruit training school (KNM *Harald Haarfagre*), the naval medical branch and the naval bases (*Haakonsvern* and *Ramsund*)

FORCES BY ROLE
MANOEUVRE
Reconnaissance
1 ISR coy (Coastal Rangers)
COMBAT SUPPORT
1 EOD pl
EQUIPMENT BY TYPE
SUBMARINES 6
SSK 6 *Ula* with 8 single 533mm TT with *SeaHake* (DM2A3) HWT
PRINCIPAL SURFACE COMBATANTS • FRIGATES 4
FFGHM 4 *Fridtjof Nansen* with *Aegis* C2 (mod), 2 quad lnchr with NSM AShM, 1 8-cell Mk 41 VLS with RIM-162A ESSM SAM, 2 twin 324mm ASTT with *Sting Ray* mod 1 LWT, 1 76mm gun (capacity 1 med hel)
PATROL AND COASTAL COMBATANTS 13
PSOH 1 *Nordkapp* with 1 57mm gun (capacity 1 med tpt hel)
PCFG 6 *Skjold* with 8 single lnchr with NSM AShM, 1 76mm gun
PBF 6 CB90N (capacity 20 troops)
MINE WARFARE • MINE COUNTERMEASURES 4
MSC 2 *Alta* with 1 twin *Simbad* lnchr with *Mistral* SAM
MHC 2 *Oksoy* with 1 twin *Simbad* lnchr with *Mistral* SAM
LOGISTICS AND SUPPORT 6
AGI 1 *Marjata* IV
AGS 2: 1 *HU Sverdrup* II; 1 *Eger* (*Marjata* III) with 1 hel landing platform
AORH 1 *Maud* (BMT *Aegir*) (capacity 2 med hel)
AXL 2 *Reine*

Coast Guard

EQUIPMENT BY TYPE
PATROL AND COASTAL COMBATANTS 12
   PSOH 2: 1 *Jan Mayen* (capacity 2 med hel); 1 *Nordkapp* with 1 57mm gun (capacity 1 med tpt hel)
   PSO 5: 3 *Barentshav*; 1 *Harstad*; 1 *Svalbard* with 1 57mm gun, 1 hel landing platform
   PCC 5 *Nornen*
LOGISTICS AND SUPPORT • ATF 2 *Jarl* (leased)

Air Force 2,900; 1,400 conscript (total 4,300)

Joint Command – Norwegian National HQ
FORCES BY ROLE
FIGHTER/GROUND ATTACK
2 sqn with F-35A *Lightning* II

MARITIME PATROL
  1 sqn with P-3C *Orion*; P-8A *Poseidon*
SEARCH & RESCUE
  1 sqn with Sea King Mk43B; AW101
TRANSPORT
  1 sqn with C-130J-30 *Hercules*
TRAINING
  1 sqn with MFI-15 *Safari*
TRANSPORT HELICOPTER
  2 sqn with Bell 412SP *Twin Huey*
AIR DEFENCE
  2 bn with NASAMS III

EQUIPMENT BY TYPE
AIRCRAFT 45 combat capable
  FGA 37 F-35A *Lightning* II
  ASW 8: 3 P-3C *Orion*; 5 P-8A *Poseidon*
  TPT • Medium 4 C-130J-30 *Hercules*
  TRG 16 MFI-15 *Safari*
HELICOPTERS
  ASW (13 NH90 NFH in store)
  SAR 19: 9 AW101; 10 *Sea King* Mk43B
  MRH 18: 6 Bell 412HP; 12 Bell 412SP
AIR DEFENCE
  SAM • Medium-range NASAMS III
AIR-LAUNCHED MISSILES
  AAM • IR AIM-9L *Sidewinder*; **IIR** AIM-9X *Sidewinder* II; IRIS-T; **ARH** AIM-120B AMRAAM; AIM-120C AMRAAM
BOMBS
  Laser-guided EGBU-12 *Paveway* II
  INS/GPS guided JDAM

Special Operations Command (NORSOCOM)
FORCES BY ROLE
SPECIAL FORCES
  1 (armed forces) SF comd (2 SF gp)
  1 (navy) SF comd (1 SF gp)
EQUIPMENT BY TYPE
PATROL AND COASTAL COMBATANTS • PBF 2 IC20M

Central Support, Administration and Command 5,850; 1,550 conscripts (total 7,400)

Central Support, Administration and Command includes military personnel in all joint elements and they are responsible for logistics and CIS in support of all forces in Norway and abroad

Home Guard 400; 400 conscripts (40,000 reserves)

The Home Guard is a separate organisation, but closely cooperates with all services. The Home Guard is organised in 11 Districts with mobile Rapid Reaction Forces (3,000 troops in total) as well as reinforcements and follow-on forces (37,000 troops in total).

EQUIPMENT BY TYPE
PATROL AND COASTAL COMBATANTS • PB 11: 4 *Harek*; 2 *Gyda*; 5 *Alusafe* 1290

DEPLOYMENT

CYPRUS: UN • UNFICYP 2
EGYPT: MFO 3
IRAQ: Operation Inherent Resolve 60; 1 trg unit; **NATO** • NATO Mission Iraq 2
JORDAN: Operation Inherent Resolve 20
LITHUANIA: NATO • Enhanced Forward Presence 270; 1 armd inf coy(+); CV9030
MALI: UN • MINUSMA 29
MIDDLE EAST: UN • UNTSO 13
BALTIC SEA: NATO • SNMG 1: 50; 1 AORH
SOUTH SUDAN: UN • UNMISS 15

FOREIGN FORCES

United States US European Command 1,100; 1 (USMC) MEU eqpt set; 1 (APS) 155mm SP Arty bn eqpt set

Poland POL

Polish Zloty PLN		2021	2022	2023
GDP	PLN	2.62tr	3.09tr	
	USD	679bn	716bn	
per capita	USD	17,946	19,023	
Growth	%	5.9	3.8	
Inflation	%	5.1	13.8	
Def exp [a]	PLN	58.3bn	73.9bn	
	USD	15.1bn	17.1bn	
Def bdgt [b]	PLN	51.8bn	57.8bn	97.4bn
	USD	13.4bn	13.4bn	
USD1=PLN		3.86	4.31	

[a] NATO figure
[b] Includes military pensions

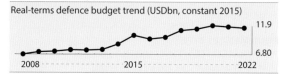
Real-terms defence budget trend (USDbn, constant 2015)

Population	38,093,101					
Age	0–14	15–19	20–24	25–29	30–64	65 plus
Male	7.6%	2.4%	2.5%	3.0%	24.8%	8.1%
Female	7.1%	2.3%	2.4%	2.9%	25.1%	11.9%

Capabilities

Territorial defence and NATO membership are central pillars of Poland's defence policy. The primary focus of the 2017–32 defence concept is to prepare the armed forces to deter Russian aggression. Russia is characterised as a direct threat to Poland and to a stable international order, a view sharpened by Russia's February 2022 invasion of Ukraine. Poland is one of the main European contributors to efforts to support Ukraine and has delivered to Ukraine a variety of defence equipment including armour and anti-armour systems. There has been a rapid increase in defence expenditure, designed to support investment projects. An extra-budgetary fund

Europe 121

will deliver funds additional to the base defence budget. The government continues to pursue a goal of permanently stationing US troops in the country. The US Army's V Corps Headquarters (Forward) was established in Poznań at the end of 2020. There are ambitious plans to boost personnel numbers to 300,000 by 2035, including 50,000 to be recruited under a new salaried one-year service scheme. This stems from plans to set up an additional heavy division in the east. Acquisition reform has been under way for some time and a central armaments agency was established in January 2022. A technical-modernisation plan, covering the period 2021–35, was released in October 2019, which extended the planning horizon from ten to 15 years. Ambitious modernisation plans are underway. F-35As are due to arrive from 2024, and land forces capabilities will be boosted by the arrival of *Abrams* main battle tanks. In 2022 agreements were signed with South Korea for the procurement of FA-50 combat aircraft, K2 MBTs and K9 self-propelled artillery pieces. *Chunmoo* MRLs will be bought, alongside US HIMARS systems. Warsaw continues plans to strengthen its domestic defence-industrial base, much of which is now consolidated in the state-owned holding company PGZ, using technology transfers and international partnering, such as the deals with South Korea. Beyond PGZ, several international defence companies have subsidiaries in Poland.

ACTIVE 114,050 (Army 58,500 Navy 6,000 Air Force 14,300 Special Forces 3,150 Territorial 3,800 Joint 28,300) Gendarmerie & Paramilitary 14,300

ORGANISATIONS BY SERVICE

Army 58,500

FORCES BY ROLE
COMMAND
  elm 1 (MNC NE) corps HQ
MANOEUVRE
  Reconnaissance
  3 recce regt
  Armoured
  1 (11th) armd cav div (2 armd bde, 1 mech bde, 1 arty regt)
  Mechanised
  1 (12th) mech div (2 mech bde, 1 (coastal) mech bde, 1 arty regt)
  1 (16th) mech div (1 armd bde, 2 mech bde, 1 arty regt, 1 AT regt)
  1 (18th) mech div (1 armd bde, 2 mech bde, 1 log regt)
  Air Manoeuvre
  1 (6th) AB bde (3 para bn)
  1 (25th) air cav bde (2 air cav bn, 2 tpt hel bn, 1 (casevac) med unit)
COMBAT SUPPORT
  2 engr regt
  2 ptn br regt
  2 chem def regt
COMBAT SUPPORT
  2 log bde
HELICOPTER
  1 (1st) hel bde (2 atk hel sqn with Mi-24D/V *Hind* D/E, 1 CSAR sqn with Mi-24V *Hind* E; PZL W-3PL *Gluszec*; 2 ISR hel sqn with Mi-2URP; 2 hel sqn with Mi-2)
AIR DEFENCE
  3 AD regt

EQUIPMENT BY TYPE
ARMOURED FIGHTING VEHICLES
  MBT 647: 10 K2; 108 *Leopard* 2A4 (being upgraded to 2PL); 105 *Leopard* 2A5; 34 *Leopard* 2PL; 28 M1A2 SEPv2 *Abrams* (on loan for trg) up to 232 PT-91 *Twardy*; 130 T-72A/T-72M1/M1R
  RECCE 407: 282 BRDM-2; 38 BWR-1 (being upgraded); 87 BRDM-2 R5
  IFV 1,567: up to 1,212 BMP-1; 4 *Borsuk* (in test); 351 *Rosomak* IFV
  APC 450
    APC (T) 6 WDSz (OP)
    APC (W) 344: 300 *Rosomak* APC (incl variants); 44 AWD RAK (arty CP)
    PPV 100 *Maxxpro*
  AUV 255: 210 *Cougar*; 45 M-ATV
ENGINEERING & MAINTENANCE VEHICLES
  AEV 106+: IWT; 65 MT-LB AEV; 33 *Rosomak* WRT; 8 MID *Bizon*
  ARV 122: 28 BPz-2; 68 MT-LB ARV; 26 WZT-3M
  VLB 119: 4 *Biber*; 103 BLG67M2; 12 MS-20 *Daglezja*
  MW 27: 17 *Bozena* 4; 6 ISM *Kroton*; 4 *Kalina* SUM
ANTI-TANK/ANTI-INFRASTRUCTURE
  MSL • MANPATS 9K11 *Malyutka* (RS-AT-3 *Sagger*); 9K111 *Fagot* (RS-AT-4 *Spigot*); *Spike*-LR
ARTILLERY 773
  SP 424: **122mm** up to 227 2S1 *Gvozdika*; **152mm** 111 M-77 *Dana*; **155mm** 86: 24 K9A1; 62 *Krab*
  MRL 122mm 179: up to 75 BM-21; 29 RM-70; 75 WR-40 *Langusta*
  MOR 170: **120mm** 80: 15 2B11; 65 M120; **SP 120mm** 90 SMK120 RAK
HELICOPTERS
  ATK 28 Mi-24D/V *Hind* D/E
  MRH 64: 7 Mi-8MT *Hip*; 3 Mi-17 *Hip* H; 1 Mi-17AE *Hip* (aeromedical); 5 Mi-17-1V *Hip*; 16 PZL Mi-2URP *Hoplite*; 24 PZL W-3W/WA *Sokol*; 8 PZL W-3PL *Gluszec* (CSAR)
  TPT 37: **Medium** 12: 6 Mi-8T *Hip*; 2 PZL W-3AE *Sokol* (aeromedical); 4 S-70i *Black Hawk*; **Light** 25 PZL Mi-2 *Hoplite*
UNINHABITED AERIAL VEHICLES 6
  CISR • Medium 6 *Bayraktar* TB2
AIR DEFENCE
  SAM 166+
    Short-range 23: 3 CAMM (*Narew*); 20 2K12 *Kub* (RS-SA-6 *Gainful*)
    Point-defence 143+: 64 9K33 *Osa*-AK (RS-SA-8 *Gecko*); GROM; *Piorun*; 79 *Poprad*
  SPAAGM 23mm 20 ZSU-23-4MP *Biala*
  GUNS 345
    SP 23mm 2 ZSU-23-4
    TOWED 23mm 343: 268 ZU-23-2; 75 ZUR-23-2KG *Jodek*-G (with GROM msl)
BOMBS • Laser-guided MAM-C/L

Navy 6,000

EQUIPMENT BY TYPE
SUBMARINES • SSK 1 *Orzeł* (ex-FSU *Kilo*)† with 6 single 533mm TT each with 53-65KE HWT/TEST-71ME
PRINCIPAL SURFACE COMBATANTS • FRIGATES 2
  FFH 2 *Pułaski* (ex-US *Oliver Hazard Perry*) (of which 1 used as training ship) with 2 triple 324mm SVTT Mk 32 ASTT with MU90 LWT, 1 Mk 15 *Phalanx* CIWS, 1 76mm gun (capacity 2 SH-2G *Super Seasprite* ASW hel)
PATROL AND COASTAL COMBATANTS 5
  CORVETTES • FSM 1 *Kaszub* with 2 quad lnchr with 9K32 *Strela*-2 (RS-SA-N-5 *Grail*) SAM, 2 twin 533mm ASTT with SET-53 HWT, 2 RBU 6000 *Smerch* 2 A/S mor, 1 76mm gun
  PSO 1 *Ślązak* (MEKO A-100) with 1 76mm gun, 1 hel landing platform
  PCFGM 3 *Orkan* (ex-GDR *Sassnitz*) with 1 quad lnchr with RBS15 Mk3 AShM, 1 quad lnchr (manual aiming) with 9K32 *Strela*-2M (RS-SA-N-5 *Grail*) SAM, 1 AK630 CIWS, 1 76mm gun
MINE WARFARE • MINE COUNTERMEASURES 21
  MCCS 1 *Kontradmiral Xawery Czernicki*
  MCO 2 *Kormoran* II
  MHO 1 *Krogulec*
  MSI 17: 1 *Gopło*; 12 *Gardno*; 4 *Mamry*
AMPHIBIOUS 8
  LANDING SHIPS • LSM 5 *Lublin* (capacity 9 tanks; 135 troops)
  LANDING CRAFT • LCU 3 *Deba* (capacity 50 troops)
LOGISTICS AND SUPPORT 26
  AGI 2 *Moma*
  AGS 8: 2 *Heweliusz*; 4 *Wildcat* 40; 2 (coastal)
  AORL 1 *Bałtyk*
  AOL 1 *Moskit*
  ARS 4: 2 *Piast*; 2 *Zbyszko*
  ATF 8: 6 *Bolko* (B860); 2 H960
  AX 1 *Wodnik* with 1 twin AK230 CIWS
  AXS 1 *Iskra*
COASTAL DEFENCE • AShM 12 NSM

Naval Aviation 1,300

FORCES BY ROLE
ANTI SUBMARINE WARFARE/SEARCH & RESCUE
  1 sqn with Mi-14PL *Haze* A; Mi-14PL/R *Haze* C
  1 sqn with PZL W-3RM *Anakonda*; SH-2G *Super Seasprite*
MARITIME PATROL
  1 sqn with An-28E/RM *Bryza*
TRANSPORT
  1 sqn with An-28TD; M-28B TD *Bryza*
  1 sqn with An-28TD; M-28B; PZL Mi-2 *Hoplite*; PZL W-3T/A
EQUIPMENT BY TYPE
AIRCRAFT
  MP 10: 8 An-28RM *Bryza*; 2 An-28E *Bryza*
  TPT • Light 4: 2 An-28TD *Bryza*; 2 M-28B TD *Bryza*
HELICOPTERS
  ASW 8: 6 Mi-14PL *Haze*; 2 SH-2G *Super Seasprite*
  SAR 8: 2 Mi-14PL/R *Haze* C; 4 PZL W-3RM *Anakonda*; 2 PZL W-3WA RM *Anakonda*

  TPT • Light 7: 4 PZL Mi-2 *Hoplite*; 1 PZL W-3A; 2 PZL-W-3T

Air Force 14,300

FORCES BY ROLE
FIGHTER
  2 sqn with MiG-29A/UB *Fulcrum*
FIGHTER/GROUND ATTACK
  3 sqn with F-16C/D Block 52+ *Fighting Falcon*
FIGHTER/GROUND ATTACK/ISR
  2 sqn with Su-22M-4 *Fitter*
SEARCH AND RESCUE
  1 sqn with Mi-2; PZL W-3 *Sokol*
TRANSPORT
  1 sqn with C-130H/E; M-28 *Bryza*
  1 sqn with C295M; M-28 *Bryza*
TRAINING
  1 sqn with PZL-130 *Orlik*
  1 sqn with M-346
  1 hel sqn with SW-4 *Puszczyk*
TRANSPORT HELICOPTER
  1 (Spec Ops) sqn with Mi-17 *Hip* H
  1 (VIP) sqn with Mi-8 *Hip*; W-3WA *Sokol*
AIR DEFENCE
  1 bde with S-125 *Newa* SC; S-200C *Vega* (RS-SA-5 *Gammon*)
EQUIPMENT BY TYPE
AIRCRAFT 94 combat capable
  FTR 28: 22 MiG-29A *Fulcrum*; 6 MiG-29UB *Fulcrum*
  FGA 66: 36 F-16C Block 52+ *Fighting Falcon*; 12 F-16D Block 52+ *Fighting Falcon*; 12 Su-22M4 *Fitter*; 6 Su-22UM3K *Fitter*
  TPT 50: **Medium** 7: 2 C-130H *Hercules*; 5 C-130E *Hercules*; **Light** 39: 16 C295M; 10 M-28 *Bryza* TD; 13 M-28 *Bryza* PT; **PAX** 4: 2 Gulfstream G550; 2 B-737-800 (VIP)
  TRG 40: 12 M-346; 28 PZL-130 *Orlik*
HELICOPTERS
  MRH 8 Mi-17 *Hip* H
  TPT 65: **Medium** 29: 9 Mi-8 *Hip*; 10 PZL W-3 *Sokol*; 10 PZL W-3WA *Sokol* (VIP); **Light** 36: 14 PZL Mi-2 *Hoplite*; 22 SW-4 *Puszczyk* (trg)
AIR DEFENCE
  SAM 18
    Long-range 1 S-200C *Vega* (RS-SA-5 *Gammon*)
    Short-range 17 S-125 *Newa* SC
  GUNS • TOWED 23mm 12 *Pilica* (with *Piorun* msl)
AIR-LAUNCHED MISSILES
  AAM • IR AIM-9 *Sidewinder*; R-60 (RS-AA-8 *Aphid*); R-73 (RS-AA-11A *Archer*); R-27T (RS-AA-10B *Alamo*); **IIR** AIM-9X *Sidwinder* II; **ARH** AIM-120C AMRAAM
  ASM AGM-65J/G *Maverick*; Kh-25 (RS-AS-10 *Karen*); Kh-29 (RS-AS-14 *Kedge*)
  ALCM • Conventional AGM-158 JASSM

Special Forces 3,150

FORCES BY ROLE
SPECIAL FORCES
  3 SF units (GROM, FORMOZA & cdo)
COMBAT SUPPORT/
  1 cbt spt unit (AGAT)
COMBAT SERVICE SUPPORT
  1 spt unit (NIL)

Territorial Defence Forces 3,800 (plus 20,000 reservists)

FORCES BY ROLE
MANOEUVRE
Other
15 sy bde
2 sy bde (forming)

Gendarmerie & Paramilitary 14,300

Border Guards 14,300
Ministry of Interior

Maritime Border Guard 2,000
EQUIPMENT BY TYPE
PATROL AND COASTAL COMBATANTS 18
PCC 2 *Kaper*
PBF 6: 2 *Strażnik*; 4 IC16M
PB 10: 2 *Wisłoka*; 2 *Baltic 24*; 1 Project MI-6
AMPHIBIOUS • LANDING CRAFT
UCAC 2 *Griffon* 2000TDX

DEPLOYMENT

BOSNIA-HERZEGOVINA: EU • EUFOR (*Operation Althea*) 38

CENTRAL AFRICAN REPUBLIC: EU • EUTM RCA 2

DEMOCRATIC REPUBLIC OF THE CONGO: UN • MONUSCO 1

IRAQ: *Operation Inherent Resolve* 150; **NATO** • NATO Mission Iraq 30

LATVIA: NATO • Enhanced Forward Presence 177; 1 tk coy

LEBANON: UN • UNIFIL 193; 1 mech inf coy

MIDDLE EAST: UN • UNTSO 4

ROMANIA: NATO • MNB-SE 220; 1 mech inf coy; *Rosomak*

SERBIA: NATO • KFOR 247; 1 inf coy; UN • UNMIK 2

SOUTH SUDAN: UN • UNMISS 1

WESTERN SAHARA: UN • MINURSO 2

FOREIGN FORCES

All NATO Enhanced Forward Presence unless stated
Canada *Operation Unifier* 40 (UKR trg)
Croatia 4
Germany MNC-NE corps HQ: 95
Italy NATO Baltic Air Policing: 135; 4 Eurofighter *Typhoon*
United Kingdom 129; 1 recce sqn; Army: 250; 1 tk sqn with *Challenger* 2; 1 SAM bty with CAMM (*Land Ceptor*)
United States: 780; 1 armd bn with M1A2 SEPv2 *Abrams*; M2A3 *Bradley*; • *Operation Atlantic Resolve* 15,000; 1 corps HQ; 2 div HQ; 2 armd bde with M1A2 SEPv2 *Abrams*; M3A3 *Bradley*; M2A3 *Bradley*; M109A6/A7; 1 AB bde with M119A3; M777A2; 2 SAM bty with M902 *Patriot* PAC3; 1 FGA sqn with 12 F-22A *Raptor* 1 CISR UAV sqn with MQ-9A *Reaper*

Portugal PRT

Euro EUR		2021	2022	2023
GDP	EUR	211bn	242bn	
	USD	250bn	256bn	
per capita	USD	24,296	24,910	
Growth	%	4.9	6.2	
Inflation	%	0.9	7.9	
Def exp [a]	EUR	3.30bn	3.33bn	
	USD	3.90bn	3.52bn	
Def bdgt	EUR	2.48bn	2.45bn	2.58bn
	USD	2.93bn	2.59bn	
USD1=EUR		0.84	0.95	

[a] NATO figure

Real-terms defence budget trend (USDbn, constant 2015)

Population	10,242,081					
Age	0–14	15–19	20–24	25–29	30–64	65 plus
Male	6.7%	2.7%	2.9%	2.8%	23.7%	8.6%
Female	6.4%	2.6%	2.7%	2.7%	25.3%	13.0%

Capabilities

Principal tasks for Portugal's all-volunteer armed forces are homeland defence, maritime security, multinational operations and responding to humanitarian disasters. Investment plans support Portugal's ambition to field rapid-reaction and maritime-surveillance capabilities for territorial defence and multinational operations. A new military programme law for 2019–30 was approved by parliament, funding the acquisition of five KC-390 aircraft, six offshore-patrol vessels, a replenishment tanker and a multi-purpose logistics ship, as well as cyber-defence and soldier-combat systems. In 2022 a modest increase to defence spending was announced, with the country aiming to boost by 2024 the proportion of GDP spent on defence. Portugal hosts NATO's cyber-security academy and the country also contributes to EU military structures. There is a close relationship with former dependencies and with the US, which operates out of Lajes air base. All three services have programmes to modernise and sustain existing equipment platforms. There is an active defence industry, though principally in relation to shipbuilding, broader maintenance tasks and the manufacture of components, small arms and light weapons.

ACTIVE 26,700 (Army 13,350 Navy 7,400 Air 5,950)
Gendarmerie & Paramilitary 24,700

RESERVE 23,500 (Army 10,000 Navy 9,000, Air Force 4,500)
Reserve obligation to age 35

ORGANISATIONS BY SERVICE

Army 13,350
5 territorial comd (2 mil region, 1 mil district, 2 mil zone)

124 THE MILITARY BALANCE 2023

FORCES BY ROLE
SPECIAL FORCES
1 SF bn
MANOEUVRE
Mechanised
1 mech bde (1 recce sqn, 1 tk regt, 1 mech inf bn, 1 arty bn, 1 AD bty, 1 engr coy, 1 sigs coy, 1 spt bn)
1 (intervention) bde (1 recce regt, 2 mech inf bn, 1 arty bn, 1 AD bty, 1 engr coy, 1 sigs coy, 1 spt bn)
Air Manoeuvre
1 (rapid reaction) bde (1 cdo bn, 1 ISR bn, 2 para bn, 1 arty bn, 1 AD bty, 1 engr coy, 1 sigs coy, 1 spt bn)
Other
1 (Azores) inf gp (2 inf bn, 1 AD bty)
1 (Madeira) inf gp (1 inf bn, 1 AD bty)
COMBAT SUPPORT
1 STA bty
1 engr bn (1 construction coy; 1 EOD unit; 1 ptn br coy; 1 CBRN coy)
1 EW coy
1 MP bn
1 psyops unit
1 CIMIC coy (joint)
1 sigs bn
COMBAT SERVICE SUPPORT
1 maint coy
1 log coy
1 tpt coy
1 med unit
AIR DEFENCE
1 AD bn

Reserves 210,000
FORCES BY ROLE
MANOEUVRE
Light
3 (territorial) def bde (on mobilisation)
EQUIPMENT BY TYPE
ARMOURED FIGHTING VEHICLES
MBT 37 Leopard 2A6
IFV 30 Pandur II MK 30mm
APC 406
    APC (T) 239: 176 M113A1; 14 M113A2; 49 M577A2 (CP)
    APC (W) 167: 9 V-150 Commando; 12 V-200 Chaimite; 146 Pandur II (incl variants)
AUV 16 VBL
ENGINEERING & MAINTENANCE VEHICLES
AEV M728
ARV 13: 6 M88A1, 7 Pandur II ARV
VLB M48
ANTI-TANK/ANTI-INFRASTRUCTURE
MSL
    SP 26: 17 M113 with TOW; 4 M901 with TOW; 5 Pandur II with TOW
    MANPATS Milan; TOW
RCL • 84mm Carl Gustaf; **106mm** 45 M40A1
ARTILLERY 320
SP 155mm 24: 6 M109A2; 18 M109A5
TOWED 62: **105mm** 39: 17 L119 Light Gun; 21 M101A1; **155mm** 24 M114A1
MOR 234: **81mm** 143; **SP 81mm** 12: 2 M125A1; 10

M125A2; **107mm** 11 M30; **SP 107mm** 18: 3 M106A1; 15 M106A2; **120mm** 50 Tampella
AIR DEFENCE
SAM • Point-defence 20+: 1 M48A2 Chaparral; 19 M48A3 Chaparral; FIM-92 Stinger
GUNS • TOWED 20mm 20 Rh 202

Navy 7,400 (incl 950 Marines)
EQUIPMENT BY TYPE
SUBMARINES 2
SSK 2 Tridente (GER Type-214) (fitted with AIP) with 8 533mm TT with UGM-84L Harpoon Block II AShM/Black Shark HWT
PRINCIPAL SURFACE COMBATANTS • FRIGATES 5
FFGHM 5:
    1 Bartolomeu Dias (ex-NLD Karel Doorman) (MLU ongoing) with 2 quad lnchr with RGM-84C Harpoon Block 1B AShM, 1 16-cell Mk 48 mod 1 VLS with RIM-7M Sea Sparrow SAM, 2 twin 324mm SVTT Mk 32 ASTT with Mk 46 LWT, 1 Goalkeeper CIWS, 1 76mm gun (capacity 1 Lynx Mk95 (Super Lynx) hel)
    1 Bartolomeu Dias (ex-NLD Karel Doorman) with 2 quad lnchr with RGM-84L Harpoon Block II AShM, 1 16-cell Mk 48 mod 1 VLS with RIM-162 ESSM SAM, 2 twin 324mm SVTT Mk 32 ASTT with Mk 46 LWT, 1 Goalkeeper CIWS, 1 76mm gun (capacity 1 Lynx Mk95 (Super Lynx) hel)
    3 Vasco Da Gama with 2 quad lnchr with RGM-84C Harpoon Block 1B AShM, 1 octuple Mk 29 GMLS with RIM-7M Sea Sparrow SAM, 2 triple 324mm SVTT Mk 32 ASTT with Mk 46 LWT, 1 Mk 15 Phalanx Block 1B CIWS, 1 100mm gun (capacity 2 Lynx Mk95 (Super Lynx) hel)
PATROL AND COASTAL COMBATANTS 22
CORVETTES • FS 2:
    1 Baptista de Andrade with 1 100mm gun, 1 hel landing platform
    1 Joao Coutinho with 1 twin 76mm gun, 1 hel landing platform
PSO 4 Viana do Castelo with 1 hel landing platform
PCC 5: 1 Cacine; 4 Tejo (ex-DNK Flyvisken)
PBR 10: 5 Argos; 4 Centauro; 1 Rio Minho
PB 1 Patrão Cego do Maio (SAR)
LOGISTICS AND SUPPORT 10
AGS 4: 2 D Carlos I (ex-US Stalwart); 2 Andromeda
AXS 6: 1 Sagres; 1 Creoula; 1 Polar; 2 Belatrix; 1 Zarco

Marines 950
FORCES BY ROLE
SPECIAL FORCES
1 SF det
MANOEUVRE
Light
1 lt inf bn
COMBAT SUPPORT
1 mor coy
1 MP coy

EQUIPMENT BY TYPE
ANTI-TANK/ANTI-INFRASTRUCTURE
  MSL • MANPATS Milan; TOW
  RCL • 84mm Carl Gustaf
  ARTILLERY • MOR 30+: 81mm some; 120mm 30

Naval Aviation
EQUIPMENT BY TYPE
HELICOPTERS • ASW 5: 4 Lynx Mk95 (Super Lynx); 1 Lynx Mk95A (Super Lynx)

Air Force 5,950
FORCES BY ROLE
FIGHTER/GROUND ATTACK
  2 sqn with F-16AM/BM Fighting Falcon
MARITIME PATROL
  1 sqn with P-3C Orion
ISR/TRANSPORT
  1 sqn with C295M
COMBAT SEARCH & RESCUE
  1 sqn with with AW101 Merlin
TRANSPORT
  1 sqn with C-130H/C-130H-30 Hercules
  1 sqn with Falcon 50
TRAINING
  1 sqn with AW119 Koala
  1 sqn with TB-30 Epsilon
EQUIPMENT BY TYPE
AIRCRAFT 35 combat capable
  FTR 30: 26 F-16AM Fighting Falcon; 4 F-16BM Fighting Falcon
  ASW 5 P-3C Orion
  ISR 7: 5 C295M (maritime surveillance), 2 C295M (photo recce)
  TPT 13: Medium 5: 2 C-130H Hercules; 3 C-130H-30 Hercules (tpt/SAR); Light 5 C295M; PAX 3 Falcon 50 (tpt/VIP)
  TRG 16 TB-30 Epsilon
HELICOPTERS
  TPT 17: Medium 12 AW101 Merlin (6 SAR, 4 CSAR, 2 fishery protection); Light 5 AW119 Koala
AIR-LAUNCHED MISSILES
  AAM • IR AIM-9L/I Sidewinder; ARH AIM-120C AMRAAM
  ASM AGM-65A Maverick
  AShM AGM-84A Harpoon
BOMBS
  Laser & INS/GPS-guided GBU-49 Enhanced Paveway II
  INS/GPS guided GBU-31 JDAM

Gendarmerie & Paramilitary 24,700

National Republican Guard 24,700
EQUIPMENT BY TYPE
PATROL AND COASTAL COMBATANTS 32
  PBF 12
  PB 20
HELICOPTERS • MRH 7 SA315 Lama

DEPLOYMENT
BOSNIA-HERZEGOVINA: EU • EUFOR (Operation Althea) 1
CENTRAL AFRICAN REPUBLIC: EU • EUTM RCA 14; UN • MINUSCA 196; 1 AB coy
IRAQ: Operation Inherent Resolve 30
MALI: EU • EUTM Mali 11
MEDITERRANEAN SEA: NATO • SNMCMG 2: 40; 1 PSO
MOZAMBIQUE: EU • EUTM Mozambique 120
SOMALIA: EU • EUTM Somalia 2

FOREIGN FORCES
United States US European Command: 250; 1 spt facility at Lajes

Romania ROM

Romanian Leu RON		2021	2022	2023
GDP	RON	1.18tr	1.40tr	
	USD	284bn	300bn	
per capita	USD	14,795	15,619	
Growth	%	5.9	4.8	
Inflation	%	5.0	13.3	
Def exp [a]	RON	22.0bn	26.4bn	
	USD	5.29bn	5.64bn	
Def bdgt [b]	RON	23.1bn	24.3bn	
	USD	5.56bn	5.19bn	
USD1=RON		4.16	4.68	

[a] NATO figure
[b] Includes military pensions

Real-terms defence budget trend (USDbn, constant 2015)

Population 18,519,899

Age	0–14	15–19	20–24	25–29	30–64	65 plus
Male	8.1%	2.7%	2.5%	2.3%	23.7%	9.0%
Female	7.7%	2.5%	2.5%	2.3%	23.9%	12.8%

Capabilities

Romania's armed forces are structured around territorial defence, support to NATO and EU missions, and contributing to regional and global stability and security. According to the National Defence Strategy 2020–2024, principal security threats include Russia's increased presence in the Black Sea, hybrid warfare, cyber-attacks, terrorism and the economic impact of the coronavirus pandemic. Under the Armata 2040 project, authorities are looking to modernise and upgrade the armed forces to NATO standards. A defence budget increase was announced in March 2022. Bucharest has signed defence cooperation agreements with regional allies and, in the aftermath of Russia's 2022 invasion of Ukraine, bolstered cooperation with the US, France, and regional allies in the Bucharest Nine organisation. There is a strategic partnership with the US. Romania

126   THE MILITARY BALANCE 2023

hosts the *Aegis* Ashore ballistic-missile-defence system at Deveselu. In May 2022, NATO's multinational Battle Group Forward Presence achieved initial operational capability. Led by France, this unit is based at Cincu. Elements of the US Army's Task Force Cougar started to arrive at Mihail Kogalniceanu air base in early 2022. There is broad training with NATO and regional allies, and Romania contributes to EU and NATO missions. The inventory is mainly composed of Soviet-era equipment, which is seen as a factor-limiting capability. Though Romanian airspace benefits from NATO's Enhanced Air Policing mission, in May 2022 the authorities indicated a plan to extend the service life of the ageing MiG-21 *Lancer* aircraft by approximately a year, following delays in transitioning to the F-16. Romania has received a number of F-16s, purchased from Portugal, and in 2023 is expected to receive the first batch of F-16s purchased from Norway. Acquisition plans include armoured vehicles, air-defence radars, surface-to-air missiles and corvettes. The *Naval Strike Missile* will be procured for coastal defence from 2024, while Bucharest has received the first elements of the HIMARS system ordered in 2018. The country's defence industry has struggled since 1989. Current production focuses on small arms and ammunition. However, Bucharest has agreed a contract with General Dynamics to produce locally a new batch of *Piranha* V armoured vehicles, and with Airbus to produce H215 helicopters. Bucharest continues to look for opportunities to boost its defence industry through offset agreements and technology transfers.

ACTIVE 71,500 (Army 35,500 Navy 6,800 Air 11,700 Joint 17,500) Gendarmerie & Paramilitary 57,000

RESERVE 55,000 (Joint 55,000)

ORGANISATIONS BY SERVICE

Army 35,500

Readiness is reported as 70–90% for NATO-designated forces (1 div HQ, 1 mech bde, 1 inf bde & 1 mtn inf bde) and 40–70% for other forces

FORCES BY ROLE
COMMAND
2 div HQ (2nd & 4th)
elm 1 div HQ (MND-SE)
SPECIAL FORCES
1 SF bde (2 SF bn, 1 para bn, 1 log bn)
MANOEUVRE
Reconnaissance
1 recce bde
2 recce regt
Mechanised
5 mech bde (1 tk bn, 2 mech inf bn, 1 arty bn, 1 AD bn, 1 log bn)
1 (MNB-SE) mech inf bde (2 armd inf bn, 1 inf bn, 1 arty bn, 1 AD bn, 1 log bn)
Light
2 mtn inf bde (3 mtn inf bn, 1 arty bn, 1 AD bn, 1 log bn)
COMBAT SUPPORT
1 MRL bde (3 MRL bn, 1 STA bn, 1 log bn)
2 arty regt
1 engr bde (4 engr bn, 1 ptn br bn, 1 log bn)
2 engr bn
3 sigs bn
1 CIMIC bn
1 MP bn
3 CBRN bn

COMBAT SERVICE SUPPORT
3 spt bn
AIR DEFENCE
3 AD regt
EQUIPMENT BY TYPE
ARMOURED FIGHTING VEHICLES
MBT 377: 220 T-55AM; 103 TR-85; 54 TR-85 M1
IFV 241: 41 MLI-84 (incl CP); 101 MLI-84M *Jderul*; 99 *Piranha* V
APC 749
  APC (T) 76 MLVM
  APC (W) 613: 69 B33 TAB *Zimbru*; 37 *Piranha* IIIC; 354 TAB-71 (incl variants); 153 TAB-77 (incl variants)
  PPV 60 *Maxxpro*
AUV 480 TABC-79 (incl variants)
ENGINEERING & MAINTENANCE VEHICLES
ARV 55: 3 MLI-84M TEHEVAC; 8 TERA-71L; 44 TERA-77L
VLB 43 BLG-67
NBC VEHICLES 109 RCH-84
ANTI-TANK/ANTI-INFRASTRUCTURE
MSL
  SP 158: 12 9P122 *Malyutka* (RS-AT-3 *Sagger*); 98 9P133 *Malyutka* (RS-AT-3 *Sagger*); 48 9P148 *Konkurs* (RS-AT-5 *Spandrel*)
  MANPATS *Spike*-LR
GUNS
  SP 100mm (23 SU-100 in store)
  TOWED 100mm 218 M-1977
ARTILLERY 1,136
  SP 122mm 40: 6 2S1 *Gvodzika*; 34 Model 89
  TOWED 447: **122mm** 96 (M-30) M-1938 (A-19); **152mm** 351: 247 M-1981; 104 M-1985
  MRL 206: **122mm** 170: 134 APR-40; 36 LAROM; **227mm** 36 M142 HIMARS
  MOR 443: **SP 82mm** 177: 92 TAB-71AR; 85 TABC-79AR; **120mm** 266 M-1982
AIR DEFENCE
SAM 96
  Short-range 48: 32 2K12 *Kub* (RS-SA-6 *Gainful*); 16 9K33 *Osa* (RS-SA-8 *Gecko*)
  Point-defence 48 CA-95
GUNS 65+
  SP 35mm 41 *Gepard*
  TOWED 24+: **14.5mm** ZPU-2; **35mm** 24 GDF-003; **57mm** S-60

Navy 6,800

EQUIPMENT BY TYPE
PRINCIPAL SURFACE COMBATANTS • FRIGATES 3
FFGH 1 *Marasesti* with 4 twin lnchr with P-22 (RS-SS-N-2C *Styx*) AShM, 2 triple 533mm ASTT with 53–65 HWT, 2 RBU 6000 *Smerch* 2 A/S mor, 4 AK630M CIWS, 2 twin 76mm guns (capacity 2 SA-316 (IAR-316) *Alouette* III hel)
FFH 2 *Regele Ferdinand* (ex-UK Type-22), with 2 triple STWS Mk.2 324mm TT, 1 76mm gun (capacity 1 SA330 (IAR-330) *Puma*)
PATROL AND COASTAL COMBATANTS 24
CORVETTES 4
  FSH 2 *Tetal* II with 2 twin 533mm ASTT with SET-53M

HWT, 2 RBU 6000 *Smerch* 2 A/S mor, 2 AK630 CIWS, 1 76mm gun (capacity 1 SA316 (IAR-316) *Alouette* III hel)
FS 2 *Tetal* I with 2 twin 533mm ASTT with SET-53M HWT, 2 RBU 2500 *Smerch* 1 A/S mor, 2 AK230 CIWS, 2 twin 76mm guns
PCFG 3 *Zborul* with 2 twin lnchr with P-22 (RS-SS-N-2C *Styx*) AShM, 2 AK630 CIWS, 1 76mm gun
PCFT 3 *Naluca* with 4 single 533mm ASTT
PCR 8: 5 *Brutar* II with 2 BM-21 MRL, 1 100mm gun; 3 *Kogalniceanu* with 2 BM-21 MRL, 2 100mm guns
PBR 6 VD141 (ex-MSR now used for river patrol)
MINE WARFARE 11
  MINE COUNTERMEASURES 10
    MSO 4 *Musca* with 2 RBU 1200 *Uragan* A/S mor, 2 AK230 CIWS
    MSR 6 VD141
  MINELAYERS • ML 1 *Corsar* with up to 120 mines, 2 RBU 1200 *Uragan* A/S mor, 2 AK230 CIWS
LOGISTICS AND SUPPORT 8
  AE 2 *Constanta* with 2 RBU 1200 *Uragan* A/S mor, 2 AK230 CIWS, 2 twin 57mm guns
  AGOR 1 *Corsar*
  AGS 2: 1 *Emil Racovita*; 1 *Catuneanu*
  AOL 1 *Tulcea*
  ATF 1 *Grozavu*
  AXS 1 *Mircea*

Naval Infantry

FORCES BY ROLE
MANOEUVRE
  Light
    1 naval inf regt
EQUIPMENT BY TYPE
ARMOURED FIGHTING VEHICLES
  AUV 14: 11 ABC-79M; 3 TABC-79M

Air Force 11,700

FORCES BY ROLE
FIGHTER
  2 sqn with MiG-21 *Lancer* C
FIGHTER/GROUND ATTACK
  1 sqn with with F-16AM/BM *Fighting Falcon*
GROUND ATTACK
  1 sqn with IAR-99 *Soim**
TRANSPORT
  1 sqn with An-30 *Clank*; C-27J *Spartan*
  1 sqn with C-130B/H *Hercules*
TRAINING
  1 sqn with IAR-99 *Soim**
  1 sqn with SA316B *Alouette* III (IAR-316B); Yak-52 (Iak-52)
TRANSPORT HELICOPTER
  2 (multi-role) sqn with IAR-330 SOCAT *Puma*
  2 sqn with SA330L/M *Puma* (IAR-330L/M)
AIR DEFENCE
  1 AD bde
COMBAT SERVICE SUPPORT
  1 engr spt regt
EQUIPMENT BY TYPE
AIRCRAFT 59 combat capable
  FTR 17: 14 F-16AM *Fighting Falcon*; 3 F-16BM *Fighting Falcon*

FGA 22: 6 MiG-21 *Lancer* B; 16 MiG-21 *Lancer* C
ISR 2 An-30 *Clank*
TPT • Medium 12: 7 C-27J *Spartan*; 4 C-130B *Hercules*; 1 C-130H *Hercules*
TRG 32: 10 IAR-99*; 10 IAR-99C *Soim**; 12 Yak-52 (Iak-52)
HELICOPTERS
  MRH 29: 21 IAR-330 SOCAT *Puma*; 8 SA316B *Alouette* III (IAR-316B)
  TPT • Medium 24: 12 SA330L *Puma* (IAR-330L); 12 SA330M *Puma* (IAR-330M)
AIR DEFENCE • SAM 17
  Long-range 8 M903 *Patriot* PAC-3 MSE
  Medium-range 13: 5 S-75M3 *Volkhov* (RS-SA-2 *Guideline*); 8 MIM-23 *Hawk* PIP III
AIR-LAUNCHED MISSILES
  AAM • IR AIM-9M *Sidewinder*; R-73 (RS-AA-11A *Archer*); R-550 *Magic* 2; *Python* 3 **IIR** AIM-9X *Sidewinder* II; **ARH** AIM-120C AMRAAM
  ASM *Spike*-ER
BOMBS
  Laser-guided GBU-12 *Paveway*;
  Laser & INS/GPS-guided GBU-54 Laser JDAM
  INS/GPS guided GBU-38 JDAM

Gendarmerie & Paramilitary ε57,000

Gendarmerie ε57,000
Ministry of Interior

DEPLOYMENT

BOSNIA-HERZEGOVINA: EU • EUFOR (*Operation Althea*) 203; 1 inf coy

CENTRAL AFRICAN REPUBLIC: EU • EUTM RCA 13

DEMOCRATIC REPUBLIC OF THE CONGO: UN • MONUSCO 8

INDIA/PAKISTAN: UN • UNMOGIP 2

IRAQ: *Operation Inherent Resolve* 30; **NATO •** NATO Mission Iraq 170

MALI: EU • EUTM Mali 25; **UN •** MINUSMA 5

MOZAMBIQUE: EU • EUTM Mozambique 6

SERBIA: NATO • KFOR 65; **UN •** UNMIK 1

SOMALIA: EU • EUTM Somalia 5

SOUTH SUDAN: UN • UNMISS 6

FOREIGN FORCES

Canada NATO Air Policing: 170; 6 F/A-18A *Hornet* (CF-18AM)
Belgium NATO Enhanced Vigilance Activities: 250; 1 mech inf coy
France NATO Enhanced Vigilance Activities: 750; 1 armd BG; 1 SAM bty with SAMP/T
Netherlands NATO Enhanced Vigilance Activities: 200; 1 air mob inf coy
Poland NATO MNB-SE 220; 1 mech inf coy; *Rosomak*
United States US European Command: 4,000; 1 air aslt bde with M119A3; M777A2; 1 *Aegis Ashore* BMD unit with 3 8-cell Mk 41 VLS with SM-3

Serbia SER

Serbian Dinar RSD		2021	2022	2023
GDP	RSD	6.27tr	6.99tr	
	USD	63.1bn	62.7bn	
per capita	USD	9,178	9,164	
Growth	%	7.4	3.5	
Inflation	%	4.1	11.5	
Def bdgt	RSD	103bn	136bn	
	USD	1.03bn	1.22bn	
USD1=RSD		99.40	111.40	

Real-terms defence budget trend (USDm, constant 2015)

Population	6,739,471					
Age	0–14	15–19	20–24	25–29	30–64	65 plus
Male	7.5%	2.8%	2.8%	3.0%	24.6%	8.1%
Female	7.0%	2.6%	2.7%	3.0%	24.5%	11.5%

Capabilities

Serbia's armed forces focus on territorial defence, internal security and limited support to peacekeeping missions. According to the 2019 National-Security Strategy, key threats include separatism, ethnic and religious extremism, climate change and further international recognition of Kosovo. The armed forces are modernising to address long-term capability shortfalls and personnel shortages. Priorities include procurements, improving availability, maintenance and readiness levels, and bolstering air-defence capability. Serbia has agreed to deepen cooperation with NATO through an Individual Partnership Action Plan. Belgrade aspires to join the EU but not NATO. Serbia also maintains a close relationship with Russia, from which it has received transfers of military equipment in recent years. However, the country has also intensified its security relations with China, purchasing Chinese military equipment, including air defence equipment. The armed forces have reduced in size over the last decade, though annual recruitment goals have not yet been met. The armed forces also lack skilled technicians to operate and maintain advanced systems and suffer from a shortage of pilots. Air force modernisation is a priority, including upgrading its MiG-29s, while there have been reports of negotiations with France and the UK over possible combat aircraft procurement. Serbia mostly trains with its Balkan neighbours, Russia and NATO countries. It contributes to EU, OSCE and UN peacekeeping missions. Serbia's defence industry focuses on missile and artillery systems, and small arms and ammunition, but the country is reliant on external suppliers for major platforms. Serbia continues to develop its defence industry, with a focus on the aerospace industry.

ACTIVE 28,150 (Army 13,250 Air Force and Air Defence 5,100 Training Command 3,000 Guards 1,600 Other MoD 5,200) Gendarmerie & Paramilitary 3,700

Conscript liability 6 months (voluntary)

RESERVE 50,150

ORGANISATIONS BY SERVICE

Army 13,250

FORCES BY ROLE
SPECIAL FORCES
1 SF bde (1 CT bn, 1 cdo bn, 1 para bn)
MANOEUVRE
  Mechanised
  1 (1st) bde (1 tk bn, 2 mech inf bn, 1 inf bn, 1 SP arty bn, 1 MRL bn, 1 AD bn, 1 engr bn, 1 log bn)
  3 (2nd, 3rd & 4th) bde (1 tk bn, 2 mech inf bn, 2 inf bn, 1 SP arty bn, 1 MRL bn, 1 AD bn, 1 engr bn, 1 log bn)
COMBAT SUPPORT
1 (mixed) arty bde (4 arty bn, 1 MRL bn, 1 spt bn)
2 ptn bridging bn
1 NBC bn
1 sigs bn
2 MP bn

Reserve Organisations
FORCES BY ROLE
MANOEUVRE
  Light
  8 (territorial) inf bde

EQUIPMENT BY TYPE
ARMOURED FIGHTING VEHICLES
  MBT 229: 197 M-84; 2 M-84AS1 (in test); 30 T-72MS
  RECCE 76: 46 BRDM-2; 30 BRDM-2M
  IFV 326: 320 M-80; 3 M80AB1
  APC 95
    APC(T) 44: 12 BTR-50 (CP); 32 MT-LB (CP)
    APC (W) 51: 39 BOV-VP M-86; 12 *Lazar-3* APC
  AUV 25 BOV M16 *Milos*
ENGINEERING & MAINTENANCE VEHICLES
  AEV IWT
  ARV M84A1; T-54/T-55
  VLB MT-55; TMM
ANTI-TANK/ANTI-INFRASTRUCTURE
  MSL
    SP 48 BOV-1 (M-83) with 9K11 *Malyutka* (RS-AT-3 *Sagger*)
    MANPATS 9K11 *Malyutka* (RS-AT-3 *Sagger*); 9K111 *Fagot* (RS-AT-4 *Spigot*); Kornet-EM
  RCL 90mm M-79
ARTILLERY 461
  SP 95: **122mm** 67 2S1 *Gvozdika*; **155mm** 18 B-52 NORA
  TOWED 132: **122mm** 78 D-30; **130mm** 18 M-46; **152mm** 36 M-84 NORA-A
  MRL 81: **128mm** 78: 18 M-63 *Plamen*; 60 M-77 *Organj*; **262mm** 3 M-87 *Orkan*
  MOR 163: **82mm** 106 M-69; **120mm** 57 M-74/M-75
AIR DEFENCE
  SAM 94+
    Short-range 77 2K12 *Kub* (RS-SA-6 *Gainful*);
    Point-defence 17+: 12 9K31M *Strela*-1M (RS-SA-9 *Gaskin*); 5 9K35M *Strela*-10M; 9K32M *Strela*-2M (RS-SA-7B *Grail*)‡; *Šilo* (RS-SA-16 *Gimlet*)
  GUNS
    SP **40mm** 20 *Pasars*-16
    TOWED **40mm** 36 Bofors L/70

Europe 129

UNINHABITED AERIAL VEHICLES
CISR • **Medium** 6 CH-92A
AIR-LAUNCHED MISSILES
ASM FT-8C

River Flotilla

The Serbian–Montenegrin navy was transferred to Montenegro upon independence in 2006, but the Danube flotilla remained in Serbian control. The flotilla is subordinate to the Land Forces

EQUIPMENT BY TYPE
PATROL AND COASTAL COMBATANTS 4
  PBR 4: 3 Type-20; 1 *Jadar*
MINE WARFARE • MINE COUNTERMEASURES 4
  MSI 4 *Nestin* with 1 quad lnchr with 9K32 *Strela*-2M (RS-SA-N-5 *Grail*) SAM
AMPHIBIOUS • LANDING CRAFT
  LCVP 4 Type-22 (1 more non-operational)
LOGISTICS AND SUPPORT 3
  AG 1 *Šabac* (deguassing vessel also used for patrol and troop transport) (capacity 80 troops)
  AGF 1 *Kozara*
  AOL 1

Air Force and Air Defence 5,100

FORCES BY ROLE
FIGHTER
  1 sqn with MiG-29 *Fulcrum*; MiG-29UB *Fulcrum* B; MiG-29SE *Fulcrum* C
FIGHTER/GROUND ATTACK
  1 sqn with J-22/NJ-22 *Orao* 1
TRANSPORT
  1 sqn with An-2; An-26; Yak-40 (Jak-40); 1 PA-34 *Seneca* V
TRAINING
  1 sqn with G-4 *Super Galeb** (adv trg/light atk); SA341/342 *Gazelle*; *Lasta* 95; Utva-75 (basic trg)
ATTACK HELICOPTER
  1 sqn with SA341H/342L *Gazelle*; (HN-42/45); Mi-24 *Hind*; Mi-35M *Hind*
TRANSPORT HELICOPTER
  2 sqn with H145M; Mi-8 *Hip*; Mi-17 *Hip* H; Mi-17V-5 *Hip*
AIR DEFENCE
  1 bde (5 bn (2 msl, 3 SP msl) with S-125M *Neva*-M (RS-SA-3 *Goa*); 2K12 *Kub* (RS-SA-6 *Gainful*); 9K32 *Strela*-2 (RS-SA-7 *Grail*); 9K310 *Igla*-1 (RS-SA-16 *Gimlet*))
  2 radar bn (for early warning and reporting)
COMBAT SUPPORT
  1 sigs bn
COMBAT SERVICE SUPPORT
  1 maint bn

EQUIPMENT BY TYPE
AIRCRAFT 51 combat capable
  FTR 14: 3 MiG-29 *Fulcrum*; 3 MiG-29UB *Fulcrum* B; 8 MiG-29SE *Fulcrum* C
  FGA up to 18 J-22/NJ-22 *Orao* 1
  ISR (10 IJ-22R *Orao* 1* in store)
  TPT • Light 8: 1 An-2 *Colt*; 4 An-26 *Curl*; 2 Yak-40 (Jak-40); 1 PA-34 *Seneca* V
  TRG 44: 19 G-4 *Super Galeb**; 11 Utva-75; 14 *Lasta* 95

HELICOPTERS
  ATK 6: 2 Mi-24 *Hind*†; 4 Mi-35M *Hind*
  MRH 52: 5 H145M; 1 Mi-17 *Hip* H; 5 Mi-17V-5 *Hip*; 2 SA341H *Gazelle* (HI-42); 26 SA341H *Gazelle* (HN-42)/SA342L *Gazelle* (HN-45); 13 SA341H *Gazelle* (HO-42)/SA342L1 *Gazelle* (HO-45)
  TPT • Medium 8 Mi-8T *Hip* (HT-40)
AIR DEFENCE
  SAM 19+
    Long-range 4 FK-3 (HQ-22)
    Short-range 15: 6 S-125M *Neva*-M (RS-SA-3 *Goa*); 9 2K12 *Kub* (RS-SA-6 *Gainful*)
    Point-defence 9K32 *Strela*-2 (RS-SA-7 *Grail*)‡; 9K310 *Igla*-1 (RS-SA-16 *Gimlet*)
  SPAAGM 30mm 6 96K6 *Pantsir*-S1 (RS-SA-22 *Greyhound*)
  GUNS • TOWED 40mm 24 Bofors L/70
AIR-LAUNCHED MISSILES
  AAM • IR R-60 (RS-AA-8 *Aphid*); R-73 (RS-AA-11A *Archer*); **SARH** R-27ER (RS-AA-10C *Alamo*); **ARH** R-77 (RS-AA-12 *Adder*)
  ASM AGM-65 *Maverick*; A-77 *Thunder*; Kh-29T (RS-AS-14B *Kedge*)

Guards 1,600

FORCES BY ROLE
MANOEUVRE
  Other
    1 (ceremonial) gd bde (1 gd bn, 1 MP bn, 1 spt bn)

Gendarmerie & Paramilitary 3,700

Gendarmerie 3,700

EQUIPMENT BY TYPE
ARMOURED FIGHTING VEHICLES
  APC • APC (W) 24: 12 *Lazar*-3; 12 BOV-VP M-86
  AUV BOV M16 *Milos*

DEPLOYMENT

CENTRAL AFRICAN REPUBLIC: EU • EUTM RCA 7; **UN** • MINUSCA 78; 1 med coy

CYPRUS: UN • UNFICYP 8

LEBANON: UN • UNIFIL 177; 1 mech inf coy

MIDDLE EAST: UN • UNTSO 1

SOMALIA: EU • EUTM Somalia 6

TERRITORY WHERE THE GOVERNMENT DOES NOT EXERCISE EFFECTIVE CONTROL

In February 2008, Kosovo declared itself independent. Serbia remains opposed to this, and while Kosovo has not been admitted to the United Nations, a number of states have recognised Kosovo's self-declared status. Data here represents the de facto situation in Kosovo. This does not imply international recognition as a sovereign state.

Europe

Kosovo Security Force 2,500; reserves 800

The Kosovo Security Force (KSF) was formed in January 2009 as a non-military organisation with responsibility for crisis response, civil protection and EOD. The new president has reaffirmed the ambition to develop a regular army following NATO standards and to join the Alliance, although NATO members are divided on this and the Alliance is formally against such a development. The KSF has been upgrading its capabilities, including the acquisition of light armoured security vehicles from the United States starting in 2021. A small detachment deployed to Kuwait in 2021, alongside the US Iowa National Guard. A military police unit was reportedly established in 2022. The NATO peace-support mission, KFOR, continues to maintain a presence in Kosovo.

EQUIPMENT BY TYPE
ARMOURED FIGHTING VEHICLES
AUV 55 M1117 *Guardian*; some *Cobra*

FOREIGN FORCES

All under Kosovo Force (KFOR) command unless otherwise specified
Albania 61
Armenia 40
Austria 244; 1 recce coy; 1 mech inf coy; 1 log coy • UNMIK 1 obs
Bulgaria 30
Canada 5
Croatia 147; 1 inf coy; 1 hel flt with Mi-8
Czech Republic 8 • UNMIK 2 obs
Denmark 35
Finland 20
Germany 68
Greece 113; 1 inf coy
Hungary 469; 1 inf coy (KTM)
Ireland 13
Italy 715; 1 arty regt BG HQ; 1 Carabinieri unit
Latvia 136; 1 inf coy
Lithuania 1
Macedonia, North 65
Moldova 41 • UNMIK 1 obs
Montenegro 1
Poland 247; 1 inf coy • UNMIK 2 obs
Romania 65 • UNMIK 1 obs
Slovenia 97; 1 mot inf coy; 1 MP unit; 1 hel unit
Sweden 3
Switzerland 186; 1 inf coy; 1 engr pl; 1 hel flt with AS332
Turkey 335; 1 inf coy • UNMIK 2 obs
Ukraine 40
United Kingdom 41
United States 561; elm 1 ARNG inf bde HQ; 1 ARNG inf bn; 1 hel flt with UH-60

Slovakia SVK

Euro EUR		2021	2022	2023
GDP	EUR	97.1bn	106bn	
	USD	115bn	112bn	
per capita	USD	21,053	20,565	
Growth	%	3.0	1.8	
Inflation	%	2.8	11.9	
Def exp [a]	EUR	1.68bn	2.14bn	
	USD	1.98bn	2.27bn	
Def bdgt	EUR	1.68bn	1.90bn	2.46bn
	USD	1.99bn	2.01bn	
USD1=EUR		0.84	0.95	

[a] NATO figure

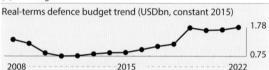
Real-terms defence budget trend (USDbn, constant 2015)

Population	5,431,252					
Age	0–14	15–19	20–24	25–29	30–64	65 plus
Male	7.7%	2.5%	2.6%	3.0%	25.5%	7.2%
Female	7.3%	2.4%	2.5%	2.8%	25.7%	10.9%

Capabilities

Slovakia is looking to modernise its armed forces and replace obsolete equipment while contributing to international crisis-management missions. A defence White Paper in September 2016 set out security priorities and a plan to increase defence capabilities. In 2017, the government approved a Long-Term Defence Development Plan. A new national-security strategy and a new defence strategy were drafted in 2020 and adopted by parliament in January 2021. A NATO and EU member state, Slovakia cooperates closely with the Visegrád Group, and there are reports that the country is considering forming a collective fighter jet pilot training programme. Bratislava has signed an agreement to enable air policing and closer integration of air-defence capabilities. A Defence Cooperation Agreement was signed with the United States in February 2022 and funds were allocated to Slovakia under the Foreign Military Financing Programme to help the country replace part of the military equipment sent to Ukraine since the Russian invasion. Germany is planning to supply 15 *Leopard* 2A4 MBTs, after Slovakia sent Infantry Fighting Vehicles to Ukraine. The air force is in the process of procuring new jet trainers in preparation for the delivery of its F-16s, expected between 2023 and 2024. US *Patriot* air defence systems arrived, after Slovakia donated S-300s to Ukraine. As part of plans to improve mechanised capabilities, agreements were signed in 2022 for the acquisition of *Patria* 8x8 armoured vehicles. CV90s will be delivered between 2025 and 2028. Slovakia has deployed a company-sized unit to NATO's Enhanced Forward Presence in Latvia and stood up the EFP Battlegroup Slovakia to assist in defending NATO's eastern flank. In June 2021, Slovakia began planning for upgrades to Sliač air base, which is to become the main operating base for the F-16, and pilot training began in April in the US. Part of Slovakia's defence-industrial base is organised within the state-controlled holding company DMD Group, including KONSTRUKTA Defence, which produces land systems. Other companies focus on maintenance, repair and overhaul services.

ACTIVE 17,950 (Army 10,300 Air 4,000 Central Staff 3,650)

ORGANISATIONS BY SERVICE

Central Staff 3,650
FORCES BY ROLE
SPECIAL FORCES
1 (5th) spec ops bn

Army 10,300
FORCES BY ROLE
MANOEUVRE
Armoured
1 (2nd) armd bde (1 recce bn, 1 tk bn, 2 armd inf bn, 1 mixed SP arty bn)
Mechanised
1 (1st) mech bde (3 armd inf bn, 1 MRL bn, 1 engr bn, 1 NBC bn)
COMBAT SUPPORT
1 MP bn
COMBAT SERVICE SUPPORT
1 spt bde (2 log bn, 1 maint bn, 1 spt bn)
EQUIPMENT BY TYPE
ARMOURED FIGHTING VEHICLES
MBT 30 T-72M
RECCE 18 BPsVI
IFV 216: 108 BMP-1; 91 BMP-2; 17 BVP-M
APC 101+
 APC (T) 72 OT-90
 APC (W) 22: 7 OT-64; 15 *Tatrapan* (6×6)
 PPV 7+ RG-32M
 AUV IVECO LMV
ENGINEERING & MAINTENANCE VEHICLES
ARV MT-55; VT-55A; VT-72B; WPT-TOPAS
VLB AM-50; MT-55A
MW *Bozena*; UOS-155 *Belarty*
ANTI-TANK/ANTI-INFRASTRUCTURE
SP 9S428 with *Malyutka* (RS-AT-3 *Sagger*) on BMP-1; 9P135 *Fagot* (RS-AT-4 *Spigot*) on BMP-2; 9P148 *Konkurs* (RS-AT-5 *Spandrel*) on BRDM-2
MANPATS 9K11 *Malyutka* (RS-AT-3 *Sagger*); 9K111-1 *Konkurs* (RS-AT-5 *Spandrel*)
RCL 84mm *Carl Gustaf*
ARTILLERY 60
SP 30: **152mm** 3 M-77 *Dana*; **155mm** 27: 16 M-2000 *Zuzana*; 11 *Zuzana-2*
MRL 30: **122mm** 4 RM-70; **122/227mm** 26 RM-70/85 MODULAR
AIR DEFENCE
SAM • Point-defence 9K310 *Igla*-1 (RS-SA-16 *Gimlet*)

Air Force 4,000
FORCES BY ROLE
FIGHTER
1 sqn with MiG-29AS/UBS *Fulcrum*
TRANSPORT
1 flt with C-27J *Spartan*
1 flt with L-410FG/T *Turbolet*
TRANSPORT HELICOPTER
1 sqn with Mi-17 *Hip* H
1 sqn with UH-60M *Black Hawk*
TRAINING
1 sqn with L-39CM/ZAM *Albatros**
AIR DEFENCE
1 bde with 2K12 *Kub* (RS-SA-6 *Gainful*)
EQUIPMENT BY TYPE
AIRCRAFT 19 combat capable
FTR 11: 9 MiG-29AS *Fulcrum*; 2 MiG-29UBS *Fulcrum*;
TPT 5: **Medium** 2 C-27J *Spartan*; **Light** 3: 1 L-410FG *Turbolet*; 2 L-410T *Turbolet*; (4 L-410UVP *Turbolet* in store)
TRG 8: 6 L-39CM *Albatros**; 2 L-39ZAM *Albatros** (1 more in store)
HELICOPTERS
ATK (15: 5 Mi-24D *Hind* D; 10 Mi-24V *Hind* E all in store)
MRH 13 Mi-17 *Hip* H (incl 4 SAR)
TPT • Medium 9 UH-60M *Black Hawk*
AIR DEFENCE • SAM
Short-range 2K12 *Kub* (RS-SA-6 *Gainful*)
AIR-LAUNCHED MISSILES
AAM • IR R-60 (RS-AA-8 *Aphid*); R-73 (RS-AA-11A *Archer*); **SARH** R-27R (RS-AA-10A *Alamo*)

DEPLOYMENT

BOSNIA-HERZEGOVINA: EU • EUFOR (*Operation Althea*) 53

CENTRAL AFRICAN REPUBLIC: EU • EUTM RCA 2

CYPRUS: UN • UNFICYP 300; 2 inf coy; 1 engr pl

IRAQ: NATO • NATO Mission Iraq 5

LATVIA: NATO • Enhanced Forward Presence 152; 1 arty bty with M-2000 *Zuzana*

MALI: EU • EUTM Mali 4

MIDDLE EAST: UN • UNTSO 2

FOREIGN FORCES

All under NATO Enhanced Vigilance Activities
Czech Republic 400; 1 mech inf bn HQ; 1 mech inf coy
Germany 480; 1 inf coy; 1 SAM bty with M902 *Patriot* PAC-3
Netherlands 125; 1 SAM bty with M902 *Patriot* PAC-3
Slovenia 101; 1 lt inf coy
United States 400; 1 SAM bty with M902 *Patriot* PAC-3

Slovenia SVN

Euro EUR		2021	2022	2023
GDP	EUR	52.2bn	58.8bn	
	USD	61.8bn	62.2bn	
per capita	USD	29,298	29,469	
Growth	%	8.2	5.7	
Inflation	%	1.9	8.9	
Def exp [a]	EUR	645m	699m	
	USD	763m	739m	
Def bdgt [b]	EUR	706m	835m	939m
	USD	836m	883m	
USD1=EUR		0.84	0.95	

[a] NATO figure
[b] Includes military pensions

Real-terms defence budget trend (USDm, constant 2015)

Population	2,101,208					
Age	0–14	15–19	20–24	25–29	30–64	65 plus
Male	7.5%	2.4%	2.4%	2.6%	25.5%	9.7%
Female	7.2%	2.2%	2.2%	2.3%	23.5%	12.5%

Capabilities

Since joining NATO and the EU in 2004, territorial defence and the ability to take part in peace-support operations have been central to Slovenia's defence strategy. In January 2020, the defence ministry published a White Paper and in February 2022 authorised the Long-Term Development Programme for the Slovenian Armed Forces 2022-35. Subsequently, the government in April adopted a Medium-Term Development Programme to serve as the guiding document for defence programming and planning. Defence spending is increasing. Short term plans are focused on developing a medium infantry battalion (rather than two battalion groups originally envisaged) and equipped with IFVs and combat support and combat service support. In September, the country withdrew from an MOU for the acquisition of 45 *Boxer* armoured vehicles. Fixed-wing and rotary-wing transport capabilities are modestly improving with new acquisitions and upgrades. There are plans to establish a cyber reserve force. Slovenia has donated military equipment to Ukraine, reportedly including MBTs. Slovenia acts as the framework nation for the NATO Mountain Warfare Centre of Excellence and in 2023 will provide units to the NATO VJTF. Italy and Hungary currently provide air policing capability under NATO arrangements. The country has contributed to EU, NATO and UN operations. Slovenia participates in NATO's Enhanced Forward Presence, where it contributes to the Canadian-led battlegroup in Latvia and to the newly-formed battlegroup in Slovakia. Its defence industry relies heavily on exports for its revenue and focuses on personal equipment, small arms and ammunition, and CBRN protection and detection.

ACTIVE 6,400 (Army 6,400)
RESERVE 750 (Army 750)

ORGANISATIONS BY SERVICE

Army 6,400
FORCES BY ROLE
Regt are bn sized
SPECIAL FORCES
 1 SF unit (1 spec ops coy, 1 CSS coy)
MANOEUVRE
 Mechanised
 1 (1st) mech inf bde (1 mech inf regt, 1 mtn inf regt, 1 cbt spt bn (1 ISR coy, 1 arty bty, 1 engr coy, 1 MP coy, 1 CBRN coy, 1 sigs coy, 1 SAM bty))
 1 (72nd) mech inf bde (2 mech inf regt, 1 cbt spt bn (1 ISR coy, 1 arty bty, 1 engr coy, 1 MP coy, 1 CBRN coy, 1 sigs coy, 1 SAM bty))
COMBAT SUPPORT
 1 EW coy
COMBAT SERVICE SUPPORT
 1 log bde (1 log regt, 1 maint regt (1 tk coy), 1 med regt)

Reserves
FORCES BY ROLE
MANOEUVRE
 Mountain
 2 inf regt (territorial – 1 allocated to each inf bde)
EQUIPMENT BY TYPE
ARMOURED FIGHTING VEHICLES
 MBT 14 M-84 (trg role) (32 more in store)
 APC 115+:
  APC (W) 115: 85 *Pandur* 6×6 (*Valuk*); 30 Patria 8×8 (*Svarun*)
  PPV *Cougar* 6×6 JERRV
 AUV 38 JLTV
ENGINEERING & MAINTENANCE VEHICLES
 ARV VT-55A
 VLB MT-55A
NBC VEHICLES 10 *Cobra* CBRN
ANTI-TANK/ANTI-INFRASTRUCTURE
 MSL • MANPATS *Spike* MR/LR
ARTILLERY 68
 TOWED • 155mm 18 TN-90
 MOR 50+: 82mm M-69; 120mm 50 MN-9/M-74
AIR DEFENCE • SAM • Point-defence 9K338 *Igla*-S (RSSA-24 *Grinch*)

Army Maritime Element 130
FORCES BY ROLE
SPECIAL FORCES
 1 SF unit
EQUIPMENT BY TYPE
PATROL AND COASTAL COMBATANTS 2
 PCC 1 *Triglav* III (RUS *Svetlyak*)
 PBF 1 *Super Dvora* MkII

Air Element 600
FORCES BY ROLE
TRANSPORT
 1 sqn with *Falcon* 2000EX; L-410 *Turbolet*; PC-6B *Turbo Porter*
TRAINING
 1 unit with Bell 206 *Jet Ranger* (AB-206); PC-9M*; Z-143L; Z-242L

TRANSPORT HELICOPTER
  1 sqn with AS532AL *Cougar*; Bell 412 *Twin Huey*
COMBAT SERVICE SUPPORT
  1 maint sqn
EQUIPMENT BY TYPE
AIRCRAFT 9 combat capable
  TPT 4: **Light** 3: 1 L-410 *Turbolet*; 2 PC-6B *Turbo Porter*
  PAX 1 *Falcon* 2000EX
  TRG 19: 9 PC-9M*; 2 Z-143L; 8 Z-242L
HELICOPTERS
  MRH 8: 5 Bell 412EP *Twin Huey*; 2 Bell 412HP *Twin Huey*; 1 Bell 412SP *Twin Huey*
  TPT 8: **Medium** 4 AS532AL *Cougar*; **Light** 4 Bell 206 *Jet Ranger* (AB-206)

DEPLOYMENT

BOSNIA-HERZEGOVINA: EU • EUFOR (*Operation Althea*) 16
IRAQ: *Operation Inherent Resolve* 3
LATVIA: NATO • Enhanced Forward Presence 42
LEBANON: UN • UNIFIL 1
MALI: EU • EUTM Mali 9
MIDDLE EAST: UN • UNTSO 3
SERBIA: NATO • KFOR 97; 1 mot inf coy; 1 MP unit; 1 hel unit
SLOVAKIA: NATO • Enhanced Vigilance Activities 101; 1 lt inf coy

Spain ESP

Euro EUR		2021	2022	2023
GDP	EUR	1.21tr	1.32tr	
	USD	1.43tr	1.39tr	
per capita	USD	30,090	29,198	
Growth	%	5.1	4.3	
Inflation	%	3.1	8.8	
Def exp [a]	EUR	12.5bn	13.1bn	
	USD	14.8bn	13.9bn	
Def bdgt [b]	EUR	12.8bn	ε13.9bn	ε17.5bn
	USD	15.1bn	ε14.7bn	
USD1=EUR		0.84	0.95	

[a] NATO figure
[b] Includes military pensions

Real-terms defence budget trend (USDbn, constant 2015)

Population 47,163,418

Age	0–14	15–19	20–24	25–29	30–64	65 plus
Male	7.0%	2.7%	2.5%	2.4%	25.5%	8.7%
Female	6.7%	2.6%	2.4%	2.4%	25.6%	11.5%

Capabilities

The 2021 National Security Strategy indicated increased effort toward strengthening capacity against hybrid threats. Following Russia's full-scale invasion of Ukraine in February 2022, the government unveiled plans to increase defence spending with the eventual goal of reaching by 2029 the NATO goal of spending 2% on defence. The National Defence Directive, issued in June 2020, updated defence policy guidelines and indicated a desire to foster an integrated approach to security alongside a drive to strengthen the national defence industry. Spain continues to support NATO, EU and UN operations abroad, and hosts one of NATO's two Combined Air Operations Centres. The armed forces are well trained and there is a routine exercise programme for both domestic and multinational exercises. The country's equipment and logistics-support capability appears to be sufficient to meet its national commitments and contribution to NATO operations and exercises. Equipment-modernisation plans include modernisation of army *Chinook* helicopters and Eurofighter combat aircraft, the acquisition of four S-80 submarines, new 8x8 armoured vehicles, and two military-communications satellites. Spain participates in the Future Combat Air System (FCAS) project together with France and Germany. Spain's defence industry manufactures across all domains and exports globally, with major firms including state-owned shipbuilder Navantia, Airbus and Santa Barbara Sistemas, belonging to General Dynamics European Land Systems. The industry is largely integrated within the European defence-industrial manufacturing base.

ACTIVE 124,150 (Army 71,900 Navy 20,500 Air 20,350 Joint 11,400) **Gendarmerie & Paramilitary 75,800**

RESERVE 14,700 (Army 8,550 Navy 3,100 Air 2,550 Other 500)

ORGANISATIONS BY SERVICE

Space
EQUIPMENT BY TYPE
SATELLITES 3
  COMMUNICATIONS 2: 1 *Spainsat*; 1 *Xtar-Eur*
  ISR 1 *Paz*

Army 71,900
The Land Forces High Readiness HQ Spain provides one NATO Rapid Deployment Corps HQ (NRDC-ESP)
FORCES BY ROLE
COMMAND
  1 corps HQ (CGTAD/NRDC-ESP) (1 int regt, 1 MP bn)
  2 div HQ
SPECIAL FORCES
  1 comd (3 spec ops bn, 1 int coy, 1 sigs coy, 1 log bn)
MANOEUVRE
  Reconnaissance
    1 armd cav regt (2 armd recce bn)
  Mechanised
    2 (10th & 11th) mech bde (1 armd regt (1 armd recce bn, 1 tk bn), 1 mech inf regt (1 armd inf bn, 1 mech inf bn), 1 lt inf bn, 1 SP arty bn, 1 AT coy, 1 AD coy, 1 engr bn, 1 int coy, 1 NBC coy, 1 sigs coy, 1 log bn)
    1 (12th) mech bde (1 armd regt (1 armd recce bn, 1 tk bn), 1 mech inf regt (1 armd inf bn, 1 mech inf bn), 1 mtn inf bn, 1 SP arty bn, 1 AT coy, 1 AD coy, 1 engr bn, 1 int coy, 1 NBC coy, 1 sigs coy, 1 log bn)

1 (1st) mech bde (1 armd regt (1 armd recce bn, 1 tk bn),
1 armd inf regt (1 armd inf bn), 1 SP arty bn, 1 AT coy,
1 AD coy, 1 engr bn, 1 int coy, 1 NBC coy, 1 sigs coy,
1 log bn)

2 (2nd/La Legion & 7th) lt mech bde (1 armd recce bn,
1 mech inf regt (2 mech inf bn), 1 lt inf bn, 1 fd arty bn,
1 AT coy, 1 AD coy, 1 engr bn, 1 int coy, 1 NBC coy,
1 sigs coy, 1 log bn)

Mountain

1 mtn comd (1 mtn inf regt (1 mtn inf bn, 1 mtn inf coy);
1 mtn inf bn)

Air Manoeuvre

1 (6th) bde (1 recce bn, 2 para bn, 1 lt inf bn, 1 fd arty bn,
1 AT coy, 1 AD coy, 1 engr bn, 1 int coy, 1 NBC coy,
1 sigs coy, 1 log bn)

Other

1 (Canary Islands) comd (1 lt inf bde (2 mech inf regt
(1 mech inf bn), 1 lt inf regt (1 lt inf bn), 1 fd arty regt,
1 AT coy, 1 engr bn, 1 int coy, 1 NBC coy, 1 sigs coy,
1 log bn); 1 EW regt; 1 spt hel bn; 1 AD regt)

1 (Balearic Islands) comd (1 inf regt (1 lt inf bn))

2 (Ceuta and Melilla) comd (1 recce regt, 1 mech inf bn, 1
inf bn, 1 arty regt (1 fd arty bn, 1 ADA bn), 1 engr bn,
1 sigs coy, 1 log bn)

COMBAT SUPPORT

1 arty comd (1 arty regt; 1 MRL regt; 1 coastal arty regt)

1 engr comd (2 engr regt, 1 bridging regt)

1 EW/sigs bde (2 EW regt, 3 sigs regt)

1 NBC regt

1 info ops regt (1 CIMIC bn; 1 Psyops bn)

1 int regt

COMBAT SERVICE SUPPORT

1 log bde (5 log regt; 1 tpt regt; 1 med regt (1 log bn,
2 med bn, 1 fd hospital bn))

HELICOPTER

1 hel comd (1 atk hel bn, 2 spt hel bn, 1 tpt hel bn, 1 sigs
bn, 1 log unit (1 spt coy, 1 supply coy))

AIR DEFENCE

1 AD comd (3 SAM regt, 1 sigs unit)

EQUIPMENT BY TYPE

ARMOURED FIGHTING VEHICLES

MBT 327: 108 *Leopard* 2A4; 219 *Leopard* 2E

ASLT 84 B1 *Centauro*

RECCE 187 VEC-M1

IFV 225: 204 *Pizarro*; 21 *Pizarro* (CP)

APC 903

    APC (T) 473: 20 Bv-206S; 453 M113 (incl variants)

    APC (W) 320 BMR-600/BMR-600M1

    PPV 110 RG-31

AUV 258 IVECO LMV

ENGINEERING & MAINTENANCE VEHICLES

AEV 27 CZ-10/25E; 1 *Pizarro* CEV (*Castor*) (in test)

ARV 51: 16 *Leopard* REC; 5 BMR REC; 4 *Centauro* REC; 14
Maxxpro MRV; 12 M113

VLB 15 M60 AVLB

MW 6 *Husky* 2G

ANTI-TANK/ANTI-INFRASTRUCTURE

MSL • MANPATS *Spike*-LR; TOW

ARTILLERY 1,552

SP 155mm 95 M109A5

TOWED 268: **105mm** 204: 56 L118 Light Gun; 148 Model
56 pack howitzer; **155mm** 64 SBT 155/52 SIAC

MOR 1,189: **81mm** 777; **SP 81mm** 10 VAMTAC with
Cardom 81mm; **120mm** 402

COASTAL DEFENCE • ARTY 155mm 19 SBT 155/52 APU
SBT V07

HELICOPTERS

ATK 18 *Tiger* HAD-E

TPT 84: **Heavy** 17: 13 CH-47D *Chinook* (HT-17D); 4 CH-
47F *Chinook*; **Medium** 48: 16 AS332B *Super Puma* (HU-21);
12 AS532UL *Cougar*; 6 AS532AL *Cougar*; 14 NH90 TTH;
Light 19: 3 Bell 212 (HU.18); 16 H135 (HE.26/HU.26)

UAV • ISR • Medium 6: 2 *Searcher* MkII-J (PASI); 4
Searcher MkIII (PASI)

AIR DEFENCE

SAM 79+

    Long-range 18 M901 *Patriot* PAC-2

    Medium-range 40 MIM-23B I-*Hawk* Phase III

    Short-range 21: 8 NASAMS; 13 *Skyguard/Aspide*

    Point-defence *Mistral*

GUNS • TOWED 35mm 67: 19 GDF-005; 48 GDF-007

AIR-LAUNCHED MISSILES • ASM *Spike*-ER

Navy 20,500 (incl Naval Aviation and Marines)

EQUIPMENT BY TYPE

SUBMARINES 2

SSK 2 *Galerna* with 4 single 533mm TT with F17 mod
2 HWT

PRINCIPAL SURFACE COMBATANTS 11

DESTROYERS • DDGHM 5 *Alvaro de Bazan* with *Aegis*
Baseline 5 C2, 2 quad lnchr with RGM-84F *Harpoon* Block
1D AShM, 6 8-cell Mk 41 VLS with SM-2 Block IIIA/
RIM-162B ESSM SAM, 2 twin 324mm SVTT Mk 32 mod
9 ASTT with Mk 46 mod 5 LWT, 1 127mm gun (capacity
1 SH-60B *Seahawk* ASW hel)

FRIGATES • FFGH 6 *Santa Maria* with 1 Mk 13 GMLS
with RGM-84C *Harpoon* Block 1B AShM, 2 triple 324mm
SVTT Mk 32 ASTT with Mk 46 mod 5 LWT, 1 *Meroka*
mod 2B CIWS, 1 76mm gun (capacity 2 SH-60B *Seahawk*
ASW hel)

AMPHIBIOUS

PRINCIPAL AMPHIBIOUS SHIPS 3:

    LHD 1 *Juan Carlos* I (capacity 18 hel or 10 AV-8B FGA
ac; 4 LCM-1E; 42 APC; 46 MBT; 900 troops)

    LPD 2 *Galicia* (capacity 6 Bell 212 or 4 SH-3D *Sea King*
hel; 4 LCM or 2 LCM & 8 AAV; 130 APC or 33 MBT;
540 troops)

    LANDING CRAFT • LCM 12 LCM 1E

LOGISTICS AND SUPPORT 2

    AORH 2: 1 *Patino* (capacity 3 Bell 212 or 2 SH-3D *Sea King*
hel); 1 *Cantabria* (capacity 3 Bell 212 or 2 SH-3D *Sea King* hel)

Europe 135

Maritime Action Force

EQUIPMENT BY TYPE
PATROL AND COASTAL COMBATANTS 23
PSOH 6 *Meteoro* (*Buques de Accion Maritima*) with 1 76mm gun
PSO 5: 3 *Alboran* each with 1 hel landing platform; 2 *Descubierta* with 1 76mm gun
PCO 4 *Serviola* with 1 76mm gun
PCC 3 *Anaga* with 1 76mm gun
PB 4: 2 P-101; 2 *Toralla*
PBR 1 *Cabo Fradera*
MINE WARFARE • MINE COUNTERMEASURES 6
MHO 6 *Segura*
LOGISTICS AND SUPPORT 30
AGI 1 *Alerta*
AGOR 2 (with ice-strengthened hull, for polar research duties in Antarctica)
AGS 3: 2 *Malaspina*; 1 *Castor*
AKR 1 *Ysabel*
AP 1 *Contramaestre Casado* with 1 hel landing platform
ASR 1 *Neptuno*
ATF 3: 1 *Mar Caribe*; 1 *Mahon*; 1 *La Grana*
AXL 10: 6 *Contramaestre*; 4 *Guardiamarina*
AXS 8

Naval Aviation 850

FORCES BY ROLE
FIGHTER/GROUND ATTACK
1 sqn with AV-8B *Harrier* II Plus
ANTI-SUBMARINE WARFARE
1 sqn with SH-60B/F *Seahawk*
TRANSPORT
1 (liaison) sqn with Cessna 550 *Citation* II; Cessna 650 *Citation* VII
TRAINING
1 sqn with Hughes 500MD8
1 flt with TAV-8B *Harrier*
TRANSPORT HELICOPTER
1 sqn with Bell 212 (HU-18)
EQUIPMENT BY TYPE
AIRCRAFT 13 combat capable **FGA** 13: 12 AV-8B *Harrier* II Plus; 1 TAV-8B *Harrier* (on lease from USMC)
TPT • Light 4: 3 Cessna 550 *Citation* II; 1 Cessna 650 *Citation* VII
HELICOPTERS
ASW 18: 12 SH-60B *Seahawk*; 6 SH-60F *Seahawk*
MRH 9 Hughes 500MD
TPT • Light 7 Bell 212 (HA-18)
AIR-LAUNCHED MISSILES
AAM • IR AIM-9L *Sidewinder*; **ARH** AIM-120 AMRAAM
ASM AGM-65G *Maverick*; AGM-114K/R *Hellfire* II
AShM AGM-119 *Penguin*

Marines 5,350

FORCES BY ROLE
SPECIAL FORCES
1 spec ops bn
MANOEUVRE
Amphibious

1 mne bde (1 recce unit, 1 mech inf bn, 2 inf bn, 1 arty bn, 1 log bn)
Other
1 sy bde (5 mne garrison gp)
EQUIPMENT BY TYPE
ARMOURED FIGHTING VEHICLES
APC • APC (W) 34: 32 *Piranha* IIIC; 1 *Piranha* IIIC (amb); 1 *Piranha* IIIC EW (EW)
AAV 18: 16 AAV-7A1/AAVP-7A1; 2 AAVC-7A1 (CP)
ENGINEERING & MAINTENANCE VEHICLES
AEV 4 *Piranha* IIIC
ARV 3: 1 AAVR-7A1; 1 M88; 1 *Piranha* IIIC
ARTILLERY 30
SP 155mm 6 M109A2
TOWED 105mm 24 Model 56 pack howitzer
ANTI-TANK/ANTI-INFRASTRUCTURE
MSL • MANPATS *Spike*-LR; TOW-2
AIR DEFENCE • SAM • Point-defence *Mistral*

Air Force 20,350

The Spanish Air Force is organised in 3 commands – General Air Command, Combat Air Command and Canary Islands Air Command

FORCES BY ROLE
FIGHTER
2 sqn with Eurofighter *Typhoon*
FIGHTER/GROUND ATTACK
5 sqn with F/A-18A/B MLU *Hornet* (EF-18A/B MLU)
MARITIME PATROL
1 sqn with P-3A/M *Orion*
ISR
1 sqn with Beech C90 *King Air*
1 sqn with Cessna 550 *Citation* V; CN235 (TR-19A)
SEARCH & RESCUE
1 sqn with AS332B/B1 *Super Puma*; CN235 VIGMA
1 sqn with AS332B *Super Puma*; CN235 VIGMA; H215 (AS332C1) *Super Puma*
1 sqn with C-212 *Aviocar*; CN235 VIGMA
TANKER/TRANSPORT
1 sqn with A400M
TRANSPORT
1 VIP sqn with A310; *Falcon* 900
1 sqn with A400M
1 sqn with C-212 *Aviocar*
2 sqn with C295
1 sqn with CN235
TRAINING
1 OCU sqn with Eurofighter *Typhoon*
1 OCU sqn with F/A-18A/B (EF-18A/B MLU) *Hornet*
1 sqn with Beech F33C *Bonanza*
1 sqn with C-212 *Aviocar*
1 sqn with PC-21
1 sqn with T-35 *Pillan* (E-26)
2 (LIFT) sqn with F-5B *Freedom Fighter*
1 hel sqn with H120 *Colibri*
1 hel sqn with S-76C
TRANSPORT HELICOPTER
1 sqn with AS332M1 *Super Puma*; AS532UL *Cougar* (VIP)
ISR UAV
1 sqn with MQ-9A *Reaper* (forming)

EQUIPMENT BY TYPE

AIRCRAFT 175 combat capable

FTR 88: 69 Eurofighter *Typhoon*; 19 F-5B *Freedom Fighter*

FGA 84: 20 F/A-18A *Hornet* (EF-18A); 52 EF-18A MLU; 12 EF-18B MLU

ASW 3 P-3M *Orion*

MP 8 CN235 VIGMA

ISR 2 CN235 (TR-19A)

EW 1 C-212 *Aviocar* (TM.12D)

TPT 73: **Heavy** 13 A400M; **Light** 51: 3 Beech C90 *King Air*; 15 Beech F33C *Bonanza*; 10 C-212 *Aviocar* (incl 9 trg); 12 C295; 8 CN235; 3 Cessna 560 *Citation* V (ISR); **PAX** 9: 2 A310; 2 A330 (to be converted to MRTT tkt/tpt configuration); 5 *Falcon* 900 (VIP)

TRG 60: 24 PC-21; 36 T-35 *Pillan* (E-26)

HELICOPTERS

TPT 43: **Medium** 21: 5 AS332B/B1 *Super Puma*; 4 AS332M1 *Super Puma*; 4 H215 (AS332C1) *Super Puma*; 2 AS532UL *Cougar* (VIP); 6 NH90 TTH; **Light** 22: 14 H120 *Colibri*; 8 S-76C

UNINHABITED AERIAL VEHICLES • CISR • Heavy 4 MQ-9A *Reaper* (unarmed)

AIR DEFENCE • SAM

Short-range *Skyguard/Aspide*

Point-defence *Mistral*

AIR-LAUNCHED MISSILES

AAM • IR AIM-9L/JULI *Sidewinder*; **IIR** IRIS-T; **SARH** AIM-7P *Sparrow*; **ARH** AIM-120B/C AMRAAM; *Meteor*

ARM AGM-88B HARM

ASM AGM-65G *Maverick*

AShM AGM-84D *Harpoon*

LACM Taurus KEPD 350

BOMBS

Laser-guided: GBU-10/-12/-16 *Paveway* II; GBU-24 *Paveway* III; BPG-2000

Laser & INS/GPS-guided EGBU-16 *Paveway* II

INS/GPS guided: GBU-38 JDAM

Emergencies Military Unit (UME) 3,500

FORCES BY ROLE

COMMAND

1 div HQ

MANOEUVRE

Other

5 Emergency Intervention bn

1 Emergency Support and Intervention regt

COMBAT SUPPORT

1 sigs bn

HELICOPTER

1 hel bn opcon Army

Gendarmerie & Paramilitary 75,800

Guardia Civil 75,800

17 regions, 54 Rural Comds

FORCES BY ROLE

SPECIAL FORCES

8 (rural) gp

MANOEUVRE

Other

15 (traffic) sy gp

1 (Special) sy bn

EQUIPMENT BY TYPE

PATROL AND COASTAL COMBATANTS 64

PSO 1 with 1 hel landing platform

PCC 2

PBF 34

PB 27

AIRCRAFT • TPT • Light 3: 2 CN235-300; 1 King Air 350i

HELICOPTERS

MRH 20: 4 AS653N3 *Dauphin*; 16 Bo-105ATH

TPT • Light 21: 8 BK-117; 13 H135

DEPLOYMENT

BOSNIA-HERZEGOVINA: EU • EUFOR (*Operation Althea*) 2

BULGARIA: NATO • Enhanced Air Policing 130; 6 Eurofighter *Typhoon*

CENTRAL AFRICAN REPUBLIC: EU • EUTM RCA 8

DJIBOUTI: EU • *Operation Atalanta* 60; 1 P-3M *Orion*

GULF OF ADEN & INDIAN OCEAN: EU • *Operation Atalanta* 220; 1 FFGHM

GULF OF GUINEA: Navy 50; 1 PCO

IRAQ: *Operation Inherent Resolve* 150; 1 trg unit; 1 hel unit with 3 NH90 TTH; **NATO •** NATO Mission Iraq 130; 1 armd inf coy

LATVIA: NATO • Enhanced Forward Presence 504; 1 armd inf coy(+); 1 arty bty; 1 cbt engr coy; 1 SAM bty with NASAMS

LEBANON: UN • UNIFIL 669; 1 mech bde HQ; 1 mech inf bn(-); 1 engr coy; 1 sigs coy; 1 log coy

MALI: EU • EUTM Mali 420; 1 hel unit with 3 NH90 TTH; **UN •** MINUSMA 1

MEDITERRANEAN SEA: NATO • SNMG 2: 200; 1 DDGHM; **NATO •** SNMCMG 2: 40; 1 MHO

MOZAMBIQUE: EU • EUTM Mozambique 2

SENEGAL: *Operation Barkhane* 65; 2 C295M

SOMALIA: EU • EUTM Somalia 20

TURKEY: NATO • *Operation Active Fence* 150; 1 SAM bty with M901 *Patriot* PAC-2

FOREIGN FORCES

United States US European Command: 3,550; 4 DDGM; 1 air base at Morón; 1 naval base at Rota

Sweden SWE

Swedish Krona SEK		2021	2022	2023
GDP	SEK	5.45tr	5.98tr	
	USD	636bn	604bn	
per capita	USD	60,816	56,361	
Growth	%	5.1	2.6	
Inflation	%	2.7	7.2	
Def bdgt	SEK	71.2bn	79.9bn	94.0bn
	USD	8.30bn	8.07bn	
USD1=SEK		8.58	9.89	

Real-terms defence budget trend (USDbn, constant 2015)

| Population | 10,483,647 |

Age	0–14	15–19	20–24	25–29	30–64	65 plus
Male	8.9%	2.9%	2.9%	3.3%	22.7%	9.6%
Female	8.4%	2.7%	2.6%	3.1%	21.9%	11.0%

Capabilities

Sweden's armed forces remain configured for territorial defence and there has been growing concern over Russia's military activity in the Baltic area. There has also been a focus on increasing cooperation with neighbours and NATO in recent years. Sweden applied for NATO membership in May 2022, three months after Russia's full-scale invasion of Ukraine. Sweden also plans to increase its defence budget to 2% of GDP. Under the 2021–25 defence bill, which was presented in October 2020, Sweden had already envisaged increased spending. Measures to enhance societal resilience and the ability to deal with civil emergencies have also been announced. In July 2019, Sweden joined the UK-led *Tempest* project for a future combat aircraft, and in 2022 signed a mutual security agreement with the UK. Concerns over readiness levels have led to greater cooperation with NORDEFCO. In May 2018, Sweden, Finland and the US signed a statement of intent to develop closer cooperation on exercises and interoperability. Sweden has started to re-garrison the island of Gotland, and is in the process of establishing five new regiments which will raise and train new infantry battalions. Readiness challenges in the air force triggered a discussion about extending the service life of the JAS-39C *Gripens* beyond their intended 2026 retirement date, not least since the air force was slated to receive a lower number of JAS-39Es than requested. Air defence has been boosted in recent years with the acquisition of the *Patriot* system. The country's export-oriented defence industry is privately owned and capable of meeting most of the armed forces' equipment needs, including for advanced combat aircraft and conventional submarines.

ACTIVE 14,600 (Army 6,850 Navy 2,350 Air 2,700 Other 2,950) Voluntary Auxiliary Organisations **21,200**

Conscript liability 4–11 months, depending on branch (selective conscription; 4,000 in total, gender neutral)

RESERVE 10,000

ORGANISATIONS BY SERVICE

Army 6,850

The army has been transformed to provide brigade-sized task forces depending on the operational requirement

FORCES BY ROLE
COMMAND
  2 bde HQ
MANOEUVRE
  Reconnaissance
  1 recce bn
  Armoured
  5 armd bn
  1 armd BG
  Mechanised
  1 mech bn
  Light
  1 mot inf bn
  1 lt inf bn
  Air Manoeuvre
  1 AB bn
  Other
  1 sy bn
COMBAT SUPPORT
  2 arty bn
  2 engr bn
  2 MP coy
  1 CBRN coy
COMBAT SERVICE SUPPORT
  1 tpt coy
AIR DEFENCE
  2 AD bn

Reserves

FORCES BY ROLE
MANOEUVRE
  Other
  40 Home Guard bn

EQUIPMENT BY TYPE
ARMOURED FIGHTING VEHICLES
  MBT 120 *Leopard* 2A5 (Strv 122)
  IFV 411: 369 CV9040 (Strf 9040; incl 54 CP); 42 Epbv 90 (OP)
  APC 1,064
    APC (T) 389: 239 Pbv 302 (incl variants); 150 BvS-10 MkII
    APC (W) 315+: some *Bastion* APC; 34 XA-180 *Sisu* (Patgb 180); 20 XA-202 *Sisu* (Patgb 202); 148 XA-203 *Sisu* (Patgb 203); 113 Patria AMV (XA-360/Patgb 360)
  PPV 360 RG-32M
ENGINEERING & MAINTENANCE VEHICLES
  AEV 6 Pionierpanzer-3 *Kodiak* (Ingbv 120)
  ARV 40: 14 Bgbv 120; 26 Bgbv 90
  VLB 3 Brobv 120
  MW 33+: *Aardvark* Mk2; 33 Area Clearing System
ANTI-TANK/ANTI-INFRASTRUCTURE
  MSL • MANPATS NLAW; RBS-55
  RCL 84mm *Carl Gustaf*

138 THE MILITARY BALANCE 2023

ARTILLERY 357

SP 155mm 35 *Archer*

MOR 322: **81mm** 201 M/86; **120mm** 81 M/41D **SP 120mm** 40 CV90 *Mjolner* (Gkpbv 90)

AIR DEFENCE

SAM 14+

Long-range 6 M903 *Patriot* PAC-3 MSE

Medium-range MIM-23B *Hawk* (RBS-97)

Short-range 8 IRIS-T SLS (RBS-98); RBS-23 BAMSE

Point-defence RBS-70

GUNS • SP 40mm 30 Lvkv 90

Navy 1,250; 1,100 Amphibious (total 2,350)

EQUIPMENT BY TYPE

SUBMARINE • SSK 5:

1 *Gotland* (fitted with AIP) with 2 single 400mm TT with Torped 431 LWT/Torped 451 LWT, 4 single 533mm TT with Torped 613 HWT/Torped 62 HWT

2 *Gotland* mod (fitted with AIP) with 2 single 400mm TT with Torped 431 LWT/Torped 451 LWT, 4 single 533mm TT with Torped 613 HWT/Torped 62 HWT

2 *Södermanland* (fitted with AIP) with 3 single 400mm TT with Torped 431 LWT/Torped 451 LWT, 6 single 533mm TT with Torped 613 HWT/Torped 62 HWT

PATROL AND COASTAL COMBATANTS 150

CORVETTES • FSG 5 *Visby* with 8 RBS15 Mk2 AShM, 4 single 400mm ASTT with Torped 45 LWT, 1 57mm gun, 1 hel landing platform

PCGT 4:

2 *Göteborg* with 4 twin lnchr with RBS15 Mk2 AShM, 4 single 400mm ASTT with Torped 431 LWT, 1 57mm gun

2 *Stockholm* with 4 twin lnchr with RBS15 Mk2 AShM, 4 single 400mm ASTT with Torped 431 LWT, 1 57mm gun

PBF 133: 100+ Combat Boat 90H (capacity 18 troops); 27 Combat Boat HS (capacity 18 troops); 6 Combat Boat 90HSM (capacity 18 troops)

PB 8 *Tapper* (Type 80)

MINE WARFARE • MINE COUNTERMEASURES 7

MCC 5 *Koster* (SWE *Landsort* mod)

MCD 2 *Spårö* (*Styrsö* mod)

AMPHIBIOUS • LANDING CRAFT 11

LCVP 8 *Trossbat*

LCAC 3 *Griffon* 8100TD

LOGISTICS AND SUPPORT 15

AG 2: 1 *Carlskrona* with 1 hel landing platform (former ML); 1 *Trosso* (spt ship for corvettes and patrol vessels but can also be used as HQ ship)

AGF 2 *Ledningsbåt* 2000

AGI 1 *Orion*

AKL 1 *Loke*

ARS 2: 1 *Belos* III; 1 *Furusund* (former ML)

AX 5 *Altair*

AXS 2: 1 *Falken*; 1 *Gladan*

Amphibious 1,100

FORCES BY ROLE

MANOEUVRE

Amphibious

2 amph bn

EQUIPMENT BY TYPE

ARTILLERY • MOR 81mm 12 M/86

COASTAL DEFENCE • AShM 8 RBS-17 *Hellfire*

Coastal Defence

FORCES BY ROLE

COASTAL DEFENCE

1 AShM bty with RBS-15

EQUIPMENT BY TYPE

COASTAL DEFENCE • AShM RBS-15

Air Force 2,700

FORCES BY ROLE

FIGHTER/GROUND ATTACK/ISR

6 sqn with JAS 39C/D *Gripen*

TRANSPORT/ISR/AEW&C

1 sqn with C-130H *Hercules* (Tp-84); KC-130H *Hercules* (Tp-84); Gulfstream IV SRA-4 (S-102B); S-100B/D *Argus*

TRAINING

1 unit with Sk-60

AIR DEFENCE

1 (fighter control and air surv) bn

EQUIPMENT BY TYPE

AIRCRAFT 98 combat capable

FGA 98: 96 JAS 39C/D *Gripen*; 2 JAS 39E *Gripen* (in test)

ELINT 2 Gulfstream IV SRA-4 (S-102B)

AEW&C 3: 1 S-100B *Argus*; 2 S-100D *Argus*

TKR/TPT 1 KC-130H *Hercules* (Tp-84)

TPT 8: **Medium** 5 C-130H *Hercules* (Tp-84); **Light** 2 Saab 340 (OS-100A/Tp-100C); **PAX** 1 Gulfstream 550 (Tp-102D)

TRG 67 Sk-60W

UNINHABITED AERIAL VEHICLES

ISR • Medium 8 RQ-7 *Shadow* (AUV 3 Örnen)

AIR-LAUNCHED MISSILES

ASM AGM-65 *Maverick* (RB-75)

AShM RB-15F

AAM • IR AIM-9L *Sidewinder* (RB-74); **IIR** IRIS-T (RB-98); **ARH** AIM-120B AMRAAM (RB-99); *Meteor*

BOMBS

Laser-Guided GBU-12 *Paveway* II

INS/GPS guided GBU-39 Small Diameter Bomb

Armed Forces Hel Wing

FORCES BY ROLE

TRANSPORT HELICOPTER

3 sqn with AW109 (Hkp 15A); AW109M (Hkp-15B); NH90 TTH (Hkp-14) (SAR/ASW); UH-60M *Black Hawk* (Hkp-16)

EQUIPMENT BY TYPE

HELICOPTERS

TPT 53: **Medium** 33: 15 UH-60M *Black Hawk* (Hkp-16); 18 NH90 TTH (Hkp-14) (of which 9 configured for ASW); **Light** 20: 12 AW109 (Hkp-15A); 8 AW109M (Hkp-15B)

Special Forces

FORCES BY ROLE

SPECIAL FORCES

1 spec ops gp

COMBAT SUPPORT

1 cbt spt gp

Other 2,950
Includes staff, logistics and intelligence personnel
FORCES BY ROLE
COMBAT SUPPORT
 1 EW bn
 1 psyops unit
COMBAT SERVICE SUPPORT
 2 log bn
 1 maint bn
 4 med coy
 1 tpt coy

DEPLOYMENT

INDIA/PAKISTAN: UN • UNMOGIP 4
IRAQ: *Operation Inherent Resolve* 2; **NATO** • NATO Mission Iraq 1
KOREA, REPUBLIC OF: NNSC • 5
MALI: EU • EUTM Mali 8; **UN** • MINUSMA 184; 1 int coy
MIDDLE EAST: UN • UNTSO 7
SERBIA: NATO • KFOR 3
SOMALIA: EU • EUTM Somalia 5
UNITED KINGDOM: *Operation Interflex* 45 (UKR trg)
WESTERN SAHARA: UN • MINURSO 1

Switzerland CHE

Swiss Franc CHF		2021	2022	2023
GDP	CHF	731bn	766bn	
	USD	800bn	807bn	
per capita	USD	92,249	92,434	
Growth	%	4.2	2.2	
Inflation	%	0.6	3.1	
Def bdgt [a]	CHF	5.20bn	5.27bn	5.30bn
	USD	5.69bn	5.55bn	
USD1=CHF		0.91	0.95	

[a] Includes military pensions

Real-terms defence budget trend (USDbn, constant 2015)

Population	8,508,698				
Age	0–14	15–19	20–24	25–29	30–64	65 plus
Male	8.0%	2.5%	2.7%	3.0%	24.6%	8.6%
Female	7.5%	2.4%	2.6%	3.0%	24.6%	10.6%

Capabilities

The conscript-based armed forces are postured for territorial defence and limited participation in international peace-support operations. The government has begun to reduce its armed forces, reflecting an assessment that in the militia-based system not all personnel would realistically be available for active service. With permanent neutrality a core feature of foreign and security policy, Switzerland is not a member of any alliances, although it joined NATO's Partnership for Peace programme in 1996 and on occasion contributes to NATO- and EU-led operations alongside its engagement in UN or OSCE missions. Switzerland does not participate in combat operations for peace-enforcement purposes and its deployments are limited in size. The 2016 armed-forces development plan emphasised improvements in readiness, training and equipment. In 2022, the defence ministry published a paper on the future of the armed forces out to the 2030s, summarising its approach to modernisation requirements for air defence and ground forces and for stronger cyber capabilities. The approach to readiness is changing to a flexible model in which different units are called up for active service gradually and on different timelines. A multi-stage selection process for aircraft to replace the F-5 *Tiger II* and F/A-18 *Hornet* was completed in June 2021 and the F-35A was chosen. The life of the *Hornet* fleet has been extended until 2030. This was approved by parliament in September 2022, after which the contract was signed. Plans for a referendum on the F-35 procurement gathered the required number of signatures but were withdrawn after the government indicated it would not diverge from the procurement timetable. The fighter-acquisition programme was capped at CHF6 billion in May 2019 and has been separated from the ground-based air-defence procurement. Previously both programmes were linked. Other priorities include upgrades to Switzerland's air-surveillance systems and to transport helicopters. Switzerland's defence industry has limited design and manufacturing capabilities, with recognised capacity in the land-vehicles sector, which has links to North American firms.

ACTIVE 19,550 (Armed Forces 19,550)
Conscript liability 260–600 compulsory service days depending on rank. 18 or 23 weeks' training (depending on branch) generally at age 20, followed by 6 refresher trg courses (3 weeks each). Alternative service available

RESERVE 123,450

Civil Defence 73,000 (51,000 Reserve)

ORGANISATIONS BY SERVICE

Armed Forces 3,100 active; 16,450 conscript (19,550 total)

Operations Command 72,600 on mobilisation
4 Territorial Regions. With the exception of military police all units are non-active
FORCES BY ROLE
COMMAND
 4 regional comd
SPECIAL FORCES
 2 SF bn
MANOEUVRE
 Armoured
 2 (1st & 11th) bde (1 recce bn, 1 tk bn, 2 armd inf bn, 1 SP arty bn, 1 engr bn, 1 sigs bn)
 Mechanised
 1 (4th) bde (2 recce bn, 2 SP arty bn, 1 ptn br bn)
 Light
 10 inf bn
 7 mtn inf bn
 1 mtn inf unit

COMBAT SUPPORT
4 engr bn
4 MP bn
1 NBC bn
1 int unit
COMBAT SUPPORT
4 engr rescue bn

EQUIPMENT BY TYPE
ARMOURED FIGHTING VEHICLES
MBT 134 Leopard 2 (Pz-87 Leo)
IFV 186: 154 CV9030CH; 32 CV9030 (CP)
APC 1,233
    APC (T) 309 M113A2 (incl variants)
    APC (W) 924 Piranha I/II/IIIC
AUV 292: 173 Eagle II; 119 Eagle III (CP)
ENGINEERING & MAINTENANCE VEHICLES
AEV 12 Kodiak
ARV 25 Büffel
VLB 9 Leopard 2 with Leguan
MW 46: 26 Area Clearing System; 20 M113A2
NBC VEHICLES 12 Piranha IIIC CBRN
ANTI-TANK/ANTI-INFRASTRUCTURE
MSL • SP 106 Piranha I TOW-2
ARTILLERY 355
SP 155mm 133 M109 KAWEST
MOR • 81mm 222 Mw-72
PATROL AND COASTAL COMBATANTS 14
PB 14 Watercat 1250
AIR DEFENCE • SAM • Point-defence FIM-92 Stinger

Air Force 18,900 on mobilisation
FORCES BY ROLE
FIGHTER
2 sqn with F-5E/F Tiger II
3 sqn with F/A-18C/D Hornet
TRANSPORT
1 sqn with Beech 350 King Air; DHC-6 Twin Otter;
    PC-6 Turbo Porter; PC-12
1 VIP Flt with Cessna 560XL Citation; CL-604
    Challenger; Falcon 900EX; PC-24
TRAINING
1 sqn with PC-7CH Turbo Trainer; PC-21
1 sqn with PC-9 (tgt towing)
1 OCU Sqn with F-5E/F Tiger II
TRANSPORT HELICOPTER
6 sqn with AS332M Super Puma; AS532UL Cougar; H135M
ISR UAV
1 sqn with Hermes 900
EQUIPMENT BY TYPE
AIRCRAFT 55 combat capable
FTR 25: 20 F-5E Tiger II; 5 F-5F Tiger II
FGA 30: 25 F/A-18C Hornet; 5 F/A-18D Hornet
TPT 23: **Light** 19: 1 Beech 350 King Air; 1 Cessna
560XL Citation; 1 DHC-6 Twin Otter; 14 PC-6
Turbo Porter; 1 PC-6 (owned by armasuisse, civil
registration); 1 PC-12 (owned by armasuisse, civil
registration); **PAX** 4: 2 CL-604 Challenger; 1 Falcon
900EX; 1 PC-24 (VIP)
TRG 40: 27 PC-7CH Turbo Trainer; 5 PC-9 (used for
target training only); 8 PC-21

HELICOPTERS
MRH 20 H135M
TPT • Medium 24: 15 AS332M Super Puma; 9
AS532UL Cougar
UNINHABITED AERIAL VEHICLES
ISR • Medium 1 Hermes 900
AIR-LAUNCHED MISSILES • AAM • IIR AIM-9X
Sidewinder II; **ARH** AIM-120B/C-7 AMRAAM

Ground Based Air Defence (GBAD)
GBAD assets can be used to form AD clusters to
be deployed independently as task forces within
Swiss territory
EQUIPMENT BY TYPE
AIR DEFENCE
SAM • Point-defence 56+: 56 Rapier; FIM-92 Stinger
GUNS 35mm 27 GDF-003/-005 with Skyguard

Armed Forces Logistic Organisation 9,650 on mobilisation
FORCES BY ROLE
COMBAT SERVICE SUPPORT
1 log bde (6 log bn; 1 tpt bn; 6 med bn)

Command Support Organisation 11,150 on mobilisation
FORCES BY ROLE
COMBAT SERVICE SUPPORT
1 spt bde

Training Command 37,350 on mobilisation
COMBAT SERVICE SUPPORT
5 trg unit

Civil Defence 73,000 (51,000 Reserve)
(not part of armed forces)

DEPLOYMENT
BOSNIA-HERZEGOVINA: EU • EUFOR (Operation Althea) 20

DEMOCRATIC REPUBLIC OF THE CONGO: UN •
MONUSCO 1

INDIA/PAKISTAN: UN • UNMOGIP 3

KOREA, REPUBLIC OF: NNSC • 5

MALI: UN • MINUSMA 5

MIDDLE EAST: UN • UNTSO 11

SERBIA: NATO • KFOR 186 (military volunteers); 1 inf
coy; 1 engr pl; 1 hel flt with AS332M Super Puma

SOUTH SUDAN: UN • UNMISS 1

WESTERN SAHARA: UN • MINURSO 2

Turkey TUR

New Turkish Lira TRY		2021	2022	2023
GDP	TRY	7.25tr	14.29tr	
	USD	818bn	853bn	
per capita	USD	9,654	9,961	
Growth	%	11.4	5.0	
Inflation	%	19.6	73.1	
Def exp [a]	TRY	117bn	138bn	
	USD	13.1bn	8.2bn	
Def bdgt [b]	TRY	84.6bn	104bn	206bn
	USD	9.55bn	6.19bn	
USD1=TRY		8.87	16.74	

[a] NATO figure

[b] Includes funding for Undersecretariat of Defence Industries; Defence Industry Support Fund; TUBITAK Defense Industries R&D Institute (SAGE); and military pensions

Real-terms defence budget trend (USDbn, constant 2015)

Population   83,047,706

Age	0–14	15–19	20–24	25–29	30–64	65 plus
Male	11.5%	4.0%	3.9%	3.7%	23.0%	4.1%
Female	11.0%	3.8%	3.7%	3.6%	22.7%	4.9%

Capabilities

Turkey has large, generally well-equipped armed forces that are primarily structured for national defence. Much recent activity has focused on internal security and cross-border operations in response to the continuing wars in Syria and Libya. The conflict with Kurdish armed groups continues. The armed forces' 2033 strategic plan aims to modernise military equipment and force structures. Turkey is a NATO member and has provided access to its airspace and facilities for operations in Iraq and Syria. However, relations with NATO allies have come under pressure after Ankara's decision to procure the Russian-made S-400 air-defence system, its operations in northern Syria, rising tensions with Greece in the eastern Mediterranean Sea, its role in Libya and its position regarding the fighting in recent years between Armenia and Azerbaijan. Following an attempted coup in July 2016, Ankara dismissed large numbers of officers from the armed forces. The armed forces train regularly, including with NATO allies. While key subcomponents are still often imported, a number of locally developed equipment designs are in production. Efforts are under way to increase military exports and Turkey has secured markets in Azerbaijan, Pakistan and Ukraine, as well as a number of African states, successfully offering cost-effective assets in specific sectors. The US government terminated Turkey's participation in the F-35 programme after deliveries under the S-400 contract began in 2019. Turkey is also developing a domestic fighter aircraft but is dependent on collaboration with external defence companies. The president has authority over defence procurement and control over Turkey's top defence companies. Turkey has signed defence-cooperation agreements with a focus on exports and technology transfer, in an effort to boost its national defence industry and achieve defence-industrial autonomy.

ACTIVE 355,200 (Army 260,200 Navy 45,000 Air 50,000) Gendarmerie & Paramilitary 156,800

Conscript liability 12 months (5.5 months for university graduates; 21 days for graduates with exemption) (reducing to 6 months)

RESERVE 378,700 (Army 258,700 Navy 55,000 Air 65,000)

Reserve service to age 41 for all services

ORGANISATIONS BY SERVICE

Space
EQUIPMENT BY TYPE
SATELLITES • ISR 2 *Gokturk*-1/2

Army ε260,200 (incl conscripts)
FORCES BY ROLE
COMMAND
  4 army HQ
  9 corps HQ
SPECIAL FORCES
  8 cdo bde
  1 mtn cdo bde
  1 cdo regt
MANOEUVRE
  Armoured
  1 (52nd) armd div (2 armd bde, 1 mech bde)
  7 armd bde
  Mechanised
  2 (28th & 29th) mech div
  14 mech inf bde
  Light
  1 (23rd) mot inf div (3 mot inf regt)
  7 mot inf bde
COMBAT SUPPORT
  2 arty bde
  1 trg arty bde
  6 arty regt
  2 engr regt
AVIATION
  4 avn regt
  4 avn bn
EQUIPMENT BY TYPE
ARMOURED FIGHTING VEHICLES
  MBT 2,378: 316 *Leopard* 2A4 (being upgraded); 170 *Leopard* 1A4; 227 *Leopard* 1A3; 100 M60A1; 650 M60A3 TTS; 165 M60TM *Firat*; 750 M48A5 T2 *Patton*
  IFV 645 ACV AIFV
  APC 6,403
    APC (T) 3,579: 823 ACV AAPC; 2,813 M113/M113A1/M113A2
    APC (W) 57 *Pars* 6×6 (incl variants)
    PPV 2,710: 360 *Edjer Yalcin* 4×4; ε2,000 *Kirpi/Kirpi*-II; ε350 *Vuran*
  AUV 1,450: ε250 *Akrep*; 800+ *Cobra*; ε400 *Cobra* II
ENGINEERING & MAINTENANCE VEHICLES
  AEV 12+: AZMIM; 12 M48 AEV; M113A2T2
  ARV 150: 12 BPz-2; 105 M48T5; 33 M88A1
  VLB 88: 36 *Leguan*; 52 Mobile Floating Assault Bridge
  MW 14+: 4 *Husky* 2G; 10 *Kirpi* PMKI; *Tamkar*; *Bozena*

ANTI-TANK/ANTI-INFRASTRUCTURE
MSL
 SP 625: 365 ACV TOW; 184 *Kaplan* STA; 76 *Pars* STA 4×4
 MANPATS 9K135 *Kornet*-E (RS-AT-14 *Spriggan*); *Eryx*; FGM-148 *Javelin*; Milan; OMTAS; Tek-Er
RCL 106mm M40A1
ARTILLERY 2,760+
SP 1,080: **155mm** 828: ε150 M44T1; 365 M52T (mod); ε280 T-155 *Firtina*; εY30 T-155 *Firtina* II; **175mm** 36 M107; **203mm** 219 M110A2
TOWED 675+: **105mm** 82: 7 *Boran* (in test); 75+ M101A1; **155mm** 557: 517 M114A1/M114A2; 40 *Panter*; **203mm** 36+ M115
MRL 98+: **122mm** ε36 T-122; **227mm** 12 M270 MLRS; **302mm** 50+ TR-300 *Kasirga* (WS-1)
MOR 907+
 SP 329+: **81mm** some; **107mm** ε150 M106; **120mm** 179
 TOWED 578+: **81mm** some; **120mm** 578 HY12
SURFACE-TO-SURFACE MISSILE LAUNCHERS
SRBM • Conventional *Bora*; MGM-140A ATACMS (launched from M270 MLRS); J-600T *Yildrim* (B-611/CH-SS-9 mod 1)
AIRCRAFT
ISR 5 Beech 350 *King Air*
TPT • Light 8: 5 Beech 200 *King Air*; 3 Cessna 421
TRG 49: 45 Cessna T182; 4 T-42A *Cochise*
HELICOPTERS
ATK 96: 18 AH-1P *Cobra*; 12 AH-1S *Cobra*; 5 AH-1W *Cobra*; 4 TAH-1P *Cobra*; 9 T129A; 48 T129B
MRH 28 Hughes 300C
TPT 226+: **Heavy** 11 CH-47F *Chinook*; **Medium** 76+: 28 AS532UL *Cougar*; 48+ S-70A *Black Hawk*; **Light** 139: 12 Bell 204B (AB-204B); ε43 Bell 205 (UH-1H *Iroquois*); 64 Bell 205A (AB-205A); 20 Bell 206 *Jet Ranger*
UNINHABITED AERIAL VEHICLES
CISR • Medium 33 *Bayraktar* TB2
ISR • Heavy *Falcon* 600/*Firebee*; **Medium** CL-89; *Gnat*
LOITERING & DIRECT ATTACK MUNITIONS
Harpy
AIR-LAUNCHED MISSILES
ASM *Mizrak*-U (UMTAS)
BOMBS
Laser-guided MAM-C/L
AIR DEFENCE
SAM
 Short-range HISAR-A/A+; HISAR-O
 Point-defence 148+: 70 *Atilgan* PMADS octuple *Stinger* lnchr, 78 *Zipkin* PMADS quad *Stinger* lnchr; FIM-92 *Stinger*
GUNS 1,404
 SP 35mm 42 *Korkut*
 TOWED 1,362: **20mm** 439 GAI-D01/Rh-202; **35mm** 120 GDF-001/-003; **40mm** 803 L/60/L/70

Navy ε45,000 (incl conscripts)
EQUIPMENT BY TYPE
SUBMARINES • SSK 12
4 *Atilay* (GER Type-209/1200) with 8 single 533mm TT with SST-4 HWT
4 *Gür* (GER Type-209/1400) with 8 single 533mm TT with UGM-84 *Harpoon* AShM/Mk 24 *Tigerfish* mod 2 HWT/ *SeaHake* mod 4 (DM2A4) HWT
4 *Preveze* (GER Type-209/1400) (MLU ongoing) with 8 single 533mm TT with UGM-84 *Harpoon* AShM/Mk 24 *Tigerfish* mod 2 HWT/*SeaHake* mod 4 (DM2A4) HWT
PRINCIPAL SURFACE COMBATANTS • FRIGATES 16
FFGHM 16:
4 *Barbaros* (GER MEKO 200 mod) with 2 quad lnchr with RGM-84C *Harpoon* Block 1B AShM, 2 8-cell Mk 41 VLS with RIM-162B ESSM SAM, 2 triple 324mm SVTT Mk 32 ASTT with Mk 46 LWT, 3 *Sea Zenith* CIWS, 1 127mm gun (capacity 1 Bell 212 (AB-212) hel)
4 *Gabya* (ex-US *Oliver Hazard Perry*) with 1 Mk 13 GMLS with RGM-84C *Harpoon* Block 1B AShM/SM-1MR Block VI SAM, 1 8-cell Mk 41 VLS with RIM-162B ESSM SAM, 2 triple 324mm SVTT Mk 32 ASTT with Mk 46 LWT, 1 Mk 15 *Phalanx* Block 1B CIWS, 1 76mm gun (capacity 1 S-70B *Seahawk*/AB-212 ASW hel)
4 *Gabya* (ex-US *Oliver Hazard Perry*) with 1 Mk 13 GMLS with RGM-84C *Harpoon* Block 1B AShM/SM-1MR Block VI SAM, 2 triple 324mm SVTT Mk 32 ASTT with Mk 46 LWT, 1 Mk 15 *Phalanx* Block 1B CIWS, 1 76mm gun (capacity 1 S-70B *Seahawk*/AB-212 ASW hel)
4 *Yavuz* (GER MEKO 200TN) with 2 quad lnchr with RGM-84C *Harpoon* Block 1B AShM, 1 octuple Mk 29 GMLS with RIM-7M *Sea Sparrow* SAM, 2 triple 324mm SVTT Mk 32 ASTT with Mk 46 LWT, 3 *Sea Zenith* CIWS, 1 127mm gun (capacity 1 Bell 212 (AB-212) hel)
PATROL AND COASTAL COMBATANTS 45
CORVETTES 10:
FSGHM 4 *Ada* with 2 quad lnchr with RGM-84C *Harpoon* Block 1B AShM, 1 Mk 49 21-cell lnchr with RIM-116 SAM, 2 twin 324mm SVTT Mk 32 ASTT with Mk 46 LWT, 1 76mm gun (capacity 1 S-70B *Seahawk* hel)
FSG 6 *Burak* (ex-FRA *d'Estienne d'Orves*) with 2 single lnchr with MM38 *Exocet* AShM, 4 single 324mm ASTT with Mk 46 LWT, 1 Creusot-Loire Mk 54 A/S mor, 1 100mm gun (1 vessel with 1 76mm gun instead)
PCFG 19:
4 *Dogan* (GER Lurssen-57) with 2 quad lnchr with RGM-84C *Harpoon* Block 1B AShM, 1 76mm gun
9 *Kilic* with 2 quad lnchr with RGM-84C *Harpoon* Block 1B AShM, 1 76mm gun
4 *Rüzgar* (GER Lurssen-57) with 2 quad lnchr with RGM-84C *Harpoon* Block 1B AShM, 1 76mm gun
2 *Yildiz* with 2 quad lnchr with RGM-84C *Harpoon* Block 1B AShM, 1 76mm gun
PCC 16 *Tuzla*
MINE WARFARE • MINE COUNTERMEASURES 15
MHO 11: 5 *Engin* (FRA *Circe*); 6 *Aydin*
MSC 4 *Seydi* (US *Adjutant*)

AMPHIBIOUS
LANDING SHIPS • LST 5:
2 *Bayraktar* with 2 Mk 15 *Phalanx* Block 1B CIWS, 1 hel landing platform (capacity 20 MBT; 250 troops)
1 *Osmangazi* with 1 Mk 15 *Phalanx* CIWS (capacity 4 LCVP; 17 tanks; 980 troops; 1 hel landing platform)
2 *Sarucabey* with 1 Mk 15 *Phalanx* CIWS (capacity 11 tanks; 600 troops; 1 hel landing platform)
LANDING CRAFT 38
LCT 21: 2 C-120/130; 11 C-140; 8 C-151
LCM 9: 1 C-310; 8 LCM 8
LCVP 8 Anadolu 16m
LOGISTICS AND SUPPORT 37
ABU 2: 1 AG5; 1 AG6 with 1 76mm gun
AGI 1 *Ufuk* (MILGEM) (capacity 1 S-70B *Seahawk* hel)
AGS 2: 1 *Cesme* (ex-US *Silas Bent*); 1 *Cubuklu*
AOR 2 *Akar* with 1 Mk 15 *Phalanx* CIWS, 1 hel landing platform
AOT 3: 2 *Burak*; 1 *Yuzbasi Gungor Durmus* with 1 hel landing platform
AOL 1 *Gurcan*
AP 1 *Iskenderun*
ASR 3: 1 *Alemdar* with 1 hel landing platform; 2 *Isin* II
ATF 9: 1 *Akbas*; 1 *Degirmendere*; 1 *Gazal*; 1 *Inebolu*; 5 *Onder*
AWT 3 *Sogut*
AXL 8
AX 2 *Pasa* (ex-GER *Rhein*)

Marines 3,000
FORCES BY ROLE
MANOEUVRE
Amphibious
1 mne bde (3 mne bn; 1 arty bn)

Naval Aviation
FORCES BY ROLE
ANTI-SUBMARINE WARFARE
2 sqn with Bell 212 ASW (AB-212 ASW); S-70B *Seahawk*
1 sqn with ATR-72-600; CN235M-100; TB-20 *Trinidad*
EQUIPMENT BY TYPE
AIRCRAFT 4 combat capable
ASW 4 ATR-72-600
MP 6 CN235M-100
TPT • Light 7: 3 ATR-72-600; 4 TB-20 *Trinidad*
HELICOPTERS
ASW 33: 9 Bell 212 ASW (AB-212 ASW); 24 S-70B *Seahawk*
UNINHABITED AERIAL VEHICLES 20
CISR 20: **Heavy** 9: 3 *Aksungur*; 8 *Anka*-S; **Medium** 9 *Bayraktar* TB2
AIR-LAUNCHED MISSILES
ASM AGM-114M *Hellfire* II
BOMBS • Laser-guided MAM-C/L

Air Force ε50,000
2 tac air forces (divided between east and west)
FORCES BY ROLE
FIGHTER/GROUND ATTACK
1 sqn with F-4E *Phantom* 2020
8 sqn with F-16C/D *Fighting Falcon*

ISR
1 sqn with F-16C/D *Fighting Falcon*
1 unit with *King Air* 350
AIRBORNE EARLY WARNING & CONTROL
1 sqn (forming) with B-737 AEW&C
EW
1 unit with CN235M EW
SEARCH & RESCUE
1 sqn with AS532AL/UL *Cougar*
TANKER
1 sqn with KC-135R *Stratotanker*
TRANSPORT
1 sqn with A400M; C-160D *Transall*
1 sqn with C-130B/E *Hercules*
1 (VIP) sqn with Cessna 550 *Citation* II (UC-35); Cessna 650 *Citation* VII; CN235M; Gulfstream 550
3 sqn with CN235M
10 (liaison) flt with Bell 205 (UH-1H *Iroquois*); CN235M
TRAINING
1 sqn with F-16C/D *Fighting Falcon*
1 sqn (display team) with NF-5A-2000/NF-5B-2000 *Freedom Fighter*
1 sqn with MFI-395 *Super Mushshak*; SF-260D
1 sqn with *Hurkus*-B; KT-IT
1 sqn with T-38A/M *Talon*
1 sqn with T-41D *Mescalero*
COMBAT/ISR UAV
1 sqn with *Akinci*
AIR DEFENCE
4 bn with S-400 (RS-SA-21 *Growler*)
4 sqn with MIM-14 *Nike Hercules*
2 sqn with *Rapier*
8 (firing) unit with MIM-23 *Hawk*
MANOEUVRE
Air Manoeuvre
1 AB bde

EQUIPMENT BY TYPE
AIRCRAFT 295 combat capable
FTR 16: up to 10 NF-5A-2000 *Freedom Fighter* (display team); up to 6 NF-5B-2000 *Freedom Fighter* (display team)
FGA 279: 19 F-4E *Phantom* 2020; 27 F-16C *Fighting Falcon* Block 30; 162 F-16C *Fighting Falcon* Block 50; 14 F-16C *Fighting Falcon* Block 50+; 8 F-16D Block 30 *Fighting Falcon*; 33 F-16D *Fighting Falcon* Block 50; 16 F-16D *Fighting Falcon* Block 50+
ISR 9: 5 Beech 350 *King Air*; 3 C-160D *Transall*; 1 CN235M (Open Skies)
EW 2 C-160D *Transall*
SIGINT 3 CN235M
AEW&C 4 B-737 AEW&C
TKR 7 KC-135R *Stratotanker*
TPT 84: **Heavy** 10 A400M; **Medium** 24: 6 C-130B *Hercules*; 13 C-130E *Hercules*; 5 C-160D *Transall*; **Light** 49: 2 Cessna 550 *Citation* II (UC-35 - VIP); 2 Cessna 650 *Citation* VII; 45 CN235M; **PAX** 1 Gulfstream 550
TRG 174: 4 *Hurkus*-B; 39 KT-IT; 3 MFI-395 *Super Mushshak*; 33 SF-260D; 70 T-38A/M *Talon*; 25 T-41D *Mescalero*
HELICOPTERS
TPT 35: **Medium** 20: 6 AS532AL *Cougar* (CSAR); 14 AS532UL *Cougar* (SAR); **Light** 15 Bell 205 (UH-1H *Iroquois*)

144 THE MILITARY BALANCE 2023

UNINHABITED AERIAL VEHICLES
  CISR • Heavy 25: 6 *Akinci*; 19 *Anka*-S
  ISR 27: **Heavy** 9: 9 *Heron*; **Medium** 18 *Gnat* 750
AIR DEFENCE • SAM 32+
  Long-range 32+: MIM-14 *Nike Hercules*; 32 S-400
  (RS-SA-21 *Growler*)
  Medium-range MIM-23 *Hawk*
  Point-defence *Rapier*
AIR-LAUNCHED MISSILES
  AAM • IR AIM-9S *Sidewinder*; *Shafrir* 2‡; **IIR** AIM-9X
  Sidewinder II; **SARH** AIM-7E *Sparrow*; **ARH** AIM-
  120A/B AMRAAM
  ARM AGM-88A HARM
  ASM AGM-65A/G *Maverick*; *Popeye* I
  LACM Coventional AGM-84K SLAM-ER
BOMBS
  Electro-optical guided GBU-8B HOBOS (GBU-15)
  Laser-guided MAM-C/-L; *Paveway* I/II
  INS/GPS guided AGM-154A JSOW; AGM-154C JSOW

Gendarmerie & Paramilitary 156,800

Gendarmerie 152,100

Ministry of Interior; Ministry of Defence in war

FORCES BY ROLE
SPECIAL FORCES
  1 cdo bde
MANOEUVRE
  Other
  1 (border) paramilitary div
  2 paramilitary bde
EQUIPMENT BY TYPE
ARMOURED FIGHTING VEHICLES
  RECCE 57+: *Akrep*; 57 *Ates*
  APC 760+
    APC (W) 560: 535 BTR-60/BTR-80; 25 *Condor*
    PPV 200+: *Edjer Yaclin* 4×4; *Kirpi*; 200 *Kirpi* II; *Vuran*
    AUV *Cobra*; *Cobra* II; Otokar *Ural*
AIRCRAFT
  ISR Some O-1E *Bird Dog*
  TPT • Light 2 Do-28D
HELICOPTERS
  ATK 13 T129B
  MRH 19 Mi-17 *Hip* H
  TPT 35: **Medium** 12 S-70A *Black Hawk*; **Light** 23: 8 Bell
  204B (AB-204B); 6 Bell 205A (AB-205A); 8 Bell 206A
  (AB-206A) *Jet Ranger*; 1 Bell 212 (AB-212)
UNINHABITED AERIAL VEHICLES
  CISR 24: **Heavy** 6 *Anka*-S; **Medium** 18 *Bayraktar* TB2
BOMBS
  Laser-guided MAM-C/L

Coast Guard 4,700

EQUIPMENT BY TYPE
PATROL AND COASTAL COMBATANTS 99
  PSOH 4 *Dost*
  PBF 50: 18 *Kaan* 15; 10 *Kaan* 19; 9 *Kaan* 29; 13 *Kaan* 33
  PB 45: 15 Damen SAR 1906; 8 *Saar* 33 (1 more non-
  operational); 4 *Saar* 35; 18 Type-80
AIRCRAFT • MP 3 CN235 MPA
HELICOPTERS • MRH 8 Bell 412EP (AB-412EP – SAR)
UNINHABITED AERIAL VEHICLES 6
  CISR • Medium 6 *Bayraktar* TB2

DEPLOYMENT

AZERBAIJAN: Army 170; 1 EOD unit

BOSNIA-HERZEGOVINA: EU • EUFOR • *Operation Althea*
242; 1 inf coy

CYPRUS (NORTHERN): ε33,800; 1 army corps HQ; 1 SF regt;
1 armd bde; 2 mech inf div; 1 mech inf regt; 1 arty regt; 1
avn comd; 287 M48A5T2; 145 ACV AIFV; 70 ACV AAPC
(incl variants); 418 M113 (incl variants); 36 M101A1; 36
M114A2; 12 M115; 30 M44T; 144 M52T1; 4 T-155; 18 T-122;
171 81mm mor; 70 M30; 135 HY-12; *Milan*; 66 ACV TOW;
219 M40A1; FIM-92 *Stinger*; 44 Rh 202; 78 GAI-D01; 16
GDF-003; 3 Cessna 185 (U-17); 2 AS532UL *Cougar*; 1 Bell
205 (UH-1H *Iroquois*); 1 PB

IRAQ: Army: 1,000; 1 cdo unit; **NATO • NATO Mission**
Iraq 86

LEBANON: UN • UNIFIL 110; 1 FFGHM

LIBYA: ε500; ACV-AAPC; *Kirpi*; 1 arty unit with T-155
Firtina; 1 AD unit with MIM-23B *Hawk*; *Korkut*; GDF-003; 1
CISR UAV unit with *Bayraktar* TB2

MEDITERRANEAN SEA: NATO • SNMG 2: 220; 1 FFGHM
• SNMCMG 2: 120; 1 MHO; 1 AOT

QATAR: Army: 300 (trg team); 1 mech inf coy; 1 arty unit;
12+ ACV AIFV/AAPC; 2 T-155 *Firtina*

SERBIA: NATO • KFOR 335; 1 inf coy; **UN • UNMIK** 2

SOMALIA: 200 (trg team); **UN • UNSOM** 1

SYRIA: ε3,000; some cdo units; 3 armd BG; 1 SAM unit;
1 gendarmerie unit

FOREIGN FORCES

Spain *Active Fence*: 150; 1 SAM bty with M901 *Patriot* PAC-2
United States US European Command: 1,700; 1 tkr sqn
with 14 KC-135; 1 spt facility at Izmir; 1 spt facility at
Ankara; 1 air base at Incirlik • US Strategic Command: 1
AN/TPY-2 X-band radar at Kürecik

United Kingdom UK

British Pound GBP		2021	2022	2023
GDP	GBP	2.32tr	2.54tr	
	USD	3.19tr	3.20tr	
per capita	USD	47,329	47,318	
Growth	%	7.4	3.6	
Inflation	%	2.6	9.1	
Def exp [a]	GBP	52.3bn	53.9bn	
	USD	71.9bn	67.7bn	
Def bdgt [b]	GBP	51.5bn	ε55.7bn	
	USD	70.9bn	ε70.0bn	
USD1=GBP		0.73	0.80	

[a] NATO figure

[b] Includes total departmental expenditure limits; costs of military operations; Armed Forces Pension Service; military aid to Ukraine; and external income earned by the MoD

Real-terms defence budget trend (USDbn, constant 2015)

Population 67,791,400

Age	0–14	15–19	20–24	25–29	30–64	65 plus
Male	8.7%	2.9%	3.0%	3.4%	23.1%	8.6%
Female	8.3%	2.8%	3.1%	3.4%	22.5%	10.2%

Capabilities

UK defence policy is based on the armed forces providing credible nuclear and conventional deterrence. The armed forces are well trained. They also have a role in supporting the management of domestic civil emergencies. Defence activity includes maintaining the nuclear deterrent and sustaining a broad range of conventional capabilities, including for counter-terrorism. The government published an Integrated Review of Security, Defence, Development and Foreign Policy (IR) in March 2021 followed by a Defence Command Paper (DCP) that set out modernisation and restructuring plans. An update of the review was underway in late 2022, in light of intervening events and particularly the war in Ukraine, with revisions to the DCP likely to follow. There was an ambition to raise defence expenditure to 3% of GDP by 2030, but by the end of 2022 a new government was committing only to 2% of GDP, amid economic headwinds. The IR and DCP underscored the intent to still play a central role in NATO while also enhancing engagement and presence in the Indo-Pacific region. The policy update will likely affect how those ambitions will be balanced. How the AUKUS defence technology accord between Australia, the UK and the US develops will also have an impact. A significant part of UK defence effort in 2022 was devoted to providing materiel and training support to Ukraine, raising some questions about the UK armed forces' own stocks and sustainment capacity. While plans to transform and ultimately grow naval capabilities were proving slow to materialise, the ambition to develop undersea surveillance capacity was accelerated. The prospects for the Future Combat Air System programme will be key to transforming air combat capability. The army has established a Deep Strike Reconnaissance Brigade. Efforts to develop greater integrated cross-domain capability centre on Strategic Command, comprising key joint-force elements, such as special forces, defence intelligence and the military component of the civil/military National Cyber Force. A new Space Command was set up within the air force in early 2021 and spending on military space capabilities is increasing. Weaknesses in defence procurement persist, not least with some troubled armoured vehicle programmes, while concerns continue over nuclear programme delivery. The UK's sophisticated defence industry is globally competitive in some areas of defence exports but cannot meet all of the UK's requirements.

ACTIVE 150,350 (Army 83,450 Navy 33,750 Air 33,150)

RESERVE 71,950 (Regular Reserve 34,750 (Army 22,700, Navy 5,750, Air 6,300); Volunteer Reserve 35,250 (Army 28,350, Navy 3,650, Air 3,250); Sponsored Reserve 1,950)
Includes both trained and those currently under training within the Regular Forces, excluding university cadet units

ORGANISATIONS BY SERVICE

Strategic Forces 1,000

Royal Navy
EQUIPMENT BY TYPE
SUBMARINES • STRATEGIC
 SSBN 4 *Vanguard* with 16 UGM-133A *Trident* II D-5/D-5LE nuclear SLBM, 4 533mm TT with *Spearfish* HWT (recent deployment practice of no more than 8 missiles/40 warheads per boat; each missile could carry up to 12 MIRV; some *Trident* D-5 capable of being configured for sub-strategic role)
MSL • SLBM • Nuclear 48 UGM-133A *Trident* II D-5

Royal Air Force
EQUIPMENT BY TYPE
RADAR • STRATEGIC 1 Ballistic Missile Early Warning System (BMEWS) at Fylingdales Moor

Space
EQUIPMENT BY TYPE
SATELLITES • COMMUNICATIONS 6: 2 *Skynet*-4; 4 *Skynet*-5

Army 79,350; 4,100 Gurkhas (total 83,450)
Regt normally bn size. Many cbt spt and CSS regt and bn have reservist sub-units
FORCES BY ROLE
COMMAND
 1 (ARRC) corps HQ
MANOEUVRE
 Armoured
 1 (3rd) armd inf div (1 armd recce/arty bde (2 armd recce regt, 1 recce regt, 2 SP arty regt, 1 fd arty regt, 1 MRL regt, 1 STA regt, 1 maint bn); 1 (12th) armd inf bde (2 tk regt, 2 armd inf bn, 1 inf bn, 1 log regt, 1 maint regt, 1 med regt); 1 (20th) armd inf bde (1 armd recce regt, 1 tk regt, 2 armd inf bn, 1 mech inf bn, 1 log regt, 1 maint regt, 1 med regt); 1 cbt engr gp (3 cbt engr regt); 1 int bn; 1 sigs bde (6 sigs regt); 1 log bde (3 log regt, 1 med regt); 1 AD gp (2 SAM regt))
 Light
 1 (1st) inf div (1 (4th) inf bde (1 recce regt, 5 inf bn); 1 (7th) lt mech inf bde (1 recce regt, 3 lt mech inf bn, 3 inf bn; 1 fd

146 THE MILITARY BALANCE 2023

arty regt; 1 cbt engr regt); 1 (11th) inf bde (2 inf bn); 1 engr bde (1 CBRN regt, 2 EOD regt, 1 (MWD) EOD search regt, 1 engr regt, 1 (air spt) engr regt, 1 log regt); 1 int bn; 1 log bde (2 log regt; 2 maint bn); 1 med bde (2 fd hospital))
1 inf bn (London)
1 inf bn (Brunei)

Air Manoeuvre
1 (16th) air aslt bde (1 recce pl, 2 para bn, 1 air aslt bn, 1 inf bn, 1 fd arty regt, 1 cbt engr regt, 1 log regt, 1 med regt)

Other
1 inf bn (trials gp)

COMBAT SUPPORT
1 (6th) cbt spt div (1 ranger bde (4 ranger bn); 1 ISR gp (1 EW regt, 1 int bn, 2 ISR UAV regt); 1 (77th) info ops bde (3 info ops gp, 1 spt gp, 1 engr spt/log gp))
1 (geographic) engr regt
1 engr bn(-) (joint GER-UK unit)
1 MP bde (2 MP regt)
1 sigs bde (1 EW regt, 2 sigs regt; 1 (ARRC) spt bn)

COMBAT SERVICE SUPPORT
1 log bde (3 log regt; 1 maint regt)

Reserves

Army Reserve 28,350 reservists
The Army Reserve (AR) generates individuals, sub-units and some full units. The majority of units are subordinate to regular-formation headquarters and paired with one or more regular units

FORCES BY ROLE
MANOEUVRE
Reconnaissance
1 recce regt
Armoured
1 armd regt
Light
1 inf bde (2 recce regt, 8 inf bn)
7 inf bn
Air Manoeuvre
1 para bn
COMBAT SUPPORT
3 arty regt
1 STA regt
1 MRL regt
3 engr regt
1 EOD regt
4 int bn
4 sigs regt
COMBAT SERVICE SUPPORT
11 log regt
3 maint regt
3 med regt
9 fd hospital
AIR DEFENCE
1 AD regt

EQUIPMENT BY TYPE
ARMOURED FIGHTING VEHICLES
MBT 227 *Challenger* 2
RECCE 145: 117 FV107 *Scimitar*; 28 *Scimitar* Mk2
IFV 388+: 388 FV510 *Warrior*; FV511 *Warrior* (CP); FV514 *Warrior* (OP); FV515 *Warrior* (CP)

APC 796
APC (T) 409 FV430 *Bulldog* (incl variants)
PPV 387 *Mastiff* (6×6)
AUV 1,588: 399 *Foxhound*; 138 FV103 *Spartan*; 63 FV105 *Sultan* (CP); 17 *Spartan* Mk2; 4 *Sultan* Mk2 (CP); 197 *Jackal*; 110 *Jackal* 2; 130 *Jackal* 2A; 380 *Panther* CLV; 150 *Ridgback*
ENGINEERING & MAINTENANCE VEHICLES
AEV 88: 56 *Terrier*; 32 *Trojan*
ARV 243: 80 *Challenger* ARRV; 12 FV106 *Samson*; 5 *Samson* Mk2; 105 FV512 *Warrior*; 41 FV513 *Warrior*
MW 64 *Aardvark*
VLB 68: 35 M3; 33 *Titan*
NBC VEHICLES 8 TPz-1 *Fuchs* NBC
ANTI-TANK/ANTI-INFRASTRUCTURE • MSL
SP *Exactor*-2 (*Spike* NLOS)
MANPATS FGM-148 *Javelin*; NLAW
ARTILLERY 598
SP 155mm 89 AS90
TOWED 105mm 114 L118 Light Gun
MRL 227mm 35 M270B1 MLRS
MOR 81mm 360 L16A1
AMPHIBIOUS • LCM 3 Ramped Craft Logistic
AIR DEFENCE • SAM 60+
Short-range CAMM (*Land Ceptor*)
Point-defence 60 FV4333 *Stormer* with *Starstreak*; *Starstreak* (LML)
UNINHABITED AERIAL VEHICLES • ISR • Medium 13 *Watchkeeper* (34 more in store)

Joint Helicopter Command
Tri-service joint organisation including Royal Navy, Army and RAF units

Army
FORCES BY ROLE
HELICOPTER
1 bde (1 atk hel regt (2 sqn with AH-64E *Apache*; 1 trg sqn with AH-64D/E *Apache*); 1 atk hel regt (2 sqn with AH-64D *Apache*); 1 regt (2 sqn with AW159 *Wildcat* AH1; 1 trg sqn with AW159 *Wildcat* AH1); 1 regt (1 sqn with SA341B *Gazelle* AH1); 1 (spec ops) sqn with AS365N3; SA341B *Gazelle* AH1; 1 sqn with Bell 212 (Brunei); 1 flt with SA341B *Gazelle* AH1 (Canada); 1 maint regt)
TRAINING
1 hel regt (1 sqn with AH-64E *Apache*; 1 sqn with AS350B *Ecureuil*; 1 sqn with Bell 212; SA341B *Gazelle* AH1)

Army Reserve
FORCES BY ROLE
HELICOPTER
1 hel regt (4 sqn personnel only)

Royal Navy
FORCES BY ROLE
ATTACK HELICOPTER
1 lt sqn with AW159 *Wildcat* AH1
TRANSPORT HELICOPTER
2 sqn with AW101 *Merlin* HC4/4A

Europe 147

Royal Air Force

FORCES BY ROLE

TRANSPORT HELICOPTER

3 sqn with CH-47D/F/SD *Chinook* HC6A/6/5
2 sqn with SA330 *Puma* HC2

TRAINING

1 OCU sqn with CH-47D/SD/F *Chinook* HC3/4/4A/6;
SA330 *Puma* HC2

EQUIPMENT BY TYPE

HELICOPTERS

ATK 50: 25 AH-64D *Apache*; 25 AH-64E *Apache*
MRH 56: 5 AS365N3; 34 AW159 *Wildcat* AH1; 17
SA341B *Gazelle* AH1
TPT 114: **Heavy** 60: 38 CH-47D *Chinook* HC6A; 14 CH-47F *Chinook* HC6; 8 CH-47SD *Chinook* HC5; **Medium** 42:
25 AW101 *Merlin* HC4/4A; 17 SA330 *Puma* HC2; **Light** 12:
9 AS350B *Ecureuil*; 3 Bell 212

Royal Navy 33,750

EQUIPMENT BY TYPE

SUBMARINES 10

STRATEGIC • SSBN 4 *Vanguard*, opcon Strategic Forces
with 16 UGM-133A *Trident* II D-5/D-5LE nuclear SLBM, 4
single 533mm TT with *Spearfish* HWT (recent deployment
practice of no more than 8 missiles/40 warheads per boat;
each missile could carry up to 12 MIRV; some *Trident* D-5
capable of being configured for sub-strategic role)

TACTICAL • SSN 6

1 *Trafalgar* with 5 single 533mm TT with UGM-109E
Tomahawk Block IV LACM/*Spearfish* HWT
5 *Astute* with 6 single 533mm TT with UGM-109E
Tomahawk Block IV LACM/*Spearfish* HWT

PRINCIPAL SURFACE COMBATANTS 20

AIRCRAFT CARRIERS 2:

CV 2 *Queen Elizabeth* with up to 3 Mk 15 *Phalanx* Block
1B CIWS (capacity 40 ac/hel, incl 24+ F-35B *Lightning*
II, 14+ *Merlin* HM2/*Wildcat* HMA2/CH-47 *Chinook* hel)

DESTROYERS 6:

DDGHM 3 *Daring* (Type-45) with 2 quad lnchr with
RGM-84D *Harpoon* Block 1C AShM, 6 8-cell *Sylver* A50
VLS with *Aster* 15/30 (*Sea Viper*) SAM, 2 Mk 15 *Phalanx*
Block 1B CIWS, 1 114mm gun (capacity 1 AW159
Wildcat/AW101 *Merlin* hel)
DDHM 3 *Daring* (Type-45) with 6 8-cell *Sylver* A50
VLS with *Aster* 15/30 (*Sea Viper*) SAM, 2 Mk 15 *Phalanx*
Block 1B CIWS, 1 114mm gun (capacity 1 AW159
Wildcat/AW101 *Merlin* hel)

FRIGATES • FFGHM 12:

3 *Duke* (Type-23) with 2 quad lnchr with RGM-84D
Harpoon Block 1C AShM, 1 32-cell VLS with *Sea Wolf*
SAM, 2 twin 324mm ASTT with *Sting Ray* LWT, 1
114mm gun (capacity either 2 AW159 *Wildcat* or 1
AW101 *Merlin* hel)
9 *Duke* (Type-23) with 2 quad lnchr with RGM-84D
Harpoon Block 1C AShM, 1 32-cell VLS with *Sea
Ceptor* SAM, 2 twin 324mm ASTT with *Sting Ray*
LWT, 1 114mm gun (capacity either 2 AW159 *Wildcat*
or 1 AW101 *Merlin* hel)

PATROL AND COASTAL COMBATANTS 26

PSO 8: 3 *River* Batch 1; 5 *River* Batch 2 with 1 hel
landing platform
PBF 2 *Cutlass*
PBI 16 *Archer* (14 in trg role, 2 deployed to Gibraltar sqn)

MINE WARFARE • MINE COUNTERMEASURES 9

MCO 6 *Hunt* (incl 4 mod *Hunt*)
MHC 3 *Sandown*

AMPHIBIOUS

PRINCIPAL AMPHIBIOUS SHIPS 2

LPD 2 *Albion* with 2 Mk 15 *Phalanx* Block 1B CIWS
(capacity 2 med hel; 4 LCU or 2 LCAC; 4 LCVP; 6 MBT;
300 troops) (of which 1 at extended readiness)

LOGISTICS AND SUPPORT 4

AGB 1 *Protector* with 1 hel landing platform
AGS 3: 1 *Scott* with 1 hel landing platform; 1 *Echo* with 1
hel landing platform; 1 *Magpie*

Royal Fleet Auxiliary

Support and miscellaneous vessels are mostly crewed
and maintained by the Royal Fleet Auxiliary (RFA),
a civilian fleet owned by the UK MoD, which has
approximately 1,900 personnel with type comd under
Fleet Commander

AMPHIBIOUS • PRINCIPAL AMPHIBIOUS SHIPS 3:

LSD 3 *Bay* (capacity 4 LCU; 2 LCVP; 24 *Challenger* 2
MBT; 350 troops)

LOGISTICS AND SUPPORT 12

AOEH 4 *Tide* (capacity 1 AW159 *Wildcat*/AW101
Merlin hel)
AORH 3: 2 *Wave* (extended readiness); 1 *Fort Victoria*
with 2 Mk 15 *Phalanx* Block 1B CIWS
AG 1 *Argus* (primary casualty-receiving ship with
secondary aviation trg ship role)
AKR 4 *Point* (not RFA manned)

Naval Aviation (Fleet Air Arm) 4,900

FORCES BY ROLE

ANTI-SUBMARINE WARFARE

3 sqn with AW101 ASW *Merlin* HM2
2 sqn with AW159 *Wildcat* HMA2

TRAINING

1 sqn with Beech 350ER *King Air*
1 sqn with G-115

EQUIPMENT BY TYPE

AIRCRAFT

TPT • Light 4 Beech 350ER *King Air* (*Avenger*)
TRG 5 G-115

HELICOPTERS

ASW 58: 28 AW159 *Wildcat* HMA2; 30 AW101 ASW
Merlin HM2

AIR-LAUNCHED MISSILES • ASM *Martlet*

148　THE MILITARY BALANCE 2023

Royal Marines 6,600

FORCES BY ROLE
MANOEUVRE
Amphibious
1 (3rd Cdo) mne bde (2 mne bn; 2 sy bn; 1 amph gp; 1 amph aslt sqn; 1 (army) arty regt; 1 (army) engr regt; 1 ISR gp (1 EW sqn; 1 cbt spt sqn; 1 sigs sqn; 1 log sqn), 1 log regt)
2 amph sqn

EQUIPMENT BY TYPE
ARMOURED FIGHTING VEHICLES
APC (T) 99 BvS-10 Mk2 *Viking* (incl 19 cabs with 81mm mor)
ANTI-TANK/ANTI-INFRASTUCTURE
MSL • MANPATS FGM-148 *Javelin*
ARTILLERY 39
TOWED 105mm 12 L118 Light Gun
MOR 81mm 27 L16A1
PATROL AND COASTAL COMBATANTS • PB 2 *Island*
AMPHIBIOUS • LANDING CRAFT 26
LCU 10 LCU Mk10 (capacity 4 *Viking* APC or 120 troops)
LCVP 16 LCVP Mk5B (capacity 35 troops)
AIR DEFENCE • SAM • Point-defence *Starstreak*

Royal Air Force 33,150

FORCES BY ROLE
FIGHTER
2 sqn with *Typhoon* FGR4/T3
FIGHTER/GROUND ATTACK
4 sqn with *Typhoon* FGR4/T3 (including one joint QTR-UK sqn)
1 sqn with *Typhoon* FGR4/T3 (aggressor)
1 sqn with F-35B *Lightning* II
ANTI-SUBMARINE WARFARE
2 sqn with P-8A *Poseidon* (MRA Mk1)
ISR
1 sqn with *Shadow* R1
ELINT
1 sqn with RC-135W *Rivet Joint*
SEARCH & RESCUE
1 sqn with Bell 412EP *Griffin* HAR-2
TANKER/TRANSPORT
2 sqn with A330 MRTT *Voyager* KC2/3
TRANSPORT
1 (VIP) sqn with AW109SP; *Falcon* 900LX (*Envoy* IV CC Mk1)
2 sqn with A400M *Atlas*
1 sqn with C-17A *Globemaster*
1 sqn with C-130J/J-30 *Hercules*
TRAINING
1 OCU sqn with A400M *Atlas*; C-17A *Globemaster*; C-130J/J-30 *Hercules*
1 OCU sqn with F-35B *Lightning* II (forming)
1 OCU sqn with *Typhoon* FGR4/T3
1 OCU sqn with RC-135W *Rivet Joint*
1 sqn with EMB-500 *Phenom* 100
2 sqn with *Hawk* T2
1 sqn with T-6C *Texan* II
2 sqn with G-115E *Tutor*

COMBAT/ISR UAV
1 sqn with MQ-9A *Reaper*
EQUIPMENT BY TYPE
AIRCRAFT 201 combat capable
FGA 153: 26 F-35B *Lightning* II; 121 *Typhoon* FGR4; 6 *Typhoon* T3; (10 *Typhoon* FGR4 in store)
ASW 9 P-8A *Poseidon* (MRA Mk1)
ISR 6 *Shadow* R1
ELINT 3 RC-135W *Rivet Joint*
AEW&C 3 E-3D *Sentry*
TKR/TPT 10: 3 A330 MRTT *Voyager* KC2 (of which 1 equipped for VIP tpt); 7 A330 MRTT Voyager KC3
TPT 44: **Heavy** 28: 20 A400M *Atlas*; 8 C-17A *Globemaster*; **Medium** 14: 1 C-130J *Hercules*; 13 C-130J-30 *Hercules*; **PAX** 2 *Falcon* 900LX (*Envoy* IV CC Mk1)
TRG 144: 5 EMB-500 *Phenom* 100; 86 G-115E *Tutor*; 28 *Hawk* T2*; 11 *Hawk* T1* (Red Arrows) (ε60 more in store); 14 T-6C *Texan* II
HELICOPTERS
MRH 4: 1 AW139; 3 Bell 412EP *Griffin* HAR-2
TPT • Light 1 AW109SP
UNINHABITED AERIAL VEHICLES
CISR • Heavy 11: 10 MQ-9A *Reaper*; 1 MQ-9B *Sky Guardian* (*Protector* RG Mk1)
AIR-LAUNCHED MISSILES
AAM • IR AIM-9L/L(I) *Sidewinder*; **IIR** ASRAAM; **ARH** AIM-120C-5 AMRAAM; *Meteor*
ASM AGM-114 *Hellfire*; *Brimstone*; *Dual-Mode Brimstone*; *Brimstone* II
LACM *Storm Shadow*
BOMBS
Laser-guided GBU-10 *Paveway* II; GBU-24 *Paveway* III
Laser & INS/GPS-guided Enhanced *Paveway* II/III; *Paveway* IV

Royal Air Force Regiment

FORCES BY ROLE
MANOEUVRE
Other
6 sy sqn

No. 1 Flying Training School (Tri-Service Helicopter Training)

FORCES BY ROLE
TRAINING
1 hel sqn with H135 (*Juno* HT1); H145 (*Jupiter*)
3 hel sqn with H135 (*Juno* HT1)

EQUIPMENT BY TYPE
HELICOPTERS
MRH 7 H145 (*Jupiter*)
TPT • Light 31: 2 AW109E; 29 H135 (*Juno* HT1)

Volunteer Reserve Air Forces

(Royal Auxiliary Air Force/RAF Reserve)
MANOEUVRE
Other
5 sy sqn
COMBAT SUPPORT
2 int sqn

Europe 149

COMBAT SERVICE SUPPORT
1 med sqn
1 (air movements) sqn
1 (HQ augmentation) sqn
1 (C-130 Reserve Aircrew) flt

UK Special Forces

Includes Royal Navy, Army and RAF units

FORCES BY ROLE
SPECIAL FORCES
1 (SAS) SF regt
1 (SBS) SF regt
1 (Special Reconnaissance) SF regt
1 SF BG (based on 1 para bn)
AVIATION
1 wg (includes assets drawn from 3 Army hel sqn, 1
RAF tpt sqn and 1 RAF hel sqn)
COMBAT SUPPORT
1 sigs regt

Reserve

FORCES BY ROLE
SPECIAL FORCES
2 (SAS) SF regt
EQUIPMENT BY TYPE
ARMOURED FIGHTING VEHICLES
AUV 24 *Bushmaster* IMV
ANTI-TANK/ANTI-INFRASTRUCTURE • MSL
MANPATS FGM-148 *Javelin*; NLAW

DEPLOYMENT

ASCENSION ISLAND: 20

ATLANTIC (NORTH)/CARIBBEAN: 140; 1 PSO; 1 AOEH

ATLANTIC (SOUTH): 40; 1 PSO

BAHRAIN: *Operation Kipion* 1,000; 1 FFGHM; 2 MCO; 2 MHC; 1 LSD; 1 naval facility

BELIZE: BATSUB 12

BRITISH INDIAN OCEAN TERRITORY: 40; 1 navy/marine det

BRUNEI: 2,000; 1 (Gurkha) lt inf bn; 1 jungle trg centre; 1 hel sqn with 3 Bell 212

BULGARIA: NATO • Enhanced Vigilance Activities 120; 1 lt mech inf coy

CANADA: BATUS 400; 1 trg unit; 1 hel flt with SA341 *Gazelle* AH1

CYPRUS: 2,260; 2 inf bn; 1 SAR sqn with 4 Bell 412 *Griffin* HAR-2; 1 radar (on det); *Operation Shader* 450: 1 FGA sqn with 10 *Typhoon* FGR4; 1 A330 MRTT *Voyager*; 2 C-130J-30 *Hercules*; UN • UNFICYP (*Operation Tosca*) 253; 2 inf coy

DEMOCRATIC REPUBLIC OF THE CONGO: UN • MONUSCO 3

EGYPT: MFO 2

ESTONIA: NATO • Enhanced Forward Presence (*Operation Cabrit*) 1,750; 1 armd BG; 1 inf BG; 1 SP arty bty; 1 MRL bty; 1 cbt engr coy

FALKLAND ISLANDS: 1,200: 1 inf coy(+); 1 sigs unit; 1 AD det with CAMM (*Land Ceptor*); 1 PSO; 1 ftr flt with 4 *Typhoon* FGR4; 1 tkr/tpt flt with 1 A330 MRTT *Voyager*; 1 A400M; 1 hel flt with 2 *Chinook*

GERMANY: 185

GIBRALTAR: 600 (including Royal Gibraltar regt); 1 PSO; 2 PBI

IRAQ: *Operation Shader* 100; **NATO** • NATO Mission Iraq 12

KENYA: BATUK 350; 1 trg unit

KUWAIT: *Operation Shader* 50; 1 CISR UAV sqn with 8 MQ-9A *Reaper*

LIBYA: UN • UNSMIL (*Operation Tramal*) 1

MALI: UN • MINUSMA (*Operation Newcombe*) 256; 1 recce regt(-)

NEPAL: 60 (Gurkha trg org)

NIGERIA: 80 (trg team)

OMAN: 90

PACIFIC OCEAN: 60; 2 PSO

POLAND: Army 250; 1 tk sqn with *Challenger* 2; 1 SAM bty with CAMM (*Land Ceptor*); **NATO** • Enhanced Forward Presence 129; 1 recce sqn

QATAR: 200; 1 FGA sqn with 12 *Typhoon* FGR4

SAUDI ARABIA: 50 (radar det)

SERBIA: NATO • KFOR 41

SOMALIA: 65 (trg team); **UN** • UNSOM (*Operation Praiser*) 2; **UN** • UNSOS (*Operation Catan*) 10

SOUTH SUDAN: UN • UNMISS (*Operation Vogul*) 4

UNITED ARAB EMIRATES: 200; 1 tpt/tkr flt with C-17A *Globemaster*; A400M *Atlas*; A330 MRTT *Voyager* (on rotation)

FOREIGN FORCES

Canada Air Task Force Prestwick (ATF-P) 55; 3 C-130J-30 *Hercules* (CC-130J); *Operation Unifier* 170 (UKR trg)
Denmark *Operation Interflex* 120 (UKR trg)
Finland *Operation Interflex* 20 (UKR trg)
Lithuania *Operation Interflex* 15 (UKR trg)
Netherlands *Operation Interflex* 90 (UKR trg)
New Zealand *Operation Interflex* 149 (UKR trg)
Sweden *Operation Interflex* 45 (UKR trg)
United States
US European Command: 10,000; 1 FGA wg at RAF Lakenheath (2 FGA sqn with 23 F-15E *Strike Eagle*, 1 FGA sqn with 21 F-35A *Lightning* II; 1 FGA sqn with F-35 *Lightning* II (forming)); 1 ISR sqn at RAF Mildenhall with OC-135/RC-135; 1 tkr wg at RAF Mildenhall with 15 KC-135R/T *Stratotanker*; 1 spec ops gp at RAF Mildenhall (1 sqn with 8 CV-22B *Osprey*; 1 sqn with 8 MC-130J *Commando* II) • US Strategic Command: 1 AN/FPS-132 Upgraded Early Warning Radar and 1 *Spacetrack* radar at Fylingdales Moor

Chapter Five
Russia and Eurasia

- Russia's full-scale invasion of Ukraine failed in its initial objectives and exposed significant shortcomings in several areas of the Russian armed forces, including strategy, command and control, training, logistics and industrial supply. By year's end, Russia had resorted to using Iranian uninhabited aerial vehicles (UAVs) and direct attack munitions due to the Russian armed forces' heavy use of its own ballistic and cruise missiles and the continued threat posed by Ukraine's air defences.

- The performance of some Russian weapons has been underwhelming. Russia's tanks and infantry fighting vehicles proved vulnerable to modern anti-armour systems while some air-launched weapons, such as its cruise missiles, were not as successful as they were in Syria. Most notably, the Raduga Kh-101 (RS-AS-23A *Kodiak*) air-launched cruise missile failed to meet expectations.

- Russia's decision to 'partially' mobilise shows that the plan to produce a full-time service component, of contractors, failed when confronted with a high-intensity war. The mobilisation process has highlighted institutional and infrastructure shortcomings as well as problems in training.

- The heavy losses to Russia's equipment inventory, particularly its armour and artillery, raises significant questions over the direction of Russia's state armament programme; the country needs to reconstitute its ground forces' combat capability while they are at war, balancing current needs against existing and future development plans.

- Both Russia and Ukraine have suffered significant casualties. Ukraine mobilised early, and Western training assistance is intended to produce a steady stream of trained troops, though the training package lasts weeks instead of months. The battlefield successes of Ukraine's troops have shown the benefits of the training delivered with Western assistance after 2014 and Kyiv's plan – also with Western assistance – to develop a professional non-commissioned officer cadre.

- Western materiel support has reshaped Ukraine's artillery capabilities. But much legacy-equipment remains and ammunition-supply for these will be a key near-term constraint. However, Kyiv's forces are now able to strike faster and further and have shown the capability to integrate real-time targeting into this process through the use of small UAVs.

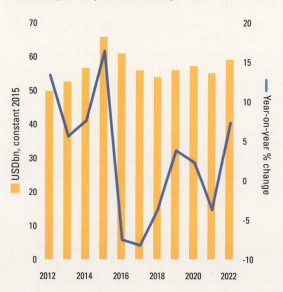

Russia real-terms total military expenditure, 2012–22 (USDbn, constant 2015)

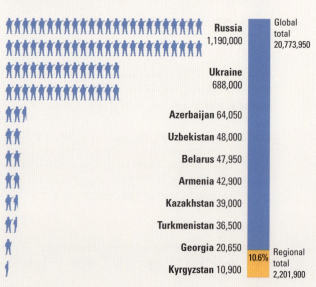

Active military personnel – top 10
(25,000 per unit)

Russia 1,190,000
Ukraine 688,000
Azerbaijan 64,050
Uzbekistan 48,000
Belarus 47,950
Armenia 42,900
Kazakhstan 39,000
Turkmenistan 36,500
Georgia 20,650
Kyrgyzstan 10,900

Global total 20,773,950
Regional total 2,201,900
10.6%

Regional defence policy and economics	152 ▶
Arms procurements and deliveries	169 ▶
Armed forces data section	171 ▶

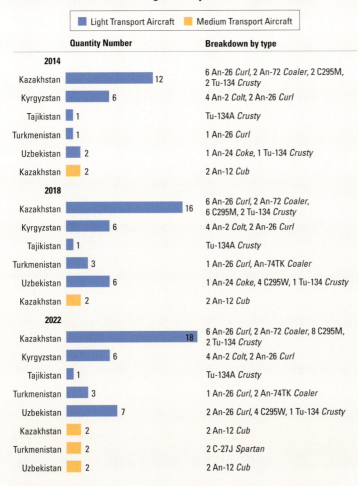

Central Asia: medium and light transport air fleets, 2014–22*

Ukraine's artillery transformation

2021			
Self Propelled			
122mm		2S1 *Gvozdika*	292
152mm		2S3 *Akatsiya*	249
		2S5 *Giantsit-S*	18
		2S19 *Msta-S*	35
155mm		2S3 *Akatsiya*	18
203mm		2S7 *Pion*	13
Towed			
122mm		D-30	129
152mm		2A36 *Giantsit-B*	180
		2A65 *Msta-B*	130
		D-20	130
MRL			
122mm		9P138	18
		BM-21	191
220mm		9P140 *Uragan*	70
300mm		9A52 *Smerch*	83
		Vilkha	
2022			
Self Propelled			
122mm		2S1 *Gvozdika*	120
152mm		M-77 *Dana*	18
		Dana-M2	1+
		2S3 *Akatsiya*	140
		2S5 *Giantsit-S*	10
		2S19 *Msta-S*	35
155mm		M-2000 *Zuzana*	6
		M109A3GN	50
		M109L	20
		Krab	53
		PzH 2000	22
		Caesar	17
203mm		2S7 *Pion*	20
Towed			
105mm		L119/M119A3	30
		M101	3+
122mm		D-30	60
130mm		M-46	18
152mm		2A36 *Giantsit-B*	90
		2A65 *Msta-B*	80
		D-20	60
155mm		M777A2	132
		FH-70	20
Gun/Mor			
120mm		2B16 NONA-K	
MRL			
122mm		RM-70 *Vampir*	20
		*Tornado-*G/BM-21	100
220mm		*Bureviy*/9P140 *Uragan*	40
227mm		M142 HIMARS	20
		M270A1/B1 MLRS	11
300mm		9A52 *Smerch*	40
		*Vilkha-*M	
		Vilkha	

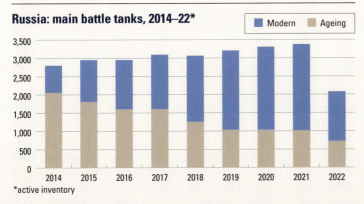

Russia: main battle tanks, 2014–22*

*active inventory

Russia and Eurasia

The chaotic collapse of the Soviet Union in 1991 was followed by the creation of 15 new states from the former Soviet republics. These states continued to count large numbers of Russians within their new borders. Ethnic tensions, often accompanied by friction with Moscow, are a legacy of the Soviet empire's dissolution. Russia's full-scale invasion of Ukraine has roots in the break-up of the Soviet Union. More broadly, though, the war is the most egregious example of the problematic relations between Russia and what it sometimes refers to as its 'near abroad'. It also owes much to the failure of Russia's efforts during 2021 and earlier to exercise influence over those parts of Ukraine it did not already control, as well as its government, and to Vladimir Putin's world view, made apparent in his July 2021 extended text entitled 'On the Historical Unity of Russians and Ukrainians'. In this document, Putin described Russians and Ukrainians as 'one people'. However, the invasion has served only to cement Ukraine's identity as an independent state. Moscow's travails in its ill-judged and ill-executed invasion, furthermore, will make relationships with its other neighbouring countries more problematic. The war on Ukraine has led to a decline in Russia's influence over many of them and may inhibit its ability to manage regional disputes.

The most westerly of the former Soviet republics that remains outside NATO is Moldova. The country's pro-European government is struggling with pro-Russian opposition and allegations of Russian disinformation operations. The government declared a state of emergency on the same day as Russia's 2022 invasion of Ukraine, with which it shares a border. Russian ground forces remain in the pro-Moscow Moldovan breakaway region of Transnistria because of a civil war in 1992. Russia has hinted that it could use its forces in Transnistria against Ukraine. On 23 June 2022 Moldova gained candidate status from the European Union, in response to Russia's aggression against Ukraine. Kyiv was also given candidate status at the same time. Meanwhile, Belarus has been pulled further into Russia's orbit. At the start of the year, Belarus was complicit in Russia's invasion, and by the end of the year its training grounds were being used to drill newly mobilised Russian troops. But the Belarusian armed forces themselves stayed out of the fight, instead serving a useful purpose for Moscow by 'fixing' elements of Ukraine's forces on its northern border as well as reportedly supplying equipment to Russia.

Sporadic fighting also recurred in September 2022 between Armenia and Azerbaijan over the disputed territory of Nagorno-Karabakh. Armenia is a member of the Russian-led Collective Security Treaty Organization (CSTO), and Azerbaijan is a former member, but Moscow has been unable to force a lasting peace between the two. September 2022 also saw border clashes between two other CSTO members: Kyrgyzstan and Tajikistan. The latter dispute also stems from contested territory and the lack of an agreed border. Both countries have also suffered from internal upheaval. In Tajikistan a civil war began in the immediate aftermath of the collapse of the Soviet Union, lasting from 1992 to 1997, that also involved Russian ground forces. Kyrgyzstan, meanwhile, has seen three revolutions in the past two decades.

Perhaps the most notable shift has been in Moscow's relationships with Kazakhstan and Uzbekistan. In recent years, Kazakhstan has started to modernise its armed forces, with its land forces introducing equipment of Turkish origin and even signing an agreement with Turkey in late 2022 to develop 'long-term strategic cooperation'. In January, in the wake of fomented protests designed to unseat him, Kazakhstan's President Qasym-Jomart Toqaev requested assistance from the CSTO. Russia deployed elements of its airborne forces to secure Toqaev in power. Toqaev has not, however, supported Russia's war in Ukraine. Indeed, Kazakhstan sent humanitarian aid to Ukraine, and in June Toqaev refused to recognise – in Putin's presence – the independence of the Luhansk and Donetsk 'people's republics'; the foreign minister of Uzbekistan was reported as using a similar formulation in March, though he was out of office by mid-year. Regardless, Russia's influence over its former republics – it retains military installations in some – cannot be taken for granted by Moscow. Moreover, Russia's remaining influence in Central Asia must also contend with the financial heft of China, with Beijing building economic ties with all the former Soviet republics in the region.

RUSSIA

Russia's full-scale invasion of Ukraine has proven a defining event for the Russian armed forces, 14 years after they fought an unsatisfactory short war against Georgia and subsequently launched the 'New Look' military-modernisation process. The war on Ukraine has also proven a defining chapter of President Vladimir Putin's leadership. The operation had been telegraphed. Russian troops had assembled close to the border with Ukraine in April 2021, to exert pressure on Ukraine, and in late year began to return. These forces remained in position for some weeks. Western open-source analysts – and rapidly declassified US intelligence assessments – indicated after mid-February that some troops were deploying from their assembly areas into assault formations. Early on 24 February, the latest invasion began. Even in the early phases, instead of rapidly extinguishing Ukrainian resistance, Russia suffered a series of reversals. Since then, Moscow has become bogged down in an often-attritional war that has highlighted failings in its political and high-level military decision-making, while highlighting structural weaknesses in its armed forces, particularly its ground forces. At the same time, the course and conduct of the war is leading to renewed focus on the effectiveness and future of various modernisation initiatives pursued in recent years, such as the Battalion Tactical Group concept. It also raises questions over Russia's military culture and organisation and the degree to which Moscow can learn and implement lessons, as well as the future of the equipment-modernisation plans pursued under the latest State Armament Programme.

The war: overconfidence and underestimation

Russian forces advanced along multiple axes in the initial phase of the operation, estimated to involve 127 Battalion Tactical Groups and 150,000 personnel as well as additional Russian-led proxy forces. The aim was apparently to quickly topple Volodymyr Zelenskyy's government in a far larger version of the 2014 Crimean operation with a rapid assault focused on seizing leadership centres in Kyiv, while Ukraine's armed forces and society would be effectively paralysed by shaping operations and a push on multiple axes by ground forces from the north, the east and the south. However, the campaign was flawed before its execution. There were poor intelligence assessments of the attitudes of the Ukrainian population, combined with an underestimation of the combat capability of Ukraine's armed forces and an overestimation of the capability of the Russian armed forces. Russia hoped for a swift victory; its forces were not prepared for the long haul.

At the start of the war, Russia's advances lacked the massed artillery fires traditionally associated with its ground forces, while Ukrainian critical national infrastructure was not targeted extensively. The forces deployed in the initial attacks do not appear to have been prepared for, or supplied for, sustained high-intensity fighting. Initially poorly coordinated, and with inadequate air-, fire- and logistics-support, these formations suffered very heavy losses in both personnel and equipment, and many were rendered combat ineffective within the first month of operations. Moreover, political imperatives to demonstrate success on the battlefield meant that battle-weary units were given little or no time to recover and reset, instead being rapidly thrown back into the fighting.

Russia's comparative success in fighting Ukrainian forces in 2014–15 likely resulted in considerable overconfidence, as did the air-led campaign in Syria. The deployment in Syria allowed the air force to rotate crews and gain experience in operations at-reach and test new weapons, but it was nonetheless conducted in a permissive air environment. Meanwhile, Russia's annual large-scale exercises (each year there is one of the *Kavkaz*, *Tsentr*, *Zapad* and *Vostok* drills) with their extensive use of tube and rocket artillery and combat aviation – *Zapad* 2021 was the largest for some years, involving multiple military districts and large groups of forces – may have led to a distorted assessment of capability and readiness both by outside observers and by the Russian armed forces. Similar doubts remain about the value of smaller combat-readiness inspections. Such exercises, whether deliberately or otherwise, masked the structural problems that have now been exposed in Ukraine. Perhaps more fundamentally, while peacetime training and maintenance were nominally improved and made more realistic at the same time, in practice poor oversight, corruption and rapid turnover in both contract and conscript personnel seriously hindered the qualitative development of individual soldiers.

154 THE MILITARY BALANCE 2023

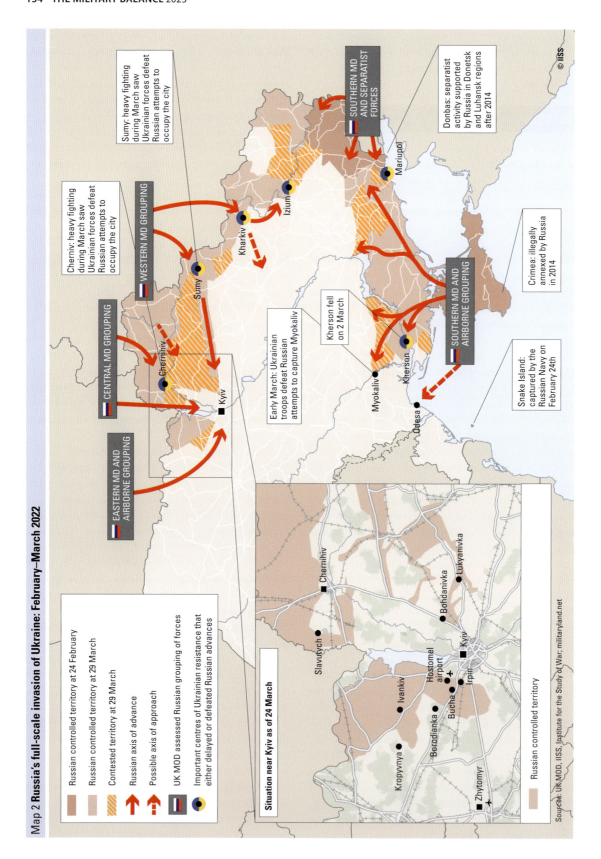

Map 2 Russia's full-scale invasion of Ukraine: February–March 2022

Russia and Eurasia 155

Map 3 **Russia's full-scale invasion of Ukraine: April–October 2022**

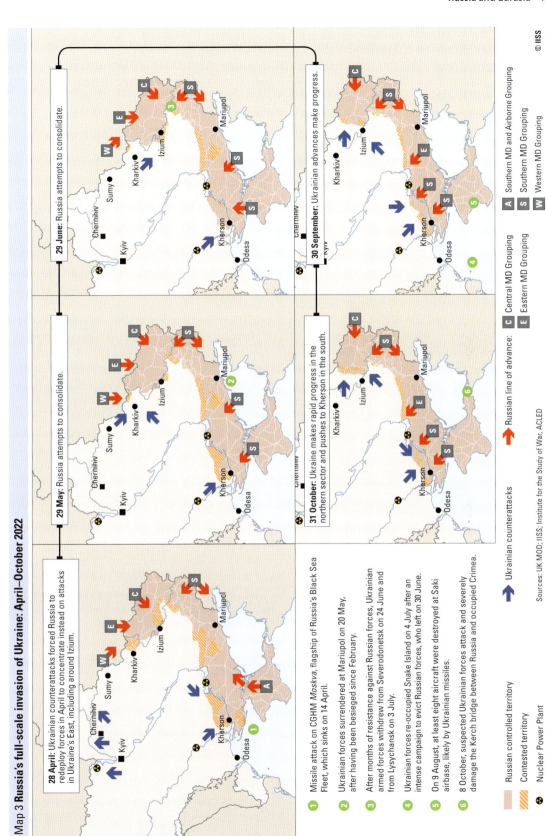

Moreover, Russia's forces have had to take account of large-scale personnel losses, including among the more experienced personnel that participated in the opening phase of the invasion. The subsequent inflow of reservists, and later of mobilised personnel, has exposed weaknesses in training, with many newly arrived personnel seemingly lacking both adequate equipment and enough ammunition, amidst infrastructure that appears to be failing to cope with the increased number of trainees. And the war has highlighted long-standing problems related to command and control at both junior and higher command levels, with inflexibility proving an important weakness.

There are indications of some adaptation following the initial failings of the campaign. Commanders were replaced and there has been a move to improve and unify operational command and control; once Ukrainian forces had defeated Russia's push to Kyiv, forces were redeployed to Ukraine's east. Subsequently, Russian forces were concentrated on two axes, with efforts focused on the two 'self-proclaimed' Luhansk and Donetsk people's republics (LPR and DPR). Russian tactics were also revised, with far greater reliance on artillery. However, this has highlighted another challenge relating to ammunition supply. Estimates by some analysts suggest Russian forces have at times expended more than ten times the ammunition on a daily basis compared to the Ukrainians and, while it is difficult to verify such claims, it is clear that the supply of ammunition became a more significant factor as 2022 wore on.

Initial Russian operations included heliborne assaults, and these seemed to follow the pattern of recent experimentation with such capability, but Russia's drills had not adequately prepared its forces for actions against a determined and well-armed opponent. And though the air war has been immensely destructive for Ukraine, Russia's relatively haphazard application of airpower, including missile strikes, did not allow it to gain control of the air. These failures forced Russia's helicopters and ground-attack aircraft to adopt unconventional weapons-release tactics, its fixed-wing aircraft to engage targets from greater range and commanders to use large numbers of long-range stand-off weapons. And both Russian and Ukrainian helicopters and ground-attack aircraft have, at least close to the front lines, been flown at extremely low-level in order to minimise the threat from air defences.

The way Russia has employed its precision-guided weapons, coupled with problems in increasing production, means there was by late year a lack of such systems, while there have been reliability issues with those in the inventory. Russia's defence industry may have been slowly improving, but it remains bedevilled by inefficiencies. These include multiple plants producing varied types of combat aircraft. In terms of personnel, it has an ageing workforce and – while there is little firm information on their background beyond some reporting – the flight of thousands of Russians from the country after February will not help matters. There also appears to have been a failure to appreciate the need for near-real time intelligence, surveillance and reconnaissance (ISR), integrated with the targeting cycle. And in late summer, when Ukrainian forces employed offensive manoeuvre operations in regaining swathes of territory in the north and south, Russia's troops did not have an answer either tactically or operationally.

While these are issues recognised by many in the armed forces and in the defence industry, they appear not to be acknowledged within decision-making circles, which remain conservative in nature. Moreover, Moscow's practice of simply replacing senior staff, or moving commanders from one military district to another, has not addressed the underlying issues of leadership culture in the Russian armed forces. A rigidly hierarchical structure remains embedded in military education and tradition. Also, continued revelations of entrenched corruption in the armed forces will almost certainly not help to improve mutual trust; in advanced Western armed forces this is seen as a key feature in assisting effective military leadership at all levels. Achieving change in Russia will require political will, combined with fundamental improvements in education and training.

Ground Forces, Airborne Forces and Naval Infantry

Russia's initial invasion employed around 75% of its total deployable ground-combat forces. Many of the formations engaged in February suffered heavy attrition in the months that followed. This initially forced the Russian armed forces to turn to a variety of sources to find new personnel in order to sustain operations, including reservists, mercenaries and conscripts from the Donetsk and Luhansk regions, before ultimately opting for widespread mobilisation in Russia. Older armoured fighting vehicles and artillery pieces were taken out of store and reactivated to replace combat losses. These measures have, for now, proved just about sufficient to maintain an 'army in being' in Ukraine. However, attempts to generate the operational and strategic reserve forces needed to restart large-scale offensive operations on the ground appear to have been repeatedly thwarted by the battlefield pressure applied by Ukrainian forces. It is likely that Ukrainian forces will try to maintain this pressure, looking to prevent Russia gaining the space to reset its forces before spring 2023.

The current focus on short-term operational requirements also raises questions about the future shape and sustainability of Russian ground-combat power. Under the New Look military-modernisation process, which started in 2008, the ground forces were, by 2022, the least modernised of all the armed forces, and they were the source of most of the formations employed. Between 2012 and 2022, and particularly after 2014, Russia's Ground Forces, Airborne Forces and Naval Infantry had attempted to balance their relatively low budgetary priority with a requirement to generate an increasing amount of deployable ground-combat power. This resulted in a series of compromises, with advanced-equipment programmes, such as the *Armata*, *Kurganets* and *Bumerang* universal combat platforms, delayed and most formations expected to deploy understrength by using limited numbers of contract service personnel in task-organised Battalion Tactical Groups.

The invasion of Ukraine has laid bare many of the limitations of this approach. Against a determined adversary, many formations appear to have struggled to effectively conduct core military tasks, such as reconnaissance or combined-arms operations, a problem concealed to some extent by the relatively high level of performance of a small number of select units in Ukraine in 2014, and then in Syria. The exhaustion of surviving contract personnel, and the influx of inadequately trained and equipped reservists, conscripts and draftees, suggests that these performance levels are unlikely to improve in the short term. At the same time, the impact of economic sanctions imposed on Russia and restricted access to foreign technology is likely to curtail future re-equipment plans, even if the ground forces enjoy a larger share of the procurement budget than they have in previous years.

If the compromise policies of the past decade are ultimately deemed a failure by Russian military and political leadership, it is unclear what alternative approaches might realistically be adopted in their stead. Both a larger, conscript-based, mass-mobilisation model and a substantially smaller higher-quality force would pose problems in terms of both resourcing and sustainment. Such a model may also not fit with the Russian government's apparent objectives.

In the short term, the prospects for the project to deliver new equipment to the ground forces is unclear. *Armata* remains in test, and other equipment that has arrived during the last decade, such as the TOS-1 multiple-rocket launcher and *Typhoon* protected patrol vehicle, has been seen in Ukraine and in some cases observed as destroyed. The armed forces have lost significant numbers of all types of their in-service main battle tanks, and bringing out of store older types is a gap-filler solution at best when confronted with modern anti-armour systems. But the course of the war has forced some innovation. It is likely that improving command and control and integrating new strike systems, such as the *Lancet*-3 loitering munition, will be prioritised. These were not procured in large volumes before the war and were operated only by special forces, but by late 2022 they were being more widely used. Even with increased budgets, it will be challenging to keep the military forces supplied for the ongoing conflict in Ukraine, and that is before taking into account issues related to industrial capacity and the impact of Western sanctions on component supplies.

Weapons failings

While Russian land-attack cruise missiles were used with comparative success during Moscow's intervention in Syria, this has not so far been the case in Ukraine. Most notably, the Raduga Kh-101 (RS-AS-23A *Kodiak*) air-launched cruise missile has failed to meet expectations. The problems do not appear to have been limited to the missile and extend to the launch aircraft. Furthermore, stocks of the Kh-101 have been depleted. As of the fourth quarter of 2022, the inventory was potentially as low as 25% of the pre-war holding. The Novator 3M14 (RS-SS-N-30A *Sagaris*) naval land-attack cruise missile may have recorded a somewhat more reliable performance. The Russian armed forces have long recognised the need to increase the quality and quantity of precision-guided munitions but have so far failed to achieve this. There remains also an inability to knit together ISR and command and

Figure 7 Recapitalising Russia's bomber inventory

Russia has long held ambitions to recapitalise its bomber fleets, but efforts so far have been piecemeal. Ambition has risked overreaching capacity in industrial, technical and economic terms. As of 2022, Moscow was following three paths simultaneously: upgrading current types, restarting manufacture of one design, and supporting the research and development of a new bomber. The Tupolev Tu-22M3 *Backfire* C, Tu-95MS *Bear* H and Tu-160 *Blackjack* A are all the subject of upgrade programmes, while the last is also re-entering production as the Tu-160M *Blackjack* B. Tupolev is also working on the Item 80 design to meet the Aerospace Forces' (VKS) Future Long-Range Aviation Complex (PAK DA) project. A prototype of this design, almost certainly a subsonic low-observable flying wing, could be flown possibly by the middle of this decade. Meanwhile, after a three-decade gap in production, the first new-build Tu-160 was flown for the first time at the beginning of 2022. The modernised Tu-160M is being built at the Gorbunov production site in Kazan, and the design to meet the PAK DA requirement will likely be built there too. However, it remains unclear whether Russia has the economic and industrial capacity to sustain all its currently planned bomber projects.

Next-generation *Blackjack*

The Tu-160M draws on upgrade programmes implemented for the *Blackjack* A, but with a new airframe and aerostructures. The VKS has ten aircraft on order for delivery by 2027, and a notional ambition to field up to 50 Tu-160Ms by the mid-2030s.

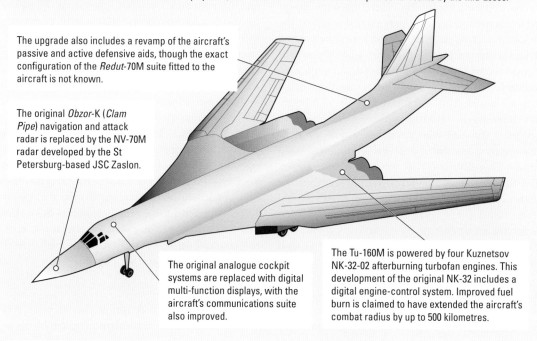

The upgrade also includes a revamp of the aircraft's passive and active defensive aids, though the exact configuration of the *Redut*-70M suite fitted to the aircraft is not known.

The original *Obzor*-K (*Clam Pipe*) navigation and attack radar is replaced by the NV-70M radar developed by the St Petersburg-based JSC Zaslon.

The original analogue cockpit systems are replaced with digital multi-function displays, with the aircraft's communications suite also improved.

The Tu-160M is powered by four Kuznetsov NK-32-02 afterburning turbofan engines. This development of the original NK-32 includes a digital engine-control system. Improved fuel burn is claimed to have extended the aircraft's combat radius by up to 500 kilometres.

Kh-101 (RS-AS-23A *Kodiak*)

The aircraft may be able to carry several long-range land-attack cruise missile (LACM) designs, with the most obvious system the Raduga Kh-101/102 (RS-AS-23A/B *Kodiak*) which is already operated with the Tu-160. The Kh-BD (Item 506) is also in development by Raduga and is intended to provide a yet-longer-range LACM. The Kh-BD could be based on an extended-length Kh-101/102. As well as subsonic LACMs, the aircraft's weapons suite could also include high-speed missiles now reportedly in development.

PAK DA, Item 80

A Tupolev patent published in March 2022 provides possible insight into the configuration of the VKS's next bomber. The patent illustration showed a twin-engine flying wing, with the patent related to the engine intake duct. Tupolev was awarded a 36-month bomber study contract in 2009, with the programme given the go-ahead in 2013. However, while the 2014 decision to return the Tu-160 to production appeared to show a near-term shift in priorities, an initial operational capability for the low-observable design at around the end of this decade remains possible, at least notionally.

©IISS

control at the tactical level to make better use of its artillery. Even when operating the same Soviet-era equipment, Ukraine's use of artillery has generally been more effective than Russia's. This is likely down to a closer linkage and better use of ISR-roled uninhabited aerial vehicles (UAVs), combined with the adoption of digital tactical command and control systems.

Inadequate command and control

The repeated setbacks have also prompted numerous changes in the military leadership, and the failures following February resulted in the gradual centralisation of operational command. Setbacks during the third quarter of 2022, including defeats in the Kharkiv and Kherson regions, prompted the appointment of General of the Army Sergei Surovikin as the overall commander. The defeat in the Kharkiv region showed that many new units, especially volunteer battalions, were not well integrated with the regular army units, and a loss of effective command and control was still a regular problem. This has rendered offensive operations and counter-attacks more difficult, with the effect that some Russian offensive actions have been predictable, with an increasing reliance on artillery and little emphasis on manoeuvre.

To mobilise or not

Having avoided declaring mobilisation for over six months, Russia's hand was finally forced in September 2022, following the collapse of its position in the Kharkiv region. The 21 September announcement by Putin was likely prompted by a recognition that overall defeat was an increasing possibility. According to official statements, the goal was to call up 300,000 reservists, but some Russian commentators put the figure at nearer to one million. Mobilisation was implemented too late, with those called up receiving as little as two weeks' training before being deployed to make up for combat losses in existing units. Prior to mobilisation, and since in parallel to it, Russia has also used 'volunteer battalions' as well as private military companies, the largest of which is Wagner Group.

Naval forces

Russia adopted a new Maritime Doctrine on 31 July 2022, replacing the 2015 document. Notably, the revised document identified the United States and NATO as 'threats'; in the previous volume the

US had been described as only a 'rival'. The 2022 document was also more ideological, with echoes of Soviet-era rhetoric. Maritime dominance was held to be the aim of the US, with the additional goal of reducing Russia's ability to exploit and develop maritime resources. The doctrine also recognised the challenge of Russia's lack of overseas naval bases, and the sanctions-based constraints on its shipbuilding capacity.

Nonetheless, the document identified building 'modern aircraft carriers' as a priority. But the practicality of this is a different matter: for years, Russia's surface-ship programme has funded only comparatively small warships. The revised doctrine reflected the adversarial relations between Russia, the US and NATO, but lacked realism concerning the state of Russian naval shipbuilding.

Russia's navy suffered some spectacular setbacks in 2022 and its impact on the invasion of Ukraine has been less than might have been expected. The Black Sea Fleet has exhibited poor command direction and slow responsiveness to threats as well as questionable operational readiness. Nevertheless, it continued to exert influence through at least a partial and distant blockade plus the use of both surface and submarine platforms to launch land-attack cruise-missile strikes against Ukrainian targets.

In the run-up to the opening of hostilities, there was a significant massing of Russian naval forces in the Mediterranean, including from the Northern, Baltic and Pacific fleets, as well as activity in northern European waters, ostensibly for exercises but no doubt for strategic signalling and to exert pressure. There was also reinforcement of the Black Sea Fleet with a number of amphibious ships, including a Project 11711 *Ivan Gren*-class vessel and several Project 775 *Ropucha*-class landing ships.

After 24 February, this reinforced amphibious capability played only a limited role, in part because of the known hazards of such operations in the area, the fact that the land war did not advance as Moscow planned, and also subsequently the innovative approaches Ukraine employed to put Russian naval vessels at risk. Russian shipping in the Mediterranean may have had some deterrent effect with, for example, the Project 1164 *Slava*-class cruisers from the Northern and Pacific fleets shadowing NATO aircraft-carrier formations in the area for a time. However, Turkey's decision to close to warships the transit route into and out of the Black Sea has likely affected Russia's ability both to support its Mediterranean presence and to reinforce its forces in the Black Sea itself.

The most attention-grabbing Russian naval setback was the sinking of the then Black Sea Fleet flagship, the Project 1164 *Slava*-class cruiser *Moskva*. Poor operational tactics in the use of the vessel and questions over the readiness and effectiveness of both the crew and the ship's systems appear to have contributed to the sinking. This raises new questions over the combat effectiveness of the other large legacy Soviet-era surface combatants on which the Russian fleet continues to rely for the bulk of its blue-water operations and power-projection missions.

The navy also lost a Project 1171 *Alligator*-class landing ship alongside in the port of Berdyansk in March 2022 plus a number of minor war vessels in different attacks. The attack with uncrewed air and surface vehicles at the end of October on the naval base at Sevastopol appeared to cause damage to the new Black Sea Fleet flagship, the Project 11356 *Grigorovich*-class frigate *Admiral Makarov*. Again, Ukraine's use of novel capabilities and combinations of capabilities, as well as audacious tactics, has hampered Black Sea Fleet operations. That said, the Russian Navy continued to display an ability to conduct operations on a global basis. These included several, albeit relatively limited, joint manoeuvres with the Chinese navy in the Western Pacific, including in the waters around Japan.

There were a number of important additions to the submarine-fleet inventory. The second Project 955A *Borey*-A nuclear-powered ballistic-missile submarine (SSBN) and the second Project 08851 *Yasen*-M nuclear-powered guided-missile submarine, which were commissioned at the end of 2021, have both joined the Pacific Fleet, boosting its capabilities. A third Project 08551 *Yasen*-M was undergoing sea trials in mid-2022. July saw the commissioning of the new nuclear-powered special-mission submarine *Belgorod*, although there remains continuing uncertainty over the operational status of the *Poseidon* nuclear-powered and potentially nuclear-tipped large uninhabited underwater vehicle that it is designed to carry. The final Project 941UM *Typhoon*-class SSBN, which had for some time essentially been a reserve asset for training and trials, now appears to have been retired.

Otherwise, additions to the fleet have been limited, reflecting the continuing poor performance of the naval-industrial base. This has no doubt been exacerbated by additional Western sanctions. The ambition outlined in the new maritime doctrine only served to highlight the fitful and accident-prone modernisation of the sole aircraft carrier, *Admiral Kuznetsov*; the timing of its completion was uncertain as was the vessel's likely combat effectiveness even if it does return to the fleet.

DEFENCE ECONOMICS

Russia

Assessments of Russian defence spending in 2022 have to consider the situation before the start of the 'special military operation' against Ukraine on 24 February 2022, and the circumstances after that date. After growing by 2.3% on average in 2017–19, the economic fallout of the coronavirus pandemic caused a 2.7% contraction in Russia's real GDP in 2020. The economic recovery got off to a strong start in 2021, with real GDP growing by 4.7%, but, following the invasion of February 2022, contractions of 3.4% and 2.3% are projected for 2022 and 2023.

After increasing rapidly in the early years (2011–15) of the State Armament Programme (SAP) to 2020, military expenditure slowed and declined in real terms in 2016–18 before recovering to a modest extent in 2019. Growth in real terms in 2019 and 2020 was followed by a decline in 2021 when inflation rose to 6.7% from an average of 3.6% in 2017–20. With the exception of 2020, when Russian GDP dipped amid the coronavirus pandemic, the proportion of GDP allocated to total military spending fell below 4% in recent years until the revised 2022 budget following the invasion of Ukraine.

The scale of the annual state defence order (SDO) for 2021 and 2022 has not been revealed but appears to be approximately RUB1.5 trillion (USD21.4 billion) in both years, which means it is declining in real terms.

Monitoring Russian military spending in 2022 was complicated by a Ministry of Finance decision to limit the publication of data on the implementation of the federal budget and, from April, only provide figures for total income and expenditure. The Federal Treasury initially followed suit but later resumed publication of detailed figures, issuing a report of spending during the first half of the year and then in July. During January–July, Russia's core 'National Defence' budget amounted to RUB2.89tr (USD41.3bn), more than 19% of total budget expenditure, compared with the 14.8% set out in budget law for 2022. Total military spending amounted to RUB3.68tr (USD52.6bn), almost one-quarter of the total and an

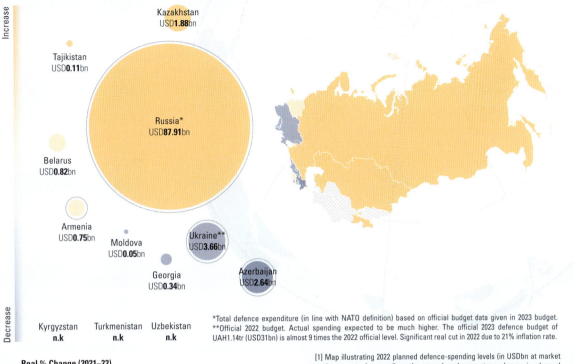

▲ Map 4 **Russia and Eurasia: regional defence spending** (USDbn, %ch yoy)[1]

estimated 4.5% of GDP. However, this total did not reflect the full cost to Russia of the war with Ukraine, as the evidence suggested that various aspects of the conflict were funded from other sections of the budget. The share of GDP was probably nearer to 6–7% at a time when the Russian economy was under pressure from sanctions and living standards were being depressed. Beyond equipment and operational costs, Russia was also reportedly seeking to increase the size of its armed forces.

The submission of the draft Russian 2023 budget to the State Duma on 30 September did offer more transparency in revealing that, as expected, final allocations for defence in 2022 were much higher than initially budgeted. The original core 2022 budget of RUB3.50tr (USD50.0bn) was revised upward to RUB4.68tr (USD66.9bn), with corresponding total military expenditure increasing from an estimated RUB4.98tr (USD71.1bn) to RUB6.15tr (USD87.9bn). Using purchasing-power-parity rates of conversion to better reflect the lower costs of production and labour in Russia, total Russian military expenditure is estimated to be USD192bn in 2022, the third largest globally behind the United States and China. The official projection for 2023 shows that military expenditure will be maintained at this higher level,

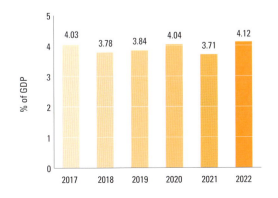

▼ Figure 8 **Russia: defence expenditure** as % of GDP

162 THE MILITARY BALANCE 2023

Table 9 Russia: defence expenditure, 2015–22 (trillion roubles, current prices)

Year	'National Defence' ('ND')		Annual state defence order (SDO)		Total military expenditure[1]		
	RUB (trillion)	% of GDP	RUB (trillion)[2]	% of 'ND'	RUB (trillion)	% of GDP	% change real terms
2022R[3]	4.680	3.13	n.k.	n.k.	6.153	4.12	+7.3
2022B[3]	3.502	2.68	1.500	42.8	4.975	3.80	-1.6
2021	3.573	2.73	1.500	42.0	4.859	3.71	-6.5
2020	3.169	2.87	1.500	47.3	4.460	4.04	+5.2
2019	2.997	2.73	1.500	50.1	4.211	3.84	+3.8
2018	2.827	2.72	1.450	51.3	3.928	3.78	-3.6
2017	2.666[4]	2.90	1.400	52.5	3.704[4]	4.03	-8.2
2016	2.982[4]	3.48	1.600	53.7	3.831[4]	4.47	-7.4
2015	3.181	3.83	1.800	56.6	4.026	4.85	+16.5

1. According to NATO definition. GDP figures from IMF World Economic Outlook, October 2022. 2. Approximate; the annual SDO is classified, but every a few years an approximate total is released. 3. 2022B shows the initial 2022 budget, and 2022R shows the revised budget following the invasion of Ukraine. 4. Excludes a one-off payment to reduce accumulated debts of defence-industry enterprises under the scheme of state-guaranteed credits. If this debt payment is included, the total share of GDP rises to 5.4% in 2016 and 4.2% in 2017.

with the core budget held at RUB4.98tr (USD71.1bn) and total funding reaching an estimated RUB6.65tr (USD95.0bn).

Weapons procurement

Due to the war and the imposition of sanctions, less information is available on the development and procurement of new weapons than in previous years. But the limited evidence suggests that many new systems are behind schedule and the rate of production of the latest weapons and other military hardware has fallen. The fulfilment of the main success indicator used, the share of modern weapons in the active stock of the armed forces, is now less frequently cited.

The SDO is now based on the SAP to 2027. President Vladimir Putin signed off on it in early 2018, with total funding of approximately USD19tr plus an additional USD1tr for infrastructure relating to the deployment of new systems. It is claimed that work is under way on its successor for 2024–33, but no details have been provided. Its drafting must now be extremely difficult given the current highly uncertain military and economic circumstances, rendering any forecasting and planning highly problematic.

However, some details of new systems have become available. Former chief of Roscosmos Dmitri Rogozin in early 2022 claimed that the new, long-overdue *Sarmat* heavy intercontinental ballistic missile would be deployed by the end of 2022, though it had only had one flight test, in April, and will need more than that (some analysts estimate at least ten) before it can be approved for service, though it remains unclear whether war exigencies will lead

Russia to curtail this test schedule. Deployment looks more likely in late 2023 or 2024. Testing of the new *Tsirkon* hypersonic missile for surface ships and submarines continues, with optimistic claims that it will enter service in 2022–23. While it was reported last year that a contract had been signed with Almaz-Antey for the delivery of ten new S-500 air-defence systems, scheduled to start in the first half of 2022, there have been no reports of its deployment. Still, there have been claims that some elements of it are in production. The medium-range S-350 *Vityaz* (RS-SA-28) air-defence system is reported to have been first deployed in 2020, but the available evidence suggests that very few have entered service. Only six 'fifth generation' Su-57 *Felon* fighters had been supplied by September 2022 under the present contract, and the rate of production is such that the supply of a planned 76 by the end of 2027 is beginning to look in doubt. Development of the new *Checkmate* fighter continues, with a first flight test planned for 2024. But it remains unclear who will buy it, as the Russian air force appears to have no interest in acquiring the aircraft.

Naval deliveries have been limited in 2022 and include the new strategic *Borey*-A-class submarine *Knyaz Oleg*; the multi-role *Yasen*-M (*Severodvinsk* II) boat *Krasnoyarsk*; and two Project 677 *Lada*-class (*Petersburg*) diesel-electric submarines, *Kronstadt* and *Velikiye Luki*. The Project 09582 special-purpose submarine *Belgorod* was handed over to the navy in July 2022 and will enter service with the Pacific Fleet. It is associated with the future *Poseidon* nuclear-powered and potentially nuclear-tipped large uninhabited underwater vehicle still under development. The main new surface ships will be the Project 22350 (*Gorshkov*) frigate *Admiral Golovko*, likely to be the first ship equipped with the *Tsirkon* missile, and the Project 20380 (*Steregushchiy* II) corvette *Rezkiy*. As for the *Admiral Kuznetsov* aircraft carrier under repair and limited modernisation, delays keep arising and it is now unlikely that it will return to service before the end of 2024. There is little evidence of anything but very limited building of the new *Armata* tank and some Russian military specialists think that it will never enter serial production given its high unit cost and considerations that it would offer capability outcomes too marginal to justify its adoption. This may also apply to the new *Kurganets* and *Bumerang* armoured vehicles, now not often mentioned in the specialist military media.

Defence industry

It has become difficult to follow the development of the Russian defence industry in quantitative terms as published data has become increasingly scarce, especially since the start of the war.

By the summer of 2022 there were mounting reports of defence companies working with two or three shifts in sectors such as munitions, armoured vehicles, artillery systems and high-precision missiles. This followed government measures in the summer facilitating the transfer of companies to defence work on a temporary basis and requiring some workers to perform overtime or night work and delay holidays in order to 'optimise' work on orders for the armed forces. Repair facilities also appear to have become more active than usual, and Prime Minister Mikhail Mishustin in early September approved a decree for the quick establishment of two new tank and armoured-vehicle repair facilities, one near Moscow and the other in the Rostov region.

There are reports that sanctions are disrupting the work of defence enterprises, though some of these have turned out to be misleading. They include a report that the vast Uralvagonzavod tank and rail-wagon works had ceased military production because of an inability to obtain imported components. In reality, batches of new tanks and armoured vehicles were still being delivered several months after the start of the war, including T-90M *Proryv* tanks in early September. The ground forces also took delivery of some BREM-1M armoured recovery vehicles, and batches of modernised BMP-1K, BRM-1K and BMP-3 infantry fighting vehicles, but overall for the ground forces, combat losses in Ukraine dwarfed 2022

delivery numbers. Moreover, as stocks of imported systems and components have become exhausted, the manufacture of some products has come to a halt. They include the *Ansat* helicopter, which has a Pratt & Whitney power unit, and the Czech L-410 small transport plane assembled in Russia, which has General Electric turboprop engines.

Analysis of Russian weapons captured in Ukraine has revealed extensive use of foreign electronic components. Now that sanctions on integrated circuits and many other components have been tightened, there is a question as to the ability of the defence industry to maintain the output of some weapons. However, it is likely that quite large reserve stocks of imported components were built up, following long-established Soviet practice. Belarus, meanwhile, has been an important source of supply of electronic components suitable for use in military hardware; its role may increase. The Russian government is engaged in a vigorous import-substitution campaign, but rapid results are unlikely. It may prove difficult to obtain suitable advanced production equipment in some cases, for example for integrated circuits. Russia's sole volume producer of microchips, Mikron, is able to produce only at the 180–190-nanometre level, with a modest annual output by international standards. Taiwan was fabricating more advanced chips and processors to Russian designs, but sanctions will be restricting Russia's ability to secure such technologies from abroad.

Notable organisational changes in the defence industry in 2022 include completion of the merger of the Sukhoi and MiG design bureaus, in June 2022, while the United Aircraft Corporation is in the process of converting from a holding company to a fully integrated single company. In July 2022 there was a significant change of official personnel. Yuri Borisov, deputy prime minister responsible for oversight of the defence industry since May 2018, was replaced by the industry minister since 2012, Denis Manturov, who retains that ministerial post. Borisov became director general of Roscosmos, replacing Rogozin.

The diversification of the defence industry into civil high-technology fields continues with a 26.7% share of civil and dual-use output in 2021, a modest increase on the 25.6% of 2020. The Rosatom nuclear corporation is at the fore in diversification: its civil share was 42% in 2020 with a goal of 48% by the end of 2022 and 53% in 2024. That process for much of the defence industry, however, may be pushed off

Table 10 Russia: Volume of military-technical cooperation and arms exports (USD billion, current)

	2016	2017	2018	2019	2020	2021
FSVTS military-technical cooperation	15.0	15.0	15.0	15.2	15.6	14.6
Inc 'Rosoboronexport'	13.0	13.4	13.7	11.0	13.0	(13.0)[1]
TsAMTO arms sales	11.2	12.0	14.3	12.4	11.1	
% of world arms sales	14.1	14.8	18.7	15.5	13.0	

1. Rosoboronexport's claimed approximate total, possibly overstated. FSVTS: Federal Service for Military-Technical Cooperation. TsAMTO: Centre for the Analysis of the World Trade in Arms, Moscow. The centre measures all arms exports in terms of current US dollars. Note, the centre has revised its data for 2016–19 on the basis of new information presenting a slightly more modest volume for Russia.

course by the war and sanctions. Given the scale of equipment losses during the war, it may prove necessary to increase the state defence order over the next few years, reducing the scope for diversification.

There have been mounting reports that the defence industry is facing a shortage of labour, especially personnel with higher education, including IT specialists. In June 2022, Borisov said that about 400,000 workers were needed, including 120,000 graduates. Meeting this challenge may well necessitate increased salaries and wages.

Arms exports

In recent years, the value of Russian arms exports has been maintained at a stable level, notwithstanding the imposition of sanctions on some countries opting to buy weapons from Russia and the impact of the coronavirus pandemic. In fact, the volume of sales increased in 2020. Russia's own measure of export volumes relates to so-called military-industrial cooperation, which includes sales of weapons and other military equipment, components, licence sales, repairs, servicing and training. The annual volume is reported by the Federal Service for Military-Technical Cooperation (FSVTS). The valuation of Russian arms exports is becoming more complex, as there is increasing reliance on payment in national currencies rather than US dollars and on non-transparent barter and offset deals.

Russia's share of the global arms market has been declining when valued in current US dollars. Prospects for 2022 are uncertain. Speaking in August, Aleksandr Mikheev, head of Rosoboronexport, said that sales had reached USD5.4bn, suggesting that the annual total may turn out to be less than in 2021. Some potential purchases appear to be on hold as importers fear falling foul of US sanctions. A deal with Turkey to buy a second batch of S-400 (RS-SA-21 *Growler*) air-defence systems has been signed in principle, but the issue of part localisation of production in Turkey has not been resolved. There have been reports in the Russian media that the fulfilment of some export contracts is being delayed – aircraft for Algeria and artillery systems for Vietnam being examples – to prioritise production for the domestic armed forces, while the Philippines cancelled a contract for 16 Mi-17 helicopters to avoid US sanctions.

Indeed, Russia has been resorting to arms imports to meet urgent needs posed by its invasion of Ukraine, particularly Iranian *Shahed* 136 direct-attack munitions. Russia seriously lags in strike uninhabited aerial vehicle development. It is held back by an inability to develop and manufacture in quantity suitable small piston engines, with their import blocked by sanctions. There have also been claims that North Korea has sent munitions but, contrary to the expectations of some commentators, there is no evidence of China supplying weapons to Russia.

Regional defence economics

The war in Ukraine has had a dramatic economic impact on countries in Central Asia. Inflation rates, already high in 2021, rose even further in all countries primarily due to increased food prices. Balancing this are the 'unexpected spillovers' that the IMF identifies as the relocation of workers and firms from Russia with associated money and capital inflows which strengthened the consumption component of GDP. Furthermore, the spike in oil prices has bolstered the revenues of the oil exporters in the region – Azerbaijan, Kazakhstan and Turkmenistan. The short-term outlook, however, does face downside risks through the exposure of these economies to that of Russia. Several countries rely on remittances, primarily from Russia, which are threatened by the impact of sanctions on Russia's economy and indeed the cost of war. Russian real GDP is estimated to have contracted by 3.4% in 2022 with a further 2.3% contraction in 2023.

Defence spending in the region is difficult to ascertain for certain countries – for example Kyrgyzstan and Turkmenistan – but of the countries that *The Military Balance* assesses, it is evident that there has been strong growth in recent years. Armenia's defence budget has grown from USD435m in 2017 to USD749m in 2022 and is projected to increase to USD1.1bn in 2023. As a proportion of GDP, the country allocated 4.4% on average to defence between 2017 and 2022, spiking to 5.57% in 2023. Growth is also evident in Azerbaijan where spending increased from USD1.5bn in 2017 to USD2.6bn in 2022 and reaching USD3.1bn in 2023, thus maintaining a 3:1 ratio with Armenia's defence budget over this period. Growth in Kazakhstan's budget has also been significant, from USD1.3bn in 2017 to USD1.9bn in 2022. Across the region, high rates of inflation erode increases, or result in cuts, in defence spending in real terms, an issue that will be exacerbated until the elevated rates seen in 2021 and 2022 start to abate.

The economic impact on Ukraine following Russia's invasion has been severe. Real GDP is projected to have contracted by 35% in 2022 while inflation rose from 9.4% in 2021 to 20.6% in 2022. Projections for 2023 are difficult due to the high levels of uncertainty around the trajectory of the war in the short term. The instability caused by the war means it is difficult to determine the actual level of military spending in Ukraine in 2022. The original 2022 budget came to UAH131bn (USD3.6bn), presenting a 10.8% real cut from 2021 owing to the spike in the inflation rate. Actual spending was expected to be much higher. Indeed, the official 2023 defence budget of UAH1.14tr (USD31bn) is almost nine times the 2022 official level.

UKRAINE

Russia first invaded Ukraine in 2014. The seizure of Crimea in March 2014, and Russia's subsequent fomenting of discord and political and military support for proxy forces in Donetsk and Luhansk regions, provided the impetus for significant changes in Ukraine's armed forces. Up to then, they had been significantly degraded through disinvestment in the post-Soviet period.

Reform activities after 2014 were designed to improve not only the capability of Ukraine's armed forces, but also its defence and security institutions. These reforms were designed to produce armed forces and a defence sector more aligned with Western military standards, and that were capable of territorial defence. Volunteer battalions were formed, and territorial-defence units were established. But

moves to empower and strengthen resilience in local administrations and develop civil-defence measures were also important. The 2016 Strategic Defence Bulletin outlined reform plans and guided the strategic development of the armed forces. Defence assistance by Western states since 2014 significantly aided the development of institutions by boosting capability in areas such as cyber security and supplying limited amounts of military equipment, including *Javelin* anti-armour systems and counter-battery radars.

Defence education has also been important. Since 2008, NATO has delivered a Defence Education Enhancement Programme (DEEP) that has been used as a framework to deliver training assistance in a number of countries, ranging from Armenia to Tunisia. A number of NATO trust funds, headed by individual member states, also delivered targeted assistance in defence-transformation initiatives. DEEP projects in Ukraine included assistance to Ukrainian forces in developing professional military education capacity, as well as plans to develop professional non-commissioned officers. Some Western states also delivered training assistance in Ukraine, including at the Yaroviv training centre. This led to the generation of a force that had since 2014–15 cycled a large number of personnel through the front lines in Ukraine's east, with those personnel out of regular service going into reserve. It also sparked a culture change that included the development of a group of officers and non-commissioned officers who are more empowered than their predecessors to take decisions on the battlefield.

As 2022 wore on, and Ukrainian losses mounted, continued training support became more important. Mobilisation has led to a significant influx of recruits. However, with many training grounds in Ukraine under threat, and given the Western decision not to deploy training troops to Ukraine itself, this expanded training initiative saw the development of plans to train Ukrainians in European countries. Since mid-year, the United Kingdom has led a training programme that at its inception aimed to train 10,000 Ukrainian personnel by the end of 2022; it also includes instructors from NATO allies and partners. Training includes modules on weapons skills, basic patrolling and combat tactics, and battlefield first aid in a compressed five-week package. According to the UK Ministry of Defence, this has, over time, also seen Ukrainians bringing with them their battlefield experiences, which have brought mutual benefits for

Figure 9 **Ukraine: selected Ukrainian main battle tank (MBT) upgrades**

Ukraine inherited a large fleet of main battle tanks (MBTs) from the former Soviet army, after the dissolution of the Soviet Union in December 1991. (Ukraine had earlier declared independence in August 1991.) This fleet included examples of all three of the major Soviet MBT families in frontline service in 1991: the T-64, T-72, and T-80. Ukraine's post-Soviet inventory has included a notably large fleet of T-64 series vehicles, as the primary factory for the construction of T-64s – and the home of its design bureau – was (and still is) located in Kharkiv. The country has continued to develop upgrades for all three of these Soviet-era MBT families, with the most recent examples shown below. The heritage of the T-72AMT and T-64BM2 *Bulat* is readily apparent; the base-T-84, meanwhile, is a variant of the Soviet T-80 and was designed in Kharkiv in the 1990s. Prior to Russia's full-scale invasion of Ukraine in February 2022, these upgrades were principally carried out at the Kharkiv, Kyiv, and Lviv Armoured Plants. Combat losses, and vehicles captured from Russian forces and received from Eastern European operators of Soviet-era tank fleets, mean that Ukraine's tank fleet is now in transition, while authorities look to improve overall capability with more modern armour, including from foreign suppliers.

T-64BM2 *Bulat*

Upgrades:
- Thermal-imaging gunner's sight
- Improved fire-control systems
- *Nizh* explosive reactive armour
- Bar armour
- Upgraded 1,000 hp engine
- Improved communications and GPS systems

T-84 *Oplot*-M

Upgrades:
- New welded turret
- Thermal-imaging gunner's sight
- Thermal-imaging commander's panoramic periscope
- Improved fire-control systems
- *Duplet* explosive reactive armour
- *Varta* soft-kill active protection system
- Upgraded 1,200 hp engine
- Auxiliary power unit

T-72AMT

Upgrades:
- Improved fire-control systems
- *Nizh* explosive reactive armour
- Bar armour
- Improved communications and GPS systems

©IISS

Western training personnel. The European Union also launched a training initiative in October that will see Ukrainian personnel trained in Germany and Poland.

Adaptation and innovation

During 2022, the Ukrainian armed forces that had developed since 2014 blunted Russia's attempt to seize the capital and occupy other cities, including Kharkiv and Mykolaiv. The post-2014 Ukrainian forces, which had been developed for what Kyiv termed anti-terrorist operations and, after 2018, joint-forces operations, were in 2022 faced with a different type of war due to the geographic scope of Russia's assault and the greater numbers of artillery and (at least initially) personnel among the assault troops. By late year this force had regained territory in the north and forced a Russian retreat from Kherson in the south by drawing upon its strengths and exploiting the weaknesses of the Russian ground forces. Combat losses of personnel and equipment mounted on both sides during the year, but Ukrainian forces were able to gain advantage in several important areas through adaptation, flexibility and innovation.

Communications

The provision of robust communications systems, including the much-reported *Starlink*, has been an important factor. The distribution of these systems – reportedly down to company level and below – has given Ukrainian commanders the capacity to correct artillery fire by aerial surveillance and to maintain operational control of distributed units, including those on the offensive. It was reported that these were important in maintaining control of forces in efforts to regain territory around Kharkiv and Kherson, among others. There was concern that these signals failed at times, such as when Ukrainian forces moved into previously occupied territory. This highlighted the importance of counter-jamming activity and the measures data providers may be taking to prevent the exploitation of any captured material by Russian troops. At the same time, many Russian troops relied on what turned out to be vulnerable systems, including commercial radios and mobile phones; Ukraine's security services regularly published intercepted calls for propaganda purposes.

Transport

The rapid increase in personnel strength after mobilisation, and the wide front of operations and related mobility and supply demands, created issues around the supply of transport vehicles. The civilian car market has become the main source for increasing the mobility of these formations. Here, too, private funding has been vital. Limited funds, even before this latest invasion, meant that the Ukrainian forces were already using pickups, jeeps, minibuses and minivans, as well as cars. This was partly down to insufficient funds to acquire more suitable vehicles, but also the limited availability of four-wheel-drive vehicles on the second-hand market, including in Europe. Dry conditions during the offensive in Kharkiv somewhat hid the weaknesses of such vehicles, but mobility challenges increase as weather conditions change, raising requirements for military-style vehicles or civilian 4x4 vehicles through winter and into the spring.

Aerial reconnaissance and surveillance

While some foreign and Ukrainian uninhabited aerial vehicles are available, commercial quadcopters have also proved their utility at the tactical level. Ukrainian specialists consider these to primarily be the DJI Mavic 3, DJI Matrice 300 and 30, as well as the Autel Evo 2, including a version with a thermal-imaging camera. These have been primarily supplied by charitable foundations and volunteer organisations or purchased by individual servicemen and their families. While such devices have proven vulnerable to Russian electronic-warfare interference, small-arms fire and weather conditions, as well as operator error, they have rapidly proliferated in the Ukrainian armed forces. The quadcopters have been important in enabling junior commanders to deploy organic reconnaissance assets and have improved information sharing on a horizontal basis (between units) as well as vertically (with higher-formation headquarters). They have helped increase the effectiveness of Ukrainian artillery, principally mortars and towed- and self-propelled artillery, and have also been used to deliver munitions directly onto targets. Moreover, they have had an important psychological effect in being used to directly target troops, including in ostensibly defensive positions.

Artillery

Ukraine's inventory of legacy Soviet-era artillery systems has been depleted by combat loss, overuse and also because the high rate of fire has caused ammunition-supply issues. Foreign assistance has supplied large numbers of 152-millimetre shells, but foreign stocks are reducing too. Ukrainian analysts have said that the limited numbers of artillery pieces, coupled with ammunition challenges and the wide operational front, have caused Ukraine's artillery forces to be dispersed, with engagements conducted by small units rather than batteries and higher formations. In these instances, accuracy was of increased importance and, even in distributed operations, the arrival of more precise artillery pieces from abroad has helped decentralised operations to remain effective. Precision-guided Western-made projectiles such as the GPS-guided M982 *Excalibur* and SMArt 155, suitable for newly supplied 155mm systems, are said to have been particularly important. Given the central role of rocket artillery to the capabilities of both Russia and Ukraine, the arrival in Kyiv's inventory of the M142 HIMARS and M270 MLRS systems has been important. Ukraine's widespread use of GMLRS missiles has turned these systems into a key part of offensive operations and, because of the increased range they offer over Ukraine's legacy systems, has enabled Ukrainian forces to hold at risk Russian command posts, supply depots and other targets previously out of range. It has also reportedly enabled Ukraine to assign to these assets some tasks previously performed by tactical aircraft.

Anti-armour weapons

Western deliveries of anti-armour weapons have expanded Ukraine's inventories of these systems, ranging from lightweight disposable grenade launchers to more advanced NLAWs and *Javelins*; small numbers of the latter had been supplied after 2018. Some Ukrainian specialists claim that the outcome of this has been a significant loss of Russian armour as well as an apparent shift in the way these forces operate, now looking to avoid close-quarters battle and instead focusing on long-range engagements, often from concealed locations. In turn, this has encouraged Ukrainian anti-tank units to actively search for enemy armoured vehicles using mobile teams with four-wheel-drive vehicles and buggies employing anti-armour weapons, including the *Stugna*-P, *Corsar*, 9K111 *Fagot* (RS-AT-4 *Spigot*) and the Western-supplied FGM-148 *Javelin*. At the same time, the groups use grenade launchers and NLAWs in close combat.

Aviation

Although Russia has proven unable to establish control of the air, its aerospace forces and missile strikes have forced Ukraine's aviation forces to disperse in order to survive, in turn increasing supply and maintenance demands. Although Ukraine has lost a number of aircraft and helicopters, it has succeeded in maintaining a level of effective capability. Western-supplied equipment has been important. Although there has been no supply of Soviet-era aircraft, weapons have been sent, including AGM-88 HARM anti-radiation missiles, which have been employed by Ukrainian aircraft against Russian air defences. Moreover, Ukraine managed to retain some S-300 and *Buk* air-defence systems and has used them to defend rear areas. This has led Russia to largely abandon attempts to penetrate deep into Ukrainian airspace with crewed aircraft and switch to stand-off munitions; in turn, Russia's frequent use of systems like cruise missiles (along with increasingly effective Ukrainian defences) has reduced the available numbers of these systems. This pattern was established before the receipt of modern Western surface-to-air missiles, such as NASAMS and IRIS-T. On the battlefield, man-portable air-defence systems (MANPADs) have become Ukraine's primary air-defence assets. Indeed, the threat from MANPADS has forced tactical adaptation on both sides, with ground-attack aircraft and helicopters having to not only fly extremely low but also adopt novel 'lofted launch' tactics for unguided missiles, reducing the effectiveness of these attacks.

Arms procurements and deliveries – Russia and Eurasia

Significant events in 2022

UKRAINE'S DEFENCE INDUSTRY

FEBRUARY

Russia's armed forces have attacked defence-industrial facilities across Ukraine following Moscow's full-scale invasion. Targets have included facilities in the land, sea and aerospace sectors, including plants capable of repairing armoured vehicles and also missile production facilities. While many facilities have suffered visible damage, the precise impact on defence-industrial capacity is less clear. Continued Ukrainian combat capability indicates that local maintenance, repair and overhaul (MRO) capacity persists, even if some defence equipment newly supplied in 2022 has been repaired outside Ukraine. Meanwhile, plans to reorganise UkrOboronProm, the state-owned conglomerate, have been postponed indefinitely. The company is now seeking to provide MRO capabilities for much of the NATO-standard equipment donated to Ukraine both in the short term and as part of a post-war development plan. Plans include the licensed production of foreign systems and a Ukraine Startup Fund; the latter will encompass 13 development initiatives including for new armed UAVs, new vehicles and dual-use technology.

KAZAKHSTAN'S DEFENCE-INDUSTRIAL AMBITIONS

JULY

Kazakhstan's defence minister informed parliament of plans to increase both defence exports and the share of domestically produced products in the armed forces' inventory. This followed a series of earlier defence-industrial announcements. In May, Kazakhstan Engineering (KE) – owned since 2019 by the Ministry of Industry and Infrastructural Development – signed a memorandum of understanding with Turkish Aerospace Industries (TAI) to set up a final assembly line for the *Anka* uninhabited air vehicle (UAV). There are reports that a contract for three aircraft was signed in October 2021, with deliveries due in 2023. In February, the ministry announced a series of initiatives, including the assembly of Mi-171Sh helicopters (the assembly of other variants began in 2019) and the establishment of an Airbus maintenance centre. Kazakhstan's defence-industrial modernisation process has so far seen agreements with foreign firms, typically through joint ventures, rather than the local design of platforms. This strategy has had some success, with several dozen Airbus H145 helicopters and over 100 *Arlan* 4x4 protected patrol vehicles delivered to Kazakh customers so far. Export contracts are rarer, though in August, Eurocopter Kazakhstan Engineering (an Airbus–KE joint venture) began delivering H125 helicopters to Kyrgyzstan's Ministry of Emergency Situations, following an export contract signed with Kyrgyzstan in March.

RUSSIAN DEFENCE EXPORTS

AUGUST

Rosoboronexport claimed that it had signed agreements worth more than USD14.5bn during the Army-2022 exhibition. Companies from Belarus, China, India, Iran and Thailand travelled to the show, notwithstanding international sanctions on Russia. The war in Ukraine, and sanctions on Russia, have raised questions over the future of Russia's defence exports. There is the potential for sanctions to be imposed on prospective purchasers, while Russia's customers may also make judgements on the effectiveness of its military equipment and combat losses may make Moscow prioritise domestic deliveries over exports. In August, the Philippines announced it was cancelling a November 2021 contract with Russian Helicopters for 16 Mi-17 medium transport helicopters worth PHP12.7bn (USD257.84m). Similarly, Egypt's 2018 contract for Su-35 combat aircraft seems to have been either postponed or cancelled. Continued sanctions will likely make it harder for Russia to export defence materiel. This may lead Moscow to attempt to secure exports by setting more flexible terms, offering yet more advanced equipment or looking to find new customers.

RUSSIA LOOKS TO SECURE DEFENCE-INDUSTRY WORKFORCE

SEPTEMBER

President Vladimir Putin signed legislation outlining harsher prison sentences for desertion, looting and evading mobilisation. These measures include a sentence of up to ten years for violating the terms of a contract under the state defence order, causing damage worth at least 5% of the order's contract value, or failing to fulfil it. Earlier, in August, it had been reported that Rostec was preventing key managers from travelling on holiday. While this was ostensibly intended to help fulfil the state defence order, it may also have been designed to stop personnel fleeing the country. The loss in Ukraine of large amounts of Russia's most modern equipment is likely fuelling anxiety over defence production. Moreover, Russia's efforts to substitute domestic for foreign defence components since 2014 have seen limited success, and analysis of defence equipment damaged and destroyed in Ukraine has pointed to continued dependencies, including in microelectronics. Tighter international sanctions after February will increase the challenge for Russia in maintaining the development and production of defence equipment.

170   THE MILITARY BALANCE 2023

Table 11 — Selected equipment donations to Ukraine, February–September 2022

Country	Armoured fighting vehicles		Artillery		Missiles				Air defence	
	MBT	IFV, APC and AUV	MRL	Howitzer	MANPATS*	MANPADS	Coastal defence	Air-launched	Short- to long-range SAM	SPAAG
Australia		Western		Western						
Canada		Western		Western						
Croatia										
Czech Republic	Soviet	Soviet	Soviet	Soviet						
Denmark		Western					Western			
Estonia				Both	Western					
France		Western		Western		Western				
Germany			Western	Western		Both			Western	Western
Greece		Western (pending)								
Italy		Western		Western		Western				
Latvia						Western				
Lithuania				Western		Western				
Macedonia, North	Soviet									
Netherlands		Western		Western		Western		Western		
Norway		Western	Western (pending)	Western		Western				
Poland	Soviet	Soviet	Soviet	Both		Soviet		Soviet		
Portugal		Western								
Slovakia		Soviet	Soviet						Soviet	
Slovenia		Soviet								
Spain		Western								
Sweden								Western (pending)		
United Kingdom		Western	Western	Western	Western	Western	Western			
United States		Western	Western	Western	Western	Western		Western	Western	Western (pending)

*crew operated

Origin of equipment:

	Delivered	Pending
Western	(blue)	(light blue)
Soviet/Warsaw Pact era	(red)	n/a
Both	(orange)	n/a

Armenia ARM

Armenian Dram AMD		2021	2022	2023
GDP	AMD	6.98tr	8.04tr	
	USD	13.9bn	17.7bn	
per capita	USD	4,701	5,972	
Growth	%	5.7	7.0	
Inflation	%	7.2	8.5	
Def bdgt [a]	AMD	312bn	340bn	501bn
	USD	622m	749m	
USD1=AMD		501.36	454.30	

[a] Includes imported military equipment, excludes military pensions

Real-terms defence budget trend (USDm, constant 2015)

Population 3,000,756

Age	0–14	15–19	20–24	25–29	30–64	65 plus
Male	9.6%	2.9%	3.0%	3.4%	24.3%	5.6%
Female	8.6%	2.6%	2.7%	3.4%	25.8%	8.1%

Capabilities

The armed forces' focus is defence and maintenance of the territorial integrity of the state. The country is involved in a longstanding dispute with Azerbaijan over Nagorno-Karabakh. Fighting flared again in September 2022, the worst since the short war in September 2020. The goal of moving the armed forces from a conscript to a contract-based force remains an ambition, though with no timetable apparent. The 2020 National Security Strategy unsurprisingly identified Azerbaijan as Armenia's primary security concern, while also highlighting the role it claims Turkey plays in supporting Azerbaijan's policy aims. The country retains close ties with Russia, and irrespective of Moscow's invasion of Ukraine, Russia was viewed still as Armenia's strategic partner as of late 2022. Yerevan has also begun to build defence relations with India. The 2021 delivery of counter-battery radars was followed in September 2022 with an order that included the *Pinaka* multiple rocket launcher and anti-tank weapons. Armenia is a member of the CSTO, with military doctrine continuing to be influenced by Russian thinking. Armenia is also engaged in a NATO Individual Partnership Action Plan. Personnel train regularly and take part in annual CSTO exercises and in bilateral drills with Russia. Equipment is mainly of Russian origin. Agreements have been reached in recent years to purchase modern Russian systems, though only in small quantities. Serviceability and maintenance of mainly ageing aircraft have been a problem for the air force. There is some capacity to manufacture defence equipment for the domestic market, including electro-optics, light weapons and UAVs, but Armenia is reliant on Russia for other equipment platforms and military systems. The government has set the goal of further developing its domestic defence industry, while also looking to improve the quality of systems fielded.

ACTIVE 42,900 (Army 40,000 Air/AD Aviation Forces (Joint) 1,100 other Air Defence Forces 1,800) **Paramilitary 4,300**
Conscript liability 24 months

RESERVE
Some mobilisation reported, possibly 210,000 with military service within 15 years

ORGANISATIONS BY SERVICE

Army ε40,000
FORCES BY ROLE
SPECIAL FORCES
  1 SF bde
MANOEUVRE
  Mechanised
  1 (Special) corps (1 recce bn, 1 tk bn(-), 5 MR regt, 1 sigs bn, 1 maint bn)
  1 (2nd) corps (1 recce bn, 1 tk bn, 2 MR regt, 1 lt inf regt, 1 arty bn)
  1 (3rd) corps (1 recce bn, 1 tk bn, 5 MR regt, 1 arty bn, 1 MRL bn, 1 sigs bn, 1 maint bn)
  1 (5th) corps (2 MR regt)
  Other
  1 indep MR trg bde
COMBAT SUPPORT
  1 arty bde
  1 MRL bde
  1 AT regt
  1 AD bde
  2 AD regt
  2 (radiotech) AD regt
  1 engr regt
SURFACE-TO-SURFACE MISSILE
  1 SRBM regt

EQUIPMENT BY TYPE
Available estimates should be treated with caution following losses suffered in the fighting since late 2020 in Nagorno-Karabakh
ARMOURED FIGHTING VEHICLES
  MBT 109: 3 T-54; 5 T-55; ε100 T-72A/B; 1 T-90A
  RECCE 12 BRM-1K (CP)
  IFV 140: 100 BMP-1; 25 BMP-1K (CP); 15 BMP-2
  APC 150
    APC (T) 20 MT-LB
    APC (W) 130: 108 BTR-60 (incl variants); 18 BTR-70; 4 BTR-80
  AUV *Tigr*
ENGINEERING & MAINTENANCE VEHICLES
  AEV MT-LB
  ARV BREhM-D; BREM-1
ANTI-TANK/ANTI-INFRASTRUCTURE
  MSL • SP 22+: 9 9P148 *Konkurs* (RS-AT-5 *Spandrel*); 13 9P149 *Shturm* (RS-AT-6 *Spiral*); 9K129 *Kornet-E* (RS-AT-14 *Spriggan*)
ARTILLERY 225
  SP 37: **122mm** 9 2S1 *Gvozdika*; **152mm** 28 2S3 *Akatsiya*
  TOWED 122: **122mm** 60 D-30; **152mm** 62: 26 2A36 *Giatsint*-B; 2 D-1; 34 D-20
  MRL 54: **122mm** up to 50 BM-21 *Grad*; **273mm** 2 WM-80; **300mm** 2 9A52 *Smerch*
  MOR 120mm 12 M120

SURFACE-TO-SURFACE MISSILE LAUNCHERS
SRBM • Conventional 14: 7+ 9K72 *Elbrus* (RS-SS-1C *Scud B*); 3+ 9K79 *Tochka* (RS-SS-21 *Scarab*); 4 9K720 *Iskander-E*
UNINHABITED AERIAL VEHICLES
ISR • Light *Krunk*
AIR DEFENCE
SAM
Medium-range 2K11 *Krug* (RS-SA-4 *Ganef*); S-75 *Dvina* (RS-SA-2 *Guideline*); 9K37M *Buk-M1* (RS-SA-11 *Gadfly*)
Short-range 2K12 *Kub* (RS-SA-6 *Gainful*); S-125 *Pechora* (RS-SA-3 *Goa*); 9K331MKM *Tor-M2KM*
Point-defence 9K33 *Osa* (RS-SA-8 *Gecko*); 9K35M *Strela*-10 (RS-SA-13 *Gopher*); 9K310 *Igla*-1 (RS-SA-16 *Gimlet*); 9K38 *Igla* (RS-SA-18 *Grouse*); 9K333 *Verba* (RS-SA-29 *Gizmo*); 9K338 *Igla-S* (RS-SA-24 *Grinch*)
GUNS
SP 23mm ZSU-23-4 *Shilka*
TOWED 23mm ZU-23-2

Air and Air Defence Aviation Forces 1,100
1 Air & AD Joint Command
FORCES BY ROLE
GROUND ATTACK
1 sqn with Su-25/Su-25UBK *Frogfoot*
EQUIPMENT BY TYPE
AIRCRAFT 17 combat capable
FGA 4 Su-30SM *Flanker H*
ATK 13: up to 12 Su-25 *Frogfoot*; 1 Su-25UBK *Frogfoot*
TPT 4: **Heavy** 3 Il-76 *Candid*; **PAX** 1 A319CJ
TRG 14: 4 L-39 *Albatros*; 10 Yak-52
HELICOPTERS
ATK 7 Mi-24P *Hind*
ISR 4: 2 Mi-24K *Hind*; 2 Mi-24R *Hind* (cbt spt)
MRH 14: 10 Mi-8MT (cbt spt); 4 Mi-8MTV-5 *Hip*
C2 2 Mi-9 *Hip G* (cbt spt)
TPT • Light 7 PZL Mi-2 *Hoplite*
AIR DEFENCE • SAM • Long-range S-300PT (RS-SA-10 *Grumble*); S-300PS (RS-SA-10B *Grumble*)
AIR-LAUNCHED MISSILES
AAM • IR R-73 (RS-AA-11A *Archer*); **SARH** R-27R (RS-AA-10A *Alamo*)

Gendarmerie & Paramilitary 4,300

Police
FORCES BY ROLE
MANOEUVRE
Other
4 paramilitary bn
EQUIPMENT BY TYPE
ARMOURED FIGHTING VEHICLES
RECCE 5 BRM-1K (CP)
IFV 45: 44 BMP-1; 1 BMP-1K (CP)
APC • APC (W) 24 BTR-60/BTR-70/BTR-152
ABCV 5 BMD-1

Border Troops
Ministry of National Security
EQUIPMENT BY TYPE
ARMOURED FIGHTING VEHICLES
RECCE 3 BRM-1K (CP)
IFV 35 BMP-1
APC • APC (W) 23: 5 BTR-60; 18 BTR-70
ABCV 5 BMD-1

DEPLOYMENT
LEBANON: UN • UNIFIL 31
SERBIA: NATO • KFOR 40

FOREIGN FORCES
Russia 3,500: 1 mil base with (1 MR bde; 74 T-72; 80 BMP-1; 80 BMP-2; 12 2S1; 12 BM-21); 1 ftr sqn with 18 MiG-29 *Fulcrum*; 4 Su-30SM *Flanker* H; 1 hel sqn with 11 Mi-24P *Hind*; 4 Mi-8AMTSh *Hip*; 4 Mi-8MT *Hip*; 2 SAM bty with S-300V (RS-SA-12 *Gladiator/Giant*); 1 SAM bty with *Buk*-M1-2 (RS-SA-11 *Gadfly*)

Azerbaijan AZE

Azerbaijani New Manat AZN		2021	2022	2023
GDP	AZN	92.9bn	119bn	
	USD	54.6bn	70.1bn	
per capita	USD	5,398	6,842	
Growth	%	5.6	3.7	
Inflation	%	6.7	12.2	
Def bdgt [a]	AZN	4.59bn	4.49bn	
	USD	2.70bn	2.64bn	
USD1=AZN		1.70	1.70	

[a] Official defence budget. Excludes a significant proportion of procurement outlays.

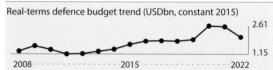
Real-terms defence budget trend (USDbn, constant 2015)

Population	10,353,296					
Age	0–14	15–19	20–24	25–29	30–64	65 plus
Male	11.7%	3.7%	3.4%	4.1%	23.6%	3.2%
Female	10.5%	3.2%	2.9%	3.8%	25.1%	4.9%

Capabilities

The armed forces' principal focus is territorial defence. There was renewed fighting between Azerbaijani and Armenian forces in September 2022, two years after a six-week war between the two over Nagorno-Karabakh. Russia has been the traditional defence partner for Azerbaijan, but more recently it has bought from Israel and forged a strategic relationship with Turkey. In June 2021, Baku and Ankara signed the 'Shusha Declaration', which included cooperation if either nation is threatened by a third state. Both parliaments ratified the accord in early 2022. Pakistan has also begun to emerge as a defence-industrial partner. Azerbaijan maintains a defence relationship with NATO, concluding in 2019 a fifth cycle of its NATO Individual Partnership Action Plan. Readiness within Azerbaijan's conscript-based armed services varies between units. Azerbaijan has taken part in multilateral exercises and its forces also train bilaterally with Turkey. The two air forces held *TurAz Eagle 2022* in September, while Azerbaijani personnel also took part in the multinational *Efes-2022* drill held in Turkey. The armed forces have little expeditionary capability. Defence modernisation and procurement has been a focus in the past decade, intended to replace the ageing inventory of mainly Soviet-era equipment.

Recent orders include air-defence and artillery systems and wheeled and tracked armoured vehicles, predominantly of Russian origin. In recent years there has been significant procurement and industrial cooperation with Israel, focused on UAVs and guided weapons, and increasingly with Turkey as a key defence partner. Azerbaijan's limited but growing defence-industrial capabilities are centred on the Ministry of Defence Industry, which manages and oversees the production of small arms and light weapons. While the country is reliant on external suppliers for major defence-equipment platforms and systems, some defence companies have started to export to foreign markets.

ACTIVE 64,050 (Army 44,500 Navy 1,750 Air 8,650 Other 9,150) Gendarmerie & Paramilitary 15,000

Conscript liability 18 months (12 for graduates)

RESERVE 300,000

Some mobilisation reported; 300,000 with military service within 15 years

ORGANISATIONS BY SERVICE

Army 44,500

FORCES BY ROLE
COMMAND
  5 corps HQ
SPECIAL FORCES
  5 cdo bde
MANOEUVRE
  Mechanised
  4 MR bde
  Light
  17 MR bde
COMBAT SUPPORT
  2 arty bde
  1 MRL bde
  1 engr bde
  1 sigs bde
COMBAT SERVICE SUPPORT
  1 log bde
SURFACE TO SURFACE MISSILE
  1 SRBM bde

EQUIPMENT BY TYPE
ARMOURED FIGHTING VEHICLES
  MBT 497: 404 T-72A/AV/B/SIM2; 93 T-90S
  RECCE 7 BRM-1K
  IFV 325: 64 BMP-1; 101 BMP-2; 46 BMP-3; 7 BTR-80A; 107 BTR-82A
  APC 506
    APC (T) 336 MT-LB
    APC (W) 142: 10 BTR-60; 132 BTR-70
    PPV 28: 14 *Marauder*; 14 *Matador*
  AUV 121: 35 *Cobra*; 86 *Sand Cat*
  ABCV 20 BMD-1
ENGINEERING & MAINTENANCE VEHICLES
  AEV IMR-2; MT-LB
  ARV BREM-L *Brelianka*
  MW *Bozena*; GW-3 (minelayer)

ANTI-TANK/ANTI-INFRASTRUCTURE
MSL
  SP 18 9P157-2 *Khrizantema-S* (RS-AT-15 *Springer*); *Cobra* with *Skif*; 23 *Sand Cat* with *Spike*-ER; 7 *Sand Cat* with *Spike*-LR
  MANPATS 9K11 *Malyutka* (RS-AT-3 *Sagger*); 9K111 *Fagot* (RS-AT-4 *Spigot*); 9K111-1 *Konkurs* (RS-AT-5 *Spandrel*); 9K115 *Metis* (RS-AT-7 *Saxhorn*); 9K135 *Kornet* (RS-AT-14 *Spriggan*) (reported); *Spike*-LR
  GUNS • TOWED 85mm some D-44
ARTILLERY 1,251
  SP 153: **122mm** 68 2S1 *Gvozdika*; **152mm** 68: 14 2S3 *Akatsiya*; 18 2S19 *Msta-S*; 36 *Dana*-M1M; **155mm** 5 ATMOS 2000; **203mm** 12 2S7 *Pion*
  TOWED 551: **122mm** 423 D-30; **130mm** 36 M-46; **152mm** 92: 49 2A36 *Giatsint*-B; 43 D-20
  GUN/MOR 120mm 17 2S31 *Vena*
  MRL 282: **107mm** 71 T-107; **122mm** 130: 78 BM-21 *Grad*; 16 IMI *Lynx*; 18 RM-70 *Vampir*; 18 T-122; **128mm** 10 RAK-12; **220mm** 17 TOS-1A; **300mm** 36: 30 9A52 *Smerch*; 6 *Polonez*; **302mm** 18 T-300 *Kasirga*
  MOR 248: **120mm** 230: 5 *Cardom*; 27 M-1938 (PM-38); 198 2S12; **SP 120mm** 18 *Sand Cat* with *Spear*
SURFACE-TO-SURFACE MISSILE LAUNCHERS
  SRBM • Conventional 7: 4 IAI LORA; 3 9K79-1 *Tochka-U* (RS-SS-21B *Scarab*)
AIR DEFENCE
  SAM
    Short-range 9K33-1T *Osa*-1T (RS-SA-8 *Gecko*)
    Point-defence 9K35 *Strela*-10 (RS-SA-13 *Gopher*); 9K32 *Strela* (RS-SA-7 *Grail*)‡; 9K34 *Strela*-3 (RS-SA-14 *Gremlin*); 9K310 *Igla*-1 (RS-SA-16 *Gimlet*); 9K338 *Igla-S* (RS-SA-24 *Grinch*)
  GUNS
    SP 23mm ZSU-23-4
    TOWED 23mm ZU-23-2

Navy 1,750

EQUIPMENT BY TYPE
PATROL AND COASTAL COMBATANTS 11
  CORVETTES • FS 1 *Kusar* (ex-FSU *Petya* II) with 2 RBU 6000 *Smerch* 2 A/S mor, 2 twin 76mm gun
  PSO 1 *Luga* (*Wodnik* 2) (FSU Project 888; additional trg role)
  PCC 3: 2 *Petrushka* (FSU UK-3; additional trg role); 1 *Shelon* (ex-FSU Project 1388M)
  PB 3: 1 *Araz* (ex-TUR AB 25); 1 *Bryza* (ex-FSU Project 722); 1 *Poluchat* (ex-FSU Project 368)
  PBF 3 *Stenka*
MINE WARFARE • MINE COUNTERMEASURES 4
  MHC 4: 2 *Korund* (Project 1258 (*Yevgenya*)); 2 *Yakhont* (FSU *Sonya*)
AMPHIBIOUS 5
  LSM 2: 1 Project 770 (FSU *Polnochny* A) (capacity 6 MBT; 180 troops); 1 Project 771 (*Polnochny* B) (capacity 6 MBT; 180 troops)
  LCM 3: 2 T-4 (FSU); 1 *Vydra*† (FSU) (capacity either 3 MBT or 200 troops)
LOGISTICS AND SUPPORT • ATF 2 *Neftegaz* (Project B-92) (ex-Coast Guard)

174 THE MILITARY BALANCE 2023

Marines
FORCES BY ROLE
MANOEUVRE
Amphibious
1 mne bn

Air Force and Air Defence 8,650
FORCES BY ROLE
FIGHTER
1 sqn with MiG-29 *Fulcrum* A; MiG-29UB *Fulcrum* B
GROUND ATTACK
1 regt with Su-25 *Frogfoot*; Su-25UB *Frogfoot* B
TRANSPORT
1 sqn with Il-76TD *Candid*
TRAINING
1 sqn with L-39 *Albatros*
ATTACK/TRANSPORT HELICOPTER
1 regt with Bell 407; Bell 412; Ka-32 *Helix* C; MD-530; Mi-8 *Hip*; Mi-17-1V *Hip*; Mi-24 *Hind*; Mi-35M *Hind*

EQUIPMENT BY TYPE
AIRCRAFT 52 combat capable
FTR 14: 11 MiG-29 *Fulcrum* A; 3 MiG-29UB *Fulcrum* B
ATK 38: 33 Su-25 *Frogfoot*; 5 Su-25UB *Frogfoot* B
TPT • Heavy 2 Il-76TD *Candid*
TRG 22: 12 L-39 *Albatros*; 10 *Super Mushshak*
HELICOPTERS
ATK 44: 20 Mi-24 *Hind*; 24 Mi-35M *Hind*
MRH 33: 1 Bell 407; 3 Bell 412; 1 MD-530; 28 Mi-17-1V *Hip*
TPT 11: **Medium** 11: 3 Ka-32 *Helix* C; 8 Mi-8 *Hip*
UNINHABITED AERIAL VEHICLES
CISR • Medium *Bayraktar* TB2
ISR 7+: **Heavy** 3+ *Heron*; **Medium** 4+ *Aerostar*
AIR DEFENCE • SAM
Long-range S-200 *Vega* (RS-SA-5 *Gammon*); S-300PMU2 (RS-SA-20 *Gargoyle*)
Medium-range S-75 *Dvina* (RS-SA-2 *Guideline*); 9K37M *Buk*-M1 (RS-SA-11 *Gadfly*); *Buk*-MB; ε24 S-125-2TM *Pechora*-2TM; *Barak*-LRAD
Short-range *Abisr* (*Barak*-MRAD)
AIR-LAUNCHED MISSILES
AAM • IR R-27T (RS-AA-10B *Alamo*); R-60 (RS-AA-8 *Aphid*); R-73 (RS-AA-11A *Archer*); **SARH** R-27R (RS-AA-10A *Alamo*)
ASM *Barrier*-V
BOMBS
Laser-guided MAM-L

Gendarmerie & Paramilitary ε15,000

State Border Service ε5,000
Ministry of Internal Affairs
EQUIPMENT BY TYPE
ARMOURED FIGHTING VEHICLES
IFV 168 BMP-1/BMP-2
APC • APC (W) 19 BTR-60/70/80
AIRCRAFT • TPT • Light 40 An-2 *Colt* (modified for use as decoys)
UNINHABITED AERIAL VEHICLES
ISR • Medium 7+: 4+ *Hermes* 450; 3+ *Hermes* 900
LOITERING & DIRECT ATTACK MUNITIONS
Harop; *Skystriker* (two variants)

Coast Guard
The Coast Guard was established in 2005 as part of the State Border Service
EQUIPMENT BY TYPE
PATROL AND COASTAL COMBATANTS 19
PCG 6 *Sa'ar* 62 with 1 8-cell *Typhoon* MLS-NLOS lnchr with *Spike* NLOS SSM, 1 hel landing platform
PBF 9: 1 Project 205 (FSU *Osa* II); 6 *Shaldag* V; 2 Silver Ships 48ft
PB 4: 2 Baltic 150; 1 *Point* (US); 1 *Grif* (FSU *Zhuk*)
LOGISTICS AND SUPPORT 3
ATF 3 *Neftegaz* (Project B-92) (also used for patrol duties)

Internal Troops 10,000+
Ministry of Internal Affairs
EQUIPMENT BY TYPE
ARMOURED FIGHTING VEHICLES
APC • APC (W) 7 BTR-60/BTR-70/BTR-80

DEPLOYMENT

SOUTH SUDAN: UN • UNMISS 1

FOREIGN FORCES
Turkey 170; 1 EOD unit

TERRITORY WHERE THE GOVERNMENT DOES NOT EXERCISE EFFECTIVE CONTROL

The status of Nagorno-Karabakh is disputed by Armenia and Azerbaijan. Renewed clashes occurred in September 2022 following a short war in September–November 2020. The fighting in 2020 saw Azerbaijan's forces regain most of the territory lost prior to a 1994 ceasefire. This had brought an uneasy cessation to the first outbreak of hostilities following the 1991 collapse of the Soviet Union. Data presented here represents the de facto situation and does not imply international recognition.

Nagorno-Karabakh ε5,000
Available estimates vary with reference to military holdings in Nagorno-Karabakh and must be treated with caution due to the heavy levels of attrition in the 2020 conflict and subsequent clashes.
FORCES BY ROLE
MANOEUVRE
Mechanised
1 MR div(-)
1 mtn div(-)
EQUIPMENT BY TYPE
ARMOURED FIGHTING VEHICLES
MBT 22: ε20 T-72AV/B; 1 T-72 SIM2; 1 T-90S
RECCE BRDM-2
IFV 150: ε50 BMP-1; ε100 BMP-2
ANTI-TANK/ANTI-INFRASTRUCTURE
MSL • MANPATS 9K111-1 *Konkurs* (RS-AT-5 *Spandrel*)
RCL 73mm SPG-9

ARTILLERY
   TOWED 122mm some D-30
   MRL 122mm some BM-21 *Grad*
AIR DEFENCE
   SAM
      Short-range 9K331 *Tor*-M1 (RS-SA-15 *Gauntlet*)
      Point-defence 9K33 *Osa* (RS-SA-8 *Gecko*); 9K310 *Igla*-1 (RS-SA-16 *Gimlet*); 9K38 *Igla* (RS-SA-18 *Grouse*)
   GUNS
      SP 23mm ZSU-23-4
      TOWED 23mm ZU-23-2

FOREIGN FORCES
Russia 1,960; 1 MR bde(-) (peacekeeping)

Belarus BLR

Belarusian Ruble BYN		2021	2022	2023
GDP	BYN	173bn	195bn	
	USD	68.2bn	79.7bn	
per capita	USD	7,295	8,567	
Growth	%	2.3	-7.0	
Inflation	%	9.5	16.5	
Def bdgt	BYN	1.63bn	2.00bn	
	USD	640m	818m	
USD1=BYN		2.54	2.44	

Real-terms defence budget trend (USDm, constant 2015)

Population	9,413,505				
Age	0–14	15–19	20–24	25–29	30–64	65 plus
Male	8.2%	2.5%	2.5%	2.9%	24.8%	5.6%
Female	7.8%	2.4%	2.3%	2.7%	27.0%	11.2%

Capabilities

Located between Russia and NATO European members, the main task of Belarus's armed forces is maintaining territorial integrity, though the army has also been used for internal security tasks. As of late 2022, the country was working on a revised national state security concept to address what the regime views as changes in the security environment over the last decade. The current military doctrine was approved in July 2016 and identified as security challenges 'hybrid methods' and 'colour revolutions'. A further plan for the development of the armed forces until 2030 was approved in late 2019. Belarus is a member of the CSTO and reportedly may apply for membership of the Shanghai Cooperation Organisation. Russia remains the country's principal defence partner, with Belarus vocal in support of Moscow's war in Ukraine. Russian forces used Belarusian territory to launch attacks on Ukraine. In June 2022, Russia suggested that Belarussian armed forces could be provided at least notionally with a nuclear-capable delivery system, either in the form of the 9M723 (RS-SS-26 *Stone*) short-range ballistic missile or through an air-delivered munition. Despite Moscow's invasion of Ukraine joint training continued with Russian forces during 2022, including air defence exercises, and military training areas were being used in late year to train newly-mobilised Russian troops. The forces remain conscript-based and train regularly with other CSTO partners. As of the fourth quarter of 2022, Belarus had not imposed mobilisation, despite the war on its borders. There has been increased emphasis on the training of territorial-defence troops to allow them to operate more effectively with the regular forces. There is a small heavy-airlift fleet that could be supplemented by civil transport aircraft, and Minsk has a special-forces brigade trained for the air-assault role. There is no requirement to independently deploy and sustain the armed forces, but it could be possible for elements assigned to the CSTO. Russia continues to be Minsk's main defence-equipment supplier. There is a renewed emphasis on air defence, with Minsk expressing interest in 2021 in acquiring additional systems from Russia. The local defence industry manufactures vehicles, guided weapons and electronic-warfare systems, among other equipment. However, there is no capacity to design or manufacture modern combat aircraft. The sector also undertakes upgrade work for foreign customers.

ACTIVE 47,950 (Army 11,700 Air 11,300 Special Operations Forces 6,150 Joint 18,800) **Gendarmerie & Paramilitary 110,000**
Conscript liability 18 months; 12 months for graduates (alternative service option)

RESERVE 289,500
(Joint 289,500 with mil service within last 5 years)

ORGANISATIONS BY SERVICE

Army 11,700
FORCES BY ROLE
COMMAND
   2 comd HQ (West & North West)
MANOEUVRE
   Mechanised
   4 mech bde
COMBAT SUPPORT
   2 arty bde
   1 engr bde
   1 engr regt
   2 sigs regt
EQUIPMENT BY TYPE
ARMOURED FIGHTING VEHICLES
   MBT 497: 477 T-72B; 20 T-72B3 mod
   RECCE 132 BRM-1
   IFV 937: 906 BMP-2; 31+ BTR-82A
   APC • APC (T) 58 MT-LB
   AUV *Tigr*
ENGINEERING & MAINTENANCE VEHICLES
   AEV BAT-2; IMR-2; MT-LB
   ARV 2 BREM-K
   VLB 24: 20 MTU-20; 4 MT-55A
   MW UR-77
NBC VEHICLES BRDM-2RKhB; *Cayman* NRBC *Chimera*; RKhM-4; RKhM-K
ANTI-TANK/ANTI-INFRASTRUCTURE • MSL
   SP 160: 75 9P148 *Konkurs* (RS-AT-5 *Spandrel*); 85 9P149 *Shturm* (RS-AT-6 *Spiral*)
   MANPATS 9K111 *Fagot* (RS-AT-4 *Spigot*); 9K111-1 *Konkurs* (RS-AT-5 *Spandrel*); 9K115 *Metis* (RS-AT-7 *Saxhorn*)
ARTILLERY 583
   SP 333: **122mm** 125 2S1 *Gvozdika*; **152mm** 208: 125 2S3 *Akatsiya*; 71 2S5; 12 2S19 *Msta*-S

TOWED 152mm 72 2A65 *Msta-B*
MRL 164: **122mm** 128 BM-21 *Grad;* **220mm** 36 9P140 *Uragan*
MOR 120mm 14 2S12
AIR DEFENCE
    SAM Point-defence 2K22 *Tunguska* (RS-SA-19 *Grison*)
    GUNS • SP 23mm ZU-23-2 (tch)

Air Force and Air Defence Forces 11,300
FORCES BY ROLE
FIGHTER
    2 sqn with MiG-29/S/UB *Fulcrum* A/C/B
GROUND ATTACK
    2 sqn with Su-25K/UBK *Frogfoot* A/B
TRANSPORT
    1 base with An-24 *Coke*; An-26 *Curl*; Il-76 *Candid*;
    Tu-134 *Crusty*
TRAINING
    Some sqn with L-39 *Albatros*
ATTACK HELICOPTER
    Some sqn with Mi-24 *Hind*
TRANSPORT HELICOPTER
    Some (cbt spt) sqn with Mi-8 *Hip*; Mi-8MTV-5 *Hip*;
    Mi-26 *Halo*
EQUIPMENT BY TYPE
AIRCRAFT 71 combat capable
    FTR 34: 28 MiG-29 *Fulcrum* A/MiG-29S *Fulcrum* C;
    6 MiG-29UB *Fulcrum* B
    FGA 4 Su-30SM *Flanker* H; (21 Su-27/UB *Flanker* B/C
    non-operational/stored)
    ATK 22 Su-25K/UBK *Frogfoot* A/B
    TPT 8: **Heavy** 2 Il-76 *Candid* (+9 civ Il-76 available for mil
    use); **Light** 6: 1 An-24 *Coke*; 4 An-26 *Curl*; 1 Tu-134 *Crusty*
    TRG 11+: Some L-39 *Albatros*; 11 Yak-130 *Mitten**
HELICOPTERS
    ATK 12 Mi-24 *Hind*
    TPT 26: **Heavy** 6 Mi-26 *Halo*; **Medium** 20: 8 Mi-8 *Hip*;
    12 Mi-8MTV-5 *Hip*
AIR-LAUNCHED MISSILES
    AAM • IR R-60 (RS-AA-8 *Aphid*); R-73 (RS-AA-11A
    Archer) **SARH** R-27R (RS-AA-10 *Alamo* A)
    ASM Kh-25 (RS-AS-10 *Karen*); Kh-29 (RS-AS-14 *Kedge*)
    ARM Kh-58 (RS-AS-11 *Kilter*) (likely WFU)

Air Defence
AD data from Uzal Baranovichi EW radar
FORCES BY ROLE
AIR DEFENCE
    1 bde S-300PS (RS-SA-10B *Grumble*)
    3 regt with S-300PS (RS-SA-10B *Grumble*)
    1 bde with 9K37 *Buk* (RS-SA-11 *Gadfly*); 9K331ME
    Tor-M2E (RS-SA-15 *Gauntlet*)
    1 regt with 9K331ME *Tor*-M2E (RS-SA-15 *Gauntlet*)
    2 regt with 9K33 *Osa* (RS-SA-8 *Gecko*)
EQUIPMENT BY TYPE
AIR DEFENCE • SAM
    Long-range S-300PS (RS-SA-10B *Grumble*)
    Medium-range 9K37 *Buk* (RS-SA-11 *Gadfly*)
    Short-range 21 9K331ME *Tor*-M2E (RS-SA-15 *Gauntlet*)
    Point-defence 9K33 *Osa* (RS-SA-8 *Gecko*); 9K35
    Strela-10 (RS-SA-13 *Gopher*)

Special Operations Command 6,150
FORCES BY ROLE
SPECIAL FORCES
    1 SF bde
MANOEUVRE
    Mechanised
    2 mech bde
EQUIPMENT BY TYPE
ARMOURED FIGHTING VEHICLES
    RECCE 13+ *Cayman* BRDM
    APC • APC (W) 217: ε64 BTR-70M1; 153 BTR-80
    AUV 12 CS/VN3B mod
ARTILLERY 114
    TOWED 122mm 24 D-30
    GUN/MOR • TOWED 120mm 18 2B23 NONA-M1
ANTI-TANK/ANTI-INFRASTRUCTURE • MSL
    MANPATS 9K111 *Fagot* (RS-AT-4 *Spigot*); 9K111-1 *Konkurs*
    (RS-AT-5 *Spandrel*); 9K115 *Metis* (RS-AT-7 *Saxhorn*)

Joint 18,800 (Centrally controlled units and MoD staff)
FORCES BY ROLE
SURFACE-TO-SURFACE MISSILE
    1 SRBM bde
COMBAT SUPPORT
    1 arty bde
    1 MRL bde
    2 engr bde
    1 EW unit
    1 NBC regt
    1 ptn bridging regt
    2 sigs bde
EQUIPMENT BY TYPE
ARMOURED FIGHTING VEHICLES
    APC • APC (T) 20 MT-LB
NBC VEHICLES BRDM-2RKhB; RKhM-4; RKhM-K
ARTILLERY 112
    SP 152mm 36 2S5 *Giatsint-S*
    TOWED 152mm 36 2A65 *Msta-B*
    MRL 300mm 42: 36 9A52 *Smerch*; 6 *Polonez*
SURFACE-TO-SURFACE MISSILE LAUNCHERS
    SRBM • Conventional 96: 36 9K79 *Tochka* (RS-SS-21
    Scarab); 60 9K72 *Elbrus* (RS-SS-1C *Scud* B)

Gendarmerie & Paramilitary 110,000
State Border Troops 12,000
Ministry of Interior
Militia 87,000
Ministry of Interior
Internal Troops 11,000

DEPLOYMENT
LEBANON: UN • UNIFIL 5

FOREIGN FORCES
Russia 10,000; 1 SSM bn with *Iskander*-M; 1 FGA sqn(-)
with Su-34; Su-35S; 1 atk flt with MiG-31K; 2 SAM bn
with S-400; 1 radar station at Baranovichi (*Volga* system;
leased); 1 naval comms site

Georgia GEO

Georgian Lari GEL		2021	2022	2023
GDP	GEL	60.2bn	73.5bn	
	USD	18.7bn	25.2bn	
per capita	USD	5,014	6,770	
Growth	%	10.4	9.0	
Inflation	%	9.6	11.6	
Def bdgt	GEL	900m	918m	1.26bn
	USD	279m	314m	
FMA (US)	USD	35m	25m	25m
USD1=GEL		3.22	2.92	

Real-terms defence budget trend (USDm, constant 2015)

Population	4,935,518				
Age	0–14	15–19	20–24	25–29	30–64	65 plus
Male	9.6%	2.7%	2.9%	3.4%	22.4%	6.9%
Female	9.0%	2.5%	2.5%	3.1%	24.5%	10.7%

Capabilities

Georgia's main security preoccupations concern Russian military deployments and the breakaway regions of Abkhazia and South Ossetia, concerns heightened by Russia's February 2022 invasion of Ukraine. The country has the goal of joining NATO, and a package of 'tailored support measures' were agreed at the alliance's 2022 Madrid Summit in response to the invasion of Ukraine. Bilateral security cooperation with the US continues with the Georgia Defense Readiness Program (GDRP) succeeded by the Georgia Defense and Deterrence Enhancement Initiative, signed in October 2021. The GDRP was intended to bring nine Georgian infantry battalions to a NATO-standard. Forces take part in several NATO multinational exercises. Georgia's armed forces have limited expeditionary logistic capability. The backbone of the armed forces' military equipment remains legacy Soviet-era systems, though the aim is to increasingly replace these. The Major Systems Acquisitions Strategy 2019–25 outlines efforts to procure new equipment in several areas, though funding availability will be key to meeting aspirations. Plans have included boosting special-forces capacity and anti-armour and air-defence capability. The country has begun to develop a defence-industrial base, and this is intended mainly to support the armed forces. The State Military Scientific-Technical Center has demonstrated some maintenance, repair, overhaul and design capabilities for the production of light armoured vehicles. A combat training centre is being developed under the NATO–Georgia Joint Training and Evaluation Centre. Conscription was reinstated with revised terms and increased pay in early 2017.

ACTIVE 20,650 (Army 19,050 National Guard 1,600)
Gendarmerie & Paramilitary 5,400
Conscript liability 12 months

ORGANISATIONS BY SERVICE

Army 15,000; 4,050 conscript (total 19,050)

FORCES BY ROLE
SPECIAL FORCES
  1 SF bde
MANOEUVRE
  Mechanised
  1 (4th) mech inf bde (1 armd bn, 2 mech inf bn, 1 SP arty bn)
  Light
  1 (1st) inf bde (1 mech inf bn, 3 inf bn)
  1 (2nd) inf bde (3 inf bn, 1 fd arty bn)
  1 (3rd) inf bde (3 inf bn, 1 SP arty bn)
  Amphibious
  2 mne bn (1 cadre)
COMBAT SUPPORT
  1 (5th) arty bde (1 fd arty bn; 1 MRL bn)
  1 (6th) arty bde (1 SP arty bn; 1 MRL bn)
  1 engr bde
  1 engr bn
  1 sigs bn
  1 SIGINT bn
  1 MP bn
COMBAT SERVICE SUPPORT
  1 med bn

EQUIPMENT BY TYPE
ARMOURED FIGHTING VEHICLES
  MBT 123: 23 T-55AM2; 100 T-72B/SIM1
  RECCE 41: 1 BRM-1K; 40+ *Didgori*-2
  IFV 71: 25 BMP-1; 46 BMP-2
  APC 221
    APC (T) 69+: 3+ *Lazika*; 66 MT-LB
    APC (W) 152+: 25 BTR-70; 19 BTR-80; 40+ *Didgori*-1; 3+ *Didgori*-3; 65 *Ejder*
  AUV 10+: ATF *Dingo*; *Cobra*; 10 *Cougar*
ENGINEERING & MAINTENANCE VEHICLES
  ARV IMR-2
ANTI-TANK/ANTI-INFRASTRUCTURE
  MSL • MANPATS 9K111 *Fagot* (RS-AT-4 *Spigot*); 9K111-1 *Konkurs* (RS-AT-5 *Spandrel*); FGM-148 *Javelin*
  GUNS • TOWED ε40: 85mm D-44; 100mm T-12
ARTILLERY 240
  SP 67: 122mm 20 2S1 *Gvozdika*; 152mm 46: 32 M-77 *Dana*; 13 2S3 *Akatsiya*; 1 2S19 *Msta-S*; 203mm 1 2S7 *Pion*
  TOWED 71: 122mm 58 D-30; 152mm 13: 3 2A36 *Giatsint*-B; 10 2A65 *Msta*-B
  MRL 122mm 37: 13 BM-21 *Grad*; 6 GradLAR; 18 RM-70
  MOR 120mm 65: 14 2S12 *Sani*; 33 M-75; 18 M120
AIR DEFENCE • SAM
  Short-range *Spyder*-SR
  Point-defence *Grom*; *Mistral*-2; 9K32 *Strela*-2 (RS-SA-7 *Grail*)‡; 9K35 *Strela*-10 (RS-SA-13 *Gopher*); 9K36 *Strela*-3 (RS-SA-14 *Gremlin*); 9K310 *Igla*-1 (RS-SA-16 *Gimlet*)

Aviation and Air Defence Command 1,300 (incl 300 conscript)

1 avn base, 1 hel air base

EQUIPMENT BY TYPE
AIRCRAFT 5 combat capable
  ATK 5: 3 Su-25KM *Frogfoot*; 2 Su-25UB *Frogfoot* B (2 Su-25 *Frogfoot* in store)
  TPT • Light 9: 6 An-2 *Colt*; 2 Yak-40 *Codling*

HELICOPTERS
ATK 6 Mi-24 *Hind*
TPT 18: **Medium** 17 Mi-8T *Hip*; **Light** 1+ Bell 205 (UH-1H *Iroquois*) (up to 8 more in store)
UNINHABITED AERIAL VEHICLES
ISR • **Medium** 1+ *Hermes* 450
AIR DEFENCE • SAM
Medium-range 9K37 *Buk*-M1 (RS-SA-11 *Gadfly*) (1–2 bn)
Point-defence 8 9K33 *Osa*-AK (RS-SA-8B *Gecko*) (two bty); 9K33 *Osa*-AKM (6–10 updated SAM systems)

National Guard 1,600 active reservists opcon Army

FORCES BY ROLE
MANOEUVRE
  Light
    2 inf bde

Gendarmerie & Paramilitary 5,400

Border Police 5,400
EQUIPMENT BY TYPE
HELICOPTERS
TPT • **Medium** 3 Mi-8MTV-1 *Hip*

Coast Guard
HQ at Poti. The Navy was merged with the Coast Guard in 2009 under the auspices of the Georgian Border Police, within the Ministry of the Interior
EQUIPMENT BY TYPE
PATROL AND COASTAL COMBATANTS 24
  PCC 2 *Ochamchira* (ex-US *Island*)
  PBF 7: 4 *Ares* 43m; 1 *Kaan* 33; 1 *Kaan* 20; 1 Project 205P (*Stenka*)
  PB 15: 1 *Akhmeta*; 2 *Dauntless*; 2 *Dilos* (ex-GRC); 1 *Kutaisi* (ex-TUR AB 25); 2 *Point*; 7 *Zhuk* (3 ex-UKR)

DEPLOYMENT

CENTRAL AFRICAN REPUBLIC: EU • EUTM RCA 35
MALI: EU • EUTM Mali 1

TERRITORY WHERE THE GOVERNMENT DOES NOT EXERCISE EFFECTIVE CONTROL

Following the August 2008 war between Russia and Georgia, the areas of Abkhazia and South Ossetia declared themselves independent. Data presented here represents the de facto situation and does not imply international recognition as sovereign states.

FOREIGN FORCES

Russia ε4,000; 1 mil base at Gudauta (Abkhazia) with 1 MR bde(-); 1 SAM regt with S-300PS; 1 mil base at Djava/Tskhinvali (S. Ossetia) with 1 MR bde(-)

Kazakhstan KAZ

Kazakhstani Tenge KZT		2021	2022	2023
GDP	KZT	84.0tr	103tr	
	USD	197bn	224bn	
per capita	USD	10,306	11,591	
Growth	%	4.1	2.5	
Inflation	%	8.0	14.0	
Def bdgt	KZT	655bn	859bn	
	USD	1.54bn	1.88bn	
USD1=KZT		425.91	457.73	

Real-terms defence budget trend (USDbn, constant 2015): 1.11–1.85 (2008–2022)

Population 19,398,331

Age	0–14	15–19	20–24	25–29	30–64	65 plus
Male	12.5%	3.6%	3.1%	3.7%	21.4%	3.2%
Female	13.2%	3.4%	3.0%	3.6%	23.4%	5.8%

Capabilities

Kazakhstan's October 2017 military doctrine indicates a change in focus from countering violent extremism towards a wider concern for border security and hybrid threats. In 2022, this doctrine was updated by consolidating the authority of the president's office, enhancing the capabilities of the National Guard to respond to domestic disorder, strengthening of cyber and information capabilities across all security agencies, and creating a new military territorial directorate. Kazakhstan entered a bilateral military agreement with Uzbekistan in September 2017 to cooperate on training and education, countering violent extremism and reducing militant movements in their region. There has traditionally been a close defence relationship with Russia, reinforced by CSTO and SCO membership. Moscow operates a radar station at Balkash. In January 2022, Russian troops led a brief CSTO mission to the country following anti-government protests. Kazakhstan takes part in regional and CSTO exercises, including anti-terror drills. However, Kazakhstan also in 2022 sent humanitarian aid to Ukraine and did not recognise the independence of the Luhansk and Donetsk 'people's republics.' By regional standards, the armed forces are relatively sizeable and well equipped, following the acquisition of significant amounts of new and upgraded materiel in recent years, primarily from Russia. Russia has supplied Kazakhstan with S-300PS self-propelled surface-to-air missile systems as part of a Joint Air-Defence Agreement, boosting its long-range air-defence capability. Kazakhstan is expanding its indigenous defence industry, and joint ventures and the production of rotary-wing and medium-lift fixed-wing aircraft are envisaged with European companies. In 2021 following a two-day summit of the CSTO and in light of instability in Taliban-led Afghanistan, it was announced that Kazakhstan's military-industrial complex will be used to expand the CSTO's defense capabilities. However, Kazakhstan announced in August 2022 that it would suspend arms exports for one year.

ACTIVE 39,000 (Army 20,000 Navy 3,000 Air 12,000 MoD 4,000) **Gendarmerie & Paramilitary 31,500**
Conscript liability 12 months (due to be abolished)

Russia and Eurasia **179**

ORGANISATIONS BY SERVICE

Army 20,000

4 regional comd: Astana, East, West and Southern

FORCES BY ROLE

MANOEUVRE

Armoured

2 tk bde

2 mech bde

1 aslt bde

Mechanised

1 naval inf bde

1 (peacekeeping) inf regt

Air Manoeuvre

4 air aslt bde

COMBAT SUPPORT

3 arty bde

1 SSM unit

3 cbt engr regt

EQUIPMENT BY TYPE

ARMOURED FIGHTING VEHICLES

MBT 350 T-72BA

TSV 3 BMPT

RECCE 100: 40 BRDM-2; 60 BRM-1

IFV 413: 280 BMP-2; 70 BTR-80A; 63 BTR-82A

APC 340

APC (T) 50 MT-LB

APC (W) 152: 2 BTR-3E; 150 BTR-80

PPV 138: 138 *Arlan*

AUV 17+: 17 *Cobra; SandCat*

ENGINEERING & MAINTENANCE VEHICLES

AEV MT-LB

ANTI-TANK/ANTI-INFRASTRUCTURE

MSL

SP 6+: HMMWV with 9K111-1 *Konkurs* (RS-AT-5 *Spandrel*); 6 9P149 *Shturm* (MT-LB with RS-AT-6 *Spiral*)

MANPATS 9K111 *Fagot* (RS-AT-4 *Spigot*); 9K111-1 *Konkurs* (RS-AT-5 *Spandrel*); 9K115 *Metis* (RS-AT-7 *Saxhorn*)

GUNS 100mm 20 MT-12

ARTILLERY 490

SP 126: **122mm** 66: 60 2S1 *Gvozdika*; 6 *Semser*; **152mm** 60 2S3M *Akatsiya*

TOWED 194: **122mm** 100 D-30; **152mm** 94: 70 2A65 *Msta-B*; 24 D-20

MRL 107: **122mm** 80 BM-21 *Grad*; **220mm** 3 TOS-1A; **300mm** 24: 6 BM-30 *Smerch*; 18 IMI *Lynx* (with 50 msl)

MOR 63+: **82mm** some; **SP 120mm** 18 *Cardom*; **120mm** 45 2B11 *Sani*/M120

SURFACE-TO-SURFACE MISSILE LAUNCHERS

SRBM • Conventional 12 9K79 *Tochka* (RS-SS-21 *Scarab*)

Navy 3,000

EQUIPMENT BY TYPE

PATROL AND COASTAL COMBATANTS 14

PCGM 3 *Kazakhstan* with 1 4-cell lnchr with 4 *Barrier-VK* SSM, 1 *Arbalet-K* lnchr with 4 9K38 *Igla* (RS-SA-18 *Grouse*), 1 AK630 CIWS

PCC 1 *Kazakhstan* with 1 122mm MRL

PBF 3 *Sea Dolphin*

PB 7: 3 *Archangel*; 1 *Dauntless*; 1 *Lashyn*; 1 *Turk* (AB 25); 1 Other

MINE WARFARE • MINE COUNTERMEASURES 1

MCC 1 *Alatau* (Project 10750E)

LOGISTICS AND SUPPORT • AGS 1 *Zhaik*

Air Force 12,000 (incl Air Defence)

FORCES BY ROLE

FIGHTER

1 sqn with MiG-29/MiG-29UB *Fulcrum* A/B

2 sqn with MiG-31B/MiG-31BM *Foxhound* A/C

FIGHTER/GROUND ATTACK

1 sqn with MiG-27 *Flogger* D; MiG-23UB *Flogger* C

1 sqn with Su-27/Su-27UB *Flanker* B/C

1 sqn with Su-27/Su-30SM *Flanker* B/H

GROUND ATTACK

1 sqn with Su-25 *Frogfoot*

TRANSPORT

1 unit with Tu-134 *Crusty*; Tu-154 *Careless*

1 sqn with An-12 *Cub*, An-26 *Curl*, An-30 *Clank*, An-72 *Coaler*, C295M

TRAINING

1 sqn with L-39 *Albatros*

ATTACK HELICOPTER

5 sqn with Mi-24V *Hind*

TRANSPORT HELICOPTER

Some sqn with Bell 205 (UH-1H *Iroquois*); H145; Mi-8 *Hip*; Mi-17V-5 *Hip*; Mi-171Sh *Hip*; Mi-26 *Halo*

AIR DEFENCE

1 bty with 9K317M2 Buk-M2E (RS-SA-17 *Grizzly*)

2 bty with S-75M *Volkhov* (RS-SA-2 *Guideline*)

1 bty with S-125-1T

1 bty with S-200 *Angara* (RS-SA-5 *Gammon*)

10 bty with S-300PS (RS-SA-10 *Grumble*)

Some regt with 2K12 *Kub* (RS-SA-6 *Gainful*)

EQUIPMENT BY TYPE

AIRCRAFT 120 combat capable

FTR 45: 12 MiG-29 *Fulcrum* A; 2 MiG-29UB *Fulcrum* B; 31 MiG-31/MiG-31BM *Foxhound*

FGA 61: 12 MiG-27 *Flogger* D; 2 MiG-23UB *Flogger* C; 20 Su-27 *Flanker*; 4 Su-27UB *Flanker*; 23 Su-30SM *Flanker* H

ATK 14: 12 Su-25 *Frogfoot*; 2 Su-25UB *Frogfoot*

ISR 1 An-30 *Clank*

TPT 21: **Medium** 2 An-12 *Cub*; **Light** 18: 6 An-26 *Curl*, 2 An-72 *Coaler*; 8 C295; 2 Tu-134 *Crusty*; **PAX** 1 Tu-154 *Careless*

TRG 19: 17 L-39 *Albatros*; 2 Z-242L

HELICOPTERS

ATK 32: 20 Mi-24V *Hind* (some upgraded); 12 Mi-35M *Hind*

MRH 26: 20 Mi-17V-5 *Hip*; 6 Mi-171Sh *Hip*

TPT 16: **Heavy** 4 Mi-26 *Halo*; **Light** 12: 4 Bell 205 (UH-1H *Iroquois*); 8 H145

UNINHABITED AERIAL VEHICLES

CISR • Heavy 2 *Wing Loong* (GJ-1)

AIR DEFENCE • SAM

Long-range 43+: 3 S-200 *Angara* (RS-SA-5 *Gammon*); 40+ S-300PS (RS-SA-10B *Grumble*)

Medium-range 15: 3 9K317M2 *Buk*-M2E (RS-SA-17 *Grizzly*); 12 S-75M *Volkhov* (RS-SA-2 *Guideline*)

Short-range 3+: some 2K12 *Kub* (RS-SA-6 *Gainful*); 3 S-125-1T

Point-defence 9K35 *Strela*-10 (RS-SA-13 *Gopher*)

AIR-LAUNCHED MISSILES

AAM • IR R-27T (RS-AA-10B *Alamo*); R-60 (RS-AA-8 *Aphid*); R-73 (RS-AA-11A *Archer*); **SARH** R-27ER (RS-AA-10C *Alamo*); R-27R (RS-AA-10A *Alamo*); R-33 (RS-AA-9A *Amos*); **ARH** R-77 (RS-AA-12A *Adder* – on MiG-31BM)

ASM Kh-25 (RS-AS-10 *Karen*); Kh-29 (RS-AS-14 *Kedge*)

ARM Kh-27 (RS-AS-12 *Kegler*); Kh-58 (RS-AS-11 *Kilter*)

Gendarmerie & Paramilitary 31,500

National Guard ε20,000

Ministry of Interior

EQUIPMENT BY TYPE
ARMOURED FIGHTING VEHICLE
APC
APC (W) Kamaz-43629 *Vystrel*
PPV *Ural*-VV
AIRCRAFT
TPT • Medium 1 Y-8F-200WA

State Security Service 2,500

Border Service ε9,000

Ministry of Interior

EQUIPMENT BY TYPE
AIRCRAFT 6: **Light** 5: 3 An-26 *Curl*; 1 An-74T; 1 An-74TK; **PAX** 1 SSJ-100
HELICOPTERS • TPT • Medium 15: 1 Mi-171; 14 Mi-171Sh

Coast Guard

EQUIPMENT BY TYPE
PATROL AND COASTAL COMBATANTS 25
PBF 12: 2 *Aibar* (Project 0210); 8 FC-19; 2 *Saygak*
PB 13: 7 *Almaty*; 6 *Sardar*

DEPLOYMENT

LEBANON: UN • UNIFIL 9

WESTERN SAHARA: UN • MINURSO 6

Kyrgyzstan KGZ

Kyrgyzstani Som KGS		2021	2022	2023
GDP	KGS	723bn	853bn	
	USD	8.54bn	9.75bn	
per capita	USD	1,283	1,435	
Growth	%	3.7	3.8	
Inflation	%	11.9	13.5	
Def bdgt	KGS	n.k	n.k	
	USD	n.k	n.k	
USD1=KGS			84.69	87.45

Population	6,071,750

Age	0–14	15–19	20–24	25–29	30–64	65 plus
Male	15.3%	4.2%	3.7%	4.1%	19.2%	2.4%
Female	14.5%	4.0%	3.6%	4.0%	21.0%	3.9%

Capabilities

Kyrgyzstan has started to expand its ties with its neighbours on issues such as defence-industrial cooperation, though it remains generally dependent on Russian assistance for its defence requirements. Kyrgyzstan is a member of both the CSTO and the SCO. However, Kyrgyzstan cancelled CSTO command staff exercises at the last minute in 2022 following heightened border tensions with Tajikistan. Moscow maintains a military presence, including a squadron of Su-25SM ground-attack aircraft at Kant air base, which it has leased since 2003. Plans were reported in 2020 to add air-defence systems and UAVs to the Russian air base. In 2020, Kyrgyzstan increased its annual fees, reportedly because Russian forces are using more land than outlined in the 2003 agreement. Talks are ongoing over a possible second Russian base. Joint training is held with regional countries, including on anti-terror drills, but combat readiness remains an issue. In 2021, Indian and Kyrgyz special forces held the eighth iteration of bilateral exercises that focus on high-altitude and mountain operations in the broader context of counter-terrorism missions. Kyrgyzstan has a limited capability to deploy externally, and personnel have been deployed to OSCE and UN missions. The armed forces possess ageing land equipment and limited air capabilities, relying instead on Russian support, training and deployments. There is little local defence industry, although in 2018 Kazakhstan and Kyrgyzstan discussed defence-industrial cooperation. Defence ties with India have increased and a joint working group has been formed on defence cooperation. Reports in 2019 that India might provide a credit line to enable Kyrgyzstan to make defence purchases have yet to transpire. Reports in 2020 indicated discussions with Russia over the transfer of air-defence equipment and helicopters.

ACTIVE 10,900 (Army 8,500 Air 2,400) Gendarmerie & Paramilitary 9,500

Conscript liability 18 months

ORGANISATIONS BY SERVICE

Army 8,500

FORCES BY ROLE
SPECIAL FORCES
1 SF bde

MANOEUVRE
Mechanised
2 MR bde
1 (mtn) MR bde
COMBAT SUPPORT
1 arty bde
1 AD bde
EQUIPMENT BY TYPE
ARMOURED FIGHTING VEHICLES
MBT 150 T-72
RECCE 39: 30 BRDM-2; 9 BRDM-2M
IFV 320: 230 BMP-1; 90 BMP-2
APC • APC (W) 55: 25 BTR-70; 20 BTR-70M; 10 BTR-80
ANTI-TANK/ANTI-INFRASTRUCTURE
MSL • MANPATS 9K11 *Malyutka* (RS-AT-3 *Sagger*); 9K111 *Fagot* (RS-AT-4 *Spigot*); 9K111-1 *Konkurs* (RS-AT-5 *Spandrel*)
RCL 73mm SPG-9
GUNS 100mm 36: 18 MT-12/T-12; 18 M-1944
ARTILLERY 228
SP 122mm 18 2S1 *Gvozdika*
TOWED 123: 122mm 107: 72 D-30; 35 M-30 (M-1938); 152mm 16 D-1
GUN/MOR 120mm 12 2S9 NONA-S
MRL 21: 122mm 15 BM-21; 220mm 6 9P140 *Uragan*
MOR 120mm 54: 6 2S12; 48 M-120
AIR DEFENCE
SAM • Point-defence 9K32 *Strela*-2 (RS-SA-7 *Grail*)‡; 9K35 *Strela*-10 (RS-SA-13 *Gopher*)
GUNS 48
SP 23mm 24 ZSU-23-4
TOWED 57mm 24 S-60

Air Force 2,400
FORCES BY ROLE
FIGHTER
1 regt with L-39 *Albatros**
TRANSPORT
1 regt with An-2 *Colt*; An-26 *Curl*
ATTACK/TRANSPORT HELICOPTER
1 regt with Mi-24 *Hind*; Mi-8 *Hip*
AIR DEFENCE
2 bty with S-125 *Neva*-M1 (RS-SA-3 *Goa*)
1 bty with S-75M3 *Dvina* (RS-SA-2 *Guideline*)
EQUIPMENT BY TYPE
AIRCRAFT 4 combat capable
TPT • Light 6: 4 An-2 *Colt*; 2 An-26 *Curl*
TRG 4 L-39 *Albatros**
HELICOPTERS
ATK 2 Mi-24 *Hind*
MRH 4 Mi-8MT *Hip*
TPT • Medium 8 Mi-8 *Hip*
AIR DEFENCE • SAM
Medium-range 6 S-75M3 *Dvina* (RS-SA-2 *Guideline*)
Short-range 8 S-125M1 *Neva*-M1 (RS-SA-3 *Goa*)

Gendarmerie & Paramilitary 9,500
Border Guards 5,000 (KGZ conscript, RUS officers)
EQUIPMENT BY TYPE
ARMOURED FIGHTING VEHICLES
AUV 54 *Tigr*

Internal Troops 3,500

National Guard 1,000

DEPLOYMENT
SOUTH SUDAN: UN • UNMISS 1
SUDAN: UN • UNISFA 2

FOREIGN FORCES
Russia ε500 Military Air Forces: 13 Su-25SM *Frogfoot*; 2 Mi-8 *Hip*

Moldova MDA

Moldovan Leu MDL		2021	2022	2023
GDP	MDL	242bn	278bn	
	USD	13.7bn	14.0bn	
per capita	USD	5,285	5,529	
Growth	%	13.9	0.0	
Inflation	%	5.1	28.5	
Def bdgt	MDL	914m	902m	
	USD	51.7m	45.5m	
USD1=MDL		17.69	19.80	

Real-terms defence budget trend (USDm, constant 2015)

Population	3,287,326					
Age	0–14	15–19	20–24	25–29	30–64	65 plus
Male	9.4%	3.0%	2.8%	3.3%	24.5%	6.0%
Female	8.8%	2.8%	2.6%	3.1%	24.8%	9.0%

Capabilities

The primary role of Moldova's armed forces is to maintain territorial integrity, though their size means they would be unable to offer more than very limited resistance to a determined adversary. The country is constitutionally neutral. Tensions with Russia over the breakaway region of Transnistria, which Moscow supports, worsened following Russia's February 2022 invasion of Ukraine. Russia alleged its 'peace-keeping' forces in Transnistria had been threatened, a claim Moldova rejected, instead arguing it was a Russian attempt to destabilise the government. A state of emergency was declared after the February 2022 invasion of Ukraine. Moldova continues to build relations with European states and with NATO. The June 2022 NATO Summit in Madrid agreed measures to support Moldova's 'national resilience and civil preparedness'. A Long-Term Military Capabilities Development Plan was

182 THE MILITARY BALANCE 2023

approved in March 2020, covering the period to 2030, with a review of the goals to be concluded by the end of 2022. There is an emphasis on improving land forces mobility and in developing more capable ground-based air defence. The services exercise regularly with NATO states. Moldova has no requirement or capability to independently deploy and support its forces overseas, though personnel again deployed to the NATO-led KFOR mission during 2022. The country has no defence-industrial capabilities beyond the basic maintenance of front-line equipment. The country aims to move to an all-professional army and end conscription. The goal of achieving this by the end of 2021, however, was not met.

ACTIVE 5,150 (Army 3,250 Air 600 Logistic Support 1,300) Gendarmerie & Paramilitary 900

Conscript liability 12 months (3 months for university graduates)

RESERVE 58,000 (Joint 58,000)

ORGANISATIONS BY SERVICE

Army 1,300; 1,950 conscript (total 3,250)

FORCES BY ROLE
SPECIAL FORCES
1 SF bn
MANOEUVRE
Light
3 mot inf bde
1 lt inf bn
Other
1 gd bn
COMBAT SUPPORT
1 arty bn
1 engr bn
1 NBC coy
1 sigs bn
EQUIPMENT BY TYPE
ARMOURED FIGHTING VEHICLES
APC 153
APC (T) 61: 9 BTR-D; 52 MT-LB (variants)
APC (W) 92: 12 BTR-80; 80 TAB-71
ABCV 44 BMD-1
ANTI-TANK/ANTI-INFRASTRUCTURE
MSL • MANPATS 9K111 *Fagot* (RS-AT-4 *Spigot*); 9K111-1 *Konkurs* (RS-AT-5 *Spandrel*)
RCL 73mm SPG-9
GUNS 100mm 31 MT-12
ARTILLERY 219
TOWED 67: 122mm 16 M-30 (M-1938); 152mm 51: 20 2A36 *Giatsint*-B; 31 D-20
GUN/MOR • SP 120mm 9 2S9 NONA-S
MRL 220mm 11 9P140 *Uragan*
MOR 132: 82mm 75 BM-37; 120mm 57: 50 M-1989; 7 PM-38
AIR DEFENCE • GUNS • TOWED 39: 23mm 28 ZU-23; 57mm 11 S-60

Air Force 600 (incl 250 conscripts)

FORCES BY ROLE
TRANSPORT
1 sqn with An-2 *Colt*; Mi-8MTV-1/PS *Hip*; Yak-18
AIR DEFENCE
1 regt with S-125M1 *Neva*-M1 (RS-SA-3 *Goa*)
EQUIPMENT BY TYPE
AIRCRAFT
TPT • Light 3: 2 An-2 *Colt*; 1 Yak-18 *Max*
HELICOPTERS
TPT • Medium 6: 2 Mi-8PS *Hip*; 4 Mi-8MTV-1 *Hip*
AIR DEFENCE • SAM • Short-range 3 S-125M1 *Neva*-M1 (RS-SA-3 *Goa*)

Gendarmerie & Paramilitary 900

Special Police Brigade 900
Ministry of Interior

DEPLOYMENT

CENTRAL AFRICAN REPUBLIC: UN • MINUSCA 4

LEBANON: UN • UNIFIL 4

MALI: EU • EUTM Mali 1

SERBIA: NATO • KFOR 41; **UN** • UNMIK 1

SOUTH SUDAN: UN • UNMISS 3

TERRITORY WHERE THE GOVERNMENT DOES NOT EXERCISE EFFECTIVE CONTROL

Data presented here represents the de facto situation in the territory of Transnistria and does not imply international recognition.

FOREIGN FORCES

Russia ε1,500 (including 400 peacekeepers); 7 Mi-24 *Hind*/ Mi-8 *Hip*

Russia RUS

Russian Rouble RUB		2021	2022	2023
GDP	RUB	131tr	149tr	
	USD	1.78tr	2.13tr	
per capita	USD	12,219	14,665	
Growth	%	4.7	-3.4	
Inflation	%	6.7	13.8	
Def exp [a]	RUB	4.86tr	6.15tr	
	USD	66.0bn	87.9bn	
Def bdgt	RUB	3.58tr	4.68tr	4.98tr
	USD	48.5bn	66.9bn	
USD1=RUB		73.66	70.00	

[a] Calculated to be comparable with NATO definition of defence expenditure

Real-terms defence budget trend (USDbn, constant 2015)

Population 142,021,981

Age	0–14	15–19	20–24	25–29	30–64	65 plus
Male	8.8%	2.7%	2.3%	2.6%	24.5%	5.4%
Female	8.3%	2.5%	2.2%	2.5%	27.0%	11.2%

Capabilities

Russia supports large conventional military forces and retains the world's second-largest nuclear arsenal. However, its 2022 full-scale invasion of Ukraine exposed weaknesses in terms of leadership, planning, personnel, and equipment, particularly in the ground and airborne forces, when faced with a committed opponent. A lack of airborne intelligence, surveillance and reconnaissance systems has also been evident. Russian ground forces, in particular, have suffered heavy personnel and equipment losses. Estimates of personnel losses vary widely but some units became combat ineffective. The ground forces have lost a large number of main battle tanks and armoured fighting vehicles, while the conflict also exposed the relative vulnerability of VDV units and their armour when faced with an opponent well-equipped with heavier assets. The navy and air force have also suffered reverses, including the sinking of the *Slava*-class cruiser *Moskva* and losses of modern combat aircraft and helicopters. The invasion of Ukraine reflects the armed forces' role in Russia's foreign policy. Military aims are guaranteeing sovereignty and territorial integrity as well as maintaining and increasing Russia's influence in its near abroad and further afield. An updated National Security Policy was adopted in June 2021 extending beyond core military concerns to include countering the influence of the US and its allies. The 2021–2025 Defence Plan was also agreed, though this remains classified. The defence ministry has also been working on a follow-on to the State Armament Programme (SAP) 2027, SAP 2033. It remains unclear how far the current SAP and its successor will need to be re-shaped to accommodate the costs of the Ukraine war, including Russia's considerable equipment losses. Russia is a leading member of both the CSTO and the SCO. An updated CSTO security strategy is planned, to cover 2026–2030. Moscow, as of October 2022, was having to continue to manage tensions within the CSTO resulting from member states' differing responses to the Armenia—Azerbaijan conflict in 2020, renewed skirmishes between the two in September 2022 and also stemming from the war in Ukraine. In January 2022, Russian forces briefly deployed to Kazakhstan, after Almaty appealed to the CSTO in the wake of anti-government protests. Prior to the February 2022 invasion of Ukraine, volunteers outweighed conscripts in the armed forces. Defence reforms launched in 2008 had emphasised the shift from a conscript-based mass-mobilisation army to smaller, more professional ground forces. However, the limits of Russia's professionalisation process have become evident in Ukraine. Setbacks and losses in Ukraine led President Vladimir Putin to introduce a partial mobilisation in September 2022, a move in itself that appeared to have been poorly executed initially. The armed forces can independently deploy and sustain forces on a global scale, although likely only in modest size at extended distances. Ground force losses in Ukraine, however, may further limit the size, and the competency, of the units Moscow is able to deploy. Russia continues to modernise its nuclear and conventional weapons. The SAP 2020 was broadly successful, although several of the more ambitious procurement goals were not met. SAP 2027 continues the emphasis on modernisation, though some aims are more modest. Russia can design, develop, and manufacture advanced nuclear and conventional weaponry. Its defence-industrial base suffered from a lack of investment in the 1990s, and more recently from the loss of access to Ukrainian components. Tighter Western sanctions after the February 2022 invasion of Ukraine will further restrict the supply of foreign components. The defence-aerospace sector has been notably successful in terms of exports, particularly of combat aircraft and surface-to-air missile systems.

ACTIVE 1,190,000 (Army 550,000 Navy 145,000 Air 165,000 Strategic Rocket Force 50,000 Airborne 40,000 Special Operations Forces 1,000 Railway Forces 29,000 1st & 2nd Army Corps 30,000 Command and Support 180,000) **Gendarmerie & Paramilitary 559,000**

Conscript liability 12 months (conscripts now can opt for contract service immediately, which entails a 24-month contract)

RESERVE 1,500,000 (all arms)

Some 1,500,000 with service within last 5 years; reserve obligation to age 50

ORGANISATIONS BY SERVICE

Strategic Deterrent Forces ε80,000 (incl personnel assigned from the Navy and Aerospace Forces)

Navy
EQUIPMENT BY TYPE
SUBMARINES • STRATEGIC • SSBN 11:
  6 *Delfin* (Project 667BDRM (*Delta* IV)) with 16 R-29RMU2 *Sineva*/R-29RMU2.1 *Layner* (RS-SS-N-23 *Skiff*) nuclear SLBM, 4 single 533mm TT with 53-65K HWT/SET-65K HWT/USET-80K *Keramika* HWT
  3 *Borey* (Project 955 (*Dolgorukiy*)) with 16 *Bulava* (RS-SS-N-32) nuclear SLBM, 6 single 533mm TT with USET-80K *Keramika* HWT/UGST *Fizik* HWT
  2 *Borey*-A (Project 955A) with 16 *Bulava* (RS-SS-N-32) nuclear SLBM, 6 single 533mm TT with USET-80K *Keramika* HWT/UGST *Fizik* HWT

Strategic Rocket Forces 50,000

3 Rocket Armies operating silo and mobile launchers organised in 12 divs. Regt normally with 6 to 10 silos or 9 mobile launchers, and one control centre

FORCES BY ROLE
SURFACE-TO-SURFACE MISSILE
1 ICBM regt with RS-12M *Topol* (RS-SS-25 *Sickle*)
8 ICBM regt with RS-12M2 *Topol*-M (RS-SS-27 mod 1)
2 ICBM regt with RS-18 (RS-SS-19 *Stiletto*)
1 ICBM regt with RS-18 with Avangard HGV (RS-SS-19 mod 4 *Stiletto*)
8 ICBM regt with RS-20 (RS-SS-18 *Satan*)
14 ICBM regt with RS-24 *Yars* (RS-SS-27 mod 2)
7 ICBM regt with *Yars*-S

EQUIPMENT BY TYPE
SURFACE-TO-SURFACE MISSILE LAUNCHERS
ICBM • Nuclear 339: 9 RS-12M *Topol* (RS-SS-25 *Sickle*) (mobile single warhead); 60 RS-12M2 *Topol*-M (RS-SS-27 mod 1) silo-based (single warhead); 18 RS-12M2 *Topol*-M (RS-SS-27 mod 1) road mobile (single warhead); up to 20 RS-18 (RS-SS-19 *Stiletto*) (mostly mod 3, 6 MIRV per msl) (being withdrawn); ε6 RS-18 with *Avangard* HGV (RS-SS-19 mod 4 *Stiletto*); 46 RS-20 (RS-SS-18 *Satan*) (mostly mod 5, 10 MIRV per msl); ε99 RS-24 *Yars* (RS-SS-27 mod 2; ε3 MIRV per msl) road mobile; ε18 RS-24 *Yars* (RS-SS-27 mod 2; ε3 MIRV per msl) silo-based; ε63 *Yars*-S (ε3 MIRV per msl) road mobile
COUNTERSPACE • DE • Laser *Peresvet*

Long-Range Aviation Command

FORCES BY ROLE
BOMBER
1 sqn with Tu-160/Tu-160 mod *Blackjack*
3 sqn with Tu-95MS/MS mod *Bear*

EQUIPMENT BY TYPE
AIRCRAFT
BBR 76: 9 Tu-160 *Blackjack* with Kh-55SM (RS-AS-15B *Kent*) nuclear LACM; 7 Tu-160 mod *Blackjack* with Kh-55SM (RS-AS-15B *Kent*)/Kh-102 (RS-AS-23B *Kodiak*) nuclear LACM; 42 Tu-95MS *Bear* H with Kh-55SM (RS-AS-15B *Kent*) nuclear LACM; 18 Tu-95MS mod *Bear* H with Kh-55SM (RS-AS-15B *Kent*)/Kh-102 (RS-AS-23B *Kodiak*) nuclear LACM

Space Command

EQUIPMENT BY TYPE
SATELLITES 89
COMMUNICATIONS 32: 4 *Blagovest*; 1 *Garpun*; 3 *Globus*-M (*Raduga*-1M); 6 *Meridian*; 3 *Meridian*-M; 15 *Rodnik*-S (*Strela*-3M)
POSITIONING, NAVIGATION & TIMING 27: 3 GLONASS-K1; 24 GLONASS-M
ISR 10: 3 *Bars*-M; 2 GEO-IK-2; 1 *Neitron*; 2 *Persona*; 2 *Resurs*-P
ELINT/SIGINT 8: 6 *Lotos*-S; 1 *Pion*-NKS; 1 *Tselina*-2

EARLY WARNING 5 *Tundra* (EKS)
RENDEZVOUS & PROXIMITY OPERATIONS 7: 6 *Nivelir*; 1 *Olymp*-K (*Luch*)
MISSILE DEFENCE some S-500 (entering service)
RADAR 12; Russia leases ground-based radar stations in Baranovichi (Belarus) and Balkhash (Kazakhstan). It also has radars on its own territory at Lekhtusi (St Petersburg); Armavir (Krasnodar); Olenegorsk (Murmansk); Mishelevka (Irkutsk); Kaliningrad; Pechora (Komi); Yeniseysk (Krasnoyarsk); Baranul (Altayskiy); Orsk (Orenburg); and Gorodets/Kovylkino (OTH)

Aerospace Defence Command

FORCES BY ROLE
AIR DEFENCE
2 AD div HQ
4 SAM regt with S-300PM1/PM2 (RS-SA-20 *Gargoyle*)
5 SAM regt with S-400 (RS-SA-21 *Growler*); 96K6 *Pantsir*-S1 (RS-SA-22 *Greyhound*)

EQUIPMENT BY TYPE
AIR DEFENCE
SAM • Long-range 186: 90 S-300PM1/PM2 (RS-SA-20 *Gargoyle*); 96 S-400 (RS-SA-21 *Growler*)
SPAAGM 30mm 36 96K6 *Pantsir*-S1 (RS-SA-22 *Greyhound*)
MISSILE DEFENCE 68 53T6 (RS-AB-4A *Gazelle*)
RADAR 1 BMD engagement system located at Sofrino (Moscow)

Army ε550,000 (incl ε100,000 conscripts & up to 300,000 mobilised personnel)

FORCES BY ROLE
As a result of heavy losses suffered during the invasion of Ukraine, almost all of the manoeuvre formations listed are currently significantly understrength and some are now effectively only cadre-sized until mobilised personnel can be drafted into them.
COMMAND
12 army HQ
1 corps HQ
SPECIAL FORCES
8 (Spetsnaz) SF bde
1 (Spetsnaz) SF regt
MANOEUVRE
Reconnaissance
2 recce bde
Armoured
1 (4th) tk div (1 armd recce bn, 2 tk regt, 1 MR regt, 1 arty regt, 1 AD regt)
1 (47th) tk div (1 tk regt)
1 (90th) tk div (1 armd recce bn, 2 tk regt, 1 MR regt, 1 arty regt)
1 tk bde (1 armd recce bn, 3 tk bn, 1 MR bn, 1 arty bn, 1 MRL bn, 2 AD bn, 1 engr bn, 1 EW coy, 1 NBC coy)
1 (3rd) MR corps (1 MR div, 1 MR bde, 1 SP arty bde, 1 fd arty regt)
2 (3rd & 144th) MR div (1 armd recce bn, 1 tk regt, 2 MR regt, 1 arty regt)
1 (19th) MR div (2 MR regt, 1 arty regt)
1 (20th) MR div (2 MR regt, 1 arty regt)
1 (127th) MR div (1 tk regt, 2 MR regt, 1 arty regt, 1 AD regt)

1 (150th) MR div (1 armd recce bn, 2 tk regt, 2 MR regt; 1 arty regt, 1 AD regt)

11 (BMP) MR bde (1 armd recce bn, 1 tk bn, 3 armd inf bn, 2 arty bn, 1 MRL bn, 1 AT bn, 2 AD bn, 1 engr bn, 1 EW coy, 1 NBC coy)

Mechanised
1 (2nd) MR div (1 armd recce bn, 1 tk regt, 2 MR regt, 1 arty regt, 1 AD regt)

1 (42nd) MR div (1 armd recce bn, 3 MR regt, 1 arty regt)

8 (BTR/MT-LB) MR bde (1 recce bn, 1 tk bn, 3 mech inf bn, 2 arty bn, 1 MRL bn, 1 AT bn, 2 AD bn, 1 engr bn,1 EW coy, 1 NBC coy)

2 MR bde (4–5 mech inf bn, 1 arty bn, 1 AD bn, 1 engr bn)

3 (lt/mtn) MR bde (1 recce bn, 2 mech inf bn, 1 arty bn)

1 (18th) MGA div (1 tk bn, 2 MGA regt, 1 arty regt, 2 AD bn)

SURFACE-TO-SURFACE MISSILE
12 SRBM/GLCM bde with 9K720 *Iskander*-M (RS-SS-26 *Stone*/RS-SSC-7 *Southpaw*) (3+ brigades also with 9M729 (RS-SSC-8 *Screwdriver*))

COMBAT SUPPORT
9 arty bde
1 hy arty bde
4 MRL bde
4 engr bde
7 engr regt
1 ptn br bde
5 EW bde
5 NBC bde
10 NBC regt

COMBAT SERVICE SUPPORT
11 log bde

AIR DEFENCE
16 AD bde

EQUIPMENT BY TYPE
Surface-to-surface missile systems may have very limited numbers of available missiles remaining.

ARMOURED FIGHTING VEHICLES
MBT 1,800: 150 T-62M/MV; 400 T-72B/BA; 500 T-72B3; 250 T-72B3M; 100 T-80BV/U; 100 T-80BVM; 200 T-90A; 100 T-90M; (5,000 T-62M/T-62MV/T-72/T-72A/T-72B/T-80B/T-80BV/T-80U/T-90/T-90A in store)

TSV ε9 BMPT

RECCE 700 BRM-1K (CP); (1,000+ BRDM-2/-2A in store)

IFV 4,150: 500 BMP-1/-1AM; 2,350 BMP-2/-2M; 400 BMP-3/-3M; 100 BTR-80A; 800 BTR-82A/AM; (4,000 BMP-1/-2 in store)

APC 5,350+

  APC (T) 3,050+: some BMO-T; 3,000 MT-LB; 50+ MT-LB VM1K; (2,000 MT-LB in store)

  APC (W) 2,300: 800 BTR-60 (all variants); 200 BTR-70 (all variants); 1,300 BTR-80; (4,000 BTR-60/70 in store)

  PPV *Typhoon*-K 4×4; *Typhoon*-K 6×6

AUV IVECO LMV; *Linza*; *Tigr*; *Tigr*-M; *Tigr*-M SpN; *Vystrel*

ENGINEERING & MAINTENANCE VEHICLES
AEV BAT-2; IMR; IMR-2; IMR-3; IRM; MT-LB

ARV BMP-1; BREM-1/64/K/L; BTR-50PK(B); M1977; MTP-LB; RM-G; T-54/55; VT-72A

VLB KMM; MT-55A; MTU; MTU-20; MTU-72; PMM-2

MW BMR-3M; GMX-3; MCV-2 (reported); MTK; MTK-2; UR-77

ANTI-TANK/ANTI-INFRASTRUCTURE
MSL

  SP 9P149 with 9K114 *Shturm* (RS-AT-6 *Spiral*); 9P149M with 9K132 *Shturm*-SM (RS-AT-9 *Spiral*-2); 9P157-2 with 9K123 *Khrizantema* (RS-AT-15 *Springer*); 9P163-3 with 9M133 *Kornet* (RS-AT-14 *Spriggan*); 9K128-1 *Kornet*-T (RS-AT-14 *Spriggan*)

  MANPATS 9K111M *Fagot* (RS-AT-4 *Spigot*); 9K111-1 *Konkurs* (RS-AT-5 *Spandrel*); 9K115 *Metis* (RS-AT-7 *Saxhorn*); 9K115-1 *Metis*-M (RS-AT-13); 9K115-2 *Metis*-M1 (RS-AT-13); 9K135 *Kornet* (RS-AT-14 *Spriggan*)

RCL 73mm SPG-9

GUNS • TOWED 100mm 520 MT-12 (**100mm** 1,000 T-12/MT-12 in store)

ARTILLERY 4,458
SP 1,678: **122mm** 130 2S1 *Gvozdika*; **152mm** 1,493: 700 2S3/2S3M *Akatsiya*; 85 2S5 *Giatsint*-S; 400 2S19/2S19M1 *Msta*-S; 300 2S19M2/2S33 *Msta*-SM; 8 2S35 *Koalitsiya*-SV (in test); **203mm** 55 2S7M *Malka* (4,260 in store: **122mm** 2,000 2S1 *Gvozdika*; **152mm** 2,000: 1,000 2S3 *Akatsiya*; 850 2S5 *Giatsint*-S; 150 2S19 *Msta*-S; **203mm** 260 2S7 *Pion*)

TOWED 220: **152mm** 220: 20+ D-1 (M-1943); 100 D-20; 100 2A65 *Msta*-B (7,190 in store: **122mm** 4,500: 2,500 D-30; 2,000 M-30 (M-1938); **130mm** 350 M-46; **152mm** 2,300: 600 2A36 *Giatsint*-B; 400 2A65 *Msta*-B; 500 D-1 (M-1943); 750 D-20; 100 M-1937 (ML-20); **203mm** 40 B-4M)

GUN/MOR 160

  SP 120mm 75: 27 2S23 NONA-SVK; 48 2S34

  TOWED 120mm 85 2B16 NONA-K

MRL 886: **122mm** 610: 450 BM-21 *Grad*; 160 9K51M *Tornado*-G; **220mm** 156+: 150 9P140 *Uragan*; 6 9K512 *Uragan*-1M; some TOS-1A; **300mm** 120: 100 9A52 *Smerch*; 20 9K515 *Tornado*-S; (3,220 in store: **122mm** 2,420: 2,000 BM-21 *Grad*; 420 9P138; **132mm** 100 BM-13; **220mm** 700 9P140 *Uragan*)

MOR 1,514: **82mm** 800+ 2B14; **120mm** 675 2S12 *Sani*; **240mm** 39 2S4 *Tulpan* (1,300 in store: **120mm** 950: 500 2S12 *Sani*; 450 M-1938 (PM-38); **160mm** 150 M-160; **SP 240mm** 200 2S4 *Tulpan*)

SURFACE-TO-SURFACE MISSILE LAUNCHERS
SRBM 200:

  Dual-capable 200: 50 9K79-1 *Tochka*-U (RS-SS-21B *Scarab*); 150 9K720 *Iskander*-M (RS-SS-26 *Stone*)

GLCM • Dual-capable Some 9M728 (RS-SSC-7 *Southpaw*); some 9M729 (RS-SSC-8 *Screwdriver*)

UNINHABITED AERIAL VEHICLES
ISR • Heavy Tu-243 *Reys*/Tu-243 *Reys* D (service status unclear); **Light** BLA-07; *Pchela*-1; *Pchela*-2

LOITERING & DIRECT ATTACK MUNITIONS
Geran 1 (*Shahed* 131); *Geran* 2 (*Shahed* 136); (multiple systems below 20kg in weight)

AIR DEFENCE
SAM 1,520+

  Long-range S-300V (RS-SA-12A/B *Gladiator*/*Giant*); S-300V4 (RS-SA-23)

  Medium-range 350: ε200 9K37M1-2 *Buk*-M1-2 (RS-SA-11 *Gadfly*); ε90 9K317 *Buk*-M2 (RS-SA-17 *Grizzly*); ε60 9K317M *Buk*-M3 (RS-SA-27)

  Short-range 120+ 9K331/9K331M/9K331MU *Tor*-M1/M2/M2U (RS-SA-15 *Gauntlet*) (9M338 msl entering service)

186 THE MILITARY BALANCE 2023

Point-defence 800+: 400 9K33M3 *Osa-AKM* (RS-SA-8B *Gecko*); 400 9K35M3 *Strela-10* (RS-SA-13 *Gopher*); 9K310 *Igla-1* (RS-SA-16 *Gimlet*); 9K34 *Strela-3* (RS-SA-14 *Gremlin*); 9K38 *Igla* (RS-SA-18 *Grouse*); 9K333 *Verba* (RS-SA-29 *Gizmo*); 9K338 *Igla-S* (RS-SA-24 *Grinch*)
SPAAGM 30mm 250+ 2K22M *Tunguska* (RS-SA-19 *Grison*)
GUNS
SP 23mm ZSU-23-4
TOWED 23mm ZU-23-2; **57mm** S-60

Navy ε145,000 (incl conscripts)

4 major fleet organisations (Northern Fleet, Pacific Fleet, Baltic Fleet, Black Sea Fleet) and Caspian Sea Flotilla

EQUIPMENT BY TYPE
SUBMARINES 51
STRATEGIC • SSBN 11:
6 *Delfin* (Project 667BDRM (*Delta* IV)) with 16 R-29RMU2 *Sineva*/R-29RMU2.1 *Layner* (RS-SS-N-23 *Skiff*) nuclear SLBM, 4 single 533mm TT with 53-65K HWT/SET-65K HWT/USET-80K *Keramika* HWT
3 *Borey* (Project 955 (*Dolgorukiy*)) with 16 *Bulava* (RS-SS-N-32) nuclear SLBM, 6 single 533mm TT with USET-80K *Keramika* HWT/UGST *Fizik* HWT
2 *Borey*-A (Project 955A) with 16 *Bulava* (RS-SS-N-32) nuclear SLBM, 6 single 533mm TT with USET-80K *Keramika* HWT/UGST *Fizik* HWT
TACTICAL 40
SSGN 9:
6 *Antey* (Project 949A (*Oscar* II)) (2 more non-operational, in long-term refit) with 24 single SM-225A lnchr with 3M45 *Granit* (RS-SS-N-19 *Shipwreck*) dual-capable AShM, 2 single 650mm TT each with T-65 HWT/RPK-7 (RS-SS-N-16 *Stallion*) ASW msl, 4 single 553mm TT with 53-65K HWT/SET-65K HWT/USET-80K *Keramika* HWT
1 *Yasen* (Project 885 (*Severodvinsk* I)) with 8 4-cell SM-346 VLS with 3M14K (RS-SS-N-30A *Sagaris*) dual-capable LACM/3M54K1 (RS-SS-N-27) AShM/3M54K (RS-SS-N-27B *Sizzler*) AShM/3M55 *Oniks* (RS-SS-N-26 *Strobile*) AShM (3M54K/K1 operational status unclear); 10 single 533mm TT with USET-80K *Keramika* HWT/UGST *Fizik* HWT
2 *Yasen*-M (Project 08851 (*Severodvinsk* II)) with 8 4-cell SM-346 VLS with 3M14K (RS-SS-N-30A *Sagaris*) dual-capable LACM/3M54K1 (RS-SS-N-27) AShM/3M54K (RS-SS-N-27B *Sizzler*) AShM/3M55 *Oniks* (RS-SS-N-26 *Strobile*) AShM (3M54K/K1 operational status unclear); up to 10 single 533mm TT with UGST *Fizik* HWT
SSN 10:
1 *Kalmar* (Project 667BDR (*Delta* III)) with 2 single 400mm TT with SET-72 LWT, 4 single 533mm TT with 53-65K HWT/SET-65K HWT/USET-80K *Keramika* HWT (re-roled SSBN)
2 *Kondor* (Project 945A (*Sierra* II)) with 4 single 533mm TT with TEST-71M HWT/USET-80K *Keramika* HWT (unclear if dual-capable 3M14 (RS-SS-N-30A *Sagaris*) has replaced 3M10 *Granat* (RS-SS-N-21 *Sampson*) nuclear LACM which

is possibly withdrawn; AShM capability unconfirmed), 4 single 650mm TT with 65-73 HWT
2 *Schuka* (Project 671RTMK (*Victor* III)) with 4 single 533mm TT with 53-65K HWT/SET-65K HWT/USET-80K *Keramika* HWT (unclear if dual-capable 3M14 (RS-SS-N-30A *Sagaris*) has replaced 3M10 *Granat* (RS-SS-N-21 *Sampson*) nuclear LACM which is possibly withdrawn; AShM capability unconfirmed), 2 single 650mm TT with 65-73 HWT
3 *Schuka*-B (Project 971 (*Akula* I)) (5 more non-operational, return to service significantly delayed) with 4 single 533mm TT with 53-65K HWT/TEST-71M HWT/USET-80K *Keramika* HWT (unclear if dual-capable 3M14 (RS-SS-N-30A *Sagaris*) has replaced 3M10 *Granat* (RS-SS-N-21 *Sampson*) nuclear LACM which is possibly withdrawn; AShM capability unconfirmed), 4 single 650mm TT with 65-73 HWT/RPK-7 (RS-SS-N-16 *Stallion*) ASW msl
2 *Schuka*-B (Project 971/09711 (*Akula* II)) with 4 single 533mm TT with 53-65K HWT/TEST-71M HWT/USET-80K *Keramika* HWT (unclear if dual-capable 3M14 (RS-SS-N-30A *Sagaris*) has replaced 3M10 *Granat* (RS-SS-N-21 *Sampson*) nuclear LACM which is possibly withdrawn; AShM capability unconfirmed), 4 single 650mm TT with 65-73 HWT/RPK-7 (RS-SS-N-16 *Stallion*) ASW msl
(1 *Barracuda* (Project 945 (*Sierra* I)) (in reserve) with 6 single 533mm TT with TEST-71M HWT/USET-80K *Keramika* HWT (unclear if dual-capable 3M14 (RS-SS-N-30A *Sagaris*) has replaced 3M10 *Granat* (RS-SS-N-21 *Sampson*) nuclear LACM which is possibly withdrawn; AShM capability unconfirmed))
SSK 21:
10 *Paltus* (Project 877 (*Kilo*)) (1 more non-operational, in long-term refit) with 6 single 533mm TT with 53-65K HWT/TEST-71M HWT/USET-80K *Keramika* HWT
10 *Varshavyanka* (Project 06363 (*Improved Kilo*)) with 6 single 533mm TT with 3M14K *Kalibr*-PL (RS-SS-N-30A *Sagaris*) dual-capable LACM/3M54K (RS-SS-N-27B *Sizzler*) AShM/3M54K1 (RS-SS-N-27) AShM/53-65K HWT/TEST-71M HWT/USET-80K *Keramika* HWT (3M54K/K1 operational status unclear)
1 *Lada* (Project 677 (*Petersburg*)) (in test) with 6 single 533mm TT with 3M14K *Kalibr*-PL (RS-SS-N-30A *Sagaris*) dual-capable LACM/3M54K (RS-SS-N-27B *Sizzler*) AShM/3M54K1 (RS-SS-N-27) AShM/USET-80K *Keramika* HWT (3M54K/K1 operational status unclear)
PRINCIPAL SURFACE COMBATANTS 31
AIRCRAFT CARRIERS • CV 1 *Admiral Kuznetsov* (in extended refit) with 12 single SM-233A lnchr with 3M45 *Granit* (RS-SS-N-19 *Shipwreck*) AShM, 24 8-cell 3S95 VLS with 3K95 *Kinzhal* (RS-SA-N-9 *Gauntlet*) SAM, 2 RBU 12000 *Udav* 1 A/S mor, 8 3M87 *Kortik* CIWS with 9M311 SAM (RS-CADS-N-1), 6 AK630M CIWS (capacity 18–24 Su-33 *Flanker* D/MiG-29KR/KUBR Ftr/FGA ac; 15 Ka-27 *Helix* ASW hel, 2 Ka-31R *Helix* AEW hel)
CRUISERS 3:
CGHMN 1 *Orlan* (Project 11442 (*Kirov* I)) (1 other non-operational; undergoing extensive refit and planned

to return to service in 2023) with 20 single SM-233 lnchr with 3M45 *Granit* (RS-SS-N-19 *Shipwreck*) AShM, 6 6-cell B-203A VLS with S-300F *Fort* (RS-SA-N-6 *Grumble*) SAM, 6 6-cell B-203A VLS with S-300FM *Fort*-M (RS-SA-N-20 *Gargoyle*) SAM, 16 8-cell 3S95 VLS with 3K95 *Kinzhal* (RS-SA-N-9 *Gauntlet*) SAM, 2 quintuple 533mm TT with RPK-6M *Vodopad*-NK (RS-SS-N-16 *Stallion*) A/S msl, 1 RBU 6000 *Smerch* 2 A/S mor, 2 RBU 1000 *Smerch* 3 A/S mor, 6 3M87 *Kortik* CIWS with 9M311 SAM (RS-CADS-N-1), 1 twin 130mm gun (capacity 3 Ka-27 *Helix* ASW hel)

CGHM 2 *Atlant* (Project 1164 (*Slava*)) with 8 twin SM-248 lnchr with 3M70 *Vulkan* (RS-SS-N-12 mod 2 *Sandbox*) AShM, 8 octuple VLS with S-300F *Fort* (RS-SA-N-6 *Grumble*) SAM/S-300FM *Fort* M (RS-SA-N-20 *Gargoyle*) SAM, 2 twin ZIF-122 lnchr with 4K33 *Osa*-M (RS-SA-N-4 *Gecko*) SAM, 2 quintuple 533mm PTA-53-1164 ASTT with SET-65K HWT, 2 RBU 6000 *Smerch* 2 A/S mor, 6 AK630 CIWS, 1 twin 130mm gun (capacity 1 Ka-27 *Helix* ASW hel)

DESTROYERS • DDGHM 11:

3 *Sarych* (Project 956 (*Sovremenny* I)) (1 more non-operational) with 2 quad lnchr with 3M80 *Moskit* (RS-SS-N-22 *Sunburn*) AShM, 2 twin 3S90 lnchr with 9M317 *Yezh* (RS-SA-N-7B) SAM, 2 twin DTA-53-956 533mm TT with 53-65K HWT/SET-65K HWT, 2 RBU 1000 *Smerch* 3 A/S mor, 4 AK630 CIWS, 2 twin 130mm guns (capacity 1 Ka-27 *Helix* ASW hel)

6 *Fregat* (Project 1155 (*Udaloy* I)) with 2 quad lnchr with URK-5 *Rastrub*-B (RS-SS-N-14 *Silex*) AShM/ASW, 8 8-cell 3S95 VLS with 3K95 *Kinzhal* (RS-SA-N-9 *Gauntlet*) SAM, 2 quad 533mm ChTA-53-1155 ASTT with 53-65K HWT/SET-65K HWT, 2 RBU 6000 *Smerch* 2 A/S mor, 4 AK630 CIWS, 2 100mm guns (capacity 2 Ka-27 *Helix* ASW hel)

1 *Fregat* (Project 1155 (*Udaloy* I)) with 2 8-cell 3S14 UKSK VLS with with 3M14T *Kalibr*-NK (RS-SS-N-30A *Sagaris*) dual-capable LACM/3M54T (RS-SS-N-27B *Sizzler*) AShM/3M54T1 (RS-SS-N-27) AShM/3M55 *Oniks* (RS-SS-N-26 *Strobile*) AShM (3M54T/T1 operational status unclear), 2 quad lnchr with 3M24 *Uran* (RS-SS-N-25 *Switchblade*) AShM, 2 quad 533mm ChTA-53-1155 ASTT with 53-65K HWT/SET-65K HWT, 2 RBU 6000 *Smerch* 2 A/S mor, 4 AK630 CIWS, 1 100mm gun (capacity 2 Ka-27 *Helix* ASW hel)

1 *Fregat* (Project 11551 (*Udaloy* II)) (in refit) with 2 quad lnchr with 3M80 *Moskit* (RS-SS-N-22 *Sunburn*) AShM, 8 8-cell 3S95 VLS with 3K95 *Kinzhal* (RS-SA-N-9 *Gauntlet*) SAM, 2 3M87 *Kortik* CIWS with 9M311 SAM (RS-CADS-N-1), 2 RBU 6000 *Smerch* 2 A/S mor, 1 twin 130mm gun (capacity 2 Ka-27 *Helix* ASW hel)

FRIGATES 16

FFGHM 14:

3 Project 11356 (*Grigorovich*) with 1 8-cell 3S14 UKSK VLS with 3M14T *Kalibr*-NK (RS-SS-N-30A *Sagaris*) dual-capable LACM/3M54T (RS-SS-N-27B *Sizzler*) AShM/3M54T1 (RS-SS-N-27) AShM/3M55 *Oniks* (RS-SS-N-26 *Strobile*) AShM/91RT2 A/S msl (3M54T/T1 operational status unclear),

2 12-cell 3S90.1 VLS with 9M317 *Yezh* (RS-SA-N-7B) SAM/9M317M *Yezh* (RS-SA-N-7C) SAM, 2 twin DTA-53-11356 533mm TT with 53-65K HWT/SET-65K HWT, 1 RBU 6000 A/S mor, 2 AK630 CIWS, 1 100mm gun (capacity 1 Ka-27 *Helix* ASW hel)

1 *Jastreb* (Project 11540 (*Neustrashimyy*)) (1 other non-operational, in long-term refit) with 2 quad lnchr with 3M24 *Uran* (RS-SS-N-25 *Switchblade*) AShM, 4 8-cell 3S95 VLS with 3K95 *Kinzhal* (RS-SA-N-9 *Gauntlet*), 6 single 533mm ASTT with RPK-6M *Vodopad*-NK (RS-SS-N-16 *Stallion*) A/S msl, 1 RBU 6000 *Smerch* 2 A/S mor, 2 3M87 *Kortik* CIWS with 9M311 SAM (RS-CADS-N-1), 1 100mm gun (capacity 1 Ka-27 *Helix* ASW hel)

1 Project 20380 (*Steregushchiy* I) with 2 quad lnchr with 3M24 *Uran* (RS-SS-N-25 *Switchblade*) AShM, 2 quad 324mm SM-588 ASTT with MTT LWT, 1 3M87 *Kortik*-M CIWS with 9M311 SAM (RS-CADS-N-1), 2 AK630 CIWS, 1 100mm gun (capacity 1 Ka-27 *Helix* ASW hel)

6 Project 20380 (*Steregushchiy* II) with 2 quad lnchr with 3M24 *Uran* (RS-SS-N-25 *Switchblade)* AShM, 3 4-cell 3S97 VLS with 3K96-3 *Redut* (RS-SA-N-28) SAM, 2 quad 324mm SM-588 ASTT with MTT LWT, 2 AK630 CIWS, 1 100mm gun (capacity 1 Ka-27 *Helix* ASW hel)

1 Project 20385 (*Gremyashchiy*) with 1 8-cell 3S14 UKSK VLS with 3M14T *Kalibr*-NK (RS-SS-N-30A *Sagaris*) dual-capable LACM/3M54T (RS-SS-N-27B *Sizzler*) AShM/3M54T1 (RS-SS-N-27) AShM/3M55 *Oniks* (RS-SS-N-26 *Strobile*) AShM (3M54T/T1 operational status unclear), 4 4-cell 3S97 VLS with 3K96-2 *Poliment-Redut* (RS-SA-N-28) SAM, 2 quad 324mm TT with MTT LWT, 2 AK630 CIWS, 1 100mm gun (capacity 1 Ka-27 *Helix* ASW hel)

2 Project 22350 (*Gorshkov*) with 2 8-cell 3S14 UKSK VLS with 3M14T *Kalibr*-NK (RS-SS-N-30A *Sagaris*) dual-capable LACM/3M54T (RS-SS-N-27B *Sizzler*) AShM/3M54T1 (RS-SS-N-27) AShM/3M55 *Oniks* (RS-SS-N-26 *Strobile*) AShM (3M54T/T1 operational status unclear), 4 8-cell 3S97 VLS with 3K96-2 *Poliment-Redut* (RS-SA-N-28) SAM, 2 quad 324mm TT with MTT LWT, 2 3M89 *Palash* CIWS (RS-CADS-N-2), 1 130mm gun (capacity 1 Ka-27 *Helix* ASW hel)

FFGM 2:

1 *Burevestnik* (Project 1135 (*Krivak* I))† with 1 quad lnchr with URK-5 *Rastrub*-B (RS-SS-N-14 *Silex*) AShM/ASW, 1 twin ZIF-122 lnchr with *Osa*-M (RS-SA-N-4 *Gecko*) SAM, 2 quad 533mm ChTA-53-1135 ASTT with 53-65K HWT/SET-65K HWT, 2 RBU 6000 *Smerch* 2 A/S mor, 2 twin 76mm guns

1 *Burevestnik* M (Project 1135M (*Krivak* II)) with 1 quad lnchr with URK-5 *Rastrub*-B (RS-SS-N-14 *Silex*) AShM/ASW, 2 twin ZIF-122 lnchr with 4K33 *Osa*-M (RS-SA-N-4 *Gecko* SAM), 2 quad 533mm ChTA-53-1135 ASTT with 53-65K HWT/SET-65K HWT, 2 RBU 6000 *Smerch* 2 A/S mor, 2 100mm guns

188 THE MILITARY BALANCE 2023

PATROL AND COASTAL COMBATANTS 128
  CORVETTES 42
    FSGM 14

      9 *Buyan*-M (Project 21631 (*Sviyazhsk*)) with 1 8-cell 3S14 UKSK VLS with 3M14T *Kalibr*-NK (RS-SS-N-30A *Sagaris*) dual-capable LACM/3M54T (RS-SS-N-27B *Sizzler*) AShM/3M54T1 (RS-SS-N-27) AShM/3M55 *Oniks* (RS-SS-N-26 *Strobile*) AShM (3M54T/T1 operational status unclear), 2 sextuple 3M47 *Gibka* lnchr with *Igla*-1M (RS-SA-N-10 *Grouse*) SAM, 1 AK630M-2 CIWS, 1 100mm gun

      1 Karakurt (Project 22800 (*Uragan*)) with 1 8-cell 3S14 UKSK VLS with 3M14T *Kalibr*-NK (RS-SS-N-30A *Sagaris*) dual-capable LACM/3M54T (RS-SS-N-27B *Sizzler*) AShM/3M54T1 (RS-SS-N-27) AShM/3M55 *Oniks* (RS-SS-N-26 *Strobile*) AShM (3M54T/T1 operational status unclear), 2 Pantsir-M with 57E6 SAM, 1 76mm gun

      1 Project 11661K (*Gepard* I) with 2 quad lnchr with 3M24 *Uran* (RS-SS-N-25 *Switchblade*) AShM, 1 twin ZIF-122 lnchr with 4K33 *Osa*-M (RS-SA-N-4 *Gecko*) SAM, 2 AK630 CIWS, 1 76mm gun

      1 Project 11661K (*Gepard* II) with 1 8-cell VLS with 3M14T *Kalibr*-NK (RS-SS-N-30A *Sagaris*) dual-capable LACM/3M54T (RS-SS-N-27B *Sizzler*) AShM/3M54T1 (RS-SS-N-27) AShM/3M55 *Oniks* (RS-SS-N-26 *Strobile*) AShM (3M54T/T1 operational status unclear), 1 3M89 *Palash* CIWS with 9M337 *Sosna*-R SAM (RS-CADS-N-2), 1 76mm gun

      2 *Sivuch* (Project 1239 (*Dergach*)) with 2 quad lnchr with 3M80 *Moskit* (RS-SS-N-22 *Sunburn*) AShM, 1 twin ZIF-122 lnchr with 4K33AM *Osa*-MA2 (RS-SA-N-4 *Gecko*) SAM, 2 AK630M CIWS, 1 76mm gun

    FSG 2 Karakurt (Project 22800 (*Uragan*)) with 1 8-cell 3S14 VLS with 3M14T *Kalibr*-NK (RS-SS-N-30A *Sagaris*) dual-capable LACM/3M54T (RS-SS-N-27B *Sizzler*) AShM/3M54T1 (RS-SS-N-27) AShM/3M55 *Oniks* (RS-SS-N-26 *Strobile*) AShM (3M54T/T1 operational status unclear), 2 AK630M CIWS, 1 76mm gun

    FSM 26:

      2 *Albatros* (Project 1124 (*Grisha* III)) with 1 twin ZIF-122 lnchr with 4K33 *Osa*-M (RS-SA-N-4 *Gecko*) SAM, 2 twin 533mm DTA-53-1124 ASTT, 2 RBU 6000 *Smerch* 2 A/S mor, 1 twin 57mm gun

      18 *Albatros* (Project 1124M (*Grisha* V)) with 1 twin ZIF-122 lnchr with 4K33 *Osa*-M (RS-SA-N-4 *Gecko*) SAM, 2 twin 533mm DTA-53-1124 ASTT, 1 RBU 6000 *Smerch* 2 A/S mor, 1 AK630 CIWS, 1 76mm gun

      6 Project 1331M (*Parchim* II) with 2 quad lnchr with 9K32 *Strela*-2 (RS-SA-N-5 *Grail*) SAM, 2 twin 533mm ASTT, 2 RBU 6000 *Smerch* 2 A/S mor, 1 AK630 CIWS, 1 76mm gun

  PSOH 4 Project 22160 (*Bykov*) with 1 76mm gun (capacity 1 Ka-27 *Helix* ASW hel)

  PCGM 10:

    9 *Ovod*-1 (Project 1234.1 (*Nanuchka* III)) with 2 triple lnchr with P-120 *Malakhit* (RS-SS-N-9 *Siren*) AShM, 1 twin ZIF-122 lnchr with 4K33 *Osa*-M (RS-SA-N-4 *Gecko*) SAM, 1 AK630 CIWS, 1 76mm gun

    1 *Ovod*-1 (Project 1234.1 (*Nanuchka* III)) with 4 quad lnchr with 3M24 *Uran* (RS-SS-N-25 *Switchblade*) AShM, 1 twin lnchr with 4K33 *Osa*-M (RS-SA-N-4 *Gecko*) SAM, 1 AK630 CIWS, 1 76mm gun

  PCFG 23:

    5 *Molnya* (*Tarantul* II) with 2 twin lnchr with P-22 *Termit*-R (RS-SS-N-2D *Styx*) AShM, 2 AK630M CIWS, 1 76mm gun

    17 *Molnya* (*Tarantul* III) with 2 twin lnchr with 3M80 *Moskit* (RS-SS-N-22 *Sunburn*) AShM, 2 AK630M CIWS, 1 76mm gun

    1 *Molnya* (*Tarantul* III) with 2 twin lnchr with 3M80 *Moskit* (RS-SS-N-22 *Sunburn*) AShM, 1 3K89 *Palash* (RS-CADS-N-2) CIWS, 1 76mm gun

  PCM 3 *Buyan* (Project 21630 (*Astrakhan*)) with 1 sextuple lnchr with 3M47 *Gibka* lnchr with *Igla*-1M (RS-SA-N-10 *Grouse*) SAM, 1 A-215 *Grad*-M 122mm MRL, 1 100mm gun

  PCF 1 *Molnya* (*Tarantul* III) with 2 AK630M CIWS, 1 76mm gun

  PBF 14: 12+ *Raptor* (capacity 20 troops); 2 *Mangust*

  PBR 4 *Shmel* with 1 17-cell BM-14 MRL, 1 76mm gun

  PB 27 *Grachonok*

MINE WARFARE • MINE COUNTERMEASURES 43

  MCC 6 *Alexandrit* (Project 12700)

  MHI 7 *Sapfir* (Project 10750 (*Lida*)) with 1 AK630 CIWS

  MHO 2 *Rubin* (Project 12660 (*Gorya*)) with 2 quad lnchr with 9K32 *Strela*-2 (RS-SA-N-5 *Grail*) SAM, 1 AK630 CIWS, 1 76mm gun

  MSC 20: 19 *Yakhont* (Project 1265 (*Sonya*)) with 4 AK630 CIWS (some with 2 quad lnchr with 9K32 *Strela*-2 (RS-SA-N-5 *Grail*) SAM); 1 *Korund*-E (Project 1258E (*Yevgenya*))

  MSO 8: 7 *Akvamaren*-M (Project 266M (*Natya*)); 1 *Agat* (Project 02668 (*Natya* II)) (all with 2 quad lnchr (manual aiming) with 9K32 *Strela*-2 (RS-SA-N-5 *Grail*) SAM, 2 RBU 1200 *Uragan* A/S mor, 2 twin AK230 CIWS

AMPHIBIOUS

  LANDING SHIPS • LST 20:

    12 Project 775 (*Ropucha* I/II) with 2 twin 57mm guns (capacity either 10 MBT and 190 troops or 24 APC (T) and 170 troops)

    3 Project 775M (*Ropucha* III) with 2 AK630 CIWS, 1 76mm gun (capacity either 10 MBT and 190 troops or 24 APC (T) and 170 troops)

    3 *Tapir* (Project 1171 (*Alligator*)) with at least 2 twin lnchr with 9K32 *Strela*-2 (RS-SA-N-5 *Grail*) SAM, 2 twin 57mm guns (capacity 20 tanks; 300 troops)

    2 Project 11711 (*Gren*) with 1 AK630M-2 CIWS, 2 AK630M CIWS (capacity 1 Ka-29 *Helix* B hel; 13 MBT/36 AFV; 300 troops)

  LANDING CRAFT 26

    LCM 24: 8 *Akula* (Project 1176 (*Ondatra*)) (capacity 1 MBT); 5 *Dyugon* (Project 21820) (capacity 5 APC or 100 troops); 11 *Serna* (Project 11770) (capacity 2 APC or 100 troops)

    LCAC 2 *Zubr* (Project 12322 (*Pomornik*)) with 2 22-cell 140mm MS-227 *Ogon* MRL, 2 AK630 CIWS (capacity 230 troops; either 3 MBT or 10 APC(T))

Russia and Eurasia 189

LOGISTICS AND SUPPORT 281

SSAN 9:

1 *Belgorod* (Project 22870 (*Oscar* II mod))

2 *Halibut* (Project 18511 (*Paltus*))

3 *Kashalot* (Project 1910 (*Uniform*))

1 *Nelma* (Project 1851 (X-*Ray*))

1 *Orenburg* (*Delta* III Stretch)

1 *Podmoskovye* (Project 09787)

(1 non-operational *Losharik* (Project 10831 (*Norsub*-5)) reportedly damaged by fire in 2019)

SSA 1 *Sarov* (Project 20120)

ABU 12: 8 *Kashtan*; 4 Project 419 (*Sura*)

AE 9: 6 *Muna*; 1 *Dubnyak*; 2 *Akademik Kovalev* (Project 20181) with 1 hel landing platform

AEM 2: 1 *Kalma*-3 (Project 1791R); 1 *Lama*

AFS 2 *Longvinik* (Project 23120)

AG 1 *Potok*

AGB 5: 1 *Dobrynya Mikitich*; 1 *Ilya Muromets*; 2 *Ivan Susanin*; 1 *Vladimir Kavraisky*

AGE 3: 2 *Seliger*; 1 *Tchusovoy*

AGHS 6 Project 23040G

AGI 14: 2 *Alpinist*; 2 *Dubridium* (Project 1826); 1 *Moma*; 7 *Vishnya*; 2 *Yuri Ivanov*

AGM 1 *Marshal Nedelin*

AGOR 7: 1 *Akademik Alexandrov* (Project 20183); 1 *Akademik Krylov*; 2 *Sibiriyakov*; 2 *Vinograd*; 1 *Yantar*

AGS 67: 8 *Biya*; 16+ *Finik*; 7 *Kamenka*; 5 *Moma*; 8+ *Onega*; 6 *Baklan* (Project 19920); 4 *Baklan* (Project 19920B); 4 *Vaygach*; 9+ *Yug*

AGSH 1 *Samara*

AH 3 *Ob*†

AK 3: 2 *Irgiz*; 1 *Pevek*

AOL 8: 2+ *Dubna*; 3 *Uda*; 3+ *Altay* (mod)

AOR 4: 3 *Boris Chilikin*; 1 *Akademik Pashin* (Project 23130)

AORL 2: 1 *Kaliningradneft*; 1 *Olekma*

AOS 1 *Luza*

AOTL 1 *Platforma-Arktika* (Project 03182) with 1 hel landing plafform

AR ε7 *Amur*

ARC 5: 4 *Emba*; 1 Improved *Klasma*

ARS 33: 1 *Kommuna*; 5 *Goryn*; 4 *Mikhail Rudnitsky*; 22 Project 23040; 1 *Zvezdochka* (Project 20180)

AS 3 Project 2020 (*Malina*)

ASR 2: 1 *Elbrus*; 1 *Igor Belousov*

ATF 54: 1 *Okhotsk*; 1 *Baklan*; ε3 *Katun*; 3 *Ingul*; 1 *Neftegaz*; 10 *Okhtensky*; 13 *Prometey*; 3 Project 23470 with 1 hel landing platform; 1 *Prut*; 4 *Sliva*; 14 *Sorum*

ATS 5 Project 22870

AWT 1 *Manych*

AXL 9: 7 *Petrushka*; 2 *Smolny* with 2 RBU 2500 *Smerch* 1 A/S mor, 2 twin 76mm guns

Naval Aviation ε31,000

FORCES BY ROLE

FIGHTER

1 regt with MiG-31B/BS/BM *Foxhound*

1 regt with Su-27/Su-27UB *Flanker*

1 regt with Su-33 *Flanker* D; Su-25UTG *Frogfoot*

FIGHTER/GROUND ATTACK

1 regt with MiG-29KR/KUBR *Fulcrum*

1 regt with MiG-31BM *Foxhound*; Su-24M/M2/MR *Fencer*

ANTI-SURFACE WARFARE/ISR

2 regt with Su-24M/MR *Fencer*; Su-30SM

ANTI-SUBMARINE WARFARE

1 regt with Il-38/Il-38N *May**; Il-18D; Il-20RT *Coot* A; Il-22 *Coot* B

2 sqn with Il-38/Il-38N *May**; Il-18D; Il-20RT *Coot* A; Il-22 *Coot* B

1 regt with Ka-27/Ka-29 *Helix*

1 sqn with Ka-27/Ka-29 *Helix*

2 sqn with Tu-142MK/MZ/MR *Bear* F/J*

1 unit with Ka-31R *Helix*

MARITIME PATROL/TRANSPORT

1 regt with An-26 *Curl*; Be-12 *Mail**; Ka-27 *Helix*; Mi-8 *Hip*

SEARCH & RESCUE/TRANSPORT

1 sqn with An-12PS *Cub*; An-26 *Curl*; Tu-134

TRANSPORT

1 sqn with An-12BK *Cub*; An-24RV *Coke*; An-26 *Curl*; An-72 *Coaler*; An-140

2 sqn with An-26 *Curl*; Tu-134

TRAINING

1 sqn with L-39 *Albatros*; Su-25UTG *Frogfoot*

1 sqn with An-140; Tu-134; Tu-154; Il-38 *May*

ATTACK/TRANSPORT HELICOPTER

1 sqn with Mi-24P *Hind*; Mi-8 *Hip*

TRANSPORT HELICOPTER

1 sqn with Mi-8 *Hip*

AIR DEFENCE

4 AD div HQ

1 SAM regt with S-300PM1 (RS-SA-20 *Gargoyle*); S-300PS (RS-SA-10B *Grumble*)

1 SAM regt with S-300PM1 (RS-SA-20 *Gargoyle*); S-400 (RS-SA-21 *Growler*); 96K6 *Pantsir*-S1 (RS-SA-22 *Greyhound*)

1 SAM regt with S-300PS (RS-SA-10B *Grumble*)

1 SAM regt with S-300PS (RS-SA-10B *Grumble*); S-400 (RS-SA-21 *Growler*); 96K6 *Pantsir*-S1 (RS-SA-22 *Greyhound*)

4 SAM regt with S-400 (RS-SA-21 *Growler*); 96K6 *Pantsir*-S1 (RS-SA-22 *Greyhound*)

EQUIPMENT BY TYPE

AIRCRAFT 207 combat capable

FTR 67: 10 MiG-31B/BS *Foxhound*; 22 MiG-31BM *Foxhound* C; 17 Su-33 *Flanker* D; 18 Su-27/Su-27UB *Flanker*

FGA 45: 19 MiG-29KR *Fulcrum*; 3 MiG-29KUBR *Fulcrum*; up to 19 Su-30SM *Flanker* H; 4 Su-30SM2 Flanker H

ATK 35: up to 30 Su-24M *Fencer*; 5 Su-25UTG *Frogfoot* (trg role)

ASW 44: 12 Tu-142MK/MZ *Bear* F; 10 Tu-142MR *Bear* J (comms); 15 Il-38 *May*; 7 Il-38N *May*

MP 7: 6 Be-12PS *Mail**; 1 Il-18D

ISR 10 Su-24MR *Fencer* E*

SAR 4: 3 An-12PS *Cub*; 1 Be-200ES

ELINT 4: 2 Il-20RT *Coot* A; 2 Il-22 *Coot* B

TPT 49: **Medium** 2 An-12BK *Cub*; **Light** 45: 1 An-24RV *Coke*; 24 An-26 *Curl*; 6 An-72 *Coaler*; 4 An-140; 9 Tu-134; 1 Tu-134UBL; **PAX** 2 Tu-154M *Careless*

TRG 4 L-39 *Albatros*

HELICOPTERS

ATK 8 Mi-24P *Hind*

ASW 52: 30 Ka-27PL *Helix*; 22 Ka-27M *Helix*

EW 8 Mi-8 *Hip* J

190   THE MILITARY BALANCE 2023

AEW 2 Ka-31R *Helix*
SAR 16 Ka-27PS *Helix* D
TPT 41: **Medium** 35: 27 Ka-29 *Helix*; 4 Mi-8T *Hip*; 4 Mi-8MT *Hip*; **Light** 6 Ka-226T
AIR DEFENCE
SAM • Long-range 200: 56 S-300PM1 (RS-SA-20 *Gargoyle*); 40 S-300PS (RS-SA-10B *Grumble*); 104 S-400 (RS-SA-21 *Growler*)
SPAAGM 30mm 30 96K6 *Pantsir*-S1 (RS-SA-22 *Greyhound*)
AIR-LAUNCHED MISSILES
AAM • IR R-27T/ET (RS-AA-10B/D *Alamo*); R-60 (RS-AA-8 *Aphid*); R-73 (RS-AA-11A *Archer*); R-74M (RS-AA-11B *Archer*); **ARH** R-77-1 (RS-AA-12B *Adder*); **SARH** R-27R/ER (RS-AA-10A/C *Alamo*); R-33 (RS-AA-9A *Amos*)
ARM Kh-25MP (RS-AS-12A *Kegler*); Kh-31P (RS-AS-17A *Krypton*); Kh-58 (RS-AS-11 *Kilter*)
ASM Kh-59 (RS-AS-13 *Kingbolt*); Kh-59M (RS-AS-18 *Kazoo*); Kh-29T (RS-AS-14 *Kedge*)
AShM Kh-31A (RS-AS-17B *Krypton*)

Naval Infantry (Marines) ε30,000

FORCES BY ROLE

As a result of heavy losses suffered during the invasion of Ukraine, almost all of the manoeuvre formations listed are currently significantly understrength and some are now effectively only cadre-sized until mobilised personnel can be drafted into them.

COMMAND
3 corps HQ
SPECIAL FORCES
4 (OMRP) SF unit
11 (PDSS) cbt diver unit
MANOEUVRE
Reconnaissance
1 recce bde
Mechanised
1 MR div (1 tk regt, 2 MR regt; 1 SAM regt)
2 MR bde
1 MR regt
6 naval inf bde
1 naval inf regt
SURFACE-TO-SURFACE MISSILE
1 SRBM/GLCM bde with 9K720 *Iskander*-M (RS-SS-26 *Stone*/RS-SSC-7 *Southpaw*)
COMBAT SUPPORT
2 arty bde
2 engr regt
AIR DEFENCE
1 SAM regt with 9K33 *Osa* (RS-SA-8 *Gecko*); *Strela*-1/*Strela*-10 (RS-SA-9 *Gaskin*/RS-SA-13 *Gopher*)

EQUIPMENT BY TYPE
ARMOURED FIGHTING VEHICLES
MBT 220: 170 T-72B/B3/B3M; 50 T-80BV/BVM
IFV 1,010: 300 BMP-2; 70 BMP-3; 40 BMP-3F; 600 BTR-82A
APC 300
  APC (T) 250 MT-LB
  APC (W) 50 BTR-80
AUV *Vystrel*

ANTI-TANK/ANTI-INFRASTRUCTURE
MSL
SP 60+: 60 9P148 with 9K111-1 *Konkurs* (RS-AT-5 *Spandrel*); 9P149 with 9K114 *Shturm* (RS-AT-6 *Spiral*); 9P157-2 with 9K123 *Khrisantema* (RS-AT-15 *Springer*)
MANPATS 9K111-1 *Konkurs* (RS-AT-5 *Spandrel*); 9K135 *Kornet* (RS-AT-14 *Spriggan*)
GUNS 100mm T-12
ARTILLERY 395
SP 171: **122mm** 85 2S1 *Gvozdika*; **152mm** 86: 50 2S3 *Akatsiya*; 36 2S19M1 *Msta*-S
TOWED 152mm 100: 50 2A36 *Giatsint*-B; 50 2A65 *Msta*-B
GUN/MOR 66
SP 120mm 42: 12 2S23 NONA-SVK; 30 2S9 NONA-S
TOWED 120mm 24 2B16 NONA-K
MRL 58: **122mm** 36 BM-21 *Grad*/*Tornado*-G; **220mm** 18 9P140 *Uragan*; **300mm** 4+ 9A52 *Smerch*
SURFACE-TO-SURFACE MISSILE LAUNCHER
SRBM • Dual-capable 12 9K720 *Iskander*-M (RS-SS-26 *Stone*)
GLCM • Dual-capable Some 9M728 (RS-SSC-7 *Southpaw*)
AIR DEFENCE
SAM
Short-range 12+ *Tor*-M2DT
Point-defence 70+: 20 9K33 *Osa* (RS-SA-8 *Gecko*); 50 9K31 *Strela*-1/9K35 *Strela*-10 (RS-SA-9 *Gaskin*/RS-SA-13 *Gopher*); 9K338 *Igla*-S (RS-SA-24 *Grinch*)
GUNS • SP 23mm 60 ZSU-23-4

Coastal Missile and Artillery Forces 2,000

FORCES BY ROLE
COASTAL DEFENCE
5 AShM bde
1 AShM regt

EQUIPMENT BY TYPE
COASTAL DEFENCE
ARTY • SP 130mm ε36 A-222 *Bereg*
AShM 96+: 40 3K60 *Bal* (RS-SSC-6 *Sennight*); 56 3K55 *Bastion* (RS-SSC-5 *Stooge*); some 4K44 *Redut* (RS-SSC-1 *Sepal*); some 4K51 *Rubezh* (RS-SSC-3 *Styx*)

Aerospace Forces ε165,000 (incl conscripts)

A joint CIS Unified Air Defence System covers RUS, ARM, BLR, KAZ, KGZ, TJK, TKM and UZB

FORCES BY ROLE
BOMBER
3 regt with Tu-22M3 *Backfire* C
3 sqn with Tu-95MS/MS mod *Bear*
1 sqn with Tu-160/Tu-160 mod *Blackjack*
FIGHTER
1 sqn with MiG-29/MiG-29UB *Fulcrum* (Armenia)
2 regt with MiG-31BM *Foxhound* C
1 regt with MiG-31BM *Foxhound* C; Su-35S *Flanker* M
1 regt with Su-27/Su-27SM/Su-27UB *Flanker* B/J/C; Su-30M2 *Flanker* G
2 regt with Su-30SM *Flanker* H

FIGHTER/GROUND ATTACK

1 regt with MiG-31BM *Foxhound* C; Su-27SM *Flanker* J; Su-30M2 *Flanker* G; Su-30SM *Flanker* H; Su-35S *Flanker* M

1 regt with Su-27SM *Flanker* J; Su-35S *Flanker* M

1 regt with Su-35S *Flanker* M; Su-30SM *Flanker* H

1 regt with Su-27SM3 *Flanker*; Su-30M2 *Flanker* G

1 regt with Su-25 *Frogfoot*; Su-30SM *Flanker* H

GROUND ATTACK

1 regt with MiG-31K

1 regt with Su-24M/M2 *Fencer*; Su-34 *Fullback*

1 regt with Su-24M *Fencer*; Su-25SM *Frogfoot*

3 regt with Su-25SM/SM3 *Frogfoot*

1 sqn with Su-25SM *Frogfoot* (Kyrgyzstan)

3 regt with Su-34 *Fullback*

GROUND ATTACK/ISR

1 regt with Su-24M/MR *Fencer*

ISR

3 sqn with Su-24MR *Fencer*

1 flt with An-30 *Clank*

AIRBORNE EARLY WARNING & CONTROL

1 sqn with A-50/A-50U *Mainstay*

TANKER

1 sqn with Il-78/Il-78M *Midas*

TRANSPORT

6 regt/sqn with An-12BK *Cub*; An-148-100E; An-26 *Curl*; Tu-134 *Crusty*; Tu-154 *Careless*; Mi-8 *Hip*

1 regt with An-124 *Condor*; Il-76MD *Candid*

1 regt with An-124 *Condor*; Il-76MD/MD-90A *Candid*

1 regt with An-12BK *Cub*; Il-76MD *Candid*

1 sqn with An-22 *Cock*

3 regt with Il-76MD *Candid*

ATTACK/TRANSPORT HELICOPTER

1 bde with Ka-52A *Hokum* B; Mi-28N *Havoc* B; Mi-35 *Hind*; Mi-26 *Halo*; Mi-8MTV-5 *Hip*

1 bde with Ka-52A *Hokum* B; Mi-26 *Halo*; Mi-8 *Hip*

1 bde with Mi-28N *Havoc* B; Mi-35 *Hind*; Mi-26 *Halo*; Mi-8 *Hip*

2 regt with Ka-52A *Hokum* B; Mi-28N *Havoc* B; Mi-35 *Hind*; Mi-8 *Hip*

1 regt with Ka-52A *Hokum* B; Mi-24P *Hind*; Mi-8MTPR-1 *Hip*; Mi-8 *Hip*

1 regt with Ka-52A *Hokum* B; Mi-8 *Hip*

1 regt with Mi-28N *Havoc* B; Mi-35 *Hind*; Mi-8 *Hip*

1 regt with Mi-28N *Havoc* B; Mi-24P *Hind*; Mi-35 *Hind*; Mi-8 *Hip*

2 regt with Mi-24P *Hind*; Mi-8 *Hip*

2 sqn with Mi-24P *Hind*; Mi-8 *Hip*

AIR DEFENCE

9 AD div HQ

4 regt with 9K37M1-2 *Buk*-M1-2 (RS-SA-11 *Gadfly*); 9K317 *Buk*-M2 (RS-SA-17 *Grizzly*); S-300V (RS-SA-12 *Gladiator/Giant*)

1 bde with S-300PS (RS-SA-10B *Grumble*)

2 regt with S-300PS (RS-SA-10B *Grumble*)

6 regt with S-300PM1/PM2 (RS-SA-20 *Gargoyle*)

12 regt with S-400 (RS-SA-21 *Growler*); 96K6 *Pantsir*-S1 (RS-SA-22 *Greyhound*)

EQUIPMENT BY TYPE

AIRCRAFT 1,153 combat capable

BBR 137: 60 Tu-22M3 *Backfire* C; 1 Tu-22MR *Backfire*† (1 in overhaul); 33 Tu-95MS *Bear*; 27 Tu-95MS mod *Bear*; 7 Tu-160 *Blackjack*; 7 Tu-160 mod *Blackjack*; 2 Tu-160M *Blackjack* (in test)

FTR 185: 70 MiG-29/MiG-29UB *Fulcrum*; 85 MiG-31BM *Foxhound* C; 12 Su-27 *Flanker* B; 18 Su-27UB *Flanker* C

FGA 410+: 15 MiG-29SMT *Fulcrum*; 2 MiG-29UBT *Fulcrum*; 6 MiG-35S/UB *Fulcrum* (in test); 47 Su-27SM *Flanker* J; 24 Su-27SM3 *Flanker*; 19 Su-30M2 *Flanker* G; ε80 Su-30SM *Flanker* H; ε105 Su-34 *Fullback*; 7+ Su-34 mod *Fullback*; 99 Su-35S *Flanker* M; 6 Su-57 *Felon*

ATK 262: 12 MiG-31K; 70 Su-24M/M2 *Fencer*; 40 Su-25 *Frogfoot*; ε125 Su-25SM/SM3 *Frogfoot*; 15 Su-25UB *Frogfoot*

ISR 58: 4 An-30 *Clank*; up to 50 Su-24MR *Fencer**; 2 Tu-214ON; 2 Tu-214R

EW 3 Il-22PP *Mute*

ELINT 31: 14 Il-20M *Coot* A; 5 Il-22 *Coot* B; 12 Il-22M *Coot* B

AEW&C 10: 3 A-50 *Mainstay*; 7 A-50U *Mainstay*

C2 8: 2 Il-80 *Maxdome*; 1 Il-82; 4 Tu-214SR; 1 Tu-214PU-SBUS

TKR 15: 5 Il-78 *Midas*; 10 Il-78M *Midas*

TPT 446: **Heavy** 125: 11 An-124 *Condor*; 4 An-22 *Cock*; 98 Il-76MD *Candid*; 3 Il-76MD-M *Candid*; 9 Il-76MD-90A *Candid*; **Medium** 65 An-12BK *Cub*; **Light** 224: ε113 An-26 *Curl*; 25 An-72 *Coaler*; 5 An-140; 27 L-410; 54 Tu-134 *Crusty*; **PAX** 32: 15 An-148-100E; 17 Tu-154 *Careless*

TRG 262: 35 DA42T; 118 L-39 *Albatros*; 109 Yak-130 *Mitten**

HELICOPTERS

ATK 361+: ε105 Ka-52A *Hokum* B; 100 Mi-24D/V/P *Hind*; 80+ Mi-28N *Havoc* B; 13 Mi-28UB *Havoc*; ε60 Mi-35 *Hind*

EW ε20 Mi-8MTPR-1 *Hip*

TPT 313: **Heavy** 33 Mi-26/Mi-26T *Halo*; **Medium** 280 Mi-8/AMTSh/AMTSh-VA/MT/MTV-5/MTV-5-1 *Hip*

TRG 69: 19 Ka-226U; 50 *Ansat*-U

UNINHABITED AERIAL VEHICLES

CISR • **Heavy** some *Inokhodets*; **Medium** *Forpost* R; *Mohajer* 6

ISR • **Medium** *Forpost* (*Searcher* II)

AIR DEFENCE

SAM 714:

Long-range 584: 160 S-300PS (RS-SA-10B *Grumble*); 150 S-300PM1/PM2 (RS-SA-20 *Gargoyle*); 20 S-300V (RS-SA-12 *Gladiator/Giant*); 6 S-350 *Vityaz* (RS-SA-28); 248 S-400 (RS-SA-21 *Growler*)

Medium-range 80 9K37M1-2 *Buk*-M1-2/9K317 *Buk*-M2 (RS-SA-11 *Gadfly*/RS-SA-17 *Grizzly*)

SPAAGM 30mm 50 96K6 *Pantsir*-S1/S2 (RS-SA-22 *Greyhound*)

AIR-LAUNCHED MISSILES

AAM • **IR** R-27T/ET (RS-AA-10B/D *Alamo*); R-73 (RS-AA-11A *Archer*); R-74M (RS-AA-11B *Archer*); R-60T (RS-AA-8 *Aphid*); **SARH** R-27R/ER (RS-AA-10A/C *Alamo*); R-33 (RS-AA-9A *Amos*); **ARH** R-77-1 (RS-AA-12B *Adder*); R-37M (RS-AA-13A *Axehead*); **PRH** R-27P/EP (RS-AA-10E/F *Alamo*)

ARM Kh-25MP (RS-AS-12A *Kegler*); Kh-31P/PM (RS-AS-17A/C *Krypton*); Kh-58 (RS-AS-11 *Kilter*)

ASM Item 305/LMUR; Kh-25ML (RS-AS-12B *Kegler*); Kh-29 (RS-AS-14 *Kedge*); Kh-38; Kh-59 (RS-AS-13 *Kingbolt*) Kh-59M (RS-AS-18 *Kazoo*); *Kinzhal* (RS-AS-24 *Killjoy*); 9M114 *Kokon* (RS-AT-6 *Spiral*); 9M120 *Ataka* (RS-AT-9

Spiral 2); 9M120-1 *Vikhr* (RS-AT-16 *Scallion*)
AShM Kh-22 (RS-AS-4 *Kitchen*); Kh-31A/AM (RS-AS-17B/D *Krypton*); Kh-32 (RS-AS-4A mod); Kh-35U (RS-AS-20 *Kayak*)
LACM
Nuclear Kh-55SM (RS-AS-15B *Kent*); Kh-102 (RS-AS-23B *Kodiak*)
Conventional Kh-101 (RS-AS-23A *Kodiak*); Kh-555 (RS-AS-22 *Kluge*)
BOMBS
INS/GLONASS-guided KAB-500S
Laser-guided KAB-500L; KAB-1500L
TV-guided *Ghaem*-5; KAB-500KR; KAB-1500KR; KAB-500OD; UPAB 1500

Airborne Forces ε40,000

FORCES BY ROLE
As a result of heavy losses suffered during the invasion of Ukraine, almost all of the manoeuvre formations listed are currently significantly understrength and some are now effectively only cadre-sized until mobilised personnel can be drafted into them.
SPECIAL FORCES
1 (AB Recce) SF bde
MANOEUVRE
Air Manoeuvre
2 AB div (1 tk bn, 3 para/air aslt regt, 1 arty regt, 1 AD regt)
2 AB div (2 para/air aslt regt, 1 arty regt, 1 AD regt)
1 indep AB bde
2 air aslt bde
EQUIPMENT BY TYPE
ARMOURED FIGHTING VEHICLES
MBT 50 T-72B3/B3M
IFV 120 BTR-82AM
APC 700+
APC (T) 700: 600 BTR-D; 100 BTR-MDM
PPV *Typhoon*-VDV
ABCV 850: 600 BMD-2; 250 BMD-4M
AUV GAZ *Tigr*; UAMZ *Toros*
ENGINEERING & MAINTENANCE VEHICLES
ARV BREM-D; BREhM-D
ANTI-TANK/ANTI-INFRASTRUCTURE
MSL
SP 100 BTR-RD
MANPATS 9K111 *Fagot* (RS-AT-4 *Spigot*); 9K113 *Konkurs* (RS-AT-5 *Spandrel*); 9K115 *Metis* (RS-AT-7 *Saxhorn*); 9K115-1 *Metis*-M (RS-AT-13); 9K135 *Kornet* (RS-AT-14 *Spriggan*)
RCL 73mm SPG-9
GUNS • SP 125mm 36+ 2S25 *Sprut*-SD
ARTILLERY 550+
TOWED 122mm 140 D-30
GUN/MOR • SP 120mm 210: 180 2S9 NONA-S; 30 2S9 NONA-SM; (500 2S9 NONA-S in store)
MOR • TOWED 200+ **82mm** 150 2B14; **120mm** 50+ 2B23 NONA-M1
AIR DEFENCE
SAM • Point-defence 30+: 30 *Strela*-10MN (RS-SA-13 *Gopher*); 9K310 *Igla*-1 (RS-SA-16 *Gimlet*); 9K38 *Igla* (RS-

SA-18 *Grouse*); 9K333 *Verba* (RS-SA-29 *Gizmo*); 9K338 *Igla*-S (RS-SA-24 *Grinch*); 9K34 *Strela*-3 (RS-SA-14 *Gremlin*)
GUNS • SP 23mm 150 BTR-ZD

Special Operations Forces ε1,000

FORCES BY ROLE
SPECIAL FORCES
2 SF unit

Railway Forces ε29,000

4 regional commands
FORCES BY ROLE
COMBAT SERVICE SUPPORT
10 (railway) tpt bde

1st & 2nd Army Corps ε30,000

Formations drawn from the Russian-backed 'Donetsk People's Republic' and 'Luhansk People's Republic' and integrated into the Russian command structure
FORCES BY ROLE
MANOEUVRE
Mechanised
7 MR bde
15 MR regt
COMBAT SUPPORT
2 arty bde
EQUIPMENT BY TYPE
ARMOURED FIGHTING VEHICLES
MBT T-64A; T-72A; T-72B
IFV BMP-1; BMP-2
APC
APC (T) MT-LB
APC (W) BTR-60/-70/-80
ARTILLERY
SP 122mm 2S1 *Gvozdika*
TOWED 122mm D-30; **152mm** 2A36 *Giatsint*-B; D-1 (M-1943); D-20
MRL 122m BM-21 *Grad*
MOR 120mm 2S12 *Sani*

Russian Military Districts

5 military districts each with a unified Joint Strategic Command. Organisational data presented here represents peacetime assignments rather than operational deployments resulting from Russia's full-scale invasion of Ukraine.

Western Military District

HQ at St Petersburg

Army
FORCES BY ROLE
COMMAND
3 army HQ
SPECIAL FORCES
2 (Spetsnaz) SF bde
MANOEUVRE
Reconnaissance
1 recce bde
Armoured
2 tk div

1 MR corps
3 MR div
Mechanised
1 MR div
3 MR bde
SURFACE-TO-SURFACE MISSILE
3 SRBM/GLCM bde with *Iskander*-M
COMBAT SUPPORT
2 arty bde
1 (hy) arty bde
1 MRL bde
1 engr bde
3 engr regt
1 ptn br bde
1 EW bde
1 NBC bde
2 NBC regt
COMBAT SERVICE SUPPORT
3 log bde
AIR DEFENCE
4 AD bde

Baltic Fleet

EQUIPMENT BY TYPE
SUBMARINES • TACTICAL • SSK 1
PRINCIPAL SURFACE COMBATANTS 6: 1 **DDGHM**;
5 **FFGHM** (1 more non-operational, in long-term refit)
PATROL AND COASTAL COMBATANTS 35: 3
FSGM; 2 **FSG**; 6 **FSM**; 4 **PCGM**; 7 **PCFG**; 12 **PBF**; 1 **PB**
MINE WARFARE • MINE COUNTERMEASURES
11: 1 **MCC**; 4 **MSC**; 6 **MHI**
AMPHIBIOUS 13: 4 **LST**; 7 **LCM**; 2 **LCAC**

Naval Aviation

FORCES BY ROLE
FIGHTER
1 regt with Su-27 *Flanker* B
ANTI-SURFACE WARFARE/ISR
1 regt with Su-24M/MR *Fencer*; Su-30SM *Flanker* H
TRANSPORT
1 sqn with An-26 *Curl*; Tu-134 *Crusty*
ATTACK/TRANSPORT HELICOPTER
1 regt with Ka-27/Ka-29 *Helix*; Mi-24P *Hind*;
Mi-8 *Hip*
AIR DEFENCE
2 SAM regt with S-400 (RS-SA-21 *Growler*); 96K6
Pantsir-S1 (RS-SA-22 *Greyhound*)

Naval Infantry

FORCES BY ROLE
COMMAND
1 corps HQ
MANOEUVRE
Mechanised
1 MR div
1 MR regt
1 naval inf bde
SURFACE-TO-SURFACE MISSILE
1 SRBM/GLCM bde with *Iskander*-M
COMBAT SUPPORT
1 arty bde

Coastal Artillery and Missile Forces

FORCES BY ROLE
COASTAL DEFENCE
1 AShM regt

Military Air Force

6th Air Force & Air Defence Army

FORCES BY ROLE
FIGHTER
1 regt with Su-30SM *Flanker* H
1 regt with MiG-31BM *Foxhound* C; Su-35S *Flanker* M
1 regt with Su-27SM *Flanker* J; Su-35S *Flanker* M
GROUND ATTACK
1 regt with Su-34 *Fullback*
ISR
1 sqn with Su-24MR *Fencer* E; An-30 *Clank*
TRANSPORT
1 regt with An-12 *Cub*; An-26 *Curl*; Tu-134 *Crusty*
ATTACK HELICOPTER
1 bde with Ka-52A *Hokum* B; Mi-28N *Havoc* B;
Mi-35 *Hind*; Mi-26 *Halo*; Mi-8MTV-5 *Hip*
1 regt with Mi-24P/Mi-35 *Hind*; Mi-28N *Havoc* B;
Mi-8 *Hip*
1 regt with Mi-24P *Hind*; Ka-52A *Hokum* B; Mi-8
Hip; Mi-8PPA *Hip*
AIR DEFENCE
3 SAM regt with S-300PM1/PM2 (RS-SA-20 *Gargoyle*)
4 SAM regt with S-400 (RS-SA-21 *Growler*); 96K6
Pantsir-S1 (RS-SA-22 *Greyhound*)

Airborne Forces

FORCES BY ROLE
SPECIAL FORCES
1 (AB Recce) SF bde
MANOEUVRE
Air Manoeuvre
3 AB div

Northern Fleet Military District

HQ at Severomorsk

Northern Fleet

EQUIPMENT BY TYPE
SUBMARINES 26
STRATEGIC 8 **SSBN** (of which 2 in refit)
TACTICAL 19: 5 **SSGN**; 8 **SSN**; 5 **SSK**
PRINCIPAL SURFACE COMBATANTS 10: 1 **CV** (in
refit); 1 **CGHMN**; 1 **CGHM**; 5 **DDGHM** (1 more in
reserve); 2 **FFGHM**
PATROL AND COASTAL COMBATANTS 16: 6
FSM; 2 **PCGM**; 8 **PB**
MINE WARFARE • MINE COUNTERMEASURES 8:
1 **MHO**; 1 **MSO**; 6 **MSC**
AMPHIBIOUS 8: 6 **LST**; 2 **LCM**

Naval Aviation

FORCES BY ROLE
FIGHTER
1 regt with Su-33 *Flanker* D; Su-25UTG *Frogfoot*

FIGHTER/GROUND ATTACK
1 regt with MiG-29KR/KUBR *Fulcrum*
FIGHTER/GROUND ATTACK/ISR
1 regt with MiG-31BM *Foxhound* C; Su-24M/M2/MR *Fencer*
ANTI-SUBMARINE WARFARE
1 regt with Il-38/Il-38N *May*; Il-20RT *Coot* A; Tu-134
1 regt with Ka-27/Ka-29 *Helix*
1 sqn with Tu-142MK/MZ/MR *Bear* F/J
AIR DEFENCE
5 SAM regt with S-300PS (RS-SA-10B *Grumble*); S-300PM1 (RS-SA-20 *Gargoyle*); S-400 (RS-SA-21 *Growler*); 96K6 *Pantsir*-S1 (RS-SA-22 *Greyhound*)

Naval Infantry
FORCES BY ROLE
COMMAND
1 corps HQ
MANOEUVRE
Mechanised
2 MR bde
1 naval inf bde
COMMAND
1 engr regt

Coastal Artillery and Missile Forces
FORCES BY ROLE
COASTAL DEFENCE
1 AShM bde

Central Military District
HQ at Yekaterinburg

Army
FORCES BY ROLE
COMMAND
2 army HQ
SPECIAL FORCES
2 (Spetsnaz) SF bde
MANOEUVRE
Armoured
1 tk div
3 MR bde
Mechanised
3 (lt/mtn) MR bde
SURFACE-TO-SURFACE MISSILE
2 SRBM/GLCM bde with *Iskander*-M
COMBAT SUPPORT
2 arty bde
1 MRL bde
1 engr bde
3 engr regt
1 EW bde
2 NBC bde
2 NBC regt

COMBAT SERVICE SUPPORT
2 log bde
AIR DEFENCE
3 AD bde

Military Air Force

14th Air Force & Air Defence Army
FORCES BY ROLE
FIGHTER
2 regt with MiG-31BM *Foxhound* C
GROUND ATTACK
1 regt with Su-34 *Fullback*
1 sqn with Su-25SM *Frogfoot* (Kyrgyzstan)
ISR
1 sqn with Su-24MR *Fencer* E
TRANSPORT
1 regt with An-12 *Cub*; An-26 *Curl*; Tu-134 *Crusty*; Tu-154; Mi-8 *Hip*
ATTACK/TRANSPORT HELICOPTER
1 bde with Mi-24P *Hind*; Mi-8 *Hip*
1 regt with Mi-24P *Hind*; Mi-8 *Hip*
1 sqn with Mi-24P *Hind*; Mi-8 *Hip* (Tajikistan)
AIR DEFENCE
1 regt with S-300PS (RS-SA-10B *Grumble*)
1 bde with S-300PS (RS-SA-10B *Grumble*)
1 regt with S-300PM2 (RS-SA-20 *Gargoyle*)
4 regt with S-400 (RS-SA-21 *Growler*); 96K6 *Pantsir*-S1 (RS-SA-22 *Greyhound*)

Airborne Troops
FORCES BY ROLE
MANOEUVRE
Air Manoeuvre
1 AB bde

Southern Military District
HQ at Rostov-on-Don

Army
FORCES BY ROLE
COMMAND
3 army HQ
SPECIAL FORCES
3 (Spetsnaz) SF bde
1 (Spetsnaz) SF regt
MANOEUVRE
Reconnaissance
1 recce bde
Armoured
3 MR div
1 MR bde
1 MR bde (Armenia)
1 MR bde (South Ossetia)
Mechanised
1 MR div
1 MR bde
1 MR bde (Abkhazia)
1 (lt/mtn) MR bde
SURFACE-TO-SURFACE MISSILE
3 SRBM/GLCM bde with *Iskander*-M

COMBAT SUPPORT
3 arty bde
1 MRL bde
1 engr bde
1 EW bde
1 NBC bde
2 NBC regt
COMBAT SERVICE SUPPORT
2 log bde
AIR DEFENCE
3 AD bde

Black Sea Fleet

The Black Sea Fleet is primarily based in Crimea, at Sevastopol, Karantinnaya Bay and Streletskaya Bay

EQUIPMENT BY TYPE
SUBMARINES • TACTICAL 6 **SSK**
PRINCIPAL SURFACE COMBATANTS 5: 3 **FFGHM**; 2 **FFGM**
PATROL AND COASTAL COMBATANTS 32: 8 **FSGM**; 6 **FSM**; 3 **PSOH**; 5 **PCFG**; 6 **PB**; 4 **PBF**
MINE WARFARE • MINE COUNTERMEASURES 10: 3 **MCC**; 1 **MHO**; 5 **MSO**; 1 **MSC**
AMPHIBIOUS 8: 6 **LST**; 2 **LCM**

Naval Aviation
FORCES BY ROLE
FIGHTER
ANTI-SURFACE WARFARE/ISR
  1 regt with Su-24M/MR *Fencer*; Su-30SM *Flanker* H
MARITIME PATROL/TRANSPORT
  1 regt with Ka-27 *Helix*; An-26 *Curl*; Be-12PS *Mail*; Mi-8 *Hip*
  TPT • Medium Mi-8 *Hip*

Naval Infantry
FORCES BY ROLE
COMMAND
  1 corps HQ
MANOEUVRE
  Mechanised
  2 naval inf bde
COMBAT SUPPORT
  1 arty regt
  1 engr regt
AIR DEFENCE
  1 SAM regt

Coastal Artillery and Missile Forces
FORCES BY ROLE
COASTAL DEFENCE
  2 AShM bde

Caspian Sea Flotilla
EQUIPMENT BY TYPE
PATROL AND COASTAL COMBATANTS 15: 3 **FSGM**; 1 **PCFG**; 3 **PCM**; 3 **PB**; 1 **PBF**; 4 **PBR**
MINE WARFARE • MINE COUNTERMEASURES 3: 2 **MSC**; 1 **MHI**
AMPHIBIOUS 9 **LCM**

Naval Infantry
FORCES BY ROLE
MANOEUVRE
  Mechanised
  1 naval inf regt

Military Air Force

4th Air Force & Air Defence Army
FORCES BY ROLE
FIGHTER
  1 regt with Su-30SM *Flanker* H
  1 sqn with MiG-29 *Fulcrum*; Su-30SM *Flanker* H (Armenia)
FIGHTER/GROUND ATTACK
  1 regt with Su-27/Su-27SM *Flanker* B/J; Su-30M2 *Flanker* G
  1 regt with Su-27SM3 *Flanker*; Su-30M2 *Flanker* G
GROUND ATTACK
  1 regt with Su-24M *Fencer*; Su-25SM *Frogfoot*
  2 regt with Su-25SM/SM3 *Frogfoot*
  1 regt with Su-34 *Fullback*
GROUND ATTACK/ISR
  1 regt with Su-24M/MR *Fencer* D/E
TRANSPORT
  1 regt with An-12 *Cub*/Mi-8 *Hip*
ATTACK/TRANSPORT HELICOPTER
  1 bde with Mi-28N *Havoc* B; Mi-35 *Hind*; Mi-8 *Hip*; Mi-26 *Halo*
  1 regt with Mi-28N *Havoc* B; Mi-35 *Hind*; Mi-8 *Hip*
  2 regt with Ka-52A *Hokum* B; Mi-28N *Havoc* B; Mi-35 *Hind*; Mi-8AMTSh *Hip*
  1 sqn with Mi-24P *Hind*; Mi-8 *Hip* (Armenia)
AIR DEFENCE
  1 SAM regt with 9K317 *Buk*-M2 (RS-SA-17 *Grizzly*)
  1 SAM regt with S-300PM1 (RS-SA-20 *Gargoyle*)
  3 SAM regt with S-400 (RS-SA-21 *Growler*); 96K6 *Pantsir*-S1 (RS-SA-22 *Greyhound*)

Airborne Forces
FORCES BY ROLE
MANOEUVRE
  Air Manoeuvre
  1 AB div

Eastern Military District

HQ at Khabarovsk

Army
FORCES BY ROLE
COMMAND
  4 army HQ
SPECIAL FORCES
  1 (Spetsnaz) SF bde
MANOEUVRE
  Armoured
  1 tk bde
  1 MR div
  6 MR bde
  Mechanised
  2 MR bde
  1 MGA div

196 THE MILITARY BALANCE 2023

SURFACE-TO-SURFACE MISSILE
4 SRBM/GLCM bde with *Iskander*-M
COMBAT SUPPORT
4 arty bde
1 MRL bde
1 engr bde
1 EW bde
1 NBC bde
4 NBC regt
COMBAT SERVICE SUPPORT
4 log bde
AIR DEFENCE
5 AD bde

Pacific Fleet
EQUIPMENT BY TYPE
SUBMARINES 17
STRATEGIC 3 **SSBN**
TACTICAL 15: 4 **SSGN** (2 more non-operational in long-term refit); 2 **SSN** (3 more non-operational in long-term refit); 9 **SSK**
PRINCIPAL SURFACE COMBATANTS 10: 1 **CGHM**; 5 **DDGHM**; 4 **FFGHM**
PATROL AND COASTAL COMBATANTS 28: 8 **FSM**; 4 **PCGM**; 10 **PCFG**; 6 **PB**
MINE WARFARE 11: 2 **MCC**; 2 **MSO**; 7 **MSC**
AMPHIBIOUS 9: 4 **LST**; 5 **LCM**

Naval Aviation
FORCES BY ROLE
FIGHTER
1 sqn with MiG-31BS/BM *Foxhound* A/C
ANTI-SUBMARINE WARFARE
1 sqn with Ka-27/Ka-29 *Helix*
2 sqn with Il-38/Il-38N *May*; Il-18D; Il-22 *Coot* B
1 sqn with Tu-142MK/MZ/MR *Bear* F/J
TRANSPORT
1 sqn with An-12BK *Cub*; An-26 *Curl*; Tu-134
AIR DEFENCE
1 SAM regt with S-400 (RS-SA-21 *Growler*); 96K6 *Pantsir*-S1 (RS-SA-22 *Greyhound*)

Naval Infantry
FORCES BY ROLE
MANOEUVRE
Mechanised
2 naval inf bde

Coastal Artillery and Missile Forces
FORCES BY ROLE
COASTAL DEFENCE
2 AShM bde

Military Air Force

11th Air Force & Air Defence Army
FORCES BY ROLE
FIGHTER/GROUND ATTACK
1 regt with MiG-31BM *Foxhound* C; Su-27SM *Flanker* J; Su-30M2 *Flanker* G; Su-30SM *Flanker* H; Su-35S *Flanker* M

1 regt with Su-35S *Flanker* M; Su-30SM *Flanker* H
1 regt with Su-25 *Frogfoot*; Su-30SM *Flanker* H
GROUND ATTACK
1 regt with Su-24M/M2 *Fencer* D/D mod; Su-34 *Fullback*
1 regt with Su-25SM *Frogfoot*
ISR
1 sqn with Su-24MR *Fencer* E
TRANSPORT
1 regt with An-12 *Cub*; An-26 *Curl*; Tu-134 *Crusty*/Tu-154 *Careless*
ATTACK/TRANSPORT HELICOPTER
1 bde with Ka-52A *Hokum* B; Mi-8 *Hip*; Mi-26 *Halo*
1 regt with Ka-52A *Hokum* B; Mi-8 *Hip*; Mi-26 *Halo*
1 regt with Mi-24P *Hind*; Mi-8 *Hip*
AIR DEFENCE
1 regt with 9K37M *Buk*-M1-2 (RS-SA-11 *Gadfly*);
1 regt with S-300V (RS-SA-12 *Gladiator/Giant*); S-400 (RS-SA-21 *Growler*)
4 regt with S-300PS (RS-SA-10B *Grumble*); S-400 (RS-SA-21 *Growler*); 96K6 *Pantsir*-S1 (RS-SA-22 *Greyhound*)

Airborne Forces
FORCES BY ROLE
MANOEUVRE
Air Manoeuvre
2 air aslt bde

Gendarmerie & Paramilitary 559,000

Border Guard Service ε160,000
Subordinate to Federal Security Service
FORCES BY ROLE
10 regional directorates
MANOEUVRE
Other
7 frontier gp
EQUIPMENT BY TYPE
ARMOURED FIGHTING VEHICLES
IFV/APC (W) 1,000 BMP/BTR/
AUV BPM-97
ARTILLERY 90
SP 122mm 2S1 *Gvozdika*
GUN/MOR • SP 120mm 2S9 NONA-S
MOR 120mm 2S12 *Sani*
PATROL AND COASTAL COMBATANTS 205
PSOHM 2 *Nerey* (*Krivak* III) with 1 twin ZIF-122 lnchr with 4K33 *Osa*-M (RS-SA-N-4 *Gecko*) SAM, 2 quad PTA-53-1135 533mm TT lnchr, 2 RBU 6000 *Smerch* 2 A/S mor, 1 100mm gun (capacity 1 Ka-27 *Helix* A ASW hel)
PSO 6: 4 *Komandor*; 2 *Okean* (Project 22100) with 1 76mm gun, 1 hel landing platform
PCM 1 *Okhotnik* (Project 22460) with 1 sextuple GMLS with *Igla*-1M (RS-SA-N-10 *Grouse*) SAM, 1 AK630 CIWS
PCO 29: 8 *Alpinist* (Project 503); 1 *Sprut*; 13 *Okhotnik* (Project 22460) with 1 AK630M CIWS, 1 hel landing platform; 8 *Purga* with 1 hel landing platform

PCC 33: 4 *Molnya* II (*Pauk* II); 6 *Svetlyak* (Project 10410); 13 *Svetlyak* (Project 10410) with 1 AK630M CIWS, 1 76mm gun; 8 *Svetlyak* (Project 10410) with 2 AK630M CIWS; 1 *Svetlyak* (Project 10410) with 1 AK630M CIWS; 1 *Yakhont*

PCR 1 *Slepen* (*Yaz*) with 1 AK630 CIWS, 2 100mm guns

PBF 87: 57 *Mangust*; 3 *Mirazh* (Project 14310); 4 *Mustang*-2 (Project 18623); 21 *Sobol*; 2 *Sokzhoi*

PBR 27: 4 *Ogonek*; 8 *Piyavka* with 1 AK630 CIWS; 15 *Moskit* (*Vosh*) with 1 AK630 CIWS, 1 100mm gun

PB 18: 6 *Gyuys* (Project 03050); 2 *Morzh* (Project 1496M); 10 *Lamantin* (Project 1496M1)

LOGISTICS AND SUPPORT 34

AE 1 *Muna*

AGB 2 *Ivan Susanin* (primarily used as patrol ships) with 2 AK630 CIWS, 1 76mm gun, 1 hel landing platform

AK 8 *Pevek*

AKSL 5 *Kanin*

AO 3: 1 *Ishim* (Project 15010); 2 *Envoron*

ATF 15: 14 *Sorum* (primarily used as patrol ships) with 2 AK230M CIWS; 1 *Sorum* (primarily used as patrol ship)

AIRCRAFT • TPT ε86: 70 An-24 *Coke*/An-26 *Curl*/An-72 *Coaler*/Il-76 *Candid*/Tu-134 *Crusty*/Yak-40 *Codling*; 16 SM-92

HELICOPTERS: ε200 Ka-27PS *Helix*/Mi-24 *Hind*/Mi-26 *Halo*/Mi-8 *Hip*

Federal Guard Service ε40,000–50,000

Org include elm of ground forces (mech inf bde and AB regt)

FORCES BY ROLE

MANOEUVRE

Mechanised

1 mech inf regt

Air Manoeuvre

1 AB regt

Other

1 (Presidential) gd regt

Federal Security Service Special Purpose Centre ε4,000

FORCES BY ROLE

SPECIAL FORCES

2 SF unit (Alfa and Vympel units)

National Guard ε335,000

FORCES BY ROLE

MANOEUVRE

Other

10 paramilitary div (2–5 paramilitary regt)

17 paramilitary bde (3 mech bn, 1 mor bn)

36 indep paramilitary rgt

90 paramilitary bn (incl special motorised units)

COMBAT SUPPORT

1 arty regt

TRANSPORT

8 sqn

EQUIPMENT BY TYPE

ARMOURED FIGHTING VEHICLES

RECCE some BRDM-2A

IFV/APC (W) 1,600 BMP-2/BTR-70M/BTR-80/

BTR-82A/BTR-82AM

PPV *Ural*-VV

AUV *Patrol*-A; *Tigr*

ARTILLERY 35

TOWED 122mm 20 D-30

MOR 120mm 15 M-1938 (PM-38)

PATROL AND COASTAL COMBATANTS 5

PBF 3 BK-16 (Project 02510)

PB 2+ *Grachonok*

AIRCRAFT

TPT 29: **Heavy** 9 Il-76 *Candid*; **Medium** 2 An-12 *Cub*; **Light** 18: 12 An-26 *Curl*; 6 An-72 *Coaler*

HELICOPTERS

TPT 71: **Heavy** 10 Mi-26 *Halo*; **Medium** 60+: 60 Mi-8 *Hip*; some Mi-8AMTSh *Hip*; **Light** 1 Ka-226T

Wagner Group ε10,000

Elements of Russian private military company 'Wagner' and associates integrated into the Russian command structure within Ukraine.

DEPLOYMENT

ARMENIA: 3,500: 1 mil base with (1 MR bde; 74 T-72; 80 BMP-1; 80 BMP-2; 12 2S1; 12 BM-21); 1 ftr sqn with 18 MiG-29 *Fulcrum*; 4 Su-30SM *Flanker* H; 1 hel sqn with 11 Mi-24P *Hind*; 4 Mi-8AMTSh *Hip*; 4 Mi-8MT *Hip*; 2 AD bty with S-300V; 1 AD bty with *Buk*-M1-2)

AZERBAIJAN: 1,960; 1 MR bde(-) (peacekeeping)

BELARUS: 10,000; 1 SSM bn with *Iskander*-M; 1 FGA sqn(-) with Su-34; Su-35S; 1 atk flt with MiG-31K; 2 SAM bn with S-400; 1 radar station at Baranovichi (*Volga* system; leased); 1 naval comms site

CENTRAL AFRICAN REPUBLIC: UN • MINUSCA 14

CYPRUS: UN • UNFICYP 6

DEMOCRATIC REPUBLIC OF THE CONGO: UN • MONUSCO 9

GEORGIA: ε4,000; Abkhazia: 1 mil base with 1 MR bde(-); 1 SAM regt with S-300PS; South Ossetia: 1 mil base with 1 MR bde(-)

KAZAKHSTAN: 1 radar station at Balkash (*Dnepr* system; leased)

KYRGYZSTAN: ε500; 13 Su-25SM *Frogfoot*; 2 Mi-8 *Hip*

MEDITERRANEAN SEA: 2 SSK; 1 FFGHM; 1 FFGM; 1 AGI

MIDDLE EAST: UN • UNTSO 4

MOLDOVA: Transnistria ε1,500 (including 400 peacekeepers): 2 MR bn; 7 Mi-24 *Hind*; some Mi-8 *Hip*

SOUTH SUDAN: UN • UNMISS 2

SUDAN: UN • UNISFA 2

SYRIA: 4,000: 1 inf BG; 3 MP bn; 1 engr unit; ε10 T-72B3; ε20 BTR-82A; BPM-97; *Typhoon*-K; *Tigr*; 12 2A65; 4 9A52 *Smerch*; 10 Su-24M *Fencer* D; 6 Su-34; 6 Su-35S *Flanker* M; 1 A-50U *Mainstay*; 1 Il-20M; 12 Mi-24P/Mi-35M *Hind*; 4 Mi-8AMTSh *Hip*; 1 AShM bty with 3K55 *Bastion*; 1 SAM bty with S-400; 1 SAM bty with *Pantsir*-S1/S2; air base at Latakia; naval facility at Tartus

TAJIKISTAN: ε3,000; 1 (201st) mil base with 1 MR bde(-); 1 hel sqn with 4 Mi-24P *Hind*; 4 Mi-8MTV *Hip*; 2 Mi-8MTV-5-1 *Hip*; 1 SAM bn with 8 S-300PS

UKRAINE: Donetsk, Kherson, Luhansk & Zaporizhzhia: ε150,000; Crimea: ε25,000; 1 recce bde, 2 naval inf bde(-); 1 air aslt regt(-); 1 arty bde; 1 NBC regt; 1 AShM bde with 3K60 *Bal*; 3K55 *Bastion*; 1 FGA regt with Su-24M/MR; Su-30SM; 1 FGA regt with Su-27SM/SM3; Su-30M2; 1 atk regt with Su-24M/Su-25SM; 1 atk/tpt hel regt; 1 ASW hel regt; 2 AD regt with S-400; *Pantsir*-S1; 1 Fleet HQ located at Sevastopol; 2 radar stations located at Sevastopol (*Dnepr* system) and Mukachevo (*Dnepr* system)

WESTERN SAHARA: UN • MINURSO 13

Tajikistan TJK

Tajikistani Somoni TJS		2021	2022	2023
GDP	TJS	99.0bn	112bn	
	USD	8.75bn	9.98bn	
per capita	USD	906	1,015	
Growth	%	9.2	5.5	
Inflation	%	9.0	8.3	
Def bdgt [a]	TJS	ε1.06bn	ε1.19bn	
	USD	ε94.0m	ε107m	
USD1=TJS		11.31	11.18	

[a] Excludes budget for law enforcement

Population	9,119,347					
Age	0–14	15–19	20–24	25–29	30–64	65 plus
Male	15.5%	4.7%	4.5%	4.2%	19.2%	1.6%
Female	14.9%	4.6%	4.3%	4.1%	20.0%	2.3%

Capabilities

The Tajik armed forces have little capacity to deploy other than token forces and most equipment is of Soviet-era origin. Regional security and terrorism remain key security concerns, given the border with Afghanistan. Tajikistan has been building its capability by hosting CSTO counter-terrorism exercises and by taking part in exercises, organised by US CENTCOM, focused on scenarios including counter-terrorism. Tajikistan is a member of the CSTO and the SCO, and the armed forces also conduct exercises with Russian troops based at Russia's 201st military base. In 2021, bilateral military exercises and CSTO joint drills concerned scenarios focused on the border with Afghanistan. Reports in early 2019 indicated that there may be a Chinese military facility in eastern Tajikistan, though this remains unconfirmed by either Beijing or Dushanbe. In 2021, reports indicated that China was to fund an outpost for Tajikistan's police special forces near to the border with Afghanistan. Though the pre-existing base is still officially denied by Beijing and Dushanbe, there were reports that full control of the facility would be transferred to Beijing and future rent will be waived in exchange for military aid from China. In 2018, India and Tajikistan agreed to strengthen defence cooperation, in particular on counter-terrorism and there were reports in 2021 of agreements on security cooperation with Iran. Border deployments have been stepped up recently in response to concerns about regional and border security and terrorism. In late 2016, a Military Cooperation Plan was signed with Russia. Moscow has indicated that Tajikistan is to receive military equipment, including aircraft. Some personal equipment has been donated by the US. Barring maintenance facilities, Tajikistan has only minimal defence-industrial capacity, though in 2022, Iran reportedly opened a UAV production line in the country.

ACTIVE 8,800 (Army 7,300 Air Force/Air Defence 1,500) **Gendarmerie & Paramilitary 7,500**
Conscript liability 24 months

RESERVE 20,000 (Army 20,000)

ORGANISATIONS BY SERVICE

Army 7,300
FORCES BY ROLE
MANOEUVRE
  Mechanised
  3 MR bde
  Air Manoeuvre
  1 air aslt bde
COMBAT SUPPORT
  1 arty bde
AIR DEFENCE
  1 SAM regt
EQUIPMENT BY TYPE
ARMOURED FIGHTING VEHICLES
  MBT 38: 28 T-72 Ural/T-72A/T-72AV/T-72B; 3 T-72B1; 7 T-62/T-62AV/T-62AM
  RECCE 31: 9 BRDM-2; 22 BRDM-2M
  IFV 23: 8 BMP-1; 15 BMP-2
  APC 36
    APC (W) 23 BTR-60/BTR-70/BTR-80
    PPV 13 VP11
  AUV 24 CS/VN3B mod; *Tigr*
ARTILLERY 40
  SP 122mm 3 2S1 *Gvozdika*
  TOWED 122mm 13 D-30
  MRL 122mm 14 BM-21 *Grad*
  MOR 10+: SP 82mm CS/SS4; 120mm 10
AIR DEFENCE
  SAM
    Medium-range 3 S-125 *Pechora*-2M (RS-SA-26)
    Short-range 5 S-125M1 *Neva*-M1 (RS-SA-3 *Goa*)
    Point-defence 9K32 *Strela*-2 (RS-SA-7 *Grail*)‡
  GUNS
    SP 23mm 8 BTR-ZD
    TOWED 23mm ZU-23M1

Air Force/Air Defence 1,500
FORCES BY ROLE
TRANSPORT
  1 sqn with Tu-134A *Crusty*
ATTACK/TRANSPORT HELICOPTER
  1 sqn with Mi-24 *Hind*; Mi-8 *Hip*; Mi-17TM *Hip* H

EQUIPMENT BY TYPE
AIRCRAFT
TPT • **Light** 1 Tu-134A *Crusty*
TRG 4+: 4 L-39 *Albatros*; some Yak-52
HELICOPTERS
ATK 4 Mi-24 *Hind*
TPT • **Medium** 11 Mi-8 *Hip*/Mi-17TM *Hip* H

Gendarmerie & Paramilitary 7,500

Internal Troops 3,800

National Guard 1,200

Emergencies Ministry 2,500

Border Guards

FOREIGN FORCES

China ε300 (trg)
Russia ε3,000; 1 (201st) mil base with 1 MR bde(-); 1 hel sqn with 4 Mi-24P *Hind*; 4 Mi-8MTV *Hip*; 2 Mi-8MTV-5-1 *Hip*; 1 SAM bn with 8 S-300PS

Turkmenistan TKM

Turkmen New Manat TMT		2021	2022	2023
GDP	TMT	218bn	261bn	
	USD	62.2bn	74.4bn	
per capita	USD	10,111	11,929	
Growth	%	4.6	1.2	
Inflation	%	15.0	17.5	
Def bdgt	TMT	n.k	n.k	
	USD	n.k	n.k	
USD1=TMT		3.50	3.50	
Population	5,636,011			

Age	0–14	15–19	20–24	25–29	30–64	65 plus
Male	12.6%	3.8%	4.0%	4.6%	21.9%	2.7%
Female	12.2%	3.8%	3.9%	4.6%	22.5%	3.5%

Capabilities

Turkmenistan has concerns over potential spillover from security challenges in Afghanistan, but its armed forces lack significant capabilities and equipment. Ashgabat has maintained a policy of neutrality since 1995 and confirmed this commitment in its 2016 military doctrine. This aimed to increase the armed forces' defensive capability in order to safeguard national interests and territorial integrity. Turkmenistan is not a member of the CSTO or the SCO. In 2022, Turkmenistan participated in the Organization of Turkic States (OTS) with observer status. The summit agreed to continue regular security cooperation and called for closer defence industrial and military cooperation. While the ground forces are shifting from a Soviet-era divisional structure to a brigade system, progress is slow. The armed forces are largely conscript-based and reliant on Soviet-era equipment and doctrine, and the government has stated a requirement to improve conditions of service. Turkmenistan has participated in multinational exercises and is reported to have restarted joint exercises with Russia and Uzbekistan, but has limited capacity to deploy externally and maintains no international deployments. In October 2019, in Saint Petersburg, Turkmenistan and four other Caspian littoral states signed a memorandum of understanding on military cooperation, among other discussions, including on maritime security. There are plans to strengthen the border guard with new equipment and facilities. Plans to bolster the naval forces have resulted in some procurements, leading to a modest improvement in the naval presence in the Caspian Sea. There has been limited procurement of systems such as UAVs, including from China and Turkey. A 2021 military parade also featured a range of new military equipment, including C-27J *Spartan*, EMB-314 *Super Tucano* and and M-346FA aircraft and *Bayraktar* TB2 UAVs. Apart from maintenance facilities, Turkmenistan has little domestic defence industry, but is building a number of patrol vessels of Turkish design under licence.

ACTIVE 36,500 (Army 33,000 Navy 500 Air 3,000)
Gendarmerie & Paramilitary 20,000
Conscript liability 24 months

ORGANISATIONS BY SERVICE

Army 33,000

5 Mil Districts

FORCES BY ROLE
SPECIAL FORCES
1 spec ops regt
MANOEUVRE
Armoured
1 tk bde
Mechanised
1 (3rd) MR div (1 tk regt; 3 MR regt, 1 arty regt)
1 (22nd) MR div (1 tk regt; 1 MR regt, 1 arty regt)
4 MR bde
1 naval inf bde
Other
1 MR trg div
SURFACE-TO-SURFACE MISSILE
1 SRBM bde with 9K72 *Elbrus* (RS-SS-1C *Scud* B)
COMBAT SUPPORT
1 arty bde
1 (mixed) arty/AT regt
1 MRL bde
1 AT regt
1 engr regt
AIR DEFENCE
2 SAM bde
EQUIPMENT BY TYPE†
ARMOURED FIGHTING VEHICLES
MBT 654: 4 T-90S; 650 T-72/T-72UMG
RECCE 260+: 200 BRDM-2; 60 BRM-1; Nimr *Ajban*
IFV 1,050: 600 BMP-1/BMP-1M; 4 BMP-1UM; 430 BMP-2; 4 BMP-2D; 4 BMP-3; 4 BTR-80A; 4 BTR-80 *Grom*
APC 907+
APC (W) 870+: 120 BTR-60 (all variants); 300 BTR-70; 450 BTR-80
PPV 37+: 28+ *Kirpi*; 9+ Titan-DS; some *Typhoon*-K
AUV 12+: 8 Nimr *Ajban* 440A; 4+ *Cobra*
ABCV 8 BMD-1

200 THE MILITARY BALANCE 2023

ANTI-TANK/ANTI-INFRASTRUCTURE
MSL

SP 58+: 8 9P122 *Malyutka*-M (RS-AT-3 *Sagger* on BRDM-2); 8 9P133 *Malyutka*-P (RS-AT-3 *Sagger* on BRDM-2); 2 9P148 *Konkurs* (RS-AT-5 *Spandrel* on BRDM-2); 36 9P149 *Shturm* (RS-AT-6 *Spiral* on MT-LB); 4+ *Baryer* (on *Karakal*)

MANPATS 9K11 *Malyutka* (RS-AT-3 *Sagger*); 9K111 *Fagot* (RS-AT-4 *Spigot*); 9K111-1 *Konkurs* (RS-AT-5 *Spandrel*); 9K115 *Metis* (RS-AT-7 *Saxhorn*)

GUNS 100mm 60 MT-12/T-12

ARTILLERY 769

SP 122mm 40 2S1

TOWED 457: **122mm** 350 D-30; **130mm** 6 M-46; **152mm** 101: 17 D-1; 72 D-20; 6 2A36 *Giatsint-B*; 6 2A65 *Msta-B*

GUN/MOR 120mm 17 2S9 NONA-S

MRL 158: **122mm** 92: 18 9P138; 70 BM-21 *Grad*; 4 BM-21A; RM-70; **220mm** 60 9P140 *Uragan*; **300mm** 6 9A52 *Smerch*

MOR 97: **82mm** 31; **120mm** 66 M-1938 (PM-38)

SURFACE-TO-SURFACE MISSILE LAUNCHERS
SRBM • Conventional 16 9K72 *Elbrus* (RS-SS-1C *Scud* B)

AIR DEFENCE
SAM

Short-range: FM-90 (CH-SA-4); 2K12 *Kub* (RS-SA-6 *Gainful*)

Point-defence 53+: 40 9K33 *Osa* (RS-SA-8 *Gecko*); 13 9K35 *Strela*-10 mod (RS-SA-13 *Gopher*); 9K38 *Igla* (RS-SA-18 *Grouse*); 9K32M *Strela*-2M (RS-SA-7 *Grail*)‡; 9K34 *Strela*-3 (RS-SA-14 *Gremlin*); *Mistral* (reported); QW-2 (CH-SA-8)

GUNS 70

SP 23mm 48 ZSU-23-4

TOWED 22+: **23mm** ZU-23-2; **57mm** 22 S-60

AIR-LAUNCHED MISSILES
ASM CM-502KG; AR-1

Navy 500
EQUIPMENT BY TYPE
PATROL AND COASTAL COMBATANTS 5

CORVETTES • FSGM 1 *Deñiz Han* with 4 twin lnchr with *Otomat* AShM, 1 16-cell CLA VLS with VL MICA, 1 Roketsan ASW Rocket Launcher System A/S mor, 1 *Gokdeniz* CIWS, 1 76mm gun, 1 hel landing platform

PCFG 2 *Edermen* (RUS *Molnya*) with 4 quad lnchr with 3M24E *Uran-E* (RS-SS-N-25 *Switchblade*) AShM, 2 AK630 CIWS, 1 76mm gun

PCGM 2 *Arkadag* (TUR *Tuzla*) with 2 twin lnchr with *Otomat* AShM, 2 twin *Simbad-RC* lnchr with *Mistral* SAM, 1 Roketsan ASW Rocket Launcher System A/S mor

LOGISTICS AND SUPPORT• AGHS 1 (Dearsan 41m)

Air Force 3,000
FORCES BY ROLE
FIGHTER

2 sqn with MiG-29A/S/UB *Fulcrum*

GROUND ATTACK

1 sqn with Su-25 *Frogfoot*
1 sqn with Su-25MK *Frogfoot*
1 sqn with M-346FA*

TRANSPORT

1 sqn with An-26 *Curl*; Mi-8 *Hip*; Mi-24 *Hind*

TRAINING

1 unit with EMB-314 *Super Tucano**
1 unit with L-39 *Albatros*

AIR DEFENCE

1 bty with FD-2000 (CH-SA-9)
1 bty with KS-1C (CH-SA-12)
3 bty with S-125 *Neva*-M1 (RS-SA-3 *Goa*)
1 bty with S-125 *Pechora*-2M (RS-SA-26)
2 bty with S-200 *Angara* (RS-SA-5 *Gammon*)

EQUIPMENT BY TYPE
AIRCRAFT 65 combat capable

FTR 24: 22 MiG-29A/S *Fulcrum*; 2 MiG-29UB *Fulcrum*

ATK 31: 19 Su-25 *Frogfoot*; 12 Su-25MK *Frogfoot*

TPT 5: **Medium** 2 C-27J *Spartan*; **Light** 3: 1 An-26 *Curl*; 2 An-74TK *Coaler*

TRG 12: 5 EMB-314 *Super Tucano**; 5 M-346FA*; 2 L-39 *Albatros*

HELICOPTERS

ATK 10 Mi-24P *Hind* F

MRH 2+ AW139

TPT 11+: **Medium** 8: 6 Mi-8 *Hip*; 2 Mi-17V-V *Hip*; **Light** 3+ AW109

UNINHABITED AERIAL VEHICLES

CISR 3+: **Heavy** CH-3A; WJ-600; **Medium** 3+ *Bayraktar* TB2

ISR 3+: **Medium** 3+ *Falco* **Light** *Orbiter*-2

LOITERING & DIRECT ATTACK MUNITIONS
Skystriker

AIR DEFENCE • SAM

Long-range 18: 2 2K11 *Krug* (RS-SA-4 *Ganef*); 4 FD-2000 (CH-SA-9); 12 S-200 *Angara* (RS-SA-5 *Gammon*);

Medium-range 8: 4 S-125 *Pechora*-2M (RS-SA-26); 4 KS-1A (CH-SA-12)

Short-range 12: 12 S-125M1 *Neva*-M1 (RS-SA-3 *Goa*); some S-125-2BM *Pechora*

AIR-LAUNCHED MISSILES

AAM • IR R-60 (RS-AA-8 *Aphid*); R-73 (RS-AA-11A *Archer*)

BOMBS

Laser-guided MAM-C; MAM-L

Gendarmerie & Paramilitary 20,000

Internal Troops ε15,000
EQUIPMENT BY TYPE
ARMOURED FIGHTING VEHICLES

IFV 2+ *Lazar*-3

APC • PPV 9: 4+ *Survivor* II; 5 *Titan-DS*

AUV 4+ Plasan *Stormrider*

Federal Border Guard Service ε5,000
EQUIPMENT BY TYPE
ARMOURED FIGHTING VEHICLES

APC • PPV 8: 4+ *Kirpi*; 4+ *Survivor* II

AUV 6+ *Cobra*

ARTILLERY • MRL 122mm 4 BM-21A

AIR DEFENCE

GUNS • TOWED • 23mm ZU-23-2

PATROL AND COASTAL COMBATANTS 33

PCGM 8 *Arkadag* (TUR *Tuzla*) with 2 twin lnchr with *Otomat* AShM, 2 twin *Simbad*-RC lnchr with *Mistral* SAM, 1 Roketsan ASW Rocket Launcher System A/S mor

PBFG 6 *Nazya* (Dearsan 33) with 2 single lnchr with *Marte* Mk2/N AShM

PBF 18: 10 *Bars*-12; 5 *Grif*-T; 3 *Sobol*

PB 1 *Point*

AMPHIBIOUS • **LCM** 1 Dearsan LCM-1

HELICOPTERS

MRH 2 AW139

TPT 3+: **Medium** some Mi-8 *Hip*; **Light** 3 AW109

Ukraine UKR

Ukrainian Hryvnia UAH		2021	2022	2023
GDP [a]	UAH	5.46tr	n.k	
	USD	200bn	n.k	
per capita	USD	4,862	n.k	
Growth	%	3.4	ε-35.0	
Inflation	%	9.4	ε20.6	
Def bdgt [b]	UAH	118bn	131bn	1.14tr
	USD	4.30bn	3.55bn	
FMA (US)	USD	115m	115m	165m
USD1=UAH		27.34	36.93	

[a] Limited IMF economic data available for Ukraine in 2022

[b] Official budget (including military pensions). Actual spending expected to be much higher in 2022 following Russian invasion in February. Significant uplift announced for 2023.

Real-terms defence budget trend (USDbn, constant 2015)

Population	43,528,136				
Age	0–14	15–19	20–24	25–29	30–64	65 plus
Male	8.3%	2.5%	2.3%	2.9%	24.4%	6.0%
Female	7.8%	2.4%	2.2%	2.8%	26.8%	11.7%

Capabilities

After absorbing the initial assault of Russia's February 2022 invasion, Ukrainian forces halted Russia's apparent attempt to seize Kyiv. By late-year Ukraine's forces were on the offensive, retaking territory in the Donetsk region and also around Kherson in the south and to the east of Kharkiv further north. Ukraine has received considerable support from Western states in the form of military materiel, most notably the US. This support has included the supply of main battle tanks, tube and rocket artillery, anti-armour and anti-air weapons. Intelligence support has also been forthcoming from some of these states. Substantial numbers of Ukrainian personnel have been killed or wounded, and equipment losses have been significant, but Ukrainian forces have also inflicted heavy losses on Russian forces. In response, at the end of September 2022, to Russian President Vladimir Putin's illegal annexation of several regions and claims that these were now Russian, Ukrainian President Volodymyr Zelenskyy announced Ukraine's application to join NATO. This move is unlikely to succeed in the near term, but it may have had an immediate propaganda value. General mobilisation was declared on 24 February: 18–60-year-old men were not allowed to leave the country, while women between 18–60 in certain professions also had to register for military service. After the invasion, substantial numbers of civilians volunteered for defence duties. At the outset of the war Ukraine's equipment inventory consisted predominantly of Soviet-era weaponry, though more modern ground equipment from Western sources has increasingly supplemented the inventory. After the February invasion there have been repeat deliveries of Turkish-manufactured UAVs while numerous countries have provided portable anti-armour and anti-air weapons. Western states have also started to provide heavier weapons, including main battle tanks and artillery, as well as training on these systems. A number of Western states are now offering training assistance to Ukrainian troops in their own nations, with this ranging from basic training and combat skills to training on new equipment. There is also some maintenance support. Since 2014, Western-delivered training support developed combat and command skills, including relating to NCOs. Ukraine's development of an NCO cadre after 2014 has proven valuable. In 2021, Ukraine replaced its Military Doctrine with a new Military Security Strategy, which built on the 2020 National Security Strategy. Part of the reform programme included the establishment of several new commands, including a Joint Forces Command. The war will spur Kyiv's ambition to replace its Soviet-era equipment, though the country will need considerable financial support in meeting this goal, as it will with wider reconstruction costs. Ukraine has a broad defence-industrial base, operating in all sectors, though its capability remains shaped, and limited, by its Soviet heritage. The condition of its defence-industrial facilities is unclear; many have been subject to Russian attacks. Ongoing combat, and Ukraine's mobilisation, means that equipment, forces and personnel assessments in the data sections should be treated with caution.

ACTIVE 688,000 (Army 250,000 Navy 13,000 Air Force 37,000 Airborne 30,000 Special Operations Forces 3,000 Territorial Defence 350,000)

Gendarmerie & Paramilitary 250,000

Conscript liability Army, Air Force 18 months, Navy 2 years. Minimum age for conscription raised from 18 to 20 in 2015

RESERVE 400,000 (Joint 400,000)

Military service within 5 years

ORGANISATIONS BY SERVICE

Army ε250,00

4 regional HQ

FORCES BY ROLE

MANOEUVRE

Reconnaissance

5 recce bn

Armoured

2 tk bde

Mechanised

9 mech bde

2 mtn bde

Light

4 mot inf bde

1 (volunteer) lt inf regt

SURFACE-TO-SURFACE MISSILES

1 SSM bde

202 THE MILITARY BALANCE 2023

COMBAT SUPPORT
5 arty bde
1 MRL bde
1 MRL regt
1 STA regt
1 engr bde
1 engr regt
1 ptn br regt
1 EW regt
1 EW bn
2 EW coy
1 CBRN regt
4 sigs regt

COMBAT SERVICE SUPPORT
1 engr spt bde
3 maint regt
1 maint coy

HELICOPTERS
4 avn bde

AIR DEFENCE
4 AD regt

Reserves

FORCES BY ROLE
MANOEUVRE
Armoured
3 tk bde
Mechanised
4 mech bde
Light
1 mot inf bde
1 lt inf bde
COMBAT SUPPORT
2 arty bde

EQUIPMENT BY TYPE

Warsaw Pact calibre artillery and missile systems may have limited or no available ammunition.

ARMOURED FIGHTING VEHICLES
MBT 953: 28 M-55S; 30 T-62M/MV; 250 T-64BV/BV mod 2017; 50 T-64BM *Bulat*; 500 T-72AV/AV mod 2021/B1/B3/M1/M1R/PT-91 *Twardy*; 80 T-80BV/BVM/U/UK; 10 T-90A; 5 T-84 *Oplot*
RECCE 200: 150 BRDM-2/-2L1/-2T; 50 BRM-1K (CP)
IFV 770: 500 BMP-1/-1AK/-2; 40 BMP-3; 60 BTR-3DA/-3E1/-4E/-4MV1; 80 BTR-82A; 35 BVP M-80A; 55 PbV-501; YPR-765
APC 1,159
　APC (T) 550: 350 M113A1/AS4/G3DK/G4DK; 200 MT-LB
　APC (W) 239: 39 ACSV; 200 BTR-60/-70/-80; XA-180 *Sisu*
　PPV 370: 50 *Kozak*-2/-2M; 240 *Maxxpro*; 80 *Varta*
AUV 95: 30 *Dingo* 2; 35 FV103 *Spartan*; 30 *Novator*; Roshel *Senator*
ENGINEERING & MAINTENANCE VEHICLES
AEV 40 BAT-2; MT-LB
ARV 10+: 10 BPz-2; BREM-1; BREM-M; BREM-2; BREM-64; BTS-4; IMR-2; VT-72M4CZ
VLB 17 *Biber*; MTU-20

ANTI-TANK/ANTI-INFRASTRUCTURE
MSL
　SP 9P148 *Konkurs* (RS-AT-5 *Spandrel*); 9P148 with *Stugna*-P; 9P149 with 9K114 *Shturm* (RS-AT-6 *Spiral*); M1064A1 HMMWV with TOW; *Brimstone*; *Brimstone* II
　MANPATS 9K111 *Fagot* (RS-AT-4 *Spigot*); 9K113 *Konkurs* (RS-AT-5 *Spandrel*); *Corsar*; FGM-148 *Javelin*; NLAW; *Stugna*-P
GUNS 100mm ε200 MT-12/T-12
ARTILLERY 1,536
SP 512: **122mm** 120 2S1 *Gvozdika*; **152mm** 204: 140 2S3 *Akatsiya*; 10 2S5 *Giatsint*-S; 35 2S19 *Msta*-S; 1+ *Dana*-M2; 18 M-77 *Dana*; **155mm** 168: 17 *Caesar*; 53 *Krab*; 50 M109A3GN/A4/A5Oe; 20 M109L; 6 M-2000 *Zuzana*; 22 PzH 2000; **203mm** 20 2S7 *Pion*
TOWED 493: **105mm** 33: 30 L119 Light Gun/M119A3; 3+ M101; **122mm** 60 D-30; **130mm** 18 M-46; **152mm** 230: 90 2A36 *Giatsint*-B; 80 2A65 *Msta*-B; 60 D-20; **155mm** 152: 20 FH 70; 132 M777A2
GUN/MOR • 120mm • TOWED 2B16 NONA-K
MRL 231: **122mm** 120: 100 9K51M *Tornado*-G/BM-21 *Grad*; 20 RM-70 *Vampir*; **220mm** 40 *Bureivy*/9P140 *Uragan*; **227mm** 31: 20 M142 HIMARS; 11 M270A1/B1 MLRS; **300mm** 40+: *Vilkha/Vilkha-M*; 40 9A52 *Smerch*
MOR 300: **120mm** 300: 100 2S12 *Sani*; 140 EM-120; some Krh/92; 60 M120-15; **SP 120mm** BTR-3M2
SURFACE-TO-SURFACE MISSILE LAUNCHERS
SRBM • Conventional some 9K79 *Tochka* (RS-SS-21 *Scarab*)
COASTAL • DEFENCE AShM RBS-17 *Hellfire*
HELICOPTERS
ATK ε35 Mi-24/Mi-35 *Hind*
TPT • Medium ε15 Mi-8 *Hip*
LOITERING & DIRECT ATTACK MUNITIONS
(Multiple systems below 20kg in weight)
AIR DEFENCE
SAM 81+
　Long-range Some S-300V (RS-SA-12A *Gladiator*)
　Short-range 10: 4 *Crotale* NG; 6 9K330 *Tor*-M (RS-SA-15 *Gauntlet*)
　Point-defence 9K33 *Osa*-AKM (RS-SA-8 *Gecko*); 9K35 *Strela*-10 (RS-SA-13 *Gopher*); 9K38 *Igla* (RS-SA-18 *Grouse*); 6 FV4333 *Stormer* with *Starstreak*; *Martlet*; *Mistral*; *Piorun*; *Starstreak*
　SPAAGM 30mm 75 2K22 *Tunguska* (RS-SA-19 *Grison*)
GUNS
　SP 23mm ZSU-23-4 *Shilka*; **35mm** 30 *Gepard*
　TOWED 23mm ZU-23-2; **57mm** S-60
AIR-LAUNCHED MISSILES • ASM *Barrier*-V

Navy ε13,000
After Russia's annexation of Crimea, HQ shifted to Odessa. Several additional vessels remain in Russian possession in Crimea

EQUIPMENT BY TYPE
PATROL AND COASTAL COMBATANTS 13
PCC 3 *Slavyansk* (ex-US *Island*)
PBG 3 *Gyurza*-M (Project 51855) with 2 *Katran*-M RWS with *Barrier* SSM
PBF 7: 6 Defiant 40; 1 *Kentavr*-LK

Russia and Eurasia 203

LOGISTICS AND SUPPORT 8
ABU 1 Project 419 (*Sura*)
AG 1 *Bereza*
AGI 1 *Muna*
AKL 1
AWT 1 *Sudak*
AXL 3 *Petrushka*

Naval Aviation ε1,000

EQUIPMENT BY TYPE
FIXED-WING AIRCRAFT
ASW (2 Be-12 *Mail* non-operational)
TPT • Light (2 An-26 *Curl* in store)
HELICOPTERS
ASW 7+: 4+ Ka-27 *Helix* A; 1 Mi-14PS *Haze* A; 2 Mi-14PL *Haze* C
TPT • Medium 1 Ka-29 *Helix*-B
TRG 1 Ka-226
UNINHABITED AERIAL VEHICLES
CISR • Medium *Bayraktar* TB2
BOMBS • Laser-guided MAM-C/-L

Naval Infantry ε4,000

FORCES BY ROLE
MANOEUVRE
Reconnaissance
1 recce bn
Light
1 nav inf bde
1 nav inf bde(-)
EQUIPMENT BY TYPE
ARMOURED FIGHTING VEHICLES
MBT T-64BV
IFV BMP-1; BMP-3
APC
APC (T) MT-LB
APC (W) BTR-60; BTR-80
PPV ε40 *Mastiff*; *Varta*
ANTI-TANK/ANTI-INFRASTRUCTURE
GUNS 100mm MT-12
ARTILLERY
SP 122mm 2S1 *Gvozdika*
TOWED 152mm 2A36 *Giatsint*-B
AIR DEFENCE
GUNS • SP 23mm ZSU-23-4

Coastal Defence ε1,500

FORCES BY ROLE
COASTAL DEFENCE
1 arty bde
1 MRL regt
EQUIPMENT BY TYPE
ARTILLERY
TOWED 152mm D-20
MRL 220mm 9P140 *Uragan*
COASTAL DEFENCE
AShM *Maritime Brimstone*; RGM-84 *Harpoon*; RK-360MC *Neptun*

Air Forces 37,000

4 Regional HQ

FORCES BY ROLE
FIGHTER
4 bde with MiG-29 *Fulcrum*; Su-27 *Flanker* B; L-39 *Albatros*
FIGHTER/GROUND ATTACK
2 bde with Su-24M *Fencer*; Su-25 *Frogfoot*
ISR
2 sqn with Su-24MR *Fencer* E*
TRANSPORT
3 bde with An-24 *Curl*; An-26 *Coke*; An-30 *Clank*; Il-76 *Candid*; Tu-134 *Crusty*
TRAINING
Some sqn with L-39 *Albatros*
TRANSPORT HELICOPTER
Some sqn with Mi-8 *Hip*; Mi-9 *Hip*; PZL Mi-2 *Hoplite*
AIR DEFENCE
6 bde with S-300PS/PT (RS-SA-10 *Grumble*)
3 regt with S-300PS/PT (RS-SA-10 *Grumble*)
3 regt with 9K37M *Buk*-M1 (RS-SA-11 *Gadfly*)

EQUIPMENT BY TYPE
AIRCRAFT 79 combat capable
FTR 50: ε20 MiG-29 *Fulcrum*; ε30 Su-27 *Flanker* B
ATK 20: ε5 Su-24M *Fencer* D; ε20 Su-25 *Frogfoot*
ISR 12: 3 An-30 *Clank*; ε9 Su-24MR *Fencer* E*
TPT 26: **Heavy** 4 Il-76 *Candid*; **Medium** 1 An-70; **Light** ε21: 3 An-24 *Coke*; ε17 An-26 *Curl*; 1 Tu-134 *Crusty*
TRG ε31 L-39 *Albatros*
HELICOPTERS
C2 ε14 Mi-9 *Hip*
MRH ε25 Mi-17 *Hip* H
TPT 25: **Medium** ε20 Mi-8 *Hip*; **Light** ε5 PZL Mi-2 *Hoplite*
UNINHABITED AERIAL VEHICLES
CISR • Medium *Bayraktar* TB2
ISR • Heavy some Tu-141 *Strizh*
AIR DEFENCE
SAM 271:
Long-range 208: 200 S-300PS/PT (RS-SA-10 *Grumble*); 8 S-300PMU (RS-SA-10 *Grumble*)
Medium-range 63: 60 9K37M *Buk*-M1 (RS-SA-11 *Gadfly*); 3+ IRIS-T SLM
Short-range NASAMS
GUNS • TOWED 23mm some ZU-23-2
AIR-LAUNCHED MISSILES
AAM • IR R-27ET (RS-AA-10D *Alamo*); R-60 (RS-AA-8 *Aphid*); R-73 (RS-AA-11A *Archer*); **SARH** R-27R (RS-AA-10A *Alamo*); R-27ER (RS-AA-10C *Alamo*)
ASM Kh-25 (RS-AS-10 *Karen*); Kh-29 (RS-AS-14 *Kedge*)
ARM AGM-88 HARM; Kh-25MP (RS-AS-12A *Kegler*); Kh-58 (RS-AS-11 *Kilter*)
BOMBS • Laser-guided MAM-C/-L

Airborne Assault Troops ε30,000

FORCES BY ROLE
MANOEUVRE
Reconnaissance
1 recce bn
Air Manoeuvre
1 AB bde
4 air aslt bde
1 air aslt regt
2 air mob bde
1 air mob bde (forming)

COMBAT SUPPORT
1 SP arty bn

EQUIPMENT BY TYPE

ARMOURED FIGHTING VEHICLES

MBT T-80BV mod

IFV BTR-3E1; BTR-4 *Bucephalus*

APC 166

APC (T) 30 BTR-D

APC (W) 93+: BTR-80; 10 *Dozor*-B; 27+ *Oncilla*; 56+ VAB

PPV 43+ *Kirpi*

ABCV 70: 20 BMD-1†; 50 BMD-2

AUV 56+: 56 *Bushmaster*; IVECO LMV; KrAZ *Spartan*; MLS *Shield*; *Novator*

ANTI-TANK/ANTI-INFRASTRUCTURE

MSL • MANPATS 9K111 *Fagot* (RS-AT-4 *Spigot*); 9K111-1 *Konkurs* (RS-AT-5 *Spandrel*); NLAW

ARTILLERY

SP 122mm 2S1 *Gvozdika*; **152mm** 2S3 *Akatsiya*

TOWED • 122mm D-30

MRL 122mm BM-21 *Grad*

GUN/MOR • SP • 120mm 30 2S9 NONA-S

MOR 120mm 2S12 *Sani*

AIR DEFENCE

SAM • Point-defence 9K35M *Strela*-10M; *Piorun*

GUNS • SP 23mm some ZU-23-2 (truck mounted)

Special Operations Forces ε3,000

FORCES BY ROLE

SPECIAL FORCES

2 SF regt

1 (volunteer) SF regt

1 SF bn

1 spec ops regt

1 spec ops bn

Territorial Defence Force ε350,000

FORCES BY ROLE

MANOEUVRE

Light

30 (territorial def) inf bde

Gendarmerie & Paramilitary 250,000

National Guard ε90,000

Ministry of Internal Affairs; 5 territorial comd

FORCES BY ROLE

MANOEUVRE

Mechanised

1 mech inf bde

Light

1 mot inf bde(-)

2 mot inf regt

2 inf bde

Other

3 sy bde

1 sy regt

EQUIPMENT BY TYPE

ARMOURED FIGHTING VEHICLES

MBT T-64; T-64BV; T-64BM; T-72; T-90M

IFV BMP-2; BTR-3; BTR-3E1; BTR-4 *Bucephalus*; BTR-4E

APC

APC (W) BTR-70; BTR-80

PPV Streit *Cougar*; Streit *Spartan*; *Kozak*-2; *Varta*

AUV *Novator*

ANTI-TANK/ANTI-INFRASTRUCTURE

MSL • MANPATS NLAW

RCL 73mm SPG-9

ARTILLERY

TOWED 122mm D-30

MOR 120mm some

AIRCRAFT

TPT • Light 24: 20 An-26 *Curl*; 2 An-72 *Coaler*; 2 Tu-134 *Crusty*

HELICOPTERS • TPT 14: **Medium** 11: 4 H225M; 7 Mi-8 *Hip*; **Light** 3: 2 H125; 1 Mi-2MSB

AIR DEFENCE

SAM • Point-defence 9K38 *Igla* (RS-SA-18 *Grouse*); *Piorun*

GUNS • SP 23mm some ZU-23-2 (tch)

Border Guard ε60,000

FORCES BY ROLE

MANOEUVRE

Other

1 (mobile) sy bn

19 sy bn

EQUIPMENT BY TYPE

ARMOURED FIGHTING VEHICLES

APC • PPV *Kozak*-2

Maritime Border Guard

The Maritime Border Guard is an independent subdivision of the State Commission for Border Guards and is not part of the navy

EQUIPMENT BY TYPE

PATROL AND COASTAL COMBATANTS 21

PCT 1 *Molnya* (*Pauk* I) with 4 single 406mm TT, 2 RBU 1200 *Uragan* A/S mor, 1 76mm gun

PCC 4 *Tarantul* (*Stenka*)

PB 12: 11 *Zhuk*; 1 *Orlan*

PBR 4 *Shmel* with 1 76mm gun

LOGISTICS AND SUPPORT • AGF 1

AIRCRAFT • TPT Medium An-8 *Camp*; **Light** An-24 *Coke*; An-26 *Curl*; An-72 *Coaler*

HELICOPTERS • ASW: Ka-27 *Helix* A

National Police ε100,000

Ministry of Internal Affairs

DEPLOYMENT

SERBIA: NATO • KFOR 40

TERRITORY WHERE THE GOVERNMENT DOES NOT EXERCISE EFFECTIVE CONTROL

Russia annexed the Ukrainian region of Crimea in March 2014, having occupied the territory the previous month. It has been used by Russia as a basing area since the start of its full-scale invasion of Ukraine in February 2022. Data presented here represents the de facto situation and does not imply international recognition.

FOREIGN FORCES

Russia Donetsk, Kherson, Luhansk & Zaporizhzhia, ε150,000; Crimea: ε25,000; 1 recce bde(-), 2 naval inf bde(-); 1 air aslt regt; 1 arty bde; 1 NBC bde; 1 AShM bde with 3K60 *Bal*; 3K55 *Bastion*; 1 FGA regt with Su-24M/MR; Su-30SM; 1 FGA regt with Su-27SM/SM3; Su-30M2; 1 atk regt with Su-24M/Su-25SM; 1 atk sqn(-) with Su-34; 1 atk/tpt hel regt; 1 ASW hel regt; 1 AD regt with S-300PM; 1 AD regt with S-400; 1 Fleet HQ located at Sevastopol; 2 radar stations located at Sevastopol (*Dnepr* system) and Mukachevo (*Dnepr* system)

Uzbekistan UZB

Uzbekistani Som UZS		2021	2022	2023
GDP	UZS	735tr	866tr	
	USD	69.2bn	79.1bn	
per capita	USD	2,002	2,243	
Growth	%	7.4	5.2	
Inflation	%	10.8	11.2	
Def exp	UZS	n.k	n.k	
	USD	n.k	n.k	
USS1=UZS		10615.12	10942.97	
Population	31,104,937			

Age	0–14	15–19	20–24	25–29	30–64	65 plus
Male	11.6%	3.8%	4.1%	4.8%	22.6%	2.8%
Female	11.1%	3.7%	3.9%	4.8%	23.2%	3.7%

Capabilities

Uzbekistan introduced a new military doctrine in early 2018, which highlighted increased concern over terrorism and the potential impact of conflicts including in Afghanistan. It noted a requirement for military modernisation. The doctrine also focuses on border security and hybrid-warfare concerns. Uzbekistan is a member of the SCO but suspended its CSTO membership in 2012. Uzbekistan is a member of the Organization of Turkic States, and the 2022 Summit Communique called for closer defence industrial cooperation and a common security concept. It maintains bilateral defence ties with Moscow. However, in 2022 Uzbekistan sent humanitarian aid to Ukraine and did not recognise the independence of the Luhansk and Donetsk 'people's republics.' In late 2018 a defence-cooperation agreement was reported with India. Military cooperation is developing with Turkey. Bilateral exercises were held in 2021, and in 2022 the two countries signed an agreement on military cooperation. The armed forces are army-dominated and conscript-based. Uzbekistan has a limited capacity to deploy its forces externally and does not have any international deployments. A sizeable air fleet was inherited from the Soviet Union, but minimal recapitalisation in the intervening period has substantially reduced the active inventory. Logistical and maintenance shortcomings hinder aircraft availability. Uzbekistan is reliant on foreign suppliers for advanced military equipment and procured equipment including military helicopters and armoured personnel carriers from Russia in 2019. Meetings took place with India in 2020 to advance defence cooperation (three defence-related MOUs were signed in 2019) and in 2021 the leaders of Pakistan and Uzbekistan signed an agreement on defence cooperation. A State Committee for the Defence Industry was established in late 2017 to organise domestic industry and defence orders. The 2018 doctrine calls for improvements to the domestic defence industry. In recent years, Uzbekistan's defence industry has showcased domestically produced light-armoured vehicles.

ACTIVE 48,000 (Army 24,500 Air 7,500 Joint 16,000)

Gendarmerie & Paramilitary 20,000

Conscript liability 12 months

ORGANISATIONS BY SERVICE

Army 24,500

4 Mil Districts; 2 op comd; 1 Tashkent Comd

FORCES BY ROLE

SPECIAL FORCES

1 SF bde

MANOEUVRE

Armoured

1 tk bde

Mechanised

11 MR bde

Air Manoeuvre

1 air aslt bde

1 AB bde

Mountain

1 lt mtn inf bde

COMBAT SUPPORT

3 arty bde 1 MRL bde

EQUIPMENT BY TYPE

ARMOURED FIGHTING VEHICLES

MBT 340: 70 T-72; 100 T-64B/MV; 170 T-62

RECCE 19: 13 BRDM-2; 6 BRM-1

IFV 370: 270 BMP-2; ε100 BTR-82A

APC 388

APC (T) 50 BTR-D

APC (W) 259: 24 BTR-60; 25 BTR-70; 210 BTR-80

PPV 79: *Cougar* 4×4; 24 *Ejder Yalcin*; 50 *Maxxpro+*; 5 *Typhoon*-K 4×4

ABCV 129: 120 BMD-1; 9 BMD-2

AUV 11+: 7 *Cougar*; 4+ M-ATV; some *Tigr*-M

ENGINEERING & MAINTENANCE VEHICLES

ARV 20 *Maxxpro* ARV

ANTI-TANK/ANTI-INFRASTRUCTURE

MSL • MANPATS 9K11 *Malyutka* (RS-AT-3 *Sagger*); 9K111 *Fagot* (RS-AT-4 *Spigot*)

GUNS 100mm 36 MT-12/T-12

ARTILLERY 487+

SP 83+: **122mm** 18 2S1 *Gvozdika*; **152mm** 17+: 17 2S3 *Akatsiya*; 2S5 *Giatsint*-S (reported); **203mm** 48 2S7 *Pion*

TOWED 200: **122mm** 60 D-30; **152mm** 140 2A36 *Giatsint*-B

GUN/MOR 120mm 54 2S9 NONA-S

MRL 108: **122mm** 60: 36 BM-21 *Grad*; 24 9P138; **220mm** 48 9P140 *Uragan*

MOR 120mm 42: 5 2B11 *Sani*; 19 2S12 *Sani*; 18 M-120

AIR DEFENCE • SAM

Point-defence QW-18 (CH-SA-11)

Air Force 7,500

FORCES BY ROLE

FIGHTER

1 sqn with MiG-29/MiG-29UB *Fulcrum* A/B

GROUND ATTACK

1 sqn with Su-25/Su-25BM *Frogfoot*

TRANSPORT

1 regt with Il-76 *Candid*; An-12 *Cub*; An-26 *Curl*; C295W; Tu-134 *Crusty*

TRAINING

1 sqn with L-39 *Albatros*

ATTACK/TRANSPORT HELICOPTER

1 regt with Mi-24 *Hind*; Mi-26 *Halo*; Mi-35M *Hind*; Mi-8 *Hip*

AIR DEFENCE

1 bty with FD-2000 (CH-SA-9)
1 bty with S-125-2M *Pechora*-2M (RS-SA-26)
2 bty with S-125M1 *Neva*-M1 (RA-SA-3 *Goa*)

EQUIPMENT BY TYPE

AIRCRAFT 24 combat capable

FTR 12 MiG-29/MiG-29UB *Fulcrum* A/B; (18 more in store); (26 Su-27/Su-27UB *Flanker* B/C in store)

ATK 12: 12 Su-25/Su-25BM *Frogfoot*; (15 Su-24 *Fencer* in store)

TPT 11: **Heavy** 2 Il-76 *Candid*; **Medium** 2 An-12 *Cub*; **Light** 7: 2 An-26 *Curl*; 4 C295W; 1 Tu-134 *Crusty*

TRG 6 L-39 *Albatros*

HELICOPTERS

ATK 41: 29 Mi-24 *Hind*; 12 Mi-35M *Hind*

TPT 69: **Heavy** 9: 8 H225M *Caracal*; 1 Mi-26 *Halo*; **Medium** 52 Mi-8 *Hip*; **Light** 8 AS350 *Ecureuil*

AIR DEFENCE • SAM 18

Long-range 4 FD-2000 (CH-SA-9)
Medium-range 4 S-125-2M *Pechora*-2M (RS-SA-26)
Short-range 10 S-125M1 *Neva*-M1 (RS-SA-3 *Goa*)

AIR-LAUNCHED MISSILES

AAM • IR R-60 (RS-AA-8 *Aphid*); R-73 (RS-AA-11A *Archer*); **IR/SARH** R-27 (RS-AA-10 *Alamo*)
ASM Kh-25 (RS-AS-10 *Karen*)
ARM Kh-25MP (RS-AS-12A *Kegler*); Kh-28 (RS-AS-9 *Kyle*); Kh-58 (RS-AS-11 *Kilter*)

Gendarmerie & Paramilitary up to 20,000

Internal Security Troops up to 19,000

Ministry of Interior

National Guard 1,000

Ministry of Defence

an IISS strategic dossier

MISSILE TECHNOLOGY: ACCELERATING CHALLENGES

The IISS Strategic Dossier *Missile Technology: Accelerating Challenges* examines the ballistic- and cruise-missile developments of the world's most prominent users and producers; the impact of development and procurement programmes on regional and strategic stability; the arms-control processes designed to restrain proliferation; and the trajectory of future technological developments, particularly Mach 5+ systems.

Missile Technology: Accelerating Challenges focuses on the missile forces of China, Russia and the United States, given the quantitative and qualitative dimensions of their arsenals, and prominent producers and operators of ballistic and cruise missiles in Asia, Europe and the Middle East.

The dossier examines the prospects for arms- and export-control mechanisms and confidence-building measures in an increasingly competitive environment characterised by accelerating proliferation and deteriorating global security.

DOWNLOAD FREE
https://go.iiss.org/MDISD

Chapter Six
Asia

- China's People's Liberation Army (PLA) held naval and air exercises to the north, southwest and east of Taiwan for three days in early August 2022, at the time of the visit to Taiwan of then-speaker of the US House of Representatives, Nancy Pelosi. After this, PLA assets have more frequently crossed the Taiwan Strait 'median line'.
- In China, 2022 saw continued deliveries of the Chengdu J-20 combat aircraft. Since at least 2021, the air force has been taking delivery of J-20s fitted with a domestic afterburning turbofan, the Shenyang WS-10C, replacing the Russian Saturn AL-31F variant.
- China began fielding JL-3 (CH-SS-N-20) ballistic missiles on its submarines. According to the Pentagon, newer longer-ranged missiles like the JL-3 give 'the PLAN the ability to target the continental United States from littoral waters.'
- By late October, North Korea had launched some 40 ballistic missiles – more than in any previous year. US and South Korean officials claimed that North Korea was in the final stages of planning its first nuclear test since 2017.
- Concerns were raised in India about potential dependence on Russia for defence supplies. Deliveries of S-400 systems continued, but only because of US congressional support for ensuring 'India's immediate defense needs' by waiving CAATSA sanctions in this specific case.
- Japan's government completed reviews of its National Security Strategy, National Defense Program Guidelines and Medium-Term Defense Program. Prime Minister Kishida Fumio set 2027 as a target for the defence budget to reach 2% of GDP.
- The new Australian government announced a Defence Strategic Review to deliver recommendations in early 2023. Meanwhile, discussions continued with the UK and US over the provision of a new fleet of conventionally armed, nuclear-powered submarines and other advanced military capabilities.
- Overall regional defence budget growth was below trend in real terms compared to the previous decade. This is partially a result of constrained government spending, but also related to the effect of inflation on the spending power of defence budgets.

Asia defence spending, 2022 – top 5

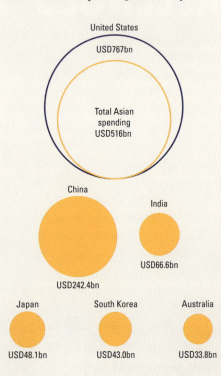

United States USD767bn
Total Asian spending USD516bn
China USD242.4bn
India USD66.6bn
Japan USD48.1bn
South Korea USD43.0bn
Australia USD33.8bn

Active military personnel – top 10
(25,000 per unit)

Country	Personnel
China	2,035,000
India	1,463,700
North Korea	1,280,000
Pakistan	651,800
South Korea	555,000
Vietnam	482,000
Indonesia	395,500
Thailand	360,850
Myanmar	356,000
Sri Lanka	255,000

Global total 20,773,950

44.2% Regional total 9,177,730

Regional defence policy and economics 210
Arms procurements and deliveries 226
Armed forces data section 229

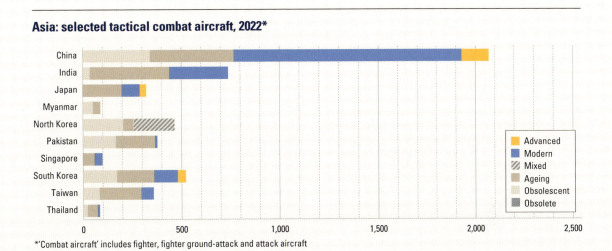

Asia: selected tactical combat aircraft, 2022*

*'Combat aircraft' includes fighter, fighter ground-attack and attack aircraft

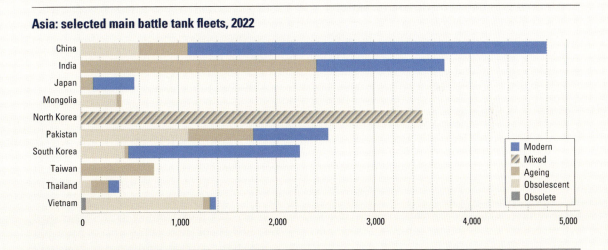

Asia: selected main battle tank fleets, 2022

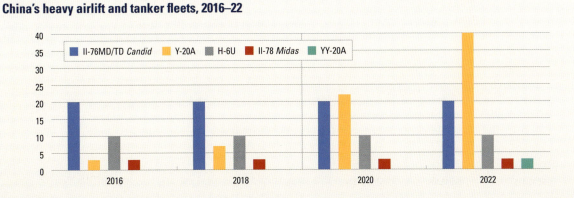

China's heavy airlift and tanker fleets, 2016–22

Asia

Russia's full-scale invasion of Ukraine in February 2022 further complicated the challenges faced by some Asia-Pacific defence establishments at a time when the region's security outlook was already deteriorating as a result of growing Chinese threats to Taiwan. Fears that developments in Ukraine might provide an opportunity for China to invade Taiwan while the United States and other Western powers were distracted proved unrealistic in the short term, but the war highlighted the danger of major inter-state conflict resulting from the failure of diplomacy and deterrence. In addition, Russia's lack of success in its initial offensive and the successes of the Western-backed Ukrainian armed forces provided reasons for Asia-Pacific armed forces to reassess their own capabilities and requirements.

Focus on dependence on Russian weapons

Almost immediately, the war in Ukraine posed challenges for Asian countries reliant on military equipment supplied by Russia. The considerable strengthening of US and European Union sanctions against Russia's defence-industrial sector following the invasion quickly affected India's defence procurement. In May, New Delhi reportedly halted negotiations for additional Ka-31 naval airborne early-warning helicopters and suspended plans to upgrade Su-30MKI combat aircraft with Russian assistance. Deliveries of S-400 systems continued, but only because of US congressional support for ensuring 'India's immediate defense needs' by waiving CAATSA (Countering American Adversaries Through Sanctions Act) sanctions in this specific case. Although important equipment has also recently come from contracts with French, UK and US suppliers, there remain considerable dependencies in all domains on Russian suppliers. Absent any significant weakening of sanctions, India will need to consider alternative sources for some of its equipment purchases, as well as for spares and support for many of its Soviet- and Russian-origin systems, while bolstering its co-development and co-production of defence systems with foreign partners. India's aim remains to produce more defence materiel itself, and the government has redoubled its efforts in this area,

but India's defence industry remains largely unable to deliver advanced-weapons systems in significant numbers and on time. Speaking in July 2022, India's chief of army staff, General Manoj Pande, stressed that India's dependence on imported arms was 'a matter of concern'. Along with some other Asian countries, such as Myanmar, Vietnam was similarly affected, and it seemed likely that the new obstacles to importing Russian arms would reinforce Hanoi's drive to widen the range of military equipment and technology it imports from other sources. The 'Vietnam Defence 2022' exhibition scheduled for Hanoi in December 2022 seemed designed to attract a wide range of potential suppliers to Vietnam.

Sino-Russian collaboration

Russian military equipment and technology have been important for the modernisation of China's People's Liberation Army (PLA): key examples during the last decade include Su-35 combat aircraft and S-400 air-defence systems, and assistance for China's development of a ballistic missile early-warning system. In the past two decades, however, China's defence industry has produced increasing volumes of advanced equipment itself as part of Beijing's military modernisation ambitions. Indeed, since the 2014 crisis over Ukraine and the Western sanctions against Russia following its annexation of Crimea, bilateral defence-industrial interdependence has grown, with China becoming a vital source for components that Russia cannot now obtain from the West and, more importantly, a major partner in joint projects to develop air-defence systems and engines for combat aircraft. The 'no limits' bilateral relationship declared by the two countries' leaders in early February 2022 may exaggerate the depth and potential of contemporary Sino-Russian relations, and a formal Sino-Russian military alliance or direct Chinese military support for Russia's war in Ukraine both seem unlikely prospects. Nevertheless, the bilateral partnership is now closer and includes an increasingly strong military dimension that goes beyond defence-industrial cooperation. In October 2021, the *Joint Sea–2021* bilateral exercise brought the two countries' navies together in the Sea of Japan,

Map 5 — China and Russia: selected military cooperation activities, 2019–22

Military cooperation between China and Russia has increased in recent years. Between 2013 and 2015, exercises took place annually, but since then they have gradually increased in number. 2022 saw the two countries' military cooperation increase in frequency with a number of joint air or naval patrols and joint exercises. These have included airlift, manoeuvring and live-fire drills, predominantly taking place in and above waters to the west of Japan, with limited instances in the Arabian Sea and Pacific Ocean. The joint exercises have not entered Japanese territorial waters. While the two countries likely use this military cooperation as a form of political signalling, such as of their 'no limits' friendship following Russia's war in Ukraine, the depth of this bilateral military cooperation, including its utility in terms of developing combat capability and interoperability, remains unclear.

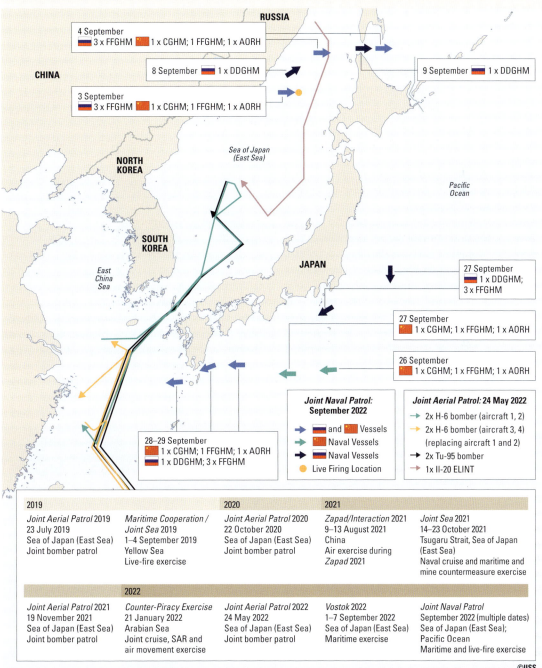

2019	2020	2021		2022	
Joint Aerial Patrol 2019 23 July 2019 Sea of Japan (East Sea) Joint bomber patrol	**Maritime Cooperation / Joint Sea 2019** 1–4 September 2019 Yellow Sea Live-fire exercise	**Joint Aerial Patrol 2020** 22 October 2020 Sea of Japan (East Sea) Joint bomber patrol	**Zapad/Interaction 2021** 9–13 August 2021 China Air exercise during Zapad 2021	**Joint Sea 2021** 14–23 October 2021 Tsugaru Strait, Sea of Japan (East Sea) Naval cruise and maritime and mine countermeasure exercise	
Joint Aerial Patrol 2021 19 November 2021 Sea of Japan (East Sea) Joint bomber patrol	**Counter-Piracy Exercise** 21 January 2022 Arabian Sea Joint cruise, SAR and air movement exercise	**Joint Aerial Patrol 2022** 24 May 2022 Sea of Japan (East Sea) Joint bomber patrol	**Vostok 2022** 1–7 September 2022 Sea of Japan (East Sea) Maritime exercise	**Joint Naval Patrol** September 2022 (multiple dates) Sea of Japan (East Sea); Pacific Ocean Maritime and live-fire exercise	

©IISS

with the participating Chinese flotilla led by a Type-055 cruiser. In early September 2022, around 2,000 Chinese personnel along with air, land and naval equipment took part in Russia's *Vostok 2022* exercise. In addition, in November 2021 and May 2022 the Chinese and Russian air forces conducted their third and fourth 'joint strategic patrols' in the Asia-Pacific region. Nonetheless, how far these ties advance combat capability remains unclear.

Defending Taiwan

These developments occurred against the background of growing strategic tensions between China on one side and the US and its allies on the other. Chinese pressure on Taiwan increasingly made the island a focal point of these tensions. In March 2022, Commander of US Indo-Pacific Command Admiral John Aquilino said that Russia's actions had reinforced concerns that China might attack Taiwan and called for the US to re-examine its policy of 'strategic ambiguity' towards defending the island. That policy broadly prevailed despite President Joe Biden's indications during 2021–22 that the US was willing to defend Taiwan militarily. Meanwhile, PLA aircraft have continued to cross the notional 'median line' in the Taiwan Strait. While Taipei claimed these flights were supposed to intimidate Taiwan and wear down its air defences' effectiveness by provoking frequent alerts and scrambles, some of them may have had genuine training purposes or supported PLA efforts to track US and other submarines. Nonetheless, these flights appear to have increased in frequency after US House of Representatives Speaker Nancy Pelosi visited Taiwan on 2 August.

Major PLA naval and air exercises held to the north, southwest and east of Taiwan for three days in early August 2022 were widely viewed as a measure of Beijing's strong disapproval of Pelosi's visit. However, the exercises, which were some of the largest organised by the PLA in Taiwan's vicinity, would have required months of planning and may have been part of Beijing's overall drive to improve China's military. It is also possible that the annual August exercises were adapted in light of Pelosi's visit or that the PLA was executing a pre-planned contingency response, or a blend of the two. Following the exercises, President Tsai Ing-wen identified flights by Chinese-operated uninhabited aerial vehicles (UAVs) over the Kinmen and Matsu islands as among Beijing's 'grey-zone tactics'. On 1 September, Taiwan's armed forces shot down an 'unidentified civilian drone' that entered airspace near Shiyu, an islet in the Kinmen group only ten kilometres from China's coast. Meanwhile, the Biden administration – perhaps taking to heart early lessons from the war in Ukraine – reinforced its encouragement of Taiwan's development of 'asymmetric' or 'porcupine' defence capabilities suited to slowing down any Chinese invasion attempt. By September 2022, the US Defense Security Cooperation Agency was listing a number of approved sales of defence equipment and support services to Taipei since Biden took office, the most recent including contractor support for Taiwan's PAVE PAWS long-range surveillance radar system together with additional RGM-84L *Harpoon* Block II coastal-defence systems and AIM-9X *Sidewinder* II air-to-air missiles. However, these sales remain subject to congressional approval in the US.

Taiwan: lessons from 2022

For Taiwan, 2022 presented an opportunity to learn how to prepare for and respond to an armed attack, as well as measures to deter Beijing in a worsening political and military-security environment across the Taiwan Strait. In her 'Double-Ten' National Day speech, President Tsai Ing-wen outlined a number of ambitions: increase Taiwan's defence budget each year, ramp up production of precision-guided missiles and naval vessels, work to acquire asymmetric warfare capabilities, make progress in domestic aircraft and shipbuilding (including the indigenous submarine programme), establish a defence-mobilisation agency to train reservists and broaden public awareness of Taiwan's self-defence needs.

Taipei and its armed forces have watched closely both the successes and the failures of Russia's armed forces in Ukraine, as well as Ukraine's military and civil response, for any potential lessons that may be helpful in a possible Taiwan contingency. The armed forces' continued balancing of asymmetric and conventional capabilities reflects the need to respond to both grey-zone and full-scale invasion threats posed by the PLA. While US President Joe Biden has on several occasions mentioned the United States' unequivocal military support for Taiwan in any armed attack launched by the PLA, Taipei and Washington reportedly disagree about how much focus should be placed on the development of asymmetric capabilities; according to specialists, the US would prefer to see Taipei prioritise these.

The PLA's exercises following Speaker of the House Nancy Pelosi's visit to Taipei in August 2022 created a 'new normal' for PLA activity across the strait. This has included regular air and naval incursions across the Taiwan Strait 'median line', which Beijing has said does not exist. The PLA has also begun integrating uninhabited aerial vehicles (UAVs) into its air defence identification zone incursions and has leveraged civilian UAV technology to conduct surveillance of islands close to the Chinese mainland. On one such occasion, Taiwanese soldiers were filmed throwing stones to ward off the UAV, apparently uncertain of how to respond. Later, Taiwanese armed forces shot down a PLA UAV, likely in an attempt to set a precedent against further provocation.

Nevertheless, lessons learned from the war in Ukraine may be more helpful than any gleaned from the post-Pelosi exercises. For instance, plans have been discussed to raise the duration of conscription from four months to one year. Similarly, Taipei is developing a centralised approach to civil-defence preparedness. This has until now been a largely bottom-up process and a meagre area of work for few in Taiwanese civil society. Nonetheless, these efforts remain nascent and, so far, Taiwan lacks the same level of investment in civil defence that Ukraine looked to develop following Russia's 2014 assault and annexation of Crimea.

Japan and South Korea modernise at pace

The war in Ukraine as well as Taiwan-related developments influenced thinking about defence policy by the new Japanese government led by Kishida Fumio, who became prime minister in October 2021, reinforcing the view that a tougher posture was needed to deter 'grey-zone' coercion as well as larger-scale aggression. In November, the Cabinet approved a supplementary budget which boosted annual defence spending to JPY6.17 trillion (USD48.1bn) for 2022.

In late 2021, Kishida's administration started reviewing the country's National Security Strategy, National Defense Program Guidelines and Medium-Term Defense Program. These reviews were completed at the end of 2022 and may yield substantial increases in defence spending. In his keynote address to the IISS Shangri-La Dialogue in June 2022, Kishida said that no military option, including 'counter-strike capabilities' to deter missile attacks, would be ruled out. Tokyo's annual *Defense of Japan* White Paper, published in July 2022, said that Japan's security environment was 'growing increasingly severe at an unprecedented pace', meaning Japan needed to strengthen its defence capabilities 'dramatically'. The White Paper emphasised Tokyo's particular concern over China's efforts to 'change the status quo by coercion in the East China Sea and South China Sea', its deepening ties 'with Russia, an aggressor nation', and Beijing's threats to reunify with Taiwan 'by force'. In August the defence ministry requested a budget for FY2023 that was 1.1% larger than that for 2022 and included funding for a joint next-generation combat-aircraft programme with the UK; additional F-35A and F-35B *Lightning* II fighter ground-attack aircraft; Joint Strike Missiles to arm the F-35A; AGM-158B JASSM-ER air-to-surface missiles; continued modifications to the two *Izumo*-class helicopter carriers to allow shipborne F-35B operations; large-scale production of indigenously developed Type-12 coastal-defence missiles; and continued research on hypersonic missiles. In addition, the Japan Self-Defense Forces continued to strengthen their deterrent posture by establishing additional forces on Kyushu and the southwestern island chain: during 2022, these were scheduled to include surface-to-air- and anti-ship-missile as well as electronic-warfare and radar units.

Tokyo expressed concern over the new phase of North Korea's ballistic-missile tests that started in September 2021. These initially included tests of a new submarine-launched ballistic missile but by the end of the year there had also been claims of a hypersonic-glide-vehicle test and an apparent land-attack cruise-missile launch. By late October 2022, North Korea had launched some 40 ballistic missiles – more than in any previous year. While these were predominantly shorter-range types, they also included – for the first time since 2017 – a series of intercontinental ballistic missile-related launches in March and May as well as an overflight of Japan by a claimed new intermediate-range ballistic missile in October. US and South Korean officials repeatedly claimed during 2022 that Kim Jong-un's regime was in the final stages of planning a seventh nuclear test, its first since 2017. Under President Yoon Suk-yeol, elected in May 2022, South Korea continued to combine economic incentives and military deterrence in response to the missile and nuclear challenges from Pyongyang. However, the Yoon administration was less conciliatory than its predecessor and stressed the development of independent national military capabilities and strengthened military cooperation with the US. In July, Yoon publicly emphasised the importance of South Korea's 'Kill Chain' system, which would involve pre-emptive strikes against key North Korean targets. The president also announced that a joint-service Strategic Command would be established by 2024 to take responsibility for Seoul's 'three-axis' strategic deterrence and defence, comprising 'Kill Chain' and two other systems: Korea Massive Punishment and Retaliation (under which conventionally armed ballistic missiles would be launched in response to an attack by North Korea, potentially targeting its senior leaders as well as nuclear and missile installations and long-range artillery) and Korean Air and Missile Defense. Developing all three systems will depend in large measure on South Korea's space and missile capabilities. The lifting of US-imposed 'missile guidelines' in 2021 has allowed Seoul to accelerate its development of ballistic missiles with two-ton warheads which could, in combination with enhanced surveillance, provide a powerful precision-strike capability. In July 2021, Seoul contracted the US private-sector company SpaceX to launch five surveillance satellites by 2025. Separately, in June, the Korea Aerospace Research Institute achieved its first satellite launch using the domestically produced KSLV-2 rocket.

From 22 August to 1 September South Korean and US forces held their largest joint exercise since 2017; it was also the first in five years to involve joint field training, which had been paused due to the previous South Korean administration's policy of seeking dialogue with Pyongyang and restrictions related to the coronavirus pandemic. Details of Exercise *Ulchi Freedom Shield* were classified, but one significant feature was that for the first time the US Forces Korea commander shared control with a South Korean senior officer. The US has set such experience for South Korean military commanders as one of many requirements to be fulfilled before South Korea can assume command responsibility for its armed forces in wartime. During the exercise, President Yoon ordered the armed forces to accelerate their 'updating' of operational plans to counter the North Korean threat.

Budgetary constraints slow Southeast Asian capability improvements

Southeast Asian states facing Chinese pressure on their South China Sea interests continued efforts to enhance their naval and air capabilities. In the Philippines, a new administration led by President Ferdinand Marcos Jr was elected in May 2022. A spokesman for the country's Department of National Defense emphasised in August that all major military-modernisation contracts agreed by the previous administration would proceed. These included the purchase of two multi-role missile-armed HDC-3100 frigates and six offshore patrol vessels from South Korea, *BrahMos* anti-ship missiles from India and additional S-70i helicopters from Poland. Nevertheless, because of budgetary constraints the new administration launched a review of the armed forces' modernisation programme and some projects were halted, including mooted plans to acquire conventionally-powered submarines.

Although some domestic critics claimed that efforts to strengthen Indonesia's navy and air force were not effective responses to Beijing's 'grey-zone' strategy in the South China Sea (which included a Chinese survey vessel mapping the seabed inside Jakarta's exclusive economic zone (EEZ) for seven weeks during 2021), Jakarta's defence plans continued to be among Southeast Asia's most expansive. In February 2022, defence minister Prabowo Subianto signed agreements with France covering the purchase of 42 *Rafale* combat aircraft and two *Scorpène*-class submarines. These agreements represented significant changes in the country's defence procurement: an earlier plan to buy Su-35 aircraft from Russia was apparently abandoned owing to fears over the potential imposition of US sanctions, and it seemed likely that Jakarta would cancel a project to acquire a second batch of three Type 209/1400 submarines from South Korea. Also in February, the US government conditionally approved the sale to Indonesia of up to 36 F-15EX aircraft. However, these major procurement plans – combined with other recent contracts, including one for six FREMM and two *Maestrale*-class frigates ordered from Italy, and another for two A400M transport aircraft – threatened to overwhelm Indonesia's defence budget, which in 2021 required a presidentially approved USD2.06 billion special supplement to cover equipment and defence-industrial costs. By July 2022, it was reported that the defence ministry was struggling to find the funds to honour existing contracts.

Malaysia also experienced Beijing's 'grey-zone' tactics, particularly off the coasts of Sabah and Sarawak states, such as in October 2021 when Chinese vessels including a survey ship entered its EEZ. However, there was no perceived acute threat to Malaysia's security and continuing budgetary restrictions impeded efforts to modernise its military capabilities. Procurement priorities remained confined to new light combat aircraft, long- and medium-range air defence radars, maritime patrol aircraft and medium-altitude long-endurance UAVs, but near-term acquisitions mainly focused on less expensive equipment. In March 2022, defence minister Hishammuddin Hussein said that current procurement projects for the army included armoured personnel carriers for use by the Malaysian battalion with the United Nations Interim Force in Lebanon, 155-millimetre self-propelled howitzers, logistic-support bridges and light anti-tank weapons. New naval equipment 'in the pipeline' included a second batch of three Littoral Mission Ships, three AW139 utility helicopters and 'about 13' fast interceptor craft. Hishammuddin also announced plans to acquire 24 new helicopters from 2026 and highlighted the conversion of three CN235 transport aircraft to maritime patrol configuration with funding from the US government's regional Maritime Security Initiative.

Thailand is not a claimant in the South China Sea but is concerned about the region's increasingly tense maritime security environment and continues efforts to enhance its naval capabilities. Submarine acquisition remains a priority, although this project faces major challenges. Bangkok suspended plans to buy two additional S26T *Yuan*-class submarines on order from China (along with other defence-equipment contracts) in April 2020 owing to the financial constraints imposed by the coronavirus pandemic. During March 2022, Thailand's navy confirmed that construction in China of the first boat had stopped following Germany's refusal – due to the EU's arms embargo on Beijing – to supply the MTU396 diesel engines needed to power its electric generators. It was reported that China had offered to transfer two ex-PLA Navy (PLAN) submarines to Thailand instead, but naval acquisitions director-general Rear Admiral Apichai Sompolgrunk said in April that, though it was too early to talk of cancelling the contract, only the *Yuan*-class boat was acceptable. In August 2022, it was reported that the China Shipbuilding & Offshore International Co. was offering replacement engines. Thailand's air force also faced re-equipment challenges. In January, the Cabinet approved in principle a plan to acquire four F-35As in FY2023, to be followed by a further four of the same type. However, in August objections from Thailand's House Budget Scrutiny Committee, in light of the country's economic downturn, cut initial proposed procurement to two aircraft. Another potential impediment was that the purchase needed approval from the US government: some analysts thought this might not be granted because of Thailand's close defence relations with China and the information-security requirements associated with the sale of the F-35.

A brief incursion by one of Myanmar's combat aircraft into Thai airspace in June highlighted the dangers that this neighbour's internal conflict posed for Thailand's security, despite the generally equable relations between the two countries' governments. Since May 2021, airstrikes and artillery fire in Myanmar's Kayin and Kayah states have also forced thousands of displaced people to cross the border into Thailand. Meanwhile, fighting between forces loyal to the State Administration Council (SAC) junta (including the *Pyusawhti* militias as well as the Tatmadaw, Myanmar's armed forces) and opposition groups comprising the People's Defence Forces aligned with the pro-democracy National Unity Government and some of the country's ethnic armed organisations was increasingly widespread across the country. Economic weakness and the Tatmadaw's preoccupation with internal-security threats meant that efforts to improve conventional military capabilities were no longer prioritised to the extent they had been before the February 2021 military coup. Until early 2022, the country's main military-equipment suppliers had been Russia and Ukraine, and the war in Ukraine and international sanctions have raised questions over the durability of these supplier relationships and where else Myanmar might look for its defence equipment. Although the Tatmadaw has a long-standing aversion to overly heavy reliance on Beijing, in December 2021 Myanmar's navy took delivery of an ex-PLAN Type-035B (*Ming*) submarine from China. And reports indicated that Myanmar was strengthening its military relations with North Korea, though it was unclear what the implications might be in terms of equipment supplies. Nonetheless, there were reports in September that Myanmar was to receive Su-30SM combat aircraft from Russia, under a 2018 contract.

Australia's new government and defence policy

Although Australia had a new Labor government following elections in May 2022, there was considerable continuity in defence policy. During the election campaign, Labor indicated its support for the then-government's defence-spending increases, [Labour have since released their own budget in October] in the March 2022 budget; it also agreed with the country's major investments in new frigates and nuclear-powered submarines (SSNs), the latter to be provided through the trilateral AUKUS arrangement with the UK and US. However, these are long-term programmes (the first SSN not being delivered until the mid-2040s, according to Richard Marles, the new defence minister) and the new government inherited a major challenge in terms of how to improve Australia's defence capability to deter fast-emerging threats during the current decade. Responding to this challenge, in August the government announced a Defence Strategic Review that will examine 'force structure, force posture and preparedness, and investment prioritisation' and deliver recommendations to the government in early 2023. The government is also due to announce by March 2023 the type of SSN that Australia will acquire, and there may be a decision by then on whether an interim non-nuclear submarine capability will be needed during the 2030s, pending the commissioning of SSNs. Meanwhile, in late August, Marles announced that Australian submariners would train aboard British *Astute*-class SSNs.

DEFENCE ECONOMICS

Macroeconomics

While Asia's recovery from the coronavirus pandemic continued through 2022, GDP remained lower than pre-pandemic levels in two-thirds of the region's economies, with mounting headwinds calling into doubt future prospects for growth. Real GDP growth had recovered to 6.5% in 2021. However, a new wave of infections and consequent lockdowns, coupled with the impact of Russia's invasion of Ukraine on 24 February 2022, quickly saw expectations for 2022 diminished. In October 2021, the IMF was forecasting real GDP growth of 5.7% for the Asia-Pacific in 2022, but this was subsequently revised down to 4.9% in April 2022 and further to 4.0% in October 2022 as a result of mounting impediments to growth, largely in China.

The economic problems facing the Asia-Pacific region are broadly similar to those faced elsewhere, though their impact varies. As much of the world adjusts to living with COVID-19, sporadic and severe lockdowns have continued in China because of Beijing's then zero tolerance approach to outbreaks. This in turn has had a significant impact on economic growth in Asia's largest economy, with knock-on effects for the rest of the region. Similarly, the impact of the war in Ukraine was initially less severe than in other regions, though increases in energy and food prices within the region served to dampen demand, both directly and indirectly through their influence on both domestic and foreign consumers. Inflation began to rise through the second half of 2022, but it remains low in most Asian economies. In general, Asia's commodity exporters find themselves in a stronger position than its importers given these pressures, though the negative effect upon growth is expected to be felt throughout the region.

Higher energy prices and other key commodities have also had an immediate impact on government finances in a number of Asian states because of the tendency for the region's emerging economies to provide related subsidies to their populations. For example, Indonesia initially earmarked USD10.2 billion for energy subsidies in its 2022 budget, but by mid-year had been forced to increase this total to USD33.8bn. Wider inflationary pressures have had a similar impact in Malaysia, where the Ministry of Finance announced in June that the overall subsidies

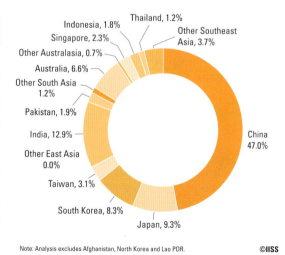

▲ Figure 10 **Asia: defence spending by country and sub-region, 2022**

bill for energy, basic foodstuffs, agriculture and welfare would reach its highest-ever level in 2022 at USD17.9bn. Combined with a need to rein in budget deficits, which proliferated through the pandemic, this new and unexpected spending has placed considerable strain on government budgets and left little headroom for expansionary policy in alternative areas.

Defence spending

Against the backdrop of these mounting economic and fiscal challenges, overall defence budget growth in the region was significantly below trend in real terms compared to the previous decade. This is partially a result of constrained government spending, but also related to the effect of inflation on the spending power of defence budgets. Where significant growth did occur, it was generally the result of the approval of large special budgets for defence, such as in Japan and Taiwan. This suggests that, as in Europe, strategic factors have enabled defence-spending trends to overcome wider budgetary constraints. However, trends are far from universal, with Southeast Asian budgets particularly likely to come under pressure in the short term as a result of fiscal consolidation and competing priorities for strained government resources.

The limited real-terms growth in Asia-Pacific military spending over the course of 2022 hides the fact that a number of countries announced significant increases to their defence budgets earlier in the year, before inflationary pressures began to mount. In February, India announced a 2022–23 defence budget of INR5.25 trillion (USD66.6bn), a 4.4% increase over the revised figure for 2021–22. Perhaps more crucially, the new budget made progress in rebalancing resources towards modernisation, with the capital budget – which provides funding for research and development (R&D) and procurement – increasing by 12.7%. As recently as 2013–14, capital spend accounted for 31% of India's budget. However, rising pay and pension costs, combined with lower rates of top-line growth, saw that share drop to 23% by 2018–19. The new budget takes the share of spending dedicated to capital investment back to 29%, close to previous highs.

India's new budget also continued the recent practice of prioritising domestic programmes and suppliers within its procurement plans, with 68% of the capital budget earmarked for indigenous manufacturers, up from 58% in 2021–22. The R&D budget is also being used to support the local

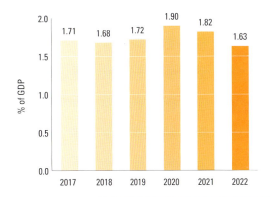

▲ Figure 11 **Asia: regional defence spending** as % of GDP (average)

defence sector. Government officials stated that 25% of spending earmarked for this purpose in 2022–23 will be opened up to private industry. Most of this amount had traditionally been funnelled through state-owned agencies like the Defence Research and Development Organisation.

In Japan, the re-election of the Liberal Democratic Party in October 2021 also appears to have reinvigorated efforts to raise defence spending. Having campaigned on a platform that included the pledge to double defence spending as a proportion of GDP to 2%, the Kishida government is now reportedly working on ways to realise this ambition, or at least heavily augment current resources for defence. In the immediate term, this included the approval of the 'Defense-Strengthening Acceleration Package', which ostensibly added JPY773.8bn (USD6.0bn) to the FY2022 budget in order to accelerate a number of projects initially earmarked for inclusion in the FY2023 budget. In effect, this provided the Japan Ministry of Defense with a 15.6% nominal uplift in spending for FY2022, a significant development for a country where annual increases in core spending have averaged less than 1% over the last decade. Reports in late 2022 suggest that this practice of raising defence expenditure through the use of supplemental appropriations is likely to be retained over the coming years; it seems likely to be the main method used to raise spending towards 2% of GDP, a target that Prime Minister Kishida Fumio is seeking to reach by 2027.

Taiwan's use of supplemental budgets to bolster defence spending was also expanded in 2022 with the approval of new special appropriation aimed at enhancing navy and air force capabilities. Specifically, the new budget will provide TWD237bn (USD8.1bn)

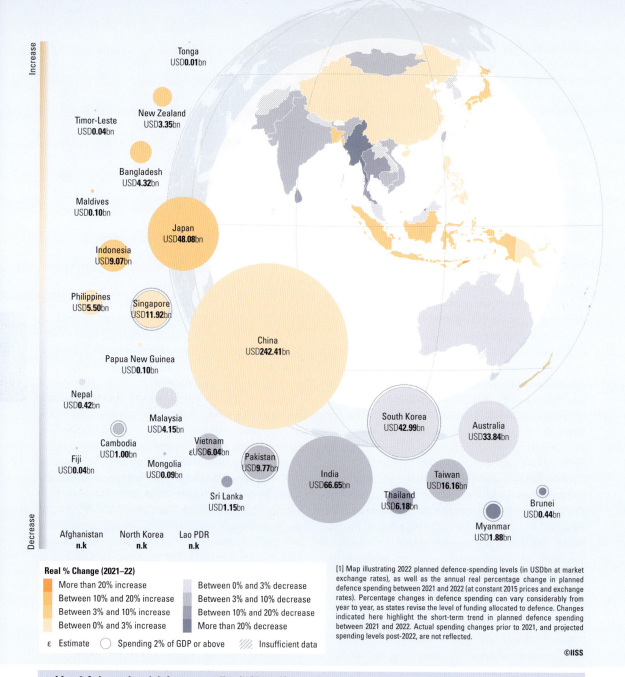

▲ Map 6 **Asia: regional defence spending** (USDbn, %ch yoy)[1]

between 2022 and 2026 for new ships, shore-based anti-ship missiles and air-defence systems that are set to be developed and manufactured by the local defence sector. This funding comes on top of the previously approved TWD247bn (USD8.5bn) special budget for the procurement of 66 F-16V combat aircraft with a further TWD40bn (USD1.4bn) appropriated for this acquisition in 2022. When taken alongside the Ministry of National Defense's annual core budget, overall defence spending for 2022 represents a 20.5% increase in spending over the previous two years. This was followed in August by the announcement that the Cabinet had approved a further large increase in core spending for 2023 which, when combined with ongoing special budget appropriations, will see a further 19.6% increase next year.

In May, Australia elected a Labor government for the first time in almost nine years. Initially

▲ Figure 12 **Asia: sub-regional real-terms defence-spending growth, 2021–22** (USDbn, constant 2015)

this created a degree of uncertainty around future funding for defence, following a period under the Liberal/National coalition where core defence spending had risen by 79% since 2013. However, the new government has been explicit in its support for maintaining defence spending at levels above 2% of GDP. It announced plans for a Defence Strategic Review which will make recommendations to government in early 2023. Meanwhile, the new government backed the enhanced investments in the Australian Defence Force outlined in the 2016 White Paper and reaffirmed in the 2020 Strategic Update, firmly suggesting that spending will continue to rise in the coming years in line with those long-term plans. The Labor government's first budget, which was released in October 2022, maintained funding for defence largely in line with the Strategic Update, while future decisions will likely be shaped by the upcoming Defence Strategic Review. The budget also announced AUD900 million (USD638m) and AUD470m (USD333m) in overseas assistance for Pacific Island nations and Southeast Asia respectively.

Defence industry

The new Labor government will also continue with plans for the new trilateral strategic agreement between Australia, the United Kingdom and the United States – referred to as AUKUS – which intends to provide Australia with a new fleet of conventionally armed, nuclear-powered submarines and other advanced military capabilities such as hypersonic missiles. Coupled with the announcement in May that Australia would acquire another seven MQ-28A *Ghost Bat* uninhabited aerial vehicles (bringing the Royal Australian Air Force's planned total order to ten) to be made locally by Boeing Australia, it is apparent that investment in the local defence sector continues to increase, with local companies moving up the value chain through their development and production of systems and platforms. This move aligns with Australia's Defence Export Strategy, released in 2018, which aims to turn the country into one of the top ten global exporters of defence equipment by 2028.

Over the course of 2022, the defence-industrial relationship between Japan and the UK continued to strengthen, most notably in relation to cooperation on future combat aircraft development. With both countries making progress on their respective projects but acutely aware of the attendant costs, London and Tokyo are exploring potential collaboration. After announcements on cooperation around engines and sensor technology, both countries launched, with Italy in December, the 'Global Combat Air Programme'. Speaking during a visit to the UK in May, Prime Minister Kishida stated that the work could become the cornerstone of a much closer UK–Japan bilateral defence relationship; Japanese and UK companies are already cooperating in a number of key areas.

In August, Vietnam unveiled reforms aimed at developing the local defence sector and increasing equipment self-sufficiency. The new policies will focus on restructuring the existing defence industrial base, encouraging greater cooperation with civil industry and international partners. The most significant changes are likely to relate to reform and restructuring within the General Department of Defence Industry (GDDI), a state-owned network of around 60 manufacturing facilities and research institutes in Vietnam, in an attempt to expand its existing capabilities.

India continued its import substitution drive, against the backdrop of potential shortages of spare parts for Russian military equipment in light of the war in Ukraine. New Delhi announced a new list of 780 'strategically important' components that it intends to produce domestically. The list included parts for Russian-designed T-90 main battle tanks and Su-30MKI combat aircraft at a time when concern has been growing over the ability to source components from Russia. Reports from India, citing defence officials, suggest that the conflict has added impetus to plans to upgrade the air force's Su-30MKI fleet with an indigenous radar, cockpit avionics and flight-control computer in order to reduce dependence upon Russia and offset potential challenges in sustaining the inventory.

South Korea arguably had the region's most significant industrial success in 2022 with the framework agreements for the sale to Poland of 1,000 K2 main battle tanks, 672 K9 self-propelled howitzers and 48 FA-50 light combat aircraft. The initial contracts for 180 K2 tanks and 212 K9 artillery pieces, finalised in August, were valued at USD6.06bn, while Korea Aerospace Industries (KAI) announced the signed FA-50 deal would be worth a further USD3.31bn. Even if additional orders do not materialise as expected, the agreements between Poland and Korea represent by some distance the largest defence export deal secured by an Asian country. Earlier in July, South Korea had celebrated the first flight of the indigenously developed KF-21 combat aircraft, further advancing the country's growing industrial capabilities and expanding its equipment portfolio to multi-role combat aircraft. These deals highlighted the maturity of South Korea's defence industry and the price point and perceived quality of its products, but they also raised potential prioritisation challenges (particularly for the land sector) for a domestic defence sector that must also meet local modernisation requirements.

CHINA

In 2022, the People's Liberation Army (PLA) continued its plan to build a modernised army by 2027 and to 'basically achieve' defence and armed forces modernisation by 2035. Xi Jinping started 2022, after his new year's speech, by signing a mobilisation order for military training, instructing the armed forces to 'redouble their efforts to better combine training with combat operations, and strengthen systematic training and the use of technologies to develop an elite force that is capable of fighting and winning wars'. In March, Xi stressed the importance of operating the armed forces in accordance with the law, calling for advances in military legislation, stepping up enforcement of laws and regulations, strengthening troop management and enhancing oversight.

The 20th Party Congress

In late October, the 20th National Congress of the Communist Party of China took stock of the PLA's achievements since 2017 and set the agenda for the next five years. The PLA is still aiming towards its 2027 and 2035 targets. The 20th Party Congress work report included a mention of the 2027 goal, which was officially announced by Xi in 2020; it is important as 2027 marks the centenary of the foundation of the PLA's antecedent. It was the first time that a party congress work report contained an explicit reference to this goal. The report also stated that following reforms the PLA had by 2022 become a 'much more modern and capable fighting force'.

For the next five years, it continued, the PLA should focus on measures including maintaining political loyalty to the Party, intensifying training and enhancing combat preparedness, establishing 'a strong system of strategic deterrence', speeding the development of uninhabited and 'intelligent' combat capabilities and promoting the coordinated development and application of network information systems. The latter suggests that the goal of 'informatisation' has not yet been achieved and that 'intelligentisation' remains an ambition. Informatisation is generally held to refer to efforts to improve technical sophistication (likened by the Pentagon to 'net-centric' capability) while intelligentisation may refer to the idea that military systems will be improved by the integration of automation, big data and artificial intelligence.

Additionally, the report said that the command system for joint operations required improvement, and that the PLA's systems and capacity for reconnaissance and early warning, joint strikes, battlefield support and integrated logistics support also needed to be enhanced. Moreover, further efforts were required in areas such as joint and force-on-force training, military–civil fusion, and hastening the development of modern logistics. The text mentioned accelerating progress towards certain objectives, but language like this is common in Party documents and therefore does not signal an ambition to speed up the drive to achieve military modernisation by 2035. Two notable deductions from the work report's section on the PLA are that informatisation remains a work in progress and that the PLA has been directed to focus more on strategic capabilities and deterrence, including in the use of emerging and disruptive technologies and 'new-domain forces'.

Xi's speech at the Party Congress signalled little new in terms of China's approach to Taiwan. However, the Party's constitution was amended to include a line to 'resolutely oppose and deter Taiwan independence'. This represents a shift from the previous revision in 2017 where there was a pledge to 'facilitate national unification'. However, the work report also shifted tone slightly to be conciliatory to China's Taiwan compatriots, and instead made clear that the option of taking all measures necessary to ensure reunification was 'directed solely at interference by outside forces and the few separatists seeking Taiwan independence'.

The Party Congress also unveiled a new Central Military Commission (CMC) line-up. Personnel changes mirrored wider changes in the Politburo standing and central committees that broke with long-held norms around retirement age and promotional ladders. The new CMC is less diverse, lacking PLA Navy (PLAN) and PLA Air Force (PLAAF) representation, and puts the army back at the centre of PLA decision-making. While Admiral Miao Hua remains as a member of the CMC, his background is in the PLA Army (PLAA) prior to transferring to the PLAN as political commissar. Only three members of the former CMC remain. Zhang Youxia was promoted to first vice chairman, while He Weidong was promoted to the second-ranking vice chairman, having previously served on the Joint Operations Command Center, as commander of the Eastern Theatre Command and deputy commander of the Western Theatre Command and commander of the Western Theatre Command Army. While Zhang brings his experience from the Sino-Vietnam war in 1979, he has been in command positions for recent Taiwan- and Doklam-related activities. Li Shangfu will likely become the new minister of national defence, despite being sanctioned by the US government in 2018 while he was head of the Equipment Development Department. The new chief of the Joint Staff Department, Liu Zhenli, fought in the Sino-Vietnam war but has not served in any joint position.

Later in the year, China's military training went beyond national exercises in what some analysts called a 'fourth Taiwan Strait crisis'. Following a visit by then Speaker of the US House of Representatives Nancy Pelosi to Taiwan, China's drills, which began on 3 August, were widely viewed as a measure of Beijing's strong disapproval of Pelosi's visit. Components of these drills included anti-submarine warfare, joint-service logistic support, in-flight refuelling, aircraft-carrier and submarine operations and the firing of a range of ballistic missiles, including DF-15B (CH-SS-6 Mod 3) missiles launched to Taiwan's north, east and south. The PLAN held exercises off the coast of Taiwan's main ports in six locations, though it did not enter into Taiwan's territorial seas. The PLA's army- and navy-aviation forces conducted numerous large-scale incursions into Taiwan's air defence identification zone (ADIZ), crossing over the politically sensitive Taiwan Strait median line. Since August, the latter has become a more routine occurrence. Amphibious exercises were absent from the exercises that followed Pelosi's visit, as the PLA likely calibrated its response to limit misunderstanding.

PLA Army

Having completed its organisational transition to a combined-arms battalion- and brigade-based structure, the PLAA now appears to be focused on training and developing the skills necessary to use these new formations effectively, both as an individual service and in conjunction with other elements of the PLA.

The army has almost certainly paid close attention to the performance of Russian and Ukrainian ground forces during Russia's invasion of Ukraine, in relation to equipment, organisations and operational concepts. This may ultimately lead to some further changes in force design, but the perceived lessons of the campaign will likely take some time to digest before practical changes occur.

As in 2021, PLAA brigades continued to participate in established annual exercise series, such as *Stride*. However, these exercises again received less coverage in China's media than they had before 2020. Official reporting contrasts the progress achieved in these exercises over the last decade with persistent shortfalls in some areas. It also suggests that at least some brigades are participating in the same exercise series over multiple consecutive years, implying an iterative, long-term approach to skills transfer.

Although the army played a lower-profile role than other PLA services in the large-scale exercises following Pelosi's visit to Taiwan, it has increased both the profile and the frequency of its amphibious training. However, most publicised exercises still appear to be conducted at the brigade level or below, and the scale at which the PLAA physically participates in the larger annual theatre-level exercises remains unclear in open sources.

While modern equipment platforms now comprise the majority of the army's armoured-vehicle and tube-artillery inventories, it continues to operate ageing and sometimes obsolescent systems in a number of its combat brigades. The continued presence of such systems would likely hinder these brigades' ability to effectively conduct the kind of mechanised and 'informationised' operations envisaged by the PLA. The apparent acceptance of short-term risk in this area may reflect an understanding among the PLAA leadership that training personnel across the force to use newly issued equipment effectively is an ongoing, and perhaps lengthy, process.

Exports of Chinese ground combat systems have previously been focused on cheaper, light- to medium-weight armoured fighting vehicles and artillery systems. In recent years, however, there have been a number of export successes with more advanced heavy armour and sophisticated tactical missile and air- and missile-defence systems, including directed-energy systems. Customers have included armed forces in Asia, the Middle East and Africa, such as those of Bangladesh, Myanmar, Nigeria, Pakistan, Saudi Arabia and Thailand.

At Airshow China 2022 (commonly known as the Zhuhai Airshow), NORINCO advertised a full mechanised brigade concept, designated as the 'New-Generation Army Brigade Combat Team' and including uninhabited aerial and ground systems in a number of roles. This included an Urban Combat Module – a particular focus of PLAA uninhabited-systems development work.

Ground-combat systems were not the primary focus of the air show, but a significant number of air-defence systems were displayed, including export variants of some of the PLA's most advanced medium- or long-range surface-to-air missile systems, such as the HQ-9BE, and several new short-range air- and missile-defence systems, including the H-11 and the FK-3000 SPAAGM.

PLA Navy

In September 2022, the PLAN marked the tenth anniversary of the commissioning of its first aircraft carrier, *Liaoning*. A second carrier, a near-copy called *Shandong*, followed in 2019. In June 2022, Beijing launched its third carrier, *Fujian*.

Over the past decade, the PLAN's development of its carrier operations has been steady and incremental, perhaps even cautious. The latest carrier represents something of a step change. While it is unlikely to be fully commissioned before 2025 (the Pentagon estimated it will commission in 2024 in its 2022 report on Chinese military capability), it is larger than the earlier vessels at an estimated 85,000 tonnes full load displacement and is configured for catapult-assisted but arrested recovery-aircraft operation (possibly utilising an electromagnetic aircraft launch system), allowing for a larger and more comprehensive embarked air group.

Flight-testing of the Xian KJ-600 airborne early-warning and control aircraft appears to be well advanced. When embarked, this will provide considerably greater mission performance than the available helicopter types. The development of a new low-observable aircraft, apparently based on the Shenyang J-31 and unofficially dubbed the Shenyang J-35, could in future also complement the existing Shenyang J-15 carrier-based fixed-wing combat aircraft aboard the new carrier.

Deployments of the other two carriers during 2022 also hinted that Beijing is now focusing on developing the skills needed for integrated carrier group operations. The assumption remains that further, and possibly even larger, carriers will follow by the end of this decade and into the 2030s.

More broadly, the PLAN made further strides in 2022 in fielding new, high-capability surface units that will add to its maturing capacity to deploy a blue-water naval capability. A further three Type-055 (*Renhai*) cruisers appear to have joined the fleet since December 2021, bringing the total in service to seven. Three additional Type-052D mod (*Luyang* III mod) destroyers also entered service.

The rapid construction and induction into service of the Type-075 (*Yushen*) large-deck amphibious ships also point to efforts being directed at rectifying shortfalls in this area of capability. The second ship commissioned at the end of 2021 and the third in October 2022. Exercises in August 2022 also appeared to provide further evidence of China's plans to incorporate civilian car ferries into its amphibious-lift capacity.

The PLAN also undertook a number of joint exercises with Russian navy units. However, while these involved significant numbers of vessels, attracted considerable attention and were no doubt meant to send a diplomatic message, they remained relatively limited in scope and operational ambition. Another notable deployment was that of the space- and missile-tracking ship *Yuan Wang* 5 (part of the Strategic Support Force) into the Indian Ocean, including a port visit to Hambantota in Sri Lanka.

International attention has also remained focused on the continuing assertive use by Beijing of its other maritime-security agencies, the China Coast Guard and the maritime militia. Among improvements in the coastguard's capabilities has been the transfer of all Type-056 corvettes from the PLAN, modified by the removal of air-defence and anti-ship missile systems, significantly enhancing the coastguard's inventory of ocean-deployable units.

PLA Air Force

The PLAAF played a notable role in what appeared to be Beijing's display of displeasure over Pelosi's visit to Taiwan at the beginning of August 2022. The increase in PLAAF activity near Taiwan also likely provided the air force with a valuable opportunity, and an excuse, to package comparatively large formations in an operationally relevant environment.

While the scope of the air force's ongoing combat aircraft recapitalisation is readily apparent, with older types being replaced by modern platforms, less easily observed is the extent of the progress being made in the training and skills required for joint and integrated air operations. This remains a focus of PLAAF attention, as does improving and shortening the training syllabus for combat aircraft aircrew.

Deliveries of the Chengdu J-20 and J-10C *Firebird*, and Shenyang J-16 combat aircraft, continued during 2022. As of the fourth quarter of 2022, development of a two-seat variant of the J-20 is also ongoing with one or two aircraft in flight test. The PLAAF has, since at least 2021, been taking delivery of J-20s fitted with a domestic afterburning turbofan, the Shenyang WS-10C, replacing the Russian *Saturn* AL-31F variant used originally. The PLAAF also appears to be looking at further upgrades for its Shenyang J-11B *Flanker* L aircraft.

Engine upgrades are also being introduced in the PLAAF's Xian Y-20 heavy transport. The Y-20 was introduced into service using a version of the Russian Soloviev D-30KP, which has a late-1960s design heritage. It is being replaced by the Shenyang WS-20, a more modern and more powerful engine. Indeed, the Y-20 transport aircraft, and the YY-20A tanker variant, are now starting to be built fitted with the WS-20 rather than the Russian powerplant. The YY-20A will be used to replace the H-6U tanker variant of the H-6 *Badger* and likely also the Ilyushin Il-78 *Midas* tanker. In August 2022 the PLAAF released footage of a YY-20A being used to refuel J-16s.

With the emergence in early December of the Northrop Grumman B-21 *Raider* bomber in the United States, it remained to be seen whether this might prompt Beijing to show the Xian H-20 bomber now assessed to be in development. Still possibly under wraps is a fighter-bomber design alluded to by the US Defense Intelligence Agency.

At Airshow China 2022, a variant of the turbojet-powered *Wing Loong*-10 uninhabited aerial vehicle (UAV) was displayed with the designation WZ-10 and in PLAAF markings. This supports earlier commercial satellite imagery suggesting that the type has now entered PLA service, but in an intelligence, surveillance and reconnaissance (ISR)/electronic-warfare role rather than the combat ISR role advertised for the *Wing Loong*-10 export variants. There was also a display featuring the FH-97 'loyal wingman' UAV, depicted operating with J-20 on display screens. This suggests that the PLAAF may be considering operating these assets in similar roles to those being considered by advanced Western air forces for such assets.

PLA Rocket Force

The modernisation and expansion of China's conventional and nuclear missile forces continues at a steady pace. In 2021, the discovery by non-government analysts of three intercontinental ballistic missile (ICBM) silo fields in northern China was seen to potentially signify a significant change in China's nuclear-force structure and posture. According to the United States' annual military report on China, the People's Liberation Army Rocket Force (PLARF) is projected to increase the number of warheads it possesses from around 400 to 1,500 by 2035 and increase its number of deployed strategic-range launchers by at least 300. If China were to significantly expand the size of its ICBM forces but continue its historic policy of nuclear ambiguity, this could have significant implications for strategic stability with the United States and possible knock-on effects for bilateral Russian–US arms control. Meanwhile, the PLARF continues to add additional brigades of conventional missiles to its force structure and modernise its equipment, underlining the importance the PLARF continues to place on these systems for regional deterrence and war-fighting purposes.

Construction at the Hami, Ordos and Yumen silo fields progressed significantly between 2021 and 2022, and most temporary shelters that have been used to conceal excavation and construction work have been removed, revealing reinforced silo hatches. Although US government reports have estimated that China's ICBM force has increased from 100 to 300 launchers and from 150 to 300 missiles, satellite imagery analysis of the silo fields does not appear to display evidence that these silos have been filled. Moreover, additional construction work will be required to support the necessary infrastructure for these to become fully operational. Once ready, however, China is likely to fill these silos with either the solid-fuel DF-41 (CH-SS-20) or the DF-31A (CH-SS-10 Mod 2), both of which can reach targets on the United States' eastern seaboard. Although the DF-5A/B variants (CH-SS-4 Mod 2/3 respectively) are also capable of striking targets at similar ranges, both systems are liquid-fuelled, and their lengthy fuelling process means that they can be vulnerable to pre-emptive attack.

Whether the PLARF will fill all of these silos is a matter of debate among analysts. Some specialists have suggested that the gradual evolvement of the PLARF's force structure reflects statements from China's leadership, such as Xi's directive at the Communist Party of China's 20th Party Conference to 'establish a strong system of strategic deterrence'. The increasingly tense Sino-US security relationship is likely an important reason for China's apparent slow drift from its historic restraint in deploying a small nuclear force. Although Chinese policymakers have not provided an official explanation for the developments to its nuclear force structure and posture, some Chinese officials have noted that China's nuclear forces will be influenced by changes in the international security environment. Finally, some specialists have suggested that assessments of changes to the PLARF's force structure should be considered alongside broader changes in other branches of the PLA, given qualitative and quantitative developments in the PLAAF and PLAN.

In addition to improving its nuclear forces, the PLARF continues to expand, improve and modernise its conventional missile capabilities, evidenced by the expansion in the number of brigades operating medium- and intermediate-range ballistic missiles (MRBM and IRBM respectively). Although the DF-21C/-D (CH-SS-5 Mod 4/5) MRBM had been the primary instrument for the PLARF's conventional mission, it appears to have been superseded in this role by the DF-26 (CH-SS-18) IRBM since the missile reached initial operational capability in 2016. It is assessed that at least six brigades have been equipped with the DF-26 (CH-SS-18), with a significant increase in launchers noted in US government reports between 2019 and 2020. Although the DF-26 is a dual-capable system, meaning it can be equipped with either a nuclear or a conventional warhead, most of these systems are believed to have a conventional mission.

China has also begun to deploy its new DF-17 (CH-SS-22) medium-range hypersonic boost-glide vehicle and at least two brigades have been identified as being equipped with the DF-17 since the system was unveiled in 2019. It is possible that the PLARF will continue increasing the number of brigades operating this system, especially among units that are based in eastern China, considering current deployments. At the same time, the number of short-range ballistic-missile launchers possessed by the PLARF, such as the DF-11A (CH-SS-7 Mod 2), has gradually decreased according to US government assessments.

Finally, while China's ballistic missiles are a focus of attention from analysts and policymakers, the PLARF also operates several types of ground-launched cruise missiles (GLCM), including the CJ-100 (CH-SSC-13). However, there is very little open-source information available on the service status of the PLARF's GLCMs and their deployment.

DEFENCE ECONOMICS

Despite the economic challenges posed by ongoing lockdowns and the country's zero-tolerance approach to COVID-19, China's defence-budget growth remained in line with recent trends in 2022. In February, Beijing announced that it would raise defence spending by 7% for 2022 in nominal terms, taking military spending to CNY1.45 trillion (USD238 billion) from CNY1.36tr (USD224bn). Taking into account the funding of local militias, the budget increased to CNY1.47tr (USD242bn) in 2022. The new budget represented a marginal acceleration in growth from the 6.9% increase approved in 2021 but remains largely in line with the average 7.3% nominal growth seen over the previous five years.

As a result of this sustained and robust growth in Chinese military spending, the 7% increase for 2022 represents a CNY95bn (USD16bn) boost in funding for the People's Liberation Army (PLA), the largest-ever annual increase in absolute terms. Growth in real terms, however, has stalled in the last five years.

As a proportion of overall government spending, Chinese military expenditure had declined in the early 2000s, dropping from 9.0% in 2000 down to 5.2% by the time Xi Jinping became president in 2013. Since that time, this decline has been arrested, suggesting an increased focus on ensuring the PLA receives the resources it requires. Officially, the 2022 budget represents around 5.4% of overall government spending, slightly below the 5.5% spent in 2021. The official 2022 defence budget comes to 1.2% of GDP, a level at which it has hovered throughout President Xi's ten years in power, yet still well below the global average of around 2%.

There remains, however, significant debate over the extent to which the official budget represents the entirety of the country's spending on defence, with additional funding thought to be provided from other sources. A key example is through the government's long-standing commitment to the policy of military–civil fusion, which aims to leverage technological advances between the civil and military functions. Ostensibly, this creates the potential for substantial levels of research and development spending, not specifically counted as part of the defence budget, to feed into military programmes through investments made in parallel domains such as aeroengines and advanced electronics.

A further transparency problem exists with regard to how even the official defence budget is spent. Priorities for the 2022 budget were not laid out, but a communique on China's 14th Five-Year Plan issued in October 2020 outlined plans to 'make major strides in the modernization of national defense and the armed forces' and in 'building a modernised military by 2027'. Data contained within the country's 2019 defence White Paper also showed spending on military equipment – which includes procurement and support – had increased from 33.2% of total spending in 2010 to 41.1% by 2017, as the government sought to direct more funding towards technological modernisation.

This prioritisation of modernisation has been a hallmark of Xi's leadership, with the PLA reduced in size by 300,000 personnel between 2015 and 2017 in order to channel more funding into equipment. News that emerged in 2021 of a pay increase of up to 40% for some military personnel is likely to have precluded any further growth in the share of spending directed towards equipment given the resultant increase in personnel expenses. Nevertheless, with the president having outlined plans to largely complete the modernisation of the PLA by 2035 as part of the 19th National Congress of the Communist Party of China in 2017, the focus on technological advancement will remain over the coming years.

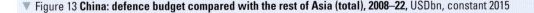

Figure 13 **China: defence budget compared with the rest of Asia (total), 2008–22**, USDbn, constant 2015

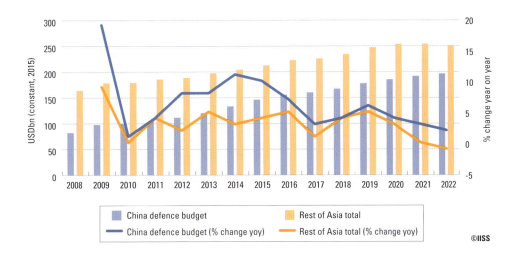

Arms procurements and deliveries – Asia

Significant events in 2022

MARCH — CHINA ISSUES NEW PROCUREMENT REGULATIONS

New procurement regulations, set by the Central Military Commission (CMC), entered into force in March. The new statute empowers the CMC to regulate, manage and supervise the PLA's procurement activities and gives the PLA and CMC greater control over various stages of procurement together with the defence industrial base. It followed other recent initiatives. In January 2021, revised regulations were published focusing, among other measures, on management and maintenance as well as research and development, reportedly also clarifying the military tasks allocated to units. Subsequently, regulations issued in November 2021 focused on improving procurement processes while new procedures on testing military equipment were issued in February 2022.

APRIL — INDIA OFFSET PROGRAMMES TROUBLE

New Delhi announced that as of the end of 2021, 21 foreign defence contractors had been penalised since January 2016 for not fulfilling offset obligations on time. The contracts include the 2016 deal for 36 *Rafale* fighter ground-attack aircraft, and contracts for Mi-17V-5 *Hip* multi-role helicopters, *Heron* UAVs and *Harop* loitering munitions. Reforms to offsets were introduced in 2020 that require the original equipment manufacturer to submit offset plans a year before each contract is signed rather than at the point of signature. Meanwhile, offset obligations for government-to-government agreements have been lifted.

AUGUST — SOUTH KOREA: DEFENCE EXPORT SUCCESS

South Korea secured defence export contracts worth KRW23.99tr (USD18.88bn) from January–November 2022, with August the most profitable month. Starting in January with the UAE's purchase of the *Cheongung* medium-range self-propelled surface-to-air missile system for KRW4.29tr (USD3.38bn), export deals were signed in February with Egypt for the K9 *Thunder* 155mm self-propelled artillery systems for KRW2tr (USD1.57bn), and in June with the Philippines for six offshore patrol vessels worth KRW744.9bn (USD586.4m). In August, Poland signed contracts for 212 K9s and 180 K2 *Black Panther* main battle tanks worth a combined KRW7.7tr (USD6.06bn). Then, in September and November, Warsaw signed contracts for 48 FA-50 *Fighting Eagle* fighter ground-attack aircraft and 218 *Chunmoo* multiple rocket launchers worth KRW4.21tr (USD3.31bn) and KRW5.05tr (USD3.97bn) respectively. Almost all of these contracts include the participation of local defence industry, and South Korea's willingness to offer this is likely a key attraction. However, these contracts are leading to prioritisation challenges for South Korean defence industries, which also have to fulfil local orders.

SEPTEMBER — PHILIPPINES: MODERNISATION CONTINUES

In Manila, the House of Representatives allocated PHP45bn (USD833.5m) to its FY2023 plan for the last phase of the Philippines' 15-year-long defence modernisation programme, Horizon Three, covering the period 2023–28. The new government is continuing pre-existing plans on condition that any unsigned contracts left from the Horizon Two phase (2018–22) will go through a prioritisation review. However, due to budget constraints, several important projects including diesel-electric powered submarines will not now be pursued. During the first (2013–17) and second Horizon phases, equipment was mainly acquired from Israel, South Korea and the United States. While these suppliers are likely to remain prominent, the 2022 deal with India for the *BrahMos* anti-ship missile suggests that the Philippines is also looking elsewhere.

Asia 227

Table 12 — Philippines: selected aerospace procurement since 2010

Contract Date	Equipment	Type	Quantity	Value (USD millions)		Prime Contractor	Deliveries	Phase*	Service
Mar 2013	AW109	Light transport helicopter	3	PHP1.33bn (USD31.33m)		AgustaWestland	Dec 2013	Horizon 1	Navy
Feb 2014	AW109E *Power*	Multi-role helicopter (MRH)	2				Jul 2015		
Nov 2013	AW109E *Power*	MRH	8	PHP3.44bn (USD81.04m)		AgustaWestland	Dec 2014–Dec 2015	Horizon 1	Air Force
Jan 2014	C-212 *Aviocar* (NC-212i)	Light transport aircraft	2	PHP814m (USD18.34m)		Dirgantara Indonesia (DI)	Jun 2018	Horizon 1	Air Force
Feb 2014	C295	Light transport aircraft	3	PHP5.39bn (USD121.41m)	M	Airbus	Mar 2015–Dec 2015	Horizon 1	Air Force
Mar 2014	Bell 412EP	MRH	8	USD105.9m		Bell (formerly Bell Helicopter)	2015	Horizon 1	Air Force
Mar 2014	FA-50PH *Fighting Eagle*	Fighter ground-attack aircraft	12	USD421.64m		Korea Aerospace Industries (KAI)	Nov 2015–May 2017	Horizon 1	Air Force
Mar 2016	AW159 *Wildcat*	Anti-submarine warfare helicopter	2	PHP5.36bn (USD112.92m)		Leonardo (formerly Finmeccanica)	May 2019	Horizon 1	Navy
Nov 2017	EMB-314 *Super Tucano* (A-29B)	Training aircraft***	6	PHP4.97bn (USD98.56m)		Embraer	Sep–Oct 2020	Horizon 2	Air Force
c. 2018	*Hermes* 450	Medium intelligence, surveillance and reconnaissance uninhabited air vehicle	4	PHP8.47bn (USD160.84m)		Elbit Systems	2019–20	Horizon 2	Air Force
	Hermes 900		9						
Dec 2018	C295M	Light transport aircraft	1	EUR28.81m (USD34.04m)	M	Airbus	Sep 2019	Horizon 2	Air Force
c. 2019	C295M	Light transport aircraft	3	PHP5.29bn (USD102.10m)	M	Airbus	Mar 2022–ongoing	Horizon 2	Air Force
c. 2019	*Spyder*-MR	Medium-range self-propelled surface-to-air missile system	9	PHP6.85bn (USD132.19m)		Rafael Advanced Defense Systems	Sep 2022–ongoing	Horizon 2	Air Force
Apr 2019	S-70i *Black Hawk*	Medium transport helicopter	16	USD241.46m		PZL Mielec	Nov 2020–Dec 2021	Horizon 2	Air Force
Jul 2020	T129B	Attack helicopter	6	PHP13.73bn (USD276.62m)		Turkish Aerospace Industries (TAI)	Mar 2020–ongoing	Horizon 2	Air Force
Feb 2022	S-70i *Black Hawk*	Medium transport helicopter	32	USD624m		PZL Mielec	2023–26**	Horizon 2	Air Force

*Horizon 1 (2013–17); Horizon 2 (2018–22); Horizon 3 (2023–28) – excluding equipment that was second-hand, donated or given in an assistance or aid programme

**Planned

***Combat capable

M = multinational

228 THE MILITARY BALANCE 2023

Table 13 ☪ Pakistan: selected naval procurement since 2000

In 2000, the Pakistan Navy (PN) largely comprised platforms of French and UK origin with a handful of Chinese-designed patrol craft. Today, many of the navy's key vessels have been, or are being, replaced by Chinese-designed ships. Indeed, a 2005 deal for *Sword*-class frigates – based on the Chinese navy's Type-053H3 (*Jiangwei* II) design – heralded the construction of the first new-build principal surface combatants for the PN since its establishment in 1947. The fourth vessel was built in Pakistan by the state-owned Karachi Shipyards & Engineering Works (KSEW) shipyard.

This provided a template for subsequent purchases from China, with the first vessels built at a Chinese shipyard and subsequent platforms at KSEW. This pattern has been reflected in procurements from China by the other armed services, coming at a time when Pakistan's economic and strategic relationship with China has deepened significantly. But while China may now be the predominant naval supplier, Pakistan's shipbuilding sector is benefiting from other ties: the most recent deal was for Turkish-designed corvettes, two of which will also be built at KSEW.

Contract Date	Equipment	Type	Quantity	Value (USD millions)	Contractor	Deliveries	Notes
2002	*Jurrat*	Patrol boat with surface-to-surface missiles	2	n.k.	Karachi Shipyards & Engineering Works (KSEW); Marsun	2006	Based on the M39 design by Thai firm Marsun
c. 2003	M16 Fast Assault Boat	Patrol boat	4	n.k.	KSEW; Marsun	2004	
2005	*Sword* (F-22P) (Type-053H3 derivative (*Jiangwei* II))	Frigate	4	600	Hudong–Zhonghua Shipbuilding	2009–13	Fourth vessel built in Pakistan. Contract includes six Z-9C hel
2006	MRTP-33	Fast patrol boat	2	n.k.	Yonca-Onuk Shipyard	2007–08	
2007	*Madadgar*	Light oiler	2	20	KSEW	2011	
2010	*Azmat*	Patrol craft with surface-to-surface missiles (PCG)	2	n.k.	China Shipbuilding Industry Corporation (CSIC); KSEW	2012–14	Second vessel built in Pakistan
2010	*Alamgir* (ex-US *Oliver Hazard Perry*)	Frigate	1	0	Government surplus	2010	
2013	*Azmat*	PCG	1	n.k.	KSEW	2017	
2013	*Moawin*	Fleet replenishment oiler	1	n.k.	Savunma Teknolojileri ve Mühendislik (STM)	2018	Built at KSEW
2014	*Azmat*	PCG	1	n.k.	KSEW	2022	
2015	*Hangor* (*Yuan*)	Attack submarine	8	n.k.	China State Shipbuilding Corporation (CSSC); KSEW	2022–28	Four built in China, four in Pakistan
2017	*Yarmook* (Damen OPV 1900)	Corvette	2	n.k.	Damen Schelde Naval Shipbuilding (DSNS)	2020	Constructed in Romania
2017	*Tughril* (Type-054AP (*Jiangkai* II))	Frigate	4	n.k.	CSSC	2021–Ongoing	
2018	*Babur* (*Ada* (MILGEM))	Corvette	4	1,000	ASFAT	2023–24	Two built in Pakistan, two in Turkey
2020	Indigenously Designed Gunboat	Patrol boat	1+	n.k.	KSEW	2023*	
c. 2021	OPV 2600	Frigate	2	n.k.	DSNS	n.k.	

*planned

Afghanistan AFG

New Afghan Afghani AFN		2021	2022	2023
GDP [a]	AFN	n.k	n.k	
	USD	n.k	n.k	
per capita	USD	n.k	n.k	
Growth	%	n.k	n.k	
Inflation	%	n.k	n.k	
Def bdgt [b]	AFN	ε172bn	n.k	
	USD	n.k	n.k	
USD1=AFN		n.k	n.k	

[a] IMF economic data unavailable for Afghanistan from 2021
[b] Security expenditure. Includes expenditure on Ministry of Defence, Ministry of Interior, Ministry of Foreign Affairs, National Security Council and the General Directorate of National Security. Also includes donor funding.

Real-terms defence budget trend (USDbn, constant 2015)

Population	38,346,720					
Age	0–14	15–19	20–24	25–29	30–64	65 plus
Male	20.3%	5.2%	5.3%	4.6%	14.0%	1.3%
Female	19.7%	5.0%	5.1%	4.4%	13.6%	1.5%

Capabilities

Over one year after the collapse of the former Afghan National Security and Defence Forces (ANSDF), it remains difficult to assess the strength and capability of the Afghan Taliban's armed forces and the extent to which they have been able to use the foreign-supplied equipment seized from former government forces. US authorities indicate that the Taliban administration is reorganising its MOD structure, and they have also retained some formation structures used by the ANSDF, particularly in regions outside Kabul. They have been able to employ some armoured vehicles and a small number of Soviet-era helicopters for troop movements as well as – according to the Taliban – low numbers of Western-supplied helicopters and an An-32 and Cessna 208. It is likely that, over time, the Taliban's ability to maintain in service its Western-derived equipment will reduce, because of sanctions and limited supplies of spares. While it appears that the Taliban have tried to recruit former ANSDF personnel, including pilots and maintainers, the success of these initiatives is unclear, not least because of continued attacks against former members of the ANSDF. And the Taliban policy on female education is another disincentive to those who might otherwise return to the country. The government's priority for its forces is internal and border security. It has prioritised operations against the National Resistance Front in the mountainous east of the country, as well as intelligence-led operations against Islamic State terrorist cells. The lack of international recognition and continued financial challenges will likely inhibit efforts to modernise the security forces.

ACTIVE 100,000 (Taliban 100,000)

ORGANISATIONS BY SERVICE

Taliban ε100,000
The Taliban has announced plans to expand their regular armed forces to 150,000 personnel

FORCES BY ROLE
SPECIAL FORCES
 3 spec ops bn
MANOEUVRE
 Light
 8 inf corps
EQUIPMENT BY TYPE
ARMOURED FIGHTING VEHICLES
 MBT T-62M†
 APC • PPV Maxxpro
 AUV MSFV
ARTILLERY
 TOWED 122mm D-30
 MRL 122mm BM-21
 MOR 82mm 2B14
AIRCRAFT • TPT • Light 2: 1 An-32 Cline; 1 Cessna 208B Grand Caravan
HELICOPTERS
 ATK 4 Mi-35 Hind
 MRH 14: 8 MD-530F; 6 Mi-17 Hip H
 TPT • **Medium** 4 UH-60A Black Hawk

Australia AUS

Australian Dollar AUD		2021	2022	2023
GDP	AUD	2.18tr	2.43tr	
	USD	1.64tr	1.72tr	
per capita	USD	63,464	66,408	
Growth	%	4.9	3.8	
Inflation	%	2.8	6.5	
Def bdgt [a]	AUD	45.5bn	47.8bn	51.7bn
	USD	34.2bn	33.8bn	
USD1=AUD		1.33	1.41	

[a] Includes pensions

Real-terms defence budget trend (USDbn, constant 2015)

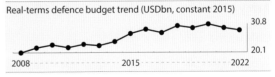

Population	26,141,369					
Age	0–14	15–19	20–24	25–29	30–64	65 plus
Male	9.6%	3.1%	3.5%	3.8%	22.1%	7.6%
Female	9.0%	2.9%	3.2%	3.6%	22.8%	8.8%

Capabilities

The Australian Defence Force (ADF) is capable, well trained and well equipped. It also has considerable recent operational experience. In 2016, the government published Australia's third defence White Paper in seven years. This identified China's growing regional role, regional military modernisation and inter-state rivalry as

230 THE MILITARY BALANCE 2023

among the influences shaping defence policy. A 'Strategic Update' to the White Paper, published in July 2020, outlined plans to adjust Australia's defence posture in order to develop a more powerful and self-reliant military deterrent. The document pointed to an increased prospect of war in Australia's region, claimed that a ten-year 'strategic warning time' could no longer be assumed, and highlighted potential threats from 'grey-zone activities'. In August 2022, the new Labor government announced a Defence Strategic Review to examine military posture, structures and investments. This is due to report in early 2023. The country's primary ally is the US, but it is also forging closer defence ties with India, Japan, South Korea and the UK, while remaining committed to the Five Power Defence Arrangements and to its close defence relations with New Zealand. A defence agreement was signed with Fiji in 2022, and there are plans for closer defence cooperation with Papua New Guinea. The AUKUS partnership, signed in September 2021, will see the UK and US assist Australia in developing a conventionally-armed, nuclear-powered submarine capability and other defence and security technologies. The plan is to build the nuclear-powered submarines in Adelaide, though some doubt has been cast on the timeline for delivering the first Australian-built boat, raising questions over what interim capability may be required. Australia is also building frigates and patrol ships, based on European designs. Strategic air- and sea-lift platforms give the capability to move and sustain deployments. Combat-air, maritime-patrol and armoured-vehicle capabilities are also being boosted, and more closely integrating Australia's armed forces – and their modern platforms – is a priority. Australia imports most of its significant defence equipment but possesses an increasingly capable defence industry. Its largest naval shipbuilders are ASC and Austal, whose US subsidiary, Austal USA, builds vessels for the US Navy.

ACTIVE 59,800 (Army 29,400 Navy 15,500 Air 14,900)

RESERVE 29,750 (Army 20,100 Navy 3,950 Air 5,700)
Integrated units are formed from a mix of reserve and regular personnel. All ADF operations are now controlled by Headquarters Joint Operations Command (HQJOC)

ORGANISATIONS BY SERVICE

Space
EQUIPMENT BY TYPE
SATELLITES • COMMUNICATIONS 1 *Optus* C1 (dual use for civil/mil comms)

Army 29,400
FORCES BY ROLE
COMMAND
1 (1st) div HQ (1 sigs regt)
MANOEUVRE
Mechanised
3 mech inf bde (1 armd cav regt, 1 mech inf bn, 1 lt mech inf bn, 1 arty regt, 1 cbt engr regt, 1 sigs regt, 1 CSS bn)
Amphibious
1 (2nd RAR) amph bn
Aviation
1 (16th) avn bde (1 regt (2 ISR hel sqn), 1 regt (3 tpt hel sqn), 1 regt (2 spec ops hel sqn, 1 avn sqn))
COMBAT SUPPORT
1 (6th) cbt spt bde (1 STA regt (1 STA bty, 2 UAV bty, 1 CSS bty), 1 AD/FAC regt (integrated), 1 engr regt (2 construction sqn, 1 EOD sqn), 1 EW regt, 1 int bn)

COMBAT SERVICE SUPPORT
1 (17th) CSS bde (3 log bn, 3 med bn, 1 MP bn)

Special Operations Command
FORCES BY ROLE
SPECIAL FORCES
1 (SAS) SF regt
1 (SF Engr) SF regt
2 cdo regt
COMBAT SUPPORT
3 sigs sqn (incl 1 reserve sqn)
COMBAT SERVICE SUPPORT
1 CSS sqn

Reserve Organisations 20,100 reservists
FORCES BY ROLE
COMMAND
1 (2nd) div HQ
MANOEUVRE
Reconnaissance
3 (regional force) surv unit (integrated)
Light
1 (4th) inf bde (1 recce regt, 2 inf bn, 1 engr regt, 1 spt bn)
1 (5th) inf bde (1 recce bn, 4 inf bn, 1 engr regt, 2 spt bn)
1 (9th) inf bde (1 recce sqn, 2 inf bn, 1 spt bn)
1 (11th) inf bde (1 recce regt, 3 inf bn, 1 engr regt, 1 spt bn)
1 (13th) inf bde (1 recce sqn, 2 inf bn, 1 spt bn)
COMBAT SUPPORT
1 arty regt
1 sigs regt
COMBAT SERVICE SUPPORT
1 trg bde
EQUIPMENT BY TYPE
ARMOURED FIGHTING VEHICLES
MBT 59 M1A1 *Abrams*
RECCE 25 *Boxer* CRV (incl variants)
IFV 221 ASLAV-25 (incl 100 variants)
APC • APC (T) 416 M113AS4
AUV 1,950: ε950 *Bushmaster* IMV; 1,000 *Hawkei*
ENGINEERING & MAINTENANCE VEHICLES
ARV 45: 15 ASLAV-F; 17 ASLAV-R; 13 M88A2
VLB 5 *Biber*
MW 20: 12 *Husky*; 8 MV-10
ANTI-TANK/ANTI-INFRASTRUCTURE
MSL • MANPATS FGM-148 *Javelin*
RCL • 84mm *Carl Gustaf*
ARTILLERY 264
TOWED 155mm 48 M777A2
MOR 81mm 216: 40 L16; 176 M252A1
AIR DEFENCE • SAM • Point-defence RBS-70
AMPHIBIOUS 15 LCM 8 (capacity either 1 MBT or 200 troops)
HELICOPTERS
ATK 22 *Tiger*
MRH 2 AW139 (leased)
TPT 89: **Heavy** 14 CH-47F *Chinook*; **Medium** 75: 41 NH90 TTH (MRH90); 34 S-70A *Black Hawk*
UNINHABITED AERIAL VEHICLES
ISR • Medium 15 RQ-7B *Shadow* 200
AIR-LAUNCHED MISSILES
ASM AGM-114M *Hellfire*

Navy 15,500

Fleet Comd HQ located at Sydney. Navy HQ located at Canberra

EQUIPMENT BY TYPE
SUBMARINES 6
  SSK 6 *Collins* with 6 single 533mm TT with UGM-84C *Harpoon* Block 1B AShM/Mk 48 ADCAP mod 7 HWT
PRINCIPAL SURFACE COMBATANTS 11
  DESTROYERS • DDGHM 3 *Hobart* with *Aegis* Baseline 8.1 C2, 2 quad lnchr with RGM-84L *Harpoon* Block II AShM, 6 8-cell Mk 41 VLS with SM-2 Block IIIB SAM/RIM-162A ESSM SAM, 2 twin 324mm SVTT Mk 32 mod 9 ASTT with MU90 LWT/Mk 54 LWT, 1 MK 15 *Phalanx* Block 1B CIWS, 1 127mm gun (capacity 1 MH-60R *Seahawk*)
  FRIGATES • FFGHM 8 *Anzac* (GER MEKO 200) with 2 quad lnchr with RGM-84L *Harpoon* Block II AShM, 1 8-cell Mk 41 VLS with RIM-162B ESSM SAM, 2 triple 324mm SVTT Mk 32 mod 5 ASTT with MU90 LWT, 1 127mm gun (capacity 1 MH-60R *Seahawk* ASW hel)
PATROL AND COASTAL COMBATANTS 15
  PCO 15: 10 *Armidale* (*Bay* mod); 5 *Cape* (of which 2 leased)
MINE WARFARE • MINE COUNTERMEASURES 4
  MHC 4 *Huon*
AMPHIBIOUS
  PRINCIPAL AMPHIBIOUS SHIPS 3
    LHD 2 *Canberra* (capacity 18 hel; 4 LCM-1E; 110 veh; 12 M1 *Abrams* MBT; 1,000 troops)
    LSD 1 *Choules* (ex-UK *Bay*) (capacity 1 med hel; 24 MBT; 350 troops)
  LANDING CRAFT • LCM 12 LCM-1E
LOGISTICS AND SUPPORT 11
  AGHS 2 *Leeuwin* with 1 hel landing platform
  AGS 2 *Paluma*
  AORH 2 *Supply* (ESP *Cantabria*) (capacity 1 MH-60R *Seahawk*)
  AX 1 *Sycamore* (capacity 1 med hel) (operated by private company, Teekay Shipping; multi-role aviation training vessel)
  AXS 1 *Young Endeavour*
  The following vessels are operated by a private company, DMS Maritime:
  ASR 2: 1 *Besant*; 1 *Stoker*
  AXL 1 *Seahorse Mercator*

Naval Aviation 1,450

FORCES BY ROLE
ANTI SUBMARINE WARFARE
  1 sqn with NH90 TTH (MRH90)
  1 sqn with MH-60R *Seahawk*
TRAINING
  1 OCU sqn with MH-60R *Seahawk*
  1 sqn with H135
EQUIPMENT BY TYPE
HELICOPTERS
  ASW 24 MH-60R *Seahawk*
  TPT 21: **Medium** 6 NH90 TTH (MRH90) (operated on rotational basis); **Light** 15 H135
AIR-LAUNCHED MISSILES
  ASM AGM-114M *Hellfire*

Clearance Diving Branch

FORCES BY ROLE
SPECIAL FORCES
  2 diving unit

Air Force 14,900

FORCES BY ROLE
FIGHTER/GROUND ATTACK
  1 sqn with F/A-18F *Super Hornet*
  2 sqn with F-35A *Lightning* II
  1 sqn with F-35A *Lightning* II (forming)
ANTI SUBMARINE WARFARE
  1 sqn with P-8A *Poseidon*
ELECTRONIC WARFARE
  1 sqn with EA-18G *Growler*
ISR
  1 (FAC) sqn with PC-21
  1 sqn with AP-3C *Orion*
AIRBORNE EARLY WARNING & CONTROL
  1 sqn with E-7A *Wedgetail*
TANKER/TRANSPORT
  1 sqn with A330 MRTT (KC-30A)
TRANSPORT
  1 VIP sqn with B-737BBJ; *Falcon* 7X
  1 sqn with C-17A *Globemaster* III
  1 sqn with C-27J *Spartan*
  1 sqn with C-130J-30 *Hercules*
TRAINING
  1 OCU sqn with F-35A *Lightning* II
  1 sqn with Beech 350 *King Air*
  2 sqn with PC-21
  2 (LIFT) sqn with *Hawk* MK127*

EQUIPMENT BY TYPE
AIRCRAFT 136 combat capable
  FGA 80: 24 F/A-18F *Super Hornet*; 56 F-35A *Lightning* II
  ASW 12 P-8A *Poseidon*
  EW 13: 2 AP-3C *Orion* mod; 11 EA-18G *Growler**
  AEW&C 6 E-7A *Wedgetail*
  TKR/TPT 7 A330 MRTT (KC-30A)
  TPT 47: **Heavy** 8 C-17A *Globemaster* III; **Medium** 22: 10 C-27J *Spartan*; 12 C-130J-30 *Hercules*; **Light** 12 Beech 350 *King Air*; **PAX** 5: 2 B-737BBJ (VIP); 3 *Falcon* 7X (VIP)
  TRG 82: 33 *Hawk* Mk127*; 49 PC-21
AIR-LAUNCHED MISSILES
  AAM • IIR AIM-9X *Sidewinder* II; ASRAAM; **ARH** AIM-120B/C-5/C-7 AMRAAM
  ARM AGM-88B HARM; AGM-88E AARGM
  AShM AGM-84A *Harpoon*
  ALCM • Conventional AGM-158A JASSM
BOMBS
  Laser-guided *Paveway* II
  Laser & INS/GPS-guided GBU-54 Laser JDAM; *Paveway* IV
  INS/GPS-guided AGM-154C JSOW; JDAM; JDAM-ER

DEPLOYMENT

EGYPT: MFO (*Operation Mazurka*) 27

IRAQ: *Operation Inherent Resolve* (*Okra*) 110; 1 SF gp; **NATO • NATO Mission Iraq** 2

MALI: UN • MINUSMA 1

MALAYSIA: 120; 1 inf coy (on 3-month rotational tours); 1 P-8A *Poseidon* (on rotation)
MIDDLE EAST: UN • UNTSO (*Operation Paladin*) 11
PHILIPPINES: *Operation Augury* 100 (trg team)
SOUTH SUDAN: UN • UNMISS (*Operation Aslan*) 15
UNITED ARAB EMIRATES: *Operation Accordion* 400: 1 tpt det with 2 C-130J-30 *Hercules*

FOREIGN FORCES

Singapore 230: 1 trg sqn at Pearce with PC-21 trg ac; 1 trg sqn at Oakey with 12 AS332 *Super Puma*; AS532 *Cougar*
United States US Pacific Command: 1,700; 1 SEWS at Pine Gap; 1 comms facility at NW Cape; 1 SIGINT stn at Pine Gap • US Strategic Command: 1 detection and tracking radar at Naval Communication Station Harold E. Holt

Bangladesh BGD

Bangladeshi Taka BDT		2021	2022	2023
GDP	BDT	35.3tr	39.8tr	
	USD	416bn	461bn	
per capita	USD	2,498	2,734	
Growth	%	6.9	7.2	
Inflation	%	5.6	6.2	
Def bdgt	BDT	344bn	373bn	400bn
	USD	4.06bn	4.32bn	
USD1=BDT		84.81	86.30	

Real-terms defence budget trend (USDbn, constant 2015)

Population 165,650,475

Age	0–14	15–19	20–24	25–29	30–64	65 plus
Male	13.1%	4.4%	4.5%	4.2%	19.4%	3.4%
Female	12.6%	4.3%	4.5%	4.4%	21.2%	3.9%

Capabilities

Bangladesh has limited military capability, which is optimised for border and domestic security, including domestic disaster relief. A defence-modernisation plan is under way, called Forces 2030, although acquisitions have been limited. Bangladesh has relied on Chinese and Russian aid and credit to overcome its limited procurement funding. It has increased defence collaboration with India. Increased tensions on its border with Myanmar may result in enhancements to border security. The country has a long record of UN peacekeeping deployments. A naval-recapitalisation and -expansion programme, including local manufacture of patrol boats, is underway to better protect the country's large EEZ. There are plans to recapitalise the combat air fleet, and there has also been recent investment in the fixed-wing training inventory. Airlift capability has improved with the addition of C295Ws and ex-UK C-130Js. Substantial efforts have also been made to strengthen the shipbuilding industry and work has begun on a new submarine-support facility. The armed forces reportedly retain extensive commercial interests, including in real estate, banks and other businesses.

ACTIVE 163,050 (Army 132,150 Navy 16,900 Air 14,000) Gendarmerie & Paramilitary 63,900

ORGANISATIONS BY SERVICE

Army 132,150
FORCES BY ROLE
COMMAND
  10 inf div HQ
SPECIAL FORCES
  1 cdo bde (2 cdo bn)
MANOEUVRE
  Armoured
  1 armd bde
  3 indep armd regt
  Light
  25 inf bde
  2 (composite) bde
COMBAT SUPPORT
  10 arty bde
  1 engr bde
  1 sigs bde
AVIATION
  1 avn regt (1 avn sqn; 1 hel sqn)
AIR DEFENCE
  1 AD bde
EQUIPMENT BY TYPE
ARMOURED FIGHTING VEHICLES
  MBT 276: 174 Type-59/-59G(BD); 58 Type-69/-69G; 44 Type-90-II (MBT-2000)
  LT TK 8+: 8 Type-62; some VT-5
  RECCE 8+ BOV M11
  APC 545
    APC (T) 134 MT-LB
    APC (W) 330 BTR-80
    PPV 81+ *Maxxpro*
  AUV 138: 36 *Cobra*; 102 *Cobra* II
ENGINEERING & MAINTENANCE VEHICLES
  AEV MT-LB
  ARV 3+: T-54/T-55; Type-84; 3 Type-654
  VLB MTU
ANTI-TANK/ANTI-INFRASTRUCTURE
  MSL • MANPATS 9K115-2 *Metis* M1 (RS-AT-13)
  RCL 106mm 238 M40A1
ARTILLERY 907+
  SP 155mm 18 NORA B-52
  TOWED 363+: 105mm 170 Model 56 pack howitzer; 122mm 131: 57 Type-54/54-1 (M-30); 20 Type-83; 54 Type-96 (D-30), 130mm 62 Type-59-1 (M-46)
  MRL 54: 122mm 36+ WS-22; 302mm 18 T-300
  MOR 472: 81mm 11 M29A1; 82mm 366 Type-53/type-87/M-31 (M-1937); 120mm 95 AM-50/UBM 52
AMPHIBIOUS • LANDING CRAFT 3: 1 LCT; 2 LCVP
AIRCRAFT • TPT • Light 7: 1 C295; 5 Cessna 152; 1 PA-31T *Cheyenne*
HELICOPTERS
  MRH 2 AS365N3 *Dauphin*
  TPT 7: **Medium** 3 Mi-171Sh **Light** 4: 2 Bell 206L-4 *Long Ranger* IV; 2 Bell 407GXi

Asia 233

AIR DEFENCE
SAM
Short-range FM-90 (CH-SA-4)
Point-defence FN-16 (CH-SA-14); QW-2 (CH-SA-8)
GUNS • TOWED 174: **35mm** 8 GDF-009 (with *Skyguard*-3); **37mm** 132 Type-65/74; **57mm** 34 Type-59 (S-60)

Navy 16,900

EQUIPMENT BY TYPE
SUBMARINES 2
SSK 2 *Nabajatra* (ex-PRC Type-035G (*Ming*)) with 8 single 533mm TT
PRINCIPAL SURFACE COMBATANTS • FRIGATES 6
FFGHM 3:
1 *Bangabandhu* (ROK modified *Ulsan*) with 2 twin lnchr with *Otomat* Mk2 AShM, 1 octuple FM-90N (CH-SA-N-4) SAM, 2 triple ILAS-3 (B-515) 324mm TT with A244/S LWT, 1 76mm gun (capacity 1 AW109E hel)
2 *Umar Farooq* (ex-PRC Type-053H3 (*Jiangwei* II)) with 2 quad lnchr with YJ-83 AShM, 1 octuple GMLS with HHQ-7 (CH-SA-N-4) SAM, 2 FQF 3200 A/S mor, 1 twin 100mm gun (capacity 1 hel)
FFG 3:
2 *Abu Bakr* (ex-PRC Type-053H2 (*Jianghu* III)) with 2 twin lnchr with C-802A AShM, 2 RBU 1200 *Uragan* A/S mor, 2 twin 100mm gun
1 *Osman* (ex-PRC Type-053H1 (*Jianghu* I)) with 2 quad lnchr with C-802 (CH-SS-N-6) AShM, 2 RBU 1200 *Uragan* A/S mor, 2 twin 100mm gun
PATROL AND COASTAL COMBATANTS 46
CORVETTES 6
FSGM 4 *Shadhinota* (PRC C13B) with 2 twin lnchr with C-802 (CH-SS-N-6) AShM, 1 octuple lnchr with FL-3000N (HHQ-10) (CH-SA-N-17) SAM, 1 76mm gun, 1 hel landing platform
FSG 2 *Bijoy* (ex-UK *Castle*) (of which 1 damaged in 2020 Beirut port explosion) with 2 twin lnchr with C-704 AShM, 1 76mm gun, 1 hel landing platform
PSOH 2 *Somudra Joy* (ex-US *Hero*) with 1 76mm gun, hel landing platform
PCFG 4 *Durdarsha* (ex-PRC *Huangfeng*) with 4 single lnchr with HY-2 (CH-SS-N-2 *Safflower*) AShM
PCG 2 *Durjoy* with 2 twin lnchr with C-704 AShM, 1 76MM gun
PCO 8: 1 *Madhumati* (*Sea Dragon*) with 1 57mm gun; 5 *Kapatakhaya* (ex-UK *Island*); 2 *Durjoy* with 2 triple 324mm ASTT, 1 76mm gun
PCC 8: 2 *Meghna* with 1 57mm gun (fishery protection); 1 *Nirbhoy* (ex-PRC *Hainan*) with 4 RBU 1200 *Uragan* A/S mor; 2 twin 57mm gun; 5 *Padma*
PBFG 5 *Durbar* (PRC *Hegu*) with 2 single lnchr with SY-1 (CH-SS-N-1 *Scrubbrush*) AShM
PBF 4 *Titas* (ROK *Sea Dolphin*)
PB 7: 1 *Barkat* (ex-PRC *Shanghai* III); 2 *Karnaphuli*; 1 *Salam* (ex-PRC *Huangfen*); 3 *Shaheed Daulat* (PRC *Shanghai* II)
MINE WARFARE • MINE COUNTERMEASURES 5
MSO 5: 1 *Sagar*; 4 *Shapla* (ex-UK *River*)
AMPHIBIOUS
LANDING SHIPS • LSL 1
LANDING CRAFT 14

LCU 4 (of which 2†)
LCT 2
LCM 5 *Darshak* (*Yuchin*)
LCVP 3†
LOGISTICS AND SUPPORT 11
AG 1
AGHS 2: 1 *Agradoot*; 1 *Anushandhan*
AGS 2 *Darshak*
AOR 2 (coastal)
AOT 1 *Khan Jahangir Ali*
AR 1†
ATF 1†
AX 1 *Shaheed Ruhul Amin*

Naval Aviation
EQUIPMENT BY TYPE
AIRCRAFT • MP 4 Do-228NG
HELICOPTERS • TPT • Light 2 AW109E *Power*

Special Warfare and Diving Command 300

Air Force 14,000
FORCES BY ROLE
FIGHTER
1 sqn with MiG-29/MiG-29UB *Fulcrum*
FIGHTER/GROUND ATTACK
1 sqn with F-7MB/FT-7B *Airguard*
1 sqn with F-7BG/FT-7BG *Airguard*
1 sqn with F-7BGI/FT-7BGI *Airguard*
GROUND ATTACK
1 sqn with Yak-130 *Mitten**
TRANSPORT
1 sqn with An-32 *Cline*
1 sqn with C-130B/J *Hercules*
1 sqn with L-410UVP
TRAINING
1 sqn with K-8W *Karakorum**; L-39ZA *Albatros**
1 sqn with PT-6
TRANSPORT HELICOPTER
1 sqn with AW139; Mi-17 *Hip* H; Mi-17-1V *Hip* H; Mi-171Sh
1 sqn with Mi-17 *Hip* H; Mi-17-1V *Hip* H; Mi-171Sh
1 sqn with Bell 212
1 trg sqn with Bell 206L *Long Ranger*; AW119 *Koala*
EQUIPMENT BY TYPE
AIRCRAFT 88 combat capable
FTR 53: 9 F-7MB *Airguard*; 11 F-7BG *Airguard*; 12 F-7BGI *Airguard*; 5 FT-7B *Airguard*; 4 FT-7BG *Airguard*; 4 FT-7BGI *Airguard*; 6 MiG-29 *Fulcrum*; 2 MiG-29UB *Fulcrum* B
TPT 16: **Medium** 8: 4 C-130B *Hercules*; 4 C-130J *Hercules*; **Light** 8: 3 An-32 *Cline*†; 2 C295W; 3 L-410UVP
TRG 81: 4 DA40NG; 12 G 120TP; 15 K-8W *Karakorum**; 7 L-39ZA *Albatros**; 30+ PT-6; 13 Yak-130 *Mitten**
HELICOPTERS
MRH 16: 2 AW139 (SAR); 12 Mi-17 *Hip* H; 2 Mi-17-1V *Hip* H (VIP)
TPT 19: **Medium** 11 Mi-171Sh; **Light** 8: 2 Bell 206L *Long Ranger*; 4 Bell 212; 2 AW119 *Koala*
AIR-LAUNCHED MISSILES
AAM • IR R-73 (RS-AA-11A *Archer*); PL-5; PL-7; **SARH** R-27R (RS-AA-10A *Alamo*)

Gendarmerie & Paramilitary 63,900

Ansars 20,000+
Security Guards

Rapid Action Battalions 5,000
Ministry of Home Affairs
FORCES BY ROLE
MANOEUVRE
  Other
    14 paramilitary bn

Border Guard Bangladesh 38,000
FORCES BY ROLE
MANOEUVRE
  Amphibious
    1 rvn coy
  Other
    54 paramilitary bn

Coast Guard 900
EQUIPMENT BY TYPE
PATROL AND COASTAL COMBATANTS 23
  PSO 4 *Syed Nazrul* (ex-ITA *Minerva*) with 1 hel landing platform
  PCC 5 *Sobuj Bangla* (*Padma* mod)
  PB 9: 1 *Ruposhi Bangla*; 4 *Shaheed Daulat*; 2 *Shetgang*; 2 *Sonadia*
  PBR 5 *Pabna*

DEPLOYMENT

CENTRAL AFRICAN REPUBLIC: UN • MINUSCA 1,382; 1 cdo coy; 1 inf bn; 1 med coy; 1 hel coy
DEMOCRATIC REPUBLIC OF THE CONGO: UN • MONUSCO 1,637; 1 inf bn; 1 engr coy; 1 avn sqn; 1 hel coy
LEBANON: UN • UNIFIL 118; 1 FSGM
MALI: UN • MINUSMA 1,297; 1 mech inf bn; 1 engr coy; 1 sigs coy
SOUTH SUDAN: UN • UNMISS 1,628; 1 inf bn; 2 rvn coy; 2 engr coy
SUDAN: UN • UNISFA 508; 1 inf bn
WESTERN SAHARA: UN • MINURSO 27; 1 fd hospital

Brunei BRN

Brunei Dollar BND		2021	2022	2023
GDP	BND	18.8bn	25.4bn	
	USD	14.0bn	18.5bn	
per capita	USD	32,573	42,939	
Growth	%	-1.6	1.2	
Inflation	%	1.7	2.5	
Def bdgt	BND	610m	598m	
	USD	454m	435m	
USD1=BND		1.34	1.37	

Real-terms defence budget trend (USDm, constant 2015)

Population	478,054					
Age	0–14	15–19	20–24	25–29	30–64	65 plus
Male	11.3%	3.5%	4.1%	4.6%	22.0%	3.3%
Female	10.7%	3.5%	4.2%	4.9%	24.5%	3.4%

Capabilities

The Royal Brunei Armed Forces are professional and well trained. In May 2021, the government published Brunei's fourth defence White Paper in 17 years, within the context of the Vision Brunei 2035 framework. C4ISR capabilities are being improved to offset the forces' relatively small size, and the White Paper advocates procurements to strengthen airspace control and harden C4 systems. Under a long-standing bilateral arrangement, which currently extends to 2025, Brunei continues to host a British military presence including a Gurkha infantry battalion, a helicopter-flight and a jungle-warfare school. Brunei has a close defence relationship with Singapore and hosts a permanent Singapore Armed Forces training facility. There are regular bilateral exercises with Singapore and other Southeast Asian countries. The armed forces also take part in multinational exercises organised by the ADMM-Plus. Brunei has limited capacity to deploy forces abroad without assistance, but has nevertheless maintained a small deployment to UNIFIL in Lebanon since 2008. Brunei has no domestic defence industry and imports all its military equipment. In 2010, the Centre of Science and Technology Research and Development was established to conduct defence-technology research and provide engineering and support services to the armed forces.

ACTIVE 7,200 (Army 4,400 Navy 1,200 Air 1,100 Special Forces 500) **Gendarmerie & Paramilitary 400–500**

RESERVE 700 (Army 700)

ORGANISATIONS BY SERVICE

Army 4,400
FORCES BY ROLE
MANOEUVRE
  Light
    3 inf bn

COMBAT SUPPORT
1 cbt spt bn (1 armd recce sqn, 1 engr sqn)

Reserves 700
FORCES BY ROLE
MANOEUVRE
Light
1 inf bn
EQUIPMENT BY TYPE
ARMOURED FIGHTING VEHICLES
LT TK 20 FV101 *Scorpion* (incl FV105 *Sultan* CP)
APC • APC (W) 45 VAB
ENGINEERING & MAINTENANCE VEHICLES
ARV 2 *Samson*
ARTILLERY • MOR 81mm 24

Navy 1,200
FORCES BY ROLE
SPECIAL FORCES
1 SF sqn
EQUIPMENT BY TYPE
PATROL AND COASTAL COMBATANTS 9
 CORVETTES • FSG 4 *Darussalam* with 2 twin lnchr with MM40 *Exocet* Block 2 AShM, 1 57mm gun, 1 hel landing platform
 PCC 4 *Ijtihad*
 PBF 1 *Mustaed*
AMPHIBIOUS • LANDING CRAFT • LCM 4: 2 *Teraban*; 2 *Cheverton Loadmaster*

Air Force 1,100
FORCES BY ROLE
MARITIME PATROL
1 sqn with CN235M
TRAINING
1 sqn with Bell 206B *Jet Ranger* II
TRANSPORT HELICOPTER
1 sqn with Bell 214 (SAR)
1 sqn with S-70i *Black Hawk*
AIR DEFENCE
1 sqn with *Mistral*
1 sqn with *Rapier*
EQUIPMENT BY TYPE
AIRCRAFT
 TPT • Light 1 CN235M
 TRG 4 PC-7
HELICOPTERS
 TPT 15: Medium 13: 1 Bell 214 (SAR); 12 S-70i *Black Hawk*; Light 2 Bell 206B *Jet Ranger* II
AIR DEFENCE • SAM • Point-defence *Mistral*; *Rapier*

Special Forces Regiment ε500
FORCES BY ROLE
SPECIAL FORCES
1 SF regt

Gendarmerie & Paramilitary 400–500

Gurkha Reserve Unit 400–500
FORCES BY ROLE
MANOEUVRE
Light
2 inf bn(-)

DEPLOYMENT
LEBANON: UN • UNIFIL 30

FOREIGN FORCES
Singapore 1 trg camp with infantry units on rotation; 1 trg school; 1 hel det with AS332 *Super Puma*
United Kingdom 2,000; 1 (Gurkha) inf bn; 1 jungle trg centre; 1 hel sqn with 3 Bell 212

Cambodia CAM

Cambodian Riel KHR		2021	2022	2023
GDP	KHR	109tr	119tr	
	USD	26.3bn	28.3bn	
per capita	USD	1,662	1,771	
Growth	%	3.0	5.1	
Inflation	%	2.9	5.2	
Def bdgt [a]	KHR	4.25tr	4.21tr	
	USD	1.02bn	1.00bn	
USD1=KHR		4154.25	4199.86	

[a] Defence and security budget

Real-terms defence budget trend (USDm, constant 2015)

Population	16,713,015				
Age	0–14	15–19	20–24	25–29	30–64	65 plus
Male	15.2%	4.3%	3.8%	4.1%	19.3%	1.8%
Female	14.8%	4.4%	4.0%	4.4%	20.8%	3.2%

Capabilities
Despite their name, which reflects Cambodia's formal status as a constitutional monarchy, the Royal Cambodian Armed Forces (RCAF) are essentially the modern manifestation of the armed forces of the former People's Republic of Kampuchea, and were established in 1979 following Vietnam's invasion. Cambodia faces no direct external military threats, besides border clashes with Thailand which last occurred in 2011. Relations have developed since then and a seventh meeting on border issues took place in September 2022, the same month as reports that both sides had resumed talks on overlapping maritime border claims. There were reports in November 2022 of an agreement on demining activities on the border. Internally, security concerns include civil unrest and transnational threats that can generate instability, such as drug trafficking. Skirmishes on the border with Thailand provided little indication of capacity for high-intensity combat. However, Cambodia has contributed personnel to UN peacekeeping missions, including UNMISS in South Sudan. Cambodia's most important international defence links are with China's and Vietnam's armed forces. While traditionally reliant on Russia for defence equipment, China has emerged

236 THE MILITARY BALANCE 2023

as a key supplier in recent years. Training ties have also developed with China and exercises have grown in scale. Cambodia lacks significant resources for personnel training, which is partly financed by Chinese military assistance. In response to deepening Chinese military influence in Cambodia, the US imposed an arms embargo on Cambodia in December 2021. Funds for equipment purchases are limited, although the 2022 National Defence White Paper stated that modernisation of the RCAF is the top priority. There is no domestic defence industry, with Cambodia possessing no ability to design and manufacture modern equipment for its armed forces.

ACTIVE 124,300 (Army 75,000 Navy 2,800 Air 1,500 Provincial Forces 45,000) Gendarmerie & Paramilitary 67,000

Conscript liability 18 months service authorised but not implemented since 1993

ORGANISATIONS BY SERVICE

Army ε75,000

6 Military Regions (incl 1 special zone for capital)

FORCES BY ROLE
SPECIAL FORCES
  1 (Spec Ops Comd) AB/SF Bde
MANOEUVRE
  Light
  2 (2nd & 3rd Intervention) inf div (3 inf bde)
  5 (Intervention) indep inf bde
  8 indep inf bde
  Other
  1 (70th) sy bde (4 sy bn)
  17 (border) sy bn
COMBAT SUPPORT
  2 arty bn
  4 fd engr regt
COMBAT SERVICE SUPPORT
  1 (construction) engr regt
  2 tpt bde
AIR DEFENCE
  1 AD bn

EQUIPMENT BY TYPE
ARMOURED FIGHTING VEHICLES
  MBT 200+: 50 Type-59; 150+ T-54/T-55
  LT TK 20+: Type-62; 20 Type-63
  RECCE 20+ BRDM-2
  IFV 70 BMP-1
  APC 230+
    APC (T) M113
    APC (W) 230: 200 BTR-60/BTR-152; 30 OT-64
  AUV 27: 12 Dongfeng *Mengshi*; 15 *Tiger* 4×4
ENGINEERING & MAINTENANCE VEHICLES
  ARV T-54/T-55
  MW *Bozena*; RA-140 DS
ANTI-TANK/ANTI-INFRASTRUCTURE
  RCL 82mm B-10; **107mm** B-11
ARTILLERY 486+
  SP 155mm 12 SH-1
  TOWED 400+: **76mm** ZIS-3 (M-1942)/**122mm** D-30/
  122mm M-30 (M-1938)/**130mm** Type-59-I
  MRL 74+: 107mm Type-63; **122mm** 48+: 8 BM-21; ε20
  PHL-81; some PHL-90B; 20 RM-70; **132mm** BM-13-16

(BM-13); **140mm** 20 BM-14-16 (BM-14); **300mm** 6 PHL-03
MOR 82mm M-37; **120mm** M-43; **160mm** M-160
AIR DEFENCE
  SAM • Point-defence FN-6 (CH-SA-10); FN-16 (CH-SA-14) (reported)
  GUNS • TOWED 14.5mm ZPU-1/ZPU-2/ZPU-4; **37mm** M-1939; **57mm** S-60

Navy ε2,800 (incl 1,500 Naval Infantry)

EQUIPMENT BY TYPE
PATROL AND COASTAL COMBATANTS 13
  PBF 4 Project 205P (*Stenka*)
  PB 7: 3 (PRC 20m); 4 (PRC 46m)
  PBR 2 *Kaoh Chhlam*
AMPHIBIOUS • LANDING CRAFT 1
  LCU 1 Type-067 (*Yunnan*)
LOGISTICS AND SUPPORT • AFDL 1

Naval Infantry 1,500

FORCES BY ROLE
MANOEUVRE
  Light
  1 (31st) nav inf bde
COMBAT SUPPORT
  1 arty bn

Air Force 1,500

FORCES BY ROLE
ISR/TRAINING
  1 sqn with P-92 *Echo*
TRANSPORT
  1 VIP sqn (reporting to Council of Ministers) with
    An-24RV *Coke*; AS350 *Ecureuil*; AS355F2 *Ecureuil* II
  1 sqn with BN-2 *Islander*; Y-12 (II)
TRANSPORT HELICOPTER
  1 sqn with Mi-17 *Hip* H; Mi-8 *Hip*; Z-9

EQUIPMENT BY TYPE
AIRCRAFT
  TPT • Light 9: 2 MA60; 5 P-92 *Echo* (pilot trg/recce);
  2 Y-12 (II) (2 An-24RV *Coke*; 1 BN-2 *Islander* in store)
  TRG (5 L-39C *Albatros** in store)
HELICOPTERS
  MRH 14: 3 Mi-17 *Hip* H; 11 Z-9
  TPT 4: **Heavy** (2 Mi-26 *Halo* in store); **Light** 4: 2 AS350 *Ecureuil*; 2 AS355F2 *Ecureuil* II

Provincial Forces 45,000+

Reports of at least 1 inf regt per province, with varying numbers of inf bn (with lt wpn)

Gendarmerie & Paramilitary 67,000

Police 67,000 (including gendarmerie)

DEPLOYMENT

CENTRAL AFRICAN REPUBLIC: UN • MINUSCA 225; 1 engr coy
LEBANON: UN • UNIFIL 180; 1 EOD coy
MALI: UN • MINUSMA 289: 2 engr coy; 1 EOD coy
SOUTH SUDAN: UN • UNMISS 84; 1 MP coy
SUDAN: UN • UNISFA 1

China, People's Republic of PRC

Chinese Yuan Renminbi CNY		2021	2022	2023
GDP	CNY	114tr	123tr	
	USD	17.7tr	20.3tr	
per capita	USD	12,562	14,340	
Growth	%	8.1	3.2	
Inflation	%	0.9	2.2	
Def exp	CNY	ε1.84tr	ε1.95tr	
	USD	ε285bn	ε319bn	
Def bdgt [a]	CNY	1.38tr	1.47tr	
	USD	214bn	242bn	
USD1=CNY		6.45	6.08	

[a] Central Expenditure budget including local militia funding

Real-terms defence budget trend (USDbn, constant 2015)

Population	1,418,451,639				
Age	0–14	15–19	20–24	25–29	30–64	65 plus
Male	8.9%	2.9%	3.0%	3.6%	26.3%	6.3%
Female	7.8%	2.4%	2.6%	3.3%	25.6%	7.3%

Capabilities

China's People's Liberation Army (PLA) is the world's largest armed force, with an increasingly advanced equipment inventory. Its operational effectiveness, however, remains hampered by training and doctrine issues. China's 2019 defence White Paper did not significantly alter the strategic direction laid out in the 2015 edition and was focused more on updating the progress of PLA modernisation efforts. In 2021, amendments to the National Defense Law were enacted, which handed responsibility for defence mobilisation fully to the Central Military Commission and removed the role of the State Council. A major restructuring process is now mostly complete and the Strategic Support Force continues to develop China's cyber, space and information-dominance capabilities. China does not maintain any formal alliances, but it does have a number of key defence relationships with regional states and through its membership of the SCO and has also worked to develop defence ties with several African and Middle Eastern states. In February 2022, China and Russia announced a friendship with 'no limits', though China has been reluctant to assist Russia militarily in its war on Ukraine. Improving readiness for combat operations is a key objective of the current reforms; the PLA currently lacks any significant recent combat experience and its training has traditionally suffered from over-scripted and unrealistic exercises. Though these weaknesses are acknowledged, it is unclear how effective the newly established structures will be at generating and controlling high-intensity combined-arms capabilities. In 2021, the PLA's conscription pattern changed from once to twice a year, with the aim of improving force readiness. Recruitment maintains a particular focus on college graduates and those skilled in science and engineering. The requirement for out-of-area operations is relatively new for the PLA; the navy is the only service to have experience in extended deployments, assisted by its support base in Djibouti. Major platform inventories in all the services comprise a mix of modern, older and obsolescent designs as modernisation efforts continue. China has an extensive defence-industrial base, capable of producing advanced equipment across all domains, although questions persist over quality and reliability.

ACTIVE 2,035,000 (Ground Forces 965,000 Navy 260,000 Air Force 395,000 Strategic Missile Forces 120,000 Strategic Support Force 145,000 Other 150,000) **Gendarmerie & Paramilitary 500,000**
Conscript liability Selective conscription; all services 24 months

RESERVE ε510,000

ORGANISATIONS BY SERVICE

Strategic Missile Forces 120,000+

People's Liberation Army Rocket Force

The People's Liberation Army Rocket Force organises and commands its own troops to launch nuclear counter-attacks with strategic missiles and to conduct operations with conventional missiles. Organised as launch brigades subordinate to 6 army-level missile bases.

FORCES BY ROLE
SURFACE-TO-SURFACE MISSILE
  1 ICBM bde with DF-4
  3 ICBM bde with DF-5A/B
  1 ICBM bde with DF-31
  1 ICBM bde with DF-31A
  5 ICBM bde with DF-31A(G)
  2 ICBM bde with DF-41
  6 IRBM bde with DF-26
  3 MRBM bde with DF-17 with HGV
  2 MRBM bde with DF-21A/E
  1 MRBM bde with DF-21C/D
  2 SRBM bde with DF-11A/DF-15B
  2 SRBM bde with DF-16
  3 GLCM bde with CJ-10/CJ-10A/CJ-100
  8 SSM bde (forming)

EQUIPMENT BY TYPE
SURFACE-TO-SURFACE MISSILE LAUNCHERS
  ICBM • Nuclear 140: ε10 DF-4 (CH-SS-3); ε20 DF-5A/B (CH-SS-4 Mod 2/3); ε8 DF-31 (CH-SS-10 Mod 1); ε24 DF-31A (CH-SS-10 Mod 2); ε54 DF-31A(G) (CH-SS-10 Mod 3); ε24 DF-41 (CH-SS-20)
  IRBM • Dual-capable 110+ DF-26 (CH-SS-18)
  MRBM 94: **Nuclear** ε40 DF-21A/E (CH-SS-5 Mod 2/6); **Conventional** 54: ε24 DF-17 with HGV (CH-SS-22); ε30 DF-21D (CH-SS-5 Mod 5 – ASBM)
  SRBM • Conventional 225: ε108 DF-11A (CH-SS-7 Mod 2); ε81 DF-15B (CH-SS-6 Mod 3); ε36 DF-16 (CH-SS-11 Mod 1/2)
  GLCM • Conventional 108: ε54 CJ-10/CJ-10A (CH-SSC-9 mod 1/2); ε54 CJ-100 (CH-SSC-13 *Splinter*)

Navy

EQUIPMENT BY TYPE
SUBMARINES • STRATEGIC 6
  SSBN 6 Type-094 (*Jin*) with up to 12 JL-2 (CH-SS-N-14)/ JL-3 (CH-SS-N-20) strategic SLBMs, 6 single 533mm TT with Yu-6 HWT

238　THE MILITARY BALANCE 2023

Defensive

EQUIPMENT BY TYPE
RADAR • STRATEGIC: 4+ large phased array radars; some detection and tracking radars

Space

EQUIPMENT BY TYPE
SATELLITES 207
COMMUNICATIONS 11: 2 *Shen Tong*-1; 4 *Shen Tong*-2; 2 *Feng Huo*-1; 3 *Feng Huo*-2
POSITIONING, NAVIGATION & TIMING 45: 3 *Beidou*-2(M); 5 *Beidou*-2(G); 7 *Beidou*-2(IGSO); 24 *Beidou*-3(M); 3 *Beidou*-3(G); 3 *Beidou*-3(ISGO)
METEOROLOGY/OCEANOGRAPHY 8: 2 *Yunhai*-1; 6 *Yunhai*-2
ISR 55: 2 *Jianbing*-5; 4 *Jianbing*-6; 4 *Jianbing*-7; 5 *Jianbing*-9; 3 *Jianbing*-10; 3 *Jianbing*-11/-12; 3 *Jianbing*-16; 4 *LKW*; 4 *Tianhui*-2; 3 *Yaogan*-29; 2 *Yaogan*-34; 15 *Yaogan*-35; 3 *Yaogan*-36
ELINT/SIGINT 81: 30 *Chuangxin*-5 (*Yaogan*-30); 15 *Jianbing*-8; 3 *Qianshao*-3; 10 *Shijian*-6 (5 pairs – reported ELINT/SIGINT role); 7 *Shijian*-11 (reported ELINT/SIGINT role); 12 *Yaogan*-31; 4 *Yaogan*-32
EARLY WARNING 5: 5 *Huoyan*-1
RENDEZVOUS & PROXIMITY OPERATIONS 2: 1 *Shijian*-17; 1 *Shijian*-21
REUSABLE SPACECRAFT 1 CSSHQ
COUNTERSPACE • MSL SC-19 (reported)

Army ε965,000

FORCES BY ROLE
COMMAND
13 (Group) army HQ
SPECIAL FORCES
15 spec ops bde
MANOEUVRE
　Armoured
　33 (cbd arms) armd bde
　Mechanised
　2 (high alt) mech inf div (3 (cbd arms) mech regt, 1 arty regt, 1 AD regt)
　17 (cbd arms) mech inf bde
　2 indep mech inf regt
　Light
　2 (high alt) inf div (3 (cbd arms) inf regt, 1 arty regt, 1 AD regt)
　25 (cbd arms) inf bde
　Air Manoeuvre
　2 air aslt bde
　Amphibious
　6 amph aslt bde
　Other
　1 (OPFOR) armd bde
　1 mech gd div (1 armd regt, 2 mech inf regt, 1 arty regt, 1 AD regt)
　1 sy gd div (4 sy regt)
　16 (border) sy bde
　15 (border) sy regt
　1 (border) sy gp

COMBAT SUPPORT
15 arty bde
9 engr/NBC bde
5 engr bde
5 NBC bde
1 engr regt
COMBAT SERVICE SUPPORT
13 spt bde
COASTAL DEFENCE
19 coastal arty/AShM bde
AVIATION
1 mixed avn bde
HELICOPTER
12 hel bde
TRAINING
4 hel trg bde
AIR DEFENCE
15 AD bde

Reserves

The People's Liberation Army Reserve Force is being restructured, and the army component reduced. As a result some of the units below may have been re-roled or disbanded

FORCES BY ROLE
MANOEUVRE
　Armoured
　2 armd regt
　Light
　18 inf div
　4 inf bde
　3 indep inf regt
COMBAT SUPPORT
　3 arty div
　7 arty bde
　15 engr regt
　1 ptn br bde
　3 ptn br regt
　10 chem regt
　10 sigs regt
COMBAT SERVICE SUPPORT
　9 log bde
　1 log regt
AIR DEFENCE
　17 AD div
　8 AD bde
　8 AD regt
EQUIPMENT BY TYPE
ARMOURED FIGHTING VEHICLES
MBT 4,800: 600 ZTZ-59/-59-II/-59D; 200 ZTZ-79; 300 ZTZ-88A/B; 1,000 ZTZ-96; 1,500 ZTZ-96A; 600 ZTZ-99; 600 ZTZ-99A
LT TK 1,250: 750 ZTD-05; 500 ZTQ-15
ASLT 1,200 ZTL-11
IFV 7,700: 400 ZBD-04; 1,900 ZBD-04A; 3,000 ZBL-08; 600 ZBD-86; 650 ZBD-86A; 550 ZSL-92; 600 ZSL-92B
APC 3,900
　APC (T) 2,250: 500 ZSD-63; 1,750 ZSD-89/-89A
　APC (W) 1,650: 700 ZSL-92A; 900 ZSL-10; 50 ZSL-93
AAV 750 ZBD-05
AUV Dongfeng Mengshi; *Tiger* 4×4

ENGINEERING & MAINTENANCE VEHICLES

ARV Type-73; Type-84; Type-85; Type-97; Type-654

VLB MTU; TMM; GQL-110A (Type-84A); GQL-111 (HZQL75); GQL-321 (HZQL22); GQL-410; High Altitude VLB; HZQL-18; ZGQ-84

MW Type-74; Type-79; Type-81-II; Type-84

ANTI-TANK/ANTI-INFRASTRUCTURE

MSL

SP 1,125: 450 HJ-8 (veh mounted); 200 HJ-10; 25 HJ-10A; 450 ZSL-02B

MANPATS HJ-73D; HJ-8A/C/E; HJ-11; HJ-12

RCL 3,966: **75mm** PF-56; **82mm** PF-65 (B-10); PF-78; **105mm** PF-75; **120mm** PF-98

GUNS 1,788

SP 480: **100mm** 250 PTL-02; **120mm** 230 PTZ-89

TOWED • 100mm 1,308 PT-73 (T-12)/PT-86

ARTILLERY 9,550+

SP 3,180: **122mm** 2,110: 300 PLZ-89; 550 PLZ-07A; 150 PLZ-07B; 300 PCL-09; 600 PLL-09; 60 PCL-161; 120 PCL-171; 30 PCL-181 **152mm** 150 PLZ-83A/B; **155mm** 920: 320 PLZ-05; 600 PCL-181; (600 in store: **122mm** 400 PLZ-89; **152mm** 200 PLZ-83A)

TOWED 900: **122mm** 300 PL-96 (D-30); **130mm** 100 PL-59 (M-46)/PL-59-I; **152mm** 500 PL-66 (D-20); (4,700 in store: **122mm** 3,000 PL-54-1 (M-1938)/PL-83/PL-60 (D-74)/PL-96 (D-30); **152mm** 1,700 PL-54 (D-1)/PL-66 (D-20))

GUN/MOR 120mm 1,250: 450 PLL-05; 800 PPZ-10

MRL 1,320+ **107mm** PH-63; **122mm** 1,095: 200 PHL-81/PHL-90; 350 PHL-11; 375 PHZ-89; 120 PHZ-11; 30 PHL-20; 10+ PHL-21; 10 PHL-161; **300mm** 175 PHL-03; **370mm** 50+ PHL-19; (1,000 in store: **122mm** 1,000 PHL-81)

MOR 2,800: **82mm** PP-53 (M-37)/PP-67/PP-82/PP-87; **SP 82mm** PCP-001; **100mm** PP-89

COASTAL DEFENCE

AShM HY-1 (CH-SSC-2 *Silkworm*); HY-2 (CH-SSC-3 *Seersucker*); HY-4 (CH-SSC-7 *Sadsack*); YJ-62

PATROL AND COASTAL COMBATANTS 25

PB 25: 9 *Huzong*; 16 *Shenyang*

AMPHIBIOUS • LANDING CRAFT • LCM 255: 3+ *Yugong*; 50+ *Yunnan* II; 100+ *Yupen*; 2+ *Yutu*; approx. 100 *Yuwei*

LOGISTICS AND SUPPORT 22

AK 6+ *Leizhuang*

AKR 1 *Yunsong* (capacity 1 MBT; 1 med hel)

ARC 1

AOT 11: 1 *Fuzhong*; 8 *Fubing*; 2 *Fulei*

ATF 2 *Huntao*

AX 1 *Haixun* III

AIRCRAFT • TPT 6: **Medium** 4: 2 Y-8; 2 Y-9; **Light** 2 Y-7

HELICOPTERS

ATK 320+: 200 WZ-10; 120+ WZ-19

MRH 208: 22 Mi-17 *Hip* H; 3 Mi-17-1V *Hip* H; 38 Mi-17V-5 *Hip* H; 25 Mi-17V-7 *Hip* H; ε120 Z-9WZ

TPT 452: **Heavy** 125: 9 Z-8A; 96 Z-8B; ε20 Z-8L; **Medium** 259: 140 Mi-171; 19 S-70C2 (S-70C) *Black Hawk*; ε100 Z-20; **Light** 68: 15 H120 *Colibri*; 53 Z-11

UNINHABITED AERIAL VEHICLES

CISR • Heavy 5+ CH-4B

ISR • Heavy BZK-005; BZK-009 (reported); **Medium** BZK-006 (incl variants); BZK-007; BZK-008

LOITERING & DIRECT ATTACK MUNITIONS

Harpy

AIR DEFENCE

SAM 754+

Medium-range 250 HQ-16A/B (CH-SA-16)

Short-range 504: 24 9K331 *Tor*-M1 (RS-SA-15 *Gauntlet*); 30 HQ-6D (CH-SA-6); 200 HQ-7A/B (CH-SA-4); 200 HQ-17 (CH-SA-15); 50 HQ-17A (CH-SA-15)

Point-defence HN-5A/B (CH-SA-3); FN-6 (CH-SA-10); QW-1 (CH-SA-7); QW-2 (CH-SA-8)

SPAAGM 25mm 270 PGZ-04A

GUNS 7,126+

SP 126: **30mm** some PGL-19; **35mm** 120 PGZ-07; **37mm** 6 PGZ-88

TOWED 7,000+: **25mm** PG-87; **35mm** PG-99 (GDF-002); **37mm** PG-55 (M-1939)/PG-65/PG-74; **57mm** PG-59 (S-60); **100mm** PG-59 (KS-19)

AIR-LAUNCHED MISSILES

AAM • IR TY-90

ASM AKD-8; AKD-9; AKD-10

Navy ε260,000

The PLA Navy is organised into five service arms: submarine, surface, naval aviation, coastal defence and marine corps, as well as other specialised units. There are three fleets, one each in the Eastern, Southern and Northern theatre commands

EQUIPMENT BY TYPE

SUBMARINES 59

STRATEGIC • SSBN 6 Type-094 (*Jin*) with up to 12 JL-2 (CH-SS-N-14)/JL-3 (CH-SS-N-20) strategic SLBMs, 6 single 533mm TT with Yu-6 HWT

TACTICAL 53

SSN 6:

2 Type-093 (*Shang* I) with 6 single 533mm TT with YJ-82 (CH-SS-N-7) AShM or YJ-18 (CH-SS-N-13) AShM/Yu-3 HWT/Yu-6 HWT

4 Type-093A (*Shang* II) with 6 single 533mm TT with YJ-82 (CH-SS-N-7) AShM or YJ-18 (CH-SS-N-13) AShM/Yu-3 HWT/Yu-6 HWT

(3 Type-091 (*Han*) in reserve with 6 single 533mm TT with YJ-82 (CH-SS-N-7) AShM/Yu-3 HWT)

SSK 46:

2 Project 636 (Improved *Kilo*) with 6 single 533mm TT with TEST-71ME HWT/53-65KE HWT

8 Project 636M (Improved *Kilo*) with 6 single 533mm TT with TEST-71ME HWT/53-65KE HWT/3M54E *Klub*-S (RS-SS-N-27B *Sizzler*) AShM

4 Type-035B (*Ming*) with 8 single 533mm TT with Yu-3 HWT/Yu-4 HWT

12 Type-039(G) (*Song*) with 6 single 533mm TT with YJ-82 (CH-SS-N-7) AShM or YJ-18 (CH-SS-N-13) AShM/Yu-3 HWT/Yu-6 HWT

4 Type-039A (*Yuan*) (fitted with AIP) with 6 533mm TT with YJ-82 (CH-SS-N-7) AShM or YJ-18 (CH-SS-N-13) AShM/Yu-3 HWT/Yu-6 HWT

16+ Type-039B (*Yuan*) (fitted with AIP) with 6 533mm TT with YJ-82 (CH-SS-N-7) AShM or YJ-18 (CH-SS-N-13) AShM/Yu-3 HWT/Yu-6 HWT

(10 Type-035(G) (*Ming*) in reserve with 8 single 533mm TT with Yu-3 HWT/Yu-4 HWT)

SSB 1 Type-032 (*Qing*) (SLBM trials)

PRINCIPAL SURFACE COMBATANTS 92

AIRCRAFT CARRIERS • CV 2:

1 Type-001 (*Kuznetsov*) with 3 18-cell GMLS with HHQ-10 (CH-SA-N-17) SAM, 2 RBU 6000 *Smerch* 2 A/S mor, 3 H/PJ-11 CIWS (capacity 18–24 J-15 ac; 17 Ka-28/Ka-31/Z-8S/Z-8JH/Z-8AEW hel)

1 Type-002 (*Kuznetsov* mod) with 3 18-cell GMLS with HHQ-10 (CH-SA-N-17) SAM, 2 RBU 6000 *Smerch* 2 A/S mor, 3 H/PJ-11 CIWS (capacity 32 J-15 ac; 12 Ka-28/Ka-31/Z-8S/Z-8JH/Z-8AEW hel)

CRUISERS • CGHM 7 Type-055 (*Renhai*) with 14 8-cell VLS (8 fore, 6 aft) with YJ-18A (CH-SS-N-13) AShM/HHQ-9B (CH-SA-N-21) SAM/Yu-8 A/S msl, 1 24-cell GMLS with HHQ-10 (CH-SA-N-17) SAM, 2 triple 324mm ASTT with Yu-7 LWT, 1 H/PJ-11 CIWS, 1 130mm gun (capacity 2 med hel)

DESTROYERS 42

DDGHM 40:

2 *Hangzhou* (Project 956EM (*Sovremenny* II)) with 2 quad lnchr with 3M80MVE *Moskit*-E (RS-SS-N-22B *Sunburn*) AShM, 2 single 3S90E lnchr with 9M38E M-22E *Shtil* (RS-SA-N-7 *Gadfly*) SAM, 2 twin 533mm DTA-53-956 ASTT with SET-65KE HWT/53-65KE HWT, 2 RBU 1000 *Smerch* 3 A/S mor, 2 *Kashtan* (RS-CADS-N-1) CIWS, 1 twin 130mm gun (capacity 1 Z-9C/Ka-28 *Helix* A hel)

2 *Hangzhou* (Project 956E (*Sovremenny* III)) with 2 quad lnchr with YJ-12A AShM, 4 8-cell H/AJK-16 VLS with HHQ-16 (CH-SA-N-16) SAM/Yu-8 A/S msl, 2 triple 324mm ASTT with Yu-7 LWT, 4 AK630M CIWS, 2 twin 130mm gun (capacity 1 Z-9C/Ka-28 *Helix* A hel)

1 Type-051B (*Luhai*) with 4 quad lnchr with YJ-12A AShM, 4 8-cell H/AJK-16 VLS with HHQ-16 (CH-SA-N-16) SAM/Yu-8 A/S msl, 2 triple 324mm ASTT with Yu-7 LWT, 2 H/PJ-11 CIWS, 1 twin 100mm gun (capacity 2 Z-9C/Ka-28 *Helix* A hel)

2 Type-052 (*Luhu*) with 4 quad lnchr with YJ-83 AShM, 1 octuple lnchr with HHQ-7 (CH-SA-N-4) SAM, 2 triple 324mm ASTT with Yu-7 LWT, 2 FQF 2500 A/S mor, 2 H/PJ-12 CIWS, 1 twin 100mm gun (capacity 2 Z-9C hel)

2 Type-052B (*Luyang* I) (in refit) with 4 quad lnchr with YJ-83 AShM, 2 single 3S90E lnchr with 9M317E *Shtil*-1 (RS-SA-N-7B) SAM, 2 triple 324mm ASTT with Yu-7 LWT, 2 H/PJ-12 CIWS, 1 100mm gun (capacity 1 Ka-28 *Helix* A hel)

6 Type-052C (*Luyang* II) (of which 1 in refit) with 2 quad lnchr with YJ-62 AShM, 8 8-cell VLS with HHQ-9 (CH-SA-N-9) SAM (CH-SA-N-9), 2 triple 324mm ASTT with Yu-7 LWT, 2 H/PJ-12 CIWS, 1 100mm gun (capacity 2 Ka-28 *Helix* A hel)

10 Type-052D (*Luyang* III) with 8 8-cell VLS with YJ-18A (CH-SS-N-13) AShM/HHQ-9B (CH-SA-N-21) SAM/Yu-8 A/S msl, 1 24-cell GMLS with HHQ-10 (CH-SA-N-17) SAM, 2 triple 324mm ASTT with Yu-7 LWT, 1 H/PJ-12 CIWS, 1 130mm gun (capacity 2 Ka-28 *Helix* A hel)

3 Type-052D (*Luyang* III) with 8 octuple VLS with YJ-18A (CH-SS-N-13) AShM/HHQ-9B (CH-SA-N-21) SAM/Yu-8 A/S msl, 1 24-cell GMLS with HHQ-10 (CH-SA-N-17) SAM, 2 triple 324mm ASTT with Yu-7 LWT, 1 H/PJ-11 CIWS, 1 130mm gun (capacity 2 Ka-28 *Helix* A hel)

12 Type-052D mod (*Luyang* III mod) with 8 octuple VLS with YJ-18A (CH-SS-N-13) AShM/HHQ-9B (CH-SA-N-21) SAM/Yu-8 A/S msl, 1 24-cell GMLS with HHQ-10 (CH-SA-N-17) SAM, 2 triple 324mm ASTT with Yu-7 LWT, 1 H/PJ-11 CIWS, 1 130mm gun (capacity 2 Z-9/Z-20 hel)

DDGM 2 Type-051C (*Luzhou*) with 2 quad lnchr with YJ-83 AShM; 6 6-cell B-204 VLS with S-300FM *Rif*-M (RS-SA-N-20 *Gargoyle*) SAM, 2 H/PJ-12 CIWS, 1 100mm gun, 1 hel landing platform

FRIGATES • FFGHM 41

2 Type-053H3 (*Jiangwei* II) with 2 quad lnchr with YJ-83 AShM, 1 octuple lnchr with HHQ-7 (CH-SA-N-4) SAM, 2 RBU 1200 A/S mor, 1 twin 100mm gun (capacity 1 Z-9C hel)

6 Type-053H3 (*Jiangwei* II Upgrade) with 2 quad lnchr with YJ-83 AShM, 1 8-cell GMLS with HHQ-10 (CH-SA-N-17) SAM, 2 RBU 1200 A/S mor, 1 twin 100mm gun (capacity 1 Z-9C hel)

2 Type-054 (*Jiangkai*) with 2 quad lnchr with YJ-83 AShM, 1 24-cell GMLS with HHQ-10 (CH-SA-N-17) SAM, 2 triple 324mm ASTT with Yu-7 LWT, 2 RBU 1200 A/S mor, 4 AK630 CIWS, 1 100mm gun (capacity 1 Ka-28 *Helix* A/Z-9C hel)

31 Type-054A (*Jiangkai* II) with 2 quad lnchr with YJ-83 AShM, 4 8-cell VLS with Yu-8 A/S msl/HHQ-16 (CH-SA-N-16) SAM, 2 triple 324mm ASTT with Yu-7 LWT, 2 FQF 3200 A/S mor, 2 H/PJ-11/12 CIWS, 1 76mm gun (capacity 1 Ka-28 *Helix* A/Z-9C hel)

PATROL AND COASTAL COMBATANTS 142+

CORVETTES • FSGM 50 Type-056A (*Jiangdao*) with 2 twin lnchr with YJ-83 AShM, 1 8-cell GMLS with HHQ-10 (CH-SA-N-17) SAM, 2 triple 324mm ASTT with Yu-7 LWT, 1 76mm gun, 1 hel landing platform

PCFG ε60 Type-022 (*Houbei*) with 2 quad lnchr with YJ-83 AShM, 1 H/PJ-13 CIWS

PCG 22: 4 Type-037-II (*Houjian*) with 2 triple lnchr with YJ-8 (CH-SS-N-4) AShM; 18 Type-037-IG (*Houxin*) with 2 twin lnchr with YJ-8 (CH-SS-N-4) AShM

PCC some Type-037-IS (*Haiqing*) with 2 FQF-3200 A/S mor

PB up to 10 Type-062-1 (*Shanghai* III)

MINE WARFARE • MINE COUNTERMEASURES 57:

MCO 20: 4 Type-081 (*Wochi*); 9+ Type-081A (*Wochi* mod); 7+ Type-082II (*Wozang*)

MSC 16: 4 Type-082 (*Wosao* I); 12 Type-082-II (*Wosao* II)

MSD 21 Type-529 (*Wonang*) (operated by *Wozang* MCO)

AMPHIBIOUS

PRINCIPAL AMPHIBIOUS SHIPS 11:

LHD 3 Type-075 (*Yushen*) with 2 24-cell GMLS with HHQ-10 (CH-SA-N-17) SAM, 2 H/PJ-11 CIWS (capacity 3 *Yuyi* LCAC; 800 troops; at least 60 AFVs; 28 hel)

LPD 8 Type-071 (*Yuzhao*) with 4 AK630 CIWS, 1 76mm gun (capacity 4 *Yuyi* LCAC plus supporting vehicles; 800 troops; 60 armoured vehs; 4 hel)

LANDING SHIPS 49

LST 28:

4 Type-072-IIG (*Yukan*) (capacity 2 LCVP; 10 tk; 200 troops)

9 Type-072-II/III (*Yuting* I) (capacity 10 tk; 250 troops; 2 hel)

9 Type-072A (*Yuting* II) (capacity 4 LCVP; 10 tk; 250 troops)

6 Type-072B (*Yuting* II) (capacity 4 LCVP; 10 tk; 250 troops)

LSM 21:

1 Type-073-II (*Yudeng*) with 1 twin 57mm gun (capacity 5 tk or 500 troops)

10 Type-073A (*Yunshu*) (capacity 6 tk)

7 Type-074 (*Yuhai*) (capacity 2 tk; 250 troops)

3 Type-074 (mod)

LANDING CRAFT 60

LCU 11 Type-074A (*Yubei*) (capacity 10 tanks or 150 troops)

LCM ε30 Type-067A (*Yunnan*)

LCAC 19: 15+ Type-726 (*Yuyi*); 4 *Zubr*

LOGISTICS AND SUPPORT 153

ABU 1 Type-744A

AFS 2: 1 Type-904 (*Dayun*); 1 Type-904A (*Danyao* I)

AFSH 2 Type-904B (*Danyao* II)

AG 7: 6 *Kanhai*; 1 *Kanwu*

AGB 2 Type-272 (*Yanrao*) with 1 hel landing platform

AGE 7: 2 Type-909 (*Dahua*) with 1 hel landing platform (weapons test platform); 1 *Kantan*; 3 Type-636 (*Shupang*); 1 *Yuting* I (naval rail gun test ship)

AGI 19: 1 *Dadie*; 1 Type-815 (*Dongdiao*) with 1 hel landing platform; 9 Type-815A (*Dongdiao*) with 1 hel landing platform; 8 FT-14

AGOR 2 *Dahua*

AGOS 4 *Dongjian*

AGS 8 Type-636A (*Shupang*) with 1 hel landing platform

AH 8: 5 *Ankang*; 1 Type-920 (*Anwei*); 2 *Anshen*

AOEH 2 Type-901 (*Fuyu*) with 2 H/PJ-13 CIWS

AORH 10: 2 Type-903 (*Fuchi*); 7 Type-903A (*Fuchi* II); 1 *Fusu*

AOT 22: 4 *Fubai*; 16 Type-632 (*Fujian*); 2 *Fuxiao*

AP 4: 2 *Daguan*; 2 *Darong*

ARC 2 *Youlan*

ARS 18: 1 *Dadao*; 1 *Dadong*; 1 Type-922III (*Dalang* II); 3 Type-922IIIA (*Dalang* III); 3 *Dasan*; 4 *Datuo*; 2 *Dazhou*; 3 *Hai Jiu* 101 with 1 hel landing platform

ASR 6: 3 Type-926 (*Dalao*); 3 Type-925 (*Dajiang*) (capacity 2 Z-8)

ATF 14: ε11 *Hujiu*; 3 *Tuqiang*

AWT 8: 4 *Fujian*; 3 *Fushi*; 1 *Jinyou*

AX 4:

1 Type-0891A (*Dashi*) with 2 hel landing platforms

1 *Daxin* with 2 FQF 1200 A/S mor, 1 57mm gun, 1 hel landing platform

1 Type-927 (*Qi Ji Guang*) with 1 76mm gun, 1 hel landing platform

1 *Yudao*

ESD 1 *Donghaidao*

COASTAL DEFENCE • AShM 72 YJ-12/YJ-62 (3 regt)

Naval Aviation 26,000

FORCES BY ROLE

Naval aviation fighter/ground-attack units adopted brigade structure in 2017

BOMBER

2 regt with H-6DU/G/J

FIGHTER/GROUND ATTACK

1 bde with J-10A/S *Firebird*; Su-30MK2 *Flanker G*

1 bde with J-11B/BS *Flanker* L

1 bde with J-11B/BS *Flanker* L; JH-7A *Flounder*

1 bde with J-8F *Finback*; JH-7A *Flounder*

2 regt with J-15 *Flanker*

GROUND ATTACK

1 bde with JH-7 *Flounder*

ANTI-SUBMARINE WARFARE

2 regt with KQ-200

ELINT/ISR/ASW

1 regt with Y-8JB/X; Y-9JZ; KQ-200

AIRBORNE EARLY WARNING & CONTROL

3 regt with Y-8J; KJ-200; KJ-500

TRANSPORT

1 regt with Y-7H; Y-8C; CRJ-200/700

TRAINING

1 regt with CJ-6A

1 regt with HY-7

2 regt with JL-8

1 regt with JL-9G

1 regt with JL-9

1 regt with JL-10

1 regt with Z-9C

HELICOPTER

1 regt with Ka-27PS; Ka-28; Ka-31

1 regt with AS365N; Z-9C/D; Z-8J/JH

1 regt with Y-7G; Z-8; Z-8J; Z-8S; Z-9C/D

AIR DEFENCE

2 SAM bde with HQ-9; HQ-9B: HQ-6A

EQUIPMENT BY TYPE

AIRCRAFT 456 combat capable

BBR 45: 27 H-6G/G mod; 18 H-6J

FTR 24 J-8F *Finback*

FGA 179: 16 J-10A *Firebird*; 7 J-10S *Firebird*; 72 J-11B/BS *Flanker* L; ε60 J-15 *Flanker*; 24 Su-30MK2 *Flanker G*

ATK 120: 48 JH-7; 72 JH-7A *Flounder*

ASW 20+ KQ-200

ELINT 13: 4 Y-8JB *High New* 2; 3 Y-8X; 6 Y-9JZ

AEW&C 24: 6 KJ-200 *Moth*; 14+ KJ-500; 4 Y-8J *Mask*

TKR 5 H-6DU

TPT 38: **Medium** 6 Y-8C; **Light** 28: 20 Y-5; 2 Y-7G; 6 Y-7H; **PAX** 4: 2 CRJ-200; 2 CRJ-700

TRG 118: 38 CJ-6; 12 HY-7; 16 JL-8*; 28 JL-9*; 12 JL-9G*; 12 JL-10*

HELICOPTERS

ASW 33: 14 Ka-28 *Helix A*; 14 Z-9C; 5 Z-18F

AEW 12: 9 Ka-31; 3 Z-18 AEW

MRH 18: 7 AS365N; 11 Z-9D

SAR 11: 3 Ka-27PS; 4 Z-8JH; 2 Z-8S; 2 Z-9S

TPT 42: **Heavy** 34: 8 SA321 *Super Frelon*; 9 Z-8; 13 Z-8J; 4 Z-18; **Medium** 8 Mi-8 *Hip*

242 THE MILITARY BALANCE 2023

UNINHABITED AERIAL VEHICLES
ISR Heavy BZK-005; **Medium** BZK-007
AIR DEFENCE • SAM
Long-range 32: 16 HQ-9 (CH-SA-9); 16 HQ-9B (CH-SA-21)
Short-range HQ-6A (CH-SA-6)
AIR-LAUNCHED MISSILES
AAM • IR PL-5; PL-8; PL-9; R-73 (RS-AA-11A *Archer*);
IR/SARH R-27 (RS-AA-10 *Alamo*); **SARH** PL-11; **ARH**
R-77 (RS-AA-12A *Adder*); PL-12 (CH-AA-7A *Adze*)
ASM KD-88
AShM Kh-31A (RS-AS-17B *Krypton*); YJ-12; YJ-61;
YJ-8K; YJ-83K; YJ-9
ARM Kh-31P (RS-AS-17A *Krypton*); YJ-91
BOMBS
Laser-guided: LS-500J
TV-guided: KAB-500KR; KAB-1500KR

Marines ε35,000

FORCES BY ROLE
SPECIAL FORCES
1 spec ops bde
MANOEUVRE
Mechanised
3 mne bde
Amphibious
3 mne bde
HELICOPTER
1 bde (forming) with Z-8C

EQUIPMENT BY TYPE
ARMOURED FIGHTING VEHICLES
LT TK 80+: ε80 ZTD-05; some ZTQ-15
ASLT ε50 ZTL-11
IFV ε150 ZBL-08
AAV ε240 ZBD-05
ANTI-TANK/ANTI-INFRASTRUCTURE
MSL • MANPATS HJ-73; HJ-8
RCL 120mm Type-98
ARTILLERY 40+
SP 122mm 40+: 20+ PLZ-07; 20+ PLZ-89
MRL 107mm PH-63
MOR 82mmε
HELICOPTERS
TPT • Heavy 5 Z-8C
AIR DEFENCE • SAM • Point-defence HN-5 (CH-SA-3);
FN-6 (CH-SA-10); QW-2 (CH-SA-8)

Air Force 395,000

FORCES BY ROLE
BOMBER
1 regt with H-6M
2 regt with H-6H
4 regt with H-6K
1 bde with H-6N (forming)
FIGHTER
1 bde with J-7 *Fishcan*
5 bde with J-7E *Fishcan*
5 bde with J-7G *Fishcan*
1 bde with J-8F/H *Finback*

2 bde with J-11A/Su-27UBK *Flanker*
3 bde with J-11A/J-11B/Su-27UBK *Flanker*
2 bde with J-11B/BS *Flanker* L
FIGHTER/GROUND ATTACK
5 bde with J-10A/S *Firebird*
1 bde with J-10B/S *Firebird*
6 bde with J-10C/S *Firebird*
1 bde with Su-35 *Flanker* M; Su-30MKK *Flanker* G
6 bde with J-16 *Flanker*
2 bde with Su-30MKK *Flanker* G
5 bde with J-20A
GROUND ATTACK
5 bde with JH-7A *Flounder*
ELECTRONIC WARFARE
4 regt with Y-8CB/DZ/G/XZ; Y-9G/XZ
ISR
1 regt with JZ-8F *Finback**
1 bde with JZ-8F *Finback**
AIRBORNE EARLY WARNING & CONTROL
1 regt with KJ-500
1 regt with KJ-200 *Moth*; KJ-2000; Y-8T
SEARCH & RESCUE
4 bde with Y-5; Mi-171E; Z-8
1 regt with Y-5; Mi-171E; Z-8
TANKER
1 bde with H-6U
TRANSPORT
1 (VIP) regt with A319; B-737; CRJ-200/700
1 (VIP) regt with Tu-154M; Tu-154M/D
1 regt with Il-76MD/TD *Candid*
1 regt with Il-76MD *Candid*; Il-78 *Midas*
1 regt with Y-7
2 regt with Y-9
2 regt with Y-20/YY-20A
TRAINING
5 bde with CJ-6/6A/6B; Y-5
3 bde with J-7; JJ-7A
14 bde with JJ-7A; JL-8; JL-9; JL-10; J-10A/S
1 trg bde with Y-7; Y-8C
TRANSPORT HELICOPTER
1 (VIP) regt with AS332 *Super Puma*; H225
ISR UAV
2 bde with GJ-1; GJ-2
1 regt with WZ-7
AIR DEFENCE
1 SAM div (3 SAM regt)
24 SAM bde

EQUIPMENT BY TYPE
AIRCRAFT 2,566 combat capable
BBR 176: ε12 H-6A (trg role); ε60 H-6H/M; ε100 H-6K; 4+ H-6N
FTR 446: 50 J-7 *Fishcan*; 119 J-7E *Fishcan*; 120 J-7G *Fishcan*;
30 J-8F/H *Finback*; 95 J-11; 32 Su-27UBK *Flanker*
FGA 1,182+: 220 J-10A *Firebird*; 55 J-10B *Firebird*; 220
J-10C *Firebird*; 70 J-10S *Firebird*; 130 J-11B/BS *Flanker* L;
250 J-16 *Flanker*; 140+ J-20A; 73 Su-30MKK *Flanker* G; 24
Su-35 *Flanker* M
ATK 120 JH-7A *Flounder*
EW 31: ε12 J-16D *Flanker**; 4 Y-8CB *High New* 1; 2 Y-8DZ;
6 Y-8G *High New* 3; 2 Y-8XZ *High New* 7; 3 Y-9G; 2 Y-9XZ
ELINT 4 Tu-154M/D *Careless*
ISR 48: 24 JZ-8 *Finback**; 24 JZ-8F *Finback**

AEW&C 28: 4 KJ-200 *Moth*; 20 KJ-500; 4 KJ-2000

C2 5: 2 B-737; 3 Y-8T *High New* 4

TKR 13: 10 H-6U; 3 Il-78 *Midas*

TKR/TPT 8 YY-20A

TPT 271: **Heavy** 70: 20 Il-76MD/TD *Candid*; 50 Y-20; **Medium** 60: 30 Y-8C; 30 Y-9; **Light** 111: 70 Y-5; 41 Y-7/Y-7H; **PAX** 30: 3 A319; 9 B-737 (VIP); 5 CRJ-200; 5 CRJ-700; 8 Tu-154M *Careless*

TRG 1,012+: 400 CJ-6/-6A/-6B; 12+ HY-7; 50 JJ-7*; 150 JJ-7A*; 350 JL-8*; 30 JL-9*; 50+ JL-10*

HELICOPTERS

MRH 22: 20 Z-9; 2 Mi-17V-5 *Hip* H

TPT 31+: **Heavy** 18+ Z-8; **Medium** 13+: 6+ AS332 *Super Puma* (VIP); 3 H225 (VIP); 4+ Mi-171

UNINHABITED AERIAL VEHICLES

CISR • Heavy 12+ GJ-1; some GJ-2; GJ-11 (in test)

ISR • Heavy 14+: 12+ WZ-7; 2+ WZ-8; some WZ-10 (EW/ISR)

AIR DEFENCE

SAM 862+

Long-range 638+: 180 HQ-9 (CH-SA-9); 80 HQ-9B (CH-SA-21); 130+ HQ-22; 32 S-300PMU (RS-SA-10 *Grumble*); 64 S-300PMU1 (RS-SA-20 *Gargoyle*); 120 S-300PMU2 (RS-SA-20 *Gargoyle*); 32 S-400 (RS-SA-21B *Growler*)

Medium-range 150 HQ-12 (CH-SA-12)

Short-range 74+: 50+ HQ-6A (CH-SA-6); 24 HQ-6D (CH-SA-6)

GUNS • TOWED • 57mm PG-59 (S-60)

AIR-LAUNCHED MISSILES

AAM • IR PL-5B/C; PL-8; R-73 (RS-AA-11A *Archer*); **IIR** PL-10 (CH-AA-9); **IR/SARH** R-27 (RS-AA-10 *Alamo*); **SARH** PL-11; **ARH** PL-12 (CH-AA-7A *Adze*); PL-12A (CH-AA-7B *Adze*); PL-15 (CH-AA-10); R-77 (RS-AA-12A *Adder*); R-77-1 (RVV-SD) (RS-AA-12B *Adder*)

ASM AKD-9; AKD-10; KD-88; Kh-29 (RS-AS-14 *Kedge*); Kh-31A (RS-AS-17B *Krypton*); Kh-59M (RS-AS-18 *Kazoo*)

AShM YJ-12

ARM Kh-31P (RS-AS-17A *Krypton*); YJ-91 (Domestically produced Kh-31P variant)

ALCM • Conventional CJ-20; YJ(KD)-63

BOMBS

Laser-guided: LS-500J; LT-2

TV-guided: KAB-500KR; KAB-1500KR

Airborne Corps

FORCES BY ROLE

SPECIAL FORCES

1 spec ops bde

MANOEUVRE

Air Manoeuvre

5 AB bde

1 air aslt bde

COMBAT SERVICE SUPPORT

1 spt bde

TRANSPORT

1 bde with Y-5; Y-7; Y-8; Y-12

HELICOPTER

1 regt with WZ-10K; Z-8KA; Z-9WZ

EQUIPMENT BY TYPE

ARMOURED FIGHTING VEHICLES

ABCV 180 ZBD-03

APC • APC (T) 4 ZZZ-03 (CP)

AUV CS/VN3 mod

ANTI-TANK/ANTI-INFRASTRUCTURE

SP some HJ-9

ARTILLERY 162+

TOWED 122mm ε54 PL-96 (D-30)

MRL 107mm ε54 PH-63

MOR 54+: **82mm** some; **100mm** 54

AIRCRAFT • TPT 40: **Medium** 6 Y-8; **Light** 34: 20 Y-5; 2 Y-7; 12 Y-12D

HELICOPTERS

ATK 8 WZ-10K

CSAR 8 Z-8KA

MRH 12 Z-9WZ

TPT • Medium Z-20K

AIR DEFENCE

SAM • Point-defence QW-1 (CH-SA-7)

GUNS • TOWED 25mm 54 PG-87

Strategic Support Force ε175,000

The Strategic Support Force reports to the Central Military Commission and is responsible for the PLA's space and cyber capabilities

EQUIPMENT BY TYPE

LOGISTICS AND SUPPORT • AGM 4 Type-718 (*Yuan Wang*) (space and missile tracking)

Theatre Commands

Eastern Theatre Command

Eastern Theatre Ground Forces

71st Group Army

(1 spec ops bde, 4 armd bde, 1 mech inf bde, 1 inf bde, 1 arty bde, 1 engr/NBC bde bde, 1 spt bde, 1 hel bde, 1 AD bde)

72nd Group Army

(1 spec ops bde, 1 armd bde, 1 mech inf bde, 2 inf bde, 2 amph bde, 1 arty bde, 1 engr bde, 1 NBC bde, 1 spt bde, 1 hel bde, 1 AD bde)

73rd Group Army

(1 spec ops bde, 1 armd bde, 1 mech inf bde, 2 inf bde, 2 amph bde, 1 arty bde, 1 engr/NBC bde, 1 spt bde, 1 hel bde, 1 AD bde)

Eastern Theatre Navy

Coastal defence from south of Lianyungang to Dongshan (approx. 35°10′N to 23°30′N), and to seaward; HQ at Ningbo; support bases at Fujian, Zhoushan, Ningbo

16 **SSK**; 16 **DDGHM**; 18 **FFGHM**; 19 **FSGM**; ε30 **PCFG/PCG**; ε22 **MCMV**; 3 **LPD**; ε22 **LST/M**

Eastern Theatre Navy Aviation

1st Naval Aviation Division

(1 AEW&C regt with KJ-500: 1 ASW regt with KQ-200)

Other Forces

(1 bbr regt with H-6DU/G/J; 1 FGA bde with JH-7; 1 FGA bde with Su-30MK2; J-10A; 1 hel regt with Ka-27PS; Ka-28; Ka-31)

Eastern Theatre Air Force

10th Bomber Division
(1 bbr regt with H-6H; 1 bbr regt with H-6K; 1 bbr regt with H-6M)

26th Special Mission Division
(1 AEW&C regt with KJ-500; 1 AEW&C regt with KJ-200/KJ-2000/Y-8T)

Fuzhou Base
(1 ftr bde with J-7E; 1 FGA bde with J-10C; 1 ftr bde with J-11A/B; 1 FGA bde with J-16; 1 FGA bde with Su-30MKK; 2 SAM bde)

Shanghai Base
(1 ftr bde with J-11B; 1 FGA bde with J-10A; 2 FGA bde with J-16; 1 FGA bde with J-20A; 1 atk bde with JH-7A; 1 trg bde with J-10/JL-10; 2 SAM bde)

Other Forces
(1 ISR bde with JZ-8F; 1 SAR bde; 1 Flight Instructor Training Base with CJ-6; JL-8; JL-9; JL-10)

Other Forces

Marines
(2 mne bde)

Southern Theatre Command

Southern Theatre Ground Forces

74th Group Army
(1 spec ops bde, 1 armd bde, 1 mech inf bde, 2 inf bde, 2 amph bde, 1 arty bde, 1 engr bde, 1 NBC bde, 1 spt bde, 1 hel bde, 1 AD bde)

75th Group Army
(1 spec ops bde, 2 armd bde, 1 mech inf bde, 3 inf bde, 1 air aslt bde, 1 arty bde, 1 engr/NBC bde, 1 spt bde, 1 AD bde)

Other Forces
(1 (composite) inf bde (Hong Kong); 1 hel sqn (Hong Kong), 1 AD bn (Hong Kong))

Southern Theatre Navy

Coastal defence from Dongshan (approx. 23°30′N) to VNM border, and to seaward (including Paracel and Spratly islands); HQ at Zhanjiang; support bases at Yulin, Guangzhou

6 **SSBN**; 2 **SSN**; 15 **SSK**; 1 **CV**; 3 **CGHM**; 14 **DDGHM**; 12 **FFGHM**; 21 **FSGM**; ε30 **PCFG/PCG**; ε16 **MCMV**; 2 **LHD**; 5 **LPD**; ε21 **LST/M**

Southern Theatre Navy Aviation

3rd Naval Aviation Division
(1 ASW regt with KQ-200; 1 AEW&C regt with KJ-500)

Other Forces
(1 bbr regt with H-6DU/G/J; 1 FGA regt with J-15; 1 FGA bde with J-11B; 1 FGA bde with J-11B; JH-7A; 1 tpt/hel regt with Y-7G; Z-8; Z-8J; Z-8S; Z-9C/D; 1 SAM bde)

Southern Theatre Air Force

8th Bomber Division

(2 bbr regt with H-6K)

20th Special Mission Division
(3 EW regt with Y-8CB/DZ/G/XZ; Y-9G/XZ)

Kunming Base
(1 FGA bde with J-10A; 1 FGA bde with J-10C; 1 trg bde with JJ-7A; 1 SAM bde)

Nanning Base
(1 ftr bde with J-11A; 1 FGA bde with J-10A; 1 FGA bde with J-16; 1 FGA bde with J-20A; 1 FGA bde with Su-35; 1 FGA bde with Su-30MKK; 1 atk bde with JH-7A; 3 SAM bde)

Other Forces
(1 tkr bde with H-6U; 1 SAR bde; 1 UAV bde)

Other Forces

Marines
(1 spec ops bde; 2 mne bde)

Western Theatre Command

Western Theatre Ground Forces

76th Group Army
(1 spec ops bde, 4 armd bde, 2 inf bde, 1 arty bde, 1 engr/NBC bde, 1 spt bde, 1 hel bde, 1 AD bde)

77th Group Army
(1 spec ops bde, 2 armd bde, 1 mech inf bde; 3 inf bde, 1 arty bde, 1 engr bde, 1 NBC bde, 1 spt bde, 1 hel bde, 1 AD bde)

Xinjiang Military District
(1 spec ops bde, 3 (high alt) mech div, 1 (high alt) inf div, 2 mech inf regt, 1 arty bde, 1 AD bde, 1 engr regt, 1 hel bde)

Xizang Military District
(1 spec ops bde; 1 mech inf bde; 2 inf bde; 1 arty bde, 1 AD bde, 1 engr/NBC bde, 1 hel bde)

Western Theatre Air Force

4th Transport Division
(2 tpt regt with Y-9; 1 tpt regt with Y-20A)

Lanzhou Base
(1 ftr bde with J-11A/B; 1 ftr bde with J-7E; 1 FGA bde with J-10C; 1 FGA bde with J-16; 1 SAM bde)

Urumqi Base
(1 ftr bde with J-8F/H; 1 FGA bde with J-20A; 1 atk bde with JH-7A; 2 SAM bde)

Lhasa Base
(1 SAM bde)

Xi'an Flying Academy
(1 trg bde with JJ-7A; 1 trg bde with JL-9A; 2 trg bde with JL-8; 1 trg bde with Y-7; Y-8)

Other Forces
(1 SAR regt)

Northern Theatre Command

Northern Theatre Ground Forces

78th Group Army
(1 spec ops bde, 4 armd bde, 1 mech inf bde, 1 inf bde, 1 arty bde, 1 engr/NBC bde, 1 spt bde, 1 hel bde, 1 AD bde)

79th Group Army
(1 spec ops bde, 4 armd bde, 1 mech inf bde, 1 inf bde,

1 arty bde, 1 engr bde, 1 NBC bde, 1 spt bde, 1 hel bde, 1 AD bde)

80th Group Army
(1 spec ops bde, 1 armd bde; 2 mech inf bde, 3 inf bde, 1 arty bde, 1 engr/NBC bde, 1 spt bde, 1 hel bde, 1 AD bde)

Northern Theatre Navy
Coastal defence from the DPRK border (Yalu River) to south of Lianyungang (approx 35°10′N), and to seaward; HQ at Qingdao; support bases at Lushun, Qingdao.
4 **SSN**; 15 **SSK**; 1 **CV**; 4 **CGHM**; 10 **DDGHM**; 2 **DDGM**; 11 **FFGHM**; 10 **FSGM**; ε18 **PCFG/PCG**; ε18 **MCMV**; ε7 **LST/M**

Northern Theatre Navy Aviation
2nd Naval Air Division
(1 EW/ISR/ASW regt with KQ-200; Y-8JB/X; Y-9JZ; 1 AEW&C regt with Y-8J; KJ-200; KJ-500)

Other Forces
(1 FGA regt with J-15; 1 FGA bde with JH-7A; J-8F; 1 hel regt with AS365N; Z-8J/JH; Z-9C/D1 tpt regt with Y-7H/Y-8C/CRJ-200/CRJ-700; 1 trg regt with CJ-6A; 2 trg regt with JL-8; 1 trg regt with HY-7; 1 trg regt with JL-9G; 1 trg regt with JL-9; 1 trg regt with JL-10)

Northern Theatre Air Force
16th Special Mission Division
(1 EW regt with Y-8CB/G; 1 ISR regt with JZ-8F; 1 UAV regt with WZ-7)

Dalian Base
(1 ftr bde with J-7; 2 ftr bde with J-7E; 1 ftr bde with J-11B; 1 FGA bde with J-10C; 1 FGA bde with J-10B; 1 FGA bde with J-16; 1 FGA bde with J-20A; 1 atk bde with JH-7A; 3 SAM bde)

Jinan Base
(1 ftr bde with J-7G; 1 FGA bde with J-10C; 1 atk bde with JH-7A; 2 SAM bde)

Harbin Flying Academy
(1 trg bde with CJ-6; Y-5; 1 trg bde with H-6; HY-7; 2 trg bde with JL-8; 1 trg bde with JL-9)

Other Forces
(1 SAR bde)

Other Forces
Marines
(2 mne bde; 1 hel bde)

Central Theatre Command

Central Theatre Ground Forces
81st Group Army
(1 spec ops bde, 2 armd bde, 1 (OPFOR) armd bde, 2 mech inf bde, 1 inf bde, 1 arty bde, 1 engr/NBC bde, 1 spt bde, 1 avn bde, 1 AD bde)

82nd Group Army
(1 spec ops bde, 4 armd bde, 1 mech bde, 2 inf bde, 1 arty bde, 1 engr bde, 1 NBC bde, 1 spt bde, 1 hel bde, 1 AD bde)

83rd Group Army
(1 spec ops bde, 2 armd bde, 4 mech inf bde, 1 air aslt bde, 1 arty bde, 1 engr/NBC bde, 1 spt bde, 1 AD bde)

Other Forces
(2 (Beijing) gd div)

Central Theatre Air Force
13th Transport Division
(1 tpt regt with Y-20A; 1 tpt regt with Il-76MD/TD; 1 tpt regt with Il-76MD; Il-78)

34th VIP Transport Division
(1 tpt regt with A319; B-737; CRJ200/700; 1 tpt regt with Tu-154M; Tu-154M/D; 1 tpt regt with Y-7; 1 hel regt with AS332; H225)

36th Bomber Division
(1 bbr regt with H-6K; 1 bbr regt with H-6H)

Datong Base
(3 ftr bde with J-7E/G; 1 ftr bde with J-11A/B; 2 FGA bde with J-10A; 1 FGA bde with J-10C; 1 SAM div; 4 SAM bde)

Wuhan Base
(2 ftr bde with J-7E/G; 1 ftr bde with J-11A; 1 FGA bde with J-20A; 1 trg bde with J-7/JJ-7A; 3 SAM bde)

Shijiazhuang Flying Academy
(3 trg bde with JL-8; 1 trg bde with JL-8; JL-10)

Airborne Corps
(5 AB bde; 1 air aslt bde; 1 tpt bde; 1 hel regt)

Other Forces
(1 bbr bde with H-6N; 1 SAR bde)

Gendarmerie & Paramilitary 500,000+ active

People's Armed Police ε500,000
In 2018 the People's Armed Police (PAP) divested its border-defence, firefighting, gold, forest, hydropower and security-guard units. In addition to the forces listed below, PAP also has 32 regional commands, each with one or more mobile units

FORCES BY ROLE
MANOEUVRE
Other
1 (1st Mobile) paramilitary corps (3 SF regt; 9 (mobile) paramilitary units; 1 engr/CBRN unit; 1 hel unit)
1 (2nd Mobile) paramilitary corps (2 SF unit; 9 (mobile) paramilitary units; 1 engr/CBRN unit; 1 hel unit)

China Coast Guard (CCG)
In 2018 the CCG was moved from the authority of the State Oceanic Administration to that of the People's Armed Police. The CCG is currently reorganising its pennant-number system, making it problematic to assess the number of vessels that entered service since 2019.

EQUIPMENT BY TYPE
PATROL AND COASTAL COMBATANTS 546
  PSOH 42:
    2 *Zhaotou* with 1 76mm gun (capacity 2 med hel)
    3 Type-053H2G (*Jiangwei* I) (capacity 1 med hel) (ex-PLAN)
    7 Type-054 mod (*Zhaoduan*) with 1 76mm gun (capacity 1 med hel)
    4 *Shuoshi* II (capacity 1 med hel)
    2 *Shucha* I (capacity 1 med hel)
    10 *Shucha* II (capacity 1 med hel)
    12 *Zhaoyu* (capacity 1 med hel)
    1 *Zhaochang* (capacity 1 med hel)
    1 *Zhongyang* (capacity 1 med hel)

PSO 49:
9 Type-718B (*Zhaojun*) with 1 76mm gun, 1 hel landing platform
1 Type-922 (*Dalang* I) (ex-PLAN)
1 Type-625C (*Hai Yang*) (ex-PLAN)
1 Type-053H (*Jianghu* I) (ex-PLAN)
1 Type-636A (*Kanjie*) with 1 hel landing platform (ex-PLAN)
6 *Shusheng* with 1 hel landing platform
3 *Shuwu*
3 *Tuzhong* (ex-PLAN)
4 Type-056 mod (*Zhaogao*) with 1 hel landing platform
1 Type-918 (*Wolei*) (ex-PLAN)
1 *Xiang Yang Hong* 9 (ex-PLAN)
4 *Zhaolai* with 1 hel landing platform
14 *Zhaotim*
PCOH 22 Type-056 (*Jiangdao*) (ex-PLAN) with 1 76mm gun
PCO 29: 1 *Shuke* I; 4 *Shuke* II; 14 *Shuke* III; 3 *Shuyou*; 4 *Zhaodai*; 3 *Zhaoming*
PCC 104: 25+ Type-618B-II; 45 *Hailin* I/II; 1 *Shuzao* II; 14 *Shuzao* III; 10 *Zhongeng*; 2 *Zhongmel*; 7 *Zhongsui*
PB/PBF 300+
AMPHIBIOUS • LANDING SHIPS 2
LST 2 Type-072-II (*Yuting* I) (ex-PLAN; used as hospital vessels and island supply)
LOGISTICS AND SUPPORT 27
AG 6: 5+ *Kaobo*; 1 *Shutu*
AGB 1 Type-210 (*Yanbing*) (ex-PLAN)
AGOR 9: 4 *Haijian*; 3 *Shuguang* 04 (ex-PLAN); w2 *Xiang Yang Hong* 9
ATF 11
AIRCRAFT
MP 1+ MA60H
TPT • Light Y-12 (MP role)
HELICOPTERS
TPT • Light Z-9

Maritime Militia

Composed of full- and part-time personnel. Reports to PLA command and trains to assist PLAN and CCG in a variety of military roles. These include ISR, maritime law enforcement, island supply, troop transport and supporting sovereignty claims. The Maritime Militia operates a variety of civilian vessels including fishing boats and oil tankers.

DEPLOYMENT

DEMOCRATIC REPUBLIC OF THE CONGO: UN • MONUSCO 233; 1 engr coy; 1 fd hospital

DJIBOUTI: 240; 1 mne coy(-); 1 med unit; 2 ZTL-11; 8 ZBL-08; 1 LPD; 1 ESD

GULF OF ADEN: 1 DDGHM; 1 FFGHM; 1 AORH

LEBANON: UN • UNIFIL 419; 2 engr coy; 1 med coy

MALI: UN • MINUSMA 430; 1 engr coy; 1 fd hospital

MIDDLE EAST: UN • UNTSO 5

SOUTH SUDAN: UN • UNMISS 1,054; 1 inf bn; 1 engr coy; 1 fd hospital

SUDAN: UN • UNISFA 87; 1 hel flt with 2 Mi-171

TAJIKISTAN: ε300 (trg)

WESTERN SAHARA: UN • MINURSO 11

Fiji FJI

Fijian Dollar FJD		2021	2022	2023
GDP	FJD	8.90bn	10.5bn	
	USD	4.30bn	4.86bn	
per capita	USD	4,749	5,341	
Growth	%	-5.1	12.5	
Inflation	%	0.2	4.7	
Def bdgt	FJD	95m	94m	109m
	USD	45.8m	43.6m	
USD1=FJD		2.07	2.16	

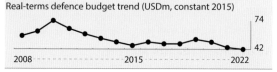
Real-terms defence budget trend (USDm, constant 2015)

Population	943,737					
Age	0–14	15–19	20–24	25–29	30–64	65 plus
Male	13.1%	4.1%	3.7%	3.9%	22.1%	3.8%
Female	12.6%	4.0%	3.5%	3.8%	21.0%	4.4%

Capabilities

The Republic of Fiji Military Forces (RFMF) are an infantry-dominated defence force with a small naval element. The RFMF has intervened heavily in Fiji's domestic politics and after a third coup in 2006, democracy was effectively suspended until 2014. Guidelines issued in 2018 emphasised the need to confront non-traditional threats such as climate change, terrorism and transnational crime. The RFMF is developing a deployable-force headquarters, funded by Australia, which will also administer and train personnel for peacekeeping and HA/DR roles. Engagement in international peacekeeping operations is an important source of revenue for the government. Fiji's principal defence relationships are with Australia and New Zealand, with which the RFMF regularly conducts training and maritime patrols. A status of forces agreement was signed with Australia in October 2022. Defence relations with China, South Korea and the US are growing, with all three countries providing training or donating equipment. The RFMF is attempting to improve the quality of senior NCOs and to raise standards across the rest of the force. Fiji has no significant defence industry and is only able to carry out basic equipment maintenance domestically. Significant upgrade and maintenance work is usually conducted in Australia.

ACTIVE 4,040 (Army 3,700 Navy 340)

RESERVE ε6,000

(to age 45)

ORGANISATIONS BY SERVICE

Army 3,700 (incl 300 recalled reserves)
FORCES BY ROLE
SPECIAL FORCES
1 spec ops coy
MANOEUVRE
Light
3 inf bn
COMBAT SUPPORT
1 arty bty
1 engr bn
COMBAT SUPPORT
1 log bn

Reserves 6,000
FORCES BY ROLE
MANOEUVRE
Light
5 inf bn
EQUIPMENT BY TYPE
ARMOURED FIGHTING VEHICLES
AUV 10 *Bushmaster* IMV
ARTILLERY • MOR 81mm 12

Navy 340
EQUIPMENT BY TYPE
PATROL AND COASTAL COMBATANTS 4:
PCO 1 *Guardian* (AUS *Bay* mod)
PB 3: 1 *Kula* (AUS *Pacific*); 2 *Levuka*
LOGISTICS AND SUPPORT 2
AGHS 2: 1 *Kacau*; 1 *Volasiga*

DEPLOYMENT

EGYPT: MFO 170; elm 1 inf bn
IRAQ: UN • UNAMI 174; 2 sy unit
LEBANON: UN • UNIFIL 1
MIDDLE EAST: UN • UNTSO 2
SOUTH SUDAN: UN • UNMISS 3
SYRIA/ISRAEL: UN • UNDOF 150; 1 inf coy

India IND

Indian Rupee INR		2021	2022	2023
GDP	INR	237tr	273tr	
	USD	3.18tr	3.47tr	
per capita	USD	2,280	2,466	
Growth	%	8.7	6.8	
Inflation	%	5.5	6.9	
Def bdgt [a]	INR	5.03tr	5.25tr	
	USD	67.5bn	66.6bn	
USD1=INR		74.50	78.80	

[a] Includes defence civil estimates, which include military pensions

Real-terms defence budget trend (USDbn, constant 2015)

Population	1,389,637,446					
Age	0–14	15–19	20–24	25–29	30–64	65 plus
Male	13.2%	4.6%	4.7%	4.6%	21.3%	3.2%
Female	11.9%	4.2%	4.2%	4.1%	20.5%	3.7%

Capabilities

India continues to modernise its armed forces, though progress in some areas remains slow. The armed forces are orientated against both Pakistan and China. India is looking to improve military infrastructure on its northern border. Mutual reaffirmation of the 2003 ceasefire agreement between India and Pakistan reduced conflict across the Line of Control in the disputed region of Kashmir. There is growing focus on Indian Ocean security. Indian forces participate in numerous bilateral and multilateral exercises, and the country is one of the main troop contributors to UN peacekeeping operations. In April 2022, it was announced after the annual US-India 2+2 talks that India would join the Combined Maritime Forces multinational maritime partnership as an associate member. Large numbers of paramilitary forces remain employed in the internal-security role. A Joint Armed Forces Doctrine was issued in 2017. It set out doctrine for Indian nuclear command and control, and envisaged an 'emerging triad' of space, cyber and special-operations capabilities complementing conventional land, sea and air capabilities. India continues to develop its nuclear capabilities. Army doctrine issued in late 2018 identified requirements including for 'integrated battle groups' and improved cyber, information-warfare and electronic-warfare capabilities. In 2020 the first Chief of Defence Staff was appointed. India operates significant quantities of equipment of Soviet as well as Russian origin and there is cooperation with Russia on missile developments. In 2022 concerns were raised over dependence on Russia for some weapons and spare parts, after Russia's full-scale invasion of Ukraine. Recent imports of foreign equipment have primarily been from the US and France. However, the overall capability of India's large conventional forces is limited by inadequate logistics, maintenance and shortages of ammunition, spare parts and maintenance personnel. Though modernisation continues, many equipment projects have seen delays and cost overruns, particularly indigenous systems. The government's 'Make in India' policy aims to strengthen the defence-industrial base.

248 THE MILITARY BALANCE 2023

ACTIVE 1,463,700 (Army 1,237,000 Navy 73,850 Air 139,850 Coast Guard 13,000) Gendarmerie & Paramilitary 1,608,150

RESERVE 1,155,000 (Army 960,000 Navy 55,000 Air 140,000) Gendarmerie & Paramilitary 941,000
Army first-line reserves (300,000) within 5 years of full-time service, further 500,000 have commitment to age 50

ORGANISATIONS BY SERVICE

Strategic Forces Command

Strategic Forces Command (SFC) is a tri-service command established in 2003. The commander-in-chief of SFC, a senior three-star military officer, manages and administers all strategic forces through army, navy and air-force chains of command

FORCES BY ROLE
SURFACE-TO-SURFACE MISSILE
  1 SRBM bde with *Agni* I
  1 IRBM bde with *Agni* II/III
  2 SRBM bde with SS-250 *Prithvi* II
EQUIPMENT BY TYPE
SURFACE-TO-SURFACE MISSILE LAUNCHERS 54
  ICBM • Nuclear *Agni* V (in test)
  IRBM • Nuclear ε4 *Agni* III; *Agni* IV (entering service)
  MRBM • Nuclear ε8 *Agni* II
  SRBM • Nuclear 54: ε12 *Agni* I; ε42 SS-250 *Prithvi* II; some SS-350 *Dhanush* (naval testbed)
SUBMARINES • STRATEGIC • SSBN 1 *Arihant* with 4 1-cell VLS with K-15 *Sagarika* SLBM, 6 533mm TT
AIR-LAUNCHED MISSILES • ALCM • Nuclear *Nirbhay* (likely nuclear capable; in development)
Some Indian Air Force assets (such as *Mirage* 2000H or Su-30MKI) may be tasked with a strategic role

Space

EQUIPMENT BY TYPE
SATELLITES 25
  NAVIGATION, POSITIONING, TIMING: 7 IRNSS
  COMMUNICATIONS: 2 GSAT-7/-7A
  ISR 15: 9 *Cartosat*; 6 RISAT
  ELINT/SIGINT 1 EMISAT

Army 1,237,000

6 Regional Comd HQ (Northern, Western, Central, Southern, Eastern, Southwestern), 1 Training Comd (ARTRAC)

FORCES BY ROLE
COMMAND
  4 (strike) corps HQ
  10 (holding) corps HQ
SPECIAL FORCES
  8 SF bn
MANOEUVRE
  Armoured
  2 armd div (3 armd bde, 1 arty bde (2 arty regt))
  1 armd div (3 armd bde, 1 SP arty bde (2 SP arty regt))
  8 indep armd bde

  Mechanised
  6 (RAPID) mech inf div (1 armd bde, 2 mech inf bde, 1 arty bde)
  2 indep mech bde
  Light
  15 inf div (2–5 inf bde, 1 arty bde)
  1 inf div (forming)
  7 indep inf bde
  12 mtn div (3-4 mtn inf bde, 1 arty bde)
  2 indep mtn bde
  Air Manoeuvre
  1 para bde
SURFACE-TO-SURFACE MISSILE
  1 IRBM bde with *Agni* II/III
  1 SRBM bde with *Agni* I
  2 SRBM bde with SS-250 *Prithvi* II
  3 GLCM regt with PJ-10 *Brahmos*
COMBAT SUPPORT
  3 arty div (2 arty bde, 1 MRL bde)
  2 indep arty bde
  4 engr bde
ATTACK HELICOPTER
  1 atk hel sqn
HELICOPTER
  25 hel sqn
AIR DEFENCE
  8 AD bde

Reserve Organisations

Reserves 300,000 reservists (first-line reserve within 5 years full-time service); **500,000 reservists** (commitment until age 50) (total 800,000)

Territorial Army 160,000 reservists (only 40,000 regular establishment)
FORCES BY ROLE
MANOEUVRE
  Light
  42 inf bn
COMBAT SUPPORT
  6 (Railway) engr regt
  2 engr regt
  1 sigs regt
COMBAT SERVICE SUPPORT
  6 ecological bn
EQUIPMENT BY TYPE
ARMOURED FIGHTING VEHICLES
  MBT 3,740: 122 *Arjun*; 2,418 T-72M1; ε1,200 T-90S (ε1,100 various models in store)
  RECCE *Ferret* (used for internal-security duties along with some indigenously built armd cars)
  IFV 3,100: 700 BMP-1; 2,400 BMP-2 *Sarath* (incl some BMP-2K CP)
  APC 369+
    APC (W) 163: 157+ OT-64; 6 TASL IPMV
    PPV 206+: 165 *Casspir*; 27 *Kalyani* M4; some TASL QRFV; 14+ *Yukthirath* MPV
ENGINEERING & MAINTENANCE VEHICLES
  AEV BMP-2; FV180
  ARV 730+: T-54/T-55; 156 VT-72B; 222 WZT-2; 352 WZT-3

VLB AM-50; BLG-60; BLG T-72; *Kartik*; MTU-20; MT-55; *Sarvatra*

MW 24 910 MCV-2

ANTI-TANK/ANTI-INFRASTRUCTURE

MSL

SP 110 9P148 *Konkurs* (RS-AT-5 *Spandrel*)

MANPATS 9K113 *Konkurs* (RS-AT-5 *Spandrel*); *Milan* 2

RCL 3,000+: **84mm** *Carl Gustaf*; **106mm** 3,000+ M40A1 (10 per inf bn)

ARTILLERY 9,743+

SP 155mm 100 K9 *Vajra*-T

TOWED 3,095+: **105mm** 1,350+: 600+ IFG Mk1/Mk2/Mk3; up to 700 LFG; 50 M-56; **122mm** 520 D-30; **130mm** ε600 M-46 (500 in store) **155mm** 625: ε300 FH-77B; ε200 M-46 (mod); 125 M777A2

MRL 228: **122mm** ε150 BM-21/LRAR **214mm** 36 *Pinaka*; **300mm** 42 9A52 *Smerch*

MOR 6,320+: **81mm** 5,000+ E1; **120mm** ε1,500 AM-50/E1; **SP 120mm** E1

SURFACE-TO-SURFACE MISSILE LAUNCHERS

IRBM • Nuclear some *Agni*-III (entering service)

MRBM • Nuclear ε12 *Agni*-II

SRBM • Nuclear 42: ε12 *Agni*-I; ε30 250 *Prithvi* II

GLCM • Conventional 15 PJ-10 *Brahmos*

HELICOPTERS

ATK 5 LCH *Prachand*

MRH 342: 79 *Dhruv*; 12 *Lancer*; 74 *Rudra*; 117 SA315B *Lama* (*Cheetah*); 60 SA316B *Alouette* III (*Chetak*)

UNINHABITED AERIAL VEHICLES

ISR • Medium 25: 13 *Nishant*; 12 *Searcher* Mk I/II

AIR DEFENCE

SAM 748+

Medium-range ε48 *Akash*

Short-range 180 2K12 *Kub* (RS-SA-6 *Gainful*)

Point-defence 500+: 50+ 9K33AKM *Osa-AKM* (RS-SA-8 *Gecko*); 200 9K31 *Strela*-1 (RS-SA-9 *Gaskin*); 250 9K35 *Strela*-10 (RS-SA-13 *Gopher*); 9K310 *Igla*-1 (RS-SA-16 *Gimlet*); 9K38 *Igla* (RS-SA-18 *Grouse*)

SPAAGM 30mm up to 80 2K22 *Tunguska* (RS-SA-19 *Grison*)

GUNS 2,315+

SP 23mm 75 ZSU-23-4; ZU-23-2 (truck-mounted);

TOWED 2,240+: **20mm** Oerlikon (reported); **23mm** 320 ZU-23-2; **40mm** 1,920 L40/70

Navy 73,850 (incl 7,000 Naval Avn and 1,200 Marines)

Fleet HQ New Delhi. Commands located at Mumbai, Vishakhapatnam, Kochi and Port Blair

EQUIPMENT BY TYPE

SUBMARINES 16

STRATEGIC • SSBN 1 *Arihant* with 4 1-cell VLS with K-15 *Sagarika* SLBM, 6 533mm TT

TACTICAL 15

SSK 15:

3 *Shishumar* (GER T-209/1500) with 8 single 533mm TT with SUT mod 1 HWT

1 *Shishumar* (GER T-209/1500) with 8 single 533mm TT with UGM-84L *Harpoon* II AShM/SUT mod 1 HWT

7 *Sindhughosh* (FSU *Kilo*) with 6 single 533mm TT with 3M54E1/E *Klub*-S (RS-SS-N-27A/B) (*Klub*-S

AShM variant unclear) AShM/53-65KE HWT/TEST-71ME HWT/SET-65E HWT

4 *Kalvari* (FRA *Scorpène*) with 6 533mm TT with SM39 *Exocet* Block 2 AShM

PRINCIPAL SURFACE COMBATANTS 28

AIRCRAFT CARRIERS • CV 2

1 *Vikramaditya* (ex-FSU *Kiev* mod) with 3 8-cell VLS with *Barak*-1 SAM, 4 AK630M CIWS (capacity 12 MiG-29K/KUB *Fulcrum* FGA ac; 6 Ka-28 *Helix* A ASW hel/Ka-31 *Helix* B AEW hel)

1 *Vikrant* with 3 AK630M CIWS (to be fitted with *Barak* 8 SAM) (capacity 30 aircraft including MiG-29K/KUB *Fulcrum*, Ka-31 *Helix* B, MH-60R *Seahawk*, *Dhruv*)

DESTROYERS 10

DDGHM 7:

2 *Delhi* (Project 15) with 4 quad lnchr with 3M24E *Uran*-E (RS-SS-N-25 *Switchblade*) AShM, 2 single 3S90E lnchr with 9M38E M-22E *Shtil* (RS-SA-N-7 *Gadfly*) SAM, 4 8-cell VLS with *Barak*-1 SAM, 5 single 533mm ASTT with SET-65E HWT/*Varunastra* HWT, 2 RBU 6000 *Smerch* 2 A/S mor; 2 AK630 CIWS, 1 100mm gun (capacity either 2 *Dhruv* hel/*Sea King* Mk42A ASW hel)

1 *Delhi* (Project 15) with 4 quad lnchr with 3M24E *Uran*-E (RS-SS-N-25 *Switchblade*) AShM, 2 single 3S90E lnchr with 9M38E M-22E *Shtil* (RS-SA-N-7 *Gadfly*) SAM, 5 single 533mm ASTT with SET-65E HWT/*Varunastra* HWT, 2 RBU 6000 *Smerch* 2 A/S mor; 2 AK630 CIWS, 1 100mm gun (capacity either 2 *Dhruv* hel/*Sea King* Mk42A ASW hel)

3 *Kolkata* (Project 15A) with 2 8-cell UVLM VLS with *Brahmos* AShM, 4 8-cell VLS with *Barak*-8 SAM; 2 twin 533mm TT with SET-65E HWT/*Varunastra* HWT, 2 RBU 6000 *Smerch* 2 A/S mor, 4 AK630M CIWS, 1 76mm gun (capacity 2 *Dhruv*/*Sea King* Mk42B hel)

1 *Visakhapatnam* (Project 15B) with 2 8-cell UVLM VLS with *Brahmos* AShM, 4 8-cell VLS with *Barak*-8 SAM; 2 twin 533mm TT with *Varunastra* HWT, 2 RBU 6000 *Smerch* 2 A/S mor, 4 AK630M CIWS, 1 76mm gun (capacity 2 *Dhruv*/*Sea King* Mk42B hel)

DDGM 3:

1 *Rajput* (FSU *Kashin*) with 2 twin lnchr with P-27 *Termit*-R (RS-SS-N-2D *Styx*) AShM, 2 twin ZIF-101 lnchr with 4K91 M-1 *Volnya* (RS-SA-N-1 *Goa*) SAM, 5 single 533mm PTA-51-61ME ASTT with SET-65E HWT/*Varunastra* HWT, 2 RBU 6000 *Smerch* 2 A/S mor, 2 AK630M CIWS, 1 76mm gun (capacity Ka-28 *Helix* A hel)

2 *Rajput* (FSU *Kashin*) with 1 8-cell UVLM VLS with *Brahmos* AShM, 2 twin lnchr with P-27 *Termit*-R (RS-SS-N-2D *Styx*) AShM, 2 8-cell VLS with *Barak*-1 SAM, 1 twin ZIF-101 lnchr with 4K91 M-1 *Volnya* (RS-SA-N-1 *Goa*) SAM, 5 single 533mm ASTT with SET-65E HWT/*Varunastra* HWT, 2 RBU 6000 *Smerch* 2 A/S mor, 4 AK630M CIWS, 1 76mm gun (capacity 1 Ka-28 *Helix* A hel)

FRIGATES 16

FFGHM 12:

3 *Brahmaputra* (Project 16A) with 4 quad lnchr with 3M24E *Uran*-E (RS-SS-N-25 *Switchblade*) AShM,

3 8-cell VLS with *Barak*-1 SAM, 2 triple ILAS-3 (B-515) 324mm ASTT with A244 LWT, 4 AK630M CIWS, 1 76mm gun (capacity 2 SA316B *Alouette* III (*Chetak*)/*Sea King* Mk42 ASW hel)

3 *Shivalik* (Project 17) with 1 8-cell 3S14E VLS with 3M54TE *Klub*-N (RS-SS-N-27B *Sizzler*) AShM/*Brahmos* AShM, 4 8-cell VLS with *Barak*-1 SAM, 1 single 3S90E lnchr with 9M317E *Shtil*-1 (RS-SA-N-7B) SAM, 2 triple 324mm ILAS-3 (B-515) ASTT, 2 RBU 6000 *Smerch* 2 A/S mor, 2 AK630M CIWS, 1 76mm gun (capacity 1 *Sea King* Mk42B ASW hel)

3 *Talwar* I with 1 8-cell 3S14E VLS with 3M54TE *Klub*-N (RS-SS-N-27B *Sizzler*) AShM, 1 single 3S90E lnchr with 9M317E *Shtil*-1 (RS-SA-N-7B) SAM, 2 twin 533mm DTA-53-11356 ASTT with SET-65E HWT/*Varunastra* HWT, 2 RBU 6000 *Smerch* 2 A/S mor, 2 *Kashtan* (RS-CADS-N-1) CIWS, 1 100mm gun (capacity 1 *Dhruv*/Ka-28 *Helix* A ASW hel)

3 *Talwar* II with 1 8-cell UVLM VLS with *Brahmos* AShM, 1 single 3S90E lnchr with 9M317E *Shtil*-1 (RS-SA-N-7B) SAM, 2 twin 533mm DTA-53-11356 ASTT with SET-65E HWT/*Varunastra* HWT, 2 RBU 6000 *Smerch* 2 A/S mor, 2 AK630M CIWS, 1 100mm gun (capacity 1 *Dhruv*/Ka-28 *Helix* A ASW hel)

FFH 4 *Kamorta* (Project 28) with 2 twin 533mm ITTL ASTT with *Varunastra* HWT, 2 RBU 6000 *Smerch* 2 A/S mor, 2 AK630 CIWS, 1 76mm gun (capacity 1 *Dhruv*/Ka-28 *Helix* A ASW hel)

PATROL AND COASTAL COMBATANTS 164
CORVETTES • FSGM 7:

3 *Khukri* (Project 25) with 2 twin lnchr with P-27 *Termit*-R (RS-SS-N-2D *Styx*) AShM, 2 twin lnchr (manual aiming) with 9K32M *Strela*-2M (RS-SA-N-5 *Grail*) SAM, 2 AK630M CIWS, 1 76mm gun, 1 hel landing platform (for *Dhruv*/SA316 *Alouette* III (*Chetak*))

4 *Kora* (Project 25A) with 4 quad lnchr with 3M24E *Uran*-E (RS-SS-N-25 *Switchblade*) AShM, 1 quad lnchr (manual aiming) with 9K32M *Strela*-2M (RS-SA-N-5 *Grail*) SAM, 2 AK630M CIWS, 1 76mm gun, 1 hel landing platform (for *Dhruv*/SA316 *Alouette* III (*Chetak*))

PSOH 10: 4 *Saryu* with 2 AK630M CIWS, 1 76mm gun (capacity 1 *Dhruv*); 6 *Sukanya* with 4 RBU 2500 A/S mor (capacity 1 SA316 *Alouette* III (*Chetak*))

PCFGM 7:

5 *Veer* (FSU *Tarantul*) with 4 single lnchr with P-27 *Termit*-R (RS-SS-N-2D *Styx*) AShM, 2 quad lnchr (manual aiming) with 9K32M *Strela*-2M (RS-SA-N-5 *Grail*), 2 AK630M CIWS, 1 76mm gun

2 *Prabal* (mod *Veer*) each with 4 quad lnchr with 3M24E *Uran*-E (RS-SS-N-25 *Switchblade*) AShM, 1 quad lnchr (manual aiming) with 9K32M *Strela*-2M (RS-SA-N-5 *Grail*) SAM, 2 AK630M CIWS, 1 76mm gun

PCMT 1 *Abhay* (FSU *Pauk* II) with 1 quad lnchr (manual aiming) with 9K32M *Strela*-2M (RS-SA-N-5 *Grail*) SAM, 2 twin 533mm DTA-53 ASTT with SET-65E, 2 RBU 1200 *Uragan* A/S mor, 1 AK630M CIWS, 1 76mm gun

PCC 15: 4 *Bangaram*; 10 *Car Nicobar*; 1 *Trinkat* (SDB Mk5)

PCF 4 *Tarmugli* (*Car Nicobar* mod)

PBF 120: 9 Immediate Support Vessel (Rodman 78); 14 Immediate Support Vessel (Craftway); 15 Plascoa 1300 (SPB); 5 *Super Dvora*; 77 Solas Marine Interceptor

AMPHIBIOUS
PRINCIPAL AMPHIBIOUS VESSELS • LPD 1 *Jalashwa* (ex-US *Austin*) with 1 Mk 15 *Phalanx* CIWS (capacity up to 6 med spt hel; either 9 LCM or 4 LCM and 2 LCAC; 4 LCVP; 930 troops)

LANDING SHIPS 8
LSM 3 *Kumbhir* (FSU *Polnochny* C) (capacity 5 MBT or 5 APC; 160 troops)
LST 5: 2 *Magar* (capacity 15 MBT or 8 APC or 10 trucks; 500 troops); 3 *Magar* mod (capacity 11 MBT or 8 APC or 10 trucks; 500 troops)

LANDING CRAFT 12
LCT 8 LCU Mk-IV (capacity 1 *Arjun* MBT/2 T-90 MBT/4 IFV/160 troops)
LCM 4 LCM 8 (for use in *Jalashwa*)

LOGISTICS AND SUPPORT 41
AFD 2: 1 FDN-1; 1 FDN-2
AGOR 1 *Sagardhwani* with 1 hel landing platform
AGHS 7: 1 *Makar*; 6 *Sandhayak*
AGM 1 *Dhruv*
AO 4 GSL 1,000T Fuel Barge
AOL 10: 1 *Ambika*; 2 *Poshak*; 7 *Purak*
AOR 1 *Jyoti* with 1 hel landing platform
AORH 3: 1 *Aditya* (based on *Deepak* (1967) Bremer Vulkan design); 2 *Deepak* with 4 AK630 CIWS
AP 3 *Nicobar* with 1 hel landing platform
ASR 1
ATF 1
AWT 3 *Ambuda*
AX 1 *Tir*
AXS 4: 2 *Mhadei*; 2 *Tarangini*

Naval Aviation 7,000

FORCES BY ROLE
FIGHTER/GROUND ATTACK
2 sqn with MiG-29K/KUB *Fulcrum*
ANTI-SUBMARINE WARFARE
1 sqn with Ka-28 *Helix* A
1 sqn with *Sea King* Mk42B
MARITIME PATROL
4 sqn with BN-2 *Islander*; Do-228-101
1 sqn with Do-228
1 sqn with Il-38SD *May*
2 sqn with P-8I *Neptune*
AIRBORNE EARLY WARNING & CONTROL
1 sqn with Ka-31 *Helix* B
SEARCH & RESCUE
1 sqn with SA316B *Alouette* III (*Chetak*); *Sea King* Mk42C
4 sqn with *Dhruv* MkI/MkIII
TRANSPORT
1 sqn with Do-228-101; HS-748M (HAL-748M)
TRAINING
1 sqn with Do-228
1 sqn with HJT-16 *Kiran* MkI/II, *Hawk* Mk132*
1 hel sqn with *Sea King* Mk42B
TRANSPORT HELICOPTER
1 sqn with UH-3H *Sea King*

ISR UAV
3 sqn with *Heron; Searcher* MkII
EQUIPMENT BY TYPE
AIRCRAFT 74 combat capable
FTR 42 MiG-29K/KUB *Fulcrum*
ASW 15: 3 Il-38SD *May*; 12 P-8I *Neptune*
MP 12+ Do-228-101
TPT 37:
Light 27: 17 BN-2 *Islander*; 10 Do-228
PAX 10 HS-748M (HAL-748M)
TRG 29: 6 HJT-16 *Kiran* MkI; 6 HJT-16 *Kiran* MkII;
17 *Hawk* Mk132*
HELICOPTERS
ASW 36: 12 Ka-28 *Helix* A; 6 MH-60R *Seahawk*; 18 *Sea King* Mk42B
MRH 73: 10 *Dhruv* MkI; 16 *Dhruv* MkIII; 24 SA316B *Alouette* III (*Chetak*); 23 SA319 *Alouette* III
AEW 11 Ka-31 *Helix* B
TPT • Medium 11: 5 *Sea King* Mk42C; up to 6 UH-3H *Sea King*
UNINHABITED AERIAL VEHICLES
ISR 10: **Heavy** 4 *Heron;* **Medium** 6 *Searcher* Mk II
AIR-LAUNCHED MISSILES
AAM • IR R-550 *Magic/Magic* 2; R-73 (RS-AA-11A *Archer*); **IR/SARH** R-27 (RS-AA-10 *Alamo*); **ARH**: R-77 (RS-AA-12A *Adder*)
AShM AGM-84 *Harpoon* (on P-8I ac); Kh-35 (RS-AS-20 *Kayak*)
BOMBS • TV-guided KAB-500KR/OD

Marines ε1,200 (Additional 1,000 for SPB duties)

After the Mumbai attacks, the Sagar Prahari Bal (SPB), with 80 PBF, was established to protect critical maritime infrastructure

FORCES BY ROLE
SPECIAL FORCES
1 (marine) cdo force
MANOEUVRE
Amphibious
1 amph bde

Air Force 139,850

5 regional air comds: Western (New Delhi), Southwestern (Gandhinagar), Eastern (Shillong), Central (Allahabad), Southern (Trivandrum). 2 support comds: Maintenance (Nagpur) and Training (Bangalore)

FORCES BY ROLE
FIGHTER
3 sqn with MiG-29 *Fulcrum*; MiG-29UB *Fulcrum*
FIGHTER/GROUND ATTACK
4 sqn with *Jaguar* IB/IS
6 sqn with MiG-21 *Bison*
3 sqn with *Mirage* 2000E/ED/I/IT (2000H/TH – secondary ECM role)
2 sqn with *Rafale* DH/EH
11 sqn with Su-30MKI *Flanker*
2 sqn with *Tejas*
ANTI SURFACE WARFARE
1 sqn with *Jaguar* IM

ISR
1 unit with Gulfstream IV SRA-4
AIRBORNE EARLY WARNING & CONTROL
1 sqn with Il-76TD *Phalcon*
TANKER
1 sqn with Il-78 *Midas*
TRANSPORT
1 sqn with C-130J-30 *Hercules*
1 sqn with C-17A *Globemaster* III
5 sqn with An-32/An-32RE *Cline*
1 (comms) sqn with B-737; B-737BBJ; EMB-135BJ
4 sqn with Do-228; HS-748
1 sqn with Il-76MD *Candid*
1 flt with HS-748
TRAINING
1 OCU sqn with Su-30MKI *Flanker*
ATTACK HELICOPTER
1 sqn with AH-64E *Apache Guardian*
1 sqn with LCH *Prachand*
2 sqn with Mi-25 *Hind*; Mi-35 *Hind*
TRANSPORT HELICOPTER
5 sqn with *Dhruv*
7 sqn with Mi-17/Mi-17-1V *Hip* H
12 sqn with Mi-17V-5 *Hip* H
2 sqn with SA316B *Alouette* III (*Chetak*)
1 flt with Mi-26 *Halo*
2 flt with SA315B *Lama* (*Cheetah*)
2 flt with SA316B *Alouette* III (*Chetak*)
ISR UAV
5 sqn with *Heron; Searcher* MkII
SURFACE-TO-SURFACE MISSILE
2 GLCM sqn with PJ-10 *Brahmos*
AIR DEFENCE
6 sqn with 9K33M3 *Osa*-AKM (RS-SA-8B *Gecko*)
8 sqn with *Akash*
2 sqn with *Barak*-8 MR-SAM
25 sqn with S-125M *Pechora*-M (RS-SA-3B *Goa*)
2 sqn with S-400 (RS-SA-21 *Growler*)
10 flt with 9K38 *Igla*-1 (RS-SA-18 *Grouse*)
EQUIPMENT BY TYPE
AIRCRAFT 800 combat capable
FTR 61: 54 MiG-29 *Fulcrum* (incl 12+ MiG-29UPG); 7 MiG-29UB *Fulcrum* B
FGA 523: 109 MiG-21 *Bison*; 37 MiG-21U/UM *Mongol*; 38 *Mirage* 2000E/I (2000H); 10 *Mirage* 2000ED/IT (2000TH); 8 *Rafale* DH; 28 *Rafale* EH; 263 Su-30MKI *Flanker* H; 30 *Tejas*
ATK 115: 28 *Jaguar* IB; 79 *Jaguar* IS; 8 *Jaguar* IM
ISR 3 Gulfstream IV SRA-4
AEW&C 5: 2 EMB-145AEW *Netra* (1 more in test); 3 Il-76TD *Phalcon*
TKR 6 Il-78 *Midas*
TPT 243: **Heavy** 28: 11 C-17A *Globemaster* III; 17 Il-76MD *Candid*; **Medium** 10 C-130J-30 *Hercules*; **Light** 141: 47 An-32; 55 An-32RE *Cline*; 35 Do-228; 4 EMB-135BJ; **PAX** 64: 1 B-707; 4 B-737; 3 B-737BBJ; 56 HS-748
TRG 308: 101 *Hawk* Mk132*; 90 HJT-16 *Kiran* MkI/IA; 42 HJT-16 *Kiran* MkII; 75 PC-7 *Turbo Trainer* MkII
HELICOPTERS
ATK 43: 22 AH-64E *Apache Guardian*; 4 LCH *Prachand*; 17 Mi-25/Mi-35 *Hind*

MRH 402: 60 *Dhruv*; 35 Mi-17 *Hip* H; 45 Mi-17-1V *Hip* H; 148 Mi-17V-5 *Hip* H; 59 SA315B *Lama* (*Cheetah*); 39 SA316B *Alouette* III (*Chetak*); 16 *Rudra*

TPT • Heavy 16: 15 CH-47F *Chinook*; 1 Mi-26 *Halo*

UNINHABITED AERIAL VEHICLES

ISR • Heavy 9 *Heron*; **Medium** some *Searcher* MkII

LOITERING & DIRECT ATTACK MUNITIONS

Harop

AIR DEFENCE • SAM

Long-range 16 S-400 (RS-SA-21 *Growler*)

Medium-range 72: ε64 *Akash*; 8 Barak-8 (MRSAM)

Short-range S-125M *Pechora*-M (RS-SA-3B *Goa*); *Spyder*-SR

Point-defence 9K33M3 *Osa*-AKM (RS-SA-8 *Gecko*); 9K38 *Igla* (RS-SA-18 *Grouse*)

AIR-LAUNCHED MISSILES

AAM • IR R-60 (RS-AA-8 *Aphid)*; R-73 (RS-AA-11A *Archer*) R-550 *Magic*; **IIR** *Mica* IR; **IR/SARH** R-27 (RS-AA-10 *Alamo*); **SARH** Super 530D **ARH** R-77 (RS-AA-12A *Adder*); *Mica* RF

AShM AGM-84 *Harpoon*; AM39 *Exocet*; Kh-31A (RS-AS-17B *Krypton*)

ASM AASM; AGM-114L/R *Hellfire*; Kh-29 (RS-AS-14 *Kedge*); Kh-59 (RS-AS-13 *Kingbolt*); Kh-59M (RS-AS-18 *Kazoo*); AS-30; *Popeye* II (*Crystal Maze*)

ARM Kh-25MP (RS-AS-12A *Kegler*); Kh-31P (RS-AS-17A *Krypton*)

ALCM

Conventional SCALP-EG

Nuclear *Nirbhay* (likely nuclear capable; in development)

BOMBS

INS/SAT guided *Spice*

Laser-guided *Griffin*; KAB-500L; *Paveway* II

TV-guided KAB-500KR

SURFACE-TO-SURFACE MISSILE LAUNCHERS

GLCM • Conventional PJ-10 *Brahmos*

Coast Guard 13,000

EQUIPMENT BY TYPE

PATROL AND COASTAL COMBATANTS 140

PSOH 27: 2 *Sankalp* (capacity 1 *Chetak/Dhruv* hel); 4 *Samar* with 1 76mm gun (capacity 1 *Chetak/Dhruv* hel); 11 *Samarth*; 7 *Vikram* (capacity 1 *Dhruv* hel); 3 *Vishwast* (capacity 1 *Dhruv* hel)

PSO 3 *Samudra Prahari* with 1 hel landing platform

PCC 44: 20 *Aadesh*; 8 *Rajshree* (Flight I); 4 *Rajshree* (Flight II) 5 *Rani Abbakka*; 7 *Sarojini Naidu*

PBF 66: 6 C-154; 2 C-141; 11 C-143; 47 C-401

AMPHIBIOUS • UCAC 17: 5 H-181 (*Griffon* 8000TD); 12 H-187 (*Griffon* 8000TD)

AIRCRAFT • MP 23 Do-228-101

HELICOPTERS • MRH 37: 4 *Dhruv* MkI; 16 *Dhruv* MkIII; 17 SA316B *Alouette* III (*Chetak*)

Gendarmerie & Paramilitary 1,608,150

Rashtriya Rifles 65,000

Ministry of Defence. 15 sector HQ

FORCES BY ROLE

MANOEUVRE

Other

65 paramilitary bn

Assam Rifles 65,150

Ministry of Home Affairs. Security within northeastern states, mainly army-officered; better trained than BSF

FORCES BY ROLE

Equipped to roughly same standard as an army inf bn

COMMAND

7 HQ

MANOEUVRE

Other

46 paramilitary bn

EQUIPMENT BY TYPE

ARTILLERY • MOR 81mm 252

Border Security Force 263,900

Ministry of Home Affairs

FORCES BY ROLE

MANOEUVRE

Other

192 paramilitary bn

EQUIPMENT BY TYPE

Small arms, lt arty, some anti-tank weapons

ARTILLERY • MOR 81mm 942+

AIRCRAFT • TPT some (air spt)

HELICOPTERS • MRH 2 Mi-17V-5 *Hip*

Central Industrial Security Force 144,400 (lightly armed security guards)

Ministry of Home Affairs. Guards public-sector locations

Central Reserve Police Force 324,800

Ministry of Home Affairs. Internal-security duties, only lightly armed, deployable throughout the country

FORCES BY ROLE

MANOEUVRE

Other

215 paramilitary bn

15 (rapid action force) paramilitary bn

10 (CoBRA) paramilitary bn

6 (Mahila) paramilitary bn (female)

2 sy gp

COMBAT SUPPORT

5 sigs bn

Defence Security Corps 31,000

Provides security at Defence Ministry sites

Indo-Tibetan Border Police 89,450

Ministry of Home Affairs. Tibetan border security SF/guerrilla-warfare and high-altitude-warfare specialists

FORCES BY ROLE

MANOEUVRE

Other

56 paramilitary bn

National Security Guards 12,000

Anti-terrorism contingency deployment force, comprising elements of the armed forces, CRPF and Border Security Force

Railway Protection Forces 70,000

Sashastra Seema Bal 79,450

Guards the borders with Nepal and Bhutan

FORCES BY ROLE
MANOEUVRE
Other
73 paramilitary bn

Special Frontier Force 10,000

Mainly ethnic Tibetans

Special Protection Group 3,000

Protection of ministers and senior officials

State Armed Police 450,000

For duty primarily in home state only, but can be moved to other states. Some bn with GPMG and army-standard infantry weapons and equipment

FORCES BY ROLE
MANOEUVRE
Other
144 (India Reserve Police) paramilitary bn

Reserve Organisations

Civil Defence 500,000 reservists

Operate in 225 categorised towns in 32 states. Some units for NBC defence

Home Guard 441,000 reservists (547,000 authorised str)

In all states except Arunachal Pradesh and Kerala; men on reserve lists, no trg. Not armed in peacetime. Used for civil defence, rescue and firefighting provision in wartime; 6 bn (created to protect tea plantations in Assam)

DEPLOYMENT

CYPRUS: UN • UNFICYP 1

DEMOCRATIC REPUBLIC OF THE CONGO: UN • MONUSCO 1,891; 2 inf bn; 1 med coy

LEBANON: UN • UNIFIL 895; 1 inf bn; 1 med coy

MIDDLE EAST: UN • UNTSO 2

SOMALIA: UN • UNSOM 1

SOUTH SUDAN: UN • UNMISS 2,396; 2 inf bn; 1 engr coy; 1 sigs coy; 1 fd hospital

SUDAN: UN • UNISFA 325; 1 mech inf bn(-)

SYRIA/ISRAEL: UN • UNDOF 198; 1 inf pl, 1 MP pl, 1 log coy(-)

WESTERN SAHARA: UN • MINURSO 3

FOREIGN FORCES

Total numbers for UNMOGIP mission in India and Pakistan
Argentina 3
Croatia 8
Italy 2
Korea, Republic of 7
Mexico 1
Philippines 5
Romania 2
Sweden 4
Switzerland 3
Thailand 6
Uruguay 3

Indonesia IDN

Indonesian Rupiah IDR		2021	2022	2023
GDP	IDR	16971tr	18988tr	
	USD	1.19tr	1.29tr	
per capita	USD	4,361	4,691	
Growth	%	3.7	5.3	
Inflation	%	1.6	4.6	
Def bdgt	IDR	120tr	133tr	132tr
	USD	8.41bn	9.06bn	
FMA (US)	USD	14m	14m	14m
USD1=IDR		14293.37	14725.86	

Real-terms defence budget trend (USDbn, constant 2015)

Population	277,329,163					
Age	0–14	15–19	20–24	25–29	30–64	65 plus
Male	12.6%	4.3%	4.1%	3.9%	21.7%	3.4%
Female	12.0%	4.1%	3.9%	3.7%	22.2%	4.0%

Capabilities

The Tentara Nasional Indonesia (Indonesian National Armed Forces) are the largest armed forces in Southeast Asia. They have traditionally been concerned primarily with internal security and counter-insurgency. The army remains the dominant service and is deployed operationally for counter-insurgency tasks in West Papua and in a counter-terrorist role in central Sulawesi. A modernisation plan, adopted in 2010, called for establishing a 'Minimum Essential Force' including strengthened naval and air forces by 2024. The 2015 defence White Paper outlined Indonesia's 'Global Maritime Fulcrum' policy and advocated building up maritime, satellite and UAV capabilities. Some of these objectives were reflected in the 2020–24 State Defence Policy document. In 2018, Indonesia expanded its forces in the country's east and established a third naval fleet command and a third air-force regional command in that region. A new army reserve division and a third marine corps group were also established in the east. Indonesia has no formal defence alliances but there are a number of defence-cooperation agreements with regional and extra-regional partners. China has supplied some military equipment, including armed UAVs.

254   THE MILITARY BALANCE 2023

The armed forces have contributed to UN and other international peacekeeping operations and exercise regularly with Australian and US armed forces as well as those of other Southeast Asian states. The TNI's inventory comprises equipment from diverse international sources, and the country uses technology-transfer agreements to develop its national defence industry which has significant capabilities in specific areas, including naval construction and the manufacture of transport aircraft and helicopters. Indonesia consolidated its five leading defence firms into the state-owned Defend ID in 2022 as part of plans to achieve more than 40% localisation in defence production.

ACTIVE 395,500 (Army 300,400 Navy 65,000 Air 30,100) Gendarmerie & Paramilitary 280,000
Conscription liability 24 months selective conscription authorised (not required by law)

RESERVE 400,000
Army cadre units; numerical str n.k., obligation to age 45 for officers

ORGANISATIONS BY SERVICE

Army ε300,400

Mil Area Commands (KODAM)
15 comd (I, II, III, IV, V, VI, IX, XII, XIII, XIV, XVI, XVII, XVIII, Jaya & Iskandar Muda)
FORCES BY ROLE
MANOEUVRE
Mechanised
3 armd cav bn
8 cav bn
1 mech inf bde (1 cav bn, 3 mech inf bn)
1 mech inf bde (3 mech inf bn)
3 indep mech inf bn
Light
1 inf bde (3 cdo bn)
1 inf bde (2 cdo bn, 1 inf bn)
1 inf bde (1 cdo bn, 2 inf bn)
2 inf bde (3 inf bn)
3 inf bde (1 cdo bn, 1 inf bn)
3 inf bde (2 inf bn)
24 indep inf bn
20 indep cdo bn
COMBAT SUPPORT
1 SP arty bn
11 fd arty bn
11 cbt engr bn
COMBAT SERVICE SUPPORT
4 construction bn
AVIATION
1 composite avn sqn
HELICOPTER
1 hel sqn with Bo-105; Bell 205A; Bell 412; Bell 412EPI *Twin Huey*; AH-64E *Apache Guardian*
1 hel sqn Mi-35P *Hind*; Mi-17V-5 *Hip* H
AIR DEFENCE
1 AD regt (2 ADA bn, 1 SAM unit)
9 ADA bn
3 SAM unit

Special Forces Command (KOPASSUS)
FORCES BY ROLE
SPECIAL FORCES
3 SF gp (total: 2 cdo/para unit, 1 CT unit, 1 int unit)

Strategic Reserve Command (KOSTRAD)
FORCES BY ROLE
COMMAND
3 div HQ
MANOEUVRE
Armoured
2 tk bn
Mechanised
1 mech inf bde (3 mech inf bn)
Light
2 inf bde (3 cdo bn)
1 inf bde (2 inf bn)
Air Manoeuvre
3 AB bde (3 AB bn)
COMBAT SUPPORT
2 arty regt (1 SP arty bn; 1 MRL bn; 1 fd arty bn)
1 fd arty bn
2 cbt engr bn
AIR DEFENCE
3 AD bn
EQUIPMENT BY TYPE
ARMOURED FIGHTING VEHICLES
MBT 103: 42 *Leopard* 2A4; 61 *Leopard* 2RI
LT TK 350: 275 AMX-13 (partially upgraded); 15 PT-76; 60 FV101 *Scorpion-90*
ASLT 7 *Babak*
RECCE 142: 55 *Ferret* (13 upgraded); 69 *Saladin* (16 upgraded); 18 VBL
IFV 64: 22 *Black Fox*; 42 *Marder* 1A3
APC 860+
    APC (T) 267: 75 AMX-VCI; 34 BTR-50PK; 15 FV4333 *Stormer*; 143 M113A1-B
    APC (W) 593+: 376 *Anoa*; some *Barracuda*; 40 BTR-40; 45 FV603 *Saracen* (14 upgraded); 100 LAV-150 *Commando*; 32 VAB-VTT
    PPV some *Casspir*
AUV 39: 14 APR-1; 3 *Bushmaster*; 22 *Commando Ranger*; *Komodo* 4×4
ENGINEERING & MAINTENANCE VEHICLES
AEV 4: 3 PiPz-2RI *Dachs*; 1 M113A1-B-GN
ARV 15+: 2 AMX-13; 6 AMX-VCI; 3 BREM-2; 4 BPz-3 *Buffel*; *Stormer*; T-54/T-55
VLB 19: 10 AMX-13; 3 BPR *Biber*-1; 4 M3; 2 *Stormer*
ANTI-TANK/ANTI-INFRASTRUCTURE
MSL • MANPATS FGM-148 *Javelin*; SS.11; *Milan*; 9K11 *Malyutka* (RS-AT-3 *Sagger*)
RCL 90mm M67; **106mm** M40A1
RL 89mm LRAC
ARTILLERY 1,243+
SP 92: **105mm** 20 AMX Mk61; **155mm** 72: 54 CAESAR; 18 M109A4
TOWED 133+: **105mm** 110+: some KH-178; 60 M101; 50 M-56; **155mm** 23: 5 FH-88; 18 KH-179
MRL 127mm 63 ASTROS II Mk6
MOR 955: **81mm** 800; **120mm** 155: 75 Brandt; 80 UBM 52

Asia 255

AMPHIBIOUS
LANDING SHIPS • LST 2 ADRI LI with 1 hel landing platform (capacity 8 MBT; 500 troops)
LANDING CRAFT • LCU 17: 1 ADRI XXXII; 4 ADRI XXXIII; 1 ADRI XXXIX; 1 ADRI XL; 3 ADRI XLI; 2 ADRI XLIV; 2 ADRI XLVI; 2 ADRI XLVIII; 1 ADRI L
AIRCRAFT • TPT • Light 9: 1 BN-2A *Islander*; 6 C-212 *Aviocar* (NC-212); 2 *Turbo Commander* 680

HELICOPTERS
ATK 14: 8 AH-64E *Apache Guardian*; 6 Mi-35P *Hind*
MRH 51: 12 H125M *Fennec*; 17 Bell 412 *Twin Huey* (NB-412); 6 Bell 412EPI *Twin Huey*; 16 Mi-17V-5 *Hip H*
TPT • Light 29: 7 Bell 205A; 20 Bo-105 (NBo-105); 2 H120 *Colibri*
TRG up to 19 Hughes 300C

AIR DEFENCE
SAM • Point-defence 95+: 2 *Kobra* (with 125 GROM-2 msl); *Starstreak*; TD-2000B (*Giant Bow* II); 51 *Rapier*; 42 RBS-70; QW-3
GUNS • TOWED 411: **20mm** 121 Rh 202; **23mm** *Giant Bow*; **40mm** 90 L/70; **57mm** 200 S-60

AIR-LAUNCHED MISSILES
ASM AGM-114 *Hellfire*

Navy ε65,000 (including Marines and Aviation)

Three fleets: East (Sorong), Central (Surabaya) and West (Jakarta). Two Forward Operating Bases at Kupang (West Timor) and Tahuna (North Sulawesi)

EQUIPMENT BY TYPE
SUBMARINES • SSK 4:
1 *Cakra* (Type-209/1300) with 8 single 533mm TT with SUT HWT
3 *Nagapasa* (Type-209/1400) with 8 single 533mm TT with *Black Shark* HWT

PRINCIPAL SURFACE COMBATANTS 7
FRIGATES 7:
FFGHM 5:
1 *Ahmad Yani* (ex-NLD *Van Speijk*) with 2 twin-cell VLS with 3M55E *Yakhont* (RS-SS-N-26 *Strobile*) AShM; 2 twin *Simbad* lnchr (manual) with *Mistral* SAM, 2 triple 324mm SVTT Mk 32 ASTT with Mk 46 LWT, 1 76mm gun (capacity 1 Bo-105 (NBo-105) hel)
2 *Ahmad Yani* (ex-NLD *Van Speijk*) with 2 twin lnchr with C-802 (CH-SS-N-6) AShM, 2 twin *Simbad* lnchr (manual) with *Mistral* SAM, 2 triple 324mm SVTT Mk 32 ASTT with Mk 46 LWT, 1 76mm gun (capacity 1 Bo-105 (NBo-105) hel)
2 *R.E. Martadinata* (SIGMA 10514) with 2 quad lnchr with MM40 *Exocet* Block 3 AShM, 2 6-cell CLA VLS with VL MICA SAM, 2 triple 324mm ILAS-3 (B-515) ASTT with A244/S LWT, 1 *Millennium* CIWS, 1 76mm gun (capacity 1 med hel)
FFHM 2 *Ahmad Yani* (ex-NLD *Van Speijk*) with 2 twin *Simbad* lnchr (manual) with *Mistral* SAM, 2 triple 324mm ASTT with Mk 46 LWT, 1 76mm gun (capacity 1 Bo-105 (NBo-105) hel)

PATROL AND COASTAL COMBATANTS 138
CORVETTES 24
FSGM 7:
3 *Bung Tomo* with 2 quad lnchr with MM40 *Exocet* Block 2 AShM, 1 18-cell VLS with *Sea Wolf* SAM, 2 triple 324mm ASTT, 1 76mm gun (capacity: 1 Bo-105 hel)
4 *Diponegoro* (SIGMA 9113) with 2 twin lnchr with MM40 *Exocet* Block 2 AShM, 2 quad *Tetral* lnchr with *Mistral* SAM, 2 triple 324mm ILAS-3 (B-515) ASTT with MU90 LWT, 1 76mm gun, 1 hel landing platform
FSGH 1 *Nala* with 2 twin lnchr with MM38 *Exocet* AShM, 1 twin Bofors ASW Rocket Launcher System 375mm A/S mor, 1 120mm gun (capacity 1 lt hel)
FS 16:
2 *Fatahillah* with 2 triple 324mm SVTT Mk 32 ASTT with Mk 46 LWT, 1 twin 375mm A/S mor, 1 120mm gun
14 *Kapitan Pattimura* (GDR *Parchim* I) with 4 single 400mm ASTT, 2 RBU 6000 *Smerch* 2 A/S mor, 1 twin 57mm gun
PCFG 3 *Mandau* with 4 single lnchr with MM38 *Exocet* AShM, 1 57mm gun
PCG 4:
2 *Sampari* (KCR-60M) with 2 twin lnchr for C-705 AShM
2 *Todak* with 2 single lnchr with C-802 (CH-SS-N-6), 1 57mm gun
PCT 2 *Andau* with 2 single 533mm TT with SUT, 1 57mm gun
PCC 14: 4 *Kakap* with 1 hel landing platform; 2 *Pandrong*; 4 *Pari*; 2 *Sampari* (KCR-60M) with 1 NG-18 CIWS; 2 *Todak* with 1 57mm gun
PBG 8: 2 *Clurit* with 2 single lnchr with C-705 AShM, 1 AK630 CIWS; 6 *Clurit* with 2 single lnchr with C-705 AShM
PBF 4 Combat Boat AL D-18
PB 79: 2 *Badau* (ex-BRN *Waspada*); 9 *Boa*; 1 *Cucut* (ex-SGP *Jupiter*); 1 *Klewang*; 4 *Kobra*; 1 *Krait*; 8 *Sibarau*; up to 32 *Sinabang* (KAL 28); 4 *Tarihu*; 13 *Tatihu* (PC-40); 4 *Viper*

MINE WARFARE • MINE COUNTERMEASURES 8
MCO 2 *Pulau Rengat*
MSC 6 *Pulau Rote* (ex-GDR *Wolgast*)

AMPHIBIOUS
PRINCIPAL AMPHIBIOUS VESSELS • LPD 6:
1 *Dr Soeharso* (ex-*Tanjung Dalpele*) (capacity 2 LCU/LCVP; 13 tanks; 500 troops; 2 AS332L *Super Puma*) (used in AH role)
4 *Makassar* (capacity 2 LCU or 4 LCVP; 13 tanks; 500 troops; 2 AS332L *Super Puma*)
1 *Semarang* (IDN *Makassar* mod) (capacity 2 LCM; 3 hels; 28 vehs; 650 troops) (used in AH role)
LANDING SHIPS • LST 25
1 *Teluk Amboina* (capacity 16 tanks; 800 troops)
4 *Teluk Bintuni* (capacity 10 MBT)
2 *Teluk Cirebon* (ex-GDR *Frosch* II)
9 *Teluk Gilimanuk* (ex-GDR *Frosch*)
5 *Teluk Lada* with 1 hel landing platform (capacity 4 LCVP; 470 troops; 15 APC; 10 MBT)
4 *Teluk Semangka* (capacity 17 tanks; 200 troops)
LANDING CRAFT 54
LCM 20
LCU 4
LCVP 30

LOGISTICS AND SUPPORT 19

AGF 1 *Multatuli* with 1 hel landing platform
AGOR 2 *Rigel* (OSV 190)
AGOS 1 *Leuser*
AGHS 1 *Dewa Kembar* (ex-UK *Hecla*)
AGS 1 *Pulau Rote* (ex-GDR *Wolgast*)
AH 1 *Dr Sudirohusodo* (*Semarang* mod) (capacity 3 med hel)
AKSL 1
AORLH (1 *Arun* (ex-UK *Rover*) damaged at sea 2018, non-operational and in repair)
AOR 2: 1 *Bontang* with 1 hel landing platform; 1 *Tarakan* with 1 hel landing platform
AOT 1 *Sorong*
AP 2: 1 *Tanjung Kambani* (troop transport) with 1 hel landing platform; 1 *Karang Pilang* (troop transport)
ATF 1 *Soputan*
AX 2 *Kadet*
AXS 3: 1 *Arung Samudera*; 1 *Bima Suci*; 1 *Dewaruci*

Naval Aviation ε1,000

EQUIPMENT BY TYPE
AIRCRAFT
MP 29: 3 C212-200; 6 CN235-220 (MPA); 14 N-22B *Searchmaster* B; 6 N-22SL *Searchmaster* L
TPT • Light 32: 1 Beech 350i *King Air* (VIP transport); 7 Beech G36 *Bonanza*; 2 Beech G38 *Baron*; 17 C-212-200 *Aviocar*; 3 TB-9 *Tampico*; 2 TB-10
HELICOPTERS
ASW 11 AS565MBe *Panther*
MRH 4 Bell 412 (NB-412) *Twin Huey*
CSAR 4 H225M *Caracal*
TPT 15: **Medium** 3 AS332L *Super Puma* (NAS322L); **Light** 12: 3 H120 *Colibri*; 9 Bo-105 (NBo-105)

Marines ε20,000

FORCES BY ROLE
SPECIAL FORCES
1 SF bn
MANOEUVRE
Amphibious
2 mne gp (1 cav regt, 3 mne bn, 1 arty regt, 1 cbt spt regt, 1 CSS regt)
1 mne gp (forming)
1 mne bde (3 mne bn)
EQUIPMENT BY TYPE
ARMOURED FIGHTING VEHICLES
LT TK 65: 10 AMX-10 PAC 90; 55 PT-76†
RECCE 21 BRDM-2
IFV 114: 24 AMX-10P; 22 BMP-2; 54 BMP-3F; 2 BTR-4; 12 BTR-80A
APC 103: **APC (T)** 100 BTR-50P; **APC (W)** 3 BTR-4M
AAV 15: 10 LVTP-7A1; 5 M113 *Arisgator*
ARTILLERY 71+
TOWED 50: **105mm** 22 LG1 MK II; **122mm** 28 M-38
MRL 122mm 21: 4 PHL-90B; 9 RM-70; 8 RM-70 *Vampir*
MOR 81mm some
AIR DEFENCE • GUNS • 40mm 5 L/60/L/70; 57mm S-60

Air Force 30,100

3 operational comd (East, Central and West) plus trg comd
FORCES BY ROLE
FIGHTER
1 sqn with F-16A/B/C/D *Fighting Falcon*
FIGHTER/GROUND ATTACK
1 sqn with F-16C/D *Fighting Falcon*
1 sqn with Su-27SK *Flanker*; Su-30MK *Flanker*
1 sqn with Su-27SKM *Flanker*; Su-30MK2 *Flanker*
2 sqn with *Hawk* Mk109*/Mk209*
1 sqn with T-50i *Golden Eagle*
GROUND ATTACK
1 sqn with EMB-314 (A-29) *Super Tucano*
MARITIME PATROL
1 sqn with B-737-200
1 sqn with CN235M-220 MPA; CN235M-110
TANKER/TRANSPORT
1 sqn with C-130B/KC-130B *Hercules*
TRANSPORT
1 VIP sqn with B-737-200; C-130H/H-30 *Hercules*; L-100-30; F-27-400M *Troopship*; F-28-1000/3000
1 sqn with C-130H/H-30 *Hercules*; L-100-30
1 sqn with C-130H *Hercules*
1 sqn with C-212 *Aviocar* (NC-212/NC-212i)
1 sqn with C295M
TRAINING
1 sqn with G 120TP
1 sqn with KT-1B
TRANSPORT HELICOPTER
2 sqn with H225M; AS332L *Super Puma* (NAS332L); NAS332 C1+ *Super Puma*; SA330J/L *Puma* (NAS330J/L)
1 VIP sqn with AS332L *Super Puma* (NAS332L); SA330SM *Puma* (NAS300SM)
1 sqn with H120 *Colibri*
ISR UAV
1 sqn with *Aerostar*
AIR DEFENCE
1 SAM unit with NASAMS II
EQUIPMENT BY TYPE
Only 45% of ac op
AIRCRAFT 107 combat capable
FTR 9: 7 F-16A *Fighting Falcon*; 2 F-16B *Fighting Falcon* (8 F-5E *Tiger* II; 4 F-5F *Tiger* II non-operational)
FGA 40: 19 F-16C *Fighting Falcon*; 5 F-16D *Fighting Falcon*; 2 Su-27SK *Flanker*; 3 Su-27SKM *Flanker*; 2 Su-30MK *Flanker* F; 9 Su-30MK2 *Flanker* G
MP 8: 3 B-737-200; 2 CN235M-220 MPA
ISR 1 C295M
TKR/TPT 1 KC-130B *Hercules*
TPT 53: **Medium** 18: 3 C-130B *Hercules*; 7 C-130H *Hercules*; 6 C-130H-30 *Hercules*; 2 L-100-30; **Light** 26: 9 C295; 9 C-212 *Aviocar* (NC-212); 3 C-212 *Aviocar* (NC-212i); 5 CN235-110; **PAX** 9: 1 B-737-200; 3 B-737-400; 1 B-737-500; 1 B-737-800BBJ; 1 F-28-1000; 2 F-28-3000
TRG 104: 15 EMB-314 (A-29) *Super Tucano*; 30 G 120TP; 7 *Hawk* Mk109*; 22 *Hawk* Mk209*; 16 KT-1B; 14 T-50i *Golden Eagle*
HELICOPTERS
TPT 37: **Heavy** 6 H225M (CSAR); **Medium** 19: 9 AS332 *Super Puma* (NAS332L) (VIP/CSAR); 1 NAS332 C1+ *Super Puma*; 1 SA330SM *Puma* (NAS330SM) (VIP); 4 SA330J

Puma (NAS330J); 4 SA330L *Puma* (NAS330L); **Light** 12 H120 *Colibri*
UNINHABITED AERIAL VEHICLES
　CISR • Heavy CH-4B (in test)
　ISR • Medium *Aerostar*
AIR-LAUNCHED MISSILES
　AAM • IR AIM-9P *Sidewinder*; R-73 (RS-AA-11A *Archer*);
　IR/SARH R-27 (RS-AA-10 *Alamo*)
　ARH R-77 (RS-AA-12A *Adder*)
　ASM AGM-65G *Maverick*; AR-2; Kh-59M (RS-AS-18 *Kazoo*); Kh-59T (RS-AS-14B *Kedge*)
　ARM Kh-31P (RS-AS-17A *Krypton*)
AIR DEFENCE
　SAM • Medium-range NASAMS II

Special Forces (Paskhasau)
FORCES BY ROLE
SPECIAL FORCES
　3 (PASKHASAU) SF wg (total: 6 spec ops sqn)
　4 indep SF coy
EQUIPMENT BY TYPE
AIR DEFENCE
　SAM • Point-defence *Chiron*; QW-3
　GUNS • TOWED 35mm 6 Oerlikon *Skyshield*

Gendarmerie & Paramilitary 280,000+

Police ε280,000 (including 14,000 police 'mobile bde' (BRIMOB) org in 56 coy, incl CT unit (Gegana))
EQUIPMENT BY TYPE
ARMOURED FIGHTING VEHICLES
　APC (W) 34 *Tactica*
AIRCRAFT • TPT • Light 6: 2 Beech 18; 2 C-212 *Aviocar* (NC-212); 1 C295; 1 Turbo Commander 680
HELICOPTERS
　MRH 1 Bell 412EP
　TPT • Light 22: 3 Bell 206 *Jet Ranger*; 19 Bo-105 (NBo-105)

KPLP (Coast and Seaward Defence Command)
Responsible to Military Sea Communications Agency
EQUIPMENT BY TYPE
PATROL AND COASTAL COMBATANTS 37
　PCO 7: 1 *Arda Dedali*; 3 *Chundamani*; 1 *Kalimasada*; 2 *Trisula*
　PB 30: 4 *Golok* (SAR); 5 *Kujang*; 6 *Rantos*; 15 (various)
LOGISTICS AND SUPPORT • ABU 1 *Jadayat*

Bakamla (Maritime Security Agency)
EQUIPMENT BY TYPE
PATROL AND COASTAL COMBATANTS 10
　PSO 4: 3 *Pulau Nipah* with 1 hel landing platform; 1 *Tanjung Datu* with 1 hel landing platform
　PB 6 *Bintang Laut* (KCR-40 mod)

Reserve Organisations

Kamra People's Security ε40,000
Report for 3 weeks' basic training each year; part-time police auxiliary

DEPLOYMENT
CENTRAL AFRICAN REPUBLIC: UN • MINUSCA 241; 1 engr coy
DEMOCRATIC REPUBLIC OF THE CONGO: UN • MONUSCO 1,037; 1 inf bn; 1 engr coy
LEBANON: UN • UNIFIL 1,106; 1 mech inf bn; 1 MP coy; 1 FSGM
MALI: UN • MINUSMA 10
SOUTH SUDAN: UN • UNMISS 3
SUDAN: UN • UNISFA 4
WESTERN SAHARA: UN • MINURSO 3

Japan JPN

Japanese Yen JPY		2021	2022	2023
GDP	JPY	541tr	552tr	
	USD	4.93tr	4.30tr	
per capita	USD	39,301	34,358	
Growth	%	1.7	1.7	
Inflation	%	-0.2	2.0	
Def bdgt	JPY	5.73tr	6.17tr	
	USD	52.2bn	48.1bn	
USD1=JPY		109.75	128.42	

Real-terms defence budget trend (USDbn, constant 2015)

Population　124,214,766

Age	0–14	15–19	20–24	25–29	30–64	65 plus
Male	6.4%	2.3%	2.5%	2.6%	21.9%	12.8%
Female	6.0%	2.2%	2.3%	2.4%	22.3%	16.3%

Capabilities

Japan's concerns over its regional security environment have heightened, as evidenced in its 2022 Defence White Paper. These principally relate to security challenges posed by a more assertive China and continued concern over North Korea. As a result, there have been defence-budget increases and defence-policy and legislative reforms designed to enable Japan to play a more active international security role and strengthen the Japan Self-Defense Forces (JSDF). Due to their defensive mandate, JSDF deployments are mostly for peacekeeping purposes. While the JSDF's offensive capacity remains weak, the navy has strengths in anti-submarine warfare and air defence. An Amphibious Rapid Deployment Brigade has also been established, tasked mainly with the defence of remote islands. The *Izumo* helicopter carrier has completed the first stage of modifications to embark and operate fixed-wing aircraft. Final conversion work will take place at the end of FY 2024. JS *Kaga* began the first stage of its conversion in March 2022, with the second stage due in FY 2026. Japan is developing capabilities in space, cyberspace and the electromagnetic spectrum to develop a 'multi-domain defence force', based on the 2018 National Defense Program Guidelines and the 2019–23 Mid-Term Defense Program. In 2020, a Space Operations Squadron was set up, with the aim of enhancing space situational-awareness capabilities.

258 THE MILITARY BALANCE 2023

The Cyber Defense Group is to expand. Enhancing ballistic missile defence remains a key priority. In December 2020, the cabinet announced that two vessels equipped with *Aegis* ballistic missile defence systems would be developed as alternatives to the cancelled land-based *Aegis* Ashore. The Ministry of Defense requested a budget for the development of the vessels for FY2023. Japan's alliance with the US remains the cornerstone of its defence policy, reflected by continued US basing, the widespread use of US equipment across all three services and regular training with US forces. Meanwhile, meetings with Germany, India, Indonesia and the UK have indicated efforts to expand security relations. In November 2020, Australia and Japan agreed in principle on a Reciprocal Access Agreement, while India and Japan inked an Acquisition and Cross-Servicing Agreement in September 2020. Negotiations for a Reciprocal Access Agreement with the UK continued in 2022, as did discussions on closer cooperation on future combat aircraft development. Japan has an advanced defence-industrial base. Defence exports have mainly consisted of components, though there are ambitions to secure more significant export deals. Japan's ongoing military-procurement drive is focused on power projection, mobility and ISR. Budget documents also note research on a hypersonic glide body, new anti-ship missiles and research on advanced radar technology.

ACTIVE 247,150 (Ground Self-Defense Force 150,700 Maritime Self-Defense Force 45,300 Air Self-Defense Force 46,950 Central Staff 4,200) Gendarmerie & Paramilitary 14,550

RESERVE 55,900 (General Reserve Army (GSDF) 46,000 Ready Reserve Army (GSDF) 8,000 Navy 1,100 Air 800)

ORGANISATIONS BY SERVICE

Space
EQUIPMENT BY TYPE
SATELLITES 11
    COMMUNICATIONS 2: 1 *Kirameki*-1; 1 *Kirameki*-2
    ISR 9 IGS

Ground Self-Defense Force 150,700
FORCES BY ROLE
COMMAND
  5 army HQ (regional comd)
SPECIAL FORCES
  1 spec ops unit (bn)
MANOEUVRE
  Armoured
  1 (7th) armd div (1 armd recce sqn, 3 tk regt, 1 armd inf regt, 1 hel sqn, 1 SP arty regt, 1 AD regt, 1 cbt engr bn, 1 sigs bn, 1 NBC bn, 1 log regt)
  1 indep tk bn
  Mechanised
  1 (2nd) inf div (1 armd recce sqn, 1 tk regt, 1 mech inf regt, 2 inf regt, 1 hel sqn, 1 SP arty regt, 1 AT coy, 1 ADA bn, 1 cbt engr bn, 1 sigs bn, 1 NBC bn, 1 log regt)
  1 (4th) inf div (1 armd recce bn, 3 inf regt, 1 inf coy, 1 hel sqn, 1 AT coy, 1 SAM bn, 1 cbt engr bn, 1 sigs bn, 1 NBC bn, 1 log regt)

1 (6th) inf div (1 recce sqn, 1 mech inf regt; 3 inf regt, 1 hel sqn, 1 SAM bn, 1 cbt engr bn, 1 sigs bn, 1 NBC bn, 1 log regt)
1 (9th) inf div (1 armd recce sqn, 1 tk bn, 3 inf regt, 1 hel sqn, 1 SAM bn, 1 cbt engr bn, 1 sigs bn, 1 NBC bn, 1 log regt)
1 (5th) inf bde (1 armd recce sqn, 1 tk bn, 3 inf regt, 1 hel sqn, 1 SP arty bn, 1 SAM coy, 1 cbt engr coy, 1 sigs coy, 1 NBC coy, 1 log bn)
1 (11th) inf bde (1 armd recce sqn, 1 tk sqn, 3 inf regt, 1 hel sqn, 1 SP arty bn, 1 SAM coy, 1 cbt engr coy, 1 sigs coy, 1 NBC coy, 1 log bn)
Light
1 (1st) inf div (1 armd recce bn, 3 inf regt, 1 hel sqn, 1 fd arty bn, 1 SAM bn, 1 cbt engr bn, 1 sigs bn, 1 NBC bn, 1 log regt)
1 (3rd) inf div (1 recce sqn, 1 tk bn, 3 inf regt, 1 hel sqn, 1 fd arty bn, 1 SAM bn, 1 cbt engr bn, 1 sigs bn, 1 NBC bn, 1 log regt)
1 (10th) inf div (1 recce sqn, 1 tk bn, 3 inf regt, 1 hel sqn, 1 fd arty regt, 1 SAM bn, 1 cbt engr bn, 1 sigs bn, 1 NBC bn, 1 log regt)
1 (8th) inf div (1 recce sqn, 3 inf regt, 1 hel sqn, 1 SAM bn, 1 cbt engr bn, 1 sigs bn, 1 NBC bn, 1 log regt)
1 (13th) inf bde (1 recce sqn, 1 tk coy, 3 inf regt, 1 hel sqn, 1 fd arty bn, 1 SAM coy, 1 cbt engr coy, 1 NBC coy, 1 sigs coy, 1 log bn)
1 (14th) inf bde (1 recce sqn, 2 inf regt, 1 hel sqn, 1 SAM coy, 1 cbt engr coy, 1 NBC coy, 1 sigs coy, 1 log bn)
1 (15th) inf bde (1 recce sqn, 1 inf regt, 1 avn sqn, 1 AD regt, 1 cbt engr coy, 1 NBC coy, 1 sigs coy, 1 log bn)
Air Manoeuvre
1 (1st) AB bde (3 AB bn, 1 fd arty bn, 1 cbt engr coy, 1 sigs coy, 1 log bn)
1 (12th) air mob inf bde (1 recce sqn, 3 inf regt, 1 avn sqn, 1 fd arty bn, 1 SAM coy, 1 cbt engr coy, 1 NBC coy, 1 sigs coy, 1 log bn)
Amphibious
1 amph bde (1 recce coy, 2 amph regt, 1 amph aslt bn, 1 log bn)
COMBAT SUPPORT
1 (1st) arty bde (1 SP arty regt (2 SP arty bn, 1 MRL bn); 1 SP arty regt (1 SP arty bn, 1 MRL bn); 3 AShM regt)
1 (Northwestern Army) arty bde (1 fd arty regt (4 fd arty bn); 1 AShM regt)
1 (Western Army) arty bde (1 fd arty regt (4 fd arty bn); 1 MRL bn; 1 AShM regt)
1 (Central Army) fd arty bn
4 engr bde
1 engr unit
1 EW bn
5 int bn
1 MP bde
1 sigs bde
COMBAT SERVICE SUPPORT
5 log unit (bde)
5 trg bde
HELICOPTER
2 sqn with MV-22B *Osprey* (forming)

Asia 259

HELICOPTER
1 hel bde (5 tpt hel sqn; 1 VIP tpt hel bn)
5 hel gp (1 atk hel bn, 1 hel bn)

AIR DEFENCE
2 SAM bde (2 SAM gp)
2 SAM gp

EQUIPMENT BY TYPE
ARMOURED FIGHTING VEHICLES
MBT 555: 105 Type-10; 130 Type-74; 320 Type-90
ASLT 141 Type-16 MCV
RECCE 111 Type-87
IFV 68 Type-89
APC 804
  APC (T) 226 Type-73
  APC (W) 578: 197 Type-82 (CP); 381 Type-96
AAV 52 AAV-7
AUV 8 *Bushmaster*

ENGINEERING & MAINTENANCE VEHICLES
ARV 63: 5 Type-11; 28 Type-78; 30 Type-90
VLB 22 Type-91
NBC VEHICLES 55: 34 Chemical Reconnaissance Vehicle; 21 NBC Reconnaissance Vehicle

ANTI-TANK/ANTI-INFRASTRUCTURE
MSL
  SP 37 Type-96 MPMS
  MANPATS Type-79 *Jyu*-MAT; Type-87 *Chu*-MAT; Type-01 LMAT
RCL • 84mm *Carl Gustaf*
ARTILLERY 1,593
  SP 167: **155mm** 136 Type-99; **203mm** 31 M110A2
  TOWED 155mm 229 FH-70
  MRL 227mm 54 M270 MLRS
  MOR 1,143: **81mm** 656 L16 **120mm** 463 RT-61; **SP 120mm** 24 Type-96
COASTAL DEFENCE • AShM 92: 30 Type-12; 62 Type-88
AIRCRAFT • TPT • Light 8 Beech 350 *King Air* (LR-2)
TILTROTOR • TPT 7+ MV-22B *Osprey*
HELICOPTERS
ATK 99: 50 AH-1S *Cobra*; 12 AH-64D *Apache*; 37 OH-1
TPT 249: **Heavy** 53: 18 CH-47D *Chinook* (CH-47J); 35 CH-47JA *Chinook*; **Medium** 43: 3 H225 *Super Puma* MkII+ (VIP); 40 UH-60L *Black Hawk* (UH-60JA); **Light** 153: 123 Bell 205 (UH-1J); 30 Enstrom 480B (TH-480B)
AIR DEFENCE
SAM 311+
  Medium-range 130: 48 Type-03 *Chu*-SAM; 4 Type-03 *Chu*-SAM Kai; 78 MIM-23B I-*Hawk*
  Short-range ε44 Type-11 *Tan*-SAM
  Point-defence 137+: 46 Type-81 *Tan*-SAM; 91 Type-93 *Kin*-SAM; Type-91 *Kei*-SAM
GUNS • SP 35mm 52 Type-87

Maritime Self-Defense Force 45,300

Surface units organised into 4 Escort Flotillas with a mix of 8 warships each. Bases at Yokosuka, Kure, Sasebo, Maizuru, Ominato. SSK organised into two flotillas with bases at Kure and Yokosuka

EQUIPMENT BY TYPE
SUBMARINES • SSK 24:
11 *Oyashio* (of which 2 in trg role) with 6 single 533mm TT with UGM-84C *Harpoon* Block 1B AShM/Type-89 HWT
12 *Soryu* (of which 9 fitted with AIP and 2 fitted with lithium-ion fuel battery) with 6 single 533mm TT with UGM-84C *Harpoon* Block 1B AShM/Type-89 HWT
1 *Taigei* with (fitted with lithium-ion fuel battery) with 6 single 533mm TT with UGM-84C *Harpoon* Block 1B AShM/Type-89 HWT/Type-18 HWT
PRINCIPAL SURFACE COMBATANTS 50
AIRCRAFT CARRIERS • CVH 4:
2 *Hyuga* with 2 8-cell Mk 41 VLS with ASROC/RIM-162B ESSM SAM, 2 triple 324mm HOS-303 ASTT with Mk 46/Type-97 LWT, 2 Mk 15 *Phalanx* Block 1B CIWS (normal ac capacity 3 SH-60 *Seahawk* ASW hel; plus additional ac embarkation up to 7 SH-60 *Seahawk* or 7 MCH-101)
2 *Izumo* (being converted to CVS) with 2 11-cell Mk 15 SeaRAM lnchr with RIM-116 SAM, 2 Mk 15 *Phalanx* Block 1B CIWS (normal ac capacity 7 SH-60 *Seahawk* ASW hel; plus additional ac embarkation up to 5 SH-60 *Seahawk*/MCH-101 hel)
CRUISERS • CGHM 4:
2 *Atago* with *Aegis* Baseline 9 C2, 2 quad lnchr with SSM-1B (Type-90) AShM, 12 8-cell Mk 41 VLS (8 fore, 4 aft) with SM-2 Block IIIA/B SAM/SM-3 Block IA/IB SAM/ASROC A/S msl, 2 triple 324mm HOS-302 ASTT with Mk 46 LWT, 2 Mk 15 *Phalanx* Block 1B CIWS, 1 127mm gun (capacity 1 SH-60 *Seahawk* ASW hel)
2 *Maya* (*Atago* mod) with *Aegis* Baseline 9 C2, w quad lnchr with SSM-1B (Type-90) AShM/SSM-2 (Type-17) AShM, 12 8-cell Mk 41 VLS (8 fore, 4 aft) with SM-2 Block IIIA/B SAM/SM-3 Block IA/IB SAM/Type-07 A/S msl, 2 triple 324mm HOS-303 ASTT with Mk 46 LWT, 2 Mk 15 *Phalanx* Block 1B CIWS, 1 127mm gun (capacity 1 SH-60 *Seahawk* ASW hel)
DESTROYERS 34
DDGHM 28:
8 *Asagiri* with 2 quad lnchr with RGM-84C *Harpoon* Block 1B AShM, 1 octuple Mk 29 lnchr with RIM-7M *Sea Sparrow* SAM, 2 triple 324mm HOS-302 ASTT with Mk 46 LWT, 1 octuple Mk 112 lnchr with ASROC, 2 Mk 15 *Phalanx* CIWS, 1 76mm gun (capacity 1 SH-60 *Seahawk* ASW hel)
4 *Akizuki* with 2 quad lnchr with SSM-1B (Type-90) AShM, 4 8-cell Mk 41 VLS with ASROC/RIM-162B ESSM SAM, 2 triple 324mm HOS-303 ASTT with Type-97 LWT, 2 Mk 15 *Phalanx* Block 1B CIWS, 1 127mm gun (capacity 1 SH-60 *Seahawk* ASW hel)
2 *Asahi* (*Akizuki* mod) with 2 quad lnchr with SSM-1B (Type-90) AShM, 4 8-cell Mk 41 VLS with RIM-162B ESSM SAM/Type-07 A/S msl, 2 triple 324mm HOS-303 ASTT with Type-12 LWT, 2 Mk 15 *Phalanx* Block 1B CIWS, 1 127mm gun (capacity 1 SH-60 *Seahawk* ASW hel)
9 *Murasame* with 2 quad lnchr with SSM-1B (Type-90) AShM, 1 16-cell Mk 48 mod 0 VLS with RIM-162C ESSM SAM, 2 triple 324mm HOS-302 ASTT

with Mk 46 LWT, 2 8-cell Mk 41 VLS with ASROC, 2 Mk 15 *Phalanx* CIWS, 2 76mm gun (capacity 1 SH-60 *Seahawk* ASW hel)

5 *Takanami* (improved *Murasame*) with 2 quad lnchr with SSM-1B (Type-90) AShM, 4 8-cell Mk 41 VLS with RIM-162B ESSM SAM/ASROC A/S msl, 2 triple 324mm HOS-302 ASTT with Mk 46 LWT, 2 Mk 15 *Phalanx* Block 1B CIWS, 1 127mm gun (capacity 1 SH-60 *Seahawk* ASW hel)

DDGM 6:

2 *Hatakaze* (trg role) with 2 quad lnchr with RGM-84C *Harpoon* Block 1B AShM, 1 Mk 13 GMLS with SM-1MR Block VI SAM, 2 triple 324mm HOS-301 ASTT with Mk 46 LWT, 1 octuple Mk 112 lnchr with ASROC, 2 Mk 15 *Phalanx* CIWS, 2 127mm gun, 1 hel landing platform

4 *Kongou* with *Aegis* Baseline 5 C2, 2 quad lnchr with RGM-84C *Harpoon* Block 1B AShM, 12 8-cell Mk 41 VLS (of which 2 only 5-cell and fitted with reload crane) with SM-2 Block IIIA/B SAM/SM-3 Block IA SAM/ASROC A/S msl, 2 triple 324mm HOS-302 ASTT with Mk 46 LWT, 2 Mk 15 *Phalanx* Block 1B CIWS, 1 127mm gun

FRIGATES 8

FFGHM 2 *Mogami* with 2 quad lnchr with SSM-2 (Type-17) AShM, 1 11-cell Mk 15 SeaRAM GMLS with RIM-116 RAM SAM, 2 triple 324mm HOS-303 ASTT with Mk 46 LWT, 1 127mm gun (capacity 1 SH-60 *Seahawk* hel) (to be fitted with Mk 41 VLS)

FFG 6 *Abukuma* with 2 quad lnchr with RGM-84C *Harpoon* Block 1B AShM, 2 triple 324mm HOS-301 ASTT with Mk 46 LWT, 1 octuple Mk 112 lnchr with ASROC A/S msl, 1 Mk 15 *Phalanx* CIWS, 1 76mm gun

PATROL AND COASTAL COMBATANTS 6

PBFG 6 *Hayabusa* with 4 SSM-1B (Type-90) AShM, 1 76mm gun

MINE WARFARE • MINE COUNTERMEASURES 22

MCCS 2:

1 *Uraga* with 1 76mm gun, 1 hel landing platform (for MCH-101 hel)

1 *Uraga* with 1 hel landing platform (for MCH-101)

MSC 17: 3 *Hirashima*; 11 *Sugashima*; 3 *Enoshima*

MSO 3 *Awaji*

AMPHIBIOUS

PRINCIPAL AMPHIBIOUS SHIPS • LHD 3 *Osumi* with 2 Mk 15 *Phalanx* CIWS (capacity for 2 CH-47 hel) (capacity 10 Type-90 MBT; 2 LCAC(L) ACV; 330 troops)

LANDING CRAFT 8

LCM 2 LCU-2001

LCAC 6 LCAC(L) (capacity either 1 MBT or 60 troops)

LOGISTICS AND SUPPORT 24

AGBH 1 *Shirase* (capacity 2 AW101 *Merlin* hel)

AGEH 1 *Asuka* (wpn trials) with 1 8-cell Mk 41 VLS (capacity 1 SH-60 *Seahawk* hel)

AGOS 3 *Hibiki* with 1 hel landing platform

AGS 3: 1 *Futami*; 1 *Nichinan*; 1 *Shonan*

AOE 5: 2 *Mashu* (capacity 1 med hel); 3 *Towada* with 1 hel landing platform

ARC 1 *Muroto*

ASR 2: 1 *Chihaya* with 1 hel landing platform; 1 Chiyoda with 1 hel landing platform

ATF 5 *Hiuchi*

AX 3:

1 *Kashima* with 2 triple 324mm HOS-301 ASTT, 1 76mm gun, 1 hel landing platform

1 *Kurobe* with 1 76mm gun (trg spt ship)

1 *Tenryu* (trg spt ship); with 1 76mm gun (capacity: 1 med hel)

Naval Aviation ε9,800

7 Air Groups

FORCES BY ROLE

ANTI SUBMARINE/SURFACE WARFARE

5 sqn with SH-60B (SH-60J)/SH-60K *Seahawk*

MARITIME PATROL

2 sqn with P-1

2 sqn with P-3C *Orion*

ELECTRONIC WARFARE

1 sqn with EP-3 *Orion*

MINE COUNTERMEASURES

1 sqn with MCH-101

SEARCH & RESCUE

1 sqn with *Shin Meiwa* US-2

2 sqn with UH-60J *Black Hawk*

TRANSPORT

1 sqn with AW101 *Merlin* (CH-101); Beech 90 *King Air* (LC-90); KC-130R *Hercules*

TRAINING

1 sqn with Beech 90 *King Air* (TC-90)

1 sqn with P-3C *Orion*

1 sqn with T-5J

1 hel sqn with H135 (TH-135); SH-60K *Seahawk*

EQUIPMENT BY TYPE

AIRCRAFT 77 combat capable

ASW 77: 33 P-1; 44 P-3C *Orion*

ELINT 5 EP-3C *Orion*

SAR 6 *Shin Meiwa* US-2

TPT 24: **Medium** 6 C-130R *Hercules*; **Light** 18: 5 Beech 90 *King Air* (LC-90); 13 Beech 90 *King Air* (TC-90) (trg)

TRG 30 T-5J

HELICOPTERS

ASW 87: 12 SH-60B *Seahawk* (SH-60J); 75 SH-60K *Seahawk*

MCM 10 MCH-101

SAR 6 UH-60J *Black Hawk*

TPT 18: **Medium** 3 AW101 *Merlin* (CH-101); **Light** 15 H135 (TH-135) (trg)

AIR-LAUNCHED MISSILES

AShM ASM-1C (Type-90)

Air Self-Defense Force 46,950

7 cbt wg

FORCES BY ROLE

FIGHTER

7 sqn with F-15J *Eagle*

3 sqn with Mitsubishi F-2

2 sqn with F-35A *Lightning* II

ELECTRONIC WARFARE

1 sqn with Kawasaki EC-1; YS-11EA

ELINT

1 sqn with RC-2; YS-11EB

AIRBORNE EARLY WARNING & CONTROL
2 sqn with E-2C/D *Hawkeye*
1 sqn with E-767
SEARCH & RESCUE
1 wg with U-125A *Peace Krypton*; UH-60J *Black Hawk*
TANKER
1 sqn with KC-46A *Pegasus* (forming)
1 sqn with KC-767J
TRANSPORT
1 (VIP) sqn with B-777-300ER
1 sqn with C-1; C-2; Gulfstream IV (U-4)
1 sqn with C-2
1 sqn with C-130H *Hercules*; KC-130H *Hercules*
Some (liaison) sqn with Gulfstream IV (U-4); T-4*
TRAINING
1 (aggressor) sqn with F-15J *Eagle*
TEST
1 wg with F-15J *Eagle*; T-4*
TRANSPORT HELICOPTER
4 flt with CH-47JA *Chinook*

EQUIPMENT BY TYPE
AIRCRAFT 519 combat capable
  FTR 200: 156 F-15J *Eagle*; 44 F-15DJ *Eagle*
  FGA 122: 64 F-2A; 27 F-2B; 31 F-35A *Lightning* II
  EW 3: 1 Kawasaki EC-1; 2 YS-11EA
  SIGINT 4: 1 RC-2; 3 YS-11EB
  AEW&C 20: 10 E-2C *Hawkeye*; 6 E-2D *Hawkeye*; 4 E-767
  SAR 26 U-125A *Peace Krypton*
  TKR/TPT 8: 2 KC-46A *Pegasus*; 2 KC-130H *Hercules*; 4 KC-767J
  TPT 54: **Medium** 34: 13 C-130H *Hercules*; 7 C-1; 14 C-2; **PAX** 20: 2 B-777-300ER (VIP); 13 Beech T-400; 5 Gulfstream IV (U-4)
  TRG 246: 197 T-4*; 49 T-7
HELICOPTERS
  SAR 37 UH-60J *Black Hawk*
  TPT • Heavy 15 CH-47JA *Chinook*
UNINHABITED AERIAL VEHICLES 1
  ISR • Heavy 1 RQ-4B *Global Hawk*
AIR-LAUNCHED MISSILES
  AAM • IR AAM-3 (Type-90); **IIR** AAM-5 (Type-04); **SARH** AIM-7 *Sparrow*; **ARH** AAM-4 (Type-99); AIM-120C5/C7 AMRAAM (limited numbers)
  AShM ASM-1 (Type-80); ASM-2 (Type-93)
BOMBS
  Laser & INS/SAT-guided GBU-54 Laser JDAM
  INS/SAT-guided GBU-38 JDAM

Air Defence
Ac control and warning. 4 wg; 28 radar sites

FORCES BY ROLE
AIR DEFENCE
  6 SAM gp (total: 24 SAM bty with M902 *Patriot* PAC-3)
  1 AD gp with Type-81 *Tan-SAM*; M167 *Vulcan*

EQUIPMENT BY TYPE
AIR DEFENCE
  SAM 146+
    Long-range 120 M902 *Patriot* PAC-3
    Short-range ε26 Air Base Defense SAM
    Point-defence Type-81 *Tan-SAM*
  GUNS • TOWED 20mm M167 *Vulcan*

Gendarmerie & Paramilitary 14,550

Coast Guard 14,550
Ministry of Land, Transport, Infrastructure and Tourism (no cbt role)

EQUIPMENT BY TYPE
PATROL AND COASTAL COMBATANTS 378
  PSOH 19: 2 *Mizuho* (capacity 2 hels); 1 *Mizuho* II (capacity 2 hels); 5 *Shikishima* (capacity 2 hels); 1 *Shunko* (capacity 2 hels); 1 *Soya* (capacity 1 hel) (icebreaking capability); 9 *Tsugaru* (*Soya* mod) (capacity 1 hel)
  PSO 48: 9 *Hateruma* with 1 hel landing platform; 3 *Hida* with 1 hel landing platform; 6 *Iwami*; 1 *Izu* with 1 hel landing platform; 1 *Kojima* (trg) with 1 hel landing platform; 1 *Miura* with 1 hel landing platform (trg role); 2 *Miyako* with 1 hel landing platform; 5 *Ojika* with 1 hel landing platform; 20 *Taketomi* with 1 hel landing platform
  PCO 13: 3 *Aso*; 9 *Katori*; 1 *Teshio*
  PCC 24: 4 *Amami*; 20 *Tokara*
  PBF 49: 24 *Hayagumo*; 2 *Mihashi*; 15 *Raizan*; 2 *Takatsuki*; 6 *Tsuruugi*
  PB 55: 4 *Asogiri*; 4 *Hamagumo*; 11 *Hayanami*; 15 *Katonami*; 1 *Matsunami*; 10 *Shimoji*; 10 *Yodo*
  PBI 170: 2 *Hakubai*; 1 *Hayagiku*; 167 *Himegiku*
LOGISTICS AND SUPPORT 18
  ABU 1 *Teshio*
  AGS 14: 6 *Hamashio*; 1 *Jinbei*; 2 *Meiyo*; 2 *Peiyo*; 1 *Shoyo*; 1 *Takuyo*; 1 *Tenyo*
  AX 3
AIRCRAFT
  MP 5 *Falcon* 2000MSA
  SAR 4 Saab 340B
  TPT 27: **Light** 25: 5 Cessna 172; 10 Beech 350 *King Air* (LR-2); 10 DHC *Dash-7* (Bombardier 300) (MP); **PAX** 2 Gulfstream V (MP)
HELICOPTERS
  MRH 4 Bell 412 *Twin Huey*
  SAR 12 S-76D
  TPT 39: **Medium** 13: 2 AS332 *Super Puma*; 11 H225 *Super Puma*; **Light** 26: 19 AW139; 4 Bell 505 *Jet Ranger* X; 3 S-76C
UNINHABITED AERIAL VEHICLES 1
  CISR • Heavy 1 MQ-9B *SeaGuardian* (unarmed)

DEPLOYMENT

ARABIAN SEA & GULF OF ADEN: Combined Maritime Forces • CTF-151: 160; 1 DDGHM

DJIBOUTI: 180; 2 P-3C *Orion*

SOUTH SUDAN: UN • UNMISS 4

FOREIGN FORCES

United States
US Pacific Command: 55,600
  Army 2,600; 1 corps HQ (fwd); 1 SF gp; 1 avn bn; 1 SAM bn with M903 *Patriot* PAC MSE
  Navy 20,000; 1 CVN; 3 CGHM; 4 DDGHM; 4 DDGM; 1 LCC; 4 MCO; 1 LHA; 2 LPD; 2 LSD; 3 FGA sqn with 10 F/A-18E *Super Hornet*; 1 FGA sqn with 10 F/A-18F *Super*

Hornet; 2 ASW sqn with 5 P-8A *Poseidon*; 1 ELINT flt with 2 EP-3E *Aries* II; 2 EW sqn with 5 EA-18G *Growler*; 1 AEW&C sqn with 5 E-2D *Hawkeye*; 2 ASW hel sqn with 12 MH-60R *Seahawk*; 1 tpt hel sqn with MH-60S *Knight Hawk*; 1 base at Sasebo; 1 base at Yokosuka

USAF: 13,000; 1 HQ (5th Air Force) at Okinawa–Kadena AB; 1 ftr wg at Misawa AB (2 ftr sqn with 22 F-16C/D *Fighting Falcon*); 1 ftr wg at Okinawa–Kadena AB (2 ftr sqn with 27 F-15C/D *Eagle*; 1 tkr sqn with 15 KC-135R *Stratotanker*; 1 AEW sqn with 2 E-3B *Sentry*; 1 CSAR sqn with 10 HH-60G *Pave Hawk*); 1 tpt wg at Yokota AB with 10 C-130J-30 *Hercules*; 3 Beech 1900C (C-12J); 1 spec ops gp at Okinawa–Kadena AB with (1 sqn with 5 MC-130J *Commando* II; 1 sqn with 5 CV-22B *Osprey*); 1 ISR sqn with RC-135 *Rivet Joint*; 1 ISR UAV flt with 5 RQ-4A *Global Hawk*

USMC 20,000; 1 mne div; 1 mne regt HQ; 1 arty regt HQ; 1 recce bn; 1 mne bn; 1 amph aslt bn; 1 arty bn; 1 FGA sqn at Iwakuni with 12 F/A-18A++/C+ *Hornet*; 2 FGA sqn at Iwakuni with 12 F-35B *Lightning* II; 1 tkr sqn at Iwakuni with 15 KC-130J *Hercules*; 2 tpt sqn at Futenma with 12 MV-22B *Osprey*

US Strategic Command: 1 AN/TPY-2 X-band radar at Shariki; 1 AN/TPY-2 X-band radar at Kyogamisaki

Korea, Democratic People's Republic of DPRK

North Korean Won KPW		2021	2022	2023
GDP	USD			
per capita	USD			
Def exp	KPW			
	USD			
USD1=KPW				

Definitive economic data not available

Population	25,955,138

Age	0–14	15–19	20–24	25–29	30–64	65 plus
Male	10.4%	3.5%	3.7%	3.9%	23.6%	3.6%
Female	9.9%	3.4%	3.6%	3.9%	24.0%	6.6%

Capabilities

Tensions on the Korean Peninsula rose in 2022, after diplomacy since 2018 had reduced overall tensions. North Korea's observed actions remain inconsistent with de-nuclearisation. 2022 saw Pyongyang conduct more ballistic missile tests than any other year on record. These included a resumption in flight tests of ICBM categorised systems and a separate IRBM overflight of Japan; these had not occurred since 2017. There remains scrutiny of North Korea's nuclear facilities, with increased concerns that the country may renew nuclear testing. Aware of the qualitative inferiority of its conventional forces, North Korea continues to invest in asymmetric capabilities, particularly the development of nuclear weapons and ballistic missile delivery systems. Pyongyang's ambitions to further diversify its shorter-range delivery systems continue. These include quasi-ballistic missiles, claimed hypersonic glide vehicles and apparent land-attack cruise missiles. North Korea is also exploring new, potentially less vulnerable basing options, such as a rail-based system and additional SLBM designs. In October there

was a reported incursion by a North Korean merchant vessel across the Northern Limit Line, and in November a North Korean missile crossed the NLL. North Korea remains diplomatically isolated. While foreign defence cooperation is restricted by international pressure and sanctions, Pyongyang has nonetheless often found ways to develop military ties. Official conscription for both men and women is often extended, sometimes indefinitely. Training is focused on fighting a short, intensive war on the peninsula, but the armed forces' overall effectiveness in a modern conflict against technologically superior opposition is unclear. Internal exercises are conducted regularly, but those publicised are staged and are not necessarily representative of wider operational capability. In May 2022 North Korea announced it had mobilised the armed forces to supply medicines, in response to the country's first acknowledged outbreak of COVID-19. North Korea's conventional forces remain reliant on increasingly obsolete equipment, with older Soviet-era and Chinese-origin equipment supplemented by a growing number of indigenous designs and upgrades, though the precise capability of these remains unclear. The overall effectiveness and serviceability of some equipment remains in doubt but there is local maintenance, repair and overhaul capacity. Local defence-industrial capacity includes the manufacture of light arms, armoured vehicles, artillery and missile systems. North Korea has exported weaponry in the past. In September 2022 Pyongyang denied any plans to supply Russia with ammunition, following US reporting that this had been requested. It is unclear whether the country would have had the capability to indigenously develop some of the technical advances it has demonstrated, including in rocket propulsion.

ACTIVE 1,280,000 (Army 1,100,000 Navy 60,000 Air 110,000 Strategic Forces 10,000) Gendarmerie & Paramilitary 189,000

Conscript liability Army 5–12 years, Navy 5–10 years, Air Force 3–4 years, followed by compulsory part-time service to age 40. Thereafter service in the Worker/Peasant Red Guard to age 60

RESERVE ε600,000 (Armed Forces ε600,000), Gendarmerie & Paramilitary 5,700,000

Reservists are assigned to units (see also Paramilitary)

ORGANISATIONS BY SERVICE

Strategic Forces ε10,000

North Korea describes its ballistic missile force as nuclear capable, although there is no conclusive evidence to verify the successful integration of a warhead with any of these systems

EQUIPMENT BY TYPE (ε)
SURFACE-TO-SURFACE MISSILE LAUNCHERS
ICBM 10+: 6+ *Hwasong*-14/-15/-15 mod 1 (all in test); 4+ *Hwasong*-17 mod 1 (in test); (Earlier *Hwasong*-13/-13 mod designs untested and presumed cancelled)
IRBM 10+ *Hwasong*-10 (*Musudan*) (status uncertain)/ *Hwasong*-12/-12 mod 1 (in test)
MRBM 17+: ε10 *Nodong* mod 1/mod 2 (ε90+ msl); some *Scud*-ER; 7+ *Pukgusong*-2 (in test)
SBRM 69+: 30+ *Hwasong*-5/-6 (RS-SS-1C/D *Scud*-B/C) (ε200+ msl); 1+ *Hwasong*-8/-8 mod 1 (in test); 9+ *Hwasong*-11 mod (in test); 6+ *Scud* (mod) (in test); 17+ KN-23 (road & rail mobile variants); 6+ KN-23 mod 1 (in test); some KN-23 mod 2 (in test)
GLCM some M-2021 (in test); some M-2021-2 (in test)

Army ε1,100,000

FORCES BY ROLE
COMMAND
10 inf corps HQ
1 (Capital Defence) corps HQ
MANOEUVRE
Armoured
1 armd div
15 armd bde
Mechanised
6 mech div
Light
27 inf div
14 inf bde
COMBAT SUPPORT
1 arty div
21 arty bde
9 MRL bde
5–8 engr river crossing/amphibious regt
1 engr river crossing bde

Special Purpose Forces Command 88,000

FORCES BY ROLE
SPECIAL FORCES
8 (Reconnaissance General Bureau) SF bn
MANOEUVRE
Reconnaissance
17 recce bn
Light
9 lt inf bde
6 sniper bde
Air Manoeuvre
3 AB bde
1 AB bn
2 sniper bde
Amphibious
2 sniper bde

Reserves 600,000

FORCES BY ROLE
MANOEUVRE
Light
40 inf div
18 inf bde

EQUIPMENT BY TYPE (ε)
ARMOURED FIGHTING VEHICLES
The Korean People's Army displayed a number of new armoured-vehicle designs at a parade in 2020, but it is unclear if any of them have entered operational service
MBT 3,500+ T-34/T-54/T-55/T-62/Type-59/*Chonma/Pokpoong/Songun*
LT TK 560+: 560 PT-76; M-1985
IFV 32 BTR-80A
APC 2,500+
  APC (T) BTR-50; Type-531 (Type-63); VTT-323
  APC (W) 2,500 BTR-40/BTR-60/M-1992/1/BTR-152/M-2010 (6×6)/M-2010 (8×8)
ANTI-TANK/ANTI-INFRASTRUCTURE
MSL
  SP 9K11 *Malyutka* (RS-AT-3 *Sagger*); M-2010 ATGM

  MANPATS 2K15 *Shmel* (RS-AT-1 *Snapper*); 9K111 *Fagot* (RS-AT-4 *Spigot*); 9K111-1 *Konkurs* (RS-AT-5 *Spandrel*)
  RCL 82mm 1,700 B-10
ARTILLERY 21,600+
  SP/TOWED 8,600:
  SP 122mm M-1977; M-1981; M-1985; M-1991; **130mm** M-1975; M-1981; M-1991; **152mm** M-1974; M-1977; M-2018; **170mm** M-1978; M-1989
  TOWED 122mm D-30; D-74; M-1931/37; **130mm** M-46; **152mm** M-1937; M-1938; M-1943
  GUN/MOR 120mm (reported)
  MRL 5,500: **107mm** Type-63; VTT-323 107mm; **122mm** BM-11; M-1977 (BM-21); M-1985; M-1992; M-1993; VTT-323 122mm; **200mm** BMD-20; **240mm** BM-24; M-1985; M-1989; M-1991; **300mm** some M-2015 (KN-SS-X-09) (in test); **600mm** some M-2019 (in test)
  MOR 7,500: **82mm** M-37; **120mm** M-43; **160mm** M-43
SURFACE-TO-SURFACE MISSILE LAUNCHERS
  SBRM 24+: 24 FROG-3/5/7; some *Toksa* (RS-SS-21B *Scarab* mod); some M-2022 (in test)
AIR DEFENCE
  SAM
    Point-defence 9K35 *Strela*-10 (RS-SA-13 *Gopher*); 9K310 *Igla*-1 (RS-SA-16 *Gimlet*); 9K32 *Strela*-2 (RS-SA-7 *Grail*)‡
  GUNS 11,000+
    SP 14.5mm M-1984; **23mm** M-1992; **37mm** M-1992; **57mm** M-1985
    TOWED 11,000: **14.5mm** ZPU-1/ZPU-2/ZPU-4; **23mm** ZU-23; **37mm** M-1939; **57mm** S-60; **85mm** M-1939 *KS-12*; **100mm** KS-19

Navy ε60,000

EQUIPMENT BY TYPE
SUBMARINES 71
  SSB 1 *8.24 Yongung* (*Gorae* (*Sinpo*-B)) (SLBM trials) with 1 *Pukguksong*-1 SLBM (status unclear)/KN-23 Mod 2 SLBM (in test)
  SSK ε20 Type-033 (*Romeo*) with 8 single 533mm TT with SAET-60 HWT
  SSC ε40 (some *Sang-O* some with 2 single 533mm TT with 53–65E HWT; some *Sang-O* II with 4 single 533mm TT with 53–65E HWT)
  SSW ε10† (some *Yugo* some with 2 single 406mm TT; some *Yeono* some with 2 single 533mm TT)
PRINCIPAL SURFACE COMBATANTS 2
  FRIGATES • FFG 2:
    1 *Najin* with 2 single lnchr with P-20 (RS-SS-N-2A *Styx*) AShM, 2 RBU 1200 *Uragan* A/S mor, 2 100mm gun, 2 twin 57mm gun
    1 *Najin* with 2 twin lnchr with *Kumsong*-3 (KN-SS-N-2 *Stormpetrel*) AShM, 2 RBU 1200 *Uragan* A/S mor, 2 100mm gun, 2 twin 57mm gun (operational status unclear)
PATROL AND COASTAL COMBATANTS 372+
  CORVETTES • FS 5: 4 *Sariwon* with 2 twin 57mm gun; 1 *Tral* with 1 85mm gun (Two *Tuman*- and two *Amnok*-class corvettes constructed since early 2010s; operational status unknown)
  PCG 10 *Soju* (FSU Project 205 mod (*Osa*)) with 4 single lnchr with P-20 (RS-SS-N-2A *Styx*) AShM

264 THE MILITARY BALANCE 2023

PCC 18:

6 Type-037 (*Hainan*) with 4 RBU 1200 A/S mor, 2 twin 57mm gun

7 *Taechong* I with 2 RBU 1200 *Uragan* A/S mor, 1 85mm gun, 1 twin 57mm gun

5 *Taechong* II with 2 RBU 1200 *Uragan* A/S mor, 1 100mm gun, 1 twin 57mm gun

PBFG 31+:

4 *Huangfeng* (Type-021) with 4 single lnchr with P-15 *Termit* (RS-SS-N-2 *Styx*) AShM, 2 twin AK230 CIWS

6 *Komar* with 2 single lnchr with P-20 (RS-SS-N-2A *Styx*) AShM

8 Project 205 (*Osa* I) with 4 single lnchr with P-20 (RS-SS-N-2A *Styx*) AShM, 2 twin AK230 CIWS

6 *Sohung* (*Komar* mod) with 2 single lnchr with P-20 (RS-SS-N-2A *Styx*) AShM

1+ *Nongo* with 2 single lnchr with P-15 *Termit* (RS-SS-N-2 *Styx*) AShM (operational status unknown)

6+ *Nongo* with 2 twin lnchr with *Kumsong*-3 (KN-SS-N-2 *Stormpetrel*) AShM (operational status unknown)

PBF 222: approx. 50 *Chong-Jin* with 1 85mm gun; 142 *Ku Song/Sin Hung/Sin Hung* (mod); approx. 30 *Sinpo*

PB 86: approx. 50 *Chaho*; 6 *Chong-Ju* with 2 RBU 1200 *Uragan* A/S mor, 1 85mm gun; 12 Type-062 (*Shanghai* II); 18 SO-1 with 4 RBU 1200 *Uragan* A/S mor, 2 twin 57mm gun

MINE WARFARE • MINE COUNTERMEASURES 20

MSC 20: 15 *Yukto* I; 5 *Yukto* II

AMPHIBIOUS

LANDING SHIPS • LSM 10 *Hantae* (capacity 3 tanks; 350 troops)

LANDING CRAFT 255

LCM 25

LCPL approx. 95 *Nampo* (capacity 35 troops)

UCAC 135 *Kongbang* (capacity 50 troops)

LOGISTICS AND SUPPORT 23:

AGI 14 (converted fishing vessels)

AS 8 (converted cargo ships)

ASR 1 *Kowan*

Coastal Defence

FORCES BY ROLE

COASTAL DEFENCE

2 AShM regt with HY-1/*Kumsong*-3 (6 sites, some mobile launchers)

EQUIPMENT BY TYPE

COASTAL DEFENCE

ARTY 130mm M-1992; SM-4-1

AShM HY-1; *Kumsong*-3

ARTILLERY • TOWED 122mm M-1931/37; **152mm** M-1937

Air Force 110,000

4 air divs. 1st, 2nd and 3rd Air Divs (cbt) responsible for N, E and S air-defence sectors respectively; 8th Air Div (trg) responsible for NE sector. The AF controls the national airline

FORCES BY ROLE

BOMBER

3 lt regt with H-5; Il-28 *Beagle*

FIGHTER

1 regt with MiG-15 *Fagot*

6 regt with J-5; MiG-17 *Fresco*

4 regt with J-6; MiG-19 *Farmer*

5 regt with J-7; MiG-21F-13/PFM *Fishbed*

1 regt with MiG-21bis *Fishbed*

1 regt with MiG-23ML/P *Flogger*

1 regt with MiG-29A/S/UB *Fulcrum*

GROUND ATTACK

1 regt with Su-25K/UBK *Frogfoot*

TRANSPORT

Some regt with An-2 *Colt*/Y-5 (to infiltrate 2 air-force sniper brigades deep into ROK rear areas); Il-62M *Classic*

TRAINING

Some regt with CJ-6; FT-2; MiG-21U/UM

TRANSPORT HELICOPTER

Some regt with Hughes 500D/E; Mi-8 *Hip*; Mi-17 *Hip* H; Mil-26 *Halo*; PZL Mi-2 *Hoplite*; Mi-4 *Hound*; Z-5

AIR DEFENCE

19 bde with S-125M1 *Pechora*-M1 (RS-SA-3 *Goa*); S-75 *Dvina* (RS-SA-2 *Guideline*); S-200 *Angara* (RS-SA-5 *Gammon*); 9K36 *Strela*-3 (RS-SA-14 *Gremlin*); 9K310 *Igla*-1 (RS-SA-16 *Gimlet*); 9K32 *Strela*-2 (RS-SA-7 *Grail*)‡

EQUIPMENT BY TYPE

AIRCRAFT 545 combat capable

BBR 80 Il-28 *Beagle*/H-5‡ (includes some Il-28 for ISR)

FTR 401+: MiG-15 *Fagot*‡; 107 MiG-17 *Fresco*/J-5‡; 100 MiG-19 *Farmer*/J-6 (incl JJ-6 trg ac); 120 MiG-21F-13 *Fishbed*/J-7; MiG-21PFM *Fishbed*; 46 MiG-23ML *Flogger*; 10 MiG-23P *Flogger*; 18+ MiG-29A/S/UB *Fulcrum*

FGA 30 MiG-21bis *Fishbed* (18 Su-7 *Fitter* in store)

ATK 34 Su-25K/UBK *Frogfoot*

TPT 205: **Heavy** 3 Il-76 (operated by state airline); **Light** ε200 An-2 *Colt*/Y-5; **PAX** 2 Il-62M *Classic* (VIP)

TRG 215+: 180 CJ-6; 35 FT-2; some MiG-21U/UM

HELICOPTERS

MRH 80 Hughes 500D/E (some armed)

TPT 206: **Heavy** 4 Mi-26 *Halo*; **Medium** 63: 15 Mi-8 *Hip*/Mi-17 *Hip* H; 48 Mi-4 *Hound*/Z-5; **Light** 139 PZL Mi-2 *Hoplite*

UNINHABITED AERIAL VEHICLES

ISR • Medium some (unidentified indigenous type); **Light** *Pchela*-1 (*Shmel*) (reported)

AIR DEFENCE • SAM 209+

Long-range 10 S-200 *Angara*† (RS-SA-5 *Gammon*)

Medium-range 179+: some *Pongae*-5 (KN-SA-X-01) (status unknown); 179+ S-75 *Dvina* (RS-SA-2 *Guideline*)

Short-range ε20 S-125M1 *Pechora*-M1† (RS-SA-3 *Goa*)

Point-defence 9K32 *Strela*-2 (RS-SA-7 *Grail*)‡; 9K36 *Strela*-3 (RS-SA-14 *Gremlin*); 9K310 *Igla*-1 (RS-SA-16 *Gimlet*)

AIR-LAUNCHED MISSILES

AAM • IR R-3 (RS-AA-2 *Atoll*)‡; R-60 (RS-AA-8 *Aphid*); R-73 (RS-AA-11A *Archer*); PL-5; PL-7; **SARH** R-23/24 (RS-AA-7 *Apex*); R-27R/ER (RS-AA-10 A/C *Alamo*) **ASM** Kh-23 (RS-AS-7 *Kerry*)‡; Kh-25 (RS-AS-10 *Karen*); Kh-29L (RS-AS-14A *Kedge*)

Gendarmerie & Paramilitary 189,000 active

Security Troops 189,000 (incl border guards, public-safety personnel)

Ministry of Public Security

Worker/Peasant Red Guard ε5,700,000 reservists

Org on a province/town/village basis; comd structure is bde–bn–coy–pl; small arms with some mor and AD guns (but many units unarmed)

Korea, Republic of ROK

South Korean Won KRW		2021	2022	2023
GDP	KRW	2072tr	2203tr	
	USD	1.81tr	1.73tr	
per capita	USD	35,004	33,592	
Growth	%	4.1	2.6	
Inflation	%	2.5	5.5	
Def bdgt	KRW	52.9tr	54.6tr	57.1tr
	USD	46.3bn	43.0bn	
USD1=KRW		1143.95	1270.29	

Real-terms defence budget trend (USDbn, constant 2015)

Population	51,844,834					
Age	0–14	15–19	20–24	25–29	30–64	65 plus
Male	6.0%	2.3%	3.1%	3.8%	27.3%	7.7%
Female	5.7%	2.1%	2.8%	3.3%	26.1%	9.9%

Capabilities

South Korea's forces are some of the best equipped and trained in the region. Defence policy remains focused on North Korea, and Seoul continues to prioritise developing new capabilities to respond to the nuclear and conventional threat from the DPRK. The new administration is replacing the 2018 Defense Reform 2.0 project with the Defense Innovation 4.0 programme. As well as redesigning overall defence policy to focus on advanced technology and cyber security, South Korea has again adopted the three-axis defence strategy comprising 'Kill Chain', 'Korea Air and Missile Defense' and 'Korea Massive Punishment and Retaliation' components which were abandoned in 2019. The 2020 defence White Paper, released in February 2021, detailed plans to tackle North Korea's missile threats through a 'four-Ds strategy' of detect, disrupt, destroy and defend. The next edition of the White Paper is expected to be released in early 2023. The long-established alliance with the US is a central element of defence strategy. The planned transfer of wartime operational control of forces to Seoul is now 'conditions based' with no firm date set. A large number of US military personnel and equipment remain stationed in South Korea, along with THAAD missile-defence systems. In 2022, South Korea and the US resumed large-scale joint military exercises that had been scaled back in recent years. A space operations centre was inaugurated in 2021. South Korea has demonstrated the capacity to support small international deployments, including contributions to UN missions and counter-piracy operations in the Arabian Sea. The equipment inventory increasingly comprises modern systems. South Korea has developed a substantial domestic defence industry which supply a large proportion of equipment requirements, although some equipment – notably the F-35 combat aircraft – is still procured from the US. Local defence companies are finding growing export success globally, though industry will have to carefully balance new export contracts against existing local orders, particularly in land systems.

ACTIVE 555,000 (Army 420,000 Navy 70,000 Air 65,000) **Gendarmerie & Paramilitary 13,500**

Conscript liability Army and Marines 18 months, Navy 20 months, Air Force 21 months

RESERVE 3,100,000

Reserve obligation of three days per year. First Combat Forces (Mobilisation Reserve Forces) or Regional Combat Forces (Homeland Defence Forces) to age 33

Reserve Paramilitary 3,000,000

Being reorganised

ORGANISATIONS BY SERVICE

Space
EQUIPMENT BY TYPE
SATELLITES • COMMUNICATIONS 2 *Anasis*

Army 420,000
FORCES BY ROLE
COMMAND
  8 corps HQ
  1 (Capital Defence) comd HQ
SPECIAL FORCES
  1 (Special Warfare) SF comd (1 SF gp; 6 spec ops bde)
  6 cdo regt
  2 indep cdo bn
MANOEUVRE
  Armoured
  7 armd bde
  1 (Capital) armd inf div (1 armd cav bn, 2 armd bde, 1 armd inf bde, 1 SP arty bde, 1 engr bn)
  1 (8th) armd inf div (1 armd cav bn, 1 armd bde, 2 armd inf bde, 1 SP arty bde, 1 engr bn)
  1 (11th) armd inf div (1 armd cav bn, 3 armd inf bde, 1 SP arty bde, 1 engr bn)
  2 tk bn
  Light
  15 inf div (1 recce bn, 1 tk bn, 3 inf bde, 1 arty bde, 1 engr bn)
  2 indep inf bde
  Air Manoeuvre
  1 air mob div (2 cdo bde)
  1 air aslt bde
  Other
  5 sy regt
SURFACE-TO-SURFACE MISSILE
  3 SSM bn
COMBAT SUPPORT
  6 arty bde
  1 MRL bde (3 MRL bn; 1 SSM bn)
  6 engr bde
  5 engr gp
  1 CBRN defence bde
  8 sigs bde

COMBAT SERVICE SUPPORT
4 log spt comd
HELICOPTER
1 (army avn) comd
AIR DEFENCE
1 ADA bde
5 ADA bn

Reserves

FORCES BY ROLE
COMMAND
1 army HQ
MANOEUVRE
Light
24 inf div

EQUIPMENT BY TYPE
ARMOURED FIGHTING VEHICLES
MBT 2,149: 1,000 K1/K1E1; 484 K1A1/K1A2; ε225 K2; ε400 M48A5; 40 T-80U
IFV 540: ε500 K21; 40 BMP-3
APC 2,566
APC (T) 2,260: 1,700 KIFV; 420 M113; 140 M577 (CP)
APC (W) 296; 20 BTR-80; 276 K806/K808
PPV 10 *MaxxPro*
ENGINEERING & MAINTENANCE VEHICLES
AEV 207 M9; K600
ARV 238+: 200 K1; K21 ARV; K288A1; M47; 38 M88A1
VLB 56 K1
ANTI-TANK/ANTI-INFRASTRUCTURE
MSL
SP *Hyeongung*
MANPATS 9K115 *Metis* (RS-AT-7 *Saxhorn*); *Hyeongung*; TOW-2A
RCL 75mm; 90mm M67; **106mm** M40A2
GUNS 58
SP 90mm 50 M36
TOWED 76mm 8 M18 *Hellcat* (AT gun)
ARTILLERY 12,128+
SP 2,330: **105mm** ε50 K105A1; **155mm** 2,280: ε1,240 K9/K9A1 *Thunder*; 1,040 M109A2 (K55/K55A1)
TOWED 3,500+: **105mm** 1,700 M101/KH-178; **155mm** 1,800+ KH-179/M114
MRL 298: **130mm** ε40 K136 *Kooryong*; **227mm** 58: 48 M270 MLRS; 10 M270A1 MLRS; **239mm** ε200 K239 *Cheonmu*
MOR 6,000: **81mm** KM29 (M29); **107mm** M30; **120mm** Hanwha 120mm mortar
SURFACE-TO-SURFACE MISSILE LAUNCHERS
SRBM • Conventional 30+: 30 *Hyonmu* IIA/IIB; MGM-140A/B ATACMS (launched from M270/M270A1 MLRS)
GLCM • Conventional *Hyonmu* III
HELICOPTERS
ATK 96: 60 AH-1F/J *Cobra*; 36 AH-64E *Apache*
MRH 175: 130 Hughes 500D; 45 MD-500
TPT 236+: **Heavy** 37: 31 CH-47D *Chinook*; 6 MH-47E *Chinook*; **Medium** 287: ε200 KUH-1 *Surion*; 87 UH-60P *Black Hawk*; **Light** 12 Bo-105
AIR DEFENCE
SAM • Point-defence *Chiron*; *Chun Ma* (*Pegasus*); FIM-92 *Stinger*; *Javelin*; *Mistral*; 9K310 *Igla-1* (RS-SA-16 *Gimlet*)
GUNS 477+
SP 317: **20mm** ε150 KIFV *Vulcan* SPAAG; **30mm** 167

K30 *Biho*; some K-808 SPAAG
TOWED 160: **20mm** 60 M167 *Vulcan*; **35mm** 20 GDF-003; **40mm** 80 L/60/L/70; M1
AIR-LAUNCHED MISSILES
ASM AGM-114R1 *Hellfire*

Navy 70,000 (incl marines)

Three separate fleet elements: 1st Fleet Donghae (East Sea/Sea of Japan); 2nd Fleet Pyeongtaek (West Sea/Yellow Sea); 3rd Fleet Busan (South Sea/Korea Strait); independent submarine command; three additional flotillas (incl SF, mine-warfare, amphibious and spt elements) and 1 Naval Air Wing (3 gp plus spt gp)

EQUIPMENT BY TYPE
SUBMARINES 19
SSB 1 *Chang Bogo* III (Batch I (GER Type-214 mod; KSS-III)) (fitted with AIP) with 6 SLBM (likely based on *Hyeonmu*-IIB), 8 single 533mm TT with K731 *White Shark*
SSK 18:
6 *Chang Bogo* I (GER Type-209/1200; KSS-1) with 8 single 533mm TT with SUT HWT/K731 *White Shark* HWT
3 *Chang Bogo* I (GER Type-209/1200; KSS-1) with 8 single 533mm TT with UGM-84 *Harpoon* AShM/SUT HWT/K731 *White Shark* HWT
9 *Chang Bogo* II (GER Type-214; KSS-2) (fitted with AIP) with 8 single 533mm TT with *Hae Sung* III LACM/*Hae Sung* I AShM/SUT HWT/K731 *White Shark* HWT
PRINCIPAL SURFACE COMBATANTS 26
CRUISERS • CGHM 3 *Sejong* (KDD-III) with *Aegis* Baseline 7 C2, 6 8-cell K-VLS with *Hae Sung* II LACM/*Red Shark* A/S msl, 4 quad lnchr with *Hae Sung* I AShM, 10 8-cell Mk 41 VLS (6 fore, 4 aft) with SM-2 Block IIIA/B SAM, 1 21-cell Mk 49 GMLS with RIM-116 RAM SAM, 2 triple 324mm SVTT Mk 32 ASTT with K745 *Blue Shark* LWT, 1 *Goalkeeper* CIWS, 1 127mm gun (capacity 2 *Lynx* Mk99/AW159 *Wildcat* hels)
DESTROYERS • DDGHM 6 *Chungmugong Yi Sun-Sin* (KDD-II) with 2 8-cell K-VLS with *Hae Sung* II LACM/*Red Shark* A/S msl, 2 quad lnchr with RGM-84 *Harpoon* AShM/*Hae Sung* I AShM, 4 8-cell Mk 41 VLS with SM-2 Block IIIA/B SAM, 1 21-cell Mk 49 GMLS with RIM-116 RAM SAM, 2 triple 324mm SVTT Mk 32 ASTT with Mk 46 LWT, 1 *Goalkeeper* CIWS, 1 127mm gun (capacity 1 *Lynx* Mk99/AW159 *Wildcat* hel)
FRIGATES 17
FFGHM 13:
4 *Daegu* (*Incheon* Batch II)† (limited serviceability due to faulty propulsion system) with 2 8-cell K-VLS with *Hae Sung* II LACM/TSLM LACM/*Haegung* (K-SAAM) SAM/*Red Shark* A/S msl, 2 quad lnchr with TSLM LACM/*Hae Sung* I AShM, 2 triple 324mm KMk. 32 ASTT with K745 *Blue Shark* LWT, 1 Mk 15 *Phalanx* Block 1B CIWS, 1 127mm gun (capacity 1 *Lynx* Mk99/AW159 *Wildcat* hel)
3 *Gwanggaeto Daewang* (KDD-I) with 2 quad lnchr with RGM-84 *Harpoon* AShM, 2 8-cell Mk 48 mod 2 VLS with RIM-7P *Sea Sparrow* SAM, 2 triple 324mm KMk. 32 ASTT with K745 *Blue Shark* LWT, 2 *Goalkeeper* CIWS, 1 127mm gun (capacity 1 *Lynx* Mk99/AW159 *Wildcat* hel)

6 *Incheon* with 2 quad lnchr with TSLM LACM/*Hae Sung* I AShM, 1 21-cell Mk 49 lnchr with RIM-116 RAM SAM, 2 triple 324mm KMk. 32 ASTT with K745 *Blue Shark* LWT, 1 Mk 15 *Phalanx* Block 1B CIWS, 1 127 mm gun (capacity 1 *Lynx* Mk99/AW159 *Wildcat* hel)

FFG 4 *Ulsan* with 2 quad lnchr with RGM-84 *Harpoon* AShM, 2 triple 324mm SVTT Mk 32 ASTT with Mk 46 LWT, 2 76mm gun

PATROL AND COASTAL COMBATANTS ε64

CORVETTES • FSG 7:

1 *Po Hang* (Flight IV) with 2 twin lnchr with RGM-84 *Harpoon* AShM, 2 triple 324mm ASTT with Mk 46 LWT, 2 76mm gun

6 *Po Hang* (Flight V/VI) with 2 twin lnchr with *Hae Sung* I AShM, 2 triple 324mm KMk. 32 ASTT with K745 *Blue Shark* LWT, 2 76mm gun

PCFG 22: 18 *Gumdoksuri* with 2 twin lnchr with *Hae Sung* I AShM, 1 76mm gun; 4 *Chamsuri* II with 1 12-cell 130mm MRL, 1 76mm gun

PBF ε35 *Sea Dolphin*

MINE WARFARE 12

MINE COUNTERMEASURES 10

MHO 6 *Kan Kyeong*

MSO 4 *Yang Yang*

MINELAYERS • ML 2:

1 *Nampo* (MLS-II) with 1 4-cell K-VLS VLS with *Haegung* (K-SAAM) SAM, 2 triple KMk. 32 triple 324mm ASTT with K745 *Blue Shark* LWT, 1 76mm gun (capacity 1 med hel)

1 *Won San* with 2 triple 324mm SVTT Mk 32 ASTT with Mk 46 LWT/K745 *Blue Shark* LWT, 1 76mm gun, 1 hel landing platform

AMPHIBIOUS

PRINCIPAL AMPHIBIOUS SHIPS 6

LHD 2:

1 *Dokdo* with 1 Mk 49 GMLS with RIM-116 RAM SAM, 2 *Goalkeeper* CIWS (capacity 2 LCAC; 10 tanks; 700 troops; 10 UH-60 hel)

1 *Marado* (*Dokdo* mod) with 1 4-cell K-VLS with K-SAAM SAM, 2 Mk 15 *Phalanx* Block 1B CIWS (capacity 2 LCAC; 6 MBT, 7 AAV-7A1, 720 troops; 7-12 hels)

LPD 4 *Cheonwangbong* (LST-II) (capacity 3 LCM; 2 MBT; 8 AFV; 300 troops; 2 med hel)

LANDING SHIPS • LST 4 *Go Jun Bong* with 1 hel landing platform (capacity 20 tanks; 300 troops)

LANDING CRAFT 25

LCU 7+ *Mulgae* I

LCT 3 *Mulgae* II

LCM 10 LCM-8

LCAC 5: 3 *Tsaplya* (capacity 1 MBT; 130 troops); 2 LSF-II (capacity 150 troops or 1 MBT & 24 troops)

LOGISTICS AND SUPPORT 11

AG 1 *Sunjin* (trials spt)

AOEH 1 *Soyangham* (AOE-II) with 1 Mk 15 *Phalanx* Block 1B CIWS (capacity 1 med hel)

AORH 3 *Chun Jee*

ARS 1 *Cheong Hae Jin*

ATS 2 *Tongyeong*

AX 3: 1 *Hansando* with 2 triple 324mm KMk. 32 ASTT

with K745 *Blue Shark* LWT, 1 76mm gun (fitted for but not with K-VLS) (capacity 2 med hels; 300 students); 2 MTB

Naval Aviation

EQUIPMENT BY TYPE

AIRCRAFT 16 combat capable

ASW 16: 8 P-3C *Orion*; 8 P-3CK *Orion*

TPT • Light 5 Cessna F406 *Caravan* II

HELICOPTERS

ASW 31: 11 *Lynx* Mk99; 12 *Lynx* Mk99A; 8 AW159 *Wildcat*

TPT 15: **Medium** 8 UH-60P *Black Hawk* **Light** 7 Bell 205 (UH-1H *Iroquois*)

Marines 29,000

FORCES BY ROLE

SPECIAL FORCES

1 SF regt

MANOEUVRE

Amphibious

2 mne div (1 recce bn, 1 tk bn, 3 mne bde, 1 amph bn, 1 arty bde, 1 engr bn)

1 mne bde (1 recce coy, 4 mne bn, 1 SP arty bn)

1 mne bde (3 mne bn, 1 fd arty bn)

1 mne BG (1 mne bn, 1 SP arty bn)

EQUIPMENT BY TYPE

ARMOURED FIGHTING VEHICLES

MBT 100: 50 K1E1/A2; 50 M48A3

AAV 166 AAV-7A1

APC • APC(W) K808

ANTI-TANK/ANTI-INFRASTUCTURE • MSL

SP *Spike* NLOS

MANPATS *Hyeongung*

ARTILLERY 238

SP • 155mm 80: ε40 K9 *Thunder*; ε20 K9A1 *Thunder*; ε20 M109A2 (K55/K55A1)

TOWED 140: **105mm** ε20 M101; **155mm** ε120 KH-179

MRL • 239mm 18 K239 *Cheonmu*

MOR 81mm KM29 (M29)

COASTAL DEFENCE • AShM RGM-84A *Harpoon* (truck mounted)

HELICOPTERS • TPT • Medium 15+ MUH-1 *Surion*

AIR DEFENCE

GUNS • Towed • 20mm M167 *Vulcan* (direct fire role)

Naval Special Warfare Flotilla

Air Force 65,000

4 Comd (Ops, Southern Combat, Logs, Trg)

FORCES BY ROLE

FIGHTER/GROUND ATTACK

1 sqn with F-4E *Phantom* II

5 sqn with F-5E/F *Tiger* II

3 sqn with F-15K *Eagle*

8 sqn with F-16C/D *Fighting Falcon* (KF-16C/D)

2 sqn with F-35A *Lightning* II

3 sqn with FA-50 *Fighting Eagle*

ISR

1 wg with KO-1

1 sqn with F-16C/D *Fighting Falcon* (KF-16C/D)

268   THE MILITARY BALANCE 2023

SIGINT
1 sqn with Hawker 800RA/XP
AIRBORNE EARLY WARNING & CONTROL
1 sqn with B-737 AEW
SEARCH & RESCUE
2 sqn with AS332L *Super Puma*; Bell 412EP; HH-47D *Chinook*; HH-60P *Black Hawk*; Ka-32 *Helix* C
TANKER
1 sqn with A330 MRTT
TRANSPORT
1 VIP sqn with B-737-300; B-747-8; CN235-220; S-92A *Superhawk*; VH-60P *Black Hawk* (VIP)
3 sqn (incl 1 spec ops) with C-130H/H-30/J-30 *Hercules*
2 sqn with CN235M-100/220
TRAINING
1 sqn with F-5E/F *Tiger* II
1 sqn with F-16C/D *Fighting Falcon*
4 sqn with KT-1
1 sqn with KT-100
3 sqn with T-50/TA-50 *Golden Eagle**
TRANSPORT HELICOPTER
1 sqn with UH-60P *Black Hawk* (Spec Ops)
ISR UAV
1 sqn with RQ-4B *Global Hawk* (forming)
SPECIAL FORCES
1 SF sqn
AIR DEFENCE
3 AD bde (total: 6 SAM bn with *Chunggung*; 2 SAM bn with M902 *Patriot* PAC-3 CRI)

EQUIPMENT BY TYPE
AIRCRAFT 602 combat capable
FTR 173: 141 F-5E *Tiger* II; 32 F-5F *Tiger* II
FGA 349: 29 F-4E *Phantom* II; 59 F-15K *Eagle*; 117 F-16C *Fighting Falcon* (KF-16C); 44 F-16D *Fighting Falcon* (KF-16D); 40 F-35A *Lightning* II; 60 FA-50 *Fighting Eagle*
AEW&C 4 B-737 AEW
ISR 24: 4 Hawker 800RA; 20 KO-1
SIGINT 6: 4 Hawker 800SIG; 2 *Falcon* 2000 (COMINT/SIGINT)
TKR/TPT 4 A330 MRTT
TPT 38: **Medium** 16: 8 C-130H *Hercules*; 4 C-130H-30 *Hercules*; 4 C-130J-30 *Hercules*; **Light** 20: 12 CN235M-100; 8 CN235M-220 (incl 2 VIP); **PAX** 2: 1 B-737-300; 1 B-747-8 (leased)
TRG 183: 83 KT-1; 49 T-50 *Golden Eagle**; 9 T-50B *Black Eagle** (aerobatics); 22 TA-50 *Golden Eagle**; ε20 KT-100
HELICOPTERS
SAR 16: 5 HH-47D *Chinook*; 11 HH-60P *Black Hawk*
MRH 3 Bell 412EP
TPT • Medium 30: 2 AS332L *Super Puma*; 8 Ka-32 *Helix* C; 3 S-92A *Super Hawk*; 7 UH-60P *Black Hawk*; 10 VH-60P *Black Hawk* (VIP)
UNINHABITED AERIAL VEHICLES • ISR 7+: **Heavy** 4 RQ-4B *Global Hawk*; **Medium** 3+: some *Night Intruder*; 3 *Searcher*
LOITERING & DIRECT ATTACK MUNITIONS
Harpy
AIR DEFENCE • SAM 120
Long-range 48 M902 *Patriot* PAC-3 CRI
Medium-range 72 *Chunggung* (KM-SAM)

AIR-LAUNCHED MISSILES
AAM • IR AIM-9 *Sidewinder*; **IIR** AIM-9X *Sidewinder* II; **SARH** AIM-7 *Sparrow*; **ARH** AIM-120B/C-5/7 AMRAAM
ASM AGM-65A *Maverick*; AGM-130
AShM AGM-84L *Harpoon* Block II; AGM-142 *Popeye*
ARM AGM-88 HARM
ALCM AGM-84H SLAM-ER; KEPD-350 *Taurus*
BOMBS
Inertial/satellite-guided GBU-31/2/8 JDAM; GBU-39 SDB; KGGB; *Spice* 2000
Laser-guided GBU-28; *Paveway* II

Gendarmerie & Paramilitary 13,500 active

Civilian Defence Corps 3,000,000 reservists (to age 50)

Coast Guard 13,500

Part of the Ministry of Maritime Affairs and Fisheries. Five regional headquarters with 19 coastguard stations and one guard unit
EQUIPMENT BY TYPE
PATROL AND COASTAL COMBATANTS 111
PSOH 16: 1 *Lee Cheong-ho* with 1 76mm gun; 1 *Sambongho*; 14 *Tae Pung Yang* with 1 med hel
PSO 21: 3 *Han Kang* with 1 76mm gun, 1 hel landing platform; 5 *Han Kang* II with 1 76mm gun, 1 hel landing pllatform; 12 *Jaemin* with 1 hel landing platform; 1 *Sumjinkang*
PCO 23 *Tae Geuk*
PCC 21: 4 *Hae Uri*; 15 *Hae Uri* II; 2 *Hae Uri* III
PB 30: 26 *Haenuri*; ε4 (various)
AMPHIBIOUS • LANDING CRAFT 8
UCAC 8: 1 BHT-150; 4 *Griffon* 470TD; 3 *Griffon* 8000TD
AIRCRAFT
MP 5: 1 C-212-400 MP; 4 CN235-110 MPA
TPT • PAX 1 CL-604
HELICOPTERS
MRH 7: 5 AS565MB *Panther*; 1 AW139; 1 Bell 412SP
SAR 3 S-92
TPT • Medium 10: 8 Ka-32 *Helix* C; 2 KUH-1 *Surion*

DEPLOYMENT

ARABIAN SEA & GULF OF ADEN: Combined Maritime Forces • CTF-151: 200; 1 DDGHM

INDIA/PAKISTAN: UN • UNMOGIP 7

LEBANON: UN • UNIFIL 254; 1 mech inf BG HQ; 1 mech inf coy; 1 inf coy; 1 log coy

SOUTH SUDAN: UN • UNMISS 277; 1 engr coy

UNITED ARAB EMIRATES: 170 (trg activities at UAE Spec Ops School)

WESTERN SAHARA: UN • MINURSO 4

FOREIGN FORCES

Sweden NNSC: 5
Switzerland NNSC: 5
United States US Pacific Command: 30,400

Army 21,500; 1 HQ (8th Army) at Pyeongtaek; 1 div HQ at Pyeongtaek; 1 armd bde with M1A2 SEPv2 *Abrams*; M2A3/M3A3 *Bradley*; M109A6; 1 (cbt avn) hel bde with AH-64D/E *Apache*; CH-47F *Chinook*; UH-60L/M *Black Hawk*; 1 MRL bde with M270A1 MLRS; 1 AD bde with M902 *Patriot* PAC-3/FIM-92A *Avenger*; 1 SAM bty with THAAD; 1 (APS) armd bde eqpt set

Navy 350

USAF 8,350; 1 HQ (7th Air Force) at Osan AB; 1 ftr wg at Kunsan AB (2 ftr sqn with 20 F-16C/D *Fighting Falcon*); 1 ftr wg at Osan AB (1 ftr sqn with 20 F-16C/D *Fighting Falcon*, 1 atk sqn with 24 A-10C *Thunderbolt* II); 1 ISR sqn at Osan AB with U-2S

USMC 200

Laos LAO

New Lao Kip LAK		2021	2022	2023
GDP	LAK	181tr	213tr	
	USD	18.5bn	16.3bn	
per capita	USD	2,513	2,172	
Growth	%	2.1	2.2	
Inflation	%	3.8	15.0	
Def bdgt	LAK	n.k.	n.k.	
	USD	n.k.	n.k.	
USD1=LAK		9753.18	13082.84	
Population	7,749,595			

Age	0–14	15–19	20–24	25–29	30–64	65 plus
Male	15.8%	4.9%	5.0%	4.5%	17.7%	2.1%
Female	15.3%	4.8%	5.0%	4.5%	18.0%	2.4%

Capabilities

The Lao People's Armed Forces (LPAF) are closely linked to the ruling Communist Party and their primary role is internal security. Their main operational experience dates from the Second Indo-China War and the 1988 border war with Thailand. Defence spending and military procurement have been constrained for the last two decades. There are military-to-military contacts including with the Cambodian, Chinese and Vietnamese armed forces, and there is defence cooperation with Russia. Training support has been provided by Russia and Vietnam. The LPAF have participated in exercises, including those organised by the ADMM-Plus, with other regional countries and international partners. However, they have made no international deployments and have little capacity for sustained operations. Laos still operates Soviet-era military equipment and relies on Russian supplies, as illustrated by ongoing deliveries of training aircraft, armoured reconnaissance vehicles and main battle tanks. The country lacks a traditional defence-industrial base and maintenance capacity is limited, reflected in a support contract with a Russian firm for helicopter maintenance in 2016.

ACTIVE 29,100 (Army 25,600 Air 3,500)
Gendarmerie & Paramilitary 100,000
Conscript liability 18 months minimum

ORGANISATIONS BY SERVICE

Space
EQUIPMENT BY TYPE
SATELLITES • ISR 1 LaoSat-1

Army 25,600
FORCES BY ROLE
4 mil regions
MANOEUVRE
Armoured
1 armd bn
Light
5 inf div
7 indep inf regt
65 indep inf coy
COMBAT SUPPORT
5 arty bn
1 engr regt
2 (construction) engr regt
AIR DEFENCE
9 ADA bn
EQUIPMENT BY TYPE
ARMOURED FIGHTING VEHICLES
MBT 25: 15 T-54/T-55; 10 T-72B1
LT TK 10 PT-76
RECCE BRDM-2M
IFV 10+ BMP-1
APC • APC (W) 50: 30 BTR-40/BTR-60; 20 BTR-152
AUV Dongfeng Mengshi 4×4; ZYZ-8002 (CS/VN3)
ENGINEERING & MAINTENANCE VEHICLES
ARV T-54/T-55
VLB MTU
ANTI-TANK/ANTI-INFRASTRUCTURE • RCL 57mm M18/A1; **75mm** M20; **106mm** M40; **107mm** B-11
ARTILLERY 62+
TOWED 62: **105mm** 20 M101; **122mm** 20 D-30/M-30 M-1938; **130mm** 10 M-46; **155mm** 12 M114
MOR 81mm; 82mm; 107mm M-1938/M2A1; **120mm** M-43
AIR DEFENCE
SAM
Short-range 6+: 6 S-125M *Pechora*-M† (RS-SA-3 *Goa*); some *Yitian* (CH-SA-13)
Point-defence 9K32M *Strela*-2M (RS-SA-7 *Grail*)‡; 9K35 *Strela*-10 (RS-SA-13 *Gopher*); 9K310 *Igla*-1 (RS-SA-16 *Gimlet*)
GUNS
SP 23mm ZSU-23-4
TOWED 14.5mm ZPU-1/ZPU-4; **23mm** ZU-23; **37mm** M-1939; **57mm** S-60

Army Marine Section ε600
EQUIPMENT BY TYPE
PATROL AND COASTAL COMBATANTS • PBR some
AMPHIBIOUS • LCM some

Air Force 3,500
FORCES BY ROLE
TRANSPORT
1 regt with MA60; MA600; Mi-17 *Hip* H

EQUIPMENT BY TYPE
AIRCRAFT 4 combat capable
 TPT • **Light** 5: 1 An-74TK *Coaler*; 2 MA60; 2 MA600
 TRG 4 Yak-130 *Mitten**
HELICOPTERS
 MRH 15: 6 Mi-17 *Hip* H; 5 Mi-17V-5 *Hip*; 4 Z-9A
 TPT 4: **Medium** 1 Ka-32T *Helix* C; **Light** 3 SA360 *Dauphin*

Gendarmerie & Paramilitary

Militia Self-Defence Forces 100,000+
Village 'home guard' or local defence

Malaysia MYS

Malaysian Ringgit MYR		2021	2022	2023
GDP	MYR	1.55tr	1.69tr	
	USD	373bn	434bn	
per capita	USD	11,408	13,108	
Growth	%	3.1	5.4	
Inflation	%	2.5	3.2	
Def bdgt	MYR	15.9bn	16.1bn	
	USD	3.83bn	4.15bn	
USD1=MYR		4.14	3.89	

Real-terms defence budget trend (USDbn, constant 2015)

Population	33,871,431					
Age	0–14	15–19	20–24	25–29	30–64	65 plus
Male	11.7%	4.0%	4.5%	4.7%	22.6%	3.8%
Female	11.0%	3.8%	4.2%	4.4%	21.3%	4.0%

Capabilities

Modernisation programmes over the past 30 years have provided the Malaysian armed forces with a limited capacity for external defence. However, the army has continued to be the dominant service, reflecting a longstanding but now outdated focus on counter-insurgency. In December 2019, the then-government tabled the country's first defence White Paper; this was reaffirmed by the new government that took office in August 2021. The White Paper identified the 'three pillars' of Malaysia's defence strategy as 'concentric deterrence' (the armed forces' protection of national interests in 'core', 'extended' and 'forward' zones); 'comprehensive defence' (involving whole-of-government and whole-of-society support for the national-defence effort); and 'credible partnerships' (involving engagement in regional and wider international defence cooperation). While the paper identified new defence challenges, including tensions in the South China Sea and cyber threats, it provided no detailed insights into future resource allocation or capability development. However, it is likely that budgetary constraints will continue to limit defence resources. Malaysian forces regularly participate in ADMM–Plus, Five Power Defence Arrangements and other exercises with regional and international partners, including the US. Malaysia has invested in synthetic military-training aids. In 2017, Malaysia began trilateral joint maritime patrols and joint Sulu-Sulawesi Seas air patrols with Indonesia and the Philippines. Much of Malaysia's military equipment is ageing and there are important capability gaps, particularly in air defence and maritime surveillance. There are plans to acquire new light combat aircraft, maritime patrol aircraft and MALE UAVs. An air force squadron was established in 2021 to operate UAVs. Funds have been earmarked for an F/A-18D sustainment and upgrade programme. Malaysia hosts Australian forces and the headquarters of the FPDA Integrated Area Defence System at RMAF Butterworth; Butterworth is set to be modernised in 2023-25. Malaysia's defence industry focuses mainly on providing maintenance, repair and overhaul services, and on naval shipbuilding and land vehicle production via offset agreements with European companies.

ACTIVE 113,000 (Army 80,000 Navy 18,000 Air 15,000) Gendarmerie & Paramilitary 22,500

RESERVE 51,600 (Army 50,000, Navy 1,000 Air Force 600) Gendarmerie & Paramilitary 244,700

ORGANISATIONS BY SERVICE

Army 80,000
2 mil region
FORCES BY ROLE
COMMAND
 5 div HQ
SPECIAL FORCES
 1 SF bde (3 SF bn)
MANOEUVRE
 Armoured
 1 tk regt
 Mechanised
 4 armd regt
 1 mech inf bde (4 mech bn, 1 cbt engr sqn)
 Light
 1 inf bde (6 inf bn, 1 arty regt)
 4 inf bde (3 inf bn, 1 arty regt)
 2 inf bde (3 inf bn)
 1 inf bde (2 inf bn, 1 arty regt)
 1 inf bde (2 inf bn)
 1 inf bde (forming)
 Air Manoeuvre
 1 (Rapid Deployment Force) AB bde (1 lt tk sqn, 4 AB bn, 1 lt arty regt, 1 engr sqn)
 Other
 2 (border) sy bde (5 bn)
COMBAT SUPPORT
 9 arty regt
 1 STA regt
 1 MRL regt
 1 cbt engr sqn
 3 fd engr regt (total: 7 cbt engr sqn, 3 engr spt sqn)
 1 construction regt
 1 int unit
 4 MP regt
 1 sigs regt
HELICOPTER
 1 hel sqn
 1 tpt sqn with S-61A-4 *Nuri* (forming)
AIR DEFENCE
 3 ADA regt

EQUIPMENT BY TYPE
ARMOURED FIGHTING VEHICLES
MBT 48 PT-91M *Twardy*
LT TK 21 *Scorpion*-90
RECCE 98: 74 SIBMAS (some†); 24 AV8 *Gempita*
IFV 212: 31 ACV300 *Adnan* (25mm *Bushmaster*);
13 ACV300 *Adnan* AGL; 46 AV8 *Gempita* IFV25; 122 AV8
Gempita IFV30 (incl 54 with *Ingwe* ATGM)
APC 629
  APC (T) 265: 149 ACV300 *Adnan* (incl 69 variants);
  13 FV4333 *Stormer* (upgraded); 63 K200A; 40 K200A1
  APC (W) 335: 35 AV8 *Gempita* APC (incl 13 CP; 3 sigs; 9
  amb); 300 *Condor* (incl variants)
  PPV 29: 9 IAG *Guardian*; 20 *Lipanbara*
ENGINEERING & MAINTENANCE VEHICLES
AEV 3 MID-M
ARV 65+: *Condor*; 15 ACV300; 4 K288A1; 22 SIBMAS; 6
WZT-4; 18 AV8 *Gempita* ARV
VLB 5+: *Leguan*; 5 PMCz-90
NBC VEHICLES 4+: 4 AV8 *Gempita*; K216A1
ANTI-TANK/ANTI-INFRASTRUCTURE • MSL
  SP 8 ACV300 *Baktar Shikan*
  MANPATS 9K115 *Metis* (RS-AT-7 *Saxhorn*); 9K115-2
  Metis-M1 (RS-AT-13); *Eryx*; *Baktar Shihan* (HJ-8); SS.11
RCL 84mm *Carl Gustaf*
ARTILLERY 438
TOWED 140: **105mm** 118: 18 LG1 MkIII; 100 Model 56
pack howitzer; **155mm** 22 G-5
MRL 36 ASTROS II (equipped with 127mm SS-30)
MOR 262: **81mm** 232; **SP 81mm** 14: 4 K281A1; 10
ACV300-S; **SP 120mm** 16: 8 ACV-S; 8 AV8 *Gempita*
AMPHIBIOUS • LANDING CRAFT
LCA 165 Damen Assault Craft 540 (capacity 10 troops)
HELICOPTERS
MRH 6 MD-530G
TPT 12: **Medium** 2 S-61A-4 *Nuri*; **Light** 10 AW109
AIR DEFENCE
  SAM • Point-defence 15+: 15 *Jernas* (*Rapier* 2000); *Anza*-II;
  HY-6 (FN-6) (CH-SA-10); 9K38 *Igla* (RS-SA-18 *Grouse*); *Starstreak*
  GUNS 52+
    SP 20mm K263
    TOWED 52: **35mm** 16 GDF-005; **40mm** 36 L40/70

Reserves

Territorial Army
Some paramilitary forces to be incorporated into a reorganised territorial organisation

FORCES BY ROLE
MANOEUVRE
  Mechanised
  4 armd sqn
  Light
  16 inf regt (3 inf bn)
  Other
  5 (highway) sy bn
COMBAT SUPPORT
  5 arty bty
  2 fd engr regt
  1 int unit
  3 sigs sqn

COMBAT SUPPORT
  4 med coy
  5 tpt coy

Navy 18,000
3 Regional Commands: MAWILLA 1 (Kuantan), MAWIL-
LA 2 (Sabah) and MAWILLA 3 (Langkawi). A fourth is being formed (Bintulu)

EQUIPMENT BY TYPE
SUBMARINES 2
SSK 2 *Tunku Abdul Rahman* (FRA *Scorpène*) with 6 single
533mm TT with SM39 *Exocet* AShM/*Black Shark* HWT
PRINCIPAL SURFACE COMBATANTS • FRIGATES 2
FFGHM 2 *Lekiu* with 2 quad lnchr with MM40 *Exocet*
Block 2 AShM, 1 16-cell VLS with *Sea Wolf* SAM, 2 triple
324mm ILAS-3 (B-515) ASTT with A244/S LWT, 1 57mm
gun (capacity 1 *Super Lynx* 300 hel)
PATROL AND COASTAL COMBATANTS 55
  CORVETTES 8
    FSG 2 *Kasturi* with 2 quad lnchr with MM40 *Exocet*
    Block 2 AShM, 2 triple 324mm ILAS-3 (B-515) ASTT
    with A244/S LWT, 1 57mm gun, 1 hel landing platform
    FSH 6 *Kedah* (GER MEKO 100) with 1 76mm gun, 1 hel
    landing platform (fitted for but not with MM40 *Exocet*
    AShM & RAM SAM)
  PCFM 4 *Laksamana* with 1 *Albatros* quad lnchr with
  Aspide SAM, 1 76mm gun
  PCF 4 *Perdana* (FRA *Combattante* II) with 1 57mm gun
  PCC 4 *Keris* (Littoral Mission Ship)
  PBF 23: 6 Gading Marine FIC; 17 *Tempur* (SWE CB90)
  PB 12: 4 *Handalan* (SWE *Spica*-M) with 1 57mm gun; 6
  Jerong (Lurssen 45) with 1 57mm gun; 2 *Sri Perlis*
MINE WARFARE • MINE COUNTERMEASURES 4
  MCO 4 *Mahamiru* (ITA *Lerici*)
LOGISTICS AND SUPPORT 14
  AFS 2: 1 *Mahawangsa* with 2 57mm guns, 1 hel landing
  platform; 1 *Sri Indera Sakti* with 1 57mm gun, 1 hel
  landing platform
  AG 3: 2 *Bunga Mas Lima* with 1 hel landing platform; 1
  Tun Azizan
  AGS 2: 1 *Dayang Sari*; 1 *Perantau*
  AP 2 *Sri Gaya*
  ASR 1 *Mega Bakti*
  ATF 1
  AX 2 *Gagah Samudera* with 1 hel landing platform
  AXS 1 *Tunas Samudera*

Naval Aviation 160
FORCES BY ROLE
ANTI-SUBMARINE WARFARE
  1 sqn with *Super Lynx* 300
TRANSPORT HELICOPTER
  1 sqn with AS555 *Fennec*
  1 sqn with AW139
EQUIPMENT BY TYPE
HELICOPTERS
  ASW 6 *Super Lynx* 300
  MRH 8: 6 AS555 *Fennec*; 2 AW139
AIR-LAUNCHED MISSILES • AShM *Sea Skua*

Special Forces

FORCES BY ROLE
SPECIAL FORCES
1 (mne cdo) SF unit

Air Force 15,000

1 air op HQ, 2 air div, 1 trg and log comd, 1 Intergrated Area Def Systems HQ

FORCES BY ROLE
FIGHTER/GROUND ATTACK
1 sqn with F/A-18D *Hornet*
1 sqn with Su-30MKM *Flanker*
2 sqn with *Hawk* Mk108*/Mk208*
MARITIME PATROL
1 sqn with Beech 200T
TANKER/TRANSPORT
2 sqn with KC-130H *Hercules*; C-130H *Hercules*; C-130H-30 *Hercules*
TRANSPORT
1 sqn with A400M *Atlas*
1 (VIP) sqn with A319CT; AW109; BD700 *Global Express*; F-28 *Fellowship*; *Falcon* 900
1 sqn with CN235M-220
TRAINING
1 unit with PC-7
TRANSPORT HELICOPTER
4 (tpt/SAR) sqn with H225M *Super Cougar*; S-70A *Black Hawk*
1 sqn with AW139
UNINHABITED AERIAL VEHICLE
1 sqn (forming)
AIR DEFENCE
1 sqn with *Starburst*
SPECIAL FORCES
1 (Air Force Commando) unit (airfield defence/SAR)

EQUIPMENT BY TYPE
AIRCRAFT 42 combat capable
FTR (8 MiG-29 *Fulcrum* (MiG-29N); 2 MiG-29UB *Fulcrum* B (MIG-29NUB) in store)
FGA 26: 8 F/A-18D *Hornet* (some serviceability in doubt); 18 Su-30MKM (some serviceability in doubt)
MP 1 CN235 MPA
ISR 3 Beech 200T
TKR/TPT 4 KC-130H *Hercules*
TPT 24: **Heavy** 4 A400M *Atlas*; **Medium** 10: 2 C-130H *Hercules*; 8 C-130H-30 *Hercules*; **Light** 6 CN235M-220 (incl 1 VIP and 2 being reconfigured); **PAX** 4: 1 A319CT (VIP); 1 BD700 *Global Express*; 1 F-28 *Fellowship*; 1 *Falcon* 900
TRG 70: 4 *Hawk* Mk108*; 12 *Hawk* Mk208*; 7 MB-339C; 30 PC-7; 17 PC-7 Mk II *Turbo Trainer*
HELICOPTERS
MRH 2 AW139 (leased)
TPT 15: **Heavy** 12 H225M *Super Cougar*; **Medium** 2 S-70A *Black Hawk*; **Light** 1 AW109
AIR DEFENCE • SAM • Point-defence *Starstreak*
AIR-LAUNCHED MISSILES
AAM • IR AIM-9 *Sidewinder*; R-73 (RS-AA-11A *Archer*); **IIR** AIM-9X *Sidewinder* II; **IR/SARH** R-27 (RS-AA-10 *Alamo*); **SARH** AIM-7 *Sparrow*; **ARH** AIM-120C AMRAAM; R-77 (RS-AA-12A *Adder*)
ASM AGM-65 *Maverick*; Kh-29T (RS-AS-14B *Kedge*); Kh-29L (RS-AS-14A *Kedge*); Kh-31P (RS-AS-17A *Krypton*); Kh-59M (RS-AS-18 *Kazoo*)
ARM Kh-31P (RS-AS-17A *Krypton*);
AShM AGM-84D *Harpoon*; Kh-31A (RS-AS-17B *Krypton*)
BOMBS
Electro-optical guided KAB-500KR; KAB-500OD
Laser-guided *Paveway* II

Gendarmerie & Paramilitary ε22,500

Police–General Ops Force 18,000

FORCES BY ROLE
COMMAND
5 bde HQ
SPECIAL FORCES
1 spec ops bn
MANOEUVRE
Other
19 paramilitary bn
2 (Aboriginal) paramilitary bn
4 indep paramilitary coy

EQUIPMENT BY TYPE
ARMOURED FIGHTING VEHICLES
APC • APC (W) AT105 *Saxon*
AUV ε30 SB-301

Malaysian Maritime Enforcement Agency (MMEA) ε4,500

Controls 5 Maritime Regions (Northern Peninsula; Southern Peninsula; Eastern Peninsula; Sarawak; Sabah), subdivided into a further 18 Maritime Districts. Supported by one provisional MMEA Air Unit

EQUIPMENT BY TYPE
PATROL AND COASTAL COMBATANTS 137
PSO 4: 1 *Arau* (ex-JPN *Nojima*) with 1 hel landing platform; 2 *Langkawi* with 1 57mm gun, 1 hel landing platform; 1 *Pekan* (ex-JPN *Ojika*) with 1 hel landing platform
PCC 5 *Bagan Datuk*
PBF 56: 16 *Penggalang* 16; 18 *Penggalang* 17 (TUR MRTP 16); 2 *Penggalang* 18; 6 *Penyelamat* 20; 14 *Tugau*
PB 72: 15 *Gagah*; 4 *Malawali*; 2 *Nusa*; 3 *Nusa* 28; 1 *Peninjau*; 7 *Ramunia*; 2 *Rhu*; 4 *Semilang*; 9 *Sipadan Steel*; 8 *Icarus* 1650; 10 *Pengawal*; 4 *Penyelamat*; 2 *Perwira*; 1 *Sugut*
LOGISTICS AND SUPPORT • AX 1 *Marlin*
AIRCRAFT • MP 2 Bombardier 415MP
HELICOPTERS
SAR 3 AW139
MRH 3 AS365 *Dauphin*

Area Security Units 3,500 reservists

(Auxiliary General Ops Force)
FORCES BY ROLE
MANOEUVRE
Other
89 paramilitary unit

Border Scouts 1,200 reservists
in Sabah, Sarawak

People's Volunteer Corps 240,000 reservists (some 17,500 armed)
RELA

DEPLOYMENT

DEMOCRATIC REPUBLIC OF THE CONGO: UN • MONUSCO 6

LEBANON: UN • UNIFIL 830; 1 mech inf bn(-); 1 sigs coy; 1 log coy; 1 maint coy; 1 tpt coy

SUDAN: UN • UNISFA 1

WESTERN SAHARA: UN • MINURSO 9

FOREIGN FORCES

Australia 130; 1 inf coy (on 3-month rotational tours); 1 P-8A *Poseidon* (rotational)

Maldives MDV

Maldivian Rufiyaa MVR		2021	2022	2023
GDP	MVR	80.2bn	90.9bn	
	USD	5.20bn	5.90bn	
per capita	USD	13,539	15,097	
Growth	%	37.0	8.7	
Inflation	%	0.2	4.3	
Def bdgt	MVR	1.42bn	1.55bn	1.49bn
	USD	92.4m	100m	
USD1=MVR		15.41	15.41	

Real-terms defence budget trend (USDm, constant 2015)

Population	390,164					
Age	0–14	15–19	20–24	25–29	30–64	65 plus
Male	11.3%	3.8%	4.8%	5.8%	23.9%	2.4%
Female	10.8%	3.3%	3.8%	4.7%	22.3%	3.0%

Capabilities

The Maldives National Defence Force (MNDF) is tasked with defence, security and civil emergency response over the wide-ranging and mostly oceanic territory of the archipelagic nation. It is therefore a maritime-centric organisation, with a littoral Coast Guard, including a small aviation wing, and a Marine Corps. There is focus on ISR, maritime security and counter-terrorist training and capability development needs. India is the MNDF's key defence partner, having supplied most of the force's major military platforms, and regularly donates surplus military equipment and offers training to MNDF personnel. In 2020 Malé signed a defence agreement with the United States and in 2021 the MNDF started capacity building work with the US Army. Training facilities are being developed, including a basic training school in 2020 and work is proceeding on the development of the Composite Training Centre on Maafilaafushi Island.

ACTIVE 4,000 (Maldives National Defence Force 4,000)

ORGANISATIONS BY SERVICE

Maldives National Defence Force 4,000

Special Forces
FORCES BY ROLE
SPECIAL FORCES
 1 SF sqn

Marine Corps
FORCES BY ROLE
SPECIAL FORCES
 1 spec ops unit
MANOEUVRE
 Mechanised
 1 mech sqn
 Amphibious
 7 mne coy
EQUIPMENT BY TYPE
ARMOURED FIGHTING VEHICLES
 IFV 2 BMP-2
 AUV 2 *Cobra*

Coast Guard
FORCES BY ROLE
SPECIAL FORCES
 1 spec ops unit
EQUIPMENT BY TYPE
PATROL AND COASTAL COMBATANTS 12
 PCC 3: 1 *Ghazee*; 1 *Shaheed Ali*; 1 *Trinkat* (*Bangaram* SDB Mk5)
 PBF 7: 5 SM50 Interceptor; 2 *Super Dvora* Mk III
 PB 2: 1 *Dhaharaat*; 1 *Kaamiyab*
AMPHIBIOUS • LANDING CRAFT 4:
 LCU 1 L301
 LCP 3
AIRCRAFT
 MP 1 Do-228
HELICOPTERS
 MRH 2 *Dhruv*

Mongolia MNG

Mongolian Tugrik MNT		2021	2022	2023
GDP	MNT	43.6tr	50.2tr	
	USD	15.3bn	15.7bn	
per capita	USD	4,483	4,542	
Growth	%	1.6	2.5	
Inflation	%	7.1	14.8	
Def bdgt	MNT	284bn	287bn	311bn
	USD	99.5m	89.8m	
FMA (US)	USD	3m	3m	3m
USD1=MNT		2849.37	3191.33	

Real-terms defence budget trend (USDm, constant 2015)

Population	3,227,863

Age	0–14	15–19	20–24	25–29	30–64	65 plus
Male	13.5%	3.7%	3.7%	3.8%	21.9%	2.1%
Female	13.0%	3.5%	3.6%	3.9%	24.1%	3.2%

Capabilities

Mongolia's latest defence-policy document, from 2015, stresses the importance of peacekeeping and anti-terrorist capabilities. The country has no formal military alliances, but pursues defence ties and bilateral training with regional states and others including India, Turkey and the US. Mongolia hosts the annual *Khaan Quest* multinational peacekeeping-training exercise. The country's main exercise partners are India and Russia, with each country running regular bilateral exercises. In 2022, Mongolia and Russia held the counter-terrorism-focused exercise *Selenga*. In 2021, NATO completed a multi-year project that involved establishing a Cyber Security Centre and Cyber Incident Response Capability. Mongolia's most significant deployment is to the UN peacekeeping mission in South Sudan. The inventory generally comprises Soviet-era equipment, supplemented by deliveries of second-hand Russian weapons. Barring maintenance facilities, there is no significant defence-industrial base.

ACTIVE 9,700 (Army 8,900 Air 800) Gendarmerie & Paramilitary 7,500

Conscript liability 12 months for males aged 18–25

RESERVE 137,000 (Army 137,000)

ORGANISATIONS BY SERVICE

Army 5,600; 3,300 conscript (total 8,900)

FORCES BY ROLE
MANOEUVRE
  Mechanised
  1 MR bde
  Light
  1 (rapid deployment) lt inf bn (2nd bn to form)
  Air Manoeuvre
  1 AB bn

COMBAT SUPPORT
1 arty regt

EQUIPMENT BY TYPE
ARMOURED FIGHTING VEHICLES
  MBT 420: 370 T-54/T-55; 50 T-72A
  RECCE 120 BRDM-2
  IFV 310 BMP-1
  APC • APC (W) 210: 150 BTR-60; 40 BTR-70M; 20 BTR-80
ENGINEERING & MAINTENANCE VEHICLES
  ARV T-54/T-55
ANTI-TANK/ANTI-INFRASTRUCTURE
  GUNS • TOWED 200: 85mm D-44/D-48; 100mm M-1944/MT-12
ARTILLERY 570
  TOWED ε300: 122mm D-30/M-30 (M-1938); 130mm M-46; 152mm ML-20 (M-1937)
  MRL 122mm 130 BM-21
  MOR 140: 120mm; 160mm; 82mm
AIR DEFENCE
  SAM Medium-range 2+ S-125-2M *Pechora*-2M (RS-SA-26)
  GUNS • TOWED 23mm ZU-23-2

Air Force 800

FORCES BY ROLE
FIGHTER
  1 sqn with MiG-29UB *Fulcrum* B
TRANSPORT
  1 sqn with An-24 *Coke*; An-26 *Curl*
ATTACK/TRANSPORT HELICOPTER
  1 sqn with Mi-8 *Hip*; Mi-171
AIR DEFENCE
  2 regt with S-60/ZPU-4/ZU-23

EQUIPMENT BY TYPE
AIRCRAFT 6 combat capable
  FTR 6 MiG-29UB *Fulcrum* B
  TPT • Light 3: 2 An-24 *Coke*; 1 An-26 *Curl*
HELICOPTERS
  TPT • Medium 12: 10 Mi-8 *Hip*; 2 Mi-171
AIR-LAUNCHED MISSILES
  IR R-73 (RS-AA-11A *Archer*)
AIR DEFENCE • GUNS • TOWED 150: 14.5mm ZPU-4; 23mm ZU-23; 57mm S-60

Gendarmerie & Paramilitary 7,500 active

Border Guard 1,300; 4,700 conscript (total 6,000)

Internal Security Troops 400; 800 conscript (total 1,200)

FORCES BY ROLE
MANOEUVRE
  Other
  4 gd unit

Construction Troops 300

DEPLOYMENT

DEMOCRATIC REPUBLIC OF THE CONGO: UN • MONUSCO 2

SOUTH SUDAN: UN • UNMISS 868; 1 inf bn

SUDAN: UN • UNISFA 4

WESTERN SAHARA: UN • MINURSO 3

Myanmar MMR

Myanmar Kyat MMK		2021	2022	2023
GDP	MMK	98.7tr	118tr	
	USD	65.2bn	59.5bn	
per capita	USD	1,217	1,105	
Growth	%	-17.9	2.0	
Inflation	%	3.6	16.2	
Def bdgt	MMK	5.16tr	3.70tr	
	USD	3.41bn	1.88bn	
USD1=MMK		1514.03	1974.80	

Real-terms defence budget trend (USDbn, constant 2015)

Population	57,526,449					
Age	0–14	15–19	20–24	25–29	30–64	65 plus
Male	12.9%	4.2%	4.2%	4.1%	21.0%	2.9%
Female	12.3%	4.1%	4.1%	4.2%	22.2%	3.7%

Capabilities

Since the country's independence struggle in the 1940s, Myanmar's large, army-dominated Tatmadaw (armed forces) has been intimately involved in domestic politics as well as internal security. Even though the National League for Democracy (NLD) won the November 2015 election, the armed forces remained politically powerful. A defence White Paper published in 2016 gave a 'statebuilding' role to the Tatmadaw, further legitimising intervention in politics. Despite the NLD winning an increased majority in the November 2020 election, the Tatmadaw declared the result illegitimate and seized power on 1 February 2021, declaring a year-long state of emergency which was extended to 31 July 2022 and then again to February 2023. The 2016 White Paper prioritised ending conflicts with domestic armed groups. However, widespread civil unrest and an escalation in clashes with ethnic-minority armed groups and People's Defence Force (PDF) groups since the coup has sharpened the Tatmadaw's focus on internal security and counter-insurgency. In response, the Tatmadaw launched a multipronged counter-insurgency campaign across 2021 and 2022. The Tatmadaw's actions have also focused attention on force health, including morale and general cohesion. The Tatmadaw has been accused of widespread human-rights abuses against non-combatants during counter-insurgency operations. These concerns intensified after the widely condemned actions aimed at the Rohingya ethnic minority in 2017. China and Russia are key partners in defence cooperation. In September 2022, Japan said it would stop from 2023 a training programme that has since 2015 seen small numbers of Myanmar military personnel attend defence educational institutions in Japan. Since the 1990s, the armed forces have attempted to develop limited conventional warfare capabilities, though these efforts have been called into question by the renewed focus on internal security and counter-insurgency. While defence-industrial capacity is limited, naval shipbuilding capability has grown, notably through the Naval Dockyard in Thanlyin, with satellite imagery revealing in December 2020 the construction of a new guided-missile frigate. The Aircraft Production and Maintenance Base in Meiktila has also engaged in final assembly and Maintenance, Repair and Overhaul (MRO) services on trainer/light attack aircraft and combat helicopters since 2010.

ACTIVE 356,000 (Army 325,000 Navy 16,000 Air 15,000) **Gendarmerie & Paramilitary 107,000**

Conscript liability 24–36 months

ORGANISATIONS BY SERVICE

Army ε325,000

14 military regions, 7 regional op comd. Following the 2021 coup, and reports of desertions, combat losses and recruitment problems, personnel figures should be treated with caution

FORCES BY ROLE
COMMAND
  20 div HQ (military op comd)
  10 inf div HQ
  34+ bde HQ (tactical op comd)
MANOEUVRE
  Armoured
  10 armd bn
  Light
  100 inf bn (coy)
  337 inf bn (coy) (regional comd)
COMBAT SUPPORT
  7 arty bn
  37 indep arty coy
  6 cbt engr bn
  54 fd engr bn
  40 int coy
  45 sigs bn
AIR DEFENCE
  7 AD bn

EQUIPMENT BY TYPE
ARMOURED FIGHTING VEHICLES
  MBT 195+: 10 T-55; 50 T-72S; 25+ Type-59D; 100 Type-69-II; 10+ Type-90-II (MBT-2000)
  LT TK 105 Type-63 (ε60 serviceable)
  ASLT 24 PTL-02 mod
  RECCE 95+: ε50 AML-90; 33 BRDM-2MS (incl CP); 12+ EE-9 *Cascavel*; MAV-1
  IFV 36+: 10+ BTR-3U; 26+ MT-LBMSh
  APC 345+
    APC (T) 305: 250 ZSD-85; 55 ZSD-90
    APC (W) 30+ ZSL-92
    PPV 10+: BAAC-87; Gaia *Thunder*; 10 MPV
  AUV MAV-2; MAV-3
ENGINEERING & MAINTENANCE VEHICLES
  ARV Type-72
  VLB MT-55A
ANTI-TANK/ANTI-INFRASTRUCTURE
  RCL 84mm *Carl Gustaf*; **106mm** M40A1
  GUNS • TOWED 60: **57mm** 6-pdr; **76mm** 17-pdr

276   THE MILITARY BALANCE 2023

ARTILLERY 440+
  SP 155mm 42: 30 NORA B-52; 12 SH-1
  TOWED 282+: **105mm** 150: 54 M-56; 96 M101; **122mm** 100
  D-30; **130mm** 16 M-46; **140mm**; **155mm** 16 Soltam M-845P
  MRL 36+: **107mm** 30 Type-63; **122mm** BM-21 *Grad*
  (reported); Type-81; **240mm** 6+ M-1985 mod
  MOR 80+: **82mm** Type-53 (M-37); **120mm** 80+: 80 Soltam;
  Type-53 (M-1943)
SURFACE-TO-SURFACE MISSILE LAUNCHERS
  SRBM • Conventional some *Hwasong*-6 (reported)
AIR DEFENCE
  SAM 4+
    Medium-range 12+: 12+ KS-1A (CH-SA-12); S-125-
    2M *Pechora*-2M (RS-SA-26); 2K12 *Kvadrat*-M
    (RS-SA-6 *Gainful*)
    Point-defence HN-5 (CH-SA-3) (reported); 9K310 *Igla*-
    1 (RS-SA-16 *Gimlet*)
  SPAAGM 30mm Some 2K22 *Tunguska* (RS-SA-19 *Grison*)
  GUNS 46
    SP 57mm 12 Type-80
    TOWED 34: **37mm** 24 Type-74; **40mm** 10 M1

Navy ε16,000

EQUIPMENT BY TYPE
SUBMARINES • SSK 2
  1 *Min Kyaw Htin* (ex-PRC Type-035B (*Ming*)) with 8
  single 533mm TT
  1 *Min Ye Thein Kha Thu* (ex-IND *Sindhughosh* (Project
  877EKM (*Kilo*))) with 6 single 533mm TT
PRINCIPAL SURFACE COMBATANTS • FRIGATES 5
  FFGHM 2 *Kyansitthar* with 2 twin lnchr with C-802 (CH-
  SS-N-6) AShM, 1 sextuple lnchr with MANPAD SAM, 2
  RDC-32 A/S mor, 3 AK630 CIWS, 1 76mm gun (capacity
  1 med hel)
  FFGM 1 *Aung Zeya* with 2 quad lnchr with DPRK AShM
  (possibly 3M24 derivative), 1 sextuple GMLS with
  MANPAD SAM; 4 AK630 CIWS, 2 RDC-32 A/S mor, 1
  76mm gun, 1 hel landing platform
  FFG 2 *Mahar Bandoola* (ex-PRC Type-053H1 (*Jianghu* I))
  with 2 quad lnchr with C-802 (CH-SS-N-6) AShM, 2
  RBU 1200 *Uragan* A/S mor, 2 twin 100mm gun
PATROL AND COASTAL COMBATANTS 81
  CORVETTES 3
    FSGHM 1 *Tabinshwethi* (*Anawrahta* mod) with 2 twin
    lnchr with C-802 (CH-SS-N-6), 1 sectuple lnchr with
    unknown MANPADs, 2 RBU 1200 *Uragan* A/S mor, 1
    76mm gun (capacity 1 med hel)
    FSG 2 *Anawrahta* with 2 twin lnchr with C-802
    (CH-SS-N-6) AShM, 2 RDC-32 A/S mor, 1 76mm gun, 1
    hel landing platform
  PSOH 2 *Inlay* with 1 twin 57mm gun
  PCG 8: 6 Type-037-IG (*Houxin*) with 2 twin lnchr with
  C-801 (CH-SS-N-4) AShM; 2 FAC(M) mod with 2 twin
  lnchr with C-802 (CH-SS-N-6) AShM, 1 AK630 CIWS
  PCT 2 *Yan Nyein Aung* (Project PGG 063) with 2 FQF 1200
  A/S mor, 2 triple 324mm TLS with *Shyena* LWT
  PCO 2 *Indaw*
  PCC 7 Type-037 (*Hainan*) with 4 RBU 1200 *Uragan* A/S
  mor, 2 twin 57mm gun

  PBG 4 *Myanmar* with 2 single lnchr with C-801
  (CH-SS-N-4) AShM
  PBF 7: 1 Type-201; 6 *Super Dvora* Mk III
  PB 32: 3 PB-90; 6 PGM 401; 6 PGM 412; 14 *Myanmar*; 3 *Swift*
  PBR 14: 4 *Sagu*; 9 Y-301†; 1 Y-301 (Imp)
AMPHIBIOUS
  PRINCIPAL AMPHIBIOUS VESSELS • LPD 1:
    1 *Moattama* (ROK *Makassar*) (capacity 2 LCVP; 2 hels;
    13 tanks; 500 troops)
  LANDING CRAFT 21: **LCU** 5; **LCM** 16
LOGISTICS AND SUPPORT 12
  ABU 1
  AGHS 2: 1 *Innya*; 1 (near shore)
  AGS 1
  AH 1 *Thanlwin*
  AK 1
  AKSL 5
  AP 1 *Chindwin*

Naval Infantry 800

FORCES BY ROLE
MANOEUVRE
  Light
  1 inf bn

Air Force ε15,000

FORCES BY ROLE
FIGHTER
  4 sqn with F-7 *Airguard*; FT-7; JF-17 *Thunder*; MiG-29
  Fulcrum; MiG-29SE/SM *Fulcrum*; MiG-29UB *Fulcrum*
GROUND ATTACK
  2 sqn with A-5C *Fantan*
TRANSPORT
  1 sqn with F-27 *Friendship*; FH-227; PC-6AB *Turbo Porter*
TRAINING
  2 sqn with G-4 *Super Galeb**; PC-7 *Turbo Trainer**; PC-9*
  1 (trg/liaison) sqn with Cessna 550 *Citation* II; Cessna
  180 *Skywagon*; K-8 *Karakorum**
TRANSPORT HELICOPTER
  4 sqn with Bell 205; Bell 206 *Jet Ranger*; Mi-17 *Hip* H;
  Mi-35P *Hind*; PZL Mi-2 *Hoplite*; PZL W-3 *Sokol*; SA316
  Alouette III
EQUIPMENT BY TYPE
AIRCRAFT 166 combat capable
  FTR 63: 21 F-7 *Airguard*; 10 FT-7; 11 MiG-29 *Fulcrum*;
  6 MiG-29SE *Fulcrum*; 10 MiG-29SM *Fulcrum*; 5 MiG-
  29UB *Fulcrum*
  FGA 6: 4 JF-17 *Thunder* (FC-1 Block 2); 2 JF-17B *Thunder*
  (FC-1 Block 2)
  ATK 21 A-5C *Fantan*
  MP 2 ATR-42
  TPT 26: **Medium** 5: 4 Y-8D; 1 Y-8F-200W **Light** 20: 1
  ATR-42; 6 Beech 1900D; 4 Cessna 180 *Skywagon*; 1 Cessna
  550 *Citation* II; 3 F-27 *Friendship*; 5 PC-6A/B *Turbo Porter*
  PAX 1+ FH-227
  TRG 96: 11 G-4 *Super Galeb**; 20 Grob G120; 24+ K-8
  *Karakorum**; 12 PC-7 *Turbo Trainer**; 9 PC-9*; 20 Yak-130
  *Mitten**
HELICOPTERS
  ATK 12 Mi-35P *Hind*

MRH 23: 3 AS365; 11 Mi-17 *Hip* H; 9 SA316 *Alouette* III
TPT 49: **Medium** 10 PZL W-3 *Sokol*; **Light** 39: 12 Bell 205; 6 Bell 206 *Jet Ranger*; 4 H120 *Colibri*; 17 PZL Mi-2 *Hoplite*
UNINHABITED AERIAL VEHICLES
 CISR • **Heavy** 4 CH-3
AIR-LAUNCHED MISSILES
 AAM • **IR** PL-5; R-73 (RS-AA-11A *Archer*); PL-5E-II; **IR/SARH** R-27 (RS-AA-10 *Alamo*); **ARH** PL-12 (CH-AA-7A *Adze*)
 AShM C-802A

Gendarmerie & Paramilitary 107,000

People's Police Force 72,000

People's Militia 35,000

Nepal NPL

Nepalese Rupee NPR		2021	2022	2023
GDP	NPR	4.28tr	4.74tr	
	USD	35.8bn	39.0bn	
per capita	USD	1,209	1,293	
Growth	%	4.2	4.2	
Inflation	%	3.6	6.3	
Def bdgt	NPR	49.2bn	51.0bn	55.0bn
	USD	413m	421m	
USD1=NPR		119.32	121.38	

Real-terms defence budget trend (USDm, constant 2015)

Population	30,666,598					
Age	0–14	15–19	20–24	25–29	30–64	65 plus
Male	13.8%	5.0%	5.1%	5.0%	17.1%	2.9%
Female	13.1%	4.7%	5.1%	5.1%	20.1%	3.0%

Capabilities

The principal role of Nepal's armed forces is maintaining territorial integrity, but they have also traditionally focused on internal security and humanitarian relief. Nepal has a history of deploying contingents to UN peacekeeping operations. Training support is provided by several countries, including China, India and the US. Following a 2006 peace accord with the Maoist People's Liberation Army, Maoist personnel underwent a process of demobilisation or integration into the armed forces. Gurkhas continue to be recruited by the British and Indian armed forces and the Singaporean police. The small air wing provides a limited transport and support capacity but mobility remains a challenge, in part because of topography. Nepal's logistic capability appears to be sufficient for internal-security operations; however, its contingents on UN peacekeeping operations appear to largely depend on contracted logistic support. Modernisation plans include a very limited increase in the size of its air force. Barring maintenance capacities there is no defence-industrial base, and Nepal is dependent on foreign suppliers for modern equipment.

ACTIVE 96,600 (Army 96,600) Gendarmerie & Paramilitary 15,000

ORGANISATIONS BY SERVICE

Army 96,600
FORCES BY ROLE
COMMAND
 2 inf div HQ
 1 (valley) comd
SPECIAL FORCES
 1 bde (1 SF bn, 1 AB bn, 1 cdo bn, 1 ranger bn, 1 mech inf bn)
MANOEUVRE
 Light
 18 inf bde (total: 62 inf bn; 32 indep inf coy)
COMBAT SUPPORT
 1 arty bde
 4 arty regt
 5 engr bn
 1 sigs bde
AIR DEFENCE
 2 AD regt
 4 indep AD coy
EQUIPMENT BY TYPE
ARMOURED FIGHTING VEHICLES
 RECCE 40 *Ferret*
 APC 253
  APC (W) 13: 8 OT-64C; 5 WZ-551
  PPV 240: 90 *Casspir*; 150 MPV
 AUV Dongfeng *Mengshi*; CS/VN3C mod 2
ARTILLERY 92+
 TOWED 105mm 22: 8 L118 Light Gun; 14 pack howitzer (6 non-operational)
 MOR 70+: 81mm; 120mm 70 M-43 (est 12 op)
AIR DEFENCE • GUNS • TOWED 32+: 14.5mm 30 Type-56 (ZPU-4); 37mm (PRC); 40mm 2 L/60

Air Wing 320
EQUIPMENT BY TYPE†
AIRCRAFT • TPT • **Light** 7: 1 BN-2T *Islander*; 1 CN235M-220; 3 M-28 *Skytruck*; 2 PA-28 *Cherokee* (trg)
HELICOPTERS
 MRH 14: 1 A139; 1 Bell 407GXP (VIP); 2 *Dhruv*; 2 *Lancer*; 3 Mi-17-1V *Hip* H; 2 Mi-17V-5 *Hip*; 1 SA315B *Lama* (*Cheetah*); 2 SA316B *Alouette* III
 TPT 3: **Medium** 1 SA330J *Puma*; **Light** 2 AS350B2 *Ecureuil*

Paramilitary 15,000

Armed Police Force 15,000
Ministry of Home Affairs

DEPLOYMENT

CENTRAL AFRICAN REPUBLIC: UN • MINUSCA 835; 1 inf bn; 1 MP pl

DEMOCRATIC REPUBLIC OF THE CONGO: UN • MONUSCO 1,154; 1 inf bn; 1 engr coy

IRAQ: UN • UNAMI 77; 1 sy unit
LEBANON: UN • UNIFIL 872; 1 mech inf bn
LIBYA: UN • UNISMIL 234; 2 sy coy
MALI: UN • MINUSMA 177; 1 EOD coy
MIDDLE EAST: UN • UNTSO 3
SOUTH SUDAN: UN • UNMISS 1,749; 2 inf bn
SUDAN: UN • UNISFA 89; 1 log coy
SYRIA/ISRAEL: UN • UNDOF 412; 1 mech inf coy; 1 inf coy; 1 log coy(-)
WESTERN SAHARA: UN • MINURSO 5

FOREIGN FORCES
United Kingdom 60 (Gurkha trg org)

New Zealand NZL

New Zealand Dollar NZD		2021	2022	2023
GDP	NZD	349bn	375bn	
	USD	247bn	243bn	
per capita	USD	48,317	47,278	
Growth	%	5.6	2.3	
Inflation	%	3.9	6.3	
Def bdgt	NZD	4.62bn	5.19bn	6.08bn
	USD	3.27bn	3.35bn	
USD1=NZD		1.41	1.55	

Real-terms defence budget trend (USDbn, constant 2015)

Population	5,053,004					
Age	0–14	15–19	20–24	25–29	30–64	65 plus
Male	10.0%	3.2%	3.3%	3.6%	22.4%	7.6%
Female	9.4%	3.1%	3.1%	3.4%	22.3%	8.6%

Capabilities

New Zealand has a strong military tradition. The New Zealand Defence Force (NZDF) is well trained and has substantial operational experience. The June 2016 defence White Paper forecasted a range of challenges likely to affect the country's security in the period to 2040, including rising tension in the South and East China seas. In December 2021 the defence ministry released the Defence Assessment 2021, discussing challenges to New Zealand's strategic defence interests, including strategic competition and climate change. This proposed a defence policy review, which was formally announced in July 2022. A policy and strategy statement is due in March 2023, with a 'future force design principles' statement following in June. The terms of reference for the review noted that the 'impetus for a comprehensive review' had sharpened since the assessment was released, making reference to Russia's 2022 invasion of Ukraine. A Defence Capability Plan will accompany the policy review. New Zealand's closest defence partner is Australia and the country has revived defence relations with the United States. The 2019 Defence Capability Plan outlined plans to acquire a sealift vessel and C-130J *Hercules* transport aircraft before 2030, as well as to expand the army to 6,000 personnel by 2035. The year before, the decision was taken to purchase four P-8 *Poseidon* maritime patrol aircraft. Replacement of the ANZAC frigates, both of which are being upgraded, has now been postponed until the 2030s. New Zealand has a small defence industry consisting of numerous private companies and subsidiaries of larger North American and European companies. These companies are able to provide some maintenance, repair and overhaul capability but significant work is contracted overseas.

ACTIVE 9,200 (Army 4,500 Navy 2,200 Air 2,500)

RESERVE 3,010 (Army 2,050 Navy 610 Air Force 350)

ORGANISATIONS BY SERVICE

Army 4,500
FORCES BY ROLE
SPECIAL FORCES
  1 SF regt
MANOEUVRE
Light
  1 inf bde (1 armd recce regt, 2 lt inf bn, 1 arty regt (2 arty bty), 1 engr regt(-), 1 MP coy, 1 sigs regt, 2 log bn)
EQUIPMENT BY TYPE
ARMOURED FIGHTING VEHICLES
  IFV 74 NZLAV-25
  AUV 5+ *Bushmaster*
ENGINEERING & MAINTENANCE VEHICLES
  AEV 7 NZLAV
  ARV 3 LAV-R
ANTI-TANK/ANTI-INFRASTRUCTURE
  MSL • MANPATS FGM-148 *Javelin*
ARTILLERY 56
  TOWED 105mm 24 L118 Light Gun
  MOR 81mm 32

Reserves

Territorial Force 1,850 reservists
Responsible for providing trained individuals for augmenting deployed forces
FORCES BY ROLE
COMBAT SERVICE SUPPORT
  3 (Territorial Force Regional) trg regt

Navy 2,200
Fleet based in Auckland. Fleet HQ at Wellington
EQUIPMENT BY TYPE
PRINCIPAL SURFACE COMBATANTS • FRIGATES 2
  FFHM 2 *Anzac* (GER MEKO 200) with 1 20-cell VLS with *Sea Ceptor* SAM, 2 triple SVTT Mk 32 324mm ASTT with Mk 46 mod 5 LWT, 1 Mk 15 *Phalanx* Block 1B CIWS, 1 127mm gun (capacity 1 SH-2G(I) *Super Seasprite* ASW hel)
PATROL AND COASTAL COMBATANTS 4
  PSOH 2 *Otago* (capacity 1 SH-2G(I) *Super Seasprite* ASW hel) (ice-strengthened hull)
  PCC 2 *Lake*

AMPHIBIOUS • LANDING CRAFT 2
  LCM 2 (operated off HMNZS *Canterbury*)
LOGISTICS AND SUPPORT • 3
  AGHS 1 *Manawanui* with 1 hel landing platform
  AKRH 1 *Canterbury* (capacity 4 NH90 tpt hel; 1 SH-2G(I) *Super Seasprite* ASW hel; 2 LCM; 16 NZLAV; 20 trucks; 250 troops)
  AORH 1 *Aotearoa* (capacity 1 NH90/SH-2G(I) hel)

Air Force 2,500
FORCES BY ROLE
MARITIME PATROL
  1 sqn with P-3K2 *Orion*
TRANSPORT
  1 sqn with B-757-200 (upgraded); C-130H *Hercules* (upgraded)
ANTI-SUBMARINE/SURFACE WARFARE
  1 (RNZAF/RNZN) sqn with SH-2G(I) *Super Seasprite*
TRAINING
  1 sqn with T-6C *Texan* II
  1 sqn with Beech 350 *King Air* (leased)
TRANSPORT HELICOPTER
  1 sqn with AW109LUH; NH90
EQUIPMENT BY TYPE
AIRCRAFT 3 combat capable
  ASW 3 P-3K2 *Orion*
  TPT 11: **Medium** 5 C-130H *Hercules* (upgraded); **Light** 4 Beech 350 *King Air* (leased); **PAX** 2 B-757-200 (upgraded)
  TRG 11 T-6C *Texan* II
HELICOPTERS
  ASW 8 SH-2G(I) *Super Seasprite*
  TPT 13: **Medium** 8 NH90; **Light** 5 AW109LUH
AIR-LAUNCHED MISSILES • **AShM** AGM-119 *Penguin* Mk2 mod7

DEPLOYMENT
EGYPT: MFO 26; 1 trg unit; 1 tpt unit
IRAQ: Operation Inherent Resolve 9
MIDDLE EAST: UN • UNTSO 8
SOUTH SUDAN: UN • UNMISS 3

Pakistan PAK

Pakistani Rupee PKR		2021	2022	2023
GDP	PKR	55.8tr	66.9tr	
	USD	348bn	376bn	
per capita	USD	1,462	1,658	
Growth	%	5.7	6.0	
Inflation	%	8.9	12.1	
Def bdgt [a]	PKR	1.65tr	1.74tr	1.97tr
	USD	10.3bn	9.8bn	
USD1=PKR		160.23	177.83	

[a] Includes defence allocations to the Public Sector Development Programme (PSDP), including funding to the Defence Division and the Defence Production Division

Real-terms defence budget trend (USDbn, constant 2015)

Population   242,923,845

Age	0–14	15–19	20–24	25–29	30–64	65 plus
Male	18.0%	5.2%	4.7%	4.2%	16.7%	2.2%
Female	17.2%	5.0%	4.4%	4.0%	16.0%	2.5%

Capabilities

The armed forces have considerable domestic political influence and are the dominant voice on defence and security policy. Pakistan's nuclear and conventional forces have traditionally been oriented and structured against a prospective threat from India. Since 2008, counter-insurgency and counter-terrorism have been the forces' main effort. Although an army-led counter-terrorism operation has improved domestic security, terrorist attacks continue. Some analysts believe that the Pakistan government considered the Taliban victory in Afghanistan a policy success. Mutual reaffirmation of the 2003 ceasefire agreement between India and Pakistan has reduced conflict across the Line of Control in the disputed region of Jammu and Kashmir. The armed forces have a major role in disaster relief. China is Pakistan's main defence partner, with all three services employing a large amount of Chinese equipment. Military cooperation with the US is limited by sanctions aiming to improve cooperation on counter-terrorism. Recruitment is good, retention is high and the forces have experienced training establishments. The army and air force have considerable operational experience from a decade of counter-insurgency operations in Pakistan's tribal areas. Funds have been directed towards improving security on the border with Afghanistan. Major investment in military nuclear programmes continues, including the testing of a nuclear-capable sea-launched cruise missile. The navy plans to increase surface combatants, patrol vessels, submarines (in collaboration with China), maritime-patrol aircraft and UAVs. This is to both improve combat capability and the protection of sea-based nuclear weapons. The air force is modernising its inventory while improving its precision-strike and ISR capabilities. The indigenous defence industry has well-developed maintenance facilities for combat aircraft and exports platforms, weapons and ammunition; there is considerable defence-industrial collaboration with China.

ACTIVE 651,800 (Army 560,000 Navy 21,800 Air 70,000) **Gendarmerie & Paramilitary 291,000**

ORGANISATIONS BY SERVICE

Strategic Forces

Operational control rests with the National Command Authority. The Strategic Plans Directorate (SPD) manages and commands all of Pakistan's military nuclear capability. The SPD also commands a reportedly 25,000-strong military security force responsible for guarding the country's nuclear infrastructure

Army Strategic Forces Command 12,000–15,000

Commands all land-based strategic nuclear forces

EQUIPMENT BY TYPE
SURFACE-TO-SURFACE MISSILE LAUNCHERS 60+
MRBM • Nuclear 30+: ε30 *Ghauri/Ghauri* II (*Hatf*-V)/*Shaheen*-II (*Hatf*-VI); *Shaheen*-III (in test)
SRBM • Nuclear 30+: ε30 *Ghaznavi* (*Hatf*-III – PRC M-11)/*Shaheen*-I (*Hatf*-IV); some *Abdali* (*Hatf*-II); some *Nasr* (*Hatf*-IX)
GLCM • Nuclear *Babur*-I/IA (*Hatf*-VII); *Ra'ad* (*Hatf*-VIII – in test)

Air Force

1–2 sqn of F-16A/B or *Mirage* 5 may be assigned a nuclear-strike role

Army 560,000

FORCES BY ROLE
COMMAND
9 corps HQ
1 (Northern) comd
SPECIAL FORCES
2 SF gp (total: 4 SF bn)
MANOEUVRE
Armoured
2 armd div
7 indep armd bde
Mechanised
2 mech inf div
1 indep mech bde
Light
18 inf div
5 indep inf bde
4 (Northern Command) inf bde
Other
2 sy div
COMBAT SUPPORT
1 arty div
14 arty bde
7 engr bde
AVIATION
1 VIP avn sqn
4 avn sqn
HELICOPTER
3 atk hel sqn
2 ISR hel sqn
2 SAR hel sqn
2 tpt hel sqn
1 spec ops hel sqn
AIR DEFENCE
1 AD comd (3 AD gp (total: 8 AD bn))

EQUIPMENT BY TYPE
ARMOURED FIGHTING VEHICLES
MBT 2,537: 300 *Al-Khalid* (MBT 2000); ε110 *Al-Khalid* I; 315 T-80UD; ε500 *Al-Zarrar*; 400 Type-69; 268 Type-85-IIAP; 44 VT-4; ε600 ZTZ-59
APC 3,545
  APC (T) 3,200: 2,300 M113A1/A2/P; ε200 *Talha*; 600 VCC-1/VCC-2; ε100 ZSD-63
  APC (W) 120 BTR-70/BTR-80
  PPV 225 *Maxxpro*
AUV 10 *Dingo* 2
ENGINEERING & MAINTENANCE VEHICLES
ARV 262+: 175 Type-70/Type-84 (W653/W653A); *Al-Hadeed*; 52 M88A1; 35 *Maxxpro* ARV; T-54/T-55
VLB M47M; M48/60
MW *Aardvark* Mk II
ANTI-TANK/ANTI-INFRASTRUCTURE
MSL
  SP M901 TOW; ε30 *Maaz* (HJ-8 on *Talha* chassis)
  MANPATS HJ-8; TOW
RCL 75mm Type-52; **106mm** M40A1 **RL 89mm** M20
GUNS 85mm 200 Type-56 (D-44)
ARTILLERY 4,619+
SP 552: **155mm** 492: 200 M109A2; ε115 M109A5; 123 M109L; ε54 SH-15; **203mm** 60 M110/M110A2
TOWED 1,629: **105mm** 329: 216 M101; 113 M-56; **122mm** 570: 80 D-30 (PRC); 490 Type-54 (M-1938); **130mm** 410 Type-59-I; **155mm** 292: 144 M114; 148 M198; **203mm** 28 M115
MRL 88+: **107mm** Type-81; **122mm** 52+: 52 *Azar* (Type-83); some KRL-122; **300mm** 36 A100
MOR 2,350+: **81mm**; **120mm** AM-50
SURFACE-TO-SURFACE MISSILE LAUNCHERS
  MRBM • Nuclear 30+: ε30 *Ghauri/Ghauri* II (*Hatf*-V)/*Shaheen*-II (*Hatf*-VI); some *Shaheen*-III (in test)
  SRBM 135+: **Nuclear** 30+: ε30 *Ghaznavi* (*Hatf*-III – PRC M-11)/*Shaheen*-I (*Hatf*-IV); some *Abdali* (*Hatf*-II); some *Nasr* (*Hatf*-IX); **Conventional** 105 *Hatf*-I
  GLCM • Nuclear some *Babur*-I/IA (*Hatf*-VII)
AIRCRAFT
TPT • Light 13: 1 Beech 350 *King Air*; 3 Cessna 208B; 1 Cessna 421; 1 Cessna 550 *Citation*; 1 Cessna 560 *Citation*; 2 *Turbo Commander* 690; 4 Y-12(II)
TRG 87 MFI-17B *Mushshak*
HELICOPTERS
ATK 42: 38 AH-1F/S *Cobra* with TOW; 4 Mi-35M *Hind*; (1 Mi-24 *Hind* in store)
MRH 115+: 10 H125M *Fennec*; 7 AW139; 26 Bell 412EP *Twin Huey*; 38+ Mi-17 *Hip* H; 2 Mi-171E *Hip*; 12 SA315B *Lama*; 20 SA319 *Alouette* III
TPT 76: **Medium** 36: 31 SA330 *Puma*; 4 Mi-171; 1 Mi-172; **Light** 40: 17 H125 *Ecureuil* (SAR); 5 Bell 205 (UH-1H *Iroquois*); 5 Bell 205A-1 (AB-205A-1); 13 Bell 206B *Jet Ranger* II
TRG 10 Hughes 300C
UNINHABITED AERIAL VEHICLES
CISR • Heavy 5 CH-4
ISR • Light *Bravo*; *Jasoos*; *Vector*

Asia 281

AIR DEFENCE
SAM 27+
Long-range some FK-3 (HQ-22)
Medium-range 27 LY-80 (CH-SA-16)
Short-range FM-90 (CH-SA-4)
Point-defence M113 with RBS-70; *Anza*-II; FN-6 (CH-SA-10); *Mistral*; QW-18 (CH-SA-11); RBS-70
GUNS • TOWED 1,933: **14.5mm** 981; **35mm** 248 GDF-002/GDF-005 (with 134 *Skyguard* radar units); **37mm** 310 Type-55 (M-1939)/Type-65; **40mm** 50 L/60; **57mm** 144 Type-59 (S-60); **85mm** 200 Type-72 (M-1939) KS-12

Navy 21,800 (incl ε3,200 Marines)

EQUIPMENT BY TYPE
SUBMARINES 8
SSK 5:
2 *Hashmat* (FRA *Agosta* 70) with 4 single 533mm ASTT with UGM-84 *Harpoon* AShM/F-17P HWT
3 *Khalid* (FRA *Agosta* 90B) (of which 2 fitted with AIP) with 4 single 533mm ASTT with SM39 *Exocet* AShM/ *SeaHake* mod 4 (DM2A4) HWT
SSW 3 MG110 (SF delivery) each with 2 single 533mm TT with F-17P HWT
PRINCIPAL SURFACE COMBATANTS • FRIGATES 8
FFGHM 6:
4 *Sword* (F-22P) with 2 quad lnchr with C-802A AShM, 1 octuple lnchr with FM-90N (CH-SA-N-4) SAM, 2 triple 324mm ASTT with ET-52C (A244/S) LWT, 2 RDC-32 A/S mor, 1 Type 730B (H/PJ-12) CIWS, 1 76mm gun (capacity 1 Z-9C *Haitun* hel)
2 *Tughril* (Type-054AP (*Jiangkai* II)) with 2 twin lnchr with CM-302 (YJ-12A) AShM, 4 8-cell H/AJK-16 VLS with LY-80N (HHQ-16 (CH-SA-N-16)) SAM, 2 triple 324mm ASTT with Yu-7 LWT, 2 H/PJ-11 CIWS, 1 76mm gun (capacity 1 Z-9C *Haitun* ASW hel)
FFGH 1 *Alamgir* (ex-US *Oliver Hazard Perry*) with 2 quad lnchr with RGM-84 *Harpoon* AShM, 2 triple 324mm ASTT with Mk 46 LWT, 1 Mk 15 *Phalanx* CIWS, 1 76mm gun
FFHM 1 *Tariq* (ex-UK *Amazon*) with 1 sextuple lnchr with LY-60N SAM, 2 triple 324mm ASTT with Mk 46 LWT, 1 Mk 15 *Phalanx* Block 1B CIWS, 1 114mm gun (capacity 1 hel)
PATROL AND COASTAL COMBATANTS 20
CORVETTES • FSH 2 *Yarmook* (Damen OPV 1900) (fitted for but not with 2 quad lnchr for AShM) with 1 Mk 15 *Phalanx* CIWS (capacity 1 hel)
PCG 4: 2 *Azmat* (FAC(M)) with 2 quad lnchr with C-802A AShM, 1 AK630 CIWS; 2 *Azmat* (FAC(M)) with 2 triple lnchr with C-602 AShM, 1 AK630 CIWS
PBG 4: 2 *Jalalat* with 2 twin lnchr with C-802 (CH-SS-N-6) AShM; 2 *Jurrat* with 2 twin lnchr with C-802 (CH-SS-N-6) AShM
PBF 4: 2 *Kaan* 15; 2 *Zarrar* (33)
PB 6: 1 *Larkana*; 1 *Rajshahi†*; 4 M16 Fast Assault Boat
MINE WARFARE • MINE COUNTERMEASURES 3
MCC 3 *Munsif* (FRA *Eridan*)
AMPHIBIOUS • LANDING CRAFT 8
LCM 2
LCAC 2 *Griffon* 8100TD
UCAC 4 *Griffon* 2000TD

LOGISTICS AND SUPPORT 9
AGS 2: 1 *Behr Masa*; 1 *Behr Paima*
AOL 2 *Madadgar*
AORH 2: 1 *Fuqing* with 1 Mk 15 *Phalanx* CIWS (capacity 1 SA319 *Alouette* III hel); 1 *Moawin* (Fleet Tanker) with 2 Mk 15 *Phalanx* CIWS, 1 hel landing platform
AOT 2 *Gwadar*
AXS 1

Marines ε3,200

FORCES BY ROLE
SPECIAL FORCES
1 cdo gp
MANOEUVRE
Amphibious
3 mne bn
AIR DEFENCE
1 AD bn

Naval Aviation

EQUIPMENT BY TYPE
AIRCRAFT 9 combat capable
ASW 9: 7 P-3B/C *Orion*; 2 ATR-72-500
MP 7: 6 F-27-200 MPA; 1 Lineage 1000
TPT 3: **Light** 2 ATR-72-500; **PAX** 1 Hawker 850XP
HELICOPTERS
ASW 11: 4 *Sea King* Mk45; 7 Z-9C *Haitun*
MRH 6 SA319B *Alouette* III
SAR 1 *Sea King* (ex-HAR3A)
TPT • **Medium** 5: 1 *Commando* Mk2A; 3 *Commando* Mk3; 1 *Sea King* (ex-HC4)
AIR-LAUNCHED MISSILES • AShM AM39 *Exocet*

Coastal Defence

FORCES BY ROLE
COASTAL Defence
1 AShM regt with *Zarb* (YJ-62)
EQUIPMENT BY TYPE
COASTAL DEFENCE • AShM *Zarb* (YJ-62)

Air Force 70,000

3 regional comds: Northern (Peshawar), Central (Sargodha), Southern (Masroor). The Composite Air Tpt Wg, Combat Cadres School and PAF Academy are Direct Reporting Units
FORCES BY ROLE
FIGHTER
3 sqn with F-7PG/FT-7PG *Airguard*
1 sqn with F-16A/B MLU *Fighting Falcon*
1 sqn with F-16A/B ADF *Fighting Falcon*
1 sqn with *Mirage* IIID/E (IIIOD/EP)
FIGHTER/GROUND ATTACK
1 sqn with JF-17 *Thunder* (FC-1 Block 1)
3 sqn with JF-17 *Thunder* (FC-1 Block 2)
1 sqn with JF-17B *Thunder* (FC-1 Block 2)
1 sqn with F-16C/D Block 52 *Fighting Falcon*
3 sqn with *Mirage* 5 (5PA)
ANTI-SURFACE WARFARE
1 sqn with *Mirage* 5PA2/5PA3 with AM-39 *Exocet* AShM
ELECTRONIC WARFARE/ELINT
1 sqn with *Falcon* 20F

Asia

AIRBORNE EARLY WARNING & CONTROL
1 sqn with Saab 2000; Saab 2000 *Erieye*
1 sqn with ZDK-03

SEARCH & RESCUE
1 sqn with Mi-171Sh; AW139 (SAR/liaison)
5 sqn with SA316 *Alouette* III
2 sqn with AW139

TANKER
1 sqn with Il-78 *Midas*

TRANSPORT
1 sqn with C-130E/H *Hercules*; L-100-20
1 sqn with CN235M-220
1 VIP sqn with B-707; Cessna 560XL *Citation Excel*;
CN235M-220; F-27-200 *Friendship*; Falcon 20E;
Gulfstream IVSP
1 (comms) sqn with EMB-500 *Phenom* 100; Y-12 (II)

TRAINING
1 OCU sqn with F-7P/FT-7P *Skybolt*
1 OCU sqn with *Mirage* III/*Mirage* 5
1 OCU sqn with F-16A/B MLU *Fighting Falcon*
2 sqn with K-8 *Karakorum**
2 sqn with MFI-17
2 sqn with T-37C *Tweet*

AIR DEFENCE
1 bty with HQ-2 (CH-SA-1); 9K310 *Igla*-1 (RS-SA-16 *Gimlet*)
6 bty with *Crotale*
10 bty with SPADA 2000

EQUIPMENT BY TYPE
AIRCRAFT 431 combat capable
FTR 151: 46 F-7PG *Airguard*; 20 F-7P *Skybolt*; 23 F-16A
MLU *Fighting Falcon*; 21 F-16B MLU *Fighting Falcon*;
9 F-16A ADF *Fighting Falcon*; 4 F-16B ADF *Fighting Falcon*;
21 FT-7; 5 FT-7PG; 2 *Mirage* IIIB
FGA 229: 12 F-16C Block 52 *Fighting Falcon*; 6 F-16D
Block 52 *Fighting Falcon*; 12+ J-10CE; 49 JF-17 *Thunder*
(FC-1 Block 1); 61 JF-17 *Thunder* (FC-1 Block 2); 15 JF-
17B *Thunder*; 7 *Mirage* IIID (*Mirage* IIIOD); 30 *Mirage*
IIIE (IIIEP); 25 *Mirage* 5 (5PA)/5PA2; 2 *Mirage* 5D
(5DPA)/5DPA2; 10 *Mirage* 5PA3 (ASuW)
ISR 10 *Mirage* IIIR* (*Mirage* IIIRP)
ELINT 2 *Falcon* 20F
AEW&C 10: 6 Saab 2000 *Erieye*; 4 ZDK-03
TKR 4 Il-78 *Midas*
TPT 35: **Medium** 16: 10 C-130E *Hercules*; 5 C-130H
Hercules; 1 L-100-20; **Light** 14: 2 Cessna 208B; 1 Cessna
560XL *Citation Excel*; 4 CN235M-220; 4 EMB-500 *Phenom*
100; 1 F-27-200 *Friendship*; 2 Y-12 (II); **PAX** 5: 1 B-707;
1 *Falcon* 20E; 2 Gulfstream IVSP; 1 Saab 2000
TRG 140: 38 K-8 *Karakorum**; 79 MFI-17B *Mushshak*;
23 T-37C *Tweet*
HELICOPTERS
MRH 29: 15 SA316 *Alouette* III; 14 AW139
TPT • Medium 4 Mi-171Sh
UNINHABITED AERIAL VEHICLES
CISR • Heavy CH-3 (*Burraq*); CH-4 (reported)
ISR • Medium *Falco*
AIR DEFENCE • SAM 190+
Medium-range 6 HQ-2 (CH-SA-1)
Short-range 184: 144 *Crotale*; ε40 SPADA 2000
Point-defence 9K310 *Igla*-1 (RS-SA-16 *Gimlet*)

AIR-LAUNCHED MISSILES
AAM • IR AIM-9L/P *Sidewinder*; U-Darter; PL-5; PL-5E-
II; **IIR** PL-10 (CH-AA-9); **SARH** Super 530; **ARH** PL-12
(CH-AA-7A *Adze*); PL-15 (CH-AA-10); AIM-120C AMRAAM
ASM AGM-65 *Maverick*; Raptor II
AShM AM39 *Exocet*; C-802
ARM MAR-1
ALCM • Nuclear *Ra'ad*
BOMBS
INS/SAT-guided FT-6 (REK)
Laser-guided *Paveway* II

Gendarmerie & Paramilitary 291,000 active

Airport Security Force 9,000
Government Aviation Division

Pakistan Coast Guards
Ministry of Interior
EQUIPMENT BY TYPE
PATROL AND COASTAL COMBATANTS 5:
PBF 4
PB 1

Frontier Corps 70,000
Ministry of Interior
FORCES BY ROLE
MANOEUVRE
Reconnaissance
1 armd recce sqn
Other
11 paramilitary regt (total: 40 paramilitary bn)
EQUIPMENT BY TYPE
ARMOURED FIGHTING VEHICLES
APC (W) 45 UR-416

Maritime Security Agency ε2,000
FORCES BY ROLE
MARITIME PATROL
1 sqn with BN-2T *Defender*
EQUIPMENT BY TYPE
PATROL AND COASTAL COMBATANTS 20
PSO 2 *Kashmir*
PCC 10: 4 *Barkat*; 4 *Hingol*; 2 *Sabqat* (ex-US *Island*)
PBF 5 Response Boat-Medium (RB-M) (ex-US)
PB 3 *Guns*
AIRCRAFT • TPT • Light 3 BN-2T *Defender*

National Guard 185,000
Incl Janbaz Force; Mujahid Force; National Cadet Corps;
Women Guards

Pakistan Rangers 25,000
Ministry of Interior

DEPLOYMENT

**ARABIAN SEA & GULF OF ADEN: Combined Maritime
Forces • CTF-151:** 1 FFGHM

CENTRAL AFRICAN REPUBLIC: UN • MINUSCA 1,310; 1 inf bn; 2 engr coy; 1 hel sqn
CYPRUS: UN • UNFICYP 3
DEMOCRATIC REPUBLIC OF THE CONGO: UN • MONUSCO 1,974; 2 inf bn; 1 hel sqn with SA330 *Puma*
MALI: UN • MINUSMA 221; 1 hel flt with 3 Mi-17; 1 fd hospital
SOMALIA: UN • UNSOS 1
SOUTH SUDAN: UN • UNMISS 286; 1 engr coy
SUDAN: UN • UNISFA 583; 1 inf bn
WESTERN SAHARA: UN • MINURSO 13

FOREIGN FORCES

Figures represent total numbers for UNMOGIP mission in India and Pakistan
Argentina 3
Croatia 8
Italy 2
Korea, Republic of 7
Mexico 1
Philippines 5
Romania 2
Sweden 4
Switzerland 3
Thailand 6
Uruguay 3

Papua New Guinea PNG

Papua New Guinea Kina PGK		2021	2022	2023
GDP	PGK	94.6bn	109bn	
	USD	27.3bn	31.4bn	
per capita	USD	3,050	3,427	
Growth	%	1.2	3.8	
Inflation	%	4.5	6.6	
Def bdgt	PGK	305m	344m	333m
	USD	88.2m	99.4m	
USD1=PGK		3.46	3.46	

Real-terms defence budget trend (USDm, constant 2015)

Population	9,593,498					
Age	0–14	15–19	20–24	25–29	30–64	65 plus
Male	19.2%	5.0%	4.5%	4.1%	16.1%	1.9%
Female	18.4%	4.8%	4.4%	3.9%	15.9%	1.9%

Capabilities

Since independence in 1975, the Papua New Guinea Defence Force (PNGDF) has suffered from underfunding and lack of capacity to perform its core roles. After personnel reductions in the 2000s, the government made efforts in the next decade to revive defence capability. A 2013 defence White Paper identified core roles including defending the state and civil-emergency assistance, but noted that 'defence capabilities have deteriorated to the extent that we have alarming gaps in our land, air and maritime borders'. The White Paper called for strengthening defence capability on an ambitious scale, with long-term plans calling for a 'division-sized force' of 10,000 personnel by 2030. The PNGDF continues to receive substantial external military assistance from Australia and also from China, which has donated equipment. In late 2018, plans to build a joint US–Australia–Papua New Guinea naval base at Lombrum were announced. In 2022 there were discussions on closer defence cooperation with Australia. The PNGDF is not able to deploy outside the country without outside assistance and there have only been small PNGDF deployments to UN peacekeeping missions. The PNGDF will receive four of the *Guardian*-class patrol boats that Australia is donating to small Pacific island nations. These will replace the four *Pacific*-class boats Australia donated in the 1980s. Papua New Guinea has no significant defence industry, though there is some local maintenance capacity.

ACTIVE 4,000 (Army 3,700 Maritime Element 200 Air 100)

ORGANISATIONS BY SERVICE

Army ε3,700

FORCES BY ROLE
SPECIAL FORCES
　1 spec ops unit
MANOEUVRE
　Light
　2 inf bn
COMBAT SUPPORT
　1 engr bn
　1 EOD unit
　1 sigs sqn
EQUIPMENT BY TYPE
ARTILLERY • **MOR** 3+: **81mm** Some; **120mm** 3

Maritime Element ε200

HQ located at Port Moresby
EQUIPMENT BY TYPE
PATROL AND COASTAL COMBATANTS • **PCO** 3 *Guardian* (AUS *Bay* mod)
AMPHIBIOUS • **LANDING CRAFT** 2
　LCT 1 *Salamaua* (ex-AUS *Balikpapan*)
　LCM 1 *Cape Gloucester*

Air Force ε100

FORCES BY ROLE
TRANSPORT
　1 sqn with CN235M-100; IAI-201 *Arava*
TRANSPORT HELICOPTER
　1 sqn with Bell 205 (UH-1H *Iroquois*)†
EQUIPMENT BY TYPE
AIRCRAFT • **TPT** • **Light** 3: 1 CN235M-100 (1 more in store); 2 IAI-201 *Arava*
HELICOPTERS • **TPT** • **Light** 3: 2 Bell 412 (leased); 1 Bell 212 (leased) (2 Bell 205 (UH-1H *Iroquois*) non-operational)

Philippines PHL

Philippine Peso PHP		2021	2022	2023
GDP	PHP	19.4tr	21.7tr	
	USD	394bn	402bn	
per capita	USD	3,576	3,597	
Growth	%	5.7	6.5	
Inflation	%	3.9	5.3	
Def bdgt [a]	PHP	279bn	295bn	333bn
	USD	5.66bn	5.46bn	
FMA (US)	USD	40m	40m	40m
USD1=PHP		49.25	53.99	

[a] Excludes military pensions

Real-terms defence budget trend (USDbn, constant 2015)

Population		114,597,229				
Age	0–14	15–19	20–24	25–29	30–64	65 plus
Male	15.7%	5.0%	4.6%	4.2%	18.4%	2.1%
Female	15.1%	4.8%	4.5%	4.1%	18.3%	3.2%

Capabilities

Despite modest increases in defence funding, mainly in response to the growing challenge posed by China to Philippine interests in the South China Sea, the capabilities and procurement plans of the Armed Forces of the Philippines (AFP), which have traditionally focused on maintaining internal security, remain limited. The National Defense Strategy 2018–22 identified policy priorities including ensuring sovereignty and territorial integrity, and internal stability. In 2019, the Philippine Space Agency was set up, and an MoU on closer collaboration with the defence department was agreed in 2022. The Philippines remains an ally of the US, which provides support for the AFP's external security role and its counter-terrorist operations. Bilateral defence relations improved in 2021 after then-president Duterte agreed to maintain the bilateral Visiting Forces Agreement. The AFP continues to host the long-running Balikatan exercise series with US forces, and to participate in ADMM-Plus exercises. In 2017 it began trilateral joint maritime patrols in the Sulu Sea with Indonesia and Malaysia to counter regional terrorist activity. The armed forces continue to be deployed on internal-security duties in the south, where Manila faces continuing challenges from insurgent groups. The second phase (2018–22) of the 'second horizon' AFP modernisation programme was approved in 2018, and projects still outstanding are set to transition to a third and final phase (2023–28). The new government has reviewed projects slated for the third phase and amid budget concerns some, such as the plan to acquire conventionally-powered submarines, are reportedly no longer a priority. The Philippine Aerospace Development Corporation, owned by the defence department since 2019, has assembled a variety of small helicopters and aircraft for the AFP, and also provides maintenance, repair and overhaul services for military aircraft.

ACTIVE 145,300 (Army 103,200 Navy 24,500 Air 17,600) Gendarmerie & Paramilitary 12,300

RESERVE 131,000 (Army 100,000 Navy 15,000 Air 16,000) Gendarmerie & Paramilitary 50,000 (to age 49)

ORGANISATIONS BY SERVICE

Army 103,200

5 Area Unified Comd (joint service), 1 National Capital Region Comd

FORCES BY ROLE
SPECIAL FORCES
  1 spec ops comd (1 ranger regt, 1 SF regt, 1 CT regt)
MANOEUVRE
  Mechanised
  1 armd div (2 mech bde (total: 3 lt armd bn, 7 armd cav coy, 4 mech inf bn), 1 cbt engr coy, 1 sigs coy, 1 avn regt)
  Light
  1 div (4 inf bde, 1 fd arty bn, 1 int bn, 1 sigs bn)
  7 div (3 inf bde, 1 fd arty bn, 1 int bn, 1 sigs bn)
  3 div (3 inf bde, 1 int bn, 1 sigs bn)
  Other
  1 (Presidential) gd gp
COMBAT SUPPORT
  1 SP arty bn
  2 MRL bty (forming)
  5 engr bde
SURFACE-TO-SURFACE MISSILE
  1 SSM bty (forming)
AIR DEFENCE
  1 AD bty

EQUIPMENT BY TYPE
ARMOURED FIGHTING VEHICLES
  LT TK 7 FV101 Scorpion
  IFV 54: 2 YPR-765; 34 M113A1 FSV; 18 M113A2 FSV
  APC 387
    APC (T) 168: 6 ACV300; 42 M113A1; 120 M113A2 (some with Dragon RWS)
    APC (W) 219: 73 LAV-150 Commando; 146 Simba
  PPV 2+ CS/VP-3
ENGINEERING & MAINTENANCE VEHICLES
  ARV ACV-300; Samson; M578; 4 M113 ARV
  VLB 2+: some GQL-111; 2 Merkava MkIV AVLB
ANTI-TANK-ANTI-INFRASTRUCTURE • RCL 75mm M20; **90mm** M67; **106mm** M40A1
ARTILLERY 272+
  SP 155mm 12 ATMOS 2000
  TOWED 220: **105mm** 204 M101/M102/Model 56 pack howitzer; **155mm** 16: 10 M114/M-68; 6 Soltam M-71
  MOR 40+: **81mm** M29; **107mm** 40 M30; **120mm** some Cardom
AIRCRAFT
  TPT • Light 4: 1 Beech 80 Queen Air; 1 Cessna 170; 1 Cessna 172; 1 Cessna P206A
HELICOPTERS
  TPT • Light 2 R-44 Raven II
UNINHABITED AERIAL VEHICLES • ISR • Medium Blue Horizon

Navy 24,500

EQUIPMENT BY TYPE
PRINCIPAL SURFACE COMBATANTS • FRIGATES 2
  FFGHM 2 Jose Rizal (HDF-3000) with 2 quad lnchr with Hae Sung I AShM, 2 twin Simbad-RC lnchr with Mistral SAM, 2 triple 324mm SEA TLS ASTT with K745 Blue

Shark LWT, 1 76mm gun (fitted for but not with 1 8-cell VLS) (capacity 1 AW159 *Wildcat*)

PATROL AND COASTAL COMBATANTS 53

CORVETTES • FS 1 *Conrado Yap* (ex-ROK *Po Hang* (Flight III)) with 2 triple 324mm SVTT Mk 32 ASTT, 2 76mm gun

PSOH 3 *Del Pilar* (ex-US *Hamilton*) with 1 76mm gun (capacity 1 Bo 105)

PCF 1 *General Mariano Alvares* (ex-US *Cyclone*)

PCO 4: 3 *Emilio Jacinto* (ex-UK *Peacock*) with 1 76mm gun; 1 *Miguel Malvar* (ex-US) with 1 76mm gun

PBFG 6 MPAC Mk3 with 1 *Typhoon* MLS-ER quad lnchr with *Spike*-ER SSM

PBF 6 MPAC Mk1/2

PB 26: 22 *Jose Andrada*; 2 *Kagitingan*; 2 *Point* (ex-US)

PBR 6 Silver Ships

AMPHIBIOUS

PRINCIPAL AMPHIBIOUS SHIPS • LPD 2:

2 *Tarlac* (IDN *Makassar*) (capacity 2 LCVP; 3 hels; 13 tanks; 500 troops)

LANDING SHIPS • LST 4:

2 *Bacolod City* (US *Besson*) with 1 hel landing platform (capacity 32 tanks; 150 troops)

2 LST-1/542 (ex-US) (capacity 16 tanks; 200 troops) (1 other permanently grounded as marine outpost)

LANDING CRAFT 15

LCM 2: 1 *Manobo*; 1 *Tagbanua* (capacity 100 tons; 200 troops)

LCT 5 *Ivatan* (ex-AUS *Balikpapan*)

LCU 4: 3 LCU Mk 6 (ex-US); 1 *Mamanwa* (ex-RoK *Mulgae* I)

LCVP 4

LOGISTICS AND SUPPORT 4

AGOR 1 *Gregorio Velasquez* (ex-US *Melville*)

AOL 1

AP 1 *Ang Pangulo*

AWT 1 *Lake Buluan*

Naval Aviation

EQUIPMENT BY TYPE

AIRCRAFT • TPT • Light 14: 5 Beech 90 *King Air* (TC-90); 3 BN-2A *Defender*; 4 Cessna 172; 2 Cessna 177 *Cardinal*

HELICOPTERS

ASW 2 AW159 *Wildcat*

TPT 13: **Medium** 4 Mi-171Sh; **Light** 9: 3 AW109; 2 AW109E; 4 Bo-105

Marines 8,300

FORCES BY ROLE

SPECIAL FORCES

1 (force recon) spec ops bn

MANOEUVRE

Amphibious

4 mne bde (total: 12 mne bn)

COMBAT SERVICE SUPPORT

1 CSS bde (6 CSS bn)

COASTAL DEFENCE

1 coastal def bde (1 AShM bn (forming); 1 SAM bn (forming))

EQUIPMENT BY TYPE

ARMOURED FIGHTING VEHICLES

APC • APC (W) 42: 19 LAV-150 *Commando*; 23 LAV-300

AAV 67: 8 AAV-7A1; 4 LVTH-6†; 55 LVTP-7

ARTILLERY 37+

TOWED 37: **105mm** 31: 23 M101; 8 M-26; **155mm** 6 Soltam M-71

MOR 107mm M30

Naval Special Operations Group

FORCES BY ROLE

SPECIAL FORCES

1 SEAL unit

1 diving unit

10 naval spec ops unit

1 special boat unit

COMBAT SUPPORT

1 EOD unit

Air Force 17,600

FORCES BY ROLE

FIGHTER

1 sqn with FA-50PH *Fighting Eagle**

GROUND ATTACK

1 sqn with EMB-314 *Super Tucano**

1 sqn with OV-10A/C *Bronco**; SF-260F/TP*

ISR

1 sqn with Cessna 208B *Grand Caravan*; *Turbo Commander* 690A

SEARCH & RESCUE

4 (SAR/Comms) sqn with Bell 205 (UH-1M *Iroquois*); AUH-76; W-3A *Sokol*

TRANSPORT

1 sqn with C-130B/H/T *Hercules*

1 sqn with C295/W; F-27-200 MPA; F-27-500 *Friendship*

1 sqn with N-22B *Nomad*; N-22SL *Searchmaster*; C-212 *Aviocar* (NC-212i)

1 VIP sqn with C295M; F-28 *Fellowship*; Gulfstream G280

TRAINING

1 sqn with SF-260FH

1 sqn with T-41B/D/K *Mescalero*

1 sqn with S-211*

1 sqn with Bell 205 (UH-1H *Iroquois*)

ATTACK HELICOPTERS

1 sqn with AH-1S *Cobra*; MD-520MG

1 sqn with AW109E

TRANSPORT HELICOPTER

2 sqn with Bell 205 (UH-1H *Iroquois*)

1 sqn with S-70i *Black Hawk*

1 (VIP) sqn with Bell 412EP *Twin Huey*; S-70A *Black Hawk* (S-70A-5)

ISR UAV

1 sqn with *Hermes* 450/900

AIR DEFENCE

2 bty with *Spyder*-MR

EQUIPMENT BY TYPE

AIRCRAFT 49 combat capable

FGA 12 FA-50PH *Fighting Eagle*

MP 3: 1 C-130T MP mod; 1 F-27-200 MPA; 1 N-22SL *Searchmaster*

ISR 11: 2 Cessna 208B *Grand Caravan*; 9 OV-10A/C *Bronco**

TPT 17: **Medium** 4: 1 C-130B *Hercules*; 2 C-130H *Hercules*; 1 C-130T *Hercules* **Light** 11: 3 C295; 1 C295M; 2 C295W;

1 F-27-500 *Friendship*; 1 N-22B *Nomad*; 1 *Turbo Commander* 690A; 2 C-212 *Aviocar* (NC-212i); **PAX** 2: 1 F-28 *Fellowship* (VIP); 1 Gulfstream G280
TRG 45: 6 EMB-314 *Super Tucano**; 12 S-211*; 7 SF-260FH; 10 SF-260TP*; 10 T-41B/D/K *Mescalero*
HELICOPTERS
ATK 4: 2 AH-1S *Cobra*; T129B
MRH 39: 8 W-3A *Sokol*; 2 AUH-76; 8 AW109E; 8 Bell 412EP *Twin Huey*; 2 Bell 412HP *Twin Huey*; 11 MD-520MG
TPT 35: **Medium** 16: 1 S-70A *Black Hawk* (S-70A-5); 15 S-70i *Black Hawk*; **Light** 19 Bell 205 (UH-1H *Iroquois*) (25 more non-operational)
UNINHABITED AERIAL VEHICLES
ISR • Medium 5: 2 *Blue Horizon* II; 1 *Hermes* 450; 2 *Hermes* 900
AIR-LAUNCHED MISSILES
AAM • IR AIM-9L *Sidewinder*
ASM AGM-65D *Maverick*; AGM-65G2 *Maverick*
BOMBS
INS/GPS-guided: GBU-49 *Enhanced Paveway* II
AIR DEFENCE • SAM
Medium-range 6 *Spyder*-MR

Gendarmerie & Paramilitary 12,300

Coast Guard 12,300
EQUIPMENT BY TYPE
Rodman 38 and Rodman 101 owned by Bureau of Fisheries and Aquatic Resources
PATROL AND COASTAL COMBATANTS 72
  PSOH 1 *Gabriela Silang* (OCEA OPV 270)
  PCO 4 *San Juan* with 1 hel landing platform
  PB 56: 4 *Boracay* (FPB 72 Mk II); 4 *Ilocos Norte*; 10 *Parola* (MRRV); 10 PCF 46; 12 PCF 50 (US *Swift* Mk1/2); 2 PCF 65 (US *Swift* Mk3); 4 Rodman 38; 10 Rodman 101
  PBR 11
LOGISTICS AND SUPPORT • ABU 1 *Corregidor*
AIRCRAFT • TPT • Light 3: 2 BN-2 *Islander*; 1 Cessna 208B *Grand Caravan* EX
HELICOPTERS • TPT • Light 4: 2 Bo-105; 2 H145

Citizen Armed Force Geographical Units
50,000 reservists
FORCES BY ROLE
MANOEUVRE
  Other 56 militia bn (part-time units which can be called up for extended periods)

DEPLOYMENT
CENTRAL AFRICAN REPUBLIC: UN • MINUSCA 3
INDIA/PAKISTAN: UN • UNMOGIP 5
SOUTH SUDAN: UN • UNMISS 2

FOREIGN FORCES
Australia *Operation Augury* 100
United States US Pacific Command: *Operation Pacific Eagle – Philippines* 200

Singapore SGP

Singapore Dollar SGD		2021	2022	2023
GDP	SGD	533bn	582bn	
	USD	397bn	424bn	
per capita	USD	72,795	79,426	
Growth	%	7.6	3.0	
Inflation	%	2.3	5.5	
Def bdgt	SGD	15.4bn	16.4bn	
	USD	11.4bn	11.9bn	
USD1=SGD		1.34	1.37	

Real-terms defence budget trend (USDbn, constant 2015)

Population	5,921,231					
Age	0–14	15–19	20–24	25–29	30–64	65 plus
Male	7.8%	3.1%	3.8%	4.3%	24.9%	6.1%
Female	7.3%	2.8%	3.5%	3.8%	25.7%	7.0%

Capabilities

The Singapore Armed Forces (SAF) are the best equipped in Southeast Asia. They are organised essentially along Israeli lines, with the air force and navy staffed mainly by professional personnel while, apart from a small core of regulars, the much larger army is based on conscripts and reservists. Although there are no publicly available defence-policy documents, it is widely presumed that the SAF's primary role is to deter attacks on the city state or interference with its vital interests – particularly its sea lines of communication – by potential regional adversaries. There is an additional focus on counter-terrorist operations. With an ageing population and declining conscript cohort, there is a significant personnel challenge, which the defence ministry is addressing by lean staffing and increased use of technology. There is routine overseas training, and plans have been announced to further improve domestic training areas. The SAF also engages extensively in bilateral and multilateral exercises with regional and international partners. Singaporean forces have gradually become more involved – albeit on a small-scale – in multinational operations. While deployments have provided some operational experience, and training standards and operational readiness are high, the army's reliance on conscripts and reservists limits its capacity for sustained operations abroad. Equipment modernisation continues, which will be further enhanced by the 'SAF 2040' vision, launched in March 2022. This outlines procurement and upgrade priorities across all domains, including the establishment of a fourth service branch – the Digital and Intelligence Service, which was established in October 2022. Plans to acquire capabilities including F-35 combat aircraft, multi-role combat vessels, uninhabited surface vessels and uninhabited aerial vehicles, offshore patrol vessels, maritime patrol aircraft and land equipment are intended to maintain Singapore's military edge over other Southeast Asian countries. There is a small but sophisticated defence industry. ST Engineering manufactures armoured vehicles, artillery and naval vessels for the SAF.

ACTIVE 51,000 (Army 40,000 Navy 4,000 Air 6,000 Digitial & Intelligence 1,000) **Gendarmerie & Paramilitary 7,400**
Conscription liability 22–24 months

RESERVE 252,500 (Army 240,000 Navy 5,000 Air 7,500)

Annual trg to age 40 for army other ranks, 50 for officers

ORGANISATIONS BY SERVICE

Army 40,000 (including 26,000 conscripts)

FORCES BY ROLE
COMMAND
3 (combined arms) div HQ
1 (rapid reaction) div HQ
4 armd bde HQ
9 inf bde HQ
1 air mob bde HQ
1 amph bde HQ
SPECIAL FORCES
1 cdo bn
MANOEUVRE
Reconnaissance
3 lt armd/recce bn
Armoured
1 armd bn
Mechanised
6 mech inf bn
Light
2 (gds) inf bn
Other
2 sy bn
COMBAT SUPPORT
2 arty bn
1 STA bn
2 engr bn
1 EOD bn
1 ptn br bn
1 int bn
2 ISR bn
1 CBRN bn
3 sigs bn
COMBAT SERVICE SUPPORT
3 med bn
2 tpt bn
3 spt bn

Reserves

Activated units form part of divisions and brigades listed above; 1 op reserve div with additional armd & inf bde; People's Defence Force Comd (homeland defence) with 12 inf bn

FORCES BY ROLE
SPECIAL FORCES
1 cdo bn
MANOEUVRE
Reconnaissance
6 lt armd/recce bn
Mechanised
6 mech inf bn
Light
ε56 inf bn
COMBAT SUPPORT
ε12 arty bn
ε8 engr bn

EQUIPMENT BY TYPE
ARMOURED FIGHTING VEHICLES
MBT 96+ *Leopard* 2SG
LT TK ε50 AMX-13 SM1 (22 AMX-10 PAC 90; ε300 AMX-13 SM1 in store)
IFV 600+: 250 *Bionix* IFV-25; 250 *Bionix* IFV-40/50; ε50 *Hunter* AFV; 50+ M113A2 *Ultra*; (22 AMX-10P)
APC 1,375+
  APC (T) 1,100+: 700+ M113A1/A2; 400+ ATTC *Bronco*
  APC (W) 135 *Terrex* ICV; (250 LAV-150/V-200 *Commando*; 30 V-100 *Commando* in store)
  PPV 140: 74 *Belrex*; 15 *MaxxPro Dash*; 51 *Peacekeeper*
ENGINEERING & MAINTENANCE VEHICLES
AEV 94: 18 CET; 54 FV180; 14 *Kodiak*; 8 M728
ARV *Bionix*; *Büffel*; LAV-150; LAV-300
VLB 72+: *Bionix*; LAB 30; *Leguan*; M2; 60 M3; 12 M60
MW 910-MCV-2; *Trailblazer*
ANTI-TANK/ANTI-INFRASTRUCTURE
MSL • MANPATS *Milan*; *Spike*-SR; *Spike*-MR
RCL 90+: **84mm** *Carl Gustaf*; **106mm** 90 M40A1
ARTILLERY 798+
SP 155mm 54 SSPH-1 *Primus*
TOWED 88: **105mm** (37 LG1 in store); **155mm** 88: 18 FH-2000; ε18 *Pegasus*; 52 FH-88
MRL 227mm 18 M142 HIMARS
MOR 638+
  SP 90+: **81mm**; **120mm** 90: 40 on *Bronco*; 50 on M113
  TOWED 548: **81mm** 500 **120mm** 36 M-65; **160mm** 12 M-58 Tampella

Navy 4,000 (incl 1,000 conscripts)

EQUIPMENT BY TYPE
SUBMARINES • SSK 4:
  2 *Archer* (ex-SWE *Västergötland*) (fitted with AIP) with 3 single 400mm TT with Torped 431, 6 single 533mm TT with *Black Shark* HWT
  2 *Challenger* (ex-SWE *Sjoormen*) with 2 single 400mm TT with Torped 431, 4 single 533mm TT with Torped 613
PRINCIPAL SURFACE COMBATANTS • FRIGATES 6
  FFGHM 6 *Formidable* with 2 quad lnchr with RGM-84 *Harpoon* AShM, 4 8-cell *Sylver* A43 VLS with *Aster* 15 SAM, 2 triple 324mm ILAS-3 (B-515) ASTT with A244/S LWT, 1 76mm gun (capacity 1 S-70B *Sea Hawk* hel)
PATROL AND COASTAL COMBATANTS 26
  CORVETTES • FSM 8 *Independence* (Littoral Mission Vessel) with 1 12-cell CLA VLS with VL MICA, 1 76mm gun, 1 hel landing platform
  PCGM 6 *Victory* with 2 quad lnchr with RGM-84C *Harpoon* Block 1B AShM, 2 8-cell VLS with *Barak*-1 SAM, 1 76mm gun
  PCO 4 *Sentinel* (*Fearless* mod) with 1 76mm gun
  PBF 8: 2 SMC Type 1; 6 SMC Type 2
MINE WARFARE • MINE COUNTERMEASURES 4
  MCC 4 *Bedok*
AMPHIBIOUS
  PRINCIPAL AMPHIBIOUS SHIPS • LPD 4 *Endurance* with 2 twin *Simbad* lnchr with *Mistral* SAM, 1 76mm gun (capacity 2 hel; 4 LCVP; 18 MBT; 350 troops)
  LANDING CRAFT • LCVP 23: ε17 FCEP; 6 FCU
LOGISTICS AND SUPPORT 5

288 THE MILITARY BALANCE 2023

ASR 1 *Swift Rescue*
ATF 2
AX 2: 1 *Avatar*; 1 *Stet Polaris*

Naval Diving Unit
FORCES BY ROLE
SPECIAL FORCES
1 SF gp
1 (diving) SF gp
COMBAT SUPPORT
1 EOD gp

Air Force 6,000 (incl 3,000 conscripts)

5 comds
FORCES BY ROLE
FIGHTER/GROUND ATTACK
2 sqn with F-15SG *Eagle*
2 sqn with F-16C/D *Fighting Falcon* (some used for ISR with pods)
ANTI-SUBMARINE WARFARE
1 sqn with S-70B *Seahawk*
MARITIME PATROL/TRANSPORT
1 sqn with F-50
AIRBORNE EARLY WARNING & CONTROL
1 sqn with G550-AEW
TANKER
1 sqn with A330 MRTT
TANKER/TRANSPORT
1 sqn with KC-130B/H *Hercules*; C-130H *Hercules*
TRAINING
1 (aggressor) sqn with F-15SG *Eagle*; F-16C/D *Fighting Falcon*
1 (FRA-based) sqn with M-346 *Master*
4 (US-based) units with AH-64D *Apache*; CH-47D *Chinook*; F-15SG: F-16C/D
1 (AUS-based) sqn with PC-21
1 hel sqn with H120 *Colibri*
ATTACK HELICOPTER
1 sqn with AH-64D *Apache*
TRANSPORT HELICOPTER
1 sqn with CH-47SD *Super D Chinook*
2 sqn with AS332M *Super Puma*; AS532UL *Cougar*
ISR UAV
1 sqn with *Hermes* 450
2 sqn with *Heron* 1
AIR DEFENCE
1 AD bn with *Mistral* (opcon Army)
3 AD bn with RBS-70; 9K38 *Igla* (RS-SA-18 *Grouse*); *Mechanised Igla* (opcon Army)
1 ADA sqn with Oerlikon
1 AD sqn with SAMP/T
1 AD sqn with *Spyder*-SR
1 radar sqn with radar (mobile)
1 radar sqn with LORADS
MANOEUVRE
Other
4 (field def) sy sqn
EQUIPMENT BY TYPE
AIRCRAFT 105 combat capable
FGA 100: 40 F-15SG *Eagle*; 20 F-16C Block 52 *Fighting Falcon*; 20 F-16D Block 52 *Fighting Falcon*; 20 F-16D Block

52+ *Fighting Falcon* (incl reserves)
MP 5 F-50 *Maritime Enforcer**
AEW&C 4 G550-AEW
TKR/TPT 11: 6 A330 MRTT; 4 KC-130B *Hercules*; 1 KC-130H *Hercules*
TPT 9: **Medium** 5 C-130H *Hercules* (2 ELINT); **PAX** 4 F-50
TRG 31: 12 M-346 *Master*; 19 PC-21
HELICOPTERS
ATK 19 AH-64D *Apache*
ASW 8 S-70B *Seahawk*
TPT 56: **Heavy** 21: 6 CH-47D *Chinook*; 10 CH-47SD *Super D Chinook*; 2+ CH-47F *Chinook*; 3+ H225M; **Medium** 30: 18 AS332M *Super Puma* (incl 5 SAR); 12 AS532UL *Cougar*; **Light** 5 H120 *Colibri* (leased)
UNINHABITED AERIAL VEHICLES
ISR 17+: **Heavy** 8+ *Heron* 1; **Medium** 9+ *Hermes* 450; **Light** some *Orbiter*-4
AIR DEFENCE
SAM 4+
Long-range 4+ SAMP/T
Short-range *Spyder*-SR
Point-defence 9K38 *Igla* (RS-SA-18 *Grouse*); *Mechanised Igla*; *Mistral*; RBS-70
GUNS 34
SP 20mm GAI-C01
TOWED 34+: **20mm** GAI-C01; **35mm** 34 GDF (with 25 *Super-Fledermaus* fire-control radar)
AIR-LAUNCHED MISSILES
AAM • **IR** AIM-9P/S *Sidewinder*; *Python* 4 (reported); **IIR** AIM-9X *Sidewinder* II; **SARH** AIM-7P *Sparrow*; **ARH** (AIM-120C5/7 AMRAAM in store in US)
ASM: AGM-65B/G *Maverick*; AGM-114K/L *Hellfire*; AGM-154A/C JSOW
AShM AGM-84 *Harpoon*; AM39 *Exocet*
BOMBS
Laser-guided GBU-10/12 *Paveway* II
Laser & INS/GPS-guided GBU-49 Enhanced Paveway II; GBU-54 Laser JDAM
INS/GPS guided GBU-31 JDAM

Digital & Intelligence Service 1,000

Formed 2022 as fourth service of the Singapore Armed Forces, consolidating existing intelligence and cyber capabilities

Gendarmerie & Paramilitary 7,400 active

Civil Defence Force 5,600 (incl conscripts); 500 auxiliaries (total 6,100)

Singapore Gurkha Contingent 1,800
Under the Police
FORCES BY ROLE
MANOEUVRE
Other
6 paramilitary coy

DEPLOYMENT

AUSTRALIA: 2 trg schools – 1 with 12 AS332M1 *Super Puma/ AS532UL Cougar* (flying trg) located at Oakey; 1 with PC-

21 (flying trg) located at Pearce. Army: prepositioned AFVs and heavy equipment at Shoalwater Bay training area

BRUNEI: 1 trg camp with inf units on rotation; 1 hel det with AS332M1 *Super Puma*

FRANCE: 200; 1 trg sqn with 12 M-346 *Master*

TAIWAN: 3 trg camp (incl inf and arty)

THAILAND: 1 trg camp (arty, cbt engr)

UNITED STATES: Trg units with F-16C/D; 12 F-15SG; AH-64D *Apache*; 6+ CH-47D *Chinook*

FOREIGN FORCES

United States US Indo-Pacific Command: 200; 1 naval spt facility at Changi naval base; 1 USAF log spt sqn at Paya Lebar air base

Sri Lanka LKA

Sri Lankan Rupee LKR		2021	2022	2023
GDP	LKR	17.7tr	23.8tr	
	USD	89.0bn	73.7bn	
per capita	USD	4,016	3,293	
Growth	%	3.3	-8.7	
Inflation	%	6.0	48.2	
Def bdgt	LKR	308bn	373bn	
	USD	1.55bn	1.15bn	
USD1=LKR		198.76	323.34	

Real-terms defence budget trend (USDbn, constant 2015)

Population	23,187,516				
Age	0–14	15–19	20–24	25–29	30–64	65 plus
Male	11.4%	4.0%	3.6%	3.5%	21.6%	4.8%
Female	11.0%	3.8%	3.4%	3.4%	23.0%	6.6%

Capabilities

Since the defeat of the Tamil Tigers, the armed forces have reoriented to a peacetime internal-security role. Support has been provided by China, in an indication of a growing military-to-military relationship. The US has eased its long-standing military trade restrictions and Japan has stated an intention to increase maritime cooperation. Sri Lanka has little capacity for force projection beyond its national territory but has sent small numbers of troops on UN missions. The navy's littoral capability, based on fast-attack and patrol boats, has been strengthened with the acquisition of offshore-patrol vessels, while the US has gifted a former US coastguard cutter and China has gifted a frigate. The army is reducing in size and there appears to have been little spending on new equipment since the end of the civil war. Sri Lanka is looking to begin a series of procurements to fill key capability gaps but ambitions are limited by budget constraints. The effect of the 2022 political and economic crisis on Sri Lanka's defence policy and procurement is unclear. Beyond maintenance facilities and limited fabrication, such as at Sri Lanka's shipyards, there is no defence-industrial base.

ACTIVE 255,000 (Army 177,000 Navy 50,000 Air 28,000) Gendarmerie & Paramilitary 62,200

RESERVE 5,500 (Army 1,100 Navy 2,400 Air Force 2,000) Gendarmerie & Paramilitary 30,400

ORGANISATIONS BY SERVICE

Army 113,000; 64,00 active reservists (recalled) (total 177,000)

Regt are bn sized

FORCES BY ROLE
COMMAND
  7 region HQ
  21 div HQ
SPECIAL FORCES
  1 indep SF bde
MANOEUVRE
  Reconnaissance
  3 armd recce regt
  Armoured
  1 armd bde(-)
  Mechanised
  1 mech inf bde
  Light
  60 inf bde
  1 cdo bde
  Air Manoeuvre
  1 air mob bde
COMBAT SUPPORT
  7 arty regt
  1 MRL regt
  8 engr regt
  6 sigs regt

EQUIPMENT BY TYPE
ARMOURED FIGHTING VEHICLES
  MBT 62 T-55A/T-55AM2
  RECCE 15 *Saladin*
  IFV 62+: 13 BMP-1; 49 BMP-2; WZ-551 20mm
  APC 211+
    APC (T) 30+: some Type-63; 30 Type-85; some Type-89
    APC (W) 181: 25 BTR-80/BTR-80A; 31 *Buffel*; 20 WZ-551; 105 *Unicorn*
ENGINEERING & MAINTENANCE VEHICLES
  ARV 16 VT-55
  VLB 2 MT-55
ANTI-TANK/ANTI-INFRASTRUCTURE
  MANPATS HJ-8
  RCL 40: **105mm** ε10 M-65; **106mm** ε30 M40
  GUNS **85mm** 8 Type-56 (D-44)
ARTILLERY 908
  TOWED 96: **122mm** 20; **130mm** 30 Type-59-I; **152mm** 46 Type-66 (D-20)
  MRL **122mm** 28: 6 KRL-122; 22 RM-70
  MOR 784: **81mm** 520; **82mm** 209; **120mm** 55 M-43
UNINHABITED AERIAL VEHICLES
  ISR • Medium 1 *Seeker*

Navy ε37,000; ε13,000 active reserves (total 50,000)

Seven naval areas

EQUIPMENT BY TYPE
PRINCIPAL SURFACE COMBATANTS • FRIGATES 1
FFH 1 *Parakramabahu* (ex-PRC Type-053H2G (*Jiangwei* I)) with 1 twin 100mm gun (capacity 1 med hel)
PATROL AND COASTAL COMBATANTS 121
PSOH 5: 2 *Gajabahu* (ex-US *Hamilton*) with 1 76mm gun (capacity 1 med hel); 1 *Sayura* (ex-IND *Sukanya*); 2 *Sayurala* (IND *Samarth*)
PCO 2: 1 *Samudura* (ex-US *Reliance);* 1 *Sagara* (IND *Vikram*) with 1 hel landing platform
PCC 3: 1 *Jayasagara*; 2 *Nandimithra* (ISR *Sa'ar* 4) with 1 76mm gun
PBF 74: 26 *Colombo*; 6 *Shaldag*; 4 *Super Dvora* Mk II; 6 *Super Dvora* Mk III; 5 *Trinity Marine*; 27 *Wave Rider*
PB 11: 2 *Mihikatha* (ex-AUS *Bay*); 2 *Prathapa* (PRC mod *Haizhui*); 3 *Ranajaya* (PRC *Haizhui*); 1 *Ranarisi* (PRC mod *Shanghai* II); 3 *Weeraya* (PRC *Shanghai* II)
PBR 26
AMPHIBIOUS
LANDING SHIPS • LSM 1 *Shakthi* (PRC *Yuhai*) (capacity 2 tanks; 250 troops)
LANDING CRAFT 5
LCM 2
LCU 2 *Yunnan*
UCAC 1 M 10 (capacity 56 troops)
LOGISTICS AND SUPPORT 3: 2 **AP**; 1 **AX**

Marines ε500

FORCES BY ROLE
MANOEUVRE
Amphibious
1 mne bn

Special Boat Service ε100

Reserve Organisations

Sri Lanka Volunteer Naval Force (SLVNF) 13,000 active reservists

Air Force 28,000 (incl SLAF Regt)

FORCES BY ROLE
FIGHTER
1 sqn with F-7BS/G; FT-7
FIGHTER/GROUND ATTACK
1 sqn with *Kfir* C-2
1 sqn with K-8 *Karakorum**
TRANSPORT
1 sqn with An-32B *Cline*; C-130K *Hercules*; Cessna 421C *Golden Eagle*
1 sqn with Beech B200 *King Air*; Y-12 (II)
TRAINING
1 wg with PT-6, Cessna 150L
ATTACK HELICOPTER
1 sqn with Mi-24V *Hind* E; Mi-35P *Hind*
TRANSPORT HELICOPTER
1 sqn with Mi-17 *Hip* H; Mi-171Sh
1 sqn with Bell 206A/B (incl basic trg), Bell 212
1 (VIP) sqn with Bell 212; Bell 412 *Twin Huey*

ISR UAV
1 sqn with *Blue Horizon* II
1 sqn with *Searcher* MkII
MANOEUVRE
Other
1 (SLAF) sy regt

EQUIPMENT BY TYPE
AIRCRAFT 13 combat capable
FTR 5: 3 F-7GS; 2 FT-7 (3 F-7BS; 1 F-7GS non-operational)
FGA 1 *Kfir* C-2 (2 *Kfir* C-2; 1 *Kfir* C-7; 2 *Kfir* TC-2; 6 MiG-27M *Flogger* J; 1 MiG-23UB *Flogger* C non-operational)
MP 1 Do-228-101
TPT 20: **Medium** 2 C-130K *Hercules*; **Light** 18: 3 An-32B *Cline*; 6 Cessna 150L; 1 Cessna 421C *Golden Eagle*; 6 Y-12 (II); 2 Y-12 (IV)
TRG 13: 7 K-8 *Karakorum**; 6 PT-6
HELICOPTERS
ATK 11: 6 Mi-24P *Hind*; 3 Mi-24V *Hind* E; 2 Mi-35V *Hind*
MRH 18: 6 Bell 412 *Twin Huey* (VIP); 2 Bell 412EP (VIP); 10 Mi-17 *Hip* H
TPT 16: **Medium** 4 Mi-171Sh; **Light** 12: 2 Bell 206A *Jet Ranger*; 2 Bell 206B *Jet Ranger*; 8 Bell 212
UNINHABITED AERIAL VEHICLES
ISR • Medium 2+: some *Blue Horizon* II; 2 *Searcher* MkII
AIR DEFENCE • GUNS • TOWED 27: **40mm** 24 L/40; **94mm** 3 (3.7in)
AIR-LAUNCHED MISSILES
AAM • IR PL-5E

Gendarmerie & Paramilitary ε62,200

Home Guard 13,000

National Guard ε15,000

Police Force 30,200; 1,000 (women) (total 31,200) 30,400 reservists

Ministry of Defence Special Task Force 3,000

Anti-guerrilla unit

Coast Guard n/k

Ministry of Defence

EQUIPMENT BY TYPE
PATROL AND COASTAL COMBATANTS 28
PCO 1 *Suraksha* (ex-IND *Vikram*) with 1 hel landing platform
PBF 22: 2 *Dvora*; 4 *Super Dvora* Mk I; 3 *Killer* (ROK); 10 (Inshore Patrol Craft); 3 (Fast Patrol Craft)
PB 4: 2 Simonneau Type-508; 2 *Samudra Raksha*
PBR 1

DEPLOYMENT

CENTRAL AFRICAN REPUBLIC: UN • MINUSCA 112; 1 hel sqn

LEBANON: UN • UNIFIL 126; 1 inf coy

MALI: UN • MINUSMA 243; 1 sy coy

SOUTH SUDAN: UN • UNMISS 66; 1 fd hospital

WESTERN SAHARA: UN • MINURSO 2

Taiwan (Republic of China) ROC

New Taiwan Dollar TWD		2021	2022	2023
GDP	TWD	21.7tr	24.2tr	
	USD	775bn	829bn	
per capita	USD	33,143	35,513	
Growth	%	6.6	3.3	
Inflation	%	2.0	3.1	
Def bdgt	TWD	453bn	472bn	586bn
	USD	16.2bn	16.2bn	
USD1=TWD		28.02	29.18	

Real-terms defence budget trend (USDbn, constant 2015)

Population	23,580,712					
Age	0–14	15–19	20–24	25–29	30–64	65 plus
Male	6.3%	2.4%	3.1%	3.5%	26.2%	7.8%
Female	6.0%	2.2%	2.9%	3.4%	26.7%	9.5%

Capabilities

Taiwan's security policy is dominated by its relationship with China and its attempts to sustain a credible military capability. Taiwan's current focus is on air defence and deterrence in coastal areas, on both sides of the island. The 2021 Quadrennial Defense Review for the first time mentioned the need to counter the PLA's 'grey zone' threat. The armed forces exercise regularly. Demographic pressure has influenced plans for force reductions and a shift towards an all-volunteer force, which the 2021 Quadrennial Defense Review credited for helping the armed forces reach its staffing goals. Nonetheless, issues with recruitment and retention have reportedly created personnel challenges for combat units, and an extension of the current four-month military conscription requirement is under consideration, with a decision due by the end of 2022. Taiwan's main security partnership is with the US. The Taiwan Relations Act from 1979 states that 'the United States shall provide Taiwan with arms of a defensive character'. In 2019, the United States approved the transfer of new F-16C/D Block 70 combat aircraft to Taiwan. Nevertheless, Taipei maintains an interest in the F-35. In 2022, Taiwan's purchase of MQ-9B UAVs was confirmed. Taiwan has allocated funding for the acquisition of HIMARS, ATACMS, SRBMs and precision-guided rockets in its defence budget. Taiwan's own defence-industrial base has strengths in aerospace, shipbuilding and missiles. The government launched a new defence-industrial policy in 2019, aimed at further strengthening independent defence-manufacturing capacities.

ACTIVE 169,000 (Army 94,000 Navy 40,000 Air 35,000) Gendarmerie & Paramilitary 11,800

Conscript liability (19–40 years) 12 months for those born before 1993; four months for those born after 1994 (alternative service available)

RESERVE 1,657,000 (Army 1,500,000 Navy 67,000 Air Force 90,000)

Some obligation to age 30

ORGANISATIONS BY SERVICE

Space
EQUIPMENT BY TYPE
SATELLITES • ISR 1 *Formosat-5*

Army 94,000 (incl ε5,000 MP)
FORCES BY ROLE
COMMAND
 3 corps HQ
 5 defence comd HQ
SPECIAL FORCES/HELICOPTER
 1 SF/hel comd (5 spec ops bn, 2 hel bde)
MANOEUVRE
 Armoured
  4 armd bde
 Mechanised
  3 mech inf bde
COMBAT SUPPORT
 3 arty gp
 3 engr gp
 3 CBRN gp
 3 sigs gp
COASTAL DEFENCE
 1 AShM bn

Reserves
FORCES BY ROLE
MANOEUVRE
 Light
  27 inf bde
EQUIPMENT BY TYPE
ARMOURED FIGHTING VEHICLES
 MBT 650: 200 M60A3; 450 CM-11 *Brave Tiger* (M48H); (100 CM-12 in store)
 LT TK ε100 M41A3/D
 IFV 173 CM-34 *Yunpao*
 APC 1,543
  APC (T) 875: 225 CM-21A1; 650 M113A1/A2
  APC (W) 668: 368 CM-32 *Yunpao*; 300 LAV-150 *Commando*
ENGINEERING & MAINTENANCE VEHICLES
 AEV 18 M9
 ARV CM-27A1; 37 M88A1
 VLB 22 M3; M48A5
NBC VEHICLES 48+: BIDS; 48 K216A1; KM453
ANTI-TANK/ANTI-INFRASTRUCTURE
 MSL
  SP M113A1 with TOW; M1045A2 HMMWV with TOW
  MANPATS FGM-148 *Javelin*; TOW
 RCL 500+: **90mm** M67; **106mm** 500+: 500 M40A1; Type-51
ARTILLERY 2,093
 SP 488: **105mm** 100 M108; **155mm** 318: 225 M109A2/A5; 48 M44T; 45 T-69; **203mm** 70 M110
 TOWED 1,060+: **105mm** 650 T-64 (M101); **155mm** 340+: 90 M59; 250 T-65 (M114); M44; XT-69; **203mm** 70 M115
 MRL 223: **117mm** 120 *Kung Feng* VI; **126mm** 103: 60 *Kung Feng* III/*Kung Feng* IV; 43 RT 2000 *Thunder*
 MOR 322+
  SP 162+: **81mm** 72+: M29; 72 M125; **107mm** 90 M106A2

TOWED 81mm 160 M29; T-75; **107mm** M30; **120mm** K5; XT-86

COASTAL DEFENCE
ARTY 54: **127mm** ε50 US Mk32 (reported); **240mm** 4 M1
AShM *Ching Feng*

HELICOPTERS
ATK 96: 67 AH-1W *Cobra*; 29 AH-64E *Apache*
MRH 38 OH-58D *Kiowa Warrior*
TPT 38: **Heavy** 8 CH-47SD *Super D Chinook*; **Medium** 30 UH-60M *Black Hawk*
TRG 29 TH-67 *Creek*

UNINHABITED AERIAL VEHICLES
ISR • Light *Mastiff* III

AIR DEFENCE
SAM • Point-defence 76+: 74 M1097 *Avenger*; 2 M48 *Chaparral*; FIM-92 *Stinger*
GUNS
SP 40mm M42
TOWED 40mm L/70

Navy 40,000

EQUIPMENT BY TYPE
SUBMARINES • SSK 4:
2 *Hai Lung* with 6 single 533mm TT with UGM-84L *Harpoon* Block II AShM/SUT HWT
2 *Hai Shih†* (ex-US *Guppy* II (used in trg role)) with 10 single 533mm TT (6 fwd, 4 aft) with SUT HWT

PRINCIPAL SURFACE COMBATANTS 26
DESTROYERS • DDGHM 4 *Keelung* (ex-US *Kidd*) with 2 quad lnchr with RGM-84L *Harpoon* Block II AShM, 2 twin Mk 26 GMLS with SM-2 Block IIIA SAM, 2 triple 324mm SVTT Mk 32 ASTT with Mk 46 LWT, 2 Mk 15 *Phalanx* Block 1B CIWS, 2 127mm gun (capacity 1 S-70 ASW hel)
FRIGATES 22
FFGHM 21:
8 *Cheng Kung* (US *Oliver Hazard Perry* mod) with 2 quad lnchr with *Hsiung Feng* II/III AShM, 1 Mk 13 GMLS with SM-1MR Block VI SAM, 2 triple 324mm SVTT Mk 32 ASTT with Mk 46 LWT, 1 Mk 15 *Phalanx* Block 1B CIWS, 1 76mm gun (capacity 2 S-70C ASW hel)
2 *Meng Chuan* (ex-US *Oliver Hazard Perry*) with 1 Mk13 GMLS with RGM-84 *Harpoon* AShM/SM-1MR Block VI SAM, 2 triple 324mm SVTT Mk 32 ASTT with Mk 46 LWT, 1 Mk 15 *Phalanx* Block 1B CIWS, 1 76mm gun (capacity 2 S-70C ASW hel)
5 *Chin Yang* (ex-US *Knox*) with 1 octuple Mk 16 lnchr with RGM-84C *Harpoon* Block 1B AShM/ASROC A/S msl, 2 triple lnchr with SM-1MR Block VI SAM, 2 twin lnchr with SM-1MR Block VI SAM, 2 twin 324mm SVTT Mk 32 ASTT with Mk 46 LWT, 1 Mk 15 *Phalanx* Block 1B CIWS, 1 127mm gun (capacity 1 MD-500 hel)
6 *Kang Ding* with 2 quad lnchr with *Hsiung Feng* II AShM, 1 quad lnchr with *Sea Chaparral* SAM, 2 triple 324mm SVTT Mk 32 ASTT with Mk 46 LWT, 1 Mk 15 *Phalanx* Block 1B CIWS, 1 76mm gun (capacity 1 S-70C ASW hel)

FFGH 1 *Chin Yang* (ex-US *Knox*) with 1 octuple Mk 112 lnchr with RGM-84C *Harpoon* Block 1B AShM, 2 twin 324mm SVTT Mk 32 ASTT with Mk 46 LWT, 1 Mk 15 *Phalanx* Block 1B CIWS, 1 127mm gun (capacity 1 MD-500 hel)

PATROL AND COASTAL COMBATANTS 44
CORVETTES • FSGM 1 *Ta Jiang* (*Tuo Jiang* mod) with 4 twin lnchr with *Hsiung Feng* II AShM, 2 twin lnchr with *Hsiung Feng* III AShM, 2 octuple lnchr with *Tien Chien* 2N (*Sea Sword* II) SAM, 1 Mk 15 *Phalanx* CIWS, 1 76mm gun, 1 hel landing platform
PCFG 1 *Tuo Jiang* (*Hsun Hai*) with 4 twin lnchr with *Hsiung Feng* II AShM, 4 twin lnchr with *Hisung Feng* III AShM, 2 triple 324mm SVTT Mk 32 ASTT, 1 Mk 15 *Phalanx* Block 1B CIWS; 1 76mm gun
PCG 10:
4 *Jin Chiang* with 2 twin lnchr with *Hsiung Feng* II AShM, 1 76mm gun
6 *Jin Chiang* with 1 twin lnchr with *Hsiung Feng* III AShM, 1 76mm gun
PCC 1 *Jin Chiang* (test platform)
PBG 31 *Kwang Hua* with 2 twin lnchr with *Hsiung Feng* II AShM

MINE WARFARE 9
MINE COUNTERMEASURES 7
MHC 6: 4 *Yung Feng*; 2 *Yung Jin* (ex-US *Osprey*)
MSO 1 *Yung Yang* (ex-US *Aggressive*)
MINELAYERS • ML 2 FMLB
COMMAND SHIPS • LCC 1 *Kao Hsiung*

AMPHIBIOUS
PRINCIPAL AMPHIBIOUS SHIPS 2
LPD 1 *Yu Shan* with 4 octuple lnchr with *Tien Chien* 2N (*Sea Sword* II) SAM, 2 Mk 15 Phalanx CIWS, 1 76mm gun (capacity 2 med hel; 4 LCM; 9 AAV-7A1; approx 500 troops)
LSD 1 *Shiu Hai* (ex-US *Anchorage*) with 2 Mk 15 *Phalanx* CIWS, 1 hel landing platform (capacity either 2 LCU or 18 LCM; 360 troops)
LANDING SHIPS
LST 6:
4 *Chung Hai* (ex-US LST-524) (capacity 16 tanks; 200 troops)
2 *Chung Ho* (ex-US *Newport*) with 1 Mk 15 *Phalanx* CIWS, 1 hel landing platform (capacity 3 LCVP, 23 AFVs, 400 troops)
LANDING CRAFT 44
LCM ε32 (various)
LCU 12 LCU 1610 (capacity 2 M60A3 or 400 troops) (minelaying capability)

LOGISTICS AND SUPPORT 9
AGOR 1 *Ta Kuan*
AOEH 1 *Panshih* with 1 quad lnchr with *Sea Chaparral* SAM, 2 Mk 15 *Phalanx* CIWS (capacity 3 med hel)
AOE 1 *Wu Yi* with 1 quad lnchr with *Sea Chaparral* SAM, 1 hel landing platform
ARS 2: 1 *Da Hu* (ex-US *Diver*); 1 *Da Juen* (ex-US *Bolster*)
ATF 4 *Ta Tung* (ex-US *Cherokee*)

Marines 10,000

FORCES BY ROLE
MANOEUVRE
Amphibious
2 mne bde
Other
1 (airfield def) sy gp
COMBAT SUPPORT
Some cbt spt unit
EQUIPMENT BY TYPE
ARMOURED FIGHTING VEHICLES
MBT 100 M60A3 TTS
AAV 202: 52 AAV-7A1; 150 LVTP-5A1
ENGINEERING & MAINTENANCE VEHICLES
ARV 2 AAVR-7
ANTI-TANK/ANTI-INFRASTRUCTURE
SP ε25 CM-25
RCL 106mm
ARTILLERY • TOWED 105mm; 155mm

Naval Aviation

FORCES BY ROLE
ANTI SUBMARINE WARFARE
2 sqn with S-70C *Seahawk* (S-70C *Defender*)
1 sqn with MD-500 *Defender*
ISR UAV
1 bn with *Chung Shyang* II
EQUIPMENT BY TYPE
HELICOPTERS
ASW 19 S-70C *Seahawk* (S-70C *Defender*)
MRH 10 MD-500 *Defender*
UNINHABITED AERIAL VEHICLES • ISR • Medium
ε28 *Chung Shyang* II

Air Force 35,000

FORCES BY ROLE
FIGHTER
3 sqn with *Mirage* 2000-5E/D (2000-5EI/DI)
FIGHTER/GROUND ATTACK
3 sqn with F-5E/F *Tiger* II
3 sqn with F-16A/B *Fighting Falcon*
3 sqn with F-16V(A/B) *Fighting Falcon*
5 sqn with F-CK-1A/B/C/D *Ching Kuo*
ANTI-SUBMARINE WARFARE
1 sqn with P-3C *Orion*
ELECTRONIC WARFARE
1 sqn with C-130HE *Tien Gian*
ISR
1 sqn with RF-5E *Tigereye*
AIRBORNE EARLY WARNING & CONTROL
1 sqn with E-2T *Hawkeye*
SEARCH & RESCUE
1 sqn with H225; UH-60M *Black Hawk*
TRANSPORT
2 sqn with C-130H *Hercules*
1 (VIP) sqn with B-727-100; B-737-800; Beech 1900; F-50; S-70C *Black Hawk*
TRAINING
1 sqn with AT-3A/B *Tzu-Chung**
1 sqn with Beech 1900
1 (basic) sqn with T-34C *Turbo Mentor*

EQUIPMENT BY TYPE
AIRCRAFT 471 combat capable
FTR 215: 84 F-5E/F *Tiger* II (some in store); 77 F-16A/B *Fighting Falcon*; 9 *Mirage* 2000-5D (2000-5DI); 45 *Mirage* 2000-5E (2000-5EI)
FGA 190: 127 F-CK-1C/D *Ching Kuo*; 63 F-16V(A/B) *Fighting Falcon*
ASW 12 P-3C *Orion*
EW 1 C-130HE *Tien Gian*
ISR 7 RF-5E *Tigereye*
AEW&C 6 E-2T *Hawkeye*
TPT 33: **Medium** 19 C-130H *Hercules*; **Light** 10 Beech 1900; **PAX** 4: 1 B-737-800; 3 F-50
TRG 96: 54 AT-3A/B *Tzu-Chung**; 42 T-34C *Turbo Mentor*
HELICOPTERS
TPT • Medium 17: 3 H225; 14 UH-60M *Black Hawk*
AIR-LAUNCHED MISSILES
AAM • IR AIM-9J/P *Sidewinder*; R-550 *Magic* 2; *Shafrir*; *Sky Sword* I; **IIR** AIM-9X *Sidewinder* II; *Mica* IR; **ARH** *Mica* RF; **ARH** AIM-120C-7 AMRAAM; *Sky Sword* II
ASM AGM-65A *Maverick*
AShM AGM-84 *Harpoon*
ARM *Sky Sword* IIA
ALCM • Conventional *Wan Chien*
BOMBS • Laser-guided GBU-12 *Paveway* II

Air Defence and Missile Command

FORCES BY ROLE
SURFACE-TO-SURFACE MISSILE
1 GLCM bde (2 GLCM bn with *Hsiung Feng* IIE)
AIR DEFENCE
1 (792) SAM bde (1 SAM bn with *Tien Kung* III; 2 ADA bn)
2 (793 & 794) SAM bde (1 SAM bn with Tien Kung II; 1 SAM bn with M902 *Patriot* PAC-3; 1 SAM bn with MIM-23 *Hawk*)
1 (795) SAM bde (1 SAM bn with M902 *Patriot* PAC-3; 2 ADA bn)
EQUIPMENT BY TYPE
SURFACE-TO-SURFACE MISSILE LAUNCHERS
GLCM • Conventional ε12 *Hsiung Feng* IIE
AIR DEFENCE
SAM 202+
Long-range 122+: 72+ M902 *Patriot* PAC-3; ε50 *Tien Kung* II
Medium-range 50 MIM-23 *Hawk*
Short-range 30 RIM-7M *Sparrow* with *Skyguard*
Point-defence *Antelope*
GUNS • 20mm some T-82; **35mm** 20+ GDF-006 with *Skyguard*
MISSILE DEFENCE *Tien Kung* III

Gendarmerie & Paramilitary 11,800

Coast Guard 11,800

EQUIPMENT BY TYPE
PATROL AND COASTAL COMBATANTS 168
PSOH 5: 1 *Chiayi*; 2 *Tainan*; 2 *Yilan*
PSO 6: 4 *Miaoli* with 1 hel landing platform; 2 *Ho Hsing*
PCF 3 *Anping* (*Tuo Jiang* mod)
PCO 14: 2 *Kinmen*; 2 *Mou Hsing*; 1 *Shun Hu* 1; 3 *Shun Hu* 7; 4 *Taichung*; 2 *Taipei*
PBF ε58 (various)
PB 82: 1 *Shun Hu* 6; ε81 (various)

FOREIGN FORCES
Singapore 3 trg camp (incl inf and arty)

Thailand THA

Thai Baht THB		2021	2022	2023
GDP	THB	16.2tr	17.3tr	
	USD	506bn	535bn	
per capita	USD	7,232	7,631	
Growth	%	1.5	2.8	
Inflation	%	1.2	6.3	
Def bdgt	THB	215bn	200bn	195bn
	USD	6.71bn	6.17bn	
FMA (US)	USD	7m	10m	10m
USD1=THB		31.98	32.40	

Real-terms defence budget trend (USDbn, constant 2015)

Population	69,648,117				
Age	0–14	15–19	20–24	25–29	30–64	65 plus
Male	8.3%	3.0%	3.2%	3.6%	24.6%	6.2%
Female	7.9%	2.9%	3.1%	3.5%	26.2%	7.7%

Capabilities

Thailand has large, well-funded armed forces and its air force is one of the best equipped and trained in Southeast Asia. Facing an increasingly unstable regional-security environment, the Royal Thai Armed Forces are moving towards a greater emphasis on deterring external threats, while continuing their longstanding internal-security role, particularly in the country's far south, where a Malay-nationalist insurgency continues. The Vision 2026 defence-modernisation plan, approved by the defence council in October 2017, outlined the armed forces' planned capability improvements for the following decade. Thailand is classed as a major non-NATO ally by the US, but it has also developed closer defence ties with China since 2014. The armed forces regularly take part in international military exercises, notably the multinational annual *Cobra Gold* series with the US and some of its allies and security partners. Personnel continue to be deployed to the UNMISS mission in South Sudan. The military-modernisation effort includes development of a submarine capability, as well as the strengthening of anti-submarine-warfare capability and procurement of new surface ships. The armoured-vehicle fleet has been recapitalised with deliveries from China and Ukraine. Saab 340 AEW&C aircraft, *Gripen* combat aircraft and a new command-and-control system have improved air capability. In January 2020, the Royal Thai Air Force (RTAF) issued a White Paper which detailed further acquisition and upgrade requirements through the 2020s, including fighters, tactical-transport and VIP aircraft. The RTAF launched a space-operations centre in August 2019, a priority identified in the National Strategy 2018–37 development programme. Under its Defence Industry Masterplan, the government indicates that expanding Thailand's presently limited defence sector could be an important way to develop military capability and improve self-reliance. The latter is of increasing importance in light of the defence budget cuts since 2020. More broadly, the government is making efforts to reform defence procurement and offsets by expanding the role of its Defence Technology Institute.

ACTIVE 360,850 (Army 245,000 Navy 69,850 Air 46,000) Gendarmerie & Paramilitary 93,700
Conscription liability 24 months

RESERVE 200,000 Gendarmerie & Paramilitary 45,000

ORGANISATIONS BY SERVICE

Army 130,000; ε115,000 conscript (total 245,000)

Cav, lt armd, recce and tk sqn are bn sized

FORCES BY ROLE
COMMAND
  4 (regional) army HQ
  3 corps HQ
SPECIAL FORCES
  1 SF div
  1 SF regt
MANOEUVRE
  Armoured
  1 (3rd) mech cav div (2 tk regt (2 tk sqn); 1 sigs bn; 1 maint bn; 1 hel sqn)
  Mechanised
  1 (1st) mech cav div (1 armd recce sqn; 2 mech cav regt (3 mech cav sqn); 1 indep mech cav sqn; 1 sigs bn; 1 maint bn; 1 hel sqn)
  1 (2nd) mech cav div (1 armd recce sqn; 2 (1st & 5th) mech cav regt (1 tk sqn, 2 mech cav sqn); 1 (4th) mech cav regt (3 mech cav sqn); 1 sigs bn; 1 maint bn; 1 hel sqn)
  1 (2nd) mech inf div (1 armd recce sqn; 1 tk bn; 3 mech inf regt (3 mech inf bn); 1 arty regt (4 arty bn); 1 engr bn; 1 sigs bn)
  1 (11th) mech inf div (2 mech inf regt (3 mech inf bn); 1 engr bn; 1 sigs bn)
  Light
  1 (1st) inf div (1 lt armd sqn; 1 ranger regt (3 ranger bn); 1 arty regt (4 arty bn); 1 engr bn; 1 sigs bn)
  1 (3rd) inf div (3 inf regt (3 inf bn); 1 arty regt (3 arty bn); 1 engr bn; 1 sigs bn)
  1 (4th) inf div (1 lt armd sqn; 2 inf regt (3 inf bn); 1 arty regt (3 arty bn); 1 engr bn; 1 sigs bn)
  1 (5th) inf div (1 lt armd sqn; 3 inf regt (3 inf bn); 1 arty regt (4 arty bn); 1 engr bn; 1 sigs bn)
  1 (6th) inf div (2 inf regt (3 inf bn); 1 arty regt (4 arty bn); 1 engr bn; 1 sigs bn)
  1 (7th) inf div (2 inf regt (3 inf bn); 1 arty regt (2 arty bn); 1 engr bn; 1 sigs bn)
  1 (9th) inf div (1 mech cav sqn; 3 inf regt (3 inf bn); 1 arty regt (3 arty bn); 1 engr bn; 1 sigs bn)
  1 (15th) inf div (1 mech cav sqn; 3 inf regt (3 inf bn); 1 engr bn; 1 sigs bn)
COMBAT SUPPORT
  1 arty div (1 arty regt (1 SP arty bn; 2 fd arty bn); 1 arty regt (1 MRL bn; 2 fd arty bn))
  1 engr div
COMBAT SERVICE SUPPORT
  4 economic development div

Asia 295

HELICOPTER
Some hel flt
ISR UAV
1 UAV bn with *Hermes* 450; *Searcher* II
AIR DEFENCE
1 ADA div (6 bn)
EQUIPMENT BY TYPE
ARMOURED FIGHTING VEHICLES
MBT 394: 53 M60A1; 125 M60A3; 105 M48A5; 49 T-84 *Oplot*; 62 VT-4; (50 Type-69 in store)
LT TK 194: 24 M41; 104 *Scorpion* (50 in store); 66 *Stingray*
RECCE 42: 10 M1127 *Stryker* RV; 32 S52 *Shorland*
IFV 220: 168 BTR-3E1; 52 VN-1 (incl variants)
APC 1,199
    APC (T) 880: *Bronco*; 430 M113A1/A3; 450 Type-85
    APC (W) 219: 9 BTR-3K (CP); 6 BTR-3C (amb); 18 *Condor*; 142 LAV-150 *Commando*; 44 M1126 *Stryker* ICV
    PPV 100 REVA
ENGINEERING & MAINTENANCE VEHICLES
ARV 69+: 2 BREM-84 *Atlet*; 13 BTR-3BR; 22 M88A1; 6 M88A2; 10 M113; 5 Type-653; 11 VS-27; WZT-4
VLB Type-84
MW *Bozena*; *Giant Viper*
ANTI-TANK/ANTI-INFRASTRUCTURE
MSL
    SP 30+: 18+ M901A5 (TOW); 12 BTR-3RK
    MANPATS M47 *Dragon*
RCL 180: **75mm** 30 M20; **106mm** 150 M40
ARTILLERY 2,579
SP 155mm 42: 16 ATMOS 2000; 6 CAESAR; 20 M109A5
TOWED 525: **105mm** 296: 24 LG1 MkII; 12 M-56; 200 M101A1; 60 L119 Light Gun; (12 M102; 32 M618A2 in store); **155mm** 229: 90 GHN-45 A1; 118 M198; 21 M-71 (48 M114 in store)
MRL 68: **122mm** 4 SR-4; **130mm** 60 PHZ-85; **302mm** 4: 1 DTI-1 (WS-1B); 3 DTI-1G (WS-32)
MOR 1,944+: **81mm/107mm/120mm** 1,867; **SP 81mm** 39: 18 BTR-3M1; 21 M125A3; SP **107mm** M106A3; **SP 120mm** 38: 8 BTR-3M2; 6+ Elbit *Spear*; 12 M1064A3; 12 SM-4A
AIRCRAFT
TPT • Light 22: 2 Beech 200 *King Air*; 2 Beech 1900C; 1 C-212 *Aviocar*; 1 C295W; 3 Cessna 182T *Skylane*; 9 Cessna A185E (U-17B); 2 ERJ-135LR; 2 *Jetstream* 41
TRG 33: 11 MX-7-235 *Star Rocket*; 22 T-41B *Mescalero*
HELICOPTERS
ATK 7 AH-1F *Cobra*
MRH 20: 8 AS550 *Fennec*; 2 AW139; 10 Mi-17V-5 *Hip* H
TPT 122: **Heavy** 5 CH-47D *Chinook*; **Medium** 11: 8 UH-60L *Black Hawk*; 3 UH-60M *Black Hawk*; **Light** 106: 27 Bell 206 *Jet Ranger*; 52 Bell 212 (AB-212); 16 Enstrom 480B; 6 H145M (VIP tpt); 5 UH-72A *Lakota*
TRG 53 Hughes 300C
UNINHABITED AERIAL VEHICLES
ISR • Medium 4+: 4 *Hermes* 450; *Searcher*; *Searcher* II
AIR DEFENCE
SAM 8+
    Short-range *Aspide*
    Point-defence 8+: 8 *Starstreak*; 9K338 *Igla*-S (RS-SA-24 *Grinch*)
GUNS 192
    SP 54: **20mm** 24 M163 *Vulcan*; **40mm** 30 M1/M42 SP

TOWED 138: **20mm** 24 M167 *Vulcan*; **35mm** 8 GDF-007 with *Skyguard* 3; **37mm** 52 Type-74; **40mm** 48 L/70; **57mm** ε6 Type-59 (S-60) (18+ more non-operational)

Navy 44,000 (incl Naval Aviation, Marines, Coastal Defence); 25,850 conscript (total 69,850)

EQUIPMENT BY TYPE
PRINCIPAL SURFACE COMBATANTS 8
AIRCRAFT CARRIERS • CVH 1 *Chakri Naruebet* with 3 sextuple *Sadral* lnchr with *Mistral* SAM (capacity 6 S-70B *Seahawk* ASW hel)
FRIGATES 7
FFGHM 3:
    2 *Naresuan* with 2 quad lnchr with RGM-84 *Harpoon* AShM, 1 8 cell Mk 41 VLS with RIM-162B ESSM SAM, 2 triple SVTT Mk 32 324mm TT with Mk 46 LWT, 1 127mm gun (capacity 1 *Super Lynx* 300 hel)
    1 *Bhumibol Adulyadej* (DW3000F) with 2 quad lnchr with RGM-84L *Harpoon* Block II AShM, 1 8-cell Mk 41 VLS with RIM-162B ESSM SAM, 2 triple 324mm SEA TLS ASTT with Mk 54 LWT, 1 Mk 15 *Phalanx* Block 1B CIWS, 1 76mm gun (capacity 1 med hel)
FFG 4:
    2 *Chao Phraya* (trg role) with 4 twin lnchr with C-802A AShM, 2 RBU 1200 *Uragan* A/S mor, 2 twin 100mm gun
    2 *Chao Phraya* with 4 twin lnchr with C-802A AShM, 2 RBU 1200 *Uragan* A/S mor, 1 twin 100mm gun, 1 hel landing platform
PATROL AND COASTAL COMBATANTS 70
CORVETTES 7:
    FSGM 2 *Rattanakosin* with 2 twin lnchr with RGM-84 *Harpoon* AShM, 1 octuple *Albatros* lnchr with *Aspide* SAM, 2 triple 324mm SVTT Mk 32 ASTT with *Stingray* LWT, 1 76mm gun
    FSG 1 *Krabi* (UK *River* mod) with 2 twin lnchr with RGM-84L *Harpoon* Block II AShM, 1 76mm gun
    FS 4:
        1 *Makut Rajakumarn* with 2 triple 324mm ASTT, 2 114mm gun
        1 *Pin Klao* (ex-US *Cannon*) (trg role) with 2 triple 324mm SVTT Mk 32 ASTT, 3 76mm gun
        2 *Tapi* with 2 triple 324mm SVTT Mk 32 ASTT with Mk 46 LWT, 1 76mm gun
PSO 1 *Krabi* (UK *River* mod) with 1 76mm gun
PCT 3 *Khamronsin* with 2 triple 324mm ASTT with *Stingray* LWT, 1 76mm gun
PCOH 2 *Pattani* (1 in trg role) with 1 76mm gun
PCO 4: 3 *Hua Hin* with 1 76mm gun; 1 M58 Patrol Gun Boat with 1 76mm gun
PCC 9: 3 *Chon Buri* with 2 76mm gun; 6 *Sattahip* with 1 76mm gun
PBF 4 M18 Fast Assault Craft (capacity 18 troops)
PB 40: 3 T-81; 5 M36 Patrol Boat; 1 T-227; 2 T-997; 23 M21 Patrol Boat; 3 T-991; 3 T-994
MINE WARFARE • MINE COUNTERMEASURES 17
MCCS 1 *Thalang*
MCO 2 *Lat Ya*
MCC 2 *Bang Rachan*
MSR 12: 7 T1; 5 T6

AMPHIBIOUS

PRINCIPAL AMPHIBIOUS SHIPS • LPD 1 *Angthong* (SGP *Endurance*) with 1 76mm gun (capacity 2 hel; 19 MBT; 500 troops)

LANDING SHIPS 2

LST 2 *Sichang* with 2 hel landing platform (capacity 14 MBT; 300 troops)

LANDING CRAFT 14

LCU 9: 3 *Man Nok*; 2 *Mataphun* (capacity either 3–4 MBT or 250 troops); 4 *Thong Kaeo*

LCM 2

UCAC 3 *Griffon* 1000TD

LOGISTICS AND SUPPORT 13

ABU 1 *Suriya*

AGOR 1 *Sok*

AGS 2: 1 *Chanthara*; 1 *Paruehatsabodi*

AOL 5: 1 *Matra* with 1 hel landing platform; 2 *Proet*; 1 *Prong*; 1 *Samui*

AOR 1 *Chula*

AORH 1 *Similan* (capacity 1 hel)

AWT 2

Naval Aviation 1,200

EQUIPMENT BY TYPE

AIRCRAFT 3 combat capable

ASW 2 P-3A *Orion* (P-3T)

ISR 9 *Sentry* O-2-337

MP 1 F-27-200 MPA*

TPT • Light 15: 7 Do-228-212; 2 ERJ-135LR; 2 F-27-400M *Troopship*; 3 N-24A *Searchmaster*; 1 UP-3A *Orion* (UP-3T)

HELICOPTERS

ASW 8: 6 S-70B *Seahawk*; 2 *Super Lynx* 300

MRH 2 MH-60S *Knight Hawk*

TPT 18: **Medium** 2 Bell 214ST (AB-214ST); **Light** 16: 6 Bell 212 (AB-212); 5 H145M; 5 S-76B

AIR-LAUNCHED MISSILES • AShM AGM-84 *Harpoon*

Marines 23,000

FORCES BY ROLE

COMMAND

1 mne div HQ

MANOEUVRE

Reconnaissance

1 recce bn

Light

2 inf regt (total: 6 bn)

Amphibious

1 amph aslt bn

COMBAT SUPPORT

1 arty regt (3 fd arty bn, 1 ADA bn)

EQUIPMENT BY TYPE

ARMOURED FIGHTING VEHICLES

LT TK 3 VN-16

IFV 14 BTR-3E1

APC • APC (W) 24 LAV-150 *Commando*

AAV 33 LVTP-7

ENGINEERING & MAINTENANCE VEHICLES

ARV 1 AAVR-7

ANTI-TANK/ANTI-INFRASTRUCTURE

MSL

SP 10 M1045A2 HMMWV with TOW

MANPATS M47 *Dragon*; TOW

RCL • SP 106mm M40A1

ARTILLERY 54

SP 155mm 6 ATMOS-2000

TOWED 48: **105mm** 36 M101A1; **155mm** 12 GC-45

AIR DEFENCE

SAM Point-defence QW-18

GUNS 12.7mm 14

Naval Special Warfare Command

Air Force ε46,000

4 air divs, one flying trg school

FORCES BY ROLE

FIGHTER

2 sqn with F-5E/5F *Tiger* II

3 sqn with F-16A/B *Fighting Falcon*

FIGHTER/GROUND ATTACK

1 sqn with *Gripen* C/D

GROUND ATTACK

1 sqn with *Alpha Jet**

1 sqn with AU-23A *Peacemaker*

1 sqn with T-50TH *Golden Eagle**

ELINT/ISR

1 sqn with DA42 MPP *Guardian*

AIRBORNE EARLY WARNING & CONTROL

1 sqn with Saab 340B; Saab 340 *Erieye*

TRANSPORT

1 (Royal Flight) sqn with A319CJ; A340-500; B-737-800

1 sqn with ATR-72; BAe-748

1 sqn with BT-67

1 sqn with C-130H/H-30 *Hercules*

TRAINING

1 sqn with CT-4A/B *Airtrainer*; T-41D *Mescalero*

1 sqn with CT-4E *Airtrainer*

1 sqn with PC-9

1 sqn with H135

TRANSPORT HELICOPTER

1 sqn with Bell 205 (UH-1H *Iroquois*)

1 sqn with Bell 412 *Twin Huey*; S-92A

EQUIPMENT BY TYPE

AIRCRAFT 122 combat capable

FTR 75: 1 F-5B *Freedom Fighter*; 20 F-5E *Tiger* II; 2 F-5F *Tiger* II (F-5E/F being upgraded); 1 F-5TH(E) *Tiger* II; 1 F-5TH(F) *Tiger* II; 36 F-16A *Fighting Falcon*; 14 F-16B *Fighting Falcon*

FGA 11: 7 *Gripen* C; 4 *Gripen* D

ATK 16 AU-23A *Peacemaker*

ISR 5 DA42 MPP *Guardian*

AEW&C 2 Saab 340 *Erieye*

ELINT 2 Saab 340 *Erieye* (COMINT/ELINT)

TPT 42: **Medium** 14: 6 C-130H *Hercules*; 6 C-130H-30 *Hercules*; 2 Saab 340B; **Light** 21: 3 ATR-72; 3 Beech 200 *King Air*; 8 BT-67; 1 *Commander* 690; 6 DA42M; **PAX** 7: 1 A319CJ; 1 A320CJ; 1 A340-500; 1 B-737-800; 3 SSJ-100-95LR (1 A310-324 in store)

TRG 87: 16 *Alpha Jet**; 13 CT-4A *Airtrainer*; 6 CT-4B *Airtrainer*; 20 CT-4E *Airtrainer*; 21 PC-9; 7 T-41D *Mescalero*; 4 T-50TH *Golden Eagle**

HELICOPTERS

MRH 11: 2 Bell 412 *Twin Huey*; 2 Bell 412SP *Twin Huey*;

1 Bell 412HP *Twin Huey*; 6 Bell 412EP *Twin Huey*
CSAR 12 H225M *Super Cougar*
TPT 23: **Medium** 3 S-92A *Super Hawk*; **Light** 20: 17 Bell 205 (UH-1H *Iroquois*); 3 H135
UNINHABITED AERIAL VEHICLES • **ISR** • **Light** U-1
AIR DEFENCE
SAM Medium-range 3+ KS-1C (CH-SA-12)
AIR-LAUNCHED MISSILES
AAM • **IR** AIM-9P/S *Sidewinder*; *Python* 3; **IIR** IRIS-T; *Python* 5 (reported); **ARH** AIM-120 AMRAAM; *Derby* (reported)
ASM AGM-65 *Maverick*
AShM RBS15F
BOMBS
Laser-guided *Paveway* II
INS/GPS-guided GBU-38 JDAM

Royal Security Command

FORCES BY ROLE
MANOEUVRE
Light
2 inf regt (3 inf bn)

Gendarmerie & Paramilitary ε93,700

Border Patrol Police 20,000

Marine Police 2,200
EQUIPMENT BY TYPE
PATROL AND COASTAL COMBATANTS 101
PCO 1 *Srinakrin*
PCC 2 *Hameln*
PB 52: 1 *Chasanyabadee*; 3 *Cutlass*; 2 M25; 2 *Ratayapibanbancha* (*Reef Ranger*); 1 *Sriyanont*; 2 *Wasuthep*; 41 (various)
PBR 46

National Security Volunteer Corps 45,000 – Reserves

Police Aviation 500
EQUIPMENT BY TYPE
AIRCRAFT 6 combat capable
ATK 6 AU-23A *Peacemaker*
TPT 16: **Light** 15: 2 CN235; 8 PC-6 *Turbo-Porter*; 3 SC-7 3M *Skyvan*; 2 Short 330UTT; **PAX** 1 F-50
HELICOPTERS
MRH 12: 6 Bell 412 *Twin Huey*; 6 Bell 429
TPT • **Light** 61: 27 Bell 205A; 14 Bell 206 *Jet Ranger*; 20 Bell 212 (AB-212)

Provincial Police 50,000 (incl ε500 Special Action Force)

Thahan Phran (Hunter Soldiers) 21,000
Volunteer irregular force
FORCES BY ROLE
MANOEUVRE
Other
22 paramilitary regt (total: 275 paramilitary coy)

DEPLOYMENT

INDIA/PAKISTAN: UN • UNMOGIP 6
SOUTH SUDAN: UN • UNMISS 281; 1 engr coy

FOREIGN FORCES

United States US Pacific Command: 100

Timor-Leste TLS

US Dollar USD		2021	2022	2023
GDP	USD	2.36bn	2.46bn	
per capita	USD	1,754	1,793	
Growth	%	1.5	3.3	
Inflation	%	3.8	7.0	
Def bdgt	USD	39.2m	44.3m	

Real-terms defence budget trend (USDm, constant 2015)

Population 1,445,006

Age	0–14	15–19	20–24	25–29	30–64	65 plus
Male	20.2%	5.3%	4.9%	3.8%	13.6%	2.0%
Female	19.1%	5.1%	4.8%	4.0%	14.9%	2.2%

Capabilities

The small Timor-Leste Defence Force (F-FDTL) has been afflicted by funding, personnel and morale challenges since it was established in 2001. The F-FDTL was reconstituted in the wake of fighting between regional factions in the security forces in 2006, but is still a long way from meeting the ambitious force-structure goals set out in the Force 2020 plan published in 2007. In 2016, the government published a Strategic Defence and Security Concept (SDSC). This outlined the roles of the F-FDTL as including the protection of the country from external threats and combating violent crime. However, this parallel internal-security role has sometimes brought it into conflict with the national police force. The SDSC also stated that the F-FDTL needs to improve its naval capabilities, owing to the size of Timor-Leste's exclusive economic zone. The origins of the F-FDTL in the Falintil national resistance force, and continuing training and doctrinal emphasis on low-intensity infantry tactics, mean that the force provides a deterrent to invasion. The F-FDTL has received training from Australian and US personnel. Australia is also donating two *Guardian*-class patrol vessels as part of its Pacific Patrol Boat Replacement programme; these are due to arrive in 2023. Maintenance capacity is limited and the country has no defence industry.

ACTIVE 2,280 (Army 2,200 Naval Element 80)

ORGANISATIONS BY SERVICE

Army 2,200
Training began in January 2001 with the aim of deploying 1,500 full-time personnel and 1,500 reservists. Authorities are engaged in developing security structures with international assistance

FORCES BY ROLE
MANOEUVRE
  Light
    2 inf bn
COMBAT SUPPORT
  1 MP pl
COMBAT SERVICE SUPPORT
  1 log spt coy

Naval Element 80
EQUIPMENT BY TYPE
PATROL AND COASTAL COMBATANTS 5
  PB 5: 2 *Dili* (ex-ROK); 2 *Shanghai* II; 1 *Kamenassa* (ex-ROK *Chamsuri*)

Air Component
EQUIPMENT BY TYPE
AIRCRAFT • TPT • Light 1 Cessna 172

Tonga TON

Tongan Pa'anga TOP		2021	2022	2023
GDP	TOP	1.07bn	1.14bn	
	USD	470m	501m	
per capita	USD	4,701	5,008	
Growth	%	-2.7	-2.0	
Inflation	%	1.4	8.5	
Def bdgt	TOP	11.6m	18.5m	20.4m
	USD	5.09m	8.15m	
USD1=TOP		2.27	2.27	

Real-terms defence budget trend (USDm, constant 2015)

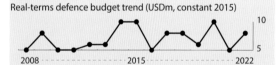

Population   105,517

Age	0–14	15–19	20–24	25–29	30–64	65 plus
Male	15.5%	5.2%	4.7%	4.0%	17.4%	3.2%
Female	15.0%	5.0%	4.5%	4.0%	17.4%	3.9%

Capabilities

His Majesty's Armed Forces (HMAF) are a battalion-sized military based around the light infantry of the Tonga Royal Guards and the Royal Tongan Marines, and a small naval patrol squadron. Maritime security is a primary concern of defence operations, although, between 2002 and 2014, HMAF also contributed platoon-sized forces to multinational peacekeeping efforts in the Solomon Islands, and then international coalition operations in Iraq and Afghanistan. Australia and the United States are Tonga's key external defence partners, but the armed forces also undertake defence cooperation activities with China, India, New Zealand and the United Kingdom.

ACTIVE 600 (Royal Guards & Land Force 140 Navy 130 Other 330)

ORGANISATIONS BY SERVICE
Royal Guard & Land Force 140
FORCES BY ROLE
MANOEUVRE
  Light
    1 inf coy(-)
  Other
    1 sy coy(-)

Navy 130
EQUIPMENT BY TYPE
PATROL AND COASTAL COMBATANTS
  PCO 2 *Guardian* (AUS *Bay* mod)
AMPHIBIOUS • LANDING CRAFT • LCM 1
LOGISTICS AND SUPPORT • AOL 1

Vietnam VNM

Vietnamese Dong VND		2021	2022	2023
GDP	VND	8399tr	9325tr	
	USD	366bn	414bn	
per capita	USD	3,718	4,163	
Growth	%	2.6	7.0	
Inflation	%	1.8	3.8	
Def bdgt	VND	ε145tr	ε136tr	
	USD	ε6.31bn	ε6.03bn	
FMA (US)	USD	10.9m	12.0m	12.0m
USD1=VND		22934.42	22534.02	

Real-terms defence budget trend (USDbn, constant 2015)

Population   103,808,319

Age	0–14	15–19	20–24	25–29	30–64	65 plus
Male	12.5%	3.8%	3.7%	4.1%	23.1%	3.0%
Female	11.2%	3.6%	3.5%	3.9%	23.3%	4.5%

Capabilities

Vietnam has a stronger military tradition, and its armed forces have more operational experience, than its neighbours. Its defence efforts and armed forces also benefit from broad popular support, particularly in the context of tensions with China over conflicting claims in the South China Sea. Vietnam adopted a new Law on National Defence in 2018 and issued a defence White Paper in 2019. The latter referred several times to Vietnam's differences with China and the need for both sides to 'put more effort into maintaining stability'. It is evident, from Hanoi's perspective, that stability will depend in good measure on Vietnam bolstering its deterrent capabilities in the South China Sea. This explains the emphasis on strengthening naval and air capabilities, including development of an advanced submarine capability and procurement of new ISR, air-defence and naval anti-surface systems to boost the capacity for anti-access/area-denial operations in Vietnam's maritime littoral. A joint vision statement on defence cooperation and a memorandum of understanding on mutual logistics support

Asia **299**

were signed with India in June 2022. While Russia has been the dominant defence supplier, Washington lifted its arms embargo on Vietnam in 2016, and New Delhi and Seoul are understood to be seeking inroads into Vietnam's defence market. Japan also signed a defence trade deal with Vietnam in September 2021 to support defence exports to the country as well as future collaboration on research and development. Long-expected orders for new combat aircraft and maritime-patrol aircraft have failed to materialise, though Vietnam ordered a Japanese-produced satellite-based surveillance system in April 2020 and jet and turboprop trainers from the Czech Republic and United States, while the US has also transferred ex-*Hamilton* class vessels to Vietnam's coastguard under the US Excess Defense Articles programme. Vietnam is developing its limited defence-industrial capacities and launched a defence-focused subsidiary to state-owned Viettel Military Industry and Telecoms Group, called Viettel High Technology Industries Corporation, which focuses on defence electronics and communications. The 2019 White Paper promoted investment in Vietnam's defence industry with the aim to become internationally competitive and join the 'global value chain' by 2030.

ACTIVE 482,000 (Army 412,000 Navy 40,000 Air 30,000) Gendarmerie & Paramilitary 40,000
Conscript liability 2 years army and air defence, 3 years air force and navy, specialists 3 years, some ethnic minorities 2 years

RESERVES Gendarmerie & Paramilitary 5,000,000

ORGANISATIONS BY SERVICE

Space
EQUIPMENT BY TYPE
SATELLITES • ISR 1 VNREDSat

Army ε412,000
8 Mil Regions (incl capital)
FORCES BY ROLE
COMMAND
 4 corps HQ
SPECIAL FORCES
 1 SF bde (1 AB bde, 1 demolition engr regt)
MANOEUVRE
 Armoured
 10 tk bde
 Mechanised
 2 mech inf div
 Light
 23 inf div
SURFACE-TO-SURFACE MISSILE
 1 SRBM bde
COMBAT SUPPORT
 13 arty bde
 1 arty regt
 11 engr bde
 1 engr regt
 1 EW unit
 3 sigs bde
 2 sigs regt
COMBAT SERVICE SUPPORT
 9 economic construction div
 1 log regt
 1 med unit

 1 trg regt
AIR DEFENCE
 11 AD bde

Reserve
FORCES BY ROLE
MANOEUVRE
 Light
 9 inf div
EQUIPMENT BY TYPE
ARMOURED FIGHTING VEHICLES
 MBT 1,383: 45 T-34; 850 T-54/T-55; 4+ T-54B mod; 70 T-62; 64 T-90S; 350 Type-59;
 LT TK 620: 300 PT-76; 320 Type-62/Type-63
 RECCE 100 BRDM-1/BRDM-2
 IFV 300 BMP-1/BMP-2
 APC 1,380+
  APC (T) 280+: Some BTR-50; 200 M113 (to be upgraded); 80 Type-63
  APC (W) 1,100 BTR-40/BTR-60/BTR-152
ENGINEERING & MAINTENANCE VEHICLES
 AEV IMR-2
 ARV BREM-1M
 VLB TMM-3
ANTI-TANK/ANTI-INFRASTRUCTURE
 MSL • MANPATS 9K11 *Malyutka* (RS-AT-3 *Sagger*); 9M14 mod
 RCL 75mm Type-56; **82mm** Type-65 (B-10); **87mm** Type-51
 GUNS
  SP 100mm SU-100; **122mm** SU-122
  TOWED 100mm T-12 (arty); M-1944
ARTILLERY 3,040+
 SP 30+: **122mm** 2S1 *Gvozdika*; **152mm** 30 2S3 *Akatsiya*; **175mm** M107
 TOWED 2,300: **105mm** M101/M102; **122mm** D-30/Type-54 (M-1938)/Type-60 (D-74); **130mm** M-46; **152mm** D-20; **155mm** M114
 MRL 710+: **107mm** 360 Type-63; **122mm** 350 BM-21 *Grad*; **140mm** BM-14
 MOR 82mm; **120mm** M-1943; **160mm** M-1943
SURFACE-TO-SURFACE MISSILE LAUNCHERS
 SRBM • Coventional 9K72/9K77 (RS-SS-1C/D *Scud* B/C)
AIR DEFENCE
 SAM • Point-defence 9K32 *Strela*-2 (RS-SA-7 *Grail*)‡; 9K310 *Igla*-1 (RS-SA-16 *Gimlet*); 9K38 *Igla* (RS-SA-18 *Grouse*)
 GUNS 12,000
  SP 23mm ZSU-23-4
  TOWED 14.5mm/30mm/37mm/57mm/85mm/100mm

Navy ε40,000 (incl ε27,000 Naval Infantry)
EQUIPMENT BY TYPE
SUBMARINES 8
 SSK 6 *Hanoi* (RUS Project 636.1 (Improved *Kilo*)) with 6 533mm TT with 3M14E *Klub*-S (RS-SS-N-30B) LACM/3M54E1/E *Klub*-S (RS-SS-N-27A/B) AShM (*Klub*-S AShM variant unclear)/53-65KE HWT/TEST-71ME HWT
 SSW 2 *Yugo* (DPRK)
PATROL AND COASTAL COMBATANTS 61
 CORVETTES 12:

300 THE MILITARY BALANCE 2023

FSGM 5:

1 BPS-500 with 2 quad lnchr with 3M24E *Uran*-E (RS-SS-N-25 *Switchblade*) AShM, 1 9K32 *Strela*-2M (RS-SA-N-5 *Grail*) SAM (manually operated), 2 twin 533mm TT, 1 RBU 1600 A/S mor, 1 AK630 CIWS, 1 76mm gun

2 *Dinh Tien Hoang* (RUS *Gepard* 3.9 (Project 11661E)) with 2 quad lnchr with 3M24E *Uran*-E (RS-SS-N-25 *Switchblade*) AShM, 1 3M89E *Palma* (*Palash*) CIWS with *Sosna*-R SAM (RS-CADS-N-2), 2 AK630M CIWS, 1 76mm gun, 1 hel landing platform

2 *Tran Hung Dao* (RUS *Gepard* 3.9 (Project 11661E)) with 2 quad lnchr with 3M24E *Uran*-E (RS-SS-N-25 *Switchblade*), 1 3M89E *Palma* (*Palash*) CIWS with *Sosna*-R SAM (RS-CADS-N-2), 2 twin 533mm TT with SET-53M HWT, 2 AK630M CIWS, 1 76mm gun, 1 hel landing platform

FSG 1 *Po Hang* (Flight III) (ex-ROK) with 2 quad lnchr with 3M24E *Uran*-E (RS-SS-N-25 *Switchblade*) AShM, 2 76mm guns

FS 6:

3 Project 159A (ex-FSU *Petya* II) with 1 quintuple 406mm ASTT, 4 RBU 6000 *Smerch* 2 A/S mor, 2 twin 76mm gun

2 Project 159AE (ex-FSU *Petya* III) with 1 triple 533mm ASTT with SET-53ME HWT, 4 RBU 2500 *Smerch* 1 A/S mor, 2 twin 76mm gun

1 *Po Hang* (Flight III) (ex-ROK) with 2 76mm guns

PCFGM 12:

4 Project 1241RE (*Tarantul* I) with 2 twin lnchr with P-15 *Termit*-R (RS-SS-N-2D *Styx*) AShM, 1 quad lnchr with 9K32 *Strela*-2M (RS-SA-N-5 *Grail*) SAM (manually operated), 2 AK630M CIWS, 1 76mm gun

8 Project 12418 (*Tarantul* V) with 4 quad lnchr with 3M24E *Uran*-E (RS-SS-N-25 *Switchblade*) AShM, 1 quad lnchr with 9K32 *Strela*-2M (RS-SA-N-5 *Grail*) SAM (manually operated), 2 AK630M CIWS, 1 76mm gun

PCO 7: 1 Project FC264; 6 TT-400TP with 2 AK630M CIWS, 1 76mm gun

PCC 6 *Svetlyak* (Project 1041.2) with 1 AK630M CIWS, 1 76mm gun

PBFG 8 Project 205 (*Osa* II) with 4 single lnchr with P-20U (RS-SS-N-2B *Styx*) AShM

PBFT 1+ *Shershen*† (FSU) with 4 single 533mm TT

PH 2 *Shtorm* (ex-FSU Project 206M (*Turya*))† with 1 twin 57mm gun

PHT 3 *Shtorm* (ex-FSU Project 206M (*Turya*))† with 4 single 533mm TT with 53-65KE HWT, 1 twin 57mm gun

PB 6: 4 *Zhuk* (mod); 2 TP-01

PBR 4 *Stolkraft*

MINE WARFARE • MINE COUNTERMEASURES 8

MSO 2 *Akvamaren* (Project 266 (*Yurka*))

MSC 4 *Sonya* (Project 1265 (*Yakhont*))

MHI 2 *Korund* (Project 1258 (*Yevgenya*))

AMPHIBIOUS

LANDING SHIPS 7

LST 2 *Tran Khanh Du* (ex-US LST 542) with 1 hel landing platform (capacity 16 Lt Tk/APC; 140 troops)

LSM 5:

1 *Polnochny* A (capacity 6 Lt Tk/APC; 200 troops)

2 *Polnochny* B (capacity 6 Lt Tk/APC; 200 troops)

2 *Nau Dinh*

LANDING CRAFT • LCM 13

8 LCM 6 (capacity 1 Lt Tk or 80 troops)

4 LCM 8 (capacity 1 MBT or 200 troops)

1 VDN-150

LOGISTICS AND SUPPORT 22

AGS 1 *Tran Dai Nia* (Damen Research Vessel 6613)

AH 1 *Khanh Hoa* (*Truong Sa* mod)

AKR 4 Damen Stan Lander 5612

AKSL 10+

AP 1 *Truong Sa*

ASR 1 *Yêt Kiêu* (Damen Rescue Gear Ship 9316)

AT 2

AWT 1

AXS 1 *Le Quy Don*

Naval Infantry ε27,000

EQUIPMENT BY TYPE

ARMOURED FIGHTING VEHICLES

LT TK PT-76; Type-63

APC • APC (W) BTR-60

Coastal Defence

FORCES BY ROLE

COASTAL DEFENCE

3 AShM bde

1 coastal arty bde

EQUIPMENT BY TYPE

COASTAL DEFENCE • AShM 4K44 *Redut* (RS-SSC-1B *Sepal*); 4K51 *Rubezh* (RS-SSC-3 *Styx*); K-300P *Bastion*-P (RS-SSC-5 *Stooge*)

ARTILLERY • MRL 160mm AccuLAR-160; **306mm** EXTRA

Navy Air Wing

FORCES BY ROLE

ASW/SAR

1 regt with H225; Ka-28 (Ka-27PL) *Helix* A; Ka-32 *Helix* C

EQUIPMENT BY TYPE

AIRCRAFT • TPT • Light 6 DHC-6-400 *Twin Otter*

HELICOPTERS

ASW 10 Ka-28 *Helix* A

TPT • Medium 4: 2 H225; 2 Ka-32 *Helix* C

Air Force 30,000

3 air div, 1 tpt bde

FORCES BY ROLE

FIGHTER/GROUND ATTACK

3 regt with Su-22M3/M4/UM *Fitter* (some ISR)

1 regt with Su-27SK/Su-27UBK *Flanker*

1 regt with Su-27SK/Su-27UBK *Flanker*; Su-30MK2 *Flanker*

2 regt with Su-30MK2 *Flanker*

TRANSPORT

2 regt with An-2 *Colt*; Bell 205 (UH-1H *Iroquois*); Mi-8 *Hip*; Mi-17 *Hip* H; M-28 *Bryza*; C295M

TRAINING

1 regt with L-39 *Albatros*

1 regt with Yak-52

ATTACK/TRANSPORT HELICOPTER

2 regt with Mi-8 *Hip*; Mi-17 *Hip* H; Mi-171; Mi-24 *Hind*

AIR DEFENCE

6 AD div HQ

2 SAM regt with S-300PMU1 (RS-SA-20 *Gargoyle*)

3 SAM regt with *Spyder*-MR
3 SAM regt with S-75 *Dvina* (RS-SA-2 *Guideline*)
4 SAM regt with S-125-2TM *Pechora*-2TM
2 SAM regt with S-125M *Pechora*-M
4 ADA regt

EQUIPMENT BY TYPE
AIRCRAFT 84 combat capable
  FGA 72: 26 Su-22M3/M4/UM *Fitter* (some ISR); 6 Su-27SK *Flanker*; 5 Su-27UBK *Flanker* B; 35 Su-30MK2 *Flanker* G
  TPT • Light 12: 6 An-2 *Colt*; 3 C295M; 1 M-28 *Bryza*; 2 C-212 *Aviocar* (NC-212i)
  TRG 59: 17 L-39 *Albatros*; 12 Yak-130 *Mitten**; 30 Yak-52
HELICOPTERS
  MRH 6 Mi-17 *Hip* H
  TPT 28: **Medium** 17: 14 Mi-8 *Hip*; 3 Mi-171; **Light** 11 Bell 205 (UH-1H *Iroquois*)
AIR DEFENCE
  SAM 98+:
    Long-range 12 S-300PMU1 (RS-SA-20 *Gargoyle*)
    Medium-range 65: ε25 S-75 *Dvina* (RS-SA-2 *Guideline*); ε30 S-125-2TM *Pechora*-2TM; ε10 *Spyder*-MR
    Short-range 21+: 2K12 *Kub* (RS-SA-6 *Gainful*); 21 S-125M *Pechora*-M (RS-SA-3 *Goa*)
    Point-defence 9K32 *Strela*-2 (RS-SA-7 *Grail*)‡; 9K310 *Igla*-1 (RS-SA-16 *Gimlet*)
  GUNS 37mm; **57mm**; **85mm**; **100mm**; **130mm**
AIR-LAUNCHED MISSILES
  AAM • IR R-60 (RS-AA-8 *Aphid*); R-73 (RS-AA-11A *Archer*); **IR/SARH** R-27 (RS-AA-10 *Alamo*); **ARH** R-77 (RS-AA-12A *Adder*)
  ASM Kh-29L/T (RS-AS-14 *Kedge*); Kh-59M (RS-AS-18 *Kazoo*)
  AShM Kh-31A (RS-AS-17B *Krypton*)
  ARM Kh-28 (RS-AS-9 *Kyle*); Kh-31P (RS-AS-17A *Krypton*)

Gendarmerie & Paramilitary 40,000+ active

Border Defence Corps ε40,000

Coast Guard

EQUIPMENT BY TYPE
PATROL AND COASTAL COMBATANTS 79+
  PSOH 2 *Hamilton* (ex-US) with 1 76mm gun (capacity 1 med hel)
  PSO 4 DN2000 (Damen 9014)
  PCO 13+: 1 *Mazinger* (ex-ROK); 9 TT-400; 3+ other
  PCC 2 *Hae Uri* (ex-ROK)
  PBF 28: 26 MS-50S; 2 *Shershen*
  PB 30: 1 MS-50; approx 14 TT-200; 14 TT-120; 1 other
LOGISTICS AND SUPPORT 5
  AFS 1
  ATF 4 Damen Salvage Tug
AIRCRAFT • MP 5 C-212-400 MPA

Local Forces ε5,000,000 reservists

Incl People's Self-Defence Force (urban units) and People's Militia (rural units); comprises static and mobile cbt units, log spt and village protection pl; some arty, mor and AD guns; acts as reserve

DEPLOYMENT

CENTRAL AFRICAN REPUBLIC: UN • MINUSCA 9

SOUTH SUDAN: UN • UNMISS 69; 1 fd hospital

SUDAN: UN • UNISFA 190; 1 engr coy

Chapter Seven
Middle East and North Africa

- Iran emerged as a key military supporter of Russia in 2022, as the latter struggled during its war in Ukraine. Iran sent *Shahed* 131 and 136 Direct Attack Munitions to Ukraine, and there was speculation that in response Russia would step up sales to Iran, potentially selling the Su-35 aircraft originally intended for Egypt. Russia has also sought Iranian assistance to circumvent Western sanctions.
- 2022 saw regional governments embrace de-escalation and engage in diplomacy in ways not seen before. These developments were motivated largely by the post-pandemic recovery and the need for a greater focus on economic affairs. However, the picture was not wholly positive: violence persisted in Libya, Syria and Yemen, while Houthi attacks on Saudi Arabia and the UAE continued.
- Ties improved between Turkey and Gulf states, and between Turkey and Israel. Ankara obtained Gulf investment pledges and Gulf boycotts of Turkish goods were lifted. This occurred within a context of strengthening defence cooperation, including maritime and air exercises, between Egypt, Greece and Cyprus, as well as between Greece and the UAE.
- To foster greater regional collective cooperation against Iran, the US has orchestrated initiatives that capitalised on warming relations between Israel and several regional states. In February, USCENTCOM launched a task force in the Gulf to conduct surveillance by using uninhabited systems and in April the US announced the creation of CTF-153, a maritime task force in the Red Sea designed to monitor the activities of Iran and its proxies.
- Amidst a challenging global economic context, regional real GDP growth is estimated to have increased from an average 4.1% in 2021 to an average 5.0% in 2022, excluding Lebanon, Libya and Syria. But regional trends mask sharp disparities driven by the surge in the oil price over 2022. Growth among oil importers is estimated to have reached 4.4% in 2022 compared to 5.2% for oil exporters and 6.5% for Gulf Cooperation Council member states. Fiscal conservatism still shaped spending decisions in 2022.

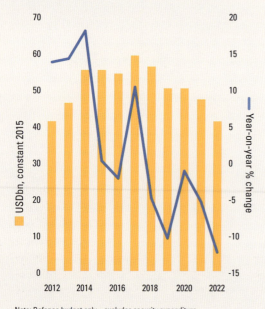

Saudi Arabia, real-terms defence budget trend, 2012–22 (USDbn, constant 2015)*

Note: Defence budget only – excludes security expenditure

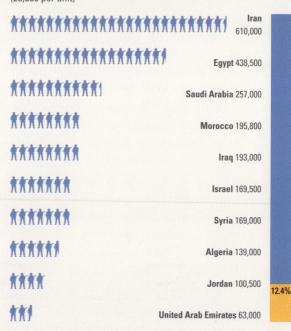

Active military personnel – top 10
(25,000 per unit)

Iran 610,000
Egypt 438,500
Saudi Arabia 257,000
Morocco 195,800
Iraq 193,000
Israel 169,500
Syria 169,000
Algeria 139,000
Jordan 100,500
United Arab Emirates 63,000

Global total 20,773,950

12.4% Regional total 2,571,750

Regional defence policy and economics 304 ▶

Arms procurements and deliveries 312 ▶

Armed forces data section 315 ▶

Middle East and North Africa: selected tactical combat aircraft, 2022*

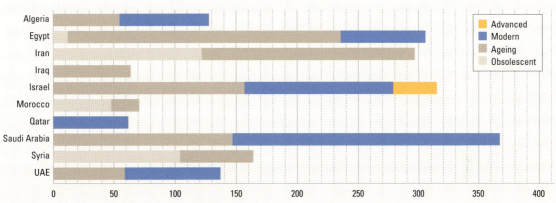

*'Combat aircraft' includes fighter, fighter ground-attack and attack aircraft

Middle East and North Africa: selected main battle tank fleets, 2022

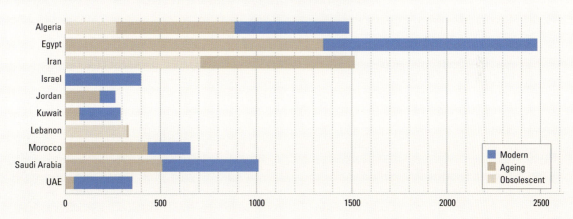

Egypt's navy: selected assets by country of origin

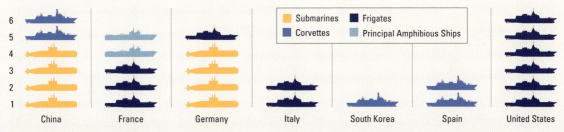

Icons are for illustrative purposes only

Middle East and North Africa

Conflict and competition in the Middle East and North Africa reached their lowest levels of intensity in a decade, as 2022 saw regional governments embrace de-escalation and engage in diplomacy in ways not seen in previous years. These developments were motivated by the post-pandemic recovery and the need for a greater focus on economic affairs. While power projection by most of the major states engaged in regional competition appeared to decline, Iran stepped up its activities, exerting influence in the war in Ukraine by supplying weapons to Russia. Indeed, broader concerns about Iran's activities and the regional repercussions of Russia's invasion of Ukraine, together with the lack of formal settlements of various crises, suggested caution over the durability of this regional de-escalation in the medium term.

Regional conflicts

Since 2011, three major civil wars have engulfed the region. Although these conflicts saw their lowest levels of violence yet in 2022, they continue to destabilise the region's economies and societies, risking military confrontation between states and continuing to cause much human suffering for civilian populations.

Yemen

In Yemen, a United Nations-brokered ceasefire was agreed in April. This froze the front lines and, though it was extended in July, ended in October. In the months leading up to April, Houthi forces had made further advances towards the south and the east. Meanwhile, United Arab Emirates-supported militias made progress pushing back Houthi advances in Shabwa and along the western coast. The forces of the UAE-backed secessionist Southern Transitional Council (STC) pushed into Abyan province. In recent years, the STC had clashed with forces loyal to the central government of president Abd Rabbo Mansour Hadi and expelled them from several regions in the south. In contrast, government forces retained the greater authority in Marib, the last major government-held city in central Yemen, thanks largely to Saudi military support. Non-governmental organisations reported a 60% decrease in civilian casualties during the ceasefire, along with greater humanitarian access and a boost to the local economy, though the reopening of roads across zones of control was limited. The Houthis had agreed to the ceasefire after months of ground attacks aimed at seizing Marib. Several thousand Houthi fighters were reportedly killed in this campaign, mainly after operations by Saudi Arabia's air force. The Houthis were believed to have only agreed to the truce because they believed it would allow them to regroup and reconstitute their forces before attempting new attacks.

Several reports, including by UN experts, indicated that Iranian provision of weaponry to the Houthis continued during the truce. Anti-Houthi forces also used the lull to regroup and prepare for new rounds of fighting but faced conflicted patrons whose interests and risk profile were more limited than during the early years of the intervention. Analysts believe that Saudi Arabia agreed to the ceasefire not only to placate the United States and the rest of the international community but also to reduce its exposure to the conflict, notably in the form of Houthi aerial attacks against the Kingdom's infrastructure. To support the political process, Riyadh also compelled president Hadi to resign in favour of a newly formed presidential council. Saudi- and Emirati-supported factions largely abided by the ceasefire, mostly out of exhaustion but also out of deference to their patrons. The Houthi decision not to extend the ceasefire in October came as the regional security situation worsened. The failure of Saudi–Iranian talks in Iraq over Yemen and large-scale popular unrest in Iran increased concerns over the potential for renewed attacks by the Houthis as well as Iran on Saudi Arabia. It was also largely interpreted as heralding new campaigns in Marib and Ta'izz. Meanwhile, the UAE maintained its support for the STC and other militias, as did Saudi Arabia with its own partners.

Libya

In Libya, violence resumed in mid-year because of a political stalemate. Long-awaited presidential elections had been scheduled for late 2021, after the formation of a unity government headed by Abdul Hamid Dbeibah. However, the postponement of the elections fuelled political divisions and led to political and militia realignments. In early 2022, two rival governments claimed authority and legitimacy: the Tripoli-based Government of National Unity led by Dbeibah and the Government of National Stability based in eastern Libya and headed by former interior minister Fathi Bashagha. Both entities relied on the support of militias: Dbeibah depended on Tripoli- and Misrata-based factions, while Bashagha could muster some support in Tripoli as well as from militias loyal to the Tobruk parliament. Khalifa Haftar, the country's most powerful warlord, was nominally supportive of Bashagha but did not commit his Libyan Arab Armed Forces (LAAF), which had failed to seize the capital in 2019–20. These factions competed over territory, particularly oil-export facilities, and institutions, including the National Oil Corporation and Libyan Central Bank.

In August, Bashagha attempted to seize power in Tripoli, mobilising several militias and obtaining political backing in the Gulf as well as Egypt. Having secured the support of Tripoli and Misrata militias, Dbeibah successfully resisted the attack. Both men, however, emerged weaker from this confrontation, unable to muster forces or attract foreign support. Importantly, Egypt, Turkey and the UAE have appeared less willing to deploy forces or provide equipment in this current round but appear ready to back more reliable and effective local partners. Dbeibah was keen to cultivate the support of Turkey, which maintained a small presence in the country, while Egypt backed the speaker of parliament and Bashagha ally Aguileh Saleh.

The Wagner Group, a Russian private military company, had been less active since the 2020 Tripoli debacle when it attempted to assault the city. But it maintained a significant presence, estimated to number between 1,500 and 2,000 troops, alongside Haftar's troops and in key locations, including oil facilities. There was no discernible reduction in this presence after Russia's full-scale invasion of Ukraine, as Libya remained a convenient pressure point for Russia against Turkey and European countries. Some of the combat aircraft previously associated with Wagner seemed to have been transferred to LAAF control. This situation led to relative quiet in the country but presaged violent competition as new contenders, courting foreign support, geared up to replace existing groups. Moreover, there were continued attempts to rearm. Crew from vessels participating in the European Union's *Operation Irini*, a maritime mission designed to intercept illicit shipments bound for Libya, boarded a number of vessels in 2022 and seized weapons and military vehicles bound for the country. The UN process, which in 2019 and 2021 seemed close to delivering a settlement, was once again under threat in late 2022.

Syria

The main battlelines in Syria did not change significantly in 2022 despite violence reaching its lowest levels since 2011. The regime of President Bashar al-Assad remained firmly in place in Damascus but remained too weak to consolidate power in the areas in the northwest and northeast that are outside its control. However, Assad's various opponents remained in disarray and heavily dependent on foreign support. Throughout the year, there were assessments that Turkey might conduct a campaign to seize further territory from the Kurdish-dominated administration in northern and eastern Syria, but US lobbying and Russian opposition seemed to forestall any Turkish plans. Instead, the greatest change occurred inside the rebel holdout of Idlib, where the jihadi group Hayat Tahrir al-Sham seized more territory from groups aligned with Ankara. The humanitarian situation remained dire, with international aid agencies securing less than half of the funding required to provide support to the population. In July, the UN Security Council agreed to keep the sole remaining cross-border humanitarian route from Turkey into Idlib open for only six months, down from 12 months in previous years. This was due to Russian opposition.

Russia's 2022 invasion of Ukraine has had some military effect in Syria. Moscow maintains a naval presence in the port of Tartus and an air base in Hmeimim, as well as an operations room and military intelligence group in Damascus that coordinates Russian activity countrywide. In the first months of Russia's invasion, there was no noticeable reduction in the size of the Russian military presence in Syria, estimated to be around 4,000 troops. But reports emerged in the autumn of increased turnover, suggesting a limited but noteworthy Russian readjustment including the relocation of one of Russia's S-300 air-defence units back to Russia.

Indeed, as Russian forces began to struggle in Ukraine, this had a direct impact on the Syrian battlefield. Turkey was a prime beneficiary of Russia's isolation and its reliance on Turkish goodwill. The prospects of Russia supporting an

Assad campaign to retake Idlib were considerably reduced. Likewise, Iran benefitted insofar as it could maintain its influence in Syria, with reduced chances of Russian pushback. Israel's reluctance to condemn the Russian invasion was partly determined by the imperative of maintaining military coordination with Russia in Syria to secure air access and avoid accidents. Israel was keen to preserve its air dominance and worried that direct Israeli military support to Ukraine would lead to Russian pushback in Syria. Nonetheless, the IDF was troubled by the increase in defence cooperation between Iran and Russia. It was feared that Iranian provision of uninhabited aerial vehicles (UAVs) to Russia would allow Tehran to test its capabilities on a contested battlefield, while the increased ties between the two also raised concerns that Russia could reciprocate and provide Iran with defence technologies previously denied to it and align itself with Tehran on critical security issues.

Within this environment, there was no real progress in reforming and modernising the Syrian Arab Army and the wider security apparatus. The worsening economic climate in Syria and the continued existence of pro-regime militias keen to preserve their autonomy precluded any prospect of consolidation. This led to sustained violence in many regions across the country: the Islamic State (ISIS) insurgency remained active in the Badiya desert region and in Deir ez-Zor and increasingly in the south. The regime was also unable to stabilise the region bordering Jordan. Moscow had guaranteed the regional deal that led in 2018 to the dismantlement and abandonment by their foreign sponsors of rebel groups operating there. Moscow, however, did not deploy military police units, provide stabilisation funds or encourage reconciliation. This failure caused security to deteriorate.

Iraq

In contrast to Libya, Syria and Yemen, violence in Iraq increased in 2022. Civil unrest, which peaked in 2019, took a back seat as political competition increased between parties backed by militias. This was notably the case between Moqtada al-Sadr, a prominent and popular Shia cleric with nationalistic appeal, and an array of Iranian-backed militias. This escalated into several armed confrontations in Baghdad and elsewhere, though the violence was ultimately contained. Intensified violence in northern Iraq was perhaps of greater significance. There,

Turkey continued to fight Kurdish separatists of the Kurdistan Workers' Party (PKK) through ground and aerial operations, which caused civilian casualties as well as protests from Baghdad over the violation of Iraqi sovereignty. Kurdish separatists of the Free Life Party of Kurdistan (PJAK) in Iraq were also the target of intense Iranian attacks.

There were also more attacks by Iranian-aligned groups against US military targets in Iraq and Syria. In parallel with diplomatic paralysis over Iran's nuclear programme and in the context of regional tensions, Iranian-backed groups launched missile and UAV attacks against small US bases in northern Iraq and Syria, including Al-Tanf in August. This precipitated US retaliation against militia leaders.

Regional effects of Russia's 2022 invasion of Ukraine

Many states in the region have preferred to remain neutral in the war in Ukraine or have only mildly condemned the Russian invasion without taking measures against Moscow or reducing their engagement. Over the past decade, Russia had emerged as a security interlocutor as well as a possible alternative to the US in the eyes of several countries who were unnerved by fluctuations in US policy and appreciative of Vladimir Putin's ostensibly effective statecraft. Several countries – notably Algeria and Syria, but also Egypt, Iraq and other smaller states – have been traditional customers of Russian weaponry as well as defence partners, at times also conducting joint exercises with Russian armed forces. Even US regional allies had evoked the possibility of acquiring Russian weapons systems, such as the S-400 air-defence system. Russian military trainers and private military companies, including the Wagner Group, have operated in several countries in the region, including Libya, Syria and Sudan.

However, Russian prestige and credibility diminished in 2022, in comparison with a high point in 2015–16, when Moscow successfully intervened in the Syrian civil war. Russia's operational and military setbacks in Ukraine and the relatively poor performance of its weapons systems have damaged its reputation across the region. It is widely considered that Russia will struggle to innovate in the technological domain and to maintain its export capability given its internal demands and shortages. Concerns about incurring Western sanctions were also thought to be a deterrent for most countries. Importantly, the rapid growth of Russian–Iranian defence relations has caused significant unease, particularly among Gulf governments. In recent years, Iran had hoped that Russia would help it recapitalise its armed forces. But Moscow, then seen as the senior partner, was reluctant and unwilling to upset Israel and Gulf countries and risk Western disapproval. The Ukraine conflict has made Russia more dependent on Iranian goodwill: Moscow has acquired Iranian UAVs and deployed them in Ukraine. Tehran has supplied the Shahed-131 and Shahed-136 direct-attack munitions and the Mohajer-6 UAV to Russia as Moscow has attempted to fill gaps in its inventory resulting from the invasion. As of November 2022, the initial batch of the *Shahed* systems appeared to have almost been exhausted in Russia's attacks. They have been used to supplement Moscow's inventory of land-attack cruise missiles, which has depleted considerably since it launched its 2022 invasion on 24 February. Russia has also sought Iranian assistance to circumvent Western sanctions.

Regional competition

There was a trend towards regional de-escalation in 2022. In the Gulf region, Iran was engaged in separate diplomatic discussions with two of its main rivals, Saudi Arabia and the UAE. A key motivation for the governments of Saudi Arabia and the UAE was the need to avoid becoming entangled in US–Iran or Israel–Iran escalation, especially as talks over Iran's nuclear programme seemed inconclusive. Additionally, they both sought to reduce aerial attacks from Yemen. The UAE was the target of several waves of UAV and missile strikes in January and February and the Saudi city of Jeddah was hit in March during the Saudi Arabian Grand Prix. The bilateral discussions had limited positive impact, with Iran unwilling to make firm security commitments until an agreement with the US had been reached.

More notable detentes occurred between Saudi Arabia and the UAE and between Saudi Arabia and Turkey. Turkey's economic problems were the proximate cause of this rapprochement, which helped alleviate its regional isolation. Ankara obtained Gulf investment pledges and the Gulf boycotts of Turkish goods were lifted. This also opened the way to renewed discussions over defence procurement, notably those concerning Turkish UAVs. Likewise, Turkish–Israeli relations improved markedly. Facing isolation in the Eastern Mediterranean, Turkey was keen to restore political ties with Israel. This took place within a context of strengthening defence cooperation, including maritime and air exercises, between Cyprus, Egypt and Greece as well as between Greece and the UAE.

A maritime agreement between Israel and Lebanon, brokered by the US, also served to reduce tensions. The two countries have not delineated their land borders and there have been regular confrontations. However, the prospect of exploiting offshore energy resources seemed to underpin the agreement in October by both countries to delineate their maritime border. In the months prior to the agreement, Hizbullah had threatened Israeli ships and exploration vessels operating in the hitherto contested area, deploying surveillance UAVs and alluding to the possession of armed UAVs. However, domestic pressure in Lebanon, where the prospect of energy wealth seemed to improve an otherwise dire economic outlook, trumped Hizbullah's scepticism. There was hope that the agreement would reduce tensions between Lebanon and Israel, but Hizbullah as well as other Iran- and Syria-aligned groups rejected this prospect. The breakthrough happened as Lebanon continued to face economic and political turmoil. This put significant pressure on the armed forces to preserve domestic stability, with some help from Western and Arab governments.

The rivalry between Algeria and Morocco worsened substantially in 2022. Morocco obtained increased access to defence technology thanks to improving ties with the US, and especially Israel – with whom it signed a normalisation agreement in 2020. It now boasts the most diverse UAV fleet in the region, comprising Chinese, Israeli, Turkish and US equipment. Rabat deployed UAVs against the Polisario Front in the contested Western Sahara region. Morocco reportedly sought to buy the Israeli-made *Barak* MX air- and missile-defence system in 2022. For Algeria, the prospect of a better-armed Morocco, benefitting from Western alliances, has raised alarms given its dependence on Russian weaponry.

To foster conditions for greater regional collective cooperation against Iran, the US has orchestrated initiatives that capitalised on warming relations between Israel and several regional states. In February, US Central Command launched a task force in the Gulf to conduct surveillance by using uninhabited systems. In March, the Negev Summit in Israel brought together the US, Israeli, Egyptian, Moroccan, Bahraini and Emirati foreign ministers. In April, the US announced the creation of CTF-153, a maritime task force in the Red Sea designed to monitor the activities of Iran and its proxies in the region. Over the spring and summer, the US organised regional discussions about air-defence cooperation. However, political and operational obstacles hindered an agreement. Perhaps the most significant hurdles were the absence of a peace agreement between Saudi Arabia and Israel and political disagreements related to Red Sea issues. Inventories comprising different weapons systems and states having diverse weapons procurement priorities were equally significant factors.

DEFENCE ECONOMICS

Macroeconomics

The region's economies have generally been shielded from the slowdown in global economic activity in 2022. The year before, a tentative economic recovery across the world saw real GDP grow by 6% following the near 3% contraction in 2020 linked to the coronavirus pandemic. In contrast, real GDP growth in 2022 is projected to reach just 3.2%, inhibited by the economic fallout of Russia's full-scale invasion of Ukraine – which contributed to high rates of inflation and a cost-of-living crisis in several regions. The lingering coronavirus pandemic and the negative impact on Chinese economic activity is also weighing heavily on the economic outlook.

Amid this challenging context, regional real GDP growth is projected to increase from an average 4.1% in 2021 to an average 5.0% in 2022, excluding Lebanon, Libya and Syria. The Middle East and North Africa is highly exposed to global food prices, particularly the price of wheat, but inflation rates in several regional states are lower than those being experienced in Europe, Russia and Latin America. The most notable exceptions to this are inflation rates in Iran and Yemen, which reached 40.0% and 43.8% in 2022 respectively. Conversely, inflation in Gulf Cooperation Council (GCC) states is expected to be just 3.6% in 2022. Regional trends therefore mask sharp disparities driven by the surge in the oil price over 2022: real GDP growth among oil importers is expected to reach 4.4% in 2022 compared with 5.2% for the region's oil exporters and 6.5% for the GCC.

Indeed, higher oil prices are offering these countries a chance to transcend the two policy trade-offs that the war in Ukraine has sharpened for most of the world: 'between tackling inflation and safeguarding the recovery; and between supporting the vulnerable and rebuilding fiscal buffers', as the IMF put it. Brent crude prices jumped to levels in excess of USD120 a barrel in March, but they then stabilised to pre-invasion levels by the end of the year mainly because of a strong dollar, an increase in interest rates and fears of recession impacting oil demand. Throughout 2022, oil prices have stayed at levels beyond the amount needed by some Gulf states to balance their budgets. In 2022, this fiscal breakeven price ranged between USD60 and USD80 a barrel for Oman, Saudi Arabia and the UAE and was between USD48–55 a barrel for Kuwait and Qatar, with Bahrain being the exception at USD128 a barrel. In late September 2022, days after prices dipped close to USD80 a barrel for the first time since the beginning of the year, OPEC+ (OPEC members plus ten leading non-OPEC oil exporters) announced an agreement for the biggest oil production cut since the start of the coronavirus pandemic in a move likely designed to keep oil prices at elevated levels.

Defence spending and procurement

Defence spending in the Middle East and North Africa reached USD187 billion in 2022, up from USD173bn in 2021 (excluding Foreign Military Financing allocations from the US) largely due to a surge in spending in Iran. However, Iran's 40% inflation rate meant that regional spending in real terms continued to contract in line with the trend seen in the region since 2018. The strengthening of the oil price in 2021 was not reflected in the spending decisions for 2022 made by several of the region's oil exporters that continued to pursue a fiscally conservative stance.

This subdued regional trend covers significant disparities. The notable real reductions in defence spending between 2021 and 2022 in Saudi Arabia (-12.4%), Israel (-5.6%), Algeria (-3.7%) and Oman (-3.0%) were partially offset by growth in Iran (+30.0%), Qatar (+28.8%), Iraq (10.3%) and Egypt (+2.9%). It has been suggested that Saudi Arabia's reduced share could be linked to the Kingdom's ambition to diversify its economy through the development of local industry and plans to increase domestic weapons procurement and reduce dependence on expensive imports. Other factors should not be overlooked, such as the completion of existing equipment delivery contracts, a possible reduction in the level of spending on military operations in Yemen and a strained diplomatic relationship between Riyadh and Washington, traditionally the Kingdom's main arms supplier. Economic recovery in Saudi Arabia and other oil exporters may, along with the rise in oil prices

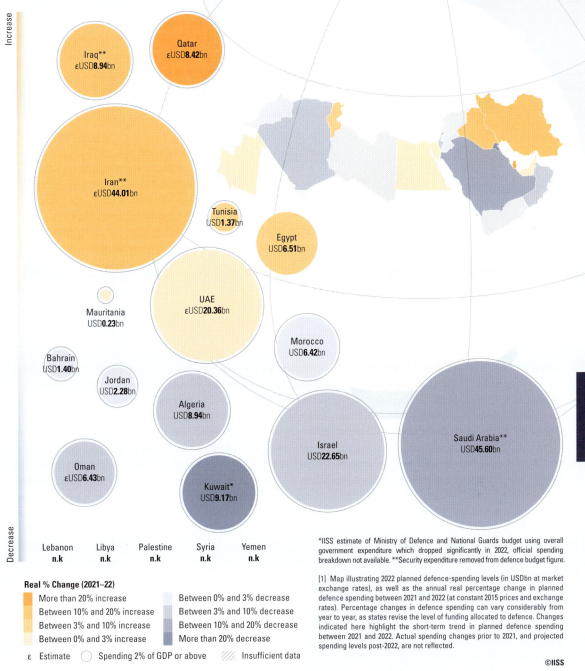

▲ Map 7 **Middle East and North Africa: regional defence spending** (USDbn, %ch yoy)[1]

in 2022, enable increased investment over the next few years. In October 2022, Saudi Arabia announced plans to boost public spending by 18% in 2023.

Over the last decade, the upward trend in defence spending in certain regional states can be linked to renewed tensions and associated threat perceptions as well as to major modernisation cycles in certain countries. Real-terms increases in Qatari defence spending averaged 12% annually between 2011 and 2022. They were driven at various points by heightened security concerns amid the diplomatic crisis with its neighbours over the period, and a

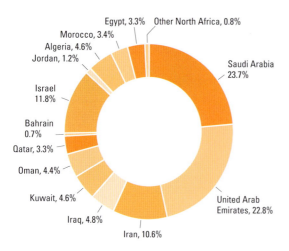

Note: Analysis excludes Lebanon, Libya, Palestinian Authority, Syrian Arab Republic and Yemen. ©IISS

▲ Figure 14 **Middle East and North Africa: defence spending by country and sub-region, 2022**

procurement drive from 2015 that included 108 combat aircraft, such as the F-15 from the United States, and the Eurofighter *Typhoon* and the *Rafale* from the UK and France respectively. Qatar's air force will be one of the most modern and diverse in the region once all three types are in service. However, the volume and speed of these acquisitions raises questions over Qatar's ability to crew and maintain the aircraft. Modernisation programmes in Kuwait and Egypt have also driven budget growth, while recent defence budget uplifts in Morocco were made against the backdrop of rising tensions with Algeria in 2021. Rabat procured attack helicopters and fighter jets from the US in 2019–2020 and armed uninhabited aerial vehicles (UAVs) from Turkey in 2021.

In Egypt and other regional states, another important recent trend has been a diversification of arms suppliers and defence partners. While Cairo historically procured from Washington, it has increasingly turned to Europe (mainly France but also Germany and Italy). While most of their crewed air platforms still come from these traditional Western suppliers, regional states have increasingly turned to other sources for UAVs and air defence systems. Over the past few years, for armed UAVs, Egypt turned to China (2018), Saudi Arabia to China (2017), the UAE to China (2017 and 2019), and Morocco to Turkey (2021). In January 2022, the UAE and South Korea also inked a preliminary agreement for the acquisition of surface-to-air missile systems a day before Houthi forces launched a UAV and missile attack on Abu Dhabi. Some regional markets remain focused on US and European suppliers. For instance, Kuwait is growing its fleet with US helicopters and F/A-18E/F *Super Hornets* and Eurofighter *Typhoons* and also its air defence such as with the notification by the US Defense Security Cooperation Agency in October 2022 of a potential US sale of the NASAMS III air defence system. Several countries may be tempted to branch out to other partners to move towards relative autonomy, which is increasingly supported by the development of regional defence-industrial and technological bases.

The outlook for the region will hinge on the response of oil producers to higher oil prices as they make their budgetary decisions. The spike in prices means that fiscal balances in the Gulf have moved from an average deficit of 5% of GDP during 2015–21 to a projected surplus of around 5% of GDP for 2022 and that countries will remain in surplus in 2023 and 2024. However, Gulf states may continue to adopt fiscally cautious behaviour. The volatility in oil prices and vulnerability to global shocks create significant budgetary uncertainty in the major defence-spending states in the Gulf. As a result, countries may prefer to continue improving resilience through economic diversification, reducing fiscal breakeven points, and shoring up reserves in the short term.

If countries do implement increases for defence in the short term, these will likely benefit investment spending or enable a resumption of delayed procurement programmes or one-off capital projects that support modernisation and domestic development efforts. The countries spending the most – Saudi Arabia and the UAE – have ambitious defence-industrial ambitions, so higher government revenues

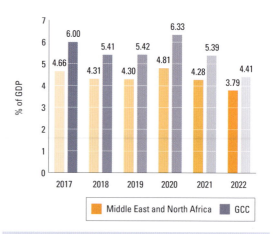

▲ Figure 15 **Middle East and North Africa: defence spending** as % of GDP (average)

may enable much-needed investment in defence R&D to bolster domestic production capabilities. However, governments will likely want to avoid higher recurring costs that result in a sustained increase in the defence budget, for instance changes in force structure. The Middle East and North Africa remains home to most of the world's countries with the highest military burden, including Oman (where spending accounts for 5.9% of GDP), Kuwait (5.0%) and Saudi Arabia (4.5%). The region's average is 3.8% of GDP to defence, which is well above the global average of 1.7% in 2022, meaning that the cost of defence is already higher here compared with other regions.

Defence industry

Continued initiatives to produce military equipment domestically and increasingly localise arms procurement are notable trends. This is apparent chiefly in Gulf states, led by the UAE and followed by Saudi Arabia, although more recently Egypt, Jordan, Morocco and Qatar have followed suit. Rabat, for example, is developing its aircraft maintenance capability. The development of a defence-industrial and technological base is most advanced in the UAE, notably with the EDGE Group. Its success is supported by demanding offset policies and diversification of partners. This has included turning to countries willing to consider technology transfer, such as South Africa, or looking to acquire know-how by acquiring or closely working with foreign firms.

The nascent localisation of regional defence procurements is also noteworthy as countries turn to their neighbours to buy military equipment or develop joint projects. The region's only credible arms provider would have been Israel until recently. Prior to 2021, there had already been numerous cases of intra-regional military assistance and arms transfers, and also to African countries, particularly of armoured personnel carriers. Meanwhile, the UAE has started exporting its weapons, such as *Al Tariq* guided bombs (re-branded Denel-designed *Umbani* guided bombs) sold to Egypt in 2020. However, the growth in intra-regional defence-industrial cooperation became particularly evident in 2021 with the memorandum of understanding between Saudi Arabia's General Authority for Military Industries and the UAE's Tawazun Economic Council signed at that year's IDEX show. This is designed to boost defence-industrial capability, explore the prospects for joint projects and identify areas of cooperation in defence R&D. It is particularly important to improve in this area, as one of the identified roadblocks to the development of domestic capabilities has been the low regional investment in defence R&D. At the same time, regional states are becoming more willing to showcase their wares as they look to defence sales as a way of boosting local industrial capacity. IDEX has been established since the early 1990s in the UAE; the Egypt Defence Expo is hosted in Cairo; Jordan hosts SOFEX; Morocco the Marrakesh Airshow; and Saudi Arabia joined in early 2022 with its first World Defense Show, held outside Riyadh.

Arms procurements and deliveries – Middle East and North Africa

Significant events in 2022

UAE: TAWAZUN ECONOMIC COUNCIL EXPANDS

FEBRUARY

Tawazun Economic Council (TEC) signed an agreement with L3Harris Technologies to create the Intelligence Software Center (ISC) and the Electro-Optical Center of Excellence (EOCE) in the UAE. This is part of a scheme whereby, since 2018, foreign companies have been encouraged to establish UAE-based regional headquarters, termed a 'landed' company, to increase local defence-industrial capability. Saab launched its UAE-based landed company in December 2017 (officially approved by the TEC in 2019), with both Raytheon Technologies and Thales following in 2019. Airbus signed a memorandum of understanding to set up a landed company in November 2021. TEC had managed UAE offset programmes since it was established in 1992, but from 2021 the organisation oversees the entire military acquisition processes and is able to formulate procurement policies and legislation, authorise procurement budgets and organise defence R&D programmes.

SAMI SECURES CONTRACTS AT WDS

MARCH

State-owned Saudi Arabian Military Industries (SAMI) signed several deals with foreign firms during the first World Defense Show (WDS) exhibition near Riyadh. SAMI announced that it had secured SAR7bn (USD1.87bn) from three Saudi banks to help achieve localisation goals. This will include work on two agreements signed at the show: with MBDA and NIMR Automotive. The former seeks to establish an MRO facility in Saudi Arabia, and there are plans for local production. The deal with NIMR will lead to the production of *Jais* 4x4 armoured vehicles in the Kingdom. At the show, SAMI and its subsidiaries were also awarded SAR7.65bn (USD2.04bn) worth of contracts for equipment and services for the Saudi armed forces. SAMI was formed in 2017 with ambitions to become a 'top 25' defence company by 2030 and for Saudi Arabia to localise over 50% of its equipment spending within the country.

OMAN: INDUSTRIAL COLLABORATION

JULY

Oman signed agreements with Rolls-Royce, Lockheed Martin, FNSS and INDRA. The Royal Air Force of Oman (RAFO) will localise engine maintenance and repair capability for its *Hawk* aircraft with the assistance of Rolls-Royce, while Lockheed Martin will help the air force operate satellite-based aircraft tracking systems for its C-130J *Hercules* and F-16C/D *Fighting Falcon* fleets. Turkey's FNSS will help establish an armoured-vehicle modernisation and maintenance facility, likely as a follow-up to Oman's 2016 order for *Pars* III 6x6 and 8x8 vehicles. Meanwhile, Spanish firm Indra will set up an Earth observation centre in Oman. No timelines have been released. Oman has long planned to strengthen its defence-industrial base through international collaboration. For instance, in October 2016, the Omani State General Reserve Fund (SGRF) purchased a 32.2% stake in Escribano Mechanical & Engineering (Escribano M&E) for EUR18m (USD19.9m). The plan was that the firm would establish an Oman-based joint venture, Escribano Middle East, as part of Oman's drive to help establish its defence-industrial base through technology transfer. However, in January 2022, Escribano M&E bought back this 32% share for undisclosed reasons, again becoming a 100% Spanish-owned firm.

ISRAEL: DEFENCE EXPORTS REFORM

AUGUST

New defence export regulations were put before the legislature. Under these proposals, Israeli defence contractors would undergo a simpler licensing process for 'unclassified' products, with more exports permitted to more countries. Israel is looking to expand the numbers of countries and equipment that are exempt from marketing licence requirements, to 127 countries and 8,200 products from 111 and 5,500 respectively. In April, Israel announced that annual defence exports in 2021 had risen by 30% from 2020, reaching USD11.3bn. The top three sectors were missiles, rockets and air defence systems (20%), training and instruction services (15%) and uninhabited systems (9%). The top three export destinations were Europe (41%), Asia-Pacific (34%) and North America (12%). Israel forecasts that exports will rise in 2022 as Russia's invasion of Ukraine has boosted defence spending in Europe and elsewhere, while the Abraham Accords have opened new markets in the Gulf to all Israeli companies, not just in the defence sector.

Middle East and North Africa 313

Table 14 — Qatar: selected procurement since 2010

Contract Date	Equipment	Type	Quantity	Contractor	Deliveries
Apr 2013	*Leopard* 2A7+	Main battle tank	62	🇩🇪 Krauss-Maffei Wegmann (KMW)	2015–20
	PzH 2000	155mm self-propelled artillery	24		2015–16
Aug 2014	AH-64E *Apache Guardian*	Attack helicopter	24	🇺🇸 Boeing	2019–20
Dec 2014	*Patriot*	Long-range surface-to-air missile (SAM) system	10	🇺🇸 Raytheon	2018–ongoing
Jun 2015	C-17A *Globemaster* III	Heavy transport aircraft	4	🇺🇸 Boeing	2016
May 2015	*Rafale*	Fighter ground-attack aircraft (FGA ac)	24	🇫🇷 Dassault Aviation	Feb 2019–ongoing
c. 2016	BP-12A (CH-SS-14 Mod 2)	Short-range ballistic missile launcher	≥8	🇨🇳 China Aerospace Science and Industry Corporation (CASIC)	c. 2017
Sep 2016	*Marte*-ER *Exocet* MM40 Blk III	Land-based anti-ship missile launcher	n.k.	M MBDA	2022*
Feb 2017	AN/FPS-132 Upgraded Early Warning Radar	Ballistic missile early warning radar	1	🇺🇸 Raytheon Technologies	2026*
Aug 2017	*Al Zubarah*	Frigate	4	🇮🇹 Fincantieri	Oct 2021–ongoing
	Musherib	Corvette	2		
	LPD	Amphibious assault ship	1		
Dec 2017	*Rafale*	FGA ac	12	🇫🇷 Dassault Aviation	n.k.
Dec 2017	Eurofighter *Typhoon*	FGA ac	24	🇬🇧 BAE Systems	Aug 2022–2024*
	Hawk Mk167	Training aircraft	9		Sep 2021–ongoing
Dec 2017	F-15QA	FGA ac	48	🇺🇸 Boeing	Oct 2021–ongoing
Mar 2018	*Bayraktar* TB2	Medium combat intelligence, surveillance and reconnaissance uninhabited aerial vehicle	6	🇹🇷 Baykar	est. 2019
Mar 2018	*Kirpi*	Protected patrol vehicle	50	🇹🇷 BMC	est. 2020–21
	Amazon		35		
Mar 2018	NH90 TTH	Medium transport helicopter	16	🇮🇹 Leonardo (formerly Finmeccanica)	Dec 2021–2025*
	NH90 NFH	Anti-submarine warfare helicopter	12		Mar 2022–2025*
	H125 (AS350) *Ecureuil***	Light transport helicopter	16		est. 2018–21
Jul 2019	MIM-104 *Patriot*	Long-range SAM system	n.k.	🇺🇸 Raytheon Technologies	n.k.
	NASAMS II	Short-range SAM system			
c. 2020	*Fuwairit* (TUR Anadolu Shipyard LCT)	Landing craft tank	1	🇹🇷 Anadolu Shipyard	Feb 2022
	Broog (Anadolu Shipyard LCM)	Landing craft medium	2		
	16m (Anadolu Shipyard LCVP)	Landing craft vehicles and personnel	1		
Dec 2020	*Gepard*	35mm self-propelled air defence artillery	15	🇩🇪 Rheinmetall Air Defence (formerly Oerlikon Contraves)	2021–ongoing
c. 2021	M-346	Training aircraft	6	🇮🇹 Leonardo (formerly Finmeccanica)	n.k.

*Planned

**In training configuration

M = multinational

Map 8 — Egypt: defence industry

During the Cold War, Egypt's defence industries licence-built foreign equipment but the country did not possess significant indigenous design capacity. Over two decades later Egypt's defence industry has made little progress in this regard despite spending significant sums on acquisition, particularly in the last decade.

Egypt's defence industry is mostly grouped under three entities that broadly correspond to the air, land and maritime domains. The Ministry of Military Production is a stand-alone government ministry established in 1954 that today oversees the production of armoured vehicles, artillery, small arms and ammunition. The *Fahd* APC, based on a German chassis and powerpack, has been exported in small numbers to states in the Middle East and North Africa and in Sub-Saharan Africa. A 2022 deal with South Korea for the licensed production of an estimated 200 K9 howitzers will be carried out by the Abu Zaabal Tank Repair Factory (Factory 200) that assembled M1 *Abrams* tanks from 1992 to 2018.

Established in 1975, the Arab Organization for Industrialization (AOI) was originally a joint effort by Egypt, Kuwait, Qatar and Saudi Arabia to develop a pan-Arab defence industry. Following Egypt's peace treaty with Israel in 1979, the other nations withdrew, leaving AOI as a solely Egyptian entity owned by the Ministry of Defense. AOI factories subsequently licence-built French *Alpha Jet* training aircraft and *Gazelle* helicopters and Brazilian *Tucano* turboprop training aircraft, as well as various missiles. The production of 120 Chinese K-8 training aircraft was completed in 2010 in Helwan, with a high level of indigenisation reported, and the site now serves as a maintenance, repair and overhaul (MRO) facility for the aircraft.

Established in 2003, the Marine Industry & Services Organisation is the smallest of the three groups and is focused on shipbuilding and maritime services. Alexandria Shipyard is licence-building three of four French *Gowind* frigates and in 2020 announced that it was going to build a MEKO A200 frigate. The navy plans to acquire at least three from Germany.

Today many of the factories that had production lines in previous decades have now either switched to MRO or have diversified their business to produce civil products. Military factories have been active in the civil sector since the 1980s; continued focus and activity in this sector may continue to complicate Cairo's ambitions to further develop indigenous defence production, including the development of complex equipment, without foreign assistance.

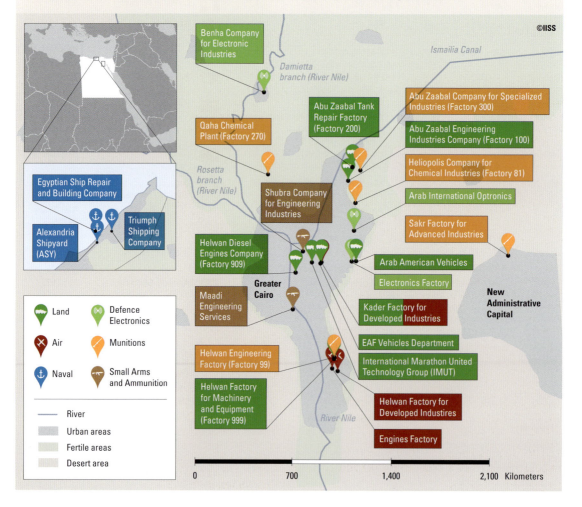

Middle East and North Africa   315

Algeria ALG

Algerian Dinar DZD		2021	2022	2023
GDP	DZD	22.0tr	27.2tr	
	USD	163bn	187bn	
per capita	USD	3,660	4,151	
Growth	%	3.5	4.7	
Inflation	%	7.2	9.7	
Def bdgt	DZD	1.23tr	1.30tr	
	USD	9.09bn	8.94bn	
USD1=DZD		135.34	145.33	

Real-terms defence budget trend (USDbn, constant 2015)

10.4

4.09

2008 -------------------- 2015 -------------------- 2022

Population	44,178,884

Age	0–14	15–19	20–24	25–29	30–64	65 plus
Male	14.9%	3.8%	3.3%	3.9%	21.6%	3.2%
Female	14.2%	3.6%	3.1%	3.7%	21.1%	3.5%

Capabilities

Algeria's armed forces are among the best equipped in North Africa. The armed forces' primary roles relate to securing territorial integrity, internal security and regional stability. The army retains a key political position since its instrumental role in 2019 in ending President Abdelaziz Bouteflika's two decades in power. Algeria is part of the African Union's North African Regional Capability Standby Force, hosting the force's logistics base in Algiers. There are discussions with neighbours about regional security challenges such as counter-terrorism and there is close security cooperation with Tunisia. A November 2020 referendum approved a change to the constitution enabling Algeria to send forces on UN peacekeeping missions. Tensions with Morocco, which increased once more in 2021, have persisted into 2022. The conscript-based force exercises regularly, although standards are difficult to judge from open sources. There is an ongoing attempt to professionalise the armed forces, which was reflected in the reduction of conscript liability from 18 to 12 months in 2014. Military logistics capability appears sufficient to support internal deployments. Army and air force inventories consist of a core of modern, primarily Russian-sourced equipment, though China has also supplied equipment, including self-propelled artillery. The extent to which Russia's invasion of Ukraine has affected the supply of spare parts to Algeria is unclear, though these are likely to become evident the longer that conflict continues. Algiers has recapitalised around half of its fixed-wing combat-aircraft inventory and the navy has invested in its submarine and frigate fleet. Local industry and the services are capable of equipment maintenance. Algeria is largely dependent on foreign suppliers for new equipment, but it has in recent years made investments towards developing a domestic defence industry. This has led to joint ventures with foreign partners, such as Italy's Leonardo and Germany's Rheinmetall.

ACTIVE 139,000 (Army 110,000 Navy 15,000 Air 14,000) Gendarmerie & Paramilitary 187,200

Conscript liability 12 months

RESERVE 150,000 (Army 150,000) to age 50

ORGANISATIONS BY SERVICE

Space
EQUIPMENT BY TYPE
SATELLITES 4
  COMMUNICATIONS 1 ALCOMSAT
  ISR 3 ALSAT

Army 35,000; 75,000 conscript (total 110,000)
FORCES BY ROLE
6 Mil Regions
MANOEUVRE
  Armoured
  2 (1st & 8th) armd div (3 tk regt; 1 mech regt, 1 arty gp)
  2 indep armd bde
  Mechanised
  2 (12th & 40th) mech div (1 tk regt; 3 mech regt,
    1 arty gp)
  4 indep mech bde
  Light
  1 indep mot bde
  Air Manoeuvre
  1 AB div (4 para regt; 1 SF regt)
COMBAT SUPPORT
  2 arty bn
  1 AT regt
  4 engr bn
AIR DEFENCE
  7 AD bn
EQUIPMENT BY TYPE
ARMOURED FIGHTING VEHICLES
  MBT 1,485: 270 T-55AMV; 290 T-62; 325 T-72M1/M1M; 600+ T-90SA
  TSV 26+: 13+ BMPT; 13+ BMPT-62
  RECCE 70: 44 AML-60; 26 BRDM-2
  IFV 980: ε220 BMP-2; 760 BMP-2M with 9M133 *Kornet* (RS-AT-14 *Spriggan*)
  APC 1,307+
    APC (T) VP-6
    APC (W) 1,305: 250 BTR-60; 150 BTR-80; 150 OT-64; 55 M3 Panhard; ε600 *Fuchs* 2; 100 *Fahd*
    PPV 2+: 2 *Marauder*; some *Maxxpro*
  AUV Nimr *Ajban*; Nimr *Ajban* LRSOV
ENGINEERING & MAINTENANCE VEHICLES
  AEV IMR-2
  ARV BREM-1
  VLB MTU-20
  MW M58 MICLIC
ANTI-TANK/ANTI-INFRASTRUCTURE
  SP 92: 64 9P133 with 9M113 *Konkurs* (RS-AT-5 *Spandrel*); 28 9P163-3 *Kornet*-EM (RS-AT-14 *Spriggan*)
  MSL • MANPATS 9K11 *Malyutka* (RS-AT-3 *Sagger*); 9K111 *Fagot* (RS-AT-4 *Spigot*); 9K111-1 *Konkurs* (RS-AT-5 *Spandrel*); 9K115-2 *Metis*-M1 (RS-AT-13); 9K135 *Kornet*-E (RS-AT-14 *Spriggan*); Luch *Skif*; Milan
  RCL 180: **82mm** 120 B-10; **107mm** 60 B-11
  GUNS 100mm 10 T-12

ARTILLERY 1,127

SP 224: **122mm** 140 2S1 *Gvozdika*; **152mm** 30 2S3 *Akatsiya*; **155mm** ε54 PLZ-45

TOWED 393: **122mm** 345: 160 D-30 (incl some truck mounted SP); 25 D-74; 100 M-1931/37; 60 M-30; **130mm** 10 M-46; **152mm** 20 M-1937 (ML-20); **155mm** 18 PLL-01

MRL 180: **122mm** 48 BM-21 *Grad*; **140mm** 48 BM-14; **220mm** 36: 18+ SR5; ε18 TOS-1A; **240mm** 30 BM-24; **300mm** 18 9A52 *Smerch*

MOR 330+: **82mm** 150 M-37; **120mm** 120 M-1943; W86; **SP 120mm** Nimr *Hafeet* with SM5; SM4; W86 (SP); **160mm** 60 M-1943

SURFACE-TO-SURFACE MISSILE LAUNCHERS

SRBM 12 *Iskander*-E

AIR DEFENCE

SAM

Point-defence 68+: ε48 9K33M *Osa* (RS-SA-8B *Gecko*); ε20 9K31 *Strela*-1 (RS-SA-9 *Gaskin*); 9K32 *Strela*-2 (RS-SA-7A/B *Grail*)‡; QW-2 (CH-SA-8)

SPAAGM 30mm 38 96K6 *Pantsir*-S1 (RS-SA-22 *Greyhound*); *Pantsir*-SM

GUNS ε425

SP 23mm ε225 ZSU-23-4

TOWED 200: **14.5mm** 100: 60 ZPU-2; 40 ZPU-4; **23mm** 100 ZU-23-2

Navy ε15,000

EQUIPMENT BY TYPE

SUBMARINES • SSK 6:

2 *Paltus* (FSU Project 877 (*Kilo*)) with 6 single 533mm TT with TEST-71ME HWT

4 *Varshavyanka* (RUS Project 636.1 (Improved *Kilo*)) with 6 single 533mm TT with 3M14E *Klub*-S (RS-SS-N-30B) LACM/3M54E1/E *Klub*-S (RS-SS-N-27A/B) AShM (*Klub*-S AShM variant unclear)/TEST-71ME HWT

PRINCIPAL SURFACE COMBATANTS • FRIGATES 5

FFGHM 5:

3 *Adhafer* (C-28A) with 2 quad lnchr with C-802A AShM, 1 octuple lnchr with FM-90 (CH-SA-N-4) SAM, 2 triple 324mm ASTT, 2 Type-730B (H/PJ-12) CIWS, 1 76mm gun (capacity 1 hel)

2 *Erradii* (MEKO A200AN) with 2 octuple lnchrs with RBS15 Mk3 AShM, 4 8-cell VLS with *Umkhonto*-IR SAM, 2 twin 324mm TT with MU90 LWT, 1 127mm gun (capacity 1 *Super Lynx* 300)

ATROL AND COASTAL COMBATANTS 28

CORVETTES • FS 3 *Mourad Rais* (FSU Project 1159 (*Koni*)) with 2 twin 533mm TT, 2 RBU 6000 *Smerch* 2 A/S mor, 2 twin 76mm gun

PCGM 3 *Rais Hamidou* (FSU Project 1234E (*Nanuchka* II)) with 4 quad lnchr with 3M24E *Uran*-E (RS-SS-N-25 *Switchblade*) AShM, 1 twin lnchr with 4K33 *Osa*-M (RS-SA-N-4 *Gecko*) SAM, 1 AK630 CIWS, 1 twin 57mm gun

PCG 4: 3 *Djebel Chenoua* with 2 twin lnchr with C-802 (CH-SS-N-6) AShM, 1 AK630 CIWS, 1 76mm gun; 1 *Rais Hassen Barbiar* (*Djebel Chenoua* mod) with 2 twin lnchr with C-802 (CH-SS-N-6) AShM, 1 Type-730 (H/PJ-12) CIWS, 1 76mm gun

PBFG 9 Project 205 (ex-FSU *Osa* II) (or which 3†) with 4 single lnchr with P-20U (RS-SS-N-2B *Styx*) AShM

PB 9 *Kebir* with 1 76mm gun

MINE WARFARE • MINE COUNTERMEASURES 2

MCC 2 *El-Kasseh* (ITA *Gaeta* mod)

AMPHIBIOUS

PRINCIPAL AMPHIBIOUS SHIPS • LHD 1 *Kalaat Beni Abbes* with 1 8-cell *Sylver* A50 VLS with *Aster* 15 SAM, 1 76mm gun (capacity 5 med hel; 3 LCVP; 15 MBT; 350 troops)

LANDING SHIPS 3:

LSM 1 *Polnochny* B with 1 twin AK230 CIWS (capacity 6 MBT; 180 troops)

LST 2 *Kalaat beni Hammad* (capacity 7 MBT; 240 troops) with 1 med hel landing platform

LANDING CRAFT • LCVP 3

LOGISTICS AND SUPPORT 3

AGS 1 *El Idrissi*

AX 1 *Daxin* with 2 AK230 CIWS, 1 76mm gun, 1 hel landing platform

AXS 1 *El Mellah*

Naval Infantry ε7,000

FORCES BY ROLE

SPECIAL FORCES

1 cdo bn

MANOEUVRE

Amphibious

8 naval inf bn

EQUIPMENT BY TYPE

ARMOURED FIGHTING VEHICLES

APC • APC(W) BTR-80

Naval Aviation

EQUIPMENT BY TYPE

HELICOPTERS

MRH 9: 3 AW139 (SAR); 6 *Super Lynx* 300

SAR 9: 5 AW101 SAR; 4 *Super Lynx* Mk130

Coastal Defence

FORCES BY ROLE

COASTAL DEFENCE

1 AShM regt with 4K51 *Rubezh* (RS-SSC-3 *Styx*); CM-302 (YJ-12E)

EQUIPMENT BY TYPE

COASTAL DEFENCE

AShM 4K51 *Rubezh* (RS-SSC-3 *Styx*); CM-302 (YJ-12E)

Coast Guard ε500

EQUIPMENT BY TYPE

PATROL AND COASTAL COMBATANTS 74

PBF 6 *Baglietto* 20

PB 68: 6 *Baglietto Mangusta*; 12 *Jebel Antar*; 40 *Deneb*; 4 *El Mounkid*; 6 *Kebir* with 1 76mm gun

LOGISTICS AND SUPPORT 9

AR 1 *El Mourafek*

ARS 3 *El Moundjid*

AXL 5 *El Mouderrib* (PRC *Chui-E*) (2 more in reserve†)

Air Force 14,000

FORCES BY ROLE
FIGHTER
    4 sqn with MiG-29S/UB *Fulcrum*
FIGHTER/GROUND ATTACK
    3 sqn with Su-30MKA *Flanker* H
GROUND ATTACK
    2 sqn with Su-24M/MK *Fencer* D
ELINT
    1 sqn with Beech 1900D
MARITIME PATROL
    2 sqn with Beech 200T/300 *King Air*
ISR
    1 sqn with Su-24MR *Fencer* E*
TANKER
    1 sqn with Il-78 *Midas*
TRANSPORT
    1 sqn with C-130H/H-30 *Hercules*; L-100-30
    1 sqn with C295M
    1 sqn with Gulfstream IV-SP; Gulfstream V
    1 sqn with Il-76MD/TD *Candid*
TRAINING
    2 sqn with Z-142
    1 sqn with Yak-130 *Mitten**
    2 sqn with L-39C *Albatros*; L-39ZA *Albatros**
    1 hel sqn with PZL Mi-2 *Hoplite*
ATTACK HELICOPTER
    3 sqn with Mi-24 *Hind* (one re-equipping with Mi-28NE *Havoc*)
TRANSPORT HELICOPTER
    1 sqn with AS355 *Ecureuil*
    5 sqn with Mi-8 *Hip*; Mi-17 *Hip* H
    1 sqn with Ka-27PS *Helix* D; Ka-32T *Helix*
ISR UAV
    1 sqn with *Seeker* II
AIR DEFENCE
    3 ADA bde
    3 SAM regt with S-125M/M1 *Pechora*-M/M1 (RS-SA-3 *Goa*); 2K12 *Kub* (RS-SA-6 *Gainful*); S-300PMU2 (RS-SA-20 *Gargoyle*)

EQUIPMENT BY TYPE
AIRCRAFT 184 combat capable
    FTR 23 MiG-29S/UB *Fulcrum*
    FGA 73: 14 MiG-29M/M2 *Fulcrum*; 59 Su-30MKA *Flanker* H
    ATK 33 Su-24M/MK *Fencer* D
    ISR 3 Su-24MR *Fencer* E*
    TKR 6 Il-78 *Midas*
    TPT 67: **Heavy** 11: 3 Il-76MD *Candid* B; 8 Il-76TD *Candid*; **Medium** 18: 8 C-130H *Hercules*; 6 C-130H-30 *Hercules*; 2 C-130J *Hercules*; 2 L-100-30; **Light** 32: 3 Beech C90B *King Air*; 5 Beech 200T *King Air*; 6 Beech 300 *King Air*; 12 Beech 1900D (electronic surv); 5 C295M; 1 F-27 *Friendship*; **PAX** 6: 1 A340; 4 Gulfstream IV-SP; 1 Gulfstream V
    TRG 99: 36 L-39ZA *Albatros**; 7 L-39C *Albatros*; 16 Yak-130 *Mitten**; 40 Z-142
HELICOPTERS
    ATK 72: 30 Mi-24 *Hind*; 42+ Mi-28NE/UB *Havoc*
    SAR 3 Ka-27PS *Helix* D
    MRH 85: 8 AW139 (SAR); 3 Bell 412EP; 74 Mi-8 *Hip*

(med tpt)/Mi-17 *Hip* H
    TPT 62: **Heavy** 14 Mi-26T2 *Halo*; **Medium** 4 Ka-32T *Helix*; **Light** 44: 8 AW119KE *Koala*; 8 AS355 *Ecureuil*; 28 PZL Mi-2 *Hoplite*
UNINHABITED AERIAL VEHICLES
    CISR • Heavy CH-3; CH-4; *Yabhon United*-30
    ISR • Medium *Seeker* II; *Yabhon Flash*-20
AIR DEFENCE • SAM
    Long-range 32+ S-300PMU2 (RS-SA-20 *Gargoyle*)
    Medium-range 20+ 9K317 *Buk*-M2E (RS-SA-17 *Grizzly*)
    Short-range 36+: 2K12 *Kvadrat* (RS-SA-6 *Gainful*); 12 S-125M; *Pechora*-M (RS-SA-3 *Goa*); 24 S-125M1 *Pechora*-M1 (RS-SA-3 *Goa*)
AIR-LAUNCHED MISSILES
    AAM • IR R-60 (RS-AA-8 *Aphid*); R-73 (RS-AA-11A *Archer*); **IR/SARH** R-40/46 (RS-AA-6 *Acrid*); R-23/24 (RS-AA-7 *Apex*); R-27 (RS-AA-10 *Alamo*); **ARH** R-77 (RS-AA-12A *Adder*)
    ASM Kh-25 (RS-AS-10 *Karen*); Kh-29 (RS-AS-14 *Kedge*); Kh-59ME (RS-AS-18 *Kazoo*); ZT-35 *Ingwe*; 9M120 *Ataka* (RS-AT-9)
    AShM Kh-31A (RS-AS-17B *Krypton*)
    ARM Kh-25MP (RS-AS-12A *Kegler*); Kh-31P (RS-AS-17A *Krypton*)

Gendarmerie & Paramilitary ε187,200

Gendarmerie 20,000

Ministry of Defence control; 6 regions

EQUIPMENT BY TYPE
ARMOURED FIGHTING VEHICLES
    RECCE AML-60
    APC • APC (W) 210: 100 TH-390 *Fahd*; 110 Panhard M3
HELICOPTERS • TPT • Light 12+: 12 AW109; Some PZL Mi-2 *Hoplite*

National Security Forces 16,000

Directorate of National Security. Equipped with small arms

Republican Guard 1,200

EQUIPMENT BY TYPE
ARMOURED FIGHTING VEHICLES
    RECCE AML-60

Legitimate Defence Groups ε150,000

Self-defence militia, communal guards (60,000)

DEPLOYMENT

DEMOCRATIC REPUBLIC OF THE CONGO: UN •
MONUSCO 2

Bahrain BHR

Bahraini Dinar BHD		2021	2022	2023
GDP	BHD	14.6bn	16.4bn	
	USD	38.9bn	43.5bn	
per capita	USD	26,136	28,692	
Growth	%	2.2	3.4	
Inflation	%	-0.6	3.5	
Def bdgt [a]	BHD	526m	526m	
	USD	1.40bn	1.40bn	
FMA (US)	USD	3.0m	4.0m	4.0m
USD1=BHD		0.38	0.38	

[a] Excludes funds allocated to the Ministry of the Interior and the National Security Agency

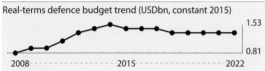

Real-terms defence budget trend (USDbn, constant 2015)

Population	1,540,558					
Age	0–14	15–19	20–24	25–29	30–64	65 plus
Male	9.2%	3.5%	4.8%	6.3%	34.5%	1.9%
Female	9.0%	3.0%	3.4%	3.9%	18.6%	1.8%

Capabilities

Bahrain is a member of the GCC and occupies a key strategic position between regional rivals Iran and Saudi Arabia. The principal roles of the armed forces are territorial defence and internal-security support. Bahrain's most critical security relationship is with Saudi Arabia, but it also has a strong defence relationship with the US and has been a US major non-NATO ally since 2002. The US 5th Fleet is headquartered in Bahrain, as is the US-led Combined Maritime Forces (CMF) and the UK-led International Maritime Security Construct. Bahrain has periodically commanded CMF task forces. The armed forces carried out a limited expeditionary deployment in support of the Saudi-led intervention in Yemen, notably by the special forces. Bahrain also signed a security cooperation agreement with Israel in February 2022. As part of a major air-force modernisation, Bahrain is in the process of acquiring new F-16V fighters and upgrading its existing F-16s to that configuration, as well as acquiring the *Patriot* air- and missile-defence system. In recent years there have been modest additions to Bahrain's naval forces in the form of an ex-UK patrol ship and former-US patrol vessels, as well as upgrades to other craft. The armed forces have organic maintenance support, but there is little in the way of a defence-industrial base beyond the limited maintenance support provided by the Arab Shipbuilding and Repair Yard.

ACTIVE 8,200 (Army 6,000 Navy 700 Air 1,500)
Gendarmerie & Paramilitary 11,260

ORGANISATIONS BY SERVICE

Army 6,000

FORCES BY ROLE
SPECIAL FORCES
  1 SF bn
MANOEUVRE
  Armoured
  1 armd bde(-) (1 recce bn, 2 armd bn)
  Mechanised
  1 inf bde (2 mech bn, 1 mot bn)
  Light
  1 (Amiri) gd bn
COMBAT SUPPORT
  1 arty bde (1 hvy arty bty, 2 med arty bty, 1 lt arty bty, 1 MRL bty)
  1 engr coy
COMBAT SERVICE SUPPORT
  1 log coy
  1 tpt coy
  1 med coy
AIR DEFENCE
  1 AD bn (1 ADA bty, 2 SAM bty)
EQUIPMENT BY TYPE
ARMOURED FIGHTING VEHICLES
  MBT 100 M60A3; (80 more in store)
  RECCE 22 AML-90
  IFV 67: 25 YPR-765 PRI; 42 AIFV-B-C25
  APC 303+
    APC (T) 303: 300 M113A2; 3 AIFV-B
    APC (W) *Arma* 6×6
  AUV M-ATV
ENGINEERING & MAINTENANCE VEHICLES
  ARV 53 *Fahd* 240
ANTI-TANK/ANTI-INFRASTRUCTURE
  MSL
    SP 5 AIFV-B-*Milan*; HMMWV with BGM-71A TOW; 9P163-3 *Kornet*-EM (RS-AT-14 *Spriggan*)
    MANPATS BGM-71A TOW; *Kornet*-EM (RS-AT-14 *Spriggan*)
  RCL 31: **106mm** 25 M40A1; **120mm** 6 MOBAT
ARTILLERY 175
  SP 82: **155mm** 20 M109A5; **203mm** 62 M110A2
  TOWED 36: **105mm** 8 L118 Light Gun; **155mm** 28 M198
  MRL 13: **220mm** 4 SR5; **227mm** 9 M270 MLRS
  MOR 44: **81mm** 12 L16; SP 81mm 20 VAMTAC with EIMOS; **SP 120mm** 12 M113A2
SURFACE-TO-SURFACE MISSILE LAUNCHERS
  SRBM • Conventional MGM-140A ATACMS (launched from M270 MLRS)
AIR DEFENCE
  SAM 13+
    Medium-range 6 MIM-23B I-*Hawk*
    Short-range 7 *Crotale*
    Point-defence 9K338 *Igla*-S (RS-SA-24 *Grinch*) (reported); FIM-92 *Stinger*; RBS-70
  GUNS 24: **35mm** 12 GDF-003/-005; **40mm** 12 L/70

Navy 700

EQUIPMENT BY TYPE
PRINCIPAL SURFACE COMBATANTS • FRIGATES 1
  FFGHM 1 *Sabha* (ex-US *Oliver Hazard Perry*) with 1 Mk 13 GMLS with RGM-84C *Harpoon* Block 1B AShM/SM-1MR Block VI SAM, 2 triple 324mm SVTT Mk 32 ASTT with Mk 46 LWT, 1 Mk 15 *Phalanx* Block 1B CIWS, 1 76mm gun (capacity 1 Bo-105 hel)

PATROL AND COASTAL COMBATANTS 25

PSO 1 *Al Zubara* (ex-UK *River* (OPV) Batch 1 (mod)) with 1 hel landing platform

PCFG 4 *Ahmed el Fateh* (GER Lurssen 45m) with 2 twin lnchr with MM40 *Exocet* AShM, 1 76mm gun

PCG 2 *Al Manama* (GER Lurssen 62m) with 2 twin lnchr with MM40 *Exocet* AShM, 2 76mm guns, 1 hel landing platform

PCF 5 *Al-Gurairiyah* (ex-US *Cyclone*)

PB 6: 2 *Al Jarim* (US *Swift* FPB-20); 2 *Al Riffa* (GER Lurssen 38m); 2 *Mashhoor* (US Swiftships 35m)

PBF 7 Mk V FPB

AMPHIBIOUS • LANDING CRAFT 9

LCM 7: 1 *Loadmaster*; 4 *Mashtan*; 2 *Dinar* (ADSB 42m)

LCVP 2 *Sea Keeper*

Naval Aviation

EQUIPMENT BY TYPE
HELICOPTERS • TPT • Light 2 Bo-105

Air Force 1,500

FORCES BY ROLE
FIGHTER
2 sqn with F-16C/D *Fighting Falcon*

FIGHTER/GROUND ATTACK
1 sqn with F-5E/F *Tiger* II

TRANSPORT
1 (Royal) flt with B-737–800; B-767; B-747; BAe-146; Gulfstream II; Gulfstream IV; Gulfstream 450; Gulfstream 550; S-92A

TRAINING
1 sqn with *Hawk* Mk129*
1 sqn with T-67M *Firefly*

ATTACK HELICOPTER
2 sqn with AH-1E/F *Cobra*; TAH-1P *Cobra*

TRANSPORT HELICOPTER
1 sqn with Bell 212 (AB-212); Bell 412EP *Twin Huey*
1 sqn with UH-60M *Black Hawk*
1 (VIP) sqn with Bo-105; S-70A *Black Hawk*; UH-60L *Black Hawk*

EQUIPMENT BY TYPE
AIRCRAFT 38 combat capable
FTR 12: 8 F-5E *Tiger* II; 4 F-5F *Tiger* II
FGA 20: 16 F-16C Block 40 *Fighting Falcon*; 4 F-16D Block 40 *Fighting Falcon*
MRH 2+ Bell 412EP *Twin Huey*
TPT 14: **Medium** 2 C-130J *Hercules*; **PAX** 12: 1 B-737-800 (VIP); 1 B-767 (VIP); 2 B-747 (VIP); 1 Gulfstream II (VIP); 1 Gulfstream IV (VIP); 1 Gulfstream 450 (VIP); 1 Gulfstream 550 (VIP); 2 BAe-146-RJ85 (VIP); 1 BAe-146-RJ100 (VIP); 1 BAe-146-RJ170 (VIP); (1 B-727 in store)
TRG 9: 6 *Hawk* Mk129*; 3 T-67M *Firefly*

HELICOPTERS
ATK 28: 10 AH-1E *Cobra*; 12 AH-1F *Cobra*; 6 AH-1Z *Viper*
TPT 27: **Medium** 13: 3 S-70A *Black Hawk*; 1 S-92A (VIP); 1 UH-60L *Black Hawk*; 8 UH-60M *Black Hawk*; **Light** 14: 11 Bell 212 (AB-212); 3 Bo-105
TRG 6 TAH-1P *Cobra*

AIR-LAUNCHED MISSILES
AAM • IR AIM-9P *Sidewinder*; **SARH** AIM-7 *Sparrow*; **ARH** AIM-120B/C AMRAAM
ASM AGM-65D/G *Maverick*; some TOW
BOMBS
Laser-guided GBU-10/12 *Paveway* II

Gendarmerie & Paramilitary ε11,260

Police 9,000

Ministry of Interior

EQUIPMENT BY TYPE
ARMOURED FIGHTING VEHICLES
APC • PPV Otokar ISV
AUV *Cobra*
HELICOPTERS
MRH 2 Bell 412 *Twin Huey*
ISR 2 Hughes 500
TPT • Light 1 Bo-105

National Guard ε2,000

FORCES BY ROLE
MANOEUVRE
Other
3 paramilitary bn

EQUIPMENT BY TYPE
ARMOURED FIGHTING VEHICLES
APC • APC (W) *Arma* 6×6; *Cobra*

Coast Guard ε260

Ministry of Interior

PATROL AND COASTAL COMBATANTS 55
PBF 26: 2 *Ares* 18; 3 *Response Boat-Medium* (RB-M); 4 *Jaris*; 6 *Saham*; 6 *Fajr*; 5 *Jarada*
PB 29: 6 *Haris*; 1 *Al Muharraq*; 10 *Deraa* (of which 4 *Halmatic* 20, 2 *Souter* 20, 4 Rodman 20); 10 *Saif* (of which 4 *Fairey Sword*, 6 *Halmatic* 160); 2 *Hawar*
AMPHIBIOUS • LANDING CRAFT • LCU 1 *Loadmaster* II

FOREIGN FORCES

United Kingdom *Operation Kipion* 1,000; 1 FFGHM; 2 MCO; 2 MHO; 1 LSD; 1 naval facility

United States US Central Command 4,700; 1 HQ (5th Fleet); 10 PCFG; 4 MCO; 1 ESB; 1 ASW sqn with 2 P-8A *Poseidon*; 1 EP-3E *Aries* II; 2 SAM bty with M902/M903 *Patriot* PAC-3/PAC-3 MSE

Egypt EGY

Egyptian Pound EGP		2021	2022	2023
GDP	EGP	6.66tr	7.74tr	
	USD	423bn	469bn	
per capita	USD	4,144	4,504	
Growth	%	3.3	6.6	
Inflation	%	4.5	8.5	
Def bdgt	EGP	76.2bn	86.0bn	
	USD	4.84bn	5.21bn	
FMA (US)	USD	1.30bn	1.30bn	1.30bn
USD1=EGP		15.74	16.50	

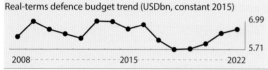

Real-terms defence budget trend (USDbn, constant 2015)

Population	107,770,524					
Age	0–14	15–19	20–24	25–29	30–64	65 plus
Male	17.9%	4.5%	4.2%	3.8%	18.3%	2.6%
Female	16.9%	4.3%	4.0%	3.6%	17.3%	2.5%

Capabilities

Egypt's armed forces are the second-largest in the region and are focused principally on maintaining territorial integrity and internal security, including tackling ISIS-affiliated groups in northern Sinai. The armed forces remain deeply involved in the civilian economy and retain a central role in Egyptian politics. Egypt and the US maintain a strong strategic partnership, which has seen significant US equipment deliveries and ongoing foreign military assistance. Defence relations have developed with Russia and other states such as France, particularly regarding procurement. National military training is supplemented by regular bilateral and multinational exercises. Egypt has a developing capacity to deploy independently beyond its borders. It contributes to UN missions, has intervened militarily in Libya and sent some combat aircraft to support the Saudi-led coalition in Yemen. The navy's two *Mistral*-class amphibious assault ships have bolstered its regional deployment capacity, although Egypt currently lacks the range of maritime helicopters to fully utilise these vessels' capabilities. The armed forces' inventory primarily comprises obsolete Soviet-era systems and newer Western-origin equipment though an extensive recapitalisation programme has also included the delivery of Russian multi-role fighters, attack helicopters and SAM systems. However, it is possible that the threat of sanctions by the US and others may have led some acquisitions from Russia to stall. Combat aircraft have also been sourced from France and armed UAVs from China. Naval recapitalisation includes submarines (from Germany) and frigates (from France, Germany and Italy). The diversity of the inventory risks complicating military maintenance and sustainment. Egypt has an established domestic defence industry, although it does not have the capability to fully develop platforms. This has resulted in a number of licensed- and co-production agreements with foreign companies, including the local assembly of M1A1 main battle tanks from US-supplied kits, production of Chinese-designed K-8 jet trainers and of frigates with French assistance.

ACTIVE 438,500 (Army 310,000 Navy 18,500 Air 30,000 Air Defence Command 80,000) Gendarmerie & Paramilitary 397,000

Conscription liability 12–36 months (followed by refresher training over a period of up to 9 years)

RESERVE 479,000 (Army 375,000 Navy 14,000 Air 20,000 Air Defence Command 70,000)

ORGANISATIONS BY SERVICE

Space
EQUIPMENT BY TYPE
SATELLITES 2
  COMMUNICATIONS 1 TIBA-1
  ISR 1 *Egyptsat*-A

Army ε310,00 (incl ε200,00 conscripts)
FORCES BY ROLE
SPECIAL FORCES
  5 cdo gp
  1 counter-terrorist unit
  1 spec ops unit
MANOEUVRE
  Armoured
  4 armd div (2 armd bde, 1 mech bde, 1 arty bde)
  4 indep armd bde
  1 Republican Guard bde
  Mechanised
  8 mech div (1 armd bde, 2 mech bde, 1 arty bde)
  4 indep mech bde
  Light
  1 inf div
  2 indep inf bde
  Air Manoeuvre
  2 air mob bde
  1 para bde
SURFACE-TO-SURFACE MISSILE
  1 SRBM bde with FROG-7
  1 SRBM bde with 9K72 *Elbrus* (RS-SS-1C *Scud*-B)
COMBAT SUPPORT
  15 arty bde
  6 engr bde (3 engr bn)
  2 spec ops engr bn
  6 salvage engr bn
  24 MP bn
  18 sigs bn
COMBAT SERVICE SUPPORT
  36 log bn
  27 med bn
EQUIPMENT BY TYPE
ARMOURED FIGHTING VEHICLES
  MBT 2,480: 1,130 M1A1 *Abrams*; 300 M60A1; 850 M60A3; 200 T-62 (840 T-54/T-55; 300 T-62 all in store)
  RECCE 412: 300 BRDM-2; 112 *Commando Scout*
  IFV 690: 390 YPR-765 25mm; 300 BMP-1
  APC 5,244+
    APC (T) 2,700: 2,000 M113A2/YPR-765 (incl variants); 500 BTR-50; 200 OT-62

APC (W) 1,560: 250 BMR-600P; 250 BTR-60; 410 *Fahd-30/TH* 390 *Fahd*; 650 *Walid*

PPV 984+: 535 *Caiman*; some REVA III; some REVA V LWB; 360 RG-33L; 89 RG-33 HAGA (amb); ST-500

AUV 173+: *Panthera* T6; 173 *Sherpa Light Scout*; ST-100

ENGINEERING & MAINTENANCE VEHICLES

ARV 367+: *Fahd* 240; BMR 3560.55; 12 *Maxxpro* ARV; 220 M88A1; 90 M88A2; M113 ARV; 45 M578; T-54/55 ARV

VLB KMM; MTU; MTU-20

MW *Aardvark* JFSU Mk4

ANTI-TANK/ANTI-INFRASTRUCTURE • MSL

SP 352+: 52 M901, 300 YPR-765 PRAT; HMMWV with TOW-2

MANPATS 9K11 *Malyutka* (RS-AT-3 *Sagger*) (incl BRDM-2); HJ-73; Luch *Corsar* (reported); *Milan*; *Stugna*-P (reported); TOW-2

ARTILLERY 4,468

SP 492+: **122mm** 124+: 124 SP 122; D-30 mod; **130mm** M-46 mod; **155mm** 368: 164 M109A2; 204 M109A5

TOWED 962: **122mm** 526: 190 D-30M; 36 M-1931/37; 300 M-30; **130mm** 420 M-46; **155mm** 16 GH-52

MRL 450: **122mm** 356: 96 BM-11; 60 BM-21; 50 *Sakr*-10; 50 *Sakr*-18; 100 *Sakr*-36; **130mm** 36 K136 *Kooryong*; **140mm** 32 BM-14; **227mm** 26 M270 MLRS; **240mm** (48 BM-24 in store)

MOR 2,564: **81mm** 50 M125A2; **82mm** 500; **SP 107mm** 100: 65 M106A1; 35 M106A2; **120mm** 1,848: 1,800 M-1943; 48 Brandt; **SP 120mm** 36 M1064A3; **160mm** 30 M-160

SURFACE-TO-SURFACE MISSILE LAUNCHERS

SRBM • Conventional 42+: 9 FROG-7; 24 *Sakr*-80; 9 9K72 *Elbrus* (RS-SS-1C *Scud*-B)

UNINHABITED AERIAL VEHICLES

ISR • Medium R4E-50 *Skyeye*; ASN-209

AIR DEFENCE

SAM 45+

Point-defence 45 *Sinai*-23 with *Ayn al-Saqr*; *Ayn al-Saqr*; FIM-92 *Stinger*; 9K38 *Igla* (RS-SA-18 *Grouse*); 9K338 *Igla*-S (RS-SA-24 *Grinch*) (reported)

GUNS 860

SP 23mm 120 ZSU-23-4; **57mm** 40 ZSU-57-2

TOWED 700: **14.5mm** 300 ZPU-4; **23mm** 200 ZU-23-2; **57mm** 200 S-60

Navy ε8,500 (incl 2,000 Coast Guard); 10,000 conscript (total 18,500)

EQUIPMENT BY TYPE

SUBMARINES • SSK 8

4 Type-033 (PRC *Romeo*) with 8 single 533mm TT with UGM-84C *Harpoon* Block 1B AShM/Mk 37 HWT

4 Type-209/1400 with 8 single 533mm TT with UGM-84L *Harpoon* Block II AShM/*SeaHake* mod 4 (DM2A4) HWT

PRINCIPAL SURFACE COMBATANTS • FRIGATES 12

FFGHM 8:

1 *Al-Aziz* (GER MEKO A200) with 4 quad lnchr with MM40 *Exocet* Block 3 AShM, 4 8-cell CLA with VL MICA NG SAM, 1 127mm gun (capacity 1 med hel)

4 *Alexandria* (ex-US *Oliver Hazard Perry*) with 1 Mk 13 GMLS with RGM-84C *Harpoon* Block 1B AShM/SM-1MR Block VI SAM, 2 triple 324mm ASTT with Mk 46 LWT, 1 Mk 15 *Phalanx* CIWS, 1 76mm gun (capacity 2 SH-2G *Super Seasprite* ASW hel)

2 *El Fateh* (*Gowind* 2500) with 2 quad lnchrs with MM40 *Exocet* Block 3 AShM, 1 16-cell CLA VLS with VL MICA SAM, 2 triple 324mm ASTT with MU90 LWT, 1 76mm gun (capacity 1 med hel)

1 *Tahya Misr* (FRA *Aquitaine* (FREMM)) with 2 quad lnchr with MM40 *Exocet* Block 3 AShM, 2 8-cell *Sylver* A43 VLS with *Aster* 15 SAM, 2 twin 324mm B-515 ASTT with MU90 LWT, 1 76mm gun (capacity 1 med hel)

FFGH 2 *Damyat* (ex-US *Knox*) with 1 octuple Mk 16 GMLS with RGM-84C *Harpoon* Block 1B AShM/ASROC, 2 twin 324mm SVTT Mk 32 TT with Mk 46 LWT, 1 Mk 15 *Phalanx* CIWS, 1 127mm gun (capacity 1 SH-2G *Super Seasprite* ASW hel)

FFHM 2 *Al-Galala* (ITA *Bergamini* (FREMM)) with 2 8-cell *Sylver* A50 VLS with *Aster* 15/30 SAM, 2 twin 324mm B-515 ASTT with MU90 LWT, 1 127mm gun, 1 76mm gun (fitted for but not with *Otomat* (*Teseo*) Mk2A AShM) (capacity 2 med hel)

PATROL AND COASTAL COMBATANTS 73

CORVETTES 5

FSGM 2 *Abu Qir* (ESP *Descubierta*) (of which 1†) with 2 quad lnchr with RGM-84C *Harpoon* Block 1B AShM, 1 octuple *Albatros* lnchr with *Aspide* SAM, 2 triple 324mm SVTT Mk 32 ASTT with *Sting Ray* LWT, 1 twin 375mm Bofors ASW Rocket Launcher System A/S mor, 1 76mm gun

FSG 2 *Najim Al Zaffer* (PRC Type-053HE (*Jianghu* I)) with 2 twin lnchr with HY-2 (CH-SS-N-2 *Safflower*) AShM, 4 RBU 1200 A/S mor, 2 twin 57mm guns

FS 1 *Shabab Misr* (ex-RoK *Po Hang*) with 2 76mm guns

PCFGM 4 *Ezzat* (US *Ambassador* Fast Missile Craft) with 2 quad lnchr with RGM-84L *Harpoon* Block 1B AShM, 1 21-cell Mk49 lnchr with RIM-116B RAM Block 1A SAM, 1 Mk15 mod 21 Block 1B *Phalanx* CIWS 1 76mm gun

PCFG 8:

1 Project 12418 (RUS *Tarantul* IV) with 2 twin lnchr with 3M80E *Moskit* (RS-SS-N-22A *Sunburn*), 2 AK630 CIWS, 1 76mm gun

6 *Ramadan* with 4 single lnchr with *Otomat* Mk2 AShM, 1 76mm gun

1 *Tiger* with 2 twin lnchr with RGM-84 *Harpoon* AShM, 1 76mm gun

PCF 4 *Tiger* with 1 76mm gun

PCC 15: 5 *Al-Nour* (ex-PRC *Hainan*) (3 more in reserve†) with 2 triple 324mm TT, 4 RBU 1200 A/S mor, 2 twin 57mm guns; 1 Lurssen 41m; 9 *Omar Ibn El Khattab* (GER OPB 40)

PBFGM 8 Project 205 (ex-YUG *Osa* I) (of which 3†) with 4 single lnchr with P-20 (RS-SS-N-2A *Styx*) AShM, 1 9K32 *Strela*-2 (RS-SA-N-5 *Grail*) SAM (manual aiming)

PBFG 9:

4 Type-024 (PRC *Hegu*) (2 additional vessels in reserve) with 2 single lnchr with SY-1 (CH-SS-N-1 *Scrubbrush*) AShM

5 *October* (FSU *Komar*) (of which 1†) with 2 single lnchr with *Otomat* Mk2 AShM (1 additional vessel in reserve)

PBFM 4 *Shershen* (FSU) with 1 9K32 *Strela*-2 (RS-SA-N-5 *Grail*) SAM (manual aiming), 1 12-tube BM-24 MRL

322 THE MILITARY BALANCE 2023

PBF 10:
6 *Kaan* 20 (TUR MRTP 20)
4 Project 205 (ex-FIN *Osa* II)
PB 6:
4 Type-062 (ex-PRC *Shanghai* II)
2 *Shershen* (FSU) (of which 1†) with 4 single 533mm
TT, 1 8-tube BM-21 MRL
MINE WARFARE • MINE COUNTERMEASURES 14
MHC 5: 2 *Al Siddiq* (ex-US *Osprey*); 3 *Dat Assawari*
(US Swiftships)
MSI 2 *Safaga* (US Swiftships)
MSO 7: 3 *Assiout* (FSU T-43); 4 *Aswan* (FSU *Yurka*)
AMPHIBIOUS
PRINCIPAL AMPHIBIOUS SHIPS • LHD 2 *Gamal
Abdel Nasser* (FRA *Mistral*) (capacity 16 med hel; 2 LCT
or 4 LCM; 13 MBTs; 50 AFVs; 450 troops)
LANDING CRAFT 15:
LCT 2 EDA-R
LCM 13: 4 CTM NG; 9 *Vydra* (FSU) (capacity either 3
MBT or 200 troops)
LOGISTICS AND SUPPORT 23
AE 1 *Halaib* (ex-GER *Westerwald*)
AKR 3 *Al Hurreya*
AOT 7 *Ayeda* (FSU *Toplivo*) (1 more in reserve)
AR 1 *Shaledin* (ex-GER *Luneberg*)
ARS 2 *Al Areesh*
ATF 5 *Al Maks*† (FSU *Okhtensky*)
AX 4: 1 *El Horriya* (also used as the presidential yacht);
1 *Al Kousser*; 1 *Intishat*; 1 other

Coastal Defence

Army tps, Navy control
EQUIPMENT BY TYPE
COASTAL DEFENCE
ARTY 100mm; 130mm SM-4-1; **152mm**
AShM 4K87 (RS-SSC-2B *Samlet*); *Otomat* MkII

Naval Aviation

All aircraft operated by Air Force
AIRCRAFT • TPT • Light 4 Beech 1900C
(maritime surveillance)
UNINHABITED AERIAL VEHICLES
ISR • Light 2 S-100 *Camcopter*

Coast Guard 2,000

EQUIPMENT BY TYPE
PATROL AND COASTAL COMBATANTS 89
PBF 14: 6 *Crestitalia*; 5 *Swift Protector*; 3 *Peterson*
PB 75: 5 *Nisr*; 12 *Sea Spectre* MkIII; 25 Swiftships;
21 *Timsah*; 3 Type-83; 9 *Peterson*

Air Force 20,000; 10,000 conscript (total 30,000)

FORCES BY ROLE
FIGHTER
1 sqn with F-16A/B *Fighting Falcon*
8 sqn with F-16C/D *Fighting Falcon*
1 sqn with *Mirage* 2000B/C
FIGHTER/GROUND ATTACK
1 sqn with *Mirage* 5E2
2 sqn with *Rafale* DM/EM
3 sqn with MiG-29M/M2 *Fulcrum*

ANTI-SUBMARINE WARFARE
1 sqn with SH-2G *Super Seasprite*
MARITIME PATROL
1 sqn with Beech 1900C
ELECTRONIC WARFARE
1 sqn with Beech 1900 (ELINT); *Commando* Mk2E (ECM)
ELECTRONIC WARFARE/TRANSPORT
1 sqn with C-130H/VC-130H *Hercules*
AIRBORNE EARLY WARNING
1 sqn with E-2C *Hawkeye*
SEARCH & RESCUE
1 unit with AW139
TRANSPORT
1 sqn with An-74TK-200A
1 sqn with C-130H/C-130H-30 *Hercules*
1 sqn with C295M
1 sqn with DHC-5D *Buffalo*
1 sqn with B-707-366C; B-737-100; Beech 200 *Super
King Air*; *Falcon* 20; Gulfstream III; Gulfstream IV;
Gulfstream IV-SP
TRAINING
1 sqn with *Alpha Jet**
1 sqn with DHC-5 *Buffalo*
3 sqn with EMB-312 *Tucano*
1 sqn with Grob 115EG
ε6 sqn with K-8 *Karakorum**
1 sqn with L-39 *Albatros*; L-59E *Albatros**
ATTACK HELICOPTER
1 sqn with Mi-24V
2 sqn with AH-64D *Apache*
1 sqn with Ka-52A *Hokum* B
2 sqn with SA-342K *Gazelle* (with HOT)
1 sqn with SA-342L *Gazelle*
TRANSPORT HELICOPTER
1 sqn with CH-47C/D *Chinook* 1 sqn with Mi-8
1 sqn with Mi-8/Mi-17-V1 *Hip*
1 sqn with S-70 *Black Hawk*; UH-60A/L *Black Hawk*
UAV
Some sqn with R4E-50 *Skyeye*; *Wing Loong* I
EQUIPMENT BY TYPE
AIRCRAFT 509 combat capable
FTR 32: 26 F-16A *Fighting Falcon*; 6 F-16B *Fighting Falcon*
FGA 274: 138 F-16C *Fighting Falcon*; 37 F-16D *Fighting
Falcon*; 2 *Mirage* 2000B; 15 *Mirage* 2000C; 12 *Mirage* 5E2;
ε46 MiG-29M/M2 *Fulcrum*; 16 *Rafale* DM; 8 *Rafale* EM
ELINT 2 VC-130H *Hercules*
ISR 12: ε6 AT-802 *Air Tractor**; 6 *Mirage* 5R (5SDR)*
AEW&C 7 E-2C *Hawkeye*
TPT 82: **Heavy** 2 Il-76MF *Candid*; **Medium** 24: 21
C-130H *Hercules*; 3 C-130H-30 *Hercules*; **Light** 45: 3
An-74TK-200A; 1 Beech 200 *King Air*; 4 Beech 1900
(ELINT); 4 Beech 1900C; 24 C295M; 9 DHC-5D *Buffalo*
(being withdrawn) **PAX** 11: 1 B-707-366C; 3 *Falcon* 20; 2
Gulfstream III; 1 Gulfstream IV; 4 Gulfstream IV-SP
TRG 329: 36 *Alpha Jet**; 54 EMB-312 *Tucano*; 74 Grob
115EG; 120 K-8 *Karakorum**; 10 L-39 *Albatros*; 35 L-59E*
HELICOPTERS
ATK 104: 45 AH-64D *Apache*; up to 46 Ka-52A *Hokum* B;
ε13 Mi-24V *Hind* E
ASW 10 SH-2G *Super Seasprite* (opcon Navy)
ELINT 4 *Commando* Mk2E (ECM)

MRH 77: 2 AW139 (SAR); 5 AW149; 65 SA342K *Gazelle* (some with HOT); 5 SA342L *Gazelle* (opcon Navy)
TPT 96: **Heavy** 19: 3 CH-47C *Chinook*; 16 CH-47D *Chinook*; **Medium** 77: 2 AS-61; 24 *Commando* (of which 3 VIP); 40 Mi-8T *Hip*; 3 Mi-17-1V *Hip*; 4 S-70 *Black Hawk* (VIP); 4 UH-60L *Black Hawk* (VIP)
TRG 17 UH-12E
UNINHABITED AERIAL VEHICLES
CISR • Heavy 4+ *Wing Loong* I
ISR • Medium R4E-50 *Skyeye*
AIR LAUNCHED MISSILES
AAM • IR AIM-9M/P *Sidewinder*; R-73 (RS-AA-11A *Archer*); R-550 *Magic*; 9M39 *Igla-V*; **IIR** Mica IR; **ARH** Mica RF; R-77 (RS-AA-12 *Adder*); **SARH** AIM-7F/M *Sparrow*; R-530
ASM AASM; AGM-65A/D/F/G *Maverick*; AGM-114F/K *Hellfire*; AS-30L; HOT; LJ-7 (AKD-10); 9M120 *Ataka* (RS-AT-9)
LACM SCALP EG
AShM AGM-84L *Harpoon* Block II; AM39 *Exocet*; Kh-35U (RS-AS-20 *Kayak*)
ARM *Armat*; Kh-25MP (RS-AS-12A *Kegler*)
BOMBS
Laser-guided GBU-10/12 *Paveway* II
INS/SAT-guided *Al Tariq*

Air Defence Command 80,000 conscript; 70,000 reservists (total 150,000)

FORCES BY ROLE
AIR DEFENCE
5 AD div HQ (geographically based)
3 SAM bty with S-300V4 (RS-SA-23)
4 SAM bty with 9K37M1-2/9K317 Buk-M1-2/M2E (RS-SA-11 *Gadfly*/RS-SA-17 *Grizzly*)
11 SAM bty with MIM-23B I-*Hawk*
38 SAM bty with S-75M *Volkhov* (RS-SA-2 *Guideline*)
10 SAM bty with S-125-2M *Pechora*-2M (RS-SA-26)
Some SAM bty with 2K12 *Kub* (RS-SA-6 *Gainful*)
2 SAM bty with 9K331/9K331ME *Tor*-M1/M2E (RS-SA-15 *Gauntlet*)
14 SAM bty with *Crotale*
12 SAM bty with M48 *Chaparral*
30 SAM bty with S-125M *Pechora*-M (RS-SA-3 *Goa*)
18 AD bn with RIM-7M *Sea Sparrow* with *Skyguard*/GDF-003 with *Skyguard*
12 ADA bde (total: 100 ADA bn)

EQUIPMENT BY TYPE
AIR DEFENCE
SAM 777
Long-range ε18 S-300V4 (RS-SA-23)
Medium-range 323+: 40+ 9K37M1-2/9K317 *Buk*-M1-2/M2E (RS-SA-11 *Gadfly*/RS-SA-17 *Grizzly*); ε33 MIM-23B I-*Hawk*; ε210 S-75M *Volkhov* (RS-SA-2 *Guideline*); ε40 S-125-2M *Pechora*-2M (RS-SA-26)
Short-range 300+: 56+ 2K12 *Kub* (RS-SA-6 *Gainful*); 10 9K331 *Tor*-M1 (RS-SA-15 *Gauntlet*); 10+ 9K331ME *Tor*-M2E (RS-SA-15 *Gauntlet*); 24+ *Crotale*; 80 RIM-7M *Sea Sparrow* with *Skyguard*; ε120 S-125M *Pechora*-M (RS-SA-3 *Goa*)
Point-defence 136+: 50 M1097 *Avenger*; 50+ M48 *Chaparral*; 36+ Sinai-23 with *Ayn al-Saqr*

GUNS 910
SP • 23mm 230 ZSU-23-4 *Shilka*
TOWED 680: **35mm** 80 GDF-005 with *Skyguard*; **57mm** 600 S-60

Gendarmerie & Paramilitary ε397,000 active

Central Security Forces ε325,000

Ministry of Interior; includes conscripts
ARMOURED FIGHTING VEHICLES
APC • APC (W) *Walid*
AUV *Sherpa Light Scout*

National Guard ε60,000

Lt wpns only
FORCES BY ROLE
MANOEUVRE
Other
8 paramilitary bde (cadre) (3 paramilitary bn)
EQUIPMENT BY TYPE
ARMOURED FIGHTING VEHICLES
APC • APC (W) 250 *Walid*

Border Guard Forces ε12,000

Ministry of Interior; lt wpns only
FORCES BY ROLE
MANOEUVRE
Other
18 Border Guard regt

DEPLOYMENT

CENTRAL AFRICAN REPUBLIC: UN • MINUSCA 1,025; 1 inf bn; 1 tpt coy

DEMOCRATIC REPUBLIC OF THE CONGO: UN • MONUSCO 11

MALI: UN • MINUSMA 1,052; 1 spec ops coy; 1 sy bn; 1 MP coy

SOUTH SUDAN: UN • UNMISS 5

SUDAN: UN • UNISFA 3

WESTERN SAHARA: UN • MINURSO 22

FOREIGN FORCES

Australia MFO (*Operation Mazurka*) 27
Canada MFO 55
Colombia MFO 275; 1 inf bn
Czech Republic MFO 18; 1 C295M
Fiji MFO 170; elm 1 inf bn
France MFO 1
Italy MFO 75; 3 PB
New Zealand MFO 26; 1 trg unit; 1 tpt unit
Norway MFO 3
United Arab Emirates ε300: 12 F-16E/F *Fighting Falcon*; *Wing Loong* I UAV; *Wing Loong* II UAV (status uncertain)
United Kingdom MFO 2
United States MFO 426; elm 1 ARNG inf bn; 1 ARNG spt bn (1 EOD coy, 1 medical coy, 1 hel coy)
Uruguay MFO 41 1 engr/tpt unit

Iran IRN

Iranian Rial IRR		2021	2022	2023
GDP	IRR	66775tr	99764tr	
	USD	1.59tr	1.97tr	
per capita	USD	18,739	23,034	
Growth	%	4.7	3.0	
Inflation	%	40.1	40.0	
Def bdgt [a]	IRR	1180tr	2225tr	
	USD	28.1bn	44.0bn	
USD1=IRR		42000.00	50545.67	

[a] Excludes Law Enforcement Forces (NAJA)

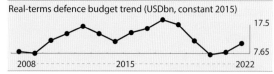

Real-terms defence budget trend (USDbn, constant 2015)

Population	86,758,304					
Age	0–14	15–19	20–24	25–29	30–64	65 plus
Male	12.1%	3.6%	3.3%	3.8%	25.0%	3.0%
Female	11.6%	3.4%	3.1%	3.6%	24.2%	3.4%

Capabilities

Iran is a major regional military power, with a military doctrine that combines territorial defence, through national mobilisation and a substantial missile arsenal, with an asymmetric defence strategy. To achieve the last objective, Iran exerts military pressure using a range of regional allies and proxies, mainly via their relationship with the Islamic Revolutionary Guard Corps (IRGC) Quds Force, as well as by the supply of weapons. During the fourth quarter of 2022, state security forces were struggling to control widespread protests, following the death of a 22-year-old woman in police custody. Tehran has also emerged as a weapons supplier to Russia, with the provision of armed uninhabited aerial vehicles and direct attack munitions for use in the latter's war with Ukraine. Iran initially denied any transfers, then in early November 2022 said what it claimed were a small number of systems had been provided prior to Russia's full-scale invasion. Iran has a key relationship with Syria and has developed influence in weaker regional states like Iraq, Lebanon and Yemen through a network of non-state groups, such as Hizbullah and Houthi forces. Tehran retains the region's largest short- and medium-range ballistic-missile inventory, has developed land-attack cruise missiles, and has a substantial inventory of a variety of UAVs. The rest of the conventional armed forces, although large by regional standards, struggle with an increasingly obsolescent equipment inventory that ingenuity and asymmetric-warfare techniques can only partially offset. Tehran's support for Russia in Ukraine, however, has the potential to offer a conduit to access more modern weaponry. The division of capability between the regular military services and the IRGC hampers effective command and control. The IRGC's operational primacy, coupled with the regular armed forces' dependence on conscript personnel, has also focused combat experience in IRGC formations. In regional terms, Iran has a well-developed defence-industrial base, which has displayed the capacity to support and sustain equipment. While unable to meet national needs for all major weapons, the domestic industry continues to produce equipment, including surface-to-air missile systems and an array of ISR- and armed-UAVs.

ACTIVE 610,000 (Army 350,000 Islamic Revolutionary Guard Corps 190,000 Navy 18,000 Air 37,000 Air Defence 15,000) Gendarmerie & Paramilitary 40,000

Armed Forces General Staff coordinates two parallel organisations: the regular armed forces and the Islamic Revolutionary Guard Corps
Conscript liability 18–21 months (reported, with variations depending on location in which service is performed)

RESERVE 350,000 (Army 350,000, ex-service volunteers)

ORGANISATIONS BY SERVICE

Army 130,000; 220,000 conscript (total 350,000)

FORCES BY ROLE
5 corps-level regional HQ
COMMAND
 1 cdo div HQ
 4 armd div HQ
 2 mech div HQ
 4 inf div HQ
SPECIAL FORCES
 1 cdo div (3 cdo bde)
 6 cdo bde
 1 SF bde
MANOEUVRE
 Armoured
 8 armd bde
 Mechanised
 14 mech bde
 Light
 12 inf bde
 Air Manoeuvre
 1 AB bde
 Aviation
 Some avn gp
COMBAT SUPPORT
 5 arty gp

EQUIPMENT BY TYPE
Totals incl those held by IRGC Ground Forces. Some equipment serviceability in doubt
ARMOURED FIGHTING VEHICLES
 MBT 1,513+: 480 T-72S; 150 M60A1; 75+ T-62; 100 *Chieftain* Mk3/Mk5; 540 T-54/T-55/Type-59/*Safir-74*; 168 M47/M48
 LT TK 80+: 80 *Scorpion*
 RECCE 35 EE-9 *Cascavel*
 IFV 610+: 210 BMP-1; 400 BMP-2 with 9K111 *Fagot* (RS-AT-4 *Spigot*); BMT-2 *Cobra*
 APC 640+
  APC (T) 340: 140 *Boragh* with 9K111 *Fagot* (RS-AT-4 *Spigot*); 200 M113
  APC (W) 300+: 300 BTR-50/BTR-60; *Rakhsh*
  PPV *Toofan*
ENGINEERING & MAINTENANCE VEHICLES
 ARV 20+: BREM-1 reported; 20 *Chieftain* ARV; M578; T-54/55 ARV reported
 VLB 15 *Chieftain* AVLB
 MW *Taftan* 1

Middle East and North Africa 325

ANTI-TANK/ANTI-INFRASTRUCTURE
MSL • MANPATS 9K11 *Malyutka* (RS-AT-3 *Sagger*);
9K111 *Fagot* (RS-AT-4 *Spigot*); 9K111-1 *Konkurs* (RS-AT-5
Spandrel/Towsan-1); *Almaz*; *Dehleavieh* (*Kornet*); I-*Raad*;
Saeqhe 1; *Saeqhe* 2; *Toophan*; *Toophan* 2
RCL 200+: **75mm** M20; **82mm** B-10; **106mm** ε200 M40;
107mm B-11
ARTILLERY 6,798+
SP 292+: **122mm** 60+: 60 2S1 *Gvozdika*; *Raad*-1 (*Thunder*
1); **155mm** 150+: 150 M109A1; *Raad*-2 (*Thunder* 2);
170mm 30 M-1978; **175mm** 22 M107; **203mm** 30 M110
TOWED 2,030+; **105mm** 150: 130 M101A1; 20 M-56;
122mm 640: 540 D-30; 100 Type-54 (M-30); **130mm** 985
M-46; **152mm** 30 D-20; **155mm** 205: 120 GHN-45; 70
M114; 15 Type-88 WAC-21; **203mm** 20 M115
MRL 1,476+: **107mm** 1,300: 700 Type-63; 600 HASEB *Fadjr*
1; **122mm** 157: 7 BM-11; 100 BM-21 *Grad*; 50 *Arash/Hadid/
Noor*; **240mm** 19+: ε10 *Fadjr* 3; 9 M-1985; **330mm** *Fadjr* 5
MOR 3,000: **81mm**; **82mm**; **107mm** M30; **120mm** HM-
15; HM-16; M-65
SURFACE-TO-SURFACE MISSILE LAUNCHERS
SRBM • Conventional ε30 CH-SS-8 (175 msl); *Shahin*-1/
Shahin-2; *Nazeat*; *Oghab*
AIRCRAFT • TPT 17 **Light** 16: 10 Cessna 185; 2 F-27
Friendship; 4 *Turbo Commander* 690; **PAX** 1 *Falcon* 20
HELICOPTERS
ATK 50 AH-1J *Cobra*
TPT 167: **Heavy** ε20 CH-47C *Chinook*; **Medium** 69: 49
Bell 214; 20 Mi-171; **Light** 78: 68 Bell 205A (AB-205A); 10
Bell 206 *Jet Ranger* (AB-206)
UNINHABITED AERIAL VEHICLES
CISR • Medium *Mohajer* 6; *Kaman* 12
ISR • Medium *Ababil* 2; *Ababil* 3; *Mohajer* 3; *Mohajer* 4;
Light *Mohajer* 2
AIR DEFENCE
SAM
Short-range FM-80 (CH-SA-4)
Point-defence 9K36 *Strela*-3 (RS-SA-14 *Gremlin*); 9K32
Strela-2 (RS-SA-7 *Grail*)‡; *Misaq* 1 (QW-1); *Misaq* 2
(QW-18); 9K338 *Igla-S* (RS-SA-24 *Grinch*) (reported);
HN-5A (CH-SA-3)
GUNS 1,122
SP 180: **23mm** 100 ZSU-23-4; **57mm** 80 ZSU-57-2
TOWED 942+: **14.5mm** ZPU-2; ZPU-4; **23mm** 300
ZU-23-2; **35mm** 92 GDF-002; **37mm** M-1939; **40mm** 50
L/70; **57mm** 200 S-60; **85mm** 300 M-1939
BOMBS
Laser-guided *Qaem*
Electro-optical guided *Qaem*

Islamic Revolutionary Guard Corps 190,000

Islamic Revolutionary Guard Corps Ground Forces 150,000

Controls Basij paramilitary forces. Lightly staffed in
peacetime. Primary role: internal security; secondary role:
external defence, in conjunction with regular armed forces
FORCES BY ROLE
COMMAND
31 provincial corps HQ (2 in Tehran)

SPECIAL FORCES
3 spec ops div
1 AB bde
MANOEUVRE
Armoured
2 armd div
3 armd bde
Light
8+ inf div
5+ inf bde
EQUIPMENT BY TYPE
LOITERING & DIRECT ATTACK MUNITIONS
Shahed 131; *Shahed* 136

Islamic Revolutionary Guard Corps Naval Forces 20,000+ (incl 5,000 Marines)

FORCES BY ROLE
COMBAT SUPPORT
Some arty bty
Some AShM bty with HY-2 (CH-SSC-3 *Seersucker*) AShM
EQUIPMENT BY TYPE
In addition to the vessels listed, the IRGC operates a
substantial number of patrol boats with a full-load dis-
placement below 10 tonnes, including *Boghammar*-class
vessels and small *Bavar*-class wing-in-ground effect
air vehicles
PATROL AND COASTAL COMBATANTS 129
PCGM 1 *Shahid Soleimani* with 2 twin lnchr with
Ghader AShM, 2 single lnchr with C-704 (*Nasr*)
AShM, 2 3-cell VLS & 4 single cell VLS (likely fitted
with SAM), 1 hel landing platform
PBFG 56:
5 C14 with 2 twin lnchr with C-701 (*Kosar*)/C-704
(*Nasr*) AShM
10 Mk13 with 2 single lnchr with C-704 (*Nasr*)
AShM, 2 single 324mm TT
10 *Thondor* (PRC *Houdong*) with 2 twin lnchr with
C-802A (*Ghader*) AShM, 2 AK230 CIWS
25 *Peykaap* II (IPS-16 mod) with 2 single lnchr
with C-701 (*Kosar*) AShM/C-704 (*Nasr*), 2 single
324mm TT
6 *Zolfaghar* (*Peykaap* III/IPS-16 mod) with 2 single
lnchr with C-701 (*Kosar*)/C-704 (*Nasr*) AShM
PBG 1 *Shahid Rouhi* with 2 twin lnchr with C-704
(*Nasr*) AShM
PBFT 15 *Peykaap* I (IPS -16) with 2 single 324mm TT
PBF 35: 15 *Kashdom* II; 10 *Tir* (IPS-18); ε10 *Pashe*
(MIG-G-1900)
PB 21: ε20 *Ghaem*; 1 *Shahid Nazeri*
AMPHIBIOUS
LANDING SHIPS • LST 3 *Hormuz* 24 (*Hejaz* design
for commercial use)
LANDING CRAFT • LCT 2 *Hormuz* 21
(minelaying capacity)
LOGISTICS AND SUPPORT • AP 3 *Naser*
COASTAL DEFENCE • AShM C-701 (*Kosar*); C-704
(*Nasr*); C-802 (*Noor*); HY-2 (CH-SSC-3 *Seersucker*)
HELICOPTERS
MRH 5 Mi-171 *Hip*
TPT • Light some Bell 206 (AB-206) *Jet Ranger*

326 THE MILITARY BALANCE 2023

UNINHABITED AERIAL VEHICLES
CISR • Medium *Mohajer 6*
BOMBS
Laser-guided *Qaem*
Electro-optical guided *Qaem*

Islamic Revolutionary Guard Corps Marines 5,000+

FORCES BY ROLE
MANOEUVRE
Amphibious
1 mne bde

Islamic Revolutionary Guard Corps Aerospace Force 15,000

Controls Iran's strategic-missile force

FORCES BY ROLE
FIGHTER/GROUND ATTACK
1 sqn with Su-22M4 *Fitter K*; Su-22UM-3K *Fitter G*
TRAINING
1 sqn with EMB-312 *Tucano**

EQUIPMENT BY TYPE
SURFACE-TO-SURFACE MISSILE LAUNCHERS
MRBM • Conventional up to 50: *Emad-1* (*Shahab-3* mod); *Ghadr-1/-2* (*Shahab-3* mod); *Sajjil-2*; *Shahab-3* (IR-SS-7) (mobile & silo); *Khorramshahr* (in devt)
SRBM • Conventional up to 100: *Fateh-110*; *Fateh-313*; *Khalij Fars* (*Fateh-110* mod ASBM); *Qiam-1/-1* mod; *Shahab-1/-2* (*Scud* variants; service status uncertain); *Zelzal*; *Zolfaghar* (IR-SS-1)
GLCM • Conventional some *Ya'ali* (*Quds-1*)
AIRCRAFT 23 combat capable
FGA 8: up to 7 Su-22M4 *Fitter K*; 1+ Su-22UM-3K *Fitter G*
TRG 15 EMB-312 *Tucano**
UNINHABITED AERIAL VEHICLES
CISR • Heavy *Shahed* 129; **Medium** *Shahed* 181; *Shahed* 191
ISR • Medium *Ababil* 3; *Mohajer* 4; *Shahed* 123
AIR DEFENCE
SAM
Medium-range *Ra'ad/3rd Khordad*; *Talash/15th Khordad*
Point-defence *Misaq 1* (QW-1); *Misaq 2* (QW-18)
BOMBS
Laser-guided *Sadid*
Electro-optical guided *Sadid*

Islamic Revolutionary Quds Force 5,000

Navy 18,000

HQ at Bandar Abbas

EQUIPMENT BY TYPE
In addition to the vessels listed, the Iranian Navy operates a substantial number of patrol boats with a full-load displacement below 10 tonnes
SUBMARINES • TACTICAL 17
SSK 1 *Taregh* (RUS *Paltus* (Project 877EKM (*Kilo*))) (2 more non-operational) with 6 single 533mm TT
SSC 1 *Fateh* with 4 single 533mm TT with C-704 (*Nasr*-1) AShM/*Valfajr* HWT

SSW 15: 14 *Ghadir* (*Yono*) with 2 single 533mm TT with *Jask*-2 (C-704 (*Nasr*)) AShM/*Valfajr* HWT (additional vessels in build); 1 *Nahang*
PATROL AND COASTAL COMBATANTS 68
CORVETTES 7
FSGM 3 *Jamaran* (UK Vosper Mk 5 derivative – 1 more undergoing sea trials) with 2 twin lnchr with C-802 (*Noor*) (CH-SS-N-6) AShM, 2 single lnchr with SM-1 SAM, 2 triple 324mm SVTT Mk 32 ASTT, 1 76mm gun, 1 hel landing platform
FSG 4:
2 *Alvand* (UK Vosper Mk 5) with 2 twin lnchr with C-802 (CH-SS-N-6) AShM, 2 triple 324mm SVTT Mk 32 ASTT, 1 114mm gun
1 *Alvand* (UK Vosper Mk 5) with 2 twin lnchr with C-802 (CH-SS-N-6) AShM, 2 triple 324mm SVTT Mk 32 ASTT, 1 AK630M CIWS, 1 114mm gun
1 *Bayandor* (US PF-103) with 2 twin lnchr with C-802 (CH-SS-N-6) AShM, 2 triple 324mm SVTT Mk 32 ASTT, 1 76mm gun
PCFG 15: up to 10 *Kaman* (FRA *Combattante* II) with 1 twin lnchr with C-802 (*Noor*) (CH-SS-N-6) AShM, 1 76mm gun; 5+ *Sina* with 1 twin lnchr with C-802 (*Noor*) (CH-SS-N-6) AShM, 1 76mm gun
PBG 9:
3 *Hendijan* with 2 twin lnchr with C-802 (*Noor*) (CH-SS-N-6) AShM
3 *Kayvan* with 2 single lnchr with C-704 (*Nasr*) AShM
3 *Parvin* with 2 single lnchr with C-704 (*Nasr*) AShM
PBFT 3 *Kajami* (semi-submersible) with 2 324mm TT
PBF 1 MIL55
PB 33: 9 C14; 8 *Hendijan*; 6 MkII; 10 MkIII
MINE WARFARE • MINE COUNTERMEASURES •
MCC 1 *Shahin*
AMPHIBIOUS
LANDING SHIPS 12
LST 3 *Hengam* with 1 hel landing platform (capacity 9 tanks; 225 troops)
LSM 3 *Farsi* (ROK) (capacity 9 tanks; 140 troops)
LSL 6 *Fouque*
LANDING CRAFT 11
LCT 2
LCU 1 *Liyan 110*
UCAC 8: 2 *Wellington* Mk 4; 4 *Wellington* Mk 5; 2 *Tondar* (UK *Winchester*)
LOGISTICS AND SUPPORT 18
AE 2 *Delvar*
AFD 2 *Dolphin*
AG 1 *Hamzah* with 2 single lnchr with C-802 (*Noor*) (CH-SS-N-6) AShM
AK 3 *Delvar*
AKR 1 *Makran*
AORH 2 *Bandar Abbas*
AWT 5: 4 *Kangan*; 1 *Delvar*
AX 2 *Kialas*
COASTAL DEFENCE • AShM C-701 (*Kosar*); C-704 (*Nasr*); C-802 (*Noor*); C-802A (*Ghader*); *Ra'ad* (reported)

Middle East and North Africa **327**

Marines 2,600

FORCES BY ROLE
MANOEUVRE
Amphibious
2 mne bde

Naval Aviation 2,600

EQUIPMENT BY TYPE
AIRCRAFT
TPT 16: **Light** 13: 5 Do-228; 4 F-27 *Friendship*; 4 *Turbo Commander* 680; **PAX** 3 *Falcon* 20 (ELINT)
HELICOPTERS
ASW ε10 SH-3D *Sea King*
MCM 3 RH-53D *Sea Stallion*
TPT • **Light** 17: 5 Bell 205A (AB-205A); 2 Bell 206 *Jet Ranger* (AB-206); 10 Bell 212 (AB-212)
UNINHABITED AERIAL VEHICLES
CISR • **Heavy** *Shahed* 129
BOMBS
Laser-guided *Sadid*
Electro-optical guided *Sadid*

Air Force 37,000

FORCES BY ROLE
Serviceability probably about 60% for US ac types and about 80% for PRC/Russian ac. Includes IRGC AF equipment
FIGHTER
1 sqn with F-7M *Airguard;* JJ-7*
2 sqn with F-14 *Tomcat*
2 sqn with MiG-29A/UB *Fulcrum*
FIGHTER/GROUND ATTACK
1 sqn with *Mirage* F-1B/E
1 sqn with F-5E/F *Tiger* II
5 sqn with F-4D/E *Phantom* II
3 sqn with F-5E/F *Tiger* II
GROUND ATTACK
1 sqn with Su-24MK *Fencer* D
MARITIME PATROL
1 sqn with P-3F *Orion*
ISR
1 (det) sqn with RF-4E *Phantom* II*
SEARCH & RESCUE
Some flt with Bell 214C (AB-214C)
TANKER/TRANSPORT
1 sqn with B-707; B-747; B-747F
TRANSPORT
1 sqn with B-707; *Falcon* 50; L-1329 *Jetstar*; Bell 412
2 sqn with C-130E/H *Hercules*
1 sqn with F-27 *Friendship*; *Falcon* 20
1 sqn with Il-76 *Candid*; An-140 (Iran-140 *Faraz*)
TRAINING
1 sqn with Beech F33A/C *Bonanza*
1 sqn with F-5B *Freedom Fighter*
1 sqn with PC-6
1 sqn with PC-7 *Turbo Trainer*
Some units with MFI-17 *Mushshak*; TB-21 *Trinidad*; TB-200 *Tobago*
TRANSPORT HELICOPTER
1 sqn with CH-47 *Chinook*

Some units with Bell 206A *Jet Ranger* (AB-206A); *Shabaviz* 2-75; *Shabaviz* 2061

EQUIPMENT BY TYPE
AIRCRAFT 312 combat capable
FTR 180+: 20 F-5B *Freedom Fighter*; 54+ F-5E/F *Tiger* II; 24 F-7M *Airguard*; up to 41 F-14 *Tomcat*; 35 MiG-29A/UB *Fulcrum*; up to 6 *Azarakhsh* (reported)
FGA 80: 62 F-4D/E *Phantom* II; 2 *Mirage* F-1BQ; 10 *Mirage* F-1EQ; up to 6 *Saegheh* (reported)
ATK 29 Su-24MK *Fencer* D
ASW 3 P-3F *Orion*
ISR: 6+ RF-4E *Phantom* II*
TKR/TPT 3: ε1 B-707; ε2 B-747
TPT 116: **Heavy** 12 Il-76 *Candid*; **Medium** ε19 C-130E/H *Hercules*; **Light** 75: 11 An-74TK-200; 5 An-140 (Iran-140 *Faraz*); 10 F-27 *Friendship*; 1 L-1329 *Jetstar*; 10 PC-6B *Turbo Porter*; 8 TB-21 *Trinidad*; 4 TB-200 *Tobago*; 3 *Turbo Commander* 680; 14 Y-7; 9 Y-12; **PAX** 10: ε1 B-707; 1 B-747; 4 B-747F; 1 *Falcon* 20; 3 *Falcon* 50
TRG 126: 25 Beech F33A/C *Bonanza*; 14 JJ-7*; 25 MFI-17 *Mushshak*; 12 *Parastu*; 15 PC-6; 35 PC-7 *Turbo Trainer*
HELICOPTERS
MRH 2 Bell 412
TPT 34+: **Heavy** 2+ CH-47 *Chinook*; **Medium** 30 Bell 214C (AB-214C); **Light** 2+: 2 Bell 206A *Jet Ranger* (AB-206A); some *Shabaviz* 2-75 (indigenous versions in production); some *Shabaviz* 2061
AIR-LAUNCHED MISSILES
AAM • **IR** PL-2A‡; PL-7; R-60 (RS-AA-8 *Aphid*); R-73 (RS-AA-11A *Archer*); AIM-9J *Sidewinder;* **IR/SARH** R-27 (RS-AA-10 *Alamo*); **SARH** AIM-7E-2 *Sparrow*; **ARH** AIM-54 *Phoenix*†
ASM AGM-65A *Maverick*; Kh-25 (RS-AS-10 *Karen*); Kh-25ML (RS-AS-10 *Karen*); Kh-29L/T (RS-AS-14A/B *Kedge*)
AShM C-801K
ARM Kh-58 (RS-AS-11 *Kilter*)
BOMBS
Electro-optical guided GBU-87/B *Qassed*

Air Defence Force 15,000

FORCES BY ROLE
AIR DEFENCE
16 bn with MIM-23B I-*Hawk/Shahin*
4 bn with S-300PMU2 (RS-SA-20 *Gargoyle*)
5 sqn with FM-80 (CH-SA-4); *Rapier*; HQ-2 (CH-SA-1); S-200 *Angara* (RS-SA-5 *Gammon*); 9K331 *Tor*-M1 (RS-SA-15 *Gauntlet*)
EQUIPMENT BY TYPE
AIR DEFENCE
SAM 410
Long-range 42+: 10 S-200 *Angara* (RS-SA-5 *Gammon*); 32 S-300PMU2 (RS-SA-20 *Gargoyle*); *Bavar*-373
Medium-range 59+: ε50 MIM-23B I-*Hawk/Shahin*; 9 HQ-2 (CH-SA-1); *Talash*/15th *Khordad*
Short-range 279: 250 FM-80 (CH-SA-4); 29 9K331 *Tor*-M1 (RS-SA-15 *Gauntlet*)
Point-defence 30+: 30 *Rapier*; *Misaq* 1 (QW-1); *Misaq* 2 (QW-18)
GUNS • **TOWED 23mm** ZU-23-2; **35mm** GDF-002

Middle East and North Africa

Gendarmerie & Paramilitary 40,000–60,000

Law-Enforcement Forces 40,000–60,000 (border and security troops); 450,000 on mobilisation (incl conscripts)

Part of armed forces in wartime

EQUIPMENT BY TYPE
PATROL AND COASTAL COMBATANTS • PB ε90
AIRCRAFT • TPT • Light 2+: 2 An-140; some Cessna 185/Cessna 310
HELICOPTERS • TPT • Light ε24 AB-205 (Bell 205)/AB-206 (Bell 206) *Jet Ranger*

Basij Resistance Force ε600,000 on mobilisation
Paramilitary militia with claimed membership of 12.6 million; ε600,000 combat capable

DEPLOYMENT

GULF OF ADEN AND SOMALI BASIN: Navy: 1 FSGM; 1 AKR
MALI: UN • MINUSMA 2
SYRIA: 1,500

Iraq IRQ

Iraqi Dinar IQD		2021	2022	2023
GDP	IQD	300tr	410tr	
	USD	207bn	283bn	
per capita	USD	5,021	6,696	
Growth	%	7.7	9.3	
Inflation	%	6.0	6.5	
Def bdgt [a]	IQD	10.8tr	12.6tr	
	USD	7.4bn	8.7bn	
FMA (US)	USD	250m	250m	100m
USD1=IQD		1450.00	1450.00	

[a] Excludes MInistry of the Interior and National Security Council budget

Real-terms defence budget trend (USDbn, constant 2015)

Population	40,462,701					
Age	0–14	15–19	20–24	25–29	30–64	65 plus
Male	18.3%	5.4%	4.7%	4.0%	16.3%	1.6%
Female	17.5%	5.2%	4.6%	3.9%	16.4%	2.0%

Capabilities

The armed forces' capabilities and morale have generally improved since the collapse of several divisions in the face of the ISIS advance in the north in 2014, but there remains concern about Baghdad's ability to independently sustain this level of operational effectiveness. The continuing reliance on a relatively small number of key formations for offensive operations, particularly the well-regarded Counter-Terrorism Service (CTS), resulted in these forces suffering disproportionately high levels of attrition. An organic aviation capability for the CTS has been mooted. Meanwhile, the nature of the relationship between the official government forces, Kurdish Peshmerga forces and the Popular Mobilisation Units militias remains uncertain. The government's most critical security relationship has been with the US, on whom Iraqi forces remain largely dependent for training and ISR support, as well as contractor maintenance. Political pressure from nationalist and Iran-aligned political parties, and continuing attacks on US forces by Iranian-supported militia units have strained this relationship in recent years. The US-led combat mission designed to help Iraqi forces tackle ISIS ended in December 2021 with troops under Combined Joint Task Force – Inherent Resolve moving to an 'advise, assist and enable' role. The NATO Mission Iraq is focused on training and capacity building. The armed forces' inventory comprises a heterogenous mix of Soviet-era and Russian equipment combined with newer European- and US-sourced platforms, but significant shortcomings remain in logistics support. Barring military maintenance facilities, Iraq's defence industry has only limited capacity, focusing on the manufacture of light weapons and ammunition.

ACTIVE 193,000 (Army 180,000 Navy 3,000 Air 5,000 Air Defence 5,000) **Gendarmerie & Paramilitary 266,000**

ORGANISATIONS BY SERVICE

Army ε180,000
Includes Counter Terrorism Service

FORCES BY ROLE
SPECIAL FORCES
 3 SF bde
 1 ranger bde (3 ranger bn)
MANOEUVRE
Armoured
 1 (9th) armd div (2 armd bde, 2 mech bde, 1 engr bn, 1 sigs regt, 1 log bde)
Mechanised
 3 (5th, 8th & 10th) mech div (4 mech inf bde, 1 engr bn, 1 sigs regt, 1 log bde) 1 (7th) mech div (2 mech inf bde, 1 inf bde, 1 engr bn, 1 sigs regt, 1 log bde)
Light
 1 (6th) mot div (3 mot inf bde, 1 inf bde, 1 engr bn, 1 sigs regt, 1 log bde)
 1 (14th) mot div (2 mot inf bde, 3 inf bde, 1 engr bn, 1 sigs regt, 1 log bde)
 1 (1st) inf div (2 inf bde)
 1 (11th) inf div (3 lt inf bde, 1 engr bn, 1 sigs regt, 1 log bde)
 1 (15th) inf div (5 inf bde)
 1 (16th) inf div (2 inf bde)
 1 (17th Cdo) inf div (4 inf bde, 1 engr bn, 1 sigs regt, 1 log bde)
 1 inf bde
Other
 1 (PM SF) sy div (3 inf bde)
HELICOPTER
 1 atk hel sqn with Mi-28NE *Havoc*
 1 atk hel sqn with Mi-35M *Hind*
 1 sqn with Bell 205 (UH-1H *Huey* II)
 3 atk hel sqn with Bell T407; H135M
 3 sqn with Mi-17 *Hip* H; Mi-171Sh
 1 ISR sqn with SA342M *Gazelle*
 2 trg sqn with Bell 206; OH-58C *Kiowa*
 1 trg sqn with Bell 205 (UH-1H *Huey* II)
 1 trg sqn with Mi-17 *Hip*

EQUIPMENT BY TYPE
ARMOURED FIGHTING VEHICLES
  MBT 391+: ε100 M1A1 *Abrams;* 168+ T-72M/M1; ε50 T-55; 73 T-90S
  RECCE 53: 18 BRDM 2; 35 EE-9 *Cascavel;*
  IFV 650: ε400 BMP-1; ε90 BMP-3M; ε60 BTR-4 (inc variants); 100 BTR-80A
  APC 1,592+
    APC (T) 900: ε500 M113A2/*Talha;* ε400 MT-LB
    PPV 692+: 12 *Barracuda;* 250 *Caiman; Gorets*-M; ε400 ILAV *Badger; Mamba;* 30 *Maxxpro*
    AUV 420+: ε400 *Akrep;* 20 *Commando;* M-ATV
ENGINEERING & MAINTENANCE VEHICLES
  ARV 222+: 180 BREM; 35+ M88A1/2; 7 *Maxxpro* ARV; T-54/55 ARV; Type-653; VT-55A
NBC VEHICLES 20 *Fuchs* NBC
ANTI-TANK/ANTI-INFRASTRUCTURE
  MSL • MANPATS 9K135 *Kornet* (RS-AT-14 *Spriggan*) (reported)
ARTILLERY 1,064+
  SP 48+: **152mm** 18+ Type-83; **155mm** 30: 6 M109A1; 24 M109A5
  TOWED 60+: **130mm** M-46/Type-59; **152mm** D-20; Type-83; **155mm** ε60 M198
  MRL 6+: **122mm** some BM-21 *Grad;* **220mm** 6+ TOS-1A
  MOR 950+: **81mm** ε500 M252; **120mm** ε450 M120; **240mm** M-240
HELICOPTERS
  ATK 35: 11 Mi-28NE *Havoc;* 4 Mi-28UB *Havoc;* 20+ Mi-35M *Hind*
  MRH 63+: 4+ SA342 *Gazelle;* 17 Bell IA407; 23 H135M; ε19 Mi-17 *Hip* H/Mi-171Sh
  ISR 10 OH-58C *Kiowa*
  TPT • Light 44: 16 Bell 205 (UH-1H *Huey* II); 10 Bell 206B3 *Jet Ranger;* ε18 Bell T407
UNINHABITED AERIAL VEHICLES
  CISR • Heavy 12 CH-4
AIR-LAUNCHED MISSILES • ASM 9K114 *Shturm* (RS-AT-6 *Spiral*); AGR-20A APKWS; AR-1; *Ingwe*
BOMBS
  INS/GPS-guided FT-9

Navy 3,000

EQUIPMENT BY TYPE
PATROL AND COASTAL COMBATANTS 32
  PCF (2 *Musa ibn Nusayr* (ITA *Assad*) with 1 76mm gun non-operational)
  PCO 2 *Al Basra* (US *River Hawk*)
  PCC 4 *Fateh* (ITA *Diciotti*)
  PB 20: 12 Swiftships 35; 5 *Predator* (PRC 27m); 3 *Al Faw*
  PBR 6: 2 Type-200; 4 Type-2010

Marines 1,000

FORCES BY ROLE
MANOEUVRE
  Amphibious
  2 mne bn

Air Force ε5,000

FORCES BY ROLE
FIGHTER/GROUND ATTACK
  2 sqn with F-16C/D *Fighting Falcon*
GROUND ATTACK
  1 sqn with Su-25/Su-25K/Su-25UBK *Frogfoot*
  1 sqn with L-159A; L-159T1
ISR
  1 sqn with CH-2000 *Sama;* SB7L-360 *Seeker*
  1 sqn with Cessna 208B *Grand Caravan;* Cessna AC-208B *Combat Caravan**
  1 sqn with Beech 350 *King Air*
TRANSPORT
  1 sqn with An-32B *Cline*
  1 sqn with C-130E/J-30 *Hercules*
TRAINING
  1 sqn with Cessna 172, Cessna 208B
  1 sqn with *Lasta*-95
  1 sqn with T-6A
  1 sqn with T-50IQ *Golden Eagle**
EQUIPMENT BY TYPE
AIRCRAFT 90 combat capable
  FGA 34: 26 F-16C *Fighting Falcon;* 8 F-16D *Fighting Falcon;*
  ATK 30: 10 L-159A; 1 L-159T1; ε19 Su-25/Su-25K/Su-25UBK *Frogfoot*†
  ISR 10: 2 Cessna AC-208B *Combat Caravan**; 2 SB7L-360 *Seeker;* 6 Beech 350ER *King Air*
  TPT 29: **Medium** 15: 3 C-130E *Hercules;* 6 C-130J-30 *Hercules;* 6 An-32B *Cline* (of which 2 combat capable); **Light** 14: 1 Beech 350 *King Air;* 5 Cessna 208B *Grand Caravan;* 8 Cessna 172
  TRG 57+: 8 CH-2000 *Sama;* 10+ *Lasta*-95; 15 T-6A; 24 T-50IQ *Golden Eagle**
AIR-LAUNCHED MISSILES
  AAM • IR AIM-9L/M *Sidewinder;* **SARH** AIM-7M *Sparrow*
  ASM AGM-114 *Hellfire*
BOMBS
  Laser-guided GBU-10 *Paveway* II; GBU-12 *Paveway* II

Air Defence Command ε5,000

FORCES BY ROLE
AIR DEFENCE
  1 SAM bn with 96K6 *Pantsir*-S1 (RS-SA-22 *Greyhound*)
  1 SAM bn with M1097 *Avenger*
  1 SAM bn with 9K338 *Igla*-S (RS-SA-24 *Grinch*)
  1 ADA bn with ZU-23-2; S-60
EQUIPMENT BY TYPE
AIR DEFENCE
  SAM
    Point-defence M1097 *Avenger;* 9K338 *Igla*-S (RS-SA-24 *Grinch*)
  SPAAGM 30mm 24 96K6 *Pantsir*-S1 (RS-SA-22 *Greyhound*)
  GUNS • TOWED 23mm ZU-23-2; **57mm** S-60

Gendarmerie & Paramilitary ε266,000

Iraqi Federal Police ε36,000

Territorial Interdiction Force ε50,000
FORCES BY ROLE
MANOEUVRE
  Other
    4 sy bde
    11 sy bde (forming)

Popular Mobilisation Forces ε180,000
Includes Badr Organisation; Kataib Hizbullah; Kataib Imam Ali; Kataib Sayyid al-Shuhada

EQUIPMENT BY TYPE
ARMOURED FIGHTING VEHICLES
  MBT T-55; T-72B; T-72 *Rakhsh*
  IFV BMP-1 mod (23mm gun); BMP-2
  APC • PPV *Toophan*
ANTI-TANK/ANTI-INFRASTRUCTURE
  MANPATS *Dehlavieh* (*Kornet*); *Toophan*
ARTILLERY
  TOWED • **130mm** M-46; **152mm** D-20
  MRL • **122mm** HM-20
AIR DEFENCE
  SAM • **Short-range** *Saqr*-1 (358) (reported)
  GUNS • **SP 23mm** BMP-1 mod (ZU-23-2 on BMP-1 chassis)

FOREIGN FORCES

Australia Operation Inherent Resolve (*Okra*) 110 • NATO Mission Iraq 2
Belgium Operation Inherent Resolve (*Valiant Phoenix*) 6 • NATO Mission Iraq 7
Canada NATO Mission Iraq 16
Croatia Operation Inherent Resolve 3 • NATO Mission Iraq 8
Czech Republic Operation Inherent Resolve 60
Denmark Operation Inherent Resolve 39 • NATO Mission Iraq 125
Estonia Operation Inherent Resolve 10 • NATO Mission Iraq 40
Fiji UNAMI 174; 2 sy unit
Finland Operation Inherent Resolve 75; 1 trg unit • NATO Mission Iraq 5
France Operation Inherent Resolve 6 • NATO Mission Iraq 3
Germany Operation Inherent Resolve 70 • NATO Mission Iraq 15
Greece NATO Mission Iraq 2
Hungary Operation Inherent Resolve 133 • NATO Mission Iraq 3
Italy Operation Inherent Resolve (*Prima Parthica*) 650; 1 inf regt; 1 trg unit; 1 hel sqn with 4 NH90 • NATO Mission Iraq 610
Latvia Operation Inherent Resolve 6 • NATO Mission Iraq 1
Lithuania Operation Inherent Resolve 6 • NATO Mission Iraq 34
Luxembourg NATO Mission Iraq 1
Nepal UNAMI 77; 1 sy unit
Netherlands Operation Inherent Resolve 150; 2 trg units • NATO Mission Iraq 2
New Zealand Operation Inherent Resolve 9
Norway Operation Inherent Resolve 60; 1 trg unit • NATO Mission Iraq 2
Poland Operation Inherent Resolve 150 • NATO Mission Iraq 30
Portugal Operation Inherent Resolve 30
Romania Operation Inherent Resolve 30 • NATO Mission Iraq 170
Slovakia NATO Mission Iraq 5
Slovenia Operation Inherent Resolve 3
Spain Operation Inherent Resolve 150; 1 trg units; 1 hel unit • NATO Mission Iraq 130
Sweden Operation Inherent Resolve 2 • NATO Mission Iraq 1
Turkey Army 1,000; 1 cdo unit • NATO Mission Iraq 86
United Kingdom Operation Inherent Resolve (*Shader*) 100 • NATO Mission Iraq 12
United States Operation Inherent Resolve 2,000; 1 mech bde(-); 1 atk hel bn with AH-64E *Apache*; MQ-1C Gray Eagle; 1 spec ops hel bn with MH-47G Chinook; MH-60M *Black Hawk*; 1 CISR UAV sqn with MQ-9A *Reaper* • NATO Mission Iraq 12

Israel ISR

New Israeli Shekel ILS		2021	2022	2023
GDP	ILS	1.58tr	1.74tr	
	USD	489bn	527bn	
per capita	USD	52,152	55,359	
Growth	%	8.6	6.1	
Inflation	%	1.5	4.5	
Def bdgt	ILS	65.9bn	63.9bn	
	USD	20.4bn	19.4bn	
FMA (US)	USD	3.30bn	3.30bn	3.30bn
USD1=ILS		3.23	3.30	

Real-terms defence budget trend (USDbn, constant 2015)

Population   8,914,885

Age	0–14	15–19	20–24	25–29	30–64	65 plus
Male	13.4%	4.2%	3.9%	3.6%	19.7%	5.5%
Female	12.8%	4.0%	3.7%	3.4%	19.1%	6.7%

Capabilities

The Israel Defense Forces (IDF) are organised for territorial defence, short-term interventions in neighbouring states and limited regional power projection. In recent years this has included air-to-ground missions in Syria, while the navy is tasked with interdicting illicit shipments and delivering maritime security as Israel's littoral becomes more economically important to the country. Israel is widely believed to possess a nuclear-weapons capability. Following the 2015 Plan *Gideon*, the IDF adopted a new five-year *Tnufa* (Momentum) programme in 2020. It seeks to improve areas of relative superiority, such as technology and intelligence, to ensure swifter and more decisive operations against future threats. The new government approved a defence budget in mid-2021, following two years without a new budget, which has enabled the plan to progress. The US remains Israel's key defence partner, as well as a significant source of funding, and is instrumental in several of the IDF's equipment programmes, particularly in missile defence and combat aviation. Israel also maintains discreet ties with a number of Arab states, has recently normalised relations with several Gulf states and has even started selling defence and security equipment to the region. Personnel quality and training are generally at a high standard, despite the IDF's continuing reliance on national service. A task force tasked with examining the number of combat roles open to women reported to service chiefs in 2022; additional roles will be opened to women, including some additional special forces positions. Ground-forces training is being overhauled, with new training centres under construction. *Edge of Tomorrow*, a new MOD and industry technology-driven project, is designed to improve situational awareness and networking. Given its mission-set, the IDF's logistics capabilities are likely limited to sustaining operations within Israel itself or in immediately neighbouring territories. The largely asymmetric nature of the threats the IDF has faced in recent years has focused modernisation efforts on force-protection, missile-defence and precision-strike capabilities. Israel maintains a broad defence-industrial base, with world-class capabilities in armoured vehicles, uninhabited systems, guided-weapons, radars and sensors, and cyber security.

ACTIVE 169,500 (Army 126,000 Navy 9,500 Air 34,000) Gendarmerie & Paramilitary 8,000

Conscript liability Officers 48 months, other ranks 32 months, women 24 months (Jews and Druze only; Christians, Circassians and Muslims may volunteer)

RESERVE 465,000 (Army 400,000 Navy 10,000 Air 55,000)

Annual trg as cbt reservists to age 40 (some specialists to age 54) for male other ranks, 38 (or marriage/pregnancy) for women

ORGANISATIONS BY SERVICE

Strategic Forces

Israel is widely believed to have a nuclear capability – delivery means include F-15I and F-16I ac, *Jericho* 2 IRBM and, reportedly, *Dolphin/Tanin*-class SSKs with LACM

FORCES BY ROLE
SURFACE-TO-SURFACE MISSILE
3 IRBM sqn with *Jericho* 2

EQUIPMENT BY TYPE
SURFACE-TO-SURFACE MISSILE LAUNCHERS
IRBM • **Nuclear**: ε24 *Jericho* 2

Strategic Defences

FORCES BY ROLE
AIR DEFENCE
3 bty with *Arrow* 2 ATBM with *Green Pine/Super Green Pine* radar and *Citrus Tree* command post
10 bty with *Iron Dome* (incl reserve bty)
4 bty with M901 *Patriot* PAC-2
2 bty with *David's Sling*

Space

EQUIPMENT BY TYPE
SATELLITES 10
COMMUNICATIONS 3 *Amos*
ISR 7: 1 EROS; 5 *Ofeq* (5, 7, 9, 10 & 16); 1 TecSAR-1 (*Polaris*)

Army 26,000; 100,000 conscript (total 126,000)

Organisation and structure of formations may vary according to op situations. Equipment includes that required for reserve forces on mobilisation

FORCES BY ROLE
COMMAND
3 (regional comd) corps HQ
2 armd div HQ
1 (Multidimensional) div HQ
5 (territorial) inf div HQ
1 (home defence) comd HQ
SPECIAL FORCES
1 spec ops bde (3 spec ops unit)
MANOEUVRE
Reconnaissance
1 indep recce bn
Armoured
3 armd bde (1 recce coy, 3 a rmd bn, 1 AT coy, 1 cbt engr bn)
1 (Multidimensional) armd inf/ISR bn
Mechanised
3 mech inf bde (3 mech inf bn, 1 cbt spt bn, 1 sigs coy)
1 mech inf bde (1 recce bn, 4 mech inf bn, 1 cbt spt bn)
1 indep mech inf bn
Light
2 indep inf bn
Air Manoeuvre
1 para bde (3 para bn, 1 cbt spt bn, 1 sigs coy)
Other
1 armd trg bde (3 armd bn)
1 (Border Protection) sy bde (5 ISR bn; 4 sy bn)
COMBAT SUPPORT
3 arty bde
1 engr bde (3 engr bn, 3 EOD coy)
1 CBRN bn
1 int bde (3 int bn)
1 int unit
1 SIGINT unit
2 MP bn

Reserves 400,000+ on mobilisation

FORCES BY ROLE
COMMAND
3 armd div HQ
1 AB div HQ
MANOEUVRE
Armoured
9 armd bde
Mechanised
8 mech inf bde
Light
16 (territorial/regional) inf bde
Air Manoeuvre
4 para bde
Mountain
1 mtn inf bde
1 mtn inf bn

332   THE MILITARY BALANCE 2023

COMBAT SUPPORT
5 arty bde
COMBAT SERVICE SUPPORT
6 log unit
EQUIPMENT BY TYPE
ARMOURED FIGHTING VEHICLES
MBT ε400 *Merkava* MkIV (ε700 *Merkava* MkIII; ε200
Merkava MkIV all in store)
APC 1,190+
APC (T) 1,190: ε290 *Namer*; 500 M113A2; ε400 *Nagmachon*
(*Centurion* chassis); *Nakpadon* (5,100: ε100 *Achzarit*
(modified T-55 chassis); 5,000 M113A1/A2 all in store)
APC (W) some *Eitan*
AUV *Ze'ev*
ENGINEERING & MAINTENANCE VEHICLES
AEV D9R; *Namer*; *Puma*
ARV *Nemmera*; M88A1; M113 ARV
VLB *Alligator* MAB; M48/60; MTU
NBC VEHICLES ε8 TPz-1 *Fuchs* NBC
ANTI-TANK/ANTI-INFRASTRUCTURE • MSL
SP M113 with *Spike*; *Tamuz* (*Spike* NLOS)
MANPATS IMI MAPATS; *Spike* SR/MR/LR/ER
ARTILLERY 530
SP 250: **155mm** 250 M109A5 (**155mm** 30 M109A2;
175mm 36 M107; **203mm** 36 M110 all in store)
TOWED (**155mm** 171: 40 M-46 mod; 50 M-68/M-71; 81
M-839P/M-845P all in store)
MRL 30: **227mm** 30 M270 MLRS; **306mm** IMI *Lynx*
(**160mm** 50 LAR-160; **227mm** 18 M270 MLRS; **290mm** 20
LAR-290 all in store)
MOR 250: **81mm** 250 (**81mm** 1,100; **120mm** 650; **160mm**
18 Soltam M-66 all in store)
AIR DEFENCE • SAM • Point-defence *Machbet*; FIM-
92 *Stinger*

Navy 7,000; 2,500 conscript (total 9,500)

EQUIPMENT BY TYPE
SUBMARINES 5
SSK 5:
3 *Dolphin* (GER HDW design) with 6 single 533mm
TT with UGM-84C *Harpoon* Block 1B AShM/*SeaHake*
(DM2A3) HWT/*SeaHake* mod 4 (DM2A4) HWT/
Kaved HWT, 4 single 650mm TT with dual-capable
LACM (reported)
2 *Tanin* (GER HDW design) (fitted with AIP) with 6
single 533mm TT with UGM-84C *Harpoon* Block
1B AShM/*SeaHake* (DM2A3) HWT/*SeaHake* mod 4
(DM2A4) HWT/*Kaved* HWT, 4 single 650mm TT
with dual-capable LACM (reported)
PATROL AND COASTAL COMBATANTS 49
CORVETTES • FSGHM 7:
2 *Eilat* (*Sa'ar* 5) with 2 quad lnchr with RGM-84
Harpoon AShM/*Gabriel* V AShM, 4 8-cell VLS with
Barak-1 SAM (being upgraded to *Barak*-8), 2 triple
324mm TT with Mk 46 LWT, 1 Mk 15 *Phalanx* CIWS
(capacity 1 AS565SA *Panther* ASW hel)

1 *Eilat* (*Sa'ar* 5) with 2 quad lnchr with RGM-84
Harpoon AShM/*Gabriel* V AShM, 4 8-cell VLS with
Barak-8 SAM, 2 triple 324mm TT with Mk 46 LWT,
1 Mk 15 *Phalanx* CIWS (capacity 1 AS565SA *Panther*
ASW hel)
4 *Magen* (*Sa'ar* 6) with 2 quad lnchr with *Gabriel* V AShM,
2 20-cell VLS with *Tamir* (*C-Dome*) SAM, 4 8-cell VLS
with *Barak* LRAD, 2 triple 324mm ASTT with Mk 54
LWT (capacity 1 AS565SA *Panther* ASW hel)
PCGM 8 *Hetz* (*Sa'ar* 4.5) with 2 quad lnchr with RGM-
84 *Harpoon* AShM (can also be fitted with up to 6 single
lnchr with *Gabriel* II AShM), 2 8-cell VLS with *Barak*-1
SAM, (can be fitted with 2 triple 324mm Mk32 TT with
Mk46 LWT), 1 Mk 15 *Phalanx* CWIS, 1 76mm gun
PBF 34: 5 *Shaldag*; 3 *Stingray*; 9 *Super Dvora* Mk I (SSM
& TT may be fitted); 4 *Super Dvora* Mk II (SSM & TT
may be fitted); 6 *Super Dvora* Mk II-I (SSM & TT may be
fitted); 4 *Super Dvora* Mk III (SSM & TT may be fitted); 3
Super Dvora Mk III (SSM may be fitted)
AMPHIBIOUS • LANDING CRAFT • LCVP 3 *Manta*
LOGISTICS AND SUPPORT • AG 1 *Bat Yam* (ex-GER
Type-745)

Naval Commandos ε300

FORCES BY ROLE
SPECIAL FORCES
1 cdo unit

Air Force 34,000

Responsible for Air and Space Coordination
FORCES BY ROLE
FIGHTER & FIGHTER/GROUND ATTACK
1 sqn with F-15A/B/D *Eagle* (*Baz*)
1 sqn with F-15B/C/D *Eagle* (*Baz*)
1 sqn with F-15I *Ra'am*
5 sqn with F-16C/D *Fighting Falcon* (*Barak*)
4 sqn with F-16I *Fighting Falcon* (*Sufa*)
2 sqn with F-35I *Adir*
ANTI-SUBMARINE WARFARE
1 sqn with AS565SA *Panther* (missions flown by IAF but
with non-rated aircrew)
ELECTRONIC WARFARE
1 sqn with RC-12D *Guardrail*; Beech A36 *Bonanza* (*Hofit*);
Beech 200/200T/200CT *King Air*
AIRBORNE EARLY WARNING & CONTROL
1 sqn with Gulfstream G550 *Eitam*; Gulfstream G550 *Shavit*
TANKER/TRANSPORT
1 sqn with C-130E/H *Hercules*; KC-130H *Hercules*
1 sqn with C-130J-30 *Hercules*
1 sqn with KC-707
TRAINING
1 OPFOR sqn with F-16C/D *Fighting Falcon* (*Barak*)
1 sqn with F-35I *Adir*
1 sqn with M-346 *Master* (*Lavi*)
ATTACK HELICOPTER
1 sqn with AH-64A *Apache* (*Peten*)
1 sqn with AH-64D *Apache* (*Sarat*)

TRANSPORT HELICOPTER
2 sqn with CH-53D *Sea Stallion*
2 sqn with S-70A *Black Hawk*; UH-60A *Black Hawk*
1 medevac unit with CH-53D *Sea Stallion*

UAV
2 ISR sqn with *Hermes* 450
1 ISR sqn with *Heron* (*Shoval*); *Heron* TP (*Eitan*)
1 ISR sqn with *Heron* (*Shoval*) (MP role)
1 ISR sqn with *Orbiter* 4 (*Nitzotz*)

AIR DEFENCE
3 bty with *Arrow* 2/3
10 bty with *Iron Dome*
4 bty with M901 *Patriot* PAC-2
2 bty with *David's Sling*

SPECIAL FORCES
1 SF wg (2 SF unit, 1 CSAR unit, 1 int unit)

SURFACE-TO-SURFACE MISSILE
3 IRBM sqn with *Jericho* 2

EQUIPMENT BY TYPE
AIRCRAFT 345 combat capable
FGA 315: 16 F-15A *Eagle* (*Baz*); 6 F-15B *Eagle* (*Baz*); 17 F-15C *Eagle* (*Baz*); 19 F-15D *Eagle* (*Baz*); 25 F-15I *Ra'am*; ε50 F-16C *Fighting Falcon* (*Barak*); 49 F-16D *Fighting Falcon* (*Barak*); 97 F-16I *Fighting Falcon* (*Sufa*); 36 F-35I *Adir*
ISR 7: 6 RC-12D *Guardrail*; 1 Gulfstream G550 *Oron*
ELINT 3 Gulfstream G550 *Shavit*
AEW 2 Gulfstream G550 *Eitam*
TKR/TPT 10: 4 KC-130H *Hercules*; 6 KC-707
TPT 65: **Medium** 18: 5 C-130E *Hercules*; 6 C-130H *Hercules*; 7 C-130J-30 *Hercules*; **Light** 47: 3 AT-802 *Air Tractor*; 9 Beech 200 *King Air*; 8 Beech 200T *King Air*; 5 Beech 200CT *King Air*; 22 Beech A36 *Bonanza* (*Hofit*)
TRG 66: 16 Grob G-120; 30 M-346 *Master* (*Lavi*)*; 20 T-6A
HELICOPTERS
ATK 43: 26 AH-64A *Apache* (*Peten*); 17 AH-64D *Apache* (*Sarat*)
ASW 7 AS565SA *Panther* (missions flown by IAF but with non-rated aircrew)
ISR 12 OH-58B *Kiowa*
TPT 80: **Heavy** 25 CH-53D *Sea Stallion*; **Medium** 49: 39 S-70A *Black Hawk*; 10 UH-60A *Black Hawk*; **Light** 6 Bell 206 *Jet Ranger*
UNINHABITED AERIAL VEHICLES
ISR 3+: **Heavy** 3+: *Heron* (*Shoval*); 3 *Heron* TP (*Eitan*); RQ-5A *Hunter*; **Medium** *Hermes* 450; *Hermes* 900 (22+ *Searcher* MkII in store); **Light** *Orbiter* 4 (*Nitzotz*); (an unknown number of ISR UAVs are combat capable)
LOITERING & DIRECT ATTACK MUNITIONS
Harop; *Harpy*
SURFACE-TO-SURFACE MISSILE LAUNCHERS
IRBM • **Nuclear** ε24 *Jericho* 2
AIR DEFENCE
SAM 40+:
Long-range M901 *Patriot* PAC-2
Medium-range some *David's Sling*
Short-range up to 40 *Iron Dome*
Point-defence *Machbet*
GUNS • **TOWED 20mm** M167 *Vulcan*
MISSILE DEFENCE • **SAM** 24 *Arrow* 2/*Arrow* 3;

AIR-LAUNCHED MISSILES
AAM • **IR** AIM-9 *Sidewinder*; *Python* 4; **IIR** *Python* 5; **ARH** AIM-120C AMRAAM
ASM AGM-114 *Hellfire*; AGM-62B *Walleye*; AGM-65 *Maverick*; *Delilah* AL; *Popeye* I/II; *Spike* NLOS
BOMBS
IIR guided *Opher*
Laser-guided *Griffin*; *Lizard*; *Paveway* II
INS/GPS-guided GBU-31 JDAM; GBU-39 Small Diameter Bomb (*Barad Had*); *Spice*

Airfield Defence 3,000 active (15,000 reservists)

Gendarmerie & Paramilitary ε8,000

Border Police ε8,000

FOREIGN FORCES

UNTSO unless specified. UNTSO figures represent total numbers for mission

Argentina 3
Australia 11
Austria 4
Belgium 1
Bhutan 5 • UNDOF 3
Canada 4
Chile 3
China 5
Czech Republic UNDOF 4
Denmark 10
Estonia 3
Fiji 2 • UNDOF 150; 1 inf coy
Finland 14
Ghana UNDOF 6
India 2 • UNDOF 198; 1 inf pl; 1 MP pl; 1 log coy(-)
Ireland 12 • UNDOF 130; 1 inf coy
Latvia 1
Nepal 3 • UNDOF 412; 1 mech inf coy; 1 inf coy; 1 log coy(-)
Netherlands 12 • UNDOF 1
New Zealand 8
Norway 13
Poland 4
Russia 4
Serbia 1
Slovakia 2
Slovenia 3
Sweden 7
Switzerland 11
United States 2 • US Strategic Command; 100; 1 AN/TPY-2 X-band radar at Mount Keren
Uruguay UNDOF 212; 1 mech inf coy
Zambia 1

Jordan JOR

Jordanian Dinar JOD		2021	2022	2023
GDP	JOD	32.1bn	34.1bn	
	USD	45.3bn	48.1bn	
per capita	USD	4,412	4,666	
Growth	%	2.2	2.4	
Inflation	%	1.3	3.8	
Def bdgt [a]	JOD	1.28bn	1.37bn	
	USD	1.80bn	1.93bn	
FMA (US)	USD	425m	350m	400m
USD1=JOD		0.71	0.71	

[a] Excludes expenditure on public order and safety

Real-terms defence budget trend (USDbn, constant 2015)

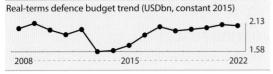

Population	10,998,531					
Age	0–14	15–19	20–24	25–29	30–64	65 plus
Male	16.4%	5.1%	5.0%	4.7%	19.4%	1.9%
Female	15.5%	4.9%	4.4%	4.0%	16.6%	2.0%

Capabilities

The Jordanian Armed Forces are structured to provide border security and an armoured response to conventional threats, and they have recently focused on tackling narcotics- and weapons-smuggling from Syria. Efforts to restructure, review modernisation requirements and increase efficiency are ongoing. In recent years, Jordan has withdrawn some equipment from service, particularly aircraft, likely due to budgetary pressure. There has been no recent public statement of defence policy, but regional instability remains a key concern, principally the ongoing war in Syria. Jordan is a major non-NATO ally of the US and there is a close bilateral defence relationship. The country has developed a bespoke special-forces training centre and has hosted training for numerous state and non-state military forces. A training centre for female personnel was inaugurated in mid-2021 and aims to boost the number of women in the armed forces to 3% of the total by the end of 2024. Personnel are relatively well trained, particularly aircrew and special forces, who are highly regarded internationally. Jordanian forces are able to independently deploy regionally and have participated in ISAF operations in Afghanistan and in coalition air operations over Syria and Yemen; additional second-hand transport aircraft were recently acquired. Jordan's inventory largely comprises older systems and procurements have typically been in small numbers, second-hand or donations. Although the state-owned Jordan Design and Development Bureau (JODDB, formerly KADDB) has demonstrated the capacity to upgrade vehicles, the army has largely recapitalised its armoured-vehicle fleet with second-hand armour from European countries. JODDB has produced some light-armoured vehicles for domestic use through agreements with foreign suppliers, but the company currently has little export profile.

ACTIVE 100,500 (Army 86,000 Navy 500 Air 14,000)
Gendarmerie & Paramilitary 15,000

RESERVE 65,000 (Army 60,000 Joint 5,000)

ORGANISATIONS BY SERVICE

Army 86,000

FORCES BY ROLE
SPECIAL FORCES
1 (Royal Guard) SF gp (1 SF regt, 1 SF bn, 1 CT bn)
1 spec ops bde (3 spec ops bn)
MANOEUVRE
  Armoured
  2 armd bde
  Mechanised
  8 mech bde
  Light
  2 (Border Gd) inf bde
  1 (Border Gd) inf gp
  Air Manoeuvre
  1 AB bde (3 AB bn)
COMBAT SUPPORT
4 arty bde
4 AD bde
1 MRL bn
1 engr bn
COMBAT SERVICE SUPPORT
1 log bn

EQUIPMENT BY TYPE
ARMOURED FIGHTING VEHICLES
  MBT 266: ε80 FV4034 *Challenger* 1 (*Al Hussein*); 4+ *Leclerc*; 182 M60A3 (ε300 FV4034 *Challenger* 1 (*Al Hussein*) in store)
  ASLT 80 B1 *Centauro* (61 more in store)
  IFV 399: 13 AIFV-B-C25; 50 *Marder* 1A3; 336 YPR-765 PRI
  APC 968+
    APC (T) 729: 370 M113A1/A2 Mk1J; 269 M577A2 (CP); 87 YPR-765 PRCO (CP); 3 AIFV-B
    PPV 239: some *Al-Wahsh*; 45 *Caiman*; 25 *Marauder*; 25 *Matador*; 100 *MaxxPro*; 44 *Nomad/Thunder*
  AUV 35 *Cougar*
ENGINEERING & MAINTENANCE VEHICLES
  ARV 85+: *Al Monjed*; 5 BPz-1; FV4204 *Chieftain* ARV; 32 M88A1; 30 M578; 18 YPR-806
  MW 12 *Aardvark* Mk2
ANTI-TANK/ANTI-INFRASTRUCTURE • MSL
  SP 115: 70 M901; 45 AIFV-B-*Milan*
  MANPATS FGM-148 *Javelin*; TOW/TOW-2A; 9K135 *Kornet* (RS-AT-14 *Spriggan*); Luch *Corsar*; Stugna-P
ARTILLERY 1,397
  SP 506: **155mm** 358 M109A1/A2; **203mm** 148 M110A2
  TOWED 84: **105mm** 66: 54 M102; 12 M119A2; **155mm** 18 M114
  MRL 30: **227mm** 12 M142 HIMARS; **273mm** 18 WM-80
  MOR 777: **81mm** 359; **SP 81mm** 50; **107mm** 50 M30; **120mm** 300 Brandt **SP 120mm** 18 *Agrab* Mk2
AIR DEFENCE
  SAM • Point-defence 92+: 92 9K35 *Strela*-10 (RS-SA-13 *Gopher*); 9K36 *Strela*-3 (RS-SA-14 *Gremlin*); 9K310 *Igla*-1 (RS-SA-16 *Gimlet*); 9K38 *Igla* (RS-SA-18 *Grouse*); 9K338 *Igla*-S (RS-SA-24 *Grinch*)
  GUNS • SP 108: **23mm** 48 ZSU-23-4 Shilka; **35mm** 60 *Gepard*

Navy ε500

EQUIPMENT BY TYPE
PATROL AND COASTAL COMBATANTS 9
PBF 2 Response Boat-Medium (RB-M)
PB 7: 4 *Abdullah* (US *Dauntless*); 3 *Al Hussein* (UK *Vosper* 30m)

Marines

FORCES BY ROLE
MANOEUVRE
Amphibious
1 mne unit

Air Force 14,000

FORCES BY ROLE
FIGHTER/GROUND ATTACK
2 sqn with F-16AM/BM *Fighting Falcon*
ISR
1 sqn with AT-802U *Air Tractor*
1 sqn with Cessna 208B
TRANSPORT
1 sqn with C-130E *Hercules*
TRAINING
1 OCU with F-16AM/BM *Fighting Falcon*
1 sqn with PC-21
1 sqn with Grob 120TP
1 hel sqn with R-44 *Raven* II
ATTACK HELICOPTER
2 sqn with AH-1F *Cobra* (with TOW)
TRANSPORT HELICOPTER
1 sqn with AS332M *Super Puma;* UH-60A *Black Hawk*
1 sqn with UH-60A *Black Hawk*
1 sqn with UH-60M *Black Hawk*
1 sqn with Mi-26T2 *Halo*
1 (Royal) flt with VH-60M *Black Hawk;* AW139
ISR UAV
1 sqn with S-100 *Camcopter*
AIR DEFENCE
2 bde with MIM-23B Phase III I-*Hawk*

EQUIPMENT BY TYPE
AIRCRAFT 57 combat capable
FGA 47: 33 F-16AM *Fighting Falcon*; 14 F-16BM *Fighting Falcon*
ATK (2 AC235 in store, offered for sale)
ISR 10 AT-802U *Air Tractor**
TPT 11: **Medium** 3 C-130E *Hercules* (1 C-130B *Hercules*; 4 C-130H *Hercules* in store); **Light** 7: 5 Cessna 208B; 2 M-28 *Skytruck* (2 C295M in store, offered for sale); **PAX** 1 CL-604 *Challenger*
TRG 26: 14 Grob 120TP; 12 PC-21; (12 *Hawk* Mk63* in store, offered for sale)

HELICOPTERS
ATK 12 AH-1F *Cobra* (17 more in store, offered for sale)
MRH 14: 3 AW139; 11 H135M (Tpt/SAR) (6 MD-530F in store, offered for sale)
TPT 49: **Heavy** 4 Mi-26T2 *Halo*; **Medium** 33: 10 AS332M *Super Puma* (being WFU); 8 UH-60A *Black Hawk*; 12 UH-60M *Black Hawk*; 3 VH-60M *Black Hawk*; (8 UH-60L in store, offered for sale); **Light** 12 R-44 *Raven* II; (13 Bell 205 (UH-1H *Iroquois*) in store, offered for sale)
UNINHABITED AERIAL VEHICLES
CISR • Heavy (some CH-4B in store, offered for sale)
ISR • Light up to 10 S-100 *Camcopter*
AIR DEFENCE
SAM • Medium-range 24 MIM-23B Phase III I-*Hawk*
GUNS • TOWED 40mm 22 L/70 (with *Flycatcher* radar)
AIR-LAUNCHED MISSILES
AAM • IR AIM-9J/N/P *Sidewinder;* **SARH** AIM-7 *Sparrow;* **ARH** AIM-120C AMRAAM
ASM AGM-65D/G *Maverick;* BGM-71 TOW
BOMBS
Laser-guided GBU-10/12 *Paveway* II

Gendarmerie & Paramilitary ε15,000 active

Gendarmerie ε15,000 active

3 regional comd
FORCES BY ROLE
SPECIAL FORCES
2 SF unit
MANOEUVRE
Other
10 sy bn
EQUIPMENT BY TYPE
ARMOURED FIGHTING VEHICLES
APC • APC (W) 25+: AT105 *Saxon* (reported); 25+ EE-11 *Urutu*
AUV AB2 *Al-Jawad*

DEPLOYMENT

CENTRAL AFRICAN REPUBLIC: UN • MINUSCA 10

DEMOCRATIC REPUBLIC OF THE CONGO: UN • MONUSCO 11

MALI: UN • MINUSMA 322; 1 mech inf coy(+)

SOUTH SUDAN: UN • UNMISS 5

FOREIGN FORCES

France *Operation Inherent Resolve* (*Chammal*) 300; 4 *Rafale* F3
Germany *Operation Inherent Resolve* 150; 1 A400M
United States Central Command: *Operation Inherent Resolve* 3,000; 1 FGA sqn with 18 F-15E *Strike Eagle*; 1 CISR sqn with 12 MQ-9A *Reaper*

Kuwait KWT

Kuwaiti Dinar KWD		2021	2022	2023
GDP	KWD	41.2bn	55.7bn	
	USD	136bn	184bn	
per capita	USD	28,665	38,123	
Growth	%	1.3	8.7	
Inflation	%	3.4	4.3	
Def bdgt [a]	KWD	2.93bn	ε2.78bn	
	USD	9.64bn	ε9.17bn	
USD1=KWD		0.30	0.30	

[a] Includes National Guard

Real-terms defence budget trend (USDbn, constant 2015)

Population	3,068,155					
Age	0–14	15–19	20–24	25–29	30–64	65 plus
Male	12.3%	3.3%	4.8%	7.1%	28.8%	1.4%
Female	11.3%	3.1%	3.7%	4.3%	17.8%	1.8%

Capabilities

Kuwait's armed forces are postured to provide territorial defence through a strategy of holding out against any superior aggressor until allied forces can be mobilised to assist. Kuwait is a member of the GCC, but its key defence relationship has been with the US since 1991. Washington designated Kuwait a major non-NATO ally in 2004, and a bilateral defence-cooperation agreement provides for a range of joint activities and mentoring, and the stationing and pre-positioning of US personnel and equipment. The US drawdown of forces from CENTCOM in 2021 means that, in future, greater emphasis for Kuwait's defence may be placed upon the country's own capabilities, as well as those of its regional GCC allies. The planned new defence ministry headquarters complex could presage improved command and control capacity. The focus on national defence means that Kuwait has little expeditionary sustainment capacity, although it did make a small air contribution to the Saudi-led coalition at the beginning of the Yemen conflict. Improvements in air and missile defence continue to receive priority, given Kuwait's proximity to Iran, and the Emirate has begun to receive new air combat platforms and is modernising its land forces armour component, although COVID-19 has delayed these plans. There is some organic maintenance capacity, though this is bolstered by contractor support. Kuwait lacks a domestic defence-industrial base and is reliant on imports, albeit with offset requirements to help stimulate the country's wider industrial sector.

ACTIVE 17,500 (Army 11,500 Navy 2,000 Air 2,500 Emiri Guard 1,500) Gendarmerie & Paramilitary 7,100

Conscript liability 12 months, males 18–35 years

RESERVE 23,700 (Joint 23,700)

Reserve obligation to age 40; 1 month annual trg

ORGANISATIONS BY SERVICE

Army 11,500
FORCES BY ROLE
SPECIAL FORCES
  1 SF unit
  1 cdo bde
MANOEUVRE
  Armoured
  3 armd bde
  Mechanised
  2 mech inf bde
COMBAT SUPPORT
  1 arty bde
  1 engr bde
  1 MP bn
COMBAT SERVICE SUPPORT
  1 log gp
  1 fd hospital

Reserve
FORCES BY ROLE
MANOEUVRE
  Mechanised
  1 bde

EQUIPMENT BY TYPE
ARMOURED FIGHTING VEHICLES
  MBT 293: 218 M1A2/A2K *Abrams*; 75 M-84AB (75 more in store)
  IFV 537: 76 BMP-2; 122 BMP-3; 103 BMP-3M; 236 *Desert Warrior*† (incl variants)
  APC 260
    APC (T) 260: 230 M113A2; 30 M577 (CP)
    APC (W) (40 TH 390 *Fahd* in store)
  AUV 300 *Sherpa Light Scout*
ENGINEERING & MAINTENANCE VEHICLES
  ARV 19+: 19 M88A1/2; Type-653A; *Warrior*
  MW *Aardvark* Mk2
NBC VEHICLES 12 *Fuchs*-2 NBC
ARTY 193
  SP 155mm 88: 37 M109A3; 51 PLZ-45
  MRL 300mm 27 9A52 *Smerch*
  MOR 78: **81mm** 60; **107mm** 6 M30; **120mm** ε12 RT-F1
ANTI-TANK/ANTI-INFRASTRUCTURE
  MSL
    SP 74: 66 HMMWV TOW; 8 M901
    MANPATS 9K135 *Kornet* (RS-AT-14 *Spriggan*); TOW-2
  RCL 84mm *Carl Gustaf*
AIR DEFENCE
  SAM • **Point-defence** *Starburst*; FIM-92 *Stinger*

Navy ε2,000 (incl 500 Coast Guard)
EQUIPMENT BY TYPE
PATROL AND COASTAL COMBATANTS 20
  PCFG 2:
    1 *Al Sanbouk* (GER Lurssen TNC 45m) with 2 twin lnchr with MM40 *Exocet* AShM, 1 76mm gun
    1 *Istiqlal* (GER Lurssen TNC 57m) with 2 twin lnchr with MM40 *Exocet* AShM, 1 76mm gun

PBF 10 *Al Nokatha* (US Mk V PBF)
PBG 8 *Um Almaradim* (FRA *Combattante* 1 derivative)
with 2 twin lnchr with *Sea Skua* AShM
AMPHIBIOUS • LANDING CRAFT 8
LCT 2 *Assafar* (ADSB 64m)
LCM 1 *Abhan* (ADSB 42m)
LCVP 5 ADSB 16m
LOGISTICS AND SUPPORT • AG 1 *Sawahil* with 1 hel landing platform

Air Force 2,500

FORCES BY ROLE
FIGHTER/GROUND ATTACK
2 sqn with F/A-18C/D *Hornet*
TRANSPORT
1 sqn with C-17A *Globemaster* III; KC-130J *Hercules*;
L-100-30
TRAINING
1 OCU sqn with F/A-18C/D *Hornet*
1 OCU sqn (forming) with Eurofighter *Typhoon*
1 unit with EMB-312 *Tucano**; *Hawk* Mk64*
ATTACK HELICOPTER
2 sqn with AH-64D *Apache*
1 atk/trg sqn with SA342 *Gazelle* with HOT
TRANSPORT HELICOPTER
1 sqn with AS532 *Cougar*; H225M; SA330 *Puma*
1 (VIP) sqn with S-92A

EQUIPMENT BY TYPE
AIRCRAFT 53 combat capable
FGA 39: 6 Eurofighter *Typhoon*; 26 F/A-18C *Hornet*; 7
F/A-18D *Hornet*
TKR/TPT 3 KC-130J *Hercules*
TPT 5: **Heavy** 2 C-17A *Globemaster* III; **Medium** 3 L-100-30
TRG 14: 6 EMB-312 *Tucano**; 8 *Hawk* Mk64* (10 EMB-312 *Tucano** in store)
HELICOPTERS
ATK 16 AH-64D *Apache*
MRH 13 SA342 *Gazelle* with HOT
TPT 19: **Heavy** 6+ H225M; **Medium** 13: 3 AS532 *Cougar*;
7 SA330 *Puma*; 3 S-92A (SAR/VIP)
AIR-LAUNCHED MISSILES
AAM • IR AIM-9L *Sidewinder*; R-550 *Magic*; **SARH**
AIM-7F *Sparrow*; **ARH** AIM-120C7 AMRAAM
ASM AGM-65G *Maverick*; AGM-114K *Hellfire*; HOT
AShM AGM-84D *Harpoon* Block IC

Air Defence Command

FORCES BY ROLE
AIR DEFENCE
1 SAM bde (7 SAM bty with M902 *Patriot* PAC-3)
1 SAM bde (6 SAM bty with *Skyguard*/*Aspide*)
EQUIPMENT BY TYPE
AIR DEFENCE
SAM 47
Long-range 35 M902 *Patriot* PAC-3
Short-range 12 *Aspide* with *Skyguard*
GUNS • TOWED 35mm 12+ Oerlikon GDF

Emiri Guard 1,500

FORCES BY ROLE
MANOEUVRE
Other
1 (Emiri) gd bde

Gendarmerie & Paramilitary ε7,100 active

National Guard ε6,600 active

FORCES BY ROLE
SPECIAL FORCES
1 SF bn
MANOEUVRE
Reconnaissance
1 armd car bn
Other
3 security bn
COMBAT SUPPORT
1 MP bn

EQUIPMENT BY TYPE
ARMOURED FIGHTING VEHICLES
RECCE 20 VBL
IFV ε150 *Pandur* (incl variants)
APC 67+
APC (W) 27+: 5+ *Desert Chameleon*; 22 S600 (incl variants)
PPV 40 Otokar ISV
AUV 120 *Sherpa Light Scout*
ENGINEERING & MAINTENANCE VEHICLES
ARV *Pandur*
HELICOPTERS
TPT • Heavy 3 H225M

Coast Guard 500

EQUIPMENT BY TYPE
PATROL AND COASTAL COMBATANTS 32
PBF 12 *Manta*
PB 20: 3 *Al Shaheed*; 4 *Inttisar* (Austal 31.5m); 3 *Kassir*
(Austal 22m); 10 *Subahi*
AMPHIBIOUS • LANDING CRAFT
LCU 4: 2 *Al Tahaddy*; 1 *Saffar*; 1 other
LOGISTICS AND SUPPORT • AG 1 *Sawahil*

FOREIGN FORCES

Canada *Operation Inherent Resolve* (*Impact*) 200

Italy *Operation Inherent Resolve* (*Prima Parthica*) 300; 4
Typhoon; 1 MQ-9A *Reaper*; 1 C-27J Spartan; 1 KC-767A;
1 SAM bty with SAMP/T

United Kingdom *Operation Inherent Resolve* (*Shader*) 50;
1 CISR UAV sqn with 8 MQ-9A *Reaper*

United States Central Command: 10,000; 1 ARNG armd
bn; 1 ARNG (cbt avn) hel bde; 1 spt bde; 1 CISR UAV sqn
with MQ-9A *Reaper*; 1 (APS) armd bde eqpt set; 1 (APS)
inf bde eqpt set

Lebanon LBN

Lebanese Pound LBP		2021	2022	2023
GDP [a]	LBP	n.k	n.k	
	USD	n.k	n.k	
per capita	USD	n.k	n.k	
Growth	%	n.k	n.k	
Inflation	%	n.k	n.k	
Def bdgt [b]	LBP	n.k	n.k	
	USD	n.k	n.k	
FMA (US)	USD	120m	160m	150m
USD1=LBP		n.k	n.k	

[a] No IMF economic data available for Lebanon from 2021

[b] No defence budget published since 2020

Real-terms defence budget trend (USDbn, constant 2015)

Population	5,296,814

Age	0–14	15–19	20–24	25–29	30–64	65 plus
Male	10.0%	3.7%	3.6%	3.8%	25.1%	3.7%
Female	9.5%	3.6%	3.5%	3.6%	24.9%	5.0%

Capabilities

The ability of the Lebanese Armed Forces (LAF) to fulfil its missions remains under strain from Hizbullah's position in national politics, from the spillover effects of the Syrian conflict, the severe and prolonged economic depression and crisis in governance. The latter was highlighted and indeed exacerbated by the port explosion in Beirut on 4 August 2020. The LAF is reliant on outside assistance to continue its operations. In August 2021, the UN Security Council ordered the UNIFIL peacekeeping mission to provide the LAF with food, fuel and medicine, and a number of governments have provided other assistance. The economic crisis has left the government struggling to pay wages to troops without foreign assistance, while inflation has eroded the value of salaries. This has likely hampered plans, since 2017, for the LAF to gradually boost its presence in the south of the country and has led to fears that troops may have to supplement their wages with other employment. Training and operational assistance have traditionally been provided by the US, as well as by France, Germany, Italy and the UK. Reconstruction has started at the Beirut naval base with German funding. The base was damaged in the 2020 port explosion. LAF operations several years ago against ISIS demonstrated an improved capability, but how much of this remains is unclear. The LAF has no requirement and minimal capability for extraterritorial deployment. It remains dependent on foreign support to replace and modernise its ageing equipment inventory. Barring limited organic maintenance facilities, Lebanon has no significant domestic defence industry.

ACTIVE 60,000 (Army 56,600 Navy 1,800 Air 1,600)

Gendarmerie & Paramilitary 20,000

ORGANISATIONS BY SERVICE

Army 56,600

FORCES BY ROLE

5 regional comd (Beirut, Bekaa Valley, Mount Lebanon, North, South)

SPECIAL FORCES

1 cdo regt

MANOEUVRE

Armoured

1 armd regt

Mechanised

11 mech inf bde

Air Manoeuvre

1 AB regt

Amphibious

1 mne cdo regt

Other

1 Presidential Guard bde

6 intervention regt 4 border sy regt

COMBAT SUPPORT

2 arty regt

1 cbt spt bde (1 engr regt, 1 AT regt, 1 sigs regt; 1 log bn)

1 MP gp

COMBAT SERVICE SUPPORT

1 log bde

1 med gp

1 construction regt

EQUIPMENT BY TYPE

MBT 334: 92 M48A1/A5; 10 M60A2; 185 T-54; 47 T-55

RECCE 55 AML

IFV 56: 24 AIFV-B-C25; 32 M2A2 *Bradley*

APC 1,378

APC (T) 1,274 M113A1/A2 (incl variants)

APC (W) 96: 86 VAB VCT; 10 VBPT-MR *Guarani*

PPV 8 *Maxxpro*

ENGINEERING & MAINTENANCE VEHICLES

ARV 3 M88A1; M113 ARV; T-54/55 ARV (reported)

VLB MTU-72 reported

MW *Bozena*

ARTILLERY 641

SP 155mm 12 M109A2

TOWED 313: **105mm** 13 M101A1; **122mm** 35: 9 D-30; 26 M-30; **130mm** 15 M-46; **155mm** 250: 18 M114A1; 218 M198; 14 Model-50

MRL 122mm 11 BM-21

MOR 305: **81mm** 134; **82mm** 112; **120mm** 59: 29 Brandt; 30 M120

ANTI-TANK/ANTI-INFRASTRUCTURE

MSL

SP 35 VAB with HOT

MANPATS *Milan*; TOW

RCL 106mm 113 M40A1

UNINHABITED AERIAL VEHICLES

ISR • Medium 8 *Mohajer* 4

AIR DEFENCE

SAM • Point-defence 9K32 *Strela*-2M (RS-SA-7B *Grail*)‡

GUNS • TOWED 77: **20mm** 20; **23mm** 57 ZU-23-2

Navy 1,800

EQUIPMENT BY TYPE
PATROL AND COASTAL COMBATANTS 13
  PCC 1 *Trablous*
  PBF 1
  PB 11: 1 *Aamchit* (ex-GER *Bremen*); 1 *Al Kalamoun* (ex-FRA *Avel Gwarlarn*); 7 *Tripoli* (ex-UK *Attacker/Tracker* Mk 2); 1 *Naquora* (ex-GER *Bremen*); 1 *Tabarja* (ex-GER *Bergen*)
AMPHIBIOUS • LANDING CRAFT
  LCT 2 *Sour* (ex-FRA EDIC – capacity 8 APC; 96 troops)

Air Force 1,600

4 air bases

FORCES BY ROLE
GROUND ATTACK
  1 sqn with Cessna AC-208 *Combat Caravan**
  1 sqn with EMB-314 *Super Tucano**
ATTACK HELICOPTER
  1 sqn with SA342L *Gazelle*
TRANSPORT HELICOPTER
  4 sqn with Bell 205 (UH-1H *Iroquois/Huey* II)
  1 sqn with SA330/IAR330SM *Puma*
  1 trg sqn with R-44 *Raven* II
EQUIPMENT BY TYPE
AIRCRAFT 9 combat capable
  ISR 3 Cessna AC-208 *Combat Caravan**
  TRG 9: 3 *Bulldog*; 6 EMB-314 *Super Tucano**
HELICOPTERS
  MRH 14: 1 AW139; 5 MD530F+; 8 SA342L *Gazelle* (5 SA342L *Gazelle*; 5 SA316 *Alouette* III; 1 SA318 *Alouette* II all non-operational)
  TPT 41: **Medium** 13: 3 S-61N (fire-fighting); 10 SA330/IAR330 *Puma*; **Light** 28: 18 Bell 205 (UH-1H *Iroquois*); 6 Bell 205 (UH-1H *Huey* II); 4 R-44 *Raven* II (basic trg) (11 Bell 205; 7 Bell 212 all non-operational)
AIR LAUNCHED MISSILES
  ASM AGM-114 *Hellfire*; AGR-20A APKWS

Gendarmerie & Paramilitary ε20,000 active

Internal Security Force ε20,000

Ministry of Interior
FORCES BY ROLE
Other Combat Forces
  1 (police) judicial unit
  1 regional sy coy
  1 (Beirut Gendarmerie) sy coy
EQUIPMENT BY TYPE
ARMOURED FIGHTING VEHICLES
  APC • APC (W) 60 V-200 *Chaimite*

Customs

EQUIPMENT BY TYPE
PATROL AND COASTAL COMBATANTS 7
  PB 7: 5 *Aztec*; 2 *Tracker*

FOREIGN FORCES

Unless specified, figures refer to UNTSO and represent total numbers for the mission

Argentina 3 • UNIFIL 2
Armenia UNIFIL 31
Australia 11
Austria 4 • UNIFIL 171: 1 log coy
Bangladesh UNIFIL 118: 1 FSGM
Belarus UNIFIL 5
Belgium 1
Bhutan 5
Brazil UNIFIL 9
Brunei UNIFIL 30
Cambodia UNIFIL 180: 1 EOD coy
Canada 4 (*Operation Jade*)
Chile 3
China, People's Republic of 5 • UNIFIL 419: 2 engr coy; 1 med coy
Colombia UNIFIL 1
Croatia UNIFIL 1
Cyprus UNIFIL 2
Denmark 10
El Salvador UNIFIL 52: 1 inf pl
Estonia 3 • UNIFIL 1
Fiji 2 • UNIFIL 1
Finland 14 • UNIFIL 161; 1 inf coy
France UNIFIL 571: 1 mech inf bn(-); VBL; VBCI; VAB; *Mistral*
Germany UNIFIL 82: 1 FSGM
Ghana UNIFIL 874: 1 recce coy; 1 mech inf bn
Greece UNIFIL 109: 1 FFGHM
Guatemala UNIFIL 2
Hungary UNIFIL 16
India 2 • UNIFIL 895: 1 inf bn; 1 med coy
Indonesia UNIFIL 1,106: 1 mech inf bn; 1 MP coy; 1 FSGM
Ireland 12 • UNIFIL 338: 1 mech inf bn(-)
Italy MIBIL 160 • UNIFIL 868: 1 mech bde HQ; 1 mech inf bn; 1 MP coy; 1 sigs coy; 1 hel bn
Kazakhstan UNIFIL 9
Kenya UNIFIL 3
Korea, Republic of UNIFIL 254: 1 mech inf BG HQ; 1 mech inf coy; 1 inf coy; 1 log coy
Latvia 1
Macedonia, North UNIFIL 3
Malaysia UNIFIL 830: 1 mech inf bn(-); 1 sigs coy; 1 log coy; 1 maint coy; 1 med coy
Malta UNIFIL 9
Moldova UNIFIL 4
Nepal 3 • UNIFIL 872: 1 mech inf bn
Netherlands 12 • UNIFIL 1
New Zealand 8
Nigeria UNIFIL 2
Norway 13
Peru UNIFIL 1
Poland 4 • UNIFIL 193; 1 mech inf coy
Qatar UNIFIL 1
Russia 4
Serbia 1 • UNIFIL 177; 1 mech inf coy
Sierra Leone UNIFIL 3

340 THE MILITARY BALANCE 2023

Slovakia 2
Slovenia 3 • UNIFIL 1
Spain UNIFIL 669: 1 mech bde HQ; 1 mech inf bn(-); 1 engr coy; 1 sigs coy; 1 log coy
Sri Lanka UNIFIL 126: 1 inf coy
Sweden 7
Switzerland 11
Tanzania UNIFIL 124: 1 MP coy
Turkey UNIFIL 110: 1 FFGHM
United States 2
Uruguay UNIFIL 1
Zambia 1 • UNIFIL 2

Libya LBY

Libyan Dinar LYD		2021	2022	2023
GDP	LYD	176bn	195bn	
	USD	39.0bn	40.8bn	
per capita	USD	5,813	6,026	
Growth	%	28.3	-18.5	
Inflation	%	2.8	5.5	
Def bdgt	LYD	n.k.	n.k.	
	USD	n.k.	n.k.	
USD1=LYD		4.51	4.78	

Population	7,137,931

Age	0–14	15–19	20–24	25–29	30–64	65 plus
Male	17.0%	4.2%	3.7%	3.4%	20.9%	1.9%
Female	16.3%	4.0%	3.5%	3.3%	19.5%	2.3%

Capabilities

The formation of a new Government of National Unity, in March 2021, unified the Tripoli-based Government of National Accord (GNA) and the Tobruk-based House of Representatives. A UN-backed ceasefire, agreed in October 2020, is intended to see the deployment of monitors, while a follow-up resolution agreed in April 2021 called for all foreign forces and mercenaries to withdraw. Libyan elections, originally scheduled for December 2021, have been postponed due to the lack of consensus between the two factions on an electoral constitutional framework. Despite President Mohamed Al-Menfi's efforts to unify government institutions and the military forces of the GNA and the Libyan Arab Armed Forces (LAAF), controlled by General Khalifa Haftar, the situation on the ground remains unstable. Forces affiliated to both have relatively low levels of training though the presence in these formations of units from the former Gadhafi-era army has over the years bolstered their military capability. The GNA-affiliated forces have since 2016 benefited from several military advisory and training programmes, including EUNAVFOR–MED maritime-security training for the Libyan Navy and Coast Guard. EUNAVFOR Operation Irini continues to monitor the implementation of the UN arms embargo, and in 2022 again seized military materiel bound for Libya. Foreign-military involvement increased in 2020. Both the GNA and the LAAF continue to be supported by foreign military forces, private military contractors and mercenaries. There are also reports of Syrian combatants paid to fight for both sides and of continued activity by Russia's Wagner Group. LAAF troops have combat experience from fighting ISIS in the eastern coastal region and have allegedly received training and combat support from

external actors in the region. Equipment is mainly of Russian or Soviet origin, including items from the former Libyan armed forces, and suffers from varying degrees of obsolescence. The country has no domestic defence-industrial capability.

Forces loyal to the Government of National Unity
(Tripoli-based)

ACTIVE n.k.

ORGANISATIONS BY SERVICE

Ground Forces n.k.

EQUIPMENT BY TYPE
ARMOURED FIGHTING VEHICLES
  MBT T-55; T-72
  IFV BMP-2
  APC
    APC (T) ACV-AAPC; Steyr 4K-7FA
    APC (W) *Mbombe-6*
    PPV *Al-Wahsh*; *Kirpi-2*; *Vuran*
  AUV Lenco *Bearcat* G3; Nimr *Ajban*
ENGINEERING & MAINTENANCE VEHICLES
  ARV *Centurion* 105 AVRE
ANTI-TANK/ANTI-INFRASTRUCTURE • MSL
  SP 9P157-2 *Khrizantema-S* (RS-AT-15 *Springer*)
  MANPATS 9K115 *Metis* (RS-AT-7 *Saxhorn*)
ARTILLERY
  SP 155mm *Palmaria*
  TOWED 122mm D-30
AIR DEFENCE
  SAM • Point-defence QW-18 (CH-SA-11)
  GUNS • SP 14.5mm ZPU-2 (on tch); **23mm** ZU-23-2 (on tch)

Navy n.k.

A number of intact naval vessels remain in Tripoli, although serviceability is questionable

EQUIPMENT BY TYPE
PATROL AND COASTAL COMBATANTS 3+
  CORVETTES • FSGM (1 *Al Hani* (ex-FSU Project 1159 (*Koni*)) in Malta for refit since 2013 with 2 twin lnchr with P-22 (RS-SS-N-2C *Styx*) AShM, 1 twin lnchr with 4K33 *Osa*-M (RS-SA-N-4 *Gecko*) SAM, 2 twin 406mm ASTT, 1 RBU 6000 *Smerch* 2 A/S mor, 2 AK230 CIWS, 2 twin 76mm gun)
  PBFG 1 *Sharaba* (FRA *Combattante* II) with 4 single lnchr with *Otomat* Mk2 AShM, 1 76mm gun†
  PB 2+ PV30
AMPHIBIOUS
  LANDING SHIPS • LST 1 *Ibn Harissa* (capacity 1 hel; 11 MBT; 240 troops)
LOGISTICS AND SUPPORT 2
  AFD 1
  ARS 1 *Al Munjed* (YUG *Spasilac*)†

Air Force n.k.

EQUIPMENT BY TYPE
AIRCRAFT 3+ combat capable
  FGA 2 MiG-23BN
  ATK 1 J-21 *Jastreb*†
  TRG 9+: 3 G-2 *Galeb**; ε5 L-39ZO*; 1+ SF-260ML*
HELICOPTERS
  ATK Mi-24 *Hind*
  TPT • Medium Mi-17 *Hip*
AIR-LAUNCHED MISSILES • AAM • IR R-3 (RS-AA-2 *Atoll*)‡; R-60 (RS-AA-8 *Aphid*); R-24 (RS-AA-7 *Apex*)

Paramilitary n.k.

Coast Guard n.k.

EQUIPMENT BY TYPE
PATROL AND COASTAL COMBATANTS 10
  PCC 1 Damen Stan 2909 with 1 sextuple 122mm MRL
  PBF 6: 4 *Bigliani*; 2 *Fezzan* (ex-ITA *Corrubia*)
  PB 3: 1 *Burdi* (Damen Stan 1605); 1 *Hamelin*; 1 *Ikrimah* (FRA RPB 20)

FOREIGN FORCES

Italy MIASIT 90
Nepal UNSMIL 235; 2 sy coy
Turkey ε500; ACV-AAPC; *Kirpi*; 1 arty unit with T-155 *Firtina*; 1 AD unit with MIM-23B *Hawk*; *Korkut*; GDF-003; 1 CISR UAV unit with *Bayraktar TB2*
United Kingdom UNSMIL 1
United States UNSMIL 1

TERRITORY WHERE THE RECOGNISED AUTHORITY DOES NOT EXERCISE EFFECTIVE CONTROL

Data here represents the de facto situation. This does not imply international recognition

ACTIVE n.k.

ORGANISATIONS BY SERVICE

Libyan Arab Armed Forces n.k.

EQUIPMENT BY TYPE
ARMOURED FIGHTING VEHICLES
  MBT T-55; T-62; T-72
  RECCE BRDM-2; EE-9 *Cascavel*
  IFV BMP-1; *Ratel*-20
  APC
    APC (T) M113
    APC (W) *Al-Mared*; BTR-60PB; *Mbombe*-6; Nimr *Jais*; *Puma*
    PPV *Al-Wahsh*; *Caiman*; Streit *Spartan*; Streit *Typhoon*; *Vuran*; Titan-DS
  AUV *Panthera* T6; *Panthera* F9; *Terrier* LT-79

ANTI-TANK/ANTI-INFRASTRUCTURE
  MSL
    SP 9P157-2 *Khrizantema*-S (status unknown)
    MANPATS 9K11 *Malyutka* (RS-AT-3 *Sagger*); 9K111 *Fagot* (RS-AT-4 *Spigot*); 9K111-1 *Konkurs* (RS-AT-5 *Spandrel*); 9K135 *Kornet* (RS-AT-14 *Spriggan*); *Milan*
  RCL: 106mm M40A1; **84mm** *Carl Gustaf*
ARTILLERY
  SP 122mm 2S1 *Gvodzika*; **155mm** G5
  TOWED 122mm D-30
  MRL 107mm Type-63; **122mm** BM-21 *Grad*
  MOR M106
AIR DEFENCE
  SAM
    Short-range 2K12 *Kvadrat* (RS-SA-6 *Gainful*)
    Point-defence 9K338 *Igla*-S (RS-SA-24 *Grinch*)
  GUNS • SP 14.5mm ZPU-2 (on tch); **23mm** ZSU-23-4 *Shilka*; ZU-23-2 (on tch)

Navy n.k.

EQUIPMENT BY TYPE
PATROL AND COASTAL COMBATANTS 7+
  PB: 7+: 2 *Burdi* (Damen Stan 1605); 1 *Burdi* (Damen Stan 1605) with 1 73mm gun; 2 *Ikrimah* (FRA RPB20); 1 *Hamelin*; 1+ PV30
LOGISTICS AND SUPPORT • AFD 1

Air Force n.k.

EQUIPMENT BY TYPE
AIRCRAFT 49 combat capable
  FTR 14: 2 MiG-23ML *Flogger* G; up to 12 MiG-29 *Fulcrum* (operator uncertain)
  FGA 13: ε10 MiG-21MF *Fishbed*; 1 *Mirage* F-1AD; 1 *Mirage* F-1ED; 1 Su-22UM3 *Fitter* G
  ATK up to 4 Su-24M *Fencer* D (operator uncertain)
  TRG 19: ε10 L-39ZO *Albatros**; 1+ MiG-21UM *Mongol* B; 8 SF-260ML*
HELICOPTERS
  ATK Mi-24/35 *Hind*
  TPT • Medium 3: up to 3 H215 (AS332L) *Super Puma*; Mi-8/Mi-17 *Hip*
AIR-LAUNCHED MISSILES • AAM • IR R-3 (RS-AA-2 *Atoll*)‡; R-27T (RS-AA-10B *Alamo*); R-60 (RS-AA-8 *Aphid*); R-73 (RS-AA-11A *Archer*)

FOREIGN FORCES

Wagner Group 2,000

Mauritania MRT

Mauritanian Ouguiya MRU		2021	2022	2023
GDP	MRU	360bn	366bn	
	USD	9.89bn	10.1bn	
per capita	USD	2,333	2,328	
Growth	%	2.4	4.0	
Inflation	%	3.8	7.1	
Def bdgt	MRU	7.77bn	8.33bn	
	USD	213m	229m	
USD1=MRU		36.44	36.30	

Real-terms defence budget trend (USDm, constant 2015)

Population	4,161,925

Age	0–14	15–19	20–24	25–29	30–64	65 plus
Male	18.3%	5.1%	4.5%	3.9%	14.5%	1.8%
Female	18.2%	5.2%	4.7%	4.3%	17.0%	2.4%

Capabilities

The country's small and modestly equipped armed forces are tasked with maintaining territorial integrity and internal security. In light of the regional threat from extremist Islamist groups, border security is also a key role for the armed forces, which are accustomed to counter-insurgency operations in the desert. In early 2021, the cabinet approved a draft decree establishing a defence area along the northern border to counter incursions by the Polisario Front. This followed the group's closure of a border crossing for several weeks in late 2020. The country is a member of the G5 Sahel group and in late 2021 the armed forces of Mauritania and Senegal signed an agreement to jointly patrol offshore gas fields. Both countries have also conducted joint riverine patrols along their border. Mauritania's armed forces take part in the *Flintlock* US-led special-operations exercise and also train with France's armed forces. Deployment capabilities are limited, but the armed forces have demonstrated mobility and sustainment in desert regions. A new naval base has been constructed by a Chinese firm in the south, possibly designed to enable improved protection of offshore gas fields. Mauritania has a limited and ageing equipment inventory, but the navy has recently received some new patrol vessels from China. Despite recent acquisitions, including small ISR aircraft, aviation resources are insufficient considering the country's size. Naval equipment is geared toward coastal-surveillance missions and China's donation of a landing ship has helped establish a basic sealift capability. There is no domestic defence industry.

ACTIVE 15,850 (Army 15,000 Navy 600 Air 250)
Gendarmerie & Paramilitary 5,000
Conscript liability 24 months

ORGANISATIONS BY SERVICE

Army 15,000
FORCES BY ROLE
6 mil regions

MANOEUVRE
Reconnaissance
1 armd recce bn
Armoured
1 armd bn
Light
7 mot inf bn
8 (garrison) inf bn
Air Manoeuvre
1 cdo/para bn
Other
2 (camel corps) bn
1 gd bn
COMBAT SUPPORT
3 arty bn
4 ADA bty
1 engr coy
EQUIPMENT BY TYPE
ARMOURED FIGHTING VEHICLES
MBT 35 T-54/T-55
RECCE 70: 20 AML-60; 40 AML-90; 10 *Saladin*
APC • APC (W) 32: 5 FV603 *Saracen*; 7 *Bastion* APC; ε20 Panhard M3
AUV 12 *Cobra*
ENGINEERING & MAINTENANCE VEHICLES
ARV T-54/55 ARV reported
ANTI-TANK/ANTI-INFRASTRUCTURE
MSL • MANPATS *Milan*
RCL • **106mm** ε90 M40A1
ARTILLERY 180
TOWED 80: **105mm** 36 HM-2/M101A1; **122mm** 44: 20 D-30; 24 D-74
MRL 10: **107mm** 4 Type-63; **122mm** 6 Type-81
MOR 90: **81mm** 60; **120mm** 30 Brandt
AIR DEFENCE
SAM • **Point-defence** ε4 9K31 *Strela*-1 (RS-SA-9 *Gaskin*) (reported); 9K32 *Strela*-2 (RS-SA-7 *Grail*)‡
GUNS • TOWED 82: **14.5mm** 28: 16 ZPU-2; 12 ZPU-4; **23mm** 20 ZU-23-2; **37mm** 10 M-1939; **57mm** 12 S-60; **100mm** 12 KS-19

Navy ε600
EQUIPMENT BY TYPE
PATROL AND COASTAL COMBATANTS 17
PCO 1 *Voum-Legleita*
PCC 7: 1 *Abourbekr Ben Amer* (FRA OPV 54); 1 *Arguin*; 2 *Conejera*; 1 *Limam El Hidrami* (PRC); 2 *Timbédra* (PRC *Huangpu* mod)
PB 9: 1 *El Nasr*† (FRA *Patra*); 4 *Mandovi*; 2 *Saeta*-12; 2 *Megsem Bakkar* (FRA RPB20 – for SAR duties)
AMPHIBIOUS • LANDING SHIPS 1
LSM 1 *Nimlane* (PRC)

Fusiliers Marins
FORCES BY ROLE
MANOEUVRE
Amphibious
1 mne unit

Air Force 250

EQUIPMENT BY TYPE
AIRCRAFT 2 combat capable
　ISR 2 Cessna 208B *Grand Caravan*
　TPT 14: **Light** 13: 1 Beech 350 *King Air*; 2 BN-2 *Defender*;
　1 C-212; 2 CN235; 3 G1; 2 PA-31T *Cheyenne* II; 2 Y-12(II);
　PAX 1 BT-67 (with sensor turret)
　TRG 9: 3 EMB-312 *Tucano*; 2 EMB-314 *Super Tucano**; 4
　SF-260E
HELICOPTERS
　MRH 3: 1 SA313B *Alouette* II; 2 Z-9
　TPT • **Light** 2 AW109

Gendarmerie & Paramilitary ε5,000 active

Gendarmerie ε3,000
Ministry of Interior
FORCES BY ROLE
MANOEUVRE
　Other
　　6 regional sy coy
EQUIPMENT BY TYPE
PATROL AND COASTAL COMBATANTS • PB 2
Rodman 55M

National Guard 2,000
Ministry of Interior

Customs
EQUIPMENT BY TYPE
PATROL AND COASTAL COMBATANTS • PB 2:
1 *Dah Ould Bah* (FRA *Amgram* 14); 1 *Yaboub Ould Rajel* (FRA RPB18)

DEPLOYMENT

CENTRAL AFRICAN REPUBLIC: UN • MINUSCA 464; 1 inf bn(-)
MALI: UN • MINUSMA 7
SOMALIA: UN • UNSOS 1

Morocco MOR

Moroccan Dirham MAD		2021	2022	2023
GDP	MAD	1.28tr	1.37tr	
	USD	143bn	143bn	
per capita	USD	3,934	3,896	
Growth	%	7.9	0.8	
Inflation	%	1.4	6.2	
Def bdgt [a]	MAD	58.6bn	61.7bn	63.5bn
	USD	6.52bn	6.41bn	
FMA (US)	USD	10m	10m	10m
USD1=MAD		8.99	9.62	

[a] Includes autonomous defence spending (SEGMA) and Treasury funding for "Acquisitions and Repair of Equipment for Royal Armed Forces"

Real-terms defence budget trend (USDbn, constant 2015)

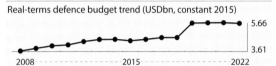

Population	36,738,229					
Age	0–14	15–19	20–24	25–29	30–64	65 plus
Male	13.4%	4.3%	3.9%	3.8%	20.8%	3.8%
Female	12.9%	4.2%	3.9%	3.8%	21.3%	4.0%

Capabilities

Regional security challenges are a key concern for Morocco's armed forces. A 30-year ceasefire between Morocco and the Polisario Front ended in late 2020 and the UN has reported that hostilities have resumed, albeit at a low-level. Morocco maintains defence ties with France and the US, receiving military training and equipment from both. However, although the US Trump administration recognised Moroccan claims to Western Sahara, the Biden administration has come under pressure in Congress to reverse the policy and to find an alternative location for the *African Lion* exercises, which in 2022 saw exercise activity in Ghana, Morocco, Senegal, and Tunisia. There is also close cooperation with NATO, and in 2016 Morocco was granted access to the Alliance's Interoperability Platform in order to strengthen the defence and security sectors and bring the armed forces up to NATO standards. Defence ties have developed with Israel, and Morocco is reportedly procuring an Israeli-developed air defence system. In 2017, Morocco rejoined the African Union. The armed forces have gained experience from UN peacekeeping deployments and from multinational exercises. Conscription was reintroduced in early 2019. The armed forces have some capacity to deploy independently within the region and on UN peacekeeping missions in sub-Saharan Africa, although they lack heavy sealift and airlift capabilities. Morocco has also deployed overseas in a combat role, contributing F-16 aircraft to the Saudi-led coalition intervention in Yemen from 2015 to early 2019. The inventory primarily comprises ageing French and US equipment, though there are plans to re-equip all the services and to invest significantly in the navy. Morocco operates two Earth-observation satellites, meeting some surveillance requirements. Morocco relies on imports and donations for major defence equipment. However, its relative stability has attracted Western defence companies, such as Airbus, Safran and Thales, to establish aerospace manufacturing and servicing facilities in the country.

344   THE MILITARY BALANCE 2023

ACTIVE 195,800 (Army 175,000 Navy 7,800 Air 13,000) **Gendarmerie & Paramilitary 50,000**
Conscript liability 12 months for men aged 19–25

RESERVE 150,000 (Army 150,000)
Reserve obligation to age 50

ORGANISATIONS BY SERVICE

Space
EQUIPMENT BY TYPE
SATELLITES • ISR 2 *Mohammed* VI

Army 175,000
FORCES BY ROLE
2 comd (Northern Zone, Southern Zone)
MANOEUVRE
  Armoured
  1 armd bde
  11 armd bn
  Mechanised
  3 mech inf bde
  Mechanised/Light
  8 mech/mot inf regt (2–3 bn)
  Light
  1 lt sy bde
  3 (camel corps) mot inf bn
  35 lt inf bn
  4 cdo unit
  Air Manoeuvre
  2 para bde
  2 AB bn
  Mountain
  1 mtn inf bn
COMBAT SUPPORT
  11 arty bn
  7 engr bn
AIR DEFENCE
  2 AD gp

Royal Guard 1,500
FORCES BY ROLE
MANOEUVRE
  Other
  1 gd bn
  2 cav sqn
EQUIPMENT BY TYPE
ARMOURED FIGHTING VEHICLES
  MBT 656: 222 M1A1SA *Abrams*; 220 M60A1 *Patton*; 120 M60A3 *Patton*; 40 T-72B; 54 Type-90-II (MBT-2000); (ε200 M48A5 *Patton* & ε60 T-72B in store)
  LT TK 116: 5 AMX-13; 111 SK-105 *Kuerassier*
  ASLT 80 AMX-10RC
  RECCE 284: 38 AML-60-7; 190 AML-90; 40 EBR-75; 16 *Eland*
  IFV 238: 10 AMX-10P; 30 *Ratel* Mk3-20; 30 *Ratel* Mk3-90; 45 VAB VCI; 123 YPR-765

  APC 1,225
    APC (T) 905: 400 M113A1/A2; 419 M113A3; 86 M577A2 (CP)
    APC (W) 320 VAB VTT
  AUV 36 *Sherpa Light Scout*
ENGINEERING & MAINTENANCE VEHICLES
  ARV 85+: 10 *Greif*; 55 M88A1; M578; 20 VAB-ECH
ANTI-TANK/ANTI-INFRASTRUCTURE
  MSL
    SP 80 M901
    MANPATS 9K11 *Malyutka* (RS-AT-3 *Sagger*); HJ-8L; M47 *Dragon*; Milan; TOW
  RCL 106mm 350 M40A1
  GUNS • SP 36: **90mm** 28 M56; **100mm** 8 SU-100
ARTILLERY 2,321
  SP 359: **105mm** 5 AMX Mk 61; **155mm** 294: ε4 CAESAR; ε130 M109A1/A1B/A2/A3/A4; 70 M109A5; 90 Mk F3; **203mm** 60 M110
  TOWED 118: **105mm** 50: 30 L118 Light Gun; 20 M101; **130mm** 18 M-46; **155mm** 50: 30 FH-70; 20 M114
  MRL 47: **122mm** 35 BM-21 *Grad*; **300mm** 12+ PHL-03
  MOR 1,797: **81mm** 1,100 Expal model LN; **SP 107mm** 36 M106A2; **120mm** 550 Brandt; **SP 120mm** 110: 20 (VAB APC); 91 M1064A3
UNINHABITED AERIAL VEHICLES
  ISR • Medium R4E-50 *Skyeye*
AIR DEFENCE
  SAM 55+
    Medium-range 18 *Tianlong*-50
    Short-range 6+: DK-9 (CH-SA-5); ε6 VL-MICA (reported)
    Point-defence 37+: 37 M48 *Chaparral*; 9K38 *Igla* (RS-SA-18 *Grouse*)
  SPAAGM 30mm 12 2K22M *Tunguska*-M (RS-SA-19 *Grison*)
  GUNS 390
    SP 20mm 60 M163 *Vulcan*
    TOWED 330: **14.5mm** 200: 150–180 ZPU-2; 20 ZPU-4; **20mm** 40 M167 *Vulcan*; **23mm** 75–90 ZU-23-2; **35mm** some PG-99

Navy 7,800 (incl 1,500 Marines)
EQUIPMENT BY TYPE
PRINCIPAL SURFACE COMBATANTS • FRIGATES 4
  FFGHM 2:
    1 *Mohammed* VI (FRA FREMM) with 2 quad lnchr with MM40 *Exocet* Block 3 AShM, 2 8-cell *Sylver* A43 VLS with *Aster* 15 SAM, 2 triple 324mm ILAS-3 (B-515) ASTT with MU90 LWT, 1 76mm gun (capacity 1 AS565SA *Panther*)
    1 *Tarik ben Ziyad* (NLD SIGMA 10513) with 2 twin lnchr with MM40 *Exocet* Block 3 AShM, 1 12-cell CLA VLS with VL MICA SAM, 2 triple 324mm ILAS-3 (B-515) ASTT with MU90 LWT, 1 76mm gun (capacity 1 AS565SA *Panther*)
  FFGH 2 *Mohammed* V (FRA *Floreal*) with 2 single lnchr with MM38 *Exocet* AShM, 1 76mm gun (fitted for but not with *Simbad* SAM) (capacity 1 AS565SA *Panther*)
PATROL AND COASTAL COMBATANTS 52
  CORVETTES 3

FSGHM 2 *Sultan Moulay Ismail* (NLD SIGMA 9813) with 2 twin lnchr with MM40 *Exocet* Block 2/3 AShM, 1 12-cell CLA VLS with VL MICA SAM, 2 triple 324mm ILAS-3 (B-515) ASTT with MU90 LWT, 1 76mm gun (capacity 1 AS565SA *Panther*)

FSM 1 *Lt Col Errhamani* (ESP *Descubierto*) with 1 octuple *Albatros* lnchr with *Aspide* SAM, 2 triple 324mm ASTT with Mk46 LWT, 1 76mm gun

PSO 1 *Bin an Zaran* (OPV 70) with 1 76mm gun

PCG 4 *Cdt El Khattabi* (ESP *Lazaga* 58m) with 4 single lnchr with MM38 *Exocet* AShM, 1 76mm gun

PCO 5 *Rais Bargach* (under control of fisheries dept)

PCC 12:
    4 *El Hahiq* (DNK *Osprey* 55, incl 2 with customs)
    6 *LV Rabhi* (ESP 58m B-200D)
    2 *Okba* (FRA PR-72) each with 1 76mm gun

PB 27: 6 *El Wacil* (FRA P-32); 10 VCSM (RPB 20); 10 Rodman 101; 1 other *(UK Bird)*

AMPHIBIOUS

LANDING SHIPS • LST 3 *Ben Aicha* (FRA *Champlain* BATRAL) with 1 hel landing platform (capacity 7 tanks; 140 troops)

LANDING CRAFT 2:
    LCT 1 *Sidi Ifni*
    LCM 1 CTM (FRA CTM-5)

LOGISTICS AND SUPPORT 9

AG 1 Damen 3011
AGHS 1 *Dar Al Beida* (FRA BHO2M)
AGOR 1 *Abou Barakat Albarbari*† (ex-US *Robert D. Conrad*)
AGS 1 Damen Stan Tender 1504
AK 2
AX 1 *Essaouira*
AXS 2

Marines 1,500

FORCES BY ROLE
MANOEUVRE
  Amphibious
    2 naval inf bn

Naval Aviation

EQUIPMENT BY TYPE
AIRCRAFT • MP 2 Beech 350ER *King Air*
HELICOPTERS • ASW/ASUW 3 AS565SA *Panther*

Air Force 13,000

FORCES BY ROLE
FIGHTER/GROUND ATTACK
  2 sqn with F-5E/F-5F *Tiger* II
  3 sqn with F-16C/D *Fighting Falcon*
  1 sqn with *Mirage* F-1C (F-1CH)
  1 sqn with *Mirage* F-1E (F-1EH)
ELECTRONIC WARFARE
  1 sqn with EC-130H *Hercules*; *Falcon* 20 (ELINT)
MARITIME PATROL
  1 flt with Do-28
TANKER/TRANSPORT
  1 sqn with C-130/KC-130H *Hercules*
TRANSPORT
  1 sqn with CN235

1 VIP sqn with B-737BBJ; Beech 200/300 *King Air*; *Falcon* 50; Gulfstream II/III/V-SP/G550

TRAINING
  1 sqn with *Alpha Jet**
  1 sqn T-6C
ATTACK HELICOPTER
  1 sqn with SA342L *Gazelle* (some with HOT)
TRANSPORT HELICOPTER
  1 sqn with Bell 205A (AB-205A); Bell 206 *Jet Ranger* (AB-206); Bell 212 (AB-212)
  1 sqn with CH-47D *Chinook*
  1 sqn with SA330 *Puma*

EQUIPMENT BY TYPE
AIRCRAFT 90 combat capable
FTR 22: 19 F-5E *Tiger* II; 3 F-5F *Tiger* II
FGA 49: 15 F-16C *Fighting Falcon*; 8 F-16D *Fighting Falcon*; 15 *Mirage* F-1C (F-1CH); 11 *Mirage* F-1E (F-1EH)
ELINT 1 EC-130H *Hercules*
TKR/TPT 2 KC-130H *Hercules*
TPT 47: **Medium** 17: 4 C-27J *Spartan*; 13 C-130H *Hercules*; **Light** 19: 4 Beech 100 *King Air*; 2 Beech 200 *King Air*; 1 Beech 200C *King Air*; 2 Beech 300 *King Air*; 3 Beech 350 *King Air*; 5 CN235; 2 Do-28; **PAX** 11: 1 B-737BBJ; 2 *Falcon* 20; 2 *Falcon* 20 (ELINT); 1 *Falcon* 50 (VIP); 1 Gulfstream II (VIP); 1 Gulfstream III; 1 Gulfstream V-SP; 2 Gulfstream G550
TRG 80: 12 AS-202 *Bravo*; 19 *Alpha Jet**; 2 CAP-10; 24 T-6C *Texan*; 9 T-34C *Turbo Mentor*; 14 T-37B *Tweet*
HELICOPTERS
MRH 19 SA342L *Gazelle* (7 with HOT, 12 with cannon)
TPT 76: **Heavy** 10 CH-47D *Chinook*; **Medium** 24 SA330 *Puma*; **Light** 42: 24 Bell 205A (AB-205A); 11 Bell 206 *Jet Ranger* (AB-206); 3 Bell 212 (AB-212); 4 Bell 429
UNINHABITED AERIAL VEHICLES
CISR
  Heavy *Wing Loong* (reported)
  Medium *Bayraktar* TB2 (reported)
ISR • Heavy *Heron*
AIR-LAUNCHED MISSILES
AAM • IR AIM-9J *Sidewinder*; R-550 *Magic*; *Mica* IR; **IIR** AIM-9X *Sidewinder* II; **ARH** AIM-120C7 AMRAAM; *Mica* RF
ASM AASM; AGM-65 *Maverick*; HOT
ARM AGM-88B HARM
BOMBS
Laser-guided *Paveway* II
Laser & INS/GPS-guided GBU-54 Laser JDAM
INS/GPS-guided GBU-31 JDAM

Gendarmerie & Paramilitary 50,000 active

Gendarmerie Royale 20,000

FORCES BY ROLE
MANOEUVRE
  Air Manoeuvre
    1 para sqn
  Other
    1 paramilitary bde
    4 (mobile) paramilitary gp
    1 coast guard unit

TRANSPORT HELICOPTER
1 sqn
EQUIPMENT BY TYPE
PATROL AND COASTAL COMBATANTS • PB 15
Arcor 53
AIRCRAFT • TRG 2 R-235 *Guerrier*
HELICOPTERS
  MRH 14: 3 SA315B *Lama*; 2 SA316 *Alouette* III; 3 SA318 *Alouette* II; 6 SA342K *Gazelle*
  TPT 8: **Medium** 6 SA330 *Puma*; **Light** 2 SA360 *Dauphin*

Force Auxiliaire 30,000 (incl 5,000 Mobile Intervention Corps)

Customs/Coast Guard
EQUIPMENT BY TYPE
PATROL AND COASTAL COMBATANTS
  PB 36: 4 *Erraid*; 18 *Arcor* 46; 14 (other SAR craft)

DEPLOYMENT
CENTRAL AFRICAN REPUBLIC: UN • MINUSCA 777; 1 inf bn
DEMOCRATIC REPUBLIC OF THE CONGO: UN • MONUSCO 926; 1 inf bn; 1 fd hospital
SOUTH SUDAN: UN • UNMISS 2
SUDAN: UN • UNISFA 3

Oman OMN

Omani Rial OMR		2021	2022	2023
GDP	OMR	33.0bn	41.9bn	
	USD	85.9bn	109bn	
per capita	USD	18,966	23,542	
Growth	%	3.0	4.4	
Inflation	%	1.5	3.1	
Def bdgt [a]	OMR	2.47bn	2.47bn	
	USD	6.43bn	6.43bn	
USD1=OMR		0.38	0.38	

[a] Excludes security funding

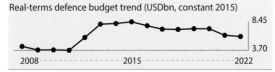
Real-terms defence budget trend (USDbn, constant 2015)

Population 3,764,348

Age	0–14	15–19	20–24	25–29	30–64	65 plus
Male	15.3%	4.0%	4.7%	5.6%	22.4%	1.8%
Female	14.6%	3.8%	4.1%	4.4%	17.2%	2.1%

Capabilities
The principal task for Oman's armed forces is ensuring territorial integrity, with a particular focus on maritime security, given the country's long coastline. Oman maintains important but carefully calibrated relations with the US while it continues to develop its defence agreements with the UK, a country with which Muscat has a close and long-standing defence and security relationship. Oman does not host a significant permanent presence of US or other foreign forces, in contrast to other GCC states, but UK forces are frequently deployed to the country for training and Oman has been developing its naval exercises with these and other partner countries. In addition, both the US and the UK make use of Omani air- and naval-logistics facilities, most notably the port at Duqm, where the UK has a Joint Logistics Support Base. Oman has also been seeking to strengthen ties with Asian states; there was another joint exercise with India and also a meeting with senior Chinese defence officials. Whilst Oman is a member of the GCC, it has not participated in the Saudi-led coalition's operations in Yemen and has largely followed a semi-independent regional policy. Although Muscat has recently maintained the highest level of defence spending as a percentage of GDP in the GCC, the defence budget was reduced in 2021. Nonetheless, Oman has recently recapitalised its core air- and naval-systems inventory, including combat aircraft and patrol and high-speed support vessels, and is now looking to do the same in the land domain. Oman has very limited indigenous defence-industrial capacity, but it has begun local production of various types of ammunition and is looking to boost organic support capability, particularly in the air and land sectors.

ACTIVE 42,600 (Army 25,000 Navy 4,200 Air 5,000 Foreign Forces 2,000 Royal Household 6,400) **Gendarmerie & Paramilitary 4,400**

ORGANISATIONS BY SERVICE

Army 25,000
FORCES BY ROLE
(Regt are bn size)
MANOEUVRE
  Armoured
  1 armd bde (2 armd regt, 1 recce regt)
  Light
  1 inf bde (5 inf regt, 1 arty regt, 1 fd engr regt, 1 engr regt, 1 sigs regt)
  1 inf bde (3 inf regt, 2 arty regt)
  1 indep inf coy (Musandam Security Force)
  Air Manoeuvre
  1 AB regt
COMBAT SERVICE SUPPORT
  1 tpt regt
AIR DEFENCE
  1 ADA regt (2 ADA bty)
EQUIPMENT BY TYPE
ARMOURED FIGHTING VEHICLES
  MBT 117: 38 *Challenger* 2; 6 M60A1 *Patton*; 73 M60A3 *Patton*
  LT TK 37 FV101 *Scorpion*
  RECCE 12 *Pars* III 6×6 (Recce)
  IFV 72 *Pars* III 8×8 IFV
  APC 262
    APC (T) 10 FV4333 *Stormer*
    APC (W) 252: 15 AT-105 *Saxon*; 15 *Pars* III 6×6 (incl 10 CP; 1 trg); 47 *Pars* III 8×8 (38 CP; 8 amb; 1 trg); 175 *Piranha* (incl variants);
  AUV 143: 6 FV103 *Spartan*; 13 FV105 *Sultan* (CP); 124 VBL
ENGINEERING & MAINTENANCE VEHICLES
  AEV 6 *Pars* III AEV

Middle East and North Africa **347**

ARV 19: 4 *Challenger* ARV; 2 M88A1; 8 *Pars* III ARV; 2 *Piranha* ARV; 3 *Samson*

ANTI-TANK/ANTI-INFRASTRUCTURE • MSL
SP 8 VBL with TOW
MANPATS FGM-148 *Javelin*; *Milan*; BGM-71 TOW/TOW-2A

ARTILLERY 245
SP 155mm 24 G-6
TOWED 108: **105mm** 42 L118 Light Gun; **122mm** 30 D-30; **130mm** 24: 12 M-46; 12 Type-59-I; **155mm** 12 FH-70
MOR 113: **81mm** 69; **SP 81mm** VAMTAC with A3MS; **107mm** 20 M30; **120mm** 12 Brandt; **SP 120mm** 12 *Pars* III AMV

AIR DEFENCE
SAM • Point-defence *Mistral* 2; *Javelin*; 9K32 *Strela-2* (RS-SA-7 *Grail*)‡
GUNS 26: **23mm** 4 ZU-23-2; **35mm** 10 GDF-005 (with *Skyguard*); **40mm** 12 L/60 (Towed)

Navy 4,200

EQUIPMENT BY TYPE
PRINCIPAL SURFACE COMBATANTS • FRIGATES 3
FFGHM 3 *Al-Shamikh* with 2 twin lnchr with MM40 *Exocet* Block 3 AShM, 2 6-cell CLA VLS with VL MICA SAM, 1 76mm gun
PATROL AND COASTAL COMBATANTS 11
CORVETTES • FSGM 2:
2 *Qahir Al Amwaj* with 2 quad lnchr with MM40 *Exocet* AShM, 1 octuple lnchr with *Crotale* SAM, 1 76mm gun, 1 hel landing platform
PCFG 1 *Dhofar* with 2 quad lnchr with MM40 *Exocet* AShM, 1 76mm gun
PCO 4 *Al Ofouq* with 1 76mm gun, 1 hel landing platform
PCC 3 *Al Bushra* (FRA P-400) with 1 76mm gun
PBF 1 1400 FIC
AMPHIBIOUS
LANDING SHIPS • LST 1 *Nasr el Bahr*† with 1 hel landing platform (capacity 7 tanks; 240 troops) (in refit since 2017)
LANDING CRAFT 5: 1 **LCU**; 1 **LCT**; 3 **LCM**
LOGISTICS AND SUPPORT 8
AGS 1 *Al Makhirah*
AK 1 *Al Sultana*
AP 2 *Shinas* (commercial tpt – auxiliary military role only) (capacity 56 veh; 200 tps)
AX 1 *Al-Mabrukah*
AXS 1 *Shabab Oman* II
EPF 2 *Al Mubshir* (High Speed Support Vessel 72) with 1 hel landing platform (capacity 260 troops)

Air Force 5,000

FORCES BY ROLE
FIGHTER/GROUND ATTACK
2 sqn with F-16C/D Block 50 *Fighting Falcon*
1 sqn with *Hawk* Mk103; *Hawk* Mk203; *Hawk* Mk166
1 sqn with *Typhoon*
MARITIME PATROL
1 sqn with C295MPA

TRANSPORT
1 sqn with C-130H/J/J-30 *Hercules*
1 sqn with C295M
TRAINING
1 sqn with MFI-17B *Mushshak*; PC-9*; Bell 206 (AB-206) *Jet Ranger*
TRANSPORT HELICOPTER
4 (med) sqn; Bell 212 (AB-212); NH-90; *Super Lynx* Mk300 (maritime/SAR)
AIR DEFENCE
2 sqn with NASAMS

EQUIPMENT BY TYPE
AIRCRAFT 63 combat capable
FGA 35: 17 F-16C Block 50 *Fighting Falcon*; 6 F-16D Block 50 *Fighting Falcon*; 12 *Typhoon*
MP 4 C295MPA
TPT 12: **Medium** 6: 3 C-130H *Hercules*; 2 C-130J *Hercules*; 1 C-130J-30 *Hercules* (VIP); **Light** 4 C295M; **PAX** 2 A320-300
TRG 43: 4 *Hawk* Mk103*; 7 *Hawk* Mk166; 12 *Hawk* Mk203*; 8 MFI-17B *Mushshak*; 12 PC-9*
HELICOPTERS
MRH 15 *Super Lynx* Mk300 (maritime/SAR)
TPT 26+ **Medium** 20 NH90 TTH; **Light** 6: 3 Bell 206 (AB-206) *Jet Ranger*; 3 Bell 212 (AB-212)
AIR DEFENCE • SAM
Short-range NASAMS
MSL
AAM • IR AIM-9/M/P *Sidewinder*; **IIR** AIM-9X *Sidewinder* II; **ARH** AIM-120C7 AMRAAM
ASM AGM-65D/G *Maverick*
AShM AGM-84D *Harpoon*
BOMBS
Laser-guided EGBU-10 *Paveway* II; EGBU-12 *Paveway* II
INS/GPS-guided GBU-31 JDAM

Royal Household 6,400

(incl HQ staff)
FORCES BY ROLE
SPECIAL FORCES
2 SF regt

Royal Guard Brigade 5,000

FORCES BY ROLE
MANOEUVRE
Other
1 gd bde (1 armd sqn, 2 gd regt, 1 cbt spt bn)

EQUIPMENT BY TYPE
ARMOURED FIGHTING VEHICLES
ASLT 9 *Centauro* MGS (9 VBC-90 in store)
IFV 14 VAB VCI
APC • APC (W) ε50 Type-92
ANTI-TANK/ANTI-INFRASTRUCTURE
MSL • MANPATS *Milan*
ARTILLERY • MRL 122mm 6 Type-90A
AIR DEFENCE
SAM • Point-defence *Javelin*
GUNS • SP 9: **20mm** 9 VAB VDAA

Middle East and North Africa

348 THE MILITARY BALANCE 2023

Royal Yacht Squadron 150
EQUIPMENT BY TYPE
LOGISTICS AND SUPPORT 3
 AP 1 *Fulk Al Salamah* (also veh tpt) with up to 2 AS332 *Super Puma* hel

Royal Flight 250
EQUIPMENT BY TYPE
AIRCRAFT • TPT • PAX 7: 1 747-400; 1 747-8; 1 B-747SP; 1 A319; 1 A320; 2 Gulfstream IV
HELICOPTERS • TPT • Medium 6 EC225LP *Super Puma*

Gendarmerie & Paramilitary 4,400 active

Tribal Home Guard 4,000
org in teams of ε100

Police Coast Guard 400
EQUIPMENT BY TYPE
PATROL AND COASTAL COMBATANTS 32
 PCO 2 *Haras*
 PBF 3 *Haras* (US Mk V PBF)
 PB 27: 3 Rodman 101; 1 *Haras* (SWE CG27); 3 *Haras* (SWE CG29); 14 Rodman 58; 1 D59116; 5 *Zahra*

Police Air Wing
EQUIPMENT BY TYPE
AIRCRAFT • TPT • Light 4: 1 BN-2T *Turbine Islander*; 2 CN235M; 1 Do-228
HELICOPTERS • TPT • Light 5: 2 Bell 205A; 3 Bell 214ST (AB-214ST)

FOREIGN FORCES
United Kingdom 90

Palestinian Territories PT

New Israeli Shekel ILS		2021	2022	2023
GDP	USD			
per capita	USD			
Growth	%			
Inflation	%			
USD1=ILS				

Population	4,997,349					
Age	**0–14**	**15–19**	**20–24**	**25–29**	**30–64**	**65 plus**
Male	19.0%	5.7%	5.0%	4.4%	14.9%	1.7%
Female	18.0%	5.5%	4.9%	4.4%	14.9%	1.8%

Capabilities
The Palestinian Territories remain effectively divided between the Palestinian Authority-run West Bank and Hamas-run Gaza. Each organisation controls its own security forces, principally the National Security Forces (NSF) in the West Bank and the Izz al-Din al-Qassam Brigades in Gaza. Both have generally proved effective at maintaining internal security in their respective territories. The Palestinian Authority has received support from the EU, Jordan and the US. Israel claims that a small number of Izz al-Din al-Qassam Brigades personnel have received military training in Iran and Syria. None of the Palestinian security organisations conduct external military deployments, and they lack a formal military-logistics structure. Both Hamas and the Palestinian Authority lack heavy military equipment, although the former has retained a substantial arsenal of improvised rocket and mortar capabilities, as well as some portable guided weapons. During renewed conflict in mid-2021, Hamas demonstrated a loitering-munition capability as well as new missiles with a claimed range of 250 km. No formal defence industry exists, although Hamas can acquire light or improvised weapons, either smuggled into Gaza or of local construction or assembly.

ACTIVE 0 Gendarmerie & Paramilitary n.k.
Precise personnel-strength figures for the various Palestinian groups are not known

ORGANISATIONS BY SERVICE
There is little available data on the status of the organisations mentioned below. Following internal fighting in June 2007, Gaza has been under the de facto control of Hamas, while the West Bank is controlled by the Palestinian Authority. In October 2017, both sides agreed a preliminary reconciliation deal on control of Gaza.

Gendarmerie & Paramilitary

Palestinian Authority n.k.

Presidential Security ε3,000

Special Forces ε1,200

Police ε9,000

National Security Force ε10,000
FORCES BY ROLE
MANOEUVRE
 Other
 9 paramilitary bn

Preventative Security ε4,000

Civil Defence ε1,000

The al-Aqsa Brigades n.k.
Profess loyalty to the Fatah group that dominates the Palestinian Authority

Hamas n.k.

Izz al-Din al-Qassam Brigades ε15,000–20,000
FORCES BY ROLE
COMMAND
 6 bde HQ (regional)
MANOEUVRE
 Other
 1 cdo unit (Nukhba)
 27 paramilitary bn
 100 paramilitary coy
 COMBAT SUPPORT Some engr units
COMBAT SERVICE SUPPORT
 Some log units

EQUIPMENT BY TYPE
ANTI-TANK/ANTI-INFRASTRUCTURE • MSL
• **MANPATS** 9K11 *Malyutka* (RS-AT-3 *Sagger*) (reported); *Dehlavieh* (*Kornet*) (reported)
ARTILLERY
MRL • *Qassam* rockets (multiple calibres); **122mm** some; **240mm** some *Fadjr* 3 (reported); **330mm** some *Fadjr* 5 (reported)
MOR some (multiple calibres)
SURFACE-TO-SURFACE MISSILE LAUNCHERS
SRBM • **Conventional** some *Ayyash*-250

Martime Police ε600

Qatar QTR

Qatari Riyal QAR		2021	2022	2023
GDP	QAR	654bn	806bn	
	USD	180bn	221bn	
per capita	USD	68,622	82,887	
Growth	%	1.6	3.4	
Inflation	%	2.3	4.5	
Def bdgt [a]	QAR	ε22.8bn	ε30.6bn	
	USD	ε6.26bn	ε8.42bn	
USD1=QAR		3.64	3.64	

[a] Defence budget estimate derived from Defence and Security allocation in the 'Public Budget Statement'

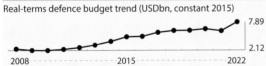
Real-terms defence budget trend (USDbn, constant 2015)

Population 2,508,182

Age	0–14	15–19	20–24	25–29	30–64	65 plus
Male	6.6%	2.3%	5.7%	10.0%	51.5%	0.9%
Female	6.5%	1.7%	1.8%	2.6%	10.0%	0.5%

Capabilities

Qatar is attempting to transform its military capabilities and regional defence standing based on significant equipment acquisitions, including platforms with power-projection capability. The scale of the equipment plan is increasing personnel requirements and suggests that Qatar will need significant assistance to integrate and operate its new capabilities. Combat-aircraft procurements are dramatically increasing the size of the air force, where Qatar faces most questions about its ability to develop and sustain the necessary personnel, infrastructure and maintenance capacity. The diplomatic crisis with several of its GCC neighbours brought Qatar and Turkey closer together in their limited but significant defence cooperation, which includes a small Turkish military presence in-country. The crisis appears not to have affected the significant Qatar–US military relationship, including the presence of forces from the US and other Western states at Al-Udeid airbase and the key US-run coalition air-operations centre. Qatar has begun deploying its own *Patriot* air- and missile-defence systems and an AN/FPS-132 early-warning radar. The Italian Navy is supporting training for new Italian-built vessels among other naval enhancements. A joint Qatar–UK Eurofighter *Typhoon* squadron, which is helping to build Qatari capabilities on the aircraft, deployed to Qatar in October 2022 to support Doha's staging of the FIFA World Cup. Qatar currently has a limited indigenous defence-industrial capability, including in ship repair.

ACTIVE 16,500 (Army 12,000 Navy 2,500 Air 2,000)
Gendarmerie & Paramilitary up to 5,000
Conscript liability 12 months, males 18–35 years. Voluntary national service for women

ORGANISATIONS BY SERVICE

Space
EQUIPMENT BY TYPE
SATELLITES • COMMUNICATIONS 1 *Es'hail*-2

Army 12,000 (including Emiri Guard)
FORCES BY ROLE
SPECIAL FORCES
1 SF coy
MANOEUVRE
Armoured
1 armd bde (1 tk bn, 1 mech inf bn, 1 mor sqn, 1 AT bn)
Mechanised
3 mech inf bn
1 (Emiri Guard) bde (3 mech regt)
COMBAT SUPPORT
1 SP arty bn
1 fd arty bn
EQUIPMENT BY TYPE
ARMOURED FIGHTING VEHICLES
MBT 62 *Leopard* 2A7+
ASLT 48: 12 AMX-10RC; 36 *Piranha* II 90mm
RECCE 32 *Fennek*
IFV 40 AMX-10P
APC 418
  APC (T) 30 AMX-VCI
  APC (W) 168: 8 V-150 *Chaimite*; 160 VAB
  PPV 220+: 170+ *Ejder Yalcin*; 50 *Kirpi*-2; RG-31
AUV 30+: 14 *Dingo* 2; NMS; 16 VBL
ENGINEERING & MAINTENANCE VEHICLES
AEV 6 *Wisent* 2
ARV 3: 1 AMX-30D; 2 *Piranha*
ANTI-TANK/ANTI-INFRASTRUCTURE
MSL
  SP 24 VAB VCAC HOT; *Ejder Yalcin* with *Stugna-P*; NMS with *Stugna-P*
  MANPATS FGM-148 *Javelin*; *Milan*; *Kornet*-EM
RCL 84mm *Carl Gustaf*
ARTILLERY 89+
  SP 155mm 24 PzH 2000
  TOWED 155mm 12 G-5
  MRL 8+: **107mm** PH-63; **122mm** 2+ (30-tube); **127mm** 6 ASTROS II Mk3
  MOR 45: **81mm** 26 L16; **SP 81mm** 4 VAB VPM 81; **120mm** 15 Brandt

350 THE MILITARY BALANCE 2023

SURFACE-TO-SURFACE MISSILE LAUNCHERS
  SRBM • Conventional 8+ BP-12A (CH-SS-14 mod 2)
AIR DEFENCE
  SAM • Point-defence NMS with *Igla*
  GUNS • SP 35mm 15 *Gepard*

Navy 2,500 (incl Coast Guard)
EQUIPMENT BY TYPE
PRINCIPAL SURFACE COMBATANTS • FRIGATES 1
  FFGHM 1 *Al Zubarah* with 2 quad lnchr with MM40
  Exocet Block 3 AShM, 2 8-cell *Sylver* A50 VLS with *Aster*
  30 SAM, 1 21-cell Mk 49 GMLS with RIM-116 RAM
  SAM, 1 76mm gun (capacity 1 med hel)
PATROL AND COASTAL COMBATANTS 13
  CORVETTES • FSGM 2 *Musherib* with 2 twin lnchr
  with MM40 *Exocet* Block 3 AShM, 1 8-cell CLA VLS with
  VL MICA SAM, 1 76mm gun
  PCFGM 4 *Barzan* (UK *Vita*) with 2 quad lnchr with
  MM40 *Exocet* Block 3 AShM, 1 sextuple *Sadral* lnchr
  with *Mistral* SAM, 1 *Goalkeeper* CIWS, 1 76mm gun
  PCFG 3 *Damsah* (FRA *Combattante* III) with 2 quad lnchr
  with MM40 *Exocet* AShM, 1 76mm gun
  PBF 3 MRTP 16
  PB 1 MRTP 34
AMPHIBIOUS 4
  LCT 1 *Fuwairit* (TUR Anadolu Shipyard LCT)
  LCM 2 *Broog* (TUR Anadolu Shipyard LCM)
  LCVP 1 Anadolu 16m
LOGISTICS AND SUPPORT • AX 2 *Al Doha* with 1 hel
landing platform

Coast Guard
EQUIPMENT BY TYPE
PATROL AND COASTAL COMBATANTS 12
  PBF 4 DV 15
  PB 8: 4 *Crestitalia* MV-45; 3 *Halmatic* M160; 1 other

Coastal Defence
FORCES BY ROLE
COASTAL DEFENCE
  1 bty with 3 quad lnchr with MM40 *Exocet* AShM
EQUIPMENT BY TYPE
COASTAL DEFENCE • AShM 12 MM40 *Exocet*
AShM

Air Force 2,000
FORCES BY ROLE
FIGHTER/GROUND ATTACK
  1 sqn with Eurofighter *Typhoon*
  1 sqn with Eurofighter *Typhoon* (personnel only) (joint
  QTR-UK unit)
  1 sqn with F-15QA
  1 sqn with *Rafale* DQ/EQ
ANTI-SUBMARINE WARFARE
  1 sqn with NH90 NFH (forming)
TRANSPORT
  1 sqn with C-17A *Globemaster* III; C-130J-30 *Hercules*
  1 sqn with A340; B-707; B-727; *Falcon* 900
TRAINING
  1 sqn with *Hawk* Mk167

  1 sqn with M-346
  1 sqn with PC-21; *Super Mushshak*
ATTACK HELICOPTER
  1 sqn with SA341 *Gazelle*; SA342L *Gazelle* with HOT
TRANSPORT HELICOPTER
  1 sqn with AW139
  1 sqn with NH90 TTH (forming)
EQUIPMENT BY TYPE
AIRCRAFT 62 combat capable
  FGA 62: 4 Eurofighter *Typhoon*; 22 F-15QA; 9 *Rafale* DQ;
  27 *Rafale* EQ; (9 *Mirage* 2000ED; 3 *Mirage* 2000D in store)
  TPT 18: **Heavy** 8 C-17A *Globemaster* III; **Medium** 4
  C-130J-30 *Hercules*; **PAX** 6: 1 A340; 2 B-707; 1 B-727; 2
  Falcon 900
  TRG 37: 5 *Hawk* Mk167; 3 M-346; 21 PC-21; 8 *Super
  Mushshak*; (6 *Alpha Jet* in store)
HELICOPTERS
  ATK 24 AH-64E *Apache*
  ASW 3 NH90 NFH
  MRH 34: 21 AW139 (incl 3 for medevac); 2 SA341
  Gazelle; 11 SA342L *Gazelle*
  TPT 3: **Medium** 2 NH90 TTH; **Light** 1 H125 *Ecureuil*
  (trg config)
UNINHABITED AERIAL VEHICLES
  CISR • Medium 6 *Bayraktar* TB2
AIR DEFENCE • SAM
  Long-range 34 M903 *Patriot* PAC-3 MSE
  Medium-range NASAMS III
  Point-defence FIM-92 *Stinger*; FN-6 (CH-SA-10); *Mistral*
RADAR 1 AN/FPS-132 Upgraded Early Warning Radar
AIR-LAUNCHED MISSILES
  AAM • IR R-550 *Magic* 2; **IIR** AIM-9X Sidewinder II;
  ASMRAAM; **ARH** AIM-120C-7 AMRAAM; *Meteor*;
  Mica RF
  ASM *Apache*; AGM-114R *Hellfire*; AGR-20A APKWS; HOT
  AShM AM39 *Exocet*

Gendarmerie & Paramilitary up to 5,000

Internal Security Force up to 5,000

DEPLOYMENT

LEBANON: UN • UNIFIL 1

FOREIGN FORCES

Turkey 300 (trg team); 1 mech coy; 1 arty unit
United Kingdom 200; 1 FGA sqn with 12 *Typhoon* FGR4
United States US Central Command: 10,000; CAOC; 1
ISR sqn with 4 RC-135 *Rivet Joint*; 1 ISR sqn with 4 E-8C
JSTARS; 2 tkr sqn with 12 KC-135R/T *Stratotanker*; 1 tpt
sqn with 4 C-17A *Globemaster*; 4 C-130H/J-30 *Hercules*; 2
SAM bty with M902/M903 *Patriot* PAC-3/PAC-3 MSE • US
Strategic Command: 1 AN/TPY-2 X-band radar

Saudi Arabia SAU

Saudi Riyal SAR		2021	2022	2023
GDP	SAR	3.13tr	3.79tr	
	USD	834bn	1.01tr	
per capita	USD	23,507	27,941	
Growth	%	3.2	7.6	
Inflation	%	3.1	2.7	
Def bdgt [a]	SAR	190bn	171bn	
	USD	50.7bn	45.6bn	
USD1=SAR		3.75	3.75	

[a] Military budget only - excludes security budget

Real-terms defence budget trend (USDbn, constant 2015)

Population 35,354,380

Age	0–14	15–19	20–24	25–29	30–64	65 plus
Male	12.2%	4.0%	3.9%	4.3%	30.0%	2.1%
Female	11.8%	3.8%	3.6%	3.6%	18.8%	1.9%

Capabilities

Saudi Arabia is the leading member of the GCC, with the largest and best equipped armed forces in the group. In addition to traditional objectives relating to territorial integrity and internal security, the Kingdom has displayed an increasing willingness to use the armed forces as part of a more assertive regional foreign policy, most notably in Yemen. Whilst operations in Yemen have allowed the armed forces to gain combat experience, they have also exposed areas of comparative weakness and capability gaps, especially in the application of precision airpower, air–ground coordination and logistics support. Meanwhile, cruise-missile and UAV attacks on Saudi oil infrastructure have exposed capability weaknesses with the Kingdom's air- and missile-defence capabilities. Saudi Arabia's most critical defence relationship continues to be with the US, although recent frictions including over the Ukraine war, related particularly to oil production, led to a review of that relationship in Washington. Issues including aspects of Saudi Arabia's military campaign in Yemen have also sharpened focus in the US over defence sales to the country more generally. Riyadh has over the years sought to mitigate any dependence on Washington by also maintaining security relationships with other states such as France and the UK, while relationships with China – including equipment sales – as well as India and others have been strengthened. Equipment recapitalisation continues, with orders for combat aircraft, corvettes and multi-mission surface combatants, despite concerns about austerity. There is currently only a modest domestic defence-industrial base, mainly in the assembly and overhaul of land systems. However, Riyadh continues to reaffirm and pursue an intention to spend 50% of its defence outlays locally as part of its Vision 2030 initiative and established the state-owned Saudi Arabian Military Industries to oversee local defence production.

ACTIVE 257,000 (Army 75,000 Navy 13,500 Air 20,000 Air Defence 16,000 Strategic Missile Forces 2,500 National Guard 130,000) Gendarmerie & Paramilitary 24,500

ORGANISATIONS BY SERVICE

Army 75,000

FORCES BY ROLE
MANOEUVRE
Armoured
4 armd bde (1 recce coy, 3 tk bn, 1 mech bn, 1 fd arty bn, 1 AD bn, 1 AT bn, 1 engr coy, 1 log bn, 1 maint coy, 1 med coy)
Mechanised
5 mech bde (1 recce coy, 1 tk bn, 3 mech bn, 1 fd arty bn, 1 AD bn, 1 AT bn, 1 engr coy, 1 log bn, 1 maint coy, 1 med coy)
Light
2 lt inf bde
Other
1 (Al-Saif Al-Ajrab) gd bde
1 (Royal Guard) gd regt (3 lt inf bn)
Air Manoeuvre
1 AB bde (2 AB bn, 3 SF coy)
Aviation
1 comd (3 hel gp)
COMBAT SUPPORT
3 arty bde

EQUIPMENT BY TYPE
MBT 1,010: 140 AMX-30; ε500 M1A2/A2S *Abrams*; ε370 M60A3 *Patton*
RECCE 300 AML-60/AML-90
IFV 860: 380 AMX-10P; 380 M2A2 *Bradley*; 100 VAB Mk3
APC 1,340
    APC (T) 1,190 M113A4 (incl variants)
    APC (W) 150 Panhard M3; (ε40 AF-40-8-1 *Al-Fahd* in store)
AUV 1,200+: 100 *Didgori* (amb); 1,000+ M-ATV; *Al-Shibl* 2; 100 *Sherpa Light Scout*; Terradyne *Gurkha*
ENGINEERING & MAINTENANCE VEHICLES
AEV 15 M728
ARV 275+: 8 ACV ARV; AMX-10EHC; 55 AMX-30D; *Leclerc* ARV; 122 M88A1; 90 M578
VLB 10 AMX-30
MW *Aardvark* Mk2
NBC VEHICLES 10 TPz-1 *Fuchs* NBC
ANTI-TANK/ANTI-INFRASTRUCTURE
MSL
    SP 290+: 90+ AMX-10P (HOT); 200 VCC-1 ITOW; M-ATV with *Milan*
    MANPATS *Hyeongung*; Luch *Corsar* (reported); Luch *Skif* (reported); *Stugna*-P (reported); TOW-2A
RCL 84mm *Carl Gustaf*; **90mm** M67; **106mm** M40A1
ARTILLERY 833
SP 155mm 224: 60 AU-F-1; 110 M109A1B/A2; 54 PLZ-45
TOWED 172: **105mm** 62 LG1; (100 M101/M102 in store); **155mm** 110: 50 M114; 60 M198; **203mm** (8 M115 in store)
MRL 70: **127mm** 60 ASTROS II Mk3; **220mm** 10 TOS-1A
MOR 367: **SP 81mm** 70; **107mm** 150 M30; **120mm** 147: 110 Brandt; 37 M12-1535; **SP 120mm** M113A4 with 2R2M
HELICOPTERS
ATK 35: 11 AH-64D *Apache*; 24 AH-64E *Apache*

MRH 21: 6 AS365N *Dauphin* 2 (medevac); 15 Bell 406CS *Combat Scout*

TPT 90: **Heavy** 4+ CH-47F *Chinook*; **Medium** 67: 22 UH-60A *Black Hawk* (4 medevac); 36 UH-60L *Black Hawk*; 9 UH-60M *Black Hawk*; **Light** 19 Schweizer 333

AIR DEFENCE • SAM

Short-range *Crotale*

Point-defence FIM-92 *Stinger*

Navy 13,500

Navy HQ at Riyadh; Eastern Fleet HQ at Jubail; Western Fleet HQ at Jeddah

EQUIPMENT BY TYPE

PRINCIPAL SURFACE COMBATANTS • FRIGATES 8

FFGHM 8:

2 *Al-Jubail* (ESP *Avante* 2200) with 2 quad lnchr with RGM-84L *Harpoon* Block II AShM, 2 8-cell Mk 41 VLS with RIM-162B ESSM SAM, 2 triple 324mm ASTT with Mk 46 LWT, 1 76mm gun (capacity 1 med hel)

3 *Al Riyadh* (FRA *La Fayette* mod) with 2 quad lnchr with MM40 *Exocet* Block 2 AShM, 2 8-cell *Sylver* A43 VLS with *Aster* 15 SAM, 4 single 533mm TT with F17P HWT, 1 76mm gun (capacity 1 AS365N *Dauphin* 2 hel)

3 *Madina* (FRA F-2000) (1 more damaged in 2017 and non-operational) with 2 quad lnchr with *Otomat* Mk2 AShM, 1 octuple lnchr with *Crotale* SAM, 4 single 533mm TT with F17P HWT, 1 100mm gun (capacity 1 AS365N *Dauphin* 2 hel)

PATROL AND COASTAL COMBATANTS 53

CORVETTES • FSG 4 *Badr* (US *Tacoma*) with 2 quad lnchr with RGM-84C *Harpoon* Block 1B AShM, 2 triple 324mm ASTT with Mk 46 LWT, 1 Mk 15 *Phalanx* CIWS, 1 76mm gun

PCFG 9 *Al Siddiq* (US 58m) with 2 twin lnchr with RGM-84C *Harpoon* Block 1B AShM, 1 Mk 15 *Phalanx* CIWS, 1 76mm gun

PBF 21 HSI 32

PB 19: 17 (US) *Halter Marine* 24m; 2 *Plascoa* 2200

MINE WARFARE • MINE COUNTERMEASURES 3

MHC 3 *Al Jawf* (UK *Sandown*)

AMPHIBIOUS • LANDING CRAFT 5

LCU ε2 *Al Qiaq* (US LCU 1610) (capacity 120 troops)

LCM 3 LCM 6 (capacity 80 troops)

LOGISTICS AND SUPPORT 1

AORH 1 *Boraida* (mod FRA *Durance*) (1 more non-operational and in drydock since 2017) (capacity either 2 AS365F *Dauphin* 2 hel or 1 AS332C *Super Puma*)

Naval Aviation

EQUIPMENT BY TYPE

HELICOPTERS

MRH 34: 6 AS365N *Dauphin* 2; 15 AS565; 13 Bell 406CS *Combat Scout*

TPT • Medium 12 AS332B/F *Super Puma*

AIR-LAUNCHED MISSILES

AShM AM39 *Exocet*; AS-15TT

Marines 3,000

FORCES BY ROLE

SPECIAL FORCES

1 spec ops regt with (2 spec ops bn)

EQUIPMENT BY TYPE

ARMOURED FIGHTING VEHICLES

RECCE *Bastion Patsas*

APC • APC (W) 135 BMR-600P

Air Force 20,000

FORCES BY ROLE

FIGHTER

4 sqn with F-15C/D *Eagle*

FIGHTER/GROUND ATTACK

3 sqn with F-15S/SA *Eagle*

3 sqn with *Typhoon*

GROUND ATTACK

3 sqn with *Tornado* IDS; *Tornado* GR1A

AIRBORNE EARLY WARNING & CONTROL

1 sqn with E-3A *Sentry*

1 sqn with Saab 2000 *Erieye*

ELINT

1 sqn with RE-3A/B; Beech 350ER *King Air*

TANKER

1 sqn with KE-3A

TANKER/TRANSPORT

1 sqn with KC-130H/J *Hercules*

1 sqn with A330 MRTT

TRANSPORT

3 sqn with C-130H *Hercules*; C-130H-30 *Hercules*; CN-235; L-100-30HS (hospital ac)

2 sqn with Beech 350 *King Air* (forming)

TRAINING

1 OCU sqn with F-15SA *Eagle*

3 sqn with *Hawk* Mk65*; *Hawk* Mk65A*; *Hawk* Mk165*

1 sqn with *Jetstream* Mk31

1 sqn with MFI-17 *Mushshak*; SR22T

2 sqn with PC-9; PC-21

TRANSPORT HELICOPTER

4 sqn with AS532 *Cougar* (CSAR); Bell 212 (AB-212); Bell 412 (AB-412) *Twin Huey* (SAR)

EQUIPMENT BY TYPE

AIRCRAFT 455 combat capable

FTR 81: 56 F-15C *Eagle*; 25 F-15D *Eagle*

FGA 221: up to 66 F-15S *Eagle* (being upgraded to F-15SA configuration); 84 F-15SA *Eagle*; 71 *Typhoon*

ATK 66 *Tornado* IDS

ISR 14+: 12 *Tornado* GR1A*; 2+ Beech 350ER *King Air*

AEW&C 7: 5 E-3A *Sentry*; 2 Saab 2000 *Erieye*

ELINT 2: 1 RE-3A; 1 RE-3B

TKR/TPT 15: 6 A330 MRTT; 7 KC-130H *Hercules*; 2 KC-130J *Hercules*

TKR 7 KE-3A

TPT 47+: **Medium** 36: 30 C-130H *Hercules*; 3 C-130H-30 *Hercules*; 3 L-100-30; **Light** 11+: 10+ Beech 350 *King Air*; 1 *Jetstream* Mk31

TRG 194: 24 *Hawk* Mk65* (incl aerobatic team); 16 *Hawk* Mk65A*; 35 *Hawk* Mk165*; 20 MFI-17 *Mushshak*; 20 PC-9; 55 PC-21; 24 SR22T

HELICOPTERS

MRH 15 Bell 412 (AB-412) *Twin Huey* (SAR)

TPT 30: **Medium** 10 AS532 *Cougar* (CSAR); **Light** 20 Bell 212 (AB-212)

UNINHABITED AERIAL VEHICLES
CISR • Heavy some *Wing Loong* I (reported); some CH-4
ISR • Medium some *Falco*
AIR-LAUNCHED MISSILES
AAM • IR AIM-9P/L *Sidewinder*; **IIR** AIM-9X *Sidewinder* II; IRIS-T; **SARH** AIM-7 *Sparrow*; AIM-7M *Sparrow*; **ARH** AIM-120C AMRAAM
ASM AGM-65 *Maverick*; AR-1; *Brimstone*
AShM AGM-84L *Harpoon* Block II
ARM ALARM
ALCM *Storm Shadow*
BOMBS
Laser-guided GBU-10/12 *Paveway* II; *Paveway* IV
Laser & INS/GPS-guided GBU-54 Laser JDAM
INS/GPS-guided GBU-31 JDAM; FT-9

Royal Flt

EQUIPMENT BY TYPE
AIRCRAFT • TPT 24: **Medium** 8: 5 C-130H *Hercules*; 3 L-100-30; **Light** 3: 1 Cessna 310; 2 Learjet 35; **PAX** 13: 1 A340; 1 B-737-200; 2 B-737BBJ; 2 B-747SP; 4 BAe-125-800; 2 Gulfstream III; 1 Gulfstream IV
HELICOPTERS • TPT 3+: **Medium** 3: 2 AS-61; 1 S-70 *Black Hawk*; **Light** some Bell 212 (AB-212)

Air Defence Forces 16,000

FORCES BY ROLE
AIR DEFENCE
6 bn with M902 *Patriot* PAC-3
17 bty with *Shahine*/AMX-30SA
16 bty with MIM-23B I-*Hawk*

EQUIPMENT BY TYPE
AIR DEFENCE
SAM 817+
Long-range 108 M902 *Patriot* PAC-3
Medium-range 128 MIM-23B I-*Hawk*
Short-range 181: 40 *Crotale*; 141 *Shahine*
Point-defence 400+: LMM; 400 M1097 *Avenger*; *Mistral*
GUNS 218
SP • 20mm 90 M163 *Vulcan*
TOWED 128: **35mm** 128 GDF Oerlikon; **40mm** (150 L/70 in store)
DE • Laser *Silent Hunter*

Strategic Missile Forces 2,500

EQUIPMENT BY TYPE
MSL • TACTICAL
IRBM 10+ DF-3 (CH-SS-2) (service status unclear)
MRBM Some DF-21 (CH-SS-5 – variant unclear) (reported)

National Guard 130,000

FORCES BY ROLE
MANOEUVRE
Mechanised
5 mech bde (1 recce coy, 3 mech inf bn, 1 SP arty bn, 1 cbt engr coy, 1 sigs coy, 1 log bn)
Light
5 inf bde (3 combined arms bn, 1 arty bn, 1 log bn)
3 indep lt inf bn

Other
1 (Special Security) sy bde (3 sy bn)
1 (ceremonial) cav sqn
COMBAT SUPPORT
1 MP bn

EQUIPMENT BY TYPE
ARMOURED FIGHTING VEHICLES
ASLT 239: 204 LAV-AG (90mm); 35 LAV 700 (105mm)
IFV 1,235: ε635 LAV-25; ε600 LAV 700 (incl variants)
APC 778
APC (W) 514: 116 LAV-A (amb); 30 LAV-AC (ammo carrier); 296 LAV-CC (CP); 72 LAV-PC
PPV 264 *Aravis*; some *Arive*
ENGINEERING & MAINTENANCE VEHICLES
AEV 58 LAV-E
ARV 111 LAV-R; V-150 ARV
MW MV5; MV10
ANTI-TANK/ANTI-INFRASTRUCTURE
MSL
SP 182 LAV-AT
MANPATS TOW-2A; M47 *Dragon*
RCL • 106mm M40A1
ARTILLERY 363+
SP 155mm up to 136 CAESAR
TOWED 108: **105mm** 50 M102; **155mm** 58 M198
MOR 119+: **81mm** some; **SP 120mm** 119: 107 LAV-M; 12 LAV-M with NEMO
HELICOPTERS
ATK 12 AH-64E *Apache*
MRH 35: 23 AH-6i *Little Bird*; 12 MD530F (trg role)
TPT • Medium ε50 UH-60M *Black Hawk*
AIR DEFENCE
SAM 73
Short-range 5 VL MICA
Point-defence 68 MPCV
GUNS • TOWED • 20mm 30 M167 *Vulcan*
AIR-LAUNCHED MISSILES
ASM AGM-114R *Hellfire* II

Gendarmerie & Paramilitary 24,500+ active

Border Guard 15,000

FORCES BY ROLE
Subordinate to Ministry of Interior. HQ in Riyadh. 9 subordinate regional commands
MANOEUVRE
Other
Some mobile def (long-range patrol/spt) units
2 border def (patrol) units
12 infrastructure def units
18 harbour def units
Some coastal def units
COMBAT SUPPORT
Some MP units

EQUIPMENT BY TYPE
ARMOURED FIGHTING VEHICLES
APC • PPV *Caprivi* Mk1/Mk3
PATROL AND COASTAL COMBATANTS 106
PCC 13+ OPB 40
PBF 85: 4 *Al Jouf*; 2 *Sea Guard*; 79 Plascoa FIC 1650

PB 8: 6 Damen Stan Patrol 2606; 2 *Al Jubatel*
AMPHIBIOUS • LANDING CRAFT • UCAC 8: 5 *Griffon* 8000; 3 other
LOGISTICS AND SUPPORT 4: 1 **AXL**; 3 **AO**

Facilities Security Force 9,000+

Subordinate to Ministry of Interior

General Civil Defence Administration Units

EQUIPMENT BY TYPE
HELICOPTERS • TPT • Medium 10 Boeing *Vertol* 107

Special Security Force 500

EQUIPMENT BY TYPE
ARMOURED FIGHTING VEHICLES
  APC • APC (W) UR-416
  AUV 60+: *Gurkha* LAPV; 60 *Kozak*-5

DEPLOYMENT

YEMEN: *Operation Restoring Hope* 2,500; 2 armd BG; M60A3; M2A2 *Bradley*; M113A4; M-ATV; 2+ M902 *Patriot* PAC-3

FOREIGN FORCES

France 50 (radar det)
Greece 100: 1 SAM bty with M901 *Patriot* PAC-2
United Kingdom 50 (radar det)
United States US Central Command: 2,000; 1 FGA sqn with 12 F-16C *Fighting Falcon*

Syria SYR

Syrian Pound SYP		2021	2022	2023
GDP	SYP			
	USD			
per capita	USD			
Growth	%			
Inflation	%			
Def exp	SYP			
	USD			
USD1=SYP				

Definitive economic data not available

Population	21,563,800					
Age	**0–14**	**15–19**	**20–24**	**25–29**	**30–64**	**65 plus**
Male	17.0%	4.9%	4.7%	4.1%	17.2%	2.0%
Female	16.2%	4.7%	4.7%	4.3%	17.8%	2.3%

Capabilities

The protracted civil war has significantly depleted the combat capabilities of the Syrian armed forces and transformed them into an irregularly structured militia-style organisation focused on internal security. Various nominally pro-government militias, often formed around local or religious identity, are reportedly funded by local businessmen or foreign powers, raising questions over capability and morale as well as loyalty. There are allegations that some elements of the Syrian Arab Army are involved in the production and distribution of illegal narcotics to other countries in the region, the Gulf and Europe. There is no published defence doctrine or White Paper with the conflict instead dictating ad hoc requirements. Opposition groups maintain control over parts of the country. Most formal pre-war structures and formations exist in name only, as resources have been channelled into the irregular network of military organisations that form the regime's most effective military capabilities. Russia has been the regime's principal ally and has provided essential combat support and assistance, as well as replacement equipment. Russia is also involved in efforts to reconstitute the army's pre-war divisions, although some Russian equipment has been withdrawn following Russia's invasion of Ukraine. Iran and Hizbullah also continue to assist in the provision and training of militias and other ground forces but reports allege a lack of coordination, with Russia supporting some formations and Iran/Hizbullah others. Overall levels of training remain poor but combat experience has improved proficiency in select regular and irregular military formations. The armed forces lack the requisite capabilities for external deployment, although they remain able to redeploy moderate numbers of formations and capabilities within the country. Logistics support for major internal operations away from established bases remains a challenge. Before the civil war, Syria did not have a major domestic defence industry, although it possessed facilities to overhaul and maintain its existing systems. It did, however, possess some capacity in focused areas, such as ballistic missiles and chemical weapons. International efforts continue to verify destruction of chemical-weapons stockpiles and production facilities.

ACTIVE 169,000 (Army 130,000 Navy 4,000 Air 15,000 Air Defence 20,000) **Gendarmerie & Paramilitary 100,000**

Conscript liability 30 months (there is widespread avoidance of military service)

ORGANISATIONS BY SERVICE

Army ε130,000

FORCES BY ROLE
The Syrian Arab Army combines conventional formations, special forces and auxiliary militias. The main fighting units are the 4th Division, the Republican Guard, the Special Forces (including the former Tiger Forces) and the brigades assigned to the 5th Assault Corps; they receive the most attention and training. Most other formations are under-strength, at an estimated 500–1,000 personnel in brigades and regiments, but Russia has been assisting in the reconstruction and re-equipment of some divisions.

COMMAND
  5 corps HQ
SPECIAL FORCES
  3 SF div(-)
MANOEUVRE
  Mechanised
  2 (4th & Republican Guard) mech div
  1 (1st) mech div (being reconstituted)
  10 mech div(-)
  7 mech bde (assigned to 5th Assault Corps)
  1 (16th) indep mech bde
  2 indep inf bde(-)
  Amphibious
  1 mne unit
COMBAT SUPPORT
  2 SSM bde

EQUIPMENT BY TYPE

Attrition during the civil war has severely reduced equipment numbers for almost all types. It is unclear how much remains available for operations

ARMOURED FIGHTING VEHICLES
  MBT T-55A; T-55AM; T-55AMV; T-62; T-62M; T-72; T-72AV; T-72B; T-72B3; T-72M1; T-90; T-90A
  RECCE BRDM-2
  IFV BMP-1; BMP-2; BTR-82A
  APC
    APC (T) BTR-50
    APC (W) BTR-152; BTR-60; BTR-70; BTR-80
  APC IVECO LMV

ENGINEERING & MAINTENANCE VEHICLES
  ARV BREM-1 reported; T-54/55
  VLB MTU; MTU-20
  MW UR-77

ANTI-TANK/ANTI-INFRASTRUCTURE • MSL
  SP 9P133 *Malyutka*-P (BRDM-2 with RS-AT-3C *Sagger*); 9P148 *Konkurs* (BRDM-2 with RS-AT-5 *Spandrel*)
  MANPATS 9K111 *Fagot* (RS-AT-4 *Spigot*); 9K111-1 *Konkurs* (RS-AT-5 *Spandrel*); 9K115 *Metis* (RS-AT-7 *Saxhorn*); 9K115-2 *Metis*-M (RS-AT-13); 9K135 *Kornet* (RS-AT-14 *Spriggan*); *Milan*

ARTILLERY
  SP 122mm 2S1 *Gvozdika*; **152mm** 2S3 *Akatsiya*
  TOWED 122mm D-30; M-30 (M1938); **130mm** M-46; **152mm** D-20; ML-20 (M-1937); **180mm** S-23
  GUN/MOR 120mm 2S9 NONA-S
  MRL 107mm Type-63; **122mm** BM-21 *Grad*; **140mm** BM-14; **220mm** 9P140 *Uragan*; **300mm** 9A52 *Smerch*; **330mm** some (also improvised systems of various calibres)
  MOR 82mm some; **120mm** M-1943; **160mm** M-160; **240mm** M-240

SURFACE-TO-SURFACE MISSILE LAUNCHERS
  SRBM • Conventional 8K14 (RS-SS-1C *Scud*-B); 9K72 *Elbrus* (RS-SS-1D *Scud* C) 9K72-1 (RS-SS-1E *Scud* D); *Scud* lookalike; 9K79 *Tochka* (RS-SS-21 *Scarab*); *Fateh*-110/M-600

UNINHABITED AERIAL VEHICLES
  ISR • Medium *Mohajer* 3/4; **Light** *Ababil*
AIR DEFENCE
  SAM
    Medium-range 9K37 *Buk* (RS-SA-11 *Gadfly*); 9K317 *Buk*-M2 (RS-SA-17 *Grizzly*)
    Point-defence 9K31 *Strela*-1 (RS-SA-9 *Gaskin*); 9K33 *Osa* (RS-SA-8 *Gecko*); 9K35 *Strela*-10 (RS-SA-13 *Gopher*); 9K32 *Strela*-2 (RS-SA-7 *Grail*)‡; 9K38 *Igla* (RS-SA-18 *Grouse*); 9K36 *Strela*-3 (RS-SA-14 *Gremlin*); 9K338 *Igla*-S (RS-SA-24 *Grinch*)
  SPAAGM 30mm 96K6 *Pantsir*-S1 (RS-SA-22 *Greyhound*)
  GUNS
    SP 23mm ZSU-23-4; **57mm** ZSU-57-2
    TOWED 23mm ZU-23-2; **37mm** M-1939; **57mm** S-60; **100mm** KS-19

Navy ε4,000

Some personnel are likely to have been drafted into other services

EQUIPMENT BY TYPE
PATROL AND COASTAL COMBATANTS 31:
  CORVETTES • FS 1 Project 159AE (*Petya* III)† with 1 triple 533mm ASTT with SAET-60 HWT, 4 RBU 2500 *Smerch* 1 A/S mor, 2 twin 76mm gun
  PBFG 22:
    16 Project 205 (*Osa* I/II)† with 4 single lnchr with P-22 (RS-SS-N-2C *Styx*) AShM
    6 *Tir* with 2 single lnchr with C-802 (CH-SS-N-6) AShM
  PB 8 *Zhuk*†
MINE WARFARE • MINE COUNTERMEASURES 7
  MHC 1 Project 1265 (*Sonya*) with 2 quad lnchr with 9K32 *Strela*-2 (RS-SA-N-5 *Grail*)‡ SAM, 2 AK630 CIWS
  MSO 1 *Akvamaren*-M (FSU Project 266M (*Natya*)) with 2 quad lnchr with 9K32 *Strela*-2 (RS-SA-N-5 *Grail*)‡ SAM
  MSI 5 *Korund* (Project 1258 (*Yevgenya*))
AMPHIBIOUS • LANDING SHIPS • LSM 3 *Polnochny* B (capacity 6 MBT; 180 troops)
LOGISTICS AND SUPPORT • AX 1 *Al Assad*

Coastal Defence

FORCES BY ROLE
COASTAL DEFENCE
  1 AShM bde with P-35 (RS-SSC-1B *Sepal*); P-15M *Termit*-R (RS-SSC-3 *Styx*); C-802; K-300P *Bastion* (RS-SSC-5 *Stooge*)

EQUIPMENT BY TYPE
COASTAL DEFENCE • AShM P-35 (RS-SSC-1B *Sepal*); P-15M *Termit*-R (RS-SSC-3 *Styx*); C-802; K-300P *Bastion* (RS-SSC-5 *Stooge*)

Naval Aviation

All possibly non-operational after vacating base for Russian deployment

EQUIPMENT BY TYPE
HELICOPTERS • ASW 9: 4 Ka-28 *Helix* A; 5 Mi-14 *Haze*

Air Force ε15,000(-)

FORCES BY ROLE
FIGHTER
  2 sqn with Mig-23MF/ML/MLD/UM *Flogger*
  2 sqn with MiG-29A/UB/SM *Fulcrum*
FIGHTER/GROUND ATTACK
  4 sqn with MiG-21MF/bis *Fishbed*; MiG-21U *Mongol* A
  2 sqn with MiG-23BN/UB *Flogger*
GROUND ATTACK
  4 sqn with Su-22M3/M4 *Fitter* J/K
  1 sqn with Su-24MK *Fencer* D
  1 sqn with L-39ZA/ZO *Albatros**
TRANSPORT
  1 sqn with An-24 *Coke*; An-26 *Curl*; Il-76 *Candid*
  1 sqn with *Falcon* 20; *Falcon* 900
  1 sqn with Tu-134B-3
  1 sqn with Yak-40 *Codling*
ATTACK HELICOPTER
  3 sqn with Mi-24D/P *Hind* D/F
  2 sqn with SA342L *Gazelle*

TRANSPORT HELICOPTER
6 sqn with Mi-8 *Hip*/Mi-17 *Hip* H

EQUIPMENT BY TYPE
Heavy use of both fixed- and rotary-wing assets has likely reduced readiness and availability to very low levels. It is estimated that no more than 30–40% of the inventory is operational

AIRCRAFT 184 combat capable

FTR 55: ε25 MiG-23MF/ML/MLD/UM *Flogger*; ε30 MiG-29A/SM/UB *Fulcrum*

FGA 79: ε50 MiG-21MF/bis *Fishbed* J/L; 9 MiG-21U *Mongol* A; ε20 MiG-23BN/UB *Flogger*

ATK 30: 20 Su-22M3/M4 *Fitter* J/K; ε10 Su-24MK *Fencer* D

TPT 23: **Heavy** 3 Il-76 *Candid*; **Light** 13: 1 An-24 *Coke*; 6 An-26 *Curl*; 2 PA-31 *Navajo*; 4 Yak-40 *Codling*; **PAX** 7: 2 *Falcon* 20; 1 *Falcon* 900; 4 Tu-134B-3

TRG 20+: ε20 L-39ZA/ZO *Albatros**; some MBB-223 *Flamingo*†

HELICOPTERS

ATK 20+: ε20 Mi-24D *Hind* D; some Mi-24P *Hind* F

MRH 40: ε20 Mi-17 *Hip* H; ε20 SA342L *Gazelle*

TPT • Medium ε10 Mi-8 *Hip*

AIR-LAUNCHED MISSILES

AAM • IR R-60 (RS-AA-8 *Aphid*); R-73 (RS-AA-11 *Archer*); **IR/SARH**; R-23/24 (RS-AA-7 *Apex*); R-27 (RS-AA-10 *Alamo*); **ARH**; R-77 (RS-AA-12A *Adder*)

ASM Kh-25 (RS-AS-10 *Karen*); Kh-29T/L (RS-AS-14 *Kedge*); HOT

ARM Kh-31P (RS-AS-17A *Krypton*)

Air Defence Command ε20,000(-)

FORCES BY ROLE
AIR DEFENCE

4 AD div with S-125M/M1 *Pechora*-M/M1 (RS-SA-3 *Goa*); S-125-2M *Pechora*-2M (RS-SA-26); 2K12 *Kub* (RS-SA-6 *Gainful*); S-75 *Dvina* (RS-SA-2 *Guideline*)

3 AD regt with S-200 *Angara* (RS-SA-5 *Gammon*); S-300PMU2 (RS-SA-20 *Gargoyle*)

EQUIPMENT BY TYPE
AIR DEFENCE • SAM

Long-range S-200 *Angara* (RS-SA-5 *Gammon*); 20 S-300PMU2 (RS-SA-20 *Gargoyle*)

Medium-range 36+: S-75 *Dvina* (RS-SA-2 *Guideline*); ε36 S-125-2M *Pechora*-2M (RS-SA-26)

Short-range 2K12 *Kub* (RS-SA-6 *Gainful*); S-125M/M1 *Pechora*-M/M1 (RS-SA-3 *Goa*)

Point-defence 9K32 *Strela*-2/2M (RS-SA-7A/B *Grail*)‡

Gendarmerie & Paramilitary ε100,000

National Defence Force ε50,000
An umbrella of disparate regime militias performing a variety of roles, including territorial control

Other Militias ε50,000
Numerous military groups fighting for the Assad regime, including Afghan, Iraqi, Pakistani and sectarian organisations. Some receive significant Iranian support

FOREIGN FORCES

Hizbullah 7,000–8,000

Iran 1,500

Russia 4,000: 1 inf BG; 3 MP bn; 1 engr unit; ε10 T-72B3; ε20 BTR-82A; BPM-97; 12 2A65; 4 9A52 *Smerch*; 10 Su-24M *Fencer*; 6 Su-34; 6 Su-35S; 1 A-50U; 1 Il-20M; 12 Mi-24P/Mi-35M *Hind*; 4 Mi-8AMTSh *Hip*; 1 AShM bty with 3K55 *Bastion* (RS-SSC-5 *Stooge*); 1 SAM bty with S-400 (RS-SA-21 *Growler*); 1 SAM bty with *Pantsir*-S1/S2; air base at Latakia; naval facility at Tartus

TERRITORY WHERE THE GOVERNMENT DOES NOT EXERCISE EFFECTIVE CONTROL

Data here represents the de facto situation for selected armed opposition groups and their observed equipment

Syrian Democratic Forces ε50,000
A coalition of predominantly Kurdish rebel groups in de facto control of much of northeastern Syria. Kurdish forces from the YPG/J (People's Protection Units/Women's Protection Units) provide military leadership and main combat power, supplemented by Arab militias and tribal groups.

EQUIPMENT BY TYPE
ARMOURED FIGHTING VEHICLES

MBT T-55; T-72 (reported)

IFV BMP-1

APC • PPV *Guardian*

AUV M-ATV

ANTI-TANK/ANTI-INFRASTRUCTURE

MSL • MANPATS 9K111-1 *Konkurs* (RS-SA-5 *Spandrel*)

RCL 73mm SPG-9; **90mm** M-79 *Osa*

ARTILLERY

MRL 122mm BM-21 *Grad*; 9K132 *Grad*-P

MOR 82mm 82-BM-37; M-1938; **120mm** M-1943; improvised mortars of varying calibre

AIR DEFENCE • GUNS

SP 14.5mm ZPU-4 (tch); ZPU-2 (tch); ZPU-1 (tch); 1 ZPU-2 (tch/on T-55); **23mm** ZSU-23-4 *Shilka*; ZU-23-2 (tch); **57mm** S-60

TOWED 14.5mm ZPU-2; ZPU-1; **23mm** ZU-23-2

Syrian National Army & National Front for Liberation ε70,000
In late 2019 the Syrian National Army (SNA) and the National Front for Liberation (NLF) began to merge under the SNA umbrella. The SNA formed in late 2017 from Syrian Arab and Turkmen rebel factions operating under Turkish command in the Aleppo governate and northwestern Syria, including Afrin province. The NLF is a coalition of surviving Islamist and nationalist rebel factions formed in 2018 operating in northwestern Syria, particularly in and around Idlib.

EQUIPMENT BY TYPE
ARMOURED FIGHTING VEHICLES

MBT T-54; T-55; T-62

IFV BMP-1

ANTI-TANK/ANTI-INFRASTRUCTURE
  MSL • MANPATS 9K11 *Malyutka* (RS-AT-3 *Sagger*); 9K111 *Fagot* (RS-AT-4 *Spigot*); 9K113 *Konkurs* (RS-T-5 *Spandrel*); 9K115 *Metis* (RS-AT-7); 9K115-2 *Metis*-M (RS-AT-13 *Saxhorn* 2); 9K135 *Kornet* (RS-AT-14 *Spriggan*); BGM-71 TOW; *Milan*
  RCL 73mm SPG-9; **82mm** B-10
ARTILLERY
  TOWED 122mm D-30
  MRL 107mm Type-63; **122mm** 9K132 *Grad*-P; BM-21 *Grad*; *Grad* (6-tube tech)
  MOR 82mm 2B9 *Vasilek*; improvised mortars of varying calibre
AIR DEFENCE
  SAM • Point-defence MANPADS some
  GUNS
    SP 14.5mm ZPU-4 (tch); ZPU-2 (tch); ZPU-1 (tch); **23mm** ZU-23-2 (tch); ZSU-23-4 *Shilka*; **57mm** AZP S-60
    TOWED 14.5mm ZPU-1; ZPU-2; ZPU-4; **23mm** ZU-23-2

Hayat Tahrir al-Sham (HTS) ε10,000

HTS was formed by Jabhat Fateh al-Sham (formerly known as Jabhat al-Nusra) in January 2017 by absorbing other hardline groups. It is designated a terrorist organisation by the US government.

EQUIPMENT BY TYPE
ANTI-TANK/ANTI-INFRASTRUCTURE
  MSL • MANPATS 9K11 *Malyutka* (RS-AT-3 *Sagger*); 9K113 *Konkurs* (RS-AT-5 *Spandrel*); 9K115-2 *Metis*-M (RS-AT-13); 9K135 *Kornet* (RS-AT-14 *Spriggan*)
  RCL 73mm SPG-9; **106mm** M-40
ARTILLERY
  MRL 107mm Type-63
  MOR 120mm some; improvised mortars of varying calibres
AIR DEFENCE
  SAM
    Point-defence 9K32M *Strela*-2M (RS-SA-7B *Grail*)‡
  GUNS
    SP 14.5mm ZPU-1; ZPU-2; **23mm** ZU-23-2; **57mm** S-60

Guardians of Religion (Huras al-Din) ε2,500

An al-Qaeda-affiliated group operating in Idlib province. It is designated a terrorist organisation by the US government.

FOREIGN FORCES

Turkey ε3,000; 3 armd BG; some cdo units; 1 gendarmerie unit
United States *Operation Inherent Resolve* 900; 1 armd inf coy; 1 mne bn(-)

Tunisia TUN

Tunisian Dinar TND		2021	2022	2023
GDP	TND	131bn	144bn	
	USD	46.8bn	46.3bn	
per capita	USD	3,897	3,816	
Growth	%	3.3	2.2	
Inflation	%	5.7	8.1	
Def bgt	TND	3.44bn	4.00bn	
	USD	1.23bn	1.28bn	
FMA (US)	USD	85m	85m	45m
USD1=TND		2.79	3.11	

Real-terms defence budget trend (USDbn, constant 2015)

Population	11,896,972					
Age	0–14	15–19	20–24	25–29	30–64	65 plus
Male	12.9%	3.4%	3.0%	3.4%	22.4%	4.5%
Female	12.1%	3.2%	3.0%	3.5%	23.5%	5.0%

Capabilities

The armed forces' main tasks are to ensure territorial sovereignty and internal security and, while they have limited capacities, a modernisation process is underway. Instability in Libya and Islamist terrorist groups operating from there continue to pose a security concern. In the light of terrorist attacks, the armed forces are engaged in counter-terrorism operations and have been tasked with securing sensitive industrial sites. Designated a major non-NATO ally by the US in 2015, Tunisia benefits from defence and security cooperation with US AFRICOM and also with France and NATO. A ten-year military-cooperation agreement signed with the US in 2020 will provide more training and after-sales support. In 2019, Tunisia sent a C-130 transport aircraft to support the UN's MINUSMA peacekeeping mission in Mali and maintains a deployment to the mission. A helicopter unit was deployed to the Central African Republic in 2021 to join the UN MINUSCA mission there, followed by a battalion of troops in 2022. Tunisia is a member of the Saudi-led Islamic Military Counter Terrorism Coalition. The armed forces are involved in multinational exercises, notably those led by the US, and was one of the hosts for the 2022 *African Lion* exercise. Overall military capability is limited by the ageing equipment inventory, although Tunisia has been the recipient of surplus US systems, including armed utility helicopters. The country has limited defence-industrial capabilities but has recently manufactured a small number of patrol boats for the navy.

ACTIVE 35,800 (Army 27,000 Navy 4,800 Air 4,000)
Gendarmerie & Paramilitary 12,000
Conscript liability 12 months selective

ORGANISATIONS BY SERVICE

Army 5,000; 22,000 conscript (total 27,000)

358 THE MILITARY BALANCE 2023

FORCES BY ROLE
SPECIAL FORCES
  1 SF bde
  1 (Sahara) SF bde
MANOEUVRE
  Reconnaissance
  1 recce regt
  Mechanised
  3 mech bde (1 armd regt, 2 mech inf regt, 1 arty regt,
    1 AD regt, 1 engr regt, 1 sigs regt, 1 log gp)
COMBAT SUPPORT
  1 engr regt

EQUIPMENT BY TYPE
ARMOURED FIGHTING VEHICLES
  MBT 84: 30 M60A1; 54 M60A3
  LT TK 48 SK-105 *Kuerassier*
  RECCE 60: 40 AML-90; 20 FV601 *Saladin*
  APC 480
    APC (T) 140 M113A1/A2
    APC (W) 110 Fiat 6614
    PPV 230: 4 *Bastion* APC: 71 *Ejder Yalcin*; 146 *Kirpi*;
    9 *Vuran*
ENGINEERING & MAINTENANCE VEHICLES
  ARV 11: 5 *Greif*; 6 M88A1
ANTI-TANK/ANTI-INFRASTRUCTURE • MSL
  SP 35 M901 ITV TOW
  MANPATS *Milan*; TOW
ARTILLERY 276
  TOWED 115: **105mm** 48 M101A1/A2; **155mm** 67: 12
  M114A1; 55 M198
  MOR 161: **81mm** 95; **SP 107mm** 48 M106; **120mm**
  18 Brandt
AIR DEFENCE
  SAM • Point-defence 26 M48 *Chaparral*; RBS-70
  GUNS 112
    SP 40mm 12 M42
    TOWED • 20mm 100 M-55

Navy ε4,800

EQUIPMENT BY TYPE
PATROL AND COASTAL COMBATANTS 37
  PSO 4 *Jugurtha* (Damen Stan MSOPV 1400) (of which 2
  with 1 hel landing platform)
  PCFG 3 *La Galite* (FRA *Combattante* III) with 2 quad
  lnchr with MM40 *Exocet* AShM, 1 76mm gun
  PCC 3 *Bizerte* (FRA PR 48)
  PCFT 6 *Albatros* (GER Type-143B) with 2 single 533mm
  TT, 2 76mm guns
  PBF 2 20m Fast Patrol Boat
  PB 19: 5 *Istiklal*; 3 *Utique* (ex-PRC Type-062 (*Haizhui* II)
  mod); 5 *Joumhouria*; 6 V Series
LOGISTICS AND SUPPORT 7:
  ABU 3: 2 *Tabarka* (ex-US *White Sumac*); 1 *Sisi Bou Said*
  AGE 1 *Hannibal*
  AGS 1 *Khaireddine* (ex-US *Wilkes*)
  AWT 1 *Ain Zaghouan* (ex-ITA *Simeto*)
  AX 1 *Salambo* (ex-US *Conrad*, survey)

Air Force 4,000

FORCES BY ROLE
FIGHTER/GROUND ATTACK
  1 sqn with F-5E/F-5F *Tiger* II
TRANSPORT
  1 sqn with C-130B/H/J-30 *Hercules*; G.222; L-410 *Turbolet*
  1 liaison unit with S-208A
TRAINING
  2 sqn with L-59 *Albatros**; MB-326B; SF-260
  1 sqn with MB-326K; MB-326L
TRANSPORT HELICOPTER
  2 sqn with AS350B *Ecureuil*; AS365 *Dauphin* 2; AB-205
    (Bell 205); SA313; SA316 *Alouette* III; UH-1H *Iroquois*;
    UH-1N *Iroquois*
  1 sqn with HH-3E

EQUIPMENT BY TYPE
AIRCRAFT 23 combat capable
  FTR 11: 9 F-5E *Tiger* II; 2 F-5F *Tiger* II
  ATK 3 MB-326K
  ISR 12 *Maule* MX-7-180B
  TPT 18: **Medium** 13: 5 C-130B *Hercules*; 1 C-130H
  Hercules; 2 C-130J-30 *Hercules*; 5 G.222; **Light** 5: 3 L-410
  Turbolet; 2 S-208A
  TRG 32: 9 L-59 *Albatros**; 4 MB-326B; 3 MB-326L; 14 SF-
  260; 2 T-6C *Texan* II
HELICOPTERS
  MRH 34: 1 AS365 *Dauphin* 2; 6 SA313; 3 SA316 *Alouette*
  III; 24 OH-58D *Kiowa Warrior*
  SAR 11 HH-3E
  TPT 39: **Medium** 8 UH-60M *Black Hawk*; **Light** 31: 6
  AS350B *Ecureuil*; 15 Bell 205 (AB-205); 8 Bell 205 (UH-
  1H *Iroquois*); 2 Bell 212 (UH-1N *Iroquois*)
AIR-LAUNCHED MISSILES
  AAM • IR AIM-9P *Sidewinder*
  ASM AGM-114R *Hellfire*

Gendarmerie & Paramilitary 12,000

National Guard 12,000
Ministry of Interior

EQUIPMENT BY TYPE
ARMOURED FIGHTING VEHICLES
  ASLT 2 EE-11 *Urutu* FSV
  APC 29+
    APC (W) 16 EE-11 *Urutu* (anti-riot); VAB Mk3
    PPV 13 Streit *Typhoon*
  AUV IVECO LMV
PATROL AND COASTAL COMBATANTS 24
  PCC 6 *Rais el Blais* (ex-GDR *Kondor* I)
  PBF 7: 4 *Gabes*; 3 *Patrouiller*
  PB 11: 5 *Breitla* (ex-GDR *Bremse*); 4 Rodman 38;
    2 *Socomena*
HELICOPTERS
  MRH 8 SA318 *Alouette* II/SA319 *Alouette* III
  TPT • Light 3 Bell 429

DEPLOYMENT

CENTRAL AFRICAN REPUBLIC: UN • MINUSCA 324; 1 inf coy; 1 hel flt with 3 Bell 205

DEMOCRATIC REPUBLIC OF THE CONGO: UN • MONUSCO 10

MALI: UN • MINUSMA 88; 1 tpt flt with C-130J-30

SOUTH SUDAN: UN • UNMISS 2

SUDAN: UN • UNISFA 2

United Arab Emirates UAE

Emirati Dirham AED		2021	2022	2023
GDP	AED	1.54tr	1.85tr	
	USD	420bn	504bn	
per capita	USD	41,205	47,793	
Growth	%	3.8	5.1	
Inflation	%	0.2	5.2	
Def bdgt [a]	AED	ε70.4bn	ε74.8bn	
	USD	ε19.2bn	ε20.4bn	
USD1=AED		3.67	3.67	

[a] Defence budget estimate derived from central MoD expenditure and a proportion of the Federal Services section of the Abu Dhabi budget

Real-terms defence budget trend (USDbn, constant 2015)

Population		9,915,803				
Age	0–14	15–19	20–24	25–29	30–64	65 plus
Male	8.3%	2.8%	2.8%	4.8%	48.8%	1.4%
Female	7.9%	2.4%	2.3%	3.1%	15.1%	0.4%

Capabilities

The UAE's armed forces are arguably the best trained and most capable of all GCC states. Iran remains a key defence concern, for reasons including the continuing dispute with Tehran over ownership of islands in the Strait of Hormuz, as well as attacks both on tankers off the UAE coast and on oil infrastructure. However, the UAE has shown a growing willingness to take part in operations and project power and influence further abroad, including by sending an F-16 detachment to Afghanistan in the early-to-mid 2010s, and involvement in the conflict in Libya. The UAE also continues to be involved in the Yemen conflict as part of the Saudi-led coalition. In 2022 it was the target of missile and UAV attacks, and the UAE continues to seek to enhance its air defences against such threats. Experience gained in Yemen-related operations has offered combat lessons, not least in limited amphibious operations, and has demonstrated the country's developing approach to both the use of force and the acceptance of military risk. The UAE hosts a French base and is diversifying its security relationships, including with China, although these are complicating ties with the US, which remains the country's key extra-regional defence partner. A new defence agreement with Washington came into force in May 2019 and the US Air Force continues to maintain a substantial force at the Al Dhafra airbase. The armed forces have an advanced inventory of modern equipment across the domains, including its air and missile defences, and are taking steps to upgrade their airborne ISR capabilities. An enhanced defence relationship with Israel reportedly includes the supply of an advanced Israeli air defence system. The UAE continues to develop its domestic defence-industrial base, having consolidated its leading defence firms into the state-owned EDGE Group in 2019, but the country remains reliant on external providers for many major weapons systems.

ACTIVE 63,000 (Army 44,000 Navy 2,500 Air 4,500 Presidential Guard 12,000)

Conscript liability 16–24 months, males 18–30 years dependent on education level. Voluntary service enrolment for women

ORGANISATIONS BY SERVICE

Space
EQUIPMENT BY TYPE
SATELLITES 4
  COMMUNICATIONS 3 *Yahsat*
  ISR 1 *FalconEye*

Army 44,000
FORCES BY ROLE
MANOEUVRE
  Armoured
  2 armd bde
  Mechanised
  2 mech bde
  Light
  1 inf bde
COMBAT SUPPORT
  1 arty bde (3 SP arty regt)
  1 engr gp

EQUIPMENT BY TYPE
ARMOURED FIGHTING VEHICLES
  MBT 303: 45 AMX-30; 258 *Leclerc*
  LT TK 76 FV101 *Scorpion*
  RECCE 49 AML-90
  IFV 395: 160 BMP-3; 235 *Rabdan*
  APC 1,656
    APC (T) 136 AAPC (incl 53 engr plus other variants)
    APC (W) 185: 45 AMV 8×8 (one with BMP-3 turret); 120 EE-11 *Urutu*; 20 VAB
    PPV 1,335: ε460 *Caiman*; ε680 *Maxxpro* LWB; 150 Nimr *Hafeet* 630A (CP); 45 Nimr *Hafeet (Amb)*
  AUV 674+: MCAV-20; 650 M-ATV; Nimr *Ajban*; Nimr *Jais*; 24 VBL
ENGINEERING & MAINTENANCE VEHICLES
  AEV 53+: 53 ACV-AESV; *Wisent*-2
  ARV 158: 8 ACV-AESV Recovery; 4 AMX-30D; 85 BREM-L; 46 *Leclerc* ARV; 15 *Maxxpro* ARV
  NBC VEHICLES 32: 8 Fuchs 2 BIO-RS; 16 *Fuchs* 2 NBC-RS; 8 Fuchs 2 NBC-CPS (CP)
ANTI-TANK/ANTI-INFRASTRUCTURE
  MSL
    SP 135: 20 HOT; 115 Nimr *Ajban* 440A with *Kornet*-E (RS-AT-14 *Spriggan*)
    MANPATS FGM-148 *Javelin*; *Milan*; TOW
  RCL 84mm *Carl Gustaf*

360   THE MILITARY BALANCE 2023

ARTILLERY 649
  SP 155mm 181: 78 G-6; 85 M109A3; 18 Mk F3
  TOWED 99: **105mm** 73 L118 Light Gun; **130mm** 20
  Type-59-I; **155mm** 6 AH-4
  MRL 124: **122mm** 74: 48 *Firos*-25 (est 24 op); 2 *Jobaria*;
  220mm 24 SR5; **227mm** 32 M142 HIMARS; **239mm** 12
  K239 *Chunmoo*; **300mm** 6 9A52 *Smerch*
  MOR 251: **81mm** 134: 20 Brandt; 114 L16; **120mm** 21
  Brandt; **SP 120mm** 96 RG-31 MMP *Agrab* Mk2
SURFACE-TO-SURFACE MISSILE LAUNCHERS
  SRBM • Conventional 6 *Hwasong*-5 (up to 20 msl);
  MGM-168 ATACMS (launched from M142 HIMARS)
UNINHABITED AERIAL VEHICLES
  ISR • Medium *Seeker* II
AIR DEFENCE
  SAM • Point-defence *Mistral*

Navy 2,500

EQUIPMENT BY TYPE
PATROL AND COASTAL COMBATANTS 43
  CORVETTES 7
    FSGHM 6 *Baynunah* with 2 quad lnchr with MM40
    Exocet Block 3 AShM, 1 8-cell Mk 56 VLS with RIM-
    162 ESSM SAM, 1 21-cell Mk 49 GMLS with RIM-
    116C RAM Block 2 SAM, 1 76mm gun
    FSGM 1 *Abu Dhabi* with 2 twin lnchr with MM40
    Exocet Block 3 AShM, 1 76mm gun
  PCFGM 2 *Mubarraz* (GER Lurssen 45m) with 2 twin
  lnchr with MM40 *Exocet* AShM, 1 sextuple *Sadral* lnchr
  with *Mistral* SAM, 1 76mm gun
  PCGM 4:
    2 *Muray Jib* (GER Lurssen 62m) with 2 quad lnchr
    with MM40 *Exocet* Block 2 AShM, 1 octuple lnchr
    with *Crotale* SAM, 1 *Goalkeeper* CIWS, 1 76mm gun,
    1 hel landing platform
    2 *Ghantut* (*Falaj* 2) with 2 twin lnchr with MM40
    Exocet Block 3 AShM, 2 3-cell VLS with VL-MICA
    SAM, 1 76mm gun, 1 hel landing platform
  PCFG 6 *Ban Yas* (GER Lurssen TNC-45) with 2 twin
  lnchr with MM40 *Exocet* Block 3 AShM, 1 76mm gun
  PBFG 12 *Butinah* (*Ghannatha* mod) with 4 single lncher
  with *Marte* Mk2/N AShM
  PBF 12: 6 *Ghannatha* with 1 120mm NEMO mor
  (capacity 42 troops); 6 *Ghannatha* (capacity 42 troops)
MINE WARFARE • MINE COUNTERMEASURES 1
  MHO 1 *Al Murjan* (ex-GER *Frankenthal* Type-332)
AMPHIBIOUS
  LANDING SHIPS • LST 3 *Alquwaisat* with 1 hel
  landing platform
  LANDING CRAFT 18
    LCM 5: 3 *Al Feyi* (capacity 56 troops); 2 (capacity 40
    troops and additional vehicles)
    LCP 4 Fast Supply Vessel (multi-purpose)
    LCT 9: 7 ADSB 64m; 1 *Al-Saadiyat* with 1 hel landing
    platform; 1 *Al Shareeah* (LSV 75m) with 1 hel landing
    platform
LOGISTICS AND SUPPORT 3:
  AFS 2 *Rmah* with 4 single 533mm TT
  AX 1 *Al Semeih* with 1 hel landing platform

Air Force 4,500

FORCES BY ROLE
FIGHTER/GROUND ATTACK
  3 sqn with F-16E/F Block 60 *Fighting Falcon*
  3 sqn with *Mirage* 2000-9DAD/EAD/RAD
AIRBORNE EARLY WARNING AND CONTROL
  1 flt with *GlobalEye*
SEARCH & RESCUE
  2 flt with AW109K2; AW139
TANKER
  1 flt with A330 MRTT
TRANSPORT
  1 sqn with C-17A *Globemaster*
  1 sqn with C-130H/H-30 *Hercules*; L-100-30
  1 sqn with CN235M-100
TRAINING
  1 sqn with Grob 115TA
  1 sqn with *Hawk* Mk102*
  1 sqn with PC-7 *Turbo Trainer*
  1 sqn with PC-21
TRANSPORT HELICOPTER
  1 sqn with Bell 412 *Twin Huey*

EQUIPMENT BY TYPE
AIRCRAFT 156 combat capable
  FGA 137: 54 F-16E Block 60 *Fighting Falcon* (*Desert
  Eagle*); 24 F-16F Block 60 *Fighting Falcon* (13 to remain in
  US for trg); 15 *Mirage* 2000-9DAD; 44 *Mirage* 2000-9EAD
  MP 2 DHC-8 *Dash* 8 MPA
  ISR 7 *Mirage* 2000 RAD*
  SIGINT 1 *Global* 6000
  AEW&C 3 *GlobalEye*
  TPT/TKR 3 A330 MRTT
  TPT 26: **Heavy** 8 C-17A *Globemaster* III; **Medium** 6: 3
  C-130H *Hercules*; 1 C-130H-30 *Hercules*; 2 L-100-30; **Light**
  16: 5 C295W; 5 CN235; 2 P.180 *Avanti* (MEDEVAC)
  TRG 79: 12 Grob 115TA; 12 *Hawk* Mk102*; 30 PC-7 *Turbo
  Trainer*; 25 PC-21
HELICOPTERS
  MRH 21: 12 AW139; 9 Bell 412 *Twin Huey*
  TPT • Light 4: 3 AW109K2; 1 Bell 407
UNINHABITED AERIAL VEHICLES
  CISR • Heavy *Wing Loong* I; *Wing Loong* II
  ISR • Heavy RQ-1E *Predator* XP
AIR-LAUNCHED MISSILES
  AAM • IR AIM-9L *Sidewinder*; R-550 *Magic*; **IIR** AIM-
  9X *Sidewinder* II; **IIR/ARH** *Mica*; **ARH** AIM-120B/C
  AMRAAM
  ASM AGM-65G *Maverick*; LJ-7; *Hakeem* 1/2/3 (A/B)
  ARM AGM-88C HARM
  ALCM *Black Shaheen* (*Storm Shadow*/SCALP EG variant)
BOMBS
  Laser-guided GBU-12/-58 *Paveway* II
  Laser & INS/GPS-guided GBU-54 Laser JDAM
  INS/SAT-guided *Al Tariq*

Air Defence

FORCES BY ROLE
AIR DEFENCE
 2 AD bde (3 bn with *Barak* LRAD: M902 *Patriot* PAC-3)
 3 (short range) AD bn with *Crotale*; *Mistral*; *Rapier*;
  RBS-70; *Javelin*; 9K38 *Igla* (RS-SA-18 *Grouse*); 96K6
  Pantsir-S1 (RS-SA-22)
 2 SAM bty with THAAD

EQUIPMENT BY TYPE
AIR DEFENCE
 SAM 81+
  Long-range 39+: 2+ *Barak* LRAD: 37 M902 *Patriot*
  PAC-3
  Short-range *Crotale*
  Point-defence 9K38 *Igla* (RS-SA-18 *Grouse*); RBS-70;
  Rapier; *Mistral*
  SPAAGM 30mm 42 96K6 *Pantsir*-S1 (RS-SA-22)
  GUNS • Towed 35mm GDF-005
 MISSILE DEFENCE 12 THAAD

Presidential Guard Command 12,000

FORCES BY ROLE
SPECIAL FORCES
 1 SF bn
 1 spec ops bn
MANOEUVRE
 Reconaissance
 1 recce sqn
 Mechanised
 1 mech bde (1 tk bn, 4 mech inf bn, 1 AT coy, 1 cbt engr
 coy, 1 CSS bn)
 Amphibious
 1 mne bn

EQUIPMENT BY TYPE
ARMOURED FIGHTING VEHICLES
 MBT 50 *Leclerc*
 IFV 290: 200 BMP-3; 90 BTR-3U *Guardian*
ANTI-TANK/ANTI-INFRASTRUCTURE
 MSL • SP HMMWV with 9M133 *Kornet*
 (RS-AT-14 *Spriggan*)

Joint Aviation Command

FORCES BY ROLE
GROUND ATTACK
 1 sqn with *Archangel*; AT802 *Air Tractor*
ANTI-SURFACE/ANTI-SUBMARINE WARFARE
 1 sqn with AS332F *Super Puma*; AS565 *Panther*
TRANSPORT
 1 (Spec Ops) gp with AS365F *Dauphin* 2; H125M *Fennec*;
 AW139; Bell 407MRH; Cessna 208B *Grand Caravan*;
 CH-47C/F *Chinook*; DHC-6-300/400 *Twin Otter*; UH-
 60L/M *Black Hawk*
ATTACK HELICOPTER
 1 gp with AH-64D *Apache*

EQUIPMENT BY TYPE
AIRCRAFT 37 combat capable
 ATK 23 *Archangel*
 ISR ε6 AT802 *Air Tractor**

TPT • Light 14: 2 Beech 350 *King Air*; 7 Cessna 208B
 Grand Caravan*; 1 DHC-6-300 *Twin Otter*; 4 DHC-6-400
 Twin Otter
HELICOPTERS
 ATK 28 AH-64D *Apache*
 ASW 7 AS332F *Super Puma* (5 in ASuW role)
 MRH 53+: 4 AS365F *Dauphin* 2 (VIP); 9 H125M *Fennec*; 7
 AS565 *Panther*; 3 AW139 (VIP); 20 Bell 407MRH; 4 SA316
 Alouette III; 6+ UH-60M *Black Hawk* (ABH)
 TPT 66: **Heavy** 22 CH-47F *Chinook*; **Medium** 44: 11 UH-
 60L *Black Hawk*; up to 33 UH-60M *Black Hawk*
AIR-LAUNCHED MISSILES
 ASM AGM-114 *Hellfire*; *Cirit*; *Hydra*-70; HOT
 AShM AS-15TT; AM39 *Exocet*

Gendarmerie & Paramilitary

Critical Infrastructure and Coastal Protection Agency (CICPA)

Ministry of Interior

EQUIPMENT BY TYPE
PATROL AND COASTAL COMBATANTS 115
 PSO 1 *Al Wtaid*
 PCM 2 *Arialah* (Damen Sea Axe 6711) with 1 11-cell
 Mk 15 SeaRAM GMLS with RIM-116C RAM Block 2
 SAM, 1 57mm gun, 1 hel landing platform
 PCC 1 *Shujaa* (Damen Stan Patrol 5009)
 PBF 58: 6 *Baglietto* GC23; 3 *Baglietto* 59; 15 DV-15;
 34 MRTP 16
 PB 53: 2 *Protector*; 16 (US Camcraft 65); 5 (US
 Camcraft 77); 6 Watercraft 45; 12 *Halmatic Work*;
 12 *Al Saber*

DEPLOYMENT

EGYPT: ε300 12 F-16E/F *Fighting Falcon*; *Wing Loong* I UAV;
Wing Loong II UAV (status uncertain)

SOMALIA: 180

FOREIGN FORCES

Australia 400; 1 tpt det with 2 C-130J-30 *Hercules*
France 650: 1 armd BG (1 tk coy, 1 armd inf coy; 1 aty bty);
Leclerc; VBCI; CAESAR; 7 *Rafale* F3; • EMASOH;
1 *Atlantique*-2
Korea, Republic of 170 (trg activities at UAE Spec Ops
School)
United Kingdom 200; 1 tkr/tpt flt with C-17A *Globemaster*;
C-130J *Hercules*; A330 MRTT *Voyager*
United States 5,000; 1 ISR sqn with 4 U-2S; 1 AEW&C
sqn with 4 E-3B/G *Sentry*; 1 tkr sqn with 12 KC-10A; 1 ISR
UAV sqn with RQ-4 *Global Hawk*; 2 SAM bty with M902/
M903 *Patriot* PAC-3/PAC-3 MSE

Yemen, Republic of YEM

Yemeni Rial YER		2021	2022	2023
GDP	YER	20.6tr	30.2tr	
	USD	19.9bn	27.6bn	
per capita	USD	644	874	
Growth	%	-1.0	2.0	
Inflation	%	45.7	43.8	
Def bdgt	YER	n.k	n.k	
	USD	n.k	n.k	
USD1=YER		1035.48	1092.84	

Population	30,984,689

Age	0–14	15–19	20–24	25–29	30–64	65 plus
Male	18.3%	5.8%	5.1%	4.5%	15.4%	1.4%
Female	17.6%	5.6%	5.0%	4.4%	15.1%	1.8%

Capabilities

There appears to be little prospect that any of the competing forces in Yemen's civil war will be able to gain a decisive upper hand in the near term, with successive offensives by various factions failing to significantly alter the situation on the ground. After President Hadi resigned in April 2022, a Saudi-brokered deal agreed a ceasefire and established the Presidential Leadership Council (PLC) under new President al-Alimi that has included the Southern Transitional Council (STC). The new unity government only appears to exercise limited control over the forces nominally allied together against the Houthis, and the end of the ceasefire in October meant a resumption of open hostilities. Irregular forces, such as Tareq Saleh's National Resistance and those of the UAE-backed STC are reportedly better paid and equipped than government forces. The UAE has largely drawn down its own forces and focused its support on the STC and other non-government forces fighting the Houthis, while the remaining members of the Saudi-led coalition continue to provide air support for the PLC administration. The conflict appears to have been sustained by a combination of large existing stockpiles of weapons and ammunition, and external supplies, despite UN embargoes. There is no domestic defence industry, barring some limited maintenance and workshop facilities.

ACTIVE 40,000 (Government forces 40,000)

ORGANISATIONS BY SERVICE

Government forces ε40,000 (incl militia)

Despite the establishment of the Presidential Leadership Council, central government control over the forces nominally allied together against the Houthis remains limited.

FORCES BY ROLE
MANOEUVRE
  Mechanised
  up to 20 bde(-)
EQUIPMENT BY TYPE
ARMOURED FIGHTING VEHICLES
  MBT Some M60A1; T-34†; T-54/55; T-62; T-72
  RECCE some BRDM-2
  IFV BMP-2; BTR-80A; *Ratel*-20

APC
  APC (W) BTR-60
  PPV Streit *Cougar*; Streit *Spartan*
  AUV M-ATV
ANTI-TANK/ANTI-INFRASTRUCTURE
  MSL • MANPATS 9K11 *Malyutka* (RS-AT-3 *Sagger*); M47 *Dragon*; TOW
  GUNS • SP 100mm SU-100†
ARTILLERY • SP 122mm 2S1 *Gvozdika*
AIRCRAFT • ISR 6 AT-802 *Air Tractor**
AIR DEFENCE • GUNS • TOWED 14.5mm ZPU-4; **23mm** ZU-23-2

DEPLOYMENT

MALI: UN • MINUSMA 2

FOREIGN FORCES

All *Operation Restoring Hope* unless stated
Saudi Arabia 2,500: 2 armd BG; M60A3; M2A2 *Bradley*; M113A4; M-ATV; AH-64 *Apache*; M902 *Patriot* PAC-3
Sudan 650; 1 mech BG; T-72AV; BTR-70M *Kobra* 2

TERRITORY WHERE THE GOVERNMENT DOES NOT EXERCISE EFFECTIVE CONTROL

Insurgent forces 20,000 (incl Houthi and tribes)

The Houthi-run de facto administration has controlled northern Yemen since 2015 and is supported by a combination of Houthi tribal militias and elements of the Yemeni armed forces that had been loyal to former president Ali Abdullah Saleh. Following a break between the Houthis and Saleh in late 2017 that resulted in the latter's death, Saleh's former forces have become further split between those that remained affiliated with the Houthis and those who have joined his son and nephew to fight against them. Houthi forces receive material support from Iran, with several clandestine weapons shipments of Iranian origin intercepted in recent years. As well as fighting within Yemen, Houthi forces have launched missile and UAV attacks on targets in Saudi Arabia and the UAE.

FORCES BY ROLE
MANOEUVRE
  Mechanised
  up to 20 bde(-)
EQUIPMENT BY TYPE
ARMOURED FIGHTING VEHICLES
  MBT T-55; T-72
  IFV BMP-2; BTR-80A
  APC • APC (W) Some BTR-40; BTR-60
  AUV M-ATV
ARTILLERY
  MRL • 122mm BM-21 *Grad*; **210mm** *Badr*
ANTI-TANK/ANTI-INFRASTRUCTURE
  MSL • MANPATS 9K111-1 *Konkurs* (RS-AT-5B *Spandrel/Towsan*-1); 9K115 *Metis* (RS-AT-7 *Saxhorn*); *Dehlavieh* (*Kornet*); *Toophan*
  RCL 82mm B-10

SURFACE-TO-SURFACE MISSILE LAUNCHERS
　MRBM • Conventional *Kheibar Shekan* (reported)
　SRBM • Conventional *Borkan*-2H (*Qiam*-1); *Borkan*-3; *Falaq*; *Fateh*-110; *Khalij Fars*
　GLCM • Conventional *Quds*-1; *Quds*-2; *Quds*-3
COASTAL DEFENCE • AShM C-801; C-802
HELICOPTERS
　MRH 1 Mi-17 *Hip* H
　TPT • Light 1 Mi-8 *Hip*
UNINHABITED AERIAL VEHICLES
　ISR • Medium *Sammad*-1

LOITERING & DIRECT ATTACK MUNITIONS
　Qasef-1; *Qasef*-2K; *Sammad*-2; *Sammad*-3; *Waed* (*Shahed*-136)
AIR DEFENCE
　SAM
　　Short-range *Saqr*-1 (358)
　　Point-defence 9K32 *Strela*-2 (RS-SA-7 *Grail*)‡; 9K34 *Strela*-3 (RS-SA-14 *Gremlin*); *Misaq*-1 (QW-1); *Misaq*-2 (QW-18)
　GUNS • TOWED 20mm M167 *Vulcan*; **23mm** ZU-23-2

Chapter Eight
Latin America and the Caribbean

- The low risk of state-on-state conflict in Latin America and the Caribbean means that armed forces and defence investments remain limited, relative to the size of the region's economies and populations. Lacklustre economic performance, an absence of major external security threats and persistently high rates of inflation have resulted in a constrained budgetary environment for defence, with 2022 funding at the same level as 2009 in real terms.

- Brazil remains the region's foremost military power, with its most sophisticated domestic defence industry. It still has the largest defence budget in Latin America, though its share of regional spending fell from 57% in 2010 to 45% in 2022. Defence-industrial modernisation is being helped by technology offset terms associated with key defence programmes focused on air and maritime capabilities, such as the *Gripen* contract with Saab and the PROSUB submarine modernisation contract with French defence firm Naval Group.

- Brazil's army is engaged in a plan to modernise its armoured forces. There are two sub-programmes, for wheeled and tracked vehicles. In July, initial contracts were awarded for the modernisation of nine EE-9 *Cascavel* M VII 6x6 armoured reconnaissance vehicles; the plan is to upgrade 98 by 2031. However, the plan to eventually acquire *Centauro* II vehicles for the 8x8 medium wheeled armoured combat vehicle project hit delays in December, when a court objected to the proposed deal for a total of 98.

- Argentina's share of regional defence spending fell from 11% in 2015 to 5% in 2021 before increasing slightly to 7% in 2022. Hopes of recapitalising its combat air inventory faded at the end of the year, after suggestions that Buenos Aires was interested in the JF-17.

- The arrival of a new government in Colombia raised questions over the future of key procurement plans, notably the replacement of the country's ageing *Kfir* combat aircraft fleet, though the programme was reactivated in September.

Latin America and the Caribbean defence spending, 2022 – top 5, including US Foreign Military Financing

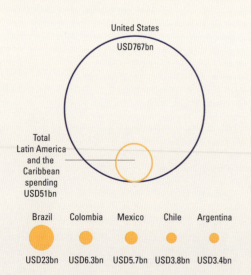

Active military personnel – top 10
(25,000 per unit)

Brazil	366,500	
Colombia	255,950	
Mexico	216,000	
Venezuela	123,000	
Peru	81,000	
Argentina	72,100	
Chile	68,500	
Dominican Republic	56,050	
Cuba	49,000	
Ecuador	41,250	

Global total 20,773,950

Regional total 1,488,330 — 7.2%

Regional defence policy and economics 366 ▶

Arms procurements and deliveries 373 ▶

Armed forces data section 376 ▶

Latin America and the Caribbean: selected tactical combat aircraft, 2022

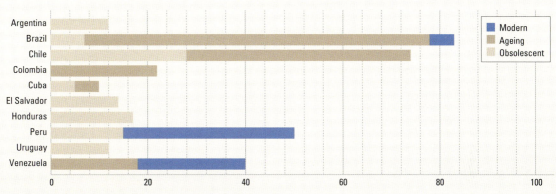

*'Combat aircraft' includes fighter, fighter ground-attack and attack aircraft

Latin America and the Caribbean: selected main battle tank fleets, 2022

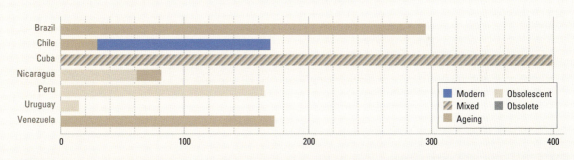

Latin America and the Caribbean: defence spending as % of GDP (average), 2008-22

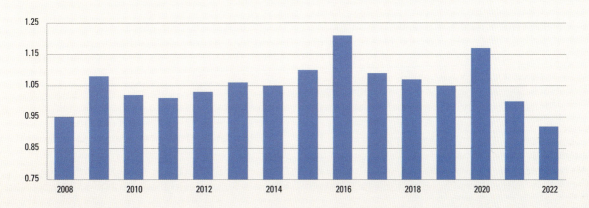

Latin America and the Caribbean

Non-state threats in the region have in recent decades led to significant investment in security capacities. Insecurity and violence persist, but this is generally the result of organised criminal activity, some political violence and, in some cases, attempts by groups to supplant state institutions. However, the still-limited risk of state-on-state conflict in Latin America and the Caribbean means that armed forces and defence investments remain small relative to the size of the region's economies and populations. High levels of coronavirus-related spending in 2020–21 and the regional economic shock caused by the pandemic, combined with the global rise in inflation and other effects of the war in Ukraine, such as supply-chain disruptions, mean that there will be less fiscal space for states looking to increase defence expenditure. As a result, it is likely that priorities, in the short term at least, will focus on continuing existing modernisation plans, particularly in countries where there are readily apparent capability gaps. And there will be continued investment by many regional defence establishments in internal-security capabilities, particularly in those states suffering from high levels of drug-related organised crime, such as Mexico, or from low-level insurgencies, such as Colombia and Peru.

Perhaps the most significant challenge to internal security is seen in **Mexico**, where authorities continue attempts to tackle drug cartels in various regions. Although there have been some procurements in recent years, notably of naval vessels and helicopters, it is possible that these continued internal-security requirements could take priority over improving the armed forces' limited war-fighting capabilities. Indeed, organisational reform has recently been a focus of the administration, including the plan to place the National Guard under military control (which faced legal objections in late 2022) and to extend until 2028 the mandate for the armed forces to remain engaged in domestic security duties. Analysts understand that the National Guard has not reached its full personnel complement or deployment targets but its presence across the country will continue expanding, particularly in regions most prone to drug-related violence such as the north and along the Pacific coast.

Brazil remains the region's foremost military power, with the region's most sophisticated domestic defence industry. Defence-industrial modernisation is being helped by technology-offset terms associated with key defence programmes, such as the *Gripen* contract with Saab and the PROSUB submarine-modernisation contract with French firm Naval Group. Military modernisation is focused on the air force and navy, but despite having the region's largest defence budget, fiscal constraints continue to force procurement trade-offs. An example is the decision to purchase additional *Gripen* combat aircraft (eventually taking the total to over 60) but at the cost of reducing its planned fleet of locally built KC-390 medium transport aircraft to just 19. Four *Gripens* will be added to the original contract for 36, and negotiations are under way for an additional batch of 26. The first aircraft are now in flight test in Brazil. Meanwhile, the navy's first *Scorpène*-class submarine, the *Riachuelo* (S40), was commissioned in September 2022, with three more to follow along with a nuclear-powered attack submarine (the region's first) later in the decade. As part of this PROSUB programme, significant investment has been made in manufacturing and operational-related infrastructure. For its part, the army is engaged in a significant series of programmes intended to modernise its armoured vehicles. Nonetheless, the country faces few serious internal or external threats, though there were entreaties by supporters of Jair Bolsonaro, the defeated candidate in the presidential elections, for the armed forces to intervene following his loss, in a bid to halt the transfer of power. The country will continue to remain active in international security tasks, such as humanitarian and peacekeeping missions. But it is reportedly unlikely to repeat its deployment to Haiti, where it led the MINUSTAH mission in the last decade, amid calls for an international presence to help stabilise Haiti in the midst of continued instability and violence.

Modernisation plans in **Argentina** remain largely dependent on the country's economic outlook. Principal capability gaps are the lack of fast-jet combat aircraft as well as submarines, with its two ageing boats currently non-operational and reactivation increasingly unlikely. Argentine defence officials reportedly visited China and Pakistan in 2022 seeking information about the JF-17 combat aircraft. But such a purchase would very likely prove difficult in budgetary terms without some form of special funding arrangement, given the declining defence budget and increasing inflation. In recent years there were reports that Buenos Aires was interested in obtaining second-hand aircraft from abroad, and that the United Kingdom had vetoed the export of UK-sourced components given reported Argentinian interest in the South Korean FA-50 aircraft. Also, there was tension with Chile in 2022 amid a dispute over the two countries' Antarctic maritime boundaries. In contrast to its neighbour, **Chile** has undertaken one of the most comprehensive military modernisation processes in Latin America over the past two decades. Concerns that there may have been tension between the administration of Gabriel Boric and the armed forces appear to have dissipated, and the president has ordered deployments into some southern regions affected by territorial disputes with indigenous groups. The armed forces are adjusting to the law passed in 2019 that sets a new framework for defence financing, which was previously reliant on copper revenues; the new framework sets financing plans for four-year periods. Similar to Chile, the arrival of a new government in **Colombia** raised questions for observers over the future of key procurement plans, notably the replacement of the country's ageing *Kfir* combat aircraft fleet. However, there appears a

willingness to proceed, and it has been reported that ex-European F-16s could be a potential replacement (these have also been suggested for Argentina) and there have been reports of negotiations with South Korea for FA-50 aircraft. Meanwhile, the government has also begun a rapprochement with Venezuela, including the re-establishment of military ties, which had been suspended since 2019. Colombia continues to face the threat of low-intensity guerrilla warfare, although it is not certain that this would escalate to levels seen before the 2016 peace deal with the Revolutionary Armed Forces of Colombia (FARC) guerrilla group.

Peru has faced a similar situation with regards to the Shining Path terrorist group, which continues to have a localised presence in areas such as the Valley of the Apurímac, Ene and Mantaro rivers (VRAEM) region despite the armed forces scoring some notable successes against them in recent years. Some limited modernisation efforts are under way, such as a requirement for a fleet of new 8x8 armoured personnel carriers, although the upgrade of Peru's equipment inventory has been complicated by limited funding in recent years, the diverse nature of the current inventory and also by the war in Ukraine. **Venezuela**'s economic crisis appears to have plateaued since 2020, though it remains subject to sanctions, which will limit the source of any military modernisation aspirations. Venezuela remains the region's most important client state for Russian, Chinese and Iranian weapons.

Brazil's armoured-vehicle recapitalisation plans

In recent years, Brazil's army has taken a series of ambitious decisions in the hope of strengthening its armoured firepower, protection and mobility. These projects are intended to not only upgrade and replace capabilities that are in many cases ageing but also contribute to the development of the local defence technological and industrial base. The army has received several types of tracked vehicles from the US as part of the Excess Defense Articles programme, has modernised and refurbished existing vehicles and has launched projects to acquire wheeled and tracked platforms and upgrade vehicles already in service. Two key projects are under way, both run by the Army Projects Office: the Army Strategic Programme for Armoured Forces (Programa Estratégico do Exército Forças Blindadas (Prg EE F Bld)) and the Army Strategic Programme for Obtaining Full Operational

Capability (Programa Estratégico do Exército Obtenção da Capacidade Operacional Plena (Prg EE OCOP)).

Modernisation programmes
The armoured forces programme comprises two sub-programmes, one for wheeled vehicles (SPrg Vtr Rodas) and another for tracked vehicles (SPrg Vtr Lagartas). Brazil has acquired a significant number of the Iveco VBTP-MR *Guarani* 6x6 armoured personnel carrier (APC) as part of the wheeled-vehicles programme. Around 600 of these have been delivered to date from the manufacturing plant in Brazil. Vehicles have been contracted in tranches, such as the contract for 1,580 announced in 2016. A number of variants are being pursued, including ambulance, APC, 120mm mortar carrier, engineering, communications, reconnaissance

and fire-direction vehicles. Analysts understand that a batch of 6x6 truck-based armoured recovery vehicles is being acquired through the US Foreign Military Sales programme to support the *Guarani* fleet.

On 7 July 2022, a consortium comprising Akaer Engenharia, Opto Space and Defence and Universal was awarded a contract for the modernisation of an initial nine EE-9 *Cascavel* M VII 6x6 armoured reconnaissance vehicles. The contract is reportedly valued at BRL74.6 million (USD14.6m) and was awarded by the Manufacturing Directorate. The plan is to gradually modernise 98 vehicles by 2031 with upgrades including a new powerpack; new communications; optronics for the driver, commander and gunner; an anti-tank guided missile (ATGM) launcher; an electric gun- and turret-drive system; as well as refurbishment of the 90mm cannon. An additional 103 vehicles could be modernised depending on available funds.

In 2021 the army received the first 32 LMV-BR 4x4 armoured vehicles under a reported BRL67.8m (USD17.2m) contract signed in November 2019 with Iveco to fulfil the army's VBMT-LSR project for wheeled light multirole vehicles. The plan is to acquire additional vehicles in several variants, including to carry ATGMs, and the artillery-observation role.

The 8x8 medium wheeled cavalry armoured combat vehicle project, known as the VBC Cav-MSR 8x8, achieved a major milestone on 25 November. It was announced that the *Centauro* II (combining the Iveco VBM 8x8 wheeled armoured platform and the Leonardo HITFACT MkII 120mm modular protected turret) from the CIO consortium (comprising Iveco Defence Vehicles and Leonardo Electronics) had been selected over proposals from NORINCO and General Dynamics Land Systems-Canada. It was suggested that a contract would be placed in early December for an initial two vehicles for evaluation in Brazil in 2023, with a further seven to be

acquired for additional trials, followed by production vehicles in tranches. The Materiel Directorate of the army's Logistics Command had earlier issued the request for proposals (RFP) on 20 July. An additional 89 vehicles in serial production configuration will be later acquired in different tranches and another 123 vehicles may be acquired at a later date, depending on budget availability.

The VBC OAP 155mm SR project will lead to the acquisition of up to 36 truck-mounted 155mm 52-calibre artillery systems. Guidelines for the project were approved in July 2021 and initial requirements were reportedly unveiled in April 2022. A request for information / request for quotations consultation process began in mid-August 2022 and was scheduled to end in November.

The SPrg Vtr Lagartas project is intended to refurbish and upgrade 116 of the existing 220 *Leopard* 1A5BR main battle tanks (MBTs) from 2023. Options include refurbishing the chassis and adding new features including an electric gun and turret drive system; battle management system; fire-control system; and driver and commander optronics. An RFP for this modernisation project may be issued in late 2022 or early 2023. The *Leopard* 1A5BR fleet will be replaced later by a medium MBT with a 120mm cannon under the VBC CC project. Initial requirements for the future MBT were released in February 2020.

The army also wants to replace its ageing M113BR APCs. To meet this requirement, the VBC Fuz project was set up to acquire a tracked platform with a crewed turret fitted with a medium-calibre automatic cannon and 7.62mm and 12.7mm machine guns. The Fifth Regional Maintenance Park modernised 150 M113B APCs to the M113BR standard between 2011 and 2016. A further 236 M113Bs were modernised at the facility between 2016 and 2019 via the US FMS programme, with the assistance of BAE Systems. This plant will soon begin modernising the third and final batch of 150 M113Bs.

DEFENCE ECONOMICS

Macroeconomics

Even before the additional shocks brought on by the war in Ukraine in 2022, the region's recovery from the economic effects of the coronavirus pandemic was losing momentum, according to the International Monetary Fund (IMF). The 7.0% economic contraction in the Caribbean and Latin America was the sharpest in the world and more severe than the global slowdown of 3.0% in 2020. However, there was a strong recovery in

2021, with regional real GDP growth surging to 6.9% as countries moved ahead with vaccination programmes, trading partners returned to growth, commodity prices rose, and external financing conditions remained accommodative, which kept the cost of borrowing low.

A lower rate of growth for 2022 would be expected in all regions as GDP levels return to trend, but the recovery in Latin America was inhibited by structural problems including low productivity and high inequality. With the war in Ukraine continuing, the region now faces challenges stemming from slower growth in the US and China combined with the supply-chain disruptions and soaring inflation that have stemmed from the war. Regional governments are also limited in their fiscal and monetary options, having increased deficits and debt to fund the support measures intended to counter the economic impact of the pandemic. Moreover, any positive economic effect from higher commodity prices is countered by rising inflation, higher interest rates and the negative impact on crucial trading partners.

Regional real GDP growth is projected to come to 3.5% in 2022 and slow to 1.7% in 2023. The regional trend masks variances in economic performance and outlook across the region. The relatively quick and effective vaccine rollout in Chile, combined with extensive policy support, resulted in a rapid recovery in 2021 and its outlook is stronger than many of its neighbours due to strong consumer activity. Colombia is also on a strong economic footing, having recovered to pre-pandemic levels of output in early 2022. The outlook there is strengthened by higher prices for oil, coal and metals. Real GDP growth in Argentina reached a sizeable 10.4% in 2021, after contracting by 9.9% in 2020, and the projected 4.0% growth rate in 2022 was among the strongest in the region. However, inflation will continue to have a dampening effect on growth.

Coming into 2022, Brazil looked to be on a solid path to regaining pre-pandemic levels of output, but the country faced challenges from high inflation which restricted real incomes, from stalling investment growth and from domestic political uncertainty after the presidential election. Meanwhile, Mexico suffered a severe 8.1% real GDP contraction in 2020 and has struggled to achieve sizeable growth since. Mexico's economy is more exposed to global shocks as its manufacturing sector is more globally integrated and therefore more vulnerable to supply-chain disruptions. Finally, Caribbean countries with high tourism-dependence saw significant contractions in output in 2022, and it may take until 2024 for them to recover as global travel struggles to return to pre-pandemic levels.

High rates of inflation are a pervasive issue across the region while increased unemployment has also resulted in a rise in regional inequality and poverty. According to the Economic Commission for Latin America and the Caribbean, the number of people in poverty in the region reached 209 million in 2020, 22m more than in 2019. High rates of inequality have fuelled protests in recent years, with some driven by perceptions of social injustice.

The wave of demonstrations across the region since late 2019 stalled in 2020 because of pandemic-related restrictions on public activity. These re-emerged as the underlying drivers of unrest have intensified with the easing of pandemic restrictions. According to the IMF, countries in the region must simultaneously tackle three major challenges: 'ensuring the sustainability of public finances; raising potential growth; and doing it in a manner that promotes social cohesion and addresses social inequities'.

Defence spending

Lacklustre economic performance, an absence of major external security threats and persistently high rates of inflation have resulted in a constrained budgetary environment for defence, with 2022 funding at the same level as 2009 in real terms. Widespread social challenges and pressing internal-security concerns create conflicting spending pressures and, as a result, regional defence spending has stagnated in recent years. Budgets have also fallen significantly in US dollar terms, as several currencies – including the Argentine peso, the Brazilian real and the Chilean peso – have been severely devalued against the dollar since 2018.

Regional spending is further muted by the stable but low growth trend in the Brazilian defence budget. This remains the largest in Latin America even though its share of regional spending fell from 57% in 2010 to 45% in 2022. The Brazilian defence budget has fluctuated between USD22 billion and USD27bn in real terms for the last decade with the country generally spending between 1.3% and 1.5% of GDP. This is somewhat higher than the regional average of 0.9% of GDP but well below the global average of 1.7% of GDP.

After a sizeable cut to the 2020 defence budget was reversed, Brazilian funding reached BRL114bn (USD22.2bn) that year, which marked a 1.9% real increase over 2019 levels. However, growth rates have been subdued ever since with spending effectively static, resulting in cuts in real terms of 9.7% and 6.0% in 2021 and 2022 respectively. The 2023 budget of BRL121bn (USD24.0bn) does little to counter this trend, with inflation expected to come to 5%, though former Minister of Defence Paulo Sérgio Nogueria de Oliveira was looking to increase the defence budget to 2% of GDP. Speaking to the House Foreign Affairs Committee of the Brazilian Congress in July 2022, he highlighted the need to invest in R&D, military training and surveillance in the Amazon as well as the need to engage more in international security.

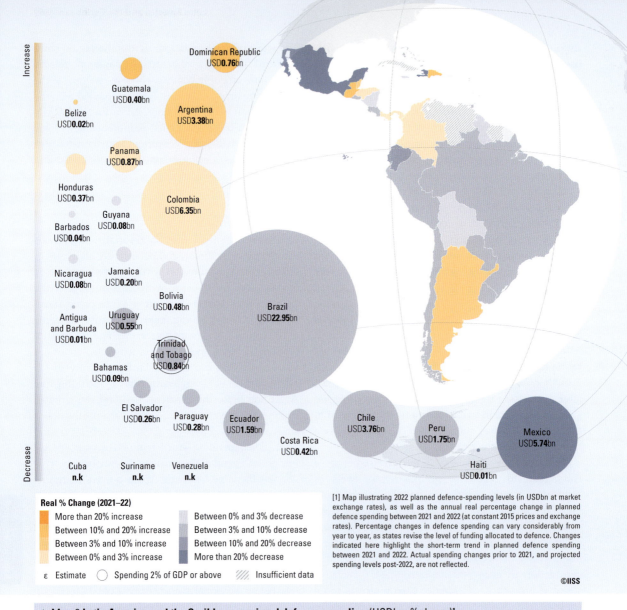

▲ Map 9 **Latin America and the Caribbean: regional defence spending** (USDbn, %ch yoy)[1]

Speaking alongside the minister, the commanders of the air force and the army asked the committee for more funds for defence and highlighted the challenges that the constrained budgetary environment had created over the previous eight years. According to the air force commander, despite closing four air bases and three maintenance facilities, personnel spending still needed to reduce in order to fund investments. The army commander asked that any cuts to defence be minimised so the progress of strategic projects was not impeded.

Despite a constrained budgetary environment, Brazil is pursuing several modernisation and acquisition programmes. They include the PROSUB submarine-development programme and the purchase of 36 Saab *Gripen* combat aircraft (both with technology-transfer terms); four MEKO frigates; a medium-range air-defence system; main battle tanks; transport aircraft; and offshore patrol vessels.

Inflation in Colombia has not been as severe as in many of its neighbours, reaching 3.5% in 2021 compared with the regional average of 8.2% (excluding Venezuela). This means the country managed real defence budget growth in 2020 and 2021 whereas other countries saw contractions. Despite inflation rising to 9.7% in 2022, the country still managed to implement real growth in the 'defence and police' budget, which reached USD10.5bn. Approximately 57% of this budget is allocated to defence with the remaining 43% allocated to the National Police. The 2023 budget is expected to show a stronger increase for 'defence and police' to USD11.6bn, although the Ministry of Finance was considering a small reduction to the defence budget that would reportedly impact investment in new systems and equipment.

It had been suggested that the outlook for Colombia's defence budget would be subdued with the election in June 2022 of a new president, Gustavo Petro, focused on pursuing 'total peace' for Colombia with a strong accent on social development. Petro reportedly stated during the election campaign that he would not prioritise the purchase of combat aircraft or military hardware. However, the programme to replace Colombia's ageing *Kfir* fighter ground-attack aircraft was reactivated in September 2022. Reports suggest that the disparity with Venezuela's inventory was a driver behind the decision, although relations between the two countries have improved recently after eight years of political conflict.

Argentina's defence budget plummeted in both real and US dollar terms between 2017 and 2021. Inflation has averaged 50% since 2018, which has created further pressure for devaluation of a currency that has already fallen from 17 pesos to the dollar in 2017 to 125 pesos to the dollar in 2022. Argentina's share of regional spending fell from 11% in 2015 to 5% in 2021 before increasing slightly to 7% in 2022. The 2022 defence budget increase to USD3.4bn was the first real-term increase for four years and investment has increased from an average of 2.1% of the budget over 2010–20 to 5.3% in 2021 and 5.9% in 2022. The government is also planning to spend USD684m on new combat aircraft and related infrastructure, a programme that has been stymied by UK embargo restrictions in the past.

Defence budget movements in Mexico have been volatile in recent years, with an 8% real cut in 2019 followed by sharp increases in 2020 and 2021 of 13% and 10% respectively to reach USD6.7bn in 2021. The 2022 budget fell back slightly to USD5.7bn. The recent increases derive from the increasing role that defence forces have played in domestic security, taking on functions previously allocated to internal security forces. In 2022, the president unveiled a plan to bring the National Guard under military control, though this was subject to legal challenge in late year. These factors are likely to drive future increases in the defence budget but could result in conflicting funding priorities and perhaps mask any reductions for core defence capabilities.

Defence industry

Brazil has been keen to develop indigenous defence industrial capabilities through successive national defence strategies since 2005 that have aimed to progress from off-the-shelf foreign purchases to the pursuit of programmes that would boost domestic capabilities and enable import substitution. Brazil has looked to leverage technology transfer and industrial participation in its foreign procurement contracts in order to develop domestic industry. This has resulted in a defence industrial base with the capability to produce large-scale naval and air platforms as well as

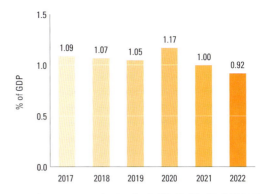

▲ Figure 17 **Latin America and the Caribbean: regional defence spending** as % of GDP (average)

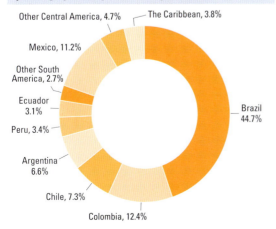

▼ Figure 16 **Latin America and the Caribbean: defence spending by country and sub-region, 2022**

Note: Analysis excludes Cuba, Suriname and Venezuela ©IISS

372　THE MILITARY BALANCE 2023

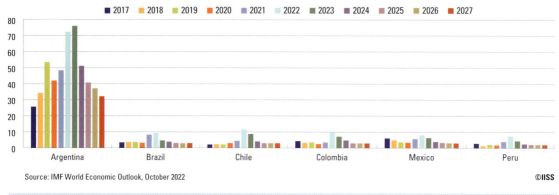

▲ Figure 18 **Latin America: selected countries, inflation (%), 2017–27**

rockets and artillery. The country has also developed capabilities in the uninhabited arena with Akaer, a domestic company, developing the *Albatross* family of medium-altitude long-endurance uninhabited aerial vehicles (MALE UAVs).

According to Brazil's defence minister, the country's defence industry makes up 4.8% of GDP and supports almost 3m direct and indirect jobs. He also stated that the Brazilian defence-industrial base extends to more than 1,100 companies, of which 142 are strategic. Embraer – Brazil's primary defence aerospace company – reported a 31% drop in company-wide revenues in 2020 but revenue growth returned in 2021, reaching 11%. Nevertheless, the defence and security sector saw revenues fall in 2021 following the agreement with the air force to reduce the number of KC-390 transport aircraft on order from 29 to 19.

Beyond Brazil, the lack of any significant and sustained growth in defence spending and the low levels of funding allocated by the major regional players to investment (procurement and R&D) – at between 2% and 10% of annual defence expenditure – constrains the development of indigenous capabilities in Latin America. Colombia's offset policy has yet to result in a wide-ranging or advanced domestic defence capability, with the country still heavily reliant on foreign imports for major programmes. One area of development is in space systems, with Colombia's air force inaugurating a space operations centre on 28 July 2022. It plans to launch a new satellite in 2022 or 2023. Mexico, meanwhile, has established a small defence industry capable of producing small arms and light weapons, 4x4 tactical patrol vehicles, UAVs, fast interceptor craft and coastal and ocean patrol vessels.

Latin America and the Caribbean 373

Arms procurements and deliveries – Latin America and the Caribbean

Significant events in 2022

ENAER PRESENTS NEW TRAINING-AIRCRAFT DESIGN

APRIL

Aerospace firm *Empresa Nacional de Aeronáutica de Chile* (ENAER), owned by the Chilean Air Force (FACh), presented a model of a *Pillán* II turboprop training aircraft that will replace the 1980s-era T-35 *Pillán* in FACh service. ENAER has completed the concept-design phase and plans for a first flight in 2025 and certification in 2026. Over 80 T-35 *Pilláns* remain in service, and as such the *Pillán* II represents an export opportunity for Chile. Since being established in 1984, ENAER has largely focused on maintenance, repair and overhaul (MRO) for the FACh and other customers. It also makes subcomponents for aircraft such as the Dassault *Falcon* business jet and the Airbus C295 transport aircraft. The T-35 *Pillán* was one of three aircraft manufactured by ENAER after the firm was established in 1984, and it was exported to Spain and six Latin American states.

PERU RATIFIES MOU WITH ISRAEL

AUGUST

The Peruvian government finally ratified a memorandum of understanding (MoU) with the Israeli government that was signed in July 2008. The plan is to develop defence-industrial cooperation, including in procurement and in technology transfer. Israeli investment in Peru's defence industry has so far been limited, with the main development being the opening in 2011 of a Peruvian production line for Israeli small arms. Peru spent USD61.8m on *Spike* LR anti-tank missiles in 2009, followed in the mid-2010s by an order for *Spike*-ER and a handful of armoured vehicles. Most of Peru's defence industry is state-owned and, while defence spending has been stagnant for the past decade, it is possible that foreign investment and cooperation could facilitate equipment recapitalisation. Currently, much equipment (particularly in the army) is obsolescent and there has been relatively little recent investment.

COLOMBIA FRIGATE AGREEMENT

SEPTEMBER

Representatives from Colombian Navy-owned COTECMAR and Dutch shipbuilder Damen Schelde Naval Shipbuilding signed a design contract for a frigate based on Damen's SIGMA 10514 design. Colombia's *Plataforma Estratégica de Superficie* (PES) [Strategic Surface Platform] programme was first announced in 2015, with the aim of acquiring two batches of four frigates to be commissioned between 2027 and 2035. Seven years later, the requirement has been reduced to five vessels. Due to the complexity of modern frigate design, Colombia had planned from the beginning to seek a partnership with a foreign company. Bogota took the same approach with Project Orión, the programme for offshore patrol vessels that it had begun in 2008 in partnership with Chile and German company Fassmer. Colombia is the third export customer for the SIGMA 10514 design, following sales to Indonesia and Mexico. Both contracts involved local construction and technology transfer.

BRAZIL CUTS AEROSPACE PROGRAMMES

OCTOBER

Embraer announced that it had agreed with the Brazilian Air Force (FAB) to cut the number of KC-390s on order from 22 to 19. In May, the chief of the FAB told reporters that he had begun talks with Embraer to reduce the number of aircraft from 22 to 15. The FAB and Embraer had previously agreed in February to cut the order under the 2014 contract from 28 to 22 aircraft and stretch deliveries from 2027 out to 2034. The coronavirus pandemic and other financial pressures mean that the service cannot presently afford all the aircraft it originally ordered. However, the FAB also wants to prioritise a second batch of 26 *Gripen* combat aircraft and modify the original 2014 *Gripen* order to increase numbers from 36 to 40. Similarly, the tri-service H-XBR programme to acquire 50 H225M helicopters will be cut by three (one from each service), in order to fund in-service support for the army as well as the procurement of H125 helicopters, for training, by the FAB and navy. The FAB also announced that it would cancel work, that it had started in early 2021, with Embraer on an armed UAV and a light transport aircraft.

Latin America and the Caribbean

Table 15 Peru: selected procurement since 2010

Since 2010, Peru has acquired defence equipment from over 15 countries. A reduction in defence spending since 2013 and recent budgetary pressures resulting from the coronavirus pandemic have meant that much acquisition has been relatively small scale and that some programmes, such as new frigates for the navy and 8x8 armoured vehicles for the army, have been postponed or scaled down. Indeed, the largest single acquisition since 2010 has been the army's procurement of 24 Mi-171Sh transport helicopters from Russia for USD528 million.

Although replacements were examined for the air force's ageing *Mirage* 2000 and MiG-29 fighter aircraft in the early 2010s, there has been little progress since – likely because of the relatively high cost of any potential acquisition. Nonetheless, some second-hand aircraft, including utility

helicopters, SH-2 *Seasprite* helicopters and KC-130H tanker aircraft, were acquired from the Netherlands, New Zealand and Spain respectively.

Similarly, apart from the procurement of Israeli and Russian anti-tank missiles in the 2000s, and Chinese multiple rocket launchers and Russian helicopters in the 2010s, the army has seen relatively little investment and continues to operate largely obsolescent equipment. In contrast, the navy has acquired improved systems. A 2012 naval cooperation agreement with South Korea has so far seen the donation of two *Po Hang*-class corvettes as well as the licensed-production of two landing platform dock (LPD) vessels at state-owned shipyard SIMA, located in Callao. The shipyard will likely also be involved in building new offshore patrol vessels (OPVs). A number of foreign designs have been linked to this requirement.

Contract Date	Equipment	Type	Quantity	Value (USD millions)	Contractor	Deliveries	Service
Feb 2010	Fokker 60	Maritime patrol aircraft; Light transport aircraft	2; 2	n.k.	Netherlands government surplus	2010	Navy
Jul 2010	Mi-35P *Hind* E; Mi-171Sh *Hip*	Attack helicopter; Medium transport helicopter	2; 6	107.9	Russian Helicopters	2011	Air Force
Jun 2011	DHC-6-400 *Twin Otter*	Light transport aircraft	12	67	Viking Air	2011–15	Air Force
c. 2012	*Río Itaya*	Patrol boat	1	1.09	SIMA Peru	2013	Coast Guard
Jan 2012	*Griffon* 2000TD	Utility craft air cushioned	5	13.27	Griffon Hoverwork	2013	Navy
Nov 2012	KT-1P	Training aircraft	20	208.87	Korea Aerospace Industries (KAI)	2014–17	Air Force
Dec 2012	H145	Light transport helicopter	5	n.k.	Airbus	2013–14	Police
Aug 2013	*Pisco*	Landing platform dock	2	137.14	SIMA Peru	2018–ongoing	Navy
Nov 2013	C-27J *Spartan*	Medium transport aircraft	2	132.81	Alenia Aermacchi	2015	Air Force
Dec 2013	*Río Pativilca*	Coastal patrol craft	6	n.k.	SIMA Peru	2016–21	Navy
Dec 2013	Mi-171Sh *Hip*	Medium transport helicopter	24	528	Ulan-Ude Aviation Plant (U-UAZ)	2014–16	Army
Dec 2013	PHL-90B	122mm multiple rocket launcher	27	38.58	NORINCO	2015	Army
c. 2014	*Angamos* (GER Type-209/1200)	Attack submarine upgrade	4	470.63	SIMA Peru	tbd	Navy
Apr 2014	PerúSAT-1	ISR satellite	1	199.01	Airbus	2016	Ministry of Defence
Jul 2014	LAV II	Armoured personnel carrier (wheeled)	32	67	General Dynamics Land Systems-Canada (GDLS-C)	2015-16	Marines
Jul 2014	*Tacna* (ex-NLD *Amsterdam*)	Fleet replenishment oiler with a hangar	1	69.1	Netherlands government surplus	2014	Navy

Date	Designation	Type	Quantity	Value (US$m)	Country	Supplier	Delivery	Operator
Oct 2014	Fokker 50	Light transport aircraft	2	n.k.	Netherlands	Netherlands government surplus	2014	Navy
Oct 2014	SH-2G *Super Seasprite*	Anti-submarine warfare helicopter upgrade	5	n.k.	Canada	General Dynamics Mission Systems-Canada	2018–22	Navy
Dec 2014	*Carrasco*	Oceanographic research vessel	1	105.24	Spain	Freire Shipyard	2017	Navy
Dec 2014	C-27J *Spartan*	Medium transport aircraft	2	132.88	Italy	Finmeccanica	2015–17	Air Force
Dec 2014	SH-2G *Super Seasprite*	Anti-submarine warfare helicopter	5	24.93	New Zealand	New Zealand government surplus	2018–22	Navy
c. 2014	Cessna 172	Light transport aircraft	7	n.k.	United States	Textron Aviation	2015	Air Force
c. 2014	*Spike*-ER	Man-portable anti-tank missile systems	36	n.k.	Israel	Rafael Advanced Defense Systems	2015–16	Army
Apr 2015	Bell 412SP *Twin Huey*	Multi-role helicopter	3	11.98	Netherlands	Netherlands government surplus	2015	Navy
Oct 2015	*Ferré* (ex-ROK *Po Hang*)	Corvette	1	0	Republic of Korea	Republic of Korea government surplus	2016	Navy
Jan 2016	RAM Mk3	Armoured reconnaissance vehicle	7	1.74	Israel	IAI RAMTA	2017	Navy
Jun 2019	Enstrom F-28	Training helicopter	4	4.11	United States	Enstrom Helicopter Corporation	2021–ongoing	Air Force
Dec 2019	Mi-171Sh *Hip*	Medium transport helicopter	2	43.7	Belarus	Belspetsvneshtechnika	2021	Police
Oct 2020	Combat Boat 90HSM	Fast patrol boat	2	n.k.	Peru	SIMA Peru	tbd	Navy
Dec 2020	KC-130H *Hercules*	Tanker/transport aircraft	2	28.53	Spain	Spain government surplus	2021	Air Force
Apr 2021	*Ferré* (ex-ROK *Po Hang*)	Corvette	1	0	Republic of Korea	Republic of Korea government surplus	2022	Navy

M = multinational

Antigua and Barbuda ATG

East Caribbean Dollar XCD		2021	2022	2023
GDP	XCD	3.97bn	4.57bn	
	USD	1.47bn	1.69bn	
per capita	USD	14,809	16,787	
Growth	%	5.3	6.0	
Inflation	%	1.6	8.5	
Def bdgt [a]	XCD	20.0m	20.5m	
	USD	7.40m	7.59m	
USD1=XCD		2.70	2.70	

[a] Budget for the Ministry of Legal Affairs, Public Safety, Immigration & Labour

Real-terms defence budget trend (USDm, constant 2015)

Population   100,335

Age	0–14	15–19	20–24	25–29	30–64	65 plus
Male	11.2%	3.6%	4.0%	3.8%	20.3%	4.1%
Female	10.9%	3.6%	4.1%	4.0%	24.8%	5.5%

Capabilities

The Antigua and Barbuda Defence Force (ABDF) focuses on internal security and disaster relief, and also contributes to regional counter-narcotics efforts. It comprises a light-infantry element, which carries out internal-security duties, and a coastguard, which is tasked with fishery protection and counter-narcotics. Antigua and Barbuda is a member of the Caribbean Community and the Caribbean Regional Security System. There are defence ties with the UK and the US. The ABDF has participated in US SOUTHCOM's *Tradewinds* disaster-response exercise, though it has no independent capacity to deploy forces other than in its immediate neighbourhood. There is no heavy land-forces equipment, while the coastguard maintains ex-US patrol vessels and a number of smaller boats. Aside from limited maintenance facilities, there is no indigenous defence industry.

ACTIVE 180 (Army 130 Coast Guard 50)
(all services form combined Antigua and Barbuda Defence Force)
RESERVE 80 (Joint 80)

ORGANISATIONS BY SERVICE

Army 130
FORCES BY ROLE
MANOEUVRE
  Light
  1 inf bn HQ
  1 inf coy
COMBAT SERVICE SUPPORT
  1 spt gp (1 engr unit, 1 med unit)

Coast Guard 50
EQUIPMENT BY TYPE
PATROL AND COASTAL COMBATANTS • PB 2: 1 *Dauntless*; 1 *Swift*

Argentina ARG

Argentine Peso ARS		2021	2022	2023
GDP	ARS	46.3tr	81.8tr	
	USD	487bn	631bn	
per capita	USD	10,617	13,622	
Growth	%	10.4	4.0	
Inflation	%	48.4	72.4	
Def bdgt	ARS	246bn	438bn	827bn
	USD	2.59bn	3.38bn	
USD1=ARS		95.09	129.63	

Real-terms defence budget trend (USDbn, constant 2015)

Population   46,245,668

Age	0–14	15–19	20–24	25–29	30–64	65 plus
Male	12.2%	3.9%	3.8%	3.6%	20.6%	5.3%
Female	11.5%	3.7%	3.6%	3.5%	21.0%	7.2%

Capabilities

Argentina's armed forces have sufficient training and equipment to fulfil internal-security tasks, although any power-projection ambition is limited by funding shortfalls. The armed forces principally focus on border security, surveillance and counter-narcotics operations, and there is some cooperation with Bolivia and Paraguay. In 2020, the government repealed 2018 legislation, passed under the previous administration, that had allowed greater latitude in deploying the armed forces to tackle external challenges including from organised-crime groups. There is military cooperation with the US and the armed forces participate in multinational exercises and bilateral peacekeeping exercises with neighbour Chile. There are limited deployment capabilities, and the equipment inventory is increasingly obsolete, with modernisation hampered by funding problems. The air force faces significant equipment-availability challenges and the navy has seen its capability decline in areas such as anti-submarine warfare, mine warfare and airborne early warning, although it has received new investment in the way of offshore patrol vessels. Argentina possesses an indigenous defence-manufacturing and maintenance capacity covering land, sea and air systems, although industry fortunes have dipped in recent years because of a lack of investment. Recent international procurement ambitions have been hampered by the UK's refusal to provide export licences for UK-built defence-related components.

ACTIVE 72,100 (Army 42,800 Navy 16,400 Air 12,900) **Gendarmerie & Paramilitary 31,250**

ORGANISATIONS BY SERVICE

Army 42,800
Regt and gp are usually bn-sized
FORCES BY ROLE
MANOEUVRE
  Mechanised

1 (1st) div (1 armd bde (1 armd recce regt, 3 tk regt, 1 mech inf regt, 1 SP arty gp, 1 cbt engr bn, 1 int coy, 1 sigs sqn, 1 log coy), 1 (3rd) jungle bde (2 jungle inf regt, 2 jungle inf coy, 1 arty gp, 1 engr coy, 1 int coy, 1 sigs coy, 1 log coy, 1 med coy); 1 (12th) jungle bde (2 jungle inf regt, 1 jungle inf coy, 1 arty gp, 1 engr bn, 1 int coy, 1 sigs coy, 1 log coy, 1 med coy), 2 engr bn, 1 sigs bn, 1 log coy)

1 (3rd) div (1 armd bde (1 armd recce sqn, 3 tk regt, 1 mech inf regt, 1 SP arty gp, 1 cbt engr coy, 1 int coy, 1 sigs sqn, 1 log coy); 1 mech bde (1 armd recce regt, 1 tk regt, 2 mech inf regt, 1 SP arty gp, 1 cbt engr bn, 1 int coy, 1 sigs coy, 1 log coy); 1 mech bde (1 armd recce regt, 1 tk regt, 2 mech inf regt, 1 SP arty gp, 1 cbt engr bn, 1 int coy, 1 sigs coy, 1 log coy); 1 int bn, 1 sigs bn, 1 log coy, 1 AD gp (2 AD bn))

1 (Rapid Deployment Force) div (1 SF gp; 1 mech bde (1 armd recce regt, 3 mech inf regt, 1 arty gp, 1 MRL gp, 1 cbt engr coy, 1 sigs coy,1 log coy); 1 AB bde (1 recce sqn, 2 para regt, 1 air aslt regt, 1 arty gp, 1 cbt engr coy, 1 sigs coy, 1 log coy))

Light

1 (2nd) mtn inf div (1 mtn inf bde (1 recce regt, 3 mtn inf regt, 1 mtn inf coy, 2 arty gp, 1 cbt engr bn, 1 sigs coy, 1 log coy); 1 mtn inf bde (1 recce regt, 3 mtn inf regt, 1 mtn inf coy, 1 arty gp, 1 cbt engr bn, 1 sigs coy, 1 log coy); 1 mtn inf bde (1 recce regt, 2 mtn inf regt, 2 arty gp, 1 cbt engr bn, 1 sigs coy, 1 construction coy, 1 log coy), 1 arty gp, 1 AD bn, 1 sigs bn)

1 mot cav regt (presidential escort)

COMBAT SUPPORT

1 engr bn

1 CBRN coy

1 sigs gp (1 EW bn, 1 sigs bn, 1 maint bn)

1 sigs bn

1 sigs coy

COMBAT SERVICE SUPPORT

3 maint bn

HELICOPTER

1 avn gp (bde) (1 avn bn, 1 tpt hel bn, 1 atk/ISR hel sqn)

EQUIPMENT BY TYPE

ARMOURED FIGHTING VEHICLES

MBT 231: 225 TAM, 6 TAM S21

LT TK 117: 107 SK-105A1 *Kuerassier*; 6 SK-105A2 *Kuerassier*; 4 *Patagón*

RECCE 47 AML-90

IFV 232: 118 VCTP (incl variants); 114 M113A2 (20mm cannon)

APC 278

  APC (T) 274: 70 M113A1-ACAV; 204 M113A2

  APC (W) 4 WZ-551B1

ENGINEERING & MAINTENANCE VEHICLES

ARV *Greif*

ANTI-TANK/ANTI-INFRASTRUCTURE

MSL • SP 3 M1025 HMMWV with TOW-2A

RCL 105mm 150 M-1968

ARTILLERY 1,108

SP 155mm 42: 23 AMX F3; 19 VCA 155 *Palmaria*

TOWED 172: **105mm** 64 Model 56 pack howitzer; **155mm** 108: 28 CITEFA M-77/CITEFA M-81; 80 SOFMA L-33

MRL 8: 105mm 4 SLAM *Pampero*; **127mm** 4 CP-30

MOR 886: **81mm** 492; **SP 107mm** 25 M106A2; **120mm** 330 Brandt; **SP 120mm** 39 TAM-VCTM

AIRCRAFT

TPT • Light 13: 1 Beech 80 *Queen Air*; 3 C-212-200 *Aviocar*; 4 Cessna 208EX *Grand Caravan*; 1 Cessna 500 *Citation* (survey); 1 Cessna 550 *Citation Bravo*; 2 DHC-6 *Twin Otter*; 1 *Sabreliner* 75A (*Gaviao* 75A)

TRG 5 T-41 *Mescalero*

HELICOPTERS

MRH 5: 4 SA315B *Lama*; 1 Z-11

TPT 62: **Medium** 3 AS332B *Super Puma*; **Light** 59: 1 Bell 212; 25 Bell 205 (UH-1H *Iroquois* – 6 armed); 5 Bell 206B3; 13 UH-1H-II *Huey* II; 15 AB206B1

AIR DEFENCE

SAM • Point-defence RBS-70

GUNS • TOWED 229: **20mm** 200 GAI-B01; **30mm** 21 HS L81; **35mm** 8 GDF-002 (*Skyguard* fire control)

Navy 16,400

Commands: Surface Fleet, Submarines, Naval Avn, Marines

FORCES BY ROLE

SPECIAL FORCES

1 (diver) SF gp

EQUIPMENT BY TYPE

SUBMARINES • SSK

1 *Santa Cruz* (GER TR-1700) (non-operational, undergoing MLU since 2015) with 6 single 533mm TT with SST-4 HWT

1 *Salta* (GER T-209/1100) (non-operational since 2013) with 8 single 533mm TT with Mk 37/SST-4 HWT)

PRINCIPAL SURFACE COMBATANTS 5

DESTROYERS • DDH 1 *Hercules* (UK Type-42) (utilised as a fast troop-transport ship), with 1 114mm gun (capacity 2 SH-3H *Sea King* hel)

FRIGATES • FFGHM 4 *Almirante Brown* (GER MEKO 360) (of which 1†) with 2 quad lnchr with MM40 *Exocet* AShM, 1 octuple *Albatros* lnchr with *Aspide* SAM, 2 triple ILAS-3 (B-515) 324mm TT with A244/S LWT, 1 127mm gun (capacity 1 AS555 *Fennec* hel)

PATROL AND COASTAL COMBATANTS 24

CORVETTES 9:

  FSGH 6 *Espora* (GER MEKO 140) with 2 twin lnchr with MM38 *Exocet* AShM, 2 triple 324mm ILAS-3 (B-515) ASTT with A244/S LWT, 1 76mm gun (capacity 1 AS555 *Fennec* hel)

  FSG 3 *Drummond* (FRA A-69) (of which 2†) with 2 twin lnchr with MM38 *Exocet* AShM, 2 triple 324mm ILAS-3 (B-515) ASTT with A244/S LWT, 1 100mm gun

PSOH 4 *Bouchard* (FRA OPV 87) (of which 1 ex-FRA *L'Adroit*) (capacity 1 hel)

PSO 1 *Teniente Olivieri* (ex-US oilfield tug)

PCFGT 1 *Intrepida* (GER Lurssen 45m) with 2 single lnchr with MM38 *Exocet* AShM, 2 single 533mm TT with SST-4 HWT, 1 76mm gun

PCF 1 *Intrepida* (GER Lurssen 45m) with 1 76mm gun

PCO 1 *Murature* (ex-US *King* – trg/river-patrol role) with 2 105mm gun

PB 7: 4 *Baradero* (ISR *Dabur*); 2 *Punta Mogotes* (ex-US *Point*); 1 *Zurubi*

Latin America and the Caribbean **377**

Latin America and the Caribbean

378 THE MILITARY BALANCE 2023

AMPHIBIOUS 6 LCVP
LOGISTICS AND SUPPORT 16
ABU 3 Red
AFS 4 Puerto Argentina (ex-RUS Neftegaz)
AGB 1 Almirante Irizar (damaged by fire in 2007; returned to service in mid-2017)
AGHS 3: 1 Austral (ex-GER Sonne); 1 Cormoran; 1 Puerto Deseado (ice-breaking capability, used for polar research)
AGOR 1 Commodoro Rivadavia
AK 2 Costa Sur (capacity 4 LCVP)
AOR 1 Patagonia (ex-FRA Durance) with 1 hel platform
AXS 1 Libertad

Naval Aviation 2,000

EQUIPMENT BY TYPE
AIRCRAFT 16 combat capable
FGA (5 Super Etendard Modernisé non-operational and undergoing modernisation; 11 Super Etendard in store)
ASW 6: 2 S-2T Tracker; 4 P-3B Orion†
TPT • Light 7 Beech 200F/M King Air
TRG 10 T-34C Turbo Mentor*
HELICOPTERS
ASW 2 SH-3H (ASH-3H) Sea King
MRH 1 AS555 Fennec
TPT • Medium 6: 2 S-61T; 4 UH-3H Sea King
AIR-LAUNCHED MISSILES
AAM • IR R-550 Magic
AShM AM39 Exocet

Marines 2,500

FORCES BY ROLE
MANOEUVRE
Amphibious
1 (fleet) force (1 cdo gp, 1 (AAV) amph bn, 1 mne bn, 1 arty bn, 1 ADA bn)
1 (fleet) force (2 mne bn, 2 navy det)
1 force (1 mne bn)
EQUIPMENT BY TYPE
ARMOURED FIGHTING VEHICLES
RECCE 12 ERC-90F Sagaie
APC • APC (W) 31 VCR
AAV 11 LVTP-7
ENGINEERING & MAINTENANCE VEHICLES
ARV AAVR 7
ANTI-TANK/ANTI-INFRASTRUCTURE
RCL 105mm 30 M-1974 FMK-1
ARTILLERY 89
TOWED 19: **105mm** 13 Model 56 pack howitzer; **155mm** 6 M114
MOR 70: **81mm** 58; **120mm** 12
AIR DEFENCE
SAM • Point-defence RBS-70
GUNS 40mm 4 Bofors 40L

Air Force 12,900

4 Major Comds – Air Operations, Personnel, Air Regions, Logistics, 8 air bde

Air Operations Command

FORCES BY ROLE
GROUND ATTACK
2 sqn with A-4/OA-4 (A-4AR/OA-4AR) Skyhawk

2 (tac air) sqn with EMB-312 Tucano (on loan for border surv/interdiction)
ISR
1 sqn with Learjet 35A
SEARCH & RESCUE/TRANSPORT HELICOPTER
2 sqn with Bell 212; Bell 412; Mi-171; SA-315B Lama
TANKER/TRANSPORT
1 sqn with C-130H Hercules; KC-130H Hercules; L-100-30
TRANSPORT
1 sqn with Beech A200 King Air (UC-12B Huron); Cessna 182 Skylane
1 sqn with DHC-6 Twin Otter; Saab 340
1 sqn with F-28 Friendship
1 sqn with Learjet 35A; Learjet 60
1 (Pres) flt with B-737-700; B-757-23ER; S-70A Black Hawk, S-76B
TRAINING
1 sqn with AT-63 Pampa II
1 sqn with EMB-312 Tucano
1 sqn with Grob 120TP
1 sqn with IA-63 Pampa III*
1 sqn with T-6C Texan II
1 hel sqn with Hughes 369; SA-315B Lama
TRANSPORT HELICOPTER
1 sqn with Hughes 369; MD-500; MD-500D

EQUIPMENT BY TYPE
AIRCRAFT 22 combat capable
ATK 12: 10 A-4 (A-4AR) Skyhawk (of which 6†); 2 OA-4 (OA-4AR) Skyhawk (of which 1†)
ELINT 1 Learjet 35A
TKR/TPT 2 KC-130H Hercules
TPT 25: Medium 4: 3 C-130H Hercules; 1 L-100-30; **Light** 17: 3 Beech A200 King Air (UC-12B Huron); 4 Cessna 182 Skylane; 2 DHC-6 Twin Otter; 3 Learjet 35A (of which 2 test and calibration and 1 medevac); 1 Learjet 60 (VIP); 1 PA-28-236 Dakota; 3 Saab 340 (jointly operated with LADE); **PAX** 4: 1 B-737; 1 B-737-700; 1 B-757-23ER; 1 F-28 Fellowship
TRG 46: 2 AT-63 Pampa II* (LIFT); 11 EMB-312 Tucano; 9 Grob 120TP; 8 IA-63 Pampa III*; 6 P2002JF Sierra; 10 T-6C Texan II (8 EMB-312 Tucano in store)
HELICOPTERS
MRH 29: 6 Bell 412EP; 11 Hughes 369; 3 MD-500; 4 MD-500D; 5 SA315B Lama
TPT 12: **Medium** 3: 2 Mi-171E; 1 S-70A Black Hawk (VIP); **Light** 9: 7 Bell 212; 2 S-76B (VIP)
AIR DEFENCE
GUNS 88: 20mm: 86 Oerlikon/Rh-202 with 9 Elta EL/M-2106 radar; **35mm**: 2 GDF-001 with Skyguard radar
AIR-LAUNCHED MISSILES
AAM • IR AIM-9L Sidewinder; R-550 Magic; Shafrir 2‡

Gendarmerie & Paramilitary 31,250

Gendarmerie 18,000

Ministry of Security

FORCES BY ROLE
COMMAND
7 regional comd
SPECIAL FORCES
1 SF unit

MANOEUVRE
Other
17 paramilitary bn
Aviation
1 (mixed) avn bn
EQUIPMENT BY TYPE
ARMOURED FIGHTING VEHICLES
APC (W) 87: 47 *Grenadier*; 40 UR-416
ARTILLERY • MOR 81mm
AIRCRAFT
TPT 13: **Light** 12: 3 Cessna 152; 3 Cessna 206; 1 Cessna 336; 1 PA-28 *Cherokee*; 2 PC-6B *Turbo Porter*; 2 PC-12; **PAX** 1 Learjet 35
HELICOPTERS
MRH 2 MD-500C
TPT • **Light** 17: 3 AW119 *Koala*; 2 Bell 206 *Jet Ranger* (AB-206); 7 AS350 *Ecureuil*; 1 H135; 1 H155; 3 R-44 *Raven* II
TRG 1 S-300C

Prefectura Naval (Coast Guard) 13,250

Ministry of Security
EQUIPMENT BY TYPE
PATROL AND COASTAL COMBATANTS 71
PCO 7: 1 *Correa Falcon*; 1 *Delfin*; 5 *Mantilla* (F30 *Halcón* – undergoing modernisation)
PCC 1 *Mariano Moreno*
PB 58: 1 *Dorado*; 25 *Estrellemar*; 2 *Lynch* (US *Cape*); 18 *Mar del Plata* (Z-28); 1 *Surel*; 8 Damen Stan 2200; 3 Stan Tender 1750
PBF 4 *Shaldag* II
PBR 1 *Tonina*
LOGISTICS & SUPPORT 11
AAR 1 *Tango*
AFS 1 *Prefecto Garcia*
AG 2
ARS 1 *Prefecto Mansilla*
AX 5: 1 *Mandubi*; 4 other
AXS 1 *Dr Bernardo Houssay*
AIRCRAFT
MP 1 Beech 350ER *King Air*
TPT • **Light** 6: 5 C-212 *Aviocar*; 1 Beech 350ER *King Air*
TRG 2 Piper PA-28 *Archer* III
HELICOPTERS
SAR 3 AS565MA *Panther*
MRH 1 AS365 *Dauphin* 2
TPT 7: **Medium** 3: 1 H225 *Puma*; 2 SA330L (AS330L) *Puma*; **Light** 4: 2 AS355 *Ecureuil* II; 2 Bell 206 (AB-206) *Jet Ranger*
TRG 4 S-300C

DEPLOYMENT

CENTRAL AFRICAN REPUBLIC: UN • MINUSCA 2
CYPRUS: UN • UNFICYP 251; 2 inf coy; 1 hel flt with 2 Bell 212
INDIA/PAKISTAN: UN • UNMOGIP 3
LEBANON: UN • UNIFII 2
MIDDLE EAST: UN • UNTSO 3
WESTERN SAHARA: UN • MINURSO 3

Bahamas BHS

Bahamian Dollar BSD		2021	2022	2023
GDP	BSD	11.2bn	12.7bn	
	USD	11.2bn	12.7bn	
per capita	USD	28,792	32,246	
Growth	%	13.7	8.0	
Inflation	%	2.9	5.7	
Def bdgt	BSD	95.4m	94.5m	146m
	USD	95.4m	94.5m	
USD1=BSD		1.00	1.00	

Real-terms defence budget trend (USDm, constant 2015)

Population	355,608					
Age	0–14	15–19	20–24	25–29	30–64	65 plus
Male	10.9%	3.6%	3.8%	4.0%	22.7%	3.7%
Female	10.6%	3.5%	3.7%	3.9%	23.7%	5.7%

Capabilities

The Royal Bahamas Defence Force (RBDF) is primarily a naval force tasked with disaster relief, maritime security and counter-narcotics duties. Its single commando squadron is tasked with base protection and internal security. The Bahamas is a member of the Caribbean Community and is looking to strengthen cooperative partnerships with its neighbours in maritime law enforcement. The RBDF maintains training relationships with the UK and US. The RBDF has participated in US SOUTHCOM's *Tradewinds* disaster-response exercise. There is little independent capacity to deploy abroad, aside from recent regional disaster-relief efforts. The RBDF's Sandy Bottom Project, the largest-ever capital investment in the service, includes the acquisition of patrol craft and the development of bases and port facilities. The maritime wing is focused around patrol vessels and smaller patrol boats, while the air wing has a small inventory of light aircraft. Apart from limited maintenance facilities, the Bahamas has no indigenous defence industry.

ACTIVE 1,500

ORGANISATIONS BY SERVICE

Royal Bahamas Defence Force 1,500
FORCES BY ROLE
MANOEUVRE
Amphibious
1 mne coy (incl marines with internal- and base-security duties)
EQUIPMENT BY TYPE
PATROL AND COASTAL COMBATANTS 21
PCC 2 *Bahamas*
PB 19: 4 *Arthur Dion Hanna* (Damen Stan Patrol 4207); 2 *Dauntless*; 4 *Lignum Vitae* (Damen 3007); 1 *Safe 33*; 4 *Safe 44*; 2 *Sea Ark 12m*; 2 *Sea Ark 15m*
LOGISTICS & SUPPORT • AKR 1 *Lawrence Major* (Damen 5612)

AIRCRAFT • TPT • Light 3: 1 Beech A350 *King Air*; 1 Cessna 208 *Caravan*; 1 P-68 *Observer*

FOREIGN FORCES

Guyana Navy: Base located at New Providence Island

Barbados BRB

Barbados Dollar BBD		2021	2022	2023
GDP	BBD	9.71bn	11.6bn	
	USD	4.85bn	5.79bn	
per capita	USD	16,817	20,004	
Growth	%	0.7	10.5	
Inflation	%	3.1	9.9	
Def bdgt [a]	BBD	79.6m	84.8m	
	USD	39.8m	42.4m	
USD1=BBD		2.00	2.00	

[a] Defence & security expenditure

Real-terms defence budget trend (USDm, constant 2015)

Population 302,674

Age	0–14	15–19	20–24	25–29	30–64	65 plus
Male	8.5%	3.0%	3.0%	3.1%	24.4%	6.3%
Female	8.5%	3.0%	3.1%	3.2%	25.3%	8.7%

Capabilities

Maritime security and resource protection are the main tasks of the Barbados Defence Force (BDF), but it has a secondary public-safety role in support of the police force. The BDF has undertaken counter-narcotics work, while troops have also been tasked with supporting law enforcement. There are plans to improve disaster-relief capabilities. Barbados is a member of the Caribbean Community, and the Caribbean Regional Security System is headquartered there. The BDF has participated in US SOUTHCOM's *Tradewinds* disaster-response exercise. There is limited capacity to deploy independently within the region, such as on hurricane-relief duties. The inventory consists principally of a small number of patrol vessels. Apart from limited maintenance facilities, Barbados has no indigenous defence industry.

ACTIVE 610 (Army 500 Coast Guard 110)

RESERVE 430 (Joint 430)

ORGANISATIONS BY SERVICE

Army 500
FORCES BY ROLE
MANOEUVRE
  Light
    1 inf bn (cadre)

Coast Guard 110
HQ located at HMBS Pelican, Spring Garden
EQUIPMENT BY TYPE
PATROL AND COASTAL COMBATANTS 6
  PB 6: 1 *Dauntless*; 2 *Enterprise* (Damen Stan 1204); 3 *Trident* (Damen Stan Patrol 4207)

Belize BLZ

Belize Dollar BZD		2021	2022	2023
GDP	BZD	4.85bn	5.35bn	
	USD	2.43bn	2.68bn	
per capita	USD	5,638	6,096	
Growth	%	16.3	3.5	
Inflation	%	3.2	6.6	
Def bdgt [a]	BZD	40.0m	46.6m	
	USD	20.0m	23.3m	
FMA (US)	USD	1.0m	0.0m	0.0m
USD1=BZD		2.00	2.00	

[a] Excludes funds allocated to Coast Guard and Police Service

Real-terms defence budget trend (USDm, constant 2015)

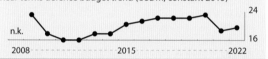

Population 412,387

Age	0–14	15–19	20–24	25–29	30–64	65 plus
Male	16.1%	5.4%	5.1%	4.1%	17.2%	2.3%
Female	15.4%	5.0%	4.5%	3.9%	18.6%	2.5%

Capabilities

Belize maintains a small Defence Force (BDF) and coastguard to provide national security, particularly control of the borders with Guatemala and Mexico. In 2022, a new National Security Strategy underscored priorities of maintaining sovereignty and territorial integrity; reducing trans-national, cross-border and other violent crime; counter-terrorism; and reducing risk from natural human-caused hazards. The UK has a long-standing security relationship with Belize and maintains a small training unit there, and the BDF also trains with US SOUTHCOM. Overall training levels are limited but generally sufficient for the BDF's tasks. Belize is a member of the Caribbean Community. The BDF does not deploy internationally and logistics support is adequate for border-security missions. The conventional equipment inventory is limited and there is no significant domestic defence industry.

ACTIVE 1,500 (Army 1,500) Gendarmerie & Paramilitary 550

RESERVE 700 (Joint 700)

ORGANISATIONS BY SERVICE

Army ε1,500
FORCES BY ROLE
SPECIAL FORCES
  1 SF unit

MANOEUVRE
Light
2 inf bn (3 inf coy)
COMBAT SERVICE SUPPORT
1 spt gp
EQUIPMENT BY TYPE
ANTI-TANK/ANTI-INFRASTRUCTURE • RCL 84mm
Carl Gustaf
ARTILLERY • MOR 81mm 6

Air Wing
EQUIPMENT BY TYPE
AIRCRAFT
TPT • Light 2: 1 BN-2B *Defender*†; 1 Cessna 182 *Skylane*†
TRG 1 T-67M-200 *Firefly*
HELICOPTERS
TPT • Light 3: 2 Bell 205 (UH-1H *Iroquois*); 1 Bell 407

Reserve
FORCES BY ROLE
MANOEUVRE
Light
1 inf bn (3 inf coy)

Gendarmerie & Paramilitary 550

Coast Guard 550
EQUIPMENT BY TYPE
All operational patrol vessels under 10t FLD

FOREIGN FORCES
United Kingdom BATSUB 12

Bolivia BOL

Bolivian Boliviano BOB		2021	2022	2023
GDP	BOB	279bn	298bn	
	USD	40.7bn	43.4bn	
per capita	USD	3,449	3,631	
Growth	%	6.1	3.8	
Inflation	%	0.7	3.2	
Def bdgt	BOB	3.26bn	3.30bn	
	USD	476m	481m	
USD1=BOB		6.86	6.86	

Real-terms defence budget trend (USDm, constant 2015)

Population	12,054,379					
Age	0–14	15–19	20–24	25–29	30–64	65 plus
Male	15.2%	5.0%	4.5%	4.1%	18.4%	3.1%
Female	14.6%	4.9%	4.4%	4.0%	18.3%	3.6%

Capabilities
The armed forces are constitutionally tasked with maintaining sovereignty and territorial defence, though principal tasks are counter-narcotics and internal and border security. Joint task forces have been formed and dispatched to border regions to combat smuggling, and a series of border posts have been established. Airspace control is an emerging strategic priority. The armed forces have also been playing a greater role in disaster-relief operations, with a new dedicated joint command established in 2022.There is defence-technology cooperation with Russia, and China remains a significant supplier of military materiel. Bolivia cooperates with Peru and Paraguay on countering illicit trafficking and on providing disaster relief. The armed forces have stressed the need to improve conditions for personnel, amid greater internal deployments to border areas on counter-trafficking tasks. An aerospace R&D centre was created in 2018 in the military-engineering school, with the objective of developing munitions and ISR UAVs. There is some local maintenance, repair and overhaul capacity.

ACTIVE 34,100 (Army 22,800 Navy 4,800 Air 6,500)
Gendarmerie & Paramilitary 37,100
Conscript liability 12 months voluntary conscription for both males and females

ORGANISATIONS BY SERVICE

Army 9,800; 13,000 conscript (total 22,800)
FORCES BY ROLE
COMMAND
6 mil region HQ
10 div HQ
SPECIAL FORCES
3 SF regt
MANOEUVRE
Reconnaissance
1 mot cav gp
Armoured
1 armd bn
Mechanised
1 mech cav regt
2 mech inf regt
Light
1 (aslt) cav gp
5 (horsed) cav gp
3 mot inf regt
21 inf regt
Air Manoeuvre
2 AB regt (bn)
Other
1 (Presidential Guard) inf regt
COMBAT SUPPORT
6 arty regt (bn)
6 engr bn
1 int coy
1 MP bn
1 sigs bn
COMBAT SERVICE SUPPORT
2 log bn
AVIATION
2 avn coy

382 THE MILITARY BALANCE 2023

AIR DEFENCE
1 ADA regt
EQUIPMENT BY TYPE
ARMOURED FIGHTING VEHICLES
LT TK 54: 36 SK-105A1 *Kuerassier*; 18 SK-105A2 *Kuerassier*
RECCE 24 EE-9 *Cascavel*
APC 148+
  APC (T) 87+: 50+ M113, 37 M9 half-track
  APC (W) 61: 24 EE-11 *Urutu*; 22 MOWAG *Roland*; 15
  V-100 *Commando*
  AUV 19 *Tiger* 4×4
ENGINEERING & MAINTENANCE VEHICLES
ARV 4 *Greif*; M578 LARV
ANTI-TANK/ANTI-INFRASTRUCTURE
MSL
  SP 2 *Koyak* with HJ-8
  MANPATS HJ-8
RCL 90mm M67; 106mm M40A1
ARTILLERY 311+
TOWED 61: 105mm 25 M101A1; 122mm 36 M-30 (M-1938)
MOR 250+: 81mm 250 M29; Type-W87; 107mm M30; 120mm M120
AIRCRAFT
TPT • Light 3: 1 Fokker F-27-200; 1 Beech 90 *King Air*; 1 C-212 *Aviocar*
HELICOPTERS • MRH 6 H425
AIR DEFENCE • GUNS • TOWED 37mm 18 Type-65

Navy 4,800

Organised into six naval districts with HQ located at Puerto Guayaramerín
EQUIPMENT BY TYPE
PATROL AND COASTAL COMBATANTS 7
PBR 7: 1 *Santa Cruz*; 6 Type 928 YC
LOGISTICS AND SUPPORT 3
AG 1 *Mojo Huayna*
AH 2

Marines 1,700 (incl 1,000 Naval Military Police)

FORCES BY ROLE
MANOEUVRE
  Mechanised
  1 mech inf bn
  Amphibious
  6 mne bn (1 in each Naval District)
COMBAT SUPPORT
  4 (naval) MP bn

Air Force 6,500 (incl conscripts)

FORCES BY ROLE
GROUND ATTACK
  1 sqn with K-8WB *Karakorum*
ISR
  1 sqn with Cessna 206; Cessna 402; Learjet 25B/25D (secondary VIP role)
SEARCH & RESCUE
  1 sqn with AS332B *Super Puma*; H125 *Ecureuil*; H145

TRANSPORT
  1 (TAM) sqn with B-727; B-737; MA60
  1 (TAB) sqn with C-130A *Hercules*; MD-10-30F
  1 sqn with C-130B/H *Hercules*
  1 sqn with F-27-400M *Troopship*
  1 (VIP) sqn with Beech 90 *King Air*; Beech 200 *King Air*; Beech 1900; *Falcon* 900EX; *Sabreliner* 60; *Falcon* 50EX
  6 sqn with Cessna 152/206; IAI-201 *Arava*; PA-32 *Saratoga*; PA-34 *Seneca*
TRAINING
  1 sqn with DA40; T-25; Z-242L
  1 sqn with Cessna 152/172
  1 sqn with PC-7 *Turbo Trainer*
  1 hel sqn with R-44 *Raven* II
TRANSPORT HELICOPTER
  1 (anti-drug) sqn with Bell 205 (UH-1H *Iroquois*)
AIR DEFENCE
  1 regt with Oerlikon; Type-65
EQUIPMENT BY TYPE
AIRCRAFT 21 combat capable
TPT 77: Heavy 1 MD-10-30F; Medium 4: 1 C-130A *Hercules*; 2 C-130B *Hercules*; 1 C-130H *Hercules*; Light 64: 1 *Aero Commander* 690; 3 Beech 90 *King Air*; 2 Beech 200 *King Air*; 1 Beech 250 *King Air*; 1 Beech 350 *King Air*; 3 C-212-100; 6 Cessna 152; 2 Cessna 172; 18 Cessna 206; 3 Cessna 210 *Centurion*; 1 Cessna 402; 8 DA40; 1 F-27-400M *Troopship*; 4 IAI-201 *Arava*; 2 Learjet 25B/D; 2 MA60†; 1 PA-32 *Saratoga*; 4 PA-34 *Seneca*; 1 *Sabreliner* 60; PAX 8: 1 B-727; 3 B-737-200; 1 *Falcon* 50EX; 1 *Falcon* 900EX (VIP); 2 RJ70
TRG 35: 5 K-8WB *Karakorum**; 6 T-25; 16 PC-7 *Turbo Trainer**; 8 Z-242L
HELICOPTERS
MRH 1 SA316 *Alouette* III
TPT 35: Medium 6 H215 *Super Puma*; Light 29: 2 H125 *Ecureuil*; 19 Bell 205 (UH-1H *Iroquois*); 2 H145; 6 R-44 *Raven* II
AIR DEFENCE • GUNS • TOWED 18+: 20mm Oerlikon GAI; **37mm** 18 Type-65

Gendarmerie & Paramilitary 37,100+

National Police 31,100+

FORCES BY ROLE
MANOEUVRE
  Other
  27 frontier sy unit
  9 paramilitary bde
  2 (rapid action) paramilitary regt

Narcotics Police 6,000+

FOE (700) – Special Operations Forces

DEPLOYMENT

CENTRAL AFRICAN REPUBLIC: UN • MINUSCA 7

DEMOCRATIC REPUBLIC OF THE CONGO: UN • MONUSCO 4

SOUTH SUDAN: UN • UNMISS 5

SUDAN: UN • UNISFA 4

Brazil BRZ

Brazilian Real BRL		2021	2022	2023
GDP	BRL	8.68tr	9.66tr	
	USD	1.61tr	1.89tr	
per capita	USD	7,564	8,857	
Growth	%	4.6	2.8	
Inflation	%	8.3	9.4	
Def bdgt [a]	BRL	115bn	117bn	121bn
	USD	21.3bn	23.0bn	
USD1=BRL		5.40	5.10	

[a] Includes military pensions

Real-terms defence budget trend (USDbn, constant 2015)

Population	217,240,060					
Age	0–14	15–19	20–24	25–29	30–64	65 plus
Male	10.2%	3.9%	4.1%	3.9%	22.8%	4.4%
Female	9.8%	3.8%	4.0%	3.8%	23.7%	5.8%

Capabilities

The armed forces are among the most capable in the region. Brazil seeks to enhance its power-projection capabilities, boost surveillance of the Amazon region and coastal waters, and further develop its defence industry. Security challenges from organised crime have seen the armed forces deploy on internal-security operations. Brazil maintains military ties with most of its neighbours including personnel exchanges and joint military training with Chile and Colombia. There is also defence cooperation with France, Sweden and the US, centred on procurement, technical advice and personnel training. Brazil's air-transport fleet enables it to independently deploy forces. It contributes small contingents to several UN missions. Brazil is attempting to modernise its equipment across all domains. Major platform developments include PROSUB (one nuclear-powered and four diesel-electric submarines) and the acquisition in 2018 of a former UK helicopter carrier. Projects to boost aerospace capabilities are also underway including the FX-2 project to procure the Saab *Gripen* combat aircraft, as well as the plan to introduce the Embraer KC-390 transport aircraft. Brazil has a well-developed defence-industrial base, across all domains, with a capability to design and manufacture equipment. Aerospace firms Avibras and Embraer also export some products. Local companies are also involved in the SISFRON border-security programme. There are industrial partnerships, including technology transfers and R&D support, with France's Naval Group (PROSUB) and Sweden's Saab (FX-2 fighter).

ACTIVE 366,500 (Army 214,000 Navy 85,000 Air 67,500) **Gendarmerie & Paramilitary 395,000**

Conscript liability 12 months (can go to 18; often waived)

RESERVE 1,340,000

ORGANISATIONS BY SERVICE

Space
EQUIPMENT BY TYPE
SATELLITES • COMMUNICATIONS 1 SGDC-1 (civil–military use)

Army 102,000; 112,000 conscript (total 214,000)
FORCES BY ROLE
COMMAND
 8 mil comd HQ
 12 mil region HQ
 7 div HQ (2 with regional HQ)
SPECIAL FORCES
 1 SF bde (1 SF bn, 1 cdo bn)
 1 SF coy
MANOEUVRE
Reconnaissance
 3 mech cav regt
Armoured
 1 (5th) armd bde (1 mech cav sqn, 2 tk regt, 2 mech inf bn, 1 SP arty bn, 1 engr bn, 1 sigs coy, 1 log bn)
 1 (6th) armd bde (1 mech cav sqn, 2 tk regt, 2 mech inf bn, 1 SP arty bn, 1 AD bty, 1 engr bn, 1 sigs coy, 1 log bn)
Mechanised
 4 (1st, 3rd & 4th) mech cav bde (1 armd cav regt, 3 mech cav regt, 1 arty bn, 1 engr coy, 1 sigs coy, 1 log bn)
 1 (2nd) mech cav bde (1 armd cav regt, 2 mech cav regt, 1 SP arty bn, 1 engr coy, 1 sigs coy, 1 log bn)
 1 (3rd) mech inf bde (1 mech cav sqn, 2 mech inf bn, 1 inf bn, 1 arty bn, 1 engr coy, 1 sigs coy, 1 log bn)
 1 (11th) mech inf bde (1 mech cav regt, 3 mech inf bn, 1 arty bn, 1 engr coy, 1 sigs coy, 1 MP coy, 1 log bn)
 1 (15th) mech inf bde (3 mech inf bn, 1 arty bn, 1 engr coy, 1 log bn)
Light
 1 (4th) mot inf bde (1 mech cav sqn, 1 mot inf bn, 1 inf bn, 1 mtn inf bn, 1 arty bn, 1 sigs coy, 1 log bn)
 1 (7th) mot inf bde (3 mot inf bn, 1 arty bn)
 1 (8th) mot inf bde (1 mech cav sqn, 3 mot inf bn, 1 arty bn, 1 log bn)
 1 (10th) mot inf bde (1 mech cav sqn, 4 mot inf bn, 1 inf coy, 1 arty bn, 1 engr coy, 1 sigs coy)
 1 (13th) mot inf bde (1 mot inf bn, 2 inf bn, 1 inf coy, 1 arty bn)
 1 (14th) mot inf bde (1 mech cav sqn, 3 inf bn, 1 arty bn)
 10 inf bn
 1 (1st) jungle inf bde (1 mech cav sqn, 2 jungle inf bn, 1 arty bn)
 4 (2nd, 16th, 17th & 22nd) jungle inf bde (3 jungle inf bn)
 1 (23rd) jungle inf bde (1 cav sqn, 4 jungle inf bn, 1 arty bn, 1 sigs coy, 1 log bn)
Air Manoeuvre
 1 AB bde (1 cav sqn, 3 AB bn, 1 arty bn, 1 engr coy, 1 sigs coy, 1 log bn)
 1 (12th) air mob bde (1 cav sqn, 3 air mob bn, 1 arty bn, 1 engr coy, 1 sigs coy, 1 log bn)

384 THE MILITARY BALANCE 2023

Other
1 (9th) mot trg bde (3 mot inf bn, 1 arty bn, 1 log bn)
1 (18th) sy bde (2 sy bn, 2 sy coy)
1 sy bn
7 sy coy
3 gd cav regt
1 gd inf bn

COMBAT SUPPORT
3 SP arty bn
6 fd arty bn
1 MRL bn
1 STA bty
6 engr bn
1 engr gp (1 engr bn, 4 construction bn)
1 engr gp (4 construction bn, 1 construction coy)
2 construction bn
1 CBRN bn
1 EW coy
1 int coy
8 MP bn
2 MP coy
4 sigs bn
2 sigs coy

COMBAT SERVICE SUPPORT
5 log bn
1 tpt bn
4 spt bn

HELICOPTER
1 avn bde (3 hel bn, 1 maint bn)
1 hel bn

AIR DEFENCE
1 ADA bde (5 ADA bn)

EQUIPMENT BY TYPE
ARMOURED FIGHTING VEHICLES
MBT 296: 41 *Leopard* 1A1BE; 220 *Leopard* 1A5BR; 35 M60A3/TTS
LT TK 50 M41C
RECCE 408 EE-9 *Cascavel*
IFV 13 VBTP-MR *Guarani* 30mm
APC 1,458
    APC (T) 660: 198 M113A1; 386 M113BR; 12 M113A2; 64 M577A2
    APC (W) 798: 223 EE-11 *Urutu*; ε575 VBTP-MR *Guarani* 6×6
    AUV IVECO LMV (LMV-BR)
ENGINEERING & MAINTENANCE VEHICLES
AEV 7+: *Greif*; 2 Sabiex HART; 5 Pionierpanzer 2 *Dachs*
ARV 13+: 9 BPz-2; 4 M88A1; M578 LARV
VLB 5+: XLP-10; 5 *Leopard* 1 with *Biber*
ANTI-TANK/ANTI-INFRASTRUCTURE
MSL • MANPATS *Eryx*; *Milan*; MSS-1.2 AC
RCL 194+: **84mm** *Carl Gustaf*; **106mm** 194 M40A1
ARTILLERY 1,881
SP 169: **155mm** 169: 37 M109A3; 100 M109A5; 32 M109A5+
TOWED 431: **105mm** 336: 233 M101/M102; 40 L118 Light Gun; 63 Model 56 pack howitzer; **155mm** 95 M114
MRL 127mm 36: 18 ASTROS II Mk3M; 18 ASTROS II Mk6
MOR 1,245: **81mm** 1,168: 453 L16, 715 M936 AGR; **120mm** 77 M2
LOGISTICS AND SUPPORT • AP 1 *Jacaretinga*

HELICOPTERS
MRH 51: 22 AS565 *Panther* (HM-1); 12 AS565 K2 *Panther* (HM-1); 17 AS550A2 *Fennec* (HA-1 – armed)
TPT 41: **Heavy** 14 H225M *Caracal* (HM-4); **Medium** 12: 8 AS532 *Cougar* (HM-3); 4 S-70A-36 *Black Hawk* (HM-2); **Light** 15 AS350L1 *Ecureuil* (HA-1)
UNINHABITED AERIAL VEHICLES
ISR • Medium 1 *Nauru* 1000C
AIR DEFENCE
SAM • Point-defence RBS-70; 9K38 *Igla* (RS-SA-18 *Grouse*); 9K338 *Igla-S* (RS-SA-24 *Grinch*)
GUNS 100:
    SP 35mm 34 *Gepard* 1A2
    TOWED 66: **35mm** 39 GDF-001 towed (some with *Super Fledermaus* radar); **40mm** 27 L/70 (some with BOFI)

Navy 85,000

Organised into 9 districts with HQ I Rio de Janeiro, HQ II Salvador, HQ III Natal, HQ IV Belém, HQ V Rio Grande, HQ VI Ladario, HQ VII Brasilia, HQ VIII Sao Paulo, HQ IX Manaus

FORCES BY ROLE
SPECIAL FORCES
1 (diver) SF gp

EQUIPMENT BY TYPE
SUBMARINES • SSK 6:
1 *Riachuelo* (FRA *Scorpène*) with 6 533mm TT with SM39 *Exocet* AShM/F21 HWT
2 *Tupi* (GER T-209/1400) with 8 single 533mm TT with Mk 24 *Tigerfish* HWT
2 *Tupi* (GER T-209/1400) with 8 single 533mm TT with Mk 48 HWT
1 *Tikuna* (GER T-209/1450) with 8 single 533mm TT with Mk 24 *Tigerfish* HWT
PRINCIPAL SURFACE COMBATANTS 7
FRIGATES 7
    FFGHM 6:
      1 *Greenhalgh* (ex-UK *Broadsword*) with 4 single lnchr with MM40 *Exocet* Block 2 AShM, 2 sextuple lnchr with *Sea Wolf* SAM, 2 triple 324mm STWS Mk.2 ASTT with Mk 46 LWT (capacity 2 *Super Lynx* Mk21A hel)
      5 *Niterói* with 2 twin lnchr with MM40 *Exocet* Block 2 AShM, 1 octuple *Albatros* lnchr with *Aspide* SAM, 2 triple 324mm SVTT Mk 32 ASTT with Mk 46 LWT, 1 twin 375mm Bofors ASW Rocket Launcher System A/S mor, 1 115mm gun (capacity 1 *Super Lynx* Mk21A hel)
    FFGH 1 *Barroso* with 2 twin lnchr with MM40 *Exocet* Block 2 AShM, 2 triple 324mm SVTT Mk 32 ASTT with Mk 46 LWT, 1 115mm gun (capacity 1 *Super Lynx* Mk21A hel)
PATROL AND COASTAL COMBATANTS 44
CORVETTES • FSGH 1 *Inhaúma* with 2 twin lnchr with MM40 *Exocet* Block 2 AShM, 2 triple 324mm SVTT Mk 32 ASTT with Mk 46 LWT, 1 115mm gun (1 *Super Lynx* Mk21A hel)
PSO 3 *Amazonas* with 1 hel landing platform
PCO 6: 4 *Bracuí* (ex-UK *River*); 1 *Imperial Marinheiro* with 1 76mm gun; 1 *Parnaiba* with 1 hel landing platform

PCC 2 *Macaé* (FRA Vigilante)
PCR 5: 2 *Pedro Teixeira* with 1 hel landing platform; 3 *Roraima*
PB 23: 12 *Grajaú*; 6 *Marlim* (ITA *Meatini* derivative); 5 *Piratini* (US PGM)
PBR 4 LPR-40

MINE WARFARE • MINE COUNTERMEASURES 3
MSC 3 *Aratù* (GER *Schutze*)

AMPHIBIOUS
  PRINCIPAL AMPHIBIOUS SHIPS 2
    LPH 1 *Atlântico* (ex-UK *Ocean*) (capacity 18 hels; 4 LCVP; 40 vehs; 800 troops)
    LPD 1 *Bahia* (ex-FRA *Foudre*) (capacity 4 hels; 8 LCM, 450 troops)
  LANDING SHIPS 2
    LST 1 *Mattoso Maia* (ex-US *Newport*) with 1 Mk 15 *Phalanx* CIWS (capacity 3 LCVP; 1 LCPL; 400 troops)
    LSLH 1 *Almirante Sabóia* (ex-UK *Sir Bedivere*) (capacity 1 med hel; 18 MBT; 340 troops)
  LANDING CRAFT 16:
    LCM 12: 10 EDVM-25; 2 *Icarai* (ex-FRA CTM)
    LCT 1 *Marambaia* (ex-FRA CDIC)
    LCU 3 *Guarapari* (LCU 1610)

LOGISTICS AND SUPPORT 42
  ABU 5: 4 *Comandante Varella*; 1 *Faroleiro Mario Seixas*
  ABUH 1 *Almirante Graça Aranha* (lighthouse tender)
  AFS 1 *Potengi*
  AGHS 5: 1 *Caravelas* (riverine); 4 *Rio Tocantin*
  AGOS 2: 1 *Ary Rongel* with 1 hel landing platform; 1 *Almirante Maximiano* (capacity 2 AS350/AS355 *Ecureuil* hel)
  AGS 8: 1 *Aspirante Moura*; 1 *Cruzeiro do Sul*; 1 *Antares*; 3 *Amorim do Valle* (ex-UK *River* (MCM)); 1 *Rio Branco*; 1 *Vital de Oliveira*
  AH 5: 2 *Oswaldo Cruz* with 1 hel landing platform; 1 *Dr Montenegro*; 1 *Tenente Maximiano* with 1 hel landing platform; 1 *Soares de Meirelles*
  AOR 1 *Almirante Gastão Motta*
  AP 3: 1 *Almirante Leverger*; 1 *Paraguassu*; 1 *Pará* (all river transports)
  ARS 3 *Mearim*
  ASR 1 *Guillobel*
  ATF 2 *Tritao*
  AX 1 *Brasil* (*Niterói* mod) with 1 hel landing platform
  AXL 3 *Nascimento*
  AXS 1 *Cisne Branco*

Naval Aviation 2,100

FORCES BY ROLE
GROUND ATTACK
  1 sqn with A-4M (AF-1B) *Skyhawk*; TA-4M (AF-1C) *Skyhawk*
ANTI SURFACE WARFARE
  1 sqn with *Super Lynx* Mk21A/B
ANTI SUBMARINE WARFARE
  1 sqn with S-70B *Seahawk* (MH-16)
TRAINING
  1 sqn with Bell 206B3 *Jet Ranger* III
TRANSPORT HELICOPTER
  2 sqn with AS350 *Ecureuil* (armed)
  1 sqn with AS350 *Ecureuil* (armed); AS355 *Ecureuil* II (armed); H135 (UH-17)

  1 sqn with AS350 *Ecureuil* (armed); H225M *Caracal* (UH-15)
  1 sqn with AS332 *Super Puma*; AS532 *Cougar* (UH-14); H225M *Caracal* (UH-15)
  1 sqn with H225M *Caracal* (UH-15)

EQUIPMENT BY TYPE
AIRCRAFT 7 combat capable
  ATK 7: 5 A-4M (AF-1B) *Skyhawk*; 2 TA-4M (AF-1C) *Skyhawk*
HELICOPTERS
  ASW 18: 9 *Super Lynx* Mk21A; 3 *Super Lynx* Mk21B; 6 S-70B *Seahawk* (MH-16)
  CSAR 3 H225M *Caracal* (UH-15A)
  TPT 55: **Heavy** 8 H225M *Caracal* (UH-15); **Medium** 7: 5 AS332 *Super Puma*; 2 AS532 *Cougar* (UH-14); **Light** 40: 15 AS350 *Ecureuil* (armed); 8 AS355 *Ecureuil* II (armed); 15 Bell 206B3 *Jet Ranger* III (IH-6B); 2 H135 (UH-17)
AIR-LAUNCHED MISSILES • AShM: AM39 *Exocet*; *Sea Skua*; AGM-119 *Penguin*

Marines 16,000

FORCES BY ROLE
SPECIAL FORCES
  1 SF bn
MANOEUVRE
  Amphibious
  1 amph div (1 lt armd bn, 3 mne bn, 1 arty bn)
  1 amph aslt bn
  7 (regional) mne gp
  1 rvn bn
COMBAT SUPPORT
  1 engr bn
COMBAT SERVICE SUPPORT
  1 log bn

EQUIPMENT BY TYPE
ARMOURED FIGHTING VEHICLES
  LT TK 18 SK-105 *Kuerassier*
  APC 60
    APC (T) 30 M113A1 (incl variants)
    APC (W) 30 *Piranha* IIIC
  AAV 47: 13 AAV-7A1; 20 AAVP-7A1 RAM/RS; 2 AAVC-7A1 RAM/RS (CP); 12 LVTP-7
ENGINEERING VEHICLES • ARV 2: 1 AAVR-7; 1 AAVR-7A1 RAM/RS
ANTI-TANK/ANTI-INFRASTRUCTURE
  MSL• MANPATS RB-56 *Bill*; MSS-1.2 AC
ARTILLERY 65
  TOWED 41: **105mm** 33: 18 L118 Light Gun; 15 M101; **155mm** 8 M114
  MRL 127mm 6 ASTROS II Mk6
  MOR 81mm 18 M29
AIR DEFENCE • GUNS 40mm 6 L/70 (with BOFI)

Air Force 67,500

Brazilian airspace is divided into 7 air regions, each of which is responsible for its designated air bases. Air assets are divided among 4 designated air forces (I, II, III & V) for operations (IV Air Force temporarily deactivated)

FORCES BY ROLE

FIGHTER
  3 sqn with F-5EM/FM *Tiger* II

FIGHTER/GROUND ATTACK
  2 sqn with AMX (A-1A/B)
  1 sqn with F-5EM/FM *Tiger* II (converting to *Gripen* E (F-39E))

GROUND ATTACK/ISR
  4 sqn with EMB-314 *Super Tucano* (A-29A/B)*

MARITIME PATROL
  1 sqn with P-3AM *Orion*
  2 sqn with EMB-111 (P-95A/B/M)

ISR
  1 sqn with AMX-R (RA-1)*
  1 sqn with Learjet 35AM (R-35AM); EMB-110B (R-95)

AIRBORNE EARLY WARNING & CONTROL
  1 sqn with EMB-145RS (R-99); EMB-145SA (E-99); EMB-145SA (E-99M)

SEARCH & RESCUE
  1 sqn with C295M *Amazonas* (SC-105); UH-60L *Black Hawk* (H-60L)

TANKER/TRANSPORT
  1 sqn with C-130H/KC-130H *Hercules*; KC-390 *Millennium*

TRANSPORT
  1 VIP sqn with A319 (VC-1A); EMB-190 (VC-2); AS355 *Ecureuil* II (VH-55); H135M (VH-35); H225M *Caracal* (VH-36)
  1 VIP sqn with EMB-135BJ (VC-99B); ERJ-135LR (VC-99C); ERJ-145LR (VC-99A); Learjet 35A (VU-35); Learjet 55C (VU-55C)
  2 sqn with C-130E/H *Hercules*
  2 sqn with C295M (C-105A)
  7 (regional) sqn with Cessna 208/208B (C-98); Cessna 208-G1000 (C-98A); EMB-110 (C-95); EMB-120 (C-97)
  1 sqn with ERJ-145 (C-99A)
  1 sqn with EMB-120RT (VC-97), EMB-121 (VU-9)

TRAINING
  1 sqn with EMB-110 (C-95)
  2 sqn with EMB-312 *Tucano* (T-27) (incl 1 air show sqn)
  1 sqn with T-25A/C

TRANSPORT HELICOPTER
  1 sqn with H225M *Caracal* (H-36)
  1 sqn with AS350B *Ecureuil* (H-50); AS355 *Ecureuil* II (H-55)
  1 sqn with Bell 205 (H-1H); H225M *Caracal* (H-36)
  2 sqn with UH-60L *Black Hawk* (H-60L)

ISR UAV
  1 sqn with *Hermes* 450/900

EQUIPMENT BY TYPE

AIRCRAFT 187 combat capable
  FTR 47: 43 F-5EM *Tiger* II; 4 F-5FM *Tiger* II
  FGA 29: 15 AMX/AMX-T (A-1A/B); 8 AMX A-1M; 1 AMX A-1BM; 5 *Gripen* E (F-39E) (in test)
  ASW 9 P-3AM *Orion*

MP 18: 10 EMB-111 (P-95A *Bandeirulha*)*; 8 EMB-111 (P-95BM *Bandeirulha*)*
ISR 8: 4 AMX-R (RA-1)*; 4 EMB-110B (R-95)
ELINT 6: 3 EMB-145RS (R-99); 3 Learjet 35AM (R-35AM)
AEW&C 5: 2 EMB-145SA (E-99); 3 EMB-145SA (E-99M)
SAR 7: 3 C295M *Amazonas* (SC-105); 4 EMB-110 (SC-95B)
TKR/TPT 2 KC-130H
TPT 186: **Medium** 24: 4 C-130E *Hercules*; 16 C-130H *Hercules*; 5 KC390 *Millennium*; **Light** 153: 11 C295M (C-105A); 7 Cessna 208 (C-98); 9 Cessna 208B (C-98); 13 Cessna 208-G1000 (C-98A); 52 EMB-110 (C-95A/B/C/M); 16 EMB-120 (C-97); 4 EMB-120RT (VC-97); 5 EMB-121 (VU-9); 7 EMB-135BJ (VC-99B); 3 EMB-201R *Ipanema* (G-19); 2 EMB-202A *Ipanema* (G-19A); 4 EMB-550 Legacy 500 (IU-50); 2 ERJ-135LR (VC-99C); 7 ERJ-145 (C-99A); 1 ERJ-145LR (VC-99A); 9 Learjet 35A (VU-35); 1 Learjet 55C (VU-55); **PAX** 8: 1 A319 (VC-1A); 3 EMB-190 (VC-2); 4 Hawker 800XP (EU-93A – calibration)
TRG 211: up to 50 EMB-312 *Tucano* (T-27); 38 EMB-314 *Super Tucano* (A-29A)*; 43 EMB-314 *Super Tucano* (A-29B)*; 80 T-25A/C

HELICOPTERS
MRH 2 H135M (VH-35)
TPT 58: **Heavy** 14 H225M *Caracal* (12 H-36 & 2 VH-36); **Medium** 16 UH-60L *Black Hawk* (H-60L); **Light** 28: 24 AS350B *Ecureuil* (H-50); 4 AS355 *Ecureuil* II (H-55/VH-55)

UNINHABITED AERIAL VEHICLES
ISR 7: **Heavy** 2 *Heron* 1; **Medium** 5: 4 *Hermes* 450; 1 *Hermes* 900

AIR-LAUNCHED MISSILES
AAM • **IR** MAA-1 *Piranha*; R-550 *Magic* 2; *Python* 3; **IIR** *Python* 4; **SARH** Super 530F; **ARH** *Derby*
AShM AM39 *Exocet*
ARM MAR-1 (in development)

Gendarmerie & Paramilitary 395,000

Public Security Forces 395,000 opcon Army

State police organisation technically under army control. However, military control is reducing, with authority reverting to individual states

DEPLOYMENT

CENTRAL AFRICAN REPUBLIC: EU • EUTM RCA 6; **UN** • MINUSCA 10

CYPRUS: UN • UNFICYP 2

DEMOCRATIC REPUBLIC OF THE CONGO: UN • MONUSCO 23

LEBANON: UN • UNIFIL 9

SOUTH SUDAN: UN • UNMISS 11

SUDAN: UN • UNISFA 3

WESTERN SAHARA: UN • MINURSO 9

Chile CHL

Chilean Peso CLP		2021	2022	2023
GDP	CLP	240tr	265tr	
	USD	317bn	311bn	
per capita	USD	16,065	15,604	
Growth	%	11.7	2.0	
Inflation	%	4.5	11.6	
Def bdgt [a]	CLP	3.07tr	3.21tr	
	USD	4.04bn	3.76bn	
USD1=CLP		759.07	853.17	

[a] Includes military pensions

Real-terms defence budget trend (USDbn, constant 2015)

Population	18,430,408					
Age	0–14	15–19	20–24	25–29	30–64	65 plus
Male	10.0%	3.2%	3.5%	3.9%	23.3%	5.3%
Female	9.6%	3.1%	3.4%	3.7%	23.8%	7.3%

Capabilities

Chile's 2017 defence White Paper noted core roles of assuring sovereignty and territorial integrity, but also indicated an increasing shift towards non-traditional military roles such as disaster relief, humanitarian assistance and peacekeeping. In 2021, the armed forces were also granted authority to fight human trafficking and illegal migration in border areas. There is R&D cooperation with Brazil and Colombia, as well as exchange programmes. Defence cooperation with the US is centred on procurement, technical advice and personnel training. There is routine national training, and the armed forces participate in international exercises. Chile has a limited capacity to deploy independently beyond its borders. The plans to upgrade the country's F-16s to prolong service life have been temporarily suspended due to the lack of available funding. Capability priorities reflect a focus on littoral and bluewater surveillance. In 2020, two frigates were bought from Australia and the surface fleet has boosted its air-defence capabilities more generally, with upgrades also to the navy's ex-UK Type-23 frigates. A new multi-role amphibious vessel will enhance Chile's ability to provide logistic support and carry out HADR operations. Chile has a developed defence-industrial base, with ENAER conducting aircraft maintenance. ASMAR and FAMAE are key maritime and land firms respectively, with the former building a new icebreaker that will enhance Chile's ability to support operations in Antarctica. The air force is also currently contributing to the development of the country's first indigenously built satellite constellation.

ACTIVE 68,500 (Army 37,650 Navy 19,800 Air 11,050) **Gendarmerie & Paramilitary 44,700**

Conscript liability Army 12 months; Navy 18 months; Air Force 12 months. Legally, conscription can last for 2 years

RESERVE 19,100 (Army 19,100)

ORGANISATIONS BY SERVICE

Space
EQUIPMENT BY TYPE
SATELLITES
ISR 1 SSOT (Sistema Satelital de Observación de la Tierra)

Army 37,650
6 military administrative regions
FORCES BY ROLE
Currently being reorganised into 1 SF bde, 4 armd bde, 1 armd det, 4 mot bde, 2 mot det, 4 mtn det and 1 avn bde
COMMAND
6 div HQ
SPECIAL FORCES
1 SF bde (1 SF bn, 1 (mtn) SF gp, 1 para bn, 3 cdo coy, 1 log coy)
MANOEUVRE
Reconnaissance
4 cav sqn
2 recce sqn
2 recce pl
Armoured
1 (1st) armd bde (1 armd recce pl, 1 armd cav gp, 1 mech inf bn, 2 arty gp, 1 AT coy, 1 engr coy, 1 sigs coy)
2 (2nd & 3rd) armd bde (1 armd recce pl, 1 armd cav gp, 1 mech inf bn, 1 arty gp, 1 AT coy, 1 engr coy, 1 sigs coy)
1 (4th) armd bde (1 armd recce pl, 1 armd cav gp, 1 mech inf bn, 1 arty gp, 1 engr coy)
1 (5th) armd det (1 armd cav gp, 1 mech inf coy, 1 arty gp)
Mechanised
1 (1st) mech inf regt
Light
1 (1st) mot inf bde (1 recce coy, 1 mot inf bn, 1 arty gp, 3 AT coy, 1 engr bn)
1 (4th) mot inf bde (1 mot inf bn, 1 MRL gp, 2 AT coy, 1 engr bn)
1 (24th) mot inf bde (1 mot inf bn, 1 arty gp, 1 AT coy)
1 (Maipo) mot inf bde (3 mot inf regt, 1 arty regt)
1 (6th) reinforced regt (1 mot inf bn, 1 arty gp, 1 sigs coy)
1 (10th) reinforced regt (1 mot inf bn, 2 AT coy, 1 engr bn)
1 (11th) mot inf det (1 inf bn, 1 arty gp)
1 (14th) mot inf det (1 mot inf bn, 1 arty gp, 1 sigs coy, 1 AT coy)
4 mot inf regt
1 (3rd) mtn det (1 mtn inf bn, 1 arty gp, 1 engr coy)
1 (9th) mtn det (1 mtn inf bn, 1 engr coy, 1 construction bn)
2 (8th & 17th) mtn det (1 mtn inf bn, 1 arty coy)
COMBAT SUPPORT
1 engr regt
4 sigs bn
1 sigs coy
1 int bde (7 int gp)
2 int regt
1 MP regt

388   THE MILITARY BALANCE 2023

COMBAT SERVICE SUPPORT
1 log div (2 log regt)
4 log regt
6 log coy
1 maint div (1 maint regt)
AVIATION
1 avn bde (1 tpt avn bn, 1 hel bn, 1 spt bn)
EQUIPMENT BY TYPE
ARMOURED FIGHTING VEHICLES
MBT 170: 30 *Leopard 1V*; 140 *Leopard 2A4*
IFV 191: 173 *Marder 1A3*; 18 YPR-765 PRI
  APC 445 **APC (T)** 306 M113A1/A2
  APC (W) 139: 121 *Piranha* 6×6; 18 *Piranha* 8×8
ENGINEERING & MAINTENANCE VEHICLES
AEV 6 Pionierpanzer 2 *Dachs*
ARV 30 BPz-2
VLB 13 *Biber*
MW 8+: Bozena 5; 8 *Leopard 1 MW*
ANTI-TANK/ANTI-INFRASTRUCTURE
MSL • MANPATS *Spike*-LR; *Spike*-ER
RCL 84mm *Carl Gustaf*; **106mm** 213 M40A1
ARTILLERY 1,398
SP 155mm 48: 24 M109A3; 24 M109A5+
TOWED 239: **105mm** 191: 87 M101; 104 Model 56 pack howitzer; **155mm** 48 M-68
MRL 160mm 12 LAR-160
MOR 1,099: **81mm** 744: 295 ECIA L65/81; 192 FAMAE; 257 Soltam; **120mm** 284: 171 ECIA L65/120; 16 FAMAE; 97 M-65; **SP 120mm** 71: 35 FAMAE (on *Piranha* 6×6); 36 Soltam (on M113A2)
AIRCRAFT
TPT • Light 8: 2 C-212-300 *Aviocar*; 3 Cessna 208 *Caravan*; 3 CN235
HELICOPTERS
ISR 9 MD-530F *Lifter* (armed)
TPT 17: **Medium** 12: 8 AS532AL *Cougar*; 2 AS532ALe *Cougar*; 2 SA330 *Puma*; **Light** 5: 4 H125 *Ecureuil*; 1 AS355F *Ecureuil* II
AIR DEFENCE
SAM • Point-defence *Mistral*
GUNS 41:
  SP 20mm 17 *Piranha*/TCM-20
  TOWED 20mm 24 TCM-20

Navy 19,800

5 Naval Zones; 1st Naval Zone and main HQ at Valparaiso; 2nd Naval Zone at Talcahuano; 3rd Naval Zone at Punta Arenas; 4th Naval Zone at Iquique; 5th Naval Zone at Puerto Montt

FORCES BY ROLE
SPECIAL FORCES
1 (diver) SF comd
EQUIPMENT BY TYPE
SUBMARINES • SSK 4:
2 *O'Higgins* (*Scorpène*) with 6 single 533mm TT with SM39 *Exocet* Block 2 AShM/*Black Shark* HWT
2 *Thomson* (GER T-209/1400) (of which 1 in refit) with 8 single 533mm TT with SM39 *Exocet* Block 2 AShM/*Black Shark* HWT/SUT HWT
PRINCIPAL SURFACE COMBATANTS 8

FRIGATES • FFGHM 8:
3 *Almirante Cochrane* (ex-UK *Norfolk* Type-23) with 2 quad lnchr with RGM-84C *Harpoon* Block 1B AShM, 1 32-cell VLS with *Sea Ceptor* SAM, 2 twin 324mm ASTT with Mk 46 mod 2 LWT, 1 114mm gun (capacity 1 AS532SC *Cougar*)
2 *Almirante Latorre* (ex-AUS *Adelaide*) with 1 Mk 13 GMLS with RGM-84L *Harpoon* Block II AShM/SM-2 Block IIIA SAM, 1 8-cell Mk 41 VLS with RIM-162B ESSM SAM, 2 triple 324mm SVTT Mk 32 ASTT with MU90 LWT, 1 76mm gun (capacity 2 AS532SC *Cougars*)
2 *Almirante Riveros* (ex-NLD *Karel Doorman*) with 2 quad lnchr with MM40 *Exocet* Block 3 AShM, 1 8-cell Mk 48 VLS with RIM-7P *Sea Sparrow* SAM, 4 single 324mm SVTT Mk 32 mod 9 ASTT with Mk 46 mod 5 HWT, 1 76mm gun (capacity 1 AS532SC *Cougar*)
1 *Almirante Williams* (ex-UK *Broadsword* Type-22) with 2 quad lnchr with RGM-84 *Harpoon* AShM, 2 8-cell VLS with *Barak*-1 SAM; 2 triple 324mm ASTT with Mk 46 LWT, 1 76mm gun (capacity 1 AS532SC *Cougar*)
PATROL AND COASTAL COMBATANTS 12
PSOH 4: 2 *Piloto Pardo*; 2 *Piloto Pardo* with 1 76mm gun (ice-strengthened hull)
PCG 3:
2 *Casma* (ISR *Sa'ar* 4) with 6 single lnchr with *Gabriel* I AShM, 2 76mm guns
1 *Casma* (ISR *Sa'ar* 4) with 4 single lnchr with *Gabriel* I AShM, 2 twin lnchr with MM40 *Exocet* AShM, 2 76mm guns
PCO 5 *Micalvi*
AMPHIBIOUS
PRINCIPAL AMPHIBIOUS SHIPS • LPD 1 *Sargento Aldea* (ex-FRA *Foudre*) with 3 twin *Simbad* lnchr with *Mistral* SAM (capacity 4 med hel; 1 LCT; 2 LCM; 22 tanks; 470 troops)
LANDING SHIPS 3
LSM 1 *Elicura*
LST 2 *Maipo* (FRA *Batral*) with 1 hel landing platform (capacity 7 tanks; 140 troops)
LANDING CRAFT 3
LCT 1 CDIC (for use in *Sargento Aldea*)
LCM 2 (for use in *Sargento Aldea*)
LOGISTICS AND SUPPORT 13
ABU 1 *George Slight Marshall* with 1 hel landing platform
AFD 3
AGOR 1 *Cabo de Hornos*
AGHS 1 *Micalvi*
AOR 2: 1 *Almirante Montt* (ex-US *Henry J. Kaiser*) with 1 hel landing platform; 1 *Araucano*
AP 1 *Aguiles* (1 hel landing platform)
ATF 3: 1 *Janequeo*; 2 *Veritas*
AXS 1 *Esmeralda*

Naval Aviation 600

EQUIPMENT BY TYPE
AIRCRAFT 14 combat capable
ASW 4: 2 C295ASW *Persuader*; 2 P-3ACH *Orion*
MP 4: 1 C295MPA *Persuader*; 3 EMB-111 *Bandeirante**
ISR 7 P-68
TRG 7 PC-7 *Turbo Trainer**

Latin America and the Caribbean 389

HELICOPTERS
ASW 5 AS532SC *Cougar*
MRH 8 AS365 *Dauphin*
TPT 9: **Medium** 2 H215 (AS332L1) *Super Puma*; **Light** 7: 4 Bo-105S; 3 H125
AIR-LAUNCHED MISSILES • AShM AM39 *Exocet*

Marines 3,600
FORCES BY ROLE
MANOEUVRE
Amphibious
1 amph bde (2 mne bn, 1 cbt spt bn, 1 log bn)
2 coastal def unit
EQUIPMENT BY TYPE
ARMOURED FIGHTING VEHICLES
LT TK 15 FV101 *Scorpion*
IFV 9 NZLAV
APC • APC (W) 25 MOWAG *Roland*
AAV 12 AAV-7
ARTILLERY 39
TOWED 23: **105mm** 7 KH-178; **155mm** 16 M-71
MOR 81mm 16
COASTAL DEFENCE • AShM MM38 *Exocet*
AIR DEFENCE • SAM • Point-defence 14: 4 M998 *Avenger*; 10 M1097 *Avenger*

Coast Guard
Integral part of the Navy
EQUIPMENT BY TYPE
PATROL AND COASTAL COMBATANTS 55
PBF 26 *Archangel*
PB 29: 18 *Alacalufe* (*Protector*); 4 *Grumete Diaz* (*Dabor*); 6 *Pelluhue*; 1 *Ona*

Air Force 11,050
FORCES BY ROLE
FIGHTER
1 sqn with F-5E/F *Tiger* III+
2 sqn with F-16AM/BM *Fighting Falcon*
FIGHTER/GROUND ATTACK
1 sqn with F-16C/D Block 50 *Fighting Falcon* (*Puma*)
ISR
1 (photo) flt with; DHC-6-300 *Twin Otter*; Gulfstream IV
TANKER/TRANSPORT
1 sqn with B-737-300; C-130B/H *Hercules*; E-3D *Sentry*; KC-130R *Hercules*; KC-135 *Stratotanker*
TRANSPORT
3 sqn with Bell 205 (UH-1H *Iroquois*); C-212-200/300 *Aviocar*; Cessna O-2A; Cessna 525 *Citation* CJ1; DHC-6-100/300 *Twin Otter*; PA-28-236 *Dakota*; Bell 205 (UH-1H *Iroquois*)
1 VIP flt with B-767-300ER; B-737-500; Gulfstream IV
TRAINING
1 sqn with EMB-314 *Super Tucano**
1 sqn with Cirrus SR-22T; T-35A/B *Pillan*
TRANSPORT HELICOPTER
1 sqn with Bell 205 (UH-1H *Iroquois*); Bell 206B (trg); Bell 412 *Twin Huey*; S-70A *Black Hawk*
AIR DEFENCE
1 AD regt M163/M167 *Vulcan*
4 AD sqn with *Crotale*; NASAMS; *Mistral*; Oerlikon GDF-005

EQUIPMENT BY TYPE
AIRCRAFT 92 combat capable
FTR 48: 10 F-5E *Tigre* III+; 2 F-5F *Tigre* III+; 29 F-16AM *Fighting Falcon*; 7 F-16BM *Fighting Falcon*
FGA 10: 6 F-16C Block 50 *Fighting Falcon*; 4 F-16D Block 50 *Fighting Falcon*
ATK 16 C-101CC *Aviojet* (A-36 *Halcón*)
ISR 3 Cessna O-2A
AEW&C 2 E-3D *Sentry*
TKR 3 KC-135 *Stratotanker*
TKR/TPT 2 KC-130R *Hercules*
TPT 33: **Medium** 3: 1 C-130B *Hercules*; 2 C-130H *Hercules*; **Light** 24: 2 C-212-200 *Aviocar*; 1 C-212-300 *Aviocar*; 4 Cessna 525 *Citation* CJ1; 3 DHC-6-100 *Twin Otter*; 7 DHC-6-300 *Twin Otter*; 7 PA-28-236 *Dakota*; **PAX** 6: 1 B-737-300; 1 B-737-500 (VIP); 1 B-767-300ER (VIP); 3 Gulfstream IV (VIP/aerial photography)
TRG 57: 8 Cirrus SR-22T; 22 EMB-314 *Super Tucano**; 27 T-35A/B *Pillan*
HELICOPTERS
MRH 12 Bell 412EP *Twin Huey*
TPT 25: **Medium** 7: 1 S-70A *Black Hawk*; 6 S-70i (MH-60M) *Black Hawk*; **Light** 18: 13 Bell 205 (UH-1H *Iroquois*); 5 Bell 206B (trg)
UNINHABITED AERIAL VEHICLES
ISR • Medium 3 *Hermes* 900
AIR DEFENCE
SAM
Short-range 17: 5 *Crotale*; 12 NASAMS
Point-defence *Mistral* (including some *Mygale*/*Aspic*)
GUNS • TOWED 20mm M163/M167 *Vulcan*; **35mm** Oerlikon GDF-005
AIR-LAUNCHED MISSILES
AAM • IR AIM-9J/M *Sidewinder*; *Python* 3; *Shafrir*‡; **IIR** *Python* 4; **ARH** AIM-120C AMRAAM; *Derby*
ASM AGM-65G *Maverick*
BOMBS
Laser-guided *Paveway* II
INS/GPS guided JDAM

Gendarmerie & Paramilitary 44,700

Carabineros 44,700
Ministry of Interior; 15 zones, 36 districts, 179 *comisaria*
EQUIPMENT BY TYPE
ARMOURED FIGHTING VEHICLES
APC • APC (W) 20 MOWAG *Roland*
ARTILLERY • MOR 81mm
AIRCRAFT
TPT • Light 4: 1 Beech 200 *King Air*; 1 Cessna 208; 1 Cessna 550 *Citation* V; 1 PA-31T *Cheyenne* II
HELICOPTERS • TPT • Light 16: 5 AW109E *Power*; 1 AW139; 1 Bell 206 *Jet Ranger*; 2 BK-117; 5 Bo-105; 2 H135

DEPLOYMENT

BOSNIA-HERZEGOVINA: EU • EUFOR (*Operation Althea*) 8
CYPRUS: UN • UNFICYP 6
MIDDLE EAST: UN • UNTSO 3

Latin America and the Caribbean

Colombia COL

Colombian Peso COP		2021	2022	2023
GDP	COP	1177tr	1374tr	
	USD	314bn	343bn	
per capita	USD	6,159	6,644	
Growth	%	10.7	7.6	
Inflation	%	3.5	9.7	
Def bdgt [a]	COP	22.8tr	25.3tr	28.4tr
	USD	6.08bn	6.31bn	
FMA (US)	USD	38.5m	40.0m	38.0m
USD1=COP		3744.25	4006.34	

[a] Excludes security budget

Real-terms defence budget trend (USDbn, constant 2015)

Population 49,059,221

Age	0–14	15–19	20–24	25–29	30–64	65 plus
Male	11.6%	4.0%	4.0%	4.1%	20.5%	4.7%
Female	11.1%	3.8%	3.9%	4.1%	22.3%	5.9%

Capabilities

Colombia's armed forces have improved their training and overall capabilities in recent decades. Internal security remains a priority, and the armed forces are focused on conducting counter-insurgency and counter-narcotics operations. In response to the humanitarian and security challenge from Venezuela, Colombia has strengthened cooperation with Brazil on border controls. There are military ties with Argentina, Chile and Peru. The US is Colombia's closest international military partner, with cooperation in equipment procurement, technical advice and personnel training. In May 2018, Colombia joined NATO as a global partner. The forces train regularly, including multilateral exercises. Although the equipment inventory mainly comprises legacy systems, Colombia has the capability to independently deploy force elements beyond national borders. The navy is planning to enhance its surface warfare capabilities by acquiring five new frigates, while the army is planning to modernise its armoured vehicles. The air force has established a space operations centre and plans to launch a new earth observation satellite in 2023. New medium transport aircraft will be equipped with ISR sensors to boost reconnaissance capabilities. Colombia's defence industry is active in all domains. CIAC is developing its first indigenous UAVs, while CODALTEC is developing an air-defence system for regional export. COTECMAR has supplied patrol boats and amphibious ships for national and export markets.

ACTIVE 255,950 (Army 185,900, Navy 56,400 Air 13,650) **Gendarmerie & Paramilitary 172,400**

Conscript liability 18 months' duration with upper age limit of 24, males only

RESERVE 34,950 (Army 25,050 Navy 6,500 Air 3,400)

ORGANISATIONS BY SERVICE

Army 185,900
FORCES BY ROLE
SPECIAL FORCES
1 SF div (3 SF regt)
1 (anti-terrorist) SF bn
MANOEUVRE
Mechanised
1 (1st) mech div (1 (2nd) mech bde (2 mech inf bn, 1 mtn inf bn, 1 engr bn, 1 MP bn, 1 spt bn, 2 Gaula anti-kidnap gp); 1 (10th) mech bde (1 (urban) spec ops bn, 1 armd recce bn, 1 mech cav bn, 1 mech inf bn, 1 mtn inf bn, 3 sy bn, 2 arty bn, 1 engr bn, 1 spt bn, 2 Gaula anti-kidnap gp))
Light
1 (2nd) inf div (1 (1st) inf bde (1 mech cav bn, 2 inf bn, 1 mtn inf bn, 1 sy bn, 1 arty bn, 1 spt bn, 1 Gaula anti-kidnap gp); 1 (5th) inf bde (3 inf bn, 1 jungle inf bn, 1 sy bn, 1 arty bn, 1 engr bn, 1 spt bn, 1 Gaula anti-kidnap gp); 1 (30th) inf bde (1 mech cav bn, 2 inf bn, 1 sy bn, 1 arty bn, 1 engr bn, 1 spt bn); 1 AD bn; 1 sy gp (1 (urban) spec ops bn, 4 COIN bn, 3 sy bn); 1 (rapid reaction) sy bde)
1 (3rd) inf div (1 (3rd) inf bde (2 inf bn, 1 mtn inf bn, 1 COIN bn, 1 arty bn, 1 engr bn, 1 cbt spt bn, 1 MP bn, 1 log bn, 1 Gaula anti-kidnap gp); 1 (23rd) inf bde (1 cav gp, 1 lt inf bn, 1 jungle inf bn, 1 spt bn, 1 log bn); 1 (29th) mtn bde (1 mtn inf bn, 1 inf bn, 2 COIN bn, 1 spt bn, 1 log bn); 1 lt cav bde (2 lt cav gp); 1 mtn inf bn; 2 (rapid reaction) sy bde)
1 (4th) inf div (1 (7th) air mob bde (1 (urban) spec ops bn, 2 air mob inf bn, 1 lt inf bn, 1 COIN bn, 1 engr bn, 1 spt bn, 1 log bn, 1 Gaula anti-kidnap gp); 1 (22nd) jungle bde (1 air mob inf bn, 1 lt inf bn, 1 jungle inf bn, 1 COIN bn, 1 spt bn, 1 log bn); 1 (31st) jungle bde (1 lt inf bn, 1 jungle inf bn))
1 (5th) inf div (1 (6th) lt inf bde (2 lt inf bn, 1 mtn inf bn, 3 COIN bn, 1 EOD bn, 2 spt bn, 1 Gaula anti-kidnap gp); 1 (8th) inf bde (1 inf bn, 1 mtn inf bn, 1 arty bn, 1 engr bn, 1 spt bn, 1 Gaula anti-kidnap gp); 1 (9th) inf bde (1 (urban) spec ops bn, 2 inf bn, 1 arty bn, 1 COIN bn, 1 sy bn, 1 spt bn, 1 Gaula anti-kidnap gp); 1 (13th) inf bde (1 recce bn, 3 inf bn, 1 mtn inf bn, 1 air mob bn, 1 COIN bn, 1 arty bn, 1 engr bn, 2 MP bn, 1 spt bn, 1 Gaula anti-kidnap gp))
1 (6th) inf div (1 (12th) inf bde (1 (urban) spec ops bn, 1 inf bn, 1 jungle inf bn, 1 mtn inf bn, 1 COIN bn, 1 engr bn, 1 spt bn, 1 Gaula anti-kidnap gp); 1 (26th) jungle bde (1 jungle inf bn, 1 spt bn); 1 (27th) jungle inf bde (1 inf bn, 1 jungle inf bn, 1 sy bn, 1 arty bn, 1 engr bn, 1 spt bn); 1 (13th) mobile sy bde; 2 COIN bn)
1 (7th) inf div (1 (4th) inf bde (1 (urban) spec ops bn; 1 mech cav gp, 3 inf bn, 1 sy bn, 1 arty bn, 1 engr bn, 1 MP bn, 1 spt bn, 2 Gaula anti-kidnap gp); 1 (11th) inf bde (1 inf bn, 1 air mob bn, 1 sy bn, 1 spt bn, 2 Gaula anti-kidnap gp); 1 (14th) inf bde (2 inf bn, 1 sy bn, 1 engr bn, 1 spt bn); 1 (15th) jungle bde (1 inf bn, 2 COIN bn, 1 engr bn); 1 (17th) inf bde (2 inf bn, 1 engr bn, 1 spt bn))

Latin America and the Caribbean **391**

1 (8th) inf div (1 (16th) lt inf bde (1 recce bn, 1 inf bn, 1 spt bn, 1 Gaula anti-kidnap gp); 1 (18th) inf bde (1 (urban) spec ops bn; 1 air mob gp, 5 sy bn, 1 arty bn, 1 engr bn, 1 spt bn); 1 (28th) jungle bde (2 inf, 2 COIN, 1 spt bn); 1 (rapid reaction) sy bde, 4 COIN bn)

3 COIN mobile bde (each: 4 COIN bn, 1 spt bn)

COMBAT SUPPORT

1 cbt engr bde (1 SF engr bn, 1 (emergency response) engr bn, 1 EOD bn, 1 construction bn, 1 demining bn, 1 maint bn)

1 int bde (2 SIGINT bn, 1 log bn, 1 maint bn)

COMBAT SERVICE SUPPORT

2 spt/log bde (each: 1 spt bn, 1 maint bn, 1 supply bn, 1 tpt bn, 1 medical bn, 1 log bn)

AVIATION

1 air aslt div (1 counter-narcotics bde (4 counter-narcotics bn, 1 spt bn); 1 (25th) avn bde (4 hel bn; 5 avn bn; 1 avn log bn); 1 (32nd) avn bde (1 avn bn, 2 maint bn, 1 trg bn, 1 spt bn); 1 SF avn bn)

EQUIPMENT BY TYPE

ARMOURED FIGHTING VEHICLES

RECCE 121 EE-9 *Cascavel*

IFV 60: 28 *Commando Advanced*; 32 LAV III

APC 114

 APC (T) 54: 28 M113A1 (TPM-113A1); 26 M113A2 (TPM-113A2)

 APC (W) 56 EE-11 *Urutu*

 PPV 4+: some *Hunter* XL; 4 RG-31 *Nyala*

AUV 126 M1117 *Guardian*

ANTI-TANK/ANTI-INFRASTRUCTURE

MSL

 SP 77 *Nimrod*

 MANPATS TOW; *Spike*-ER

RCL 106mm 73 M40A1

ARTILLERY 1,796

TOWED 120: **105mm** 107: 22 LG1 MkIII; 85 M101; **155mm** 13 155/52 APU SBT-1

MOR 1,676: **81mm** 1,507; **120mm** 169

AIRCRAFT

ELINT 3: 2 Beech B200 *King Air*; 1 Beech 350 *King Air*

TPT • Light 23: 2 An-32B; 2 Beech B200 *King Air*; 3 Beech 350 *King Air*; 1 Beech C90 *King Air*; 2 C-212 *Aviocar* (Medevac); 8 Cessna 208B *Grand Caravan*; 1 Cessna 208B-EX *Grand Caravan*; 4 *Turbo Commander* 695A

HELICOPTERS

MRH 19: 8 Mi-17-1V *Hip*; 6 Mi-17MD; 5 Mi-17V-5 *Hip*

TPT 92: **Medium** 53: 46 UH-60L *Black Hawk*; 7 S-70i *Black Hawk*; **Light** 39: 24 Bell 205 (UH-1H *Iroquois*); 15 Bell 212 (UH-1N *Twin Huey*)

AIR DEFENCE • GUNS • TOWED 40mm 4 M1A1

Navy 56,400 (incl 12,100 conscript)

HQ located at Bogotá

EQUIPMENT BY TYPE

SUBMARINES 4

SSK 2 *Pijao* (GER T-209/1200) each with 8 single 533mm TT each with *SeaHake* (DM2A3) HWT

SSC 2 *Intrépido* (ex-GER T-206A) each with 8 single 533mm TT each with *SeaHake* (DM2A3) HWT

PATROL AND COASTAL COMBATANTS 58

CORVETTES 6

FSGHM 4 *Almirante Padilla* with 2 quad lnchr with *Hae Sung* I AShM, 2 twin *Simbad* lnchr with *Mistral* SAM, 2 triple 324mm ILAS-3 (B-515) ASTT each with A244/S LWT, 1 76mm gun (capacity 1 Bo-105/AS555SN *Fennec* hel)

FSG 1 *Almirante Tono* (Ex-ROK *Po Hang* (Flight IV)) 2 twin lnchr with *Hae Sung* I AShM, 2 triple 324mm ASTT with Mk 46, 2 76mm guns

FS 1 *Narino* (ex-ROK *Dong Hae*) with 2 triple 324mm SVTT Mk 32 ASTT with Mk 46 LWT

PSOH 3: 2 *20 de Julio* (CHL *Piloto Pardo*); 1 *20 de Julio* (CHL *Piloto Pardo*) with 1 76mm gun

PCR 10: 2 *Arauca* with 1 76mm guns; 8 *Nodriza* (PAF I-IV) with hel landing platform

PBR 39: 5 *Diligente*; 16 LPR-40; 3 Swiftships; 9 *Tenerife* (US Bender Marine 12m); 2 PAF-L; 4 others

AMPHIBIOUS 16

LCT 6 *Golfo de Tribuga*

LCU 2 *Morrosquillo* (LCU 1466)

UCAC 8 *Griffon* 2000TD

LOGISTICS AND SUPPORT 8

ABU 1 *Quindio*

AG 1 *Inirida*

AGHS 2: 1 *Caribe*; 1 *Roncador*

AGOR 2 *Providencia*

AGS 1 *Gorgona*

AXS 1 *Gloria*

Coast Guard

EQUIPMENT BY TYPE

PATROL AND COASTAL COMBATANTS 17

PCO 2: 1 *San Andres* (ex-US *Balsam*); 1 *Valle del Cauca Durable* (ex-US *Reliance*) with 1 hel landing platform

PCC 3 *Punta Espada* (CPV-46)

PB 12: 1 *11 de Noviembre* (CPV-40) (GER Fassmer); 2 *Castillo y Rada* (Swiftships 105); 2 *Jaime Gomez* (ex-US Peterson Mk 3); 1 *Jorge Luis Marrugo Campo*; 1 *José Maria Palas* (Swiftships 110); 3 *Point*; 2 *Toledo* (US Bender Marine 35m)

LOGISTICS AND SUPPORT • ABU 1 *Isla Albuquerque*

Naval Aviation 150

EQUIPMENT BY TYPE

AIRCRAFT

MP 3 CN235 MPA *Persuader*

ISR 1 PA-31 *Navajo* (upgraded for ISR)

TPT • Light 14: 1 Beech 360ER *King Air*; 2 Beech C90 *King Air*; 1 C-212 (Medevac); 4 Cessna 206; 3 Cessna 208 *Caravan*; 1 PA-31 *Navajo*; 1 PA-34 *Seneca*; 1 Beech 350 *King Air*

HELICOPTERS

SAR 2 AS365 *Dauphin*

MRH 9: 1 AS555SN *Fennec*; 3 Bell 412 *Twin Huey*; 4 Bell 412EP *Twin Huey*; 1 Bell 412EPI *Twin Huey*

TPT • Light 8: 1 Bell 212; 4 Bell 212 (UH-1N); 1 BK-117; 2 Bo-105

Marines 22,250

FORCES BY ROLE

SPECIAL FORCES

1 SF bde (4 SF bn)

MANOEUVRE

Amphibious
1 mne bde (1 SF (Gaula) bn, 5 mne bn, 2 rvn bn, 1 spt bn)
1 mne bde (1 SF bn, 2 mne bn, 2 rvn bn, 1 spt bn)
1 rvn bde (1 SF bn, 1 mne bn, 2 rvn bn, 1 spt bn)
1 rvn bde (4 rvn bn)
1 rvn bde (3 rvn bn)

COMBAT SERVICE SUPPORT
1 log bde (6 spt bn)
1 trg bde (7 trg bn, 1 spt bn)

EQUIPMENT BY TYPE
ARTILLERY • MOR 82: **81mm** 74; **120mm** 8
AIR DEFENCE • SAM • **Point-defence** *Mistral*

Air Force 13,650

FORCES BY ROLE
FIGHTER/GROUND ATTACK
1 sqn with *Kfir* C-10/C-12/TC-12
GROUND ATTACK/ISR
1 sqn with AC-47T; ECN235; IAI *Arava*
1 sqn with EMB-312 *Tucano**
2 sqn with EMB-314 *Super Tucano** (A-29)
GROUND ATTACK
1 sqn with AC-47T *Spooky* (*Fantasma*); Bell 205 (UH-1H *Huey* II); Cessna 208 *Grand Caravan*
1 sqn with Cessna 208 *Grand Caravan*; C-212; UH-60L *Black Hawk*
EW/ELINT
2 sqn with Beech 350 *King Air*; Cessna 208; SA 2-37; *Turbo Commander* 695
ELINT
2 sqn with Cessna 560
TRANSPORT
1 (Presidential) sqn with AW139; B-737BBJ; EMB-600 *Legacy*; Bell 412EP; F-28 *Fellowship*; UH-60L *Black Hawk*
1 sqn with B-737-400; B-737-800; Beech C90GTx *King Air*; C-130B/H *Hercules*; C-212; C295M; CN235M; KC-767
1 sqn with Beech 350C *King Air*; Bell 212; Cessna 208B; EMB-110P1 (C-95)
1 sqn with Beech C90 *King Air*
TRAINING
1 sqn with Cessna 172
1 sqn with Lancair *Synergy* (T-90 *Calima*)
1 sqn with T-6C *Texan* II
1 hel sqn with Bell 206B3
1 hel sqn with TH-67
HELICOPTER
1 sqn with AH-60L *Arpia* III
1 sqn with UH-60L *Black Hawk* (CSAR)
1 sqn with Hughes 500M
1 sqn with Bell 205 (UH-1H *Huey* II)
1 sqn with Bell 206B3 *Jet Ranger* III
1 sqn with Bell 212; Bell 205 (UH-1H *Huey* II)
ISR UAV
1 sqn with *Hermes* 450; *Hermes* 900

EQUIPMENT BY TYPE
AIRCRAFT 66 combat capable
FGA 22: 10 *Kfir* C-10; 9 *Kfir* C-12; 3 *Kfir* TC-12
ATK 6 AC-47T *Spooky* (*Fantasma*)
ISR 11: 5 Cessna 560 *Citation* II; 6 SA 2-37

ELINT 11: 3 Beech 350 *King Air*; 6 Cessna 208 *Grand Caravan*; 1 ECN235; 1 *Turbo Commander* 695
TKR/TPT 1 KC-767
TPT 74: **Medium** 10: 3 C-130B *Hercules*; 6 C-130H *Hercules*; 1 B-737F; **Light** 52: 7 ATR-42; 2 Beech 300 *King Air*; 1 Beech 350C *King Air* (medevac); 1 Beech 350i *King Air* (VIP); 2 Beech 350 *King Air* (medevac); 2 Beech C90 *King Air*; 3 Beech C90GTx *King Air*; 4 C-212; 6 C295M; 8 Cessna 172; 1 Cessna 182R; 12 Cessna 208B (medevac); 1 CN235M; 2 EMB-110P1 (C-95); **PAX** 12: 2 B-737-400; 2 B-737-800; 1 B-737BBJ (VIP); 2 ERJ-135BJ *Legacy* 600 (VIP); 2 ERJ-145; 1 F-28-1000 *Fellowship*; 1 F-28-3000 *Fellowship*; 1 Learjet 60
TRG 68: 14 EMB-312 *Tucano**; 24 EMB-314 *Super Tucano* (A-29)*; 23 Lancair *Synergy* (T-90 *Calima*); 7 T-6C *Texan* II
HELICOPTERS
MRH 18: 4 AH-60L *Arpia* III; 10 AH-60L *Arpia* IV; 1 AW139 (VIP); 1 Bell 412EP *Twin Huey* (VIP); 2 Hughes 500M
TPT 49: **Medium** 16 UH-60L *Black Hawk* (incl 1 VIP hel); **Light** 33: 10 Bell 205 (UH-1H *Huey* II); 12 Bell 206B3 *Jet Ranger* III; 11 Bell 212
TRG 60 TH-67
UNINHABITED AERIAL VEHICLES • ISR • Medium
8: 6 *Hermes* 450; 2 *Hermes* 900
AIR-LAUNCHED MISSILES
AAM • IR Python 3; **IIR** Python 4; *Python* 5; **ARH** *Derby*; I-*Derby* ER (reported)
ASM Spike-ER; *Spike*-NLOS
BOMBS
Laser-guided *Paveway* II
INS/GPS guided *Spice*

Gendarmerie & Paramilitary 172,400

National Police Force 172,400

EQUIPMENT BY TYPE
AIRCRAFT
ELINT 5 C-26B *Metroliner*
TPT • Light 42: 5 ATR-42; 3 Beech 200 *King Air*; 2 Beech 300 *King Air*; 2 Beech 1900; 1 Beech C99; 3 BT-67; 3 C-26 *Metroliner*; 3 Cessna 152; 3 Cessna 172; 9 Cessna 206; 2 Cessna 208 *Caravan*; 2 DHC-6 *Twin Otter*; 1 DHC-8; 3 PA-31 *Navajo*
HELICOPTERS
MRH 5: 2 Bell 407GXP; 1 Bell 412EP; 2 MD-500D
TPT 80: **Medium** 22: 10 UH-60A *Black Hawk*; 9 UH-60L *Black Hawk*; 3 S-70i *Black Hawk*; **Light** 58: 34 Bell 205 (UH-1H-II *Huey* II); 6 Bell 206B; 5 Bell 206L/L3/L4 *Long Ranger*; 8 Bell 212; 5 Bell 407

DEPLOYMENT

CENTRAL AFRICAN REPUBLIC: UN • MINUSCA 2

EGYPT: MFO 275; 1 inf bn

LEBANON: UN • UNIFIL 1

WESTERN SAHARA: UN • MINURSO 2

FOREIGN FORCES

United States US Southern Command: 50

Costa Rica CRI

Costa Rican Colon CRC		2021	2022	2023
GDP	CRC	40.0tr	43.8tr	
	USD	64.4bn	68.5bn	
per capita	USD	12,436	13,090	
Growth	%	7.8	3.8	
Inflation	%	1.7	8.9	
Sy Bdgt [a]	CRC	267bn	270bn	269bn
	USD	430m	423m	
FMA (US)	USD	7.5m	0.0m	0.0m
USD1=CRC		620.85	638.94	

[a] Paramilitary budget

Real-terms defence budget trend (USDm, constant 2015)

Population 5,204,411

Age	0–14	15–19	20–24	25–29	30–64	65 plus
Male	11.1%	3.6%	3.8%	4.1%	23.1%	4.4%
Female	10.6%	3.4%	3.7%	3.9%	23.1%	5.1%

Capabilities

Costa Rica's armed forces were constitutionally abolished in 1949, and the country relies on police and coastguard organisations for internal security, maritime and air domain awareness, and counter-narcotics tasks. A new National Security Strategy was adopted in 2018 in order to help tackle rising crime. Colombia and the US have provided assistance and training, focused on policing and internal-security tasks rather than conventional military operations. The Special Intervention Unit (UEI) has received specialist training from non-regional states, including the US. In May 2022, Costa Rica declared a state of emergency in the face of a cyber-attack, underscoring its limited national defences against such a threat. The Public Force, Coast Guard and Air Surveillance units have little heavy equipment, and recent modernisation has depended on donations from countries such as China and the US. Apart from limited maintenance facilities, Costa Rica has no domestic defence industry.

Gendarmerie & Paramilitary 9,950

ORGANISATIONS BY SERVICE

Gendarmerie & Paramilitary 9,950

Special Intervention Unit
FORCES BY ROLE
SPECIAL FORCES
1 spec ops unit

Public Force 9,000
11 regional directorates

Coast Guard Unit 550
EQUIPMENT BY TYPE
PATROL AND COASTAL COMBATANTS 9
PB 9: 1 *Cabo Blanco* (US *Swift* 65); 1 *Isla del Coco* (US *Swift* 105); 3 *Libertador Juan Rafael Mora* (ex-US *Island*); 2 *Point*; 1 *Primera Dama* (US *Swift* 42); 1 *Puerto Quepos* (US *Swift* 36)

Air Surveillance Unit 400
EQUIPMENT BY TYPE
AIRCRAFT • TPT • Light 14: 2 Cessna T210 *Centurion*; 4 Cessna U206G *Stationair*; 2 PA-31 *Navajo*; 2 PA-34 *Seneca*; 1 Piper PA-23 *Aztec*; 1 Cessna 182RG; 2 Y-12E
HELICOPTERS
MRH 3: 1 MD-500E; 2 MD-600N
TPT • **Light** 4 Bell 212 (UH-1N)

Cuba CUB

Cuban Peso CUP		2021	2022	2023
GDP	USD			
per capita	USD			
Growth				
Inflation				
Def exp	CUP			
	USD			
USD1=CUP				

Definitive data not available

Population 11,008,112

Age	0–14	15–19	20–24	25–29	30–64	65 plus
Male	8.4%	2.8%	3.1%	3.0%	24.9%	7.5%
Female	8.0%	2.6%	2.9%	2.8%	25.2%	9.0%

Capabilities

Cuba's armed forces are principally focused on protecting territorial integrity and rely on a mass-mobilisation system. Military capability is limited by equipment obsolescence and a largely conscript-based force. Cuba maintains military ties with China and Russia, and the latter has supplied oil and fuel following Venezuela's economic collapse. Defence cooperation with Russia is largely centred around technical and maintenance support. Cooperation with China appears to be on a smaller scale and involves training agreements and personnel exchanges. In recent years Cuba has sent medics and maintenance personnel to South Africa and has also trained some South African personnel in Cuba. The armed forces are no longer designed for expeditionary operations and have little logistical capability to support operational deployments abroad. The inventory is almost entirely composed of legacy Soviet-era systems with varying degrees of obsolescence. Serviceability appears problematic, with much equipment at a low level of availability and maintenance demands growing as fleets age. Much of the aviation fleet is reported to be in storage. Training levels are uncertain and flying hours are likely to be low due to limited availability of aircraft. It is unlikely that significant equipment recapitalisation can be financed in the near term. Cuba has little in the way of domestic defence industry, apart from some upgrade and maintenance capacity.

ACTIVE 49,000 (Army 38,000 Navy 3,000 Air 8,000)
Gendarmerie & Paramilitary 26,500
Conscript liability 2 years

RESERVE 39,000 (Army 39,000) **Gendarmerie & Paramilitary 1,120,000**
Ready Reserves (serve 45 days per year) to fill out Active and Reserve units; see also Paramilitary

ORGANISATIONS BY SERVICE

Army ε38,000

FORCES BY ROLE
COMMAND
3 regional comd HQ
3 army comd HQ
COMMAND
3 SF regt
MANOEUVRE
Armoured
1 tk div (3 tk bde)
Mechanised
2 (mixed) mech bde
Light
2 (frontier) bde
Air Manoeuvre
1 AB bde
AIR DEFENCE
1 ADA regt
1 SAM bde

Reserves 39,000

FORCES BY ROLE
MANOEUVRE
Light
14 inf bde
EQUIPMENT BY TYPE†
ARMOURED FIGHTING VEHICLES
MBT ε400 T-54/T-55/T-62
LT TK PT-76
ASLT BTR-60 100mm
RECCE BRDM-2;
AIFV ε50 BMP-1/1P
APC ε500 BTR-152/BTR-50/BTR-60
ANTI-TANK/ANTI-INFRASTRUCTURE
MSL
SP 2K16 *Shmel* (RS-AT-1 *Snapper*)
MANPATS 9K11 *Malyutka* (RS-AT-3 *Sagger*)
GUNS 600+: **57mm** 600 ZIS-2 (M-1943); **85mm** D-44
ARTILLERY 1,715+
SP 40+: **100mm** AAPMP-100; CATAP-100; **122mm** 2S1 *Gvozdika*; AAP-T-122; AAP-BMP-122; *Jupiter* III; *Jupiter* IV; **130mm** AAP-T-130; *Jupiter* V; **152mm** 2S3 *Akatsiya*
TOWED 500: **122mm** D-30; M-30 (M-1938); **130mm** M-46; **152mm** D-1; M-1937 (ML-20)
MRL • SP 175: **122mm** BM-21 *Grad*; **140mm** BM-14
MOR 1,000: **82mm** M-41; **82mm** M-43; **120mm** M-43; M-38

AIR DEFENCE
SAM
Short-range 2K12 *Kub* (RS-SA-6 *Gainful*)
Pont-defence 200+: 200 9K35 *Strela*-10 (RS-SA-13 *Gopher*); 9K33 *Osa* (RS-SA-8 *Gecko*); 9K31 *Strela*-1 (RS-SA-9 *Gaskin*); 9K36 *Strela*-3 (RS-SA-14 *Gremlin*); 9K310 *Igla*-1 (SA-16 *Gimlet*); 9K32 *Strela*-2 (RS-SA-7 *Grail*)‡
GUNS 400
SP 23mm ZSU-23-4; **30mm** BTR-60P SP; **57mm** ZSU-57-2
TOWED 100mm KS-19/M-1939/**85mm** KS-12/**57mm** S-60/**37mm** M-1939/**30mm** M-53/**23mm** ZU-23

Navy ε3,000

Western Comd HQ at Cabanas; Eastern Comd HQ at Holquin

EQUIPMENT BY TYPE
SUBMARINES • SSW 1 *Delfin*
PATROL AND COASTAL COMBATANTS 9
PCG 2 *Rio Damuji* with two single P-22 (RS-SS-N-2C *Styx*) AShM, 2 57mm guns, 1 hel landing platform
PCM 1 Project 1241PE (FSU *Pauk* II) with 1 quad lnchr (manual aiming) with 9K32 *Strela*-2 (RS-SA-N-5 *Grail*) SAM, 2 RBU 1200 A/S mor, 1 76mm gun
PBF 6 Project 205 (FSU *Osa* II)† each with 4 single lnchr (for P-20U (RS-SS-N-2B *Styx*) AShM – missiles removed to coastal-defence units)
MINE WARFARE AND MINE COUNTERMEASURES 5
MHI 3 *Korund* (Project 1258 (*Yevgenya*))†
MSC 2 *Yakhont* (FSU Project 1265 (*Sonya*))†
LOGISTICS AND SUPPORT 2
ABU 1
AX 1

Coastal Defence

EQUIPMENT BY TYPE
ARTILLERY • TOWED 122mm M-1931/37; **130mm** M-46; **152mm** M-1937
COASTAL DEFENCE • AShM 4+: *Bandera* IV (reported); 4 4K51 *Rubezh* (RS-SSC-3 *Styx*)

Naval Infantry 550+

FORCES BY ROLE
MANOEUVRE
Amphibious
2 amph aslt bn

Anti-aircraft Defence and Revolutionary Air Force ε8,000 (incl conscripts)

Air assets divided between Western Air Zone and Eastern Air Zone

FORCES BY ROLE
FIGHTER/GROUND ATTACK
3 sqn with MiG-21bis/UM *Fishbed*; MiG-29/MiG-29UB *Fulcrum*
TRANSPORT
1 (VIP) tpt sqn with An-24 *Coke*; Mi-8P *Hip*

ATTACK HELICOPTER
 2 sqn with Mi-17 *Hip* H; Mi-35 *Hind*
TRAINING
 1 (tac trg) sqn with L-39C *Albatros* (basic); Z-142 (primary)
EQUIPMENT BY TYPE
AIRCRAFT 10 combat capable
 FTR 5: 2 MiG-29 *Fulcrum*†; 3 MiG-29UB *Fulcrum*†
 FGA 5: up to 3 MiG-21bis *Fishbed*; up to 2 MiG-21UM *Fishbed*
 ISR 1 An-30 *Clank*†
 TPT 23: **Heavy** 2 Il-76 *Candid*; **Light** 9: 1 An-24 *Coke* (Aerogaviota); 3 An-26 *Curl* (Aerogaviota); 5 ATR-42-500 (Cubana & Aergaviota); **PAX** 12: 6 An-158 (Cubana); 3 Il-96-300 (Cubana); 3 Tu-204E-100 (Cubana)
 TRG 25+: up to 25 L-39 *Albatros*; some Z-142C
HELICOPTERS
 ATK 4 Mi-35 *Hind*† (8 more in store)
 MRH 8 Mi-17 *Hip* H (12 more in store)
 TPT • **Medium** 2 Mi-8P *Hip*
AIR DEFENCE • SAM
 Medium-range S-75 *Dvina* (RS-SA-2 *Guideline*); S-75 *Dvina* mod (RS-SA-2 *Guideline* – on T-55 chassis)
 Short-range S-125M/M1 *Pechora*-M/M1 (RS-SA-3 *Goa*); S-125M1 *Pechora*-M1 mod (RS-SA-3 *Goa* – on T-55 chassis)
AIR-LAUNCHED MISSILES
 AAM • **IR** R-3‡ (RS-AA-2 *Atoll*); R-60 (RS-AA-8 *Aphid*); R-73 (RS-AA-11A *Archer*); **IR/SARH** R-23/24‡ (RS-AA-7 *Apex*); R-27 (RS-AA-10 *Alamo*)
 ASM Kh-23‡ (RS-AS-7 *Kerry*)

Gendarmerie & Paramilitary 26,500 active

State Security 20,000
Ministry of Interior

Border Guards 6,500
Ministry of Interior
PATROL AND COASTAL COMBATANTS 20
 PCC 2 *Stenka*
 PB 18 *Zhuk*

Youth Labour Army 70,000 reservists

Civil Defence Force 50,000 reservists

Territorial Militia ε1,000,000 reservists

FOREIGN FORCES
United States US Southern Command: 650 (JTF-GTMO) at Guantanamo Bay

Dominican Republic DOM

Dominican Peso DOP		2021	2022	2023
GDP	DOP	5.41tr	6.17tr	
	USD	94.7bn	112bn	
per capita	USD	8,986	10,573	
Growth	%	12.3	5.3	
Inflation	%	8.2	9.0	
Def bdgt	DOP	33.2bn	41.8bn	49.9bn
	USD	582m	761m	
USD1=DOP		57.09	54.93	

Real-terms defence budget trend (USDm, constant 2015)

Population	10,694,700					
Age	0–14	15–19	20–24	25–29	30–64	65 plus
Male	13.3%	4.5%	4.5%	4.3%	20.8%	3.2%
Female	12.9%	4.4%	4.3%	4.1%	20.2%	3.6%

Capabilities
The principal tasks for the Dominican armed forces include internal- and border-security missions, as well as disaster relief. Training and operations increasingly focus on counter-narcotics and include collaboration with the police in an inter-agency task force. The US sends training teams to the country under the terms of a 2015 military-partnership agreement, and the navy has trained with French forces. The Dominican Republic has participated in US SOUTHCOM's *Tradewinds* disaster-response exercise. In response to instability in Haiti, the army has strengthened its presence along the border, establishing new surveillance posts, while the air force has carried out overflight operations; in 2022, 12,000 troops were deployed to the border. However, there is little capacity to deploy and sustain forces abroad. The army's limited number of armoured vehicles are obsolete and likely difficult to maintain. The air force operates a modest number of light fixed-wing and rotary-wing assets, and the navy a small fleet of mainly ex-US patrol craft of varying sizes. Apart from maintenance facilities, the country does not have a domestic defence industry.

ACTIVE 56,050 (Army 28,750 Navy 11,200 Air 16,100) Gendarmerie & Paramilitary 15,000

ORGANISATIONS BY SERVICE

Army 28,750
5 Defence Zones
FORCES BY ROLE
SPECIAL FORCES
 3 SF bn
MANOEUVRE
 Light
 4 (1st, 2nd, 3rd & 4th) inf bde (3 inf bn)
 2 (5th & 6th) inf bde (2 inf bn)
 Air Manoeuvre
 1 air cav bde (1 cdo bn, 1 (6th) mtn bn, 1 hel sqn with

Bell 205 (op by Air Force); OH-58 *Kiowa*; R-22; R-44 *Raven* II)
Other
1 (Presidential Guard) gd regt
1 (MoD) sy bn
COMBAT SUPPORT
1 cbt spt bde (1 lt armd bn; 1 arty bn; 1 engr bn; 1 sigs bn)
EQUIPMENT BY TYPE
ARMOURED FIGHTING VEHICLES
  LT TK 12 M41B (76mm)
  APC • APC (W) 8 LAV-150 *Commando*
ANTI-TANK/ANTI-INFRASTRUCTURE
  RCL 106mm 20 M40A1
  GUNS 37mm 20 M3
ARTILLERY 104
  TOWED 105mm 16: 4 M101; 12 *Reinosa* 105/26
  MOR 88: **81mm** 60 M1; **107mm** 4 M30; **120mm** 24 Expal Model L
HELICOPTERS
  ISR 8: 4 OH-58A *Kiowa*; 4 OH-58C *Kiowa*
  TPT • Light 6: 4 R-22; 2 R-44 *Raven* II

Navy 11,200
HQ located at Santo Domingo
FORCES BY ROLE
SPECIAL FORCES
  1 (SEAL) SF unit
MANOEUVRE
  Amphibious
  1 mne sy unit
EQUIPMENT BY TYPE
PATROL AND COASTAL COMBATANTS 17
  PCO 1 *Almirante Didiez Burgos* (ex-US *Balsam*)
  PCC 2 *Tortuguero* (ex-US *White Sumac*)
  PB 14: 1 *Altair* (Swiftships 35m); 4 *Bellatrix* (US Sewart Seacraft); 1 *Betelgeuse* (Damen Stan Patrol 2606); 2 *Canopus* (Swiftships 110); 3 *Hamal* (Damen Stan Patrol 1505); 3 *Point*
AMPHIBIOUS • LANDING CRAFT
  LCU 1 *Neyba* (ex-US LCU 1675)
LOGISTICS AND SUPPORT 1
  AX 1 *Almirante Juan Bautista Cambiaso*

Air Force 16,100
FORCES BY ROLE
GROUND ATTACK
  1 sqn with EMB-314 *Super Tucano**
SEARCH & RESCUE
  1 sqn with Bell 205 (UH-1H *Huey* II); Bell 205 (UH-1H *Iroquois*); Bell 430 (VIP); OH-58 *Kiowa* (CH-136); S-333
TRANSPORT
  1 sqn with C-212-400 *Aviocar*; PA-31 *Navajo*
TRAINING
  1 sqn with T-35B *Pillan*
AIR DEFENCE
  1 ADA bn with 20mm guns
EQUIPMENT BY TYPE
AIRCRAFT 8 combat capable
  ISR 1 AMT-200 *Super Ximango*
  TPT • Light 13: 3 C-212-400 *Aviocar*; 1 Cessna 172; 1 Cessna 182; 1 Cessna 206; 1 Cessna 207; 1 *Commander* 690; 3 EA-100; 1 PA-31 *Navajo*; 1 P2006T

TRG 12: 8 EMB-314 *Super Tucano**; 4 T-35B *Pillan*
HELICOPTERS
  ISR 9 OH-58 *Kiowa* (CH-136)
  TPT • Light 16: 8 Bell 205 (UH-1H *Huey* II); 5 Bell 205 (UH-1H *Iroquois*); 1 H155 (VIP); 2 S-333
AIR DEFENCE • GUNS 20mm 4

Gendarmerie & Paramilitary 15,000

National Police 15,000

Ecuador ECU

United States Dollar USD		2021	2022	2023
GDP	USD	106bn	115bn	
per capita	USD	5,979	6,413	
Growth	%	4.2	2.9	
Inflation	%	0.1	3.2	
Def bdgt	USD	1.59bn	1.58bn	1.67bn
FMA (US)	USD	5.0m	5.0m	5.0m

Population	17,289,554					
Age	0–14	15–19	20–24	25–29	30–64	65 plus
Male	12.7%	4.4%	4.4%	4.3%	19.7%	4.1%
Female	12.2%	4.2%	4.3%	4.2%	20.9%	4.7%

Capabilities

Ecuador's armed forces are able to fulfil internal-security tasks, although the crisis in Venezuela and resulting refugee flows have added to existing security challenges in the northern border area. These security conditions led the armed forces to create a joint task force for counter-insurgency and counter-narcotics operations. Defence cooperation with Peru includes demining efforts on the border. Quito has recently signed a new defence agreement with Colombia to increase joint operations to counter drug trafficking and illicit smuggling. Military ties with Washington have been revived, which has led to the re-establishment of bilateral training programmes and equipment donations. The armed forces train regularly and have participated in multinational military exercises. There is limited capability to deploy independently beyond national borders. The equipment inventory is derived from a variety of sources, though obsolescence and low availability is a challenge. Modernisation plans are modest in scope and are currently focused on armoured vehicles as well as maritime-patrol capabilities. Ecuador's defence industries are centred on the army's Office of Industries (DINE), which produces military equipment through army-run enterprises. The state-owned shipyard ASTINAVE has some construction, maintenance and repair capabilities, although the navy's submarines are being modernised in Chile.

ACTIVE 41,250 (Army 25,650 Navy 9,400 Air 6,200)
Paramilitary 500
Conscript liability Voluntary conscription

RESERVE 118,000 (Joint 118,000)
Ages 18–55

ORGANISATIONS BY SERVICE

Army 25,650
FORCES BY ROLE
gp are bn sized
COMMAND
4 div HQ
SPECIAL FORCES
1 (9th) SF bde (3 SF gp, 1 SF sqn, 1 para bn, 1 sigs sqn, 1 log comd)
MANOEUVRE
Mechanised
1 (11th) armd cav bde (3 armd cav gp, 1 mech inf bn, 1 SP arty gp, 1 engr gp)
1 (5th) inf bde (1 SF sqn, 2 mech cav gp, 2 inf bn, 1 cbt engr coy, 1 sigs coy, 1 log coy)
Light
1 (1st) inf bde (1 SF sqn, 1 armd cav gp, 1 armd recce sqn, 3 inf bn, 1 med coy)
1 (3rd) inf bde (1 SF gp, 1 mech cav gp, 1 inf bn, 1 arty gp, 1 hvy mor coy, 1 cbt engr coy, 1 sigs coy, 1 log coy)
1 (7th) inf bde (1 SF sqn, 1 armd recce sqn, 1 mech cav gp, 3 inf bn, 1 jungle bn, 1 arty gp, 1 cbt engr coy, 1 sigs coy, 1 log coy, 1 med coy)
1 (13th) inf bde (1 SF sqn, 1 armd recce sqn, 1 mot cav gp, 3 inf bn, 1 arty gp, 1 hvy mor coy, 1 cbt engr coy, 1sigs coy, 1 log coy)
2 (17th & 21st) jungle bde (3 jungle bn, 1 cbt engr coy, 1 sigs coy, 1 log coy)
1 (19th) jungle bde (3 jungle bn, 1 jungle trg bn, 1 cbt engr coy, 1 sigs coy, 1 log coy)
COMBAT SUPPORT
1 (27th) arty bde (1 SP arty gp, 1 MRL gp, 1 ADA gp, 1 cbt engr coy, 1 sigs coy, 1 log coy)
1 (23rd) engr bde (3 engr bn)
2 indep MP coy
1 indep sigs coy
COMBAT SERVICE SUPPORT
1 (25th) log bde (1 log bn, 1 tpt bn, 1 maint bn, 1 med bn)
9 indep med coy
AVIATION
1 (15th) avn bde (2 tpt avn gp, 2 hel gp, 1 mixed avn gp)
AIR DEFENCE
1 ADA gp
EQUIPMENT BY TYPE
ARMOURED FIGHTING VEHICLES
LT TK 25 AMX-13
RECCE 42: 10 EE-3 *Jararaca*; 32 EE-9 *Cascavel*
APC 151
APC (T) 102: 82 AMX-VCI; 20 M113
APC (W) 49: 17 EE-11 *Urutu*; 32 UR-416
ARTILLERY 486
SP 155mm 5 Mk F3
TOWED 106: **105mm** 84: 36 M101; 24 M2A2; 24 Model 56 pack howitzer; **155mm** 22: 12 M114; 10 M198
MRL 122mm 18 BM-21 *Grad*
MOR 81mm 357 M29
AIRCRAFT
TPT • Light 10: 1 Beech 200 *King Air*; 2 C-212; 1 CN235;

2 Cessna 172; 1 Cessna 206; 1 Cessna 500 *Citation* I; 1 IAI-201 *Arava*; 1 M-28 *Skytruck*
TRG 4: 2 MX-7-235 *Star Rocket*; 2 T-41D *Mescalero*
HELICOPTERS
MRH 30: 7 H125M (AS550C3) *Fennec*; 3 Mi-17-1V *Hip*; 2 SA315B *Lama*; 18 SA342L *Gazelle* (13 with HOT for anti-armour role)
TPT 13: **Medium** 9: 5 AS332B *Super Puma*; 2 Mi-171E; 2 SA330 *Puma*; **Light** 4: 2 H125 (AS350B2) *Ecureuil*; 2 H125 (AS350B3) *Ecureuil*
AIR DEFENCE
SAM • Point-defence *Blowpipe*; 9K32 *Strela*-2 (RS-SA-7 *Grail*)‡; 9K38 *Igla* (RS-SA-18 *Grouse*)
GUNS 240
SP 20mm 44 M163 *Vulcan*
TOWED 196: **14.5mm** 128 ZPU-1/-2; **20mm** 38: 28 M-1935, 10 M167 *Vulcan*; **40mm** 30 L/70/M1A1
AIR-LAUNCHED MISSILES • ASM HOT

Navy 9,400 (incl Naval Aviation, Marines and Coast Guard)
EQUIPMENT BY TYPE
SUBMARINES 2
SSK 2 *Shyri* (GER T-209/1300) with 8 single 533mm TT each with A184 mod 3 HWT
PRINCIPAL SURFACE COMBATANTS • FRIGATES 2
FFGH 2 *Moran Valverde* (ex-UK *Leander* batch II) with 1 quad lnchr with MM40 *Exocet* AShM, 2 triple 324mm ILAS-3 (B-515) ASTT with A244 LWT, 1 Mk 15 *Phalanx* CIWS, 1 twin 114mm gun (capacity 1 Bell 230 hel)
PATROL AND COASTAL COMBATANTS 9
CORVETTES • FSGM 6
5 *Esmeraldas* (ITA Tipo 550) with 2 triple lnchr with MM40 *Exocet* AShM, 1 quad *Albatros* lnchr with *Aspide* SAM, 2 triple 324mm ILAS-3 (B-515) ASTT with A244 LWT, 1 76mm gun, 1 hel landing platform
1 *Esmeraldas* (ITA Tipo 550) with 2 triple lnchr with MM40 *Exocet* AShM, 1 quad *Albatros* lnchr with *Aspide* SAM, 1 76mm gun, 1 hel landing platform
PCFG 3 *Quito* (GER Lurssen TNC-45 45m) with 4 single lnchr with MM38 *Exocet* AShM, 1 76mm gun (upgrade programme ongoing)
LOGISTICS AND SUPPORT 8
AE 1 *Calicuchima*
AG 1 *Hualcopo* (ex-PRC *Fu Yuan Yu Leng* 999) (utilised in transport ship role)
AGOS 1 *Orion* with 1 hel landing platform
AGS 1 *Sirius*
AKL 1 *Isla Bartolome* (operated by TRANSNAVE)
ATF 1 *Chimborazo*
AWT 1 *Atahualpa*
AXS 1 *Guayas*

398 THE MILITARY BALANCE 2023

Naval Aviation 380

EQUIPMENT BY TYPE
AIRCRAFT
  MP 1 CN235-300M
  ISR 3: 2 Beech 200T *King Air*; 1 Beech 300 *Catpass King Air*
  TPT • Light 3: 1 Beech 200 *King Air*; 1 Beech 300 *King Air*; 1 CN235-100
  TRG 3 T-35B *Pillan*
HELICOPTERS
  TPT • Light 9: 3 Bell 206A; 3 Bell 206B; 1 Bell 230; 2 Bell 430
UNINHABITED AERIAL VEHICLES
  ISR 4: **Heavy** 2 *Heron*; **Medium** 2 *Searcher* Mk.II

Marines 1,950

FORCES BY ROLE
SPECIAL FORCES
  1 cdo bn
MANOEUVRE
  Amphibious
  5 mne bn
EQUIPMENT BY TYPE
ARTILLERY • MOR 32+ **81mm/120mm**
AIR DEFENCE • SAM • Point-defence 9K38 *Igla* (RS-SA-18 *Grouse*)

Air Force 6,200

Operational Command

FORCES BY ROLE
FIGHTER
  1 sqn with *Cheetah* C/D
GROUND ATTACK
  1 sqn with EMB-314 *Super Tucano**

Military Air Transport Group

FORCES BY ROLE
ISR
  1 sqn with Beech 350i *King Air*; Gulfstream G-1159; *Sabreliner* 40
SEARCH & RESCUE/TRANSPORT HELICOPTER
  1 sqn with AW119 *Koala*; Bell 206B *Jet Ranger* II; H145
  1 sqn with Cessna 206; PA-34 *Seneca*
TRANSPORT
  1 sqn with C295M
  1 sqn with DHC-6-300 *Twin Otter*
  1 sqn with B-727; B-737-200; L-100-30
TRAINING
  1 sqn with DA20-C1
  1 sqn with G-120TP

EQUIPMENT BY TYPE
AIRCRAFT 17 combat capable
  TPT 19: **Medium** 1 L-100-30; (2 C-130B *Hercules*; 1 C-130H *Hercules* in store); **Light** 11: 1 Beech E90 *King Air*; 1 Beech 350i *King Air*; 3 C295M; 1 Cessna 206; 3 DHC-6 *Twin Otter*; 1 PA-34 *Seneca*; 1 *Sabreliner* 40; **PAX** 7: 2 A320 (operated by TAME); 2 B-727; 1 B-737-200; 1 *Falcon* 7X; 1 Gulfstream G-1159

  TRG 36: 11 DA20-C1; 17 EMB-314 *Super Tucano**; 8 G-120TP
HELICOPTERS • TPT • Light 13: 4 AW119 *Koala*; 6 Bell 206B *Jet Ranger* II; 3 H145
AIR-LAUNCHED MISSILES • AAM • IR *Python* 3; R-550 *Magic*; **IIR** *Python* 4
AIR DEFENCE
  SAM • Point-defence 10+: 10 9K33 *Osa* (RS-SA-8 *Gecko*); 9K310 *Igla*-1 (RS-SA-16 *Gimlet*)
  GUNS • TOWED 52: **23mm** 34 ZU-23; **35mm** 18 GDF-002 (twin)

Paramilitary 500

Coast Guard 500

EQUIPMENT BY TYPE
PATROL AND COASTAL COMBATANTS 21
  PCC 7: 3 *Isla Fernandina* (*Vigilante*); 2 *Isla San Cristóbal* (Damen Stan Patrol 5009); 2 *Isla Floreana* (ex-ROK *Hae Uri*)
  PB 13: 2 *Espada*; 2 *Manta* (GER Lurssen 36m); 1 *Point*; 4 *Rio Coca*; 4 *Isla Santa Cruz* (Damen Stan 2606)
  PBR 1 *Rio Puyango*

DEPLOYMENT

CENTRAL AFRICAN REPUBLIC: UN • MINUSCA 2

SOUTH SUDAN: UN • UNMISS 3

SUDAN: UN • UNISFA 3

WESTERN SAHARA: UN • MINURSO 2

El Salvador SLV

United States Dollar USD		2021	2022	2023
GDP	USD	28.7bn	32.0bn	
per capita	USD	4,408	4,883	
Growth	%	10.3	2.6	
Inflation	%	3.5	7.3	
Def bdgt	USD	248m	257m	

Real-terms defence budget trend (USDm, constant 2015)

Population	6,568,745					

Age	0–14	15–19	20–24	25–29	30–64	65 plus
Male	13.1%	4.1%	4.7%	4.7%	17.9%	3.5%
Female	12.5%	4.0%	4.6%	4.8%	21.7%	4.5%

Capabilities

The primary challenge for El Salvador's armed forces is tackling organised crime and narcotics trafficking in support of the National Civil Police. A Territorial Control Plan implemented in 2019 has seen mixed military and police patrols deployed to areas with high crime rates. A spike in homicide rates in early 2020 led in March to further emergency measures and led to widespread arrests. El Salvador participates in a tri-national border task force with Guatemala and

Honduras. The armed forces have long-standing training programmes, including with regional states and with the US, focused on internal security, disaster relief and support to civilian authorities. El Salvador has deployed on UN peacekeeping missions up to company strength but lacks the logistical support to sustain independent international deployments. The armed forces have received little new heavy military equipment in recent years and are dependent on an inventory of Cold War-era platforms; the majority of these are operational, indicating adequate support and maintenance. El Salvador lacks a substantive defence industry but has successfully produced light armoured vehicles based upon commercial vehicles.

ACTIVE 24,500 (Army 20,500 Navy 2,000 Air 2,000)
Paramilitary 26,000
Conscript liability 12 months (selective); 11 months for officers and NCOs

RESERVE 9,900 (Joint 9,900)

ORGANISATIONS BY SERVICE

Army 20,500
FORCES BY ROLE
SPECIAL FORCES
1 spec ops gp (1 SF coy, 1 para bn, 1 (naval inf) coy)
MANOEUVRE
Reconnaissance
1 armd cav regt (2 armd cav bn)
Light
6 inf bde (3 inf bn)
Other
1 (special) sy bde (2 border gd bn, 2 MP bn)
COMBAT SUPPORT
1 arty bde (2 fd arty bn, 1 AD bn)
1 engr comd (2 engr bn)
EQUIPMENT BY TYPE
ARMOURED FIGHTING VEHICLES
RECCE 5 AML-90 (4 more in store)
APC • APC (W) 38: 30 VAL *Cashuat* (mod); 8 UR-416
AUV 5+ *SandCat*
ANTI-TANK/ANTI-INFRASTRUCTURE
RCL 399: **106mm** 20 M40A1 (incl 16 SP); **90mm** 379 M67
ARTILLERY 229+
TOWED 66: **105mm** 54: 36 M102; 18 M-56 (FRY); **155mm** 12 M198
MOR 163+: **81mm** 151 M29; **120mm** 12+: 12 UBM 52; (some M-74 in store)
AIR DEFENCE • GUNS 35: **20mm** 31 M-55; 4 TCM-20

Navy 2,000
EQUIPMENT BY TYPE
PATROL AND COASTAL COMBATANTS 12
PB 12: 1 Bering 65; 3 Camcraft (30m); 1 Defiant 85; 1 Swiftships 77; 1 Swiftships 65; 4 Type-44 (ex-US); 1 YP 660
AMPHIBIOUS • LANDING CRAFT • LCM 4 LCM 8 (of which 3†)

Naval Inf (SF Commandos) 90
FORCES BY ROLE
SPECIAL FORCES
1 SF coy

Air Force 2,000
FORCES BY ROLE
FIGHTER/GROUND ATTACK/ISR
1 sqn with A-37B/OA-37B *Dragonfly*; O-2A/B *Skymaster*
TRANSPORT
1 sqn with Cessna 337G; IAI-202 *Arava*
TRAINING
1 sqn with R-235GT *Guerrier*; T-35 *Pillan*; T-41D *Mescalero*; TH-300; TH-300C
TRANSPORT HELICOPTER
1 sqn with Bell 205 (UH-1H *Iroquois*); Bell 407; Bell 412EP *Twin Huey*; MD-530F; UH-1M *Iroquois*
EQUIPMENT BY TYPE
AIRCRAFT 25 combat capable
ATK 14 A-37B *Dragonfly*
ISR 11: 6 O-2A/B *Skymaster**; 5 OA-37B *Dragonfly**
TPT • Light 4: 1 Cessna 337G *Skymaster*; 3 IAI-201 *Arava*
TRG 9: 5 R-235GT *Guerrier*; 3 T-35 *Pillan*; 1 T-41D *Mescalero*
HELICOPTERS
MRH 14: 4 Bell 412EP *Twin Huey* (of which 1 VIP); 8+ MD-530F; 2 UH-1M *Iroquois*
TPT• Light 9: 8 Bell 205 (UH-1H *Iroquois*); 1 Bell 407 (VIP tpt, govt owned)
TRG 3: 2 TH-300; 1 TH-300C; (4 TH-300 in store)
AIR-LAUNCHED MISSILES • AAM • IR *Shafrir‡*

Gendarmerie & Paramilitary 26,000

National Civilian Police 26,000
Ministry of Public Security
AIRCRAFT
ISR 1 O-2A *Skymaster*
TPT • Light 1 Cessna 310
HELICOPTERS
MRH 9: 2 MD-520N; 7 MD-500E
TPT • Light 3: 1 Bell 205 (UH-1H *Iroquois*); 2 R-44 *Raven* II

DEPLOYMENT

LEBANON: UN • UNIFIL 52; 1 inf pl

MALI: UN • MINUSMA 176; 1 hel sqn with 3 MD-500E

SOUTH SUDAN: UN • UNMISS 1

SUDAN: UN • UNIFSA 1

WESTERN SAHARA: UN • MINURSO 1

FOREIGN FORCES

United States US Southern Command: 1 Forward Operating Location (Military, DEA, USCG and Customs personnel)

Guatemala GUA

Guatemalan Quetzal GTQ		2021	2022	2023
GDP	GTQ	665bn	722bn	
	USD	86.0bn	91.3bn	
per capita	USD	4,688	4,880	
Growth	%	8.0	3.4	
Inflation	%	4.3	6.4	
Def bdgt	GTQ	2.63bn	3.16bn	
	USD	340m	400m	
USD1=GTQ		7.74	7.90	

Real-terms defence budget trend (USDm, constant 2015)

Population	17,703,190				
Age	0–14	15–19	20–24	25–29	30–64	65 plus
Male	16.5%	5.0%	4.7%	4.5%	16.6%	2.3%
Female	15.9%	4.9%	4.7%	4.5%	17.6%	2.8%

Capabilities

The armed forces are refocusing on border security, having drawn down their decade-long direct support for the National Civil Police in 2018 as part of the inter-agency Plan Fortaleza. Guatemala maintains an inter-agency task force with neighbouring El Salvador and Honduras. The army has trained with US SOUTHCOM, as well as with regional partners such as Brazil and Colombia. Training for conventional military operations is limited by budget constraints and the long focus on providing internal security. Guatemala has participated in UN peacekeeping missions to company level. The equipment inventory is small and ageing. The US has provided several soft-skinned vehicles to the army and helicopters to the air force, while there has been modest recapitalisation of the air force's fixed-wing transport and surveillance capacity. Aside from limited maintenance facilities, the country has no domestic defence industry.

ACTIVE 18,050 (Army 15,550 Navy 1,500 Air 1,000) Gendarmerie & Paramilitary 25,000

RESERVE 63,850 (Navy 650 Air 900 Armed Forces 62,300)

(National Armed Forces are combined; the army provides log spt for navy and air force)

ORGANISATIONS BY SERVICE

Army 15,550

15 Military Zones

FORCES BY ROLE

SPECIAL FORCES

1 SF bde (1 SF bn, 1 trg bn)
1 SF bde (1 SF coy, 1 ranger bn)
1 SF mtn bde

MANOEUVRE

Light
1 (strategic reserve) mech bde (1 inf bn, 1 cav regt, 1 log coy)
6 inf bde (1 inf bn)

Air Manoeuvre
1 AB bde with (2 AB bn)

Amphibious
1 mne bde

Other
1 (Presidential) gd bde (1 gd bn, 1 MP bn, 1 CSS coy)

COMBAT SUPPORT

1 engr comd (1 engr bn, 1 construction bn)
2 MP bde with (1 MP bn)

Reserves

FORCES BY ROLE

MANOEUVRE

Light
ε19 inf bn

EQUIPMENT BY TYPE

ARMOURED FIGHTING VEHICLES

RECCE (7 M8 in store)
APC 39
  APC (T) 10 M113 (5 more in store)
  APC (W) 29: 22 *Armadillo*; 7 V-100 *Commando*

ANTI-TANK/ANTI-INFRASTRUCTURE

RCL 120+: **75mm** M20; **105mm** 64 M-1974 FMK-1 (ARG); **106mm** 56 M40A1

ARTILLERY 149

TOWED **105mm** 76: 12 M101; 8 M102; 56 M-56
MOR 73: **81mm** 55 M1; **107mm** (12 M30 in store); **120mm** 18 ECIA

AIR DEFENCE • GUNS • TOWED 32: **20mm** 32: 16 GAI-D01; 16 M-55

Navy 1,500

EQUIPMENT BY TYPE

PATROL AND COASTAL COMBATANTS 10

PB 10: 6 *Cutlass*; 1 *Dauntless*; 1 *Kukulkan* (US *Broadsword* 32m); 2 *Utatlan* (US *Sewart*)

AMPHIBIOUS • LANDING CRAFT 3

LCT 1 *Quetzal* (COL *Golfo de Tribuga*)
LCP 2 *Machete*

LOGISTICS AND SUPPORT • AXS 3

Marines 650 reservists

FORCES BY ROLE

MANOEUVRE

Amphibious
2 mne bn(-)

Air Force 1,000

2 air comd

FORCES BY ROLE

TRANSPORT

1 sqn with Beech 90/200/300 *King Air*

1 (tactical support) sqn with Cessna 206

TRAINING

1 sqn with T-35B *Pillan*

TRANSPORT HELICOPTER

1 sqn with Bell 212 (armed); Bell 407GX; Bell 412 *Twin Huey* (armed)

EQUIPMENT BY TYPE

Serviceability of ac is less than 50%

AIRCRAFT

TPT • **Light** 16: 1 Beech 90 *King Air*; 2 Beech 200 *King Air*; 2 Beech 300 *King Air* (VIP); 2 Cessna 206; 3 Cessna 208B *Grand Caravan*; 1 DHC-6 *Twin Otter*; 2 PA-28 *Archer III*; 1 PA-31 *Navajo*; 2 PA-34 *Seneca*; (5 Cessna R172K *Hawk* XP in store)

TRG 1 SR22; (4 T-35B *Pillan* in store)

HELICOPTERS

MRH 2 Bell 412 *Twin Huey* (armed)

TPT • **Light** 6: 2 Bell 206B *Jet Ranger*; 2 Bell 212 (armed); 2 Bell 407GX

Tactical Security Group

Air Military Police

Gendarmerie & Paramilitary 25,000

National Civil Police 25,000

FORCES BY ROLE

SPECIAL FORCES

1 SF bn

MANOEUVRE

Other

1 (integrated task force) paramilitary unit (incl mil and treasury police)

DEPLOYMENT

CENTRAL AFRICAN REPUBLIC: UN • MINUSCA 4

DEMOCRATIC REPUBLIC OF THE CONGO: UN • MONUSCO 152; 1 spec ops coy

LEBANON: UN • UNIFIL 2

MALI: UN • MINUSMA 2

SOUTH SUDAN: UN • UNMISS 7

SUDAN: UN • UNISFA 3

Guyana GUY

Guyanese Dollar GYD		2021	2022	2023
GDP	GYD	1.61tr	3.09tr	
	USD	7.72bn	14.8bn	
per capita	USD	9,778	18,745	
Growth	%	23.8	57.8	
Inflation	%	3.3	7.6	
Def bdgt	GYD	14.8bn	17.6bn	
	USD	70.9m	84.6m	
USD1=GYD		208.51	208.50	

Real-terms defence budget trend (USDm, constant 2015)

Population	789,683					
Age	0–14	15–19	20–24	25–29	30–64	65 plus
Male	12.2%	5.2%	5.9%	4.2%	20.3%	3.3%
Female	11.7%	5.0%	5.6%	3.8%	18.7%	4.3%

Capabilities

The Guyana Defence Force (GDF) is focused on border control, support for law-enforcement operations and assistance to the civil power. The government is planning to restructure the GDF to improve its flexibility. Guyana is part of the Caribbean Basin Security Initiative. It has close military ties with Brazil, with whom it cooperates on border security via annual regional military exchange meetings. The country also has bilateral agreements with China, France and the US. The GDF trains regularly and takes part in bilateral and multinational exercises. A training initiative with China helped two Guyanese pilots to acquire air-combat certification although Guyana has no combat aircraft in its inventory. There is no expeditionary or associated logistics capability. Equipment is mostly composed of second-hand platforms, mainly of Brazilian and North American manufacture. The air force has expanded its modest air-transport capabilities with some second-hand utility aircraft. Apart from maintenance facilities, there is no defence-industrial sector.

ACTIVE 3,400 (Army 3,000 Navy 200 Air 200)

Active numbers combined Guyana Defence Force

RESERVE 670 (Army 500 Navy 170)

ORGANISATIONS BY SERVICE

Army 3,000

FORCES BY ROLE

SPECIAL FORCES

1 SF sqn

MANOEUVRE

Light

3 inf bn

COMBAT SUPPORT

1 arty coy

1 (spt wpn) cbt spt coy

1 engr bn

COMBAT SERVICE SUPPORT
1 spt bn

Reserve
FORCES BY ROLE
MANOEUVRE
  Amphibious
   1 inf bn
EQUIPMENT BY TYPE
ARMOURED FIGHTING VEHICLES
  RECCE 6 EE-9 *Cascavel* (reported)
ARTILLERY 54
  TOWED 130mm 6 M-46†
  MOR 48: 81mm 12 L16A1; 82mm 18 M-43; 120mm 18 M-43

Navy 200
EQUIPMENT BY TYPE
PATROL AND COASTAL COMBATANTS 5
  PCO 1 *Essequibo* (ex-UK *River* (MCM))†
  PB 4 *Barracuda* (ex-US Type-44)

Air Force 200
FORCES BY ROLE
TRANSPORT
  1 unit with Bell 206; Cessna 206; Y-12 (II)
EQUIPMENT BY TYPE
AIRCRAFT • TPT • Light 6: 2 BN-2 *Islander*; 1 Cessna 206; 2 SC.7 3M *Skyvan*; 1 Y-12 (II)
HELICOPTERS
  MRH 2: 1 Bell 412 *Twin Huey*†; 1 Bell 412EPI *Twin Huey*
  TPT • Light 2 Bell 206

Haiti HTI

Haitian Gourde HTG		2021	2022	2023
GDP	HTG	1.70tr	2.13tr	
	USD	21.0bn	20.2bn	
per capita	USD	1,765	1,673	
Growth	%	-1.8	-1.2	
Inflation	%	15.9	26.8	
Def bdgt [a]	HTG	2.99bn	1.46bn	
	USD	37.0m	13.9m	
USD1=HTG		80.85	105.49	

[a] 2021 increase in defence budget due to greater investment in infrastructure and new Covid-19 responsibilities of the Haitian Armed Forces

Real-terms defence budget trend (USDm, constant 2015)

Population	11,334,637				
Age	0–14	15–19	20–24	25–29	30–64	65 plus
Male	15.0%	5.1%	5.0%	4.7%	17.5%	2.0%
Female	15.1%	5.1%	5.0%	4.8%	18.1%	2.5%

Capabilities
Haiti possesses almost no military capability. Following the assassination of the president in 2021, violence and instability deepened and criminal groups are active in many areas. The armed forces also struggled to respond swiftly to the country's most recent earthquake, where their ability to deliver aid and shelter was tested. A small coastguard is tasked with maritime security and law enforcement and the country's army is still in the very early stages of development, though it is hoped this will eventually number around 5,000 personnel. Plans for military expansion were outlined in the 2015 White Paper on Security and Defence. A road map for the re-establishment of the Haitian armed forces was distributed to ministers in early 2017 and in March 2018 an army high command was established. The army's initial mandate is to provide disaster relief and border security. A 2018 agreement with Mexico has seen small groups of Haitian troops travel to Mexico for training, including 'train-the-trainer' tasks. Mexico will also offer police training. Ecuador and Argentina are also reported to have offered training assistance. Haiti is a member of the Caribbean Community and has participated in US SOUTHCOM's *Tradewinds* disaster-response exercise. There is no heavy military equipment, and no defence industry.

ACTIVE 700 (Army 700) Gendarmerie & Paramilitary 50

ORGANISATIONS BY SERVICE

Army ε700
FORCES BY ROLE
MANOEUVRE
  1 inf bn (forming)

Gendarmerie & Paramilitary 50

Coast Guard ε50
EQUIPMENT BY TYPE
PATROL AND COASTAL COMBATANTS
  PB 8: 5 *Dauntless*; 3 3812-VCF

Honduras HND

Honduran Lempira HNL		2021	2022	2023
GDP	HNL	684bn	768bn	
	USD	28.5bn	30.6bn	
per capita	USD	2,816	2,969	
Growth	%	12.5	3.4	
Inflation	%	4.5	8.6	
Def bdgt [a]	HNL	8.46bn	9.34bn	12.1bn
	USD	352m	371m	
USD1=HNL		24.02	25.14	

[a] Defence & national security budget

Real-terms defence budget trend (USDm, constant 2015)

Population	9,459,440				
Age	0–14	15–19	20–24	25–29	30–64	65 plus
Male	14.5%	5.3%	5.1%	4.4%	16.7%	2.5%
Female	14.1%	5.3%	5.1%	4.6%	19.0%	3.2%

Capabilities

The armed forces have been deployed in support of the police to combat organised crime and narcotics trafficking since 2011. The new government has pledged renewed focus on professionalisation, anti-corruption and human rights in the security forces. Honduras maintains diplomatic relations with Taiwan, which has supplied surplus military equipment, and also receives US security assistance. Honduras hosts a US base at Soto Cano airfield and is also part of a tri-national border-security task force with neighbouring El Salvador and Guatemala. Training remains focused on internal- and border-security requirements, and training for conventional military action is limited. Honduras does not have the capability to maintain substantial foreign deployments. Most equipment is ageing, with serviceability in doubt. There have been reports of security assistance from Israel. Apart from limited maintenance facilities, the country has no domestic defence industry.

ACTIVE 14,950 (Army 7,300 Navy 1,350 Air 2,300 Military Police 4,000) **Gendarmerie & Paramilitary 8,000**

RESERVE 60,000 (Joint 60,000; Ex-servicemen registered)

ORGANISATIONS BY SERVICE

Army 7,300

FORCES BY ROLE
SPECIAL FORCES
1 (special tac) spec ops gp (2 spec ops bn, 1 inf bn; 1 AB bn; 1 arty bn)
MANOEUVRE
Mechanised
1 inf bde (1 mech cav regt, 1 inf bn, 1 arty bn)
Light
1 inf bde (3 inf bn, 1 arty bn)
3 inf bde (2 inf bn)
1 indep inf bn
Other
1 (Presidential) gd coy
COMBAT SUPPORT
1 engr bn
1 sigs bn

EQUIPMENT BY TYPE
ARMOURED FIGHTING VEHICLES
LT TK 12 FV101 *Scorpion*
RECCE 43: 3 FV107 *Scimitar*; 40 FV601 *Saladin*
AUV 1 FV105 *Sultan* (CP)
ANTI-TANK/ANTI-INFRASTRUCTURE
RCL 50+: **84mm** *Carl Gustaf*; **106mm** 50 M40A1
ARTILLERY 118+
TOWED 28: **105mm:** 24 M102; **155mm:** 4 M198
MOR 90+: **81mm**; **120mm** 60 FMK-2; **160mm** 30 M-66

Navy 1,350

EQUIPMENT BY TYPE
PATROL AND COASTAL COMBATANTS 15
PCO 1 *General Cabañas* (ISR OPV 62 *Sa'ar*)
PB 14: 2 *Lempira* (Damen Stan Patrol 4207 – leased); 1 *Chamelecon* (Swiftships 85); 1 *Tegucigalpa* (US *Guardian* 32m); 3 *Guaymuras* (Swiftships 105); 5 *Nacaome* (Swiftships 65); 1 *Río Aguán* (Defiant 85); 1 *Río Coco* (US PB Mk III)

AMPHIBIOUS • LANDING CRAFT 3
LCT 1 *Gracias a Dios* (COL *Golfo de Tribugá*)
LCM 3: 2 LCM 8; 1 *Punta Caxinas*

Marines 1,000

FORCES BY ROLE
MANOEUVRE
Amphibious
2 mne bn

Air Force 2,300

FORCES BY ROLE
FIGHTER/GROUND ATTACK
1 sqn with A-37B *Dragonfly*
1 sqn with F-5E/F *Tiger* II
GROUND ATTACK/ISR/TRAINING
1 unit with Cessna 182 *Skylane*; EMB-312 *Tucano*; MXT-7-180 *Star Rocket*
TRANSPORT
1 sqn with Beech 200 *King Air*; C-130A *Hercules*; Cessna 185/210; IAI-201 *Arava*; PA-42 *Cheyenne*; *Turbo Commander* 690
1 VIP flt with PA-31 *Navajo*; Bell 412EP/SP *Twin Huey*
TRANSPORT HELICOPTER
1 sqn with Bell 205 (UH-1H *Iroquois*); Bell 412SP *Twin Huey*
AIR DEFENCE
1 ADA bn

EQUIPMENT BY TYPE
AIRCRAFT 17 combat capable
FTR 11: 9 F-5E *Tiger* II†; 2 F-5F *Tiger* II†
ATK 6 A-37B *Dragonfly*
TPT 17: **Medium** 1 C-130A *Hercules*; **Light** 16: 1 Beech 200 *King Air*; 2 Cessna 172 *Skyhawk*; 2 Cessna 182 *Skylane*; 1 Cessna 185; 3 Cessna 208B *Grand Caravan*; 1 Cessna 210; 1 EMB-135 *Legacy* 600; 1 IAI-201 *Arava*; 1 L-410 (leased); 1 PA-31 *Navajo*; 1 PA-42 *Cheyenne*; 1 *Turbo Commander* 690
TRG 15: 9 EMB-312 *Tucano*; 6 MXT-7-180 *Star Rocket*
HELICOPTERS
MRH 7: 1 Bell 412EP *Twin Huey* (VIP); 4 Bell 412SP *Twin Huey*; 2 Hughes 500
TPT • **Light** 6: 5 Bell 205 (UH-1H *Iroquois*); 1 H125 *Ecureuil*
AIR DEFENCE • GUNS 20mm 48: 24 M-55A2; 24 TCM-20
AIR-LAUNCHED MISSILES • AAM • IR *Shafrir*‡

Military Police 4,000

FORCES BY ROLE
MANOEUVRE
Other
8 sy bn

Gendarmerie & Paramilitary 8,000

Public Security Forces 8,000

Ministry of Public Security and Defence; 11 regional comd

DEPLOYMENT

WESTERN SAHARA: UN • MINURSO 10

FOREIGN FORCES

United States US Southern Command: 400; 1 avn bn with 4 CH-47F *Chinook*; 12 UH-60 *Black Hawk*

Jamaica JAM

Jamaican Dollar JMD		2021	2022	2023
GDP	JMD	2.30tr	2.62tr	
	USD	15.4bn	16.1bn	
per capita	USD	5,615	5,870	
Growth	%	4.6	2.8	
Inflation	%	5.9	9.0	
Def bdgt	JMD	30.9bn	33.2bn	
	USD	207m	204m	
USD1=JMD		149.70	162.61	

Real-terms defence budget trend (USDm, constant 2015)

Population	2,818,596					
Age	0–14	15–19	20–24	25–29	30–64	65 plus
Male	12.4%	4.4%	4.4%	4.0%	19.6%	4.6%
Female	12.0%	4.3%	4.3%	4.0%	20.8%	5.1%

Capabilities

The Jamaica Defence Force (JDF) is focused principally on maritime and internal security, including support to police operations. Jamaica maintains military ties, including for training purposes, with Canada, the UK and the US and is a member of the Caribbean Community. The defence force has participated in US SOUTHCOM's *Tradewinds* disaster-response exercise. Jamaica is host to the Caribbean Special Tactics Centre, which trains special-forces units from Jamaica and other Caribbean nations. The JDF does not have any capacity to support independent deployments abroad. Funds have been allocated to procure new vehicles and helicopters, and new patrol craft are being procured. Other than limited maintenance facilities, Jamaica has no domestic defence industry.

ACTIVE 5,950 (Army 5,400 Coast Guard 300 Air 250)
(combined Jamaican Defence Force)

RESERVE 2,580 (Army 2,500 Coast Guard 60 Air 20)

ORGANISATIONS BY SERVICE

Army 5,400
FORCES BY ROLE
MANOEUVRE
  Light
    4 inf bn
COMBAT SUPPORT
  1 engr regt (4 engr sqn)
  1 MP bn
  1 cbt spt bn (1 (PMV) lt mech inf coy)
COMBAT SERVICE SUPPORT
  1 spt bn (1 med coy, 1 log coy, 1 tpt coy)
EQUIPMENT BY TYPE
ARMOURED FIGHTING VEHICLES
  AUV 18 *Bushmaster*
ARTILLERY • MOR 81mm 12 L16A1

Reserves
FORCES BY ROLE
MANOEUVRE
  Light
    3 inf bn
COMBAT SERVICE SUPPORT
  1 spt bn

Coast Guard 300
EQUIPMENT BY TYPE
PATROL AND COASTAL COMBATANTS 11
  PCC 1 *Nanny of the Maroons* (Damen Fast Crew Supplier 5009)
  PBF 3
  PB 7: 3 *Honour* (Damen Stan Patrol 4207); 4 *Dauntless*

Air Wing 250
Plus National Reserve
FORCES BY ROLE
MARITIME PATROL/TRANSPORT
  1 flt with Beech 350ER *King Air*; BN-2A *Defender*
SEARCH & RESCUE/TRANSPORT HELICOPTER
  1 flt with Bell 407
  1 flt with Bell 412EP
TRAINING
  1 unit with Bell 206B3 *Jet Ranger*; Bell 505; DA40-180FP *Diamond Star*
EQUIPMENT BY TYPE
AIRCRAFT
  MP 1 Beech 350ER *King Air*
  TPT • Light 2 DA40-180FP *Diamond Star* (1 BN-2A *Defender* in store)
HELICOPTERS
  MRH 1 Bell 412EP *Twin Huey* (1 more in store)
  TPT • Light 13: 1 Bell 206B3 *Jet Ranger*; 3 Bell 407; 3 Bell 429; 6 Bell 505

Mexico MEX

Mexican Peso MXN		2021	2022	2023
GDP	MXN	26.3tr	28.8tr	
	USD	1.30tr	1.42tr	
per capita	USD	10,062	10,948	
Growth	%	4.8	2.1	
Inflation	%	5.7	8.0	
Def bdgt [a]	MXN	136bn	116bn	138bn
	USD	6.71bn	5.74bn	
FMA (US)	USD	6.0m	0.0m	0.0m
USD1=MXN		20.27	20.25	

[a] National security expenditure

Real-terms defence budget trend (USDbn, constant 2015)

Population 129,150,971

Age	0–14	15–19	20–24	25–29	30–64	65 plus
Male	12.4%	4.5%	4.3%	4.0%	20.1%	3.5%
Female	11.8%	4.2%	4.0%	4.1%	22.7%	4.4%

Capabilities

Mexico's armed forces are the most capable in Central America, though they have been committed to providing internal-security support within Mexico for nearly a decade. The National Plan for Peace and Security 2018–24 envisaged that the armed forces would hand over lead responsibility for tackling drug cartels and other organised crime to a new National Guard gendarmerie. However, recent moves suggested a broadening of the armed forces' internal role, for instance with plans to transfer the National Guard to Ministry of Defence control. There have also been strains in the US-Mexico security relationship. The US has provided equipment and training to Mexican forces under the Mérida Initiative, as well as through bilateral programmes via the Pentagon. The armed forces have a moderate capability to deploy independently, but do not do so in significant numbers. There are plans to recapitalise diverse and ageing conventional combat platforms across all three services. In 2020, Mexico brought back to service some of its ageing F-5 combat aircraft. State-owned shipyards have produced patrol craft for the navy. Army factories have produced light armoured utility vehicles for domestic use. Airbus Helicopters is expanding a manufacturing plant for sub-assemblies that it operates in Querétaro.

ACTIVE 216,000 (Army 157,500 Navy 50,500 Air 8,000) **Gendarmerie & Paramilitary 136,900**

Conscript liability 12 months (partial, selection by ballot) from age 18, serving on Saturdays; voluntary for women; conscripts allocated to reserves.

RESERVE 81,500 (National Military Service)

ORGANISATIONS BY SERVICE

Space
EQUIPMENT BY TYPE
SATELLITES • COMMUNICATIONS 2 *Mexsat*

Army 157,500
12 regions (total: 46 army zones)

FORCES BY ROLE
SPECIAL FORCES
 1 (1st) SF bde (5 SF bn)
 1 (2nd) SF bde (7 SF bn)
 1 (3rd) SF bde (4 SF bn)
MANOEUVRE
 Reconnaissance
  3 (2nd, 3rd & 4th Armd) mech bde (2 armd recce bn, 2 lt mech bn, 1 arty bn, 1 (Canon) AT gp)
  25 mot recce regt
 Light
  1 (1st) inf corps (1 (1st Armd) mech bde (2 armd recce bn, 2 lt mech bn, 1 arty bn, 1 (Canon) AT gp), 3 (2nd, 3rd & 6th) inf bde (each: 3 inf bn, 1 arty regt, 1 (Canon) AT gp), 1 cbt engr bde (3 engr bn))
  3 (1st, 4th & 5th) indep lt inf bde (2 lt inf bn, 1 (Canon) AT gp)
  92 indep inf bn
  25 indep inf coy
 Air Manoeuvre
  1 para bde with (1 (GAFE) SF gp, 3 bn, 1 (Canon) AT gp)
COMBAT SUPPORT
 1 indep arty regt

EQUIPMENT BY TYPE
ARMOURED FIGHTING VEHICLES
 RECCE 223: 19 DN-5 *Toro*; 127 ERC-90F1 *Lynx* (7 trg); 40 M8; 37 MAC-1
 IFV 390 DNC-1 (mod AMX-VCI)
 APC 309
  APC (T) 73: 40 HWK-11; 33 M5A1 half-track
  APC (W) 236: 95 BDX; 16 DN-4; 2 DN-6; 28 LAV-100 (*Pantera*); 26 LAV-150 ST; 25 MOWAG *Roland*; 44 VCR (3 amb; 5 cmd post)
 AUV 379: 100 DN-XI; 247 *SandCat*; 32 VBL
ENGINEERING & MAINTENANCE VEHICLES
 ARV 7: 3 M32 *Recovery Sherman*; 4 VCR ARV
ANTI-TANK/ANTI-INFRASTRUCTURE
 MSL • SP 8 VBL with *Milan*
 RCL • 106mm 1,187+ M40A1 (incl some SP)
 GUNS 37mm 30 M3
ARTILLERY 1,390
 TOWED 123: 105mm 123: 40 M101; 40 M-56; 16 M2A1; 14 M3; 13 NORINCO M90
 MOR 1,267: 81mm 1,100: 400 M1; 400 Brandt; 300 SB
 120mm 167: 75 Brandt; 60 M-65; 32 RT-61
AIR DEFENCE • GUNS • TOWED 80: 12.7mm 40 M55; 20mm 40 GAI-B01

Navy 50,500
Two Fleet Commands: Gulf (6 zones), Pacific (11 zones)
EQUIPMENT BY TYPE
PRINCIPAL SURFACE COMBATANTS • FRIGATES 1

406 THE MILITARY BALANCE 2023

FFGHM 1 *Benito Juárez* (Damen SIGMA 10514) with 2 quad lnchr with RGM-84L *Harpoon* Block II AShM, 1 8-cell Mk 56 VLS with RIM-162 ESSM SAM, 1 21-cell Mk 49 lnchr with RIM-116C RAM Block 2 SAM, 2 triple 324mm SVTT Mk 32 ASTT with Mk 54 LWT, 1 57mm gun (capacity 1 med hel) (fitted for but not with Mk 56 VLS with RIM-162 *Evolved SeaSparrow Missile*)

PATROL AND COASTAL COMBATANTS 128

PSOH 8:

4 *Oaxaca* with 1 76mm gun (capacity 1 AS565MB *Panther* hel)

4 *Oaxaca* (mod) with 1 57mm gun (capacity 1 AS565MB *Panther* hel)

PCOH 16:

4 *Durango* with 1 57mm gun (capacity 1 Bo-105 hel)

4 *Holzinger* (capacity 1 MD-902 *Explorer*)

3 *Sierra* with 1 57mm gun (capacity 1 MD-902 *Explorer*)

5 *Uribe* (ESP *Halcon*) (capacity 1 Bo-105 hel)

PCO 9: 6 *Valle* (US *Auk* MSF) with 1 76mm gun; 3 *Valle* (US *Auk* MSF) with 1 76mm gun, 1 hel landing platform

PCGH 1 *Huracan* (ex-ISR *Aliya*) with 4 single lnchr with *Gabriel* II AShM, 1 Mk 15 *Phalanx* CIWS

PCC 2 *Democrata*

PBF 72: 6 *Acuario*; 2 *Acuario B*; 48 *Polaris* (SWE CB90); 16 *Polaris* II (SWE IC 16M)

PB 20: 3 *Azteca*; 3 *Cabo* (ex-US *Cape Higgon*); 2 *Lago*; 2 *Punta* (US *Point*); 10 *Tenochtitlan* (Damen Stan Patrol 4207)

AMPHIBIOUS • LANDING SHIPS

LST 4: 2 *Monte Azules* with 1 hel landing platform; 1 *Papaloapan* (ex-US *Newport*) with 2 twin 76mm guns, 1 hel landing platform; 1 *Papaloapan* (ex-US *Newport*) with 1 hel landing platform

LOGISTICS AND SUPPORT 27

AGOR 2 *Altair* (ex-US *Robert D. Conrad*)

AGS 9: 5 *Arrecife*; 1 *Onjuku*; 1 *Río Hondo*; 1 *Río Tecolutla*; 1 *Río Tuxpan*

AK 1 *Río Suchiate*

AOTL 2 *Aguascalientes*

AP 2: 1 *Isla María Madre* (Damen Fast Crew Supplier 5009); 1 *Nautla*

ATF 4 *Otomi* with 1 76mm gun

ATS 4 *Kukulkan*

AX 2 *Huasteco* (also serve as troop transport, supply and hospital ships)

AXS 1 *Cuauhtemoc*

Naval Aviation 1,250

FORCES BY ROLE

MARITIME PATROL

5 sqn with MX-7-180 *Star Rocket*; T-6C+ *Texan* II

1 sqn with Beech 350ER *King Air*; CN235-300 MPA *Persuader*

TRANSPORT

1 (VIP) sqn with DHC-8 *Dash 8*

TRANSPORT HELICOPTER

2 sqn with AS555 *Fennec*; AS565MB/AS565MBe *Panther*; MD-902

5 sqn with Mi-17-1V/V-5 *Hip*

TRAINING

1 sqn with Z-242L; Z-143Lsi

EQUIPMENT BY TYPE

AIRCRAFT 3 combat capable

MP 6 CN235-300 MPA *Persuader*

ISR 2 Z-143Lsi

TPT 20: **Light** 18: 5 Beech 350ER *King Air* (4 used for ISR); 3 Beech 350i *King Air*; 4 C295M; 2 C295W; 1 DHC-8 *Dash 8*; 2 Learjet 31A; 1 Learjet 60; **PAX** 2: 1 CL-605 *Challenger*; 1 Gulfstream 550

TRG 46: 7 MX-7-180 *Star Rocket*; 13 T-6C+ *Texan* II; 26 Z-242L

HELICOPTERS

MRH 21: 2 AS555 *Fennec*; 15 Mi-17-1V *Hip*; 4 Mi-17V-5 *Hip*

SAR 14: 4 AS565MB *Panther*; 10 AS565MBe *Panther*

TPT 26: **Heavy** 3 H225M *Caracal*; **Medium** 8 UH-60M *Black Hawk*; **Light** 15: 1 AW109SP; 1 H145; 5 MD-902 (SAR role); 8 S-333

TRG 4 Schweizer 300C

Marines 21,500

FORCES BY ROLE

SPECIAL FORCES

3 SF unit

MANOEUVRE

Light

32 inf bn(-)

Air Manoeuvre

1 AB bn

Amphibious

1 amph bde (4 inf bn, 1 amph bn, 1 arty gp)

Other

1 (Presidential) gd bn (included in army above)

COMBAT SERVICE SUPPORT

2 spt bn

EQUIPMENT BY TYPE

ARMOURED FIGHTING VEHICLES

APC • APC (W) 29: 3 BTR-60 (APC-60); 26 BTR-70 (APC-70)

ANTI-TANK/ANTI-INFRASTRUCTURE

RCL 106mm M40A1

ARTILLERY 22+

TOWED 105mm 16 M-56

MRL 122mm 6 *Firos*-25

MOR 81mm some

AIR DEFENCE • SAM • Point-defence 9K38 *Igla* (RS-SA-18 *Grouse*)

Air Force 8,000

FORCES BY ROLE

FIGHTER

1 sqn with F-5E/F *Tiger* II

GROUND ATTACK/ISR

4 sqn with T-6C+ *Texan* II*

1 sqn with PC-7*

ISR/AEW

1 sqn with Beech 350ER *King Air*; EMB-145AEW *Erieye*; EMB-145RS

TRANSPORT

1 sqn with C295M; PC-6B

1 sqn with B-737; Beech 90 *King Air*

1 sqn with C-27J *Spartan*; C-130K-30 *Hercules*; L-100-30

5 (liaison) sqn with Cessna 182
1 (anti-narcotic spraying) sqn with Bell 206
1 (Presidential) gp with AS332L *Super Puma*; AW109SP; B-737; B-757; B-787; Gulfstream 150/450/550; H225; Learjet 35A; Learjet 36; *Turbo Commander* 680
1 (VIP) gp with B-737; Beech 200 *King Air*; Beech 350i *King Air*; Cessna 501 *Citation*; CL-605 *Challenger*; Gulfstream 550; Learjet 35A; S-70A-24 *Black Hawk*

TRAINING
1 sqn with Cessna 182
1 sqn with PC-7; T-6C+ *Texan* II
1 sqn with Grob G120TP

TRANSPORT HELICOPTER
4 sqn with Bell 206B; Bell 407GX
1 (anti-narcotic spraying) sqn with Bell 206
1 sqn with MD-530MF/MG
1 sqn with Mi-17 *Hip*
1 sqn with H225M *Caracal*; Bell 412EP *Twin Huey*; S-70A-24 *Black Hawk*
1 sqn with UH-60M *Black Hawk*

ISR UAV
1 unit with *Hermes* 450; *Hermes* 900; S4 *Ehécatl*

EQUIPMENT BY TYPE
AIRCRAFT 80 combat capable
FTR 5: 4 F-5E *Tiger* II; 1 F-5F *Tiger* II
ISR 2 Cessna 501 *Citation*
ELINT 8: 6 Beech 350ER *King Air*; 2 EMB-145RS
AEW&C 1 EMB-145AEW *Erieye*
TPT 99: **Medium** 7: 4 C-27J *Spartan*; 2 C-130K-30 *Hercules*; 1 L-100-30; **Light** 79: 2 Beech 90 *King Air*; 1 Beech 200 *King Air*; 1 Beech 350i *King Air*; 6 C295M; 2 C295W; 59 Cessna 182; 1 Cessna 501 *Citation*; 2 Learjet 35A; 1 Learjet 36; 3 PC-6B; 1 *Turbo Commander* 680; **PAX** 13: 6 B-737; 1 B-757; 1 B-787; 1 CL-605 *Challenger*; 2 Gulfstream 150; 1 Gulfstream 450; 1 Gulfstream 550
TRG 100: 25 Grob G120TP; 20 PC-7* (30 more possibly in store); 55 T-6C+ *Texan* II*
HELICOPTERS
MRH 41: 14 Bell 407GXP; 11 Bell 412EP *Twin Huey*; 16 Mi-17 *Hip* H
ISR 11: 3 MD-530MF; 8 MD-530MG
TPT 99: **Heavy** 12 H225M *Caracal*; **Medium** 28: 3 AS332L *Super Puma* (VIP); 2 H225 (VIP); 6 S-70A-24 *Black Hawk*; 17 UH-60M *Black Hawk* **Light** 59: 5 AW109SP; 45 Bell 206; 1 Bell 206B *Jet Ranger* II; 8 Bell 206L
UNINHABITED AERIAL VEHICLES • ISR 9: **Medium** 4: 3 *Hermes* 450; 1 *Hermes* 900; **Light** 5 S4 *Ehécatl*

Gendarmerie & Paramilitary 136,900

Federal Ministerial Police 4,500
EQUIPMENT BY TYPE
HELICOPTERS
TPT • **Light** 25: 18 Bell 205 (UH-1H); 7 Bell 212
UNINHABITED AERIAL VEHICLES
ISR • **Heavy** 2 *Dominator* XP

National Guard 115,000
Public Security Secretariat. Gendarmerie created in 2019 from elements of the Army, Navy, Air Force and Federal Police

FORCES BY ROLE
MANOEUVRE
Other
12 sy bde (3 sy bn)
EQUIPMENT BY TYPE
HELICOPTERS
MRH 5: 1+ Bell 407GX; 4 Mi-17 *Hip* H
TPT • **Medium** 7 UH-60M *Black Hawk*

Rural Defense Militia 17,400
FORCES BY ROLE
MANOEUVRE
Light
13 inf unit
13 (horsed) cav unit

DEPLOYMENT

CENTRAL AFRICAN REPUBLIC: UN • MINUSCA 2
INDIA/PAKISTAN: UN • UNMOGIP 1
MALI: UN • MINUSMA 4
WESTERN SAHARA: UN • MINURSO 4

Nicaragua NIC

Nicaraguan Gold Cordoba NIO		2021	2022	2023
GDP	NIO	493bn	564bn	
	USD	14.0bn	15.7bn	
per capita	USD	2,141	2,375	
Growth	%	10.3	4.0	
Inflation	%	4.9	9.9	
Def bdgt	NIO	2.85bn	3.05bn	
	USD	81.0m	84.9m	
USD1=NIO		35.20	35.91	

Real-terms defence budget trend (USDm constant 2015)

Population 6,301,880

Age	0–14	15–19	20–24	25–29	30–64	65 plus
Male	12.5%	4.6%	4.8%	5.0%	19.1%	2.8%
Female	12.0%	4.4%	4.7%	5.1%	21.5%	3.5%

Capabilities

Nicaragua's armed forces are primarily a territorial light-infantry force, with limited coastal-patrol capability. They are tasked with border and internal security, as well as with support for disaster-relief efforts and ecological protection. Nicaragua has renewed its training relationship with Russia and improved ties with China and Iran. Training is largely focused on key internal- and border-security tasks, although the mechanised brigade has received Russian training. The armed forces do not undertake significant international deployments and lack the logistical support for large-scale military operations, although the mechanised brigade can deploy internally. Equipment primarily consists of ageing Cold

War-era platforms. Russia has supplied some second-hand tanks and armoured vehicles to help re-equip the mechanised brigade and has supported the establishment of a repair workshop to maintain the vehicles in-country. There are maintenance facilities but no domestic defence industry.

ACTIVE 12,000 (Army 10,000 Navy 800 Air 1,200)

ORGANISATIONS BY SERVICE

Army ε10,000
FORCES BY ROLE
SPECIAL FORCES
  1 SF bde (2 SF bn)
MANOEUVRE
  Mechanised
  1 mech inf bde (1 armd recce bn, 1 tk bn, 1 mech inf bn, 1 arty bn, 1 MRL bn, 1 AT coy)
  Light
  1 regional comd (3 lt inf bn)
  1 regional comd (2 lt inf bn; 1 arty bn)
  3 regional comd (2 lt inf bn)
  2 indep lt inf bn
  Other
  1 comd regt (1 inf bn, 1 sy bn, 1 int unit, 1 sigs bn)
  1 (ecological) sy bn
COMBAT SUPPORT
  1 engr bn
COMBAT SERVICE SUPPORT
  1 med bn
  1 tpt regt
EQUIPMENT BY TYPE
ARMOURED FIGHTING VEHICLES
  MBT 82: 62 T-55 (65 more in store); 20 T-72B1MS
  LT TK (10 PT-76 in store)
  RECCE 20 BRDM-2
  IFV 17+ BMP-1
  APC • APC (W) 90+: 41 BTR-152 (61 more in store); 45 BTR-60 (15 more in store); 4+ BTR-70M
ENGINEERING & MAINTENANCE VEHICLES
  AEV IMR
  VLB TMM-3
ANTI-TANK/ANTI-INFRASTRUCTURE
  MSL
    SP 12 9P133 *Malyutka* (RS-AT-3 *Sagger*)
    MANPATS 9K11 *Malyutka* (RS-AT-3 *Sagger*)
  RCL 82mm B-10
  GUNS 281: **57mm** 174 ZIS-2; (90 more in store); **76mm** 83 ZIS-3; **100mm** 24 M-1944
ARTILLERY 766
  TOWED 12: **122mm** 12 D-30; (**152mm** 30 D-20 in store)
  MRL 151: **107mm** 33 Type-63; **122mm** 118: 18 BM-21 *Grad*; 100 *Grad* 1P (BM-21P) (single-tube rocket launcher, man portable)
  MOR 603: **82mm** 579; **120mm** 24 M-43; (**160mm** 4 M-160 in store)
  AIR DEFENCE • SAM • Point-defence 9K36 *Strela*-3 (RS-SA-14 *Gremlin*); 9K310 *Igla*-1 (RS-SA-16 *Gimlet*); 9K32 *Strela*-2 (RS-SA-7 *Grail*)‡

Navy ε800
EQUIPMENT BY TYPE
PATROL AND COASTAL COMBATANTS
  PB 12: 3 *Dabur*; 2 *Farallones*; 1 *Río Segovia* (*Zhuk* 1400ME); 4 *Rodman* 101; 2 *Soberanía* (ex-JAM Damen Stan Patrol 4207)

Marines
FORCES BY ROLE
MANOEUVRE
  Amphibious
  1 mne bn

Air Force 1,200
FORCES BY ROLE
TRANSPORT
  1 sqn with An-26 *Curl*; Beech 90 *King Air*; Cessna U206; Cessna 404 *Titan* (VIP)
TRAINING
  1 unit with Cessna 172; PA-18 *Super Cub*; PA-28 *Cherokee*
TRANSPORT HELICOPTER
  1 sqn with Mi-17 *Hip* H (armed)
AIR DEFENCE
  1 gp with ZU-23
EQUIPMENT BY TYPE
AIRCRAFT
  TPT • Light 9: 3 An-26 *Curl*; 1 Beech 90 *King Air*; 1 Cessna 172; 1 Cessna U206; 1 Cessna 404 *Titan* (VIP); 2 PA-28 *Cherokee*
  TRG 2 PA-18 *Super Cub*
HELICOPTERS
  MRH 7 Mi-17 *Hip* H (armed)†
  TPT • Medium 2 Mi-171E
AIR DEFENCE • GUNS 23mm 18 ZU-23
AIR-LAUNCHED MISSILES • ASM 9M17 *Skorpion* (RS-AT-2 *Swatter*)

Panama PAN

Panamanian Balboa PAB		2021	2022	2023
GDP	PAB	63.6bn	71.1bn	
	USD	63.6bn	71.1bn	
per capita	USD	14,664	16,173	
Growth	%	15.3	7.5	
Inflation	%	1.6	3.9	
Def bdgt [a]	PAB	830m	870m	
	USD	830m	870m	
FMA (US)	USD	2.0m	0.0m	0.0m
USD1=PAB		1.00	1.00	

[a] Public security expenditure

Real-terms defence budget trend (USDm, constant 2015)

Population	4,337,768					
Age	0–14	15–19	20–24	25–29	30–64	65 plus
Male	13.0%	3.9%	4.0%	3.9%	21.0%	4.6%
Female	12.4%	3.8%	3.9%	3.8%	20.6%	5.2%

Capabilities

Panama abolished its armed forces in 1990, but retains a border service, a police force and an air/maritime service for low-level security tasks. The primary security focus is on the southern border with Colombia, and the majority of the border service is deployed there. Both Colombia and the US have provided training and support. Training is focused on internal and border security rather than conventional military operations and there is no capability to mount significant external deployments. None of Panama's security services maintain heavy military equipment, focusing instead on light-transport, patrol and surveillance capabilities. Aside from limited maintenance facilities, the country has no domestic defence industry.

Gendarmerie & Paramilitary 27,700

ORGANISATIONS BY SERVICE

Gendarmerie & Paramilitary 27,700

National Border Service 4,000
FORCES BY ROLE
SPECIAL FORCES
  1 SF gp
MANOEUVRE
Other
  1 sy bde (5 sy bn(-))
  1 indep sy bn

National Police Force 20,000
No hvy mil eqpt, small arms only
FORCES BY ROLE
SPECIAL FORCES
  1 SF unit
MANOEUVRE
Other
  1 (presidential) gd bn(-)

National Aeronaval Service 3,700
FORCES BY ROLE
TRANSPORT
  1 sqn with Beech 250 *King Air*; C-212M *Aviocar*; Cessna 210; PA-31 *Navajo*; PA-34 *Seneca*
  1 (Presidential) flt with ERJ-135BJ; S-76C
TRAINING
  1 unit with Cessna 152; Cessna 172; T-35D *Pillan*
TRANSPORT HELICOPTER
  1 sqn with AW139; Bell 205; Bell 205 (UH-1H *Iroquois*); Bell 212; Bell 407; Bell 412EP; H145; MD-500E
EQUIPMENT BY TYPE
PATROL AND COASTAL COMBATANTS 14
  PCC 1 *Saettia*
  PB 13: 1 *Cocle* (ex-US Swift); 1 *Chiriqui* (ex-US PB MkIV); 2 *Panquiaco* (UK Vosper 31.5m); 5 *3 De Noviembre* (ex-US Point), 4 Type-200
AMPHIBIOUS • LANDING CRAFT 1
  LCU 1 *General Estaban Huertas*
LOGISTICS AND SUPPORT 2
  AG 1 *Lina María*
  AKR 1 *Manuel Amador Guerror* (Damen Stan Lander 5612)

AIRCRAFT
TPT • **Light** 17: 1 Beech 100 *King Air*; 1 Beech 250 *King Air*; 1 Beech 350 *King Air*; 2 DHC-6-400 *Twin Otter*; 3 C-212M *Aviocar*; 1 Cessna 152, 1 Cessna 172; 2 Cessna 208B; 1 Cessna 210; 1 ERJ-135BJ; 1 PA-31 *Navajo*; 2 PA-34 *Seneca*
TRG (2 T-35D *Pillan* in store)
HELICOPTERS
MRH 10: 8 AW139; 1 Bell 412EP; 1 MD-500E
TPT • **Light** 5: 1 AW109; 2 Bell 212; 2 Bell 407

Paraguay PRY

Paraguayan Guarani PYG		2021	2022	2023
GDP	PYG	264tr	293tr	
	USD	38.8bn	41.9bn	
per capita	USD	5,279	5,615	
Growth	%	4.2	0.2	
Inflation	%	4.8	9.5	
Def bdgt	PYG	1.89tr	1.93tr	2.13tr
	USD	278m	276m	
USD1=PYG		6803.27	6989.62	

Real-terms defence budget trend (USDm, constant 2015)

Population	7,356,409					
Age	0–14	15–19	20–24	25–29	30–64	65 plus
Male	11.5%	4.0%	4.2%	4.7%	21.5%	4.2%
Female	11.1%	3.9%	4.2%	4.7%	21.3%	4.6%

Capabilities

The armed forces are small by regional standards and the equipment inventory for all services is ageing and largely obsolete. The country faces internal challenges from insurgency and transnational organised crime, chiefly drug trafficking. Conscript numbers have reduced in recent years, and there are a significant number of higher ranks in the force structure. Key formations have long been under-strength. Paraguay has had a consistent if limited tradition of contributing to UN peacekeeping operations since 2001. There is only limited ability to self-sustain forces abroad, and no effective power-projection capacity. There is a small force of river-patrol craft. Armoured capability is very limited. Recent acquisitions of heavy equipment have been confined to small quantities of engineering and transport capabilities but there is a plan to upgrade the air force's fleet of training aircraft. There is some local maintenance capacity but the effectiveness of systems is limited by age. While there is some R&D and manufacturing cooperation with local research institutes, there is no traditional defence-industrial base.

ACTIVE 13,950 (Army 7,400 Navy 3,800 Air 2,750)
Gendarmerie & Paramilitary 14,800
Conscript liability 12 months

RESERVE 164,500 (Joint 164,500)

ORGANISATIONS BY SERVICE

Army 7,400

Much of the Paraguayan army is maintained in a cadre state during peacetime; the nominal inf and cav divs are effectively only at coy strength. Active gp/regt are usually coy sized

FORCES BY ROLE
MANOEUVRE
  Light
  3 inf corps (total: 6 inf div(-), 3 cav div(-), 6 arty bty)
  Other
  1 (Presidential) gd regt (1 SF bn, 1 inf bn, 1 sy bn, 1 log gp)
COMBAT SUPPORT
  1 arty bde with (2 arty gp, 1 ADA gp)
  1 engr bde with (1 engr regt, 3 construction regt)
  1 sigs bn

Reserves
FORCES BY ROLE
MANOEUVRE
  Light
  14 inf regt (cadre)
  4 cav regt (cadre)
EQUIPMENT BY TYPE
ARMOURED FIGHTING VEHICLES
  RECCE 28 EE-9 *Cascavel*
  APC • APC (W) 12 EE-11 *Urutu*
ARTILLERY 99
  TOWED 105mm 19 M101
  MOR 81mm 80
AIR DEFENCE • GUNS 22:
  SP 20mm 3 M9 half track
  TOWED 19: 40mm 13 M1A1, 6 L/60

Navy 3,800
EQUIPMENT BY TYPE
PATROL AND COASTAL COMBATANTS 18
  PCR 1 *Itaipú* (BRZ *Roraima*) with 1 hel landing platform
  PBR 17: 1 *Capitán Cabral*; 2 *Capitán Ortiz* (ROC *Hai Ou*); 2 *Novatec*; 4 Type-701 (US Sewart); 3 *Croq* 15 (AUS Armacraft); 5 others
AMPHIBIOUS • LANDING CRAFT • LCVP 3

Naval Aviation 100
FORCES BY ROLE
TRANSPORT
  1 (liaison) sqn with Cessna 150; Cessna 210 *Centurion*; Cessna 310
TRANSPORT HELICOPTER
  1 sqn with AS350 *Ecureuil* (HB350 *Esquilo*)
EQUIPMENT BY TYPE
AIRCRAFT • TPT • Light 6: 2 Cessna 150; 1 Cessna 210 *Centurion*; 2 Cessna 310
HELICOPTERS • TPT • Light 2 AS350 *Ecureuil* (HB350 *Esquilo*)

Marines 700; 200 conscript (total 900)

FORCES BY ROLE
MANOEUVRE
  Amphibious
  3 mne bn(-)
  ARTILLERY • TOWED 105mm 2 M101

Air Force 2,750
FORCES BY ROLE
GROUND ATTACK/ISR
  1 sqn with EMB-312 *Tucano**
TRANSPORT
  1 gp with C-212-200/400 *Aviocar*; DHC-6 *Twin Otter*
  1 VIP gp with Beech 58 *Baron*; Bell 427; Cessna U206 *Stationair*; Cessna 208B *Grand Caravan*; Cessna 402B; PA-32R *Saratoga* (EMB-721C *Sertanejo*)
TRAINING
  1 sqn with T-25 *Universal*; T-35A/B *Pillan*
TRANSPORT HELICOPTER
  1 gp with AS350 *Ecureuil* (HB350 *Esquilo*); Bell 205 (UH-1H *Iroquois*)
MANOEUVRE
  Air Manoeuvre
  1 AB bde
EQUIPMENT BY TYPE
AIRCRAFT 6 combat capable
  TPT 18: **Light** 17: 1 Beech 58 *Baron*; 4 C-212-200 *Aviocar*; 1 C-212-400 *Aviocar*; 3 Cessna 208B *Grand Caravan*; 2 Cessna 208 *Grand Caravan* EX; 1 Cessna 310; 1 Cessna 402B; 2 Cessna U206 *Stationair*; 1 DHC-6 *Twin Otter*; 1 PA-32R *Saratoga* (EMB-721C *Sertanejo*); **PAX** 1 Cessna 680 *Sovereign*
  TRG 21: 6 EMB-312 *Tucano**; 6 T-25 *Universal*; 6 T-35A *Pillan*; 3 T-35B *Pillan*
HELICOPTERS • TPT • Light 11: 3 AS350 *Ecureuil* (HB350 *Esquilo*); 6 Bell 205 (UH-1H *Iroquois*); 1 Bell 407; 1 Bell 427 (VIP)

Gendarmerie & Paramilitary 14,800

Special Police Service 10,800; 4,000 conscript (total 14,800)

DEPLOYMENT

CENTRAL AFRICAN REPUBLIC: UN • MINUSCA 4

CYPRUS: UN • UNFICYP 12

DEMOCRATIC REPUBLIC OF THE CONGO: UN • MONUSCO 6

SOUTH SUDAN: UN • UNMISS 2

Peru PER

Peruvian Nuevo Sol PEN		2021	2022	2023
GDP	PEN	877bn	957bn	
	USD	226bn	239bn	
per capita	USD	6,679	7,005	
Growth	%	13.6	2.7	
Inflation	%	4.0	7.5	
Def bdgt	PEN	7.05bn	6.98bn	7.31bn
	USD	1.82bn	1.75bn	
USD1=PEN		3.88	4.00	

Real-terms defence budget trend (USDbn, constant 2015)

Population 32,275,736

Age	0–14	15–19	20–24	25–29	30–64	65 plus
Male	13.4%	4.2%	3.8%	3.9%	20.2%	3.6%
Female	12.9%	4.1%	3.8%	4.0%	21.6%	4.5%

Capabilities

Peru's armed forces are primarily orientated towards preserving territorial integrity and security, focusing on counter-insurgency and counter-narcotics operations, while also strengthening their disaster-relief capabilities. The armed forces are capable of fulfilling domestic-security tasks, although they are limited by economic constraints and an increasingly ageing inventory. Peru maintains close ties with Colombia, including a cooperation agreement on air control, humanitarian assistance and counter-narcotics. The armed forces train regularly and take part in national and multilateral exercises, and Peru took part in the 2022 iteration of the RIMPAC multinational exercise. The armed forces are capable of independently deploying externally and contribute to UN missions abroad. There has been some aviation modernisation, though not across the whole fleet. Tanker/transport capabilities have been boosted with the recent acquisition of two second-hand KC-130Hs. The navy is looking to acquire new OPVs and some second-hand anti-submarine warfare helicopters but its ageing fleet of submarines have yet to finish a modernisation process. The state-owned shipyard SIMA and aviation firm SEMAN are key players in Peru's defence industry, both in terms of manufacturing and maintenance. In 2017, SEMAN completed final assembly for the last Korean-designed KT-1 trainer, and in 2018 the navy commissioned the first locally built and South Korean-designed multipurpose vessel.

ACTIVE 81,000 (Army 47,500 Navy 24,000 Air 9,500)
Gendarmerie & Paramilitary 77,000
Conscript liability 12 months voluntary conscription for both males and females

RESERVE 188,000 (Army 188,000)

ORGANISATIONS BY SERVICE

Space
EQUIPMENT BY TYPE
SATELLITES • ISR PéruSAT-1

Army 47,500
4 mil region
FORCES BY ROLE
SPECIAL FORCES
  1 (1st) SF bde (2 spec ops bn, 2 cdo bn, 1 cdo coy, 1 CT coy, 1 airmob arty gp, 1 MP coy, 1 cbt spt bn)
  1 (3rd) SF bde (1 spec ops bn, 2 cdo bn, 1 airmob arty gp, 1 MP coy)
  1 (6th) SF bde (2 spec ops bn, 2 cdo bn, 1 cdo coy, 1 MP coy)
MANOEUVRE
  Armoured
  1 (3rd) armd bde (2 tk bn, 1 armd inf bn, 1 arty gp, 1 AT coy, 1 AD gp, 1 engr bn, 1 cbt spt bn)
  1 (9th) armd bde (2 tk bn, 1 armd inf bn, 1 SP arty gp, 1 ADA gp)
  Mechanised
  1 (3rd) armd cav bde (3 mech cav bn, 1 mot inf bn, 1 arty gp, 1 AD gp, 1 engr bn, 1 cbt spt bn)
  1 (1st) cav bde (4 mech cav bn, 1 MP coy, 1 cbt spt bn)
  Light
  2 (2nd & 31st) mot inf bde (4 mot inf bn, 1 arty gp, 1 MP coy, 1 log bn)
  3 (1st, 7th & 32nd) inf bde (3 inf bn, 1 MP coy, 1 cbt spt bn)
  1 (33rd) inf bde (4 inf bn)
  1 (4th) mtn bde (1 armd regt, 3 mot inf bn, 1 arty gp, 1 MP coy, 1 cbt spt bn)
  1 (5th) mtn bde (1 armd regt, 2 mot inf bn, 3 jungle coy, 1 arty gp, 1 MP coy, 1 cbt spt bn)
  1 (6th) jungle inf bde (4 jungle bn, 1 engr bn, 1 MP coy, 1 cbt spt bn)
  1 (35th) jungle inf bde (1 SF gp, 3 jungle bn, 3 jungle coy, 1 jungle arty gp, 1 AT coy, 1 AD gp, 1 jungle engr bn)
COMBAT SUPPORT
  1 arty gp (bde) (4 arty gp, 2 AD gp, 1 sigs gp)
  1 (3rd) arty bde (4 arty gp, 1 AD gp, 1 sigs gp)
  1 (22nd) engr bde (3 engr bn, 1 demining coy)
COMBAT SERVICE SUPPORT
  1 (1st Multipurpose) spt bde
AVIATION
  1 (1st) avn bde (1 atk hel/recce hel bn, 1 avn bn, 2 aslt hel/tpt hel bn)
AIR DEFENCE
  1 AD gp (regional troops)
EQUIPMENT BY TYPE
ARMOURED FIGHTING VEHICLES
  MBT 165 T-55; (75† in store)
  LT TK 96 AMX-13
  RECCE 95: 30 BRDM-2; 15 Fiat 6616; 50 M9A1
  APC 295
    APC (T) 120 M113A1
    APC (W) 175: 150 UR-416; 25 Fiat 6614
ENGINEERING & MAINTENANCE VEHICLES
  ARV M578
  VLB GQL-111
ANTI-TANK-ANTI-INFRASTRUCTURE
  MSL
    SP 22 M1165A2 HMMWV with 9K135 *Kornet* E (RS-AT-14 *Spriggan*)
    MANPATS 9K11 *Malyutka* (RS-AT-3 *Sagger*); HJ-73C; 9K135 *Kornet* E (RS-AT-14 *Spriggan*); *Spike*-ER

412　THE MILITARY BALANCE 2023

RCL 106mm M40A1
ARTILLERY 1,025
SP 155mm 12 M109A2
TOWED 290: **105mm** 152: 44 M101; 24 M2A1; 60 M-56; 24 Model 56 pack howitzer; **122mm**; 36 D-30; **130mm** 36 M-46; **155mm** 66: 36 M114, 30 Model 50
MRL 122mm 49: 22 BM-21 *Grad*; 27 Type-90B
MOR 674+: **81mm/107mm** 350; **SP 107mm** 24 M106A1; **120mm** 300+ Brandt/Expal Model L
PATROL AND COASTAL COMBATANTS • PBR 1
Vargas Guerra
AIRCRAFT
TPT • Light 17: 2 An-28 *Cash*; 3 An-32B *Cline*; 1 Beech 350 *King Air*; 1 Beech 1900D; 4 Cessna 152; 1 Cessna 208 *Caravan*; 1 Cessna 560 *Citation*; 2 Cessna U206 *Stationair*; 1 PA-31T *Cheyenne* II; 1 PA-34 *Seneca*
TRG 4 IL-103
HELICOPTERS
MRH 7 Mi-17 *Hip* H
TPT 33: **Heavy** (3 Mi-26T *Halo* in store); **Medium** 21 Mi-171Sh; **Light** 12: 1 AW109K2; 9 PZL Mi-2 *Hoplite*; 2 R-44
TRG 4 F-28F
AIR DEFENCE
SAM • Point-defence 9K36 *Strela-3* (RS-SA-14 *Gremlin*); 9K310 *Igla-1* (RS-SA-16 *Gimlet*); 9K32 *Strela-2* (RS-SA-7 *Grail*)‡
GUNS 165
SP 23mm 35 ZSU-23-4
TOWED 23mm 130: 80 ZU-23-2; 50 ZU-23

Navy 24,000 (incl 1,000 Coast Guard)

Commands: Pacific, Lake Titicaca, Amazon River
EQUIPMENT BY TYPE
SUBMARINES • SSK 6:
4 *Angamos* (GER T-209/1200) with 8 single 533mm TT with SST-4 HWT (of which 1 in refit)
2 *Islay* (GER T-209/1100) with 8 single 533mm TT with SUT 264 HWT
PRINCIPAL SURFACE COMBATANTS • FRIGATES 7
FFGHM 7:
2 *Aguirre* (ex-ITA *Lupo*) with 8 single lnchr with *Otomat* Mk2 AShM, 1 octuple Mk 29 lnchr with RIM-7P *Sea Sparrow* SAM, 2 triple 324mm ASTT with A244 LWT, 1 127mm gun (capacity 1 Bell 212 (AB-212)/SH-3D *Sea King*)
2 *Aguirre* (ex-ITA *Lupo*) with 2 twin lnchr with MM40 *Exocet* Block 3 AShM, 1 octuple Mk 29 lnchr with RIM-7P *Sea Sparrow* SAM, 2 triple 324mm ASTT with A244 LWT, 1 127mm gun (capacity 1 Bell 212 (AB-212)/SH-3D *Sea King*)
1 *Carvajal* (ITA *Lupo* mod) with 8 single lnchr with *Otomat* Mk2 AShM, 1 octuple *Albatros* lnchr with *Aspide* SAM, 2 triple 324mm ASTT with A244 LWT, 1 127mm gun (capacity 1 Bell 212 (AB-212)/SH-3D *Sea King*)
2 *Carvajal* (ITA *Lupo* mod) with 2 twin lnchr with MM40 *Exocet* Block 3 AShM, 1 octuple *Albatros* lnchr with *Aspide* SAM, 2 triple 324mm ASTT with A244 LWT, 1 127mm gun (capacity 1 Bell 212 (AB-212)/SH-3D *Sea King*)

PATROL AND COASTAL COMBATANTS 14
CORVETTES 8
FSG 6 *Velarde* (FRA PR-72 64m) with 4 single lnchr with MM38 *Exocet* AShM, 1 76mm gun
FS 2 *Ferré* (ex-ROK *Po Hang*) with 1 76mm gun
PCR 6: 2 *Amazonas* with 1 76mm gun; 2 *Manuel Clavero*; 2 *Marañon* with 2 76mm guns
AMPHIBIOUS
PRINCIPAL AMPHIBIOUS SHIPS • LPD 1 *Pisco* (IDN *Makassar*) (capacity 2 LCM; 3 hels; 24 IFV; 450 troops)
LANDING SHIPS • LST 2 *Paita* (capacity 395 troops) (ex-US *Terrebonne Parish*)
LANDING CRAFT • UCAC 7 *Griffon* 2000TD (capacity 22 troops)
LOGISTICS AND SUPPORT 24
AG 6 *Río Napo*
AGOR 1 *Humboldt* (operated by IMARPE)
AGORH 1 *Carrasco*
AGS 5: 1 *Zimic* (ex-NLD *Dokkum*); 2 *Van Straelen*; 1 *La Macha*, 1 *Stiglich* (river survey vessel for the upper Amazon)
AH 4 (river hospital craft)
AO 2 *Noguera*
AORH 1 *Tacna* (ex-NLD *Amsterdam*)
ATF 1 *Morales*
AWT 1 *Caloyeras*
AXS 2: 1 *Marte*; 1 *Unión*

Naval Aviation ε800

FORCES BY ROLE
MARITIME PATROL
1 sqn with Beech 200T; Bell 212 ASW (AB-212 ASW); F-27 *Friendship*; Fokker 60; SH-2G *Super Seasprite*; SH-3D *Sea King*
TRANSPORT
1 flt with An-32B *Cline*; Cessna 206; Fokker 50
TRAINING
1 sqn with F-28F; T-34C/-1 *Turbo Mentor*
TRANSPORT HELICOPTER
1 (liaison) sqn with Bell 206B *Jet Ranger II*; Mi-8 *Hip*
EQUIPMENT BY TYPE
AIRCRAFT
MP 6: 4 Beech 200T; 2 Fokker 60
ELINT 1 F-27 *Friendship*
SIGINT 1 Fokker 50
MP 1 Fokker 50
TPT • Light 5: 2 An-32B *Cline*; 1 Cessna 206; 2 Fokker 60
TRG 3: 2 T-34C *Turbo Mentor*; 1 T-34C-1 *Turbo Mentor*
HELICOPTERS
ASW 10: 2 Bell 212 ASW (AB-212 ASW); 5 SH-2G *Super Seasprite*; 3 SH-3D *Sea King*
MRH 3 Bell 412SP
TPT 10: **Medium** 7: 1 Mi-8 *Hip*; 6 UH-3H *Sea King*; **Light** 3 Bell 206B *Jet Ranger* II
TRG 5 F-28F
MSL
ASM AGM-65D *Maverick*
AShM AM39 *Exocet*

Marines 4,000

FORCES BY ROLE
SPECIAL FORCES
3 cdo gp
MANOEUVRE
Light
2 inf bn
1 inf gp
Amphibious
1 mne bde (1 SF gp, 1 recce bn, 2 inf bn, 1 amph bn, 1 arty gp)
Jungle
1 jungle inf bn

EQUIPMENT BY TYPE
ARMOURED FIGHTING VEHICLES
APC • APC (W) 47+: 32 LAV II; V-100 *Commando*; 15 V-200 *Chaimite*
AUV 7 RAM Mk3
ANTI-TANK/ANTI-INFRASTRUCTURE
RCL 84mm *Carl Gustaf*; **106mm** M40A1
ARTILLERY 18+
TOWED 122mm D-30
MOR 18+: **81mm** some; **120mm** ε18
AIR DEFENCE • GUNS 20mm SP (twin)

Air Force 9,500

Divided into five regions – North, Lima, South, Central and Amazon

FORCES BY ROLE
FIGHTER
1 sqn with MiG-29S/SE *Fulcrum* C; MiG-29UBM *Fulcrum* B
FIGHTER/GROUND ATTACK
1 sqn with *Mirage* 2000E/ED (2000P/DP)
2 sqn with A-37B *Dragonfly*
1 sqn with Su-25A *Frogfoot* A; Su-25UBK *Frogfoot* B
ISR
1 (photo-survey) sqn with Learjet 36A; SA-227-BC *Metro* III (C-26B)
TRANSPORT
1 sqn with B-737; An-32 *Cline*
1 sqn with DHC-6 *Twin Otter*; DHC-6-400 *Twin Otter*; PC-6 *Turbo Porter*
1 sqn with L-100-20
TRAINING
2 (drug interdiction) sqn with EMB-312 *Tucano*
1 sqn with MB-339A*
1 sqn with Z-242
1 hel sqn with Enstrom 280FX; Schweizer 300C
ATTACK HELICOPTER
1 sqn with Mi-25†/Mi-35P *Hind*
TRANSPORT HELICOPTER
1 sqn with Mi-17-1V *Hip*
1 sqn with Bell 206 *Jet Ranger*; Bell 212 (AB-212); Bell 412 *Twin Huey*
1 sqn with Bo-105LS
AIR DEFENCE
6 bn with S-125 *Pechora* (RS-SA-3 *Goa*)

EQUIPMENT BY TYPE
AIRCRAFT 60 combat capable
FTR 19: 9 MiG-29S *Fulcrum* C; 3 MiG-29SE *Fulcrum* C; 5 MiG-29SMP *Fulcrum*; 2 MiG-29UBM *Fulcrum* B
FGA 12: 2 *Mirage* 2000ED (2000DP); 10 *Mirage* 2000E (2000P) (some†)
ATK 19: 15 A-37B *Dragonfly*; 2 Su-25A *Frogfoot* A; 2 Su-25UBK *Frogfoot* B; (8 Su-25A *Frogfoot* A; 6 Su-25UBK *Frogfoot* B in store)
ISR 5: 2 Learjet 36A; 3 SA-227-BC *Metro* III (C-26B)
TKR/TPT 2 KC-130H *Hercules*
TPT 37: **Medium** 6: 4 C-27J *Spartan*; 2 L-100-20; **Light** 29: 4 An-32 *Cline*; 7 Cessna 172 *Skyhawk*; 3 DHC-6 *Twin Otter*; 12 DHC-6-400 *Twin Otter*; 1 PA-44; 1 PC-6 *Turbo-Porter*; **PAX** 3: 2 B-737; 1 Learjet 45 (VIP)
TRG 75: 8 CH-2000; 19 EMB-312 *Tucano*†; 20 KT-1P; 10 MB-339A*; 6 T-41A/D *Mescalero*; 12 Z-242
HELICOPTERS
ATK 18: 16 Mi-25 *Hind* D†; 2 Mi-35P *Hind* E
MRH 12: 2 Bell 412 *Twin Huey*; up to 10 Mi-17-1V *Hip*
TPT 25: **Medium** 3 Mi-171Sh; **Light** 22: 8 Bell 206 *Jet Ranger*; 6 Bell 212 (AB-212); 6 Bo-105LS; 2 Enstrom 280FX
TRG 4 Schweizer 300C
AIR DEFENCE • SAM
Short-range S-125 *Pechora* (RS-SA-3 *Goa*)
Point-defence *Javelin*
AIR-LAUNCHED MISSILES
AAM • IR R-3 (RS-AA-2 *Atoll*)‡; R-60 (RS-AA-8 *Aphid*)‡; R-73 (RS-AA-11A *Archer*); R-550 *Magic*; **IR/SARH** R-27 (RS-AA-10 *Alamo*); **ARH** R-77 (RS-AA-12 *Adder*)
ASM AS-30; Kh-29L (RS-AS-14A *Kedge*)
ARM Kh-58 (RS-AS-11 *Kilter*)

Gendarmerie & Paramilitary 77,000

National Police 77,000 (100,000 reported)

EQUIPMENT BY TYPE
ARMOURED FIGHTING VEHICLES
APC (W) 120: 20 BMR-600; 100 MOWAG *Roland*
AIRCRAFT
TPT • Light 5: 1 An-32B *Cline*; 1 Beech 1900C; 3 Cessna 208B
HELICOPTERS
MRH 4 Mi-17 *Hip* H
TPT • Light 16: 5 H145; 2 Mi-171Sh; 9 UH-1H *Huey* II

General Police 43,000

Security Police 21,000

Technical Police 13,000

Coast Guard 1,000

Personnel included as part of Navy

EQUIPMENT BY TYPE
PATROL AND COASTAL COMBATANTS 45
PSOH 1 *Carvajal* (ITA *Lupo* mod) with 1 127mm gun (capacity 1 Bell 212 (AB-212)/SH-3D *Sea King*)
PCC 10: 6 *Río Pativilca* (ROK *Tae Geuk*); 4 *Río Nepeña*
PBF 1 *Río Itaya* (SWE Combat Boat 90)
PB 12: 6 *Chicama* (US *Dauntless*); 2 *Punta Sal* (Defiant 45); 1 *Río Chira*; 3 *Río Santa*
PBR 21: 1 *Río Viru*; 8 *Parachique*; 12 *Zorritos*
LOGISTICS AND SUPPORT • AH 1 *Puno*

AIRCRAFT
TPT • Light 3: 1 DHC-6 *Twin Otter*; 2 F-27 *Friendship*

Rondas Campesinas
Peasant self-defence force. Perhaps 7,000 rondas 'gp', up to pl strength, some with small arms. Deployed mainly in emergency zone

DEPLOYMENT
CENTRAL AFRICAN REPUBLIC: UN • MINUSCA 235; 1 engr coy

DEMOCRATIC REPUBLIC OF THE CONGO: UN • MONUSCO 6

LEBANON: UN • UNIFIL 1

SOUTH SUDAN: UN • UNMISS 4

SUDAN: UN • UNISFA 4

Suriname SUR

Suriname Dollar SRD		2021	2022	2023
GDP	SRD	56.2bn	79.8bn	
	USD	2.85bn	3.01bn	
per capita	USD	4,681	4,880	
Growth	%	-3.5	1.3	
Inflation	%	59.1	47.6	
Def bdgt	SRD	n.k.	n.k.	
	USD	n.k.	n.k.	
USD1=SRD		19.71	26.51	
Population	632,638			

Age	0–14	15–19	20–24	25–29	30–64	65 plus
Male	11.8%	4.2%	4.5%	4.0%	22.2%	2.9%
Female	11.4%	4.0%	4.3%	3.9%	22.8%	4.2%

Capabilities
The armed forces are principally tasked with preserving territorial integrity. They also assist the national police in internal- and border-security missions, as well as tackling transnational criminal activity and drug trafficking and have also been involved in disaster-relief and humanitarian-assistance operations. Suriname is a member of the Caribbean Disaster Emergency Management Agency and the Caribbean Basin Security Initiative. Ties with Brazil, China, India and the US have been crucial for the supply of equipment, including a limited number of armoured vehicles and helicopters, as well as training activity. The armed forces take part in US SOUTHCOM's *Tradewinds* disaster-response exercise. The armed forces are not sized or equipped for power projection. Resource challenges and limited equipment serviceability means the armed forces are constrained in providing sufficient border and coastal control and surveillance. There is no capability to design and manufacture modern military equipment and Suriname has looked to its foreign-military cooperation to improve not just trade training but also maintenance capacity.

ACTIVE 1,840 (Army 1,400 Navy 240 Air 200)
(All services form part of the army)

ORGANISATIONS BY SERVICE
Army 1,400
FORCES BY ROLE
MANOEUVRE
  Mechanised
    1 mech cav sqn
  Light
    1 inf bn (4 coy)
COMBAT SUPPORT
  1 MP bn (coy)
EQUIPMENT BY TYPE
ARMOURED FIGHTING VEHICLES
  RECCE 6 EE-9 *Cascavel*
  APC • APC (W) 15 EE-11 *Urutu*
ANTI-TANK/ANTI-INFRASTRUCTURE
  RCL 106mm M40A1
ARTILLERY • MOR 81mm 6

Navy ε240
EQUIPMENT BY TYPE
PATROL AND COASTAL COMBATANTS 12
  PB 6: 2 FPB 72 Mk II; 1 FPB 98 Mk I; 3 Rodman 101†
  PBR 6: 1 Project 414; 5 Rodman 55

Air Force ε200
EQUIPMENT BY TYPE
HELICOPTERS • MRH 3 SA316B *Alouette* III (*Chetak*)

Trinidad and Tobago TTO

Trinidad and Tobago Dollar TTD		2021	2022	2023
GDP	TTD	162bn	198bn	
	USD	24.0bn	29.3bn	
per capita	USD	17,056	20,746	
Growth	%	-0.7	4.0	
Inflation	%	1.5	5.0	
Def bdgt	TTD	5.23bn	5.66bn	5.80bn
	USD	773m	838m	
USD1=TTD		6.76	6.76	

Real-terms defence budget trend (USDm, constant 2015)

Population 1,405,646

Age	0–14	15–19	20–24	25–29	30–64	65 plus
Male	9.9%	3.3%	3.2%	3.2%	24.5%	6.1%
Female	9.5%	3.2%	3.0%	3.0%	23.9%	7.0%

Capabilities
The Trinidad and Tobago Defence Force (TTDF) focuses on border protection and maritime security, as well as counter-narcotics tasks. A larger role in law-enforcement support is planned for

the army. Trinidad and Tobago is a member of the Caribbean Community and cooperates with other countries in the region in disaster-relief efforts. There are plans to establish a joint training academy in Trinidad and a proposal for a new coastguard base in Tobago. The TTDF has taken part in US SOUTHCOM's *Tradewinds* disaster-response exercise and has sent personnel to the US and UK for training. Trinidad and Tobago has no capacity to deploy and maintain troops abroad, and apart from limited maintenance facilities, has no domestic defence industry.

ACTIVE 4,650 (Army 3,000 Coast Guard 1,600 Air Guard 50)

(All services form the Trinidad and Tobago Defence Force)

RESERVE 650

ORGANISATIONS BY SERVICE

Army ε3,000
FORCES BY ROLE
SPECIAL FORCES
  1 SF unit
MANOEUVRE
  Light
  2 inf bn
COMBAT SUPPORT
  1 engr bn
COMBAT SERVICE SUPPORT
  1 log bn
EQUIPMENT BY TYPE
ANTI-TANK/ANTI-INFRASTRUCTURE
  RCL 84mm *Carl Gustaf*
ARTILLERY • **MOR 81mm** 6 L16A1

Coast Guard 1,600
FORCES BY ROLE
COMMAND
  1 mne HQ
EQUIPMENT BY TYPE
PATROL AND COASTAL COMBATANTS 17
  PCO 3: 2 *Port of Spain* (AUS *Cape*); 1 *Nelson* II (ex-PRC *Shuke* III)
  PCC 6: 2 *Point Lisas* (Damen Fast Crew Supplier 5009); 4 *Speyside* (Damen Stan Patrol 5009)
  PB 8: 2 *Gaspar Grande*†; 6 *Scarlet Ibis* (Austal 30m)

Air Guard 50
EQUIPMENT BY TYPE
AIRCRAFT
  TPT • **Light** 2 SA-227 *Metro* III (C-26)
HELICOPTERS
  MRH 4 AW139
  TPT • **Light** 1 S-76

Uruguay URY

Uruguayan Peso UYU		2021	2022	2023
GDP	UYU	2.58tr	2.98tr	
	USD	59.3bn	71.2bn	
per capita	USD	16,735	20,018	
Growth	%	4.4	5.3	
Inflation	%	7.7	9.1	
Def bdgt	UYU	22.5bn	22.9bn	23.2bn
	USD	516m	546m	
USD1=UYU		43.57	41.93	

Real-terms defence budget trend (USDm, constant 2015)

Population	3,407,213					
Age	0–14	15–19	20–24	25–29	30–64	65 plus
Male	9.7%	3.5%	3.8%	3.9%	21.3%	6.1%
Female	9.4%	3.4%	3.7%	3.8%	22.2%	9.0%

Capabilities

Principal tasks for the armed forces are assuring sovereignty and territorial integrity. In 2019, parliament approved a new Military Law, which aims, among other measures, to reduce the number of senior officers and address promotion issues across all services. Uruguay and Argentina have a joint peacekeeping unit and conduct joint exercises. In 2018 a defence-cooperation agreement was signed with Russia, including training exchanges. There is long-established military engagement with the US. The armed forces participate regularly in multinational exercises and deployments, notably on UN missions. The arrival of ex-US Coast Guard patrol boats as part of the navy's fleet modernisation plan heralds a focus on policing and coast guard roles, while the navy is also focused on tackling personnel issues and rebuilding broader capabilities. The air force is focused on the counter-insurgency role, but ambitions to purchase a light fighter aircraft remain hampered by funding problems. The acquisition of air-defence radars may have improved the armed forces' ability to monitor domestic airspace, but the lack of interdiction capability will continue to limit the capacity to respond to contingencies. Much equipment is second-hand, and there is little capacity for independent power projection. Maintenance work is sometimes outsourced to foreign companies, such as Chile's ENAER.

ACTIVE 21,100 (Army 13,500 Navy 5,000 Air 2,600)
Gendarmerie & Paramilitary 1,400

ORGANISATIONS BY SERVICE

Army 13,500
Uruguayan units are substandard size, mostly around 30%. Div are at most bde size, while bn are of reinforced coy strength. Regts are also coy size, some bn size, with the largest formation being the 2nd armd cav regt
FORCES BY ROLE
COMMAND
  4 mil region/div HQ

MANOEUVRE
Mechanised
2 (1st & 2nd Cav) mech bde (1 armd cav regt, 2 mech cav regt)
1 (3rd Cav) mech bde (2 mech cav regt, 1 mech inf bn)
3 (2nd, 3rd & 4th Inf) mech bde (2 mech inf bn; 1 inf bn)
1 (5th Inf) mech bde (1 armd cav regt; 1 armd inf bn; 1 mech inf bn)
Light
1 (1st Inf) inf bde (2 inf bn)
Air Manoeuvre
1 para bn
COMBAT SUPPORT
1 (strategic reserve) arty regt
5 fd arty gp
1 (1st) engr bde (2 engr bn)
4 cbt engr bn
AIR DEFENCE
1 AD gp
EQUIPMENT BY TYPE
ARMOURED FIGHTING VEHICLES
MBT 15 Tiran-5
LT TK 47: 22 M41A1UR; 25 M41C
RECCE 15 EE-9 Cascavel
IFV 18 BMP-1
APC 376
    APC (T) 27: 24 M113A1UR; 3 MT-LB
    APC (W) 349: 54 Condor; 48 GAZ-39371 Vodnik; 53 OT-64; 47 OT-93; 147 Piranha
ENGINEERING & MAINTENANCE VEHICLES
AEV MT-LB
ANTI-TANK/ANTI-INFRASTRUCTURE
MSL • MANPATS Milan
RCL 106mm 69 M40A1
ARTILLERY 185
SP 122mm 6 2S1 Gvozdika
TOWED 44: **105mm** 36: 28 M101A1; 8 M102; **155mm** 8 M114A1
MOR 135: **81mm** 91: 35 M1, 56 Expal Model LN; **120mm** 44 Model SL
UNINHABITED AERIAL VEHICLES • ISR • Light 1 Charrua
AIR DEFENCE • GUNS • TOWED 14: **20mm** 14: 6 M167 Vulcan; 8 TCM-20 (w/Elta M-2106 radar)

Navy 5,000
HQ at Montevideo
EQUIPMENT BY TYPE
PATROL AND COASTAL COMBATANTS 13
PB 10: 1 Colonia (ex-US Cape); 9 Type-44
PBI 3 Rio Arapey (ex-US Marine Protector)
MINE WARFARE • MINE COUNTERMEASURES 2
MSO 2 Temerario (Kondor II)
AMPHIBIOUS 3: 2 LCVP; 1 LCM
LOGISTICS AND SUPPORT 8
AAR 2 Islas de Flores (ex-GER Hermann Helms)
ABU 1 Sirius
AG 2: 1 Artigas (GER Freiburg, general spt ship with replenishment capabilities); 1 Maldonado (also used as patrol craft)
ARS 1 Vanguardia
AXS 2: 1 Capitan Miranda; 1 Bonanza

Naval Aviation 210
FORCES BY ROLE
MARITIME PATROL
1 flt with Beech 200T*; Cessna O-2A Skymaster
SEARCH & RESCUE/TRANSPORT HELICOPTER
1 sqn with AS350B2 Ecureuil (Esquilo); Bell 412SP Twin Huey
TRANSPORT/TRAINING
1 flt with T-34C Turbo Mentor
TRAINING
1 hel sqn with Bell 412SP Twin Huey; OH-58 Kiowa
EQUIPMENT BY TYPE
AIRCRAFT 2 combat capable
ISR 4: 2 Beech 200T*; 2 Cessna O-2A Skymaster
TRG 2 T-34C Turbo Mentor
HELICOPTERS
ISR 1 OH-58 Kiowa
MRH 4: 2 Bell 412 (AB-412); 2 Bell 412SP Twin Huey
TPT • Light 1 AS350B2 Ecureuil (Esquilo)

Naval Infantry 700
FORCES BY ROLE
MANOEUVRE
Amphibious
1 mne bn(-)

Air Force 2,600
FORCES BY ROLE
FIGHTER/GROUND ATTACK
1 sqn with A-37B Dragonfly
ISR
1 flt with EMB-110 Bandeirante†
TRANSPORT
1 sqn with C-130B Hercules; C-212 Aviocar; EMB-120 Brasilia
1 (liaison) sqn with Cessna 206H; T-41D
1 (liaison) flt with Cessna 206H
TRAINING
1 sqn with PC-7U Turbo Trainer
1 sqn with Beech 58 Baron (UB-58); SF-260EU
TRANSPORT HELICOPTER
1 sqn with AS365 Dauphin; Bell 205 (UH–1H Iroquois); Bell 212
EQUIPMENT BY TYPE
AIRCRAFT 13 combat capable
ATK 12 A-37B Dragonfly
ISR 4: 1 EMB-110 Bandeirante*†; 3 O-2A Skymaster
TKR/TPT 2 KC-130H Hercules
TPT 23: **Medium** 2 C-130B Hercules; **Light** 20: 1 BAe-125-700A; 2 Beech 58 Baron (UB-58); 6 C-212 Aviocar; 9 Cessna 206H; 1 Cessna 210; 1 EMB-120 Brasilia; **PAX** 1 C-29 Hawker
TRG 17: 5 PC-7U Turbo Trainer; 12 SF-260EU
HELICOPTERS
MRH 2 AS365N2 Dauphin II
TPT • Light 8: 5 Bell 205 (UH–1H Iroquois); 3 Bell 212

Gendarmerie & Paramilitary 1,400

Guardia Nacional Republicana 1,400

DEPLOYMENT

CENTRAL AFRICAN REPUBLIC: UN • MINUSCA 3

DEMOCRATIC REPUBLIC OF THE CONGO: UN • MONUSCO 819; 1 inf bn; 1 hel sqn

EGYPT: MFO 41; 1 engr/tpt unit

INDIA/PAKISTAN: UN • UNMOGIP 3

LEBANON: UN • UNIFIL 1

SUDAN: UN • UNISFA 2

SYRIA/ISRAEL: UN • UNDOF 212; 1 mech inf coy

Venezuela VEN

Venezuelan Bolivar soberano VES		2021	2022	2023
GDP	VES	n.k	n.k	
	USD	59.5bn	82.1bn	
per capita	USD	2,157	3,052	
Growth	%	0.5	6.0	
Inflation	%	1588.5	210.0	
Def bdgt	VES [a]	n.k	n.k	
	USD	n.k	n.k	
USD1=VES		n.k	n.k	

[a] Defence budget allocations have been difficult to track since 2017 due to high levels of currency volatility and reduced transparency in public expenditure

Population	29,789,730

Age	0–14	15–19	20–24	25–29	30–64	65 plus
Male	12.9%	4.1%	3.9%	4.0%	20.9%	3.9%
Female	12.4%	4.0%	3.9%	3.9%	21.4%	4.7%

Capabilities

The armed forces and national guard are tasked with protecting sovereignty, assuring territorial integrity and assisting with internal-security and counter-narcotics operations. They have sufficient capabilities and funding to fulfil internal-security tasks and their regime-protection role, but economic challenges have affected equipment availability and training levels. Venezuela and Colombia have recently re-established military relations after tensions due to the humanitarian crisis and to the presence of irregular Colombian armed groups and resulting troop deployments near the Colombia–Venezuela border. There are close ties with China and Russia, with Caracas relying on both countries for procurements and technical support. The armed forces train regularly and civil–military cooperation has increased. Venezuela has also taken part in joint combined exercises with China, Cuba and Russia. There is little logistics capability to support deployment abroad. Equipment is relatively modern and much is of Chinese and Russian manufacture. While the economic crisis has affected the government's ability to sustain military expenditure and procurement have suffered as a consequence, there have recently been renewed, but modest, maintenance and modernisation efforts. Venezuela's defence industry is based on a series of small, state-owned companies, mainly focused on the production of small arms and munitions. Local platform production has been limited to small coastal-patrol boats.

ACTIVE 123,000 (Army 63,000 Navy 25,500 Air 11,500 National Guard 23,000) **Gendarmerie & Paramilitary 220,000**

Conscript liability 30 months selective, varies by region for all services

RESERVE 8,000 (Army 8,000)

ORGANISATIONS BY SERVICE

Army ε63,000
FORCES BY ROLE
MANOEUVRE
  Armoured
  1 (4th) armd div (1 armd bde, 1 lt armd bde, 1 AB bde, 1 arty bde)
  Mechanised
  1 (9th) mot cav div (1 mot cav bde, 1 ranger bde, 1 sy bde)
  Light
  1 (1st) inf div (1 SF bn, 1 armd bde, 1 mech inf bde, 1 ranger bde, 1 inf bde, 1 arty unit, 1 spt unit)
  1 (2nd) inf div (1 mech inf bde, 1 inf bde, 1 mtn inf bde)
  1 (3rd) inf div (1 inf bde, 1 ranger bde, 1 sigs bde, 1 MP bde)
  1 (5th) inf div (1 SF bn, 1 cav sqn, 2 jungle inf bde, 1 engr bn)
COMBAT SUPPORT
  1 cbt engr corps (3 engr regt)
COMBAT SERVICE SUPPORT
  1 log comd (2 log regt)
AVIATION
  1 avn comd (1 tpt avn bn, 1 atk hel bn, 1 ISR avn bn)

Reserve Organisations 8,000
FORCES BY ROLE
MANOEUVRE
  Armoured
  1 armd bn
  Light
  4 inf bn
  1 ranger bn
COMBAT SUPPORT
  1 arty bn
  2 engr regt
EQUIPMENT BY TYPE
ARMOURED FIGHTING VEHICLES
  MBT 173: 81 AMX-30V; 92 T-72B1
  LT TK 109: 31 AMX-13; 78 *Scorpion*-90
  RECCE 121: 42 *Dragoon* 300 LFV2; 79 V-100/V-150
  IFV 237: 123 BMP-3 (incl variants); 114 BTR-80A (incl variants)
  APC 81
    APC (T) 45: 25 AMX-VCI; 12 AMX-PC (CP); 8 AMX-VCTB (Amb)
    APC (W) 36 *Dragoon* 300
ENGINEERING & MAINTENANCE VEHICLES
  ARV 5: 3 AMX-30D; BREM-1; 2 *Dragoon* 300RV; *Samson*
  VLB *Leguan*
NBC VEHICLES 10 TPz-1 *Fuchs* NBC
ANTI-TANK/ANTI-INFRASTRUCTURE
  MSL • **MANPATS** IMI MAPATS
  RCL 106mm 175 M40A1

418 THE MILITARY BALANCE 2023

GUNS • SP 76mm 75 M18 *Hellcat*
ARTILLERY 515
  SP 60: **152mm** 48 2S19 *Msta-S*; **155mm** 12 Mk F3
  TOWED 92: **105mm** 80: 40 M101A1; 40 Model 56 pack howitzer; **155mm** 12 M114A1
  MRL 56: **122mm** 24 BM-21 *Grad*; **160mm** 20 LAR SP (LAR-160); **300mm** 12 9A52 *Smerch*
  GUN/MOR 120mm 13 2S23 NONA-SVK
  MOR 294: **81mm** 165; **SP 81mm** 21 *Dragoon* 300PM; AMX-VTT; **120mm** 108: 60 Brandt; 48 2S12
AIRCRAFT
  TPT • Light 28: 1 Beech 90 *King Air*; 1 Beech 200 *King Air*; 1 Beech 300 *King Air*; 1 Cessna 172; 6 Cessna 182 *Skylane*; 2 Cessna 206; 2 Cessna 207 *Stationair*; 1 IAI-201 *Arava*; 2 IAI-202 *Arava*; 11 M-28 *Skytruck*
HELICOPTERS
  ATK 9 Mi-35M2 *Hind*
  MRH 31: 10 Bell 412EP; 2 Bell 412SP; 19 Mi-17V-5 *Hip* H
  TPT 9: **Heavy** 3 Mi-26T2 *Halo*; **Medium** 2 AS-61D; **Light** 4: 3 Bell 206B *Jet Ranger*, 1 Bell 206L3 *Long Ranger* II

Navy ε22,300; ε3,200 conscript (total ε25,500)

EQUIPMENT BY TYPE
SUBMARINES 1
  SSK 1 *Sábalo* (in refit; 1 more non-operational) (GER T-209/1300) with 8 single 533mm TT with SST-4 HWT
PRINCIPAL SURFACE COMBATANTS • FRIGATES 2
  FFGHM 2 *Mariscal Sucre* (ITA *Lupo* mod)† (1 more non-operational) with 8 single lnchr with *Otomat* Mk2 AShM, 1 octuple *Albatros* lnchr with *Aspide* SAM, 2 triple 324mm ASTT with A244 LWT, 1 127mm gun (capacity 1 Bell 212 (AB-212) hel)
PATROL AND COASTAL COMBATANTS 9
  PSOH 3 *Guaiqueri* with 1 *Millennium* CIWS, 1 76mm gun
  PBG 3 *Federación* (UK Vosper 37m) with 2 single lnchr with *Otomat* Mk2 AShM
  PB 3 *Constitucion* (UK Vosper 37m) with 1 76mm gun
AMPHIBIOUS
  LANDING SHIPS • LST 4 *Capana* (ROK *Alligator*) capacity 12 tanks; 200 troops)
  LANDING CRAFT 3:
    LCU 2 *Margarita* (river comd)
    UCAC 1 *Griffon* 2000TD
LOGISTICS AND SUPPORT 10
  AGOR 1 *Punta Brava*
  AGS 2 *Gabriela*
  AKR 4 *Los Frailes*
  AORH 1 *Ciudad Bolívar*
  ATF 1 *Almirante Franciso de Miranda* (Damen Salvage Tug 6014)
  AXS 1 *Simón Bolívar*

Naval Aviation 500

FORCES BY ROLE
ANTI-SUBMARINE WARFARE
  1 sqn with Bell 212 ASW (AB-212 ASW)

MARITIME PATROL
  1 flt with C-212-200 MPA
TRANSPORT
  1 sqn with Beech 200 *King Air*; C-212 *Aviocar*; *Turbo Commander* 980C
TRAINING
  1 hel sqn with Bell 206B *Jet Ranger* II; TH-57A *Sea Ranger*
TRANSPORT HELICOPTER
  1 sqn with Bell 412EP *Twin Huey*; Mi-17V-5 *Hip* H
EQUIPMENT BY TYPE
AIRCRAFT 2 combat capable
  MP 2 C-212-200 MPA*
  TPT • Light 7: 1 Beech C90 *King Air*; 1 Beech 200 *King Air*; 4 C-212 *Aviocar*; 1 *Turbo Commander* 980C
HELICOPTERS
  ASW 4 Bell 212 ASW (AB-212 ASW)
  MRH 12: 6 Bell 412EP *Twin Huey*; 6 Mi-17V-5 *Hip* H
  TPT • Light 1 Bell 206B *Jet Ranger* II (trg)
  TRG 1 TH-57A *Sea Ranger*

Marines ε15,000

FORCES BY ROLE
COMMAND
  1 div HQ
SPECIAL FORCES
  1 spec ops bde
MANOEUVRE
  Amphibious
  1 amph aslt bde
  3 mne bde
  3 (rvn) mne bde
COMBAT SUPPORT
  1 cbt engr bn
  1 MP bde
  1 sigs bn
COMBAT SERVICE SUPPORT
  1 log bn
EQUIPMENT BY TYPE
ARMOURED FIGHTING VEHICLES
  LT TK 10 VN-16
  IFV 21: 11 VN-1; 10 VN-18
  APC • APC (W) 37 EE-11 *Urutu*
  AAV 11 LVTP-7
ENGINEERING & MAINTENANCE VEHICLES
  ARV 1 VS-25
  AEV 1 AAVR7
ANTI-TANK/ANTI-INFRASTRUCTURE
  RCL 84mm *Carl Gustaf*; **106mm** M40A1
ARTILLERY 30
  TOWED 105mm 18 M-56
  MRL 107mm ε10 *Fajr-1*
  MOR 120mm 12 Brandt
PATROL AND COASTAL COMBATANTS
  PBR 23: 18 *Constancia*; 2 *Manaure*; 3 *Terepaima* (*Cougar*)
AMPHIBIOUS • LANDING CRAFT • 1 LCU; 1 LCM; 12 LCVP

Coast Guard 1,000

EQUIPMENT BY TYPE
PATROL AND COASTAL COMBATANTS 25

Latin America and the Caribbean **419**

PSO 3 *Guaicamacuto* with 1 *Millennium* CIWS, 1 76mm gun (capacity 1 Bell 212 (AB-212) hel)
PB 22: 1 *Fernando Gomez de Saa* (Damen Stan Patrol 4207); 12 *Gavion*; 3 *Pagalo* (Damen Stan Patrol 2606); 4 *Petrel* (US Point); 2 *Protector*
LOGISTICS AND SUPPORT 4
  AG 1 *Los Taques* (salvage ship)
  AKSL 1
  AP 2

Air Force 11,500

FORCES BY ROLE
FIGHTER/GROUND ATTACK
  1 sqn with F-5 *Freedom Fighter* (VF-5)
  2 sqn with F-16A/B *Fighting Falcon*
  4 sqn with Su-30MKV *Flanker*
  2 sqn with K-8W *Karakorum**
GROUND ATTACK/ISR
  1 sqn with EMB-312 *Tucano**
ELECTRONIC WARFARE
  1 sqn with *Falcon* 20DC; SA-227 *Metro* III (C-26B)
TRANSPORT
  1 sqn with Y-8; C-130H *Hercules*; KC-137
  1 sqn with A319CJ; B-737
  4 sqn with Cessna T206H; Cessna 750
  1 sqn with Cessna 500/550/551; *Falcon* 20F; *Falcon* 900
  1 sqn with G-222; Short 360 *Sherpa*
TRAINING
  1 sqn with Cessna 182N; SF-260E
  2 sqn with DA40NG; DA42VI
  1 sqn with EMB-312 *Tucano**
TRANSPORT HELICOPTER
  1 VIP sqn with AS532UL *Cougar*; Mi-172
  3 sqn with AS332B *Super Puma*; AS532 *Cougar*
  2 sqn with Mi-17 *Hip* H

EQUIPMENT BY TYPE
AIRCRAFT 80 combat capable
  FTR 18: 15 F-16A *Fighting Falcon*†; 3 F-16B *Fighting Falcon*†
  FGA 22 Su-30MKV *Flanker*
  EW 4: 2 *Falcon* 20DC; 2 SA-227 *Metro* III (C-26B)
  TKR 1 KC-137
  TPT 75: **Medium** 14: 5 C-130H *Hercules* (some in store); 1 G-222; 8 Y-8; **Light** 56: 6 Beech 200 *King Air*; 2 Beech 350 *King Air*; 10 Cessna 182N *Skylane*; 12 Cessna 206 *Stationair*; 4 Cessna 208B *Caravan*; 1 Cessna 500 *Citation* I; 3 Cessna 550 *Citation* II; 1 Cessna 551; 1 Cessna 750 *Citation* X; 2 Do-228-212; 1 Do-228-212NG; 11 Quad City *Challenger* II; 2 Short 360 *Sherpa*; **PAX** 5: 1 A319CJ; 1 B-737; 1 *Falcon* 20F; 2 *Falcon* 900
  TRG 82: 24 DA40NG; 6 DA42VI; 17 EMB-312 *Tucano**; 23 K-8W *Karakorum**; 12 SF-260E
HELICOPTERS
  MRH 8 Mi-17 (Mi-17VS) *Hip* H
  TPT 22: **Medium** 14: 3 AS332B *Super Puma*; 7 AS532 *Cougar*; 2 AS532UL *Cougar*; 2 Mi-172 (VIP); **Light** 8+ Enstrom 480B

AIR-LAUNCHED MISSILES
  AAM • **IR** AIM-9L/P *Sidewinder*; R-73 (RS-AA-11A *Archer*); PL-5E; R-27T/ET (RS-AA-10B/D *Alamo*); **IR** *Python* 4; **SARH** R-27R/ER (RS-AA-10A/C *Alamo*); **ARH** R-77 (RS-AA-12 *Adder*)
  ASM Kh-29L/T (RS-AS-14A/B *Kedge*); Kh-59M (RS-AS-18 *Kazoo*)
  AShM Kh-31A (RS-AS-17B *Krypton*); AM39 *Exocet*
  ARM Kh-31P (RS-AS-17A *Krypton*)

Air Defence Command (CODAI)

Joint service command with personnel drawn from other services

FORCES BY ROLE
AIR DEFENCE
  5 AD bde
COMBAT SERVICE SUPPORT
  1 log bde (5 log gp)

EQUIPMENT BY TYPE
AIR DEFENCE
  SAM
    Long-range 12 S-300VM (RS-SA-23)
    Medium-range 53: 9 9K317M2 *Buk*-M2E (RS-SA-17 *Grizzly*); 44 S-125 *Pechora*-2M (RS-SA-26)
    Point-defence 9K338 *Igla*-S (RS-SA-24 *Grinch*); ADAMS; *Mistral*; RBS-70
  GUNS 440+
    SP 40mm 12+: 6+ AMX-13 *Rafaga*; 6 M42
    TOWED 428+: **20mm**: 114 TCM-20; **23mm** ε200 ZU-23-2; **35mm**; **40mm** 114+: 114+ L/70; Some M1

National Guard (Fuerzas Armadas de Cooperacion) 23,000

(Internal sy, customs) 9 regional comd

EQUIPMENT BY TYPE
ARMOURED FIGHTING VEHICLES
  APC • **APC (W)** 44: 24 Fiat 6614; 20 UR-416
  AUV 121 VN4
ARTILLERY • **MOR** 50 **81mm**
PATROL AND COASTAL COMBATANTS
  PB 34: 12 *Protector*; 12 *Punta*; 10 *Rio Orinoco* II
AIRCRAFT
  TPT • **Light** 34: 1 Beech 55 *Baron*; 1 Beech 80 *Queen Air*; 1 Beech 90 *King Air*; 1 Beech 200C *King Air*; 3 Cessna 152 *Aerobat*; 2 Cessna 172; 2 Cessna 402C; 4 Cessna U206 *Stationair*; 6 DA42 MPP; 1 IAI-201 *Arava*; 12 M-28 *Skytruck*
  TRG 3: 1 PZL 106 *Kruk*; 2 PLZ M2-6 *Isquierka*
HELICOPTERS
  MRH 13: 8 Bell 412EP; 5 Mi-17V-5 *Hip* H
  TPT • **Light** 18: 9 AS355F *Ecureuil* II; 4 AW109; 4 Bell 206B/L *Jet Ranger/Long Ranger*; 1 Bell 212 (AB 212); **TRG** 5 F-280C

Gendarmerie & Paramilitary ε220,000

Bolivarian National Militia ε220,000

Latin America and the Caribbean

Chapter Nine
Sub-Saharan Africa

- In West Africa, tentative improvements in the region's security achieved in recent years are now either at risk or are being rolled back. Jihadist activity is again on the rise, notably in Gulf of Guinea countries, while coups and insurrections have highlighted continued problems with civil-military relations.
- Conflict continued in the Eastern DRC, and in September an agreement was signed enabling the intervention of armed forces from East African Community (EAC) states. An initial force of Kenyan troops landed at Goma in early November; it has been reported that the Kenyan contingent alone could number up to 900.
- Though a ceasefire was signed between the Ethiopian government and Tigrayan forces at the end of the year, in 2022 Ethiopia more than quadrupled its defence budget from USD0.38bn to USD1.58bn amid the return to conflict with the Tigray People's Liberation Front. As a result, growth in East African defence spending in 2022 was faster than in other sub-regions. Combined with consistent spending in Tanzania and a 2020 jump in Uganda's defence budget, this means that the sub-region now accounts for 25.1% of total regional spending, up from 11.0% in 2010.
- Nigeria's budget has grown significantly in recent years, from NGN594bn (USD1.83bn) in 2019 to NGN1.14 trillion (USD2.78bn) in 2022, averaging 16% nominal growth between 2020 and 2022. However, the budget has been stagnant in real terms, and accounted for between 0.5% and 0.6% of GDP, well below the regional average of 1.5%.
- South Africa retains the largest defence budget in sub-Saharan Africa, but the country's share of regional spending has fallen considerably over the last decade. In 2011, South African spending accounted for 27% of the total for sub-Saharan Africa but this proportion has declined every year since, falling to just 15% in 2022.
- Two decades of underfunding have left the South African National Defence Force in a parlous state. Nevertheless, it has sustained contingents in the DRC and Mozambique and some border patrols. The air force has faced significant challenges in generating operational capability, but a new support contract for the *Gripen* has enabled the start of a process to rebuild air combat capability.

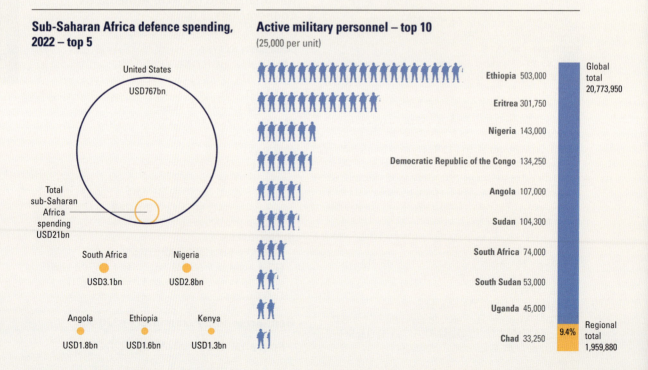

Regional defence policy and economics 422 ▶
Arms procurements and deliveries 431 ▶
Armed forces data section 433 ▶

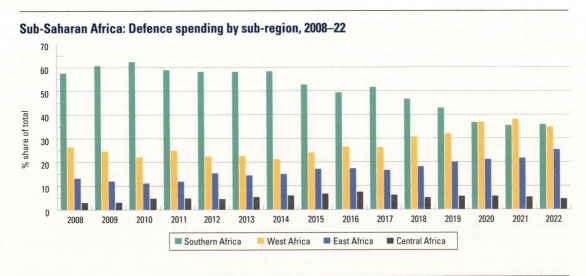

Sub-Saharan Africa: Defence spending by sub-region, 2008–22

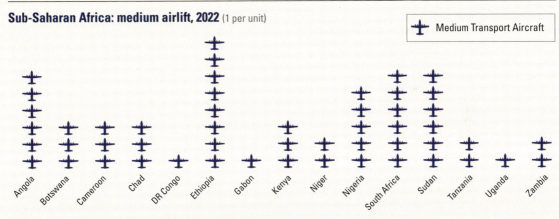

Sub-Saharan Africa: medium airlift, 2022 (1 per unit)

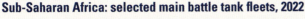

Sub-Saharan Africa: selected main battle tank fleets, 2022

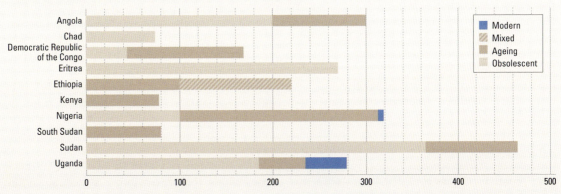

Sub-Saharan Africa

WEST AFRICA

Tentative improvements in the region's security in the latter years of the last decade are now either at risk or are being rolled back. In 2016–18, there was hope that, despite difficult security challenges, the region's governments were in the ascendant. Nigeria had regained the upper hand over Boko Haram, principally assisted by Chad and Cameroon. Cameroon, after consolidating and adapting its forces, had reduced the jihadist threat, and Mali – with the military support of the French-led *Operation Barkhane*, the EU and other countries – was on the cusp of moving beyond the 2012 coup and resulting conflict and instability.

Five years later, the security situation in the region has deteriorated. Coups and insurrections have highlighted problems not only related to civil-military relations in regional states but also in relation to military assistance from abroad. To be most effective and durable, this assistance needs to be focused as much on longer-term force health as it is on the generation of combat capability (such as through special- or rapid-reaction forces) that governments might desire to tackle more immediate threats. But requirements, and timescales, can be different for the recipient states, and in some cases choices have been made to look beyond their security partners of recent years. Indeed, assistance initiatives are also being reshaped, with France rebalancing its forces in the region, other Western states reducing security assistance, and Russia increasing its activity and influence in places. Meanwhile, jihadist activity is again on the rise, notably in Gulf of Guinea countries. Regional states are having to deal not only with political instability but also community conflicts, resource constraints and illicit trafficking. At the same time, they are also feeling the effects of the coronavirus pandemic, which hindered local industrial and agricultural production and exacerbated poverty. An April 2022 report by Oxfam said that West Africa was facing 'its worst food crisis in ten years' and that 'between 2015 and 2022, the number of people in need of emergency food assistance nearly quadrupled, from 7–27 million'. The risk for local states remains that these factors will fuel instability, including jihadist activity.

Responses have varied. Senegal has looked to maintain military professionalism and continues to receive assistance in this regard, including from France and also the United States, which in recent years has been working with the Senegalese forces on NCO development and professional military education. Togo is also pursuing modernisation and professionalisation efforts, while Benin is looking to adapt its armed forces to address non-traditional threats. Both these states have suffered terrorist attacks in recent years. There were around 20 in Benin between the end of 2021 and summer 2022, while in May 2022, eight Togolese soldiers were killed (along with 15 attackers) and 13 troops were injured. According to analysts, Côte d'Ivoire's armed forces benefit from important, but discreet, French military cooperation, and while recent jihadist attacks have generally been unsuccessful, the current government is looking to improve its military and security capacities. Plans have been announced to boost personnel numbers, while there were reports of additional armoured vehicle procurements in 2022.

There is continuing jihadist activity in Burkina Faso, Mali, Niger and the Lake Chad Basin area. Niger's armed forces are receiving additional equipment. Airlift capacity has been increased with the delivery of a second (of three) C-130H medium transport aircraft from the US, while reconnaissance and attack capabilities will be boosted by the arrival of Turkish-produced *Hurkus* light-attack aircraft. Reports currently point to only two airframes, while there are also reports indicating that protected patrol vehicles may also be procured.

The situation is worse in Mali and Burkina Faso, where the armed forces seized power in

2021 and 2022 respectively. Tensions between France and Mali worsened when the new regime in Bamako failed to implement plans for elections in early 2022, postponing them to 2024. The Malian government's decision to contract Russia's Wagner Group has seen ties deteriorate further. This decision came in the context of allegations of apparent information operations designed to foment local opposition to particularly French assistance. Wagner personnel were subsequently accused by observers of committing war crimes. Reliance on Russia may create difficulties for Malian forces, as weapons contracts may be affected by sanctions, and there may be other problems if Wagner personnel – or Russian maintenance personnel – are recalled to serve in Ukraine. France's military mission in Mali was wound down and redeployed to Niger, and other European states such as the United Kingdom curtailed their military support in the country.

Mali's armed forces have, in recent years, received a range of military equipment, from armoured vehicles and helicopters to C295 light transport aircraft, and in 2022 Bamako received some Russian ground-attack aircraft and attack helicopters. Nonetheless, with the departure of international support missions and a change in military assistance policy by the new government, any progress made in the last decade towards professionalisation is at risk if the focus of military authorities on force-health issues wanes, such as on counter-corruption initiatives.

In Nigeria and Cameroon, the break-up into factions of the former Boko Haram terrorist group has complicated the challenge for the armed forces, and analysts fear an escalation in Nigeria as presidential elections approach in 2023. Abuja continues to pursue military modernisation efforts, and the government's bid to acquire 12 AH-1Z *Viper* attack helicopters was approved in April by the US State Department (with this then sent to Congress for approval). If acquired, these could be assigned to the army's planned new light aviation formation. Although the country maintains equipment of diverse origin, and French firms have supplied many of the navy's recent procurements, in recent years China has also emerged as a significant arms supplier with CS/VP3 protected patrol vehicles and ZSD-89 tracked armoured personnel carrier among the equipment delivered.

EAST AFRICA

The Horn of Africa is more unstable than it has been for some years. Multiple conflicts – in Ethiopia, Somalia, South Sudan and Sudan – threaten the stability and development of a region already prone to high levels of displacement and migration. The population numbers more than 140 million in the narrowly defined Horn comprising Djibouti, Eritrea, Ethiopia and Somalia, and over 260m in the larger region made up of Intergovernmental Authority on Development (IGAD) states comprising the above plus Kenya, South Sudan, Sudan and Uganda. In November 2022, a peace deal was signed between the Ethiopian government and Tigrayan leaders. This raised hopes of an end to a two-year civil war that has threatened the entire Horn of Africa. The economies of Ethiopia's neighbours may not depend upon its economy, but the possibility that the conflict would worsen, or even lead to an Ethiopian collapse and potential break-up, risked the political and civil stability of the whole region. Indeed, fears were expressed that a regional refugee crisis would emerge in this eventuality.

Meanwhile, analysts assert that Eritrea has continued to act as a spoiler in the Horn by favouring Amhara over the federal government in Ethiopia since a humanitarian ceasefire was declared with Tigray in April 2022. Eritrean forces have, it has been claimed, helped Amhara forces seize, clear and hold western Tigray against Tigray Defence Force (TDF) attempts to retake it since January 2021. Meanwhile, there have also been sporadic attacks across Tigray, and reports of support for rebels in eastern Sudan. Asmara has also forged a new bilateral relationship with the new Somali president, Hassan Sheikh Mohamud, in place of the close trilateral relationship formed between Ethiopia, Eritrea and Somalia after the peace deal between Ethiopia and Eritrea in June 2018. The al-Shabaab terrorist group still poses a regional threat. In July 2022 hundreds of al-Shabaab fighters crossed the Ethiopian border from Somalia. Although Ethiopia claims to have effectively contained this threat, it illustrates the extent to which the Ethiopian security system has been challenged by the multiple conflicts in the country.

Security in the Horn of Africa is also threatened by regional tensions, particularly around the Nile and the continuing construction of the Grand Ethiopian Renaissance Dam near the border with Sudan. Ethiopia's dam is a critical issue for Egypt, with the country dependent on the Nile for 85% of its water requirements. This has led to the resurfacing of allegations of Egyptian support for armed opposition groups in Ethiopia. There have been allegations, principally on social media, of Egyptian involvement in the delivery by air of supplies into Tigray in 2022 and the unsubstantiated claim that the Ethiopian Air Force shot down one of these aircraft when the fighting reignited in northern Tigray in August. Meanwhile, Sudan's November 2020 reoccupation of the fertile al-Fashaga triangle, formerly home to many Ethiopian farmers, has created a rift between Sudan and Ethiopia just as the two were becoming more dependent on one another for their stability. Sudan's own faltering political transition means the country is ill-equipped to play a constructive role in the region.

Middle Eastern states' interest in the region is usually attributed to political and security considerations, but there are growing signs of more constructive, and mutually beneficial, economic engagement. However, Middle Eastern political rivalries continue to play out in the Horn, with the contest in Somalia between the central government and the federal states a notable example. Qatar supports the Somali central government, while the United Arab Emirates supports autonomous regions in the north. Somaliland and Puntland have also received significant support from Saudi Arabia, while Turkey has been supportive of the central state.

Meanwhile, the region's economic community, IGAD, is failing to resolve disputes between nations. Ongoing tensions between Sudan and Ethiopia and between Kenya and Somalia, coupled with external interference in the Horn, leave IGAD unable to agree on actions between states and unable to counter external influences. The current lack of unity among IGAD states, which existed previously and was both a product and an enabler of IGAD's capacity to address problems within the region (Ethiopia chaired IGAD in 2010–19), leaves the region without an effective voice or institution to address its own political and security challenges.

The war in Tigray and the Ethiopian National Defence Force

In mid-2020, before the conflict with Tigray, the Ethiopian National Defence Force (ENDF) consisted of an all-volunteer force of approximately 130,000 regular soldiers and 5,000 air force personnel. They were drawn from across the country, with a majority of the experienced senior officers from the Tigray region, and were mostly tasked with defending Ethiopia's borders. By late 2022, the ENDF had expanded to become an all-volunteer force of approximately 500,000. The army makes up the vast majority, with a largely internal role fighting the Tigray Defence Force (TDF) in the north and other armed insurgent groups across the country. Since 2021, the ENDF has also included a naval element, but no vessels have been acquired and no agreement has been publicly reached with neighbouring states on where any naval force may be based.

The loss of experienced Tigrayan leadership, who either left to join the TDF or were detained as a potential threat, was expected to seriously weaken the ENDF, and the force did indeed fail to maintain control of Tigray after an early victory in November 2020. They again failed to halt the TDF when it launched an offensive into the Amhara region in the second half of 2021. However, by early 2022 the reformation, growth and re-equipment of the ENDF allowed them to contain the TDF in Tigray. In the TDF offensive from August to September 2022, during the late rainy season, the ENDF, with the help of Amhara forces, thwarted Tigrayan attempts to re-establish a land corridor to Sudan through Western Tigray.

Prior to the Tigray war, a number of Western states were preparing to provide significant support to the regeneration of the ENDF. The conflict with Tigray caused the cancellation of these agreements, and the growth and re-equipment of the ENDF in the past year was largely supported by agreements with China, Russia and Turkey. The support from Russia and China has helped to provide conventional equipment, uniforms and vehicles. But the real turning point for the ENDF was the air force's acquisition of armed uninhabited aerial vehicles (UAVs) from China, Iran and Turkey. When weather conditions are favourable, these have allowed the ENDF to dominate remote and rocky battlespaces in Tigray, giving them a decisive tactical and operational edge over the TDF, who operate in units as a regular armed force. However, it is unclear whether the ENDF has been able to fuse intelligence and targeting to successfully operate UAVs against armed insurgent groups.

CENTRAL AND SOUTHERN AFRICA

Instability continues to mark much of the region. To the north, there are risks that the conflicts in the Central African Republic and South Sudan may spill over into surrounding regions. While piracy along the East African coast has declined, there are still risks of maritime terrorism in the region due to the insurgency in Mozambique. In the centre and south of the region, insurgencies in the Democratic Republic of the Congo (DRC) and in Mozambique contrast with the generally stable security situation elsewhere in the Southern African Development Community (SADC) region, even if Eswatini, Lesotho and Zimbabwe and potentially Angola are politically fragile.

The security situation is worsening in the DRC's eastern provinces of Ituri and North and South Kivu, despite the efforts of government forces and the United Nations mission, MONUSCO. Non-state armed groups aiming to attack Uganda (ISIS-allied Allied Democratic Forces (ADF)), Rwanda (Democratic Forces for the Liberation of Rwanda (FDLR)) and Burundi (RED-Tabara) have brought instability and led these countries to deploy forces to strike at them inside the DRC. These groups have been in the DRC for so long that they have effectively become local insurgencies. Meanwhile, M23 rebels are again active in the east, with Kinshasa accusing Rwanda of supporting them. Conflict between the local militias and with government forces as well as a plethora of illegal activities – including logging, mining and smuggling – further complicate the situation. In May 2021, the government in Kinshasa declared a 'state of siege' with the armed forces assuming control of local governments in North Kivu and Ituri, while in December 2021 Ugandan armed forces were allowed into the DRC to combat the ADF. However, government forces remain unable to tackle the nation's security challenges and MONUSCO lacks the strength, mobility and air support to be effective. Protesters in the east have demanded that MONUSCO forces withdraw from some locations, asserting it has failed to restore security. After violent demonstrations that led to the deaths of protesters and peacekeepers, the government in Kinshasa in August reportedly said it would re-evaluate the UN mission's plan to stay another two years. Meanwhile, in September 2022, an agreement was signed enabling the intervention of additional armed forces from the East African Community (EAC). A status of forces agreement was signed in Kinshasa between the EAC secretary-general and the president of the DRC. An initial force of Kenyan troops landed at Goma in early November, and it has been reported that the Kenyan contingent alone could number up to 900. The mission will be led by the DRC armed forces and the deployment was planned to last six months initially.

The insurgency in Mozambique's northern Cabo Delgado province has spread to Niassa province to the west and Nampula province to the south. Government forces and Rwandan and SADC contingents have failed to stabilise the area. But the 2,000 Rwandan troops and police deployed to Palma and the TotalEnergies gas installation on the Afungi Peninsula have largely secured the area. SADC special forces had some success, but the force is far too small and lacks air mobility and air support. Meanwhile, the South African Navy has been unable to sustain the patrols needed to stop supplies reaching insurgents by sea. South Africa is deploying an infantry battalion, but without effective air support there is little prospect of early stabilisation. Indeed, South Africa lacks the military strength to play a major role in the region or even on its periphery and faces growing risk of internal instability. The civil unrest of July 2021 in KwaZulu-Natal and Gauteng provinces saw 354 killed and led to authorities deploying some 25,000 troops to support the police. In August 2022, specialised police units were required to deal with illegal gold mining in Mpumalanga province. Both the Police Service and the Defence Force are underfunded and understrength. The latter is stretched by two external deployments (DRC and Mozambique) and border patrols. Troops were deployed internally in 2020 to help the police enforce the COVID-19 lockdown and in 2021 to deal with civil unrest.

South Africa: armed forces and defence industry

Two decades of underfunding have left the South African National Defence Force (SANDF) in a parlous state. Analysts assert that the army is understrength for the tasks set, and that much of its equipment is obsolescent and poorly maintained. Nevertheless, it has sustained contingents in the DRC and Mozambique and some border patrols.

It was also able to deploy troops to help enforce the COVID-19 lockdown in 2020 and to contain the July 2021 riots. The army is reverting to a more traditional organisational structure by re-establishing standing brigades, with a mechanised and light brigade in the process of formation with a motorised and airborne brigade to follow, and afterwards two division headquarters and additional brigades.

The air force, however, has faced significant challenges in generating operational capability. In September, the flight of one of the air force's *Gripen* combat aircraft marked the start of a process of rebuilding air combat capability, following the agreement of a support contract. However, it was unclear how many aircraft the deal covered. Other aircraft have been grounded, including most of the *Hawk* trainers, about half of the *Rooivalk* attack and *Oryx* transport helicopters and many of the AW109 utility and *Super Lynx* maritime helicopters. The only maritime-surveillance capability currently available for operations is a single C-47TP with weather radar. Only two C-130s, two C-212s and some *Caravans* are available for transport. Even most of the PC-7 Mk II trainers are grounded for lack of maintenance. As a result, the air force is facing problems in keeping operational its

three *Rooivalk* and five *Oryx* helicopters in the DRC and two *Oryx* in Mozambique, while the lack of airlift hampers troop rotation and support.

The navy is in a similar situation. Specialists say that only one frigate and one submarine have been refitted since delivery in the early 2000s and their combat systems are now largely obsolescent. The only logistics ship is ageing and in need of refit and many smaller vessels are not operational. The first of three inshore patrol vessels has been delivered and a new survey ship is under construction, but continued underfunding casts doubt on how long these can be maintained in operational status.

Meanwhile, the defence industry has been crippled by a lack of local orders, inadequate government support and problems in obtaining export permits. The state-owned Denel group is attempting to recover from the damage of 'state capture' in the mid-2010s but will find this challenging without acquisition funding for the SANDF and export support. The risk is that much of the rest of the industry may wind down, forcing the SANDF to rely on imported equipment, which will in turn present problems in supporting locally manufactured equipment in service, given dependencies related to maintenance and spares requirements.

DEFENCE ECONOMICS

Macroeconomics

The IMF estimates that after a stronger-than-expected economic performance in 2021, the global shock caused by Russia's full-scale invasion of Ukraine has disrupted the economic recovery in sub-Saharan Africa. Surging food and energy prices are straining public finances at a time when governments have limited policy response options following the costly fiscal measures enacted to counter the economic impact of the coronavirus pandemic.

The 1.6% contraction in regional real GDP in 2020 may seem mild in comparison with the global average of 3%, but this masks some of the underlying problems facing the region. Vaccination programmes continue to face challenges, not least because of the low purchasing power that countries are able to muster to fund vaccine rollouts or to sustain fiscal policies aimed at alleviating the long-term economic impact of the pandemic. According to the World Bank, governments have limited fiscal space due to the need to fund subsidies, support farmers and, in certain countries, increase spending

on security. Meanwhile, higher energy prices have had a negative impact overall, as most countries in the region are oil importers. Moreover, higher food prices are having a disproportionate impact on the most vulnerable countries.

The IMF finds that per capita incomes are expected to remain more than 4% below pre-pandemic projections until the late 2020s. Advanced economies, meanwhile, are expected to return to pre-pandemic projections of per capita GDP by 2023, further widening the inequality gap that the pandemic has already exacerbated. The progress made in recent years to reduce poverty levels in the region has been reversed, with an estimated 39 million more people falling into extreme poverty in 2020 and 2021. The much-needed expansion of skilled human capital that would, in time, serve to reduce inequality levels was hindered by the length of school closures during the pandemic.

As with all regions, inflation represents a significant cause for concern in sub-Saharan Africa. Rates were already high before the Ukraine war owing to factors such as currency depreciations, destabilising conflict and adverse weather. Supply-chain disruptions stemming from the pandemic resulted in spikes in

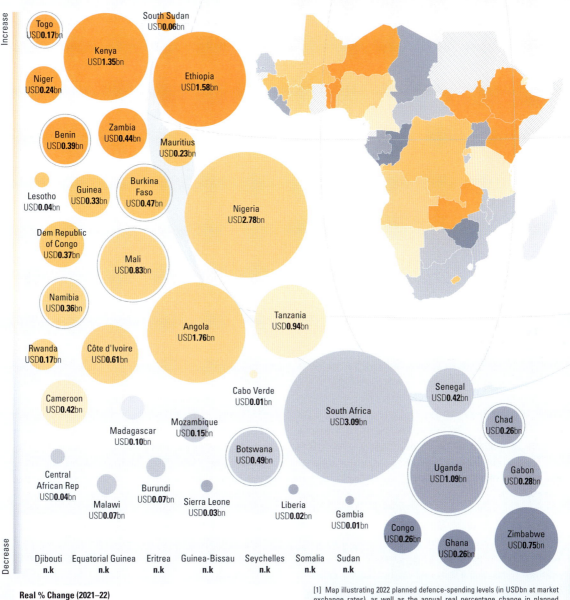

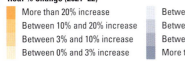

▲ Map 10 **Sub-Saharan Africa: regional defence spending** (USDbn, %ch yoy)[1]

inflation rates across the region in 2020 that persisted into 2021 and were exacerbated in 2022. Even in countries that are benefitting from higher commodity prices, such as Angola, Nigeria and South Africa, the challenges of soaring food prices and fiscal policy tightening are weighing on growth. Higher food prices are leading to growing concerns about food security in countries such as Chad, the Democratic Republic of the Congo, Eritrea, Madagascar and South Sudan. When food-security concerns are combined with poor employment prospects, the risk is that this undermines political stability.

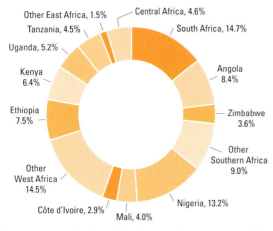

▼ Figure 19 **Sub-Saharan Africa: defence spending by country and sub-region, 2022**

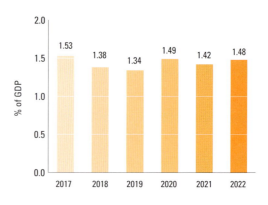

▼ Figure 20 **Sub-Saharan Africa: regional defence spending** as % of GDP (average)

Defence spending

Economic constraints have continued to subdue defence expenditure in sub-Saharan Africa, with regional spending accounting for under 1% of the global total for the last decade. After strong, double-digit real growth in 2013 and 2014, regional spending peaked at USD23.5 billion in 2014 before contracting by 4% in real terms on average every year up to and including 2019. A surge in Nigerian defence spending fuelled an uptick in regional spending in 2020 with real growth reaching 7.6%, but this was swiftly followed by a 5.3% real contraction in 2021 owing to high rates of inflation, averaging 16%. While inflation persisted at this level into 2022, regional defence spending growth was strong enough to reach 9.9% in real terms, largely due to a surge in Ethiopian spending.

South Africa retains the largest defence budget in sub-Saharan Africa, but the country's share of regional spending has fallen considerably over the last decade. In 2011, South African spending accounted for 27% of the total for sub-Saharan Africa but this proportion has declined every year since, falling to just 15% in 2022. Thus, the country may still lead the region's spending, but it now accounts for a smaller share of a market that has itself been considerably constrained over the last decade. As a proportion of GDP, South Africa's budget has fallen to 0.75% in 2022 after averaging 1% over the previous decade.

After a significant drop in 2021, the defence budget (including funding for military veterans) stabilised in 2022 at ZAR49.8bn (USD3.09bn) but still fell by 3.9% in real terms. The Medium-Term Expenditure Framework (MTEF) projects that the defence budget will continue to stagnate in the short term, with spending falling to ZAR48.6bn (USD3.02bn) in 2023 before returning to ZAR50.0bn (USD3.10bn) in 2024. Therefore, the budget does not build in any significant growth that would allow it to return to peak 2011 levels.

The Special Defence Account, used to fund the procurement of strategic and special defence equipment, has dropped significantly in recent years, from ZAR5.2bn (USD316m) in 2020 to ZAR1.5bn (USD101m) in 2021. The Treasury had indicated that the account would be closed completely by 2021/22; however, the MTEF projects that the account will hold steady at ZAR1.9bn–2bn (USD118–124m) between 2022 and 2024, offering a few more years of funding for major acquisitions. If the account is closed, investment will need to be funded from the core defence budget, of which personnel will account for a sizeable 63% over the course of the MTEF. The 2021 and 2022 budgets did outline several reforms to personnel, driven by the government's aim to stabilise debt. The reforms included freezing pay, reducing headcount, limiting reserve forces activity and capping discretionary allowances. According to the 2022 budget, the reductions to personnel will enable the Department of Defence (DoD) to address other cost pressures, including the need for investment in border safeguarding and mid-life upgrades of naval vessels.

Angolan defence spending has also been constrained in recent years. Any increases in local-currency terms between 2015 and 2021 were wiped out by depreciations in the new kwanza and soaring inflation. Over that period, real cuts to defence spending averaged 17%, as inflation rates ranged from 10% to 30% while the kwanza dropped from 120 kwanza to the dollar in 2015 to 631 to the dollar in 2021. Angola's economy, and therefore public finances, was severely affected by the 2014–16 collapse in oil prices. This placed the oil producer on a weak footing when the coronavirus pandemic emerged in 2020, creating a further economic shock. However, Russia's invasion of Ukraine in February 2022 and the subsequent spike in oil prices has benefitted Angola's GDP. With greater fiscal headroom, the government enacted a sizeable uplift to defence spending, from AOA627bn (USD993m) in 2021 to AOA790bn (USD1.76bn) in 2022, leading to the first real-terms increase in Angolan spending for seven years. The increase will help fund Angola's order of three Airbus C295 maritime-patrol aircraft in April 2022 in a deal valued at USD188.11m.

Nigeria's economy is also benefitting from higher oil prices, but slow reform of the downstream energy sector means recurrent fuel shortages and power, blackouts present a drag on output while high rates of inflation restrict consumer purchasing power according to the World Bank. The 2020 defence budget rose to NGN900bn (USD2.51bn), a 41% real increase over 2019 levels. The 2021 budget grew to NGN966bn (USD2.42bn – Nigerian naira depreciated over 2021) in 2021 and NGN1.14 trillion (USD2.78bn) in 2022. But with inflation reaching 16–17% in both years, the budget has been stagnant in real terms, accounting for between 0.5% and 0.6% of GDP. Nonetheless, Nigerian spending is still considerably higher than levels seen over the previous decade. The 2022 budget noted that funding would be allocated to settle the final payment for three JF-17 *Thunder* aircraft; the procurement of a hydrographic survey ship, a landing ship tank and three AW109 helicopters; and part-payment for the procurement of one AW139 helicopter. The Nigerian defence budget is likely to increase as instability in the north of the country worsens. Nigeria continues to pursue significant defence acquisitions, including the potential purchase of 12 AH-1Z *Viper* attack helicopters in a deal valued at USD997m (including support and spares) that was approved by the US State Department in April 2022.

Defence spending in Mali has increased every year in real terms since 2013, with funding reaching USD831m in 2022, quadruple the level reached in 2012. French forces completed their withdrawal from Mali in August following several coups in 2020 and 2021 and the shift towards Russian support by the military-led government. In August 2022, Russia delivered L-39 and Su-25 ground-attack aircraft. The country ordered C295 light transport aircraft from Airbus in December 2021.

There has been strong growth in recent years in other countries in West Africa, including Benin, Burkina Faso, Ghana and Senegal. As a result, West African spending grew to exceed the share spent by Southern African states in 2021, although in light of growth in Angola it fell back below this amount in 2022.

However, the fastest-growing sub-region in 2022 was East Africa. Ethiopia more than quadrupled its defence budget from USD0.38bn to USD1.58bn amid a return to conflict between the Tigray People's

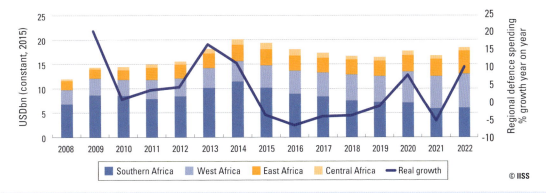

▲ Figure 21 **Sub-Saharan Africa: total defence spending by sub-region, 2008–22**

Liberation Front and the Ethiopian government. Combined with consistent spending in Tanzania and a 2020 jump in Uganda's defence budget, this means that the sub-region now accounts for 25.1% of total regional spending, up from 11.0% in 2010. In contrast, spending in Central Africa continues to stagnate, with the sub-region now accounting for 4.6% of the sub-Saharan Africa total, down from a high of 7.4% in 2016.

Defence industry

The lack of sustained growth in regional defence spending, and the low proportions allocated to investment and R&D, have continued to restrict the development of indigenous capabilities and local defence industries.

The South African DoD Strategic Plan 2020–2025 acknowledged that the economic outlook and persistently low defence budget allocations have had 'a profound adverse impact on the availability and modernisation of required defence capabilities'. This was apparent when a lack of funding and maintenance saw South Africa's *Gripen* C/Ds grounded in September 2021, with two deemed beyond economic repair. To address this, the country signed a USD30m support contract with Saab in September 2022. State-owned Denel, the country's primary defence manufacturer, was already facing a severe liquidity crisis before the pandemic, with the company struggling to pay staff wages in 2019–21. Although the company has now managed to settle salary payments, ratings agencies are cautioning that the company still faces severe liquidity constraints with downside risks amplified by the uncertainty surrounding Denel's strategic direction, together with a loss of key personnel.

Nigeria's defence-industrial base is small, with the largest concerns being the Nigerian Naval Dockyard and Proforce. Efforts to bolster indigenous capabilities have, until recent years, been restricted by economic conditions and conflicting budget priorities, such as the drive to professionalise the armed forces and the need to counter insurgent groups. These create a higher personnel and operational burden within the budget, further constricting funds for R&D. The 2020 surge in Nigerian defence spending was primarily seen in the personnel account, which grew to 80% of the entire budget, a level at which it was maintained into 2021 and 2022. As a result, capital spending has fallen from 26.6% of the budget in 2019 to 13.6% in 2022. Similarly, while allocations to the state-owned Defence Industries Corporation of Nigeria (DICON) have been maintained over the last five years as a proportion of the defence budget, allocations have fallen from 1.1% in 2016 to just 0.32% in 2022.

Angola's industrial ambitions have been restricted by low levels of investment, with no major programmes signed in recent years. The country still has ambitions for the local assembly of tactical vehicles, platform maintenance capabilities and improved naval capabilities. For its part, Uganda opened a new armoured vehicle manufacturing and assembly facility in Nakasongola in July 2022. The plant was a joint project with the STREIT Group, a company based in the United Arab Emirates.

Arms procurements and deliveries – Sub-Saharan Africa

Significant events in 2022

JULY

UGANDA: DEFENCE-INDUSTRY EXPANSION

President Yoweri Museveni opened a new armoured-vehicle production facility. Located to the east of Nakasongola air base, the factory is a joint project between the National Enterprise Corporation (NEC), owned by the Uganda People's Defence Force (UPDF), and United Arab Emirates-based STREIT Group. It will manufacture wheeled armoured vehicles for the armed forces, police and other state services. This comes four years after a plant was opened at Magamaga, in Uganda's south-east, operated by the UPDF with assistance from South African company Twiga Services and Logistics. This facility has been producing *Mamba* armoured vehicles since 2014 and in 2021 unveiled the *Chui* protected patrol vehicle. Earlier, in January 2022, a joint venture between the NEC and Russian firm Pro Heli International opened a maintenance, repair and overhaul (MRO) facility for Mi-24 *Hind* helicopters at Nakasongola air base. The intention is that the site will become an MRO centre for East Africa, as well as reducing the funds spent maintaining UPDF helicopters.

AUGUST

PROFORCE TAKES TO THE AIR

Nigerian armoured-vehicle firm Proforce signed agreements that could see it enter the aerospace sector. In April, an agreement was signed with French company Aeraccess that, according to press releases, will see 'the immediate production of drones within Nigeria'. Aeraccess manufactures small quadcopter UAVs, which have been exported to Canada and Mali among other countries. In August, the company signed a memorandum of understanding with Nigeria's National Space Research and Development Agency (NASRDA) to launch the first satellite programme involving Nigeria's private sector. NASRDA, already operates several foreign-built satellites. A Proforce press release discusses 'the potential and future of launching a satellite in Nigeria'. It is unclear whether this refers to simply building the satellite or also establishing indigenous launch services.

AUGUST

KENYA SHIPYARDS FLOATS OUT KENYAN-BUILT VESSEL

The Kisumu shipyard was commissioned on the shores of Lake Victoria by then-president Uhuru Kenyatta and a transport ship, the future MV *Uhuru* II, was floated out. The ship is being built in partnership with Dutch company Damen Schelde. It is now being fitted out and the formal launch is planned for late 2022. It is the first vessel of significant size to be constructed in the country. Owned by Kenya's National Treasury, Kenya Shipyards Limited (KSL) was established in 2020 and is run by the Kenya Defence Forces (KDF). A second shipyard was commissioned on the east coast in December 2021 and is now refitting the patrol craft KNS *Shupavu*. As well as providing extra defence-industrial capability, the two shipyards are key to the government's effort to grow the country's 'blue economy'. There may be potential to build patrol vessels for the KDF, and others, if there is sustained investment in KSL.

AUGUST

PROJECT *HOEFYSTER* TO PROCEED

State-owned company Denel has received regular bailouts in recent years and its collapse would be a significant blow to South Africa's defence-industrial capability. Under Project *Hoefyster*, Denel Land Systems was selected in 2007 to develop the *Badger* wheeled infantry fighting vehicle, based on Finnish company Patria's Armoured Modular Vehicle (AMV), to partially replace the South African Army's ageing fleet of *Ratels*. However, technical difficulties, staff shortages, COVID-19 and 'state capture' have meant that no deliveries have been made as part of the 2013 production contract. In February 2022 ARMSCOR, the defence procurement agency, recommended cancelling the programme. However, following discussions, both Denel and ARMSCOR decided that it was 'feasible' to proceed with the project provided a funding structure is agreed; this could potentially include measures such as a reconsideration of penalty charges incurred to date by Denel.

Table 16 Kenya: defence procurement since 2000

Tackling the al-Shabaab terrorist group remains a principal focus of the Kenya Defence Forces (KDF). This emphasis is reflected in the procurement of mine-resistant ambush protected vehicles (MRAPs) and helicopters. Until a recent contract for Turkish MRAPs, the KDF had purchased armoured vehicles only in relatively small batches, with the result being that the KDF and Police now operate a variety of equipment types. Meanwhile, several purchases have attracted scrutiny, including surplus Jordanian F-5 fighters and Chinese Z-9W helicopters. Kenyan media reported that auditors were investigating the procurements. The Navy has received the least investment. The delivery of a Spanish-built patrol vessel under a 2003 contract was delayed due to contractual disputes

and Kenya's suspension of payments. Overall, KDF has a varied list of suppliers, but China has delivered the most, spanning both land and air systems. For its part, US deliveries have focused on air assets and there have been more US donations than sales. At the same time, some plans have faced problems. The mooted purchase in 2017 of a squadron of AT-802L ground-attack/ISR aircraft from L-3 Communications (now L3Harris) appears to have been abandoned after elections in Kenya that year and objections to the deal in the US. The proposed maximum contract value, at up to USD418m, may also have been an issue. By way of comparison, Kenya's most expensive procurement, of three C-27J *Spartan* transport aircraft, was valued at USD197.48m.

Contract Date	Equipment	Type	Quantity	Value (USD millions)	Contractor	Deliveries	Notes
2003	*Jasiri*	Oceangoing patrol craft	1	60.58	Euromarine Industries	2012	
c. 2006	WZ-551	Wheeled armoured personnel carrier	32	n.k.	Chongqing Tiema Industries Group	2007	
2007	F-5E/F *Tiger* II	Fighter aircraft	13; 2	27.56	Government surplus	c. 2008	
c. 2009	Z-9W	Multi-role helicopter (MRH)	Up to 9	n.k.	AVIC	2010–15	
2011	*Harambee* (ex-FRA P400)	Coastal patrol craft (PCC)	1	0	Government surplus	2011	
c. 2012	G 120A	Training aircraft	6	n.k.	Grob Aircraft	2013	
2014	*Doria*	PCC	1	39.87	JGH Marine; Western Marine Shipyard	2017	Coast Guard
2014	BOV M10; NORA B-52	Armoured reconnaissance vehicle; 155mm self-propelled artillery	n.k.	n.k.	Yugoimport	2015	
2014	Cessna 208B *Grand Caravan* EX	Intelligence, surveillance and reconnaissance aircraft	1	0	Textron Aviation	c. 2016	
2015	*Springbuck* 4×4	Protected patrol vehicle (PPV)	7	2.4	DCD Protected Mobility	2016	
c. 2015	VN-4	Armoured utility vehicle	30	n.k.	Chongqing Tiema Industries Group	2016	Police
2016	Bell 205 (UH-1H *Huey* II)	Light transport helicopter	8	n.k.	Bell Helicopter	2016–17	
c. 2016	AH-1F *Cobra*	Attack helicopter	3+	n.k.	Government surplus	2017	
c. 2016	CS/VP3	PPV	25	n.k.	Poly Technologies	2017	Police
2017	AW139; AW119Kx	MRH; light transport helicopter	2; 1	44.18	Leonardo	2018	Police
2017	M-28 *Skytruck*	Light transport aircraft	3	n.k.	Government surplus	2020–Ongoing	
2018	MD-530F	MRH	6	n.k.	MD Helicopters	2020	
c. 2018	C-27J *Spartan*	Medium transport aircraft	3	197.48	Leonardo	2020	
c. 2018	AW139	MRH	3	59.24	Leonardo	c. 2020	
c. 2018	M119A2	105mm howitzer	6	0	Government surplus	2019	
c. 2020	CS/VP14	PPV	n.k.	n.k.	NORINCO	c. 2021	
c. 2020	G 120TP	Training aircraft	9	n.k.	Grob Aircraft	2021	
2021	*Hizir*	PPV	118	91.42	Katmerciler	2022–23*	

*Planned

Angola ANG

New Angolan Kwanza AOA		2021	2022	2023
GDP	AOA	47.5tr	56.0tr	
	USD	75.2bn	125bn	
per capita	USD	2,352	3,791	
Growth	%	0.8	2.9	
Inflation	%	25.8	21.7	
Def bdgt	AOA	627bn	790bn	
	USD	993m	1.76bn	
USD1=AOA		631.45	448.96	

Real-terms defence budget trend (USDbn, constant 2015)

Population 34,795,287

Age	0–14	15–19	20–24	25–29	30–64	65 plus
Male	23.7%	5.3%	4.1%	3.3%	11.5%	1.0%
Female	23.7%	5.5%	4.3%	3.6%	12.8%	1.3%

Capabilities

Though numerically one of the region's largest and best-equipped armed forces, Angola's available inventory faces maintenance and readiness challenges. The armed forces are constitutionally tasked with ensuring sovereignty and territorial integrity, and there is growing attention to the protection of offshore resources and maritime-security cooperation with regional and external powers. Defence ties with Russia continue, mainly in the form of equipment deliveries, though there are plans to boost defence-industrial cooperation. There are increasing military ties with China, and Luanda is looking for help in military modernisation, defence-industrial development and maritime security. There were discussions with US AFRICOM in 2022 on shared security concerns. Angola retains conscription, but there are also volunteer components. In recent years, force health and education have been investment priorities. The armed forces train regularly and have participated in multinational exercises. Angola is the only regional state with a strategic-airlift capacity and an order for medium-lift aircraft for transport missions and maritime surveillance was placed with Spain in 2022. Improving the military-logistics system has been identified as a key requirement. Modernisation and equipment-purchasing plans were curtailed in recent years by the fall in oil prices and a reduced defence budget. The defence industry is limited to in-service maintenance facilities, but Angola has ambitions to develop greater capacity by partnering with countries such as Brazil, China, Portugal and Russia.

ACTIVE 107,000 (Army 100,000 Navy 1,000 Air 6,000) **Gendarmerie & Paramilitary 10,000**

Conscript liability 2 years

ORGANISATIONS BY SERVICE

Army 100,000

FORCES BY ROLE
MANOEUVRE
  Armoured
    1 tk bde
  Light
    1 SF bde
    1 (1st) div (1 mot inf bde, 2 inf bde)
    1 (2nd) div (3 mot inf bde, 3 inf bde, 1 arty regt)
    1 (3rd) div (2 mot inf bde, 3 inf bde)
    1 (4th) div (1 tk regt, 5 mot inf bde, 2 inf bde, 1 engr bde)
    1 (5th) div (2 inf bde)
    1 (6th) div (1 mot inf bde, 2 inf bde, 1 engr bde)
COMBAT SUPPORT
  Some engr units
COMBAT SERVICE SUPPORT
  Some log units
EQUIPMENT BY TYPE†
ARMOURED FIGHTING VEHICLES
  MBT 300: ε200 T-55AM2; 50 T-62; 50 T-72M1
  LT TK 10 PT-76
  ASLT 9+ PTL-02 *Assaulter*
  RECCE 603: 600 BRDM-2; 3+ *Cayman* BRDM
  IFV 250 BMP-1/BMP-2
  APC 276
    APC (T) 31 MT-LB
    APC (W) 200+: ε200 BTR-152-60/-70/-80; WZ-551 (CP)
  PPV 45 *Casspir* NG2000
ENGINEERING & MAINTENANCE VEHICLES
  ARV 5+: 5 BTS-2; T-54/T-55
  MW *Bozena*
ARTILLERY 1,503+
  SP 25+: **122mm** 9+ 2S1 *Gvozdika*; **152mm** 4 2S3 *Akatsiya*; **203mm** 12 2S7 *Pion*
  TOWED 575: **122mm** 523 D-30; **130mm** 48 M-46; **152mm** 4 D-20
  MRL 153+: **122mm** 110: 70 BM-21 *Grad*; 40 RM-70; **220mm**; 3+ 9P140MB *Uragan*-M; **240mm** BM-24
  MOR 750: **82mm** 250; **120mm** 500
ANTI-TANK/ANTI-INFRASTRUCTURE
  MSL • MANPATS 9K11 (RS-AT-3 *Sagger*)
  RCL 500: 400 **82mm** B-10/**107mm** B-11†; **106mm** 100 M40†
  GUNS • SP 100mm SU-100†
AIR DEFENCE
  SAM • Point-defence 9K32 *Strela*-2 (RS-SA-7 *Grail*)‡; 9K36 *Strela*-3 (RS-SA-14 *Gremlin*); 9K310 *Igla*-1 (RS-SA-16 *Gimlet*)
  GUNS
    SP 23mm ZSU-23-4
    TOWED 450+: **14.5mm** ZPU-4; **23mm** ZU-23-2; **37mm** M-1939; **57mm** S-60

Navy ε1,000

EQUIPMENT BY TYPE
PATROL AND COASTAL COMBATANTS 24
  PCO 2 *Ngola Kiluange* with 1 hel landing platform (Ministry of Fisheries)
  PCC 5 *Rei Bula Matadi* (Ministry of Fisheries)
  PBF 8: 3 HSI 32; 5 PVC-170
  PB 9: 4 *Mandume*; 5 *Comandante Imperial Santana* (Ministry of Fisheries)

Coastal Defence

EQUIPMENT BY TYPE
COASTAL DEFENCE • AShM 4K44 *Utyos* (RS-SSC-1B *Sepal* – at Luanda)

Marines ε500

FORCES BY ROLE
MANOEUVRE
Amphibious
1 mne bn

Air Force/Air Defence 6,000

FORCES BY ROLE
FIGHTER
1 sqn with MiG-21bis/MF *Fishbed*
1 sqn with Su-27/Su-27UB/Su-30K *Flanker*
FIGHTER/GROUND ATTACK
1 sqn with MiG-23BN/ML/UB *Flogger*
1 sqn with Su-22 *Fitter D*
GROUND ATTACK
1 sqn with Su-25 *Frogfoot*
MARITIME PATROL
1 sqn with Cessna 500 *Citation 1*; C-212 *Aviocar*
TRANSPORT
3 sqn with An-12 *Cub*; An-26 *Curl*; An-32 *Cline*; An-72 *Coaler*; BN-2A *Islander*; C-212 *Aviocar*; Do-28D *Skyservant*; EMB-135BJ *Legacy* 600 (VIP); Il-76TD *Candid* MA60
TRAINING
1 sqn with Cessna 172K/R
1 sqn with EMB-312 *Tucano*
1 sqn with L-29 *Delfin*; L-39 *Albatros*
1 sqn with PC-7 *Turbo Trainer*; PC-9*
1 sqn with Z-142
ATTACK HELICOPTER
2 sqn with Mi-24/Mi-35 *Hind*; SA342M *Gazelle* (with HOT)
TRANSPORT HELICOPTER
2 sqn with AS565; SA316 *Alouette* III (IAR-316) (trg)
1 sqn with Bell 212
1 sqn with Mi-8 *Hip*; Mi-17 *Hip H*
1 sqn with Mi-171Sh
AIR DEFENCE
5 bty with S-125M1 *Pechora*-M1 (RS-SA-3 *Goa*);
5 coy with 9K35 *Strela*-10 (RS-SA-13 *Gopher*)†; 2K12-ML *Kvadrat*-ML (RS-SA-6 *Gainful*); 9K33 *Osa* (RS-SA-8 *Gecko*); 9K31 *Strela*-1 (RS-SA-9 *Gaskin*)

EQUIPMENT BY TYPE†
AIRCRAFT 97 combat capable
FTR 36: 6 Su-27/Su-27UB *Flanker*; 12 Su-30K *Flanker*; 18 MiG-23ML *Flogger*
FGA 41: 20 MiG-21bis/MF *Fishbed*; 8 MiG-23BN/UB *Flogger*; 13 Su-22 *Fitter D*
ATK 10: 8 Su-25 *Frogfoot*; 2 Su-25UB *Frogfoot*
MP 1 Cessna 500 *Citation* I
TPT 57: **Heavy** 4 Il-76TD *Candid*; **Medium** 6 An-12 *Cub*; **Light** 47: 12 An-26 *Curl*; 2 An-32 *Cline*; 8 An-72 *Coaler*; 8 BN-2A *Islander*; 2 C-212 *Aviocar*; 5 Cessna 172K; 6 Cessna 172R; 1 Do-28D *Skyservant*; 1 EMB-135BJ *Legacy* 600 (VIP); 2 MA60

TRG 54: 13 EMB-312 *Tucano*; 6 EMB-314 *Super Tucano**; 12 K-8W *Karakorum*; 6 L-29 *Delfin*; 2 L-39C *Albatros*; 5 PC-7 *Turbo Trainer*; 4 PC-9*; 6 Z-142
HELICOPTERS
ATK 56: 34 Mi-24 *Hind*; 22 Mi-35 *Hind*
MRH 63: 8 AS565 *Panther*; 4 AW139; 8 SA316 *Alouette* III (IAR-316) (incl trg); 8 SA342M *Gazelle*; 27 Mi-8 *Hip*/Mi-17 *Hip H*; 8 Mi-171Sh *Terminator*
TPT • **Light** 10: 2+ AW109E; 8 Bell 212
AIR DEFENCE • SAM 73
Short-range 28: 16 2K12-ML *Kvadrat*-ML (RS-SA-6 *Gainful*); 12 S-125M1 *Pechora*-M1 (RS-SA-3 *Goa*)
Point-defence 45: 10 9K35 *Strela*-10 (RS-SA-13 *Gopher*)†; 15 9K33 *Osa* (RS-SA-8 *Gecko*); 20 9K31 *Strela*-1 (RS-SA-9 *Gaskin*)
AIR-LAUNCHED MISSILES
AAM
IR R-3 (RS-AA-2 *Atoll*)‡; R-60 (RS-AA-8 *Aphid*); R-73 (RS-AA-11A *Archer*)
IR/SARH R-23/24 (RS-AA-7 *Apex*)‡; R-27 (RS-AA-10 *Alamo*)
ASM 9M17M *Falanga*-M (RS-AT-2 *Swatter*); HOT
ARM Kh-28 (RS-AS-9 *Kyle*)

Gendarmerie & Paramilitary 10,000

Rapid-Reaction Police 10,000

DEPLOYMENT

MOZAMBIQUE: SADC • SAMIM 18

Benin BEN

CFA Franc BCEAO XOF		2021	2022	2023
GDP	XOF	9.81tr	10.9tr	
	USD	17.7bn	17.5bn	
per capita	USD	1,417	1,367	
Growth	%	7.2	5.7	
Inflation	%	1.7	5.0	
Def bdgt	XOF	125bn	244bn	
	USD	226m	394m	
USD1=XOF		554.25	619.62	

Real-terms defence budget trend (USDm, constant 2015)

Population	13,754,688

Age	0–14	15–19	20–24	25–29	30–64	65 plus
Male	22.9%	5.3%	4.7%	3.7%	11.5%	1.1%
Female	22.5%	5.3%	4.8%	4.0%	12.9%	1.3%

Capabilities

The armed forces focus on border- and internal-security issues, as well as combating illicit trafficking. Border patrols and security have increased following concern over the regional threat from Islamist groups. Maritime security is a priority in light of continuing piracy in the Gulf of Guinea. A National Guard has been established to focus on counter-terrorism and internal security issues. There have been reports of efforts to improve soldiers' living conditions. The increased security threat in the North led to the opening of a new military base there. In July 2022, Benin signed a military cooperation agreement with Niger and security cooperation with Rwanda was boosted after a bilateral meeting in September; this might include logistical support. There is a military-cooperation agreement with France, whose Senegal-based forces have delivered training to boost Benin's border-surveillance capacity. Armoured vehicles have also been received from China. The US has provided similar training to the army and national police. Benin contributes personnel to the Multinational Joint Task Force fighting Islamist terrorist groups. There is a limited capacity to deploy beyond neighbouring states without external support. There is some maintenance capability but no defence-manufacturing sector.

ACTIVE 12,300 (Army 8,000 Navy 550 Air 250 National Guard 3,500) Gendarmerie & Paramilitary 4,800
Conscript liability 18 months (selective)

ORGANISATIONS BY SERVICE

Army ε8,000
FORCES BY ROLE
MANOEUVRE
  Armoured
  2 armd sqn
  Light
  1 (rapid reaction) mot inf bn
  8 inf bn
COMBAT SUPPORT
  2 arty bn
  1 engr bn
  1 sigs bn
COMBAT SERVICE SUPPORT
  1 log bn
  1 spt bn
EQUIPMENT BY TYPE
ARMOURED FIGHTING VEHICLES
  LT TK 18 PT-76†
  RECCE 24: 3 AML-90; 14 BRDM-2; 7 M8
  APC 34
    APC (T) 22 M113;
    APC (W) 2 *Bastion* APC
    PPV 10 *Casspir* NG
  AUV 16+: 6+ Dongfeng *Mengshi*; 10 VBL
ARTILLERY 16+
  TOWED 105mm 16: 12 L118 Light Gun; 4 M101
  MOR 81mm some; 120mm some

Navy ε550
EQUIPMENT BY TYPE
PATROL AND COASTAL COMBATANTS • PB 6:
2 *Matelot Brice Kpomasse* (ex-PRC); 3 FPB 98; 1 27m (PRC)

Air Force ε250
EQUIPMENT BY TYPE
AIRCRAFT
  TPT 3: Light 1 DHC-6 *Twin Otter*†; PAX 2: 1 B-727; 1 HS-748†
  TRG (1 LH-10 *Ellipse* non-operational)
HELICOPTERS
  TPT • Light 5: 4 AW109BA; 1 AS350B *Ecureuil*†

National Guard ε3,500
FORCES BY ROLE
MANOEUVRE
  Air Manoeuvre
  1 AB bn

Gendarmerie & Paramilitary 4,800

Republican Police ε4,800
EQUIPMENT BY TYPE
ARMOURED FIGHTING VEHICLES
  APC • PPV *Casspir* NG

DEPLOYMENT
CENTRAL AFRICAN REPUBLIC: UN • MINUSCA 6
CHAD: Lake Chad Basin Commission • MNJTF 150
DEMOCRATIC REPUBLIC OF THE CONGO: UN • MONUSCO 9
MALI: UN • MINUSMA 299; 1 mech inf coy(+)
SOUTH SUDAN: UN • UNMISS 4
SUDAN: UN • UNISFA 2

Botswana BWA

Botswana Pula BWP		2021	2022	2023
GDP	BWP	195bn	220bn	
	USD	17.6bn	18.0bn	
per capita	USD	7,337	7,348	
Growth	%	11.4	4.1	
Inflation	%	6.7	11.2	
Def bdgt [a]	BWP	5.76bn	6.06bn	
	USD	520m	495m	
USD1=BWP		11.09	12.24	

[a] Defence, Justice and Security Budget

Real-terms defence budget trend (USDm, constant 2015)

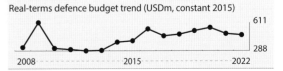

Population   2,384,246

Age	0–14	15–19	20–24	25–29	30–64	65 plus
Male	14.9%	4.6%	4.3%	4.3%	17.6%	2.4%
Female	14.7%	4.7%	4.5%	4.4%	20.4%	3.4%

436   THE MILITARY BALANCE 2023

Capabilities

The Botswana Defence Force (BDF) comprises ground forces and a small but comparatively well-equipped air wing. The BDF's primary responsibility is to ensure territorial integrity; its other tasks include tackling poaching. There is a history of involvement in peacekeeping operations. The BDF has reportedly been working on a defence doctrine that is believed to be influenced by US concepts and practices. Botswana has a good relationship with the US which provides training to the BDF. The armed forces also train with other African nations, including Namibia, with whom it holds biannual exercises. The operations centre for the Southern African Development Community (SADC) Standby Force is located in Gaborone. The BDF has deployed a small force to Mozambique, to join soldiers from other SADC countries. Recent personnel priorities include improving conditions of service and overhauling retirement ages. Recruitment into the BDF is voluntary. Some BDF military personnel have travelled to China for training. The air force has a modest airlift capacity and the BDF is able to deploy a small force by air if required. There is interest in replacing the ageing fleet of F-5 combat aircraft, though a successor type has yet to be ordered due to financial constraints. While reports suggest a limited maintenance capacity, there is no defence-manufacturing sector.

ACTIVE 9,000 (Army 8,500 Air 500)

ORGANISATIONS BY SERVICE

Army 8,500

FORCES BY ROLE

MANOEUVRE

  Armoured

  1 armd bde(-)

  Light

  2 inf bde (1 armd recce regt, 4 inf bn, 1 cdo unit, 1 engr regt, 1 log bn, 2 ADA regt)

COMBAT SUPPORT

  1 arty bde

  1 engr coy

  1 sigs coy

COMBAT SERVICE SUPPORT

  1 log gp

AIR DEFENCE

  1 AD bde(-)

EQUIPMENT BY TYPE

ARMOURED FIGHTING VEHICLES

  LT TK 45: ε20 SK-105 *Kurassier*; 25 FV101 *Scorpion*

  IFV 35+ *Piranha* V UT-30

  APC 157:

    APC (W) 145: 50 BTR-60; 50 LAV-150 *Commando* (some with 90mm gun); 45 *Piranha* III

    PPV 12 *Casspir*

  AUV 70: 6 FV103 *Spartan*; 64 VBL

ENGINEERING & MAINTENANCE VEHICLES

  ARV *Greif*; M578

  MW *Aardvark* Mk2

ANTI-TANK/ANTI-INFRASTRUCTURE

  MSL

    SP V-150 TOW

    MANPATS TOW

  RCL 84mm *Carl Gustaf*

ARTILLERY 78

  TOWED 30: **105mm** 18: 12 L118 Light Gun; 6 Model 56 pack howitzer; **155mm** 12 Soltam

  MRL 122mm 20 APRA-40

  MOR 28: **81mm** 22; **120mm** 6 M-43

AIR DEFENCE

  SAM

    Short-range 1 VL MICA

    Point-defence 9K32 *Strela-2* (RS-SA-7 *Grail*)‡; 9K310 *Igla-1* (RS-SA-16 *Gimlet*); *Javelin*; *Mistral*

  GUNS • TOWED 20mm 7 M167 *Vulcan*; **37mm** PG-65

Air Wing 500

FORCES BY ROLE

FIGHTER/GROUND ATTACK

  1 sqn with F-5A *Freedom Fighter*; F-5D *Tiger* II

ISR

  1 sqn with O-2 *Skymaster*

TRANSPORT

  2 sqn with BD-700 *Global Express*; BN-2/-2B *Defender**; Beech 200 *King Air* (VIP); C-130B *Hercules*; C-212-300/400 *Aviocar*; CN-235M-100; Do-328-110 (VIP)

TRAINING

  1 sqn with PC-7 MkII *Turbo Trainer**

TRANSPORT HELICOPTER

  1 sqn with AS350B *Ecureuil*; Bell 412EP/SP *Twin Huey*; EC225LP *Super Puma*

EQUIPMENT BY TYPE

AIRCRAFT 28 combat capable

  FTR 13: 8 F-5A *Freedom Fighter*; 5 F-5D *Tiger* II

  ISR 5 O-2 *Skymaster*

  TPT 20: **Medium** 3 C-130B *Hercules*; **Light** 16: 4 BN-2 *Defender**; 6 BN-2B *Defender**; 1 Beech 200 *King Air* (VIP); 1 C-212-300 *Aviocar*; 1 C-212-400 *Aviocar*; 2 CN-235M-100; 1 Do-328-110 (VIP); **PAX** 1 BD700 *Global Express*

  TRG 5 PC-7 MkII *Turbo Trainer**

HELICOPTERS

  MRH 7: 2 Bell 412EP *Twin Huey*; 5 Bell 412SP *Twin Huey*

  TPT 9: **Medium** 1 EC225LP *Super Puma*; **Light** 8 AS350B *Ecureuil*

DEPLOYMENT

DEMOCRATIC REPUBLIC OF THE CONGO: UN • MONUSCO 2

MOZAMBIQUE: SADC • SAMIM 359

Burkina Faso BFA

CFA Franc BCEAO XOF		2021	2022	2023
GDP	XOF	10.6tr	11.3tr	
	USD	19.1bn	18.3bn	
per capita	USD	887	825	
Growth	%	6.9	3.6	
Inflation	%	3.9	14.2	
Def bdgt	XOF	254bn	291bn	
	USD	459m	469m	
USD1=XOF		554.24	620.61	

Real-terms defence budget trend (USDm, constant 2015)

Population   21,935,389

Age	0–14	15–19	20–24	25–29	30–64	65 plus
Male	21.7%	5.5%	4.9%	3.7%	11.9%	1.4%
Female	21.0%	5.4%	4.9%	4.0%	14.0%	1.8%

Capabilities

In recent years, Burkina Faso's security forces have been challenged by an increasing terrorist threat, which has led Ouagadougou to refocus its military efforts particularly on the north of the country. In 2022, two military coups illustrated problems with military cohesion. The effect that these coups, and continuing instability, will have on Burkina Faso's defence cooperation with France remains unclear. ECOWAS missions have continued to work on processes for a transition to constitutional democracy with the new leadership. In early October, US sources reported assurances that Burkina Faso would not extend an invitation to Russia's Wagner Group, but later in the same month authorities in Ouagadougou reportedly indicated that they could review relations with Russia. In recent years, the US donated armoured vehicles and other equipment. Aviation capacity is slowly improving with the arrival of additional helicopters and more modern PPVs. Financial challenges and political instability might hinder broader capability developments. Without external support, deployment capacity is limited to neighbouring countries. While there are maintenance facilities, there is no defence-manufacturing sector.

ACTIVE 7,000 (Army 6,400 Air 600) Gendarmerie & Paramilitary 4,450

ORGANISATIONS BY SERVICE

Army 6,400

Three military regions. In 2011, several regiments were disbanded and merged into other formations, including the new 24th and 34th régiments interarmes

FORCES BY ROLE
MANOEUVRE
  Mechanised
  1 cbd arms regt
  Light
  1 cbd arms regt
  6 inf regt
  Air Manoeuvre
  1 AB regt (1 CT coy)
COMBAT SUPPORT
  1 arty bn (2 arty tp)
  1 engr bn

EQUIPMENT BY TYPE
ARMOURED FIGHTING VEHICLES
  RECCE 83: 19 AML-60/AML-90; 24 EE-9 Cascavel; 30 Ferret; 2 M20; 8 M8
  APC 138
    APC (W) 24: 13 Panhard M3; 11 Bastion APC
    PPV 114: 24 Ejder Yalcin; 6 Gila; 63 Puma M26-15; 21 Stark Motors Storm
  AUV 46+: 8+ Bastion Patsas; 38 Cobra
ENGINEERING & MAINTENANCE VEHICLES
  MW 3 Shrek-M
ANTI-TANK/ANTI-INFRASTRUCTURE
  RCL 75mm Type-52 (M20); 84mm Carl Gustaf
ARTILLERY 50+
  TOWED 14: 105mm 8 M101; 122mm 6
  MRL 9: 107mm ε4 Type-63; 122mm 5 APR-40
  MOR 27+: 81mm Brandt; 82mm 15; 120mm 12
AIR DEFENCE
  SAM • Point-defence 9K32 Strela-2 (RS-SA-7 Grail)‡
  GUNS • TOWED 42: 14.5mm 30 ZPU; 20mm 12 TCM-20

Air Force 600

FORCES BY ROLE
GROUND ATTACK/TRAINING
  1 sqn with SF-260WL Warrior*; Embraer EMB-314 Super Tucano*
TRANSPORT
  1 sqn with AT-802 Air Tractor; B-727 (VIP); Beech 200 King Air; 1 C295W; CN235-220; PA-34 Seneca; Tetras
ATTACK/TRANSPORT HELICOPTER
  1 sqn with AS350 Ecureuil; Mi-8 Hip; Mi-17 Hip H; Mi-35 Hind AW 139; UH-1Y Huey

EQUIPMENT BY TYPE
AIRCRAFT 5 combat capable
  ISR 1 DA42M (reported)
  TPT 10: Light 9: 1 AT-802 Air Tractor; 2 Beech 200 King Air; 1 C295W; 1 CN235-220; 1 PA-34 Seneca; 3 Tetras; PAX 1 B-727 (VIP)
  TRG 5: 3 EMB-314 Super Tucano*; 2 SF-260WL Warrior*
HELICOPTERS
  ATK 2 Mi-35 Hind
  MRH 3: 2 Mi-17 Hip H; 1 AW139
  TPT 3: Medium 1 Mi-8 Hip; Light 2: 1 AS350 Ecureuil; 1 UH-1H Huey

Gendarmerie & Paramilitary 4,450

National Gendarmerie 4,200
Ministry of Defence and Veteran Affairs
FORCES BY ROLE
SPECIAL FORCES
  1 spec ops gp (USIGN)
EQUIPMENT BY TYPE
ARMOURED FIGHTING VEHICLES
  APC • APC (W) some *Bastion* APC

People's Militia (R) 45,000 reservists (trained)

Security Company 250

DEPLOYMENT
CENTRAL AFRICAN REPUBLIC: UN • MINUSCA 11
DEMOCRATIC REPUBLIC OF THE CONGO: UN • MONUSCO 5
MALI: UN • MINUSMA 653; 1 mech inf bn

FOREIGN FORCES
France 300; 1 SF gp; 2 *Tiger*; 3 AS532UL; 2 H225M; 2 SA342 *Gazelle*

Burundi BDI

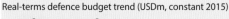

Burundi Franc BIF		2021	2022	2023
GDP	BIF	6.61tr	7.50tr	
	USD	3.35bn	3.69bn	
per capita	USD	274	293	
Growth	%	3.1	3.3	
Inflation	%	8.3	17.3	
Def bdgt	BIF	129bn	136bn	208bn
	USD	65.5m	66.7m	
USD1=BIF		1973.38	2035.18	

Real-terms defence budget trend (USDm, constant 2015)

Population 12,696,478

Age	0–14	15–19	20–24	25–29	30–64	65 plus
Male	21.7%	5.5%	4.5%	3.7%	12.9%	1.4%
Female	21.4%	5.5%	4.5%	3.7%	13.4%	1.8%

Capabilities

The political crisis in 2015 tested the cohesion of the armed forces and largely halted military-training activity with international partners. Cross-border and internal security challenges continue. There are reports of improving relations with Rwanda. Burundi signed a cooperation agreement with Russia in 2018 on counter-terrorism and joint training. The armed forces have a limited capability to deploy externally and in 2022 sent troops to the neighbouring DRC and have long-maintained a deployment in Somalia. The experience accumulated during UN operations will have increased the individual skills of those troops. Peacekeeping missions help to fund the armed forces, though financial and equipment deficiencies otherwise restrict military effectiveness. Apart from limited maintenance facilities, the country has no domestic defence-industrial capability.

ACTIVE 30,050 (Army 30,000 Navy 50) Gendarmerie & Paramilitary 1,000

ORGANISATIONS BY SERVICE

Army 30,000
FORCES BY ROLE
MANOEUVRE
  Mechanised
    2 lt armd bn (sqn)
  Light
    7 inf bn
    Some indep inf coy
COMBAT SUPPORT
  1 arty bn
  1 engr bn
AIR DEFENCE
  1 AD bn
EQUIPMENT BY TYPE
ARMOURED FIGHTING VEHICLES
  RECCE 48: 6 AML-60; 12 AML-90; 30 BRDM-2
  APC 114
    APC (W) 70: 20 BTR-40; 10 BTR-80; 10 *Fahd*-300; 9 Panhard M3; 15 Type-92; 6 *Walid*
    PPV 44: 12 *Casspir*; 12 RG-31 *Nyala*; 10 RG-33L; 10 *Springbuck* 4×4
  AUV 15 *Cougar* 4×4
ARTILLERY 120
  TOWED 122mm 18 D-30
  MRL 122mm 12 BM-21 *Grad*
  MOR 90: 82mm 15 M-43; 120mm ε75
ANTI-TANK/ANTI-INFRASTRUCTURE
  MSL • MANPATS *Milan* (reported)
  RCL 75mm Type-52 (M20)
AIR DEFENCE
  SAM • Point-defence 9K32 *Strela*-2 (RS-SA-7 *Grail*)‡
  GUNS • TOWED 150+: 14.5mm 15 ZPU-4; 135+ 23mm ZU-23/37mm Type-55 (M-1939)

Air Wing 200
EQUIPMENT BY TYPE
AIRCRAFT 1 combat capable
  TPT • Light 2 Cessna 150L†
  TRG 1 SF-260W *Warrior**
HELICOPTERS
  ATK 2 Mi-24 *Hind*
  MRH 2 SA342L *Gazelle*
TPT • Medium (2 Mi-8 *Hip* non-op)

Reserves
FORCES BY ROLE
MANOEUVRE
  Light
    10 inf bn (reported)

Navy 50
EQUIPMENT BY TYPE
PATROL AND COASTAL COMBATANTS • PB 4
AMPHIBIOUS • LCT 2

Gendarmerie & Paramilitary ε1,000

General Administration of State Security
ε1,000

DEPLOYMENT

CENTRAL AFRICAN REPUBLIC: UN • MINUSCA 766; 1 inf bn
MALI: UN • MINUSMA 1
SOMALIA: AU • ATMIS 4,000; 5 inf bn
SUDAN: UN • UNISFA 7

Cabo Verde CPV

Cape Verde Escudo CVE		2021	2022	2023
GDP	CVE	197bn	214bn	
	USD	2.11bn	2.05bn	
per capita	USD	3,749	3,600	
Growth	%	7.0	4.0	
Inflation	%	1.9	6.5	
Def bdgt	CVE	1.12bn	1.20bn	
	USD	12.0m	11.5m	
USD1=CVE		93.18	104.14	

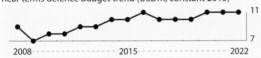

Population 596,707

Age	0–14	15–19	20–24	25–29	30–64	65 plus
Male	13.6%	4.5%	4.5%	4.5%	19.3%	2.2%
Female	13.4%	4.4%	4.5%	4.6%	20.8%	3.7%

Capabilities

Defence priorities include territorial defence, maritime security, and EEZ and airspace protection. Authorities are working to boost Coast Guard capability and presence as part of a 2017-27 coast guard strategic plan. There are plans to host the maritime coordination centre HQ for 'Zone G' of the Yaoundé maritime security architecture. There is interest in greater regional and international defence engagement, possibly including participation in UN peacekeeping missions. The armed forces take part in multinational regional exercises and cooperative activities. 2022 saw broader maritime security cooperation with the US Navy and regional partners. Security cooperation with Portugal includes training of aircrew and maintenance staff. China reportedly donated equipment, including trucks and buses,to the armed forces in 2021. Equipment capabilities remain limited and there is no defence industry, beyond maintenance facilities.

ACTIVE 1,200 (Army 1,000 Coast Guard 100 Air 100)
Conscript liability Selective conscription (14 months)

ORGANISATIONS BY SERVICE

Army 1,000
FORCES BY ROLE
MANOEUVRE
  Light
  2 inf bn (gp)
COMBAT SUPPORT
  1 engr bn
EQUIPMENT BY TYPE
ARMOURED FIGHTING VEHICLES
  RECCE 10 BRDM-2
ARTILLERY • MOR 18: 82mm 12; 120mm 6 M-1943
AIR DEFENCE
  SAM • Point-defence 9K32 *Strela* (RS-SA-7 *Grail*)‡
  GUNS • TOWED 30: 14.5mm 18 ZPU-1; 23mm 12 ZU-23

Coast Guard ε100
EQUIPMENT BY TYPE
PATROL AND COASTAL COMBATANTS 5
  PCC 2: 1 *Guardião*; 1 *Kondor I*
  PB 2: 1 *Espadarte*; 1 *Tainha* (PRC 27m)
  PBF 1 *Archangel*
AIRCRAFT • TPT • Light 1 Do-228

Air Force up to 100
FORCES BY ROLE
MARITIME PATROL
  1 sqn with An-26 *Curl*
EQUIPMENT BY TYPE
AIRCRAFT • TPT • Light 3 An-26 *Curl*†

Cameroon CMR

CFA Franc BEAC XAF		2021	2022	2023
GDP	XAF	25.2tr	27.4tr	
	USD	45.4bn	44.2bn	
per capita	USD	1,667	1,584	
Growth	%	3.6	3.8	
Inflation	%	2.3	4.6	
Def bdgt	XAF	246bn	260bn	
	USD	444m	419m	
USD1=XAF		554.25	619.61	

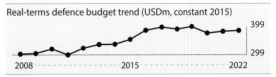

Population 29,321,637

Age	0–14	15–19	20–24	25–29	30–64	65 plus
Male	21.1%	5.4%	4.6%	3.9%	13.2%	1.5%
Female	20.8%	5.4%	4.6%	4.0%	13.7%	1.7%

440　THE MILITARY BALANCE 2023

Capabilities

Internal security is a key concern for Cameroon's armed forces, as is the cross-border challenge from Boko Haram. Cameroon is part of the Multinational Joint Task Force engaged on operations against Islamist terrorist groups. There are long-standing military ties with France, including for support and training. There is a military-assistance agreement with China and the two countries have cooperated over a floating dock at Kribi, which it is hoped will improve operational readiness. In April 2022, Cameroon signed a military cooperation agreement with Russia. The AU maintains its continental logistics base at Douala. The armed forces are considered well organised, though allegations of abuses led the US in February 2019 to halt some military assistance. Although deployments continue to UN peacekeeping operations, there is only limited organic power-projection capability without external support. Much of the equipment inventory is ageing, but infantry fighting vehicles and protected patrol vehicles have been acquired from China, France, South Africa and gifted by the US. The armed forces are improving their ISR capability with fixed-wing aircraft and small UAVs. Additional patrol vessels have in recent years improved maritime capability. Cameroon has no defence-industrial capacity, bar maintenance facilities.

ACTIVE 25,400 (Army 23,500 Navy 1,500 Air 400)
Gendarmerie & Paramilitary 9,000

ORGANISATIONS BY SERVICE

Army 23,500

5 Mil Regions

FORCES BY ROLE
MANOEUVRE
　Light
　1 rapid reaction bde (1 armd recce bn, 1 AB bn, 1 amph bn)
　1 mot inf bde (4 mot inf bn, 1 spt bn)
　5 mot inf bde (3 mot inf bn, 1 spt bn)
　6 rapid reaction bn
　4 inf bn
　Air Manoeuvre
　1 cdo/AB bn
　Other
　1 (Presidential Guard) gd bn
COMBAT SUPPORT
　1 arty regt (5 arty bty)
　5 engr regt
AIR DEFENCE
　1 AD regt (6 AD bty)
EQUIPMENT BY TYPE
ARMOURED FIGHTING VEHICLES
　ASLT 18: 6 AMX-10RC; ε12 PTL-02 mod (*Cara* 105)
　RECCE 54: 31 AML-90; 15 *Ferret*; 8 M8
　IFV 42: 8 LAV-150 *Commando* with 20mm gun; 14 LAV-150 *Commando* with 90mm gun; 12 *Ratel*-20 (Engr); ε8 Type-07P
　APC 115
　　APC (T) 12 M3 half-track
　　APC (W) 66: 45 *Bastion* APC; 21 LAV-150 *Commando*
　　PPV 37: 16 Gaia *Thunder*; 21 PKSV
　AUV 19+: 6 *Cougar* 4×4; *Panthera* T6; 5 RAM Mk3; 3 *Tiger* 4×4; 5 VBL

ENGINEERING & MAINTENANCE VEHICLES
　ARV WZ-551 ARV
ANTI-TANK/ANTI-INFRASTRUCTURE
　MSL
　　SP 24 TOW (on Jeeps)
　　MANPATS *Milan*
　RCL 53: **75mm** 13 Type-52 (M20); **106mm** 40 M40A2
ARTILLERY 106+
　SP 155mm 18 ATMOS 2000
　TOWED 52: **105mm** 20 M101; **130mm** 24: 12 M-1982 (reported); 12 Type-59 (M-46); **155mm** 8 M-71
　MRL 122mm 20 BM-21 *Grad*
　MOR 16+: **81mm** (some SP); **120mm** 16 Brandt
AIR DEFENCE • GUNS
　SP 20mm RBY-1 with TCM-20
　TOWED 54: **14.5mm** 18 Type-58 (ZPU-2); **35mm** 18 GDF-002; **37mm** 18 Type-63

Navy ε1,500

HQ located at Douala

EQUIPMENT BY TYPE
PATROL AND COASTAL COMBATANTS 16
　PCC 3: 1 *Dipikar* (ex-FRA *Flamant*); 2 *Le Ntem* (PRC *Limam El Hidrami*)
　PB 11: 2 Aresa 2400; 2 Aresa 3200; 2 Rodman 101; 4 Rodman 46; 1 *Quartier Maître Alfred Motto*†
　PBR 2 *Swift*-38
AMPHIBIOUS • LANDING CRAFT 4
　LCU 2 Type-067 (*Yunnan*)
　LCM 2: 1 Aresa 2300; 1 *Le Moungo*

Fusiliers Marin

FORCES BY ROLE
MANOEUVRE
　Amphibious
　3 mne bn

Air Force 300–400

FORCES BY ROLE
FIGHTER/GROUND ATTACK
　1 sqn with *Alpha Jet**†
TRANSPORT
　1 sqn with C-130H/H-30 *Hercules*; PA-23 *Aztec*
　1 VIP unit with AS332 *Super Puma*; AS365 *Dauphin* 2; Bell 206B *Jet Ranger*; Gulfstream III
TRAINING
　1 unit with *Tetras*
ATTACK HELICOPTER
　1 sqn with SA342 *Gazelle* (with HOT); Mi-24 *Hind*
TRANSPORT HELICOPTER
　1 sqn with Bell 206L-3; Bell 412; SA319 *Alouette* III
EQUIPMENT BY TYPE
AIRCRAFT 6 combat capable
　ISR 2 Cessna 208B *Grand Caravan*
　TPT 17: **Medium** 3: 2 C-130H *Hercules*; 1 C-130H-30 *Hercules*; **Light** 13: 1 CN235 (1 IAI-201 *Arava* in store); 2 J.300 *Joker*; 1 MA60; 2 PA-23 *Aztec*; 7 *Tetras*; **PAX** 1 Gulfstream III
　TRG 6 *Alpha Jet**†

HELICOPTERS
ATK 2 Mi-24 *Hind*
MRH 15: 1 AS365 *Dauphin* 2; 4 Bell 412 *Twin Huey*;
2 Mi-17 *Hip* H; 2 SA319 *Alouette* III; 4 SA342 *Gazelle*
(with HOT); 2 Z-9
TPT 6: **Medium** 4: 2 AS332 *Super Puma*; 2 SA330J *Puma*;
Light 2: 1 Bell 206B *Jet Ranger*; 1 Bell 206L-3 *Long Ranger*
AIR-LAUNCHED MISSILES
ASM HOT

Fusiliers de l'Air
FORCES BY ROLE
MANOEUVRE
  Other
  1 sy bn

Gendarmerie & Paramilitary 9,000

Gendarmerie 9,000
FORCES BY ROLE
MANOEUVRE
  Reconnaissance
  3 (regional spt) paramilitary gp

DEPLOYMENT
CENTRAL AFRICAN REPUBLIC: UN • MINUSCA 758; 1 inf bn
DEMOCRATIC REPUBLIC OF THE CONGO: UN • MONUSCO 4
MALI: UN • MINUSMA 2

Central African Republic CAR

CFA Franc BEAC XAF		2021	2022	2023
GDP	XAF	1.43tr	1.54tr	
	USD	2.58bn	2.49bn	
per capita	USD	525	496	
Growth	%	1.0	1.5	
Inflation	%	4.3	6.5	
Def exp	XAF	24.0bn	24.1bn	
	USD	43.2m	38.9m	
USD1=XAF		554.19	620.63	

Real-terms defence budget trend (USDm, constant 2015)

Population 5,454,533

Age	0–14	15–19	20–24	25–29	30–64	65 plus
Male	20.1%	5.6%	5.0%	4.2%	13.4%	1.5%
Female	19.1%	5.2%	4.7%	4.2%	15.2%	2.0%

Capabilities
Effective military and security organisations remain largely absent in the wake of violence in 2013 and the armed forces remain unable to fully address the country's internal-security challenges. Under the National Recovery and Peacebuilding Plan 2017–21, attempts to improve security have focused on disarmament, demobilisation and reintegration and security sector reform. The UN's MINUSCA mission remains the principal security provider in the country but has been targeted by armed groups. The UN reported that, for the first time, anti-personnel mines were discovered (and destroyed) in the country. Russia has deepened its military ties in the CAR and has donated small arms and armoured vehicles and dispatched teams of military instructors. Russian private military contractors (PMCs) are also active in the country. Apart from some equipment deliveries, the country remains under a UN arms embargo, though the terms of this were eased in late 2019. The armed forces have received training from UN forces and an EU training mission, though the EU suspended its operational training in 2021, because of concerns related to the presence of Russian PMCs. France withdrew its logistics deployment in November 2022, after suspending military cooperation with the CAR in 2021. Poor infrastructure and logistics capacity limit the armed forces' ability to provide security across the country. There is no independent capability to deploy troops externally, while the lack of financial resources and defence-industrial capacity makes equipment maintenance problematic.

ACTIVE 9,150 (Army 9,000 Air 150) Gendarmerie & Paramilitary 1,000

Conscript liability Selective conscription 2 years; reserve obligation thereafter, term n.k.

ORGANISATIONS BY SERVICE

Army ε9,000
FORCES BY ROLE
MANOEUVRE
  Light
  1 spec ops bn
  7 inf bn
  Amphibious
  1 amph coy
EQUIPMENT BY TYPE
ARMOURED FIGHTING VEHICLES
  MBT 3 T-55†
  RECCE 28: 8 *Ferret*†; 20 BRDM-2
  IFV 18 *Ratel*
  APC • APC (W) 14+: 4 BTR-152†; 10+ VAB†
  AUV *Cobra* (reported)
ARTILLERY • MOR 12+: 81mm†; 120mm 12 M-1943†
ANTI-TANK/ANTI-INFRASTRUCTURE
  RCL 106mm 14 M40†
PATROL AND COASTAL COMBATANTS • PBR 9†

Air Force 150
EQUIPMENT BY TYPE
AIRCRAFT • TPT 6: **Medium** (1 C-130A *Hercules* in store); **Light** 6: 3 BN-2 *Islander*; 1 Cessna 172RJ *Skyhawk*; 2 J.300 *Joker*
HELICOPTERS
  ATK 1 Mi-24V *Hind* E
  MRH some SA341B *Gazelle*
  TPT 2: **Medium** 1 Mi-8T *Hip*; **Light** 1 AS350 *Ecureuil*

FOREIGN FORCES

MINUSCA unless stated
Argentina 2
Bangladesh 1,382; 1 cdo coy; 1 inf bn; 1 med coy; 1 hel coy
Benin 6
Bhutan 6
Bolivia 7
Brazil 10 • EUTM RCA 6
Burkina Faso 11
Burundi 766; 1 inf bn
Cambodia 225; 1 engr coy
Cameroon 758; 1 inf bn
Colombia 2
Congo 10
Côte d'Ivoire 2
Czech Republic 3
Ecuador 2
Egypt 1,025; 1 inf bn; 1 tpt coy
France 5 • EUTM RCA 13
Gabon 4
Gambia 10
Georgia EUTM RCA 35
Ghana 13
Guatemala 4
Indonesia 241; 1 engr coy
Jordan 10
Kenya 15
Lithuania EUTM RCA 1
Macedonia, North EUTM RCA 1
Mauritania 464; 1 inf bn(-)
Mexico 2
Moldova 4
Morocco 777; 1 inf bn
Nepal 835; 1 inf bn; 1 MP pl
Niger 6
Nigeria 6
Pakistan 1,310; 1 inf bn; 2 engr coy; 1 hel sqn
Paraguay 4
Peru 235; 1 engr coy
Philippines 3
Poland EUTM RCA 2
Portugal 196; 1 AB coy • EUTM RCA 14
Romania EUTM RCA 20
Russia 14
Rwanda 2,148; 2 inf bn; 1 fd hospital
Senegal 191; 1 inf coy
Serbia 78; 1 med coy • EUTM RCA 7
Sierra Leone 7
Slovakia EUTM RCA 2
Spain EUTM RCA 8
Sri Lanka 112; 1 hel sqn
Tanzania 457; 1 inf bn(-)
Togo 10
Tunisia 324; 1 inf coy; 1 hel sqn with 3 Bell 205
United States 10
Uruguay 3
Vietnam 9
Zambia 930; 1 inf bn
Zimbabwe 3

Chad CHA

CFA Franc BEAC XAF		2021	2022	2023
GDP	XAF	6.54tr	7.62tr	
	USD	11.8bn	12.9bn	
per capita	USD	697	743	
Growth	%	-1.1	3.3	
Inflation	%	-0.8	4.9	
Def bdgt	XAF	159bn	152bn	
	USD	286m	259m	
USD1=XAF		554.24	588.59	

Real-terms defence budget trend (USDm, constant 2015)

Population 17,963,211

Age	0–14	15–19	20–24	25–29	30–64	65 plus
Male	23.6%	5.7%	4.5%	3.5%	11.2%	1.1%
Female	23.0%	5.6%	4.5%	3.5%	12.4%	1.4%

Capabilities

Chad's principal security concerns relate to instability in West Africa and the Sahel and counter-insurgency operations against Boko Haram in the Lake Chad Basin area. Although the armed forces are combat experienced, some observers judge that improvements are required in strategy and doctrine, and command and control. The country is a key contributor to the G5 Sahel and is an important component of the Multinational Joint Task Force fighting Islamist terrorist groups. There is close defence cooperation with France, which has military forces headquartered in N'Djamena. French forces also contribute to the training of some elements of the Chadian military and security forces. Chadian military skills are widely recognised by partners, though training levels are not uniform across the force. After the death of President Idriss Déby in 2021, his son became the leader of an interim administration. This body passed reform plans for the armed forces, which if implemented would increase the size of the army. However, this is now dependent on the transitional council. A lack of logistical capacity has hindered routine rotations for deployed forces. In recent years, ISR capability has been boosted by the donation of aircraft from the US, with earlier improvements in Chadian ground-attack and medium-airlift capability. Apart from maintenance facilities, there is no domestic defence-industrial capacity.

ACTIVE 33,250 (Army 27,500 Air 350 State Security Service 5,400) **Gendarmerie & Paramilitary 11,900**
Conscript liability Conscription authorised

ORGANISATIONS BY SERVICE

Army ε27,500
7 Mil Regions
FORCES BY ROLE
MANOEUVRE
  Armoured
  1 armd bn

Light
7 inf bn
COMBAT SUPPORT
1 arty bn
1 engr bn
1 sigs bn
COMBAT SERVICE SUPPORT
1 log gp
EQUIPMENT BY TYPE
Includes DGSSIE equipment
ARMOURED FIGHTING VEHICLES
MBT 74: 60 T-55; 14 ZTZ-59G
ASLT ε20 PTL-02 *Assaulter*
RECCE 265: 132 AML-60/-90; ε100 BRDM-2; 20 EE-9 *Cascavel*; 9 ERC-90D *Sagaie*; 4 ERC-90F *Sagaie*
IFV 131: 80 BMP-1; 42 BMP-1U; 9 LAV-150 *Commando* with 90mm gun
APC 149
  APC (W) 103: 4+ *Bastion* APC; 24 BTR-80; 12 BTR-3E; ε20 BTR-60; ε10 *Black Scorpion*; 25 VAB-VTT; 8 WZ-523
  PPV 46: 20 *Ejder Yalcin*; 6+ KrAZ *Cougar*; 20 Proforce *Ara* 2
  AUV 103+: 22 *Bastion Patsas*; 31+ RAM Mk3; 30 *Terrier* LT-79; *Tiger* 4×4; ε20 *Yoruk* 4×4
ARTILLERY 34+
SP 122mm 10 2S1 *Gvozdika*
TOWED 13: **105mm** 5 M2; **122mm** 8+ D-74
MRL 11+: **107mm** some PH-63; **122mm** 11: 6 BM-21 *Grad*; 5 PHL-81
MOR 81mm some; **120mm** AM-50
ANTI-TANK/ANTI-INFRASTRUCTURE
MSL • MANPATS *Eryx*; *Milan*
RCL 106mm M40A1
AIR DEFENCE
SAM
  Short-range 4 2K12 *Kub* (RS-SA-6 *Gainful*)
  Point-defence 9K310 *Igla*-1 (RS-SA-16 *Gimlet*)
GUNS
  SP 10: **23mm** 6 ZSU-23-4 *Shilka*; **37mm** 4+ M-1939 (tch)
  TOWED 14.5mm ZPU-1/-2/-4; **23mm** ZU-23-2

Air Force 350

FORCES BY ROLE
GROUND ATTACK
1 unit with PC-7; PC-9*; SF-260WL *Warrior**; Su-25 *Frogfoot*
TRANSPORT
1 sqn with An-26 *Curl*; C-130H-30 *Hercules*; Mi-17 *Hip* H; Mi-171
1 (Presidential) Flt with B-737BBJ; Beech 1900; DC-9-87; Gulfstream II
ATTACK HELICOPTER
1 sqn with AS550C *Fennec*; Mi-24V *Hind*; SA316 *Alouette* III
MANOEUVRE
Other
1 sy bn
EQUIPMENT BY TYPE
AIRCRAFT 10 combat capable
FTR (1 MiG-29S *Fulcrum* C in store)
ATK 7: 6 Su-25 *Frogfoot* (2 more in store); 1 Su-25UB *Frogfoot* B (1 more in store)

ISR 2 Cessna 208B *Grand Caravan*
TPT 10: **Medium** 3: 2 C-27J *Spartan*; 1 C-130H-30 *Hercules*; **Light** 4: 3 An-26 *Curl*; 1 Beech 1900; **PAX** 3: 1 B-737BBJ; 1 DC-9-87; 1 Gulfstream II
TRG 4: 2 PC-7 (only 1*); 1 PC-9 *Turbo Trainer**; 1 SF-260WL *Warrior**
HELICOPTERS
ATK 5 Mi-24V *Hind*
MRH 8: 3 AS550C *Fennec*; 3 Mi-17 *Hip* H; 2 SA316
TPT • Medium 2 Mi-171

State Security Service General Direction (DGSSIE) 5,400

Gendarmerie & Paramilitary 11,900 active

Gendarmerie 4,500

National and Nomadic Guard (GNNT) 7,400

Police Mobile Intervention Group (GMIP)

DEPLOYMENT

MALI: UN • MINUSMA 1,449; 1 spec ops coy; 2 inf bn
WESTERN SAHARA: UN • MINURSO 4

FOREIGN FORCES

Benin MNJTF 150
France 1,500; 1 mech inf BG; 1 FGA det with 3 *Mirage* 2000D; 1 tkr/tpt det with 1 A330 MRTT 1 C-130H; 2 CN235M

Congo, Republic of COG

CFA Franc BEAC XAF		2021	2022	2023
GDP	XAF	7.01tr	8.98tr	
	USD	12.6bn	14.5bn	
per capita	USD	2,634	2,945	
Growth	%	-0.6	4.3	
Inflation	%	2.0	3.5	
Def bdgt	XAF	174bn	164bn	173bn
	USD	313m	264m	
USD1=XAF		554.25	619.62	

Real-terms defence budget trend (USDm, constant 2015)

Population 5,546,307

Age	0–14	15–19	20–24	25–29	30–64	65 plus
Male	20.6%	5.0%	3.9%	3.5%	15.5%	1.5%
Female	20.2%	5.0%	3.9%	3.6%	15.4%	1.8%

Capabilities

Congo's small armed forces have low levels of training and limited overall capability and utilise ageing equipment. They have struggled to recover from the brief but devastating civil war in the late 1990s. France provides advisory assistance and capacity-building support in military administration and military and police capability. A military-cooperation agreement was signed with Russia in 2019. Deployment capability is limited to neighbouring countries without external support. The air force is effectively grounded for lack of spares and serviceable equipment. The navy is largely a riverine force, despite the need for maritime security on the country's small coastline. A modernisation effort is under way and several MRAPs have been bought. Maintenance facilities are limited and the country has no domestic defence-industrial capability.

ACTIVE 10,000 (Army 8,000 Navy 800 Air 1,200)
Gendarmerie & Paramilitary 2,000

ORGANISATIONS BY SERVICE

Army 8,000
FORCES BY ROLE
MANOEUVRE
  Armoured
    2 armd bn
  Light
    2 inf bn (gp) each with (1 lt tk tp, 1 arty bty)
    1 inf bn
  Air Manoeuvre
    1 cdo/AB bn
COMBAT SUPPORT
  1 arty gp (with MRL)
  1 engr bn
EQUIPMENT BY TYPE†
ARMOURED FIGHTING VEHICLES
  MBT 40: 25 T-54/T-55; 15 Type-59; (some T-34 in store)
  LT TK 13: 3 PT-76; 10 Type-62
  RECCE 25 BRDM-1/BRDM-2
  APC 133+
    APC (W) 78+: 28 AT-105 *Saxon*; 20 BTR-152; 30 BTR-60; Panhard M3
    PPV 55: 18 *Mamba*; 37 *Marauder*
ARTILLERY 56+
  SP 122mm 3 2S1 *Gvozdika*
  TOWED 15+: **122mm** 10 D-30; **130mm** 5 M-46; **152mm** D-20
  MRL 10+: **122mm** 10 BM-21 *Grad*; **140mm** BM-14; **140mm** BM-16
  MOR 28+: **82mm**; **120mm** 28 M-43
ANTI-TANK/ANTI-INFRASTRUCTURE
  RCL 57mm M18
  GUNS 15: **57mm** 5 ZIS-2 (M-1943); **100mm** 10 M-1944
AIR DEFENCE • GUNS
  SP 23mm ZSU-23-4 *Shilka*
  TOWED 14.5mm ZPU-2/-4; **37mm** 28 M-1939; **57mm** S-60; **100mm** KS-19

Navy ε800
EQUIPMENT BY TYPE
PATROL AND COASTAL COMBATANTS 8
  PCC 4 *5 Février 1979*
  PBR 4

Air Force 1,200
FORCES BY ROLE
FIGHTER/GROUND ATTACK
  1 sqn with *Mirage* F-1AZ
TRANSPORT
  1 sqn with An-24 *Coke*; An-32 *Cline*; CN235M-100
EQUIPMENT BY TYPE†
AIRCRAFT 3 combat capable
  FGA up to 3 *Mirage* F-1AZ
  TPT • Light 4: 1 An-24 *Coke*; 2 An-32 *Cline*; 1 CN235M-100
HELICOPTERS
  ATK (2 Mi-35P *Hind* in store)
  TPT • Medium (3 Mi-8 *Hip* in store)
AIR-LAUNCHED MISSILES • AAM • IR R-3 (RS-AA-2 *Atoll*)‡

Gendarmerie & Paramilitary 2,000 active

Gendarmerie 2,000
FORCES BY ROLE
MANOEUVRE
  Other
    20 paramilitary coy

Presidential Guard some
FORCES BY ROLE
MANOEUVRE
  Other
    1 paramilitary bn

DEPLOYMENT

CENTRAL AFRICAN REPUBLIC: UN • MINUSCA 10

Côte d'Ivoire CIV

CFA Franc BCEAO XOF		2021	2022	2023
GDP	XOF	38.8tr	42.6tr	
	USD	70.1bn	68.6bn	
per capita	USD	2,534	2,418	
Growth	%	7.0	5.5	
Inflation	%	4.2	5.5	
Def bdgt [a]	XOF	354bn	379bn	
	USD	638m	610m	
USD1=XOF		554.24	620.60	

[a] Defence budget only - order and security expenses excluded

Real-terms defence budget trend (USDm, constant 2015)

613
336
2008 — 2015 — 2022

Population	28,713,423

Age	0–14	15–19	20–24	25–29	30–64	65 plus
Male	18.7%	5.6%	4.7%	4.1%	15.7%	1.3%
Female	18.6%	5.6%	4.7%	4.1%	15.2%	1.6%

Capabilities

The armed forces are still regenerating and security sector reform initiatives continue. Deteriorating security in the north raises requirements relating to regional cooperation, notwithstanding tensions with Malian leaders. A 2015 law detailed defence zones and military regions and stressed the armed forces' role in assisting societal development. The Military Programme Law (LPM) for 2016–20 outlined plans to reduce military strength, though the outcome remains unclear. The 2021–25 National Development Plan indicated that efforts have been made also to improve housing allowances for paramilitary personnel. The authorities have standardised promotion and salary structures and are also looking to improve military infrastructure. The armed forces have also received new APCs and PPVs, as well as a former French patrol boat. There is close defence cooperation with France, which has a significant training mission in the country, and a new training facility, built with French assistance, was opened in 2022. The armed-forces school at Zambakro runs courses for Ivorian as well as regional personnel, and the second Higher Defence Studies course graduated in late 2021 with personnel from across the region. In 2021, with French assistance, Côte d'Ivoire opened the International Academy for the Fight Against Terrorism (AILCT) in Abidjan, to help develop regional as well as Ivorian counter-terrorist capability; aspects of the US-led *Flintlock* 2022 exercise were held there. Except for limited maintenance facilities, there is no domestic defence-industrial capability.

ACTIVE 27,400 (Army 23,000 Navy 1,000 Air 1,400 Special Forces 2,000) **Gendarmerie & Paramilitary n.k.**

Moves to restructure and reform the armed forces continue

ORGANISATIONS BY SERVICE

Army ε23,000

FORCES BY ROLE
MANOEUVRE
Armoured
1 armd bn
Light
7 inf bn
Air Manoeuvre
1 cdo/AB bn
COMBAT SUPPORT
1 arty bn
1 engr bn
COMBAT SERVICE SUPPORT
1 log bn
AIR DEFENCE
1 AD bn

EQUIPMENT BY TYPE
ARMOURED FIGHTING VEHICLES
MBT 10 T-55†
RECCE 18: 13 BRDM-2; 5 *Cayman* BRDM
IFV 10 BMP-1/BMP-2†
APC 78
    APC (W) 56: 9 *Bastion* APC; 6 BTR-80; 12 Panhard M3; 13 VAB; 16 WZ-551
    PPV 22: 21 *Springbuck* HD; 1 *Snake*
AUV 20 *Cobra* II
ENGINEERING & MAINTENANCE VEHICLES
VLB MTU
ANTI-TANK/ANTI-INFRASTRUCTURE
MSL • MANPATS 9K111-1 *Konkurs* (RS-AT-5 *Spandrel*) (reported); 9K135 *Kornet* (RS-AT-14 *Spriggan*) (reported)
RCL 106mm ε12 M40A1
ARTILLERY 36+
TOWED 4+: **105mm** 4 M-1950; **122mm** (reported)
MRL 122mm 6 BM-21
MOR 26+: **81mm**; **82mm** 10 M-37; **120mm** 16 AM-50
AIRCRAFT • TPT • Medium 1 An-12 *Cub*†
AIR DEFENCE
SAM • Point-defence 9K32 *Strela*-2 (RS-SA-7 *Grail*)‡ (reported)
GUNS 21+
    SP 20mm 6 M3 VDAA
    TOWED 15+: **20mm** 10; **23mm** ZU-23-2; **40mm** 5 L/60

Navy ε1,000

EQUIPMENT BY TYPE
PATROL AND COASTAL COMBATANTS 4
PB 4: 3 *L'Emergence*; 1 *Atchan* 2
AMPHIBIOUS • LANDING CRAFT 1
LCM 1 *Aby*

Air Force ε1,400

EQUIPMENT BY TYPE†
AIRCRAFT
TPT 3: **Light** 2: 1 An-26 *Curl*; 1 C295W; **PAX** 1 B-727
HELICOPTERS
ATK 3 Mi-24V *Hind* E
MRH 2 Mi-8P *Hip*
TPT • Medium 2 SA330L *Puma* (IAR-330L)

Special Forces ε2,000

FORCES BY ROLE
SPECIAL FORCES
 1 spec ops bde
EQUIPMENT BY TYPE
ARMOURED FIGHTING VEHICLES
 APC 16
  APC (W) 3 BTR-70MB
  PPV 13 BATT UMG

Gendarmerie & Paramilitary n.k.

Republican Guard n.k.

Gendarmerie n.k.

EQUIPMENT BY TYPE†
ARMOURED FIGHTING VEHICLES
 RECCE 3 *Cayman* BRDM
 IFV BMP-1
 APC
  APC (W) BTR-70MB; VAB
  PPV 5+ RG-31 *Nyala*; 5+ *Springbuck* HD; Streit *Spartan*
 AUV LT-79 *Terrier*
PATROL AND COASTAL COMBATANTS • PB 1 *Bian*

DEPLOYMENT

CENTRAL AFRICAN REPUBLIC: UN • MINUSCA 2
MALI: UN • MINUSMA 872; 1 mech inf bn; 1 sy coy

FOREIGN FORCES

France 900; 1 inf bn; 1 (army) hel unit with 2 SA330 *Puma*; 2 SA342 *Gazelle*; 1 (air force) hel unit with 1 AS555 *Fennec*

Democratic Republic of the Congo DRC

Congolese Franc CDF		2021	2022	2023
GDP	CDF	113tr	129tr	
	USD	56.6bn	63.9bn	
per capita	USD	603	660	
Growth	%	6.2	6.1	
Inflation	%	9.0	8.4	
Def bdgt	CDF	580bn	752bn	
	USD	291m	372m	
USD1=CDF		1990.17	2025.45	

Real-terms defence budget trend (USDm, constant 2015)

Population 108,407,721

Age	0–14	15–19	20–24	25–29	30–64	65 plus
Male	23.2%	5.2%	4.4%	3.9%	12.1%	1.1%
Female	22.9%	5.2%	4.4%	3.9%	12.2%	1.4%

Capabilities

On paper, the DRC has the largest armed forces in Central Africa. However, given the country's size and the poor levels of training, morale and equipment, they are unable to provide security throughout the country. There was renewed fighting in the east in 2022, and as part of peace initiatives led by the East African Community (EAC) an EAC military component began deploying late in the year. When conflict finally abates in the east, significant attention to wide-ranging disarmament, demobilisation and reintegration and security sector reform will be required, to continue the work intermittently undertaken over the past decade. Kinshasa has pursued several military-modernisation programmes, and a new military programme law for 2022-24 was adopted in August. The mandate of the UN's MONUSCO mission was renewed in December 2019 and the UN's Force Intervention Brigade (FIB) remains active in the east. The armed forces have incorporated a number of non-state armed groups. There remains significant scope to improve training, recruitment and retention, and there is foreign assistance in training and capacity-building. Deployment capability is limited and the lack of logistics vehicles significantly reduces transport capacity. The lack of sufficient tactical airlift and helicopters is a brake on military effectiveness and there is some reliance on MONUSCO capabilities, which are also insufficient given the geographical scale of the country. Much of the inventory is in poor repair and, while new equipment has been acquired, the absence of any defence sector apart from limited maintenance capability will also hinder military efficiency.

ACTIVE ε134,250 (Central Staffs ε14,000, Army 103,000 Republican Guard 8,000 Navy 6,700 Air 2,550)

ORGANISATIONS BY SERVICE

Army (Force Terrestre) ε103,000

The DRC has 11 Military Regions. In 2011, all brigades in North and South Kivu provinces were consolidated into 27 new regiments, the latest in a sequence of reorganisations designed to integrate non-state armed groups. The actual combat effectiveness of many formations is doubtful

FORCES BY ROLE
MANOEUVRE
 Light
  6 (integrated) inf bde
  ε3 inf bde (non-integrated)
  27+ inf regt
COMBAT SUPPORT
 1 arty regt
 1 MP bn
EQUIPMENT BY TYPE†
(includes Republican Guard eqpt)
ARMOURED FIGHTING VEHICLES
 MBT 174: 12–17 Type-59; 32 T-55; 25 T-64BV-1; 100 T-72AV
 LT TK 40: 10 PT-76; 30 Type-62
 RECCE up to 50: up to 17 AML-60; 14 AML-90; 19 EE-9 *Cascavel*
 IFV 20 BMP-1
 APC 104+:
  APC (T) 9: 3 BTR-50; 6 MT-LB
  APC (W) 95+: 30–70 BTR-60PB; 58 Panhard M3; 7 TH 390 *Fahd*

ANTI-TANK/ANTI-INFRASTRUCTURE
RCL **57mm** M18; **73mm** SPG-9; **75mm** M20;
106mm M40A1
GUNS **85mm** 10 Type-56 (D-44)
ARTILLERY 726+
SP 16: **122mm** 6 2S1 *Gvozdika*; **152mm** 10 2S3 *Akatsiya*
TOWED 125: **122mm** 77 M-30 (M-1938)/D-30/Type-60;
130mm 42 Type-59 (M-46)/Type-59-I; **152mm** 6 D-20
(reported)
MRL 57+: **107mm** 12 Type-63; **122mm** 24+: 24 BM-21
Grad; some RM-70; **128mm** 6 M-51; **130mm** 3 Type-82;
132mm 12
MOR 528+: **81mm** 100; **82mm** 400; **107mm** M30;
120mm 28: 10 Brandt; 18 other
AIR DEFENCE
SAM • **Point-defence** 9K32 *Strela*-2 (RS-SA-7 *Grail*)‡
GUNS • **TOWED** 64: **14.5mm** 12 ZPU-4; **37mm** 52
M-1939

Republican Guard 8,000

FORCES BY ROLE
MANOEUVRE
Armoured
1 armd regt
Light
3 gd bde
COMBAT SUPPORT
1 arty regt

Navy 6,700 (incl infantry and marines)

EQUIPMENT BY TYPE
PATROL AND COASTAL COMBATANTS 1
PB 1 Type-062 (PRC *Shanghai* II)†

Air Force 2,550

EQUIPMENT BY TYPE
AIRCRAFT 4 combat capable
ATK 4 Su-25 *Frogfoot*
TPT 4: **Medium** 1 C-130H *Hercules*; **Light** 1 An-26 *Curl*;
PAX 2 B-727
HELICOPTERS
ATK 7: 4 Mi-24 *Hind*; 3 Mi-24V *Hind*
TPT • **Medium** 3: 1 AS332L *Super Puma*; 2 Mi-8 *Hip*

Paramilitary

National Police Force
Incl Rapid Intervention Police (National and Provincial)

People's Defence Force

DEPLOYMENT

MOZAMBIQUE: SADC • SAMIM 1

FOREIGN FORCES

All part of MONUSCO unless otherwise specified
Algeria 2
Bangladesh 1,637; 1 inf bn; 1 engr coy; 1 avn coy; 1 hel coy

Belgium 1
Benin 9
Bhutan 2
Bolivia 4
Botswana 2
Brazil 23
Burkina Faso 5
Cameroon 4
Canada (*Operation Crocodile*) 7
China, People's Republic of 233; 1 engr coy; 1 fd hospital
Czech Republic 2
Egypt 11
France 4
Gambia 2
Ghana 19
Guatemala 152; 1 spec ops coy
India 1,891; 2 inf bn; 1 med coy
Indonesia 1,037; 1 inf bn; 1 engr coy
Jordan 11
Kenya 264
Malawi 751; 1 inf bn
Malaysia 6
Mali 4
Mongolia 2
Morocco 926; 1 inf bn; 1 fd hospital
Nepal 1,154; 1 inf bn; 1 engr coy
Niger 5
Nigeria 8
Pakistan 1,974; 2 inf bn; 1 hel sqn with SA330 *Puma*
Paraguay 6
Peru 6
Poland 1
Romania 8
Russia 9
Senegal 6
Sierra Leone 2
South Africa (*Operation Mistral*) 1,183; 1 inf bn; 1 hel sqn
Switzerland 1
Tanzania 849; 1 spec ops coy; 1 inf bn
Tunisia 10
United Kingdom 3
United States 3
Uruguay 819; 1 inf bn; 1 hel sqn
Zambia 7
Zimbabwe 3

Djibouti DJB

Djiboutian Franc DJF		2021	2022	2023
GDP	DJF	599bn	662bn	
	USD	3.37bn	3.73bn	
per capita	USD	3,365	3,666	
Growth	%	4.8	3.6	
Inflation	%	1.2	6.6	
Def exp	DJF	n.k	n.k	
	USD	n.k	n.k	
FMA (US)	USD	5m	6m	6m
USD1=DJF		177.74	177.71	

Population 957,273

Age	0–14	15–19	20–24	25–29	30–64	65 plus
Male	14.5%	4.6%	4.7%	4.5%	15.2%	1.8%
Female	14.4%	4.9%	5.5%	5.8%	21.8%	2.3%

Capabilities

Djibouti's strategic location and relative stability have led a number of foreign states to station forces in the country. The armed forces' main responsibility is internal and border security, as well as counter-insurgency operations. The 2017 defence White Paper highlighted a requirement to modernise key capabilities and while funds remain limited, recent purchases, including armed UAVs from Turkey, highlight some investment in new systems. Djibouti maintains close defence cooperation with France as it hosts its largest foreign military base. The US also operates its Combined Joint Task Force–Horn of Africa from Djibouti. Japan has based forces there for regional counter-piracy missions and the EU and NATO have at various times maintained a presence to support their operations. Djibouti also hosts an Italian base with a focus on anti-piracy activities. China's first overseas military base, including dock facilities, was officially opened in Djibouti in 2017. France and the US provide training assistance. EU NAVFOR Somalia has delivered maritime-security training to the navy and coastguard. Djibouti participates in a number of regional multinational exercises and contributes personnel to the AMISOM mission in Somalia but has limited capacity to independently deploy beyond its territory. Army equipment consists predominantly of older French and Soviet-era equipment. There are some maintenance facilities, but no defence manufacturing sector.

ACTIVE 8,450 (Army 8,000 Navy 200 Air 250)
Gendarmerie & Paramilitary 4,650

ORGANISATIONS BY SERVICE

Army ε8,000

FORCES BY ROLE
4 military districts (Tadjourah, Dikhil, Ali-Sabieh and Obock)
MANOEUVRE
  Mechanised
  1 armd regt (1 recce sqn, 3 armd sqn, 1 (anti-smuggling) sy coy)
  Light
  4 inf regt (3-4 inf coy, 1 spt coy)
  1 rapid reaction regt (4 inf coy, 1 spt coy)

  Other
  1 (Republican Guard) gd regt (1 sy sqn, 1 (close protection) sy sqn, 1 cbt spt sqn (1 recce pl, 1 armd pl, 1 arty pl), 1 spt sqn)
COMBAT SUPPORT
  1 arty regt
  1 demining coy
  1 sigs regt
  1 CIS sect
COMBAT SERVICE SUPPORT
  1 log regt
  1 maint coy
EQUIPMENT BY TYPE
ARMOURED FIGHTING VEHICLES
  ASLT 3+ PTL-02 *Assaulter*
  RECCE 23: 4 AML-60†; 17 AML-90; 2 BRDM-2
  IFV 28: 8 BTR-80A; 16-20 *Ratel*
  APC 67
    APC (W) 30+: 12 BTR-60†; 4+ AT-105 *Saxon*; 14 *Puma*
    PPV 37: 3 *Casspir*; 10 RG-33L; 24 *Puma* M26-15
  AUV 37: 10 *Cougar* 4×4 (one with 90mm gun); 2 CS/VN3B; 10 PKSV; 15 VBL
ANTI-TANK/ANTI-INFRASTRUCTURE
  RCL 106mm 16 M40A1
ARTILLERY 82
  SP 155mm 10 M109L
  TOWED 122mm 9 D-30
  MRL 12: **107mm** 2 PKSV AUV with PH-63; **122mm** 10: 6 (6-tube Toyota Land Cruiser 70 series); 2 (30-tube Iveco 110-16); 2 (30-tube)
  MOR 51: **81mm** 25; **120mm** 26: 20 Brandt; 6 RT-F1
AIR DEFENCE • GUNS 15+
  SP 20mm 5 M693
  TOWED 10: **23mm** 5 ZU-23-2; **40mm** 5 L/70

Navy ε200

EQUIPMENT BY TYPE
PATROL AND COASTAL COMBATANTS 15
  PCC 2 *Adj Ali M Houmed* (NLD Damen Stan Patrol 5009)
  PBF 2 Battalion-17
  PB 11: 1 *Plascoa*†; 1 PRC 27m; 2 Sea Ark 1739; 1 *Swari*†; 6 others
AMPHIBIOUS 2
  LANDING SHIPS • LSM 1 PRC 66m (capacity 6 light tanks)
  LANDING CRAFT • LCT 1 EDIC 700
LOGISTICS AND SUPPORT • AKR 1 *Col. Maj. Ali Gaad* (NLD Damen Stan Lander 5612)

Air Force 250

EQUIPMENT BY TYPE
AIRCRAFT
  TPT • Light 6: 1 Cessna U206G *Stationair*; 1 Cessna 208 *Caravan*; 2 Y-12E; 1 L-410UVP *Turbolet*; 1 MA60
HELICOPTERS
  ATK (2 Mi-35 *Hind* in store)
  MRH 6: 4 AS365 *Dauphin*; 1 Mi-17 *Hip* H; 1 Z-9WE
  TPT 3: **Medium** 1 Mi-8T *Hip*; **Light** 2 AS355F *Ecureuil* II
UNINHABITED AERIAL VEHICLES
  CISR • Medium 2+ *Bayraktar* TB2

BOMBS • Laser-guided MAM-L

Gendarmerie & Paramilitary ε4,650

Gendarmerie 2,000
Ministry of Defence

FORCES BY ROLE
MANOEUVRE
Other
1 paramilitary bn
EQUIPMENT BY TYPE
AFV • AUV 2 CS/VN3B
PATROL AND COASTAL COMBATANTS • PB 1

Coast Guard 150
EQUIPMENT BY TYPE
PATROL AND COASTAL COMBATANTS • PB 11: 2
Khor Angar; 9 other

National Police Force ε2,500
Ministry of Interior

DEPLOYMENT

SOMALIA: AU • ATMIS 900; 1 inf bn

FOREIGN FORCES

China 400: 1 spec ops coy; 1 mne coy; 1 med unit; 2 ZTL-11; 8 ZBL-08; 1 LPD; 1 ESD

France 1,500: 1 SF unit; 1 combined arms regt (2 recce sqn, 2 inf coy, 1 arty bty, 1 engr coy); 1 hel det with 4 SA330 *Puma*; 3 SA342 *Gazelle;* 1 LCM; 1 FGA sqn with 4 *Mirage* 2000-5; 1 SAR/tpt sqn with 1 CN235M; 3 SA330 *Puma*

Italy BMIS 150

Japan 180; 2 P-3C *Orion*

Spain *Operation Atalanta* 60; 1 P-3M *Orion*

United States US Africa Command: 4,000; 1 tpt sqn with C-130H/J-30 *Hercules*; 1 tpt sqn with 12 MV-22B *Osprey*; 2 KC-130J *Hercules*; 1 spec ops sqn with MC-130H; PC-12 (U-28A); 1 CSAR sqn with HH-60G *Pave Hawk*; 1 CISR sqn with MQ-9A *Reaper*; 1 naval air base

Equatorial Guinea EQG

CFA Franc BEAC XAF		2021	2022	2023
GDP	XAF	6.80tr	9.82tr	
	USD	12.3bn	16.9bn	
per capita	USD	8,448	11,264	
Growth	%	-3.2	5.8	
Inflation	%	-0.1	5.1	
Def exp	XAF	n.k	n.k	
	USD	n.k	n.k	
USD1=XAF		554.55	581.83	

Population	1,679,172					
Age	0–14	15–19	20–24	25–29	30–64	65 plus
Male	18.9%	5.6%	4.8%	4.1%	17.5%	2.5%
Female	17.6%	4.7%	3.9%	3.4%	14.7%	2.4%

Capabilities

The army dominates the armed forces, with internal security the principal task. Equatorial Guinea has been trying for several years to modernise its armed forces. French forces based in Gabon sometimes engage in training activities with Equatorial Guinea's armed forces. There is only limited capability for power projection and deployments are limited to neighbouring countries without external support. Recent naval investments include both equipment and onshore-infrastructure improvements at Bata and Malabo, although naval capabilities overall remain limited. An ammunition explosion in early 2021 focused attention on stockpile management. Maritime-security concerns in the Gulf of Guinea have resulted in an increased emphasis on boosting maritime-patrol capacity. There is limited maintenance capacity and no defence-industrial sector.

ACTIVE 1,450 (Army 1,100 Navy 250 Air 100)

ORGANISATIONS BY SERVICE

Army 1,100
FORCES BY ROLE
MANOEUVRE
Light
3 inf bn(-)
EQUIPMENT BY TYPE
ARMOURED FIGHTING VEHICLES
MBT 3 T-55
ASLT 6 PTL-02 *Assaulter*
RECCE 6 BRDM-2
IFV 23: 20 BMP-1; 3 WZ-551 IFV
APC 41
APC (W) 16: 10 BTR-152; 6 WZ-551
PPV 25 *Reva*
AUV Dongfeng *Mengshi*
ANTI-TANK/ANTI-INFRASTRUCTURE
MSL • MANPATS HJ-8
AIR DEFENCE
SAM Point-defence QW-2 (CH-SA-8)
GUNS • SP • 23mm ZU-23-2 (tch)

Navy ε250

EQUIPMENT BY TYPE
PRINCIPAL SURFACE COMBATANTS • FRIGATES 1
  FF 1 *Wele Nzas* with 2 MS-227 *Ogon'* 122mm MRL,
    2 AK630 CIWS, 2 76mm guns
PATROL AND COASTAL COMBATANTS 10
  CORVETTES • FSG 1 *Bata* with 2 *Katran*-M RWS with
    Barrier SSM, 2 AK630 CIWS, 1 76mm gun
  PCC 2 OPV 62
  PBF 2 *Shaldag* II
  PB 5: 1 *Daphne*†; 2 *Estuario de Muni*; 2 *Zhuk*
LOGISTICS AND SUPPORT
  AKRH 1 *Capitán David Eyama Angue Osa* with 1 76mm gun

Air Force 100

EQUIPMENT BY TYPE
AIRCRAFT 4 combat capable
  ATK 4: 2 Su-25 *Frogfoot*; 2 Su-25UB *Frogfoot* B
  TPT 4: **Light** 3: 1 An-32B *Cline*; 2 An-72 *Coaler*; **PAX** 1
    Falcon 900 (VIP)
  TRG 2 L-39C *Albatros*
HELICOPTERS
  ATK 5 Mi-24P/V *Hind*
  MRH 1 Mi-17 *Hip* H
  TPT 4: **Heavy** 1 Mi-26 *Halo*; **Medium** 1 Ka-29 *Helix*;
    Light 2 Enstrom 480

Gendarmerie & Paramilitary

Guardia Civil

FORCES BY ROLE
MANOEUVRE
  Other
    2 paramilitary coy

Coast Guard n.k.

Eritrea ERI

Eritrean Nakfa ERN		2021	2022	2023
GDP	ERN	33.2bn	35.7bn	
	USD	2.20bn	2.37bn	
per capita	USD	611	647	
Growth	%	2.9	2.6	
Inflation	%	6.6	7.4	
Def exp	ERN	n.k	n.k	
	USD	n.k	n.k	
USD1=ERN		15.07	15.08	
Population	6,209,262			

Age	0–14	15–19	20–24	25–29	30–64	65 plus
Male	18.6%	5.8%	4.5%	3.8%	14.8%	1.6%
Female	18.3%	5.8%	4.6%	4.0%	15.6%	2.4%

Capabilities

Eritrea has maintained large armed forces mainly because of its historical conflict with Ethiopia, though the easing of tensions following a 2018 peace agreement may have afforded the armed forces the opportunity to consider restructuring and recapitalisation. The full extent of Eritrea's military involvement in the conflict in the neighbouring Ethiopian province of Tigray remains unclear as does the level of ongoing support and cooperation with the Ethiopian armed forces. However, Eritrean troops were initially deployed over the border in support of Ethiopian government forces in late 2020 and subsequently re-entered the conflict in late 2022, launching a joint offensive against the Tigray Defence Forces. There were reports of mobilisation in late 2022. Maritime insecurity, including piracy, remains a challenge. It appears that the foreign military presence and related facilities at Assab, that had been used to support Gulf states' participation in the Yemen campaign, had been wound down by mid-2021. Eritrea maintains a large army due to mandatory conscription. For some, the term of service is reportedly indefinite, and significant numbers of conscripts have chosen to leave the country or otherwise evade service. These factors likely affect overall military cohesion and effectiveness. Eritrea has demonstrated limited capacity to deploy beyond its immediate borders. The armed forces' inventory primarily comprises outdated Soviet-era systems and modernisation was restricted by the UN arms embargo, until it was lifted in 2018. The arms embargo will have resulted in serviceability issues, notwithstanding allegations of external support. The navy remains capable of only limited coastal-patrol and interception operations. There is some maintenance capability, but no defence-manufacturing sector.

ACTIVE 301,750 (Army 300,000 Navy 1,400 Air 350)
Conscript liability 18 months (4 months mil trg) between ages 18 and 40

RESERVE n.k.

ORGANISATIONS BY SERVICE

Army ε300,000 (including mobilised reserves)

Div mostly bde sized

FORCES BY ROLE
COMMAND
  4 corps HQ
SPECIAL FORCES
  1 cdo div
MANOEUVRE
  Mechanised
  6 mech div
  Light
  ε50 inf div

EQUIPMENT BY TYPE
ARMOURED FIGHTING VEHICLES
  MBT 270 T-54/T-55
  RECCE 40 BRDM-1/BRDM-2
  IFV 15 BMP-1
  APC 35
    APC (T) 10 MT-LB†
    APC (W) 25 BTR-152/BTR-60
ENGINEERING & MAINTENANCE VEHICLES
  ARV T-54/T-55 reported
  VLB MTU reported

ANTI-TANK/ANTI-INFRASTRUCTURE
  MSL • MANPATS 9K11 *Malyutka* (RS-AT-3 *Sagger*); 9K111-1 *Konkurs* (RS-AT-5 *Spandrel*)
  GUNS 85mm D-44
ARTILLERY 258
  SP 45: **122mm** 32 2S1 *Gvozdika*; **152mm** 13 2S5 *Giatsint-S*
  TOWED 19+: **122mm** D-30; **130mm** 19 M-46
  MRL 44: **122mm** 35 BM-21 *Grad*; **220mm** 9 9P140 *Uragan*
  MOR 150+: **82mm** 50+; **120mm/160mm** 100+
AIR DEFENCE
  SAM • **Point-defence** 9K32 *Strela-2* (RS-SA-7 *Grail*)‡
  GUNS 70+
    SP **23mm** ZSU-23-4 *Shilka*
    TOWED **23mm** ZU-23

Navy 1,400
EQUIPMENT BY TYPE
PATROL AND COASTAL COMBATANTS 12
  PBF 9: 5 *Battalion-17*; 4 *Super Dvora*
  PB 3 *Swiftships*
AMPHIBIOUS 3
  LANDING SHIP 2
    LST 2: 1 *Chamo*† (Ministry of Transport); 1 *Ashdod*†
  LANDING CRAFT 1
    LCU 1 T-4† (in harbour service)

Air Force ε350
FORCES BY ROLE
FIGHTER/GROUND ATTACK
  1 sqn with MiG-29/MiG-29SE/MiG-29UB *Fulcrum*
  1 sqn with Su-27/Su-27UBK *Flanker*
TRANSPORT
  1 sqn with Y-12(II)
TRAINING
  1 sqn with L-90 *Redigo*
  1 sqn with MB-339CE*
TRANSPORT HELICOPTER
  1 sqn with Bell 412EP *Twin Huey*
  1 sqn with Mi-17 *Hip H*
EQUIPMENT BY TYPE
AIRCRAFT 14 combat capable
  FTR 8: 4 MiG-29 *Fulcrum*; 2 MiG-29UB *Fulcrum*; 1 Su-27 *Flanker*; 1 Su-27UBK *Flanker*
  FGA 2 MiG-29SE *Fulcrum*
  TPT • **Light** 5: 1 Beech 200 *King Air*; 4 Y-12(II)
  TRG 16+: 8 L-90 *Redigo*; 4 MB-339CE*; 4+ Z-143/Z-242
HELICOPTERS
  MRH 8: 4 Bell 412EP *Twin Huey* (AB-412EP); 4 Mi-17 *Hip H*
AIR-LAUNCHED MISSILES
  AAM • **IR** R-60 (RS-AA-8 *Aphid*); R-73 (RS-AA-11A *Archer*); **IR/SARH** R-27 (RS-AA-10 *Alamo*)

DEPLOYMENT

ETHIOPIA: Tigray: 100,000 (reported)

Ethiopia ETH

Ethiopian Birr ETB		2021	2022	2023
GDP	ETB	4.34tr	5.93tr	
	USD	99.3bn	111bn	
per capita	USD	996	1,098	
Growth	%	6.3	3.8	
Inflation	%	26.8	33.6	
Def bdgt	ETB	16.5bn	84.0bn	
	USD	377m	1.58bn	
USD1=ETB		43.73	53.29	

Real-terms defence budget trend (USDm, constant 2015)

| Population | 113,656,596 |

Age	0–14	15–19	20–24	25–29	30–64	65 plus
Male	19.7%	5.3%	4.5%	3.9%	14.8%	1.6%
Female	19.5%	5.2%	4.5%	4.0%	15.0%	1.9%

Capabilities

Ethiopia's armed forces, among the region's largest and most capable, have been engaged in fighting armed groups in and around the northern province of Tigray since November 2020. Conflict reignited in August 2022 but a peace agreement was signed in November. The conflict has created a humanitarian crisis, and there have been allegations of human-rights violations on all sides. In 2021, the conflict began to involve other ethnic groups in Ethiopia. Other military tasks include countering al-Shabaab (this group conducted a significant incursion in July 2022) and supporting regional security initiatives with deployments to the African Union presence in Somalia and also to the UN mission in South Sudan. The armed forces are experienced by regional standards, with a history of combat operations and international peacekeeping deployments. Personnel numbers have risen after a recruitment campaign, and along with reequipment this has somewhat offset the loss in 2020 of Tigrayan military leaders. The loss of Northern Command bases in the early fighting led to equipment losses though the degree of conflict-related attrition remains unclear. The country's inventory comprises mostly Soviet-era equipment, though surplus stocks have been acquired from China, Hungary, Ukraine and the US. Modern air-defence systems have been purchased from Russia and, in response to the Tigray conflict, armed UAVs have arrived from Turkey, China and reportedly Iran. There is a modest local defence-industrial base, primarily centred on small arms, with some licensed production of light armoured vehicles. There is adequate maintenance capability but only a limited capacity to support advanced platforms.

ACTIVE 503,000 (Army 500,000 Air 3,000)

ORGANISATIONS BY SERVICE

Army ε500,000
Div mostly bde sized
FORCES BY ROLE
SPECIAL FORCES
  1 cdo div

MANOEUVRE
Mechanised
5 mech inf div
Light
ε70 inf div
Other
1 (Republican Guard) gd div
EQUIPMENT BY TYPE
ARMOURED FIGHTING VEHICLES
MBT 220: ε120 T-55/T-62; ε100 T-72B/UA1
RECCE ε50 BRDM-1/BRDM-2
IFV ε20 BMP-1
APC 275+
  APC (T) ε200 ZSD-89
  APC (W) BTR-60; WZ-551
  PPV 75 Gaia *Thunder*
AUV some *Ze'ev*
ENGINEERING & MAINTENANCE VEHICLES
ARV T-54/T-55 ARV reported; 3 BTS-5B
VLB GQL-111; MTU reported
MW *Bozena*
ANTI-TANK/ANTI-INFRASTRUCTURE
MSL • MANPATS 9K11 *Malyutka* (RS-AT-3 *Sagger*); 9K111 *Fagot* (RS-AT-4 *Spigot*); 9K135 *Kornet*-E (RS-AT-14 *Spriggan*)
RCL 82mm B-10; **107mm** B-11
GUNS 85mm D-44
ARTILLERY 450+
SP 10+: 122mm 2S1 *Gvozdika*; **152mm** 10 2S19 *Msta*-S
TOWED 200+: 122mm ε200 D-30/M-30 (M-1938); **130mm** M-46; **155mm** AH2
MRL 20+: 107mm PH-63; **122mm** ε20 BM-21 *Grad*; **300mm** AR-2†
MOR 81mm M1/M29; **82mm** M-1937; **120mm** M-1944
AIR DEFENCE
SAM
  Medium-range ε4 S-75M3 Volkhov (RS-SA-2 *Guideline*)
  Short-range ε4 S-125M1 *Pechora*-M1 (RS-SA-3 *Goa*)
  Point-defence 9K32 *Strela*-2 (RS-SA-7 *Grail*)‡; 9K310 *Igla*-1 (RS-SA-16 *Gimlet*)
SPAAGM 30mm ε6 96K6 *Pantsir*-S1 (RS-SA-22 *Greyhound*)
GUNS
  SP 23mm ZSU-23-4 *Shilka*
  TOWED 23mm ZU-23; **37mm** M-1939; **57mm** S-60

Air Force 3,000
FORCES BY ROLE
FIGHTER/GROUND ATTACK
1 sqn with MiG-23BN/UB *Flogger* H/C
1 sqn with Su-27/Su-27UB *Flanker*
TRANSPORT
1 sqn with An-12 *Cub*; An-26 *Curl*; An-32 *Cline*; C-130B *Hercules*; DHC-6 *Twin Otter*; L-100-30; Yak-40 *Codling* (VIP)
TRAINING
1 sqn with L-39 *Albatros*
1 sqn with G 120TP
ATTACK/TRANSPORT HELICOPTER
2 sqn with Mi-24/Mi-35 *Hind*; Mi-8 *Hip*; Mi-17 *Hip* H; SA316 *Alouette* III
EQUIPMENT BY TYPE
AIRCRAFT 20 combat capable

FTR 11: 8 Su-27 *Flanker*; 3 Su-27UB *Flanker*
FGA 6+ MiG-23BN/UB *Flogger* H/C
ATK 3: 1 Su-25T *Frogfoot*; 2 Su-25UB *Frogfoot*
TPT 14: **Medium** 8: 3 An-12 *Cub*; 2 C-130B *Hercules*; 2 C-130E *Hercules*; 1 L-100-30; **Light** 6: 1 An-26 *Curl*; 1 An-32 *Cline*; 3 DHC-6 *Twin Otter*; 1 Yak-40 *Codling* (VIP)
TRG 24: 12 G 120TP; 12 L-39 *Albatros*
HELICOPTERS
ATK 18: 15 Mi-24 *Hind*; 3 Mi-35 *Hind*
MRH 21: 3 AW139; 6 SA316 *Alouette* III; 12 Mi-8 *Hip*/Mi-17 *Hip* H
UNINHABITED AERIAL VEHICLES
CISR • Heavy some *Wing Loong* I; **Medium** some *Mohajer* 6 (reported); some *Bayraktar* TB2
AIR-LAUNCHED MISSILES
AAM • IR R-3 (RS-AA-2 *Atoll*)‡; R-27ET (RS-AA-10D *Alamo*); R-60 (RS-AA-8 *Aphid*); R-73 (RS-AA-11A *Archer*); **SARH** R-27 (RS-AA-10 *Alamo*)
ASM Kh-25ML (RS-AS-12B *Kegler*); Kh-29T (RS-AS-14B *Kedge*); TL-2 (reported)
BOMBS
TV-guided KAB-500KR

DEPLOYMENT

SOMALIA: AU • ATMIS 4,000; 5 inf bn

SOUTH SUDAN: UN • UNMISS 1,476; 3 inf bn

SUDAN: UN • UNISFA 3

TERRITORY WHERE THE GOVERNMENT DOES NOT EXERCISE EFFECTIVE CONTROL

Political tensions between Prime Minister Abiy Ahmed's federal government and the Tigray People's Liberation Front resulted in the outbreak of open fighting in November 2020 between the newly founded Tigray Defense Forces (TDF) and the Ethiopian National Defense Force. The latter subsequently reinforced by forces from other Ethiopian regions as well as troops from the Eritrean Defence Forces. The conflict has created a humanitarian crisis, and both Tigrayan and government forces and their allies have been subject to allegations of human-rights violations. A humanitarian truce was implemented by the federal government in March 2022, and after a brief resumption of fighting in August, that saw Eritrean forces re-enter the conflict, there was a further ceasefire in November 2022.

Tigray Defense Forces (TDF)
A significant amount of Ethiopian National Defense Force heavy equipment, including long-range rocket and missile artillery, was captured by the TDF early in the conflict. It is unclear how much of this materiel remains in operation.
EQUIPMENT BY TYPE
ARMOURED FIGHTING VEHICLES
MBT T-55; T-62; T-72B
APC
  APC (T) ZSD-89
  APC (W) WZ-551

ARTILLERY
 TOWED 107mm PH-63; 122mm D-30; 130mm M-46; 155mm AH-2
 MRL 122mm BM-21
AIR DEFENCE
 SAM
  Short-range S-125M1 *Pechora*-M1 (RS-SA-3 *Goa*)
  Point-defence 9K310 *Igla*-1 (RS-SA-16 *Gimlet*)
 GUNS
  TOWED 23mm ZU-23; 37mm M-1939

FOREIGN FORCES

Eritrea Army: 100,000 (reported)

Gabon GAB

CFA Franc BEAC XAF		2021	2022	2023
GDP	XAF	11.2tr	13.8tr	
	USD	20.2bn	22.2bn	
per capita	USD	9,483	10,282	
Growth	%	1.5	2.7	
Inflation	%	1.1	3.5	
Def bdgt [a]	XAF	173bn	173bn	
	USD	312m	280m	
USD1=XAF		554.25	619.61	

[a] Includes funds allocated to Republican Guard

Real-terms defence budget trend (USDm, constant 2015)

Population 2,340,613

Age	0–14	15–19	20–24	25–29	30–64	65 plus
Male	18.0%	5.8%	5.4%	5.1%	15.5%	2.1%
Female	17.5%	5.5%	4.9%	4.3%	13.9%	2.0%

Capabilities

Oil revenues have allowed the government to support small but regionally capable armed forces, while the country has benefited from the long-term presence of French troops acting as a security guarantor. There is regular training with French forces, including with France's regionally deployed naval units, as well as with the US and other international partners. There are reports of a developing security relationship with Russia. Gabonese forces have taken part in the US Navy-led *Obangame Express* exercise. A new maritime-operations centre was built by the US in 2019. Military medicine is well regarded. The armed forces retain sufficient airlift to ensure mobility within the country, but very limited capability to project power by sea and air. Apart from limited maintenance facilities, there is no domestic defence-industrial capacity.

ACTIVE 4,700 (Army 3,200 Navy 500 Air 1,000)

Gendarmerie & Paramilitary 2,000

ORGANISATIONS BY SERVICE

Army 3,200
Republican Guard under direct presidential control
FORCES BY ROLE
MANOEUVRE
 Light
 1 (Republican Guard) gd gp (bn)
  (1 armd/recce coy, 3 inf coy, 1 arty bty, 1 ADA bty)
 8 inf coy
 Air Manoeuvre
 1 cdo/AB coy
COMBAT SUPPORT
 1 engr coy
EQUIPMENT BY TYPE
ARMOURED FIGHTING VEHICLES
 RECCE 56: 24 AML-60/AML-90; 12 EE-3 *Jararaca*; 14 EE-9 *Cascavel*; 6 ERC-90F4 *Sagaie*
 IFV 22: 12 EE-11 *Urutu* (with 20mm gun); 10 VN-1
 APC 93
  APC (W) 35: 9 LAV-150 *Commando*; 5 *Bastion* APC; 3 WZ-523; 5 VAB; 12 VXB-170; 1 *Pandur*
  PPV 58: 8 *Aravis*; 34 *Matador*; 16 VP-11
 AUV 17: 3 RAM Mk3; 14 VBL
ANTI-TANK/ANTI-INFRASTRUCTURE
 MSL • MANPATS *Milan*
 RCL 106mm M40A1
ARTILLERY 67
 TOWED 105mm 4 M101
 MRL 24: 107mm 16 PH-63; 140mm 8 *Teruel*
 MOR 39: 81mm 35; 120mm 4 Brandt
AIR DEFENCE • GUNS 41
 SP 20mm 4 ERC-20
 TOWED 37+: 14.5mm ZPU-4; 23mm 24 ZU-23-2; 37mm 10 M-1939; 40mm 3 L/70

Navy ε500
HQ located at Port Gentil
EQUIPMENT BY TYPE
PATROL AND COASTAL COMBATANTS 10
 PB 10: 1 *Patra*†; 4 *Port Gentil* (FRA VCSM); 4 Rodman 66; 1 *Vice Amiral d'Escadre Jean Léonard Mbini* (PRC 66m)
AMPHIBIOUS • LANDING CRAFT 1
 LCM 1 Mk 9 (ex-UK)

Air Force 1,000
FORCES BY ROLE
FIGHTER/GROUND ATTACK
 1 sqn with *Mirage* F-1AZ
TRANSPORT
 1 (Republican Guard) sqn with AS332 *Super Puma*; ATR-42F; *Falcon* 900; Gulfstream IV-SP/G650ER
 1 sqn with C-130H *Hercules*; CN-235M-100
ATTACK/TRANSPORT HELICOPTER
 1 sqn with Bell 412 *Twin Huey* (AB-412); SA330C/H *Puma*; SA342M *Gazelle*
EQUIPMENT BY TYPE
AIRCRAFT 8 combat capable
 FGA 6 *Mirage* F-1AZ

454 THE MILITARY BALANCE 2023

MP (1 EMB-111* in store)
TPT 6: **Medium** 1 C-130H *Hercules*; (1 L-100-30 in store);
Light 2: 1 ATR-42F; 1 CN-235M-100; **PAX** 3: 1 *Falcon* 900;
1 Gulfstream IV-SP; 1 Gulfstream G650ER
TRG 2 MB-326 *Impala* I* (4 CM-170 *Magister* in store)
HELICOPTERS
MRH 2: 1 Bell 412 *Twin Huey* (AB-412); 1 SA342M
Gazelle; (2 SA342L *Gazelle* in store)
TPT 7: **Medium** 4: 1 AS332 *Super Puma*; 3 SA330C/H
Puma; **Light** 3: 2 H120 *Colibri*; 1 H135
AIR-LAUNCHED MISSILES • AAM • IR *U-Darter*
(reported)

Gendarmerie & Paramilitary 2,000

Gendarmerie 2,000
FORCES BY ROLE
MANOEUVRE
Armoured
2 armd sqn
Other
3 paramilitary bde
11 paramilitary coy
Aviation
1 unit with AS350 *Ecureuil*; AS355 *Ecureuil* II

EQUIPMENT BY TYPE
HELICOPTERS • TPT • Light 4: 2 AS350 *Ecureuil*;
2 AS355 *Ecureuil* II

DEPLOYMENT

CENTRAL AFRICAN REPUBLIC: UN • MINUSCA 4

FOREIGN FORCES

France 350; 1 inf bn

Gambia GAM

Gambian Dalasi GMD		2021	2022	2023
GDP	GMD	105bn	120bn	
	USD	2.03bn	2.17bn	
per capita	USD	816	846	
Growth	%	4.3	5.0	
Inflation	%	7.4	11.3	
Def bdgt	GMD	834m	777m	
	USD	16.2m	14.1m	
USD1=GMD		51.60	55.07	

Population	2,413,403					

Age	0–14	15–19	20–24	25–29	30–64	65 plus
Male	19.9%	5.7%	4.9%	4.2%	13.3%	1.5%
Female	19.6%	5.6%	4.8%	4.1%	14.5%	1.9%

Capabilities

Reform of Gambia's security structure, and the armed forces, has been a key objective of the security sector reform (SSR) process that was implemented following political instability in 2016–17. The SSR process is supported by UN organisations, the AU, ECOWAS, EU, France, the UK and the US. A National Defence Policy is under development. Gambia's small forces have traditionally focused on maritime security and countering human trafficking. France, Germany, Turkey, the UK and the US have delivered military support in recent years. There is also cooperation with neighbouring states and with the AU, which maintains a technical-support mission to assist in the SSR process, including on defence reform, military reorganisation and the rule of law. The ECOMIG deployment remains in place, with its mandate extended again until the end of 2022. The armed forces participate in some multinational exercises and have deployed in support of UN missions in Africa. The equipment inventory is limited, with serviceability in doubt for some types. An order from Turkey of new APCs was reported in 2022. Gambia has no significant defence-industrial capabilities.

ACTIVE 4,100 (Army 3,500 Navy 300 National Guard 300)

ORGANISATIONS BY SERVICE

Gambian National Army 3,500
FORCES BY ROLE
MANOEUVRE
Light
4 inf bn
COMBAT SUPPORT
1 engr sqn

Air Wing
EQUIPMENT BY TYPE
AIRCRAFT
TPT 5: **Light** 2 AT-802A *Air Tractor*; **PAX** 3: 1 B-727; 1
CL-601; 1 Il-62M *Classic* (VIP)

Gambia Navy 300
EQUIPMENT BY TYPE
PATROL AND COASTAL COMBATANTS 8
PBF 4: 2 Rodman 55; 2 *Fatimah* I
PB 4: 1 *Bolong Kanta†*; 3 *Taipei* (ROC *Hai Ou*) (one
additional damaged and in reserve)

Republican National Guard 300
FORCES BY ROLE
MANOEUVRE
Other
1 gd bn (forming)

DEPLOYMENT

CENTRAL AFRICAN REPUBLIC: UN • MINUSCA 10

DEMOCRATIC REPUBLIC OF THE CONGO: UN •
MONUSCO 2

MALI: UN • MINUSMA 8

SOUTH SUDAN: UN • UNMISS 4

FOREIGN FORCES

Ghana ECOMIG 50
Nigeria ECOMIG 197
Senegal ECOMIG 250

Ghana GHA

Ghanaian New Cedi GHS		2021	2022	2023
GDP	GHS	459bn	589bn	
	USD	79.2bn	76.0bn	
per capita	USD	2,521	2,369	
Growth	%	5.4	3.6	
Inflation	%	10.0	27.2	
Def bdgt	GHS	2.10bn	2.03bn	
	USD	362m	262m	
USD1=GHS		5.80	7.75	

Real-terms defence budget trend (USDm, constant 2015)

Population 33,107,275

Age	0–14	15–19	20–24	25–29	30–64	65 plus
Male	19.2%	5.0%	4.2%	3.7%	14.7%	1.9%
Female	18.8%	4.9%	4.3%	4.0%	16.8%	2.4%

Capabilities

Ghana's armed forces are among the most capable in the region, with a long-term development plan. The ability to control its EEZ is of increasing importance, and this underpins the navy's expansion plans, including the opening of a new forward-operating base. Internal and maritime security are central military tasks, including disaster-response, along with peacekeeping missions abroad. The US delivers training and support and there is also significant and long-standing defence engagement with the UK. Air-force training, close-air support and airlift capabilities have developed in recent years. There are plans to boost training and exercises, as well as to improve military infrastructure. The army is a regular contributor to UN peacekeeping operations. Ghanaian professional military education institutions regularly train personnel from regional states. The development of forward-operating bases continues, with the principal objective of protecting energy resources. There is a limited defence-industrial base, including in maintenance, ammunition manufacturing and, more recently, armoured-vehicle production. The Defence Industries Holding Company was created in 2019 to improve defence industrial capacity.

ACTIVE 15,500 (Army 11,500 Navy 2,000 Air 2,000)

ORGANISATIONS BY SERVICE

Army 11,500
FORCES BY ROLE
COMMAND
  2 comd HQ
MANOEUVRE
  Reconnaissance
  1 armd recce regt (2 recce sqn)
  1 armd recce regt (forming)
  Light
  1 (rapid reaction) mot inf bn
  6 inf bn
  Air Manoeuvre
  2 AB coy
COMBAT SUPPORT
  1 arty regt (1 arty bty, 2 mor bty)
  1 fd engr regt (bn)
  1 sigs regt
  1 sigs sqn
COMBAT SERVICE SUPPORT
  1 log gp
  1 tpt coy
  2 maint coy
  1 med coy
  1 trg bn
EQUIPMENT BY TYPE
ARMOURED FIGHTING VEHICLES
  RECCE 3 EE-9 Cascavel
  IFV 48: 24 Ratel-90; 15 Ratel-20; 4 Piranha 25mm; 5+ Type-05P 25mm
  APC 105
    APC (W) 55+: 46 Piranha; 9+ Type-05P
    PPV 50 Streit Typhoon
  AUV 73 Cobra/Cobra II
ARTILLERY 87+
  TOWED 122mm 6 D-30
  MRL 3+: 107mm Type-63; 122mm 3 Type-81
  MOR 78: 81mm 50; 120mm 28 Tampella
ENGINEERING & MAINTENANCE VEHICLES
  AEV 1 Type-05P AEV
  ARV Piranha reported
ANTI-TANK/ANTI-INFRASTRUCTURE
  RCL 84mm Carl Gustaf
AIR DEFENCE
  SAM • Point-defence 9K32 Strela-2 (RS-SA-7 Grail)‡
  GUNS • TOWED 8+: 14.5mm 4+: 4 ZPU-2; ZPU-4; 23mm 4 ZU-23-2

Navy 2,000
Naval HQ located at Accra; Western HQ located at Sekondi; Eastern HQ located at Tema
EQUIPMENT BY TYPE
PATROL AND COASTAL COMBATANTS 18
  PCO 2 Anzone (US)
  PCC 10: 2 Achimota (GER Lurssen 57m) with 1 76mm gun; 2 Dzata (GER Lurssen 45m); 4 Snake (PRC 47m); 2 Yaa Asantewa (ex-GER Albatros)
  PBF 1 Stephen Otu (ROK Sea Dolphin)
  PB 5: 4 Flex Fighter; 1 David Hansen (US)

Special Boat Squadron
FORCES BY ROLE
SPECIAL FORCES
  1 SF unit

Air Force 2,000
FORCES BY ROLE
GROUND ATTACK
  1 sqn with K-8 Karakorum*

ISR
 1 unit with DA42
TRANSPORT
 1 sqn with BN-2 *Defender*; C295; Cessna 172
TRANSPORT HELICOPTER
 1 sqn with AW109A; Bell 412SP *Twin Huey*; Mi-17V-5 *Hip* H; SA319 *Alouette* III; Z-9EH

EQUIPMENT BY TYPE†
AIRCRAFT 4 combat capable
 ATK (3 MB-326K in store)
 TPT 10: **Light** 10: 1 BN-2 *Defender*; 3 C295; 3 Cessna 172; 3 DA42; (**PAX** 1 F-28 *Fellowship* (VIP) in store)
 TRG 4 K-8 *Karakorum**; (2 L-39ZO*; 2 MB-339A* in store)
HELICOPTERS
 MRH 10: 1 Bell 412SP *Twin Huey*; 3 Mi-17V-5 *Hip* H; 2 SA319 *Alouette* III; 4 Z-9EH
 TPT 6: **Medium** 4 Mi-171Sh; **Light** 2 AW109A

DEPLOYMENT

CENTRAL AFRICAN REPUBLIC: UN • MINUSCA 13
CYPRUS: UN • UNFICYP 1
DEMOCRATIC REPUBLIC OF THE CONGO: UN • MONUSCO 19
GAMBIA: ECOWAS • ECOMIG 50
LEBANON: UN • UNIFIL 874; 1 recce coy; 1 mech inf bn
MALI: UN • MINUSMA 141; 1 engr coy
SOMALIA: UN • UNSOM 1; **UN •** UNSOS 1
SOUTH SUDAN: UN • UNMISS 725; 1 inf bn
SUDAN: UN • UNISFA 656; 1 inf bn; 1 fd hosptial
SYRIA/ISRAEL: UN • UNDOF 6
WESTERN SAHARA: UN • MINURSO 16

Guinea GUI

Guinean Franc GNF		2021	2022	2023
GDP	GNF	157tr	185tr	
	USD	16.1bn	19.7bn	
per capita	USD	1,128	1,346	
Growth	%	3.8	4.6	
Inflation	%	12.6	12.7	
Def bdgt	GNF	2.41tr	3.06tr	
	USD	247m	327m	
USD1=GNF		9729.04	9365.60	

Population 13,237,832

Age	0–14	15–19	20–24	25–29	30–64	65 plus
Male	20.7%	5.2%	4.5%	3.7%	14.0%	1.8%
Female	20.3%	5.2%	4.5%	3.7%	14.2%	2.2%

Capabilities

Guinea's armed forces remain limited in size and conventional capacity. Special-forces troops toppled the government of former president Alpha Condé in September 2021, with their leader sworn in as interim president a month later. ECOWAS has sanctioned the new leadership and called for elections within six months, which so far have not occurred. Guinea's new leaders have discussed a far longer transition period. Before the coup, there had been plans since 2010 to bring the armed forces under political control and begin a professionalisation process. Piracy in the Gulf of Guinea is a key concern, as is illegal trafficking and fishing. A military-programme law for the period 2015–20 was not fully implemented due to funding issues. Defence cooperation in recent years with France and the US has led to financial and training assistance, including for personnel earmarked for deployment to Mali. Much of the country's military equipment is ageing and of Soviet-era vintage; serviceability will be questionable for some types. There is limited organic airlift and France was in recent years supporting the development of a light aviation observation capability. Guinea is also attempting to improve its logistics and military-health capacities. There are no significant defence-industrial capabilities.

ACTIVE 9,700 (Army 8,500 Navy 400 Air 800)
Gendarmerie & Paramilitary 2,600
Conscript liability 9–12 months (students, before graduation)

ORGANISATIONS BY SERVICE

Army 8,500
FORCES BY ROLE
MANOEUVRE
 Armoured
  1 armd bn
 Light
  1 SF bn
  5 inf bn
  1 ranger bn
  1 cdo bn
 Air Manoeuvre
  1 air mob bn
 Other
  1 (Presidential Guard) gd bn
COMBAT SUPPORT
 1 arty bn
 1 AD bn
 1 engr bn
EQUIPMENT BY TYPE
ARMOURED FIGHTING VEHICLES
 MBT 38: 30 T-34; 8 T-54
 LT TK 15 PT-76
 RECCE 27: 2 AML-90; 25 BRDM-1/BRDM-2
 IFV 2 BMP-1
 APC 59
  APC (T) 10 BTR-50
  APC (W) 30: 16 BTR-40; 8 BTR-60; 6 BTR-152
  PPV 19: 10 *Mamba*†; some *Puma* M26-15; 9 *Puma* M36
 AUV Dongfeng *Mengshi*
ENGINEERING & MAINTENANCE VEHICLES
 ARV T-54/T-55 reported
ANTI-TANK/ANTI-INFRASTRUCTURE

MSL • **MANPATS** 9K11 *Malyutka* (RS-AT-3 *Sagger*); 9K111-1 *Konkurs* (RS-AT-5 *Spandrel*)
RCL 82mm B-10
GUNS 6+: **57mm** ZIS-2 (M-1943); **85mm** 6 D-44
ARTILLERY 47+
  TOWED 24: **122mm** 12 M-1931/37; **130mm** 12 M-46
  MRL 220mm 3 9P140 *Uragan*
  MOR 20+: **82mm** M-43; **120mm** 20 M-1938/M-1943
AIR DEFENCE
  SAM • **Point-defence** 9K32 *Strela-*2 (RS-SA-7 *Grail*)‡
  GUNS • **TOWED** 24+: **30mm** M-53 (twin); **37mm** 8 M-1939; **57mm** 12 Type-59 (S-60); **100mm** 4 KS-19

Navy ε400
EQUIPMENT BY TYPE
PATROL AND COASTAL COMBATANTS 4
  PB 4: 1 *Swiftships 77*; 3 *RPB 20*

Air Force 800
FORCES BY ROLE
ISR
  1 sqn with *Tetras* (observation)
EQUIPMENT BY TYPE†
AIRCRAFT
  FGA (2 MiG-21bis *Fishbed* L; 1 MiG-21UM *Mongol* B in store)
  TPT • **Light** 4 *Tetras* (observation)
HELICOPTERS
  ATK 4 Mi-24 *Hind*
  MRH 5: 2 MD-500MD; 2 Mi-17-1V *Hip* H; 1 SA342K *Gazelle*
  TPT 2: **Medium** 1 SA330 *Puma*; **Light** 1 AS350B *Ecureuil*
AIR-LAUNCHED MISSILES
  AAM • **IR** R-3 (RS-AA-2 *Atoll*)‡

Gendarmerie & Paramilitary 2,600 active

Gendarmerie 1,000

Republican Guard 1,600

People's Militia 7,000 reservists

DEPLOYMENT
MALI: UN • MINUSMA 667; 1 mech inf bn
SOUTH SUDAN: UN • UNMISS 3
SUDAN: UN • UNISFA 1
WESTERN SAHARA: UN • MINURSO 5

Guinea-Bissau GNB

CFA Franc BCEAO XOF		2021	2022	2023
GDP	XOF	944bn	1.01tr	
	USD	1.70bn	1.62bn	
per capita	USD	918	857	
Growth	%	5.0	3.8	
Inflation	%	3.3	5.5	
Def bdgt	XOF	n.k	n.k	
	USD	n.k	n.k	
USD1=XOF		554.16	619.79	

Real-terms defence budget trend (USDm, constant 2015)

Population	2,026,778					
Age	0–14	15–19	20–24	25–29	30–64	65 plus
Male	21.5%	5.5%	4.6%	3.7%	12.3%	1.3%
Female	21.3%	5.6%	4.8%	4.1%	13.5%	1.8%

Capabilities

Guinea-Bissau's armed forces have limited capabilities and are in the midst of DDR and SSR programmes. The UN expressed concern about the armed forces' role in politics, following political disputes after the late-2019 election. Defence policy is focused mainly on tackling internal-security challenges, in particular drug trafficking. The ECOWAS and UN missions withdrew before the end of 2020. Training remains limited and there are problems with recruitment and retention, as well as in developing adequate non-commissioned-officer structures. Much of the country's military equipment is ageing and maintenance likely limits military effectiveness. There is no defence-manufacturing sector.

ACTIVE 4,450 (Army 4,000 Navy 350 Air 100)
Conscript liability Selective conscription
Personnel and eqpt totals should be treated with caution. A number of draft laws to restructure the armed services and police have been produced

ORGANISATIONS BY SERVICE

Army ε4,000
FORCES BY ROLE
MANOEUVRE
  Reconnaissance
  1 recce coy
  Armoured
  1 armd bn (sqn)
  Light
  5 inf bn
COMBAT SUPPORT
  1 arty bn
  1 engr coy

EQUIPMENT BY TYPE
ARMOURED FIGHTING VEHICLES
MBT 10 T-34
LT TK 15 PT-76
RECCE 10 BRDM-2
APC • APC (W) 55: 35 BTR-40/BTR-60; 20 Type-56 (BTR-152)
ANTI-TANK/ANTI-INFRASTRUCTURE
RCL 75mm Type-52 (M20); **82mm** B-10
GUNS 85mm 8 D-44
ARTILLERY 26+
TOWED 122mm 18 D-30/M-30 (M-1938)
MOR 8+: **82mm** M-43; **120mm** 8 M-1943
AIR DEFENCE
SAM • Point-defence 9K32 *Strela*-2 (RS-SA-7 *Grail*)‡
GUNS • TOWED 34: **23mm** 18 ZU-23; **37mm** 6 M-1939; **57mm** 10 S-60

Navy ε350

EQUIPMENT BY TYPE
PATROL AND COASTAL COMBATANTS 4
PB 4: 2 *Alfeite*†; 2 Rodman 55m

Air Force 100

EQUIPMENT BY TYPE
AIRCRAFT • TPT • Light 1 Cessna 208B

Kenya KEN

Kenyan Shilling KES		2021	2022	2023
GDP	KES	12.1tr	13.4tr	
	USD	111bn	115bn	
per capita	USD	2,219	2,255	
Growth	%	7.5	5.3	
Inflation	%	6.1	7.4	
Def bdgt [a]	KES	120bn	157bn	
	USD	1.10bn	1.35bn	
USD1=KES		109.47	116.72	

[a] Includes national intelligence funding

Real-terms defence budget trend (USDm, constant 2015)

Population 55,864,655

Age	0–14	15–19	20–24	25–29	30–64	65 plus
Male	18.7%	5.8%	4.8%	3.8%	15.4%	1.5%
Female	18.5%	5.8%	4.8%	3.8%	15.4%	1.7%

Capabilities

The armed forces are concerned with threats to regional stability and tackling security challenges, particularly from neighbouring Somalia, though there is also concern about the possibility of overspill from the conflict in Ethiopia. Kenya deployed forces to the DRC in late 2022 as part of an East African Community deployment, following rising violence in the eastern DRC. A coastguard

service was established in late 2018. The long-standing defence and security agreement with the UK was reaffirmed with a new five-year Defence Cooperation Agreement in 2021, which has included a permanent UK training unit within the country, support for maritime security and a counter-IED training centre. There are strong ties with the US, with the Cooperative Security Location Manda Bay remaining an operational base for AFRICOM. There has also been evidence of developing relationships with the Chinese and Jordanian armed forces. Regular operational deployments have increased military experience and confidence. Kenya has been a key contributor to AMISOM in Somalia, demonstrating limited capacity to project power immediately beyond its own territory. The armed forces also provide smaller contributions to other UN missions and are a leading element of the East African Standby Force. Kenya is the lead-contributor to the November 2022 EAC deployment to the eastern DRC. Kenya's armed forces regularly participate in multinational exercises. Involvement in regional security missions and multinational exercises may also foster improved levels of cooperation and interoperability. Recent equipment investments have focused on improving counter-insurgency capabilities and transport capacity to support regional deployments. There is a limited defence industry focused on equipment maintenance as well as the manufacture of small arms and ammunition.

ACTIVE 24,100 (Army 20,000 Navy 1,600 Air 2,500) **Gendarmerie & Paramilitary 5,000**

ORGANISATIONS BY SERVICE

Army 20,000

FORCES BY ROLE
SPECIAL FORCES
1 spec ops bn
1 ranger regt (1 ranger bn, 1 AB bn)
MANOEUVRE
Armoured
1 armd bde (2 armd recce bn, 2 armd bn)
Mechanised
1 mech inf bde (3 mech inf bn)
Light
3 inf bde (3 inf bn)
COMBAT SUPPORT
1 arty bde (2 arty bn, 1 ADA bn, 1 mor bty)
1 engr bde (2 engr bn)
HELICOPTER
1 air cav bn

EQUIPMENT BY TYPE
ARMOURED FIGHTING VEHICLES
MBT 78 Vickers Mk 3
RECCE 84: 72 AML-60/AML-90; 12 *Ferret*
APC 200
APC (W) 95: 52 UR-416; 31 WZ-551 (incl CP); 12 *Bastion* APC; (10 M3 Panhard in store)
PPV 105 *Puma* M26-15; CS/VP14; *Springbuck*
AUV 2+ BOV M10 (CP)
ENGINEERING & MAINTENANCE VEHICLES
ARV 7 Vickers ARV
MW *Bozena*
ARTILLERY 112
SP 155mm 3+ NORA B-52
TOWED 105mm 47: 40 L118 Light Gun; 7 Model 56 pack howitzer
MOR 62: **81mm** 50; **120mm** 12 Brandt

ANTI-TANK/ANTI-INFRASTRUCTURE
MSL • MANPATS *Milan*
RCL **84mm** *Carl Gustaf*
HELICOPTERS
MRH 42: 2 Hughes 500D†; 12 Hughes 500M†; 10 Hughes 500MD *Scout Defender*† (with TOW); 9 Hughes 500ME†; 6 MD-530F; 3 Z-9W
AIR DEFENCE • GUNS • TOWED 94: **20mm** 81: 11 Oerlikon; ε70 TCM-20; **40mm** 13 L/70
AIR-LAUNCHED MISSILES • ASM TOW

Navy 1,600 (incl 120 marines)
EQUIPMENT BY TYPE
PATROL AND COASTAL COMBATANTS 7
PCO 1 *Jasiri* with 1 AK630 CIWS, 1 76mm gun
PCF 2 *Nyayo*
PCC 3: 1 *Harambee* II (ex-FRA P400); 1 *Shujaa* with 1 76mm gun; 1 *Shujaa*
PBF 1 *Archangel*
AMPHIBIOUS • LANDING CRAFT 2
LCM 2 *Galana*
LOGISTICS AND SUPPORT • AP 2

Air Force 2,500
FORCES BY ROLE
FIGHTER/GROUND ATTACK
2 sqn with F-5E/F *Tiger* II
TRANSPORT
Some sqn with DHC-8†; F-70† (VIP); Y-12(II)†; C-27J *Spartan*; M-28 *Skytruck* (C-145A)
TRAINING
Some sqn with *Bulldog* 103/*Bulldog* 127†; EMB-312 *Tucano*†*
TRANSPORT HELICOPTER
1 sqn with SA330 *Puma*†
EQUIPMENT BY TYPE†
AIRCRAFT 32 combat capable
FTR 21: 17 F-5E *Tiger* II; 4 F-5F *Tiger* II
TPT 16: **Medium** 3 C-27J *Spartan*; **Light** 12: 3 DHC-8†; 2 M-28 *Skytruck* (C-145A); 7 Y-12(II)†; (6 Do-28D-2 in store); **PAX** 1 F-70 (VIP)
TRG 33: 8 *Bulldog* 103/127†; 11 EMB-312 *Tucano*†*; 5 G 120A; 9 G 120TP
HELICOPTERS
ATK 3 AH-1F *Cobra*
MRH 12: 3 AW139; 9 H125M (AS550) *Fennec*
TPT 19: **Medium** 11: 1 Mi-171E; 10 SA330 *Puma*†; **Light** 8 Bell 205 (UH-1H *Huey* II)
AIR-LAUNCHED MISSILES
AAM • IR AIM-9 *Sidewinder*
ASM AGM-65 *Maverick*

Gendarmerie & Paramilitary 5,000

Police General Service Unit 5,000
EQUIPMENT BY TYPE
ARMOURED FIGHTING VEHICLES
APC • PPV 25 CS/VP3
AUV 30: some Streit *Cyclone*; 30 VN-4
PATROL AND COASTAL COMBATANTS 5
PB 5 (2 on Lake Victoria)

Air Wing
EQUIPMENT BY TYPE
AIRCRAFT • TPT • **Light** 6: 2 Cessna 208B *Grand Caravan*; 3 Cessna 310; 1 Cessna 402
HELICOPTERS
MRH 3 Mi-17 *Hip* H
TPT 5: **Medium** 1 Mi-17V-5; **Light** 4: 2 AW139; 1 Bell 206L *Long Ranger*; 1 Bo-105
TRG 1 Bell 47G

Coast Guard
Ministry of Interior
EQUIPMENT BY TYPE
PATROL AND COASTAL COMBATANTS 1
PCC 1 *Doria* with 1 hel landing platform

DEPLOYMENT
CENTRAL AFRICAN REPUBLIC: UN • MINUSCA 15
DEMOCRATIC REPUBLIC OF THE CONGO: UN • MONUSCO 264; 1 inf coy(+)
LEBANON: UN • UNIFIL 3
MALI: UN • MINUSMA 9
SOMALIA: AU • AMISOM 4,000: 3 inf bn; UN • UNSOS 1
SOUTH SUDAN: UN • UNMISS 17
SUDAN: UN • UNISFA 2

FOREIGN FORCES
United Kingdom BATUK 350; 1 trg unit

Lesotho LSO

Lesotho Loti LSL		2021	2022	2023
GDP	LSL	36.6bn	40.4bn	
	USD	2.47bn	2.51bn	
per capita	USD	1,181	1,187	
Growth	%	2.1	2.1	
Inflation	%	6.0	8.1	
Def bdgt	LSL	519m	637m	
	USD	34.9m	39.6m	
USD1=LSL		14.85	16.11	

Real-terms defence budget trend (USDm, constant 2015)

Population   2,193,970

Age	0–14	15–19	20–24	25–29	30–64	65 plus
Male	16.5%	5.3%	4.7%	4.2%	16.6%	2.0%
Female	16.3%	5.2%	4.6%	4.1%	16.9%	3.4%

Capabilities

Lesotho has a small ground force and an air wing for light transport and liaison. It is a SADC member state, and a force from that organisation deployed to the country in late 2017 to support the government following the assassination of the army chief. The mission concluded at the end of November 2018. The Lesotho Defence Force (LDF) is charged with protecting territorial integrity and sovereignty and ensuring internal security. Lesotho's new government has expressed its desire to carry out defence reforms. The armed forces are comprised of volunteers. India has provided training to the LDF since 2001. In April 2020 the army was briefly deployed internally by the prime minister. The armed forces, and military facilities, were also utilised in the country's coronavirus response. There is limited capacity to deploy and sustain missions beyond national borders, though Lesotho deployed personnel to Mozambique in 2021 as part of the SADC mission. Lesotho's limited inventory is obsolescent by modern standards and there is little possibility of significant recapitalisation, although there is an aspiration to acquire light helicopters. Except for limited maintenance capacity, there is no defence-industrial base.

ACTIVE 2,000 (Army 2,000)

ORGANISATIONS BY SERVICE

Army ε2,000
FORCES BY ROLE
MANOEUVRE
  Reconnaissance
  1 recce coy
  Light
  7 inf coy
  Aviation
  1 sqn
COMBAT SUPPORT
  1 arty bty(-)
  1 spt coy (with mor)
EQUIPMENT BY TYPE
ARMOURED FIGHTING VEHICLES
  MBT 1 T-55
  RECCE 6: 4 AML-90; 2 BRDM-2†
  AUV 6 RAM Mk3
ANTI-TANK/ANTI-INFRASTRUCTURE
  RCL 106mm 6 M40
ARTILLERY 12
  TOWED 105mm 2
  MOR 81mm 10

Air Wing 110
AIRCRAFT
  TPT • Light 3: 2 C-212-300 *Aviocar*; 1 GA-8 *Airvan*
HELICOPTERS
  MRH 3: 1 Bell 412 *Twin Huey*; 2 Bell 412EP *Twin Huey*
  TPT • Light 4: 1 Bell 206 *Jet Ranger*; 3 H125
  (AS350) *Ecureuil*

DEPLOYMENT

MOZAMBIQUE: SADC • SAMIM 122

Liberia LBR

Liberian Dollar LRD		2021	2022	2023
GDP	LRD	3.51bn	3.90bn	
	USD	3.51bn	3.90bn	
per capita	USD	677	735	
Growth	%	5.0	3.7	
Inflation	%	7.8	6.9	
Def bdgt	LRD	19.6m	18.7m	
	USD	19.6m	18.7m	
USD1=LRD		1.00	1.00	

Real-terms defence budget trend (USDm, constant 2015)

Population	5,358,483					
Age	0–14	15–19	20–24	25–29	30–64	65 plus
Male	21.7%	5.5%	4.7%	3.6%	13.1%	1.4%
Female	21.2%	5.4%	4.8%	3.7%	13.5%	1.4%

Capabilities

A revised National Security Strategy was produced in 2017, reportedly clarifying the roles of Liberia's security institutions; priorities include improving infrastructure, training, operational readiness and personnel welfare. A new National Security Agency headquarters was opened in 2021. There are plans to establish an air wing; cooperation over potential Nigerian Air Force support for this was discussed in 2022. Coast Guard capabilities are set to increase after the signature, in mid-2022, of a capacity-building agreement with EU organisations, under the auspices of broader EU maritime-security support to ECOWAS states. US military assistance has in recent years focused on areas such as force health, including schemes to improve recruitment and retention, as well as maritime security and military medicine, training and the provision of spare parts. The armed forces are able to deploy and sustain small units, such as to the MINUSMA mission in Mali. The UK has in 2022 engaged in pre-deployment training to support the MINUSMA deployment. Equipment recapitalisation will depend on finances and the development of a supporting force structure but will also be dictated by the armed forces' role in national development objectives. Apart from limited maintenance-support capacities, Liberia has no domestic defence industry capacities.

ACTIVE 2,010 (Army 1,950, Coast Guard 60)

ORGANISATIONS BY SERVICE

Army 1,950
FORCES BY ROLE
MANOEUVRE
  Light
  1 (23rd) inf bde with (2 inf bn, 1 engr coy, 1 MP coy)
COMBAT SERVICE SUPPORT
  1 trg unit (forming)
ARMOURED FIGHTING VEHICLES
  APC • PPV 3+ Streit *Cougar*

Coast Guard 60

All operational patrol vessels under 10t FLD

DEPLOYMENT

MALI: UN • MINUSMA 160; 1 inf coy

SOUTH SUDAN: UN • UNMISS 1

SUDAN: UN • UNISFA 2

Madagascar MDG

Malagsy Ariary MGA		2021	2022	2023
GDP	MGA	54.7tr	62.2tr	
	USD	14.3bn	15.1bn	
per capita	USD	507	522	
Growth	%	4.3	4.2	
Inflation	%	5.8	9.8	
Def bdgt	MGA	390bn	421bn	
	USD	102m	102m	
USD1=MGA		3829.86	4116.04	

Real-terms defence budget trend (USDm, constant 2015)

Population	28,172,462				
Age	0–14	15–19	20–24	25–29	30–64	65 plus
Male	19.1%	5.3%	4.7%	4.2%	15.0%	1.7%
Female	18.8%	5.2%	4.7%	4.2%	15.0%	2.0%

Capabilities

Madagascar's principal defence aspirations include ensuring sovereignty and territorial integrity. Maritime security is also an area of focus. The army is the largest armed service. The armed forces intervened in domestic politics in 2009. Madagascar is a member of the SADC and its regional Standby Force. In 2018, the country signed an 'umbrella defence agreement' with India to explore closer defence ties and an intergovernmental agreement with Russia on military cooperation. This latter agreement was reported to have entered into force in 2022 with reports that it included arms sales, joint development of military equipment and personnel training. China has also embarked on outreach activities to foster better relations with Madagascar. There is no independent capacity to deploy and support operations beyond national borders. The equipment inventory is obsolescent, and with economic development a key government target, equipment recapitalisation is unlikely to be a key priority. A small number of second-hand transport aircraft and helicopters were acquired in 2019, modestly boosting military mobility, with new protected patrol vehicles observed at a parade in 2020.

ACTIVE 13,500 (Army 12,500 Navy 500 Air 500)
Gendarmerie & Paramilitary 8,100
Conscript liability 18 months (incl for civil purposes)

ORGANISATIONS BY SERVICE

Army 12,500+
FORCES BY ROLE
MANOEUVRE
  Light
    2 (intervention) inf regt
    10 (regional) inf regt
COMBAT SUPPORT
  1 arty regt
  3 engr regt
  1 sigs regt
COMBAT SERVICE SUPPORT
  1 log regt
AIR DEFENCE
  1 ADA regt
EQUIPMENT BY TYPE
ARMOURED FIGHTING VEHICLES
  LT TK 12 PT-76
  RECCE 73: ε35 BRDM-2; 10 FV701 *Ferret*; ε20 M3A1; 8 M8
  APC • APC (T) ε30 M3A1 half-track
  AUV 6 *Panthera* T4
ANTI-TANK/ANTI-INFRASTRUCTURE
  RCL 106mm M40A1
ARTILLERY 25+
  TOWED 17: 105mm 5 M101; 122mm 12 D-30
  MOR 8+: 82mm M-37; 120mm 8 M-43
AIR DEFENCE • GUNS • TOWED 70: 14.5mm 50 ZPU-4; 37mm 20 PG-55 (M-1939)

Navy 500 (incl some 100 Marines)
EQUIPMENT BY TYPE
PATROL AND COASTAL COMBATANTS 8
  PCC 1 *Trozona*
  PB 7 (ex-US CG MLB)
AMPHIBIOUS • LCT 1 (ex-FRA EDIC)

Air Force 500
FORCES BY ROLE
TRANSPORT
  1 sqn with An-26 *Curl*; Yak-40 *Codling* (VIP)
  1 (liaison) sqn with Cessna 310; Cessna 337 *Skymaster*; PA-23 *Aztec*
TRAINING
  1 sqn with Cessna 172; J.300 *Joker*; *Tetras*
TRANSPORT HELICOPTER
  1 sqn with SA318C *Alouette* II
EQUIPMENT BY TYPE
AIRCRAFT • TPT 22: Light 20: 1 An-26 *Curl*; 4 Cessna 172; 5 Cessna 206; 1 Cessna 310; 2 Cessna 337 *Skymaster*; 1 CN235M; 2 J.300 *Joker*; 1 PA-23 *Aztec*; 1 *Tetras*; 2 Yak-40 *Codling* (VIP); PAX 2 B-737
HELICOPTERS
  MRH 3 SA318C *Alouette* II
  TPT • Light 4: 3 AS350 *Ecureuil*; 1 BK117

Gendarmerie & Paramilitary 8,100

Gendarmerie 8,100

Malawi MWI

Malawian Kwacha MWK		2021	2022	2023
GDP	MWK	9.60tr	11.2tr	
	USD	12.0bn	11.6bn	
per capita	USD	559	523	
Growth	%	2.2	0.9	
Inflation	%	9.3	18.4	
Def bdgt	MWK	65.8bn	72.1bn	
	USD	82.3m	74.6m	
USD1=MWK		799.67	965.99	

Real-terms defence budget trend (USDm, constant 2015)

Population 20,794,353

Age	0–14	15–19	20–24	25–29	30–64	65 plus
Male	19.5%	5.6%	4.7%	4.0%	13.5%	1.7%
Female	19.8%	5.8%	4.9%	4.2%	14.2%	2.1%

Capabilities

The Malawi Defence Forces (MDF) are constitutionally tasked with ensuring sovereignty and territorial integrity. Additional tasks include providing military assistance to civil authorities and support to the police, and in recent years the army has been used to help with infrastructure development, attempts to control illegal deforestation and the government's coronavirus response. The army is the largest of the armed forces. Counter-trafficking is a role for the MDF's small air force, previously an air wing, and its naval unit. The MDF took delivery in 2022 of two transport aircraft from China, suitable for transporting personnel. Development priorities include improving combat readiness and military medicine and engineering. Malawi is a member of the SADC and its Standby Force. The armed forces have contributed to peacekeeping missions, including in Côte d'Ivoire, the DRC and Mozambique. The UK provided training and support for the deployment to the DRC (to the Force Intervention Brigade), and the UK also supports the MDF's counter-poaching operations. The armed forces have no independent capacity to deploy and support operations beyond national borders.

ACTIVE 10,700 (Army 10,500 Air Force 200)
Gendarmerie & Paramilitary 4,200

ORGANISATIONS BY SERVICE

Army 10,500
FORCES BY ROLE
MANOEUVRE
  Mechanised
  1 mech bn
  Light
  2 inf bde (2 inf bn)
  1 inf bde (1 inf bn)
  Air Manoeuvre
  1 para bn

COMBAT SUPPORT
  3 lt arty bty
  1 engr bn
COMBAT SERVICE SUPPORT
  12 log coy
EQUIPMENT BY TYPE
ARMOURED FIGHTING VEHICLES
  RECCE 58: 30 *Eland-90*; 8 FV701 *Ferret*; 20 FV721 *Fox*
  APC • PPV 31: 14 *Casspir*; 9 *Marauder*; 8 *Puma* M26-15
  AUV 8 RAM Mk3
ARTILLERY 107
  TOWED 105mm 9 L118 Light Gun
  MOR 81mm 98: 82 L16A1; 16 M3
AIR DEFENCE • GUNS • TOWED 72: **12.7mm** 32; **14.5mm** 40 ZPU-4

Navy 220
EQUIPMENT BY TYPE
PATROL AND COASTAL COMBATANTS • PB 3: 1 *Kasungu* (ex-FRA *Antares*)†; 2 *Mutharika* (PRC)

Air Force 200
EQUIPMENT BY TYPE
AIRCRAFT • TPT • Light 3: 1 Do-228; 2 MA600
HELICOPTERS • TPT 8: **Medium** 3: 1 AS532UL *Cougar*; 1 SA330H *Puma*; 1 H215 *Super Puma* **Light** 5: 1 AS350L *Ecureuil*; 4 SA341B *Gazelle*

Gendarmerie & Paramilitary 4,200

Police Mobile Service 4,200
EQUIPMENT BY TYPE
AIRCRAFT
  TPT • Light 4: 3 BN-2T *Defender* (border patrol); 1 SC.7 3M *Skyvan*
HELICOPTERS • MRH 2 AS365 *Dauphin* 2

DEPLOYMENT

DEMOCRATIC REPUBLIC OF THE CONGO: UN • MONUSCO 751; 1 inf bn
MOZAMBQIUE: SADC • SAMIM 2
SOUTH SUDAN: UN • UNMISS 6
SUDAN: UN • UNISFA 4
WESTERN SAHARA: UN • MINURSO 5

Mali MLI

CFA Franc BCEAO XOF		2021	2022	2023
GDP	XOF	10.6tr	11.4tr	
	USD	19.2bn	18.4bn	
per capita	USD	918	858	
Growth	%	3.1	2.5	
Inflation	%	3.8	8.0	
Def bdgt [a]	XOF	474bn	515bn	
	USD	855m	831m	
USD1=XOF		554.23	619.62	

[a] Defence and security budget

Real-terms defence budget trend (USDm, constant 2015)

Population 20,741,769

Age	0–14	15–19	20–24	25–29	30–64	65 plus
Male	23.8%	5.2%	3.9%	3.1%	11.2%	1.5%
Female	23.5%	5.5%	4.5%	3.7%	12.6%	1.5%

Capabilities

The armed forces remain focused on countering rebel and Islamist groups. The two military coups in August 2020 and May 2021 and the policies of Mali's new rulers have accelerated the deterioration of security relationships with Mali's external partners and with neighbouring states. At the same time, the authorities' political and security partnership with Russia has deepened. In May 2022, Mali left the G5 Sahel security partnership. The Russian private military company, Wagner Group, has been present in the country since December 2021 and has been accused of committing war crimes. Following the recent changes in government, France in 2021 suspended joint military operations and in early 2022 accelerated the withdrawal of its forces; authorities in Bamako revoked the 2014 defence cooperation agreement and the 2013 Status of Force Agreement with France. France's *Operation Barkhane* officially withdrew from Mali in August 2022. The EUTM Mali also decided to reduce its training activities. MINUSMA remains, though some contingents left or have reduced in size. The armed forces still suffer from operational deficiencies as well as broader institutional weakness though there were defence-reform plans, including under the 2015–19 military-programming law. Improvements are still required in recruitment and training, as well as in basic administrative support. Despite vehicle deliveries by external partners, and the acquisition of several aircraft from Russia, the armed forces remain under-equipped. Mali does not possess a defence-manufacturing industry and, with limited equipment and maintenance capabilities, equipment serviceability will likely be variable.

ACTIVE 21,000 (Army 19,000 Air Force 2,000)
Gendarmerie & Paramilitary 20,000

ORGANISATIONS BY SERVICE

Army ε19,000

FORCES BY ROLE
The remnants of the pre-conflict Malian army are being reformed into new combined-arms battlegroups, each of which comprises one lt mech coy, three mot inf coy, one arty bty and additional recce, cdo and cbt spt elms
MANOEUVRE
  Light
  9 mot inf bn
  1 inf coy (Special Joint Unit)
  5 inf coy (ULRI)
  Air Manoeuvre
  1 para bn
COMBAT SUPPORT
  1 engr bn
COMBAT SERVICE SUPPORT
  1 med unit

EQUIPMENT BY TYPE
ARMOURED FIGHTING VEHICLES
  LT TK 2+ PT-76
  RECCE 6+ BRDM-2
  IFV 6 VN2C
  APC 232:
    APC (W) 48+: 27 *Bastion* APC; 10+ BTR-60PB; 11 BTR-70
    PPV 186: 50 *Casspir*; 13 *Marauder*; 30 *Puma* M26-15/*Puma* M36; 24 Stark Motors *Storm Light*; 30 Streit *Cougar*; 4 Streit *Gladiator*; 5+ Streit *Python*; 30 Streit *Typhoon*†
ARTILLERY 30+
  TOWED 122mm D-30
  MRL 122mm 30+ BM-21 *Grad*

Air Force 2,000

FORCES BY ROLE
TRANSPORT
  1 sqn with BT-67; C295; Y-12E
TRAINING
  1 sqn with *Tetras*
TRANSPORT/ATTACK HELICOPTER
  1 sqn with H215; Mi-24D *Hind*; Mi-35M *Hind*

EQUIPMENT BY TYPE
AIRCRAFT 9 combat capable
  ISR 1 Cessna 208 *Caravan*
  TPT • Light 12: 1 BT-67; 2 C295; 7 *Tetras*; 2 Y-12E (1 An-24 *Coke*; 2 An-26 *Curl*; 2 BN-2 *Islander* all in store)
  TRG 9: 3 A-29 *Super Tucano**; 6 L-39C *Albratros** (6 L-29 *Delfin*; 2 SF-260WL *Warrior** all in store)
HELICOPTERS
  ATK 8: 2 Mi-24D *Hind*; 2 Mi-24P *Hind* F; 4 Mi-35M *Hind*
  TPT 8: **Medium** 7: 2 H215 (AS332L1) *Super Puma*; 4 Mi-171Sh *Hip*; 1 Mi-8T *Hip*; (1 Mi-8 *Hip* in store);
  Light (1 AS350 *Ecureuil* in store)

Gendarmerie & Paramilitary 20,000 active

Gendarmerie 6,000
FORCES BY ROLE
MANOEUVRE
  Other
  8 paramilitary coy
  1 air tpt gp (2 sy coy; 1 tpt coy)
EQUIPMENT BY TYPE

464   THE MILITARY BALANCE 2023

ARMOURED FIGHTING VEHICLES
APC • PPV 1+ RG-31 *Nyala*

National Guard 10,000

FORCES BY ROLE
MANOEUVRE
Reconnaissance
6 (camel) cav coy
Light
1 inf coy (Anti-terrorist special force)

EQUIPMENT BY TYPE
ARMOURED FIGHTING VEHICLES
APC • PPV 1+ RG-31 *Nyala*

National Police 1,000

Militia 3,000

DEPLOYMENT

DEMOCRATIC REPUBLIC OF THE CONGO: UN •
MONUSCO 4

FOREIGN FORCES

All under MINUSMA comd unless otherwise specified
Armenia 1
Austria 2 • EUTM Mali 5
Bangladesh 1,297; 1 mech inf bn; 1 engr coy; 1 sigs coy
Belgium 53 • EUTM Mali 15
Benin 299; 1 mech inf coy(+)
Bhutan 5
Bulgaria EUTM Mali 4
Burkina Faso 653; 1 mech inf bn
Burundi 1
Cambodia 289; 2 engr coy; 1 EOD coy
Cameroon 2
Canada 5
Chad 1,449; 1 SF coy; 2 inf bn
China 430; 1 sy coy; 1 engr coy; 1 fd hospital
Côte d'Ivoire 872; 1 mech inf bn; 1 sy coy
Czech Republic 5 • EUTM Mali 90
Denmark 2
Egypt 1,052; 1 SF coy; 1 sy bn; 1 MP coy
El Salvador 176; 1 hel sqn with 3 MD-500E
Estonia 2 • EUTM Mali 10
Finland 4 • EUTM Mali 12
France 26 • EUTM Mali 13
Gambia 8
Georgia EUTM Mali 1
Germany 490; 1 obs; 1 sy coy; 1 hel sqn with 5 CH-53G;
1 UAV sqn • EUTM Mali 55
Ghana 141; 1 engr coy
Greece EUTM Mali 2
Guatemala 2
Guinea 667; 1 inf bn
Hungary EUTM Mali 20
Indonesia 10

Iran 2
Ireland 12 • EUTM Mali 20
Italy 2 • EUTM Mali 12
Jordan 322; 1 mech inf coy(+)
Kenya 9
Latvia 1 • EUTM Mali 5
Liberia 160; 1 sy coy
Lithuania 45 • EUTM Mali 2
Luxembourg 2 • EUTM Mali 21
Mauritania 7
Mexico 4
Moldova EUTM Mali 2
Montenegro EUTM Mali 2
Nepal 177; 1 EOD coy
Netherlands 10 • EUTM Mali 6
Niger 873; 1 inf bn
Nigeria 78; 1 fd hospital
Norway 29
Pakistan 221; 1 hel sqn
Portugal EUTM Mali 11
Romania 5 • EUTM Mali 25
Senegal 941; 1 mech inf bn; 1 engr coy
Sierra Leone 18
Slovakia EUTM Mali 4
Slovenia EUTM Mali 9
Spain 1 • EUTM Mali 420; 1 hel unit with 3 NH90 TTH
Sri Lanka 243; 1 sy coy
Sweden 184; 1 int coy • EUTM Mali 8
Switzerland 5
Togo 733; 1 mech inf bn; 1 fd hospital
Tunisia 88; 1 tpt flt with 1 C-130J-30
United Kingdom 256; 1 recce regt(-)
United States 10

Mauritius MUS

Mauritian Rupee MUR		2021	2022	2023
GDP	MUR	465bn	520bn	
	USD	11.2bn	11.5bn	
per capita	USD	8,827	9,112	
Growth	%	4.0	6.1	
Inflation	%	4.0	10.2	
Def bdgt [a]	MUR	8.42bn	10.4bn	10.9bn
	USD	202m	230m	
USD1=MUR		41.69	45.24	

[a] Police service budget

Real-terms defence budget trend (USDm, constant 2015)

Population 1,308,222

Age	0–14	15–19	20–24	25–29	30–64	65 plus
Male	8.0%	3.5%	3.6%	3.8%	24.7%	5.3%
Female	7.6%	3.4%	3.6%	3.8%	25.4%	7.6%

Capabilities

The country has no standing armed forces; instead, responsibility for security lies with the Mauritius Police Force's Special Mobile Force (SMF), formed as a motorised infantry battalion. The SMF is tasked with ensuring internal and external territorial and maritime security. India provides support to the Mauritian National Coast Guard, which is also a branch of the police force, through training, equipment maintenance and leasing, including helicopters and light aircraft. The SMF trains along traditional military lines but has no ability to deploy beyond national borders. Apart from very limited maintenance facilities there is no defence industry.

ACTIVE NIL Gendarmerie & Paramilitary 2,550

ORGANISATIONS BY SERVICE

Gendarmerie & Paramilitary 2,550

Special Mobile Force ε1,750
FORCES BY ROLE
MANOEUVRE
Reconnaissance
2 recce coy
Light
5 (rifle) mot inf coy
COMBAT SUPPORT
1 engr sqn
COMBAT SERVICE SUPPORT
1 spt pl
EQUIPMENT BY TYPE
ARMOURED FIGHTING VEHICLES
IFV 2 VAB with 20mm gun
APC • APC (W) 12: 3 *Tactica*; 9 VAB
ARTILLERY • MOR 81mm 2

Coast Guard ε800
EQUIPMENT BY TYPE
PATROL AND COASTAL COMBATANTS 17
PCO 1 *Barracuda* with 1 hel landing platform
PCC 2 *Victory* (IND *Sarojini Naidu*)
PB 14: 10 (IND Fast Interceptor Boat); 1 P-2000; 1 SDB-Mk3; 2 *Rescuer* (FSU *Zhuk*)
AIRCRAFT • TPT • Light 4: 1 BN-2T *Defender*; 3 Do-228-101

Police Air Wing
EQUIPMENT BY TYPE
HELICOPTERS
MRH 9: 1 H125 (AS555) *Fennec*; 2 *Dhruv*; 1 SA315B *Lama* (*Cheetah*); 5 SA316 *Alouette* III (*Chetak*)

Mozambique MOZ

Mozambique New Metical MZN		2021	2022	2023
GDP	MZN	1.03tr	1.15tr	
	USD	15.8bn	17.9bn	
per capita	USD	492	542	
Growth	%	2.3	3.7	
Inflation	%	5.7	11.3	
Def bdgt	MZN	9.35bn	9.33bn	
	USD	143m	145m	
USD1=MZN		65.46	64.26	

Real-terms defence budget trend (USDm, constant 2015)

Population 31,693,239

Age	0–14	15–19	20–24	25–29	30–64	65 plus
Male	22.9%	5.4%	4.6%	3.6%	11.3%	1.4%
Female	22.3%	5.4%	4.6%	3.9%	13.1%	1.5%

Capabilities

Mozambique faces a continuing internal threat from Islamist groups that continue to challenge national defence forces, with attacks being carried out in the country's northern provinces of Cabo Delgado, Niassa and Nampula. In 2021, the Southern African Development Community (SADC) deployed a multinational force, while there has also been support from Portugal, Russia, Rwanda, and the United States. The armed forces are tasked with ensuring territorial integrity and internal security, as well as tackling piracy and human trafficking. The disarmament, demobilisation, and integration of Resistência Nacional Moçambicana (RENAMO) personnel into the military is a long-standing objective and significant numbers of RENAMO fighters have been disarmed. Mozambique has defence relationships with China, Portugal and Russia, although US forces have delivered training to the Mozambican military in response to the Islamist insurgency. Russian private military contractors were hired to advise Mozambican forces in 2019, although they have since been withdrawn. Corruption in the armed forces is reportedly a continuing concern. The armed forces have no capacity to deploy beyond Mozambique's borders without assistance. Soviet-era equipment makes up the majority of the

466　THE MILITARY BALANCE 2023

inventory and maintaining this will be problematic, not least in the absence of any local defence industry. Moreover, Mozambique's recent economic performance will likely limit the government's ability to recapitalise its inventory.

ACTIVE 11,200 (Army 10,000 Navy 200 Air 1,000)

Conscript liability 2 years

ORGANISATIONS BY SERVICE

Army ε9,000–10,000

FORCES BY ROLE
SPECIAL FORCES
3 SF bn
MANOEUVRE
Light
7 inf bn
COMBAT SUPPORT
2-3 arty bn
2 engr bn **COMBAT SERVICE SUPPORT**
1 log bn
EQUIPMENT BY TYPE†
Equipment estimated at 10% or less serviceability
ARMOURED FIGHTING VEHICLES
MBT 60+ T-54
RECCE 30 BRDM-1/BRDM-2
IFV 40 BMP-1
APC 338
APC (T) 30 FV430
APC (W) 285: 160 BTR-60; 100 BTR-152; 25 AT-105 *Saxon*
PPV 23+: 11 *Casspir*; 12 *Marauder*; some Tata Motors MRAP
AUV 9+ *Tiger* 4×4
ANTI-TANK/ANTI-INFRASTRUCTURE
MSL • MANPATS 9K11 *Malyutka* (RS-AT-3 *Sagger*); 9K111 *Fagot* (RS-AT-4 *Spigot*)
RCL 75mm; 82mm B-10; 107mm 24 B-12
GUNS 85mm 18: 6 D-48; 12 PT-56 (D-44)
ARTILLERY 126
TOWED 62: 100mm 20 M-1944; 105mm 12 M101; 122mm 12 D-30; 130mm 6 M-46; 152mm 12 D-1
MRL 122mm 12 BM-21 *Grad*
MOR 52: 82mm 40 M-43; 120mm 12 M-43
AIR DEFENCE • GUNS 290+
SP 57mm 20 ZSU-57-2
TOWED 270+: 20mm M-55; 23mm 120 ZU-23-2; 37mm 90 M-1939; (10 M-1939 in store); 57mm 60 S-60; (30 S-60 in store)

Navy ε200

EQUIPMENT BY TYPE
PATROL AND COASTAL COMBATANTS 30
PBF 26: 20+ DV 15; 2 HSI 32; 2 *Interceptor* (LKA Solas Marine); 2 *Namilti* (ex-IND C-401)
PB 4: 3 *Ocean Eagle* 43 (capacity 1 *Camcopter* S-100 UAV); 1 *Pebane* (ex-ESP *Conejera*)
UNINHABITED AERIAL VEHICLES
ISR • Light 1 S-100 *Camcopter*

Air Force 1,000

FORCES BY ROLE

FIGHTER/GROUND ATTACK
1 sqn with MiG-21bis *Fishbed*; MiG-21UM *Mongol* B
TRANSPORT
1 sqn with An-26 *Curl*; FTB-337G *Milirole*; Cessna 150B; Cessna 172; PA-34 *Seneca*
ATTACK/TRANSPORT HELICOPTER
1 sqn with Mi-24 *Hind†*
EQUIPMENT BY TYPE
AIRCRAFT 8 combat capable
FGA 8: 6 MiG-21bis *Fishbed*; 2 MiG-21UM *Mongol* B
ISR 2 FTB-337G *Milirole*
TPT 6: Light 5: 1 An-26 *Curl*; 2 Cessna 150B; 1 Cessna 172; 1 PA-34 *Seneca*; (4 PA-32 *Cherokee* non-op); PAX 1 Hawker 850XP
TRG 2 L-39 *Albatros*
HELICOPTERS
ATK 2 Mi-24V *Hind* E
MRH 2+ SA314B *Gazelle*
TPT • Medium 2 Mi-8 *Hip*

FOREIGN FORCES

Angola SAMIM 8
Austria EUTM Mozambique 1
Botswana SAMIM 359
Democratic of the Congo SAMIM 1
Estonia EUTM Mozambique 1
Finland EUTM Mozambique 4
France EUTM Mozambique 6
Greece EUTM Mozambique 8
Lesotho SAMIM 122
Lithuania EUTM Mozambique 2
Malawi SAMIM 2
Portugal EUTM Mozambqiue 120
Romania EUTM Mozambique 6
Rwanda Army: 1,500
South Africa SAMIM 1,200
Spain EUTM Mozambique 2
Tanzania SAMIM 290
Zimbabwe SAMIM 1

Namibia NAM

Namibian Dollar NAD		2021	2022	2023
GDP	NAD	182bn	201bn	
	USD	12.3bn	12.5bn	
per capita	USD	4,826	4,809	
Growth	%	2.7	3.0	
Inflation	%	3.6	6.4	
Def bdgt	NAD	5.43bn	5.85bn	
	USD	367m	363m	
USD1=NAD		14.78	16.10	

Real-terms defence budget trend (USDm, constant 2015)

Population 2,727,409

Age	0–14	15–19	20–24	25–29	30–64	65 plus
Male	17.6%	5.3%	4.8%	4.3%	15.4%	1.7%
Female	17.2%	5.2%	4.8%	4.4%	17.0%	2.3%

Capabilities

The Namibian defence authorities aim to develop a small, mobile and well-equipped professional force. According to the constitution, the primary mission of the Namibian Defence Force (NDF) is territorial defence. Secondary roles include assistance to civil authorities and supporting the AU, SADC and UN. The NDF Development Strategy 2012–22 stated that the NDF design should be based on a conventional force with a force-projection capability. The navy exercises with SADC as part of the SADC's Standing Maritime Committee and participated in the multinational UNITAS exercise for the first time in 2022. It also has conducted multinational training missions organised by US forces. Annual meetings of a permanent commission on defence and security between Namibia and Botswana were elevated in 2021 to a biannual commission, chaired by the two countries' heads of state. While the NDF receives a comparatively large proportion of the state budget, there have been recent problems in adequately funding training. A recruitment drive for officers and other ranks was announced in 2022, the first in seven years. Namibia has deployed on AU, SADC and UN missions and the NDF sent a small force to Mozambique in 2022, but there is only limited capacity for independent power projection. The NDF is equipped for the most part with ageing or obsolescent systems, but economic difficulties make recapitalisation unlikely in the near term. There is a limited defence-manufacturing sector, mainly focused on armoured vehicles, tactical communications and ammunition.

ACTIVE 9,900 (Army 9,000 Navy 900) **Gendarmerie & Paramilitary 6,000**

ORGANISATIONS BY SERVICE

Army 9,000
FORCES BY ROLE
MANOEUVRE
 Reconnaissance
  1 recce regt
 Light
  3 inf bde (total: 6 inf bn)
 Other
  1 (Presidential Guard) gd bn
COMBAT SUPPORT
 1 arty bde with (1 arty regt)
 1 AT regt
 1 engr regt
 1 sigs regt
COMBAT SERVICE SUPPORT
 1 log bn
AIR DEFENCE
 1 AD regt
EQUIPMENT BY TYPE
ARMOURED FIGHTING VEHICLES
 MBT T-54/T-55†; T-34†
 RECCE 12 BRDM-2
 IFV 7: 5 Type-05P mod (with BMP-1 turret); 2 *Wolf Turbo* 2 mod (with BMP-1 turret)
 APC 61
  APC (W) 13: 10 BTR-60; 3 Type-05P
  PPV 48: 20 *Casspir*; 28 *Wolf Turbo* 2
ENGINEERING & MAINTENANCE VEHICLES
 ARV T-54/T-55 reported
ANTI-TANK/ANTI-INFRASTRUCTURE
 RCL 82mm B-10
 GUNS 12+: 57mm ZIS-2; 76mm 12 ZIS-3
ARTILLERY 72
 TOWED 140mm 24 G-2
 MRL 122mm 8: 5 BM-21 *Grad*; 3 PHL-81
 MOR 40: 81mm; 82mm
AIR DEFENCE
 SAM • Point-defence FN-6 (CH-SA-10)
 GUNS 65
  SP 23mm 15 *Zumlac*
  TOWED 50+: 14.5mm 50 ZPU-4; 57mm S-60

Navy ε900
EQUIPMENT BY TYPE
PATROL AND COASTAL COMBATANTS 7
 PSO 1 *Elephant* with 1 hel landing platform
 PCC 3: 2 *Daures* (ex-PRC *Haiqing* (Type-037-IS)) with 2 FQF-3200 A/S mor; 1 *Oryx*
 PB 3: 1 *Brendan Simbwaye* (BRZ *Grajaú*); 2 *Terrace Bay* (BRZ *Marlim*)
AIRCRAFT • TPT • Light 1 F406 *Caravan II*
HELICOPTERS • TPT • Medium 1 S-61L

Marines ε700

Air Force
FORCES BY ROLE
FIGHTER/GROUND ATTACK
 1 sqn with F-7 (F-7NM); FT-7 (FT-7NG)
ISR
 1 sqn with O-2A *Skymaster*
TRANSPORT
 Some sqn with An-26 *Curl*; *Falcon* 900; *Learjet* 36; Y-12
TRAINING
 1 sqn with K-8 *Karakorum**

ATTACK/TRANSPORT HELICOPTER
1 sqn with H425; Mi-8 *Hip*; Mi-25 *Hind* D; SA315 *Lama* (*Cheetah*); SA316B *Alouette* III (*Chetak*)

EQUIPMENT BY TYPE
AIRCRAFT 11+ combat capable
  FTR 7: 5 F-7 (F-7NM); 2 FT-7 (FT-7NG)
  ISR 5 Cessna O-2A *Skymaster*
  TPT 6: **Light** 5: 2 An-26 *Curl*; 1 Learjet 36; 2 Y-12; **PAX** 1 *Falcon* 900
  TRG 4+ K-8 *Karakorum**
HELICOPTERS
  ATK 2 Mi-25 *Hind* D
  MRH 5: 1 H425; 1 SA315 *Lama* (*Cheetah*); 3 SA316B *Alouette* III (*Chetak*)
  TPT • Medium 1 Mi-8 *Hip*

Gendarmerie & Paramilitary 6,000

Police Force • Special Field Force 6,000 (incl Border Guard and Special Reserve Force)

DEPLOYMENT
SOUTH SUDAN: UN • UNMISS 2
SUDAN: UN • UNISFA 7

Niger NER

CFA Franc BCEAO XOF		2021	2022	2023
GDP	XOF	8.29tr	9.08tr	
	USD	15.0bn	14.6bn	
per capita	USD	595	561	
Growth	%	1.3	6.7	
Inflation	%	3.8	4.5	
Def bdgt	XOF	112bn	151bn	
	USD	203m	244m	
USD1=XOF		554.23	620.59	

Real-terms defence budget trend (USDm, constant 2015)

Population 24,484,587

Age	0–14	15–19	20–24	25–29	30–64	65 plus
Male	25.2%	5.7%	4.4%	3.2%	9.7%	1.3%
Female	24.8%	5.8%	4.6%	3.4%	10.5%	1.4%

Capabilities
Principal military roles include maintaining internal and border security, in light of the regional threat from Islamist groups. The country is a member of the G5 Sahel group and part of the Multi-National Joint Task Force fighting Boko Haram in the Lake Chad Basin. Niamey hosts air contingents from France, Germany and the US, which maintains a detachment of UAVs. France redeployed part of its *Barkhane* operation to Niger after withdrawing from Mali and has conducted joint counter-terrorism operations with Niger's armed forces. Niger's armed forces are combat experienced and relatively well trained, and there is training support from France, Italy and the US. Combat operations have also been conducted with US forces. There is limited capacity to deploy beyond neighbouring countries without external support. Operations in austere environments have demonstrated adequate sustainment and manoeuvre capacity. While there have been moves to integrate better-protected armoured vehicles, the armed forces are generally underequipped and under-resourced. Apart from limited maintenance facilities, the country has no domestic defence-industrial capability.

ACTIVE 33,100 (Army 33,000 Air 100) Gendarmerie & Paramilitary 24,500
Conscript liability Selective conscription, 2 years

ORGANISATIONS BY SERVICE

Army ε33,000
8 Mil Zones
FORCES BY ROLE
SPECIAL FORCES
  2 spec ops coy
  9 (intervention) cdo bn
MANOEUVRE
  Light
  14 (combined arms) inf bn
  Amphibious
  1 rvn coy
COMBAT SUPPORT
  1 engr coy
COMBAT SERVICE SUPPORT
  1 log gp
AIR DEFENCE
  1 AD coy
EQUIPMENT BY TYPE
ARMOURED FIGHTING VEHICLES
  RECCE 125: 35 AML-20/AML-60; 90 AML-90
  APC 151
    APC (W) 53: 11 *Bastion* APC; 22 Panhard M3; 20 WZ-551
    PPV 98+: 15 IAG *Guardian Xtreme*; 57 *Mamba* Mk7; 21 *Puma* M26-15; 5+ *Puma* M36
  AUV 10+: 3+ *Tiger* 4×4; 7 VBL; *Bastion Patsas*
ANTI-TANK/ANTI-INFRASTRUCTURE
  RCL 14: **75mm** 6 M20; **106mm** 8 M40
ARTILLERY 40+
  MRL 107mm PH-63 (tch)
  MOR 40: **81mm** 19 Brandt; **82mm** 17; **120mm** 4 Brandt
AIR DEFENCE • GUNS 39
  SP 20mm 10 Panhard M3 VDAA
  TOWED 20mm 29

Air Force 100
EQUIPMENT BY TYPE
AIRCRAFT 2 combat capable
  ATK 2 Su-25 *Frogfoot*
  ISR 6: 4 Cessna 208 *Caravan*; 2 DA42 MPP *Twin Star*
  TPT 8: **Medium** 2 C-130H *Hercules*; **Light** 5: 1 An-26 *Curl*; 2 Cessna 208 *Caravan*; 1 Do-28 *Skyservant*; 1 Do-228-201; **PAX** 1 B-737-700 (VIP)

HELICOPTERS
ATK 2 Mi-35P *Hind*
MRH 9: 2 Bell 412HP *Twin Huey*; 2 Mi-17 *Hip*; 5 SA342 *Gazelle*

Gendarmerie & Paramilitary 24,500

Gendarmerie 7,000

National Guard 9,000

National Police 8,500

DEPLOYMENT

CENTRAL AFRICAN REPUBLIC: UN • MINUSCA 6

DEMOCRATIC REPUBLIC OF THE CONGO: UN • MONUSCO 5

MALI: UN • MINUSMA 873; 1 inf bn

FOREIGN FORCES

France 1,200; 1 mech inf coy; 1 FGA det with 3 *Mirage 2000D*; 1 tkr/tpt det with 1 C-135FR; 1 C-130J-30; 1 UAV det with 6 MQ-9A *Reaper*; 1 ISR det with 1 *Atlantique* 2

Germany Operation Gazelle 200 (trg)

Italy MISIN 295; 1 inf coy; 1 engr unit; 1 CBRN unit; 1 med unit; 1 trg unit; 1 ISR unit

United States 800; 1 ISR UAV sqn with MQ-9A *Reaper*

Nigeria NGA

Nigerian Naira NGN		2021	2022	2023
GDP	NGN	176tr	207tr	
	USD	442bn	504bn	
per capita	USD	2,089	2,326	
Growth	%	3.6	3.2	
Inflation	%	17.0	18.9	
Def bdgt	NGN	966bn	1.14tr	1.25tr
	USD	2.42bn	2.78bn	
USD1=NGN		398.77	410.59	

Real-terms defence budget trend (USDbn, constant 2015)

Population   225,082,083

Age	0–14	15–19	20–24	25–29	30–64	65 plus
Male	20.9%	5.7%	4.8%	3.8%	13.8%	1.6%
Female	20.1%	5.5%	4.6%	3.7%	13.8%	1.8%

Capabilities

Nigeria is West Africa's principal military power and faces numerous security challenges, including from the Islamic State West African Province, Boko Haram and militants in the Delta. Reform initiatives have developed after relative military weaknesses were exposed during counter-insurgency operations. There have been operational changes, including attempts to implement counter-insurgency tactics, forward-operating bases and quick-reaction groups. Nigeria is part of the Multinational Joint Task Force and is a key member of the ECOWAS Standby Force. Nigeria is strengthening its cooperation with Pakistan while military and security assistance is either discussed or under way with Germany, the UK and the US. The UK bases its British Defence Staff for West Africa in Nigeria. Efforts have been made to improve training, notably in the air force with the establishment of Air Training Command and Ground Training Command. Contractors have also been used to improve training and maintenance levels. Nigeria is able to mount regional operations, though its deployment capacities remain limited. Important acquisitions have been made in every domain, including the introduction of fighter ground-attack aircraft and combat-capable trainers as well as new tanks and howitzers. Patrol boats and a number of small coastal-patrol boats have been acquired in light of security requirements in the Delta region. Nigeria is developing its defence-industrial capacity, including local production facilities for small arms and protected patrol vehicles.

ACTIVE 143,000 (Army 100,000 Navy 25,000 Air 18,000) **Gendarmerie & Paramilitary 80,000**
Reserves planned

ORGANISATIONS BY SERVICE

Army 100,000
FORCES BY ROLE
SPECIAL FORCES
  1 spec ops bn
  3 spec ops bde
  3 (mobile strike team) spec ops units
  1 ranger bn
MANOEUVRE
  Armoured
  1 (3rd) armd div (1 armd bde, 1 arty bde)
  Mechanised
  1 (1st) mech div (1 recce bn, 1 mech bde, 1 mot inf bde, 1 arty bde, 1 engr regt)
  1 (2nd) mech div (1 recce bn, 1 armd bde, 1 arty bde, 1 engr regt)
  1 (81st) composite div (1 recce bn, 1 mech bde, 1 arty bde, 1 engr regt)
  Light
  1 (6th) inf div (1 amph bde, 2 inf bde)
  1 (7th) inf div (1 spec ops bn, 1 recce bn(-), 1 armd bde, 7 (task force) inf bde, 1 arty bde, 1 engr regt)
  1 (8th Task Force) inf div (2 inf bde)
  1 (82nd) composite div (1 recce bn, 3 mot inf bde, 1 arty bde, 1 engr regt)
  1 (Multi-National Joint Task Force) bde (2 inf bn(-))
  Other
  1 (Presidential Guard) gd bde (4 gd bn)
AIR DEFENCE
  1 AD regt
EQUIPMENT BY TYPE
ARMOURED FIGHTING VEHICLES
  MBT 319+: 100 T-55†; 10 T-72AV; 31 T-72M1; 172 Vickers Mk 3; 6+ VT-4
  LT TK 154 FV101 *Scorpion*

ASLT 6+ ST-1
RECCE 312: 88 AML-60; 40 AML-90; 70 EE-9 *Cascavel*; 44 ERC-90F1 *Lynx*; 50 FV721 *Fox*; 20 FV601 *Saladin* Mk2
IFV 31: 9 BTR-4EN; 22 BVP-1
APC 865+
    APC (T) 373: 248 4K-7FA *Steyr*; 65 MT-LB; 60 ZSD-89
    APC (W) 172+: 10 FV603 *Saracen*; 110 AVGP *Grizzly* mod/*Piranha* I 6x6; 47 BTR-3UN; 5 BTR-80; some EE-11 *Urutu* (reported);
    PPV 320+: 14 *Caiman*; some *Conqueror*; 159 CS/VP3; 47 *Ezugwu*; 5+ Isotrex *Phantom* II; some *Marauder*; 7+ *Maxxpro*; 8 Proforce *Ara-1*; 13 Proforce *Ara-2*; some Proforce *Viper*; 23 REVA III 4×4; 10 Streit *Spartan*; 9 Streit *Cougar* (*Igirigi*); 25 Streit *Typhoon*
    AUV 183+: 107 *Cobra*; FV103 *Spartan*; 4+ *Tiger* 4×4; 72 VBL
ENGINEERING & MAINTENANCE VEHICLES
ARV 17+: AVGP *Husky*; 2 *Greif*; 15 Vickers ARV
VLB MTU-20; VAB
ANTI-TANK/ANTI-INFRASTRUCTURE
MSL • MANPATS *Shershen*
RCL 84mm *Carl Gustaf*; **106mm** M40A1
ARTILLERY 518+
SP 43+: **105mm** 4+ SH-5; **122mm** some SH-2; **155mm** 39 *Palmaria*
TOWED 104: **105mm** 49 M-56; **122mm** 48 D-30/D-74; **130mm** 7 M-46; (**155mm** 24 FH-77B in store)
MRL 122mm 41: 9 BM-21 *Grad*; 25 APR-21; 7 RM-70
MOR 330+: **81mm** 200; **82mm** 100; **120mm** 30+
AIR DEFENCE
SAM • Point-defence 16+: 16 *Roland*; *Blowpipe*; 9K32 *Strela*-2 (RS-SA-7 *Grail*)‡
GUNS 89+
    SP 23mm 29 ZSU-23-4 *Shilka*
    TOWED 60+: **20mm** 60+; **23mm** ZU-23; **40mm** L/70

Navy 25,000 (incl Coast Guard)

Western Comd HQ located at Apapa; Eastern Comd HQ located at Calabar; Central Comd HQ located at Brass

EQUIPMENT BY TYPE
PRINCIPAL SURFACE COMBATANTS • FRIGATES
FFGHM (1 *Aradu* (GER MEKO 360) (non-operational) with 8 single lnchr with *Otomat* Mk1 AShM, 1 octuple *Albatros* lnchr with *Aspide* SAM, 2 triple 324mm ASTT with A244/S LWT, 1 127mm gun (capacity 1 med hel))
PATROL AND COASTAL COMBATANTS 122
CORVETTES • FSM (1 *Erinomi* (UK Vosper Mk 9) (non-operational) with 1 triple lnchr with *Seacat*† SAM, 1 twin 375mm Bofors ASW Rocket Launcher System A/S mor, 1 76mm gun)
PSOH 4: 2 *Centenary* with 1 76mm gun (capacity 1 Z-9 hel); 2 *Thunder* (ex-US *Hamilton*) with 1 76mm gun
PCFG 1 *Siri* (FRA *Combattante* IIIB)† with 2 twin lnchr with MM38 *Exocet* AShM, 1 76mm gun
PCF 2 *Siri* (FRA *Combattante* IIIB) with 1 76mm gun
PCO 4 *Kyanwa* (ex-US CG *Balsam*)
PCC 4: 2 *Ekpe* (GER Lurssen 57m)† with 1 76mm gun; 2 *Kano* (Damen Fast Crew Supplier 4008)
PBF 26: 2 ARESA 1700; 4 C-*Falcon*; 12 *Manta* MkIII (Suncraft 17m); 3 *Shaldag* II; 2 *Torie* (Nautic Sentinel 17m); 3 *Wave Rider*

PB 81: 1 *Andoni*; 1 *Dorina* (FPB 98); 4 FPB 110 MkII; 8 *Okpoku* (FPB 72); 1 *Karaduwa*; 1 *Sagbama*; 2 *Sea Eagle* (Suncraft 38m); 15 *Stingray* (Suncraft 16m); 40 Suncraft 12m; 4 Swiftships; 2 *Town* (of which one laid up); 2 *Yola*†
MINE WARFARE • MINE COUNTERMEASURES 2
MCC 2 *Ohue* (ITA *Lerici* mod)†
AMPHIBIOUS 5
LANDING SHIPS • LST 1 *Kada* (NLD Damen LST 100) with 1 hel landing platform
LANDING CRAFT • LCVP 4 *Stingray* 20
LOGISTICS AND SUPPORT 2
AGHS 1 *Lana* (OSV 190)
AX 1 *Prosperity*

Naval Aviation

EQUIPMENT BY TYPE
HELICOPTERS
    MRH 2 AW139 (AB-139)
    TPT • Light 3 AW109E *Power*†

Special Boat Service 200

EQUIPMENT BY TYPE
FORCES BY ROLE
SPECIAL FORCES
    1 SF unit

Air Force 18,000

FORCES BY ROLE
Very limited op capability
FIGHTER/GROUND ATTACK
    1 sqn with F-7 (F-7NI); FT-7 (FT-7NI)
MARITIME PATROL
    1 sqn with ATR-42-500 MP; Do-128D-6 *Turbo SkyServant*; Do-228-100/200
TRANSPORT
    2 sqn with C-130H *Hercules*; C-130H-30 *Hercules*; G-222
    1 (Presidential) gp with B-727; B-737BBJ; BAe-125-800; Beech 350 *King Air*; Do-228-200; *Falcon* 7X; *Falcon* 900; Gulfstream IV/V
TRAINING
    1 unit with *Air Beetle*†
    1 unit with *Alpha Jet**
    1 unit with L-39 *Albatros*†*
    1 unit with *Super Mushshak*; DA40NG
    1 hel unit with Mi-34 *Hermit* (trg)
ATTACK HELICOPTER
    1 sqn with Mi-24/Mi-35 *Hind*†
TRANSPORT HELICOPTER
    1 sqn with H215 (AS332) *Super Puma*; (AS365N) *Dauphin*; AW109LUH; H135
EQUIPMENT BY TYPE
AIRCRAFT 62 combat capable
FTR 12: 10 F-7 (F-7NI); 2 FT-7 (FT-7NI)
FGA 3 JF-17 *Thunder* Block II
ELINT 2 ATR-42-500 MP
ISR 1 Beech 350 *King Air*
MP 1 Cessna 525 *Citation* CJ3 (operated on behalf of NIMASA)

TPT 32: **Medium** 5: 1 C-130H *Hercules* (4 more in store†); 1 C-130H-30 *Hercules* (2 more in store); 3 G.222† (2 more in store†); **Light** 18: 1 Beech 350 *King Air*; 1 Cessna 550 *Citation*; 8 Do-128D-6 *Turbo SkyServant*; 1 Do-228-100; 2 Do-228-101; 5 Do-228-200 (incl 2 VIP); **PAX** 9: 1 B-727; 1 B-737BBJ; 1 BAe 125-800; 2 *Falcon* 7X; 2 *Falcon* 900; 1 Gulfstream IV; 1 Gulfstream V

TRG 116: 58 *Air Beetle*† (up to 20 awaiting repair); 2 *Alpha Jet* A*; 10 *Alpha Jet* E*; 2 DA40NG; 12 EMB-314 *Super Tucano* (A-29B)*; 23 L-39ZA *Albatros**†; 9 *Super Mushshak*

HELICOPTERS
ATK 16: 2 Mi-24P *Hind*; 4 Mi-24V *Hind*; 3 Mi-35 *Hind*; 2 Mi-35P *Hind*; 5 Mi-35M *Hind*
MRH 11+: 6 AW109LUH; 2 Bell 412EP; 3+ SA341 *Gazelle*
TPT 24: **Medium** 12: 2 AW101; 5 H215 (AS332) *Super Puma* (4 more in store); 3 AS365N *Dauphin*; 1 Mi-171Sh; 2 Mi-171E; **Light** 11: 4 H125 (AS350B) *Ecureuil*; 1 AW109; 2 AW109M; 1 Bell 205; 3 H135

UNINHABITED AERIAL VEHICLES 5+
CISR • **Heavy** 3: 1+ CH-3; 2+ *Wing Loong* II
ISR 2: **Heavy** 1+ *Yabhon Flash*-20; **Medium** (9 *Aerostar* non-operational); **Light** 1+ *Tsaigami*

AIR-LAUNCHED MISSILES
AAM • IR R-3 (RS-AA-2 *Atoll*)‡; PL-9C
ASM AGR-20A APKWS; AR-1
BOMBS • INS/GPS guided FT-9

Gendarmerie & Paramilitary ε80,000

Security and Civil Defence Corps 80,000
EQUIPMENT BY TYPE
ARMOURED FIGHTING VEHICLES
APC 80+
APC (W) 74+: 70+ AT105 *Saxon*†; 4 BTR-3U; UR-416
PPV 6 *Springbuck* 4x4
AIRCRAFT • TPT • **Light** 4: 1 Cessna 500 *Citation* I; 2 PA-31 *Navajo*; 1 PA-31-350 *Navajo Chieftain*
HELICOPTERS • TPT • **Light** 5: 2 Bell 212 (AB-212); 2 Bell 222 (AB-222); 1 Bell 429

DEPLOYMENT

CENTRAL AFRICAN REPUBLIC: UN • MINUSCA 6
DEMOCRATIC REPUBLIC OF THE CONGO: UN • MONUSCO 8
GAMBIA: ECOWAS • ECOMIG 197
LEBANON: UN • UNIFIL 2
MALI: UN • MINUSMA 78; 1 fd hospital
SOUTH SUDAN: UN • UNMISS 14
SUDAN: UN • UNISFA 15
WESTERN SAHARA: UN • MINURSO 8

FOREIGN FORCES
United Kingdom 80 (trg teams)

Rwanda RWA

Rwandan Franc RWF		2021	2022	2023
GDP	RWF	10.9tr	12.7tr	
	USD	11.1bn	12.1bn	
per capita	USD	854	913	
Growth	%	10.9	6.0	
Inflation	%	0.8	9.5	
Def bdgt	RWF	151bn	178bn	215bn
	USD	152m	169m	
USD1=RWF		988.89	1047.46	

Real-terms defence budget trend (USDm, constant 2015)

Population	13,173,730					
Age	0–14	15–19	20–24	25–29	30–64	65 plus
Male	19.5%	5.5%	4.7%	3.8%	14.3%	1.1%
Female	19.1%	5.5%	4.7%	3.9%	16.1%	1.7%

Capabilities

Rwanda is one of the principal security actors in East Africa, with disciplined and well-trained armed forces. Their key missions are to defend territorial integrity and national sovereignty. The country fields a relatively large army, but units are lightly equipped, with little mechanisation. Rwanda signed a Mutual Defence Treaty with Kenya and Uganda in 2014 and participates in East African Community military activities. A contingent has been deployed to Mozambique since 2021, including a small marine component. The country's professional military education establishments train regional as well as Rwandan personnel. Rwanda was one of the hosts for the US-led exercise *Justified Accord* in early 2022. The lack of fixed-wing aircraft limits the armed forces' ability to independently deploy much at distance beyond personnel, though they have deployed on numerous occasions and there is also an aviation unit in South Sudan. There have been some acquisitions of modern artillery and armoured vehicles. There is limited maintenance capacity but no defence manufacturing sector.

ACTIVE 33,000 (Army 32,000 Air 1,000)
Gendarmerie & Paramilitary 2,000

ORGANISATIONS BY SERVICE

Army 32,000
FORCES BY ROLE
MANOEUVRE
Light
2 cdo bn
4 inf div (3 inf bde)
COMBAT SUPPORT
1 arty bde

EQUIPMENT BY TYPE
ARMOURED FIGHTING VEHICLES
MBT 34: 24 T-54/T-55; 10 *Tiran*-5
RECCE 90: ε90 AML-60/AML-90
IFV 38+: BMP; 13+ Ratel-23; 10 *Ratel*-60; 15 *Ratel*-90
APC 60+
  APC (W) 20+: BTR; *Buffalo* (Panhard M3); 20 WZ-551 (reported)
  PPV 40 RG-31 *Nyala*
AUV 92: 76 *Cobra/Cobra* II; 16 VBL
ENGINEERING & MAINTENANCE VEHICLES
ARV T-54/T-55 ARV reported
ANTI-TANK/ANTI-INFRASTRUCTURE
MSL • SP HJ-9A (on *Cobra*)
ARTILLERY 177+
SP 17: **122mm** 12: 6 CS/SH-1; 6 SH-3; **155mm** 5 ATMOS 2000
TOWED 35+: **105mm** some; **122mm** 6 D-30; **152mm** 29 Type-54 (D-1)†
MRL 10: **122mm** 5 RM-70; **160mm** 5 LAR-160
MOR 115: **81mm**; **82mm**; **120mm**
AIR DEFENCE SAM • Point-defence 9K32 *Strela*-2 (RS-SA-7 *Grail*)‡
GUNS ε150: **14.5mm**; **23mm**; **37mm**

Air Force ε1,000
FORCES BY ROLE
ATTACK/TRANSPORT HELICOPTER
1 sqn with Mi-17/Mi-17MD/Mi-17V-5/Mi-17-1V *Hip* H; Mi-24P/V *Hind*
EQUIPMENT BY TYPE
HELICOPTERS
ATK 5: 2 Mi-24V *Hind* E; 3 Mi-24P *Hind*
MRH 12: 1 AW139; 4 Mi-17 *Hip* H; 1 Mi-17MD *Hip* H; 1 Mi-17V-5 *Hip* H; 5 Mi-17-1V *Hip* H
TPT • Light 1 AW109S

Gendarmerie & Paramilitary
District Administration Security Support Organ ε2,000

DEPLOYMENT
CENTRAL AFRICAN REPUBLIC: UN • MINUSCA 2,148; 2 inf bn; 1 fd hospital
MOZAMBIQUE: Army 1,500
SOUTH SUDAN: UN • UNMISS 2,642; 3 inf bn; 1 hel sqn with 6 Mi-17
SUDAN: UN • UNISFA 3

Senegal SEN

CFA Franc BCEAO XOF		2021	2022	2023
GDP	XOF	15.3tr	17.1tr	
	USD	27.6bn	27.5bn	
per capita	USD	1,607	1,558	
Growth	%	6.1	4.7	
Inflation	%	2.2	7.5	
Def bdgt	XOF	263bn	263bn	
	USD	474m	423m	
USD1=XOF		554.23	620.61	

Real-terms defence budget trend (USDm, constant 2015)

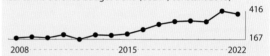

Population 17,923,036

Age	0–14	15–19	20–24	25–29	30–64	65 plus
Male	21.2%	5.5%	4.5%	3.8%	12.7%	1.4%
Female	20.4%	5.3%	4.5%	3.9%	14.8%	1.8%

Capabilities
Senegal's armed forces have strong international relationships and are experienced in foreign deployments. Their focus is internal and border security, including counter-insurgency in the country's south and tackling Islamist activity in neighbouring states, as well as combating narcotics trafficking. Under the 'Horizon 2025' programme, the defence authorities intend to reorganise and re-equip key defence organisations and renew infrastructure. Professional military education is a focus. New defence organisations are under development, reportedly including a higher war college, staff college and doctrine centre. Senegal recently procured new APCs, offshore patrol vessels, transport aircrafts and light artillery and, despite limited resources, there are plans to improve operational capabilities and training. France remains Senegal's principal defence partner and retains a military presence in the country. French military forces deliver training assistance to the armed forces and gendarmerie, including training in 2021 on the SIMBAD air-defence system that will equip new patrol ships. There is also defence cooperation with Spain and the UK, and an agreement was signed with Mauritania in 2021 regarding offshore energy-related maritime security. The US also provides security assistance, including to the national police and gendarmerie. The armed forces are able to deploy personnel using organic airlift, which has improved with the 2022 delivery of a C295, but short-notice movements of heavy equipment would be problematic without external assistance. Apart from maintenance facilities, the country has no domestic defence-industrial capability.

ACTIVE 13,600 (Army 11,900 Navy 950 Air 750)
Gendarmerie & Paramilitary 5,000
Conscript liability Selective conscription, 24 months

ORGANISATIONS BY SERVICE

Army 11,900 (incl conscripts)
7 Mil Zone HQ

Sub-Saharan Africa **473**

FORCES BY ROLE
MANOEUVRE
  Reconnaissance
  5 armd recce bn
  Light
  1 cdo bn
  6 inf bn
  Air Manoeuvre
  1 AB bn
  Other
  1 (Presidential Guard) horse cav bn
COMBAT SUPPORT
  1 arty bn
  1 engr bn
  3 construction coy
  1 sigs bn
COMBAT SERVICE SUPPORT
  1 log bn
  1 med bn
  1 trg bn

EQUIPMENT BY TYPE
ARMOURED FIGHTING VEHICLES
  ASLT 27 PTL-02 *Assaulter*
  RECCE 138: 30 AML-60; 74 AML-90; 20 BRDM-2;
  10 M8; 4 M20
  IFV 26 *Ratel*-20
  APC 102
    APC (T) 12 M3 half-track
    APC (W) 22: 2 *Oncilla;* 16 Panhard M3; 4 WZ-551 (CP)
    PPV 68: 8 *Casspir;* 39 *Puma* M26-15; 21+ *Puma* M36
  AUV 27 RAM Mk3
ENGINEERING & MAINTENANCE VEHICLES
  ARV 2 *Puma* M36 ARV
ANTI-TANK/ANTI-INFRASTRUCTURE
  MSL • MANPATS *Milan*
ARTILLERY 82
  TOWED 20: **105mm** 6 HM-2/M101; **155mm** 14: ε6
  Model-50; 8 TR-F1
  MRL 122mm 6 BM-21 *Grad* (UKR *Bastion*-1 mod)
  MOR 56: **81mm** 24; **120mm** 32
AIR DEFENCE • GUNS • TOWED 39: **14.5mm** 6 ZPU-4
(tch); **20mm** 21 M693; **40mm** 12 L/60

Navy (incl Coast Guard) 950
FORCES BY ROLE
SPECIAL FORCES
  1 cdo coy

EQUIPMENT BY TYPE
PATROL AND COASTAL COMBATANTS 10
  PCO 1 *Fouladou* (OPV 190 Mk II)
  PCC 1 *Njambour* (FRA SFCN 59m) with 2 76mm gun
  PBF 6: 3 *Anambe* (*Shaldag* II); 2 *Ferlo* (RPB 33); 1 *Lac Retba*
    (*Shaldag* V)
  PB 2: 1 *Conejera*; 1 *Kedougou*
AMPHIBIOUS • LANDING CRAFT 2
  LCT 2 EDIC 700
LOGISTICS AND SUPPORT• **AG** 1

Air Force 750
FORCES BY ROLE
MARITIME PATROL/SEARCH & RESCUE
  1 sqn with C-212 *Aviocar*; CN235; Bell 205 (UH-1H *Iroquois*)
ISR
  1 unit with BN-2T *Islander* (anti-smuggling patrols)
TRANSPORT
  1 sqn with B-727-200 (VIP); F-27-400M *Troopship*
TRAINING
  1 sqn with R-235 *Guerrier**; TB-30 *Epsilon*; KA-1S*
ATTACK/TRANSPORT HELICOPTER
  1 sqn with AS355F *Ecureuil* II; Bell 206; Mi-35P *Hind;*
  Mi-171Sh

EQUIPMENT BY TYPE
AIRCRAFT 5 combat capable
  MP 1 CN235
  TPT 11: **Light** 9: 1 BN-2T *Islander* (govt owned, mil op);
  1 C-212-100 *Aviocar*; 1 C295; 2 CN235; 2 Beech B200 *King
  Air*; 2 F-27-400M *Troopship* (3 more in store); **PAX** 2:
  1 A319; 1 B-727-200 (VIP)
  TRG 11: 4+ KA-1S*; 1 R-235 *Guerrier**; 6 TB-30 *Epsilon*
HELICOPTERS
  ATK 4: 2 Mi-24V *Hind* D; 2 Mi-35P *Hind*
  MRH 1 AW139
  TPT 8: **Medium** 2 Mi-171Sh; **Light** 6: 1 AS355F *Ecureuil* II;
  1 Bell 205 (UH-1H *Iroquois*); 2 Bell 206; 2 PZL Mi-2 *Hoplite*

Gendarmerie & Paramilitary 5,000

Gendarmerie 5,000
EQUIPMENT BY TYPE
ARMOURED FIGHTING VEHICLES
  APC 56
    APC (W) 24: 7 *Bastion* APC; 5 EE-11 *Urutu*;
    12 VXB-170†
    PPV 32: 24 *Ejder Yalcin*; 8 *Gila*
  AUV 13: 2 Bastion Patsas; 11 RAM Mk3

DEPLOYMENT

CENTRAL AFRICAN REPUBLIC: UN • MINUSCA 191;
1 inf coy

DEMOCRATIC REPUBLIC OF THE CONGO: UN •
MONUSCO 6

GAMBIA: ECOWAS • ECOMIG 250

MALI: UN • MINUSMA 941; 1 mech inf bn; 1 engr coy

SOUTH SUDAN: UN • UNMISS 3

SUDAN: UN • UNISFA 2

FOREIGN FORCES

France 400; 1 *Falcon* 50MI

Spain 65; 2 C295M

Sub-Saharan
Africa

Seychelles SYC

Seychelles Rupee SCR		2021	2022	2023
GDP	SCR	24.6bn	28.5bn	
	USD	1.46bn	2.01bn	
per capita	USD	14,861	20,266	
Growth	%	7.9	10.9	
Inflation	%	9.8	4.1	
Def exp	SCR	n.k	n.k	
	USD	n.k	n.k	
USD1=SCR		16.89	14.20	
Population	97,017			

Age	0–14	15–19	20–24	25–29	30–64	65 plus
Male	9.4%	3.1%	3.2%	3.8%	28.5%	3.8%
Female	8.9%	2.8%	2.8%	3.3%	25.2%	5.2%

Capabilities

The Seychelles maintains one of the smallest standing armed forces in the world. Its proximity to key international shipping lanes increases its strategic significance. The Seychelles People's Defence Force (PDF) primarily focuses on maritime security and counter-piracy operations. The country hosts US military forces conducting maritime-patrol activities on a rotational basis, including the operation of unarmed UAVs. India maintains strong defence ties with the Seychelles, donating equipment, providing maintenance and supporting efforts to enhance its maritime-patrol and -surveillance capability. There are plans to improve defence cooperation with China, which has already led to some equipment deliveries. The Seychelles continues to participate in and host a number of multinational maritime-security exercises. The PDF does not deploy overseas and has a limited capacity to deploy and support troops operating in the archipelago. Modern platforms in the air force and coastguard comprise donations from China, India and the UAE. There are limited maintenance facilities but no domestic defence manufacturing sector.

ACTIVE 420 (Land Forces 200; Coast Guard 200; Air Force 20)

ORGANISATIONS BY SERVICE

People's Defence Force

Land Forces 200
FORCES BY ROLE
SPECIAL FORCES
　1 SF unit
MANOEUVRE
　Light
　　1 inf coy
　Other
　　1 sy unit
COMBAT SUPPORT
　1 MP unit
EQUIPMENT BY TYPE
ARMOURED FIGHTING VEHICLES
　RECCE 6 BRDM-2†
ARTILLERY • MOR 82mm 6 M-43†
AIR DEFENCE • GUNS • TOWED 14.5mm ZPU-2†; ZPU-4†; **37mm** M-1939†

Coast Guard 200 (incl 80 Marines)
EQUIPMENT BY TYPE
PATROL AND COASTAL COMBATANTS 12
　PCO 3: 1 *Andromache* (ITA *Pichiotti 42m*); 2 *Topaz* (ex-IND *Trinkat*)
　PCC 1 *Zoroaster*
　PBF 4: 1 *Hermes* (ex-IND *Coastal Interceptor Craft*); 3 *Wave Rider*
　PB 4: 1 *Etoile* (*Shanghai* II mod); 2 *Le Vigilant* (ex-UAE *Rodman 101*); 1 *Fortune* (UK *Tyne*)

Air Force 20
EQUIPMENT BY TYPE
AIRCRAFT
　TPT • Light 5: 1 DHC-6-320 *Twin Otter*; 2 Do-228; 2 Y-12

Sierra Leone SLE

Sierra Leonean Leone SLL		2021	2022	2023
GDP	SLL	44.4tr	54.5tr	
	USD	4.15bn	4.10bn	
per capita	USD	509	494	
Growth	%	4.1	2.4	
Inflation	%	11.9	25.9	
Def bdgt	SLL	349bn	341bn	
	USD	32.6m	25.7m	
USD1=SLL		10694.21	13295.67	

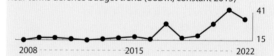
Real-terms defence budget trend (USDm, constant 2015)

Population	8,692,606

Age	0–14	15–19	20–24	25–29	30–64	65 plus
Male	20.7%	5.5%	4.8%	4.0%	13.3%	1.3%
Female	20.3%	5.5%	5.0%	4.6%	13.7%	1.4%

Capabilities

The armed forces' primary task is to ensure internal and border security and provide forces for peacekeeping missions. With international support, there remains a focus on building defence institutions, generating formal defence documentation and improving planning functions. Canada China, France, the UK, and the US are among the nations supporting military capacity-building and there were additional maritime security capacity-building activities with the US Coast Guard in 2022. UK training is also intended to boost the capacity of the police force, and of the armed forces prior to deployment abroad. Freetown's Horton Academy delivers professional military education training to national and regional personnel. Defence ties with China include personnel exchanges and support for the development of military infrastructure. The armed forces also maintain an agricultural unit active in food production. The armed forces' ability to deploy more than small units is constrained by force size and logistic-support capacity. There are plans to generate a company-sized quick-reaction force for peacekeeping missions. Limited capability in areas including air and maritime surveillance was modestly boosted by the arrival of additional inshore-patrol craft in 2020, donated by South Korea. There is limited maintenance capacity and no defence-manufacturing capability.

ACTIVE 8,500 (Joint 8,500)

ORGANISATIONS BY SERVICE

Armed Forces 8,500

FORCES BY ROLE
MANOEUVRE
Reconnaissance
1 recce unit
Light
3 inf bde (total: 12 inf bn)
COMBAT SUPPORT
1 engr regt
1 int unit
1 MP unit
1 sigs unit
COMBAT SUPPORT
1 log unit
1 fd hospital
EQUIPMENT BY TYPE
ARMOURED FIGHTING VEHICLES
APC • **PPV** 4: 3 *Casspir*; 1 *Mamba* Mk5
ANTI-TANK/ANTI-INFRASTRUCTURE
RCL 84mm *Carl Gustaf*
ARTILLERY 37
TOWED 122mm 6 PL-96 (D-30)
MOR 31: 81mm ε27; 82mm 2; 120mm 2
HELICOPTERS • MRH 2 Mi-17 *Hip* H/Mi-8 *Hip*†
AIR DEFENCE • GUNS 14.5mm 3

Maritime Wing ε200

EQUIPMENT BY TYPE
PATROL AND COASTAL COMBATANTS 2
PB 2: 1 Type-062/I (ex-PRC *Shanghai* III)†; 1 *Isle of Man*

DEPLOYMENT

CENTRAL AFRICAN REPUBLIC: UN • MINUSCA 7

DEMOCRATIC REPUBLIC OF THE CONGO: UN • MONUSCO 2

LEBANON: UN • UNIFIL 3

MALI: UN • MINUSMA 18

SOMALIA: UN • UNSOM 1; **UN** • UNSOS 1

SUDAN: UN • UNISFA 7

Somalia SOM

Somali Shilling SOS		2021	2022	2023
GDP	USD	7.63bn	8.42bn	
per capita	USD	n.k.	n.k.	
Growth	%	2.9	1.9	
Inflation	%	n.k.	n.k.	
Def bdgt	USD	n.k.	n.k.	
USD1=SOS		1.00	1.00	

*Definitive economic data unavailable

Population	12,386,248

Age	0–14	15–19	20–24	25–29	30–64	65 plus
Male	20.8%	5.3%	4.7%	3.6%	14.9%	1.1%
Female	20.9%	5.3%	4.6%	3.5%	13.8%	1.5%

Capabilities

Internal stability remains fragile following decades of conflict and insurgency, with al-Shabaab and other extremist groups still based in the country. Deployed international forces look to provide security, stabilisation and capacity-building assistance. Continued challenges have hampered a 2018 transition plan under which Somali forces were to assume security responsibility in 2021. This has required prolonged African Union support, with the African Union Transition Mission in Somalia (ATMIS) replacing the previous AMISOM in April 2022 with a UN mandate to implement a revised transitional plan by the end of 2024. The Somali National Army (SNA) remains limited in terms of both organisational and military capability, although the multi-clan US-mentored Danab Brigade, has displayed greater capability. US forces are also deployed independently to Somalia to tackle militant groups. The SNA remains reliant on external training programmes from a number of countries, organisations and private security companies to build internal capability and capacity. Turkey has established a significant military training facility in Somalia as well as providing specialist training abroad. There are reports that some troops were sent to Eritrea for training in 2021. However, wider plans to professionalise, legitimatise and unite the loose collections of clan-based militia groups that form the SNA have yet to be fully realised. Growing a domestic training capacity staff within the SNA, to enable organic continuation training remains a challenge. There is no capacity to deploy beyond national borders, while there is minimal national infrastructure available to support domestic operations. The equipment inventory is limited and eclectic, and government plans to re-establish and equip Somalia's air and maritime forces remain unfulfilled. There is no domestic defence-industrial capability.

ACTIVE 13,900 (Army 13,900)

ORGANISATIONS BY SERVICE

Army 13,900

FORCES BY ROLE
COMMAND
4 div HQ
MANOEUVRE
Light
Some cdo bn(+)
12 inf bde (3 inf bn)
2 indep inf bn

Other
1 gd bn
EQUIPMENT BY TYPE
ARMOURED FIGHTING VEHICLES
APC 73+
APC (W) 38+: 25+ AT-105 *Saxon*; 13 *Bastion* APC; Fiat 6614
PPV 35+: *Casspir*; MAV-5; 20 *Kirpi*; 9+ *Mamba* Mk5; 6 *Puma* M36; RG-31 *Nyala*
AUV 12 *Tiger* 4×4

Gendarmerie & Paramilitary

Coast Guard
All operational patrol vessels under 10t FLD

FOREIGN FORCES
Under UNSOM command unless stated
Burundi ATMIS 4,000; 5 inf bn
Djibouti ATMIS 900; 1 inf bn
Ethiopia ATMIS 4,000; 5 inf bn
Finland EUTM Somalia 12
Ghana 1 • UNSOS 1
India 1
Italy EUTM Somalia 150
Kenya ATMIS 4,000; 3 inf bn • UNSOS 1
Mauritania UNSOS 1
Pakistan UNSOS 1
Portugal EUTM Somalia 2
Romania EUTM Somalia 5
Serbia EUTM Somalia 6
Sierra Leone 1 • UNSOS 1
Spain EUTM Somalia 20
Sweden EUTM Somalia 5
Turkey Army: 200 (trg base)
Uganda 627; 1 sy bn • ATMIS 5,800; 7 inf bn • UNSOS 1
United Kingdom 2 • UNSOS 10 • Army: 65 (trg team)
United States US Africa Command: 100

TERRITORY WHERE THE GOVERNMENT DOES NOT EXERCISE EFFECTIVE CONTROL
Data presented here represents the de facto situation. This does not imply international recognition as a sovereign state. Much of this equipment is in poor repair or inoperable

Somaliland

Army ε12,500
FORCES BY ROLE
MANOEUVRE
Armoured
2 armd bde
Mechanised
1 mech inf bde
Light
14 inf bde
COMBAT SUPPORT
2 arty bde

COMBAT SERVICE SUPPORT
1 spt bn
EQUIPMENT BY TYPE†
ARMOURED FIGHTING VEHICLES
MBT T-54/55
RECCE Fiat 6616
APC • APC(W) Fiat 6614
ARTILLERY • MRL various incl BM-21 *Grad*
AIR DEFENCE • GUNS • 23mm ZU-23-2

Ministry of the Interior

Coast Guard 600
All operational patrol vessels under 10t FLD

Puntland

Army ε3,000 (to be integrated into Somali National Army)

Maritime Police Force ε1,000
EQUIPMENT BY TYPE
PATROL AND COASTAL COMBATANTS
All operational patrol vessels under 10t FLD
AIRCRAFT • TPT 4: **Light** 3 Ayres S2R; **PAX** 1 DC-3
HELICOPTERS • MRH SA316 *Alouette* III

FOREIGN FORCES
United Arab Emirates 180

South Africa RSA

South African Rand ZAR		2021	2022	2023
GDP	ZAR	6.19tr	6.62tr	
	USD	419bn	411bn	
per capita	USD	6,965	6,739	
Growth	%	4.9	2.1	
Inflation	%	4.6	6.7	
Def bdgt	ZAR	49.4bn	49.8bn	
	USD	3.34bn	3.09bn	
USD1=ZAR		14.78	16.10	

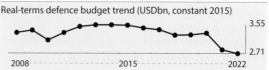
Real-terms defence budget trend (USDbn, constant 2015)

Population 57,516,665

Age	0–14	15–19	20–24	25–29	30–64	65 plus
Male	13.8%	4.2%	4.0%	4.1%	20.6%	2.7%
Female	13.8%	4.2%	4.1%	4.3%	20.4%	3.7%

Capabilities
South Africa's armed forces are on paper the most capable in the region but continuing economic and structural problems are eroding capabilities. Principal roles include maintaining territorial integrity and supporting the police service. The Department of

Defence Strategic Plan 2020–2025 is the South African National Defence Force's (SANDF) primary policy instrument. A priority for the SANDF is to arrest the decline of critical military capabilities and equipment. However, the 2020/21 Defence Annual Report said that funding constraints are affecting implementation, resulting in problems in meeting future SANDF requirements and objectives outlined in the 2015 Defence Review. The army is reverting to a more traditional structure with standing brigades being formed. South Africa contributes personnel to UN operations and remains a key component of the Force Intervention Brigade in the DRC. South Africa is a member of the SADC Standby Force and sent 1,500 personnel to Mozambique in 2021 as part of a multinational force to combat the Islamist insurgency. Troops were deployed domestically in 2021 to help counter internal unrest. Historically, South African forces have also played a key role in training and supporting other regional forces. The SANDF can independently deploy its forces and as well as peacekeeping missions it participates in national and multinational exercises. However, reduced funding has undermined modernisation ambitions, resulting in programmes being behind schedule and difficulties in maintaining and replacing obsolete equipment. The air force has had challenges in maintaining operational capabilities, but a new support contract may lead to a revival in combat aircraft availability. Naval capacity is dependent on serviceability and many vessels have been under repair or maintenance in recent years. Budget cuts are also likely to have an adverse effect on training. South Africa has the continent's most capable defence industry, including the state-owned Armaments Corporation of South Africa (ARMSCOR) and weapons manufacturer Denel, which continues to experience financial difficulties. Cuban personnel remain engaged on a project to maintain and refurbish land vehicles.

ACTIVE 74,000 (Army 38,000 Navy 6,650 Air 9,800 South African Military Health Service 7,300 Other 12,250)

RESERVE 15,050 (Army 12,250 Navy 850 Air 850 South African Military Health Service Reserve 1,100)

ORGANISATIONS BY SERVICE

Space
EQUIPMENT BY TYPE
SATELLITES • ISR 1 *Kondor*-E

Army 38,000
FORCES BY ROLE
Regt are bn sized. A new army structure is planned with 3 mixed regular/reserve divisions (1 mechanised, 1 motorised and 1 contingency) comprising 12 brigades (1 armoured, 1 mechanised, 7 motorised, 1 airborne, 1 airlanded and 1 sea landed)
COMMAND
2 bde HQ
SPECIAL FORCES
2 SF regt(-)
MANOEUVRE
Reconnaissance
1 armd recce regt
Armoured
1 tk regt(-)
Mechanised
2 mech inf bn

Light
8 mot inf bn
1 lt inf bn
Air Manoeuvre
1 AB bn
1 air mob bn
Amphibious
1 amph bn
COMBAT SUPPORT
1 arty regt
1 engr regt
1 construction regt
3 sigs regt
COMBAT SERVICE SUPPORT
1 engr spt regt
AIR DEFENCE
1 ADA regt

Reserve 12,250 reservists (under-strength)
FORCES BY ROLE
MANOEUVRE
Reconnaissance
3 armd recce regt
Armoured
4 tk regt
Mechanised
6 mech inf bn
Light
14 mot inf bn
3 lt inf bn (converting to mot inf)
Air Manoeuvre
1 AB bn
2 air mob bn
Amphibious
1 amph bn
COMBAT SUPPORT
7 arty regt
2 engr regt
AIR DEFENCE
5 AD regt
EQUIPMENT BY TYPE
ARMOURED FIGHTING VEHICLES
MBT 24 *Olifant* 2 (133 *Olifant* 1B in store)
ASLT 50 *Rooikat*-76 (126 in store)
IFV 534 *Ratel*-20/*Ratel*-60/*Ratel*-90
APC • PPV 810: 370 *Casspir*; 60 *Mamba* (refurbished); 380 *Mamba*†
ENGINEERING & MAINTENANCE VEHICLES
ARV *Gemsbok*
VLB *Leguan*
MW *Husky*
ANTI-TANK/ANTI-INFRASTRUCTURE
MSL
SP ZT-3 *Swift*
MANPATS *Milan* ADT/ER
RCL **106mm** M40A1 (some SP)

478 THE MILITARY BALANCE 2023

ARTILLERY 1,240

SP 155mm 2 G-6 (41 in store)

TOWED 155mm 6 G-5 (66 in store)

MRL 127mm 6 *Valkiri* Mk II MARS *Bataleur*; (26 *Valkiri* Mk I and 19 *Valkiri* Mk II in store)

MOR 1,226: **81mm** 1,190 (incl some SP on *Casspir* & *Ratel*); **120mm** 36

UNINHABITED AERIAL VEHICLES

ISR • Light up to 4 *Vulture*

AIR DEFENCE

SAM • Point-defence *Starstreak*

GUNS 40

SP 23mm (36 *Zumlac* in store)

TOWED 35mm 40: 22 GDF-002; 18 GDF-005A/007

Navy 6,650

Fleet HQ and Naval base located at Simon's Town; Naval stations located at Durban and Port Elizabeth

EQUIPMENT BY TYPE

SUBMARINES 2

SSK 2 *Heroine* (Type-209/1400 mod) (1 additional boat in refit since 2014, awaiting funds to complete) with 8 533mm TT with SUT 264 HWT

PRINCIPAL SURFACE COMBATANTS • FRIGATES 4

FFGHM 4 *Valour* (MEKO A200) with 2 quad lnchr with MM40 *Exocet* Block 2 AShM (upgrade to Block 3 planned); 2 16-cell VLS with *Umkhonto*-IR SAM, 1 Denel Dual Purpose Gun (DPG) CIWS, 1 76mm gun (capacity 1 *Super Lynx* 300 hel)

PATROL AND COASTAL COMBATANTS 4

PCC 3: 2 *Warrior* (ISR *Reshef*) with 1 76mm gun; 1 *Warrior* II (NLD Damen Stan Patrol 6211)

PB 1 *Tobie* (2 additional in reserve)

MINE WARFARE • MINE COUNTERMEASURES 3

MHC 3 *River* (GER *Navors*) (limited operational roles; training and dive support) (1 additional in reserve)

LOGISTICS AND SUPPORT 2

AGHS 1 *Protea* (UK *Hecla*) with 1 hel landing platform

AORH 1 *Drakensberg* (capacity 2 *Oryx* hels; 100 troops)

Maritime Reaction Squadron

FORCES BY ROLE

MANOEUVRE

Amphibious

1 mne patrol gp

1 diving gp

1 mne boarding gp

COMBAT SERVICE SUPPORT

1 spt gp

Air Force 9,800

Air Force HQ, Pretoria, and 4 op gps

Command & Control: 2 Airspace Control Sectors, 1 Mobile Deployment Wg, 1 Air Force Command Post

FORCES BY ROLE

FIGHTER/GROUND ATTACK

1 sqn with *Gripen* C/D (JAS-39C/D)

GROUND ATTACK/TRAINING

1 sqn with *Hawk* Mk120*

TRANSPORT

1 (VIP) sqn with B-737 BBJ; Cessna 550 *Citation* II; *Falcon* 50; *Falcon* 900

1 sqn with C-47TP

2 sqn with Beech 200/300 *King Air*; C-130B/BZ; C-212

ATTACK HELICOPTER

1 (cbt spt) sqn with AH-2 *Rooivalk*

TRANSPORT HELICOPTER

4 (mixed) sqn with AW109; BK-117; *Oryx*

EQUIPMENT BY TYPE

AIRCRAFT 48 combat capable

FGA 24 *Gripen* C/D (JAS-39C/D) (most non-operational)

TPT 23: **Medium** 6: 2 C-130B *Hercules*; 4 C-130BZ *Hercules*; **Light** 13: 3 Beech 200C *King Air*; 1 Beech 300 *King Air*; 3 C-47TP (maritime); 2 C-212-200 *Aviocart*; 1 C-212-300 *Aviocart*; 2 Cessna 550 *Citation* II; 1 PC-12; (9 Cessna 208 *Caravan* in store) **PAX** 4: 1 B-737BBJ; 2 *Falcon* 50; 1 *Falcon* 900

TRG 59: 24 *Hawk* Mk120*; 35 PC-7 Mk II *Astra*

HELICOPTERS

ATK 11 AH-2 *Rooivalk*

MRH 4 *Super Lynx* 300

TPT 69: **Medium** 36 *Oryx*; **Light** 33: 25 AW109; 8 BK-117

AIR-LAUNCHED MISSILES • AAM • IIR IRIS-T

BOMBS • Laser-guided GBU-12 *Paveway* II

Ground Defence

FORCES BY ROLE

MANOEUVRE

Other

12 sy sqn (SAAF regt)

South African Military Health Service 7,300

DEPLOYMENT

DEMOCRATIC REPUBLIC OF THE CONGO: UN • MONUSCO • *Operation Mistral* 1,183; 1 inf bn; 1 hel sqn

MOZAMBIQUE: SADC • SAMIM 1,200; 1 inf bn

MOZAMBIQUE CHANNEL: Navy • 1 FFGHM

South Sudan SSD

South Sudanese Pound SSP		2021	2022	2023
GDP	SSP		1.60tr	2.47tr
	USD		5.17bn	4.78bn
per capita	USD		364	328
Growth	%		5.3	6.5
Inflation	%		30.2	17.6
Def bdgt [a]	SSP		13.4bn	32.8bn
	USD		43.4m	63.5m
USD1=SSP			309.34	516.03

[a] Security and law enforcement spending

Real-terms defence budget trend (USDm, constant 2015)

Population	11,544,905					
Age	0–14	15–19	20–24	25–29	30–64	65 plus
Male	21.3%	5.6%	5.1%	4.1%	13.7%	1.4%
Female	20.5%	5.6%	4.9%	3.5%	13.2%	1.1%

Capabilities

South Sudan's civil war formally ended in 2020 and a fragile ceasefire has largely remained intact. The September 2020 peace deal built on a 2018 accord that laid out a peace framework for opposition and government forces, resulting in changes to the number and demarcation of federal states. These and other challenges remain stumbling blocks in ongoing negotiations, with the transition period extended by two years and the country's first elections since declaring independence in 2011 rescheduled to late 2024. There has been some limited progress towards unifying former rebels and the army under the banner of the South Sudan People's Defence Forces (SSPDF). However, doubts were raised, in a UN report, about the effectiveness of the disarmament, screening and training received by the 50,000 combatants, who officials claimed in February 2022 were ready for graduation after this process. The same report said that regional commanders were recruiting independently in order to strengthen their position, in violation of the peace agreement. Reports continue of the use of child soldiers, forced recruitment, and of sexual violence. There is no capacity to deploy and sustain military units beyond national borders. Equipment is primarily of Soviet origin with some light arms of Chinese origin, and there have been efforts to expand the small air force. Sanctions remain in place, with both the EU and UN arms embargoes widened in 2018 to include all types of military equipment. South Sudan has no established domestic defence industry but has reportedly sought to develop an ammunition-manufacturing capacity in recent years.

ACTIVE 53,000 (Army 53,000)

ORGANISATIONS BY SERVICE

Army ε53,000 (in training)
FORCES BY ROLE
3 military comd
MANOEUVRE
 Light
  8 inf div
COMBAT SUPPORT
 1 engr corps
EQUIPMENT BY TYPE
ARMOURED FIGHTING VEHICLES
 MBT 80+: some T-55†; 80 T-72AV†
 APC • PPV Streit *Typhoon*; Streit *Cougar*; Mamba
ANTI-TANK/ANTI-INFRASTRUCTURE
 MSL • MANPATS HJ-73; 9K115 *Metis* (RS-AT-7 *Saxhorn*)
 RCL 73mm SPG-9 (with SSLA)
ARTILLERY
 SP 122mm 2S1 *Gvozdika*; 152mm 2S3 *Akatsiya*
 TOWED 130mm Some M-46
 MRL 122mm BM-21 *Grad*; 107mm PH-63
 MOR 82mm; 120mm Type-55 look-alike
AIR DEFENCE
 SAM
  Short-range 16 S-125 *Pechora* (RS-SA-3 *Goa*)†
  Point-defence 9K32 *Strela*-2 (RS-SA-7 *Grail*)‡; QW-2
 GUNS 14.5mm ZPU-4; 23mm ZU-23-2; 37mm Type-65/74

Air Force
EQUIPMENT BY TYPE
AIRCRAFT 2 combat capable
 TPT • Light 1 Beech 1900
 TRG ε2 L-39 *Albatros**
HELICOPTERS
 ATK 5: 2 Mi-24V *Hind*; 3 Mi-24V-SMB *Hind*
 MRH 9 Mi-17 *Hip* H
 TPT 3: Medium 1 Mi-172 (VIP); Light 2 AW109 (civ livery)

FOREIGN FORCES

All UNMISS, unless otherwise indicated
Albania 2
Australia 15
Azerbaijan 1
Bangladesh 1,628; 1 inf coy; 2 rvn coy; 2 engr coy
Benin 4
Bhutan 5
Bolivia 5
Brazil 11
Cambodia 84; 1 MP unit
Canada 8
China, People's Republic of 1,054; 1 inf bn; 1 engr coy; 1 fd hospital

Ecuador 3

Egypt 5

El Salvador 1

Ethiopia 1,476; 3 inf bn

Fiji 3

Gambia 4

Germany 14

Ghana 725; 1 inf bn

Guatemala 7

Guinea 3

India 2,396; 2 inf bn; 1 engr coy; 1 sigs coy; 1 fd hospital

Indonesia 3

Japan 4

Jordan 5

Kenya 17

Korea, Republic of 277; 1 engr coy

Kyrgyzstan 1

Liberia 1

Moldova 6

Mongolia 868; 1 inf bn

Morocco 2

Namibia 2

Nepal 1,749; 2 inf bn

New Zealand 3

Nigeria 14

Norway 15

Pakistan 286; 1 engr coy

Paraguay 2

Peru 4

Philippines 2

Poland 1

Romania 6

Russia 2

Rwanda 2,642; 3 inf bn; 1 hel sqn with 6 Mi-17

Senegal 3

Sri Lanka 66; 1 fd hospital; 1 hel sqn

Switzerland 1

Tanzania 8

Thailand 281; 1 engr coy

Togo 2

Tunisia 2

Uganda 2

United Kingdom 4

United States 8

Vietnam 69

Zambia 9

Zimbabwe 14

Sudan SDN

Sudanese Pound SDG		2021	2022	2023
GDP	SDG	15.0tr	32.3tr	
	USD	35.1bn	42.8bn	
per capita	USD	772	916	
Growth	%	0.5	-0.3	
Inflation	%	359.1	154.9	
Def exp	SDG	n.k	n.k	
	USD	n.k	n.k	
USD1=SDG		425.62	756.05	

Population 47,958,856

Age	0–14	15–19	20–24	25–29	30–64	65 plus
Male	20.8%	5.9%	5.0%	3.8%	13.1%	1.6%
Female	20.1%	5.8%	4.8%	3.6%	14.0%	1.5%

Capabilities

Political uncertainty and internal division continue in Sudan in the wake of the October 2021 military coup, which replaced the civilian and military Sovereign Council formed following the 2019 ousting of President Omar al-Bashir. Though the civilian prime minister was reinstated a month after the coup, he subsequently resigned. The armed forces now control the transitional process toward democratic elections. The armed forces remain focused on internal security, though a peace deal was signed with five rebel groups in August 2020. Border issues remain a concern with neighbouring Ethiopia, and there have been reports of cross-border incursions amid the continuing conflict between Addis Ababa and Tigrayan forces. Sudan was part of the initial Saudi-led coalition intervention in Yemen, though the level of ongoing involvement in the campaign is unclear. A defence agreement with Iran in 2008 reportedly included assistance in developing the domestic arms industry. Growing defence ties with Egypt saw joint exercises take place in 2020 and 2021, and an agreement to strengthen military cooperation was signed in March 2021. The armed forces are conscript-based and will have gained operational experience from internal-security deployments and the intervention in Yemen. By regional standards, Sudan's armed forces are relatively well equipped, with significant holdings of both ageing and modern systems. A UN arms embargo remains in place, though this is limited to equipment in the Darfur region; reports continue of violations. Recent acquisitions have included Russian and Ukrainian government surplus and also new Chinese fighter ground-attack aircraft. The state-run Military Industry Corporation manufactures a range of ammunition, small arms and armoured vehicles for the domestic and export market. The majority of the corporation's products are based on older Chinese and Russian systems.

ACTIVE 104,300 (Army 100,000 Navy 1,300 Air 3,000) **Gendarmerie & Paramilitary 40,000**
Conscript liability 2 years for males aged 18–30

ORGANISATIONS BY SERVICE

Space
EQUIPMENT BY TYPE
SATELLITES • ISR 1 SRSS-1

Army 100,000+

FORCES BY ROLE
SPECIAL FORCES
5 SF coy
MANOEUVRE
Reconnaissance
1 indep recce bde
Armoured
1 armd div
Mechanised
1 mech inf div
1 indep mech inf bde
Light
15+ inf div
6 indep inf bde
Air Manoeuvre
1 air aslt bde
Amphbious
1 mne div
Other
1 (Border Guard) sy bde
COMBAT SUPPORT
3 indep arty bde
1 engr div (9 engr bn)
EQUIPMENT BY TYPE
ARMOURED FIGHTING VEHICLES
MBT 465: 20 M60A3; 60 Type-59/Type-59D; 305 T-54/T-55; 70 T-72AV; 10 *Al-Bashier* (Type-85-IIM)
LT TK 115: 70 Type-62; 45 Type-63
RECCE 206: 6 AML-90; 70 BRDM-1/2; 50–80 FV701 *Ferret*; 30–50 FV601 *Saladin*
IFV 145: 135 BMP-1/-2; 10 BTR-3
APC 405+
  APC (T) 66: 20-30 BTR-50; 36 M113
  APC (W) 339+: 50–80 BTR-152; 20 OT-62; 50 OT-64; 3+ *Rakhsh*; 10 WZ-551; WZ-523; 55-80 V-150 *Commando*; 96 *Walid*
  PPV some *Sarsar-2*; some Streit *Spartan*
  AUV 4+ Nimr *Ajban* 440A
ANTI-TANK/ANTI-INFRASTRUCTURE
MSL • MANPATS 9K11 *Malyutka* (RS-AT-3 *Sagger*); HJ-8; 9K135 *Kornet* (RS-AT-14 *Spriggan*)
RCL 106mm 40 M40A1
GUNS 76mm ZIS-3; **100mm** M-1944; **85mm** D-44
ARTILLERY 860+
SP 66: **122mm** 56 2S1 *Gvozdika*; **155mm** 10 Mk F3
TOWED 128+: **105mm** 20 M101; **122mm** 21+: 21 D-30; D-74; M-30; **130mm** 75 M-46/Type-59-I; **155mm** 12 M114A1
MRL 666+: **107mm** 477 Type-63; **122mm** 188: 120 BM-21 *Grad*; 50 *Saqr*; 18 Type-81; **302mm** 1+ WS-1
MOR 81mm; **82mm**; **120mm** AM-49; M-43; W86
AIR DEFENCE
SAM • Point-defence 4+: 9K32 *Strela-2* (RS-SA-7 *Grail*)‡; 4+ 9K33 *Osa* (RS-SA-8 *Gecko*); FN-6 (CH-SA-10)
GUNS 966+
  SP 20: **20mm** 8 M163 *Vulcan*; 12 M3 VDAA
  TOWED 946+: 740+ **14.5mm** ZPU-2/**14.5mm** ZPU-4/**37mm** Type-63/**57mm** S-60/**85mm** M-1944; **20mm** 16 M167 *Vulcan*; **23mm** 50 ZU-23-2; **37mm** 80 M-1939; (30 M-1939 unserviceable); **40mm** 60

Navy 1,300

EQUIPMENT BY TYPE
PATROL AND COASTAL COMBATANTS 11
PBR 4 *Kurmuk*
PB 7: 1 13.5m; 1 14m; 2 19m; 3 41m (PRC)
AMPHIBIOUS • LANDING CRAFT • LCVP 5
LOGISTICS AND SUPPORT 4
AG 3
AXL 1 *Petrushka* (ex-RUS)

Air Force 3,000

FORCES BY ROLE
FIGHTER
2 sqn with MiG-29SE/UB *Fulcrum*
FIGHTER/GROUND ATTACK
1 sqn with FTC-2000*
GROUND ATTACK
1 sqn with Su-24M/MR *Fencer*
1 sqn with Su-25K/Su-25UB *Frogfoot*
TRANSPORT
Some sqn with An-30 *Clank*; An-32 *Cline*; An-72 *Coaler*; An-74TK-200/300; C-130H *Hercules*; Il-76 *Candid*; Y-8
1 VIP unit with *Falcon* 20F; *Falcon* 50; *Falcon* 900; F-27; Il-62M *Classic*
TRAINING
1 sqn with K-8 *Karakorum*
ATTACK HELICOPTER
2 sqn with Mi-24/Mi-24P/Mi-24V/Mi-35P *Hind*
TRANSPORT HELICOPTER
2 sqn with Mi-8 *Hip*; Mi-17 *Hip H*; Mi-171
EQUIPMENT BY TYPE
AIRCRAFT 59 combat capable
FTR 22: 20 MiG-29SE *Fulcrum* C; 2 MiG-29UB *Fulcrum* B
FGA 6 FTC-2000G
ATK 20: 6 Su-24M/MR *Fencer*; 14 Su-25K/UB *Frogfoot*; (15 A-5 *Fantan* in store)
ISR 2 An-30 *Clank*
TPT 24: **Heavy** 1 Il-76 *Candid*; **Medium** 6: 4 C-130H *Hercules*; 2 Y-8; **Light** 13: ε3 An-26 *Curl*; 2 An-32 *Cline*; 2 An-72 *Coaler*; 4 An-74TK-200; 2 An-74TK-300; **PAX** 4: 1 *Falcon* 20F (VIP); 1 *Falcon* 50 (VIP); 1 *Falcon* 900; 1 Il-62M *Classic*
TRG 15+: 11 K-8 *Karakorum*; some SAFAT-03; 3 Utva-75
HELICOPTERS
ATK 40: 25 Mi-24 *Hind*; 2 Mi-24P *Hind*; 7 Mi-24V *Hind E*; 6 Mi-35P *Hind*
MRH ε3 Mi-17 *Hip H*
TPT 27: **Medium** 23: 21 Mi-8 *Hip*; 2 Mi-171; **Light** 4: 1 Bell 205; 3 Bo-105
TRG some SAFAT 02
UNINHABITED AERIAL VEHICLES
CISR • Heavy CH-3; CH-4
AIR DEFENCE • SAM • Medium-range: (18 S-75M *Dvina* (RS-SA-2 *Guideline*)‡ (non-operational))
AIR-LAUNCHED MISSILES • AAM • IR R-3 (RS-AA-2 *Atoll*)‡; R-60 (RS-AA-8 *Aphid*); R-73 (RS-AA-11A *Archer*); **ARH** R-77 (RS-AA-12A *Adder*)

Gendarmerie & Paramilitary 40,000

The Popular Defence Forces were officially disbanded in 2019, but it is unclear if elements still exist in some form

Rapid Support Force 40,000
EQUIPMENT BY TYPE
ARMOURED FIGHTING VEHICLES
    IFV 7 BTR-80A; WZ-523 IFV
    APC • APC (W) 20+ BTR-70M *Kobra* 2
AIR DEFENCE • GUNS
    SP 14.5mm ZPU-2 (tch)

DEPLOYMENT

YEMEN: *Operation Restoring Hope* 650; 1 mech BG; T-72AV, BTR-70M *Kobra* 2

FOREIGN FORCES

All UNISFA unless otherwise indicated
Bangladesh 508; 1 inf bn
Benin 2
Bhutan 3
Bolivia 4
Brazil 3
Burundi 7
Cambodia 1
China, People's Republic of 87; 1 hel flt with 2 Mi-171
Ecuador 3
Egypt 3
El Salvador 1
Ethiopia 3
Ghana 656; 1 inf bn; 1 fd hospital
Guatemala 3
Guinea 1
India 325; 1 mech inf bn(-)
Indonesia 4
Kenya 2
Kyrgyzstan 2
Liberia 2
Malawi 4
Malaysia 1
Mongolia 4
Namibia 7
Nepal 89; 1 log coy
Nigeria 15
Pakistan 583; 1 inf bn
Peru 4
Russia 2
Rwanda 3
Sierra Leone 7
Tanzania 2
Uganda 2
Uruguay 2
Vietnam 190; 1 engr coy
Zambia 5
Zimbabwe 9

Tanzania TZA

Tanzanian Shilling TZS		2021	2022	2023
GDP	TZS	162tr	177tr	
	USD	70.3bn	76.6bn	
per capita	USD	1,177	1,245	
Growth	%	4.9	4.5	
Inflation	%	3.7	4.0	
Def bdgt	TZS	2.08tr	2.18tr	
	USD	903m	943m	
USD1=TZS		2309.56	2314.19	

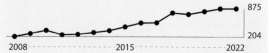
Real-terms defence budget trend (USDm, constant 2015)

Population 63,852,892

Age	0–14	15–19	20–24	25–29	30–64	65 plus
Male	21.1%	5.4%	4.6%	3.8%	13.7%	1.4%
Female	20.7%	5.3%	4.5%	3.8%	13.9%	1.9%

Capabilities

Non-state actors pose the principal threat to Tanzania's security, with terrorism, poaching and piracy of concern. A developing relationship with China has led to a series of procurements and training contracts. There are also defence-related ties with Israel, Pakistan and Russia and a military cooperation agreement was signed with the Republic of Comoros in 2022. The armed forces take part in multinational exercises in Africa and have provided some training assistance to other African forces. Training relationships also exist with extra-regional armed forces, including the US. Tanzania's contribution to the UN's Force Intervention Brigade in the eastern DRC, notably its special forces, will have provided lessons for force development. However, there is only a limited capacity to project power independently beyond the country's borders. Budget constraints have limited recapitalisation ambitions and, although heavy equipment is ageing, airlift capacity has improved with the delivery of new helicopters. There are local ammunition facilities, but otherwise Tanzania relies on imports for its military equipment.

ACTIVE 27,000 (Army 23,000 Navy 1,000 Air 3,000)
Gendarmerie & Paramilitary 1,400
Conscript liability Three months basic military training combined with social service, ages 18–23

RESERVE 80,000 (Joint 80,000)

ORGANISATIONS BY SERVICE

Army ε23,000
FORCES BY ROLE
SPECIAL FORCES
    1 SF unit
MANOEUVRE
    Armoured
    1 tk bde

Light
5 inf bde

COMBAT SUPPORT
4 arty bn
1 mor bn
2 AT bn
1 engr regt (bn)

COMBAT SERVICE SUPPORT
1 log gp

AIR DEFENCE
2 ADA bn

EQUIPMENT BY TYPE†

ARMOURED FIGHTING VEHICLES
MBT 46: 30 T-54/T-55; 15 Type-59G; 1+ VT-2
LT TK 57+: 30 FV101 *Scorpion*; 25 Type-62; 2+ Type-63A
RECCE 10 BRDM-2
APC • APC (W) 14: ε10 BTR-40/BTR-152; 4 Type-92

ANTI-TANK/ANTI-INFRASTRUCTURE
RCL 75mm Type-52 (M20)
GUNS 85mm 75 Type-56 (D-44)

ARTILLERY 344+
TOWED 130: 122mm 100: 20 D-30; 80 Type-54-1 (M-30); 130mm 30 Type-59-I
GUN/MOR 120mm 3+ Type-07PA
MRL 61+: 122mm 58 BM-21 *Grad*; 300mm 3+ A100
MOR 150: 82mm 100 M-43; 120mm 50 M-43

Navy ε1,000

EQUIPMENT BY TYPE

PATROL AND COASTAL COMBATANTS 14
PCC 2 *Mwitongo* (ex-PRC *Haiqing*)
PHT 2 Type-025 (*Huchuan*) each with 2 single 533mm ASTT
PB 10: 2 *Ngunguri*; 2 Type-062 (PRC *Shanghai* II); 2 VT 23m; 4 *Mambwe* (Damen Fast Crew Supplier 3307)

AMPHIBIOUS 3
LCT 1 *Kasa*
LCM 2 *Mbono* (ex-PRC *Yunnan*)

Air Defence Command ε3,000

FORCES BY ROLE

FIGHTER
3 sqn with F-7/FT-7; FT-5; K-8 *Karakorum**

TRANSPORT
1 sqn with Cessna 404 *Titan*; DHC-5D *Buffalo*; F-28 *Fellowship*; F-50; Gulfstream G550; Y-12 (II)

TRANSPORT HELICOPTER
1 sqn with Bell 205 (AB-205); Bell 412EP *Twin Huey*

EQUIPMENT BY TYPE†

AIRCRAFT 17 combat capable
FTR 11: 9 F-7 (F-7TN); 2 FT-7 (FT-7N)
ISR 1 SB7L-360 *Seeker*
TPT 12: Medium 2 Y-8; Light 7: 2 Cessna 404 *Titan*; 3 DHC-5D *Buffalo*; 2 Y-12(II); PAX 3: 1 F-28 *Fellowship*; 1 F-50; 1 Gulfstream G550
TRG 9: 3 FT-5 (JJ-5); 6 K-8 *Karakorum**

HELICOPTERS
MRH 1 Bell 412EP *Twin Huey*
TPT 2: Medium 1+ H225; Light 1 Bell 205 (AB-205)

AIR DEFENCE

SAM
Short-range 2K12 *Kub* (RS-SA-6 *Gainful*)†
Point-defence 9K32 *Strela*-2 (RS-SA-7 *Grail*)‡
GUNS 200
TOWED 14.5mm 40 ZPU-2/ZPU-4†; 23mm 40 ZU-23-2; 37mm 120 M-1939

Gendarmerie & Paramilitary 1,400 active

Police Field Force 1,400
18 sub-units incl Police Marine Unit

Air Wing

EQUIPMENT BY TYPE
AIRCRAFT • TPT • Light 1 Cessna U206 *Stationair*
HELICOPTERS
TPT • Light 4: 2 Bell 206A *Jet Ranger* (AB-206A); 2 Bell 206L *Long Ranger*
TRG 2 Bell 47G (AB-47G)/Bell 47G2

Marine Unit 100

EQUIPMENT BY TYPE
PATROL AND COASTAL COMBATANTS
All operational patrol vessels under 10t FLD

DEPLOYMENT

CENTRAL AFRICAN REPUBLIC: UN • MINUSCA 457; 1 inf bn(-)

DEMOCRATIC REPUBLIC OF THE CONGO: UN • MONUSCO 849; 1 spec ops coy; 1 inf bn

LEBANON: UN • UNIFIL 124; 1 MP coy

MOZAMBIQUE: SADC • SAMIM 290

SOUTH SUDAN: UN • UNMISS 8

SUDAN: UN • UNISFA 2

Togo TGO

CFA Franc BCEAO XOF		2021	2022	2023
GDP	XOF	4.67tr	5.09tr	
	USD	8.43bn	8.36bn	
per capita	USD	993	961	
Growth	%	5.3	5.4	
Inflation	%	4.3	5.6	
Def bdgt	XOF	65.6bn	106bn	
	USD	118m	173m	
USD1=XOF		554.27	608.60	

Real-terms defence budget trend (USDm, constant 2015)

Population 8,492,333

Age	0–14	15–19	20–24	25–29	30–64	65 plus
Male	19.9%	5.0%	4.2%	3.7%	14.7%	1.7%
Female	19.4%	5.0%	4.2%	3.8%	16.0%	2.5%

Capabilities

Defence authorities are increasingly concerned by the challenge from piracy and other illicit maritime activities in the Gulf of Guinea as well as jihadist activity in the north. As a result, regional cooperation is now being strengthened. In 2020 Togo adopted a new military-programming law, leading to the creation of a special-forces group. Togo plans to increase its force strength and recently acquired modern APCs while there have been unconfirmed reports of interest in armed UAVs. France continues to deliver military training, including for Togolese peacekeeping contingents. There is also a peacekeeping training centre in Lomé. The United States' Africa Contingency Operations Training and Assistance programme has provided assistance with training. The armed forces have taken part in multilateral exercises, including the US-led *Obangame Express*. Togo's deployment capabilities are limited without external support, while financial challenges limit capability development more broadly. There are some maintenance facilities but there is no defence-manufacturing sector.

ACTIVE 13,450 (Army 13,000 Navy 200 Air 250)
Gendarmerie & Paramilitary 3,000
Conscript liability Selective conscription, 2 years

ORGANISATIONS BY SERVICE

Army ε13,000
FORCES BY ROLE
MANOEUVRE
  Reconnaissance
  1 armd recce regt
  Mechanised
  1 armd bn
  Light
  2 cbd arms regt
  2 inf regt
  1 rapid reaction force
  Air Manoeuvre
  1 cdo/para regt (3 cdo/para coy)
  Other
  1 (Presidential Guard) gd regt (1 gd bn, 1 cdo bn, 2 indep gd coy)
COMBAT SUPPORT
  1 cbt spt regt (1 fd arty bty, 2 ADA bty, 1 engr/log/tpt bn)
EQUIPMENT BY TYPE
ARMOURED FIGHTING VEHICLES
  MBT 2 T-54/T-55
  LT TK 18 FV101 *Scorpion*
  RECCE 55: 3 AML-60; 7 AML-90; 36 EE-9 *Cascavel*; 6 M8; 3 M20
  IFV 20 BMP-2
  APC 86
    APC (T) 4 M3A1 half-track
    APC (W) 32: 2 *Mbombe* 4; 30 UR-416
    PPV 50 *Mamba* Mk7
  AUV 32: 29 *Bastion Patsas*; 1 FV103 *Spartan*; 2 VBL
ANTI-TANK/ANTI-INFRASTRUCTURE
  RCL 75mm Type-52 (M20)/Type-56; **82mm** Type-65 (B-10)
  GUNS 57mm 5 ZIS-2
ARTILLERY 30+
  SP 122mm 6
  TOWED 105mm 4 HM-2
  MRL 122mm PHL-81 mod (SC6 chassis)
  MOR 82mm 20 M-43
AIR DEFENCE • GUNS • TOWED 43 **14.5mm** 38 ZPU-4; **37mm** 5 M-1939

Navy ε200 (incl Marine Infantry unit)
EQUIPMENT BY TYPE
PATROL AND COASTAL COMBATANTS 3
  PBF 1 *Agou* (RPB 33)
  PB 2 *Kara* (FRA *Esterel*)

Air Force 250
FORCES BY ROLE
TRANSPORT
  1 sqn with Beech 200 *King Air*
  1 VIP unit with DC-8; F-28-1000
TRAINING
  1 sqn with TB-30 *Epsilon**
TRANSPORT HELICOPTER
  1 sqn with SA315 *Lama*; SA316 *Alouette* III; SA319 *Alouette* III; SA342L1 *Gazelle*
EQUIPMENT BY TYPE†
AIRCRAFT 3 combat capable
  TPT 5: **Light** 2 Beech 200 *King Air*; **PAX** 3: 1 DC-8; 2 F-28-1000 (VIP)
  TRG 3 TB-30 *Epsilon** (3 *Alpha Jet**; 4 EMB-326G* in store)
HELICOPTERS
  MRH 6: 2 SA315 *Lama*; 1 SA316 *Alouette* III; 1 SA319 *Alouette* III; 2 SA342L1 *Gazelle*
  TPT • Medium 2 Mi-8T *Hip* C (1 SA330 *Puma* in store)

Special Forces Group
FORCES BY ROLE
SPECIAL FORCES
 1 SF unit

Gendarmerie & Paramilitary 3,000

Gendarmerie ε3,000
Ministry of Interior
FORCES BY ROLE
2 reg sections
SPECIAL FORCES
 1 SF unit
MANOEUVRE
 Other
 1 (mobile) paramilitary sqn
ARMOURED FIGHTING VEHICLES
 APC • PPV *Mamba* Mk7

DEPLOYMENT
CENTRAL AFRICAN REPUBLIC: UN • MINUSCA 10
MALI: UN • MINUSMA 733; 1 mech inf bn; 1 fd hospital
SOUTH SUDAN: UN • UNMISS 2
WESTERN SAHARA: UN • MINURSO 3

Uganda UGA

Ugandan Shilling UGX		2021	2022	2023
GDP	UGX	153tr	171tr	
	USD	43.0bn	48.4bn	
per capita	USD	1,012	1,106	
Growth	%	6.7	4.4	
Inflation	%	2.2	6.4	
Def bdgt	UGX	4.35tr	3.87tr	3.76tr
	USD	1.22bn	1.09bn	
USD1=UGX		3562.19	3544.40	

Real-terms defence budget trend (USDm, constant 2015)

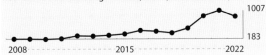

Population 46,205,893

Age	0–14	15–19	20–24	25–29	30–64	65 plus
Male	24.1%	5.7%	4.3%	3.3%	10.2%	1.0%
Female	23.5%	5.8%	4.7%	4.0%	12.0%	1.4%

Capabilities
Uganda's armed forces are well equipped and are important contributors to East African security. Operational experience and training have led to improvements in administration and planning, as well as in military skills including counter-IED and urban patrolling. The years spent targeting the Lord's Resistance Army has also given the military counter-insurgency experience. There are plans to establish a National Defence College. Uganda is one of the largest contributors to the East Africa Standby Force and in 2014 signed a Mutual Defence Treaty with Kenya and Rwanda. Training levels are adequate, particularly for the special forces, and are improving after recent experiences. There is regular training with international partners, including at Uganda's own facilities. Airlift is limited, though rotary-wing aviation has improved in recent years, partly due to US assistance. Motorised infantry formations still lack sufficient transport and logistics capacity. Mechanised forces are relatively well equipped, though equipment is disparate and ageing. Improvements include the arrival of MRAP and other protected vehicles. There is limited defence-industrial capacity, and a new armoured vehicle plant was opened in July. Uganda's 2015–19 Security Sector Development plan included the establishment of an engineering centre and a defence-research facility.

ACTIVE 45,000 (Ugandan People's Defence Force 45,000) Gendarmerie & Paramilitary 1,400

RESERVE 10,000

ORGANISATIONS BY SERVICE

Ugandan People's Defence Force ε40,000–45,000
FORCES BY ROLE
MANOEUVRE
 Armoured
 1 armd bde
 Light
 1 cdo bn
 5 inf div (total: 16 inf bde)
 1 mtn div
 Other
 1 (Special Forces Command) mot bde
COMBAT SUPPORT
 1 arty bde
AIR DEFENCE
 2 AD bn
EQUIPMENT BY TYPE†
ARMOURED FIGHTING VEHICLES
 MBT 279+: 140 T-54/T-55; 45 T-55AM2; 40 T-72A; 10 T-72B1; 44 T-90S; ZTZ-85-IIM
 LT TK ε20 PT-76
 RECCE 46: 40 *Eland-20*; 6 FV701 *Ferret*
 IFV 39: 37 BMP-2; 2+ VN2C
 APC 185
  APC (W) 58: 15 BTR-60; 20 *Buffel*; 4 OT-64; 19 *Bastion* APC
  PPV 127+: 42 *Casspir*; some *Chui*; 35 *Hizir*; 40 *Mamba*; 10 RG-33L
 AUV 15 *Cougar*
ENGINEERING & MAINTENANCE VEHICLES
 ARV 1 BTS-4; T-54/T-55 reported
 VLB MTU reported
 MW *Husky*
ARTILLERY 337+
 SP 155mm 6 ATMOS 2000
 TOWED 243+: 122mm M-30; 130mm 221; 155mm 22: 4 G-5; 18 M-839
 MRL 6+: 107mm (12-tube); 122mm 6+: BM-21 *Grad*; 6 RM-70
 MOR 82+: 81mm L16; 82mm M-43; 120mm 78 *Soltam*;
 SP 120mm 4+ *SandCat* with *Spear*

AIR DEFENCE
SAM • **Point-defence** 9K32 *Strela-2* (RS-SA-7 *Grail*)‡;
9K310 *Igla-1* (RS-SA-16 *Gimlet*)
GUNS • TOWED 20+: **14.5mm** ZPU-1/ZPU-2/ZPU-4;
37mm 20 M-1939

Marines ε400

All operational patrol vessels under 10t FLD
FORCES BY ROLE
MANOEUVRE
  Amphibious
  1 mne bn

Air Wing

FORCES BY ROLE
FIGHTER/GROUND ATTACK
  1 sqn with Su-30MK2 *Flanker*
TRANSPORT
  1 unit with Y-12
  1 VIP unit with Gulfstream 550; L-100-30
TRAINING
  1 unit with L-39ZA/ZO *Albatros**
ATTACK/TRANSPORT HELICOPTER
  1 sqn with Bell 412 *Twin Huey*; Mi-Mi-17/171E *Hip*;
    Mi-24V/P *Hind* E/F; Mi-17A1 (VIP)
EQUIPMENT BY TYPE
AIRCRAFT 13 combat capable
  FGA 6 Su-30MK2 *Flanker* (3+ MiG-21bis *Fishbed*;
    1 MiG-21UM *Mongol* B in store)
  TPT 10: **Medium** 1 L-100-30; **Light** 8: 4 Cessna 172;
    2 Cessna 208B; 2 Y-12; **PAX** 1 Gulfstream 550
  TRG 7 L-39ZA/ZO *Albatros**
HELICOPTERS
  ATK 10: ε7 Mi-24V/P *Hind* E/F; 3+ Mi-28N/UB *Havoc*
  MRH 7: 2 Bell 412 *Twin Huey*; 5 Mi-17/171E *Hip*
  TPT • Medium 1 Mi-171A1 (VIP)
AIR-LAUNCHED MISSILES
  AAM • IR R-73 (RS-AA-11A *Archer*); **SARH** R-27
    (RS-AA-10 *Alamo*); **ARH** R-77 (RS-AA-12 *Adder*)
  ARM Kh-31P (RS-AS-17A *Krypton*) (reported)

Gendarmerie & Paramilitary ε600 active

Border Defence Unit ε600
Equipped with small arms only

DEPLOYMENT

SOMALIA: AU • ATMIS 5,800; 7 inf bn; **UN** • UNSOM
627; 1 sy bn; **UN** • UNSOS 1
SOUTH SUDAN: UN • UNMISS 2
SUDAN: UN • UNISFA 2

Zambia ZMB

Zambian Kwacha ZMW		2021	2022	2023
GDP	ZMW	427bn	465bn	
	USD	21.3bn	27.0bn	
per capita	USD	1,095	1,348	
Growth	%	4.6	2.9	
Inflation	%	22.0	12.5	
Def bdgt	ZMW	5.64bn	7.63bn	8.15bn
	USD	282m	444m	
USD1=ZMW		20.02	17.19	

Real-terms defence budget trend (USDm, constant 2015)

Population	19,642,123					
Age	0–14	15–19	20–24	25–29	30–64	65 plus
Male	21.6%	5.7%	4.6%	3.8%	13.1%	1.2%
Female	21.3%	5.6%	4.6%	3.9%	13.2%	1.5%

Capabilities

The principal tasks for Zambia's armed forces are ensuring territorial integrity and border security, and there is also a commitment to international peacekeeping operations, though effectively addressing these tasks could be complicated by equipment obsolescence and a comparatively small establishment strength. Zambia faces no immediate external threat, though there is a border dispute with the Democratic Republic of the Congo. Ties have developed with China over the past decade, including in military training and weapons sales and some equipment has been procured from Israeli firms. Zambia is a member of the AU and SADC and the services have participated in exercises with international and regional partners, including for the SADC Standby Force. Zambia's largest peacekeeping contribution is to the MINUSCA operation in the Central African Republic (CAR). In April 2017, Zambia signed a defence deal with Russia for spare-parts support. The armed forces are all-volunteer. The US has provided funding and material support for army and air-force pre-deployment training for the CAR peacekeeping mission as well as general military training. The armed forces have limited capacity to independently deploy and sustain forces beyond national borders. While there is a need to modernise the inventory, funds remain limited. The country has no defence-industrial base, apart from limited ammunition production.

ACTIVE 15,100 (Army 13,500 Air 1,600)
Gendarmerie & Paramilitary 1,400

RESERVE 3,000 (Army 3,000)

ORGANISATIONS BY SERVICE

Army 13,500
FORCES BY ROLE
COMMAND
  3 bde HQ

SPECIAL FORCES
1 cdo bn
MANOEUVRE
  Armoured
  1 armd regt (1 tk bn, 1 armd recce regt)
  Light
  6 inf bn
COMBAT SUPPORT
  1 arty regt (2 fd arty bn, 1 MRL bn)
  1 engr regt

EQUIPMENT BY TYPE
Some equipment†
ARMOURED FIGHTING VEHICLES
  MBT 30: 10 T-55; 20 ZTZ-59
  LT TK 30 PT-76
  RECCE 70 BRDM-1/BRDM-2 (ε30 serviceable)
  IFV 23 *Ratel*-20
  APC • APC (W) 47+: 13 BTR-60; 20 BTR-70; 10 BTR-80;
  4+ WZ-551
  AUV 22 *Tigr*
ENGINEERING & MAINTENANCE VEHICLES
  ARV T-54/T-55 reported
ANTI-TANK/ANTI-INFRASTRUCTURE
  MSL • MANPATS 9K11 *Malyutka* (RS-AT-3 *Sagger*)
  RCL 12+: **57mm** 12 M18; **75mm** M20; **84mm** *Carl Gustaf*
ARTILLERY 194
  SP 6 Atmos M-46
  TOWED 61: **105mm** 18 Model 56 pack howitzer;
  122mm 25 D-30; **130mm** 18 M-46
  MRL 122mm 30 BM-21 *Grad* (ε12 serviceable)
  MOR 917: **81mm** 55; **82mm** 24; **120mm** 12 **SP** 120mm 6+
  Elbit *Spear* Mk2
AIR DEFENCE
  SAM • MANPAD 9K32 *Strela*-2 (RS-SA-7 *Grail*)‡
  GUNS
    SP 23mm 4 ZSU-23-4 *Shilka*
    TOWED 136: **14.5mm** ZPU-4; **20mm** 50 M-55 (triple);
    23mm ZU-23; **37mm** 40 M-1939; PG-65; **40mm** L/70;
    57mm ε30 S-60; **85mm** 16 M-1939 KS-12

Reserve 3,000

FORCES BY ROLE
MANOEUVRE
  Light
  3 inf bn

Air Force 1,600

FORCES BY ROLE
FIGHTER/GROUND ATTACK
  1 sqn with K-8 *Karakorum**
  1 sqn with L-15*
TRANSPORT
  1 sqn with MA60; Y-12(II); Y-12(IV)
  1 (VIP) unit with AW139; HS-748
  1 (liaison) sqn with Do-28
TRAINING
  1 sqn with MFI-15 *Safari*
TRANSPORT HELICOPTER
  1 sqn with Mi-17 *Hip* H
  1 (liaison) sqn with Bell 205 (UH-1H *Iroquois*/AB-205)

AIR DEFENCE
  2 bty with S-125M *Pechora*-M (RS-SA-3 *Goa*)

EQUIPMENT BY TYPE†
Very low serviceability
AIRCRAFT 21 combat capable
  TPT 19: **Medium** 2 C-27J *Spartan*; **Light** 15: 1 Cessna 208B
  Grand Caravan; 5 Do-28; 2 MA60; 3 Y-12(II); 4 Y-12(IV);
  PAX 2: 1 Gulfstream G650ER; 1 HS-748
  TRG 40: 15 K-8 *Karakorum**; 6 L-15*; 8 MFI-15 *Safari*; 11
  SF-260TW
HELICOPTERS
  MRH 9: 1 AW139; 4 Mi-17 *Hip* H; 4 Z-9
  TPT • Light 12: 9 Bell 205 (UH-1H *Iroquois*/AB-205);
  3 Bell 212
UNINHABITED AERIAL VEHICLES 3+
  ISR • Medium 3+ *Hermes* 450
AIR DEFENCE
  SAM • Short-range 6 S-125M *Pechora*-M (RS-SA-3 *Goa*)
AIR-LAUNCHED MISSILES
  AAM • IR PL-5E-II
  ASM 9K11 *Malyutka* (RS-AT-3 *Sagger*)

Gendarmerie & Paramilitary 1,400

Police Mobile Unit 700

FORCES BY ROLE
MANOEUVRE
  Other
  1 police bn (4 police coy)

Police Paramilitary Unit 700

FORCES BY ROLE
MANOEUVRE
  Other
  1 paramilitary bn (3 paramilitary coy)
EQUIPMENT BY TYPE
ARMOURED FIGHTING VEHICLES
  APC • PPV 9+: 3+ *Marauder*; 6 CS/VP3

DEPLOYMENT

CENTRAL AFRICAN REPUBLIC: UN • MINUSCA 930;
1 inf bn

DEMOCRATIC REPUBLIC OF THE CONGO: UN •
MONUSCO 7

LEBANON: UN • UNIFIL 2

MIDDLE EAST: UN • UNTSO 1

SOUTH SUDAN: UN • UNMISS 9

SUDAN: UN • UNISFA 5

Zimbabwe ZWE

Zimbabwe Dollar ZWL		2021	2022	2023
GDP	ZWL	2.91tr	14.4tr	
	USD	32.9bn	38.3bn	
per capita	USD	2,122	2,420	
Growth	%	7.2	3.0	
Inflation	%	98.5	284.9	
Def bdgt	USD	23.3bn	61.6bn	
	ZWL	287m	751m	
USD1=ZWL		81.00	82.00	

Real-terms defence budget trend (USDm, constant 2015)

Population 15,121,004

Age	0–14	15–19	20–24	25–29	30–64	65 plus
Male	18.9%	5.1%	4.7%	4.3%	14.6%	1.8%
Female	19.2%	5.3%	4.9%	4.3%	14.3%	2.8%

Capabilities

Zimbabwe's political instability and weak economy remain key challenges for the government. Principal tasks for the Zimbabwe Defence Forces include ensuring sovereignty, territorial integrity and border security, as well as providing internal-security support to the police. The armed forces take an active political role. Zimbabwe is a member of the AU and the SADC and takes part in SADC Standby Force exercises. Zimbabwe has also sent military forces as part of the SADC deployment to Mozambique. There are defence ties with China and an emergent defence relationship with Belarus, while Russia in mid-2019 reportedly said it would consider alternative payment means for military cooperation. Military leaders have identified training as a development priority. Small numbers of personnel have deployed on peacekeeping operations but there is no capacity to sustain a force far beyond national borders. Equipment recapitalisation is also a priority, though much will depend on domestic economic health and perhaps the extent to which China and Russia provide support. There are plans to revive state-owned small-arms and munitions manufacturer Zimbabwe Defence Industries, although these may be hindered by continuing UK, US and EU sanctions.

ACTIVE 29,000 (Army 25,000 Air 4,000)
Gendarmerie & Paramilitary 21,800

ORGANISATIONS BY SERVICE

Army ε25,000
FORCES BY ROLE
COMMAND
  1 SF bde HQ
  1 mech bde HQ
  5 inf bde HQ
SPECIAL FORCES
  1 SF regt
MANOEUVRE
  Armoured
  1 armd sqn
  Mechanised
  1 mech inf bn
  Light
  15 inf bn
  1 cdo bn
  Air Manoeuvre
  1 para bn
  Other
  3 gd bn
  1 (Presidential Guard) gd gp
COMBAT SUPPORT
  1 arty bde
  1 fd arty regt
  2 engr regt
AIR DEFENCE
  1 AD regt
EQUIPMENT BY TYPE
ARMOURED FIGHTING VEHICLES
  MBT 40: 30 Type-59†; 10 Type-69†
  RECCE 115: 20 *Eland*-60/90; 15 FV701 *Ferret*†; 80 EE-9 *Cascavel* (90mm)
  IFV 2+ YW307
  APC • APC (T) 30: 8 ZSD-85 (incl CP); 22 VTT-323
ENGINEERING & MAINTENANCE VEHICLES
  ARV T-54/T-55 reported; ZJX-93 ARV
  VLB MTU reported
ARTILLERY 254
  SP 122mm 12 2S1 *Gvozdika*
  TOWED 122mm 20: 4 D-30; 16 Type-60 (D-74)
  MRL 76: 107mm 16 Type-63; 122mm 60 RM-70
  MOR 146: 81mm/82mm ε140; 120mm 6 M-43
AIR DEFENCE
  SAM • Point-defence 9K32 *Strela*-2 (RS-SA-7 *Grail*)‡
  GUNS • TOWED 116: 14.5mm 36 ZPU-1/ZPU-2/ZPU-4; 23mm 45 ZU-23-2; 37mm 35 M-1939

Air Force 4,000
FORCES BY ROLE
FIGHTER
  1 sqn with F-7 II†; FT-7†
FIGHTER/GROUND ATTACK
  1 sqn with K-8 *Karakorum**
GROUND ATTACK/ISR
  1 sqn with Cessna 337/O-2A *Skymaster**
ISR/TRAINING
  1 sqn with SF-260F/M; SF-260TP*; SF-260W *Warrior**
TRANSPORT
  1 sqn with BN-2 *Islander*; CASA 212-200 *Aviocar* (VIP)
ATTACK/TRANSPORT HELICOPTER
  1 sqn with Mi-35 *Hind*; Mi-35P *Hind* (liaison); SA316 *Alouette* III; AS532UL *Cougar* (VIP)
  1 trg sqn with Bell 412 *Twin Huey*, SA316 *Alouette* III
AIR DEFENCE
  1 sqn
EQUIPMENT BY TYPE
AIRCRAFT 45 combat capable
  FTR 9: 7 F-7 II†; 2 FT-7†

ISR 2 O-2A *Skymaster*
TPT • **Light** 25: 5 BN-2 *Islander*; 7 C-212-200 *Aviocar*; 13 Cessna 337 *Skymaster**; (10 C-47 *Skytrain* in store)
TRG 33: 10 K-8 *Karakorum**; 5 SF-260M; 8 SF-260TP*; 5 SF-260W *Warrior**; 5 SF-260F
HELICOPTERS
ATK 6: 4 Mi-35 *Hind*; 2 Mi-35P *Hind*
MRH 8: 7 Bell 412 *Twin Huey*; 1 SA316 *Alouette* III
TPT • **Medium** 2 AS532UL *Cougar* (VIP)
AIR-LAUNCHED MISSILES • **AAM** • **IR** PL-2; PL-5 (reported)
AD • **GUNS** 100mm (not deployed); 37mm (not deployed); 57mm (not deployed)

Gendarmerie & Paramilitary 21,800

Zimbabwe Republic Police Force 19,500
incl air wg

Police Support Unit 2,300
EQUIPMENT BY TYPE
PATROL AND COASTAL COMBATANTS
All operational patrol vessels under 10t FLD

DEPLOYMENT

CENTRAL AFRICAN REPUBLIC: UN • MINUSCA 3

DEMOCRATIC REPUBLIC OF THE CONGO: UN • MONUSCO 3

MOZAMBIQUE: SADC • SAMIM 1

SOUTH SUDAN: UN • UNMISS 14

SUDAN: UN • UNISFA 9

Explanatory notes

The Military Balance provides an assessment of the armed forces and defence economics of 173 countries and territories. Each edition contributes to the provision of a unique compilation of data and information, enabling the reader to discern trends by studying editions as far back as 1959. The data in the current edition is accurate according to IISS assessments as of November 2022, unless specified. Inclusion of a territory, country or state in *The Military Balance*, or terminology or boundaries used in graphics or mapping, does not imply legal recognition or indicate support for any government or administration.

General arrangement and contents

The introduction is an assessment of key themes and content in the 2023 edition. An opening analytical essay examines important defence topics in 2022, such as issues around military capability assessment in light of the ongoing war in Ukraine and the performance of the armed forces of both Russia and Ukraine, and the effect of military asssistance to both from abroad. Regional chapters begin with analysis of the military and security issues that drive national defence-policy developments, and key trends in regional defence economics. In some cases there is focused text content in the form of textboxes or longer articles relating to important defence policy and capability issues, and defence economics, and then a section assessing important regional arms procurements and deliveries. Next, detailed data on regional states' military forces and equipment, and defence economics, is presented in alphabetical order. The book closes with a reference section containing comparisons of defence economics and personnel statistics.

The Military Balance wall chart

The Military Balance 2023 wall chart is an assessment of important military space assets operated by China, Russia and the US. Using text, data and graphics, the chart assesses key military and military-related spacecraft for these nations. Moreover, it includes information on the military relevance of select orbits. It also contains assessments of developments in military space technology and counterspace capabilities and includes data on selected launch vehicles, map based information on selected space launch locations, and a timeline of recent international developments related to the military use of space.

Abbreviations and definitions

Qualifier

'Up to'	Total is at most the number given, but could be lower
'Some'	Precise inventory is unavailable at time of press
'In store'	Equipment held away from front-line units; readiness and maintenance varies
Billion (bn)	1,000 million (m)
Trillion (tr)	1,000 billion
$	US dollars unless otherwise stated
ε	Estimated
*	Aircraft counted by the IISS as combat capable
(-)	Unit understrength or detached
+	Unit reinforced/total is no less than the number given
†	IISS assesses that the serviceability of equipment is in doubt[a]
‡	Missiles whose basic design is more than four decades old and which have not been significantly upgraded within the past decade)[a]

[a] Not to be taken to imply that such equipment cannot be used

Using *The Military Balance*

The country entries assess personnel strengths, organisation and equipment holdings of the world's armed forces. Force-strength and equipment-inventory data is based on the most accurate data available, or on the best estimate that can be made. In estimating a country's total capabilities, old equipment may be counted where it is considered that it may still be deployable. The data presented reflects judgements based on information available to the IISS at the time the book is compiled. Where information differs from previous editions, it is mainly because of changes in national forces, but it is sometimes because the IISS has reassessed the evidence supporting past entries.

Country entries

Information on each country is shown in a standard format, although the differing availability of information and differences in nomenclature result in some variations. Country entries include economic, demographic and military data. Population figures are based on demographic statistics taken from the US Census Bureau. Military data includes personnel numbers, conscript liability where relevant, outline organisation, number of formations and units, and an inventory of the major equipment of each service. Details of national forces stationed abroad and of foreign forces stationed within the given country are also provided.

Arms procurements and deliveries

A series of thematic tables, graphics and text follow the regional data. These are designed to illustrate key trends, principal programmes and significant events in regional defence procurements. More detailed information on defence procurements, organised by country, equipment type and manufacturing company, can be found on the IISS Military Balance+ database (*https://www.iiss.org/militarybalanceplus*). The information in this section meets the threshold for a *Military Balance* country entry and as such does not feature information on sales of small arms and light weapons.

Defence economics

Country entries include annual defence budgets (and expenditure where applicable), selected economic-performance indicators and demographic aggregates. All country entries are subject to revision each year as new information, particularly regarding actual defence expenditure, becomes available. On p. 500, there are also international comparisons of defence expenditure and military personnel, giving expenditure figures for the past three years in per capita terms and as a % of gross domestic product (GDP). The aim is to provide a measure of military expenditure and the allocation of economic resources to defence.

Individual country entries show economic performance over the past two years and current demographic data. Where this data is unavailable, information from the last available year is provided. All financial data in the country entries is shown in both national currency and US dollars at current – not constant – prices. US-dollar conversions are calculated from the exchange rates listed in the entry.

The use of market exchange rates has limitations, particularly because it does not consider the varying levels of development or the differing cost of inputs (principally personnel, equipment and investment, factors that help determine a country's military capability) specific to each country's national context. An alternative approach is to make conversions using purchasing power parity (PPP) exchange rates, which at least partially takes these cost differentials into account.

However, the suitability of PPP conversions depends on the extent to which a country is self-sufficient in developing and producing the armaments required by its armed forces. For Russia and China they are appropriate, as imported systems play almost no role in Russia's case and only a small and decreasing one in that of China. However, PPP conversions are less suitable when assessing the spending of countries such as India and Saudi Arabia, which rely heavily on imports of military equipment from relatively high-cost producers. For those countries it would be necessary to adopt a hybrid approach to determine defence expenditure in dollars, with the market exchange rate used for converting defence procurement and the PPP conversion rate applied to all other defence expenditure (personnel, operations, etc.). As such, to produce standardised international comparisons, PPP conversions would have to be applied to all countries. In the absence of defence-based PPP rates, analysts would have to use the GDP-based PPP rates that are available for all countries. However, these are also statistical estimates and, as such, difficult to apply to military expenditure because they reflect the purchasing power of the wider economy, primarily civilian goods and services.

Definitions of terms

Despite efforts by NATO and the UN to develop a standardised definition of military expenditure, many countries prefer to use their own definitions (which are often not made public). In order to present a comprehensive picture, *The Military Balance* lists three different measures of military-related spending data.

- For most countries, an official defence-budget figure is provided.
- For those countries where other military-related outlays, over and above the defence budget, are known or can be reasonably estimated, an additional measurement referred to as defence expenditure is also provided. Defence-expenditure figures will naturally be higher than official budget figures, depending on the range of additional factors included.
- For NATO countries, a defence-budget figure, as well as defence expenditure reported by NATO in local-currency terms and converted using IMF exchange rates, is quoted.

NATO's military-expenditure definition (the most comprehensive) is cash outlays of central or federal governments to meet the costs of national armed forces. The term 'armed forces' includes strategic, land, naval, air, command, administration and support forces. It also includes other forces if they are trained, structured and equipped to support defence forces and are realistically deployable. Defence expenditures are reported in four categories: Operating Costs, Procurement and Construction, Research and Development (R&D) and Other Expenditure. Operating Costs include salaries and pensions for military and civilian personnel; the cost of maintaining and training units, service organisations, headquarters and support elements; and the cost of servicing and repairing military equipment and infrastructure. Procurement and Construction expenditure covers national equipment and infrastructure spending, as well as common infrastructure programmes. R&D is defence expenditure up to the point at which new equipment can be put in service, regardless of whether new equipment is actually procured. Foreign Military Assistance (FMA) contributions are also noted – primarily the IISS tracks Foreign Military Financing (FMF) allocations from the US.

For many non-NATO countries the issue of transparency in reporting military budgets is fundamental. Not every UN member state reports defence-budget data (even fewer report real defence expenditures) to their electorates, the UN, the IMF or other multinational organisations. In the case of governments with a proven record of transparency, official figures generally conform to the standardised definition of defence budgeting, as adopted by the UN, and consistency problems are not usually a major issue. The IISS cites official defence budgets as reported by either national governments, the UN, the OSCE or the IMF.

For those countries where the official defence-budget figure is considered to be an incomplete measure of total military-related spending, and appropriate additional data is available, the IISS will use data from a variety of sources to arrive at a more accurate estimate of true defence expenditure. The most frequent instances of budgetary manipulation or falsification typically involve equipment procurement, R&D, defence-industrial investment, covert weapons programmes, pensions for retired military and civilian personnel, paramilitary forces and non-budgetary sources of revenue for the military arising from ownership of industrial, property and land assets. There will be several countries listed in *The Military Balance* for which only an official defence-budget figure is provided but where, in reality, true defence-related expenditure is almost certainly higher.

Percentage changes in defence spending are referred to in either nominal or real terms. Nominal terms relate to the percentage change in numerical spending figures, and do not account for the impact of price changes (i.e., inflation) on defence spending. By contrast, real terms account for inflationary effects, and may therefore be considered a more accurate representation of change over time.

The principal sources for national economic statistics cited in the country entries are the IMF, the OECD, the World Bank and three regional banks (the Inter-American, Asian and African Development banks). For some countries, basic economic data is difficult to obtain. GDP figures are nominal (current) values at market prices. GDP growth is real, not nominal growth, and inflation is the year-on-year change in consumer prices. When real-terms defence-spending figures are mentioned, these are measured in constant 2015 US dollars.

Units and formation strength

Company	100–200
Battalion	500–1,000
Brigade	3,000–5,000
Division	15,000–20,000
Corps or Army	50,000–100,000

General defence data
Personnel
The 'Active' total comprises all servicemen and women on full-time duty (including conscripts and long-term assignments from the Reserves). When a gendarmerie or equivalent is under control of the defence ministry, they may be included in the active total. Only the length of conscript liability is shown; where service is voluntary there is no entry. 'Reserve' describes formations and units not fully manned or operational in peacetime, but which can be mobilised by recalling reservists in an emergency. Some countries have more than one category of reserves, often kept at varying degrees of readiness. Where possible, these differences are denoted using the national descriptive title, but always under the heading of 'Reserves' to distinguish them from full-time active forces. All personnel figures are rounded to the nearest 50, except for organisations with under 500 personnel, where figures are rounded to the nearest ten.

Other forces
Many countries maintain forces whose training, organisation, equipment and control suggest that they may be used to support or replace regular military forces or be used more broadly by states to deliver militarily relevant effect. They include some forces that may have a constabulary role or are classed as gendarmerie forces, with more formal law-enforcement responsibilities. These are called 'Gendarmerie & Paramilitary' and are detailed after the military forces of each country. Their personnel numbers are not normally included in the totals at the start of each entry.

Forces by role and equipment by type
Quantities are shown by function (according to each nation's employment) and type, and represent what are believed to be total holdings, including active and reserve operational and training units. Inventory totals for missile systems relate to launchers and not to missiles. Equipment held 'in store' is not counted in the main inventory totals.

The IISS Military Balance+ assesses the relative level of capability of certain equipment platform types based on their technical characteristics. For land domain equipment, these characteristics include the level of protection, main armament, and fire control and optics. For maritime domain equipment, they include crew-to-displacement ratio, primary missile armament, sensor suites, signature reduction, and propulsion. For air domain equipment, they include avionics, weapons, signature management, and upgrades.

Platform types assessed in this fashion are described as having either an 'obsolete', 'obsolescent', 'ageing', 'modern' or 'advanced' level of capability when compared with other designs within the same category of equipment. This should not be taken as an assessment of the physical age or remaining service life of a given platform or whether it can actually be employed offensively. Examples of these assessments appear in certain graphics within *The Military Balance*.

Deployments

The Military Balance mainly lists permanent bases and operational deployments abroad, including peacekeeping operations. Domestic deployments are not included, with the exception of overseas territories. Information in the country-data sections details troop deployments and, where available, the role and equipment of deployed units. Personnel figures are not generally included for embassy staff or standing multinational headquarters.

Land forces

To make international comparison easier and more consistent, *The Military Balance* categorises forces by role and translates national military terminology for unit and formation sizes. Typical personnel strength, equipment holdings and organisation of formations such as brigades and divisions vary from country to country. In addition, some unit terms, such as 'regiment', 'squadron', 'battery' and 'troop', can refer to significantly different unit sizes in different countries. Unless otherwise stated, these terms should be assumed to reflect standard British usage where they occur.

Naval forces

Classifying naval vessels according to role is complex. A post-war consensus on primary surface combatants revolved around a distinction between independently operating cruisers, air-defence escorts (destroyers) and anti-submarine-warfare escorts (frigates). However, ships are increasingly performing a range of roles. Also, modern ship design has meant that the full-load displacement (FLD) of different warship types has evolved and in some cases overlaps. For these reasons, *The Military Balance* now classifies vessels by an assessed combination of role, equipment fit and displacement.

Air forces

Aircraft listed as combat capable are assessed as being equipped to deliver air-to-air or air-to-surface ordnance.

The definition includes aircraft designated by type as bomber, fighter, fighter/ground attack, ground attack and anti-submarine warfare. Other aircraft considered to be combat capable are marked with an asterisk (*). Operational groupings of air forces are shown where known. Typical squadron aircraft strengths can vary both between aircraft types and from country to country. When assessing missile ranges, *The Military Balance* uses the following range indicators:

- Short-range ballistic missile (SRBM): less than 1,000 km;
- Medium-range ballistic missile (MRBM): 1,000–3,000 km;
- Intermediate-range ballistic missile (IRBM): 3,000–5,000 km;
- Intercontinental ballistic missile (ICBM): over 5,000 km.

Other IISS defence data

The Military Balance+ database is integrating information on military-owned cyber capacities. The research taxonomy focuses on enablers, including indicators of capability from the armed forces. The Military Balance+ also contains data on bilateral, multilateral and notable large or important military exercises held on a national basis. More broadly, the Military Balance+ enables subscribers to view multiple years of Military Balance data, and conduct searches for complex queries more rapidly than is possible by consulting the print book.

Attribution and acknowledgements

The International Institute for Strategic Studies owes no allegiance to any government, group of governments, or any political or other organisation. Its assessments are its own, based on the material available to it from a wide variety of sources. The cooperation of governments of all listed countries has been sought and, in many cases, received. However, some data in *The Military Balance* is estimated. Care is taken to ensure that this data is as accurate and free from bias as possible. The Institute owes a considerable debt to a number of its own members, consultants and all those who help compile and check material. The Director-General and Chief Executive and staff of the Institute assume full responsibility for the data and judgements in this book. Comments and suggestions on the data and textual material contained within the book, as well as on the style and presentation of data, are welcomed and should be communicated to the Editor of *The Military Balance* at: The International Institute for Strategic Studies, Arundel House, 6 Temple Place, London, WC2R 2PG, UK, email: *milbal@iiss.org*. Copyright on all information in *The Military Balance* belongs strictly to the IISS. Application to reproduce limited amounts of data may be made to the publisher: Taylor & Francis, 4 Park Square, Milton Park, Abingdon, Oxon, OX14 4RN. Email: *society.permissions@ tandf.co.uk*. Unauthorised use of data from *The Military Balance* will be subject to legal action.

Principal land definitions

FORCES BY ROLE

Command:	free-standing, deployable formation headquarters (HQs).
Special Forces (SF):	elite units specially trained and equipped for unconventional warfare and operations in enemy-controlled territory. Many are employed in counter-terrorist roles.
Manoeuvre:	combat units and formations capable of manoeuvring. These are subdivided as follows:
Reconnaissance:	combat units and formations whose primary purpose is to gain information.
Armoured:	units and formations principally equipped with main battle tanks (MBTs) and infantry fighting vehicles (IFVs) to provide heavy mounted close-combat capability. Units and formations intended to provide mounted close-combat capability with lighter armoured vehicles, such as light tanks or wheeled assault guns, are classified as light armoured.
Mechanised:	units and formations primarily equipped with lighter armoured vehicles such as armoured personnel carriers (APCs). They have less mounted firepower and protection than their armoured equivalents, but can usually deploy more infantry.
Light:	units and formations whose principal combat capability is dismounted infantry, with few, if any, organic armoured vehicles. Some may be motorised and equipped with soft-skinned vehicles.
Air Manoeuvre:	units and formations trained and equipped for delivery by transport aircraft and/ or helicopters.
Amphibious:	amphibious forces are trained and equipped to project force from the sea.
Other Forces:	includes security units such as Presidential Guards, paramilitary units such as border guards and combat formations permanently employed in training or demonstration tasks.
Combat Support:	combat support units and formations not integral to manoeuvre formations. Includes artillery, engineers, military intelligence, nuclear, biological and chemical defence, signals and information operations.
Combat Service Support (CSS):	includes logistics, maintenance, medical, supply and transport units and formations.

EQUIPMENT BY TYPE

Light Weapons:	small arms, machine guns, grenades and grenade launchers and unguided man-portable anti-armour and support weapons have proliferated so much and are sufficiently easy to manufacture or copy that listing them would be impractical.
Crew-Served Weapons:	crew-served recoilless rifles, man-portable ATGW, MANPADs and mortars of greater than 80mm calibre are listed, but the high degree of proliferation and local manufacture of many of these weapons means that estimates of numbers held may not be reliable.
Armoured Fighting Vehicles (AFVs):	armoured combat vehicles with a combat weight of at least six metric tonnes, further subdivided as below:
Main Battle Tank (MBT):	armoured, tracked combat vehicles, armed with a turret-mounted gun of at least 100mm calibre and with a combat weight of between 35 and 75 metric tonnes.
Light Tank (LT TK):	armoured, tracked combat vehicles, armed with a turret-mounted gun of at least 75mm calibre and with a combat weight of between 15 and 40 metric tonnes.
Wheeled Assault Gun (ASLT):	armoured, wheeled combat vehicles, armed with a turret-mounted gun of at least 75mm calibre and with a combat weight of at least 15 metric tonnes.
Armoured Reconnaissance (RECCE):	armoured vehicles primarily designed for reconnaissance tasks with no significant transport capability and either a main gun of less than 75mm calibre or a combat weight of less than 15 metric tonnes, or both.
Infantry Fighting Vehicle (IFV):	armoured combat vehicles designed and equipped to transport an infantry squad and armed with a cannon of at least 20mm calibre.

Armoured Personnel Carrier (APC):	lightly armoured combat vehicles designed and equipped to transport an infantry squad but either unarmed or armed with a cannon of less than 20mm calibre.
Airborne Combat Vehicle (ABCV):	armoured vehicles designed to be deployable by parachute alongside airborne forces.
Amphibious Assault Vehicle (AAV):	armoured vehicles designed to have an amphibious ship-to-shore capability.
Armoured Utility Vehicle (AUV):	armoured vehicles not designed to transport an infantry squad, but capable of undertaking a variety of other utility battlefield tasks, including light reconnaissance and light transport.
Specialist Variants:	variants of armoured vehicles listed above that are designed to fill a specialised role, such as command posts (CP), artillery observation posts (OP), signals (sigs) and ambulances (amb), are categorised with their parent vehicles.
Engineering and Maintenance Vehicles:	includes armoured engineer vehicles (AEV), armoured repair and recovery vehicles (ARV), assault bridging (VLB) and mine-warfare vehicles (MW).
Nuclear, Biological and Chemical Defence Vehicles (NBC):	armoured vehicles principally designed to operate in potentially contaminated terrain.
Anti-Tank/Anti-Infrastructure (AT):	guns, guided weapons and recoilless rifles designed to engage armoured vehicles and battlefield hardened targets.
Surface-to-Surface Missile Launchers (SSM):	launch vehicles for transporting and firing surface-to-surface ballistic and cruise missiles.
Artillery:	weapons (including guns, howitzers, gun/howitzers, multiple-rocket launchers, mortars and gun/mortars) with a calibre greater than 100mm for artillery pieces and 80mm and above for mortars, capable of engaging ground targets with indirect fire.
Coastal Defence:	land-based coastal artillery pieces and anti-ship-missile launchers.
Air Defence (AD):	guns, directed-energy (DE) weapons and surface-to-air missile (SAM) launchers designed to engage fixed-wing, rotary-wing and uninhabited aircraft. Missiles are further classified by maximum notional engagement range: point-defence (up to 10 km); short-range (10–30 km); medium-range (30–75 km); and long-range (75 km+). Systems primarily intended to intercept missiles rather than aircraft are categorised separately as Missile Defence.

Principal naval definitions

To aid comparison between fleets, the following definitions, which do not always conform to national definitions, are used as guidance:

Submarines:	all vessels designed to operate primarily under water. Submarines with a dived displacement below 250 tonnes are classified as midget submarines (SSW); those below 500 tonnes are coastal submarines (SSC).
Principal Surface Combatants:	all surface ships designed for combat operations on the high seas, with an FLD above 2,200 tonnes. Aircraft carriers (CV), including smaller support carriers (CVS) embarking STOVL aircraft and helicopter carriers (CVH), are vessels with a flat deck primarily designed to carry fixed- and/or rotary-wing aircraft, without specialised amphibious capability. Other principal surface combatants include cruisers (C) (FLD above 9,750 tonnes), destroyers (DD) (FLD 4,500–9,749 tonnes with a primary area air-defence weapons fit and role) and frigates (FF) (FLD 2,200–9,000 tonnes and a primary anti-submarine/general-purpose weapons fit and role).
Patrol and Coastal Combatants:	surface vessels designed for coastal or inshore operations. These include corvettes (FS), which usually have an FLD between 500 and 2,199 tonnes and are distinguished from other patrol vessels by their heavier armaments. Also included in this category are offshore-patrol ships (PSO), with an FLD greater than 1,500 tonnes; patrol craft (PC), which have an FLD between 250 and 1,499 tonnes; and patrol boats (PB) with an FLD between ten and 250 tonnes. Vessels with a top speed greater than 35 knots are designated as 'fast'.

Mine warfare vessels:	all surface vessels configured primarily for mine laying (ML) or countermeasures. Countermeasures vessels are either: sweepers (MS), which are designed to locate and destroy mines in an area; hunters (MH), which are designed to locate and destroy individual mines; or countermeasures vessels (MC), which combine both roles.
Amphibious vessels:	vessels designed to transport combat personnel and/or equipment onto shore. These include aviation-capable amphibious assault ships (LHA), which can embark rotary-wing or STOVL air assets and may have a well deck for LCACs and landing craft; aviation-capable amphibious assault ships with a well dock for LCACs and landing craft (LHD), which can embark rotary-wing or STOVL assets; landing platform helicopters (LPH), which have a primary role of launch and recovery platform for rotary-wing or STOVL assets; landing platform docks (LPD), which do not have a through deck but do have a well dock and carry both combat personnel and equipment; and land ships docks (LSD) with a well dock but focused more on equipment transport. Landing ships (LS) are amphibious vessels capable of ocean passage and landing craft (LC) are smaller vessels designed to transport personnel and equipment from a larger vessel to land or across small stretches of water. Landing ships have a hold; landing craft are open vessels. Landing craft air cushioned (LCAC) are differentiated from utility craft air cushioned (UCAC) in that the former have a bow ramp for the disembarkation of vehicles and personnel.
Auxiliary vessels:	ocean-going surface vessels performing an auxiliary military role, supporting combat ships or operations. These generally fulfil five roles: replenishment (such as oilers (AO) and solid stores (AKS)); logistics (such as cargo ships (AK) and logistics ships (AFS)); maintenance (such as cable-repair ships (ARC) or buoy tenders (ABU)); research (such as survey ships (AFS)); and special purpose (such as intelligence-collection ships (AGI) and ocean-going tugs (ATF)).
Weapons systems:	weapons are listed in the following order: land-attack cruise missiles (LACM), anti-ship missiles (AShM), surface-to-air missiles (SAM), heavy (HWT) and lightweight (LWT) torpedoes, anti-submarine weapons (A/S), CIWS, guns and aircraft. Missiles with a range less than 5 km and guns with a calibre less than 57mm are generally not included.
Organisations:	naval groupings such as fleets and squadrons frequently change and are shown only where doing so would aid qualitative judgements.
Legacy platforms:	legacy-generation platforms, unless specifically modified for a new role, may be listed with their original designations although they may not conform fully with current guidance criteria.

Principal aviation definitions

Bomber (Bbr):	comparatively large platforms intended for the delivery of air-to-surface ordnance. Bbr units are units equipped with bomber aircraft for the air-to-surface role.
Fighter (Ftr):	aircraft designed primarily for air-to-air combat, which may also have a limited air-to-surface capability. Ftr units are equipped with aircraft intended to provide air superiority, which may have a secondary and limited air-to-surface capability.
Fighter/Ground Attack (FGA):	multi-role fighter-size platforms with significant air-to-surface capability, potentially including maritime attack, and at least some air-to-air capacity. FGA units are multi-role units equipped with aircraft capable of air-to-air and air-to-surface attack.
Ground Attack (Atk):	aircraft designed solely for the air-to-surface task, with limited or no air-to-air capability. Atk units are equipped with fixed-wing aircraft.
Attack Helicopter (Atk hel):	rotary-wing platforms designed for delivery of air-to-surface weapons, and fitted with an integrated fire-control system.
Anti-Submarine Warfare (ASW):	fixed- and rotary-wing platforms designed to locate and engage submarines, many with a secondary anti-surface-warfare capability. ASW units are equipped with fixed- or rotary-wing aircraft.

Explanatory Notes 497

Anti-Surface Warfare (ASuW):	ASuW units are equipped with fixed- or rotary-wing aircraft intended for anti-surface-warfare missions.
Maritime Patrol (MP):	fixed-wing aircraft and uninhabited aerial vehicles (UAVs) intended for maritime surface surveillance, which may possess an anti-surface-warfare capability. MP units are equipped with fixed-wing aircraft or UAVs.
Electronic Warfare (EW):	fixed- and rotary-wing aircraft and UAVs intended for electronic warfare. EW units are equipped with fixed- or rotary-wing aircraft or UAVs.
Intelligence/ Surveillance/ Reconnaissance (ISR):	fixed- and rotary-wing aircraft and UAVs intended to provide radar, visible-light or infrared imagery, or a mix thereof. ISR units are equipped with fixed- or rotary-wing aircraft or UAVs.
Combat/Intelligence/ Surveillance/ Reconnaissance (CISR):	aircraft and UAVs that have the capability to deliver air-to-surface weapons, as well as undertake ISR tasks. CISR units are equipped with armed aircraft and/or UAVs for ISR and air-to-surface missions.
COMINT/ELINT/ SIGINT:	fixed- and rotary-wing platforms and UAVs capable of gathering electronic (ELINT), communications (COMINT) or signals intelligence (SIGINT). COMINT units are equipped with fixed- or rotary-wing aircraft or UAVs intended for the communications-intelligence task. ELINT units are equipped with fixed- or rotary-wing aircraft or UAVs used for gathering electronic intelligence. SIGINT units are equipped with fixed- or rotary-wing aircraft or UAVs used to collect signals intelligence.
Airborne Early Warning (& Control) (AEW (&C)):	fixed- and rotary-wing platforms capable of providing airborne early warning, with a varying degree of onboard command and control depending on the platform. AEW(&C) units are equipped with fixed- or rotary-wing aircraft.
Search and Rescue (SAR):	units are equipped with fixed- or rotary-wing aircraft used to recover military personnel or civilians.
Combat Search and Rescue (CSAR):	units are equipped with armed fixed- or rotary-wing aircraft for recovery of personnel from hostile territory.
Tanker (Tkr):	fixed- and rotary-wing aircraft designed for air-to-air refuelling. Tkr units are equipped with fixed- or rotary-wing aircraft used for air-to-air refuelling.
Tanker Transport (Tkr/Tpt):	platforms capable of both air-to-air refuelling and military airlift.
Transport (Tpt):	fixed- and rotary-wing aircraft intended for military airlift. Light transport aircraft are categorised as having a maximum payload of up to 11,340 kg; medium up to 27,215 kg; and heavy above 27,215 kg. Light transport helicopters have an internal payload of up to 2,000 kg; medium transport helicopters up to 4,535 kg; heavy transport helicopters greater than 4,535 kg. PAX aircraft are platforms generally unsuited for transporting cargo on the main deck. Tpt units are equipped with fixed- or rotary-wing platforms to transport personnel or cargo.
Trainer (Trg):	fixed- and rotary-wing aircraft designed primarily for the training role; some also have the capacity to carry light to medium ordnance. Trg units are equipped with fixed- or rotary-wing training aircraft intended for pilot or other aircrew training.
Multi-Role Helicopter (MRH):	rotary-wing platforms designed to carry out a variety of military tasks including light transport, armed reconnaissance and battlefield support.
Uninhabited Aerial Vehicles (UAVs):	remotely piloted or controlled uninhabited fixed- or rotary-wing systems. Light UAVs are those weighing 20–150 kg; medium: 150–600 kg; and large: more than 600 kg.
Loitering & Direct Attack Munitions:	air vehicles with an integral warhead that share some characteristics with both UAVs and cruise missiles. They are designed to either fly directly to their target (Direct Attack), or in a search or holding pattern (Loitering).

Reference

Table 17 List of abbreviations for data sections

AAM	air-to-air missile	**ARV**	armoured recovery vehicle	**DD/G/H/M**	destroyer/with surface-to-surface missile/with hangar/with SAM
AAR	search-and-rescue vessel	**AS**	anti-submarine/submarine tender		
AAV	amphibious assault vehicle	**ASAT**	anti-satellite	**DDR**	disarmament, demobilisation and reintegration
AB	airborne	**ASBM**	anti-ship ballistic missile		
ABM	anti-ballistic missile	**ASCM**	anti-ship cruise missile	**DE**	directed energy
ABU/H	sea-going buoy tender/with hangar	**AShM**	anti-ship missile	**def**	defence
ABCV	airborne combat vehicle	**aslt**	assault	**det**	detachment
ac	aircraft	**ASM**	air-to-surface missile	**div**	division
ACS	crane ship	**ASR**	submarine rescue craft	**ECM**	electronic countermeasures
AD	air defence	**ASTT**	anti-submarine torpedo tube	**ELINT**	electronic intelligence
ADA	air-defence artillery	**ASW**	anti-submarine warfare	**elm**	element/s
adj	adjusted	**ASuW**	anti-surface warfare	**engr**	engineer
AE	auxiliary, ammunition carrier	**AT**	anti-tank	**EOD**	explosive ordnance disposal
AEM	missile support ship	**ATF**	ocean going tug	**EPF**	expeditionary fast transport vessel
AEV	armoured engineer vehicle	**ATGW**	anti-tank guided weapon	**eqpt**	equipment
AEW(&C)	airborne early warning (and control)	**Atk**	attack/ground attack	**ESB**	expeditionary sea base
AFD/L	auxiliary floating dry dock/small	**ATS**	tug, salvage and rescue ship	**ESD**	expeditionary transport dock
AFS/H	logistics ship/with hangar	**AUV**	armoured utility vehicle	**EW**	electronic warfare
AFSB	afloat forward staging base	**avn**	aviation	**excl**	excludes/excluding
AFV	armoured fighting vehicle	**AWT**	water tanker	**exp**	expenditure/expeditionary
AG	misc auxiliary	**AX/L/S**	training craft/light/sail	**FAC**	forward air control
AGB/H	icebreaker/with hangar	**BA**	Budget Authority (US)	**fd**	field
AGE/H	experimental auxiliary ship/with hangar	**Bbr**	bomber	**FF/G/H/M**	frigate/with surface-to-surface missile/with hangar/with SAM
		BCT	brigade combat team		
AGF/H	command ship/with hangar	**bde**	brigade	**FGA**	fighter/ground attack
AGHS	hydrographic survey vessel	**bdgt**	budget	**FLD**	full-load displacement
AGI	intelligence collection vessel	**BG**	battlegroup	**flt**	flight
AGM	space tracking vessel	**BMD**	ballistic-missile defence	**FMA**	Foreign Military Assistance
AGOR	oceanographic research vessel	**bn**	battalion/billion	**FRS**	fleet replacement squadron
AGOS	oceanographic surveillance vessel	**bty**	battery	**FS/G/H/M**	corvette/with surface-to-surface missile/with hangar/with SAM
AGS/H	survey ship/with hangar	**C2**	command and control		
AH	hospital ship	**C4**	command, control, communications, and computers	**Ftr**	fighter
AIP	air-independent propulsion			**FTX**	field training exercise
AK/L	cargo ship/light	**casevac**	casualty evacuation	**FY**	fiscal year
aka	also known as	**cav**	cavalry	**gd**	guard
AKEH	dry cargo/ammunition ship	**cbt**	combat	**GDP**	gross domestic product
AKR/H	roll-on/roll-off cargo ship/with hangar	**CBRN**	chemical, biological, radiological, nuclear, explosive	**GLCM**	ground-launched cruise missile
				GMLS	Guided Missile Launching System
AKS/L	stores ship/light	**cdo**	commando	**gp**	group
ALBM	air-launched ballistic missile	**C/G/H/M/N**	cruiser/with surface-to-surface missile/with hangar/with SAM/nuclear-powered	**GPS**	Global Positioning System
ALCM	air-launched cruise missile			**HA/DR**	humanitarian assistance/disaster relief
amb	ambulance				
amph	amphibious/amphibian	**CISR**	combat ISR	**hel**	helicopter
AO/S	oiler/small	**CIMIC**	civil–military cooperation	**HQ**	headquarters
AOE	fast combat support ship	**CIWS**	close-in weapons system	**HUMINT**	human intelligence
AOR/L/H	fleet replenishment oiler with RAS capability/light/with hangar	**COIN**	counter-insurgency	**HWT**	heavyweight torpedo
		comd	command	**hy**	heavy
AOT/L	oiler transport/light	**COMINT**	communications intelligence	**ICBM**	intercontinental ballistic missile
AP	transport ship	**comms**	communications	**IFV**	infantry fighting vehicle
APB	barracks ship	**coy**	company	**IIR**	imaging infrared
APC	armoured personnel carrier	**CP**	command post	**IMINT**	imagery intelligence
AR/C/D/L	repair ship/cable/dry dock/light	**CS**	combat support	**imp**	improved
ARG	amphibious ready group	**CSAR**	combat search and rescue	**indep**	independent
ARH	active radar homing	**CSS**	combat service support	**inf**	infantry
ARM	anti-radiation missile	**CT**	counter-terrorism	**info ops**	information operations
armd	armoured	**CV/H/L/N/S**	aircraft carrier/helicopter/light/nuclear powered/STOVL	**INS**	inertial navigation system
ARS/H	rescue and salvage ship/with hangar			**int**	intelligence
arty	artillery	**CW**	chemical warfare/weapons	**IOC**	Initial operating capability

IR	infrared
IRBM	intermediate-range ballistic missile
ISD	in-service date
ISR	intelligence, surveillance and reconnaissance
ISTAR	intelligence, surveillance, target acquisition and reconnaissance
LACM	land-attack cruise missile
LC/A/AC/H/M/P/T/U/VP	
	landing craft/assault/air cushion/ heavy/medium/personnel/tank/ utility/vehicles and personnel
LCC	amphibious command ship
LGB	laser-guided bomb
LHA	aviation-capable amphibious assault ship
LHD	aviation-capable amphibious assault ship with well dock
LIFT	lead-in ftr trainer
LKA	amphibious cargo ship
lnchr	launcher
LoA	letter of offer and acceptance
log	logistic
LoI	letter of intent
LP/D/H	landing platform/dock/helicopter
LRIP	low-rate initial production
LS/D/L/H/M/T	
	landing ship/dock/logistic/with hangar/medium/tank
lt	light
LWT	lightweight torpedo
maint	maintenance
MANPAD	man-portable air-defence system
MANPATS	man-portable anti-tank system
MBT	main battle tank
MC/C/CS/D/I/O	
	mine countermeasure coastal/ command and support/diving support/inshore/ocean
MCM	mine countermeasures
MCMV	mine countermeasures vessel
MD	military district
mech	mechanised
med	medium/medical
medevac	medical evacuation
MH/C/D/I/O	
	mine hunter/coastal/drone/ inshore/ocean
mil	military
MIRV	multiple independently targetable re-entry vehicle
mk	mark (model number)
ML	minelayer
MLU	mid-life update
mne	marine
mnv enh	manoeuvre enhancement
mod	modified/modification
mor	mortar
mot	motorised/motor
MoU	memorandum of understanding
MP	maritime patrol/military police
MR	motor rifle
MRBM	medium-range ballistic missile
MRH	multi-role helicopter
MRL	multiple rocket launcher

MS/C/D/I/O/R	
	mine sweeper/coastal/drone/ inshore/ocean/river
msl	missile
mtn	mountain
MW	mine warfare
n.a.	not applicable
n.k.	not known
NBC	nuclear, biological, chemical
NCO	non-commissioned officer
O & M	operations and maintenance
obs	observation/observer
OCU	operational conversion unit
OP	observation post
op/ops	operational/operations
OPFOR	opposition training force
org	organised/organisation
OPV	offshore patrol vessel
para	paratroop/parachute
PAX	passenger/passenger transport aircraft
PB/F/G/I/M/R/T	
	patrol boat/fast/with surface-to-surface missile/inshore/with SAM/ riverine/with torpedo
PC/C/F/G/H/I/M/O/R/T	
	patrol craft/coastal/fast/with surface-to-surface missile/with hangar/inshore/with CIWS missile or SAM/offshore/riverine/with torpedo
pdr	pounder
PGM	precision-guided munitions
PH/G/M/T	patrol hydrofoil/with surface-to-surface missile/with SAM/with torpedo
pl	platoon
PKO	peacekeeping operations
PNT	positioning, navigation, timing
PoR	programme of record
PPP	purchasing-power parity
PPV	protected patrol vehicle
PRH	passive radar-homing
PSO/H	peace support operations or offshore patrol ship/with hangar
psyops	psychological operations
ptn br	pontoon bridging
quad	quadruple
R&D	research and development
RCL	recoilless launcher
RDT&E	research, development, test and evaluation
recce	reconnaissance
regt	regiment
RFI	request for information
RFP	request for proposals
RL	rocket launcher
ro-ro	roll-on, roll-off
RPO	rendezvous and proximity operations
RV	re-entry vehicle
rvn	riverine
SAM	surface-to-air missile
SAR	search and rescue/synthetic aperture radar
SARH	semi-active radar homing
sat	satellite

SATCOM	satellite communications
SEAD	suppression of enemy air defence
SF	special forces
SHORAD	short-range air defence
SIGINT	signals intelligence
sigs	signals
SLBM	submarine-launched ballistic missile
SLCM	submarine-launched cruise missile
SLEP	service-life-extension programme
SP	self-propelled
Spec Ops	special operations
SPAAGM	self-propelled anti-aircraft gun and missile system
spt	support
sqn	squadron
SRBM	short-range ballistic missile
SS	submarine
SSA/N	auxiliary support submarine/ nuclear-powered
SSB/N	ballistic missile submarine/ nuclear-powered
SSC	coastal submarine
SSG	conventionally-powered attack submarine with dedicated launch tubes for guided missiles
SSGN	nuclear-powered submarine with dedicated launch tubes for guided missiles
SSK	conventionally-powered attack submarine
SSM	surface-to-surface missile
SSN	nuclear-powered attack submarine
SSR	security-sector reform
SSW	midget submarine
strat	strategic
STOVL	short take-off and vertical landing
surv	surveillance
sy	security
t	tonnes
tac	tactical
tch	technical
tk	tank
tkr	tanker
TMD	theatre missile defence
torp	torpedo
tpt	transport
tr	trillion
trg	training
TSV	tank support vehicle
TT	torpedo tube
UAV	uninhabited aerial vehicle
UCAC	utility craft air cushioned
UCAV	uninhabited combat air vehicle
UGV	uninhabited ground vehicle
utl	utility
UUV	uninhabited underwater vehicle
veh	vehicle
VLB	vehicle launched bridge
VLS	vertical launch system
VSHORAD	very short-range air defence
WFU	withdrawn from use
wg	wing

500 THE MILITARY BALANCE 2023

Table 18 International comparisons of defence expenditure and military personnel

	Defence spending (current USDm)			Defence spending per capita (current USD)			Defence spending % of GDP			Active armed forces (000)	Estimated reservists (000)	Active paramilitary (000)
	2020	2021	2022	2020	2021	2022	2020	2021	2022	2022	2022	2022
North America												
Canada	20,144	23,178	24,617	534	611	644	1.22	1.17	1.12	67	34	5
United States	774,527	759,645	766,606	2,328	2,268	2,272	3.71	3.30	3.06	1,360	817	0
Total	**794,671**	**782,823**	**791,223**	**1,431**	**1,439**	**1,458**	**2.47**	**2.24**	**2.09**	**1,426**	**852**	**5**
Europe												
Albania	222	245	286	72	79	92	1.47	1.34	1.57	8	0	0
Austria	3,466	4,200	3,643	391	473	409	0.80	0.88	0.78	23	112	0
Belgium	5,323	5,520	5,663	454	469	478	1.02	0.92	0.96	23	6	0
Bosnia-Herzegovina	168	192	169	44	50	44	0.84	0.82	0.71	11	6	0
Bulgaria	1,249	1,270	1,341	179	184	195	1.79	1.58	1.58	37	3	0
Croatia	997	1,413	1,273	236	336	304	1.74	2.09	1.84	17	21	0
Cyprus	419	571	497	331	445	384	1.70	2.06	1.86	12	50	0
Czech Republic	3,253	3,938	3,826	304	368	357	1.32	1.40	1.29	27	0	0
Denmark	4,919	5,371	5,064	838	911	855	1.38	1.35	1.31	15	44	0
Estonia	716	779	830	583	638	685	2.31	2.12	2.15	7	18	0
Finland	4,153	5,913	5,819	745	1,058	1,039	1.53	1.99	2.07	19	238	3
France	54,943	58,812	54,417	810	864	797	2.08	1.99	1.96	203	41	101
Germany	52,094	55,543	53,371	650	695	633	1.34	1.30	1.32	183	33	0
Greece	4,976	7,688	7,869	469	727	747	2.64	3.55	3.54	132	289	4
Hungary	2,175	2,620	2,992	223	269	308	1.39	1.44	1.62	32	20	0
Iceland	52	44	42	149	123	117	0.24	0.17	0.15	0	0	0
Ireland	1,187	1,269	1,170	229	243	222	0.28	0.25	0.23	8	2	0
Italy	29,696	33,479	31,120	476	537	509	1.57	1.59	1.56	161	18	176
Latvia	757	824	852	402	442	462	2.27	2.14	2.12	7	16	0
Lithuania	1,161	1,308	1,585	425	482	590	2.07	2.01	2.34	23	7	14
Luxembourg	390	412	444	620	644	683	0.53	0.47	0.54	0	0	1
Macedonia, North	188	207	229	88	97	108	1.59	1.49	1.63	8	5	8
Malta	81	85	87	177	184	188	0.54	0.49	0.51	2	0	0
Montenegro	74	91	100	121	150	166	1.65	1.55	1.63	2	3	4
Netherlands	12,594	13,883	15,228	729	801	875	1.39	1.37	1.54	34	6	7
Norway	6,476	7,503	7,433	1,184	1,362	1,338	1.79	1.56	1.47	25	40	0
Poland	12,780	13,424	13,396	334	352	352	2.13	1.98	1.87	114	0	14
Portugal	2,853	2,932	2,591	277	286	253	1.25	1.17	1.01	27	24	25
Romania	5,182	5,557	5,188	243	262	280	2.08	1.96	1.73	72	55	57
Serbia	896	1,032	1,221	128	148	181	1.68	1.64	1.95	28	50	4

Reference 501

Table 18 International comparisons of defence expenditure and military personnel

	Defence spending (current USDm)			Defence spending per capita (current USD)			Defence spending % of GDP			Active armed forces (000)	Estimated reservists (000)	Active paramilitary (000)
	2020	2021	2022	2020	2021	2022	2020	2021	2022	2022	2022	2022
Slovakia	1,847	1,992	2,008	339	366	370	1.76	1.73	1.79	18	0	0
Slovenia	605	836	883	288	397	420	1.13	1.35	1.42	6	1	0
Spain	13,744	15,126	14,669	275	320	311	1.07	1.06	1.06	124	15	76
Sweden	7,036	8,296	8,074	690	808	770	1.29	1.31	1.34	15	10	0
Switzerland	5,723	5,689	5,554	681	673	653	0.77	0.71	0.69	20	123	0
Turkey	10,885	9,547	6,188	133	116	75	1.51	1.17	0.73	355	379	157
United Kingdom*	61,473	70,870	70,029	935	1,073	1,033	2.23	2.22	2.19	150	72	0
Total	**314,753**	**348,476**	**335,152**	**412**	**471**	**467**	**1.46**	**1.47**	**1.46**	**1,948**	**1,705**	**649**
Russia and Eurasia												
Armenia	628	622	749	208	206	250	4.97	4.46	4.23	43	210	4
Azerbaijan	2,267	2,698	2,641	222	262	255	5.31	4.94	3.77	64	300	15
Belarus	601	640	818	63	68	87	0.98	0.94	1.03	48	290	110
Georgia	283	279	314	57	57	64	2.04	1.68	1.35	21	0	5
Kazakhstan	1,430	1,538	1,876	75	80	97	0.84	0.78	0.84	39	0	32
Kyrgyzstan	n.k.	n.k.	n.k.	n.k.	n.k.	n.k.	n.k.	n.k.	n.k.	11	0	10
Moldova	44	52	46	13	16	14	0.39	0.38	0.32	5	58	1
Russia [a]	42,671	48,531	66,857	301	341	471	2.87	2.73	3.13	1,190	1,500	559
Tajikistan	89	94	107	10	10	12	1.09	1.07	1.07	9	0	8
Turkmenistan*	n.k.	n.k.	n.k.	n.k.	n.k.	n.k.	n.k.	n.k.	n.k.	37	0	20
Ukraine [b]	4,353	4,298	3,547	99	98	81	2.86	2.21	n.k.	688	400	250
Uzbekistan	n.k.	n.k.	n.k.	n.k.	n.k.	n.k.	n.k.	n.k.	n.k.	48	0	20
Total**	**52,367**	**58,751**	**76,955**	**117**	**126**	**148**	**2.37**	**2.13**	**1.97**	**2,202**	**2,758**	**1,033**
Asia												
Afghanistan	2,014	n.k.	n.k.	55	n.k.	n.k.	10.00	n.k.	n.k.	100	0	0
Australia	31,418	34,185	33,841	1,234	1,324	1,295	2.31	2.09	1.96	60	30	0
Bangladesh	3,786	4,059	4,320	23	25	26	1.01	0.98	0.94	163	0	64
Brunei	439	454	435	946	964	910	3.66	3.24	2.36	7	1	1
Cambodia*	1,032	1,024	1,003	61	59	60	4.10	3.89	3.54	124	0	67
China	187,208	213,923	242,409	134	152	171	1.26	1.21	1.20	2,035	510	500
Fiji	52	46	44	55	49	46	1.16	1.07	0.90	4	6	0
India	65,307	67,498	66,645	49	50	48	2.45	2.13	1.92	1,468	1,155	1,608
Indonesia	8,116	8,407	9,059	30	31	33	0.77	0.71	0.70	396	400	280

Reference

502 THE MILITARY BALANCE 2023

Table 18 International comparisons of defence expenditure and military personnel

	Defence spending (current USDm)			Defence spending per capita (current USD)			Defence spending % of GDP			Active armed forces (000)	Estimated reservists (000)	Active paramilitary (000)
	2020	2021	2022	2020	2021	2022	2020	2021	2022	2022	2022	2022
Japan	53,758	52,198	48,079	428	419	387	1.07	1.06	1.12	247	56	14
Korea, DPR of	n.k.	n.k.	n.k.	n.k.	n.k.	n.k.	n.k.	n.k.	n.k.	1,280	600	189
Korea, Republic of	40,999	46,258	42,991	791	894	829	2.49	2.55	2.48	555	3,100	14
Laos	n.k.	n.k.	n.k.	n.k.	n.k.	n.k.	n.k.	n.k.	n.k.	29	0	100
Malaysia	3,709	3,829	4,148	114	114	122	1.10	1.03	0.96	113	52	23
Maldives	82	92	101	210	236	258	2.20	1.78	1.71	4	0	0
Mongolia	105	100	90	33	31	28	0.81	0.67	0.59	10	137	8
Myanmar	2,390	3,409	1,876	42	60	33	2.94	5.23	3.15	356	0	107
Nepal	435	413	421	14	14	14	1.29	1.15	1.08	97	0	15
New Zealand	3,287	3,269	3,353	667	655	664	1.56	1.32	1.38	9	3	0
Pakistan	9,363	10,300	9,768	40	43	40	3.12	2.96	2.59	652	0	291
Papua New Guinea	95	88	99	13	12	10	0.39	0.32	0.32	4	0	0
Philippines	5,269	5,660	5,462	48	51	48	1.47	1.45	1.37	145	131	12
Singapore	9,879	11,433	11,919	1,591	1,949	2,013	2.86	2.88	2.81	51	253	7
Sri Lanka	1,683	1,548	1,154	74	67	50	1.97	1.74	1.56	255	6	62
Taiwan	13,903	16,179	16,164	589	686	685	2.08	2.09	1.95	169	1,657	12
Thailand	6,839	6,708	6,171	99	97	89	1.37	1.33	1.16	361	200	94
Timor-Leste	42	39	44	30	28	31	2.19	1.66	1.80	2	0	0
Tonga	10	5	8	94	48	77	2.04	1.08	1.63	1	0	0
Vietnam*	5,724	6,308	6,030	58	61	58	1.67	1.73	1.46	482	5,000	40
Total **	**456,944**	**497,432**	**515,635**	**279**	**312**	**309**	**2.20**	**1.82**	**1.64**	**9,178**	**13,295**	**3,507**
Middle East and North Africa												
Algeria	9,699	9,088	8,945	226	209	202	6.69	5.59	4.78	139	150	187
Bahrain	1,405	1,399	1,399	934	916	908	4.05	3.61	3.22	8	0	11
Egypt	4,106	4,839	5,211	39	45	48	1.41	1.45	1.39	439	479	397
Iran	16,549	28,102	44,011	195	327	507	1.70	1.77	2.23	610	350	40
Iraq	10,191	7,423	8,690	262	187	215	6.01	3.71	3.16	193	0	266
Israel	17,234	20,408	19,350	1,987	2,323	2,171	4.97	4.85	4.30	170	465	8
Jordan	1,719	1,801	1,933	159	165	176	4.90	4.91	4.75	101	65	15
Kuwait	6,823	9,635	9,172	2,279	3,178	2,989	6.44	7.10	5.00	18	24	7
Lebanon	741	n.k.	n.k.	136	n.k.	n.k.	3.03	n.k.	n.k.	60	0	20
Libya	n.k.	n.k.	n.k.	n.k.	n.k.	n.k.	n.k.	n.k.	n.k.	n.k.	n.k.	n.k.
Mauritania	207	213	229	52	52	55	2.41	2.15	2.27	16	0	5
Morocco	5,961	6,521	6,413	168	182	175	4.92	4.57	4.50	196	150	50
Oman	7,483	6,431	6,431	2,059	1,741	1,709	10.12	7.49	5.90	43	0	4

Reference 503

Table 18 International comparisons of defence expenditure and military personnel

	Defence spending (current USDm)			Defence spending per capita (current USD)			Defence spending % of GDP			Active armed forces (000)	Estimated reservists (000)	Active paramilitary (000)
	2020	2021	2022	2020	2021	2022	2020	2021	2022	2022	2022	2022
Palestinian Territories	n.k.	n.k.	n.k.	n.k.	n.k.	n.k.	n.k.	n.k.	n.k.	0	0	n.k.
Qatar	6,466	6,258	8,419	2,645	2,523	3,357	4.48	3.48	3.80	17	0	5
Saudi Arabia	52,000	50,667	45,600	1,522	1,457	1,290	7.39	6.08	4.51	257	0	25
Syria	n.k.	n.k.	n.k.	n.k.	n.k.	n.k.	n.k.	n.k.	n.k.	169	0	100
Tunisia	1,153	1,231	1,283	98	104	108	2.91	2.81	2.95	36	0	12
United Arab Emirates	19,826	19,159	20,356	1,984	1,944	2,053	5.52	4.56	4.04	63	0	0
Yemen	n.k.	n.k.	n.k.	n.k.	n.k.	n.k.	n.k.	n.k.	n.k.	40	0	0
Total**	**161,564**	**173,176**	**187,442**	**921**	**1024**	**1064**	**4.81**	**4.28**	**3.79**	**2,572**	**1,683**	**1,152**
Latin America and the Caribbean												
Antigua and Barbuda	8	7	8	80	75	76	0.57	0.50	0.45	0	0	0
Argentina	2,904	2,588	3,380	64	56	73	0.75	0.53	0.54	72	0	31
Bahamas	86	95	95	254	270	266	0.88	0.85	0.74	2	0	0
Barbados	41	40	42	138	132	140	0.87	0.82	0.73	1	0	0
Belize	25	20	23	61	49	57	1.26	0.86	0.87	2	1	0
Bolivia	479	476	481	41	40	40	1.30	1.17	1.11	34	0	37
Brazil	22,234	21,293	22,951	105	100	106	1.53	1.32	1.21	367	1,340	395
Chile	4,049	4,041	3,758	223	221	204	1.60	1.28	1.21	69	19	45
Colombia	5,480	6,078	6,307	112	121	129	2.04	1.95	1.85	256	35	172
Costa Rica	457	430	423	90	84	81	0.75	0.68	0.62	0	0	10
Cuba	n.k.	n.k.	n.k.	n.k.	n.k.	n.k.	n.k.	n.k.	n.k.	49	39	27
Dominican Republic	589	582	761	56	55	71	0.75	0.61	0.68	56	0	15
Ecuador	1,545	1,593	1,581	91	93	91	1.56	1.51	1.37	41	118	1
El Salvador	172	248	257	27	38	39	0.71	0.86	0.80	25	10	26
Guatemala	366	340	400	21	20	23	0.47	0.40	0.44	18	64	25
Guyana	66	71	85	88	90	107	1.20	0.92	0.57	3	1	0
Haiti	10	37	14	1	3	1	0.07	0.18	0.07	1	0	0
Honduras	345	352	371	37	38	39	1.45	1.24	1.21	15	60	8
Jamaica	238	207	204	85	73	72	1.71	1.34	1.27	6	3	0
Mexico	5,352	6,713	5,743	42	52	44	0.49	0.52	0.40	216	82	137
Nicaragua	79	81	85	13	13	13	0.63	0.58	0.54	12	0	0
Panama	753	830	870	193	211	201	1.40	1.31	1.22	0	0	28
Paraguay	278	278	276	39	38	37	0.78	0.72	0.66	14	165	15

Reference

504 THE MILITARY BALANCE 2023

Table 18 International comparisons of defence expenditure and military personnel

	Defence spending (current USDm)			Defence spending per capita (current USD)			Defence spending % of GDP			Active armed forces (000)	Estimated reservists (000)	Active paramilitary (000)
	2020	2021	2022	2020	2021	2022	2020	2021	2022	2022	2022	2022
Peru	2,132	1,818	1,746	67	56	54	1.04	0.80	0.73	81	188	77
Suriname	n.k.	n.k.	n.k.	n.k.	n.k.	n.k.	n.k.	n.k.	n.k.	2	0	0
Trinidad and Tobago	954	773	838	789	633	596	4.46	3.22	2.86	5	1	0
Uruguay	509	516	546	150	152	160	0.95	0.87	0.77	21	0	1
Venezuela	n.k.	n.k.	n.k.	n.k.	n.k.	n.k.	n.k.	n.k.	n.k.	123	8	220
Total**	**49,150**	**49,508**	**51,245**	**115**	**109**	**109**	**1.17**	**1.00**	**0.92**	**1,488**	**2,132**	**1,269**
Sub-Saharan Africa												
Angola	1,014	993	1,760	31	30	51	1.74	1.32	1.41	107	0	10
Benin	56	226	394	4	17	29	0.36	1.27	2.24	12	0	5
Botswana	560	520	495	242	221	208	3.75	2.95	2.75	9	0	0
Burkina Faso	388	459	469	19	21	21	2.23	2.40	2.57	7	0	4
Burundi	62	65	67	5	5	5	2.02	1.95	1.81	30	0	1
Cabo Verde	12	12	12	20	20	19	0.62	0.57	0.56	1	0	0
Cameroon	407	444	419	15	16	14	1.00	0.98	0.95	25	0	9
Central African Rep	41	43	39	7	8	7	1.73	1.67	1.56	9	0	1
Chad	274	286	259	16	16	14	2.55	2.43	2.00	33	0	12
Congo	311	313	264	59	58	48	3.01	2.48	1.82	10	0	2
Côte d'Ivoire	608	638	610	22	23	6	0.99	0.91	0.89	27	0	n.k.
Dem Republic of the Congo	346	291	372	3	3	13	0.71	0.52	0.58	134	0	0
Djibouti	n.k.	n.k.	n.k.	n.k.	n.k.	n.k.	n.k.	n.k.	n.k.	8	0	5
Equatorial Guinea	n.k.	n.k.	n.k.	n.k.	n.k.	n.k.	n.k.	n.k.	n.k.	1	0	0
Eritrea	n.k.	n.k.	n.k.	n.k.	n.k.	n.k.	n.k.	n.k.	n.k.	302	n.k.	0
Ethiopia	429	377	1,576	4	3	14	0.44	0.38	1.42	503	0	0
Gabon	272	312	280	122	136	119	1.77	1.54	1.26	5	0	2
Gambia	15	16	14	7	7	6	0.82	0.79	0.65	4	0	0
Ghana	276	362	262	9	11	8	0.39	0.46	0.34	16	0	0
Guinea	211	247	327	17	19	25	1.49	1.53	1.66	10	0	3
Guinea-Bissau	n.k.	n.k.	n.k.	n.k.	n.k.	n.k.	n.k.	n.k.	n.k.	4	0	0
Kenya	1,102	1,099	1,346	21	20	24	1.09	0.99	1.17	24	0	5
Lesotho	38	35	40	19	16	18	1.84	1.42	1.58	2	0	0
Liberia	12	20	19	2	4	3	0.40	0.56	0.48	2	0	0
Madagascar	107	102	102	4	4	4	0.82	0.71	0.68	14	0	8
Malawi	69	82	75	3	4	4	0.58	0.69	0.65	11	0	4
Mali	787	855	831	40	42	40	4.50	4.47	4.51	21	0	20
Mauritius	225	202	230	163	146	176	2.06	1.81	2.00	0	0	3

Reference 505

Table 18 International comparisons of defence expenditure and military personnel

	Defence spending (current USDm)			Defence spending per capita (current USD)			Defence spending % of GDP			Active armed forces (000)	Estimated reservists (000)	Active paramilitary (000)
	2020	2021	2022	2020	2021	2022	2020	2021	2022	2022	2022	2022
Mozambique	131	143	145	4	5	5	0.93	0.91	0.81	11	0	0
Namibia	378	367	363	144	137	133	3.58	2.98	2.91	10	0	6
Niger	211	203	244	9	9	10	1.53	1.35	1.66	33	0	25
Nigeria	2,505	2,423	2,778	12	11	12	0.58	0.55	0.55	143	0	80
Rwanda	128	152	169	10	12	13	1.26	1.38	1.40	33	0	2
Senegal	346	474	423	22	29	24	1.41	1.72	1.54	14	0	5
Seychelles	n.k.	n.k.	n.k.	n.k.	n.k.	n.k.	n.k.	n.k.	n.k.	0	0	0
Sierra Leone	24	33	26	4	5	3	0.58	0.79	0.63	9	0	0
Somalia	n.k.	n.k.	n.k.	n.k.	n.k.	n.k.	n.k.	n.k.	n.k.	14	0	0
South Africa	3,321	3,342	3,090	59	59	54	0.98	0.80	0.75	74	0	15
South Sudan	92	43	64	9	4	6	1.37	0.84	1.33	53	0	0
Sudan	n.k.	n.k.	n.k.	n.k.	n.k.	n.k.	n.k.	n.k.	n.k.	104	0	40
Tanzania	803	903	943	14	15	15	1.25	1.28	1.23	27	80	1
Togo	116	118	173	13	14	20	1.53	1.40	2.07	13	0	3
Uganda	960	1,222	1,091	22	27	24	2.56	2.84	2.26	45	10	1
Zambia	358	282	444	21	15	23	1.98	1.32	1.64	15	3	1
Zimbabwe	39	287	751	3	19	50	0.17	0.87	1.96	29	0	22
Total**	**17,034**	**17,992**	**20,965**	**32**	**32**	**33**	**1.49**	**1.42**	**1.48**	**1,960**	**93**	**295**
Summary												
North America	**794,671**	**782,823**	**791,223**	**1,431**	**1,439**	**1,458**	**2.47**	**2.24**	**2.09**	**1,426**	**852**	**5**
Europe	**314,753**	**348,476**	**335,152**	**412**	**471**	**467**	**1.46**	**1.47**	**1.46**	**1,948**	**1,705**	**649**
Russia and Eurasia	**52,367**	**58,751**	**76,955**	**117**	**126**	**148**	**2.37**	**2.13**	**1.97**	**2,202**	**2,758**	**1,033**
Asia	**456,944**	**497,432**	**515,635**	**279**	**312**	**309**	**2.20**	**1.82**	**1.64**	**9,178**	**13,295**	**3,507**
Middle East and North Africa	**161,564**	**173,176**	**187,442**	**921**	**1,024**	**1,064**	**4.81**	**4.28**	**3.79**	**2,572**	**1,683**	**1,152**
Latin America and the Caribbean	**49,150**	**49,508**	**51,245**	**115**	**109**	**109**	**1.17**	**1.00**	**0.92**	**1,488**	**2,132**	**1,269**
Sub-Saharan Africa	**17,034**	**17,992**	**20,965**	**32**	**32**	**33**	**1.49**	**1.42**	**1.48**	**1,960**	**93**	**295**
Global totals	**1,846,484**	**1,928,158**	**1,978,617**	**295**	**321**	**326**	**1.96**	**1.76**	**1.67**	**20,774**	**22,517**	**7,911**

Totals may not sum precisely due to rounding. * Estimates. **Totals exclude defence-spending estimates for states where insufficient official information is available in order to enable approximate comparisons of regional defence-spending between years. Defence Spending per capita (current US$) and Defence Spending % of GDP totals are regional averages. [a] 'National Defence' budget chapter. Excludes other defence-related expenditures included under other budget lines (e.g. pensions) – see Table 5, p.191 [b] Official budget (including military pensions). Actual spending expected to be much higher in 2022 following Russian invasion in February. Significant depreciation of the Ukrainian hryvnia against the US dollar in 2022. Defence Spending as % of GDP includes US foreign military financing programmes – other figures do not.

Table 19 Index of country/territory abbreviations

AFG	Afghanistan	**GEO**	Georgia	**NOR**	Norway
ALB	Albania	**GER**	Germany	**NPL**	Nepal
ALG	Algeria	**GF**	French Guiana	**NZL**	New Zealand
ANG	Angola	**GHA**	Ghana	**OMN**	Oman
ARG	Argentina	**GIB**	Gibraltar	**PT**	Palestinian Territories
ARM	Armenia	**GNB**	Guinea-Bissau	**PAN**	Panama
ATG	Antigua and Barbuda	**GRC**	Greece	**PAK**	Pakistan
AUS	Australia	**GRL**	Greenland	**PER**	Peru
AUT	Austria	**GUA**	Guatemala	**PHL**	Philippines
AZE	Azerbaijan	**GUI**	Guinea	**POL**	Poland
BDI	Burundi	**GUY**	Guyana	**PNG**	Papua New Guinea
BEL	Belgium	**HND**	Honduras	**PRC**	China, People's Republic of
BEN	Benin	**HTI**	Haiti	**PRT**	Portugal
BFA	Burkina Faso	**HUN**	Hungary	**PRY**	Paraguay
BGD	Bangladesh	**IDN**	Indonesia	**PYF**	French Polynesia
BHR	Bahrain	**IND**	India	**QTR**	Qatar
BHS	Bahamas	**IRL**	Ireland	**ROC**	Taiwan (Republic of China)
BIH	Bosnia-Herzegovina	**IRN**	Iran	**ROK**	Korea, Republic of
BIOT	British Indian Ocean Territory	**IRQ**	Iraq	**ROM**	Romania
BLG	Bulgaria	**ISL**	Iceland	**RSA**	South Africa
BLR	Belarus	**ISR**	Israel	**RUS**	Russia
BLZ	Belize	**ITA**	Italy	**RWA**	Rwanda
BOL	Bolivia	**JAM**	Jamaica	**SAU**	Saudi Arabia
BRB	Barbados	**JOR**	Jordan	**SDN**	Sudan
BRN	Brunei	**JPN**	Japan	**SEN**	Senegal
BRZ	Brazil	**KAZ**	Kazakhstan	**SER**	Serbia
BWA	Botswana	**KEN**	Kenya	**SGP**	Singapore
CAM	Cambodia	**KGZ**	Kyrgyzstan	**SLB**	Solomon Islands
CAN	Canada	**KWT**	Kuwait	**SLE**	Sierra Leone
CAR	Central African Republic	**LAO**	Laos	**SLV**	El Salvador
CHA	Chad	**LBN**	Lebanon	**SOM**	Somalia
CHE	Switzerland	**LBR**	Liberia	**SSD**	South Sudan
CHL	Chile	**LBY**	Libya	**STP**	São Tomé and Príncipe
CIV	Côte d'Ivoire	**LKA**	Sri Lanka	**SUR**	Suriname
CMR	Cameroon	**LSO**	Lesotho	**SVK**	Slovakia
COG	Republic of Congo	**LTU**	Lithuania	**SVN**	Slovenia
COL	Colombia	**LUX**	Luxembourg	**SWE**	Sweden
CPV	Cabo Verde	**LVA**	Latvia	**SYC**	Seychelles
CRI	Costa Rica	**MDA**	Moldova	**SYR**	Syria
CRO	Croatia	**MDG**	Madagascar	**TGO**	Togo
CUB	Cuba	**MDV**	Maldives	**THA**	Thailand
CYP	Cyprus	**MEX**	Mexico	**TJK**	Tajikistan
CZE	Czech Republic	**MHL**	Marshall Islands	**TKM**	Turkmenistan
DJB	Djibouti	**MKD**	Macedonia, North	**TLS**	Timor-Leste
DNK	Denmark	**MLI**	Mali	**TON**	Tonga
DOM	Dominican Republic	**MLT**	Malta	**TTO**	Trinidad and Tobago
DPRK	Korea, Democratic People's Republic of	**MMR**	Myanmar	**TUN**	Tunisia
DRC	Democratic Republic of the Congo	**MNE**	Montenegro	**TUR**	Turkey
ECU	Ecuador	**MNG**	Mongolia	**TZA**	Tanzania
EGY	Egypt	**MOR**	Morocco	**UAE**	United Arab Emirates
EQG	Equitorial Guinea	**MOZ**	Mozambique	**UGA**	Uganda
ERI	Eritrea	**MRT**	Mauritania	**UK**	United Kingdom
ESP	Spain	**MUS**	Mauritius	**UKR**	Ukraine
EST	Estonia	**MWI**	Malawi	**URY**	Uruguay
ETH	Ethiopia	**MYS**	Malaysia	**US**	United States
FIN	Finland	**NAM**	Namibia	**UZB**	Uzbekistan
FJI	Fiji	**NCL**	New Caledonia	**VEN**	Venezuela
FLK	Falkland Islands	**NER**	Niger	**VNM**	Vietnam
FRA	France	**NGA**	Nigeria	**YEM**	Yemen, Republic of
GAB	Gabon	**NIC**	Nicaragua	**ZMB**	Zambia
GAM	Gambia	**NLD**	Netherlands	**ZWE**	Zimbabwe

Table 20 Index of countries and territories

Afghanistan AFG......................229
Albania ALB 72
Algeria ALG.........................315
Angola ANG 433
Antigua and Barbuda ATG............376
Argentina ARG......................376
Armenia ARM........................171
Australia AUS.......................229
Austria AUT.........................73
Azerbaijan AZE 172
Bahamas BHS........................379
Bahrain BHR 318
Bangladesh BGD.....................232
Barbados BRB.......................380
Belarus BLR 175
Belgium BEL 74
Belize BLZ 380
Benin BEN 434
Bolivia BOL 381
Bosnia-Herzegovina BIH..............76
Botswana BWA........................435
Brazil BRZ.........................383
Brunei BRN 234
Bulgaria BLG 77
Burkina Faso BFA....................437
Burundi BDI.........................438
Cabo Verde CPV......................439
Cambodia CAM 235
Cameroon CMR 439
Canada CAN 32
Central African Republic CAR 441
Chad CHA 442
Chile CHL..........................387
China, People's Republic of PRC.......237
Colombia COL 390
Congo, Republic of COG..............444
Costa Rica CRI......................393
Côte d'Ivoire CIV 445
Croatia CRO........................79
Cuba CUB...........................393
Cyprus CYP 80
Czech Republic CZE 82
Democratic Republic of the
Congo DRC 446
Denmark DNK 84
Djibouti DJB 448
Dominican Republic DOM..............395
Ecuador ECU........................396
Egypt EGY 320
El Salvador SLV.....................398
Equatorial Guinea EQG...............449
Eritrea ERI........................450
Estonia EST 86
Ethiopia ETH.......................451
Fiji FJI...........................246
Finland FIN 87
France FRA.........................89
Gabon GAB 453
Gambia GAM 454

Georgia GEO.........................177
Germany GER 94
Ghana GHA 455
Greece GRC 97
Guatemala GUA.......................400
Guinea GUI 456
Guinea-Bissau GNB...................457
Guyana GUY 401
Haiti HTI...........................402
Honduras HND........................402
Hungary HUN.........................101
Iceland ISL.........................102
India IND 247
Indonesia IDN.......................253
Iran IRN............................324
Iraq IRQ............................328
Ireland IRL 103
Israel ISR..........................330
Italy ITA...........................104
Jamaica JAM.........................404
Japan JPN...........................257
Jordan JOR 334
Kazakhstan KAZ......................178
Kenya KEN 458
Korea, Democratic People's
Republic of DPRK 262
Korea, Republic of ROK..............265
Kuwait KWT..........................336
Kyrgyzstan KGZ 180
Laos LAO 269
Latvia LVA 108
Lebanon LBN 338
Lesotho LSO 459
Liberia LBR.........................460
Libya LBY 340
Lithuania LTU 110
Luxembourg LUX 111
Macedonia, North MKD 112
Madagascar MDG......................461
Malawi MWI 462
Malaysia MYS 270
Maldives MDV 273
Mali MLI 463
Malta MLT 113
Mauritania MRT......................342
Mauritius MUS 465
Mexico MEX 405
Moldova MDA 181
Mongolia MNG........................274
Montenegro MNE 114
Morocco MOR 343
Mozambique MOZ......................465
Multinational Organisations.........115
Myanmar MMR 275
Namibia NAM.........................467
Nepal NPL 277
Netherlands NLD.....................116
New Zealand NZL 278
Nicaragua NIC 407

Nigeria NGA 469
Niger NER...........................468
Norway NOR..........................118
Oman OMN............................346
Pakistan PAK........................279
Palestinian Territories PT..........348
Panama PAN 408
Papua New Guinea PNG................283
Paraguay PRY 409
Peru PER............................411
Philippines PHL 284
Poland POL 120
Portugal PRT........................123
Qatar QTR 349
Romania ROM 125
Russia RUS..........................183
Rwanda RWA 471
Saudi Arabia SAU 351
Senegal SEN 472
Serbia SER 128
Seychelles SYC 474
Sierra Leone SLE 474
Singapore SGP 286
Slovakia SVK 130
Slovenia SVN........................132
Somalia SOM 475
South Africa RSA 476
South Sudan SSD 479
Spain ESP 133
Sri Lanka LKA 289
Sudan SDN 480
Suriname SUR........................414
Sweden SWE..........................137
Switzerland CHE 139
Syria SYR...........................354
Taiwan (Republic of China) ROC 291
Tajikistan TJK......................198
Tanzania TZA........................482
Thailand THA 294
Timor-Leste TLS.....................297
Togo TGO............................484
Tonga TON...........................298
Trinidad and Tobago TTO.............414
Tunisia TUN.........................357
Turkey TUR 141
Turkmenistan TKM 199
Uganda UGA 485
Ukraine UKR 201
United Arab Emirates UAE............359
United Kingdom UK...................145
United States US 35
Uruguay URY 415
Uzbekistan UZB......................205
Venezuela VEN.......................417
Vietnam VNM 298
Yemen, Republic of YEM..............362
Zambia ZMB 486
Zimbabwe ZWE........................488